Microsoft®

Excel 2010
IN DEPTH

Bill Jelen, MrExcel

MrExcel.com

800 East 96th Street
Indianapolis, Indiana 46240

MICROSOFT® EXCEL® 2010 IN DEPTH

ISBN-13: 978-0-789-74308-4

ISBN-10: 0-789-74308-6

Library of Congress Cataloging-in-Publication data is on file.

Printed in the United States of America

Third Printing: January 2012

Trademarks

All terms mentioned in this book that are known to be trademarks or service marks have been appropriately capitalized. Que Publishing cannot attest to the accuracy of this information. Use of a term in this book should not be regarded as affecting the validity of any trademark or service mark.

Warning and Disclaimer

Every effort has been made to make this book as complete and as accurate as possible, but no warranty or fitness is implied. The information provided is on an "as is" basis. The author and the publisher shall have neither liability nor responsibility to any person or entity with respect to any loss or damages arising from the information contained in this book or from the use of the CD or programs accompanying it.

Bulk Sales

Que Publishing offers excellent discounts on this book when ordered in quantity for bulk purchases or special sales. For more information, please contact

U.S. Corporate and Government Sales

1-800-382-3419

corpsales@pearsontechgroup.com

For sales outside of the U.S., please contact

International Sales

international@pearsoned.com

Associate Publisher
Greg Wiegand

Acquisitions Editor
Loretta Yates

Managing Editor
Sandra Schroeder

Project Editor
Seth Kerney

Copy Editor
Barbara Hacha

Indexer
Cheryl Lenser

Proofreaders
Apostrophe Editing Services
Debbie Williams

Technical Editor
Bob Umlas

Publishing Coordinator
Cindy Teeters

Multimedia Developer
Dan Scherf

Interior Designer
Anne Jones

Cover Designer
Anne Jones

Page Layout
Mark Shirar
Jake McFarland
Nonie Ratcliff

DEDICATION

To Bob Jelen

CONTENTS AT A GLANCE

CONTENTS

11 Using Everyday Functions: Math, Date and Time, and Text Functions **189**

14 Using Statistical Functions 389

15 Using Trig, Matrix, and Engineering Functions 503

ABOUT THE AUTHOR

Bill Jelen, Excel MVP and the host of MrExcel.com, has been using spreadsheets since 1985, and he launched the MrExcel.com website in 1998. Bill was a regular guest on Call for Help with Leo Laporte and has produced more than 1,200 episodes of his daily video podcast, Learn Excel from MrExcel. He is the author of 30 books about Microsoft Excel and writes the monthly Excel column for *Strategic Finance* magazine. You will most frequently find Bill taking his show on the road, doing half-day Power Excel seminars wherever he can find a room full of accountants or Excellers. Before founding MrExcel.com, Bill Jelen spent 12 years in the trenches — working as a financial analyst for finance, marketing, accounting and operations departments of a $500 million public company. He lives near Akron, Ohio with his wife, Mary Ellen, and his sons, Josh and Zeke.

ACKNOWLEDGMENTS

Excel 2007 and Excel 2010 brought tremendous new gains to spreadsheets. David Gainer at Microsoft led the Excel team through these two amazing versions. Thanks to all the Excel Project Managers who were happy to take the time to discuss the how or why behind a feature. The PowerPivot team of Donald Farmer, Rob Collie, and Amir Netz were tremendously helpful in getting me up to speed with PowerPivot.

Thanks to Dan Bricklin and Bob Frankston for inventing the computer spreadsheet. Thanks to Mitch Kapor for Lotus 1-2-3. Like everyone else who uses computers to make a living, I owe a debt of gratitude to these three pioneers.

I've learned that when writing a 1,000-page book, there is not much time for anything else. Thanks to Tracy Syrstad, Barb Jelen, Schar Oswald, and Scott Pierson for keeping MrExcel running while I wrote. As always, thanks to the hundreds of people answering 30,000 Excel questions a year at the MrExcel message board. Thanks to Wei Jiang and Jake Hildebrand for their programming expertise.

Michael Janscy provided great consulting help on the new statistical distribution functions.

At Pearson, Loretta Yates is an awesome acquisitions editor. If you have ever written a book for any other publisher, you are missing out by not working with Loretta Yates. Bob Umlas is the smartest Excel guy that I know and I am thrilled to have him as the technical editor for this book.

Thanks to Craig Crossman and everyone at the Computer America radio show.

Thanks to some early computing influences: Carl Bevington, Khalil Matta, Gary Kern, and Hector Guerrero. Thanks to my friend and client Jerry Kohl. Your ideas about how to make Excel sing are fantastic.

Finally, thanks to Josh Jelen, Zeke Jelen, and Mary Ellen Jelen. In particular, it was Mary Ellen who realized that things had to change if I was going to get the books done on time. Honey, you can put the whip away until Excel 15.

WE WANT TO HEAR FROM YOU!

As the reader of this book, *you* are our most important critic and commentator. We value your opinion and want to know what we're doing right, what we could do better, what areas you'd like to see us publish in, and any other words of wisdom you're willing to pass our way.

As an associate publisher for Que Publishing, I welcome your comments. You can email or write me directly to let me know what you did or didn't like about this book—as well as what we can do to make our books better.

Please note that I cannot help you with technical problems related to the topic of this book. We do have a User Services group, however, where I will forward specific technical questions related to the book.

When you write, please be sure to include this book's title and author as well as your name, email address, and phone number. I will carefully review your comments and share them with the author and editors who worked on the book.

Email:	feedback@quepublishing.com
Mail:	Greg WiegandAssociate Publisher
	Que Publishing
	800 East 96th Street
	Indianapolis, IN 46240 USA

READER SERVICES

Visit our website and register this book at www.quepublishing.com/register for convenient access to any updates, downloads, or errata that might be available for this book.

INTRODUCTION

I was amazed when Excel 2007 upped the row limit from 65,536 rows to 1.1 million rows. (Excel 2010, when combined with the PowerPivot add-in, can now sort, filter, and pivot 100 million rows!) Combine the 1 million rows with new charting, data visualizations, intelligent business diagrams, the SUMIFS function, Remove Duplicates, Page Layout view, table functionality, and Excel 2007 should have been the best-selling version of all time.

But IT departments everywhere delayed rolling out Office 2007 because the familiar menus and toolbars had been replaced by the ribbon. Suddenly, all the commands that people knew where to locate were shuffled around. This was fine for people new to Excel, but it meant some time to get up the learning curve for the 500 million people already using Excel.

It was fun to complain about why Microsoft would remove the familiar menus and toolbars from Excel 2007. We could mock them for replacing the all-important File menu with an icon so that no one could figure out how to print a document. But the Excel versions march on, and the ribbon is here to stay. When you get right down to it, there are really two things to learn about the ribbon: (1) Pivot Tables are on the Insert tab instead of the Data tab. (2) Most of the stuff that you think would be on the Insert tab is under the Insert drop-down on the Home tab. Master those two facts and the rest of the stuff is in a logical place. Besides, Microsoft replaced the mysterious wordless symbol on the File menu with the word "File" and dramatically improved that File menu into a full-screen Backstage view (see Chapter 1). You can now customize the ribbon so that you can move the PivotTable drop-down back to the Data tab where it belongs (for customizing the ribbon, see Chapter 3). And Microsoft added even more new features to Excel 2010.

New in Excel 2010

Every new Office version has a set of themes, and the new features are grouped around those themes. For Excel 2010, the themes were to improve Excel's reputation in the scientific community and to make Excel the premier tool for Business Intelligence. As a former data analyst, I love the new features for analyzing data. I also remember that while I loved wrangling large data sets into meaningful analyses, I never wanted to spend the time to make those meaningful analyses look "pretty." Excel 2010 offers new graphics improvements that make it easy to add some visual interest to your numbers.

Improvements in Business Intelligence

- **PowerPivot Add-In**—You can now sort, filter, and pivot data sets that are beyond 1 million rows. The PowerPivot tool allows you to mash up 100 million rows of data from Excel, text files, RSS Feeds, SQL Server, Oracle, and more. A new DAX expression language offers time intelligence functions that enable you to compare fiscal year-to-date sales with the parallel period from a year ago. See Chapter 24 for more about PowerPivot.

- **Pivot Table Slicers**—Filtering data in pivot tables becomes visual with graphical filters known as Slicers. In previous versions of Excel, the filter drop-downs offered the capability to choose Multiple Items, but no one reading the report could tell what was included or not included. These new graphical filters show what is in the summary report and invite people to do ad-hoc analyses by choosing new options from the slicers. See Chapter 25 for details on slicers.

- **Asymmetric Pivot Tables**—Do you need to show last year's actuals versus this year's budget? That was hard to do in previous versions of Excel, but the Named Sets command for pivot tables created from OLAP data make it easy in Excel 2010. Don't have OLAP? Run your Excel data through PowerPivot to enable Named Sets. See Chapter 24.

- **Percentage of Parent Item in Pivot Tables**—New calculations in the Show Values As drop-down allow for calculations such as Percentage of Parent row, Rank, and more.

- **AGGREGATE function**—Whereas Excel 2007 added the plural SUMIFS function, the killer function in Excel 2010 is AGGREGATE. This function is like the SUBTOTAL function on steroids. You have 19 calculation options instead of the 11 in SUBTOTAL, plus the capability to ignore hidden rows, filtered rows, or error cells. Read about Aggregate in Chapter 11.

Presentation Improvements

- **Tiny Charting with Sparklines**—Edward Tufte published his first descriptions of the intense, tiny, word-sized charts in a book in 2006. Microsoft incorporated three types of sparklines in Excel 2010. Chapter 33 will describe how to leverage sparklines. Sparklines join the Excel 2007 data visualizations. In that area, the old Data Bars feature gets a makeover with new options. See Chapter 31.

- **New SmartArt Layouts**—Fifty new business diagram layouts bring the total to more than 130 types of business diagrams that you can create with the SmartArt tools. Learn about SmartArt in Chapter 34.

- **Better Picture Tools and Background Removal**—If you need to dress up a report with a photograph, improved picture tools help to correct the picture. A fairly cool background removal tool will have you creating odd-shaped picture elements. See Chapter 35. Also in this chapter, learn about a new screen clipping tool that allows you to paste a picture of a section of any screenshot into your worksheet.

Excel Interface Improvements

- **Paste Options Flyout**—If you study the Undo command, can you guess which operation immediately precedes Undo most often? It is Paste or one of the Paste variants. The new Paste Options flyout will help you paste data with/without borders, formulas, links, column widths, and so on. Ctrl+C, Ctrl+V, Ctrl, V is becoming my favorite key sequence. See Chapter 4.

- **File Menu Becomes Backstage View**—Most ribbon tabs contain commands that you use while working in your document. The File menu contains commands that you do to the entire document when you are done with your document. The team at Microsoft figured that these commands don't require you to see the document, so all the screen real estate is taken up with a new full-screen File menu. Read about Backstage view in Chapter 1.

- **Ribbon Customizations**—This should not even be noted in the book because it has been possible to customize ribbons and toolbars for more than a decade. However, Excel 2007 offered no way in the Excel interface to customize the ribbon. Chapter 3 shows you how to customize the ribbon in Excel 2010.

Improvements for the Science Community

- **Improved Function Accuracy**—Various academic papers had attacked the accuracy of some of Excel's statistical, financial, and math functions. Microsoft hired two outside math consultancy firms to rewrite the algorithms for a number of functions and then hired a third firm to validate which algorithm was the best for each function. See Chapter 10 for a discussion of these improvements.

- **Consistency in Function Names**—The statistical function set had been a confusing jumble of functions. For every distribution, you always had to check Help to see whether the particular function was a cumulative function, left-tailed, right-tailed, and so on. You will begin to see many new functions that include the dot in their name. Those dots will lead to an easier-to-understand description of the function. For statistical distribution functions, a name like *<distribution>*.DIST will be the left-tailed cumulative distribution when the cumulative parameter is TRUE and the probability density function when the cumulative parameter is FALSE. If you need a right-tailed distribution, look for *<distribution>*.DIST.RT. For two-tailed, *<distribution>*.DIST.2T. The inverse functions will be *<distribution>*.INV. Functions based on a sample will be *<function>*.S and functions based on a population will be *<function>*.P. Excel still supports the old names, but new formulas can be created with VAR.S and VAR.P instead of the old VAR and VARS. See Chapters 10 and 14 for a description of these new function names.

- **Equation Editor**—You can now insert a variety of equations into a text box in Excel. The Equation tools support Radicals, Integrals, Matrices, brackets, functions, and symbols. You can convert the equation into a linear view for editing and then press a button to turn it back into a 2D equation.

Upgrading from Excel 2003 or Earlier

A large percentage of the people upgrading to Excel 2010 are people who skipped over Excel 2007. This book assumes that things that were new in Excel 2007 are still new to over half of the readers. If you are upgrading from Excel 2003, watch for these new features:

- **Massive Grid**—1.1 million rows and 16,000 columns. That's 17 billion cells, just on Sheet 1. Read about the big grid in Chapter 7.

- **Data Visualizations**—Icon sets, color scales, and in-cell bar charts are found on the Conditional Formatting drop-down of the Home tab. See Chapter 31 for more on these tools.

- **Better Looking Charts**—The Excel 2007 charting engine is new. The charts look better. The charting interface has improvements, but it is harder to do some things than in Excel 2003. Read about charts in Chapter 32.

- **Remove Duplicates**—You can remove duplicates with a couple of clicks using the new command on the Data tab.

- **Page Layout View**—Edit headers and footers in place using the new Page Layout view.

How This Book Is Organized

The book is organized into the following parts:

- **Part I, "Mastering the New User Interface"**—This first part of the book shows you the ribbon, Backstage View, Mini Toolbar, Quick Access Toolbar, and more.

- **Part II, "Calculating with Excel"**—This part covers what Excel does best, from formulas to functions to linking.

- **Part III, "Business Intelligence"**—Sorting, Filtering, Subtotals, Pivot Tables. These are the tools of the Excel data analyst. Learn about these tools and the new PowerPivot add-in in Part III. The chapter on VBA macros is also in this part.

- **Part IV, "Visual Presentation"**—This part covers charting, SmartArt, data visualizations, and picture tools. After you get done analyzing the data, a few features from this part will make your reports look good.

- **Part V, "Sharing Information"**—This part discusses printing and sharing your Excel workbooks by creating PDFs, or publishing to the Web.

Conventions Used in This Book

The special conventions used throughout this book are designed to help you get the most from the book as well as from Excel 2010.

Text Conventions

Different typefaces are used to convey various things throughout the book. They include those shown in Table I.1.

Table I.1   Typeface Conventions

Typeface	Description
Monospace	Screen messages appear in monospace.
Italic	New terminology appears in *italic*.
Bold	References to text you should type appear in **bold**.

Ribbon names, dialog box names, and dialog box elements are capitalized in this book (for example, Add Formatting Rule dialog, Home tab).

In this book, key combinations are represented with a plus sign. If the action you need to take is to press the Ctrl key and the T key simultaneously, the text tells you to press Ctrl+T.

There were not many changes from Excel 97 to Excel 2000 to Excel 2002 to Excel 2003. Most people upgrading to Excel 2010 will be coming from one of these versions of Excel. I will collectively refer to these versions as "legacy versions of Excel."

Special Elements

Throughout this book, you'll find tips, notes, cautions, cross-references, case studies, Excel in Practice boxes, sidebars, and Troubleshooting Tip boxes. These elements provide a variety of information, ranging from warnings you shouldn't miss to ancillary information that will enrich your Excel experience but isn't required reading.

Cross References

 See Chapter 99 for more information.

 note

Notes contain extra information or alternative techniques for performing tasks.

tip

Tips point out special features, quirks, or software tricks that will help you increase your productivity with Excel 2007.

The author has more than 1,200 Excel podcast episodes available. Certain topics in the book will refer you to a video demo in the Excel In Depth channel at YouTube.

 caution

Cautions call out potential gotchas.

Case Study: Other Elements

Sections such as Case Study, Excel in Practice, and Troubleshooting Tips are set off in boxes such as this one:

- Case studies walk you through the steps to complete a task.
- Excel in Practice boxes walk through real-life problems in Excel.
- Troubleshooting Tips boxes walk through steps to avoid certain problems or how to react when certain problems occur.

Sidebars

Historical glimpses and other information that is not critical to your understanding appear as sidebars. I imagine that if the Cliff Claven character from *Cheers* knew a lot about Excel, these would be the kinds of things he would write.

THE FILE MENU BECOMES THE BACKSTAGE VIEW

Open the File menu in Excel 2010 and you might be shocked to see that it takes up 100% of your screen real estate. This new panel is called the Backstage view and represents a significant development effort in Office 2010.

Understanding "In" Versus "Out" Commands

Microsoft added the Ribbon to Excel 2007 to make working in your spreadsheet easier. Microsoft describes the typical WYSIWYG interaction model for a command such as bolding a cell as follows:

- Scan the worksheet.
- See something you want to change.
- Find the command.
- Use the command.
- See the results on the page.

All the commands on the Home, Insert, Page Layout, Formulas, Data, Review, and View tabs of the Ribbon are commands that you use when you work in your document. Microsoft calls these commands the "In" commands.

By contrast, the commands on the File menu are not for working in the document. You use these commands after you finish the document and you are ready to do something with it. Perhaps you want to print, or email, or save the document. All the out commands share the characteristic that they don't act on a specific point in the worksheet and their results don't appear in the spreadsheet. For lack of a better term, Microsoft calls these commands the "Out" commands.

After developing the Ribbon for Excel 2007, Microsoft felt it had simplified the process of finding the In commands. But the WYSIWYG model falls apart for the Out commands:

- You can't scan the worksheet for something you want to change. The status of the Out features doesn't appear in the worksheet.

- The Out commands suffered from low discoverability. Whereas people using Excel 2007 figured that an editing command had to exist somewhere, people were not searching for the Out commands. For example, some items, such as the Document Inspector, were hidden several layers deep and rarely found.

To address these issues, Microsoft added the Backstage view to provide a consistent home for the Out commands.

Using Backstage View

To open the Backstage view, click the File menu. The Backstage view fills the screen, as shown in Figure 1.1.

Backstage is split into three sections: the narrow left navigation panel and two wider sections that provide information.

Pressing the Esc Key to Close Backstage View

To get out of Backstage and return to your worksheet, you can either press the Esc key or click another Ribbon tab.

Using the Four Quick Commands in the Left Navigation

Four commands are so important that they get their own real estate in the top of the left navigation pane: Save, Save As, Open, and Close. The Save and Close commands act as soon as you select them. The Save As and Open commands bring up another dialog box where you can save or open a document. Not much has changed in the Save As or Open dialog boxes.

At the bottom of the left navigation are two additional quick commands: Options and Exit. The Options command leads to the Excel Options dialog box.

➡ *See Chapter 6, "The Excel Options Dialog," for details on the Excel options.*

> **🔍 note**
>
> First, it is great to note that once again a File menu exists in Excel 2010. For the past 3 years, people using Excel 2007 had a version of Office in which the File menu had been replaced by a branding decoration. This led to huge frustrations as people searched the other Ribbon tabs trying to find items that used to be on the File menu. Although this frustration gave my Power Excel seminar audiences a shared common experience and a reason to laugh at Microsoft's folly, it is seriously good to see that Microsoft abandoned this idea and came back with a File menu. As late as July 2009, the technical preview of Office 2010 was sticking with the branding element instead of the File menu. Someone in the usability lab had the genius to run a test in which they tried putting the letters "F-i-l-e" on the tab instead of the Office icon. Microsoft reports that discoverability of the Backstage view increased dramatically, so it abandoned the branding decoration.

Quick
Commands

Ribbon Tabs (click to exit)

Figure 1.1
Backstage
view.

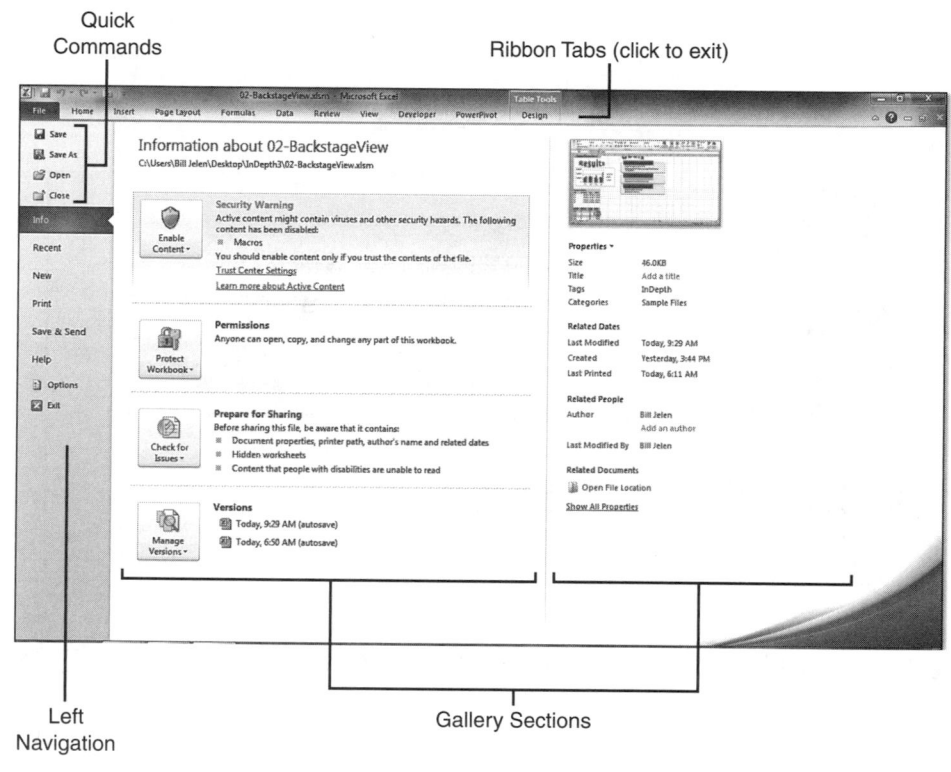

Left
Navigation

Gallery Sections

The remaining entries in the left navigation each lead to large galleries of information and commands: Info, Recent, New, Print, Save & Send, and Help. Each of these will be described in the sections that follow.

Opening Recent Files

If you have no workbook open in Excel and you go to the File menu, you start in the Recent gallery (see Figure 1.3).

In the central panel, you have a list of recent workbooks. As in Excel 2007, this list can show up to 50 documents instead of the 9 that were available in Excel 2003.

The central panel includes a vertical scrollbar so that you can scroll to more documents than are visible on your screen.

 tip

Because the commands in the Backstage view are all Out commands, they do not operate on a specific point in the spreadsheet. Thus, you do not need to actually see your spreadsheet while you use the commands. Microsoft takes the liberty of having the Backstage view fill the entire width of the screen. The screen is divided into three asymmetric parts: a narrow left navigation pane, a medium-width central command gallery, and a wide information pane on the right side.

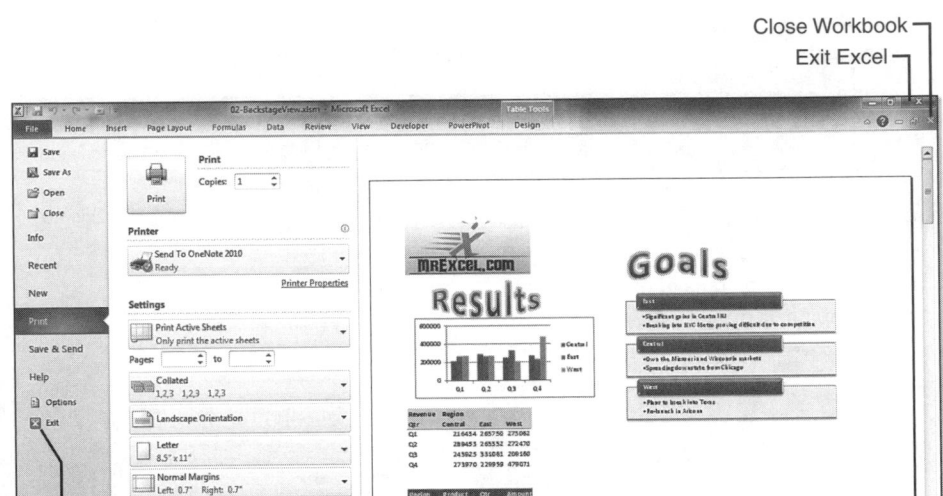

Figure 1.2
None of the visible clickable "X" elements close Backstage.

Close Workbook
Exit Excel

Exit Excel

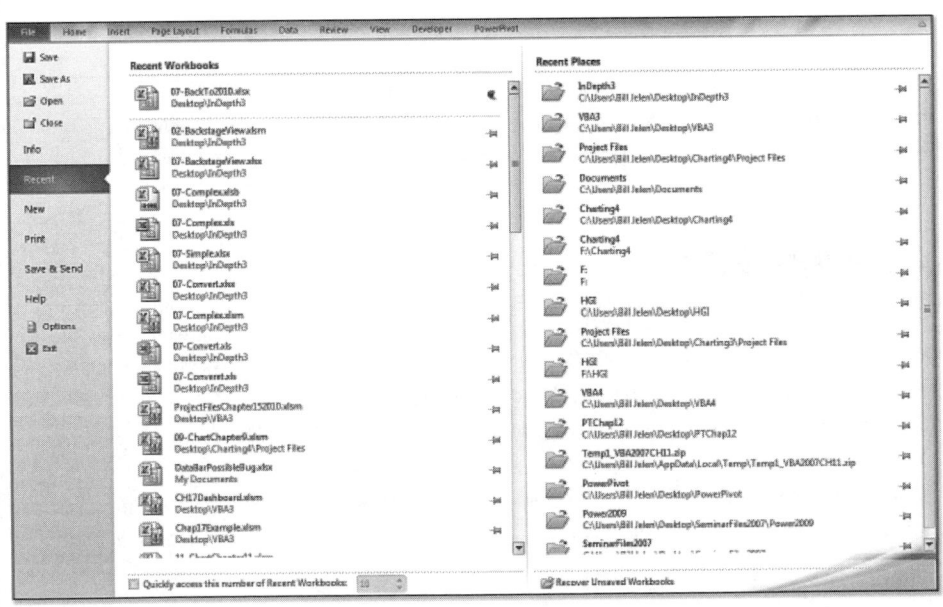

Figure 1.3
The Recent pane.

The right side of the screen includes a great new feature called Recent Places. This list shows all the folders from where you have recently opened documents. If I am currently working on next year's budget, it is likely that I will have to open other documents in the \FutureBudget\ folder. Having the list of folders on the right side is a feature that you will find yourself using frequently. When you click a folder on the right side of the screen, you are taken to the standard Excel Open dialog, but it will already be showing the selected folder.

In Figure 1.3, notice the two columns of gray pushpins. If you click one of those gray pushpins, it turns into a colored pushpin that appears to be pushed into the screen. This pins an item to either the Recent Workbooks or the Recent Places list. When an item is pinned to the list, it stays at the top of the list, no matter how many other files you might open. This is great for the files that you use for month-end reporting. Even if you happen to open 153 other files during the course of the month, when the next month-end period rolls around, you can be sure that your month-end report file is at the top of the Recent list.

tip

Initially, the Recent Workbooks list includes up to 25 documents. If you visit File, Options, Advanced, Display, you find a setting for Show This Number of Recent Documents. Dial this up to 50 documents.

One-Click Access to Recent Files

During the beta for Office 2010, many people complained that the Recent File list is now two clicks away instead of one click away. When any Excel workbook is open, clicking the File menu takes you to the Info panel instead of the Recent gallery. People complained that they had twice as many clicks to select File, Recent before they could see their recently used files.

There are two solutions for this.

First, you can easily add the Recent File List to the Quick Access Toolbar. At the right side of the Quick Access Toolbar is a drop-down arrow. Open this drop-down arrow to reveal 12 common commands you can add to the Quick Access Toolbar. (See Figure 1.4) If you choose Open Recent File from this list, you have an Open Recent File icon on your Quick Access Toolbar. Click this icon to go directly to the Recently Used File List. For people who like the keyboard accelerators, using Alt+4 invokes the fourth icon on the Quick Access Toolbar, so there is a one-keystroke method for accessing the Recently Used File list, provided it is one of the first nine icons on your Quick Access Toolbar.

tip

If you were a fan of the keyboard shortcut of Alt+F+1 to open the most recent file, you will appreciate that using this check box allows Alt+F+1 to continue to work as expected.

There is a second method for quickly accessing recent workbooks. At the bottom of the Recent Workbooks list is a check box and a Spin button. On a 900x1440 monitor, you have room for about 10 more items along the left navigation panel. This check box allows you to fill that space with recent files. Select the check box and choose any number of files. In Figure 1.5, 10 new files are shown in the left navigation.

If you have items pinned to the Recent Workbooks list, they are shown immediately after the Quick Commands in the left navigation. The rest of the space is filled with recent documents.

Open Recent File icon

QAT Drop-down

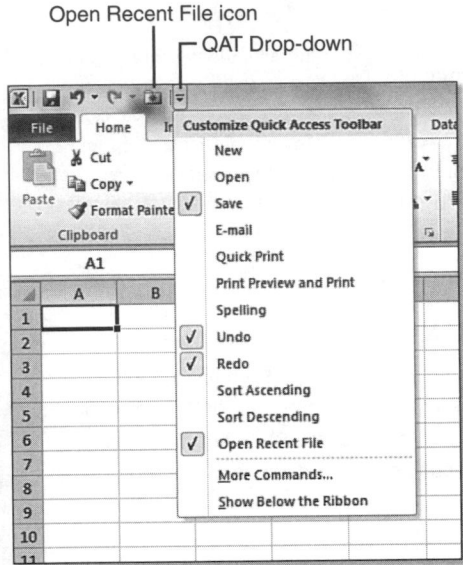

Figure 1.4
Add Open Recent Workbooks to the QAT.

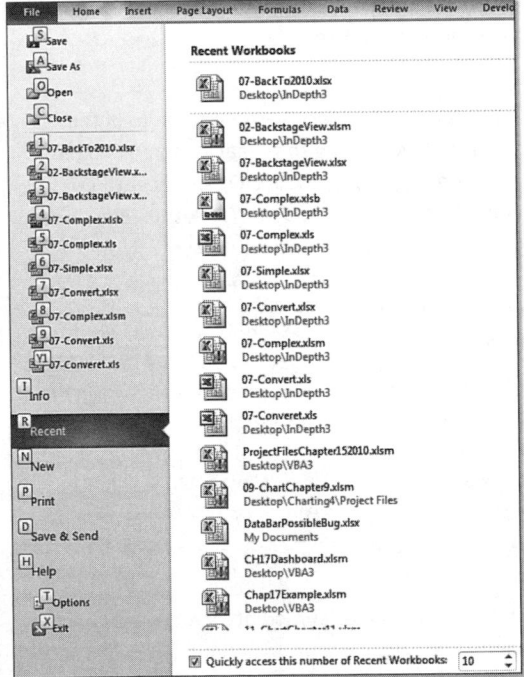

Figure 1.5
Use Alt+F+1 to access the first item pinned to your recent workbooks list.

To see a demo about the Recent Files pane, search for "Excel In Depth 1" at YouTube.

Recovering Unsaved Workbooks

As in legacy versions of Excel, the AutoSave feature can create copies of your workbook every n minutes. ("Legacy" in this book refers to Excel 2003 and earlier versions.) If an AutoSave version of your workbook exists, you can now access that file using the Recover Unsaved Workbooks icon at the bottom of the Recent Places list.

Do you ever get to the end of your workday, use the X to close Excel, and then are greeted with a barrage of Do You Want to Save questions, as shown in Figure 1.6? I frequently forget that the nth workbook that I have open is not saved. I will think that I had opened these workbooks to get information, that I had not made any significant changes, and will either start clicking Don't Save repeatedly, or will hold down Shift and click Don't Save, which is equivalent to clicking the nonexistent Don't Save to All selection.

Figure 1.6
If you accidentally click Don't Save after Excel has AutoSaved, you might be able to recover the document.

As I see that important file get closed, I realize that I just lost all my changes to that file and cringe. This is a common problem that happens to everyone sooner or later. Provided that the file was open long enough to experience an AutoSave, you may be able to get the file back.

Go to Recover Unsaved Workbooks and find the date and time of the last AutoSave. It might be within 5 minutes of the last time you edited a cell in that document. When you find the file and open it, the Information Bar reports that this is a Recovered Unsaved File (see Figure 1.7). Click Save As to give the file a name.

Figure 1.7
Excel recovers the file. You need to Save As to make the recovery permanent.

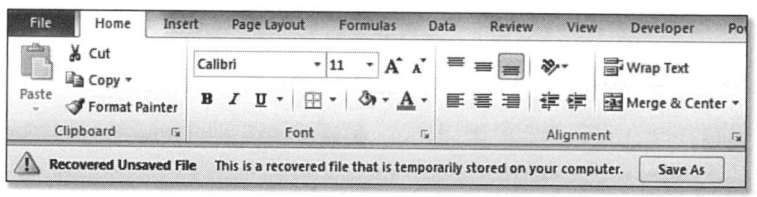

Clearing the Recent Workbooks List

If you need to clear out the Recent Workbooks List, you should visit File, Options, Advanced, Display. Set the Show This Number of Recent Documents list to zero. This is unlike the behavior in Excel 2003. In Excel 2003, to clear out the ninth item from the list, you had to reset only the number of files back to 8 and Excel would forget about number 9. In Excel 2010, if you switch from 50 files to 1 file, then back to 50 files, all 50 files will come back. The only way to clear the recent workbooks list is to set the value back to zero. You can then reset it to 50 and Excel will start collecting history again.

 caution

This raises some privacy concerns. If you are frequently working on documents that you don't want others to see, they might be able to recover them from the last autosaved version. I don't recommend it, but if you need to, you can turn off this new feature. To do this, go to File, Options, Save, and clear the Keep the Last AutoSaved Version if I Close Without Saving check box.

Getting Information About the Current Workbook

When a workbook is open and you go to the File menu, you start in the Info gallery for that workbook.

As shown in Figure 1.8, the Info pane lists all sorts of information about the current workbook. In legacy versions of Excel, much of this information might have been tough to determine without using VBA or even going out to Windows Explorer.

Some of the information is now at your fingertips in the Info gallery:

- The workbook path is shown at the top of the gallery. You can select the text in the path, and use Ctrl+C to copy and then paste the path wherever you might need to paste it.

- You can see the file size.

- You can see when the document was last modified and who modified it.

- If any special states exist, these will be reported at the top of the middle pane. Special states might include the following:

    - Macros not enabled.

    - Links not updated.

    - Checked out from SharePoint.

- You can see if the file has been AutoSaved and recover those AutoSaved versions.

- You can mark the document as final that will cause others opening the file to initially have a read-only version of the file.

- You can edit links to other documents.

- A thumbnail of the current window of the document appears in the top right in case you forgot which document you are editing.

- You can add Tags or Categories to the File.

■ Using the Check for Issues drop-down, you can run a compatibility checker to see if the workbook is compatible with legacy versions of Excel. You can run an accessibility checker to see if any parts of the document will be difficult for people with disabilities. You can run a Document Inspector to see if any private information is hidden in the file.

Figure 1.8
The Info gallery includes all of the properties of the file.

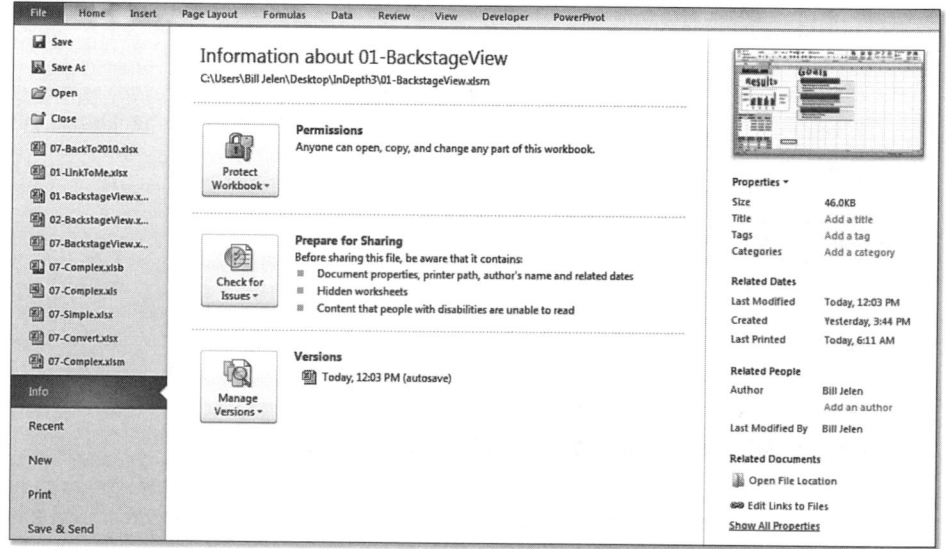

Correcting Special States Such as Disabled Macros and Links

Open a workbook that contains macros and external links. A message appears in the Information Bar that this content has not been enabled.

If you visit the Backstage view, the fact that the content has not been enabled appears at the top of the center pane (see Figure 1.9).

Figure 1.9
You see a summary that certain content is not enabled.

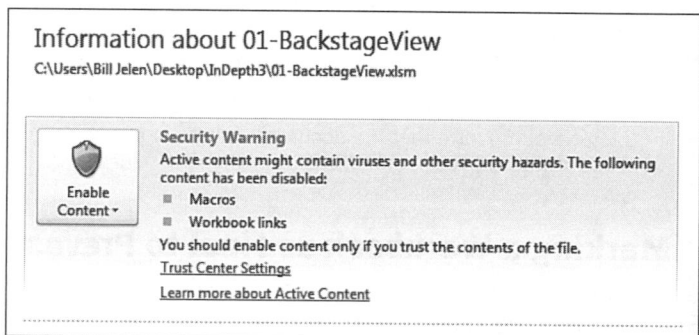

Open the Enable Content drop-down and you are presented with an easy way to make the document a trusted document (see Figure 1.10). If you choose the top item in the drop-down, all the content will be enabled and you will no longer be asked about enabling this content in this file on this computer.

note

These rules apply only to workbooks stored on a local hard drive. If the file is stored on a network, then Excel is going to ask you about enabling macros every time that you open the file.

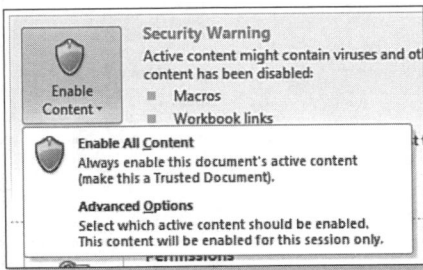

Figure 1.10
It is now easier to Trust a document using this drop-down.

Excel's Automatic Trusting of a Document

Say that you have an .xlsm workbook stored on a local hard drive. This workbook has some macros that you recorded. If you open this workbook and select to Enable Macros, then Excel assumes that you are OK with the macros and automatically enables those macros the next time.

This is a good feature. Excel asks you only once about the file. This makes it far more likely that you will actually leave the Excel Macro Security setting so that all macros are disabled with notification.

If you send the workbook to someone else and they save it on their computer, they will be presented with the Enable Macros question again, but they would be asked about it only once.

Opening a File in the Protected View Sandbox

Another new feature in Excel 2010 is the protected view. If you download a workbook from the Internet or another unsafe location, you can open the workbook, but it will default to something called Protected View. In this view, you cannot edit the workbook. Macros will not run. Links will not update. The theory is that you can actually look around the document, look for macros, look for links, and so on before you decide to trust the document.

After making sure that the document is safe, you can click the Enable Editing button in the Info bar (see Figure 1.11).

Marking a Workbook as Final to Prevent Editing

Open the Protect Workbook icon in the Info gallery to access a setting called Mark as Final (see Figure 1.12). This marks the workbook as read-only. It will prevent someone else from making changes to your final workbook.

Figure 1.11
Workbooks from
the Internet open
in a protected
sandbox.

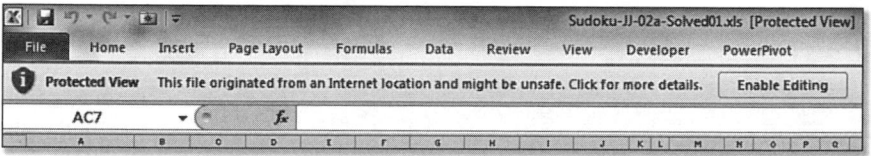

Figure 1.12
Mark a document as Read Only.

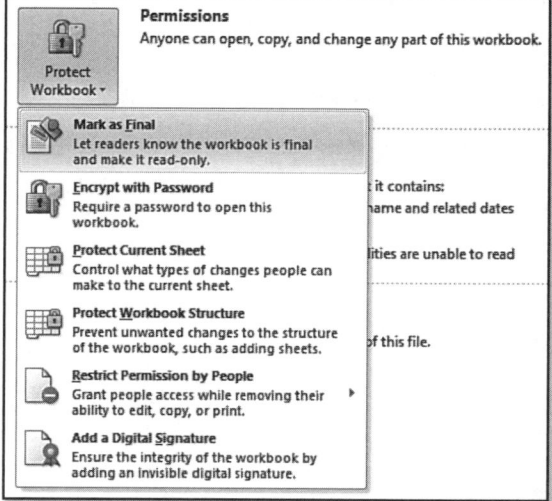

Of course, if the other person visits the Info gallery, that person can reenable editing. This feature is simply designed to warn the other people that you've marked it as final and no further changes should happen.

If you can convince everyone in your workgroup to sign up for a Windows Live ID, you can use the Restrict Permission by People setting. This layer of security allows you to define who can read, edit, and/or print the document.

Finding Hidden Content Using the Document Inspector

The Document Inspector can find a lot of hidden content, but it is not perfect. Still, finding 95% of the types of hidden content can protect you a lot of the time.

To run the Document Inspector, select File, Info, Check for Issues, Inspect Document, and click OK. The results of the Document

> **⚠ caution**
> The Document Inspector is not foolproof. Do you frequently hide settings by changing the font color to white or by using the ;;; custom number format? This won't be found by the Document Inspector. The Document Inspector also won't note that you had scrolled over outside the print area and jotted your after-work grocery list in column X.

Inspector shown in Figure 1.13 shows that the document has personal information stored in the file properties (author's name) and a hidden worksheet.

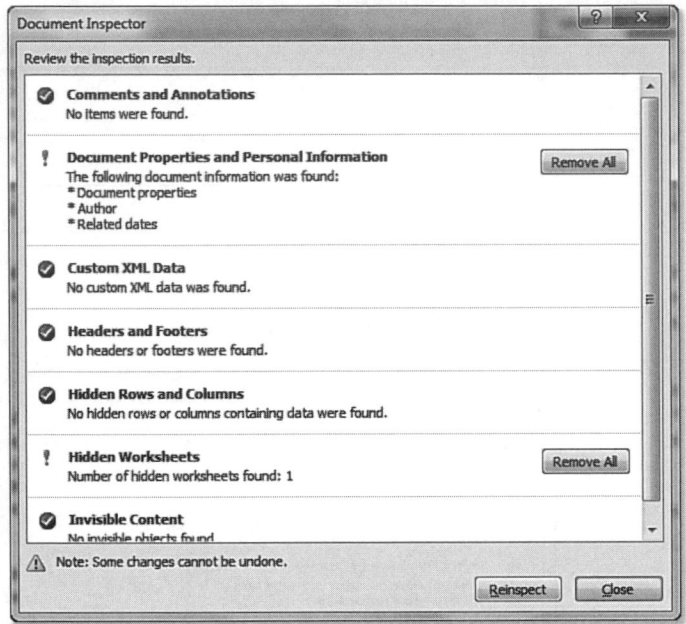

Figure 1.13
Look for hidden personal items in the workbook.

Creating a New Workbook from a Template

If your manager asks you to create a new calendar, expense report form, invoice, and so on, you should visit the New category in Backstage view. There are hundreds of templates already prebuilt on Office Online. Although the gallery initially offers Budgets, Calendars, and seven other categories, as shown in Figure 1.14, you can browse through the More Categories folder for hundreds of other types of prebuilt worksheets.

These are free for your use as a registered owner of Microsoft Excel.

 tip

If you just want a new blank workbook, use Ctrl+N and avoid the hassle of File, New, Blank Workbook, Create.

Printing and Print Preview

Print Preview has been moved to the Print category in Backstage view.

Backstage view consolidates settings that used to be in Page Setup, in the Print dialog, in Print Preview, and in the Printer Settings dialog. (See Figure 1.15)

Figure 1.14
Many pre-built templates are available for your use from Office Online.

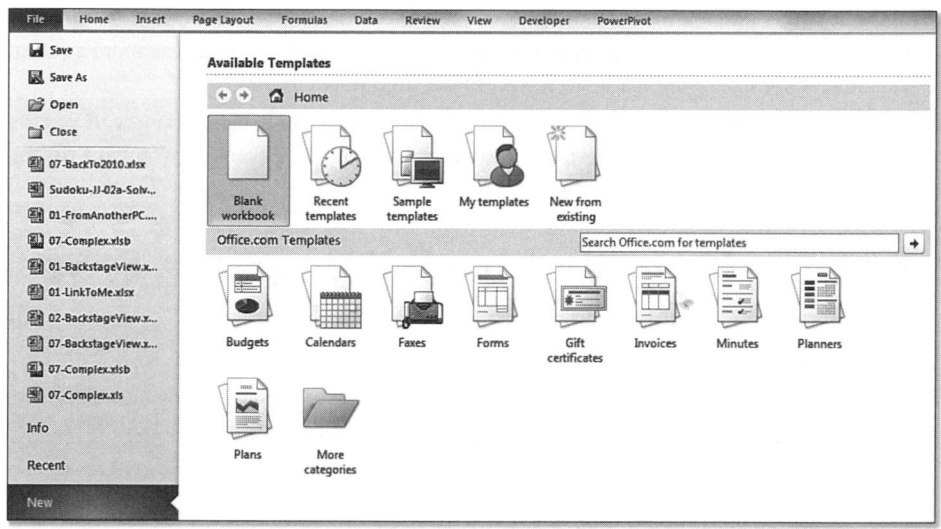

Figure 1.15
Print Preview and printer settings are combined in Backstage view.

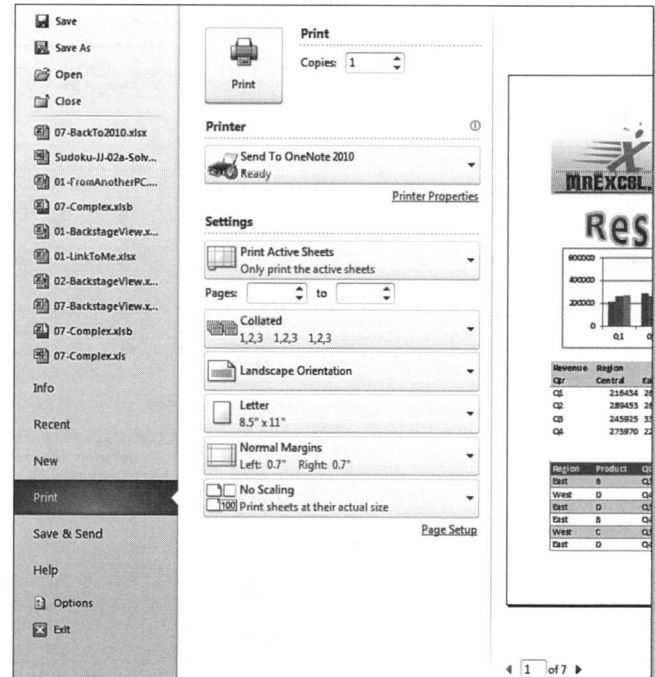

Microsoft created a brand new type of gallery for the Print section of Backstage view. Rather than have a drop-down for Orientation, this new gallery shows you the current Orientation setting. If you need to change the orientation, you can open the drop-down to access more settings. But if the setting is correct, you don't have to access the drop-down at all.

Note that Ctrl+P now brings you to the Printing gallery in Backstage view. If you want to do QuickPrint, you should add the QuickPrint icon to the Quick Access Toolbar.**Printing is covered in detail in Chapter 36, "Printing."**

Sharing Your Workbook Using Save & Send

The Save & Send gallery in Backstage view offers several categories of changes. Each item in the central pane leads to more choices in the right pane.

Figure 1.16 shows Send Using E-Mail. The right pane offers choices to attach the workbook to an email, send as PDF, send as XPS, or send as Internet Fax.

The Save to Web allows you to save your workbook to your Windows Live account.

Save to Sharepoint allows you to save your document to your company's SharePoint library.

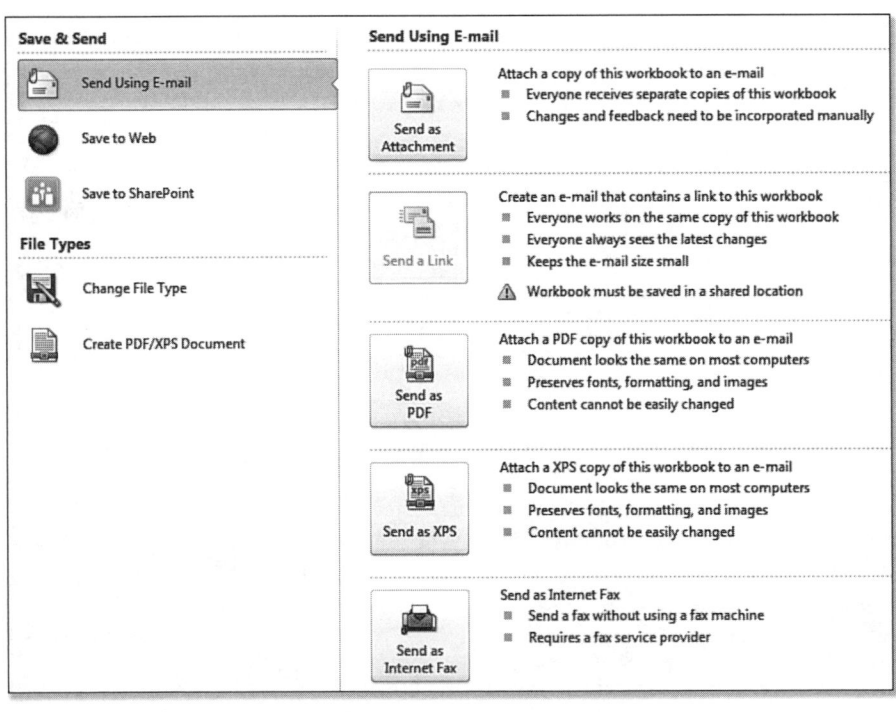

Figure 1.16
Attach your workbook to an email.

Change File Type offers to let you convert your file to an Excel 97-2003 workbook, an OpenDocument Spreadsheet, a binary workbook, or other file types (see Figure 1.17).

Finally, Create PDF/XPS Document allows you to save your workbook as an Adobe PDF file or the competing XPS format from Microsoft.

Figure 1.17
Convert your file to one of several file types.

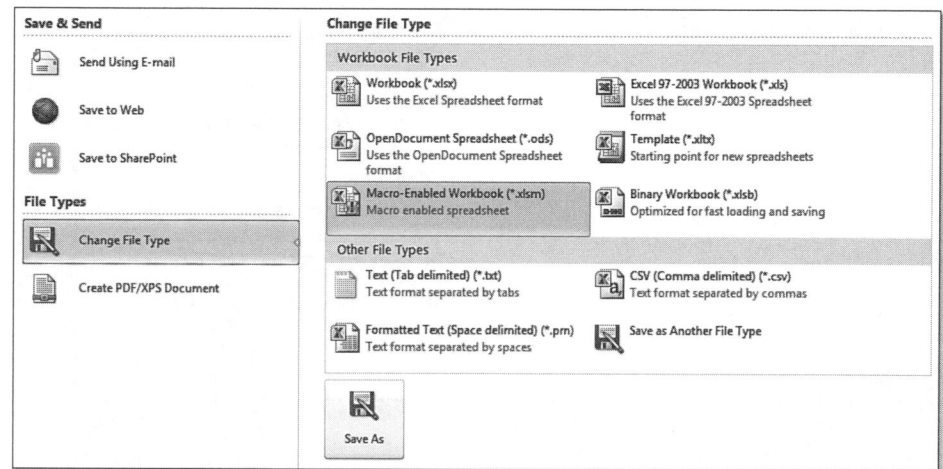

Getting Updates and Help

You can access Excel help at any time by pressing F1 or by clicking the blue question mark in the top-right corner of the Excel screen.

If you go to the Help gallery in Backstage view, you have access to Help, Getting Started, Contact Us, Options, and Check for Updates.

Help is the same as clicking the blue Question Mark icon.

Options is the same as using Options in the left navigation pane.

The right side of the screen tells you if your version of Excel has been activated or if you are in a trial. You can access your product key and product version using this panel (see Figure 1.18).

There are many benefits to the new Backstage view with only a few drawbacks. Those drawbacks, such as requiring an extra click to get to the Recent Files list, usually have workarounds. You should find that the Backstage view will receive a better welcome than the initial backlash against the Ribbon.

Support

Microsoft Office Help
Get help using Microsoft Office.

Getting Started
See what's new and find resources to help you
learn the basics quickly.

Contact Us
Let us know if you need help or how we can make
Office better.

Tools for Working With Office

Options
Customize language, display, and other program
settings.

Check for Updates
Get the latest updates available for Microsoft
Office.

Product Activation Required
Microsoft Office Professional Plus 2010
This product contains Microsoft Access, Microsoft Excel,
OneNote, Microsoft Outlook, Microsoft PowerPoint, Mic
InfoPath.

Change Product Key

⚠ This product is unlicensed. Connect to your corpora
for further assistance.

About Microsoft Excel

Version: 14.0.4723.1000 (64-bit)
Additional Version and Copyright Information
Part of Microsoft Office Professional Plus 2010
© 2010 Microsoft Corporation. All rights reserved.
Microsoft Customer Services and Support
Product ID: 02260-018-0000106-48123
Microsoft Software License Terms

Figure 1.18
Get updates, find
your current ver-
sion, or activate
Office on the Help
panel.

2

THE RIBBON INTERFACE AND QUICK ACCESS TOOLBAR

If you have upgraded directly to Excel 2010 from Excel 2003 or earlier, you are going through the shock of discovering that the familiar File, Edit, View, Insert, Format, Tools, Data, Window, and Help menus, along with the Standard and Formatting toolbars, are gone from Excel 2010.

In their place, Microsoft introduces the Ribbon.

Using the Ribbon

The Ribbon is composed of seven permanent tabs labeled Home, Insert, Page Layout, Formulas, Data, Review, and View.

Each tab is broken into rectangular groups of related commands. The group shown in Figure 2.1 is the Clipboard group.

 note

Figure 2.1 shows a bit of detail of the left side of the Home tab of the Ribbon.

The mantra of the Ribbon is to use Pictures and Words. Many people have seen the little Whisk Broom icon in previous versions of Office but never knew what it did. If you hover over the icon in Excel 2003, the ToolTip tells you that it was the Format Painter, which at least gave you a place to start looking in the Help file if you were really curious.

In Excel 2010, the same icon has the words "Format Painter" next to the icon. When you hover, the ToolTip offers paragraphs explaining what the tool does. The ToolTip offers a little-known trick: You can double-click the Format Painter to copy the formatting to many places. The ToolTip offers a link to the help topic about the Format Painter. All these steps are designed to help more people find and make use of the Format Painter tool.

In Figure 2.1, the Cut icon is a pure command. You click the icon and Excel cuts the selection onto the Clipboard.

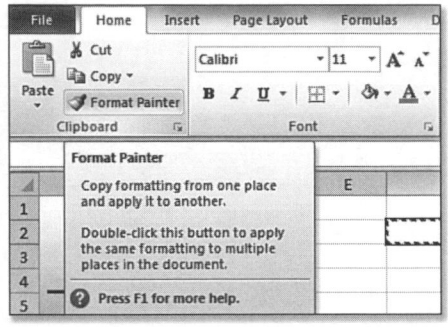

Figure 2.1
Detail of the Clipboard group of the Home tab of the Ribbon.

In contrast, the Paste and Copy icons are a new type of element in that each represents a hybrid command. Figure 2.2 is shot with the mouse pointer hovering over the Paste icon. You see that this icon is actually two icons. The top half of the icon is the actual Paste command. The bottom half of the icon is a drop-down menu offering other types of Paste commands (see Figure 2.3).

Figure 2.2
The Paste icon is actually two icons; a Paste command and a Paste drop-down.

Figure 2.3
Click the bottom of the Paste icon to access more paste options.

Using Dialog Launchers and the 80/20 Rule

The Ribbon is designed to make it easier to discover features that should be used by most people using Excel. It is not designed to hold every command available in Microsoft Excel. In many cases, even the middle-of-the-road Exceller needs to go beyond the commands on the Ribbon.

A special symbol in the lower-right corner of many Ribbon groups takes you directly to the dialog box with many more choices than those offered in the Ribbon.

Figure 2.4 shows detail of the Number group of the Home tab. In the lower-right corner is a tiny symbol. The symbol is the top-left corner of a box, with an arrow pointing downward to the right. This symbol is called a dialog launcher.

Figure 2.4
The dialog launcher takes you to additional options.

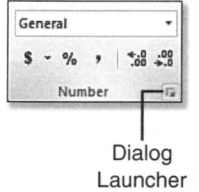

Dialog
Launcher

When you click the dialog launcher, you go to a dialog box that often offers many more choices than those available in the Ribbon. In Figure 2.5, you see the Number tab of the Format Cells dialog.

Dialog launchers are not the only way to access dialog boxes. Flyout menus and galleries offer their own way to reach dialog boxes.

Figure 2.5
Click the dialog launcher to get to the full dialog box with all the choices.

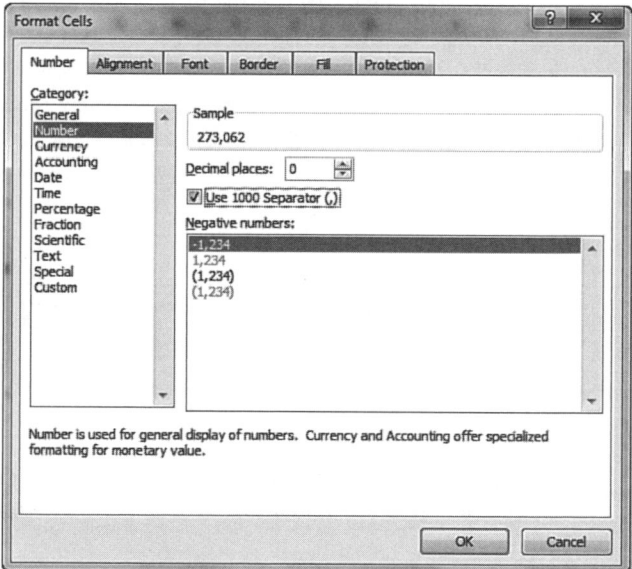

Using Flyout Menus and Galleries

The Ribbon introduces two new kinds of controls; visual flyout menus and galleries.

Figure 2.6 shows the visual flyout menu that appears when you open the Conditional Formatting drop-down on the Home tab. You can see that the initial menu continues to offer pictures and words, with words next to the icons for Data Bars, Color Scales, and Icon Sets. When you hover over a selection, a flyout menu appears with more visual choices (see Figure 2.6).

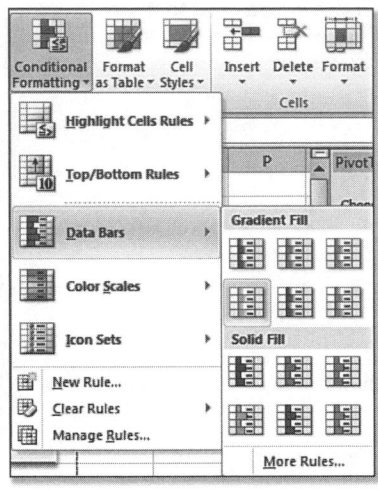

Figure 2.6
The flyout menus continue the theme of offering pictures and words.

Note the More Rules option at the bottom of the Data Bars menu. The More command occurs at the bottom of many flyout menus. When you see More, you will know that the menu is offering you only a subset of options. Click More to access all the options.

Another new element in the Ribbon is the gallery control. Galleries are used when there are dozens of options from which to choose. The gallery shows you a visual thumbnail of each choice.

In Figure 2.7, you see the first row of choices in the Table Styles gallery. Notice the three arrows at the right end of the gallery.

Figure 2.7
A gallery control starts by showing one row of thumbnails but offers three arrow controls at the right end.

You can use the up-arrow and down-arrow icons to browse through the gallery one row at a time. Or you can press the third arrow to open the entire gallery and see all the choices, as shown in Figure 2.8.

Again, at the bottom of Figure 2.8, you have additional choices for New Table Style. This leads to a dialog box with all the options around table styles.

Figure 2.8
If you open the gallery control, you can
scroll through more choices.

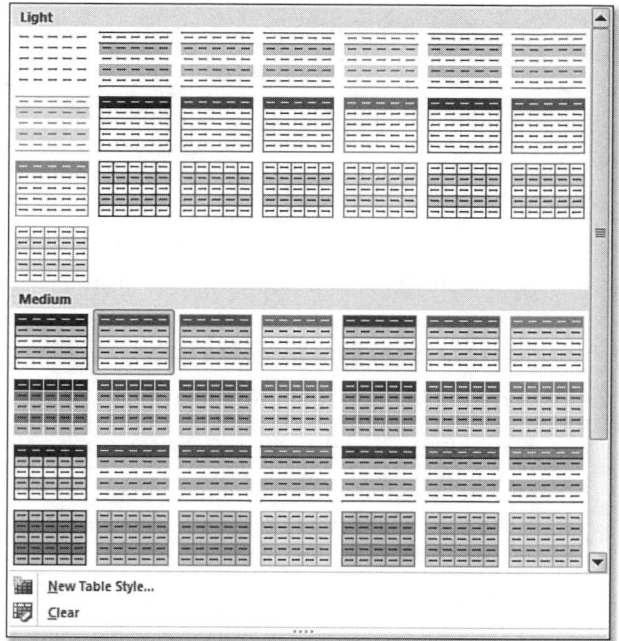

The Ribbon Is Constantly Changing

Although you start out with Ribbon tabs for File, Home, Insert, Page Layout, Formulas, Data,
Review, and View, you constantly see other tabs appearing and disappearing. Further, as you resize
your Excel window, the icons change and resize.

Harnessing Contextual Ribbon Tabs

Excel 2010 offers a whole series of commands for dealing with photographs that you insert into your
worksheet. However, 90% of the people never bother to dress up their worksheets with clip art or
pictures, so there really is no reason to show all the commands for working with photographs in the
Ribbon.

There is one persistent command in the Ribbon that deals with pictures. You can use the Picture
command on the Insert tab of the Ribbon to insert a picture.

After you use that command to insert a picture, and provided that the picture is selected, a new tab
called Picture Tools Format appears. This tab offers a gallery with all sorts of tools for changing the
appearance of the picture. See Figure 2.9 for some detail from the Picture Tools Format tab.

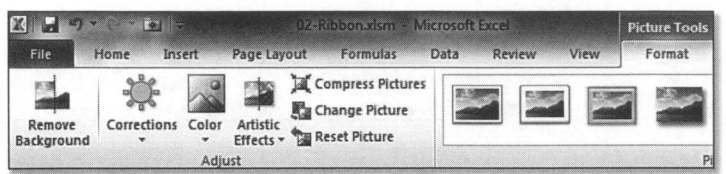

Here is the frustrating thing. As soon as you click outside of the picture, the picture is no longer selected and the Picture Tools Format tab disappears.

If you need to format an object and you cannot find the icons for formatting the object, try clicking the object to see if the contextual tabs appear.

These are the context-sensitive tabs:

- **Add-Ins**—This tab contains any menu items added through VBA macros or add-ins. This tab appears when an add-in is loaded.

- **Background Removal**—This tab is new in Excel 2010 and is used to remove the background from a photograph. To access the tab, use the Background Removal icon on the Picture Tools tab.

- **Chart Tools**—The Chart Tools tab includes three tabs: Design, Layout, and Format. The Design tab provides features to change an entire chart. By the time you get to the Format tab, you are micromanaging small aspects of a chart.

- **Drawing Tools**—This includes a Format tab for working with shapes. To access the tab, select Insert, Shapes.

- **Equation Tools**—The Design tab appears when you use the Equation Editor.

- **Header & Footer**—This tab appears when you edit the header or footer for a page in Page Layout view. To access the tab, you click View, Page Layout View and then click in either the header or footer zone. Note that there is a shortcut to Page Layout View, located to the left of the zoom slider, in the lower-right corner of the screen.

- **Ink Tools**—This tab contains Pens commands for tablet PCs.

- **Picture Tools**—This tab is available after you insert clip art or an image and select the illustration.

- **Pivot Chart Tools**—After you insert a pivot chart, four new tabs are available: Design, Layout, Format, and Analyze. The first three of these tabs are similar to the Chart Tools tabs. The fourth contains the pivot table features.

- **PivotTable Tools**—This includes two tabs: Options and Design. The major settings appear on the Options tab. Formatting options appear on the Design tab.

- **Print Preview Tools**—This small tab appears as the only tab when you are in Print Preview mode. Because Print Preview moved to the Backstage view, this tab will be very elusive.

- **Slicer Tools**—The Options tab appears whenever one of the new Excel 2010 visual filters for pivot tables is selected.

- **SmartArt Tools**—In Excel 2010, the former business diagrams has been renamed SmartArt. When you are working with organization charts or other SmartArt diagrams, two new tabs are available: Design and Format.

- **Sparkline Tools**—The Design tab appears whenever the current selection is in a sparkline. Sparklines are tiny, word-sized charts that debuted in Excel 2010.

- **Table Tools**—The Design tab allows for the formatting of a database in Excel after it has been converted to a table. In Excel 2010, tables replace Excel 2003 lists.

All these contextual tabs come and go as you select and clear certain items in Excel.

Resizing Excel Changes the Ribbon

You need a monitor with a 1440-pixel-wide resolution to see the entirety of the Ribbon. Anytime that you view the Ribbon at a smaller size, Excel starts intelligently collapsing icons on the Ribbon.

Figure 2.10 shows the Styles and the Cells group of the Home tab at a 1280 resolution. At this resolution, the Cell Styles gallery visible at 1440 resolution has already collapsed into a large drop-down icon.

Figure 2.10
At 1280 resolution, the Styles and Cells groups appear as six large drop-down icons.

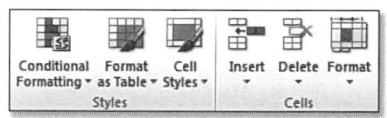

At a smaller resolution, the size of the six icons gets smaller, but you still have words, as shown in Figure 2.11.

Figure 2.11
At smaller resolutions, the icons shrink.

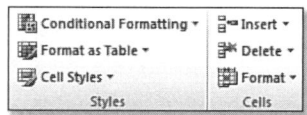

Eventually, those groups shrink into a single drop-down for the entire group, as shown in Figure 2.12.

Figure 2.12
Eventually, the entire group collapses to a single drop-down.

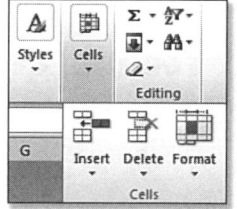

If you continue to shrink the width of the Excel window, the Ribbon disappears altogether, as shown in Figure 2.13.

Figure 2.13

Below 300 pixels of width, Microsoft figures that you are not working in the application anymore and hides the Ribbon entirely.

 To see the Ribbon changing when the window is resized, search for Excel In Depth 2 at YouTube.

Solving Common Ribbon Problems

Here are some common complaints about the Ribbon and some advice on how to best deal with these issues.

You Cannot Find a Particular Command on the Ribbon

Here are some tips for working with the Ribbon:

- Start on the Home tab. All the commands on the old Formatting toolbar are here, as well as most of the old Insert and Format menus.

- Pivot tables moved from the Data tab to the Insert tab. They don't belong here. They belong on the Data tab with all the other commands from the old Data menu.

- The four most popular commands on the Excel 2003 Insert menu are no longer on the Insert tab. Insert Cells, Insert Rows, Insert Columns, and Insert Worksheet are all now found under the Insert drop-down in the Cells group of the Home tab.

- Commands from the old Tools menu are generally found on the Review tab.

- Commands from the old Window menu are generally found on the View tab.

- Macro commands are on a Developer tab of the Ribbon that is hidden by default. See Chapter 4, "Customizing the Ribbon," for how to bring the Developer tab back.

You Still Cannot Find the Command on the Ribbon

Following are many strategies for finding the command:

- If you remember the old Excel 2003 keyboard accelerators, try typing those. For example, Alt+E+I+J still invokes Edit, Fill, Justify, even though there is no longer an Edit tab on the Ribbon.

- Right-click the Ribbon and select Customize. In the Customize dialog, select All Commands from the left drop-down. Scroll through the list of all commands until you find the command. Hover

over the command. A ToolTip appears, showing you where you can find the command. In Figure 2.14, the Justify command is located on the Home tab, in the Editing Group, under the Fill drop-down.

Figure 2.14
This ToolTip in the Customize dialog shows you where to find a command.

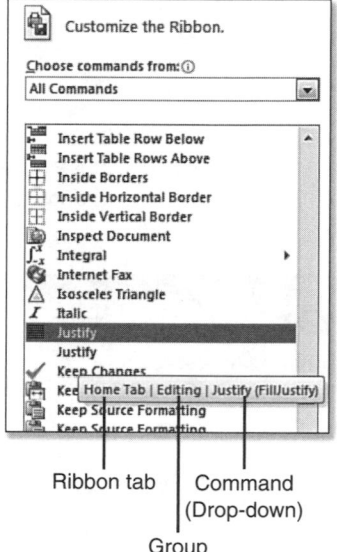

Ribbon tab | Command
(Drop-down)

Group

- Download my full-color tip card that maps every old command in the Excel 2003 menu and toolbars to a Ribbon tab. You can access the tip card at http://www.mrexcel.com/excel2007tip-card.html.

- Microsoft has an interactive Ribbon guide that can help you locate an Excel 2003 menu command on the Ribbon. Type Interactive Ribbon guide in any search engine to find the latest incarnation of the Ribbon guide.

> **note**
> Sometimes, a command truly is not in the Ribbon. If you hover over a command in the Customize dialog and it indicates that it is a command that is not in the Ribbon, you will have to use Customize to add this command to the Quick Access Toolbar or to the Ribbon.

The Ribbon Takes Up Too Many Rows

I don't want to argue with you, but the new Ribbon only appears to take up a lot of space. It does not take up more space than the Excel 2003 menu, formatting, and standard toolbars (provided you showed those toolbars on two rows).

However, you can minimize the Ribbon using one of these techniques:

Click the Caret icon on the right side of the Ribbon, just to the left of help (see Figure 2.15).

Right-click the Ribbon and select Minimize the Ribbon.

Figure 2.15
Caret icon to minimize the Ribbon.

When the Ribbon is minimized, you see only the words Home, Insert, Page Layout, and so on (see Figure 2.16). After you click a tab, the Ribbon temporarily reappears. When you finish selecting a command, the Ribbon goes back to the minimized size.

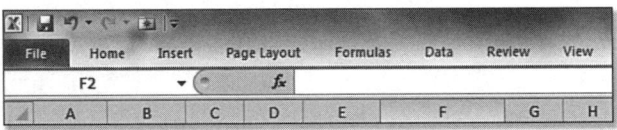

Figure 2.16
When the Ribbon is minimized, you see only the tab names.

You Do Not Like Where Something Is Located on the Ribbon

I am with you on this one. Pivot Tables belong on the Data tab, not on the Insert tab. Further, if you could take the left half of the Home tab and combine it with the right half of the Data tab, most people would hardly ever have to leave that one tab.

The great news in Excel 2010 is that you can now customize the Ribbon.

➡ *See Chapter 4 to learn more about customizing the Ribbon.*

You Cannot See All Your Favorite Commands at Once

A problem with the Ribbon is that only one-seventh of the commands are visible at any given time. You will find yourself moving from one tab to another. The alternative is to use the Quick Access Toolbar.

Using the Quick Access Toolbar

The Quick Access Toolbar is a customizable toolbar. It remains visible, no matter which tab is currently displayed. Because the Quick Access Toolbar is always visible, you can store your most used commands and have them always visible.

There are probably a handful of toolbar buttons that you use constantly. For me, the list would be Sort Ascending, Print, Filter by Selection, Align Right, Open Recent Files, and Decrease Decimal. If you tried to locate these five commands, you would find that they are spread throughout the Ribbon interface.

Luckily, the Quick Access Toolbar comes to the rescue. The Quick Access Toolbar holds up to 90 of your favorite icons. It is always visible on the screen, so you can access its icons without needing to change to a different tab.

Changing the Location of the Quick Access Toolbar

The Quick Access Toolbar is initially displayed above the left side of the ribbon. Initially, the menu offers Save, Undo, Redo, and Quick Print icons. Figure 2.17 shows the initial location and configuration of the Quick Access Toolbar.

Figure 2.17
The default location of the Quick Access Toolbar is above the Ribbon.

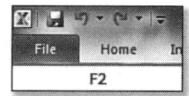

The other option is to display the Quick Access Toolbar immediately below the Ribbon. To do so, click the drop-down arrow at the right edge of the Quick Access Toolbar. Then select Show Below the Ribbon, as shown in Figure 2.18.

Figure 2.18
You can move the Quick Access Toolbar below the Ribbon.

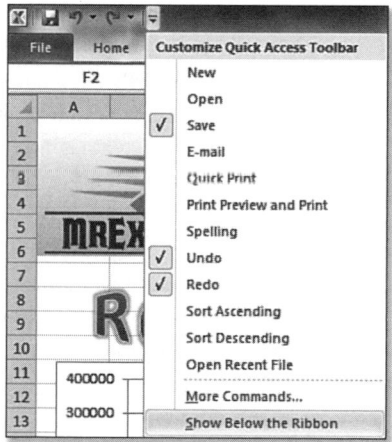

When the Quick Access Toolbar is below the Ribbon, you can use a similar method to move the Quick Access Toolbar back above the Ribbon: Click the drop-down on the right side of the Quick Access Toolbar and select Show Above the Ribbon.

Adding Favorite Commands to the Quick Access Toolbar

The drop-down shown in Figure 2.18 offers 12 popular commands that you might choose to add to the Quick Access Toolbar. Of my six desired icons, three are already available in that list.

When you find a command in the Ribbon that you are likely to use often, you can add the command to the Quick Access Toolbar. To do so, right-click any command in the Ribbon and select Add to Quick Access Toolbar. For example, to add Align Right to the Quick Access Toolbar, follow these steps:

1. Access the Home tab.

2. Right-click the Align Right icon.

3. Select Add to Quick Access Toolbar.

Items added to the Quick Access Toolbar using the right-click method are added to the right side of the Quick Access Toolbar.

Knowing Which Commands Can Be on the Quick Access Toolbar

You can add commands to the Quick Access Toolbar, but you cannot add the contents of many lists on the Ribbon. Figuring out what you can and cannot add to the Quick Access Toolbar requires a bit of experimentation.

For example, consider the Orientation icon in the Alignment group of the Home tab. You can use this icon to angle text counterclockwise. The icon also contains a drop-down that has a total of six commands: Angle Counterclockwise, Angle Clockwise, Vertical Text, Rotate Text Up, Rotate Text Down, and Alignment. If you right-click the Alignment icon and choose to add it to the Quick Access Toolbar, the entire icon, along with the drop-down of six commands, is added.

If you don't want to add the entire drop-down to the Quick Access Toolbar, you can instead open the drop-down and right-click one of the six items. Just this individual command is added to the Quick Access Toolbar.

However, other drop-downs are not drop-downs of commands. Instead, they may lead to drop-downs with list boxes. For example, consider the font size drop-down. It is possible to add the entire font size drop-down as an icon on the Quick Access Toolbar, but it is not possible to add to the Quick Access Toolbar individual items from the list. You can add the drop-down itself, but you cannot, for example, add to the Quick Access Toolbar an item that changes the font to 16 points.

If you right-click an item in a list and the context menu doesn't offer the ability to add it to the Quick Access Toolbar, this is probably not a real command.

Removing Commands from the Quick Access Toolbar

You can remove an icon from the Quick Access Toolbar by right-clicking the icon and selecting Remove from Quick Access Toolbar.

You can also remove icons by using the Excel Options dialog, as discussed in the following section.

Customizing the Quick Access Toolbar

You can make minor changes to the Quick Access Toolbar by using the context menus, but you can have far more control over the Quick Access Toolbar if you use the Customize command. You right-click the Quick Access Toolbar and select Customize Quick Access Toolbar to display the Quick Access Toolbar section of the Excel Options dialog, as shown in Figure 2.19.

The Excel Options dialog offers many features for customizing the Quick Access Toolbar:

You can choose to customize the Quick Access Toolbar for all documents on your computer or just for the current document.

You can add separators between icons to group the icons logically.

You can resequence the order of the icons on the toolbar.

You can access 1,286 commands, including the commands from every tab and commands that are not available in the Ribbon.

You can reset the Quick Access Toolbar to its original default state.

You can move the Quick Access Toolbar to appear above or below the Ribbon.

Figure 2.19
You can completely customize the Quick Access Toolbar using the Excel Options dialog.

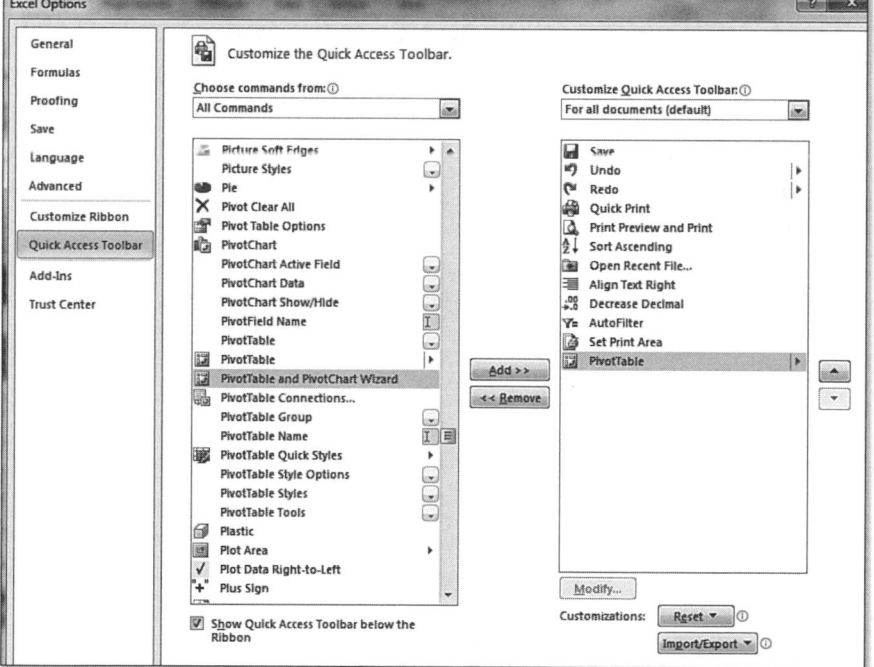

Using the Excel Options to Customize the Quick Access Toolbar for All Workbooks

In the default state, the Customize Quick Access Toolbar drop-down in the Excel Options dialog is set to For All Documents (Default). This means that any changes you make to the Quick Access Toolbar will apply to all Excel documents opened on this computer.

Initially, the Choose Commands From drop-down shows Popular commands. This drop-down lists every tab, plus two useful selections. If you select All Commands, you get an alphabetical list of every possible command. If you select Commands Not in the Ribbon, you see only the commands that you might have used in Excel 2003, but did not make it to a tab.

To add a new icon to the Quick Access Toolbar for all workbooks, follow these steps:

1. Choose the proper command subset from the Choose Commands From drop-down.

2. Select the icon in the Choose Commands From list box. You might have to scroll to see the complete list.

3. Click the Add button to add the command to the Customize Quick Access Toolbar.

The top choice in each category is a value called <Separator>. You can add this to the Customize Quick Access Toolbar list to create a vertical bar between icons on the Quick Access Toolbar.

Customizing Icons for the Current Workbook Only

Suppose you have 10 icons on your Quick Access Toolbar for all workbooks. If you add additional icons for this workbook only, the icons appear after the 10 icons for all workbooks. To add these additional icons, follow these steps.

1. Right-click the Quick Access Toolbar or most places in the Ribbon and select Customize Quick Access Toolbar.

2. With the Customize Quick Access Toolbar drop-down set to For All Documents, select the <Separator> icon at the top of the Choose Commands From list box. Click Add to add a vertical line at the end of the "all workbooks" section of the Quick Access Toolbar.

3. From the Customize Quick Access Toolbar drop-down, select For (This Workbook Name).

4. Use the Choose Commands From drop-down to find particular categories.

5. Select an icon in the Customize Quick Access Toolbar list.

6. Click the Add button.

7. Repeat steps 4–6 as needed.

8. Click OK to complete the operation.

 tip

If you are going to use icons for all workbooks and additional icons for this workbook only, you might want to end the workbook icons with a separator to help identify where the icons for this workbook only begin.

When you finish with this process, the Quick Access Toolbar shows the icons that apply to all workbooks, a vertical separator, and then icons that apply only to the current workbook.

If you have the current workbook open and then switch to another open workbook, the icons assigned to the current workbook are hidden. If you arrange the windows so that you can see many workbooks at the same time, the icons for the current workbook stay visible as long as the workbook is active.

Filling Up the Quick Access Toolbar

The Quick Access Toolbar allows about 90 icons and/or separators. This is more than will fit across the screen on most monitors. If the monitor is not large enough to display all the icons, the first 54 of them are shown onscreen, and the rest are hidden behind a double arrow at the right edge of the Quick Access Toolbar.

Rearranging Icons on the Quick Access Toolbar

You can rearrange icons on the Quick Access Toolbar by using the Excel Options dialog. Select any icon from the Customize Quick Access Toolbar list box and then use the up-arrow or down-arrow buttons on the far right side of the dialog to move the icon up or down.

Resetting the Quick Access Toolbar

If you start a new job and inherit someone else's computer, you might want to start with a fresh slate of icons on the Quick Access Toolbar. To reset the Quick Access Toolbar to the default configuration, follow these steps:

1. With the Customize Quick Access Toolbar drop-down set to For All Documents (Default), click the Reset button at the bottom of the Customize Quick Access Toolbar list box. A warning box asks if you want to reset the list for all workbooks.

2. Click OK, and the list returns to the three default icons (Save, Undo, and Repeat).

3. With the Customize Quick Access Toolbar drop-down set to For (This Workbook), click the Reset button at the bottom of the Customize Quick Access Toolbar list box. A warning box asks if you want to reset the list for this particular document.

4. Click OK, and the list clears.

Assigning VBA Macros to Quick Access Toolbar Buttons

Typically, a VBA macro is assigned to a shortcut key. In legacy versions of Excel, it was easy to customize the menu system to add commands to invoke macros. In legacy versions of Excel, more than 4,000 different icons were available for the various custom menu items.

 note

I am not sure why you would choose to use the Print icon for your macros. Considering that you used to have 4,096 choices and now have only 180 choices, this is another area where Excel 2010 does not live up to the legacy versions.

Excel 2010 offers a weak interface for adding custom macros to the Quick Access Toolbar. In the Excel Options dialog is a drop-down called Macros. If you select this group, you see all public macros in all open workbooks. You can select a macro and click Add to add that macro to the Quick Access Toolbar.

Initially, every macro added to the Quick Access Toolbar gets an identical icon. However, you can select an icon in the Customize Quick Access Toolbar list box and click the Modify button. The Modify Button dialog box that appears allows you to choose from 55 available icons for a macro. Most of these buttons are similar to icons that are already popular. For example, the Print icon is fairly well known and has a meaning. In addition to choosing from the 55 icons, you can type any text for a display name, as shown in Figure 2.20. The display name does not appear next to the button. But if you hover your mouse over the icon on the Quick Access Toolbar, you can see the display name in a ToolTip.

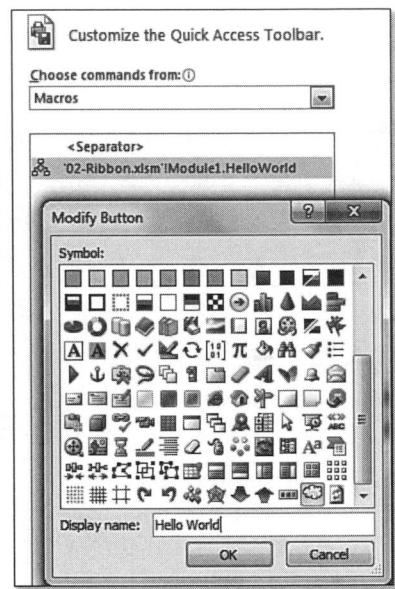

Figure 2.20
For macros, you can customize the button image and add a display name on the Quick Access Toolbar.

Troubleshooting Excel: The Downside of the Quick Access Toolbar

Although the Quick Access toolbar is cool, it has a few drawbacks compared to the legacy versions of Excel.

In legacy versions of Excel, you could choose to display an icon, words, or words and an icon for items that you added to the custom toolbar. With Excel 2010, you are pretty much limited to just icons. When Microsoft explained the need for the Ribbon, it was pretty confident that pictures and words were far superior to just pictures. It seems curious that they deprecated the ability to put words on the customizable Quick Access toolbar.

With legacy versions of Excel, holding down Shift while clicking an icon usually invoked the reverse of the icon. For example, clicking Shift+Sort Ascending would perform Sort Descending. This functionality has been removed from Excel 2010.

With legacy versions of Excel, you could easily have multiple custom toolbars, and those toolbars could be docked to any side of the screen or floating above your worksheet. With Excel 2010, you have limited customizations to the ribbon and the Quick Access Toolbar. The location of these elements must always be above the worksheet.

USING OTHER EXCEL INTERFACE IMPROVEMENTS

Although the Backstage view is likely to be the most talked-about features in the Excel 2010 interface, many of these changes added to Excel 2007 will be dramatic if you are upgrading from Excel 2003:

- **Live Preview**—You can preview formatting changes before you actually select the change.

- **Paste Options**—A newly expanded Paste Options menu will introduce many new popular shortcut key sequences to Excel.

- **Mini toolbar**—The mini toolbar appears whenever you select text. Although this may happen rarely when you edit cells in Excel, it does happen frequently when you work with charts, text boxes, and so on. The mini toolbar offers quick access to font, size, bold, italics, alignment, color, indenting, and bullets.

- **Formula bar**—The formula bar includes the capability to expand or contract itself at your whim instead of the whim of Excel.

- **Zoom slider**—The Zoom slider allows you to quickly change from seeing one page to hundreds of pages at a time.

- **Status bar**—The status bar appears at the bottom of your worksheet window. Although you probably never noticed it, the status bar in legacy versions of Excel reported the total of any selected cells. This information is now improved and expanded in Excel 2010.

- **View control**—The View control gives you one-click access to Page Break Preview mode, Normal mode, and the new Page Layout view.

- **New Sheet icon**—The New Sheet icon allows you to add new worksheets to a workbook with a single click.

Using Live Preview

Live Preview provides an answer to the question, "What would this menu selection look like in the worksheet?"

If you open a drop-down list from the Ribbon, Live Preview is often enabled. As you hover over various items in the list, the selected cells in the worksheet automatically preview what they would look like if you selected that option.

When you hover over a different selection, Live Preview quickly changes to reflect the new selection. Figure 3.1 shows a Live Preview of some text in the Copperplate Gothic Bold font.

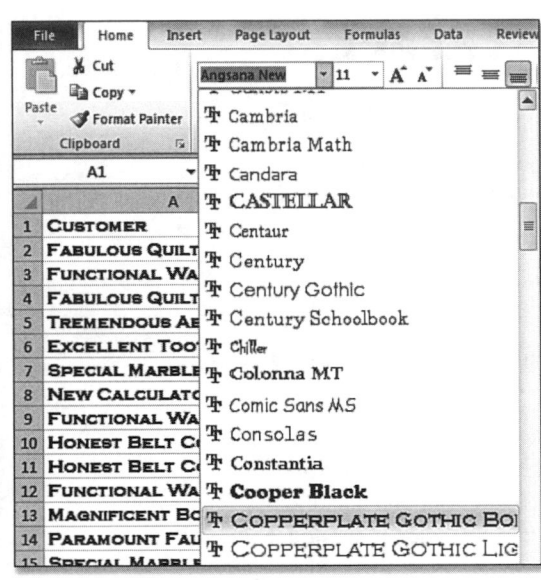

Figure 3.1
If you hover for a second over one font, Excel shows a preview of the font in the selected cells.

The preview shown with Live Preview is not permanent. If you hover over another item, the view of the workbook changes. In the process of scrolling down to the Showcard Gothic font shown in Figure 3.2, for example, Excel flips through dozens of previews of the data.

If you close the list box without clicking an item, the workbook reverts to the original style.

The Live Preview feature works with items as mundane as the font size and font face drop-downs. It also works with many features, such as table format and conditional formatting color scales.

There are a few items with which Live Preview does not work. When you try to decide on a chart type, for example, Live Preview is not enabled. This is because Excel would actually have to add an object to the sheet to show you the preview. There are also a few drop-downs where Live Preview doesn't work. Microsoft figures you know what an underline or double underline would look like, so this drop-down does not allow Live Preview.

You can choose to turn off Live Preview if it annoys you. To do this, select File, Options. The second check box in Excel options allows you to turn off Live Preview.

Figure 3.2
If you move to a new font the preview changes.

Previewing Paste Using the Paste Options Gallery

Here is a quick survey: Have you ever opened a Notepad window, pasted your data to Notepad, copied from Notepad, and then pasted to your application? This is a great way to remove formatting from a selection. If you have discovered that painful workaround, you are going to love this next feature that was added to Excel 2010.

Here is another survey: Suppose that you have to copy a column of formulas and paste it as Values. Do your fingers know how to do Ctrl+C, Alt+E+S+V+Enter? If so, you are going to love the new Ctrl+V, Ctrl, V keystrokes available in the Paste Options Gallery. If you've ever done Ctrl+C, Alt+E+S+V+Enter, Alt+E+S+T+Enter, you will love the new Context+E keyboard shortcut.

As someone who uses both of those old keyboard shortcuts frequently, I love the new Paste Options gallery. You can keep Slicers, Sparklines, even PowerPivot; the Paste Options gallery is going to be the one feature that makes a difference in my life every single hour of every single workday.

Microsoft discovered that Paste was the number one command that was immediately followed by Undo. To improve the Paste command, Microsoft added three paste options galleries to Excel 2010. These galleries support live preview and keyboard shortcuts. They should make mouse-centric and keyboard-centric people very happy.

You encounter the gallery when you have something on the Clipboard and one of these three events happens:

- You right-click a cell to access the context menu.

- You open the Paste drop-down from the Home tab.

- After performing a typical Paste operation, the old Paste Repair menu icon appears with the tip that you can press Ctrl to access the gallery.

Accessing the Gallery After Doing a Paste

Suppose that you copy a range with Ctrl+C and then Paste with Ctrl+V. The icon for the old Paste Repair appears next to the paste, but this time it notes that you can open the menu by pressing Ctrl. When you press Ctrl, you are presented with a gallery of paste options, as shown in Figure 3.3.

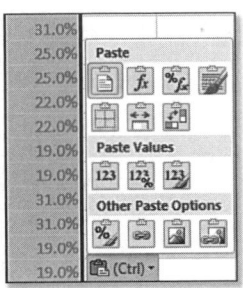

Figure 3.3
The gallery offers 14 different ways to paste the data. An elusive 15th icon appears when your pasted data includes conditional formatting.

Every one of those icons has a descriptive ToolTip and a keyboard accelerator. Figure 3.4 shows that the keyboard accelerator for doing Paste Values and then Paste Formats is E. This means that you can use my new favorite keyboard sequence: Ctrl+V to paste, Ctrl to open the paste options gallery, E to paste values and formatting.

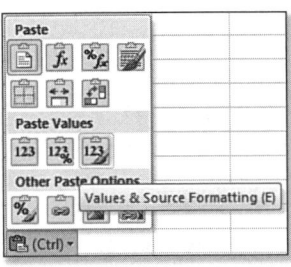

Figure 3.4
Every icon has a shortcut key.

Table 3.1 lists the shortcut keys for the icons in the gallery.

Table 3.1   Keyboard Shortcuts for Paste Options

Icon	Key	Action
	P	Paste
	F	Formulas
	O	Formulas & Number Formatting
	K	Keep Source Formatting

Icon	Key	Action
	B	No Borders
	W	Column Widths
	T	Transpose
	V	Values
	A	Values and Number Formatting
	E	Values & Source Formatting
	R	Formats
	N	Paste Link
	U	Paste as Picture
	I	Paste as Linked Picture
(Ctrl) ▾	S	Opens Paste Special

In case you have not run into some of these options before, here is a quick synopsis of each option:

- **Paste**—This is the standard paste that you would get using Ctrl+V.

- **Formulas**—asto only formulas but no formatting. This is common when you are copying down from the first row of a table that has an outline border. To prevent the top border from copying, you can paste Formulas. You then find that you have to reapply the number formatting.

- **Formulas & Number Formatting**—Copies formulas as previous formulas, along with the number formatting.

- **Keep Source Formatting**—This is particularly useful when copying from another application such as a web page. The formatting from the other application will be pasted along with the values.

- **No Borders**—Paste everything but the borders.

- **Column Widths**—Include the column widths from the copied area.

- **Transpose**—Turn the data on its side. A 12-row by 1 column copied range would paste as 1 row by 12 columns.

- **Values**—Convert formulas to values.

- **Values and Number Formatting**—Convert the formulas to values and include the number formats from the copied data.

- **Values & Source Formatting**—Convert the formulas to values and include all formatting such as cell styles, font color, number formatting, and borders.

- **Formats**—Do not bring any values, only the cell formatting. Similar to using the Format Painter but not as annoying.

- **Paste Link**—Create formulas here that point back to the copied range.

- **Paste as Picture**—Paste a picture of the original cells in this location.

- **Paste as Linked Picture**—Paste a live picture of the original cell in this location. This is the elusive Camera tool from Excel 2003.

- **Open Paste Special**—Access the old Paste Special dialog. The Paste Special dialog still offers some choices not available in the Paste Options gallery: Comments, Validation, All using Source Theme, Add, Subtract, Multiply, Divide, and Skip Blanks. Figure 3.5 shows the Paste Special dialog.

 To see a demo of the Paste Options menu, search for Excel In Depth 3 on YouTube.

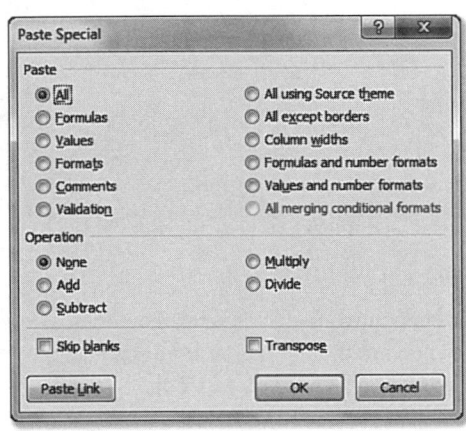

Figure 3.5
A few options in Paste Special are not covered in the Paste Options dialog.

Accessing the Paste Options Gallery from the Right-Click Menu

The Paste Options gallery appears in the right-click context menu and includes Live Preview. As shown in Figure 3.6, the top six options appear directly in the menu. A flyout menu offers all 14 options.

As you start to hover over the values options, Live Preview takes over. The rest of the context menu disappears so that you can see the worksheet. Hover over Transpose and you get a preview of what Transpose actually does (see Figure 3.7).

Hover over Formatting and you see that the formatting option copies only the cell formats and not the numbers (see Figure 3.8).

Figure 3.6
Right-click to access this menu.

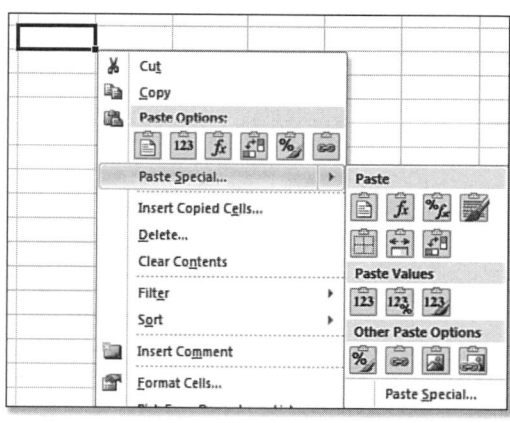

Figure 3.7
Hover over an icon to see a live preview of the paste.

▲	A	B	C	D	E	F
1						
2			Q1	Q2	Q3	Q4
3		East	25,366	26,525	20,784	20,904
4		Central	27,143	27,786	28,199	29,974
5		West	21,825	20,446	24,570	21,078
6		Total	74,334	74,757	73,553	71,956
7						
8						
9			East	Central	West	Total
10		Q1	25,366	27,143	21,825	74,334
11		Q2	26,525	27,786	20,446	74,757
12		Q3	2 Paste Options:			73,553
13		Q4	2			71,956
14						
15					Transpose (T)	
16						

Figure 3.8
Move to another icon to see how that paste would work.

▲	A	B	C	D	E	F
1						
2			Q1	Q2	Q3	Q4
3		East	25,366	26,525	20,784	20,904
4		Central	27,143	27,786	28,199	29,974
5		West	21,825	20,446	24,570	21,078
6		Total	74,334	74,757	73,553	71,956
7						
8						
9						
10						
11						
12			Paste Options:			
13						
14						
15					Formatting (R)	
16						

If you hover over Paste Special and then move out to the full gallery, all the context menu except the full gallery disappears, and Live Preview continues to work (see Figure 3.9).

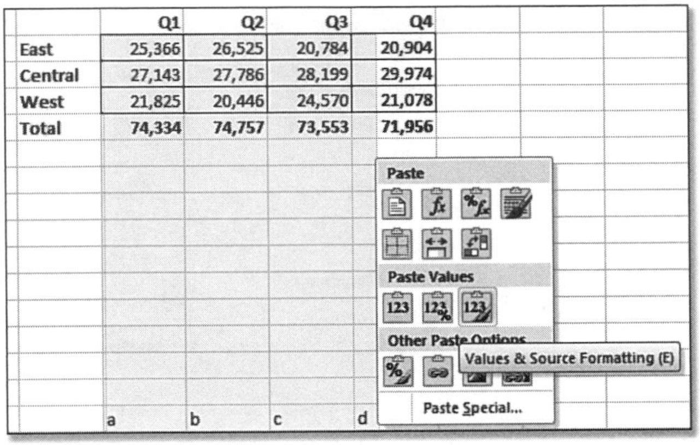

Figure 3.9
Hover over the full gallery to access all 14 options with Live Preview.

Why Keyboard-Centric People Like the Context Gallery

I am not a right-click person. I always use keyboard shortcuts instead of the mouse. I can press Alt+E+S+V+Enter before most people can even move their hand over to the mouse.

Take a close look at your keyboard. To the left of the spacebar, between the FN and Alt keys, do you have the Flying Windows key? I've memorized a few of those shortcuts, like Win+E to open Windows Explorer. Now, look over to the right of the spacebar. What do you have between Alt and Ctrl there? I have a key which I had never used before today. This key looks like the right-click menu and is the Context Menu key. When I press that key in Excel, the right-click menu appears in the worksheet.

Those six icons in the Paste Options gallery in the right-click menu each have a keyboard accelerator:

P—Normal Paste

V—Paste Values

F—Formulas

T—Transpose

R—Formats

N—Paste Link

This means that there is an even faster keyboard method for converting formulas to Values. Press Ctrl+C to Copy, press the Context key and then V to convert to values. You would probably have to use two hands, Ctrl+C with the left hand, Context with the right hand, V with the left hand. It would take a little practice until this was as fast as Ctrl+C, Ctrl+V, Ctrl, V, but it is worth a shot if you rely on keyboard shortcuts to speed your way through tasks.

Accessing the Paste Options Gallery from the Paste Drop-Down

The Paste Options gallery also appears when you open the Paste drop-down on the Home tab. Figure 3.10 shows the menu there.

Figure 3.10
The gallery replaces the old Paste drop-down in the Home tab.

Using the Mini Toolbar to Format Selected Text

The mini toolbar is a shy attendant. When you select some text, almost imperceptibly, the mini toolbar faintly appears above the text.

If you ignore the mini toolbar, it fades away. However, if you move the mouse toward the mini toolbar, the toolbar solidifies and offers you several text formatting options.

In your initial use of Excel 2010, you might not see the mini toolbar. Although you often select cells or ranges of cells, it is rare to select only a portion of a cell value in Cell Edit mode.

However, as you begin using charts, SmartArt diagrams, and text boxes, you will have the mini toolbar appearing frequently.

To use the mini toolbar, follow these steps:

 note

For those of you who started using the Values or Transpose options in the Excel 2007 Paste drop-down, you might be frustrated that these confusing array of pictures appears instead of words. After a few days of transition, you will start to get used to which pictures indicate which commands.

1. Select some text. If you select text in a cell, you must select a portion of the text in the cell by using Cell Edit mode. In a chart, SmartArt diagram, or text box, you can select any text. The mini toolbar appears faintly. On some computers and with some color schemes, "faintly" actually means "completely transparently."

2. Move the mouse pointer toward the mini toolbar, and the toolbar solidifies. The mini toolbar stays visible if your mouse is above it. After a period of inactivity, it disappears. If you move the mouse away from the mini toolbar, it fades away.

3. Make changes in the mini toolbar to affect the text you selected in step 1. The mini toolbar always has the same icons, even though some of them may not apply in the current situation.

In Figure 3.11, for example, it does not make sense to apply indenting to the SmartArt, but the icons are always there and in the same place.

Figure 3.11
The mini toolbar appears when you select text and move up and to the right.

4. When you are done formatting the selected text, you can either move the mouse away from the mini toolbar or use the Format Painter icon to apply the changes to additional text.

5. To use the Format Painter icon, click the paintbrush in the lower-right corner of the mini toolbar. Then move toward other text in the document. As shown in Figure 3.12, the mouse pointer is a black-and-white paintbrush, to indicate that you are in Format Painter mode. When you click the other text, Excel applies the same formatting to the new text.

Initially, it is difficult to see the mini toolbar. You have to move the mouse toward the upper right to get the toolbar to solidify.

In the top row, the mini toolbar offers eight controls:

- **Font name drop-down**—You open this drop-down to choose a typeface. Each of the various font names is displayed in its own font so that you can select an appropriate font easily.

- **Font Size drop-down**—This drop-down offers font sizes from 8 to 96, in several increments.

 note

Microsoft began experimenting with fading toolbars in Outlook 2003. In that version, a new message toolbar would fade into view in the lower-right corner of your screen. You could glance down and read the first line of the email. You could ignore the toolbar, and the message would be waiting for you later in your inbox. Or you could move the mouse toward the notifier, and it would stay long enough for you to click Delete or Open. I enjoyed this feature of Outlook 2003. If my attention needed to stay on the task at hand, I could ignore the notifier, and it would unobtrusively fade away. However, if I were waiting for a message, I could handle it as it came in, avoiding a buildup of messages in my Inbox.

The new mini toolbar is another feature that fades in if you move toward it and fades out if you ignore it. I expect to see more fade-in/fade-out features in future versions of Office.

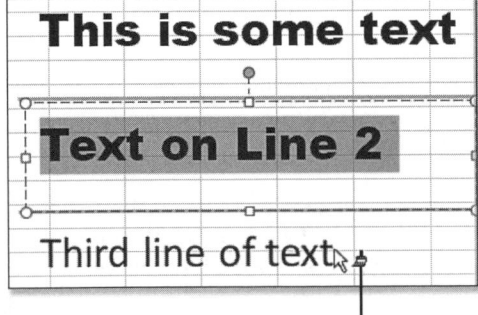

Figure 3.12
After using the mini toolbar to format some text, use the Format Painter to copy that formatting to other text.

Format Painter Mouse pointer

- **Increase Font Size icon**—You click this icon to bump the font up to the next larger size.

- **Decrease Font Size icon**—You click this icon to make the font one size smaller.

- **Decrease Indent icon**—Change the list level.

- **Increase Indent icon**—Change the list level.

- **Bring Forward icon**—Used for shapes and objects.

- **Send Backward icon**—Used for shapes and objects.

In the bottom row, the mini toolbar offers nine controls:

- **Bold icon**—Use this to toggle bold on and off. If bold is already applied, the Bold icon has a glow effect around it.

- **Italics icon**—Use this to toggle italics on and off.

- **Align Left icon**—Click this control to left-align the text.

- **Center Align icon**—Click this control to center the text.

- **Right Align icon**—Click this control to right-align the text.

- **Font Color drop-down**—Use this drop-down to select a color. A menu item at the bottom of this drop-down allows you to display the Colors dialog box.

- **Fill Color drop-down**—Use this drop-down to select a fill color.

- **Shape Outline drop-down**—Use this drop-down to change the color and style of any line in the shape.

- **Format Painter**—The format painter allows you to copy formatting from one place to another. The format painter is discussed in detail in the following section.

caution

Using the Format Painter icon is difficult to master. You get only one click to apply the formatting. If you inadvertently click a nontext element, you lose the Format Painter mouse pointer.

tip

The Format Painter command in the Clipboard group of the Home tab is a bit easier to use than the Format Painter icon. You can double-click this command to keep the application in Format Painter mode. You are then free to click multiple objects, applying the format to various elements.

Getting the Mini Toolbar Back

The shyness of the mini toolbar might be the most frustrating part of using it. If you move the mouse away from the mini toolbar, it fades away. If you immediately move back toward the mini toolbar, it comes back. If you use the mouse for some other task, such as scrolling, the mini toolbar permanently goes away. In this case, you might have to reselect the text to get the mini toolbar to come back.

Disabling the Mini Toolbar

If you are annoyed by the mini toolbar, you can turn it off for all Excel workbooks. To do this, select File, Options. The first choice in Excel Options is a check box for Show Mini Toolbar on Selection. Clear this check box.

Expanding the Formula Bar

Formulas range from very simple to very complex. As people began writing longer and longer formulas in Excel, an annoying problem began to appear: If the formula for a selected cell was longer than the formula bar, the formula bar would wrap and extend over the worksheet (see Figure 3.13). In many cases, the formula would obscure the first few rows of the worksheet. This was frustrating, especially if the selected cell was in the top few rows of the spreadsheet.

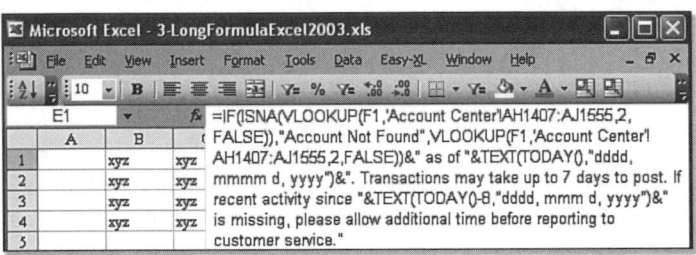

Figure 3.13
In legacy versions of Excel, the formula bar could obscure cells on a worksheet. In this case, both the active cell, B4, and the dependent cell, C4, are hidden.

Excel 2010 features a new formula bar that prevents the formula from obscuring the spreadsheet. For example, in Figure 3.14, Cell E4 contains a formula that is longer than the formula bar. Notice the two new controls at the right end of the formula bar: a scrollbar and Expand Formula Bar icon (which looks like a downward-pointing double arrow).

 tip
Clicking the % indicator to the left of the zoom slider opens the legacy Zoom dialog.

=IF(ISNA(VLOOKUP(F2,'Account Center'!AH1407:AJ1555,2,FALSE)),"Account Not Found",

	E	F	G	H	I	J	K	L	M	
	xyz	xyz	xyz							
	Account Not Found as of Monday, January 11, 2010. Transactions may take up to 7 days to post. If recen									
	xyz	xyz	xyz							

Figure 3.14
By default, Excel 2010 shows the initial portion of the formula.

You use the formula bar scrollbar to scroll through the formula, one line at a time. You use the Expand Formula Bar icon to expand the formula bar. As shown in Figure 3.15, expanding the formula bar actually moves the grid down. This way, you can see the formula bar and still see the cells in the grid, too. In expanded mode, the Expand Formula Bar icon is replaced by a double up-pointing arrow that you can use to contract the formula bar back to one line.

=IF(ISNA(VLOOKUP(F2,'Account Center'!AH1407:AJ1555,2,FALSE)),"Account Not Found",
VLOOKUP(F2,'Account Center'!AH1407:AJ1555,2,FALSE))&" as of "&TEXT(TODAY(),
"dddd, mmmm d, yyyy")&". Transactions may take up to 7 days to post. If recent activity

Figure 3.15
You can click a button to expand the formula bar.

In Figure 3.15, you are not seeing the entire formula. The line underneath the formula bar can be dragged up or down to increase the size of the formula bar, as shown in Figure 3.16.

Figure 3.16
Drag the bar underneath the formula bar to expand the formula bar even more.

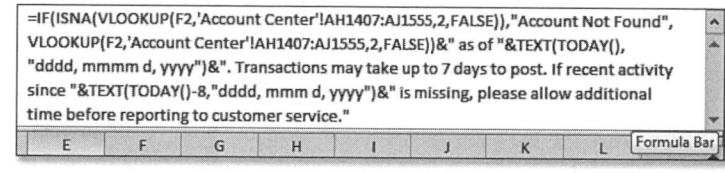

Zooming In and Out on a Worksheet

In the lower-right corner of the Excel window, a new Zoom slider allows you to zoom from 400% to 10% with lightning speed. You simply drag the slider to the right to zoom in and to the left to zoom out. The Zoom Out and Zoom In buttons on either end of the slider allow you to adjust the zoom in 10% increments.

Figure 3.17 shows the zoom control set to the maximum zoom of 400%.

Figure 3.17
You can use the Zoom slider or the Zoom Out and Zoom In buttons to change the zoom.

At the opposite end of the zoom spectrum, the 10% view shows an overview of 158 printed pages of the worksheet. As shown in Figure 3.18, you cannot make out any numbers at a 10% zoom. However, in the 40%–60% zoom range, you can see 3 to 10 pages and actually make out the numbers in the cells.

Figure 3.18
At 10% zoom, you can see 150+ pages at once.

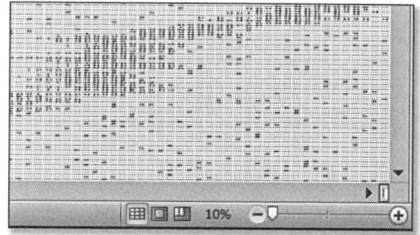

Using the Status Bar to Add Numbers

If you select several cells that contain numeric data and then look at the status bar, at the bottom of the Excel window, you can see that the status bar reports the average, count, and sum of the selected cells (see Figure 3.19).

If you need to quickly add the contents of several cells, you can select the cells and look for the total in the status bar. This feature has been in Excel for a decade, yet very few people realized it was there. In legacy versions of Excel, only the sum would appear, but you could right-click the sum to see other values, such as the average, count, minimum, and maximum.

Figure 3.19
The status bar shows the sum, average, and count of the selected cells.

As with legacy versions of Excel, in Excel 2010 you can customize which statistics are shown in the status bar. In Excel 2010, you can configure all the status bar elements. To do so, you right-click the status bar to display the Status Bar Configuration panel. In this panel, you can see the current value of all status bar icons, whether they are hidden (see Figure 3.20).

To add new items to the status bar, you click them in the Status Bar Configuration panel.

Switching Between Normal View, Page Break Preview, and Page Layout View Modes

Three shortcut icons in the status bar allow you to quickly switch between three view modes, as shown in Figure 3.21:

- **Normal View**—This mode shows worksheet cells as normal.

- **Page Break Preview**—This mode draws the page breaks with blue. You can actually drag the page breaks to new locations in Page Break preview. This mode has been available in several versions of Excel.

- **Page Layout View**—This is a new view introduced in Excel 2007. It combines the best of Page Break Preview and Print Preview modes.

tip

Because it is possible to navigate and enter formulas in any of the view modes, you might want to do actual worksheet editing in the new Page Layout View mode.

Figure 3.20
You can configure the status bar to show or hide all these indicators.

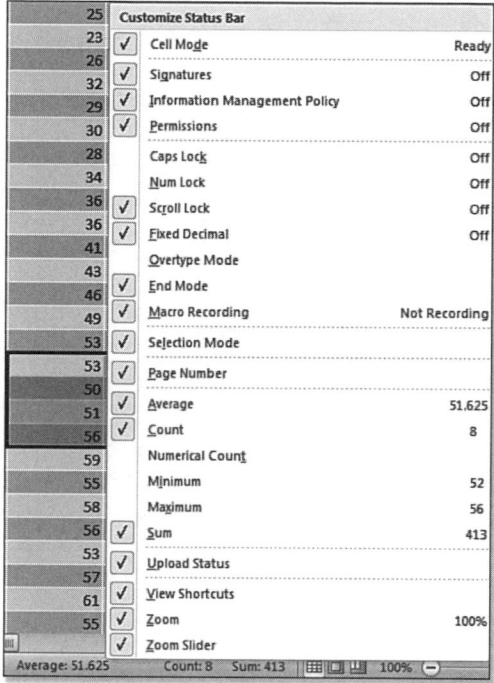

Figure 3.21
Three view shortcuts appear in the status bar.

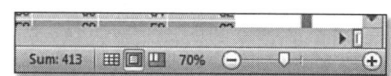

In Page Layout View mode, each page is shown, along with the margins, header, and footer. A ruler appears above the pages and to the left of the pages. (See Figure 3.22.) You can make changes in this mode in the following ways:

- To change the margins, drag the gray boxes in the ruler.

- To change column widths, drag the borders of the column headers.

- To add a header, click Click to Add Header.

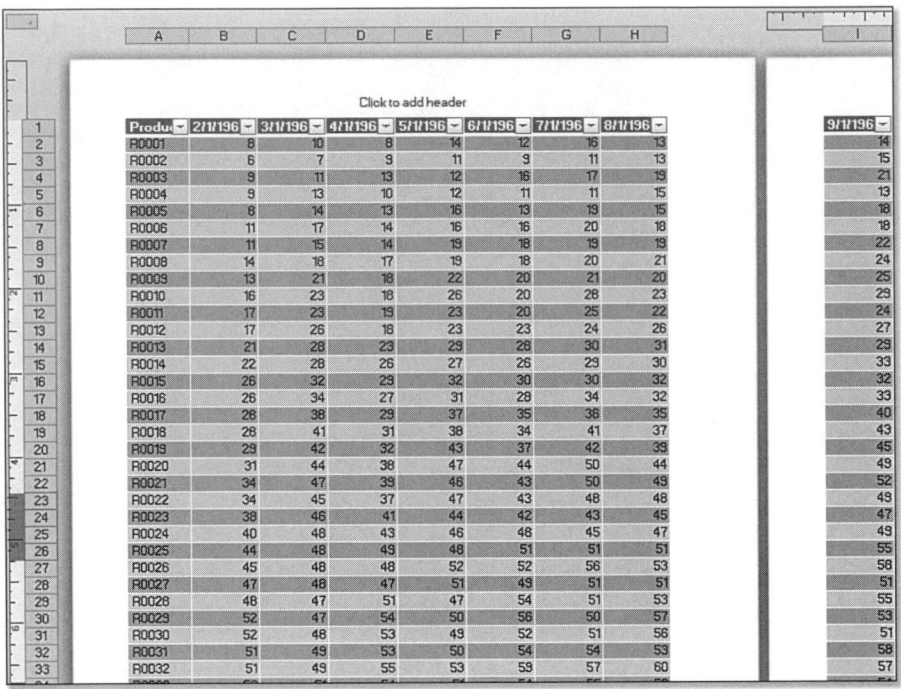

Using the New Sheet Icon to Add Worksheets

The final new control in the Excel interface is the Insert Worksheet icon. This icon appears as a small worksheet tab with a New icon. The tab appears to the right of the last worksheet tab, as shown in Figure 3.23. You click the icon to add a new worksheet to the end of the workbook.

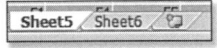

Figure 3.23
Add a new worksheet to the end of your workbook by using the New Worksheet icon.

Dragging a Worksheet to a New Location

After a worksheet has been added to the end of the workbook, you can drag the sheet to a new location in the middle of the workbook. Follow these steps to move a worksheet to a new location:

1. Click the Worksheet tab.

2. Drag the mouse left or right. The mouse pointer shows a sheet of paper under the mouse pointer.

3. Watch for the insertion triangle just above the row of sheet names. In general, the insertion triangle will indicate that the sheet is dropped to the left of the sheet you are hovering above.

4. When the insertion triangle is in the correct location, release the mouse button. The worksheet will be moved to the new location.

Inserting a Worksheet in the Middle of a Workbook

Although using the New Worksheet icon and then dragging a worksheet to a new location is easier, you can also insert a worksheet in a particular location. To insert a worksheet to the left of the current worksheet, for example, select Home, Cells, Insert, Insert Sheet. The new sheet is added before the current sheet.

Alternatively, you can right-click any sheet and select Insert. The Insert dialog appears, where you can choose to insert a worksheet or a variety of templates. The new sheet appears to the left of the selected tab.

CUSTOMIZING THE RIBBON

Customizing the Ribbon is back.

For those of you who upgraded from Excel 2003 directly to Excel 2010, you will say, "Well, of course you can customize the Ribbon." However, for those of us who lived through Excel 2007, there was no easy way to customize the Ribbon.

Starting with Excel 97 command bars, it was possible to completely customize Excel 97 through Excel 2003. You could add icons, remove icons, adjust the menu, create new toolbars, float the toolbars, and so on. Power Excellers everywhere customized their environment to match their work style.

In a blog post on June 27, 2006, Jensen Harris of Microsoft's UI team blogged that 1.3 million people were working with customized versions of Office. But—that wasn't enough. It would cost too much and take too much time to allow for customizations of the Ribbon. If you were a programmer who understood XML, you could still change the Ribbon using RibbonX. But the decision had been made that Office 2007 would not support a customizable ribbon.

Thankfully, Excel 2010 now offers a way to customize the Ribbon. Whether you want to add a few commands or design your own Ribbon tab, you will be accommodated in Excel 2010. Also, after you have designed the perfect customization, you can share that customization with others in your department.

Performing a Simple Ribbon Modification

Suppose that you generally like the Ribbon, but there is one icon that seems to be misplaced. For me, that icon is the PivotTable command. I have no idea why this is on the Insert tab instead of on the Data tab where it belongs.

Take a look at the Data tab as shown in Figure 4.1. It would make sense to have the Pivot Table command right after the Sort & Filter group and before the Data Tools group.

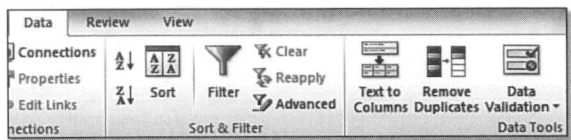

Figure 4.1
Decide where the new command should go.

To add the pivot table command to the Data tab, follow these steps:

1. Right-click the Ribbon and select Customize the Ribbon.

2. In the right list box, expand the Data tab by clicking the + sign next to Data.

3. Click the Sort & Filter entry in the right list box. The new group will go after this entry.

4. Click the New Group button at the bottom of the right list box. A New Group (Custom) item appears after Sort & Filter, as shown in Figure 4.2.

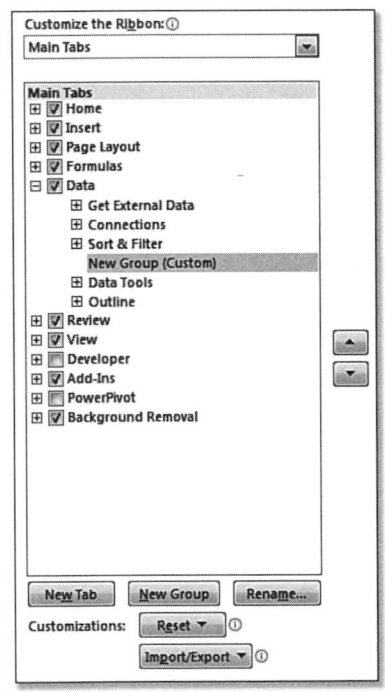

Figure 4.2
Commands have to be added to a new group.

5. While the New Group is selected, click the Rename button at the bottom of the list box. The Rename dialog appears.

6. The Rename dialog offers to let you choose an icon that does not make any sense in the current context. At the bottom, type a Display Name of "Pivot." Click OK.

7. The left list box is showing Popular Commands. Scroll through that list to find PivotTable. Click PivotTable in the left list box. Click the Add button in the center of the dialog to add PivotTable to the new custom Pivot group on the Ribbon.

8. In the drop-down above the left list box, select All Commands. The left list box changes to show an alphabetical list of all commands.

9. Scroll through the left list box until you find PivotTable and PivotChart Wizard. This is the obscure entry point to create Multiple Consolidation Range pivot tables. Select that item in the left list box.

10. Click Add in the center of the dialog. The PivotTable Wizard command is added after the regular PivotTable command.

11. While the Wizard is selected in the right list box, select Rename from the bottom of the right list box. Choose a different icon and type a new name, "Multiple Consolidation." At this point, the right side of the dialog should look like Figure 4.3.

Figure 4.3
Two new icons have been added to a new custom group on the Data tab.

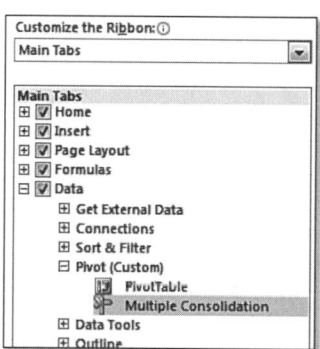

12. Click OK.

Figure 4.4 shows the new group in the Data tab of the Ribbon.

To see a demo of adding an icon to the Ribbon, search for Excel In Depth 4 at YouTube.

Figure 4.4
The results appear in the Ribbon.

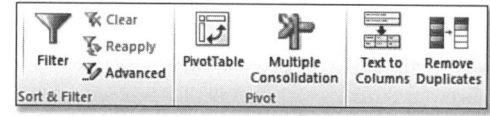

Using a More Complex Ribbon Modification

In my use of Excel 2010, I find that I am constantly bouncing back and forth between the Home tab and the Data tab. If I could add the key icons from the Data tab to the right side of the Home tab, I would not have to move from the Home tab.

Following is the list of icons that I regularly use on the Data tab:

- AZ to sort ascending

- ZA to sort descending

- The Filter button, but I would rather have the Filter by Selection button instead

- The Advanced Filter button

- PivotTable

- Text to Columns

- Remove Duplicates

- Goal Seek from the What-If Analysis drop-down

- Subtotal

Those are nine icons I would like to add to the Home tab of the Ribbon. After studying the icons, I think that I can get by with only icons and no words. This will allow me to jam several icons into a small space.

On the Home tab, I can do without the Editing group. I know keyboard shortcuts for every command in that group that I use.

Follow these steps to customize the Home tab:

1. Right-click the Ribbon and select Customize the Ribbon.

2. In the right list box, expand the Home tab.

3. Click the Editing group.

4. Click Remove in the center of the dialog to remove the Editing group.

5. Click New Group to add a custom group to the Home tab.

6. Click Rename and call the group Data.

7. From the drop-down above the left list box, select Main Tabs. The left list box now shows a list of the main ribbon tabs.

8. In the left list box, expand the Data tab by clicking the plus sign.

9. Expand the Sort and Filter group in the left list box.

10. Click Sort Ascending and click Add. Repeat for Sort Descending and Advanced (Filter).

11. In the left list box, open the Insert tab, then the Tables group, and then the PivotTable drop-down. Add the PivotTable command to the right side.

12. In the left list box, expand the Data Tools group of the Data tab. Add Text to Columns, Remove Duplicates to the right list box. Expand the What-If Analysis drop-down and add Goal Seek to the right list box.

13. In the left list box, expand the Outline group and add Subtotal to the right list box.

14. In the drop-down above the left list box, select Commands Not in the Ribbon.

15. In the left list box, find the icon labeled AutoFilter. This icon is actually Filter by Selection. In the right list box, select Sort Descending because you want to add Filter by Selection after Sort Descending. Select AutoFilter in the left list box. Click Add.

At this point, you have added nine icons to the Data group on the Home tab, as shown in Figure 4.5. You have no control over whether the icons appear as small or large. When you eventually add enough icons, those icons will appear as small.

Figure 4.5
Nine new icons appear in the Home tab.

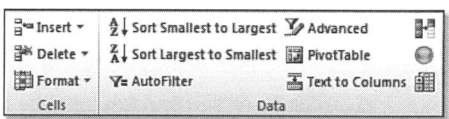

To remove the labels and leave only icons, follow these steps:

1. Right-click the Ribbon and select Customize the Ribbon.

2. In the right list box find the custom Data group in the Home tab.

3. Select the first icon and click Rename. Backspace through the name in the Modify dialog box.

4. Repeat steps 2 and 3 for the other eight icons.

5. Click OK.

 **note**

Notice that words appear next to six icons and not next to the last three icons. This is a situation where Excel is already starting to collapse the Ribbon because the screen isn't wide enough. If the monitor had a higher resolution, the last three icons would have labels as well.

The icons now appear as a small 3x3 arrangement of icons. You don't have explicit control over the arrangement of the icons. However, in the Customize dialog, you can drag an icon in a custom group to a new location. In Figure 4.6, the icons are rearranged so that the two Filter icons appear together in the second column. There was also room for the Editing Group to fit on the Home tab, so it was added back.

Figure 4.6
This has to be the most powerful group of icons ever assembled.

Hiding/Showing Ribbon Tabs

You can temporarily remove a Ribbon tab without deleting it. Notice in the screenshots so far that the Developer and PowerPivot tabs are unchecked in the Customize dialog.

Excel 2007 had an Excel Option for Show Developer Tab in the Ribbon. That command was removed from Excel 2010 because you just add a check mark next to the Developer entry in the right side of the Customize dialog.

Adding a New Ribbon Tab

To add a new Ribbon tab, follow these basic steps:

1. Right-click the Ribbon and select Customize the Ribbon.

2. Click New Tab and Rename the tab.

3. Add New Group(s) to the new tab.

4. Add commands to the new groups.

As you go through the steps to add a new Ribbon tab, you will discover how absolutely limiting the Ribbon customizations are. In Figure 4.7, the power group of nine data icons from Figure 4.6 now show up as large icons. The icons in the Font group appear as small. You have no control over which groups appear with large icons and which groups appear as small.

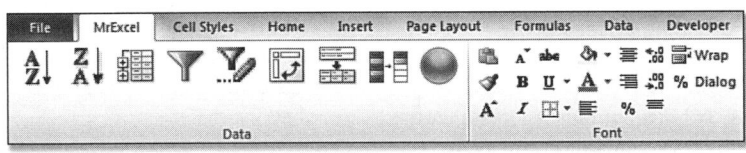

Figure 4.7
For no apparent reason, the nine small icons become nine large icons.

In a perfect world, the nine data icons would appear as small and the Cell Styles drop-down would appear as a gallery, as it does on a 1440-pixel-wide monitor. However, the cell styles always appears as a drop-down, even if it is the only thing on the entire Ribbon tab (see Figure 4.8).

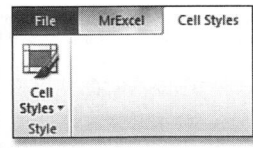

Figure 4.8
When added to a custom group, a gallery appears as a drop-down.

The workaround is to add an entire built-in group to the new Ribbon. In Figure 4.9, the Styles group from the Home tab is added as the only group in a new Ribbon tab. Because the built-in groups allow for different types of controls, the gallery appears in a wide format, as shown in Figure 4.9.

Figure 4.9
When added as a built-in group, the complete gallery appears.

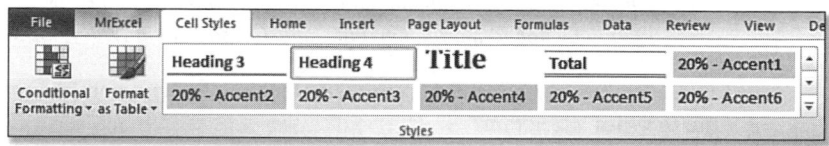

Sharing Customizations with Others

If you have developed the perfect Ribbon customization and you want everyone in your department to have the same customization, you can export all the Ribbon customizations.

To export the changes, follow these steps:

1. Right-click the Ribbon and select Customize the Ribbon.

2. Below the right list box, select Import/Export, Export All Customizations.

3. Browse to a folder and provide a name for the customization file. The file type will be .exportedUI. Click OK.

4. In Windows Explorer, find the exported .exportedUI file. Copy it to a co-worker's computer.

5. On the co-worker's computer, repeat step 1. In step 2, select to Import All Customizations. Find the file and click OK.

 note

Note that this is an all-or-nothing proposition. You cannot export your changes to the MrExcel tab without exporting your changes to the Data and Home tabs.

Resetting Customizations

It is easy to go back to the default Ribbon configuration. To do this, right-click the Ribbon and select Customize the Ribbon. Below the right list box, select Reset, Reset All Customizations. Click OK.

Questions About Ribbon Customization

Can the customizations apply to only a certain workbook?
No. The Customize the Ribbon command in Excel 2010 applies to all workbooks.

Can toolbars be docked to the side of the screen or floating as in Excel 97–2003?
No. The Ribbon always must be at the top of the screen, in a horizontal position.

Where is the Excel 2003 icon editor? Where is the list of 4,096 icons available back in Excel 2003?
Neither item is supported in Excel 2010.

How can I get complete control over the Ribbon?
Learn RibbonX and write some VBA to build your own ribbon.

> *For more information on building your own ribbon, see* RibbonX: Customizing the Office 2007 Ribbon *by Robert Martin, Ken Puls, and Teresa Hennig (Wiley, ISBN 0470191112).*

These Ribbon customizations are really lacking. Is there another option that doesn't require me to write a program?

Yes, there are a number of third-party ribbon customization programs. For example, check out a free one from Excel MVP Andy Pope at www.andypope.info/vba/ribboneditor.htm.

5

KEYBOARD SHORTCUTS

If you do a lot of typing, being able to access commands from the keyboard is faster than moving your hand to the mouse. Excel 2010 introduces new keyboard accelerators accessed using the Alt key. In addition, many of the old Alt keyboard shortcuts still work and all the old Ctrl shortcut keys are still functional. For instance, Ctrl+C still copies a selection, Ctrl+X cuts a selection, and Ctrl+V pastes a selection.

This chapter points out which of the old keyboard shortcuts still work, shows you some new shortcuts, and introduces you to the new keyboard accelerators.

Using New Keyboard Accelerators

The goal of the new Excel 2010 keyboard accelerators is to allow you to access every command by using only the keyboard. In legacy versions of Excel, many popular commands had keyboard accelerators, but other commands did not. Excel 2010 tries to ensure that every command can be invoked from the keyboard.

To access the new accelerators, press and release the Alt key. Notice that Excel places a ToolTip above each command, with an associated accelerator key.

Note that an arcane command exists in the Excel Options dialog that can cause the new keyboard accelerators not to work for you. It is possible that you turned on this setting in Excel 1995 and each successive upgrade of Excel has inherited the setting. You should check the setting before proceeding. To do so, select the Office icon and then select Excel Options. In the Advanced category, scroll to near the bottom for Lotus Compatibility. If Transition Navigation Keys is selected, then the slash character shown in the Microsoft Office Menu Key will be used instead of Alt to invoke shortcuts. If you prefer using the Alt key, you should clear the Transition Navigation Keys check box. Keep in mind that if you prefer using the slash key, you must use / in place of Alt with new keyboard accelerators.

Tiny letter ToolTips appear over each tab of the ribbon. In addition, number ToolTips appear over each icon in the Quick Access toolbar. Figure 5.1 shows the ToolTips.

Keyboard accelerators
for Ribbon tabs

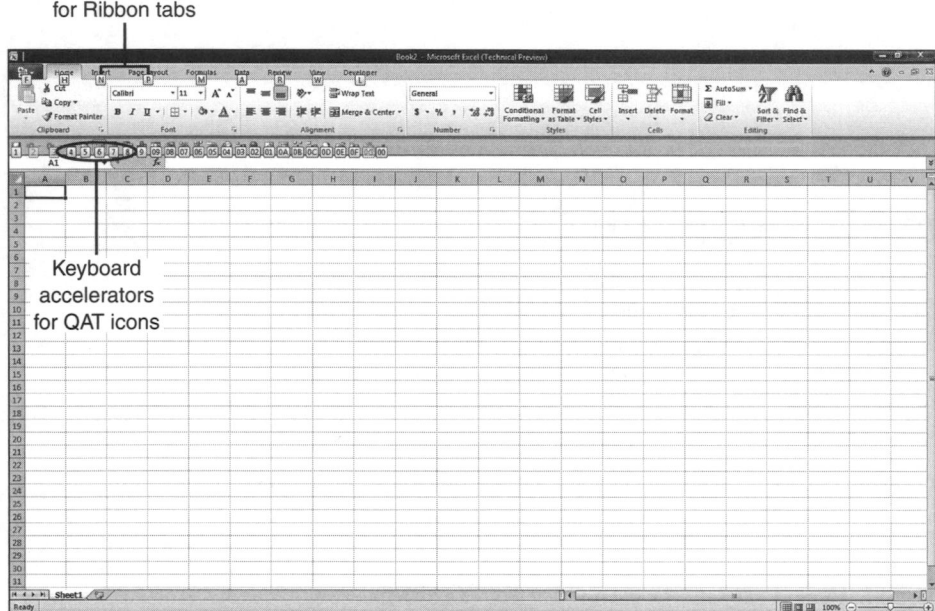

Keyboard
accelerators
for QAT icons

Figure 5.1
Type the letters in the ToolTips along the top to open various tabs. Type the numbers in the numeric keytips to access the Quick Access Toolbar.

It is possible to memorize the keytips for the ribbon tabs.

Pressing Alt+F always accesses the File menu in all Office 2010 applications.

Alt+H always accesses the Home tab in all Office 2010 applications. The accelerator definitions for each tab remain constant even if new ribbon tabs are displayed. When you activate a pivot table, the original keytip letters (F, H, N, P, M, A, R, W, L, and X) remain, and two new keytips appear for the two new tabs: JT for PivotTable Tools Options and JY for PivotTable Tools Design (see Figure 5.2).

Contextual Tab Shortcuts

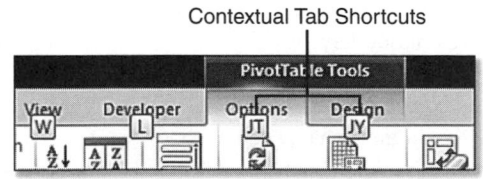

Figure 5.2
New ribbon tabs get new letters, making sure the old letters remain constant.

Unfortunately, the keytips for the Quick Access toolbar change every time you add new buttons or rearrange buttons on the Quick Access toolbar. If you want to memorize those keytips, you need to make sure you do not add a new Quick Access toolbar icon at the beginning of the list.

Selecting Icons on the Ribbon

After you press the Alt key, you can press one of the keytip letters to bring up the appropriate tab. You now see that every icon on the ribbon has a keytip.

When you choose a ribbon tab, the keytips on the Quick Access toolbar disappear, so Microsoft is free to use the letters A through Z and the numbers 0 through 9.

On very busy Ribbon tabs, some commands require two keystrokes: for example, A+C for Align Center in the Alignments Group of the Home tab, as shown in Figure 5.3. Note that after you press Alt to display the accelerators in the ToolTips, you do not have to continue holding down the Alt key.

Some shortcut keys seem to make sense: AT for Align Top, AM for Align Middle, AB for Align Bottom, AL for Align Left, W for Wrap Text, and M for Merge. Other shortcut keys seem to be assigned at random. Some take a little pondering: FA for the dialog launcher in Figure 5.3 makes sense in that it opens the legacy Format dialog and moves to the Alignment tab. Others have a historical precedent. In Excel 2003, F was used for File so O was used for Format. Similarly, in the Home tab, O now opens the Format drop-down, although since Microsoft no longer underlines the accelerator key in the menu name, O will never make sense to someone new to Excel. There might be some arcane, logical reason why 5 and 6 are used for increase and decrease indent, but it is unknown by most people.

Figure 5.3
After pressing the letter to switch to the ribbon, type the letter or letters to invoke a particular command.

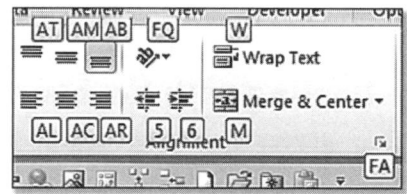

Selecting Options from a Gallery

Figure 5.4 shows the results of pressing Alt+H+T, which is the equivalent of selecting Home, Format Table. This opens the gallery of possible table styles. As you can see in Figure 5.4, you can invoke the New Table Style and New Pivot Style commands at the bottom of the gallery by pressing N and P, respectively. However, there are no letters on the table style choices in the gallery.

To select a table style using the keyboard, use the arrow keys to move through the gallery. Because this gallery is two-dimensional, you can use the up arrow, down arrow, right arrow, left arrow, Page Down, Page Up, Home, and End keys to navigate through the gallery. When you have the desired table style highlighted, press the Enter key to select it.

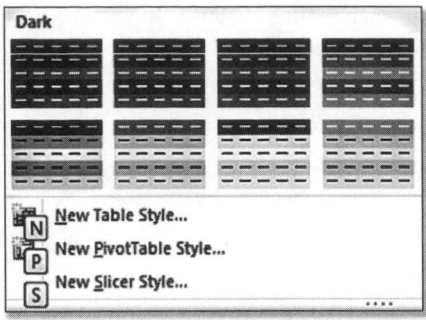

Figure 5.4
After opening a gallery, you use the arrow keys to navigate through the gallery and press Enter to select a style.

Navigating Within Drop-Down Lists

If you press Alt+H+F+S, which is the equivalent of selecting Home, Font Size, the font size in the drop-down is selected. You can either type a font size and press Enter or press the down-arrow key to open the drop-down list. You can then use the down arrow, up arrow, Page Down, Page Up, Home, and End keys to navigate to a choice in the list. When you have the desired item highlighted, press Enter to select that item.

Backing Up One Level Through a Menu

Suppose that you press Alt+H to access the Home tab and then realize you are in the wrong tab. You can press the Esc key to move back to display the ToolTips for the main menu choices.

If you want to clear the ToolTips completely, press Alt again.

Dealing with Keyboard Accelerator Confusion

If you want to select something on the Home tab in Figure 5.2, you may be frustrated because you can see the menu choices, but there are no ToolTips for most commands. For icons in the top of the ribbon, it appears that the main keytips apply to the menu items. For example, you may think that the H keytip applies to Cut. Even though you are already on the Home tab, you need to press the H key to force Excel to show the ToolTips for the individual menu items on the Home tab.

Selecting from Legacy Dialog Boxes

Some commands lead to legacy dialog boxes like the ones in previous editions of Excel. These dialog boxes do not display the Excel 2010 keytips. However, most of the dialog boxes do use the convention of having one letter of each command underlined, which is called a *hotkey* in Microsoft parlance. In this case, you can press the underlined letter to select the command.

 note

If you find the accelerator ToolTips to be confusing and unwieldy, you need to attack them one at a time. Find a task that you use regularly, such as sorting the current data set ascending by the selected column. Press the Alt key. Press A for the Data tab. Notice that A sorts ascending and D sorts descending. These should be easy enough to remember; Alt+A+A for sort ascending, and Alt+A+D for sort descending.

For example, press Alt+H+V+S instead of selecting Home, Paste, Paste Special. You are then presented with the Paste Special dialog box, as shown in Figure 5.5. To select Values and Transpose in this dialog, press V for Values and E for Transpose, because those are the letters underlined in the dialog. You can then press Enter instead of clicking the default OK button.

Figure 5.5
In a legacy dialog box, type the underlined letters to select options.

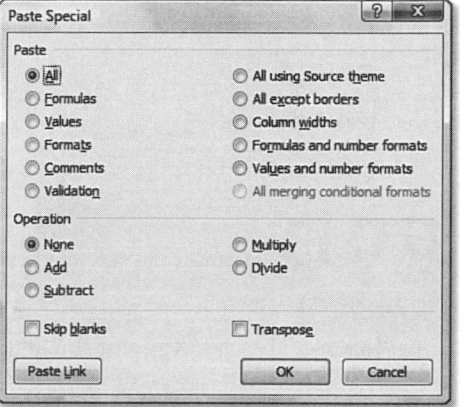

To watch a video of Legacy Dialog boxes, search for Excel In Depth 5 at YouTube.

Using the Shortcut Keys

Excel 2010 automatically recognizes all the Ctrl shortcut keys that were used in legacy versions of Excel. In fact, many of these keys are consistent across all Windows applications. Table 5.1 lists the common Windows Ctrl shortcut keys.

Table 5.1   Windows Shortcut Keys

Key Combination	Action
Ctrl+C	Copy.
Ctrl+X	Cut.
Ctrl+V	Paste.
Ctrl+Z	Undo.
Ctrl+Y	Redo.
Ctrl+A	Select all.
Ctrl+S	Save.
Ctrl+O	Open.

Key Combination	Action
Ctrl+W or Ctrl+F4	Close workbook.
Ctrl+N	New workbook.
Ctrl+P	Print.
Ctrl+B	Bold.
Ctrl+U	Underline.
Ctrl+I	Italic.
Ctrl+F	Find.

Table 5.2 illustrates the shortcut keys that you use to navigate.

Table 5.2   Shortcut Keys for Navigation

Shortcut Key	Action
Ctrl+Home	Move to Cell A1.
Ctrl+End	Move to last cell in the used range of the worksheet.
Ctrl+Page Up	Move to previous worksheet.
Ctrl+Page Down	Move to next worksheet.
Shift+F11	New Worksheet.
Alt+Tab	Switch to next program.
Alt+Shift+Tab	Switch to previous program.
Ctrl+Esc	Display Windows Start menu.
Ctrl+F5	Restore window size of current workbook.
F6	Switch to next pane in a window that has been split.
Ctrl+F6	When more than one workbook is open, switch to the next open workbook window.
Ctrl+Shift+F6	Switch to the previous workbook window.
Ctrl+F9	Minimize the window.
Ctrl+F10	Maximize the window.
Ctrl+arrow key	Move to edge of current region.
Home	Move to beginning of row.

Shortcut Key	Action
Ctrl+Backspace	Scroll to display the active cell.
F5	Display the GoTo dialog.
Shift+F5	Display the Find dialog.
Shift+F4	Find next.
Ctrl+. (period)	Move to next corner of selected range.

Table 5.3 shows the shortcut keys you use to select data and cells.

Table 5.3   Shortcut Keys for Selecting Data and Cells

Shortcut Key	Action
Ctrl+spacebar	If used outside a table, select entire column. If used inside a table, toggle between selecting the data, data and headers, and the entire column.
Shift+spacebar	Select entire row. If inside a table, toggle between selecting the table row and the entire row.
Shift+backspace	With multiple cells selected, revert selection to only the active cell.
Ctrl+Shift+*	Select the current region.
Ctrl+/	Select the array containing the active cell.
Ctrl+Shift+O (letter O)	Select all cells that contain comments.
Ctrl+\	In a selected row, select the cells that do not match the value in the active cell.
Ctrl+Shift+		In a selected column, select the cells that do not match the value in the active cell.
Ctrl+[(opening square bracket)	Select all cells directly referenced by formulas in the selection.
Ctrl+Shift+{ (opening brace)	Select all cells directly or indirectly referenced by formulas in the selection.
Ctrl+] (closing square bracket)	Select cells that contain formulas that directly reference the active cell.
Ctrl+Shift+} (closing brace)	Select cells that contain formulas that directly or indirectly reference the active cell.
Alt+; (semicolon)	Select the visible cells in the current selection.

Table 5.4 shows the shortcut keys you use to extend a selection.

Table 5.4 Shortcut Keys for Extending Selections

Shortcut Key	Action
F8	Turn Extend mode on or off. In Extend mode, EXT appears in the status line and the arrow keys extend the selection.
Shift+F8	Add another range of cells to the selection or use the arrow keys to move to the start of the range you want to add. Then press F8 and the arrow keys to select the next range.
Shift+arrow key	Extend the selection by one cell.
Ctrl+Shift+arrow key	Extend the selection to the last nonblank cell in the same column or row as the active cell.
Shift+Home	Extend the selection to the beginning of the row.
Ctrl+Shift+Home	Extend the selection to the beginning of the worksheet.
Ctrl+Shift+End	Extend the selection to the last used cell on the worksheet in the lower-right corner.
Shift+Page Down	Extend the selection down one screen.
Shift+Page Up	Extend the selection up one screen.
End+Shift+arrow key	Extend the selection to the last nonblank cell in the same column or row as the active cell.
End+Shift+Home	Extend the selection to the last used cell on the worksheet in the lower-right corner.
End+Shift+Enter	Extend the selection to the last cell in the current row.
Scroll Lock+Shift+Home	Extend the selection to the cell in the upper-left corner of the window.
Scroll Lock+Shift+End	Extend the selection to the cell in the lower-right corner of the window.

Table 5.5 shows the shortcut keys you use for entering, editing, formatting, and calculating data.

Table 5.5 Shortcut Keys for Data Entry, Formatting, and Calculating Data

Shortcut Key	Action
Enter	Complete a cell entry and select the next cell below.
Alt+Enter	Start a new line in the same cell.

Shortcut Key	Action
Ctrl+Enter	Fill the selected cell range with the current entry.
Shift+Enter	Complete a cell entry and select the next cell above.
Tab	Complete a cell entry and select the next cell to the right.
Shift+Tab	Complete a cell entry and select the previous cell to the left.
Esc	Cancel a cell entry.
Arrow keys	Move one character up, down, left, or right.
Home	Move to the beginning of the line.
F4 or Ctrl+Y	Repeat the last action.
Ctrl+Shift+F3	Create names from row and column labels.
Ctrl+D	Fill down.
Ctrl+R	Fill to the right.
Ctrl+F3	Define a name.
Ctrl+K	Insert a hyperlink.
Ctrl+; (semicolon)	Enter the date.
Ctrl+Shift+: (colon)	Enter the time.
Alt+down arrow	Display a drop-down list of the values in the current column of a range.
Ctrl+Z	Undo the last action.
= (equal sign)	Start a formula.
Backspace	In the formula bar, delete one character to the left.
Enter	Complete a cell entry from the cell or formula bar.
Ctrl+Shift+Enter	Enter a formula as an array formula.
Esc	Cancel an entry in the cell or formula bar.
Shift+F3	In a formula, display the Insert Function dialog box.
Ctrl+A	When the insertion point is to the right of a function name in a formula, display the Function Arguments dialog box.
Ctrl+Shift+A	When the insertion point is to the right of a function name in a formula, insert the argument names and parentheses.
F3	Paste a defined name into a formula.

Shortcut Key	Action
Alt+= (equal sign)	Insert an AutoSum formula with the SUM function.
Ctrl+Shift+" (quotation mark)	Copy the value from the cell above the active cell into the cell or the formula bar.
Ctrl+' (apostrophe)	Copy a formula from the cell above the active cell into the cell or the formula bar.
Ctrl+` (backtick)	Alternate between displaying cell values and displaying formulas.
F9	Calculate all worksheets in all open workbooks. When a portion of a formula is selected, calculate the selected portion and then press Enter or Ctrl+Shift+Enter (for array formulas) to replace the selected portion with the calculated value.
Shift+F9	Calculate the active worksheet.
Ctrl+Alt+F9	Calculate all worksheets in all open workbooks, regardless of whether they have changed since the last calculation.
Ctrl+Alt+Shift+F9	Recheck dependent formulas and then calculate all cells in all open workbooks, including cells not marked as needing to be calculated.
F2	Edit the active cell and position the insertion point at the end of the cell contents. If in-cell editing is turned off, moves the insertion point to the formula bar.
Alt+Enter	Start a new line in the same cell.
Backspace	Edit the active cell and then clear it or delete the preceding character in the active cell as you edit cell contents.
Delete	Delete the character to the right of the insertion point or delete the selection.
Ctrl+Delete	Delete text to the end of the line.
F7	Display the Spelling dialog box.
Shift+F2	Edit a cell comment.
Enter	Complete a cell entry and select the next cell below.
Ctrl+Z	Undo the last action.
Ctrl+Shift+Z	When the AutoCorrect smart tag is displayed, undo or redo the last automatic correction.
Delete	Clear the contents of the selected cells.
Ctrl+- (hyphen)	Delete the selected cells.

Shortcut Key	Action
Ctrl+Shift++ (plus sign)	Insert blank cells.
Alt+' (apostrophe)	Display the Style dialog box.
Ctrl+1	Display the Format Cells dialog box.
Ctrl+Shift+~	Apply the General number format.
Ctrl+Shift+$	Apply the Currency format with two decimal places (negative numbers in parentheses).
Ctrl+Shift+%	Apply the Percentage format with no decimal places.
Ctrl+Shift+^	Apply the Exponential number format with two decimal places.
Ctrl+Shift+#	Apply the Date format with the day, month, and year.
Ctrl+Shift+@	Apply the Time format with the hour and minute, and AM or PM.
Ctrl+Shift+!	Apply the Number format with two decimal places, thousands separator, and minus sign (-) for negative values.
Ctrl+B	Apply or remove bold formatting.
Ctrl+I	Apply or remove italic formatting.
Ctrl+U	Apply or remove underline.
Ctrl+5	Apply or remove strikethrough.
Ctrl+9	Hide the selected rows.
Ctrl+Shift+((opening parenthesis)	Unhide any hidden rows within the selection.
Ctrl+0 (zero)	Hide the selected columns.
Ctrl+Shift+) (closing parenthesis)	Unhide any hidden columns within the selection.
Ctrl+Shift+&	Apply the outline border to the selected cells.
Ctrl+Shift+_ (under-score)	Remove the outline border from the selected cells.

There are shortcut keys specifically for using the Border tab in the Format Cells dialog. Press Ctrl+1 to display the Format Cells dialog. Press Ctrl+PgDn until you arrive at the Border tab. Then you can use the shortcut keys shown in Table 5.6.

Table 5.6 Shortcut Keys for Borders

Shortcut Key	Action
Alt+T	Apply or remove the top border.
Alt+B	Apply or remove the bottom border.
Alt+L	Apply or remove the left border.
Alt+R	Apply or remove the right border.
Alt+H	If cells in multiple rows are selected, apply or remove the horizontal divider.
Alt+V	If cells in multiple columns are selected, apply or remove the vertical divider.
Alt+D	Apply or remove the downward diagonal border.
Alt+U	Apply or remove the upward diagonal border.

Using Excel 2003 Keyboard Accelerators

In legacy versions of Excel, most menu items included one underlined letter. In those versions, you could hold down the Alt key while pressing the underlined letter to invoke the menu item. In the Excel 2003 screen shown in Figure 5.6, you can display the Edit menu by pressing Alt+E, and you can select Edit, Fill, Justify by pressing Alt+E+I+J.

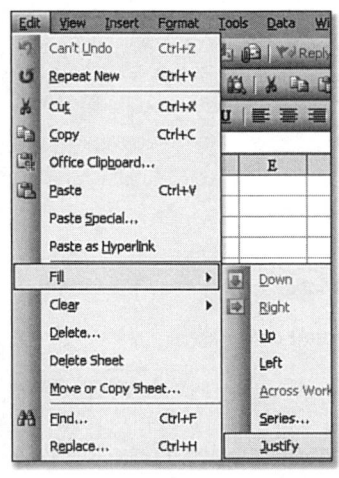

Figure 5.6
Pressing Alt+E+I+J performs Edit, Fill, Justify.

Instead of pressing Alt+E+I+J all at once, when the Edit menu is displayed, you can display the Fill flyout menu by pressing I. Then you can perform the Justify command by pressing J.

If you are a power Excel user, you probably have a few of these commands memorized, such as Alt+E+I+J for Edit, Fill, Justify; Alt+E+S+V for Edit, Paste Special, Values; and Alt+D+L for Data Validation. If you have some of these commands memorized, when you hear that the menu in Excel 2010 is completely gone, you might be worried that you have to relearn all the shortcut keys. However, there is good news for the power Excel gurus who have favorite Alt shortcut keys burned into their minds—most of them will continue to work as they did in Excel 2003.

If you were an intermediate Excel user who regularly used the Excel 2003 keyboard accelerators but had to look at the screen to use them, you should start using the new keyboard accelerators discussed at the beginning of this chapter.

Invoking an Excel 2003 Alt Shortcut

In Excel 2003, the main menus were File, Edit, View, Insert, Format, Tools, Data, Window, and Help. The keyboard accelerator commands in Excel 2003 were Alt+F, Alt+E, Alt+V, Alt+I, Alt+O, Alt+T, Alt+D, Alt+W, and Alt+H.

If you are moving from Excel 2003 to Excel 2010, you will have the best success when trying to access commands on the Edit, View, Insert, Format, Tools, and Data menus. None of the keyboard accelerators associated with Window or Help work in Excel 2010. Alt+H takes you to the Home tab instead of the few commands on the Help menu, and Alt+W takes you to the View tab.

Some of the keyboard shortcuts associated with the File menu in Excel 2003 continue to work in Excel 2010. Pressing Alt+F opens the File menu. In Excel 2003, pressing Alt+F+O performs File, Open. It happens that O is the shortcut on the File menu for Open, so pressing Alt+F+O in Excel 2010 also performs File, Open.

 tip

In Excel 2007, you had to pause briefly after typing the first letter in the legacy shortcut key sequence. For example, you pressed Alt+E, paused, then pressed S,V to Edit, Paste Special, Values. If you did not pause, the second letter was lost because Excel displayed the pop-up Office Key Sequence window. This problem has been solved in Excel 2010. You no longer have to pause between the first and second letters

For the shortcut keys Alt+E, Alt+V, Alt+I, Alt+O, Alt+T, and Alt+D, Excel switches into Office 2003 Access Key mode. In this mode, a ToolTip appears over the ribbon, indicating which letters you have typed so far (see Figure 5.7). When you have entered enough letters, the command is invoked. If you have forgotten the sequence, you can press Esc to exit the Excel 2003 Access Key mode.

Office key sequence: ALT, E.

Continue typing the key sequence from an older version of Office, or press Escape to cancel.

Figure 5.7
The Office 2003 access key ToolTip shows which keys you have used so far while entering a legacy shortcut.

Determining Which Commands Work in Legacy Mode

If you try a command that no longer works in Excel 2010, nothing happens. Several commands don't make sense in the framework of Excel 2010, so they have been deprecated.

Table 5.7 lists the legacy keyboard commands and shows which of them continue to work in Excel 2010.

Table 5.7 Excel Legacy Keyboard Commands

Works in Shortcut	Excel 2010?	Command
Alt+F+N	Yes	File, New
Alt+F+O	Yes	File, Open
Alt+F+C	Yes	File, Close
Alt+F+S	Yes	File, Save
Alt+F+A	Yes	File, Save As
Alt+F+G	No	File, Save as Web Page
Alt+F+W	No	File, Save Workspace
Alt+F+H	No	File, File Search
Alt+F+M	No	File, Permission
Alt+F+E	No	File, Check Out
Alt+F+E	No	File, Check In
Alt+F+R	No	File, Version History
Alt+F+B	No	File, Web Page Preview
Alt+F+U	No	File, Page Setup
Alt+F+T+S	No	File, Print Area, Set Print Area
Alt+F+T+C	No	File, Print Area, Clear Print Area
Alt+F+V	No	File, Print Preview
Alt+F+P	Yes as Alt+F+P+P	File, Print
Alt+F+D+M	No	File, Send To, Mail Recipient
Alt+F+D+S	No	File, Send To, Original Sender
Alt+F+D+C	No	File, Send To, Mail Recipient (for Review)
Alt+F+D+A	No	File, Send To, Mail Recipient (as Attachment)

Works in Shortcut	Excel 2010?	Command
Alt+F+D+R	No	File, Send To, Routing Recipient
Alt+F+D+E	No	File, Send To, Exchange Folder
Alt+F+D+O	No	File, Send To, Online Meeting Participant
Alt+F+D+X	No	File, Send To, Recipient Using Internet Fax Ser vice
Alt+F+I	No	File, Properties
Alt+F+1	Yes	File, 1
Alt+F+2	Yes	File, 2
Alt+F+3	Yes	File, 3
Alt+F+4	Yes	File, 4
Alt+F+5	Yes	File, 5
Alt+F+6	Yes	File, 6
Alt+F+7	Yes	File, 7
Alt+F+8	Yes	File, 8
Alt+F+9	Yes	File, 9
Alt+F+T	No	File, Sign Out
Alt+F+X	Yes	File, Exit
Alt+E+U	Yes	Edit, Undo
Alt+E+R	Yes	Edit, Repeat
Alt+E+T	Yes	Edit, Cut
Alt+E+C	Yes	Edit, Copy
Alt+E+B	Yes	Edit, Office Clipboard
Alt+E+P	Yes	Edit, Paste
Alt+E+S	Yes	Edit, Paste Special
Alt+E+H	No	Edit, Paste as Hyperlink
Alt+E+I+D	Yes	Edit, Fill, Down
Alt+E+I+R	Yes	Edit, Fill, Right
Alt+E+I+U	Yes	Edit, Fill, Up

Works in Shortcut	Excel 2010?	Command
Alt+E+I+L	Yes	Edit, Fill, Left
Alt+E+I+A	Yes	Edit, Fill, Across Worksheets
Alt+E+I+S	Yes	Edit, Fill, Series
Alt+E+I+J	Yes	Edit, Fill, Justify
Alt+E+A+A	Yes	Edit, Clear, All
Alt+E+A+F	Yes	Edit, Clear, Formats
Alt+E+A+C	Yes	Edit, Clear, Contents
Alt+E+A+M	Yes	Edit, Clear, Comments
Alt+E+D	Yes	Edit, Delete
Alt+E+L	Yes	Edit, Delete Sheet
Alt+E+M	Yes	Edit, Move or Copy Sheet
Alt+E+F	Yes	Edit, Find
Alt+E+E	Yes	Edit, Replace
Alt+E+G	Yes	Edit, Go To
Alt+E+K	Yes	Edit, Links
Alt+E+O	No	Edit, Object
Alt+E+O+V	No	Edit, Object, Convert
Alt+V+N	Yes	View, Normal
Alt+V+P	Yes	View, Page Break Preview
Alt+V+K	No	View, Task Pane
Alt+V+T+C	No	View, Toolbars, Customize
Alt+V+F	Yes	View, Formula Bar
Alt+V+S	No	View, Status Bar
Alt+V+H	Yes	View, Header and Footer
Alt+V+C	Yes	View, Comments
Alt+V+V	Yes	View, Custom Views
Alt+V+U	Yes	View, Full Screen (Caution: Use the Maximize button to return.)

Works in Shortcut	Excel 2010?	Command
Alt+V+Z	Yes	View, Zoom
Alt+I+E	Yes	Insert, Cells
Alt+I+R	Yes	Insert, Rows
Alt+I+C	Yes	Insert, Columns
Alt+I+W	Yes	Insert, Worksheet
Alt+I+H	Yes	Insert, Chart
Alt+I+S	Yes	Insert, Symbol
Alt+I+B	Yes	Insert, Page Break
Alt+I+A	Yes	Insert, Reset All Page Breaks
Alt+I+F	Yes	Insert, Function
Alt+I+N+D	Yes	Insert, Name, Define
Alt+I+N+P	Yes	Insert, Name, Paste
Alt+I+N+C	Yes	Insert, Name, Create
Alt+I+N+A	Yes	Insert, Name, Apply
Alt+I+N+L	Yes	Insert, Name, Label
Alt+I+M	Yes	Insert, Comment
Alt+I+A	Yes	Insert, Ink Annotations
Alt+I+P+C	Yes	Insert, Picture, Clip Art
Alt+I+P+F	Yes	Insert, Picture, From File
Alt+I+P+S	Yes	Insert, Picture, From Scanner or Camera
Alt+I+P+D	Yes	Insert, Picture, Ink Drawing and Writing
Alt+I+P+A	No	Insert, Picture, AutoShapes
Alt+I+P+W	No	Insert, Picture, WordArt
Alt+I+P+O	No	Insert, Picture, Organization Chart
Alt+I+G	No	Insert, Diagram
Alt+I+O	Yes	Insert, Object
Alt+I+I	Yes	Insert, Hyperlink
Alt+O+E	Yes	Format, Cells

Works in Shortcut	Excel 2010?	Command
Alt+O+R+E	Yes	Format, Row, Height
Alt+O+R+A	Yes	Format, Row, AutoFit
Alt+O+R+H	Yes	Format, Row, Hide
Alt+O+R+U	Yes	Format, Row, Unhide
Alt+O+C+W	Yes	Format, Column, Width
Alt+O+C+A	Yes	Format, Column, AutoFit Selection
Alt+O+C+H	Yes	Format, Column, Hide
Alt+O+C+U	Yes	Format, Column, Unhide
Alt+O+C+S	Yes	Format, Column, Standard Width
Alt+O+H+R	Yes	Format, Sheet, Rename
Alt+O+H+H	Yes	Format, Sheet, Hide
Alt+O+H+U	Yes	Format, Sheet, Unhide
Alt+O+H+B	Yes	Format, Sheet, Background
Alt+O+H+T	Yes	Format, Sheet, Tab Color
Alt+O+A	No	Format, AutoFormat
Alt+O+D	Yes	Format, Conditional Formatting
Alt+O+S	Yes	Format, Style
Alt+T+S	Yes	Tools, Spelling
Alt+T+R	Yes	Tools, Research
Alt+T+K	Yes	Tools, Error Checking
Alt+T+H+H	No	Tools, Speech, Speech Recognition
Alt+T+H+T	No	Tools, Speech, Show Text to Speech Toolbar
Alt+T+D	Yes	Tools, Shared Workspace
Alt+T+B	Yes	Tools, Share Workbook
Alt+T+T+H	Yes	Tools, Track Changes, Highlight Changes
Alt+T+T+A	Yes	Tools, Track Changes, Accept or Reject Changes
Alt+T+W	Yes	Tools, Compare and Merge Workbooks

Works in Shortcut	Excel 2010?	Command
Alt+T+P+P	Yes	Tools, Protection, Protect Sheet
Alt+T+P+A	Yes	Tools, Protection, Allow Users to Edit Ranges
Alt+T+P+W	Yes	Tools, Protection, Protect Workbook
Alt+T+P+S	Yes	Tools, Protection, Protect and Share Workbook
Alt+T+N+M	Yes	Tools, Online Collaboration, Meet Now
Alt+T+N+S	Yes	Tools, Online Collaboration, Schedule Meeting
Alt+T+N+W	Yes	Tools, Online Collaboration, Web Discussions
Alt+T+N+N	Yes	Tools, Online Collaboration, End Review
Alt+T+G	Yes	Tools, Goal Seek
Alt+T+E	Yes	Tools, Scenarios
Alt+T+U+T	Yes	Tools, Formula Auditing, Trace Precedents
Alt+T+U+D	Yes	Tools, Formula Auditing, Trace Dependents
Alt+T+U+E	Yes	Tools, Formula Auditing, Trace Error
Alt+T+U+A	Yes	Tools, Formula Auditing, Remove All Arrows
Alt+T+U+F	Yes	Tools, Formula Auditing, Evaluate Formula
Alt+T+U+W	Yes	Tools, Formula Auditing, Show Watch Window
Alt+T+U+M	Yes	Tools, Formula Auditing, Formula Auditing Mode
Alt+T+U+S	No	Tools, Formula Auditing, Show Formula Auditing Toolbar
Alt+T+V	Yes	Tools, Solver
Alt+T+M+M	Yes	Tools, Macro, Macros
Alt+T+M+R	Yes	Tools, Macro, Record New Macro
Alt+T+M+S	Yes	Tools, Macro, Security
Alt+T+M+V	Yes	Tools, Macro, Visual Basic Editor
Alt+T+M+E	No	Tools, Macro, Microsoft Script Editor
Alt+T+I	Yes	Tools, Add-ins

Works in Shortcut	Excel 2010?	Command
Alt+T+C	No	Tools, COM Add-ins
Alt+T+A	Yes	Tools, AutoCorrect Options
Alt+T+C	No	Tools, Customize
Alt+T+O	No	Tools, Options
Alt+T+D	No	Tools, Data Analysis
Alt+D+S	Yes	Data, Sort
Alt+D+F+F	Yes	Data, Filter, AutoFilter
Alt+D+F+S	Yes	Data, Filter, Show All
Alt+D+F+A	Yes	Data, Filter, Advanced Filter
Alt+D+O	Yes	Data, Form
Alt+D+B	Yes	Data, Subtotals
Alt+D+L	Yes	Data, Validation
Alt+D+T	Yes	Data, Table
Alt+D+E	Yes	Data, Text to Columns
Alt+D+N	Yes	Data, Consolidate
Alt+D+G+H	Yes	Data, Group and Outline, Hide Detail
Alt+D+G+S	Yes	Data, Group and Outline, Show Detail
Alt+D+G+G	Yes	Data, Group and Outline, Group
Alt+D+G+U	Yes	Data, Group and Outline, Ungroup
Alt+D+G+A	Yes	Data, Group and Outline, Auto Outline
Alt+D+G+C	Yes	Data, Group and Outline, Clear Outline
Alt+D+G+E	Yes	Data, Group and Outline, Settings
Alt+D+P	Yes	Data, PivotTable and PivotChart Report
Alt+D+D+D	Yes	Data, Import External Data, Import Data
Alt+D+D+W	Yes	Data, Import External Data, New Web Query
Alt+D+D+N	Yes	Data, Import External Data, New Database Query
Alt+D+D+E	Yes	Data, Import External Data,List

Works in Shortcut	Excel 2010?	Command
Alt+D+I+D	No	Data, List, Discard Changes and Refresh
Alt+D+I+B	No	Data, List, Hide Border of Inactive Lists
Alt+D+X+I	Yes	Data, XML, Import
Alt+D+X+E	Yes	Data, XML, Export
Alt+D+X+R	Yes	Data, XML, Refresh XML Data
Alt+D+X+X	Yes	Data, XML, XML Source
Alt+D+X+P	Yes	Data, XML, XML Map Properties
Alt+D+X+Q	Yes	Data, XML, Edit Query
Alt+D+X+A	Yes	Data, XML, XML Expansion Packs Edit Query
Alt+D+D+A	Yes	Data, Import External Data, Data Range Properties
Alt+D+D+M	Yes	Data, Import External Data, Parameters
Alt+D+I+C	Yes	Data, List, Create List
Alt+D+I+R	Yes	Data, List, Resize List
Alt+D+I+T	Yes	Data, List, Total Row
Alt+D+I+V	Yes	Data, List, Convert to Range
Alt+D+I+P	Yes	Data, List, Publish List
Alt+D+I+L	No	Data, List, View List on Server
Alt+D+I+U	No	Data, List, Unlink List
Alt+D+I+Y	No	Data, List, Synchronize
Alt+D+R	Yes	Data, Refresh Data
Alt+W+N	No	Window, New Window
Alt+W+A	No	Window, Arrange
Alt+W+B	No	Window, Compare Side by Side with filename
Alt+W+H	No	Window, Hide
Alt+W+U	No	Window, Unhide
Alt+W+S	No	Window, Split

Works in Shortcut	Excel 2010?	Command
Alt+W+F	No	Window, Freeze Panes
Alt+W+1	No	Window, 1
Alt+W+2	No	Window, 2
Alt+W+3	No	Window, 3
Alt+W+4	No	Window, 4
Alt+W+5	No	Window, 5
Alt+W+6	No	Window, 6
Alt+W+7	No	Window, 7
Alt+W+8	No	Window, 8
Alt+W+9	No	Window, 9
Alt+W+M	No	Window, More Windows
Alt+H+H	No	Help, Microsoft Excel Help
Alt+H+O	No	Help, Show the Office Assistant
Alt+H+M	No	Help, Microsoft Office Online
Alt+H+C	No	Help, Contact Us
Alt+H+L	No	Help, Lotus 1-2-3 Help
Alt+H+K	No	Help, Check for Updates
Alt+H+R	No	Help, Detect and Repair
Alt+H+V	No	Help, Activate Product
Alt+H+F	No	Help, Customer Feedback Options
Alt+H+A	No	Help, About Microsoft Office Excel

Some people liked using Alt+F+T+S in Excel 2003 for File, Print Area, Set Print Area. If you are one of those people, you will be unhappy to hear that your favorite shortcut key is not supported in Excel 2010. However, most of the powerful and common shortcut keys are still available, so there is a good chance that your knowledge of past shortcut keys will help when you upgrade to Excel 2010.

THE EXCEL OPTIONS DIALOG

In legacy versions of Excel, many options were controlled through either Tools, Options or Tools, Customize dialog boxes. Tools, Customize was the important place to turn off the adaptive menus and customize the toolbars. Tools, Options led to the busiest dialog box in Excel; the Options dialog has 173 settings on 14 tabs. In addition, the Options dialog had six buttons that would take you to further dialogs. It was a challenge to find something specific in the old Options dialog.

Excel 2010 offers a redesigned Excel Options dialog. Microsoft had the following goals for the Options dialogs for all the Office products:

- Show the most important settings earlier and more clearly, so they can be found. Most of the items you need to change are now in the General, Formulas, Proofing, and Save categories.

- Move the arcane functions to an Advanced category.

- Add ToolTip icons next to many items, so you can understand exactly what those settings do.

- Make it clear whether a setting affects all workbooks, the current workbook, or the current worksheet.

Oddly, some of the Excel options that were located on the Resources tab in Excel 2007 have been moved to the Backstage view under the Excel category.

Introducing the Excel Options Dialog

This section shows you how to display Excel options and provides an overview of what you might find on each tab. Later sections of this chapter cover each tab in detail. The entry to the Excel Options dialog is at the bottom left of the Excel Backstage view. Open the File menu and find the Options button just above the Exit button, as shown in Figure 6.1.

Click for Excel
Options here

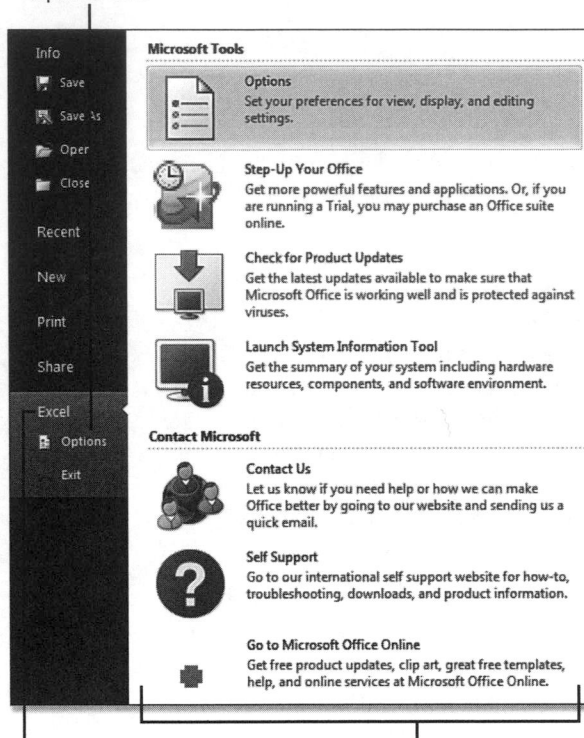

Figure 6.1
The Excel Options button is on the Backstage view.

Click for Resources here   Items formerly in
                                Options, Resource

Instead of tabs across the top, the Excel Options dialog uses ten categories of options along the left side, as shown in Figure 6.2. When you choose a category on the left, the settings for that category appear on the right.

Table 6.1 shows the general types of settings in each category.

Table 6.1   Excel Options Dialog Box Settings

Category	Type of Settings
General	The most commonly used settings, such as user interface settings, color schemes, default font for new workbooks, number of sheets in a new workbook, and customer name.
Formulas	All options for controlling calculation, error-checking rules, and formula settings. Note that options for multithreaded calculations are currently considered obscure enough to be on the Advanced tab rather than on the Formulas tab.

Category	Type of Settings
Proofing	Spell check options and a link to the AutoCorrect dialog.
Save	The default method for saving, autorecovery settings, legacy colors, and web server options.
Language	Choose editing language, ToolTip language, and Help language.
Advanced	All options that Microsoft considers arcane, including Excel 2003's editing, display, general, and Lotus compatibility settings.
Customize Ribbon	Icons to customize the Ribbon. See Chapter 3, "Using Other Excel Interface Improvements," for details on using this panel.
Quick Access Toolbar	Icons to customize the Quick Access toolbar. See Chapter 2, "The Ribbon Interface and Quick Access Toolbar," for details on using this panel.
Add-Ins	A list of available and installed add-ins and smart tags. New add-ins can be installed from the button at the bottom of this category.
Trust Center	Links to the Microsoft Trust Center, with 11 additional categories.

Excel 2007 offered a Resources category in Excel options. In Excel 2010, the items in this category have been moved to the Backstage view. Refer to Figure 6.1.

Figure 6.2
The Excel Options dialog has 10 categories along the left side.

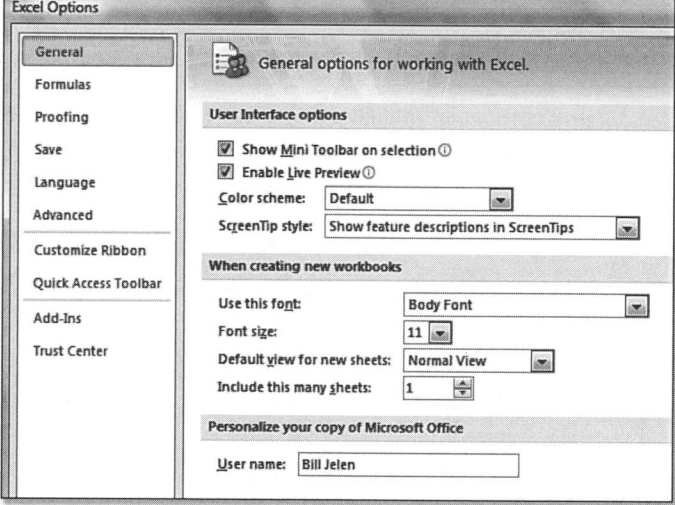

Getting Help with a Setting

Many settings appear with a small i icon. If you hover the mouse near this icon, Excel displays a super ToolTip for the setting. The ToolTip explains what happens when you choose the setting. It also provides some tips about what you need to be aware of when you turn on the setting. For example, the ToolTip in Figure 6.3 shows information about the calculation settings. It also explains that you should use the F9 key to invoke a manual calculation.

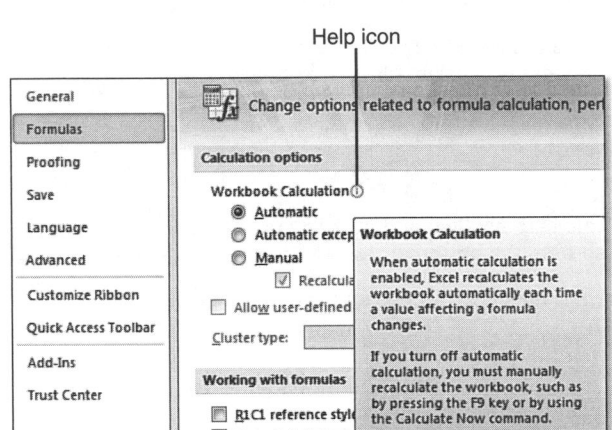

Help icon

Figure 6.3
Exploring
New Excel
2010 Options

Excel 2010 offers 28 new settings that can be grouped into categories for internationalization, performance, security, and general improvements.

Some changes you might notice in Excel 2010:

- The Excel 2007 category of Popular has been renamed to General.

- Edit Custom Lists has been removed from the General category. It is now buried in the Display section of the Advanced tab.

- Show Developer tab in the ribbon has been removed from the General category. You can now choose to show or hide the Developer tab the same as all the other ribbon tabs in the new Customize Ribbon category.

- The Customize Ribbon tab allows you to rearrange commands on the ribbon. See Chapter 3 for details on customizing the ribbon.

Using AutoRecover Options

For many versions, Excel periodically saves a version of your work every 10 minutes. If your computer crashes, the recovery pane offers to let you open the last AutoRecovered version of the file. This feature is sure to save you from retyping data that may have otherwise been lost.

Another painful situation occurs when you do not save changes and then close Excel. Yes, Excel will ask if you want to save changes for each open document, but this question usually pops up at 5:00 p.m. when you are in a hurry to get out of the office. If you are thinking about what you need to do after work and not paying attention to which files are still open, you might click No to the first document and then click No again and again without noticing that the fifth open document was one that should have been saved.

Another scenario is leaving an Excel file open overnight only to discover that Windows Update decided to restart the computer at 3:00 a.m. After being burned by this a dozen times, you can change the behavior of Windows Update to stop doing this. However, if Windows Update closed Excel without saving your documents, you can lose those AutoRecovered documents.

A new setting in Excel 2010 has Excel save the last AutoRecovered version of each open file when you close without saving. This setting is on the Save category of Excel Options and is called Keep the Last Autosaved Version if I Close Without Saving. As soon as you realize that you saved without closing, visit the AutoRecover File Location (usually %AppData%\Roaming\Microsoft\Excel\) to see if your file is there. Copy it, rename it, and paste it back to a safe location.

Another new option in the Save category is the location for storing files that you check out from a SharePoint Server. In the Save Checked Out Files To section, you can specify that files should be saved in an Office Document Cache, as well as the location for the Cache.

New Excel 2010 Options for Internationalization

Nine new options impact non-English versions of Excel 2010:

- Brazilian, Portuguese, and Spanish Proofing Options have been added to the Proofing tab. You can choose Pre-Reform and Post-Reform proofing for Portugese and a verb form for Spanish.

- Separate Language Choices for Help, ToolTips, and Display have been added to the Language tab. You can now edit in one language but have the ToolTips appear in another language. This setting is great for translators and others who must write for the home office in one language but prefer to have help and ToolTips appear in their primary language.

- Right-to-Left Language Support has been added in three places to better support languages such as Arabic and Hebrew that are read from right-to-left. The Display section of the Advanced tab offers a choice to set the Default Direction for all workbooks. You can also override that for a particular worksheet in the Display Worksheet section of the Advanced tab. Finally, the Editing section of the Advanced Tab offers a new cursor movement setting to control the cursor in right-to-left environments.

- Support for the ISO 8601 Date Format appears in the Save tab. Do not use this setting unless you have a specific need and everyone in your workgroup has Excel 2010. If you save in this format and share the workbook with Excel 2007, your dates will be lost.

New Excel 2010 Options for Performance

Many Excel features offer a lot of flash and glitter, which is fine if you have a modern computer with multiple gigabytes of RAM and a fast display processor. On an older machine, though, the animation to show columns sliding over after inserting a new column might severely hamper performance.

The following performance functions are new in Excel 2010:

 **note**

Note that this setting affects all charts that you create. You can use the Draft Mode drop-down on the Chart Tools | Design tab to change draft mode for one or all charts in the current workbook.

- Insert Charts Using Draft Mode has been added to the Chart section of the Advanced category. Excel 2010 lifts the limit on the number of points that can be shown in a single series. If you show 12 monthly points in an accounting chart, you do not need this setting. If you were a scientist showing a million points in a series, this would be a great setting until you are ready to print the final workbook. If you choose this setting, the chart will be rendered in a Draft mode. A drop-down indicator appears in the corner of the chart with options to exit Draft mode or to hide the indicator on the chart (Figure 6.4).

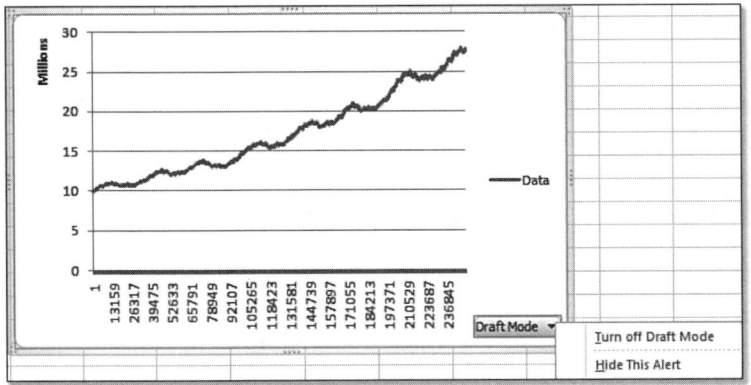

Figure 6.4
A quarter-million point chart in Draft mode renders quickly.

- Hide Draft Notification on Charts has been added to the Chart section of the Advanced category. This will globally remove the Draft Mode drop-down from charts rendered in Draft mode.

- Disable Hardware Graphics Acceleration has been added to the Display section of the Advanced category. Although Hardware Graphics Acceleration is designed to make things faster, this is not true for older PCs. The hardware cards in older Pentium III era machines actually slow things down. If you have an older PC, try turning off the hardware graphics acceleration in Excel to see if the screen renders faster.

- Disable Undo for Large PivotTable Refresh Operations has been added to the General section of the Advanced category. This setting is designed to make the refresh time faster for large pivot table data sets. Note that by default, the undo is turned off automatically when you have more than 300,000 records in the pivot cache.

- A new Image Size & Quality section has been added to the Advanced category. Most people add a photo to dress up the cover page of a document. However, you probably don't need an 8 megapixel image living in the workbook. By default, Excel compresses the image before saving the file. You can control the target output size using the drop-down in Excel options. Choices include 96 ppi, 150 ppi, and 220 ppi. The 96 ppi will look fine on your display. Use 220 ppi for images that you will print. If you want to keep your images at the original size, you can select the new Do Not Compress Images in File setting.

- Discard Editing Data has been added to the Image Size & Quality section of the Advanced category. This has both file size and privacy considerations. In the left side of Figure 6.5, an old picture of my son appears. After cropping the photo, using 96 ppi rendering and Discard Editing Data, the file size was reduced from 445K to 18K. That is a significant file size reduction. More important, it also ensures that only the cropped area of the photo is saved with the document. If you do not have editing data discarded, the next person to receive the spreadsheet can select the image, and click the Crop icon in the Picture Tools, Format ribbon tab to see the parts of the photograph that you cropped out.

- Enable Multi-Threaded Calculation is new in the General section of the Advanced category. If Excel is your primary application, leave this in the default state. If Excel is only a hobby and your computer should be using the other three processors in your quad-core CPU for running another

Figure 6.5
If you do not discard editing data, someone can later see what you cropped out of the photo.

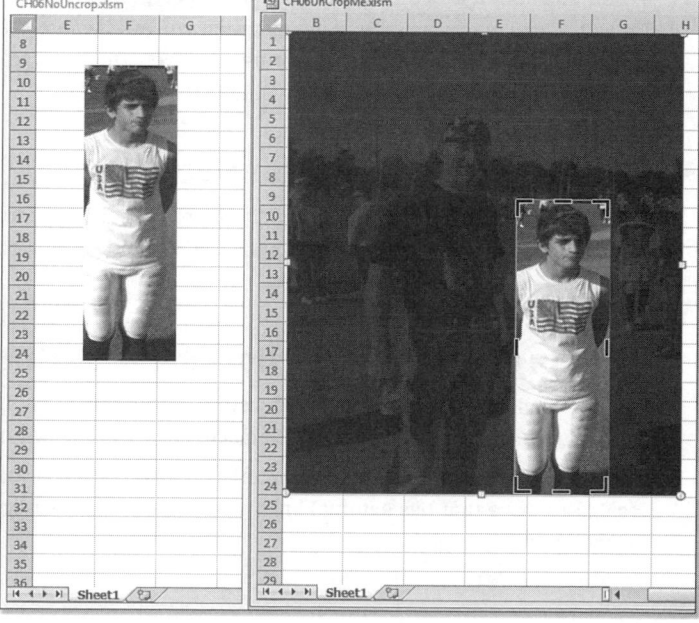

application, you can disable multithreaded calculation.

- Allow User-Defined XLL Functions to Run on a Compute Cluster is new in the Formulas category. Some companies have invested in extending Excel by designing new functions in VB. NET, C#, or C++. The theory is that if you needed a new function, you would have knocked it out in VBA. This means that people are forced to use XLL add-ins when they need better performance than VBA. If you have XLL add-ins, you can use this new setting to send XLL calculations out to a High Perfomance Computing Server. These computers have anywhere from 16 to 4,000 processors! A Microsoft whitepaper at http://download.microsoft.com/download/F/B/5/FB5A8DEE-F313-4A24-AC35-383D71FF5992/HPCServerWhitePaper.pdf describes an insurance risk model where the recalc time is 200 hours on a single processor.

 tip

Keep in mind that if you choose to Enable Content, Excel will remember that this file is a trusted document, which means you will not be required to click Enable Content the next time you open the file.

Additional Excel Features Affecting Performance

The following options, which were added in Excel 2007, also affect performance:

- Show Mini Toolbar on Selection is in the General category. This feature is popular in Word, but it rarely appears in Excel. To use it, you have to select a few characters from a cell while the cell is in Edit mode. The mini toolbar provides quick access to text formatting tools.

- Enable Live Preview is also in the General category. When you hover over a command, the worksheet previews the change before you click to select the setting.

Alert the User When a Potentially Time-Consuming Operation Occurs is in the Advanced category. When this option is set, Excel alerts you when a potentially time-consuming operation occurs. By default, Excel warns you when an operation will affect more than 35,554 cells. You can change the cell threshold or simply turn this feature off. If you are about to do a subtotals command, you need to invoke the command whether it will take a long time.

New Excel 2010 Options for Security

Excel 2010 offers seven new settings for improved security. Most of these are located in the Trust Center. To access the Trust Center, open Excel Options, click the Trust Center category, and then click the Trust Center Settings button.

Working with Trusted Document Settings

Legacy versions of Excel used the concept of a trusted folder. This means that anything stored in a particular folder will not be subject to macro security and external content settings.

Excel 2010 has a somewhat uncharacteristic easing of these rules. When you open a file from your local hard drive that has external links or macros, Excel displays a Security Warning in the Info Bar, as shown in Figure 6.6.

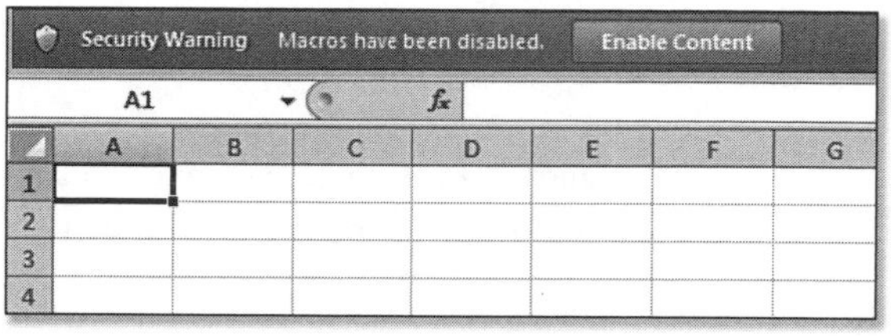

Figure 6.6
Excel alerts you when you open a file with external links or a macro.

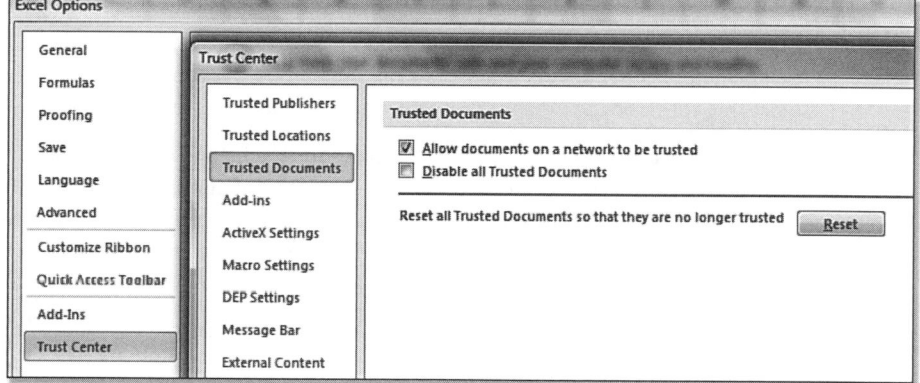

The inherent problem here is that if you open a file and discover the macros are bad, you will not want those macros to open automatically the next time. There is no way to untrust a single document other than deleting, renaming, or moving it. Instead, you have to go to the Trusted Documents category of the Trust Center where you can choose to reset the list of trusted documents (see Figure 6.7).

Figure 6.7
Use the Trusted Document category to reset a list of trusted documents.

Two additional settings in this category modify trusted document behavior. Allow Documents on a Network to Be Trusted controls whether the trusted document concept extends to files stored on a network. You might choose to trust documents on your local hard drive but not trust documents on a network. Alternatively, you might decide that your coworkers are all competent enough never to download malicious macros. In this case, the trusted document paradigm can extend to network drives. Finally, you can choose to Disable All Trusted Documents, which will force you to answer the Enable question for every document that has macros or external links.

Microsoft has been uptight about macro security for a long time. For this reason, it was initially perplexing why Microsoft would choose to turn off external links in Excel 2007. However, after years of clicking Enable repeatedly, it almost seems like the lovable behavior of a paranoid uncle. Most of us will actually miss the repeated requests if it is okay to allow external links to work.

Controlling Other Security Options

Excel 2010 offers the following new security options:

- Enable Data Execution Prevention Mode is in the new DEP Settings category of the Trust Center. Everything on a computer is stored as a series of 1s and 0s. For example, program code is a bunch of 1s and 0s, and spreadsheet data is stored as a series of 1s and 0s.

- Antivirus programs are vigilant in examining program code for viruses but may not search your spreadsheet data looking for malicious code. For this reason, hackers might use an approach where they embed the bad code in a worksheet data set and then have a virus attempt to run code that is stored in the data. This is pretty advanced stuff—you would have to be a 13-year-old computer geek to understand it.

- Windows XP SP2 introduced a set of technologies to prevent malicious code from exploiting this vulnerability. Most of the time, it makes sense to prevent anything stored in the data area of memory from being executed as program code. Some programs legitimately need to run code from the data area. Leave this setting turned on unless you have a specific program that has a DEP compatibility problem.

- Show Customer Submitted Office Live Content is a new setting in the General section of the Advanced tab. Other people can share their general-purpose templates on Office Live. Do not select this check box to prevent those documents from being available to you.

- Choose to Block or Open Certain File Types in Protected View is in the File Block Settings of the Trust Center. Excel 2010 can open many types of files, going back to Excel 2 Macrosheets. Excel 2010 is more secure than these old files. However, if you want to prevent the older files from opening, or perhaps you want to open them in Protected Mode where you can see the data but not allow any macros to run, you can adjust these settings in the new File Block Settings (see Figure 6.8).

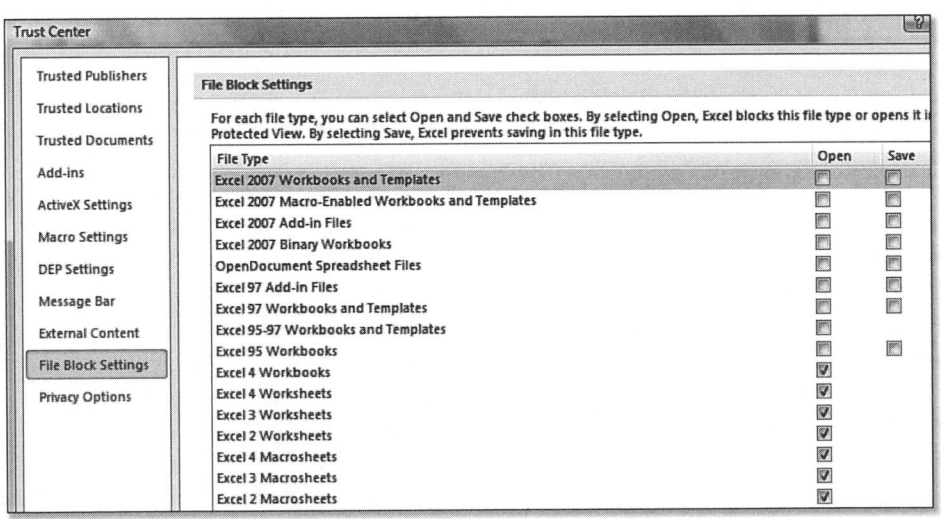

Figure 6.8
You can choose to open certain file types in Protected View to prevent malicious code from running.

- Automatically Detect Installed Office Applications to Improve Office Online Search Results is in the Privacy Section of the Trust Center. Many help topics are coming from Office Online. These topics might refer you to help topics about Outlook or PowerPoint. With this new setting, you computer will tune the Office Online results to not offer topics about Outlook if you do not have Outlook installed. This seems like a good thing, but if you do not want Microsoft to know which applications you have installed, you can prevent this information from being sent.

- Allow Research Task Pane to Check for and Install New Services is new in the Privacy section of the Trust Center. The Research pane can be displayed using Review—Research. It offers stock quotes, a dictionary, and a thesaurus. By selecting this check box, Microsoft will make additional research tools available to you as they are released.

Ten Options to Consider

Although hundreds of Excel options exist, this section provides a quick review of some options that might be helpful to you.

- Update your name in the General category. The name stored on this tab is used in cell comments and in the document properties.

- Save File in This Format in the Save category. If you regularly create macros, choose the Excel Macro-Enabled Workbook as the default format type.

- Update your Default File Location in the Save tab. Excel always wants to save new documents in your My Documents folder. However, if you always work in the C:\AccountingFiles\ folder, update the default folder to match your preferred location.

- After Pressing Enter, Move Selection Direction is the first setting in the Advanced category. If you regularly perform data entry and prefer that the cell pointer move across the spreadsheet, change this setting from Down to Right.

- Show This Number of Recent Documents has been enhanced dramatically since Excel 2003. Whereas legacy versions of Excel showed up to nine recent documents at the bottom of the File menu, Excel 2010 allows you to see up to 50 recent documents in the Recent category of the File menu. This setting can be increased up to 50 by visiting the Display section of the Advanced Category.

- Edit Custom Lists has been moved to the Display section of the Advanced category. Custom lists add functionality to the fill handle, allow custom sort orders, and control how fields are displayed in the label area of a pivot table. Type a list in the correct sequence in a worksheet. Edit Custom Lists and click Import. Excel can now automatically extend items from that list, the same as it can extend January into February, March, and so on.

- Make Excel look less like Excel by hiding interface elements in the three Display sections of the Advanced category. You can turn off the formula bar, scrollbars, sheet tabs, row and column headers, and gridlines. You can customize the ribbon to remove all main tabs except the File menu. The point is that if you design a model to be used by someone who never uses Excel, the person can open the model, plug in a few numbers, and get the result without having to see the entire Excel interface. Figure 6.9 shows an Excel screen with all elements removed.

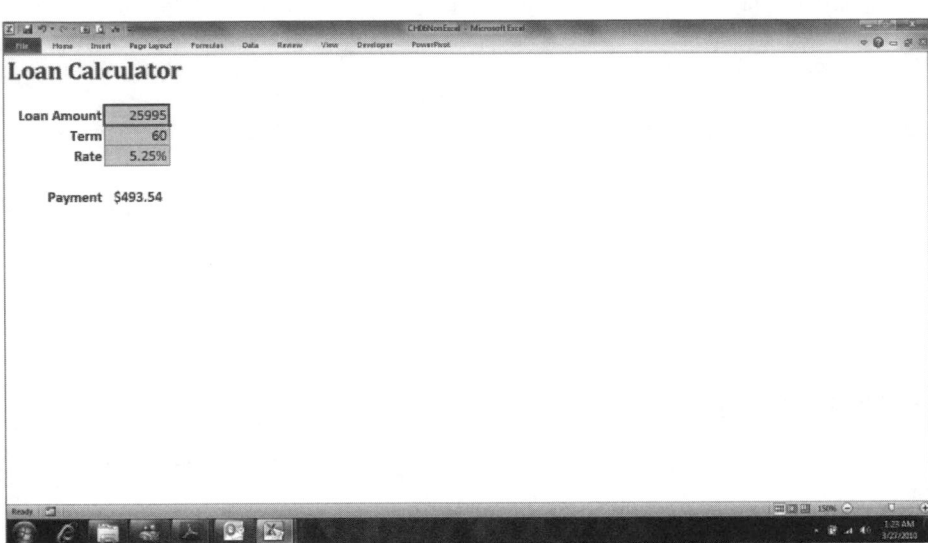

- Show Zero in Cells That Have Zero Value is in the Display Options for This Worksheet section of the Advanced Category. Occasionally people want zeros to be displayed as blanks. Although a custom number format of 0;-0;; will do this, you can change the setting globally by clearing this option.

- Group Dates in the AutoFilter Menu is in the Display Options for This Workbook section of the Advanced category. Starting with Excel 2007, date columns show a hierarchical view of years, months, days in the AutoFilter drop-down. If you like the old behavior of showing each individual date, turn off this setting.

- Add a folder on your local hard drive as a Trusted Location. Files stored in a trusted location automatically have macros enabled and external links updated. If you can trust that you will not write malicious code, then define a folder on your hard drive as a trusted location. From Excel Options, select the Trust Center category and then Trust Center Settings. In the Trust Center, select Trusted Locations, Add New Location.

Five Excel Oddities

You may rarely need any of the features presented in this section. However, in the right circumstance, they can be timesavers.

- Adjust the Gridline Color in the Display section of the Advanced category. If you are tired of gray gridlines, you can get a new outlook with bright red gridlines.

- Allow Negative Time by switching to the 1904 Date System in the General section of the Advanced category. Excel never allows a time to return a negative time. However, if you are tracking comp time and you allow people to borrow against future comp time, it might be nice to allow negative time. In this case, switch to the 1904 date system to have up to 3 years of negative time.

- Put an end to the green triangles on your account numbers stored as text. Most of the green triangle indicators are useful. However, if you have a column of text account numbers where most values are numbers, seeing thousands of green triangles can be annoying. In addition, the green triangles can hide other, more serious, problems. Clear the Numbers Formatted as Text or Preceded by an Apostrophe in the Error Checking Rules check box in the Formulas category.

 note

Note that unlike Excel 2003, the status bar can no longer be removed in the Excel 2010 interface.

- Automatically Insert a Decimal Point replicates the antique adding machines that were office fixtures in the 1970s. When working with a manual adding machine, it was frustrating to type decimal points. You could type 123456 and the adding machine would interpret the entry as 1,234.56. If you find that you are doing massive data entry of numbers in dollars and cents, you can have Excel replicate the old adding machine functionality. After enabling this setting, you can indicate how many digits of the number should be interpreted as after the decimal point. The only hassle is that you need to enter $5 as "500". The old adding machines actually had a 00 key, but those are long since gone.

- Change Dwight to Diapers using AutoCorrect Options. If you are a fan of the NBC sitcom "The Office", you might remember the 2007 episode in which Jim allegedly put a macro on Dwight's computer that automatically changed the typed word "Dwight" to "diapers." However, this doesn't require a macro. From Excel Options, choose the Proofing Category, and then click the AutoCorrect Options button. On the AutoCorrect tab, you can type new correction pairs. In this example, you would type Dwight into the Replace box and Diapers into the With box. The next time someone types Dwight and then a space, the word will automatically change to Diapers. You can also remove correction pairs by selecting the pairs and then pressing Delete. For example, if you hate that Microsoft converts (c) to ©, you can delete that entry from the list.

 To see a video demo of this trick, search for Excel In Depth 6 at YouTube.

Guide to Excel Options

Table 6.2 shows every Excel feature that you can change in the Excel Options dialog. The table shows the feature, the category where it can be modified, the section within the category, and the text of the option.

Table 6.2 Excel Options by Feature

Feature	Category	Section	Text
Mini Toolbar	General	User Interface Options	Show Mini Toolbar on Selection
Live Preview	General	User Interface Options	Enable Live Preview
Skin	General	User Interface Options	Color Scheme
Screentips	General	User Interface Options	Screentip Style
Font	General	New Workbooks	Use This Font
Font Size	General	New Workbooks	Font Size
View	General	New Workbooks	Default View for New Sheets
Worksheets	General	New Workbooks	Include This Many Sheets
Name	General	Personalize	User Name
Calculation	Formulas	Calculation Options	Workbook Calculation Automatic
Calculation	Formulas	Calculation Options	Workbook Calculation Automatic Except for Data Tables
Calculation	Formulas	Calculation Options	Calculate Workbook Manual
Calculation	Formulas	Calculation Options	Recalculate Workbook Before Saving
Circular Reference	Formulas	Calculation Options	Enable Iterative Calculation Formulas
Circular Reference	Formulas	Calculation Options	Maximum Iterations Formulas
Circular Reference	Formulas	Calculation Options	Maximum Change Formulas
HPC Cluster	Formulas	Calculation Options	Allow XLL Functions to Run on a Compute Cluster
R1C1 Style	Formulas	Working with Formulas	R1C1 Reference Style
AutoComplete	Formulas	Working with Formulas	Formula AutoComplete
Formula Style	Formulas	Working with Formulas	Use Table Names in Formulas
GetPivotData	Formulas	Working with Formulas	Use GetPivotData Functions for PivotTable References

Feature	Category	Section	Text
Error Checking	Formulas	Error Checking	Enable Background Error Checking
Error Indicators	Formulas	Error Checking	Indicate Errors Using This Color
Errors Ignored	Formulas	Error Checking	Reset Ignored Errors
Errors in Formulas	Formulas	Error Checking Rules	Error Checking Rules—Cells Containing Formulas That Result in an Error
Formulas Inconsistent in Table	Formulas	Error Checking Rules	Error Checking Rules—Inconsistent Calculated Column Formulas in Tables
Dates as Text	Formulas	Error Checking Rules	Error Checking Rules—Cells Containing Years Represented as Two Digits
Numbers as Text	Formulas	Error Checking Rules	Error Checking Rules—Numbers Formatted as Text or Preceded by an Apostrophe
Formulas—Rules Inconsistent	Formulas	Error Checking Rules	Error Checking Rules—Formulas Inconsistent with Other Formulas in the Region
Formulas—Omitted Cells	Formulas	Error Checking Rules	Error Checking Rules—Formulas Which Omit Cells in a Region
Protected Sheet with Unlocked Formulas	Formulas	Error Checking Rules	Error Checking Rules—Unlocked Cells Containing Formulas
Empty Cells in Formula	Formulas	Error Checking Rules	Error Checking Rules—Formulas Referring to Empty Cells
Table with Invalid Data	Formulas	Error Checking Rules	Error Checking Rules—Data Entered in a Table Is Invalid
AutoCorrect	Proofing	Autocorrect Options	Autocorrect Options
Spelling	Proofing	When Correcting Spelling	Spelling—Ignore Words in Uppercase
Spelling	Proofing	When Correcting Spelling—Ignore Words That Contain Numbers	

Feature	Category	Section	Text
Spelling	Proofing	When Correcting Spelling	Spelling—Ignore Internet and File Addresses
Spelling	Proofing	When Correcting Spelling	Spelling—Flag Repeated Words
Spelling	Proofing	When Correcting Spelling	Spelling—Enforce Accented Uppercase in French
Spelling	Proofing	When Correcting Spelling	Spelling—Suggest from Main
Dictionary Only			
Spelling	Proofing	When Correcting Spelling	Spelling—Custom Dictionaries
Spelling	Proofing	When Correcting Spelling	French Modes
Spelling	Proofing	When Correcting Spelling	Spanish Modes
Spelling	Proofing	When Correcting Spelling	Portuguese Modes
Spelling	Proofing	When Correcting Spelling	Brazilian Modes
Spelling	Proofing	When Correcting Spelling	Dictionary Language
File Format	Save	Save Workbooks	Save Files in This Format
AutoRecover	Save	Save Workbooks	Save AutoRecover Information Every n Minutes
AutoRecover	Save	Save Workbooks	Keep the Last Auto Recovered File if I Close Without Saving
AutoRecover	Save	Save Workbooks	AutoRecover File Location Location
Folder for Files	Save	Save Workbooks	Default File Location
ISO Dates	Save	Save Workbooks	Save Date and Time Values Using ISO 8601 Date Format (may limit precision)
AutoRecover—Disable	Save	Autorecover Exceptions	Disable AutoRecover for This Workbook Only

Feature	Category	Section	Text
Server	Save	Offline Editing Options for Document Management Server Files	Save Checked-Out Files to the Server Drafts Location Files on This Computer
Server	Save	Offline Editing Options for Document Management Server Files	Save Checked-Out Files to the Web Server
Server	Save	Offline Editing Options	Server Drafts Location or Office Document Cache for Document Management Server Files
Color	Save	Preserve Visual Appearance	Choose What Colors Will Be Seen in Legacy Versions of Excel
Languages	Language	Preferences	Choose Editing Languages
Help Language	Language	Preferences	Choose Display and Help Language
ScreenTip Language	Language	Preferences	Choose ScreenTip Language
Direction after Enter	Advanced	Editing	After Pressing Enter, Move Selection Direction
Decimal Places	Advanced	Editing	Automatically Insert a Decimal Point with n Places
Fill Handle	Advanced	Editing	Enable Fill Handle and Cell Drag and Drop
Override Alert	Advanced	Editing	Alert Before Overwriting Cells with Drag and Drop
In-Cell Editing	Advanced	Editing	Allow Editing Directly in Cell
Extend Ranges	Advanced	Editing	Extend Data Range Formats and Formulas
Percentages	Advanced	Editing	Enable Automatic Percent Entry
AutoComplete	Advanced	Editing	Enable Autocomplete for Cell Values
Mouse Wheel	Advanced	Editing	Zoom on Roll with Intellimouse

Feature	Category	Section	Text
Time Consuming Operation	Advanced	Editing	Alert the User When a Potentially Time Consuming Operation Occurs
Time Consuming Operation	Advanced	Editing	Time Consuming Is When This Number of Cells (In Thousands) Is Affected
Numeric Separators	Advanced	Editing	Use System Separators
Numeric Separators	Advanced	Editing	Decimal Separator
Numeric Separators	Advanced	Editing	Thousands Separator
Cursor Movement	Advanced	Editing	Cursor Movement Logical or Visual
Paste	Advanced	Cut, Copy, and Paste	Show Paste Options Buttons
Insert	Advanced	Cut, Copy, and Paste	Show Insert Options Buttons
Images	Advanced	Cut, Copy, and Paste	Cut, Copy, and Sort Inserted Objects with Their Parent Cells
Cropped Images	Advanced	Image Size and Quality	Discard Editing Data
Image Compression	Advanced	Image Size and Quality	Do Not Compress Images in File
Image Compression	Advanced	Image Size and Quality	Set Default Target Output to n ppi
Chart Elements	Advanced	Chart	Show Chart Element Names on Hover
Chart Data Points	Advanced	Chart	Show Data Point Values on Hover
Draft Mode	Advanced	Chart	Insert Charts Using Draft Mode
Draft Indicator	Advanced	Chart	Hide Draft Mode Notification on Charts
Recent File List	Advanced	Display	Show This Number of Recent Documents
Ruler	Advanced	Display	Ruler Units
Taskbar	Advanced	Display	Show All Windows in the Taskbar
Formula Bar	Advanced	Display	Show Formula Bar

Feature	Category	Section	Text
Screentips	Advanced	Display	Show Function Screentips
Acceleration	Advanced	Display	Disable Hardware Graphics Acceleration
Comment Display	Advanced	Display	For Cells with Comments, Show No Comments or Indicators
Comment Display	Advanced	Display	For Cells with Comments, Show Indicators Only, and Comments on Hover
Comment Display	Advanced	Display	For Cells with Comments, Show Comment and Indicators
Right-to-Left	Advanced	Display	Default Direction
Custom Lists	General	Top Options	Create Lists for Use in Sorts and Fill Sequences
Scrollbars	Advanced	Display—Workbook	Show Horizontal Scroll Bar (Affects one workbook only)
Scrollbars	Advanced	Display—Workbook	Show Vertical Scroll Bar (Workbook only)
Tabs	Advanced	Display—Workbook	Show Sheet Tabs (Workbook only)
Dates in AutoFilter	Advanced	Display—Workbook	Group Dates in the AutoFilter Menu (Workbook only)
Images, Hide	Advanced	Display—Workbook	For Objects, Show or Hide (Workbook only)
Column & Row Headers	Advanced	Display—Worksheets	Show Row and Column Headers (Affects one worksheet only)
Formulas, Show	Advanced	Display—Worksheets	Show Formulas in Cells Instead of Their Calculated Results (Worksheet)
Right-to-Left (sheet)	Advanced	Display—Worksheets	Show Sheet Right-to-Left
Page Breaks	Advanced	Display—Worksheets	Show Page Breaks (Worksheet)
Zero, Display	Advanced	Display—Worksheets	Show a Zero in Cells That Have Zero Value (Worksheet)

Feature	Category	Section	Text
Outline Symbols	Advanced	Display—Worksheets	Show Outline Symbols if an Outline is Applied (Worksheet)
Gridlines	Advanced	Display—Worksheets	Show Gridlines (Worksheet)
Gridline Color	Advanced	Display—Worksheets	Gridline Color (Worksheet)
Multi-Threaded Calculation	Advanced	General	Enable Multi-Threaded Calculation
Multi-Threaded Calculation	Advanced Threads	Formulas	Number of Calculation Threads
Links, Update	Advanced	When Calculating Workbook	Update Links to Other Documents
Precision as Displayed	Advanced	When Calculating Workbook	Set Precision as Displayed
Dates, 1904 System	Advanced	When Calculating Workbook	Use 1904 Date System
External Link Values	Advanced	When Calculating Workbook	Save External Link Values
Sound Feedback	Advanced	General	Provide Feedback with Sound
Animation Feedback	Advanced	General	Provide Feedback with Animation
DDE	Advanced	General	Ignore Other Applications That Use DDE
Links, Update	Advanced	General	Ask to Update Automatic Links
Add-In Errors	Advanced	General	Show Add-In User Interface Errors
Paper Size	Advanced	General	Scale Content for A4 or 8.5"×11" Paper Sizes
Office Live	Advanced	General	Show Customer Submitted Office Live Content
Start-Up Folder	Advanced	General	At Start-Up, Open All Files In
Web Options	Advanced	General	Web Options
Processing	Advanced	General	Enable Multi-Threaded Processing

Feature	Category	Section	Text
Pivot Undo	Advanced	General	Disable Undo for Large PivotTable refresh operations (over n thousand records)
Service Options	Advanced	General	Service Options
Menu Access Key	Advanced	Lotus Compatibility	Microsoft Office Excel Menu Key
Navigation Keys	Advanced	Lotus Compatibility	Transition Navigation Keys
Lotus Formula Evaluation	Advanced	Lotus for Worksheet	Lotus Transition Formula Evaluation
Lotus Formula	Advanced	Lotus for Worksheet	Lotus Entry Transition Formula Entry
Ribbon	Customize Ribbon	N/A	Add>>
Ribbon	Customize Ribbon	N/A	Remove
Ribbon	Customize Ribbon	N/A	New Tab
Ribbon	Customize Ribbon	N/A	New Group
Ribbon	Customize Ribbon	N/A	Rename
Ribbon	Customize Ribbon	N/A	Restore Defaults
Ribbon	Customize Ribbon	N/A	Import/Export
QAT	Quick Access Toolbar	N/A	Add>>
QAT	Quick Access Toolbar	N/A	Remove
QAT	Quick Access Toolbar	N/A	New Tab
QAT	Quick Access Toolbar	N/A	New Group
QAT	Quick Access Toolbar	N/A	Rename

Feature	Category	Section	Text
QAT	Quick Access Toolbar	N/A	Restore Defaults
QAT	Quick Access Toolbar	N/A	Import/Export
QAT Location	Quick Access Toolbar	N/A	Show QAT Below Ribbon
Add-Ins	Add-Ins	N/A	Manage Excel Add-Ins
Trust	Trust Center	N/A	Trust Center Settings

7

THE BIG GRID AND FILE FORMATS

Word leaked out in 2004 that Microsoft would be increasing the number of rows in the next version of Excel. Although no one new exactly how many rows, one thing was certain—the Excel file format would have to change. The old XLS file format was designed around cell addressing that would fit in a 2^{16} address space, hence the limit of 65,536 rows.

Excel Grid Limits

The new grid in Excel offers 1,048,576 rows—that is, 2^{20} rows—a sixteen-fold increase from 65,536 rows in Excel 2003. It offers 16,384 columns—that is, 2^{14} columns—an increase from 256 columns in Excel 2003. Overall, the new grid provides for 17.1 billion cells on each worksheet.

You can now analyze more complex data sets. For example, if you regularly analyze 2,000 items, you can analyze 2.5 years of monthly data in one Excel 2003 worksheet. In Excel 2010, you can analyze 10 years of weekly data or 43 years of monthly data. Columnwise, legacy versions of Excel could handle only 9 months of daily data going across the worksheet. Excel 2010 can handle 45 years of daily dates or 63 years of weekdays.

It is interesting to compare the size increase in the history of spreadsheets. You will see that the size increase is unprecedented. Here is a brief history of spreadsheets:

- In October 1979, VisiCalc debuted with 255 rows and 63 columns.

- In 1983, Lotus 1-2-3 debuted with 8,192 rows and 256 columns. The 2 million cells per worksheet in this version was a 13,000% increase over VisiCalc.

- In 1987, early versions of Excel offered 16,384 rows by 255 columns. This 4 million cells was double the amount offered in Lotus 1-2-3 release 2.2.

- In Excel 97, Microsoft increased Excel to offer 65,536 rows by 255 columns. This 16.7 million cells per spreadsheet was quadruple the previous limit.

- In Excel 2007, the new grid size is 1,048,576 rows by 16,384 columns. This is 17.1 billion cells, which is a 102,300% increase over the previous limit.

Why Are There Only 65,536 Rows in My Excel 2007 Spreadsheet?

When you initially install Excel 2010 and open one of your large workbooks, you might be disappointed to find only 65,536 rows in the worksheet. When this occurs, it means you are in Compatibility mode. Any time that you open an .xls format file, you are limited to the 65,536 rows that were available in legacy versions of Excel. Note that the title bar of Figure 7.1 indicates that you are in Compatibility mode.

To leave Compatibility mode, select File, and then select Convert, as shown in Figure 7.2. Excel tells you that the old file will be deleted and replaced by a new file. After the file conversion is done, Excel offers to close and reopen the file so that you are no longer in Compatibility mode.

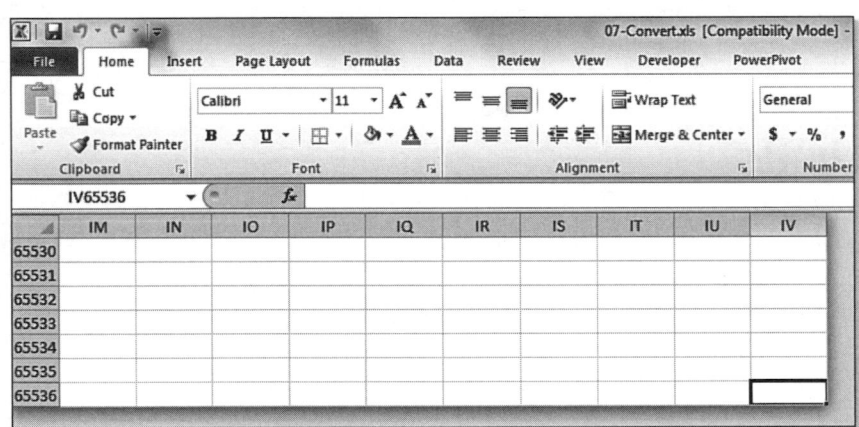

Figure 7.1
What is all the hype? There are still only 65,536 rows.

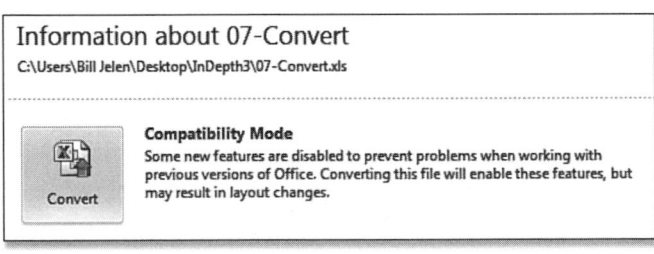

Figure 7.2
You select Convert to leave Compatibility mode.

With the bigger grid, it is far more likely that you will encounter larger files, formulas, and pivot tables. With a 102,300% increase in the file, many of the old limits in Excel 2003 no longer make sense. Because of the bigger grid, Microsoft provided relaxed limits in many areas. Limits are discussed in the next section.

There is also an unusual quirk with the big grid. Previously, columns were labeled from A to IV. Now, columns are labeled from A to XFD. This means that many three-letter words are now valid column names. In legacy versions of Excel, range names such as ROI2011 or TAX2008 would have been legal names. Now that these are actual cell addresses, those names can no longer be used in Excel 2010. Excel automatically changes such names during the conversion process. For example, a name such as YTD2012 will change to _YTD2012.

In addition, you don't have to worry about updating most formulas, because any formulas that reference the old name will change. However, if you have any VBA macros that refer to the old name, or any formulas that included the old name in double quotes in the INDIRECT function, you will have to manually fix those.

Other Limits in Excel 2010

In addition to the grid size, a number of other aspects of Excel have new limits. Table 7.1 illustrates these new limits.

Table 7.1   Excel 2010 Limits

Item	Old Limit	New Limit
PC memory Excel can use	1GB	Max allowed by Windows
Number of unique colors in a single workbook	56	4.3 billion
Number of conditional format conditions on a cell	3	Limited by available memory
Number of levels of sorting	3	64
Number of items in the AutoFilter drop-down	1,000	10,000
Number of characters that can display in one cell	1,024	32,768
Number of characters in a cell that Excel can print	1,024	32,768
Number of unique cell styles in a workbook	4,096	65,536
Maximum length of formulas	1,024 characters	8,192 characters
Number of levels of nesting in formulas	7	64
Maximum number of arguments in a function	30	255
Number of characters that can be displayed	255	32K in a cell formatted as text
Number of items that can be found with Find All	65,536	~2 billion

Item	Old Limit	New Limit
Number of columns allowed in a pivot table	255	16,384
Number of unique items in a single pivot field	32,768	~1 million
Number of fields in a pivot table	255	16,384
Number of cells that can depend on a single area before Excel must do full calculations instead of partial calculations (because it can no longer track the dependencies required to do partial calculations)	8,102	Limited by available memory
Number of different areas in a sheet that can have dependencies before Excel must do full calculations instead of partial calculations (because it can no longer track the dependencies required to do partial calculations)	65,536	Limited by available memory
Number of array formulas in a worksheet that can refer to another (given) worksheet	65,536	Limited by available memory
Number of categories that custom functions can be grouped into	32	255
Number of characters that can be updated in a nonresident external workbook reference	255	32,768
Number of rows of a column or columns that can be referred to in an array formula (full-column references allowed)	65,335	Limitation removed

As you can see in Table 7.1, Excel 2010 includes some excellent improvements.

It also has some improvements that allow people to build worse spreadsheets. Many people try to rely on nested IF functions when they should instead learn about VLOOKUP. Increasing from 7 to 64 nested functions allows people to put off learning about VLOOKUP for even longer.

> *If you've been avoiding* VLOOKUP, *you can read about it in Chapter 12, "Using Powerful Functions: Logical, Lookup, and Database Functions."*

With legacy versions of Excel, any pivot table that relied on daily dates almost always had to be built with the dates going down the side instead of across the rows. This was annoying, especially if you planned on rolling the dates up to months or quarters that would eventually fit in the 256 columns.

The number of Excel formats was a problem that was rarely encountered but that caused horrible frustration when it was hit. Now the limit will be hit much less frequently.

Even with these new limits, some areas could still be improved. For example, there is still a limit of eight levels of indentation in outlining. However, for the most part, the new limits are incredible and allow much larger analyses to happen in Excel instead of elsewhere.

Tips for Navigating the Big Grid

The navigation tips described in the following sections are not new to Excel 2010. However, with 17 billion cells, there is a better chance that you don't want to be scrolling around with the Page Up and Page Down keys.

Using Shortcut Keys to Move Around

A variety of shortcuts enable you to quickly move around a worksheet:

Shortcut	What It Does
Ctrl+Home	Move to Cell A1
Home	Move to Column A of the current row
Ctrl+End	Move to the last used cell in a worksheet
Ctrl+any arrow key	Jump to the end of a contiguous range
Ctrl+Up Arrow	Move to the first row in the data if your data has no blank cells
Ctrl+Down Arrow	Move t o the last row in the data if your data has no blank cells

Using the End Key to Navigate

The End key is one of the six keys above the arrow keys on a standard keyboard. When you press the End key, an indicator lights up in the status bar of the Excel window. When Excel is in End mode, you can press an arrow key or the Home key. Pressing an arrow key takes you to the edge of a contiguous range of cells. Pressing Home while in End mode will take you to the last used cell in the worksheet.

In Figure 7.3, pressing End and then the down arrow key causes the cell pointer to jump from C30 to C36. When the cell pointer is on the edge of a range, pressing End followed by the down arrow again causes Excel to jump over a range of blank cells and land on the starting edge of the next range. For example, pressing End+down arrow from C36 causes the cell pointer to jump to C39. Press End and then right arrow from C39 to jump the gap and land in F39.

If you press the End key to move right or down from the last cell that contains data, the cell pointer jumps to the last row or column in the spreadsheet. In a blank worksheet, you can press End+down arrow and End+right arrow to move to XFD1048576.

 To see a demo of using the End key to navigate, search for Excel In Depth 7 at YouTube.

	A	B	C	D	E	F	G	H
29	19520474	536510	682			$19,520M	$537K	682
30	517	919134	1100234			517	$919K	$1,100.2M
31	6085999	999	279608			$6,086.0M	999	$280K
32	23683765	561	1465003			$23,684M	561	$1,465.0M
33	496250	635006	154527			$496K	$635K	$155K
34	8955611	820	29070652			$8,955.6M	820	$29,071M
35	653485	334702	941			$653K	$335K	941
36	221	10030144	801			221	$10,030M	801
37								
38								
39	780696	14217683	844883			$781K	$14,218M	$845K
40	17	878	669314			17	878	$669K
41	715	558812	25648			715	$559K	$26K
42	120194	28858528	751			$120K	$28,859M	751
43	505252	13753632	64939			$505K	$13,754M	$65K
44	928282	4072000	49851			$928K	$4,072.0M	$50K
45	491	502	812856			491	502	$813K
46								

Figure 7.3
End+arrow key will cause Excel to jump over a range of blank cells or a contiguous range of cells.

Using the Current Range to Navigate

If your data has many blank cells, using Ctrl+arrow keys or Ctrl+End key will lead to frustration.

You can press Ctrl+* to select the current region. A current region starts from the current nonblank cell and extends out in all directions until Excel encounters a completely blank row, a completely blank column, or the edge of the spreadsheet.

Then you can press Ctrl+. (that is, Ctrl plus the period key) to move the active cell to each corner of the selection. From the top-left cell of a region, you can press Ctrl+* and then press Ctrl+. twice to go to the last used cell in the current region.

Using Go To to Navigate

You can press the F5 key to display the Go To dialog. Then you can type a cell address and press OK to quickly jump to that cell.

You can also use the Name box the same way you use the Go To dialog. The Name box is the drop-down area immediately to the left of the formula bar. You click in the Name box, type a valid cell address, and press Enter. Excel then jumps to that cell.

Understanding the New File Formats

Excel 2007 and Excel 2010 offer three new file formats, which are discussed in this section. Later, the section on file compatibility discusses how you can continue to share files with people using legacy versions of Excel.

A Brief History of File Formats

Excel has traditionally stored workbooks in Binary Interchange File Format (BIFF). The BIFF specification has changed occasionally over time.

In 1993, when Excel expanded to 16,384 rows, Microsoft began using BIFF5 format. In 1993, most companies did not have corporate local area networks (LANs); a file format conversion therefore usually affected just one person on one computer. If you had upgraded from Excel 4 to Excel 5, as long as you had a way to convert your Excel 4 files to Excel's new BIFF5 format, everything was fine.

In 1997, Microsoft introduced a major file change, BIFF8. This version of BIFF allowed 65,536 rows. The rise of the Internet and email meant that far more people were now sharing files. Excel 97 offered a way to save files in the old format in case you needed to share files with a person using legacy versions of Excel.

 note

Although you will generally be saving files in one of the .XLSB, .XLSSX, and .XLSM formats, there are other new file formats. The .XLAM format is used by developers to distribute add-ins. The .XLST is a template format.

All BIFF versions are proprietary formats. Figure 7.4 shows a simple Excel 2003 spreadsheet and the corresponding BIFF, as viewed in Notepad. You would certainly never be able to open a Notepad window and begin typing a new spreadsheet. Similarly, it would be very difficult for other applications to extract data from the BIFF format.

▲	A	B	C	D	E	F	G
1	308	957	16120718		308	957	$16,121M
2	908703	908	17530178		$909K	908	$17,530M
3	19520474	536510	682		$19,520M	$537K	682
4	517	919134	1100334		517	$919K	$1,100.3M
5	6085999						
6	23683765						
7	496250						
8	8955611						
9	653485						
10	221						
11	43						
12	5036						
13	370062						
14	20583642						
15	3781825						

Figure 7.4
BIFF files are difficult for other applications to read.

In Excel 2000, Microsoft flirted with a new HTML file format. By default, files were stored as XLS files in BIFF8 format. However, you could save a file as an HTML file and later open that HTML file in Excel 2000. With some limitations, most contents of the file and formatting could be successfully round-tripped from Excel to HTML and back to Excel.

This produced an interesting new paradigm: It would be possible for any program that could read or write text files to extract data from the Excel HTML file. A program other than Excel could easily read or produce this format.

Using HTML made sense in 1998–2000. The rise of the Internet made HTML a very popular format. However, although HTML is a great language for the display of information, it is not necessarily a smart language.

In 1998, the World Wide Web Consortium published the first 1.0 specification for a new language called Extensible Markup Language (XML), which presents data that any platform or application can read. Like HTML, XML is a simple text file that can be read or created with Notepad. Excel 2002 offered a way to export data in XML. Excel 2003 continued to use BIFF8 as the standard file format, but you can choose to save a workbook in XML format. When you later opened the XML file in Excel, all the formulas and formatting would be successfully round-tripped. XML in Excel 2003 did not support VBA or charts.

There are a number of advantages to XML. Because an XML file is a simple text file, any program can easily read data from it. This file format is also less prone to corruption than BIFF. If you randomly wipe out several bytes of a BIFF file, it is likely that the file will be corrupt and no longer open in Excel. If you truncate or corrupt several bytes of an XML file, the rest of the data is still readable in Excel.

Excel 2010 offers three official file formats—BIFF12, XLSX, and XLSM—described in the following sections. In addition, Excel offers support for BIFF8 and even BIFF5, in case you have files floating around from Excel 95.

Using the New Binary File Format: BIFF12

With Excel 2007's increase in rows and columns, BIFF8 would no longer work. Excel 2010 can save files in a new binary file format known as BIFF12. Files stored in BIFF12 have an `.xlsb` file extension. The Save As dialog box calls this type of file Excel Binary Workbook. For the first time, the binary workbook is not the default method for saving in Excel.

BIFF12 suffers from the same problems as all previous BIFF versions: It is difficult for other applications to read from or write to BIFF formats, and if parts of the BIFF12 file become corrupted or truncated, Excel has a difficult time successfully loading the file.

 note

If you are extremely concerned with performance issues, you might want to use BIFF12 because a large BIFF12 file loads more quickly and saves more quickly than the new XML formats. However, if you are concerned with file size issues, the new XML file formats will win.

Using the New XML File Formats: XLSX and XLSM

XML in Excel 2003 was almost an ideal solution: Files could be round-tripped from Excel to XML and back to Excel, provided that the files did not include VBA macros, charts, or other embedded images.

Excel now offers complete 100% support for every feature in the new XML file formats. Workbooks can contain charts, tables, WordArt, SmartArt, shapes, and images. For security purposes, Excel supports XML file formats that are macro free and file formats that are macro enabled. These are the two XML file formats that Excel 2010 supports:

- **XLSX**—Files stored with the `.xlsx` extension are the default file type in Excel 2010. This XML file format does not allow macros.

■ **XLSM**—Files stored with the `.xlsm` extension are XML files that allow for the inclusion of VBA macros.

The new XLSX and XLSM file formats are actually zip files, which makes it easy to look inside the file formats.

Figure 7.5 shows a worksheet that has a number of elements. It has a pivot table in Row 21, WordArt, SmartArt, sparklines, slicers, and a chart.

Figure 7.5
This workbook is saved in XLSM, one of the new XML formats.

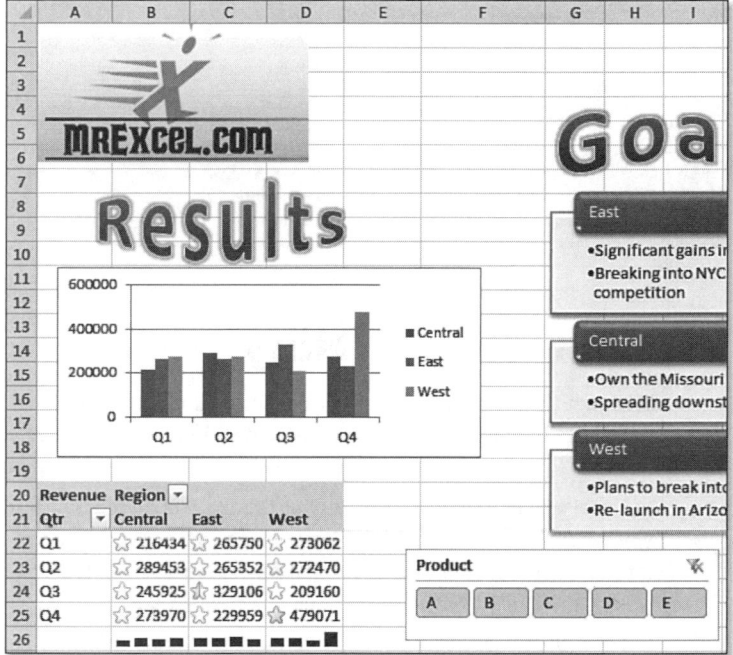

To look inside any Excel 2010 document, follow these steps:

1. In Windows Explorer, right-click the document name, which is in the format *filename*`.xlsm`, and select Rename.

2. Change the file extension to `.zip`. Windows warns you that if you change a file extension, the file may become unusable.

3. Click Yes to confirm the change.

4. Open the zip file with WinZip or any other zip utility.

As shown in Figure 7.6, inside the zip file, you can see several XML components. The embedded image is included in the zip file. All the settings and styles, drawings, and data are stored as separate XML files within the zip file. Unzipped, these components would take up 115KB. Because they are zipped files, the data is stored in 40KB.

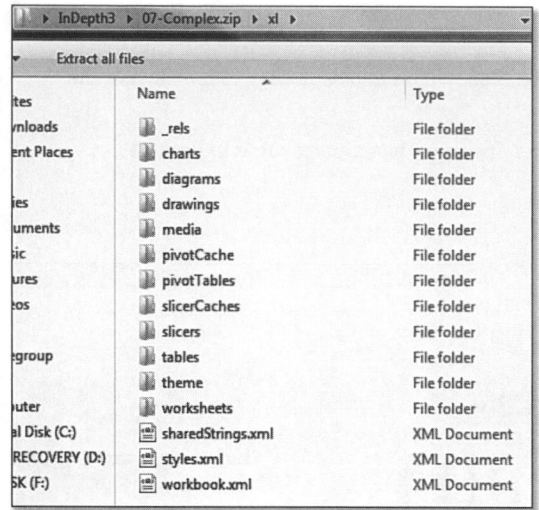

Figure 7.6
The components of the workbook are stored as XML files, zipped, and then renamed with an `.xlsx` or `.xlsm` extension.

Version Compatibility

With not just one new file format but three file formats in Excel 2010, you will face a number of problems as you try to share files with people who use legacy versions of Excel.

If you are using Excel 2010 and want to open a file created in Excel 5 through Excel 2003, your copy of Excel will gladly open the file, but the file will be in a special Compatibility mode. In this mode, you cannot use more than 65,536 rows, and you cannot use more than 256 columns. When you attempt to save the file, the Compatibility Checker will tell you what functionality will be lost.

If you start with a new spreadsheet in Excel 2010 and want to share the file with someone using Excel 5, 95, 97, or 2000, you have to use the Compatibility Checker and save the file in a legacy version of Excel.

If you start with a new spreadsheet in Excel 2010 and want to share the file with someone using Excel 2002 or Excel 2003, you can encourage that person to download the Compatibility Pack for the Microsoft Office system. This converter allows Excel 2002 and Excel 2003 to open files stored in the new XLSB, XLSM, and XLSX formats.

However, before you send the file, you should run it through the Compatibility Checker. To do so, follow these steps:

1. With the file open, go to the File menu. Excel opens in Backstage view.

2. Along the left navigation, select Info.

3. In the middle of the center pane, open the Check for Issues drop-down.

4. Select Check Compatibility. Excel displays the Compatibility Checker, as shown in Figure 7.7.

The new Select Versions to Show button allows you to filter the list to problems that would affect Excel 2007 or problems that would affect only Excel 2002–2003.

Figure 7.7
The Compatibility Checker reports on any compatibility
issues with legacy versions of Excel.

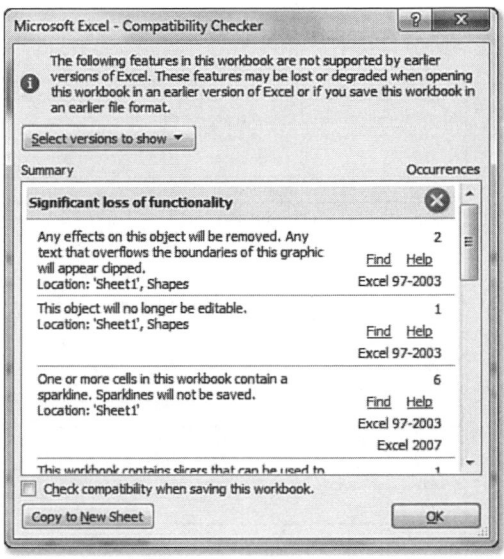

If you know this is a workbook that will always be opened by someone using Excel 2002–2007, you
can select the Check Compatibility When Saving This Workbook check box to make sure you have
not introduced any incompatibilities.

You will see two types of problems reported in the Compatibility Checker:

- **Minor Loss of Fidelity**—These issues involve formatting. If you used a color beyond the pallet of
  56 colors, it will be reported as a minor loss of fidelity. These types of issues are not considered
  serious. The person using Excel 2002, Excel 2003, or Excel 2007 will be allowed to open the file,
  edit the file, and save the file.

- **Significant Loss of Functionality**—This means that you have used a feature in Excel 2010 that
  will no longer function in legacy versions of Excel. When you have these types of issues, the file
  will open in legacy versions of Excel, but it will be forced into a read-only state.

When you have an issue reported as a Significant Loss of Functionality, you can click the Find
hyperlink. Excel closes the Compatibility Checker and takes you to the area of the worksheet that
contains the problem. If you use the method, you will constantly have to keep returning to the
Compatibility Checker to test other problems.

If many problems exist, click the Copy to New Sheet button. Excel inserts a new Compatibility
Report worksheet in the workbook. Each issue is listed, along with a count of the number of issues
and hyperlinks to help you find the problem (see Figure 7.8).

⯅ A	B	C	D	E	F
6	Significant loss of functionality			# of occurrences	Version
7					
8	Any effects on this object will be removed. Any text that overflows the boundaries of this graphic will appear clipped.			2	
9				Sheet1'!A20:D21 9	Excel 97-2003
10					
11	This object will no longer be editable.			1	
12				Sheet1'!A20:D21 9	Excel 97-2003
13					
14	One or more cells in this workbook contain a sparkline. Sparklines will not be saved.			6	
15				Sheet1'!F22:F24	Excel 97-2003
16				Sheet1'!B26:D26	Excel 2007
17					
18	This workbook contains slicers that can be used to filter PivotTables and CUBE functions within the workbook. Slicers will not be saved. Formulas that reference slicers will return a #REF! error.			1	
19				Sheet1	Excel 97-2003
20					
21	This workbook contains slicers that can be used to filter PivotTables and CUBE functions within the workbook. Slicers will not work in earlier versions of Excel.			1	
22				Sheet1	Excel 2007

Figure 7.8
If you have many significant issues, it will be easier to copy the contents of the Compatibility Checker to a new worksheet.

Opening Excel 2010 Files in Excel 2002 or 2003

If you attempt to open an Excel 2010 file in Excel 2002 or Excel 2003, you see a message that the file was created in a newer version of Excel. Excel allows you to download a converter so that you can open the file. The download process happens as part of the File Open process. It is quick. You have to do it only once per computer. Most people will not even remember downloading the utility.

After you install the Compatibility Pack, you can directly open XLSM, XLSX, and XLSB files in Excel 2003 or Excel 2002. You can also save your files back into the new format.

Minor Loss of Fidelity

Suppose that you have a simple data worksheet in Excel 2010. You might have used a few custom colors or perhaps cell styles. When you open that file in Excel 2003, you will receive a note that the custom color was converted to the closest color in the standard Excel 2003 pallet of 56 colors. Other than the formatting change, you can edit and then save the file back to an Excel 2010 format.

 note

Keep in mind that you need to get the person to pay attention to the question that pops up when they first open your file and choose to download the converter. With the malware situation today, many people will automatically choose to download nothing. For this reason, a little hand-holding over the phone as the person opens your file for the first time might be appropriate.

Significant Loss of Functionality

The Excel 2010 workbook shown previously in Figure 7.5 contain several elements that would report as a Significant Loss of Functionality in Excel 2003.

When you attempt to open this workbook in Excel 2003, Excel warns you that there is significant loss of functionality. Because of the loss of functionality, Excel forces the document to be opened as read-only. You have to use File, Save As to save the file with a new name. This prevents the original document from losing the incompatible features.

Excel 2003 does its best to deal with the incompatible features. Figure 7.9 shows the file opened in Excel 2003. The WordArt changes to boring words. The SmartArt keeps the same basic look and feel, although it is now a static shape. The slicer and the icon sets are lost. Any cells using new functions such as SUMIFS calculate with a #NAME error. Any cells beyond row 65536 are lost.

Figure 7.9
Excel does its best to render certain features in Excel 2003.

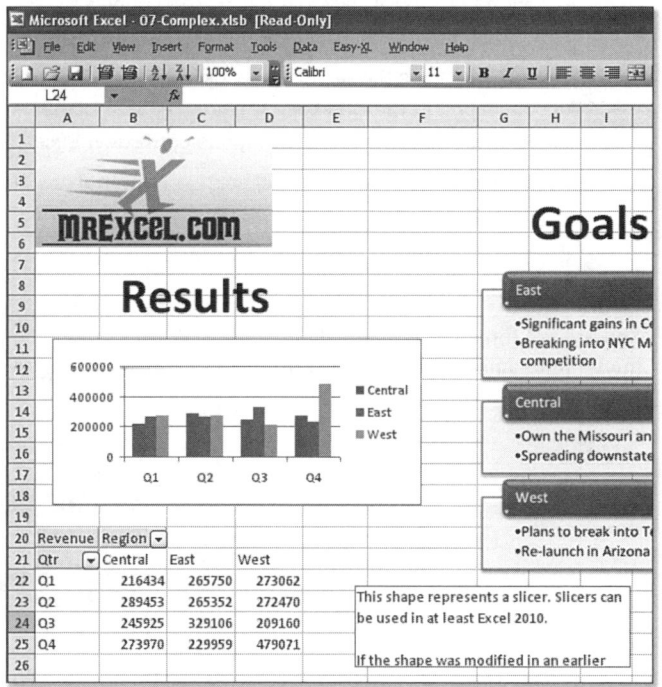

Creating Excel 2010 File Formats in Excel 2003

After you install the Office Compatibility Pack on a machine running Excel 2002 or Excel 2003, you can save files from Excel 2003 or Excel 2002 in one of the new Excel 2007–2010 file formats. The advantage is that when the file is later opened on a machine running Excel 2010, the file will not be forced into the Compatibility mode.

After you have the Compatibility Pack installed, follow these steps to save files in an Excel 2007–2010 format:

1. Open or create a workbook in Excel 2002 or Excel 2003.

2. Select File, Save As. The Save As dialog box appears.

3. Open the Save as Type drop-down and scroll to the bottom of the list. Choose one of the Excel "12" file types.

4. Type a filename.

5. Click Save. Excel runs a converter to convert the workbook to the chosen Excel 2010 format.

Opening Excel 2010 Files in Excel 2007

> **⚠ caution**
>
> Although Excel 2007 and 2010 seem fairly similar, Microsoft seems to have a freer attitude about the incompatibilities between Excel 2007 and Excel 2010. Because the files are not displaying warnings when opened in Excel 2007, there will probably be more serious problems with people unknowingly losing features when opening their Excel 2010 files on their home PC with Excel 2007.

Although both Excel 2007 and Excel 2010 support the same file formats, some new Excel 2010 features will not work in Excel 2007.

Figure 7.10 shows the same workbook opened in Excel 2007. There is no warning that you have lost any functionality and the workbook is not forced into Compatibility mode. However, the slicers are missing. The Icon Set happened to be using one of the new Excel 2010 icon styles, so the icons are missing.

If you save that file in Excel 2007 and open it in Excel 2010, the icon set and the slicer are lost. You will have to refresh the pivot table to calculate the pivot table without the slicer.

Figure 7.10
You are not forced into read-only mode, but some features are lost in Excel 2007.

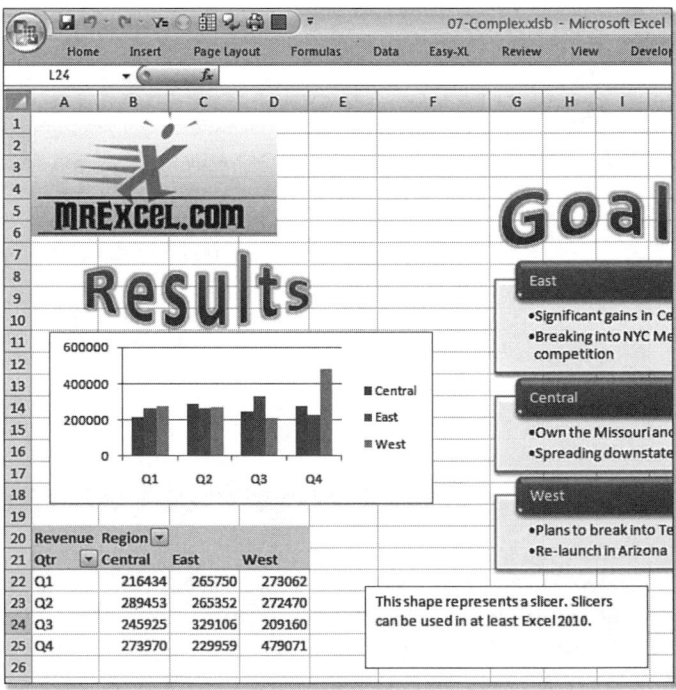

UNDERSTANDING FORMULAS

Excel's forte is performing calculations. When you use Excel, you typically use a combination of cells with numbers and cells with formulas. After you design a spreadsheet to calculate something, you can change the numbers used in the assumption cells and then watch Excel instantly calculate new results.

Getting the Most from This Chapter

Do not skip this entire chapter; one particular trick in this chapter can save you daily frustration.

I regularly entertain accountants and auditors with my Power Excel program. Although this program is a fun, laughter-filled tour through the inside tricks of Microsoft Excel, people are learning new things along the way.

I call them "gasp moments."

Imagine this setting: I am in front of 200 managerial accountants that have Excel open for 40 hours each week. You can generally figure that these folks are super-efficient with Excel. For any trick that I show, it might be already in the arsenal of half to three-quarters of the room. A lot of the people nod their heads, while others look surprised.

Universally, though, a few tricks get a universal gasp from perhaps 90 percent of the people who did not know the trick and realize just how powerful it is. I thrive on the gasp moments.

Most people reading this book believe they know Excel formulas. To a certain extent, this chapter is a primer for the person who is new to Excel. However, even the most astute person using Excel should check out these sections of the chapter:

- Everyone should read the "Double-Click the Fill Handle to Copy a Formula." Somehow, most people have learned to drag the fill handle to copy a formula. This leads to horrible frustration on long data sets, as you go flying past the end of the data. This simple but powerful trick is the one that universally amazes attendees of my seminar.

- Honestly answer this question: Do you really understand the difference between cell H1 and cell $H$1? If you think the latter has anything to do with currency, you need to review the "Overriding Relative Behavior—Absolute Cell References" section thoroughly. This isn't a trick, but one of the fundamental building blocks to building Excel worksheets. Roughly, 5 percent of the people in a Power Excel seminar do not understand this concept, and about 30 percent of the people in a community computer club presentation do not understand it. If you don't know when and why to use the dollar signs, you are in good company with 20 million other people using Excel. It is worth taking time to learn this essential technique.

- Finally, a person's age can be predicted by how that person enters formulas. There are three ways, and I believe my preferred way is the best. I probably will not convince you to change, but when you understand my way, you can enter formulas far faster than the other two ways. To get a good understanding of the alternatives, read the "Three Methods of Entering Formulas" section later in this chapter.

Introduction to Formulas

When Microsoft overhauled Excel for the 2007 version, a number of formula limits were dramatically increased. For example, the number of characters in a formula increased from 1,024 to 8,192. The number of levels of nesting for IF functions increased from 7 to 64. Thanks to those improvements, you can calculate almost anything with a formula in Excel.

 tip

Designing a formula that can be written once and then copied to a rectangular range of data is a fantastic way to use Excel more efficiently.

This chapter and Chapter 9, "Controlling Formulas," deal with formula basics. Chapters 10, "Understanding Functions," through Chapter 15, "Using Trig, Matrix, and Engineering Functions," introduce adding functions to your formulas. Chapter 16, "Connecting Worksheets, Workbooks, and External Data," introduces formulas that calculate data found on other worksheets or in other workbooks. Chapter 17, "Using Super Formulas in Excel," provides interesting examples such as 3D formulas and the all-powerful array formulas.

Because of the record-oriented nature of spreadsheets, you can generally build a formula once and then copy that formula to hundreds or thousands of cells without changing anything in the formula.

Formulas Versus Values

When looking at an Excel grid, you cannot tell the difference between a cell with a formula and one that contains numbers. To see if a cell contains a number or a formula, select the cell. Look in the formula bar. If the formula bar contains a number, as shown in Figure 8.1, you know that it is a static value. If the formula bar contains a formula, you know that the number shown in the grid is the result of a formula calculation (see Figure 8.2). Keep in mind that most formulas start with an equal sign.

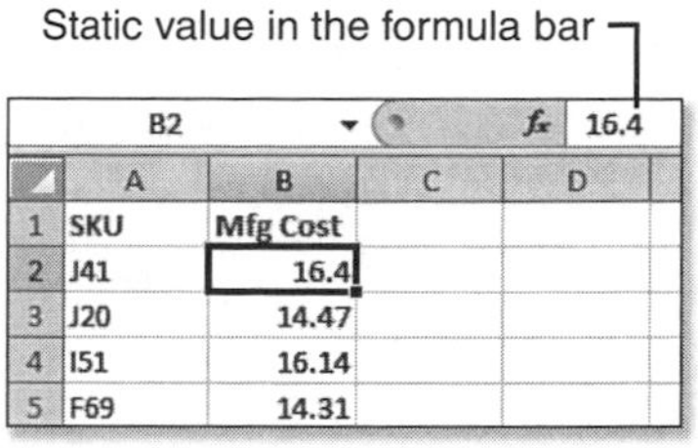

Static value in the formula bar ⌐

Figure 8.1
The formula bar reveals whether a value is a static number or a calculation. In this case, Cell B2 contains a static number.

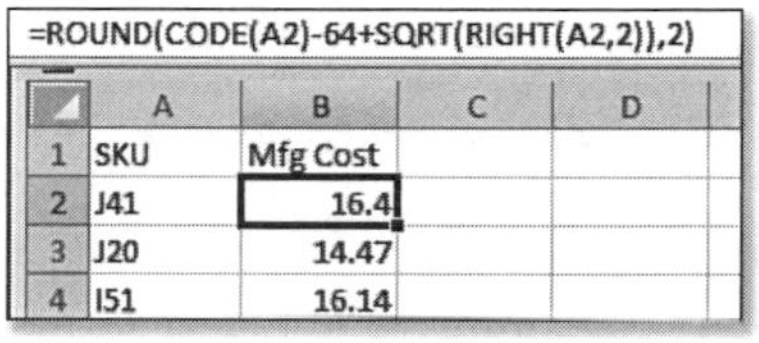

Figure 8.2
In this case, Cell B2 contains the result of a formula calculation. A formula usually starts with an equal sign.

Entering Your First Formula

Your first formula was probably a SUM function, entered with the AutoSum button. However, this discussion is talking about a pure mathematic formula that uses a value in a cell, added, subtracted, divided, or multiplied by a number or another cell.

Billions of variations of formulas can be used. Everyday life throws situations at you that can be solved with this type of formula. Keep these important points in mind as you start tinkering with your own formulas:

- Every formula starts with an equal sign.

- Entering formulas is just like typing an equation in a calculator with one exception (see the next point).

- If one of the terms in your formula is already stored in a cell in Excel, you can point to that cell's address instead of typing the number into that cell. Using this method allows you to change the value in one cell and then watch all of the formulas recalculate.

To illustrate these points, see the steps to building a basic formula included in the following example.

Building a Formula

You want to enter a formula to calculate a target sales price, as shown in Figure 8.3. Cell B2 shows the product cost. In Column C, you want to calculate the list price as two times the cost plus $3.

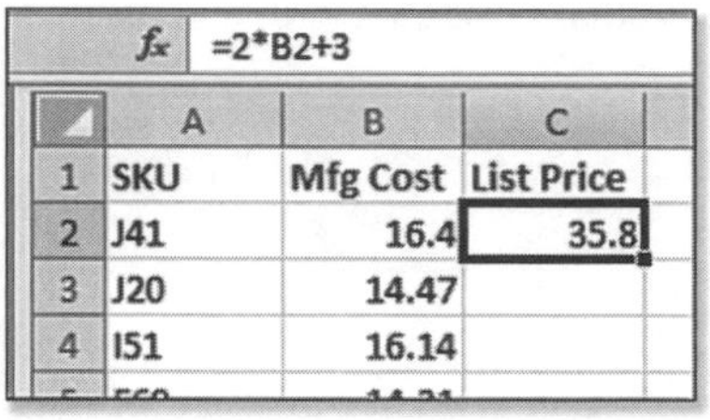

Figure 8.3
The formula in Cell C2 recalculates if the value in Cell B2 changes.

To enter a formula, follow these steps:

1. Put the cell pointer in Cell C2.

2. Type an equal sign. The equal sign tells Excel that you are starting a formula.

3. Type 2*B2 to indicate that you want to multiply two times the value in cell B2.

4. Type +3 to add three to the result. There should be no spaces in the formula. If your formula reads =2*B2+3, proceed to step 5. Otherwise, use the backspace key to correct the formula.

5. Press Enter. Excel calculates the formula in Cell C2.

By default, Excel usually moves the cell pointer down or to the right after you finish entering a formula. You should move the cell pointer back to Cell C2 to inspect the formula, as shown in Figure 8.3. Note that Excel shows a number in the grid, but the formula bar reveals the formula behind the number.

The Relative Nature of Formulas

The formula =2*B2+3 really says, "multiply two by the cell immediately to the left of me and then add three." If you need to put this formula in Cells C3 to C999, you do not need to reenter the formula 997 times. Instead, copy the formula and paste it to all the cells. As you copy, Excel copies the essence of the formula: "Multiply two by the cell to the left of me and add three." As you copy the formula to Cell C3, the formula becomes =2*B3+3. Excel handles all this automatically. Figure 8.4 shows the formula after it is copied.

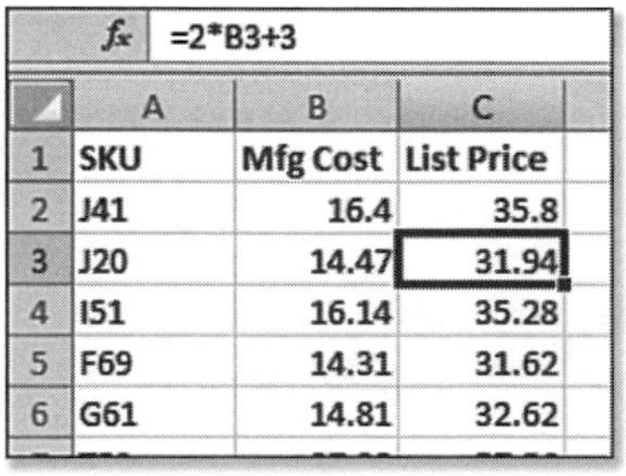

Figure 8.4
After you paste the formula, Excel automatically updates the cell reference to point to the current row.

Excel's ability to change B2 to B3 in the formula is called *relative referencing*. This is the default behavior of a reference. Sometimes, you do not want Excel to change a reference as the formula is copied, as explained in the next section.

Overriding Relative Behavior: Absolute Cell References

Relative referencing, which is Excel's ability to change a formula as it is copied, is what makes spreadsheets so useful. At times, however, you need part of a formula to always point at one particular cell. This happens a lot when you have a setting at the top of the worksheet such as a growth rate or a tax rate. It would be nice to change this cell once and have all the formulas use the new rate.

The following example sets up a sample worksheet that exhibits this problem and shows how to use an arcane notation style to solve the problem. When you see a reference with two dollar signs, such as $G$1, this indicates an absolute reference to G1. An absolute reference is a cell or range address where the row numbers and the column letters are locked and will not change during copying. Absolute references have a dollar sign before each column letter and each row number. Examples include $G$1 and $T$2:$W$99.

Suppose that you have a sales tax factor in a single cell at the top of a worksheet. After you enter the formula =C2*G1, it accurately calculates the tax in Cell D2, as shown in Figure 8.5.

However, when you copy the same formula to Cell C3, you get a zero as the result. As you can see in Figure 8.6, Excel correctly changed Cell C2 to C3 in the copied formula. However, Excel also changed G1 to G2. Because there is nothing in G2, the calculation predicts a zero.

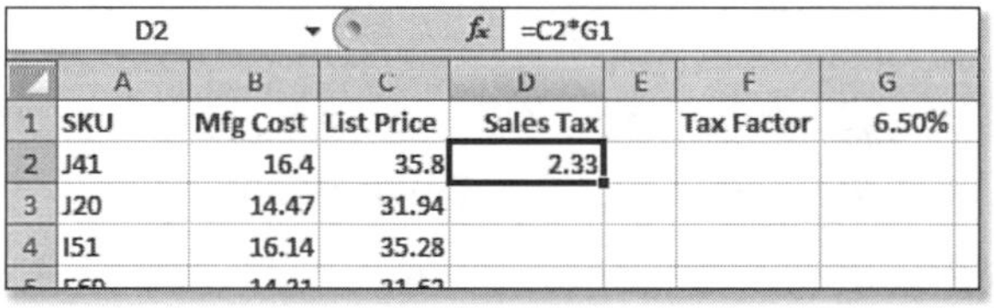

Figure 8.5
This formula works fine in Row 2.

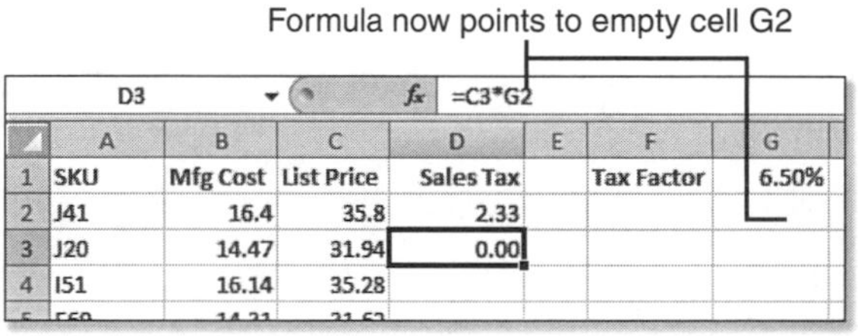

Figure 8.6
This formula fails in Row 3.

Formula now points to empty cell G2

Because the sales tax factor is only in G1, you want Excel to always point to G1. To make this happen, you need to build the original formula as =C2*$G$1. The two dollar signs tell Excel that you do not want to have the reference change as the formula is copied. The $ before the G freezes the reference to always point to Column G. The $ before the 1 freezes the reference to always point to Row 1. Now, when you copy this formula from Cell D2 to other cells in Column D, Excel changes the formula to =C3*$G$1, as shown in Figure 8.7.

To recap, a reference with two dollars signs is called an *absolute reference*.

Figure 8.7
The dollar signs in the formula make sure that the copied formula always points to Cell G1.

	D3			f_x	=C3*$G$1	
	A	B	C	D	E	F	G
1	SKU	Mfg Cost	List Price	Sales Tax		Tax Factor	6.50%
2	J41	16.4	35.8	2.33			
3	J20	14.47	31.94	2.08			
4	I51	16.14	35.28	2.29			
5	F69	14.31	31.62	2.06			

Using Mixed References to Combine Features of Relative and Absolute References

In a number of situations, you might want to build a reference that has only one dollar sign. For example, in Figure 8.8, you want to use the monthly bonus rate in Row 3, but you want to allow the column to change. In this case, the formula for Cell B19 would be =B6*B$3.

When you copy this formula, it always points to the bonus amount in Row 3, but the remaining elements of the formula are relative. For example, the formula in E21 is =E8*E$3, which multiplies Maia's April sales by the April bonus rate.

Figure 8.8
By having the dollar sign before the 3 in C$3, you lock the reference to Row 3 but allow the formula to point to Columns D, E, and so on as you copy the formula.

	B19			f_x	=B6*B$3	
	A	B	C	D	E	F	G
1	**Widget Sales Bonus Calculation**						
2							
3	Bonus	3%	2%	0%	2%	3%	1%
4							
5	$ Sold	Jan	Feb	Mar	Apr	May	Jun
6	Carolyn	6237	9009	5247	9207	7029	6435
7	Lindsay	7722	5544	6138	5445	9603	5544
8	Maia	8712	7524	6237	6336	8415	7623
9	Gabby	5148	7524	9603	5049	5643	5445
10	Max	5841	6534	8118	8910	9009	9405
11	Larry	9207	8118	6633	5148	5544	5247
12	Scarlet	4950	9603	5049	6039	9801	6039
13	Rick	8019	7920	8910	9009	8910	6831
14	Carla	6039	5841	6237	9702	7425	5346
15	Fabiano	9801	8019	6039	8316	7722	9801
16							
17							
18	Bonus	Jan	Feb	Mar	Apr	May	Jun
19	Carolyn	187.11	180.18	0.00	184.14	210.87	64.35
20	Lindsay	231.66	110.88	0.00	108.90	288.09	55.44
21	Maia	261.36	150.48	0.00	126.72	252.45	76.23

There are two kinds of mixed references. One mixed reference freezes the row number and allows the column letter to change. The other mixed reference freezes the column letter but allows the row number to change. No one has thought up clever names to distinguish between these references, so they are simply called mixed references.

To illustrate the other kind of mixed reference, as shown in Figure 8.9, say you want a single formula to multiply the daily rate from Column A by the number of days in Row 4. This formula requires both kinds of mixed references.

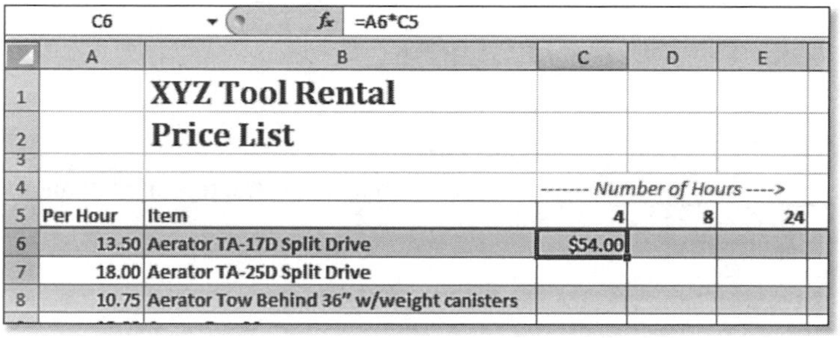

Figure 8.9
You can create a formula by using a combination of dollar signs to allow Cell C6 to be copied to all cells in the table.

In this case, you want the Cell A6 reference to always point to Column A, even when the formula is copied to the right. Therefore, the A6 portion of the formula should be entered as $A6. You also want the C5 portion of the formula to always point to Row 5, even when the formula is copied down the rows. Therefore, the C5 portion of the formula should be entered as C$5.

Using the F4 Key to Simplify Dollar Sign Entry

In the preceding section, you entered quite a few dollar signs in formulas. The good news is that you do not have to type the dollar signs! Instead, immediately after entering a reference, press the F4 key to toggle the reference from a relative reference to an absolute reference, which automatically has the dollar signs before the row and column. If you press F4 again, the reference toggles to a mixed reference with a dollar sign before the row number. When you press F4 once again, the references toggle to a mixed reference with a dollar sign before the column letter. Pressing F4 one more time returns the reference to a relative reference. You might find it easier to choose the right reference by looking at the various reference options offered by the F4 key.

The following sequence shows how the F4 key works while you are entering a formula. This particular example was included because it requires two different types of mixed references.

The important concept is that you start pressing F4 after typing a cell reference but before you type a mathematical operator.

1. Type =A6 (see Figure 8.10).

2. Before typing the asterisk to indicate multiplication, press the F4 key. On the first press of F4, the reference changes to =$A$6, as shown in Figure 8.11.

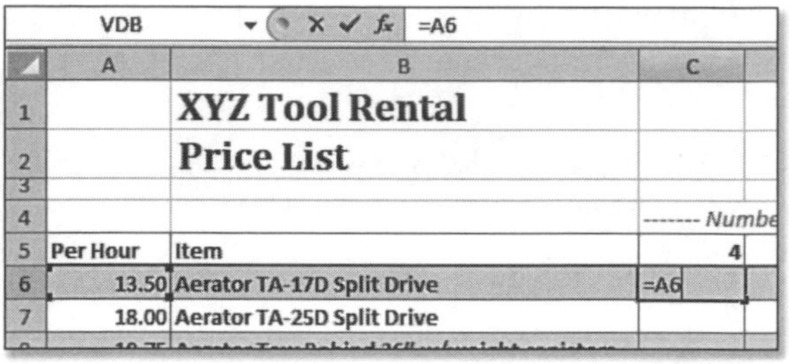

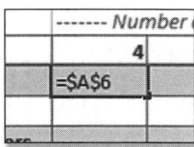

Figure 8.10
This is a relative reference: A6 without any dollar signs.

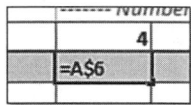

Figure 8.11
After you press F4 once, the reference changes to an absolute reference, with two dollar signs.

3. Press the F4 key again. The reference changes to A$6 to freeze the reference to Row 6, as shown in Figure 8.12.

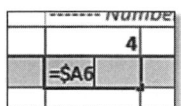

Figure 8.12
Press F4 again to switch to a mixed reference with the row number locked.

4. Press F4 one more time. Excel locks just the column, changing the reference to =$A6, as shown in Figure 8.13. This is the version of the reference that you want.

 tip

If you are having trouble remembering whether you want the dollar signs before the row, the column, or both, press F4 and then look at the formula to figure out if you are freezing the correct element—either the row or column. The item immediately after the dollar sign is the part of the address being frozen.

Figure 8.13
Press F4 again to switch to a mixed reference with the column letter locked.

5. To continue the formula, type an asterisk to indicate multiplication and then click Cell C5 with the mouse. At the point shown in Figure 8.14, you would press F4 twice to change C5 to a reference that locks only the row (that is, C$5).

6. Press Enter to accept the formula.

Figure 8.14
After clicking C5 with the mouse, press F4 twice to change this reference.

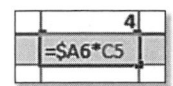

7. When you copy the formula from Cell C6 to the range C6:H36, the formula automatically multiplies the rate in Column A by the number of days in Row 5. Figure 8.15 shows the copied formula in Cell E9. The formula correctly multiplies the 55-dollar rate in Cell A9 by the three days figure in Cell E5.

Figure 8.15
By using the correct combination of row and column mixed references, you can enter this formula once and successfully copy it to the entire rectangular range.

	A	B	C	D	E
1		**XYZ Tool Rental**			
2		**Price List**			
3					
4			------- Number of Hours ---->		
5	Per Hour	Item	4	8	24
6	13.50	Aerator TA-17D Split Drive	$54.00	$108.00	$324.00
7	18.00	Aerator TA-25D Split Drive	$72.00	$144.00	$432.00
8	10.75	Aerator Tow Behind 36" w/weight canisters	$43.00	$86.00	$258.00
9	10.00	Auger One Man	$40.00	$80.00	=$A9*E$5
10	12.50	Auger Two Man	$50.00	$100.00	$300.00
11	16.25	Towable Auger	$65.00	$130.00	$390.00

VDB   =$A9*E$5

Using F4 After a Formula Is Entered

The F4 trick described in the preceding section works immediately after you enter a reference. If you try to change Cell A6 after you type the asterisk, pressing the F4 key has no effect.

However, you can still use F4 by clicking somewhere in the formula bar adjacent to the characters A6. Pressing F4 now adds dollar signs to that reference.

Using F4 on a Rectangular Range

Some functions allow you to specify a rectangular range. For example, in Figure 8.16, you would like to enter a formula to calculate month-to-date sales. One formula in Cell C29 is =SUM(B2:B29). To copy this formula, you need to change the formula to =SUM(B$2:B29).

At this point in the figure, you might be tempted to press the F4 key. However, pressing F4 now would convert the reference to the fully absolute range $B$2:$B$29. Continuing to press F4 would

> **note**
> After you press F4 again, Excel returns the reference to the relative state A6. As you continue to press F4, Excel toggles between the four modes. It is fine to toggle between them all and then choose the correct one. If you accidentally toggle past the $A6 version, just keep pressing F4 until the correct mode comes up again.

toggle to B$2:B$29, then $B2:$B29, and then B2:B29. Excel does not even attempt to go through the other 12 possible combinations of dollar signs to offer B$2:B29 eventually.

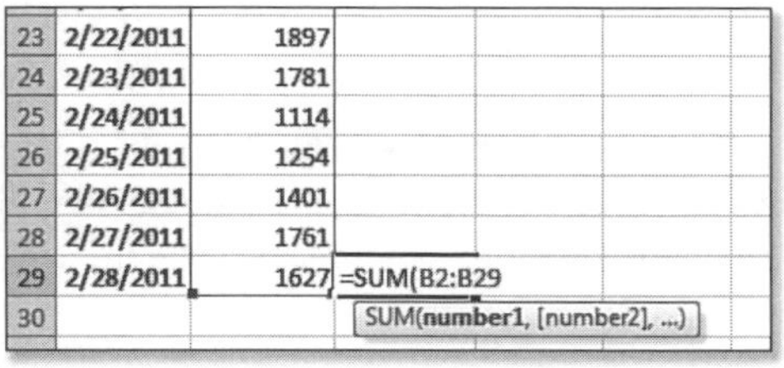

Figure 8.16
Using F4 at this point will never produce the desired result of B$2:B29.

In this case, you need to click the insertion point just before, just after, or in the middle of the characters B2 in the formula bar. If you then press F4, toggle through the various dollar sign combinations on the B2 reference. Pressing F4 twice results in the proper combination, as shown in Figure 8.17.

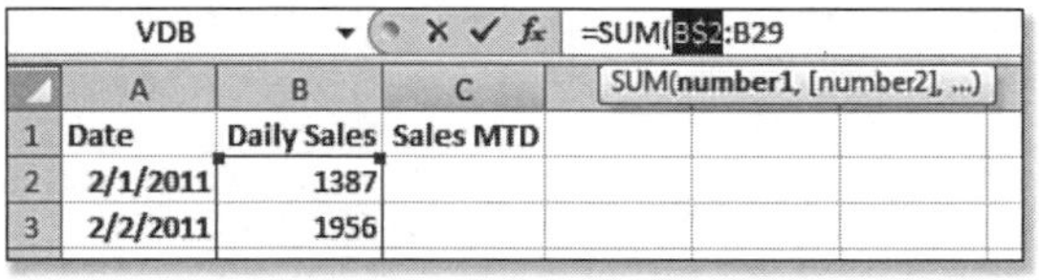

Figure 8.17
Using F4 is tricky when your reference is a rectangular range—you must click into the formula.

Three Methods of Entering Formulas

In the examples in the previous sections, you entered a formula by typing it. Although you generally need to start a formula by typing the equal sign (or the plus sign), after that point, you have three options:

- Type the complete formula as described in the previous sections.

- Type operator keys, but use the mouse to touch cell references. In this book, this is referred to as the *mouse method*.

- Type the operator keys, and then use the arrow keys to specify the cell references by navigating to the cells. In this book, this method is referred to as the *arrow key method*.

Assume you would like to multiply the merchandise total in Cell B2 by the sales tax rate in Cell F1, as shown in Figure 8.18.

Figure 8.18
You can use three methods to enter the formula
=B2*$F$1.

	VDB		▾	X ✓ fx	=	
	A	B	C	D	E	F
1	Invoice	Merch $	Tax		Rate	6.50%
2	1701	116.7	=			
3	1702	134.71				
4	1703	129.56				
5	1704	119.81				

Enter Formulas Using the Mouse Method

If you started using computers after the advent of Microsoft Windows 3.1, it is likely that you use the mouse method for entering formulas. This method is intuitive, but it requires you to move your hand between the keyboard and the mouse several times, as in this example:

1. Type =.

2. Click in Cell B2.

3. Type *.

4. Click in Cell F1.

5. Press F4 to add the dollar signs.

6. Press Enter. This usually moves the cell pointer to Cell F2.

This method requires only four keystrokes, but it requires you to move to the mouse twice. Moving to the mouse is the slowest part of entering formulas, but this method is easier than typing the entire formula if you are not a touch typist.

 tip

If you have a desktop keyboard, you can use the asterisk key on the numeric keypad to avoid pressing the Shift key.

Entering Formulas Using the Arrow-Key Method

The arrow-key method is popular with people who started using spreadsheets in the days of Lotus 1-2-3 release 2.2. It is worthwhile to learn this method because it is incredibly fast. Almost all formula entry can be accomplishing using keys on the right side of the keyboard. Here's how it works:

1. In Cell C2 type +.

2. Press the left-arrow key to move the flashing cell border to Cell B2. Note that the active cell, which is the one with a solid border, is still Cell C2. The flashing border is like a second cell pointer that you can use to point to the correct cell for the formula. As shown in Figure 8.19, the temporary formula in the formula bar reads +B2.

	VDB		▾	X ✓ fx	+B2	
	A	B	C	D	E	F
1	Invoice	Merch $	Tax		Rate	6.50%
2	1701	116.7	+B2			
3	1702	134.71				
4	1703	129.56				

Figure 8.19
By using the arrow keys during formula entry, you create a flashing border that can be used to navigate to a cell reference.

3. To accept Cell B2 as the correct reference in the formula, press either an operator key (for example, *, +), a parenthesis, or the Enter key. In this case, type *.

4. Note that the dashed cell pointer disappears, and the focus is now back to the original cell, C2.

5. Press the right-arrow key three times. The flashing cell border moves to D2, E2, and then F2. With each keypress, the temporary formula in the formula bar shows an incorrect formula (+B2*D2, +B2*E2, and +B2*F2). Figure 8.20 shows what the screen looks like after you press the right-arrow key three times.

6. Type the up-arrow key to move the flashing cell border to the correct location, Cell F1. The temporary formula in the formula bar now shows +B2*F1.

7. Press the F4 key to add dollar signs to the F1 reference.

8. Press Ctrl+Enter to accept the formula and keep the cell pointer in Cell C2.

 note

As you are moving the flashing cell border with the mouse, ignore the formula bar and watch just the flashing cell border.

 tip

Even if you are mouse-centric, you should try this method for half a day. When you get the feel for navigating by using the arrow keys, you can enter formulas much faster by using this method.

Figure 8.20
After step 4, the focus moves to the original cell. Thus, you only have to press the right-arrow key three times instead of four times to arrive at Cell F2.

Using this method requires 10 keystrokes, with no trips to the mouse. You can enter formulas that have no absolute references, mixed references, parentheses, or exponents by using just the arrow keys and the keys on the numeric keypad.

 To see a video of entering formulas using all three methods, search for Excel In Depth 8 at YouTube.

 note

Officially, every formula must start with an equal sign. However, to make former Lotus 1-2-3 users comfortable, Excel allows you to start a formula with a plus sign. Power Excel users have discovered that using a plus sign allows you to start a formula by typing on the numeric keypad. Because I routinely start formulas with the plus sign, I am often asked why I start with =+ instead of just =. Even though the formulas appear that way onscreen, I don't actually enter the =. When a formula starts with a plus sign, Excel adds an equal sign and does not remove the plus sign, so you end up with a formula that looks like =+B2*$F$1.

Entering the Same Formula in Many Cells

So far in this chapter, you have entered a formula in one cell and then copied and pasted to get the formula in many cells. To enter the same formula in many cells, you can use three alternatives:

- Preselect the entire range where the formulas need to go. Enter the formula for the first cell and press Ctrl+Enter to enter the formula in the entire selection simultaneously.

- Enter the formula in the first cell and then use the fill handle to copy the formula.

- Beginning with Excel 2007, the method is to define the range as a table. When this method is used, the new formulas are copied automatically.

Copying a Formula by Using Ctrl+Enter

This strategy works when you are entering formulas for one or more screens that are full of data:

1. If you have just a few cells, select them before entering the formula.

2. Click in the first cell and drag down to the last cell, as shown in Figure 8.21. Notice from the name box that the active cell is the first cell.

Figure 8.21
Click in the first cell and drag down to the last cell to select a range with the first cell as the active cell.

	A	B	C
1	Invoice	Merch $	Tax
2	1701	116.7	
3	1702	134.71	
4	1703	129.56	
5	1704	119.81	
6	1705	98.6	
7	1706	67.68	
8	1707	175.4	
9	1708	177.92	
10	1709	71.89	
11	1710	75.05	
12	1711	76.62	
13	1712	123.03	
14	1713	151.12	
15			

3. Enter the formula by using any of the three methods described earlier in this chapter. Even if you use the arrow-key method, Excel keeps the entire range selected. Figure 8.22 shows the formula after you press F4 to convert the F1 reference to $F$1.

4. At this point, you would normally press Enter to complete the formula. Instead, press Ctrl+Enter to enter this formula in the entire selected range. Note that Excel does not enter =B2*$F$1 in each cell. Instead, it converts the formula as if it were copied to each cell. Figure 8.23 shows the formula in Cell C20.

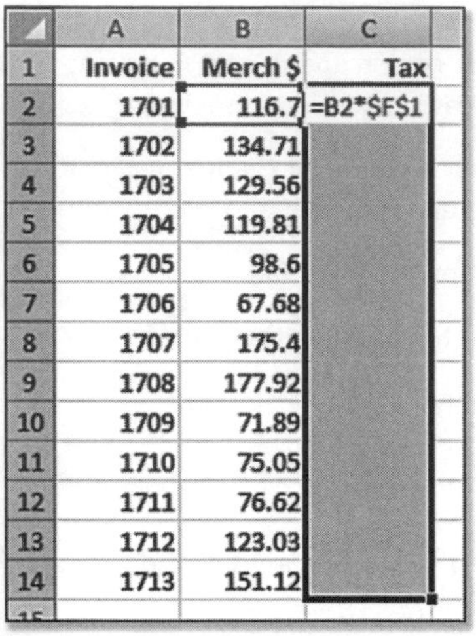

	A	B	C
1	Invoice	Merch $	Tax
2	1701	116.7	=B2*$F$1
3	1702	134.71	
4	1703	129.56	
5	1704	119.81	
6	1705	98.6	
7	1706	67.68	
8	1707	175.4	
9	1708	177.92	
10	1709	71.89	
11	1710	75.05	
12	1711	76.62	
13	1712	123.03	
14	1713	151.12	
15			

Figure 8.22
Even with a large range selected, the formula is built only in the active cell.

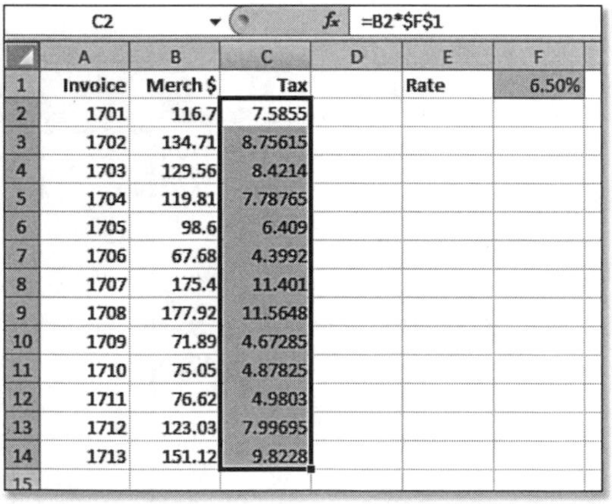

C2 f_x =B2*$F$1

	A	B	C	D	E	F
1	Invoice	Merch $	Tax		Rate	6.50%
2	1701	116.7	7.5855			
3	1702	134.71	8.75615			
4	1703	129.56	8.4214			
5	1704	119.81	7.78765			
6	1705	98.6	6.409			
7	1706	67.68	4.3992			
8	1707	175.4	11.401			
9	1708	177.92	11.5648			
10	1709	71.89	4.67285			
11	1710	75.05	4.87825			
12	1711	76.62	4.9803			
13	1712	123.03	7.99695			
14	1713	151.12	9.8228			
15						

Figure 8.23
Pressing Ctrl+Enter tells Excel to enter the formula in the active cell and to copy it to the rest of the selection.

Copying a Formula by Dragging the Fill Handle

If you want to enter a formula in one cell and then copy it to the other cells in a range, you can use the fill handle, which is the square dot in the lower-right corner of the cell pointer. There are two ways to use the fill handle:

- Drag the fill handle.
- Double-click the fill handle.

The dragging method works fine when you have less than one screen full of data:

1. Enter the formula in Cell B2.

2. Press Ctrl+Enter to accept the formula and keep the cell pointer in Cell B2.

3. Click the fill handle. You know that you are above the fill handle when the mouse pointer changes to a thick plus sign, as shown in Figure 8.24. Drag the mouse down to the last row of data, which in this case is Cell C14.

Figure 8.24
You can copy a formula by clicking and dragging the fill handle.

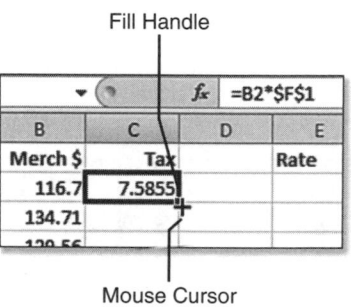

4. When you release the mouse button, the original cell is copied to all the cells in the selected range.

This method is fine for copying a formula to a few cells. However, if you have thousands or hundreds of thousands of cells, it is annoying to drag to the last row. In Excel 2003 and earlier, you would invariably end up flying past the last row. Note that Excel 2010 will automatically slow down and briefly pause at the last row. However, it is far easier to copy a formula by double-clicking the fill handle.

Double-Click the Fill Handle to Copy a Formula

In most data sets, double-clicking the fill handle is the fastest way to copy the formula. Although you will love this method, you need to understand a few shortcomings that can hamper the method when an adjacent column has blank cells among the data.

Figure 8.25 shows a table that has hundreds of rows of data. Suppose you want to copy the formula from Cell C2 down to all the rows of data in Column B.

In this particular case, Cell B2 is nonblank, and Column B contains a value in every row down to the end of the data. This is the perfect condition for using the technique of double-clicking the fill handle. Follow these steps:

1. Enter the formula in Cell B2.

2. Press Ctrl+Enter to accept the formula and keep the cell pointer in Cell B2.

3. Double-click the fill handle.

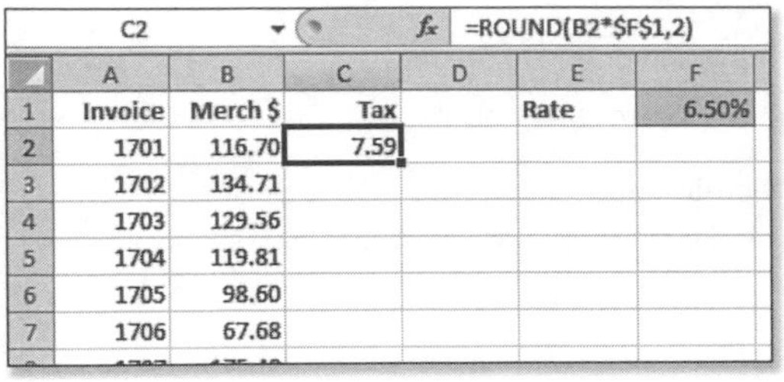

Figure 8.25
Dragging the fill handle is frustrating in a table that has hundreds of rows. The double-click method will end that frustration.

The active cell is copied down to the last row of your data, as shown in Figure 8.26.

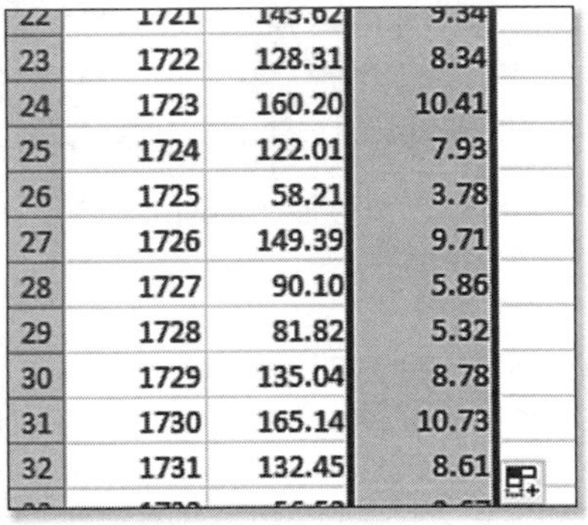

Figure 8.26
Double-click the fill handle to copy to the last row of your data.

The fill handle double-click method is fast. However, several arcane rules can trip up the data, particularly if the column to the left contains a blank cell before the end of the data. Excel will be tricked into stopping the copy early because of this blank cell. In addition, a couple of other rules exist:

- The fill handle can copy based on data in the adjacent column to the right, or even data in the current column.

- You should always type End and then press the down arrow to make sure that the formula was copied far enough.

For a complete discussion of the arcane rules, see the Excel "Troubleshooting Tip" section at the end of this chapter.

Use the Table Tool to Copy a Formula

The table tool was improved dramatically in Excel 2007. When using this tool, if you tell Excel that your current data set is a table, Excel automatically copies new formulas down to the rest of the cells in the table.

Figure 8.27 shows an Excel worksheet that has headings at the top and many rows of data below the headings.

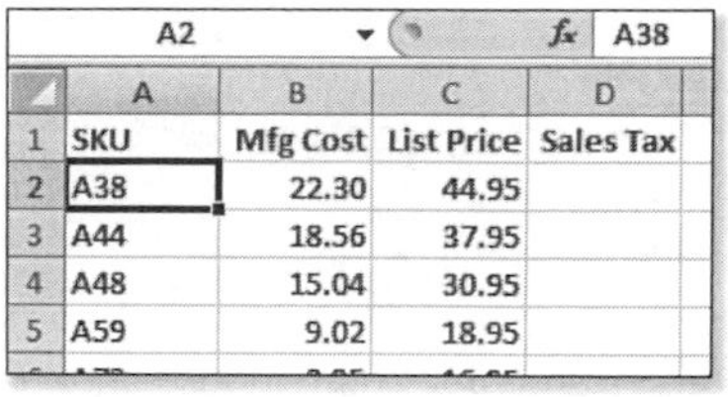

Figure 8.27
This is a typical worksheet in Excel.

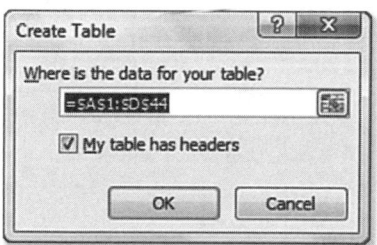

To define a range as a table, select a cell within the data set and type Ctrl+T. Excel uses its IntelliSense to guess the edges of the table. If its guess is correct, click OK in the Create Table dialog, as shown in Figure 8.28.

Figure 8.28
The Create Table dialog.

Ctrl+T is one of four entry points for creating a table. You can still use the Excel 2003 shortcut of Ctrl+L. You can choose Format as Table on the Home tab. You can choose the Table icon from the Insert tab.

As shown in Figure 8.29, after Excel recognizes the range as a table, several changes occur:

- The table is formatted with the default formatting. Depending on your preferences, this might include banded rows or columns.

- AutoFilter drop-downs are added to the headings.

- Any formulas that you enter use the headings to refer to cells within the table.

> **note**
>
> As shown in Figure 8.30, there is a lightning bolt drop-down to the right of Cell D3. This drop-down offers you the opportunity to stop Excel from automatically copying the formula down.

Figure 8.29
Defining a range as a table provides formatting and powerful features such as autofilters and natural language formulas.

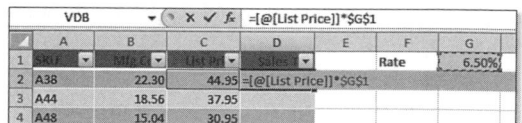

Now when you enter a formula in the table, Excel automatically copies that formula down to all rows of the table.

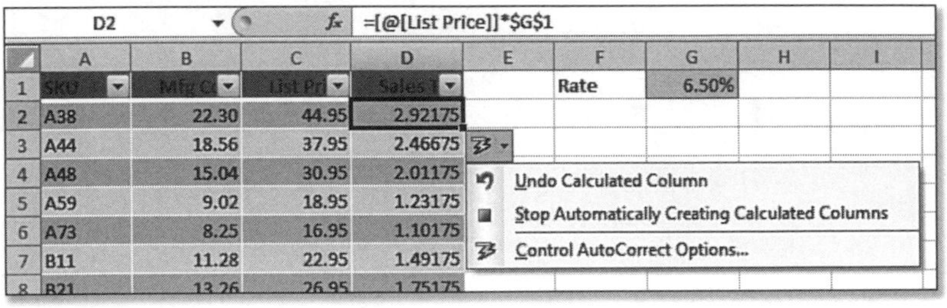

Figure 8.30
Thanks to the new Table tool in Excel 2007, a new formula entered anywhere in Column D is copied automatically to all the cells in Column D.

Troubleshooting Tip: Overcoming the Arcane Rules for Fill Handle Double-Clicking

The fill handle double-click trick is one of the best and least-known tricks that is sure to get a bunch of gasps in my Excel seminars.

Excel has an arcane set of rules it follows when you double-click the fill handle. The rules changed in Excel 2010 to make the operation work even better.

In previous versions of Excel, the fill handle would first check if the cell immediately below is non-blank. In Figure 8.31, the nonblank cell in B3 means that the fill handle would copy the formula in B2 down to B7.

If the cell just below is empty, then Excel looks to the left. If you double-click the fill handle in F2, Excel 2007 copies the formula down to row 12 based on the contiguous range in E2:E12.

If the cell to the left is empty, Excel 2007 looks to the column on the right. Double-click the fill handle in J2, and Excel copies the formula down to row 10 based on the data in K2:K10.

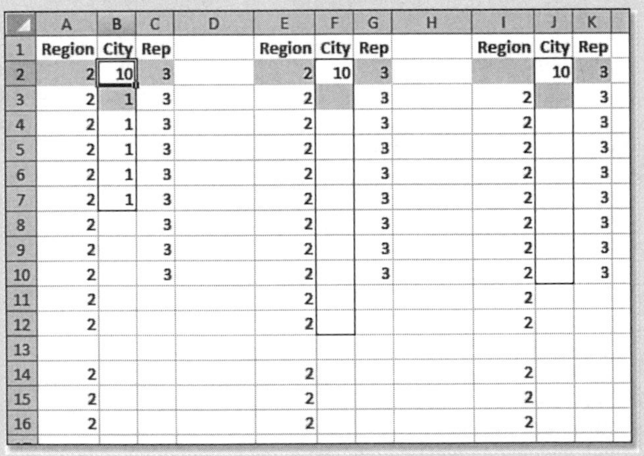

Figure 8.31
In Excel 2007 and earlier, Excel would look immediately below, then left, and then right of the active cell.

In Excel 2010, the cell immediately below the active cell still trumps all other cells. In Figure 8.32, if you double-click the fill handle in C2, Excel will see the nonblank cell in C3. In that figure, the formula will copy down to row 7 because of the filled cells in C3:C7.

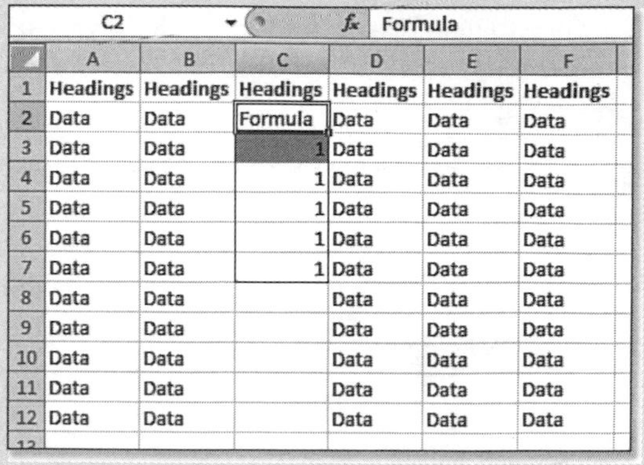

C2 fx Formula

	A	B	C	D	E	F
1	Headings	Headings	Headings	Headings	Headings	Headings
2	Data	Data	Formula	Data	Data	Data
3	Data	Data	1	Data	Data	Data
4	Data	Data	1	Data	Data	Data
5	Data	Data	1	Data	Data	Data
6	Data	Data	1	Data	Data	Data
7	Data	Data	1	Data	Data	Data
8	Data	Data		Data	Data	Data
9	Data	Data		Data	Data	Data
10	Data	Data		Data	Data	Data
11	Data	Data		Data	Data	Data
12	Data	Data		Data	Data	Data

Figure 8.32
In Excel 2010, if the cell below the active cell is nonblank, Excel copies the cell until it encounters a blank cell in the current column.

If Excel 2010 does not encounter a value immediately below the active cell, it looks at the seven cells shaded in Figure 8.33. Provided any of those cells are nonblank, Excel will launch into a new, powerful current-region algorithm.

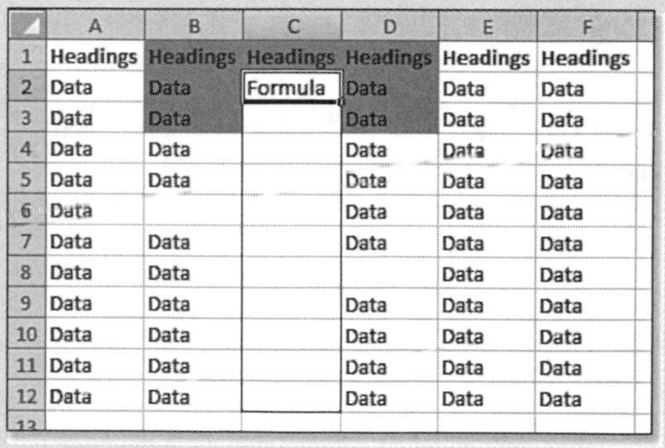

	A	B	C	D	E	F
1	Headings	Headings	Headings	Headings	Headings	Headings
2	Data	Data	Formula	Data	Data	Data
3	Data	Data		Data	Data	Data
4	Data	Data		Data	Data	Data
5	Data	Data		Data	Data	Data
6	Data			Data	Data	Data
7	Data	Data		Data	Data	Data
8	Data	Data			Data	Data
9	Data	Data		Data	Data	Data
10	Data	Data		Data	Data	Data
11	Data	Data		Data	Data	Data
12	Data	Data		Data	Data	Data

Figure 8.33
If any of the seven shaded cells around C2 are nonblank, Excel uses the entire current region to determine the last row.

Excel understands the concept of a ***current region***. If you are in a cell and press Ctrl+*, Excel extends the selection in all directions until it encounters the edge of the worksheet or a completely blank edge of the data. This concept allows Excel to extend past single blank cells and select the whole data set.

In Excel 2010, Excel looks at the current region around the active cell. In Figure 8.33, the current region is A1:F12. Excel copies the formula in C2 down to row 12 because that is how far the current region extends. This is better than the Excel 2007 algorithm that would have been fooled into stopping the copy at C5 by the blank cell in B6.

This allows Excel to find the true bottom of a column in some remarkably sparse data sets. In Figure 8.34, B2, C3, and D2 are all empty. This normally would have prevented the fill handle from copying the formula. However, in Excel 2010, Excel follows the path of C2 – D1 – E1 – F2 – F8 – E9 – E12 to find that the true bottom of the data set is row 12.

It is good to understand the arcane rules involved in the fill handle double-click trick. Although it works most of the time in Excel 2010, be aware that if you are on a computer with Excel 2007, the old rules will apply.

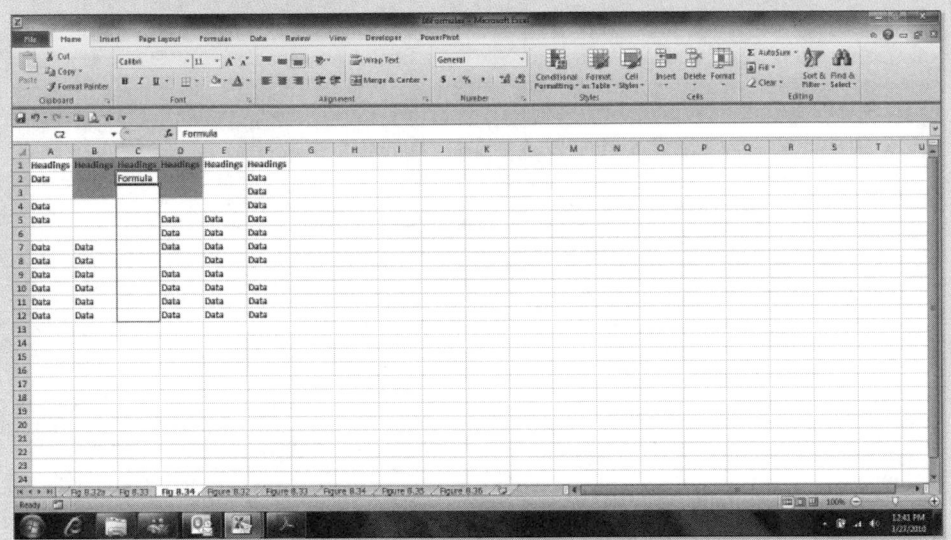

Figure 8.34
Excel 2010 accurately copies the formula down to C12.

9

CONTROLLING FORMULAS

Although you can go a long way with simple formulas, it is also possible to build extremely powerful formulas. The topics in this chapter explain the finer points of formula operators, date math, and how Excel distinguishes between cutting and copying cells referenced in formulas.

Formula Operators

Excel offers the mathematical operators shown in Table 9.1.

Table 9.1 Mathematical Operators

Operator	Description
+	Addition
-	Subtraction
*	Multiplication
/	Division or fractions
^	Exponents
()	Overriding the order of operations
-	Unary minus (for negative numbers)
&	Joining text (concatenation)
>	Greater than
<	Less than
>=	Greater than or equal to

Operator	Description
<=	Less than or equal to
<>	Not equal to
=	Equal to
,	Union operator as in SUM(A1,B2)
:	Range operator as in SUM(A1:B2)
<space>	Intersection operator as in SUM(A:J 2:4)

Order of Operations

When a formula contains many calculations, Excel evaluates the formula in a certain order. Rather than calculating from left to right as a calculator might, Excel performs certain types of calculations, such as multiplication, before calculations such as addition.

You can override the default order of operations with parentheses. If you do not use parentheses, Excel uses the following order of operations:

1. Unary minus is evaluated first.

2. Exponents are evaluated next.

3. Multiplication and division are handled next, in a left-to-right manner.

4. Addition and subtraction are handled next, in a left-to-right manner.

The following sections provide some examples of order of operations.

Unary Minus Example

The unary minus is always evaluated first. Think about when you use exponents to raise a number to a power. If you raise –2 to the second power, Excel calculates –2 × –2, which is +4. So the formula =–2^2 evaluates to 4.

If you raise –2 to the third power, Excel calculates (–2) × (–2) × (–2). Multiplying –2 by –2 results in +4, and multiplying +4 by –2 results in –8. So the simple formula =–2^3 generates –8.

You need to understand a subtle but important distinction. When Excel encounters the formula =–2^3, it evaluates the unary minus first. If you want the exponent to happen first

> **note**
>
> To see how Excel calculates the formulas you enter, first enter a formula in a cell. Next, from the Formulas tab, select Formulas, Formula Auditing, Evaluate Formula to open the Evaluate Formula dialog and watch the formula calculate in slow motion.

and then have the unary minus applied, you have to write the formula as =–(2^3). However, in a formula such as =100–2^3, the minus sign is considered to be a subtraction operator and not a unary minus sign. In this case, 2^3 is evaluated as 8, and then 8 is subtracted from 100.

Figure 9.1 shows the results of three formulas involving raising –2 to various powers.

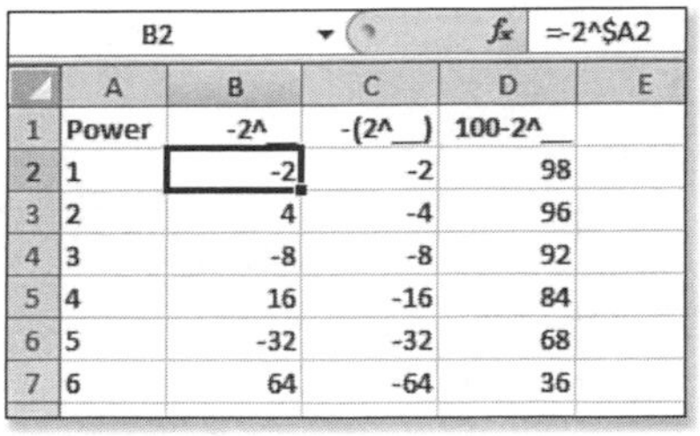

Figure 9.1
Beware of the unary minus. Three very similar formulas have different results, depending on where the minus sign occurs.

	B2			f_x	=-2^$A2
	A	B	C	D	E
1	Power	-2^	-(2^)	100-2^	
2	1	-2	-2	98	
3	2	4	-4	96	
4	3	-8	-8	92	
5	4	16	-16	84	
6	5	-32	-32	68	
7	6	64	-64	36	

Addition and Multiplication Example

The order of operations is important when you are mixing addition/subtraction with multiplication/division. For example, if you want to add 20 to 30 and then multiply by 1.06 to calculate a total with tax, the following formula leads to the wrong result:

=20+30*1.06

The result you are looking for is 53. However, the Evaluate Formula dialog shows that Excel calculates the formula =20+30*1.06 like so (see Figure 9.2):

$1.06 \times 30 = 31.8$
$31.8 + 20 = 51.8$

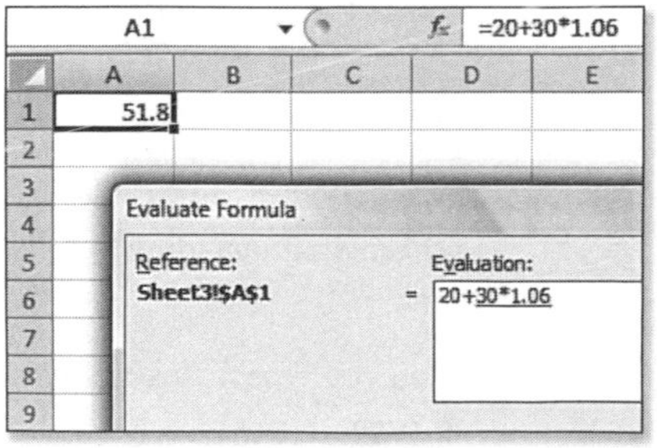

Figure 9.2
The underline indicates that Excel does the multiplication first.

	A1			f_x	=20+30*1.06
	A	B	C	D	E
1	51.8				
2					
3					

Evaluate Formula

Reference: Evaluation:
Sheet3!$A$1   =   20+30*1.06

Excel's answer is $1.20 less than expected because the formula is not written with the default order of operations in mind.

To force Excel to do the addition first, you need to enclose the addition in parentheses:

=(20+30)*1.06

Figure 9.3 shows the second step in the Evaluate Formula dialog for this formula. The addition in parentheses is done first, and then 50 is multiplied by 1.06 to get the correct answer of $53.

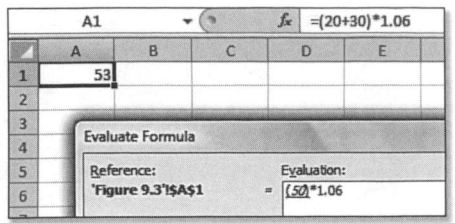

Figure 9.3
Excel evaluates the operation in parentheses first.

Stacking Multiple Parentheses

If you need to use multiple sets of parentheses when doing math by hand, you might write math formulas with square brackets and curly braces, like this:

{3-[6*4*3-(3-6)+2]/27}*14

In Excel, you use multiple sets of parentheses, as follows:

=(3-(6*4*3-(3-6)+2)/27)*14

Formulas with multiple parentheses in Excel are confusing. Excel does two things to try to improve this situation:

- As you type a formula, Excel colors the parentheses in a set order: black, forest, purple, brown, green, orange, violet, blue, forest, purple, brown, green, orange, and so on. If you bump the zoom up on your screen to 400%, you might actually be able to make out the color differences in the parentheses. However, at the normal zoom, the colors black, green, purple, and brown are all dark, and it is difficult to tell one from the other.

- When you type a closing parenthesis, Excel shows the opening parenthesis in bold for a fraction of a second. This would be more helpful if Excel kept the opening parenthesis in bold for 5 seconds or 20 seconds. However, when it is displayed for only about half a second, it is nothing more than a frustrating reminder that your reflexes are not fast enough. Figure 9.4 attempts to show the bolded condition at a ridiculously high zoom.

 tip

Remember that the first and last parentheses will always be black. Excel might repeat various shades of brown, orange, green, and purple, but it never reuses black as a parentheses color. This means if your last parenthesis in the formula is not black, you have the wrong number of parentheses.

Out of frustration with Excel's inability to highlight the matching parenthesis, I usually resort to using Notepad to make understanding complicated formulas easier. To do this, select the cell. In the formula bar, drag to select the entire formula, and then press Ctrl+C to copy it. Next, open a new Notepad window and paste the copied formula into Notepad. As shown in Figure 9.5, you can add line breaks and spaces in Notepad to visualize the formula.

Figure 9.4
This screen shot shows that after you type the fifth closing parenthesis, the tenth opening parentheses is briefly shown in bold.

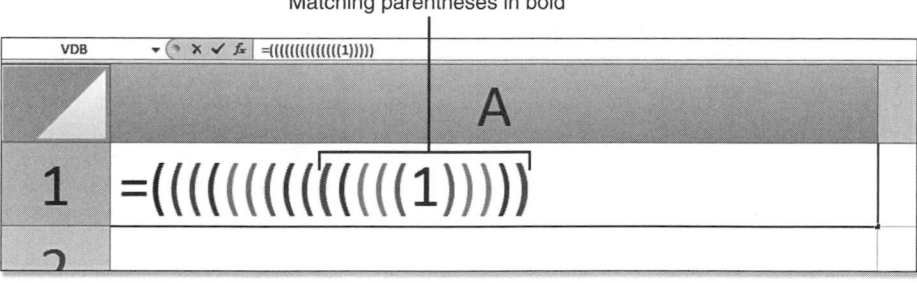

Matching parentheses in bold

Figure 9.5
You copy the formula from the formula bar and paste to a text editor, where you can actually break the formula into components.

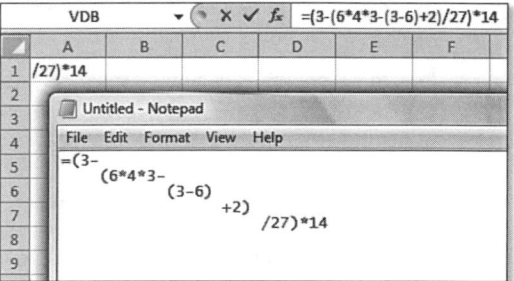

Understanding Error Messages in Formulas

Don't be frustrated when a formula returns an error result. This eventually happens to everyone. The key is to understand the difference between the various error values so that you can begin to troubleshoot the problem.

As you enter formulas, you might encounter a number of errors, including those listed next:

- **#VALUE!**—This error indicates that you are trying to do math with nonnumeric data. For example, the formula =4+"apple" returns a #VALUE! error. This error also occurs if you try to enter an array formula, but fail to use Ctrl+Shift+Enter, as described in Chapter 17, "Using Super Formulas in Excel."

- **#DIV/0!**—This error occurs when a number is divided by zero—that is, when a fraction's denominator evaluates to zero.

- **#REF!**—This error occurs when a cell reference is not valid. For example, this error can occur if one of the cells referenced in the formula has been deleted. It can also occur if you cut and paste another cell over a cell referenced in this formula. You may also get this error if you are using Dynamic Data Exchange (DDE) formulas to link to external systems and those systems are not running.

- **#N/A!**—This error occurs when a value is not available to a function or a formula. #N/A! errors most often occur because of key values not being found during lookup functions. They can occur as a result of HLOOKUP, LOOKUP, MATCH, or VLOOKUP. They can also result when an array formula has one argument that is not the same shape as the other arguments or when a function omits one or more required arguments. Interestingly, when a #N/A! error enters a range, all subsequent calculations that refer to the range have a value of #N/A!.

- **######**—This is not really an error. Instead, it means that the result is too wide to display in the current column width, so you need to make the column wider to see the actual result.

In Figure 9.6, cell E17 is a simple SUM function. It is returning a #N/A! error because Cell E11 contains the same error. Cell E11 contains the formula =D11*C11. The root cause of the problem is the VLOOKUP function in Cell D11. Because Dill cannot be found in the product table in $G$7:$H$9, the VLOOKUP function returns #N/A!.

Figure 9.6 shows only a small table, so it is relatively easy to find the earlier #N/A! errors. However, if you were totaling 100,000 rows, it can be difficult to find the one offending cell. To track down errors, follow these steps:

1. Select the cell that shows the final error. To the left of that cell, you should see an exclamation point in a yellow diamond.

> **caution**
>
> Whereas ###### usually means the column is not wide enough, Excel also uses this symbol to indicate that you are subtracting a later date from an earlier date. If making the column wider does not clear the #### signs, check the formula bar to see if your formula might be subtracting dates.

	E17		fx	=SUM(E8:E16)				
	A	B	C	D	E	F	G	H
1	Apple		4	#VALUE!	=A1+B1			
2		4	0	#DIV/0!	=A2/B2			
3		4	3	#REF!	=#REF*A3			
4		Dill		#N/A	=VLOOKUP(B4,$G$8:$H$10,2,FALSE)			
5								
6								
7	Invoice	Item	Qty	Price	Total		Apple	1
8	101	Apple	11	1	11		Banana	2
9	102	Cherry	11	4	44		Cherry	4
10	103	Banana	9	2	18			
11	104	Dill	10	#N/A	#N/A			
12	105	Apple	9	1	9			
13	106	Cherry	10	4	40			
14	107	Banana	8	2	16			
15	108	Cherry	11	4	44			
16	109	Banana	9	2	18			
17	GRAND TOTAL			⊕	#N/A			

Figure 9.6
The error in E17 is actually caused by an error two calculations earlier.

2. Hover the cursor over the yellow diamond to reveal a drop-down arrow.

3. From the drop-down menu, select Trace Error. Excel draws in red arrows pointing back to the source of the error, as shown in Figure 9.7. For example, from the original #N/A! error in Cell D11, blue arrows demonstrate what cells were causing the error.

4. Repeat steps 1-3 for the cell causing the error to trace the original root cause of the problem.

Item	Qty	Price	Total		Apple	1
Apple	11	1	11		Banana	2
Cherry	11	4	44		Cherry	4
Banana	9	2	18			
Dill	10	#N/A	#N/A			
Apple	9	1	9			
Cherry	10	4	40			
Banana	8	2	16			
Cherry	11	4	44			
Banana	9	2	18			
TAL			#N/A			

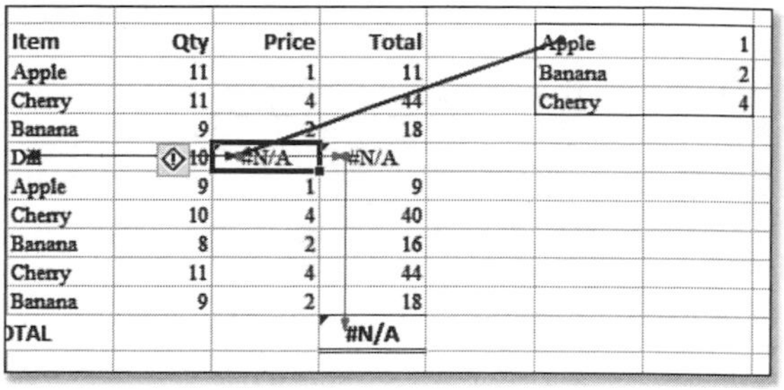

Figure 9.7
Selecting Trace Error reveals the cells leading to the error.

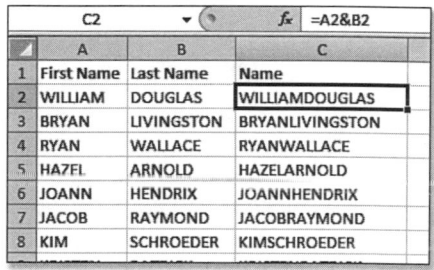

Using Formulas to Join Text

You use the ampersand (&) operator when you need to join text. In Excel the & operator is known as the concatenation operator.

For example, the formula =A2&B2 joins the text values shown in the two cells A2 and B2, as shown in Figure 9.8.

C2 fx =A2&B2

	A	B	C
1	First Name	Last Name	Name
2	WILLIAM	DOUGLAS	WILLIAMDOUGLAS
3	BRYAN	LIVINGSTON	BRYANLIVINGSTON
4	RYAN	WALLACE	RYANWALLACE
5	HAZEL	ARNOLD	HAZELARNOLD
6	JOANN	HENDRIX	JOANNHENDRIX
7	JACOB	RAYMOND	JACOBRAYMOND
8	KIM	SCHROEDER	KIMSCHROEDER

Figure 9.8
The & operator is used to join two text cells.

When using the & operator, you might want to include a space between the two items that are combined to improve the appearance of the output. For example, if the cells contain first name and last name, you might want to have a space between the names. To include a space between cells, you follow the & with a space enclosed in quotes, such as &" ". As shown in Figure 9.9, the formula =A2&" "&B2 generates a better-looking result than =A2&B2.

To watch a video of joining text, search for Excel In Depth 9 at YouTube.

caution

When you enter the formula in Figure 9.9, you have to hold down the Shift key to enter the quotation marks in " ". Many Excel users accidentally hold down the Shift key while pressing the spacebar. However, Shift+spacebar is the Excel shortcut for selecting an entire row. If your formula changes to =A2&"A:A because you pressed Shift+spacebar, you can press the Esc key and start over.

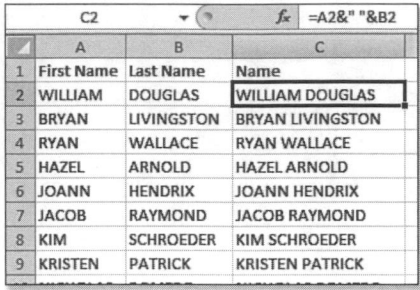

Figure 9.9
You can join cells with any text in quotation marks.

Joining Text and a Number

In many cases, you can use the & operator to join text with a number. In Figure 9.10, the formula in Cell C2 joins the words "The price is $" with the result of the calculation in Cell B2. Because Cell B2 contains an integer with no special formatting, the answer appears correctly.

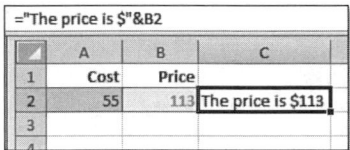

Figure 9.10
Joining text with a number works if the number is formatted with general formatting.

In Figure 9.11, Cell B2 is formatted to display a currency symbol and two decimal places. When you join this value to text in Cell C2, Excel ignores the formatting in Cell B2 and shows the result with all the decimal places. A similar problem exists when you want to join text with a date. Excel ignores the fact that the text in Cell B4 is formatted as a date and shows the underlying value in Cell C4.

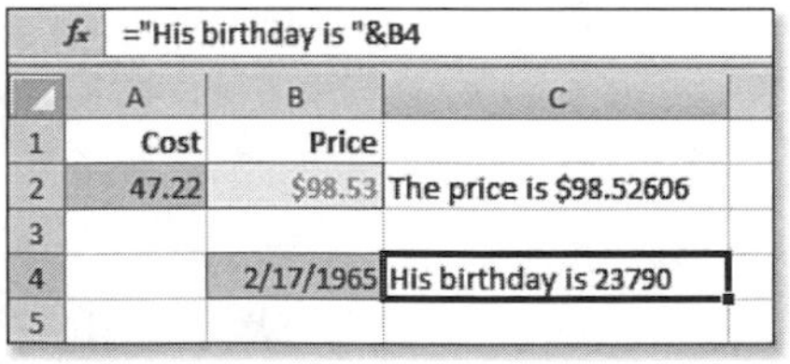

Figure 9.11
Joining text with a date or with formatted numbers rarely works well.

In this case, you need to discover the numeric formatting code associated with the original cell. To do so, follow these steps:

1. Select Cell B2.

2. Press Ctrl+1 to display the Format Cells dialog.

3. On the Number tab, choose the Custom category. This reveals the actual formatting codes for the cell.

As shown in Figure 9.12, the actual formatting code for B2 is $#,##0.00. If you repeat these steps for Cell B4, you learn that the actual formatting code is m/d/yyyy.

Figure 9.12
If you choose the Custom category, you learn the actual codes used to produce the numeric format.

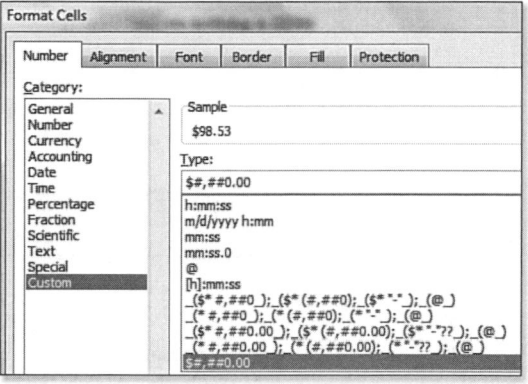

➡ *For a complete discussion of numeric formatting codes, see Chapter 30, "Formatting Worksheets."*

When you know the numeric formatting codes, you can achieve the desired effect by using those codes, enclosed in quotation marks, as the second argument of the TEXT function. In Figure 9.13, the formula in Cell C2 is ="The Answer Is "&Text(B2, "$#,##0.00"). You can use your knowledge of custom numeric formatting codes to change the look of the joined value. In Cell C4, the new formula is ="His birthday is "&TEXT(B4, "dddd mmmm d, yyyy").

Figure 9.13
Use the TEXT function to replicate formatting, as in Cell C2, or to change the formatting, as in Cell C4.

fx	="The price is $"&TEXT(B2,"#,##0.00")			
	A	B	C	D	E
1	Cost	Price			
2	47.22	$98.53	The price is $98.53		
3					
4		2/17/1965	His birthday is Wednesday February 17, 1965		
5					

Copying Versus Cutting a Formula

In Figure 9.14, the formula in Cell C7 references A7+B7. Because there are no dollar signs within the formula, those are relative references.

➡ *To learn more about relative versus absolute references, see Chapter 10, "Understanding Functions."*

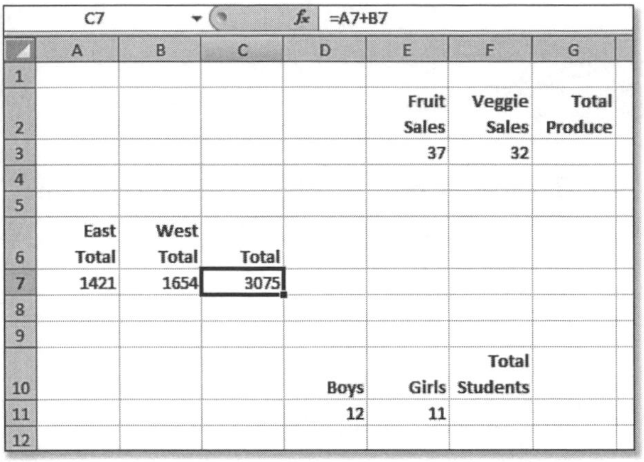

Figure 9.14
The formula in Cell C7 adds the two numbers to the left of the formula.

If you copy Cell C7 and paste it to Cell G3, the formula works perfectly, as shown in Figure 9.15.

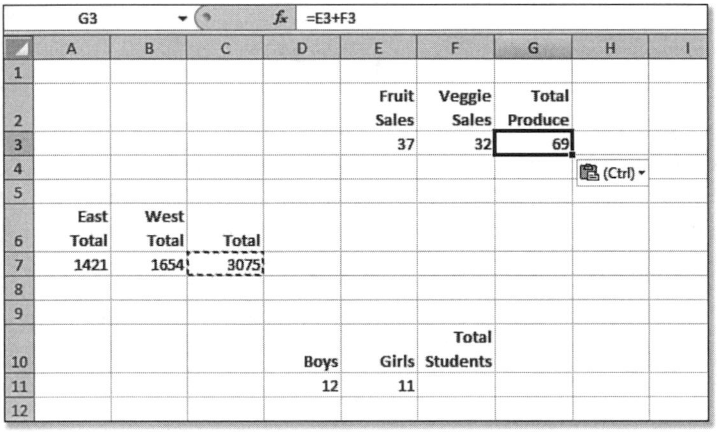

Figure 9.15
When Cell C7 is copied to Cell G3, the formula still adds the two numbers to the left of the formula.

However, if you cut Cell C7 and paste it to a new location, the formula continues to point to Cells A7+B7, as shown in Figure 9.16. Whereas cutting and copying are relatively similar in applications such as Word, they are very different in Excel. It is important to understand the effect of cutting a formula in Excel in contrast to copying the formula.

When you cut a formula, the formula continues to point to the original precedents, no matter where you paste it.

A similar rule applies to the references mentioned in a formula. For example, the formula in Cell C7 points to A7 and B7. As long as you copy Cell A7 and/or Cell B7, you can paste them anywhere without changing the formula in C7. Figure 9.17 shows the result of copying A7:B7 for 20 rows: Nothing changes in the formula.

Figure 9.16
Using cut and paste on a formula forces the formula to continue to point to the original cells.

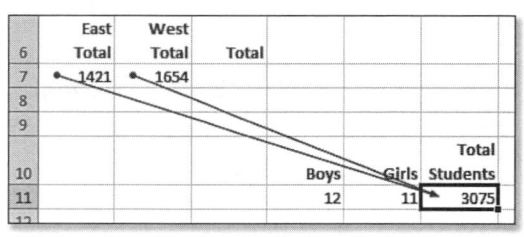

Figure 9.17
Copying the precedent cells from Cell C7 does not have any effect on Cell C7.

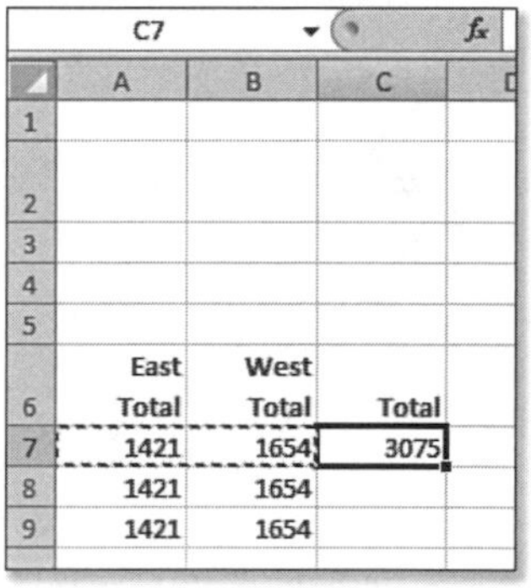

However, if you cut and paste A7:B7 to a new location such as E5:F5, the formula in Cell C7 changes. After the paste, the formula points to the new location of the pasted cells, as shown in Figure 9.18.

Figure 9.18
Cutting the precedent cells from Cell C7 causes the formula in C7 to change to reflect the new location.

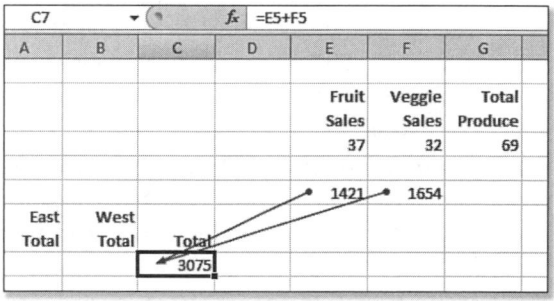

Automatically Formatting Formula Cells

The rules for formatting the result of a formula seem to be inconsistent. Suppose that you have $1.23 in Cell A1, as shown in Figure 9.19.

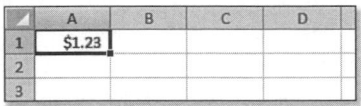

Figure 9.19
In this case, all cells are in general format, except Cell A1.

If you enter =A1+3 in another cell with general format, the result automatically inherits the currency format of Cell A1, as shown in Figure 9.20.

Note that the formatting is copied whether you use =A1+3 or =3+A1.

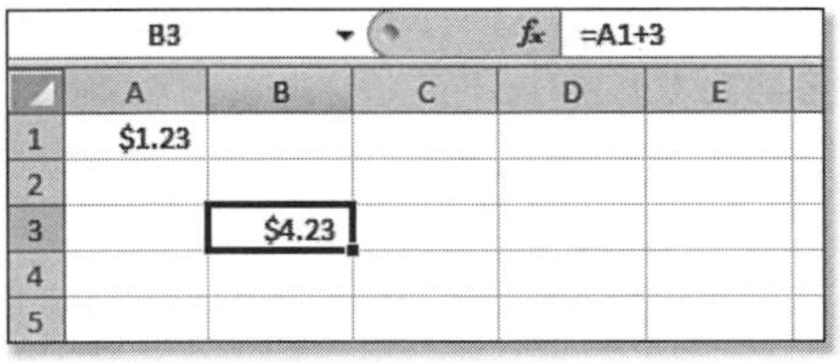

Figure 9.20
No formatting is applied to B3. Instead, Excel copies the format from Cell A1 automatically.

In Figure 9.20, Cell B3 is formatted automatically to match the only cell mentioned in the formula. It becomes harder to predict the automatic format when your formula refers to several cells, each with a different format.

Further, the result will change if you start your formula with a plus sign instead of an equal sign. Many people use the plus sign because it is easy to type on the numeric keypad. However, Microsoft probably considers using the plus sign as a Lotus transition issue and applies different rules.

In Figure 9.21, Cell A1 is formatted as currency with two decimal places. Cell A3 is formatted as number with three decimal places. Cell A5 is formatted as percent with no decimal places. Cells in columns C and F all add the three original cells. Each formula specifies A1, A3, and A5 in a different sequence. Formulas in C were entered starting with a plus sign. Formulas in F were started with an equal sign.

The resulting automatic format does not appear to follow any pattern. When you use an equal sign, either the format is copied from the first or the last cell referenced. When you use a plus sign, the format sometimes comes from the second, first, or last reference; and sometimes the format is a mix of two references.

If your formula is going to refer to multiple cells with different formatting, start the formula with an equal sign. Refer to the cell with the desired cell format first, but accept that you might have to explicitly format the resulting cell.

Figure 9.21
When a formula refers to cells with different formats, the resulting cell's format varies depending on which cell was mentioned first or last.

	A	B	C	D	E	F	G	H
1	$1.23		369.400%	+A1+A3+A5	Last + 3 decimals	$3.69	=A1+A3+A5	First
2								
3	1.234			3.694	+A3+A1+A5	First		3.694	=A3+A1+A5	First
4								
5	123%		$3.69	+A5+A1+A3	Middle		3.694	=A5+A1+A3	Last
6								
7			369.400%	+A1+A5+A3	Middle + 3 decimals		3.694	=A1+A5+A3	Last
8								
9				3.694	+A3+A5+A1	First		3.694	=A3+A5+A1	First
10								
11			$3.69	+A5+A3+A1	Last		369%	=A5+A3+A1	First
12								

Using Date Math

Dates in Excel are stored as the number of days since January 1, 1900. For example, Excel stores the date Feb-17-2011 as 40591. In Figure 9.22, Cell A1 contains the date. Cell A2 contains the formula =A1 and has been formatted to show a number.

Figure 9.22
Although Cell A1 is formatted as a date, Excel stores the date as the number of days since January 1, 1900.

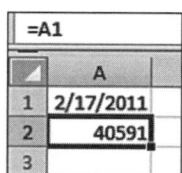

=A1

	A
1	2/17/2011
2	40591
3	

This convenient system allows you to do some pretty simple math. For example, Figure 9.23 shows a range of invoice dates in Column B. The terms for the invoice are in Column D. You can calculate the due date by adding Cells B2 and D2. Here is what actually happens in Excel's calculation engine:

1. The date in Cell B2—2/1/2011—is stored as 40575.

2. Excel adds 10 to that number to get the answer 40585.

3. Excel formats this number as a date, to yield 2/11/2011.

Figure 9.23
When the answer is formatted correctly, Excel's date math is very cool.

	A	B	C	D	E
1	Invoice	Date	Amount	Terms	Due Date
2	2011	2/1/2011	107.60	10	2/11/2011
3	2012	2/1/2011	172.99	20	2/21/2011
4	2013	2/1/2011	170.66	20	2/21/2011
5	2014	2/2/2011	193.29	30	3/4/2011

However, a frustrating problem can occur if the cell containing the formula has the wrong numeric format. For example, in Figure 9.24, the WORKDAY function in column D did not automatically convert the result to a date. It is important to recognize that dates in 2010–2013 fall in the range of 40,179 to 41,639. So, if you are expecting a date answer as the result of a formula and get a number in this range, the answer probably needs to have a date format applied.

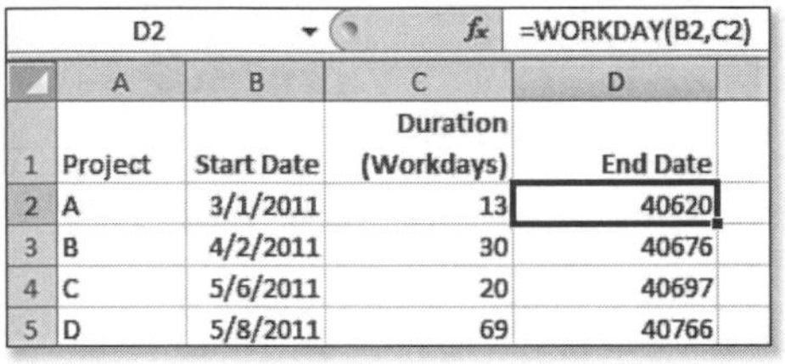

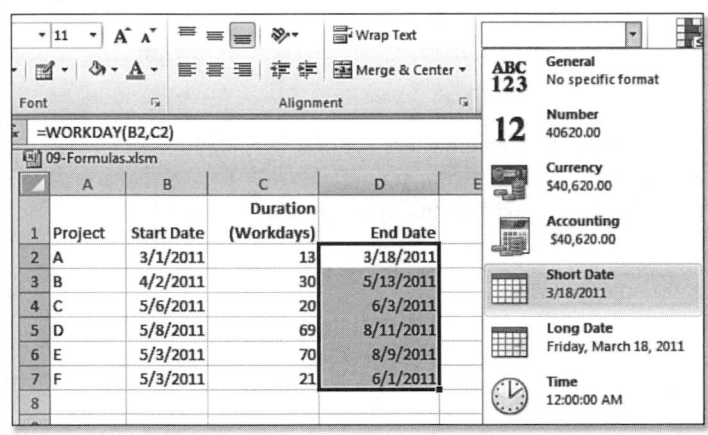

Figure 9.24
The formula appears to give the wrong answer. However, this is a formatting problem.

To apply a date format, on the Home tab use the Number drop-down to choose the Date format. The answer in Column D now appears correctly, as shown in Figure 9.25.

In general, most formulas that refer to a date cell will automatically be formatted as a date. Most formulas that contain functions from the Date category will be formatted as a date. (The WORKDAY function is one annoying exception). However, sometimes you do not want the result formatted as a date.

Figure 9.25
After you apply the Date format, the answer is displayed correctly.

For example, in Figure 9.26, you would like to count the number of days between two dates. The formula in C4 should calculate 16 days. However, because Excel automatically formatted the result as a date, the answer of 16 is shown as 1/16/1900. In this case, you need to apply a numeric format to the range containing the formula. When you select Number from the Number drop-down on the Home tab, the formula appears with the correct result (see Figure 9.27).

Anytime you are doing math between two dates, you should plan to change the format of the result to be either Number or Date, depending on the situation.

➡️ *To learn about many other useful date functions in Excel, see Chapter 11, "Using Everyday Functions: Math, Date and Time, and Text Functions."*

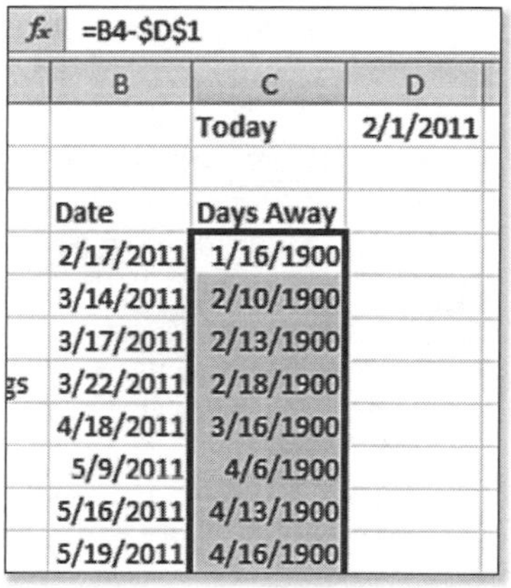

Figure 9.26
In this case, you want the answer to be formatted as a number instead of a date.

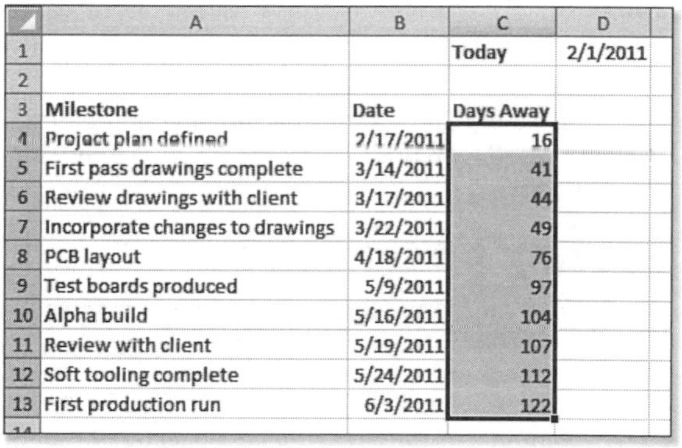

f_x	=B4-$D$1		
	B	C	D
		Today	2/1/2011
	Date	Days Away	
	2/17/2011	1/16/1900	
	3/14/2011	2/10/1900	
	3/17/2011	2/13/1900	
	3/22/2011	2/18/1900	
	4/18/2011	3/16/1900	
	5/9/2011	4/6/1900	
	5/16/2011	4/13/1900	
	5/19/2011	4/16/1900	

Figure 9.27
When you apply a numeric format, the answers are correct.

	A	B	C	D
1			Today	2/1/2011
2				
3	Milestone	Date	Days Away	
4	Project plan defined	2/17/2011	16	
5	First pass drawings complete	3/14/2011	41	
6	Review drawings with client	3/17/2011	44	
7	Incorporate changes to drawings	3/22/2011	49	
8	PCB layout	4/18/2011	76	
9	Test boards produced	5/9/2011	97	
10	Alpha build	5/16/2011	104	
11	Review with client	5/19/2011	107	
12	Soft tooling complete	5/24/2011	112	
13	First production run	6/3/2011	122	
14				

Troubleshooting Formulas

It is difficult to figure out worksheets that were set up by other people. When you receive a worksheet from a co-worker, use the information in the following sections to find and examine the formulas.

Highlighting All Formula Cells

The first technique to use when examining a new worksheet is to find all the cells that contain formulas. The following steps will identify all the formula cells in the worksheet:

1. Ensure that you have a single cell selected.

2. Press F5 to display the Go To dialog.

3. In the lower-left corner of the Go To dialog, click the Special button to display the Go To Special dialog.

4. In the Go To Special dialog, select the Formulas option button, as shown in Figure 9.28. Click OK to select all formula cells.

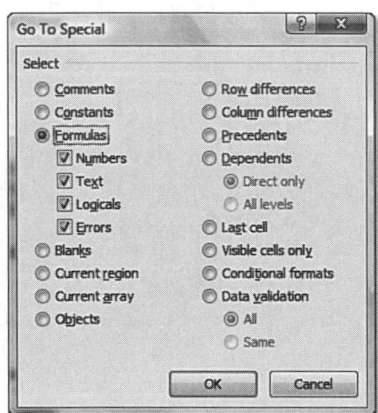

Figure 9.28
The Go To Special dialog has many incredibly powerful features.

5. To highlight all the cells that contain formulas quickly, use the Paint Bucket icon in the Home tab to mark all the formula cells, as shown in Figure 9.29.

Seeing All Formulas

For a long time, Excel has given users the ability to see all the formulas in a worksheet. The mode that provides this functionality is called *Show Formulas mode*.

On most U.S. keyboards, the key just below the Esc key in the upper-left corner of the keyboard contains a tilde (~) and also a backtick (`). In previous versions of Excel, you had to press Ctrl+` to toggle into and out of Show Formulas mode, in which each column is a little wider. Instead of showing the results of the formula, in Show Formulas mode, each cell shows the formula itself (see Figure 9.30). This keystroke had to be pressed again to return to Regular mode.

In addition to recognizing Ctrl+`, Excel 2010 offers an icon in the Formula Auditing section of the Formulas tab that enables you to toggle into and out of Show Formulas mode.

Cells containing formulas

Figure 9.29
Immediately after selecting all formulas, select the Paint Bucket icon to color the formula cells.

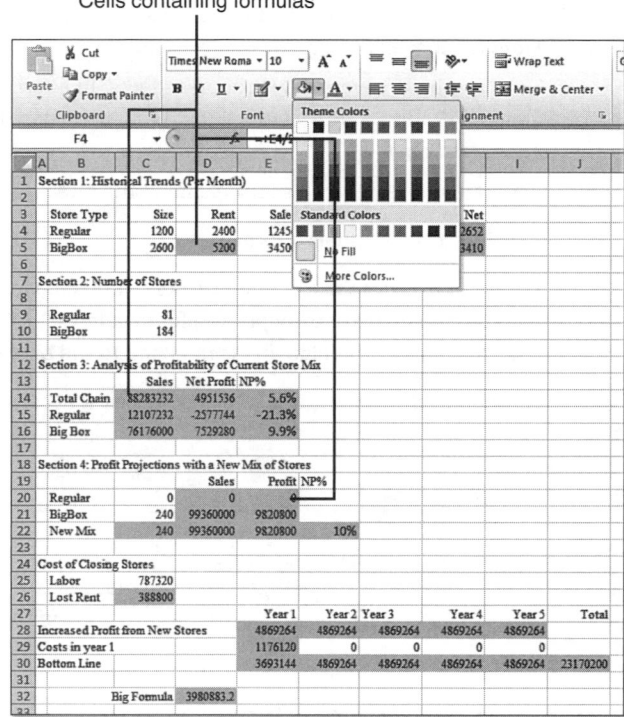

Figure 9.30
Show Formulas mode shows the formulas in the cells instead of the results. This is handy for quick formula auditing.

	A	B	C	D	E	
1	Sect					
2						
3		Store Type	Size	Rent	Sales	
4		Regular	1200	2400	12456	=+E4/2
5		BigBox	2600	=+C5*2	34500	=+E5/2
6						
7	Sect					
8						
9		Regular	81			
10		BigBox	184			
11						
12	Sect					
13			Sales	Net Profit	NP%	
14		Total Chain	=+C15+C16	=+D15+D16	=+D14/C14	
15		Regular	=(C9*E4)*12	=(C9*H4)*12	=+D15/C15	
16		Big Box	=(C10*E5)*12	=(C10*H5)*12	=+D16/C16	

Editing a Single Formula to Show Direct Precedents

It is helpful to identify cells that are used to calculate a formula. These cells are called the *precedents* of the cell.

A cell can have several levels of precedents. In a formula such as =D5+D7, there are two direct precedents: D5 and D7. However, all the direct precedents of D5 & D7 are second-level precedents of the original formula.

If you are interested in visually examing the direct precedents of a cell, follow these steps:

1. Select a cell that has a formula.

2. Press F2 to put the cell in Edit mode. In this mode, each reference of the formula is displayed in a different color. For example, the formula in Cell H5 refers to three cells. The characters F5 in the formula appear in blue and correspond to the blue box around Cell F5 in Figure 9.31.

3. Visually check the formula to ensure that it is correct.

A	B	C	D	E	F	G	H
1	Section 1: Historical Trends (Per Month)						
2							
3	Store Type	Size	Rent	Sales	Profit	Labor	Net
4	Regular	1200	2400	12456	6228	6480	-2652
5	BigBox	2600	5200	34500	17250	8640	=+F5-G5-D5

Figure 9.31
Editing a single formula lights up the direct precedent cells.

Using Formula Auditing Arrows

If you have a complicated formula, you might want to identify direct precedents and then possibly second- or third-level precedents. You can have Excel draw arrows from the current cells to all cells that make up the precedents for the current cell. To have Excel draw arrows, follow these steps:

1. From the Formula Auditing group on the Formulas tab, click Trace Precedents. Excel draws arrows from the current cell to all the cells that are directly referenced in the formula. For example, in Figure 9.32, an arrow is drawn to a worksheet icon near Cell B30. This indicates that at least one of the precedents for this cell is on another worksheet.

2. Click Trace Precedents again. Excel draws arrows from the precedent cells to the precedents of those cells. These are the second-level precedents of the original cell. Figure 9.33 shows the results of clicking Trace Precedents five times. Practically every cell on the worksheet is a precedent of Cell D32.

3. To remove the arrows, use the Remove Arrows icon in the Formula Auditing group.

tip

Although it may be impossible to follow the lines for all five levels of precedents in Figure 9.33, this figure indicates that the formula in D32 is vastly more complex than the six cells mentioned in the formula. To have a thorough understanding of what your co-worker built in this worksheet, you need to follow the logic through two dozen cells. In other words, you should not delete any of those cells if you want the formula to continue to calculate a correct result.

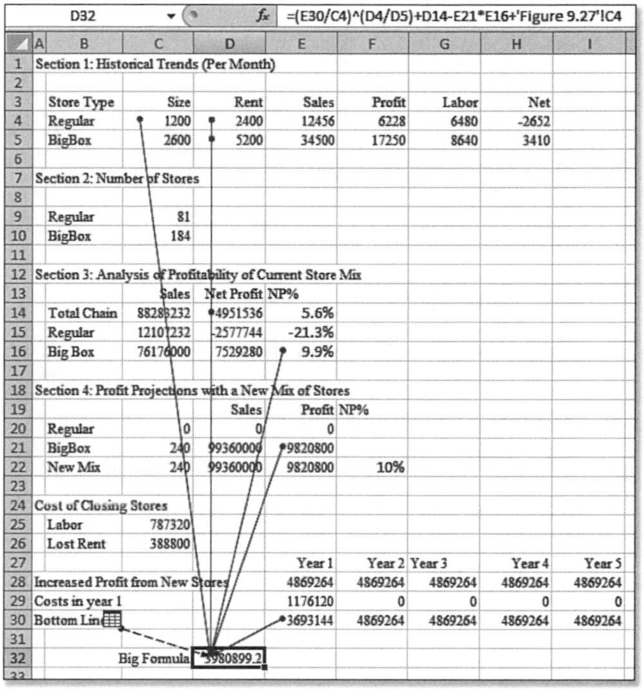

Figure 9.32
The results of trace precedents for Cell D32.

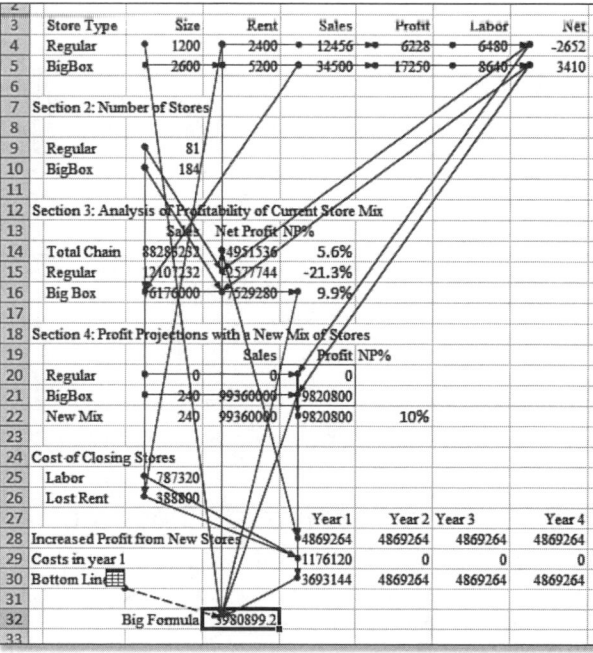

Figure 9.33
Precedents traced five times to find every precedent of the formula.

Tracing Dependents

The Formula Auditing section provides another interesting option besides the ones discussed so far in this chapter. You can use the Formula Auditing section to trace dependents so you can find all the cells on the current worksheet that depend on the active cell. Before deleting a cell, consider clicking Trace Dependents to determine whether any cells on the current sheet refer to this cell. This will prevent many #REF! errors from occurring.

 caution

Even if tracing dependents does not show any cells that are dependent on the current cell, other cells on other worksheets or on other workbooks might rely on this cell.

Using the Watch Window

If you have a large spreadsheet, you might want to watch the results of some distant cells. You can use the Watch Window icon in the Formula Auditing section of the Formulas tab to open a floating box called the *Watch Window* screen. To use the Watch Window screen, follow these steps:

1. Click the Add Watch icon. The Add Watch dialog appears.

2. In the Add Watch dialog, specify a cell to watch, as shown in Figure 9.34. After you add several cells, the Watch Window screen floats above your worksheet, showing the current value of each cell that was added to it. The Watch Window identifies the current value and the current formula of each watched cell.

 tip

To jump to a watched cell quickly, you can double-click the cell in the Watch Window screen.

In theory, this feature can be used to watch a value in a far-off section of the worksheet.

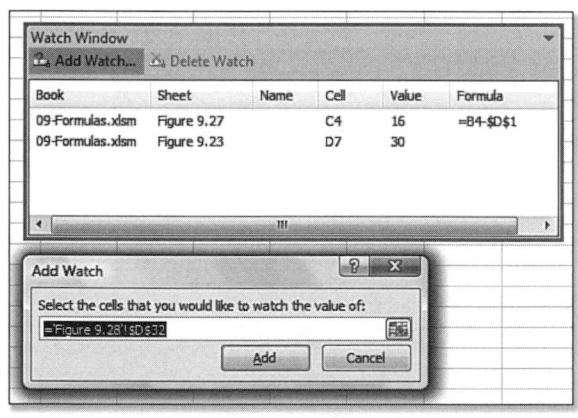

Figure 9.34
Adding a watch to the Watch Window screen.

Evaluate a Formula in Slow Motion

Most of the time, Excel calculates formulas in an instant. It will help your understanding of the formula if you could watch it being calculated in slow motion. If you need to see exactly how a formula is being calculated, follow these steps:

1. Select the cell that contains the formula in which you are interested.

2. On the Formulas tab, in the Formula Auditing group, select Evaluate Formula. The Evaluate Formula dialog appears, showing the formula. The following component of the formula is highlighted: It is the next section of the formula to be calculated.

3. If desired, click Evaluate to calculate the highlighted portion of the formula.

4. Click Step In to begin a new Evaluate section for the cell references in the underlined portion of the formula. Figure 9.35 shows the Evaluate Formula dialog after stepping in to the E30 portion of the formula.

Figure 9.35
The Evaluate Formula dialog allows you to calculate a formula in slow motion.

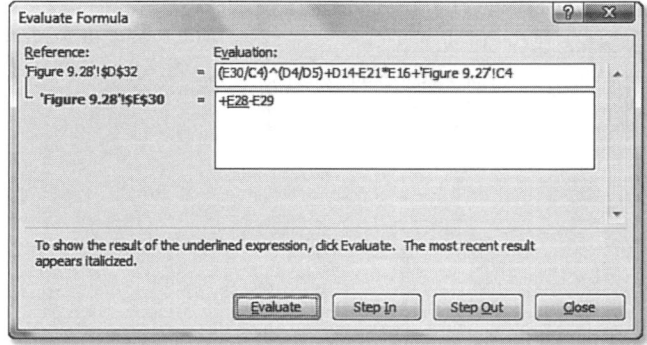

Evaluating Part of a Formula

When you do not need to evaluate an entire formula, use the Evaluate Formula feature. Follow these steps to evaluate part of a formula:

1. Use the mouse to select just the desired portion of the formula in the formula bar, as shown in Figure 9.36.

Figure 9.36
You can select a portion of the formula in the formula bar.

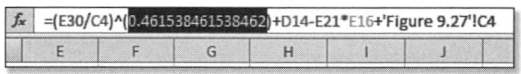

2. Press F9. Excel calculates just the highlighted portion of the formula, as shown in Figure 9.37.

Be sure to press the Esc key to exit the formula after you use this method. Instead, if you press Enter to accept the formula, that portion of the formula permanently stays in its calculated form, such as 0.407407.

Figure 9.37
Press F9 to calculate just the highlighted portion of the formula.

Excel in Practice: Moving the Formula ToolTip

As you type a formula, Excel 2010 offers a ToolTip to show the order of the arguments for a function. As shown in Figure 9.38, this ToolTip can frequently get in the way by covering nearby cells.

A cool trick is to click the ToolTip and drag it to a new location. As you continue entering the formula, the ToolTip stays in the new, detached location (see Figure 9.39).

 **tip**

If you click on the function name in the tooltip, Excel opens the Help topic for that function.

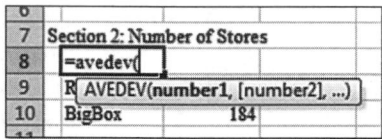

Figure 9.38
The tooltip is covering adjacent cells.

	Size	Rent	Sales	Profit	Labor	Net					
	1200	2400	12456	6228	6480	-2652					
	2600	5200	34500	17250	8640	3410					
umber of Stores											
C9:C10)+VLOOKUP(											
	81				VLOOKUP(**lookup_value**, table_array, col_index_num, [range_lookup])						
	184										

Figure 9.39
Drag the ToolTip to an out-of-the way location.

UNDERSTANDING FUNCTIONS

Excel is used on 500 million desktops around the world. People from all careers use Excel, as do many home users who use Excel's powerful features to track their finances, investments, and more. Part of Excel's versatility is its wide range of built-in functions.

Excel 2003 offered 255 built-in functions. Another 89 functions shipped with Excel but were available only to people who installed the Analysis ToolPak (ATP). Excel 2010 now offers 400 built-in functions. Although this sounds like a tremendous increase, only about seven functions will be of interest to most people:

- Excel 2010 adds the new AGGREGATE function, which is similar to SUBTOTALS but with 19 calculations instead of 11.

- Excel 2007 added the IFERROR function to reduce #N/A and DIV/0 errors.

- Excel 2007 introduced plural AVERAGEIF, SUMIFS, COUNTIFS, and AVERAGEIFS functions. The plural versions handle multiple conditions and are amazingly fast. If you've ever used SUMPRODUCT because SUMIF handles only one condition, you will love SUMIFS.

What are the other new functions? They include the following:

- International versions of NETWORKDAYS.INTL, WORKDAYS.INTL, ISO.CEILING, and ISO.FLOOR. The former workday functions assumed a work week of Monday through Friday. The new versions can handle workweeks in which the weekend is two other days.

- Thirty-eight statistical distribution functions. Some of these are truly new, and some of them are renamed versions of existing functions. In the past, some functions returned a left-tailed point distribution function and others returned a left-tailed cumulative distribution function. Some offered an Inverse function and others did not. Microsoft standardized the naming of the functions, offering consistent naming for the distribution function, for the inverse function, and so on. The old function names are still supported for compatibility with legacy versions of Excel.

- Fourteen other statistical functions. New ways to calculate Rank, Mode, Percentile, and Quartile. Consistent naming for VAR and STDDEV.

- Eighty-nine ATP functions, which are now part of the default Excel installation.

- Seven new cube functions that are useful to people who connect to a multidimensional database, such as SQL Server Analysis Services.

Microsoft also invested heavily to improve the accuracy of several functions. Over the years, various academic papers had noted that Excel was doing a poor job when the input values for certain functions started to get out into extreme ranges. For this reason, Microsoft hired three mathematical consulting firms to assist in this process. Two firms (Frontline Systems and Numerical Algorithms Group) were hired to propose new algorithms. A third firm, ScienceOps, considered the competing algorithms from the first two firms to judge which algorithm should be adopted.

What does this mean? It means that for certain input values, the following functions will return improved values in Excel 2010. It doesn't mean that every answer will be different. However, if you have a worksheet that is doing calculations near the numerical limits of the function, you might get different results when compared to computers running Excel 2007 or earlier.

- Statistical Distribution functions with improved accuracy include: BETADIST, BETAINV, BINOMDIST, CRITBINOM, CHIDIST, CHIINV, EXPONDIST, FDIST, FINV, GAMMADIST, GAMMAINV, HYPGEOMDIST, LOGNORMDIST, LOGINV, NEGBINOMDIST, NORMDIST, NORMINV, NORMSDIST, NORMSINV, POISSON, TDIST, TINV, and WEIBULL.

- Financial functions with improved accuracy include CUMIPMT, CUMPRINC, IPMT, IRR, PMT, PPMT, and XIRR.

- Math functions with improved accuracy include ASINH, CONVERT, ERF, ERFC, GAMMALN, GEOMEAN, MOD, RAND, STDEVS, and VARS.

The functions available in Excel 2010 are applicable to a wide range of industries. Financial functions help investors, bankers, and bond traders. Math and statistical functions help scientists. There are engineering functions for engineers and general-purpose functions for everyone.

No matter what you are trying to do in Excel, there are functions for you. If you cannot find a built-in function, there is a good chance that a third-party vendor sells an add-in program to Excel that adds new customized functions to Excel to assist in your particular industry. If not, you can pick up a book on programming VBA to learn how to write your own custom functions in Excel.

 Refer to Chapter 4 of VBA and Macros for Microsoft Excel 2010 *by Jelen and Syrstad (QUE, ISBN 0789743140) to learn about the 30 cool functions that you can add to Excel.*

 tip

Did you realize that function names could include a period? There were three functions in Excel 2003 that had periods: REGISTER.ID, SQL.REQUEST, and ERROR.TYPE. You might have never encountered these functions previously. In Excel 2010, 56 of the new statistical functions are implemented with a period, so you should get used to seeing functions like STDEV.S, VAR.P, PERCENTILE.EXC, and more.

Working with Functions

To use functions successfully in a worksheet, you need to follow the function syntax. Keep in mind that a formula that makes use of a function needs to start with an equal sign. You type the function name, an opening parenthesis, function arguments (separated by commas), and the closing parenthesis.

The general syntax of a function looks like this:

```
=FunctionName(Argument1,Argument2,Argument3)
```

In general, there should be no spaces anywhere in a function. Specifically, you should never use a space between the function name and the opening parenthesis. Some people like to add a space after each comma in a function, like this:

```
=FunctionName(Argument1, Argument2, Argument3)
```

Although this is not required, it does increase the readability of the final function. For what it's worth, Excel correctly calculates a formula with or without these spaces, so it's a personal choice as to whether you include them.

Parentheses are needed with every function, including functions that require no arguments. For example, these functions still require the parentheses:

```
=NOW()
=DATE()
=TODAY()
```

The arguments for a function should be entered in the correct order, as specified in this book or Excel Help. For example, the PMT() function expects the arguments to have the interest rate first, followed by the number of periods, followed by the present value. If you attempt to send the arguments in the wrong order, Excel will happily calculate the wrong result.

In many cases, you can enter arguments as numbers or as cell references. For example, all these formulas are valid:

```
=SUM(1,2,3^2,4/5,6*7)
=SUM(A1:A9,C1,D2,Sheet2!E3:M10)
=SUM(A1:A9,100,200,B3*5)
```

 note

Excel functions can return a number of errors. This happens most frequently when one of the arguments passed to the function is outside the range of what the function expects. When you receive a #NUM!, #VALUE!, or #N/A! error, you should look in Excel Help for the function. The Remarks section usually indicates exactly what problems can causes each type of error.

 note

Chapters 11 through 15 cover all of the 400 functions. This chapter covers a number of the most commonly used functions and the new functions in Excel 2010.

The Formulas Tab in Excel 2010

One way to find functions in Excel 2010 is on the Formulas tab. This tab offers Function Wizard, AutoSum, Recently Used, Financial, Logical, Text, Date & Time, Lookup & Reference, Math & Trig, and More Functions icons.

As shown in Figure 10.1, when you click the More Functions icon, a drop-down with five additional function groups—Statistical, Engineering, Cube, Information, and Compatibility—appears.

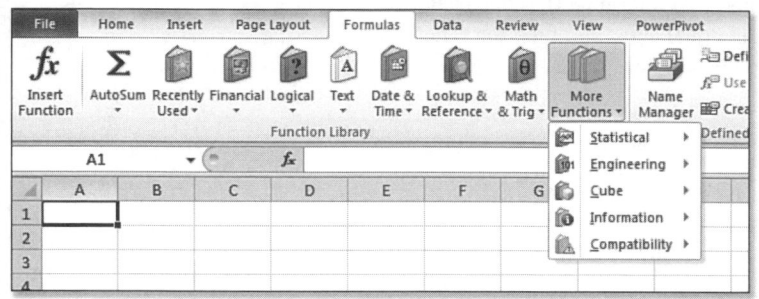

Figure 10.1
The Formulas tab contains icons for finding functions.

The Formulas tab is designed to make it easier to find the right function. You select an icon from the Ribbon, and an alphabetical list of functions in that group appears. If you hover your mouse over a function in the list, Excel displays a description of what the function does, as shown in Figure 10.2.

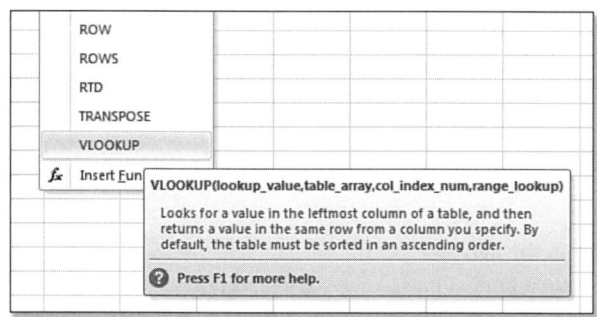

Figure 10.2
Hover over a function, and Excel displays a tip explaining what the function does.

Finding the Function You Need

The inherent problem with the Formulas tab is that you often have to guess where your desired function might be hiding. The function categories have been established in Excel for a decade, and in some cases, functions are tucked away in strange places.

For example, the SUM( ) function is a Math & Trig function. This makes sense because adding numbers is clearly a mathematical process. However, the AVERAGE( ) function is not available in the Math & Trig icon. (It is under More Functions, Statistical.) The COUNT( ) function could be math, reference, or information, but it is found under More Functions, Statistical.

By dividing the list of functions up into categories, Microsoft has made it rather difficult to find certain functions. Fortunately, as described in the following sections, you can use some tricks to make this process simpler.

Using AutoComplete to Find Functions

One feature in Excel 2010 is Formula AutoComplete. Sometimes you might remember the first letter of a function but not all the rest of the letters. For example, there are five varieties of the function you use to do averages, and they all start with A. Rather than trying to figure out whether the averaging function you need is in the Math or Statistical icon, you can just start typing =AV in a cell. Excel displays a pop-up window with all the functions that begin with AV, as shown in Figure 10.3.

Figure 10.3
Rather than use the icons on the Formulas tab, you can type =AV to display an alphabetical list of the AV functions.

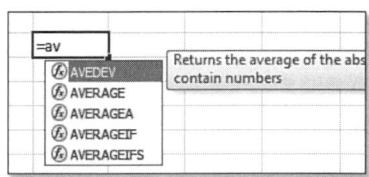

To accept a function name from the list, you can either double-click the function name or select the name and press Tab.

Using the Function Wizard to Find Functions

At the bottom of every list of functions is an icon for the Insert Function. To access the Insert Function dialog, you can also use the small fx button to the left of the formula bar, the More Functions option at the bottom of the AutoSum drop-down, or the large Function Wizard button on the Formulas tab. With 15 ways to access the Function Wizard, Microsoft is telling you that this is a good way to find functions.

Choosing any of these options to open the Function Wizard causes the Insert Function dialog to appear.

In the Excel 2003 version of the Function Wizard, Microsoft added a handy search utility. For example, if you typed Car Payment and then clicked Go, Excel would suggest PMT (the correct function) as well as PPMT, ISPMT, RATE, and others. The search functionality was a fantastic addition to Excel 2003 and should be your first stop when trying to find a function in Excel 2010.

When you choose a function in the Insert Function dialog, the dialog displays the syntax for the function, as well as a one-sentence description of the function, as shown in Figure 10.4. If you need more details, you can click the Help on This Function hyperlink in the lower-left corner of the Insert Function dialog.

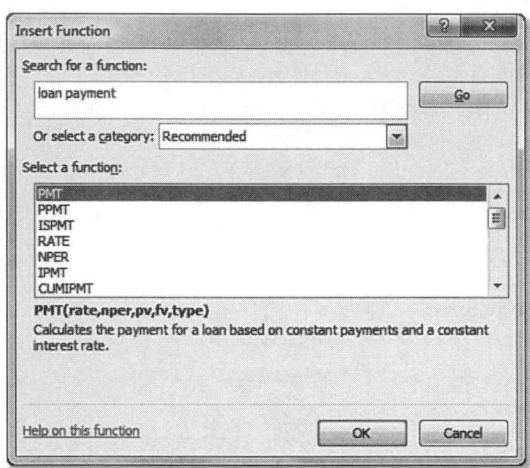

Figure 10.4
The Insert Function dialog allows you to browse the syntax and descriptions. The Help on This Function hyperlink leads to more help.

Getting Help with Excel Functions

Every Excel function has three levels of help:

- In-cell ToolTip

- Function Arguments dialog

- Excel Help

The following section discuss these levels of help. However, you are sure to find the Function Arguments dialog to be one of the best ways of getting help.

Using In-Cell ToolTips

In any cell, you can type an equal sign, a function name, and the opening parenthesis. Excel displays a ToolTip that shows the expected arguments. In many cases, this ToolTip is enough to guide you through the function. For example, I can usually remember that the function for figuring out a car loan payment is =PMT(), but I can never remember the order of the arguments. The ToolTip, as shown in Figure 10.5, is enough to remind me that rate comes first, followed by number of periods, and then the principal amount or present value. Any function names displayed in square brackets are optional, so in the example shown in Figure 10.5, you know that you may not have to enter anything for fv or type.

 tip

By the way, you can click the formula ToolTip and drag it to a new location on the worksheet. This can be useful if the ToolTip is covering cells that you need to click when building the function.

If you click on the function name in the Tool Tip, Excel will open Help for that function.

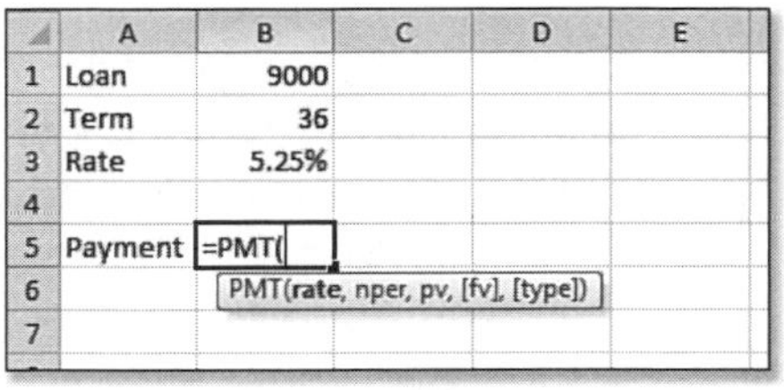

Figure 10.5
The ToolTip assists you in remembering the proper order for the arguments.

As you type each comma in the function, the next argument in the ToolTip lights up in boldface. This way, you always know which argument you are entering.

Using the Function Arguments Dialog

When you access a function through the Function Wizard or a drop-down list, Excel displays the Function Arguments dialog. This dialog is one of the best features in Excel.

> ## tip
>
> If you type =FunctionName(
> in a cell, you can press Ctrl+A anytime after the opening parenthesis to display the Function Arguments dialog.

Figure 10.6
The Function Arguments dialog helps you build a function, one step at a time.

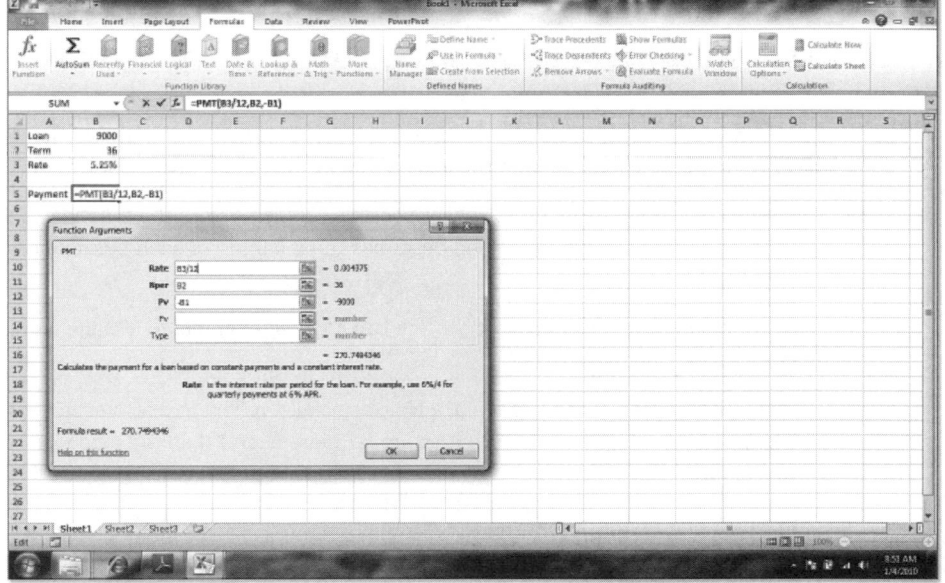

As shown in Figure 10.6, the Function Arguments dialog has many elements:

■ The one-sentence description of the function appears in the center of the dialog.

■ As you tab into the text box for each argument, the description of the argument is shown in the dialog. This description guides you as to what Excel is expecting. For example, in the dialog shown in Figure 10.6, Excel reminds you that the interest rate needs to be divided by four for quarterly payments. This reminds you to divide the APR in Cell B3 by 12.

■ To the right of each argument in the dialog is a reference button. You can click this button to collapse the dialog so you can point to the cells for that argument.

■ To the right of each text box is a label that shows the result of the entry for that argument.

■ Any arguments in bold are required. Arguments not in bold are optional.

■ After you enter the required arguments, the dialog shows the preliminary result of the formula. This is on the right side, just below the last argument text box. It appears again in the lower-left corner, just above the Help on This Function hyperlink.

■ A Help on This Function hyperlink to the Help topic for the function appears in the lower-left corner of the dialog.

Using Excel Help

The Excel Help topics for the functions are incredibly complete. You will find the following sections in each function's Help topic:

■ The function syntax appears at the top of the topic. This includes a description of each function that may be more complete than the description in the Function Arguments dialog.

■ The Remarks section helps troubleshoot possible problems with the function. It discusses specific limits for each argument and describes the meaning of each possible error that could be returned from the function.

■ Each function has an example section. You can copy an example to a blank worksheet to see the function actually working.

■ The See Also section at the bottom of a Help topic allows you to discover related functions. The logical groupings suggested by See Also are far more useful than the category groupings in the Formulas tab.

Using AutoSum

Microsoft realizes that the most common function is the SUM( ) function. It is so popular that Excel provides one-click access to the AutoSum feature.

The AutoSum icon is the large Greek letter sigma that is the second icon on the Formulas tab. You can click this icon to use AutoSum, or you can use the drop-down at the bottom of the icon to access AutoSum versions of Average, Count Numbers, Max, and Min, as shown in Figure 10.7.

Figure 10.7
The AutoSum drop-down offers the capability to average and more.

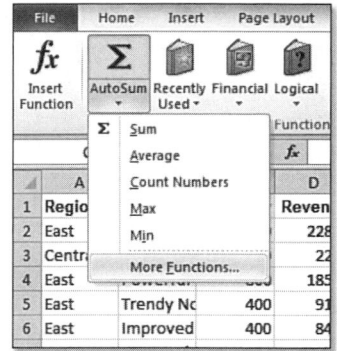

When you click the AutoSum button, Excel seeks to add up the numbers that are above or to the left of the current cell. In general, when you click the AutoSum icon, Excel guesses which cells you are trying to sum. Excel automatically types the SUM( ) formula. You should review Excel's guess to make sure that Excel chose the correct range to sum. In Figure 10.8, for example, Excel correctly guesses that you want to sum the column of revenue above the cell.

Tip
Pressing Alt+= is equivalent to clicking the AutoSum icon.

Figure 10.8
The AutoSum feature is proposing a formula to sum C2:C10.

	A	B	C	D	E	F
1	Region	Customer	Quantity	Revenue	COGS	Profit
2	East	Functiona	1000	22810	10220	12590
3	Central	Vivid Edge	100	2257	984	1273
4	East	Powerful	800	18552	7872	10680
5	East	Trendy Nc	400	9152	4088	5064
6	East	Improved	400	8456	3388	5068
7	East	Tremendc	1000	21730	9840	11890
8	Central	Improved	800	16416	6776	9640
9	Central	Wonderfu	900	21438	9198	12240
10	Central	Matchless	300	6267	2541	3726
11			=SUM(C2:C10)			
12			SUM(**number1**, [number2], ...)			
13						

SUM ▼ × ✓ ƒx =SUM(C2:C10)

Potential Problems with AutoSum

Although you should always check the range proposed by the AutoSum feature, in some cases you should be especially wary. If your headings above the data are numeric, for example, this will fool AutoSum. In Figure 10.9, the 2008 heading in C1 is numeric. This causes Excel to include the heading incorrectly in the total for Column C.

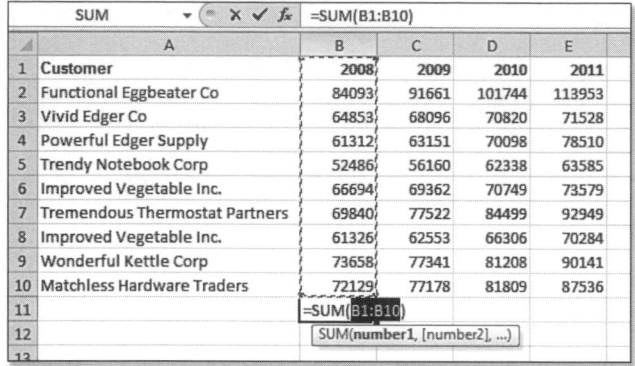

Figure 10.9
Numeric headings confuse AutoSum.

When Excel proposes the wrong range for a sum, you use your mouse to highlight the correct range before pressing Enter.

Excel avoids including other SUM() functions in an AutoSum range. If a range contains a SUM() function that references other cells, Excel prematurely stops just before the SUM() function. This problem happens only when the SUM() function references other cells. If the cell contained =7000+1878 or =H3+H4 or =SUM(7000,1878), AutoSum would include the cell.

Excel prefers to sum a column of numbers instead of a row of numbers. Figure 10.10 shows a strange anomaly. If you place the cell pointer in Cell F2 and click AutoSum, Excel correctly guesses that you want to total B2:E2. Cell F3 works fine. However, when you get to Cell F4, Excel has a choice. There are two numbers above F4 and four numbers to the left of F4. Because there are two numbers directly above, Excel tries to total those two numbers. This problem seems to happen only in the third row of the data set. After that, Excel sees that the three cells above are all summing across the rows, and AutoSum works perfectly in F5:F11.

	A	B	C	D	E	F	G
		2008	2009	2010	2011	Total	
1	Customer						
2	Functional Eggbeater Co	84093	91661	101744	113953	391451	
3	Vivid Edger Co	64853	68096	70820	71528	275297	
4	Powerful Edger Supply	61312	63151	70098	78510	=SUM(F2:F3)	
5	Trendy Notebook Corp	52486	56160	62338	63585	SUM(number1, [numbe	
6	Improved Vegetable Inc.	66694	69362	70749	73579		

Figure 10.10
Excel can choose between summing two numbers above or four numbers to the left. Excel chooses incorrectly.

Special Tricks with AutoSum

There is an amazing trick you can use with AutoSum. If you select a range of cells before clicking the AutoSum button, Excel does a much better job of predicting what to sum.

In Figure 10.10, for example, you could select F2:F10 before clicking the AutoSum button, and Excel would know to sum each row. Be careful, though, because Excel does not preview its guess before entering the formula. You should always check a formula after using AutoSum to make sure the correct range was selected.

If your selection contains a mix of blank cells and nonblank cells, Excel adds the AutoSum to only the blank cells. In Figure 10.11, for example, you select the range B2:F11 before clicking the AutoSum button.

Figure 10.11
If your selection contains a mix of blank and nonblank cells, AutoSum writes only to the blank cells.

	A	B	C	D	E	F
1	Customer	2008	2009	2010	2011	Total
2	Functional Eggbeater Co	84093	91661	101744	113953	
3	Vivid Edger Co	64853	68096	70820	71528	
4	Powerful Edger Supply	61312	63151	70098	78510	
5	Trendy Notebook Corp	52486	56160	62338	63585	
6	Improved Vegetable Inc.	66694	69362	70749	73579	
7	Tremendous Thermostat Partners	69840	77522	84499	92949	
8	Improved Vegetable Inc.	61326	62553	66306	70284	
9	Wonderful Kettle Corp	73658	77341	81208	90141	
10	Matchless Hardware Traders	72129	77178	81809	87536	
11	Total					
12						

After you click the AutoSum button, Excel correctly filled in totals for all the rows and columns, as shown in Figure 10.12.

Figure 10.12
By using AutoSum, you can add 14 SUM( ) formulas with one click.

	A	B	C	D	E	F
1	Customer	2008	2009	2010	2011	Total
2	Functional Eggbeater Co	84093	91661	101744	113953	391451
3	Vivid Edger Co	64853	68096	70820	71528	275297
4	Powerful Edger Supply	61312	63151	70098	78510	273071
5	Trendy Notebook Corp	52486	56160	62338	63585	234569
6	Improved Vegetable Inc.	66694	69362	70749	73579	280384
7	Tremendous Thermostat Partners	69840	77522	84499	92949	324810
8	Improved Vegetable Inc.	61326	62553	66306	70284	260469
9	Wonderful Kettle Corp	73658	77341	81208	90141	322348
10	Matchless Hardware Traders	72129	77178	81809	87536	318652
11	Total	606391	643024	689571	742065	2681051
12						

Using the AutoSum Drop-Down

In legacy versions of Excel, the AutoSum button was flanked by a small drop-down arrow that allowed you to use the AutoAverage, AutoMin, AutoMax, and AutoCount features. In Excel 2010, you can still click an arrow to access these features, and the drop-down arrow on the icon is more prominent than it used to be.

To see how this works, you can select a cell or range of cells. From the AutoSum drop-down, you choose another function. Excel uses the same guessing logic as with AutoSum, but it instead enters a formula for Average, Min, Max, or Count, as shown in Figure 10.13.

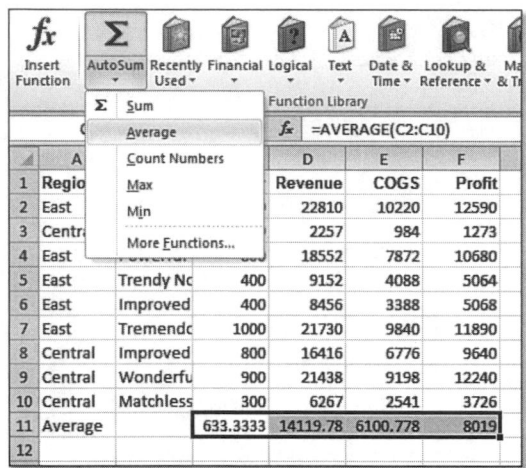

Figure 10.13
You can use the drop-down on the AutoSum icon to access the features AutoAverage, AutoMin, AutoMax, and AutoCount.

Using the New General-Purpose Functions in Excel

Excel 2010 introduces the AGGREGATE() function and includes five functions that were added in Excel 2007: IFERROR(), AVERAGEIF(), SUMIFS(), AVERAGEIFS(), and COUNTIFS(). As you will see in the following sections, these functions are a great addition to the Excel function set.

Like SUBTOTAL, but Better: AGGREGATE()

Excel 97 had introduced the SUBTOTAL function, which would look through the visible rows in a data set and do one of 11 functions. The AGGREGATE() function is similar, with two nice improvements:

- Aggregate supports 19 functions instead of 11. The first 11 functions are the same as those in the subtotal function: Average, Count, CountA, Max, Min, Product, StDev.S, StDev.P, Sum, Var.S, Var.P. The new functions are Median, Mode.Sngl, Large, Small, Percentile.Inc, Quartile.Inc, Percentile.Exc, and Quartile.Exc.

- Where the Subtotal function ignores hidden row and other subtotal functions, the options argument in aggregate allows you to ignore the following:

  - Nothing

  - Hidden rows

  - Error values

  - Both hidden rows and error values

  - Any of the above and other Subtotal and Aggregate functions

Syntax:

```
AGGREGATE(function_num, options, array, [k])
```

The addition of the new functions make the AGGREGATE function a powerful addition to the function list.

Added in Excel 2007: IFERROR()

Excel errors are not the friendliest things. No one really understands the screaming #VALUE! or #N/A! errors. With the all-capital letters and the exclamation point, they are scary looking. Furthermore, the default performance is that one single #N/A error in a column of one million good values causes the total for the column to calculate as #N/A.

For example, the VLOOKUP() function is great for converting a number to a name. Suppose that your company hires a new employee and you encounter data for the employee before anyone has updated the lookup table. This results in an #N/A! error.

> ➡ *You learn more about the* VLOOKUP() *function in Chapter 12, "Using Powerful Functions: Logical, Lookup, and Database Functions," of this book.*

You might want the table to include something friendlier than the #N/A! error. Perhaps you would like the text New Rep to appear instead of the unfriendly #N/A!. There was not an easy way to do this in legacy versions of Excel. You had to use a formula such as =IF(ISNA(VLOOKUP(A2,$AA$1:$AB$99,2,FALSE)),"New Rep", VLOOKUP(A2,$AA$1:$AB$99,2,FALSE)). This formula forces Excel to use the VLOOKUP() function once, determine if it is an #N/A error, and then calculate the VLOOKUP() function again. This is a pain for anyone using Excel. If you have to change the VLOOKUP(), you have to change it twice in the formula. Also, it takes Excel longer to calculate because it potentially has to do each good VLOOKUP() twice.

Microsoft corrected this problem in Excel 2007 by adding the IFERROR() function. With the IFERROR() function, you can use VLOOKUP() function once and then provide an alternative value or formula in case the VLOOKUP() function returns an error.

Syntax:

```
IFERROR(value,value_if_error)
```

This function returns a value you specify if a formula evaluates to an error; otherwise, it returns the result of the formula. You use the IFERROR() function to trap and handle errors in a formula.

Instead of the previous formula, you can use the following:

```
=IFERROR(VLOOKUP(A2,$AA$1:$AB$99,2,FALSE), "New Rep")
```

Using Conditional Formulas with Multiple Conditions: SUMIFS(), AVERAGEIFS(), and COUNTIFS()

When users see how easy it is to use SUMIF(), they invariably want the function to do more. One of the most frequent questions at the MrExcel message board is along the lines of, "I am using SUMIF() to get a total by region. How can I put two conditions in there to only get the total for a certain region and product?" In legacy versions of Excel, there were ways to do this, but they were difficult. You had to use either SUMPRODUCT() or an array formula. There is a lot of complexity in going from a simple SUMIF() to the complex Boolean logic required to understand SUMPRODUCT().

caution

Be careful because the syntax for SUMIFS is in a different sequence than the SUMIF function.

Thankfully, beginning with Excel 2007, Microsoft implemented versions of SUMIF(), COUNTIF(), and AVERAGEIF() that can handle not just two conditions, but unlimited conditions. Three of these newer functions add the letter S to the end of the function name, (SUMIFS(), COUNTIFS(), and AVERAGEIFS()), to signify that multiple IFs are being considered. With SUMIFS() and AVERAGEIFS(), you first specify the range to be summed or averaged. You then specify pairs of arguments. In each pair, you first specify the range to check and then the value to match in that range.

Syntax:

SUMIFS(sum_range,criteria_range1,criteria1[,criteria_range2, criteria2...])

Syntax:

COUNTIFS(criteria_range1,criteria1[,criteria_range2, criteria2...])

Syntax:

AVERAGIEIFS(average_range,criteria_range1,criteria1[,criteria_range2, criteria2...])

Functions with New Variations in Excel 2010

Several functions have new variations in Excel 2010. These are situations where Microsoft had been calculating the function in one way, whereas industry best practice had evolved to show that the function should be calculated a new way.

Calculating Multiple MODE Values

Remember back when you took a stats class? The median is the value in the center of an ordered data set. The mean is the average of the data set. The mode is the value that occurs most often in a data set.

But, what happens if two numbers are in a tie for the mode? For years, Excel returned only the first value when you used the MODE function.

The old MODE function is still in Excel with a new name of MODE.SNGL.

Excel 2010 offers a new array function called MODE.MULT. Select a vertical range of cells. Type =MODE.MULT(D1:D12). Hold down Ctrl+Shift while pressing Enter. Excel returns all of the modes in the data set, followed by #N/A values.

Calculating Workdays

Legacy versions of Excel offered NETWORKDAYS and WORKDAY functions. These functions assumed a workweek of Monday through Friday. This works fine for the United States, but other countries have workweeks that typically run on other days of the week. Excel 2010 introduces NETWORKDAYS.INTL and WORKDAY.INTL to handle other variations of 5-day or 6-day workweeks. A new weekend value is the third argument in the function; 1 represents a traditional weekend of Saturday and Sunday; 7 represents a weekend of Friday and Saturday. Double-digit values represent one-day weekends, with 1 being Sunday only through 7 being Saturday only.

Handling Ties in the RANK Function

Suppose you have 10 golfers with their scores. If you have two golfers tied for third place, the old RANK function would assign both of those golfers a rank of 3 and no golfer a rank of 4.

The RANK.EQ function is the new name for the old RANK function. It continues to calculate as before.

Excel 2010 introduces a new RANK.AVG function. In this variant, both golfers tied for third would be assigned a rank of 3.5, because this is the average of the 3 and 4 positions.

Although RANK.AVG will make statisticians and scientists happy, it will disappoint Excel gurus everywhere who need one person to be ranked 3 and another person to be ranked 4.

Calculating Percentiles and Quartiles

Statisticians disagree with Excel's method for calculating percentiles and quartiles. Excel takes the min and max value and interpolates the quartile and percentile.

The .INC version of QUARTILE, PERCENTILE, and PERCENTRANK continue to calculate using the interpolation method as in past versions of Excel. The new .EXC versions of those functions use the algorithm #6 proposed by Weibull and Gumbel in Hyndman and Fan.

Calculating CEILING and FLOOR for Negative Values

In legacy versions of Excel, =CEILING(5.1,1) would round up to 6. No one disagrees that this is the right answer. The problem is that =CEILING(-5.1,-1) would round to -6. Mathematicians argued with that answer. The ceiling function should return a value that is larger than the original value. They argued that if you move UP from -5.1, you should end up at -5.

Microsoft added =CEILING.PRECISE to always round up toward positive infinity and =FLOOR. PRECISE to always round down toward negative infinity.

Functions That Have Been Renamed

The statistical functions had been poorly named. Depending on the distribution that you are using, the naming conventions varied. For the Chi Squared distribution, the inverse function was called CHIINV. For the Binomial distribution, the inverse function was called CRITBINOM.

The existing statistical functions have been renamed. Watch for these suffixes:

- .DIST is used for the probability density function and for the left-tailed cumulative distribution function. An argument explains if the function is the PDF or the CDF.

- .INV is used for the Inverse Cumulative Distribution Function.

- .RT is used for right-tailed.

- .LT is used for left-tailed.

- .TEST is used for hypothesis testing functions.

- .P is used for functions based on a population.

- .S is used for functions based on a sample.

For the distribution function, the new names are shown in Table 10.1.

Table 10.1 New Distribution Function Names

Distribution	PDF/CDF	Right-tailed CDF	Inverse Left-Tailed CDF	Inverse Right-Tailed CDF
Beta	BETA.DIST		BETA.INV	
Binomial	BINOM.DIST		BINOM.INV	
Chi-squared	CHISQ.DIST	CHISQ.DIST.RT	CHISQ.INV	CHISQ.INV.RT
Exponential	EXPON.DIST			
F	F.DIST	F.DIST.RT	F.INV	F.INV.RT
Gamma	GAMMA.DIST		GAMMA.INV	
Hypergeometric	HYPGEOM.DIST			
Logonormal	LOGNORM.DIST		LOGNORM.INV	
Negative Binomial	NEGBINOM.DIST			
Normal	NORM.DIST		NORM.INV	
Standard Normal	NORM.S.DIST		NORM.S.INV	
Poisson	POISSON.DIST			

Distribution	PDF/CDF	Right-tailed CDF	Inverse Left-Tailed CDF	Inverse Right-Tailed CDF
Student's t	`T.DIST`	`T.DIST.RT`	`T.INV`	
Student's t (2 tailed)		`T-DIST.2T`		`T.INV.2T`
Weibull	`WEIBULL.DIST`			

For hypothesis testing, the functions are `F.TEST`, `T.TEST`, and `Z.Test`. Confidence tests are `CONFIDENCE.NORM` for the normal distribution and `CONFIDENCE.T` for the Student's t distribution.

Variance and standard deviation have always been available as functions for a sample (VAR, STDEV) and a population (VARP and STDEVP). Microsoft renamed these to be VAR.S, STDEV.S, VAR.P, STDEV.P. Microsoft also formalized the fact that the old COVAR function is based on a population by renaming it to COVARIANCE.P, and it added a sample version named COVARIANCE.S.

Using Worksheets with Legacy Function Names

With the new naming scheme, many functions are in Excel 2010 twice. The new VAR.P function will work, but Microsoft has to support the old VAR function because millions of legacy spreadsheets exist that have been using VAR.

Further, if you are creating a new workbook in Excel 2010 and that workbook will be shared with people who are using Excel 2007 or earlier, you pretty much have to keep using the old naming convention.

Still, Microsoft is hopeful that people will start using the new naming scheme. In the Statistical function drop-down, the new names appear. The old names have been moved to the Compatibility drop-down.

As you start to type a function name, the formula autocomplete always lists the new names first. The old names are listed at the end with a symbol to indicate that it is here for compatibility only (see Figure 10.14).

Figure 10.14
The old functions are listed at the end of the autocomplete list with an exclamation symbol.

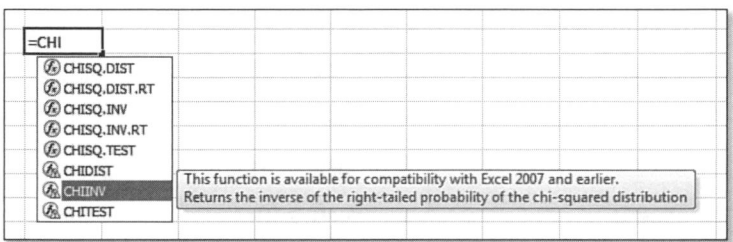

Table 10.2 compares the old and new function names.

Table 10.2 Comparison of Old and New Function Names

OLD	NEW
BETADIST	BETA.DIST
BETAINV	BETA.INV
BINOMDIST	BINOM.DIST
CHIDIST	CHISQ.DIST
CHIINV	CHISQ.INV
CHITEST	CHISQ.TEST
CONFIDENCE	CONFIDENCE.NORM
COVAR	COVARIANCE.P
CRITBINOM	BINOM.INV
EXPONDIST	EXPON.DIST
FDIST	F.DIST
FINV	F.INV
FTEST	F.TEST
GAMMADIST	GAMMA.DIST
GAMMAINV	GAMMA.INV
HYPGEOMDIST	HYPGEOM.DIST
LOGINV	LOGNORM.INV
LOGNORMDIST	LOGNORM.DIST
MODE	MODE.SNGL
NEGBINOMDIST	NEGBINOM.DIST
NORMDIST	NORM.DIST
NORMINV	NORM.INV
NORMSDIST	NORM.S.DIST
NORMSINV	NORM.S.INV
PERCENTILE	PERCENTILE.INC

OLD	NEW
PERCENTRANK	PERCENTRANK.INC
POISSON	POISSON.DIST
QUARTILE	QUARTILE.INC
RANK	RANK.EQ
STDEV	STDEV.S
STDEVP	STDEV.P
TDIST	T.DIST
TINV	T.INV
TTEST	T.TEST
VAR	VAR.S
VARP	VAR.P
WEIBULL	WEIBULL.DIST
ZTEST	Z.TEST

Cube Functions Introduced in Excel 2007

If you are creating pivot tables from OLAP data or from PowerPivot, Excel offers a Convert to Formulas command. Excel uses a series of cube functions to retrieve the data cells from the data source. The following functions were introduced in Excel 2007.

Syntax:

CUBEMEMBER(connection,member_expression[,caption])

The CUBEMEMBER() function returns a member or tuple in a cube hierarchy. You can use it to validate that the member or tuple exists in the cube.

Syntax:

CUBEMEMBERPROPERTY(connection,member_expression,property)

The CUBEMEMBERPROPERTY() function returns the value of a member property in the cube. You can use it to validate that a member name exists within the cube and to return the specified property for that member.

Syntax:

CUBERANKEDMEMBER(connection,set_expression,rank[,caption])

The CUBERANKEDMEMBER() function returns the nth, or ranked, member in a set. You can use it to return one or more elements in a set, such as the top sales performer or top 10 students.

Syntax:

CUBESET(connection,set_expression[,caption][,sort_order][,sort_by])

The CUBESET() function defines a calculated set of members or tuples by sending a set expression to the cube on the server, which creates the set. The function then returns that set to Excel. You can use CUBESET() to build dynamic reports that aggregate and filter data, by using the return value as a slicer in the CUBEVALUE() function, the CUBERANKEDMEMBER() function to choose specific members from the calculated set, and the CUBESETCOUNT() function to control the size of the set.

Syntax:

CUBESETCOUNT(set)

The CUBESETCOUNT() function returns the number of items in a set.

Syntax:

CUBEVALUE(connection,member_expression1[,member_expression2...])

The CUBEVALUE() function returns an aggregated value from a cube.

Syntax:

CUBEKPIMEMBER(connection,kpi_name,kpi_property[,caption])

The CUBEKPIMEMBER() function returns a key performance indicator (KPI) name, property, and measure, and it displays the name and property in the cell. A KPI is a quantifiable measurement, such as monthly gross profit or quarterly employee turnover, used to monitor an organization's performance.

 note

To use this function, you must have SQL Server Analysis Services 2005 or later.

Using the Former ATP Functions

In legacy versions of Excel, a variety of functions were known as the ATP functions. These functions were available only on computers that had enabled the Analysis ToolPak (ATP) add-in.

Even if you had enabled the ATP, there was a danger that you could send a workbook to a co-worker who had not enabled the ATP. If this happened, all the formulas that used any of the 89 ATP functions would change to #NAME? errors.

Although it was easy to enable the ATP in legacy versions of Excel, there was a great deal of paranoia about using these functions, sending the workbook out, and having others obtain the wrong results. For this reason, some companies instituted policies against using the ATP functions. People would write elaborate formulas to duplicate what could easily be done with the ATP.

In a smart move, Microsoft has promoted the 89 ATP functions to be part of the standard Excel package starting with Excel 2007. This means that you can safely share an Excel workbook with any other person using Excel 2007 or later, and all the functions will continue to work. However, be aware that if you are sharing a workbook with a person who is using a legacy version of Excel, the functions in the ATP may change to #NAME? errors on the other computer.

The individual functions are covered in the next five chapters of this book. However, the following alphabetical list is provided as a guide about which functions are potentially problems when sharing with people using legacy versions of Excel.

See the *"Function Reference Chapters"* section of this chapter to learn more about the functions covered in Chapters 11 to 15 of this book.

Table 10.3 lists the functions that used to be included in the ATP but are now a default part of Excel.

Table 10.3 Functions That Are Now a Default Part of Excel

ACCRINT()	ACCRINTM()	AMORDEGRC()
AMORLINC()	BESSELI()	BESSELJ()
BESSELK()	BESSELY()	BIN2DEC()
BIN2HEX()	BIN2OCT()	COMPLEX()
CONVERT()	COUPDAYBS()	COUPDAYS()
COUPDAYSNC()	COUPNCD()	COUPNUM()
COUPPCD()	CUMIPMT()	CUMPRINC()
DEC2BIN()	DEC2HEX()	DEC2OCT()
DELTA()	DISC()	DOLLARDE()
DOLLARFR()	DURATION()	EDATE()
EFFECT()	EOMONTH()	ERF()
ERFC()	ERROR.TYPE()	FACTDOUBLE()
FVSCHEDULE()	GCD()	GESTEP()
HEX2BIN()	HEX2DEC()	HEX2OCT()
IMABS()	IMAGINARY()	IMARGUMENT()
IMCONJUGATE()	IMCOS()	IMDIV()

IMEXP()	IMLN()	IMLOG10()
IMLOG2()	IMPOWER()	IMPRODUCT()
IMREAL()	IMSIN()	IMSQRT()
IMSUB()	IMSUM()	INTRATE()
ISEVEN()	ISODD()	LCM()
MDURATION()	MROUND()	MULTINOMIAL()
NETWORKDAYS()	NOMINAL()	OCT2BIN()
OCT2DEC()	ODDFPRICE()	ODDFYIELD()
ODDLPRICE()	ODDLYIELD()	PRICE()
PRICEDISC()	PRICEMAT()	QUOTIENT()
RANDBETWEEN()	RECEIVED()	SERIESSUM()
SQL.REQUEST()	SQRTPI()	TBILLEQ()
TBILLPRICE()	TBILLYIELD()	WEEKNUM()
WORKDAY()	XIRR()	XNPV()
YEARFRAC()	YIELD()	YIELDDISC()
YIELDMAT().		

Function Reference Chapters

Chapters 11 through 15 provide a fairly comprehensive reference for most of the 400 functions in Excel 2010. At the beginning of each of these chapters is an alphabetical list of the functions described, along with arguments and a short description of each function. Following the alphabetical list are examples of how to use the functions. These examples describe all the required arguments. The examples are designed to give you ideas of how to use the functions in real life.

Function coverage is broken out as follows:

- Chapter 11, "Using Everyday Functions: Math, Date and Time, and Text Functions," describes functions that many people encounter in their everyday life: some of the math functions, date functions, and text functions.

- Chapter 12, "Using Powerful Functions: Logical, Lookup, and Database Functions," describes functions that are a bit more difficult but that should be a part of your everyday arsenal. These include a series of functions for making decisions in a formula. They include the IF function and are known collectively as the *logical functions*. Chapter 12 also describes the information, lookup, and database functions.

- Chapter 13, "Using Financial Functions," describes the financial functions. The first section of the chapter includes functions that anyone can use to calculate a car loan or plan for retirement. The later sections of the chapter include functions for depreciation, business valuation, and bond investing.

- Chapter 14, "Using Statistical Functions," describes statistical functions. Many of these functions are functions that are useful everyday (for example, `AVERAGE()`, `MAX()`, `MIN()`, `RANK()`). The chapter also describes many highly specialized functions that are useful to scientists and engineers.

- Chapter 15, "Using Trig, Matrix, and Engineering Functions," describes trigonometry and engineering functions. The trigonometry functions are grouped along with the other math functions in the Math Functions icon, but they are described separately in this book because they are more specialized. The engineering functions are highly specialized.

USING EVERYDAY FUNCTIONS: MATH, DATE AND TIME, AND TEXT FUNCTIONS

Excel offers many functions for dealing with basic math, dates and times, and text. This chapter describes the functions found under the Date & Time icon and the Math & Trig icon on the Formulas tab.

A few of the new functions in Excel 2010 fall into this chapter:

- AGGREGATE—Provides a way to ignore error values, other subtotals, and/or filtered rows in 17 other functions. Whereas SUBTOTAL provided a way to ignore rows hidden in a filter for 11 functions, the AGGREGATE function adds median, mode, percentile, large, small, and quartile functions. Also, the ability to use an array gives you the possibility of extending the SUMIFS concept to min, max, median, and so on.

- CEILING.PRECISE—Corrects the way that Microsoft implemented the CEILING function for negative numbers.

- NETWORKDAYS.INTL—Extends the functionality of NETWORKDAYS to companies in which the weekend is a pair of days other than Saturday and Sunday.

- WORKDAY.INTL—Extends the functionality of WORKDAY to calendars in which the weekend is a pair of days other than Saturday and Sunday.

Table 11.1 provides an alphabetical list of all of Excel 2010's math functions. Detailed examples of these functions are provided later in this chapter.

Table 11.1 Alphabetical List of Math Functions

Function	Description
ABS(*number*)	Returns the absolute value of a number. The absolute value of a number is the number without its sign.
AGGREGATE(*function, options, array, [k]*)	Performs one of 17 functions with the ability to ignore error values, other subtotals, and/or rows hidden by a filter. New in Excel 2010.
CEILING(*number,significance*)	Returns the number rounded up, away from zero, to the nearest multiple of significance. For example, if you want to avoid using pennies in your prices and your product is priced at $4.42, you can use the formula =CEILING(4.42,0.05) to round prices up to the nearest nickel. Note that Excel calculates =CEILING(-2.1,-1) as -3, which is different than the ISO standard. See CEILING.PRECISE for an alternative.
CEILING.PRECISE(*number,significance*)	Rounds a number up to the nearest multiple of significance. New in Excel 2010 to provide compatibility with the ISO standard for computing the ceiling of a negative number.
COMBIN(*number,number_chosen*)	Returns the number of combinations for a given number of items. You use COMBIN to determine the total possible number of groups for a given number of items.
COUNTIF(*range,criteria*)	Counts the number of cells within a range that meet the given criteria.
EVEN(*number*)	Returns number rounded up to the nearest even integer. You can use this function for processing items that come in twos. For example, suppose a packing crate accepts rows of one or two items. The crate is full when the number of items, rounded up to the nearest two, matches the crate's capacity.
EXP(*number*)	Returns e raised to the power of *number*. The constant e equals 2.71828182845904, the base of the natural logarithm.
FACT(*number*)	Returns the factorial of a number. The factorial of a number is equal to $1 \times 2 \times 3 \times \ldots \times number$.
FACTDOUBLE(*number*)	Returns the double factorial of a number.
FLOOR(*number,significance*)	Rounds the number down, toward zero, to the nearest multiple of significance.

Function	Description
GCD(*number1,number2,...*)	Returns the greatest common divisor of two or more integers. The greatest common divisor is the largest integer that divides both *number1* and *number2* without a remainder.
INT(*number*)	Rounds a number down to the nearest integer.
INT(*number*)	Rounds a number down to the nearest integer.
LCM(*number1,number2,...*)	Returns the least common multiple of integers. The least common multiple is the smallest positive integer that is a multiple of all integer arguments *number1*, *number2*, and so on. You use LCM to add fractions that have different denominators.
MOD(*number,divisor*)	Returns the remainder after number is divided by divisor. The result has the same sign as divisor.
MROUND(*number,multiple*)	Returns a number rounded to the desired multiple.
MULTINOMIAL(*number1,number2,...*)	Returns the ratio of the factorial of a sum of values to the product of factorials.
ODD(*number*)	Returns number rounded up to the nearest odd integer.
PI()	Returns the number 3.14159265358979, the mathematical constant pi, accurate to 15 digits.
POWER(*number,power*)	Returns the result of a number raised to a power.
PRODUCT(*number1,number2,...*)	Multiplies all the numbers given as arguments and returns the product.
QUOTIENT(*numerator,denominator*)	Returns the integer portion of a division operation. You use this function when you want to discard the remainder of a division.
RAND()	Returns an evenly distributed random number greater than or equal to 0 and less than 1. A new random number is returned every time the worksheet is calculated.
RANDBETWEEN(*bottom,top*)	Returns a random number between the numbers specified. A new random number is returned every time the worksheet is calculated.
ROMAN(*number,form*)	Converts an Arabic numeral to Roman, as text.
ROUND(*number,num_digits*)	Rounds a number to a specified number of digits.
ROUNDDOWN(*number,num_digits*)	Rounds a number down, toward zero.

Function	Description
ROUNDUP(*number*,*num_digits*)	Rounds a number up, away from zero.
SIGN(*number*)	Determines the sign of a number. Returns 1 if the number is positive, 0 if the number is 0, and -1 if the number is negative.
SQRT(*number*)	Returns a positive square root.
SQRTPI(*number*)	Returns the square root of (*number* × pi).
SUBTOTAL(*function_num*, *ref1*,*ref2*,...)	Returns a subtotal in a list or database. It is generally easier to create a list with subtotals by using the Subtotals command (from the Data menu). After the subtotal list is created, you can modify it by editing the SUBTOTAL function.
SUM(*number1*,*number2*,...)	Adds all the numbers in a range of cells.
SUMIF(*range*,*criteria*,*sum_range*)	Adds the cells specified by the given criteria.
SUMPRODUCT(*array1*,*array2*, *array3*,...)	Multiplies corresponding components in the given arrays and returns the sum of those products.
TRUNC(*number*,*num_digits*)	Truncates a number to an integer by removing the fractional part of the number.

Table 11.2 provides an alphabetical list of all of Excel 2010's date and time functions. Detailed examples of these functions are provided later in this chapter.

Table 11.2 Alphabetical List of Date and Time Functions

Function	Description
DATE (*year*,*month*,*day*)	Returns the serial number that represents a particular date.
DATEDIF (*start_date*,*end_date*,*unit*)	Calculates the number of days, months, or years between two dates. This function is provided for compatibility with Lotus 1-2-3.
DATEVALUE (*date_text*)	Returns the serial number of the date represented by *date_text*. You use DATEVALUE to convert a date represented by text to a serial number.
DAY (*serial_number*)	Returns the day of a date, represented by a serial number. The day is given as an integer ranging from 1 to 31.

Function	Description
DAYS360 (*start_date,end_date,method*)	Returns the number of days between two dates, based on a 360-day year (that is, 12 30-day months), which is used in some accounting calculations. You use this function to help compute payments if your accounting system is based on 12 30-day months.
EDATE (*start_date,months*)	Returns the serial number that represents the date that is the indicated number of months before or after a specified date (that is, the start_date). You use EDATE to calculate maturity dates or due dates that fall on the same day of the month as the date of issue.
EOMONTH (*start_date,months*)	Returns the serial number for the last day of the month that is the indicated number of months before or after *start_date*. You use EOMONTH to calculate maturity dates or due dates that fall on the last day of the month.
HOUR (*serial_number*)	Returns the hour of a time value. The hour is given as an integer, ranging from 0 (12:00 a.m.) to 23 (11:00 p.m.).
MINUTE (*serial_number*)	Returns the minutes of a time value. The minutes are given as an integer, ranging from 0 to 59.
MONTH (*serial_number*)	Returns the month of a date represented by a serial number. The month is given as an integer, ranging from 1 (for January) to 12 (for December).
NETWORKDAYS (*start_date,end_date, holidays*)	Returns the number of whole working days between *start_date* and *end_date*. Working days exclude weekends and any dates identified in holidays. You use NETWORKDAYS to calculate employee benefits that accrue based on the number of days worked during a specific term. Weekdays are defined as Saturday and Sunday. To handle other calendars, see NETWORKDAYS.INTL.
NETWORKDAYS.INTL (*start_date,end_date, weekend, holidays*)	Returns the number of whole working days between start date and end date. Added in Excel 2010 to support calendars in which the weekend is a pair of days other than Saturday and Sunday.
NOW ()	Returns the serial number of the current date and time.
SECOND (*serial_number*)	Returns the seconds of a time value. The seconds are given as an integer in the range 0 to 59.

Function	Description
TIME (*hour,minute,second*)	Returns the decimal number for a particular time. The decimal number returned by TIME is a value ranging from 0 to 0.99999999, representing the times from 0:00:00 (12:00:00 a.m.) to 23:59:59 (11:59:59 p.m.).
TIMEVALUE (*time_text*)	Returns the decimal number of the time represented by a text string. The decimal number is a value ranging from 0 to 0.99999999, representing the times from 0:00:00 (12:00:00 a.m.) to 23:59:59 (11:59:59 p.m.).
TODAY ()	Returns the serial number of the current date. The serial number is the date/time code that Microsoft Excel uses for date and time calculations.
WEEKDAY (*serial_number,return_type*)	Returns the day of the week corresponding to a date. The day is given as an integer, ranging from 1 (for Sunday) to 7 (for Saturday), by default.
WEEKNUM (serial_num,return_type)	Returns a number that indicates where the week falls numerically within a year.
WORKDAY (*start_date,days,holidays*)	Returns a number that represents a date that is the indicated number of working days before or after a date (the starting date). Working days exclude weekends and any dates identified as holidays. You use WORKDAY to exclude weekends or holidays when you calculate invoice due dates, expected delivery times, or the number of days of work performed. To view the number as a date, format the cell as a date. Weekends are defined as Saturday and Sunday. For alternative calendars, see WORKDAY.INTL.
WORKDAY.INTL (*start_date,days, weekend,holidays*)	Returns a number that represents a date that is the indicated number of working days before or after a starting date. Added to Excel 2010 to accommodate calendar systems where the weekend is a pair of days other than Saturday and Sunday.
YEAR (*serial_number*)	Returns the year corresponding to a date. The year is returned as an integer in the range 1900 through 9999.
YEARFRAC (*start_date,end_date,basis*)	Calculates the fraction of the year represented by the number of whole days between two dates (*start_date* and *end_date*). You use the YEARFRAC worksheet function to identify the proportion of a whole year's benefits or obligations to assign to a specific term.

Table 11.3 provides an alphabetical list of all of Excel 2010's text functions. Detailed examples of these functions are provided later in this chapter.

Table 11.3   Alphabetical List of Text Functions

Function	Description
ASC (*text*)	Changes full-width (double-byte) English letters or katakana within a character string to half-width (single-byte) characters.
BAHTTEXT (*number*)	Converts a number to Thai text and adds the suffix Baht. This function was new in Excel XP.
CHAR (*number*)	Returns the character specified by *number*. You use CHAR to translate code page numbers you might get from files on other types of computers into characters.
CLEAN (*text*)	Removes all nonprintable characters from text. You use CLEAN on text imported from other applications that contains characters that may not print with your operating system. For example, you can use CLEAN to remove some low-level computer code that is frequently at the beginning and end of data files and cannot be printed.
CODE (*text*)	Returns a numeric code for the first character in a text string. The returned code corresponds to the character set used by your computer.
CONCATENATE (*text1,text2,...*)	Joins several text strings into one text string.
DOLLAR (*number,decimals*)	Converts a number to text using currency format, with the decimals rounded to the specified place. The format used is $#,##0.00_);($#,##0.00).
EXACT (*text1,text2*)	Compares two text strings and returns TRUE if they are the same, and FALSE otherwise. EXACT is case-sensitive but ignores formatting differences. You use EXACT to test text being entered into a document.
FIND (*find_text,within_text, start_num*)	Finds one text string (*find_text*) within another text string (*within_text*) and returns the number of the starting position of *find_text*, from the first character of *within_text*. You can also use SEARCH to find one text string within another, but unlike SEARCH, FIND is case-sensitive and doesn't allow wildcard characters.
FINDB (*find_text,within_ text,start_num*)	Finds one text string (*find_text*) within another text string (*within_text*) and returns the number of the starting position of find_text, based on the number of bytes each character uses, from the first character of *within_text*. You use FINDB with double-byte characters. You can also use SEARCHB to find one text string within another.
FIXED (*number,decimals,no_commas*)	Rounds a number to the specified number of decimals, formats the number in decimal format using a period and commas, and returns the result as text.

Function	Description
JIS (*text*)	Changes half-width (single-byte) English letters or katakana within a character string to full-width (double-byte) characters.
LEFT (*text,num_chars*)	Returns the first character or characters in a text string, based on the number of characters specified.
LEFTB (*text,num_bytes*)	Returns the first character or characters in a text string, based on the number of bytes specified. You use LEFTB with double-byte characters.
LEN (*text*)	Returns the number of characters in a text string.
LENB (*text*)	Returns the number of bytes used to represent the characters in a text string. You use LENB with double-byte characters.
LOWER (*text*)	Converts all uppercase letters in a text string to lowercase.
MID (*text,start_num,num_chars*)	Returns a specific number of characters from a text string, starting at the position specified, based on the number of characters specified.
MIDB (*text,start_num,num_bytes*)	Returns a specific number of characters from a text string, starting at the position specified, based on the number of bytes specified. You use MIDB with double-byte characters.
PHONETIC (*reference*)	Extracts the phonetic (furigana) characters from a text string. Furigana are a Japanese reading aid. They consist of smaller kana printed next to a kanji to indicate its pronunciation.
PROPER (*text*)	Capitalizes the first letter in a text string and any other letters in text that follow any character other than a letter. Converts all other letters to lowercase.
REPLACE (*old_text,start_num, num_chars,new_text*)	Replaces part of a text string, based on the number of characters specified, with a different text string.
REPLACEB (*old_text,start_num,num_bytes,new_text*)	Replaces part of a text string, based on the number of bytes specified, with a different text string. You use REPLACEB with double-byte characters.
REPT (*text,number_times*)	Repeats text a given number of times. You use REPT to fill a cell with a number of instances of a text string.
RIGHT (*text,num_chars*)	Returns the last character or characters in a text string, based on the number of characters specified.

Function	Description
RIGHTB (*text,num_bytes*)	Returns the last character or characters in a text string, based on the number of bytes specified. You use RIGHTB with double-byte characters.
SEARCH (*find_text,within_text, start_num*)	Returns the number of the character at which a specific character or text string is first found, beginning with *start_num*. You use SEARCH to determine the location of a character or text string within another text string so that you can use the MID or REPLACE functions to change the text.
SEARCHB (*find_text,within_text, start_num*)	Finds one text string (*find_text*) within another text string (*within_text*) and returns the number of the starting position of *find_text*. The result is based on the number of bytes each character uses, beginning with *start_num*. You use SEARCHB with double-byte characters You can also use FINDB to find one text string within another.
SUBSTITUTE (*text,old_text,new_ text,instance_num*)	Substitutes *new_text* for *old_text* in a text string. You use SUBSTITUTE when you want to replace specific text in a text string; you use REPLACE when you want to replace any text that occurs in a specific location in a text string.
T (*value*)	Returns the text referred to by *value*.
TEXT (*value,format_text*)	Converts a value to text in a specific number format.
TRIM (*text*)	Removes all spaces from text except for single spaces between words. You use TRIM on text that you have received from another application that may have irregular spacing.
UPPER (*text*)	Converts text to uppercase.
VALUE (*text*)	Converts a text string that represents a number to a number.
YEN (*number,decimals*)	Converts a number to text, using the Japanese yen currency format, with the number rounded to a specified place.

Examples of Math Functions

The most common formula in Excel is a formula to add a column of numbers. In addition to SUM, Excel offers a variety of mathematical functions.

Using SUM to Add Numbers

The SUM function is by far the most commonly used function in Excel. This function can add numbers from one or more ranges of data.

Syntax:

=SUM(*number1,number2,...*)

The SUM function adds all the numbers in a range of cells. The arguments *number1, number2,...* are 1 to 255 arguments for which you want the total value or sum.

A typical use of this function is =SUM(B4:B12). It is also possible to use =SUM(1,2,3). In the latter example, you cannot specify more than 255 individual values. In the former example, you can specify up to 255 ranges, each of which can include thousands of cells.

In Figure 11.1, cell B25 contains a formula to sum three individual cells: =SUM(B17,B19,B23).

15	Product A - East Region	10	
16	Product A - West Region	20	
17	Product A Total	**30**	
18			
19	Product B - Government Sales	15	
20			
21	Product C - East Region	10	
22	Product C - West Region	20	
23	Product C Total	**30**	
24			
25	Total	**75**	=SUM(B17,B19,B23)

Figure 11.1
A variety of SUM formulas.

It is unlikely that you will need more than 255 arguments in this function, but if you do, you can group arguments in parentheses. For example, =SUM((A10,A12),(A14,16)) would count as only 2 of the 255 allowed arguments.

If a text value that looks like a number is included in a range, the text value is not included in the result of the sum. Strangely enough, if you specify the text value directly as an argument in the function, Excel does add it to the result. For example, =SUM(1,2,"3") will be 6, yet =SUM(D4:D6) in Figure 11.1 will result in 3.

The comma is treated as a union operator. If you replace the comma with a space, Excel will find the cells that fall in the intersection of the selected ranges. In cell D17, the formula of =SUM(F13:H14 G12:G15) adds up the two cells that are in common between the two ranges.

If one cell in a referenced range contains an error, the result of the SUM function is an error. To add numbers while ignoring error cells, use the new AGGREGATE function.

It is valid to create a spearing formula. This type of formula adds the identical cell from many worksheets. For example, =SUM(Jan:Dec!B20) would add Cell B20 on all 12 sheets between January and December. If the sheet names contain spaces or other nonalphabetic characters, surround the sheet names with apostrophes: =SUM('Jan 2011:Dec 2011'!B20).

To quickly enter a SUM formula, you can press Alt+= or click the AutoSum icon on the Formulas tab. In Figure 11.2, pressing the AutoSum icon will add totals to the 13 selected blank cells all at once (see Figure 11.3).

Figure 11.2
The AutoSum icon (the Greek letter sigma) adds sum formulas to all the selected cells at once.

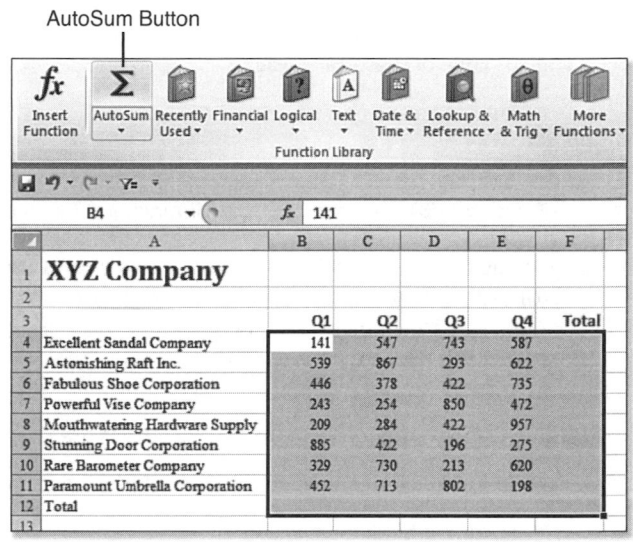

AutoSum Button

Figure 11.3
After clicking AutoSum, the total formulas are automatically entered.

A	B	C	D	E	F
XYZ Company					
	Q1	Q2	Q3	Q4	Total
Excellent Sandal Company	141	547	743	587	2018
Astonishing Raft Inc.	539	867	293	622	2321
Fabulous Shoe Corporation	446	378	422	735	1981
Powerful Vise Company	243	254	850	472	1819
Mouthwatering Hardware Supply	209	284	422	957	1872
Stunning Door Corporation	885	422	196	275	1778
Rare Barometer Company	329	730	213	620	1892
Paramount Umbrella Corporation	452	713	802	198	2165
Total	3244	4195	3941	4466	15846

Using AGGREGATE to Ignore Error Cells or Filtered Rows

One of the best new functions in Excel 2010 is the AGGREGATE function. This one function lets you perform 17 functions on a range of data while selectively ignoring error cells and/or rows hidden by a filter.

Syntax:

```
=AGGREGATE(function_num, options, array, [k])
```

Syntax:

```
=AGGREGATE(function_num, options, ref1, ref2, ...)
```

The Options argument is the interesting feature of the new function. You can choose to ignore any, all, or none of these categories:

- Error values

- Hidden rows

- Other SUBTOTAL and AGGREGATE functions

On one hand, the capability to ignore filtered rows and other AGGREGATE functions is similar to the SUBTOTAL function. The capability of AGGREGATE to ignore error values as well solves a common problem in the SUM, COUNT, and other functions. Usually, a single #N/A error cell in a range will cause most functions to return an #N/A error. The options in AGGREGATE allow you to ignore any error cells in the range.

The Options argument controls which values are ignored. This is a simple binary system, as follows:

- To ignore other subtotals, add zero. To include subtotals, add 4.

- To ignore hidden rows, add 1.

- To ignore error values, add 2.

- Thus, to ignore other subtotals, hidden rows, and error values, you would specify 3 (0+1+2) as the Option argument.

- To ignore error values but include other SUBTOTAL values, you would specify 5 (1+4) as the argument.

This calculation works out as shown in Table 11.4.

Table 11.4   Arguments for AGGREGATE Function

0	Ignore other subtotals
1	Ignore hidden rows & subtotals
2	Ignore error cells & subtotals
3	Ignore all three
4	Ignore nothing
5	Ignore hidden rows

0	Ignore other subtotals
6	Ignore error cells
7	Ignore hidden rows & error cells

In Figure 11.4, the #N/A error in cell F13 causes the SUM function in F18 to also return an #N/A. If you use a 2, 3, 5, or 7 as the second argument of AGGREGATE, you can easily sum all the other numbers as in cell F1. You can also use other function numbers to calculate MIN, MAX, COUNT, MEDIAN, MODE, PERCENTILE, and QUARTILE values.

 To see a demo of using AGGREGATE, search for "Excel In Depth 11" at YouTube.

Figure 11.4
Using a 2 or 3 as the Options argument for AGGREGATE will allow the function to ignore error cells in a range.

	B20	▾	*fx*	=AGGREGATE(14,2,(D9:D16)/((B9:B16="East")*(C9:C16="R1")),2)					
⊿	A	B	C	D	E	F	G	H	I	J
1	SUM Ignoring Errors:			255000		4530	=AGGREGATE(9,2,F9:F16)			
2	MIN Ignoring Errors:			1000		10	=AGGREGATE(5,2,F9:F16)			
3	3rd Smallest Ignoring Errors:			4000		80	=AGGREGATE(15,3,F9:F16,3)			
4	Value at 30th Percentile.exc:			4400		72	=AGGREGATE(16,3,F9:F16,0.3)			
5	Value at 30th Percentile.inc:			3400		56	=AGGREGATE(18,3,F9:F16,0.3)			
6	Value at 3rd Quartile:			40000		880	=AGGREGATE(17,3,F9:F16,3)			
7										
8	Customer	Region	Rep	Sales	Rate	Bonus				
9	Astonishing Raft Inc.	West	R3	16000	3%	480				
10	Excellent Sandal Company	East	R1	1000	1%	10				
11	Fabulous Shoe Corporation	East	R2	2000	2%	40				
12	Mouthwatering Hardware Supply	West	R4	64000	4%	2560				
13	Paramount Umbrella Corporation	West	R5	128000	#N/A	#N/A				
14	Powerful Vise Company	West	R4	32000	4%	1280				
15	Rare Barometer Company	East	R1	8000	1%	80				
16	Stunning Door Corporation	East	R2	4000	2%	80				
17										
18	SUM			255000		#N/A	=SUM(F9:F17)			
19										
20	2nd largest East R1 sale:	1000	=AGGREGATE(14,2,(D9:D16)/((B9:B16="East")*(C9:C16="R1")),2)							
21										

The function can also be used to ignore cells hidden by a Filter. Whereas the old SUBTOTAL function would allow you to do this for eleven calculation functions, the AGGREGATE function adds eight new functions to the list.

Table 11.5 shows the 19 functions available in the AGGREGATE function. This list mirrors the 11 functions available in SUBTOTAL (arranged alphabetically to match those in the SUBTOTAL function) and then eight new functions arranged in order of popularity.

Table 11.5 Functions Available in AGGREGATE

Fx #	Function
1	AVERAGE
2	COUNT
3	COUNTA
4	MAX
5	MIN
6	PRODUCT
7	STDDEV.S
8	STDDEV.P
9	SUM
10	VAR.S
11	VAR.P
12	MEDIAN
13	MODE.SNGL
14	LARGE
15	SMALL
16	PERCENTILE.INC
17	QUARTILE.INC
18	PERCENTILE.EXC
19	QUARTILE.EXC

The last six functions in this list require you to specify a value for "k" as the fourth argument. LARGE and SMALL will typically return the kth largest or smallest value from a list. Use the fourth argument in AGGREGATE to specify the value for k.

In cell F3 of Figure 11.4, the final argument of 3 specifies that you want the third smallest number in the array. For LARGE, SMALL, and QUARTILE, you should specify an integer for k. For PERCENTILE, specify a decimal between 0 and 1.

When you are trying to return results from the visible rows of a filtered data set, you can use either SUBTOTAL or AGGREGATE. In Figure 11.5, the SUM function in D1 returns the sum of the visible and hidden rows. The SUBTOTAL function in D2 returns the sum of the visible rows, the same as the AGGREGATE function in D3. The advantage of AGGREGATE is that it can return MEDIAN, LARGE, SMALL, PERCENTILE, and QUARTILE on the visible rows as well.

Figure 11.5
AGGREGATE will perform calculations on the visible items of a filtered data set.

	A	B	C	D	E	F	G
	D3	▼		f_x	=AGGREGATE(9,1,D8:D15)		
1	Total Using SUM			255000	=SUM(D8:D15)		
2	Total Using SUBTOTAL			15000	=SUBTOTAL(9,D$8:D$15)		
3	Total Using AGGREGATE			15000	=AGGREGATE(9,1,D8:D15)		
4	Median Using MEDIAN			12000	=MEDIAN(D8:D15)		
5	Median using AGGREGATE			3000	=AGGREGATE(12,1,D8:D15)		
6							
7	Customer	Regio ▼	R ▼	Sal ▼			
9	Excellent Sandal Company	East	R1	1000			
10	Fabulous Shoe Corporation	East	R2	2000			
14	Rare Barometer Company	East	R1	8000			
15	Stunning Door Corporation	East	R2	4000			

 tip

Simulating LARGEIFS, PERCENTILEIFS, QUARTILEIFS

The function arguments of 13 through 19 allow the array to be calculated on-the-fly. The formula in B20 of Figure 11.4 is a wild, over-the-top formula that seems like it would have come from the *Excel Gurus Gone Wild* book that I compiled in 2008.

The goal is to find records that match multiple criteria and then to apply the LARGE function to those matching records. The array argument starts out with the sales amounts in D9:D16. But then the sales amounts are divided by a Boolean expression.

(B9:B16="East") checks to see if the record is in the East region. (C9:C16) checks to see if the rep is R1. When you multiply these two conditions together, you will get an array of 1s and 0s. The 1 indicates both conditions are TRUE. In the figure, the result would be {0;1;0;0;0;0;1;0}.

When the formula evaluates the sales amounts divided by the array of 1s and 0s, you either end up with the sales amount or a division by zero error. In the figure, the result of 16000 divided by 0 is #DIV/0!. The result of 1000 divided by 1 is 1000, and so on. The array contains mostly #DIV/0! errors and a few actual numbers. Because the AGGREGATE function has an option to ignore error values, the result is that the function simulates doing LARGE with multiple conditions.

Using COUNT or COUNTA to Count Numbers or Nonblank Cells

A number of functions process nonblank cells. =COUNT counts all the numeric or date cells in a range. =COUNTA counts all the nonblank cells in a range.

Syntax:

=COUNT(*value1,value2,...*)

The COUNT function counts the number of cells that contain numbers and also numbers within the list of arguments. You use COUNT to get the number of numeric entries in a range or array.

 caution

COUNT and COUNTA are found in the Statistical drop-down under the More Functions icon of the Formulas tab.

The arguments value1, value2,... are 1 to 255 arguments that can contain or refer to a variety of types of data, but only numbers are counted.

Note that whereas a single error cell in a range causes the SUM function to return an error, the same condition is ignored in the COUNT function.

=COUNT(1,2,"3") results in the text entry being counted. If you refer to a range that contains text that looks like a number, the text is not included in the count.

Syntax:

=COUNTA(*value1,value2,...*)

COUNTA counts the number of cells that are not empty and the values within the list of arguments. You use COUNTA to count the number of cells that contain data in a range or an array.

The arguments *value1, value2,...* are 1 to 255 arguments representing the values you want to count. In this case, a value is any type of information, including empty text ("") but not including empty cells. If an argument is an array or a reference, empty cells within the array or reference are ignored. If you do not need to count logical values, text, or error values, you should use the COUNT function.

Note that error cells are included in the results from COUNTA.

Choosing Between COUNT and COUNTA

The key to choosing between COUNT and COUNTA is to analyze the data that you want to count. In Figure 11.6, someone has used the letter X in Column B to indicate that training has been started. In this case, you would use COUNTA to get an accurate count. Column C contains dates (which are treated as numeric). In Column C, either COUNT or COUNTA returns the correct result. Column D has a mix of text and numeric entries. If you want to

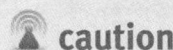

caution

Using more than 30 arguments in COUNT or COUNTA causes backward compatibility problems with legacy versions of Excel.

count how many people took the test, use COUNTA. If you want to count how many people received a numeric score, use COUNT.

Using ROUND, ROUNDDOWN, ROUNDUP, INT, TRUNC, FLOOR, FLOOR.PRECISE, CEILING, CEILING.PRECISE, EVEN, ODD, or MROUND to Remove Decimals or Round Numbers

A variety of functions—including ROUND, ROUNDDOWN, ROUNDUP, INT, TRUNC, FLOOR, FLOOR. PRECISE, CEILING, CEILING.PRECISE, EVEN, ODD, and MROUND—can be used to round a result or to remove decimals from a result.

Syntax:

=TRUNC(*number*), =INT(*number*), =EVEN(*number*), and =ODD(*number*)

Figure 11.6
Whether you use COUNT or COUNTA depends on whether your data is numeric. COUNT counts only dates and numeric entries. COUNTA counts anything that is nonblank.

	A	B	C	D
	D18		fx =COUNTA(D2:D15)	
1	NAME	Training Started	Training Completed	Test Score
2	TERRY LEBLANC			
3	LUIS CHRISTENSEN	X	3/1/2011	97
4	JENNIFER GALLOWAY	X		
5	ROSEMARY ATKINS	X	3/15/2007	85
6	GLORIA DUNLAP	X		
7	PATSY WARD			
8	CLAIRE RUSH	X	3/7/2011	Incomplete
9	MARIE HOFFMAN	X		
10	JEANNE CLEMONS			
11	MARJORIE LOPEZ	X	3/5/2011	92
12	JACOB INGRAM	X		
13	EDWARD HOOD			
14	MARTIN HAYES	X	3/9/2011	45
15	CHARLENE BURKE	X		
16				
17	COUNT:	0	5	4
18	COUNTA:	10	5	5

The TRUNC, INT, EVEN, and ODD functions always change a number to an integer. The syntax in each case is similar: The function accepts a single number or a single cell containing a number.

To remove the decimals from a result, use the =TRUNC function. This truncates a number to the integer portion of the number. For example, =TRUNC(1.9) is 1, and =TRUNC(-1.9) is –1.

To remove the decimals from a result and always round down to the next lowest integer, use =INT. For positive numbers, TRUNC and INT return identical values. A subtle difference exists between TRUNC and INT. When you have a negative number, INT rounds away from zero to produce the next lowest integer. Thus, =INT(-1.1) is –2.

EVEN rounds a number away from zero to the next even integer. For example, =EVEN(3) is 4, and =EVEN(-3) is –4. If the number is already an even integer, no adjustment is made; for example, =EVEN(6) is 6. This function is ideal for ordering products packed two to a case.

ODD rounds a number away from zero to the next odd integer. For example, =ODD(1.1) is 3, and =ODD(-3.1) is –5. If the number is already an odd integer, no adjustment is made.

Figure 11.7 compares the results of TRUNC, INT, EVEN, and ODD.

B2		▼	f_x	=INT(A2)
A	B	C	D	E
1		INT	TRUNC	EVEN	ODD

	A	B (INT)	C (TRUNC)	D (EVEN)	E (ODD)
2	2.5	2	2	4	3
3	2	2	2	2	3
4	1.5	1	1	2	3
5	1	1	1	2	1
6	0.5	0	0	2	1
7	0	0	0	0	1
8	-0.5	-1	0	-2	-1
9	-1	-1	-1	-2	-1
10	-1.5	-2	-1	-2	-3
11	-2	-2	-2	-2	-3
12	-2.5	-3	-2	-4	-3

Figure 11.7
TRUNC and INT are nearly identical, except when the numbers become negative.

Syntax:

=ROUND(*number,num_digits*), ROUNDUP(*number,num_digits*), and ROUNDDOWN (number,num_digits)

Three more functions—ROUND, ROUNDUP, and ROUNDDOWN—round a number to a specified number of decimal places. They all take the following arguments:

- *number*—This is the number you want to round.

- *num_digits*—This specifies the number of digits to which you want to round number.

With ROUND, if the number of digits is zero, the number is rounded to the nearest integer, following these rules:

- Values up to 0.49 are rounded toward zero. For example, ROUND(1.49999,0) results in 1, and ROUND(-1.49999,0) results in –1.

- Values of 0.5 and above are rounded away from zero. For example, ROUND(1.5,0) results in 2, and ROUND(-1.5,0) results in –2.

If the num_digits is positive, the number is rounded to have the specified number of decimal places. If the number of digits is negative, the number is rounded to the left of the decimal point. For example, ROUND(117,-1) is rounded to the nearest 10, or a value of 120.

To override the rounding rules, you can use ROUNDDOWN or ROUNDUP:

- The ROUNDDOWN function always rounds toward zero. For example, =ROUNDDOWN(1.999,0) rounds to 1, and =ROUNDDOWN(-19.999,0) rounds to –19. You might use this function when judging a contest in which if the entrant does not completely finish a task, he or she does not get credit for the unfinished portion of the task.

 note

Using a negative number for the number of digits provides an interesting result. If you need to round a number to the nearest thousand, you can indicate that it should be rounded to -3 decimal places. For example, ROUND(1,234,567,-3) would be 1,235,000.

- The result of the ROUNDUP function always rounds away from zero. For example, =ROUNDUP(1.01,0) rounds up to 2, and =ROUNDUP(-1.01,0) rounds to –2. You might use this function when calculating prices because if the customer uses any fractional portion of a product, he or she is charged for the complete product.

Figure 11.8 compares ROUND, ROUNDUP, and ROUNDDOWN.

Figure 11.8
These three functions always round to a power of 10.

	A	B	C	D	E
	Number	# Digits	Round	Round Up	Round Down
1	Number	# Digits	Round	Round Up	Round Down
2	314159.265359	5	314159.265360	314159.265360	314159.265350
3	314159.265359	4	314159.265400	314159.265400	314159.265300
4	314159.265359	3	314159.265	314159.266	314159.265
5	314159.265359	2	314159.27	314159.27	314159.26
6	314159.265359	1	314159.3	314159.3	314159.2
7	314159.265359	0	314159	314160	314159
8	314159.265359	-1	314160	314160	314150
9	314159.265359	-2	314200	314200	314100
10	314159.265359	-3	314000	315000	314000
11	314159.265359	-4	310000	320000	310000
12	314159.265359	-5	300000	400000	300000
13	1.500000	0	2	2	1
14	-1.500000	0	-2	-2	-1
15	1.490000	0	1	2	1
16	-1.490000	0	-1	-2	-1

Cell C2 = =ROUND(A2,B2)

Syntax:

=MROUND(*number,multiple*), =CEILING(*number,significance*), CEILING.PRECISE(*number,[significance]*), =FLOOR(*number,significance*), and =FLOOR.PRECISE(*number,[significance]*)

 caution

If you remember how they taught you to round in school, you know the rule that numbers ending in 0.5 should always round up. The Excel developers must have sat through the same curriculum as you and I did, because they implemented rounding in this manner.

However, if you have a large amount of data points that end in 0.5, you will introduce a fair amount of error in the data by using the method that we learned in school. In Figure 11.9, a million data points end with a single decimal place. Comparing the total of the points and the total of the ROUND of the data points shows a delta of 9 hundredths of a percent. In this example, the rounded values total to $52,077 more than the original values.

A set of rules known as Bankers Rounding or ASTM E29 rounding prescribes that values ending in 0.5 should always be rounded to the nearest even integer. Thus, 1.5 would round up to 2 and 2.5 would round down to 2. Column D of Figure 11.9 contrasts the Bankers Rounding method with the regular rounding method. This formula produces a result that is 91 times more accurate for this data set. The rounded values in column D are within 9.9 ten-thousandths of a percent for a total error of only $572 over the million rows of data.

=IF(MOD(B6,1)=0.5,MROUND(B6,2),ROUND(B6,0))

	A	B	C	D
1	Total	57,639,716.2	57,691,794.0	57,639,144.0
2	Difference		52,077.8	-572.2
3	Diff %		0.09035%	-0.00099%
4				
5		Random	ROUND	Round to Even
6		40.2	40	40
7		40.6	41	41
8		45.5	46	46
9		89.5	90	90
1048572		48.8	49	49
1048573		46.1	46	46
1048574				

Figure 11.9
ROUND will skew your data.

The last five functions in this group—MROUND, CEILING, CEILING.PRECISE, FLOOR, and FLOOR.PRECISE—round a number to a certain multiple. They require you to enter the number and the multiple to which to round. They all take the following arguments:

- *number*—This is the number you want to round.

- *multiple or significance*—This is the nearest multiple that you want to round toward. Note that if number is negative, *multiple* or *significance* must also be negative.

Suppose that you handle pricing for a line of products. Your general rule is to mark up the product cost, which results in a series of strange prices, such as $185.9375, as shown in Figure 11.10. To round each price to the nearest increment of $5, you would use =MROUND(C2,5). You could also use MROUND to round to the nearest quarter: =MROUND(C2,0.25).

The multiple argument in MROUND is allowed to be negative.

=MROUND(C2,5)

	A	B	C	D
	SKU	COST	LIST	PRICE
1	SKU	COST	LIST	PRICE
2	D194	87.81	185.9375	185
3	A274	14.94	34.125	35
4	B274	21.31	47.39583	45
5	A164	12.75	29.5625	30
6	F229	86.55	183.3125	185
7	A150	24.14	53.29167	55
8	A153	68.54	145.7917	145
9	D298	77.5	164.4583	165
10	F294	60.15	128.3125	130

Figure 11.10
MROUND rounds a price to a certain multiple. Here, Column D is the calculated prices rounded to the nearest $5.

In other situations, you may want to round a number up to a certain multiple. Figure 11.11 shows a requisition list. Column A shows the quantity needed, and Column B shows the item. The purchasing agent discovered a vendor who offers a significant discount, but only if you buy in complete case quantities. Column C shows the size of the case for each product. To calculate the total number to order, you need to round a number in Column A up to the nearest multiple of the case size found in Column C. You use =CEILING(A4,C4) to achieve this effect.

Figure 11.11
CEILING rounds a number up to the next multiple.

	A	B	C	D
	=CEILING(A4,C4)			
1	Orders for full cases receive a 25% discount			
2				
3	Quantity Needed	Product	Case Pack	Optimal Order
4	121	A108	8	128
5	110	A116	16	112
6	108	B108	8	112
7	172	C108	8	176
8	176	D108	8	176
9	12	E124	24	24
10	123	Z206	6	126
11	167	J312	12	168
12	30	D412	12	36

CEILING rounds away from zero. If you use =CEILING(-9,-6), the function rounds -9 to -12.

The ISO standard for calculating CEILING disagrees with Excel's calculation of CEILING for negative numbers. In Excel, the CEILING(-2.5,-1) would round the -2.5 to a lower number of -3. The ISO standard says that CEILING should always round up. If you are at -2.5, the next higher value is actually -2.

Excel 2010 introduces the new CEILING.PRECISE function. Here are the differences between CEILING and CEILING.PRECISE:

- The Significance argument is optional in CEILING.PRECISE. When omitted, the significance is assumed to be 1.

- CEILING.PRECISE(-2.5) now rounds up to -2 instead of -3.

- In Excel 2007, the number and significance had to have the same sign. Previously, =CEILING(-2,1) or =CEILING(2,-1) would have evaluated to a #NUM error. In Excel 2010, either =CEILING.PRECISE(-2.5,1) or = CEILING. PRECISE(2.5,-1) calculates without a problem. Excel 2010 still calculates =CEILING(2.5,-1) as a #NUM! error. However, strangely, =CEILING(-2.5,1) no longer returns #NUM!. Excel 2010 now returns -2 which is more like the CEILING.PRECISE result.

 caution

You should watch for one strange behavior with MROUND, FLOOR, and CEILING. If the number is negative, you must ensure that the second argument for the function is also negative. Certainly, in some situations you won't know in advance whether your numbers will be negative. If you think that your numbers might be a mix of positive and negative values, you should use =MROUND(C2,5*SIGN(C2)). This ensures that the second parameter matches the sign of the first parameter.

Figure 11.12 contrasts CEILING and CEILING.PRECISE:

The FLOOR function rounds a number to the next lowest multiple. Suppose that you employ several student workers who do piecework. They assemble products and then pack them six to a case. Your contract with the workers states that you pay only for complete cases. Column B in Figure 11.13 shows the total number of units assembled. You use =FLOOR(B6,6) to round this quantity down to the nearest multiple of six. Note that if the value is already a multiple of six, as in Cell B10, FLOOR does not change the number.

C16		▼	f_x	=CEILING.PRECISE(A16)		
A	B	C	D	E	F	G

	A	B	C	D	E	F	G
1	**CEILING EXAMPLES**						
2							
3	**Number**	**Sig.**	**Result**				
4	2.5	1	3	=CEILING(A4,B4)			
5	-2.5	-1	-3	Rounds away from zero			
6	2.5	-1	#NUM!	Invalid, signs don't match			
7	-2.5	1	-2	Would have been #NUM! in 2007			
8							
9	**CEILING.PRECISE EXAMPLES**						
10							
11	**Number**	**Sig.**	**Result**				
12	2.5	1	3	=CEILING.PRECISE(A12,B12)			
13	-2.5	-1	-2	Rounds up			
14	2.5	-1	3	Signs don't match, no problem			
15	-2.5	1	-2	Signs don't match, no problem			
16	2.5		3	=CEILING.PRECISE(A16)			
17	-2.5		-2	Significance assumed to be 1			
18							

Figure 11.12
For negative numbers, ISO.CEILING rounds toward zero.

D6		▼	f_x	=FLOOR(B6,C6)
A	B	C	D	E

	A	B	C	D	E
1	Piece Work Supply				
2	Productivity Report				
3	Workers are Paid for Complete Cases only				
4					
5	NAME	Quantity Complete	Per Case	Complete Case Quantity	
6	LAURIE	846	6	846	
7	JOE	658	6	654	
8	BRUCE	1186	6	1182	
9	MELVIN	968	6	966	
10	OLIVIA	942	6	942	
11	RODNEY	782	6	780	
12					
13					
14			-2	=FLOOR(-2.5,-1)	
15			-3	=FLOOR.PRECISE(-2.5,1)	
16					

Figure 11.13
FLOOR rounds a number down to the next multiple.

Similar to the problems with CEILING, the scientific community does not agree that floor should round toward zero for negative numbers. In cell B14 of Figure 11.13, the FLOOR of -2.5 actually rounds up to −2 instead of down to −3. You can use FLOOR.PRECISE to match the ISO standard. As shown in B15, the FLOOR.PRECISE of −2.5 is −3.

All the functions for rounding can be replaced with a clever combination of INT and ROUND functions. If you receive a spreadsheet from an old-time Lotus 1-2-3 user, you may see formulas like the ones in Figure 11.14:

- Cell B13 is equivalent to using MROUND with a multiple of 20. The formula divides 135 by 20, giving 6.75. ROUND rounds this to 7. Finally, outside the parentheses, the formula multiplies by 20 to arrive at the answer of 140.
- Cell C13 is equivalent to using FLOOR with a significance of 20. The formula divides 135 by 20, giving 6.75. The INT removes the decimal places, leaving the integer 6. The formula then multiplies this result by 20 to arrive at 120.
- Cell D13 is equivalent to using CEILING with a significance of 20. The formula divides 135 by 20, giving 6.75. Next, the formula adds just less than 0.5 to make sure that any value greater than 6 is rounded up to 7. Finally, the result is multiplied by 20 to arrive at 140.

Figure 11.14
A combination of ROUND and INT can replace any of the eight other functions used for rounding.

D13 | fx | =ROUND((A13/20)+0.49,0)*20

	A	B	C	D	E	F	G	H
1		Nearest 20	Prev 20	Next 20				
2	348	340	340	360				
3	780	780	780	780				
4	82	80	80	100				
5	480	480	480	480				
6	644	640	640	660				
7	300	300	300	300				
8	630	640	620	640				
9	454	460	440	460				
10	658	660	640	660				
11	521	520	520	540				
12	87	80	80	100				
13	135	140	120	140				
14	B13:	=ROUND((A13/20),0)*20						
15		C13:	=INT(A13/20)*20					
16			D13:	=ROUND((A13/20)+0.49,0)*20				
17								

In legacy versions of Excel, functions such as MROUND were not part of the core Excel. They were enabled when someone installed the Analysis Toolpack. Because new Excel users might never have installed the Analysis Toolpack, some people avoided using MROUND and instead wrote the formulas as shown in Figure 11.14. Now that Microsoft has elevated all the Analysis Toolpack functions to be part of the core Excel 2010 product, it is safe to use those functions.

Using SUBTOTAL Instead of SUM with Multiple Levels of Totals

Consider the data set shown in Figure 11.15. This report shows a list of invoices for each customer. Someone has manually inserted rows and used the SUM function to total each customer. Cells C5, C10, C15, and so on contain a SUM function.

It would be very difficult to enter a grand total at the bottom of this data set. You might have to enter a long formula that points only at the summary rows. In this particular case, the formula to provide a grand total for 15 customers would be possible, as shown in Figure 11.16. If you had 500 customers, however, the formula would be nearly impossible to enter.

Figure 11.15
Whoever manually summed these rows doesn't know about the Subtotal command on the Data tab.

Figure 11.16
It is difficult to enter the grand total formula.

Many accountants can teach you the old accounting trick whereby you total the entire column and divide by two to get the grand total. This is based on the assumption that every dollar is in the column twice: once on the detail row and once on the summary row. As shown in Figure 11.17, this trick does work, but it is hard to explain to your manager why it works.

The solution is to use the SUBTOTAL function. This powerful function is relatively new; it was introduced in Excel 97.

➡ *See Chapter 22, "Using Automatic Subtotals," for more information about working with subtotals.*

Syntax:

=SUBTOTAL(*function_num,ref1,ref2,...*)

Figure 11.17
The old accounting trick of adding an entire column and dividing by two works but is hard to explain.

=SUM(C2:C75)/2			
	A	B	C
1	Customer	Invoice	Revenue
66			
67	Supreme Washer Supply	1133	562.94
68	Supreme Washer Supply	1126	629.79
69	Supreme Washer Supply	1148	341.13
70	**Supreme Washer Supply**	**Total**	**1533.86**
71			
72	Well-Suited Utensil Corporation	1120	709.41
73	Well-Suited Utensil Corporation	1153	224.07
74	Well-Suited Utensil Corporation	1122	690.03
75	**Well-Suited Utensil Corporation**	**Total**	**1623.51**
76			
77	**GRAND TOTAL**		**20598.01**
78			

In its default use, SUBTOTAL works just like the SUM function, except it throws out other instances of the SUBTOTAL function within the range being summed. The SUBTOTAL function takes the following arguments:

- *function_num*—This is a number from 1 to 11. The most common function number is the number 9, which (for no apparent logical reason) is used to sum. When Microsoft introduced the SUBTOTAL function, it offered 11 options: AVERAGE, COUNT, COUNTA, MAX, MIN, PRODUCT, STDEV, STDEVP, SUM, VAR, and VARP. It just happens that SUM is the ninth item in this list when these functions are arranged alphabetically in the English language, so 9 became the function number for SUM. Although SUBTOTAL always ignores rows hidden as the result of a filter, it does not automatically ignore rows hidden with the HIDE command. To ignore rows that have been manually hidden, add 100 to the function num.

 tip

The best way to insert the SUBTOTAL function is to use the Subtotals icon on the Data tab. However, you can set up these functions manually.

- *ref1,ref2,...*—These are up to 254 ranges or references that you want to subtotal. Unlike with SUM, the references in a SUBTOTAL function cannot be 3D references.

Any other nested subtotals in the range are ignored to prevent double counting.

The SUBTOTAL function always ignores rows hidden as the result of a filter. This makes the SUBTOTAL function great in combination with autofilter, as you'll see later in this chapter, in Figure 11.19.

A feature added in Excel 2002 is that you can add 100 to the function number to prevent Excel from including rows hidden by using the Hide command. Note that this functionality works only with hidden rows. If you hide columns and attempt to subtotal in a horizontal fashion, the hidden columns are not ignored.

The arguments for SUBTOTAL are shown in Table 11.6.

Table 11.6   Function Arguments for SUBTOTAL

function_num (Includes Hidden Values)	function_num (Ignores Hidden Values)	Function
1	101	AVERAGE
2	102	COUNT
3	103	COUNTA
4	104	MAX
5	105	MIN
6	106	PRODUCT
7	107	STDEV
8	108	STDEVP
9	109	SUM
10	110	VAR
11	111	VARP

In Figure 11.18, the customer summary rows were built with the SUBTOTAL function, allowing the grand total row to be calculated with the simple formula =SUBTOTAL(9,C2:C76). In contrast, once someone has built manual subtotals using the SUM function as shown previously in Figure 11.15, the SUBTOTAL function won't work. You would have to replace SUM(with SUBTOTAL(9, to convert the existing subtotal lines to the subtotal function..

=SUBTOTAL(9,C2:C76)

	A	B	C
68	Supreme Washer Supply	1126	629.79
69	Supreme Washer Supply	1148	341.13
70	Supreme Washer Supply	Total	1533.86
71			
72	Well-Suited Utensil Corporation	1120	709.41
73	Well-Suited Utensil Corporation	1153	224.07
74	Well-Suited Utensil Corporation	1122	690.03
75	Well-Suited Utensil Corporation	Total	1623.51
76			
77	GRAND TOTAL		20598.01
78			

Figure 11.18
When you use SUBTOTAL instead of SUM for the customer totals, the problem of creating a grand total becomes simple.

Using SUBTOTAL Instead of SUM to Ignore Rows Hidden by a Filter

If you are using a filter to query a data set, you can use the SUBTOTAL function instead of the SUM function to show the total of the visible rows. In Figure 11.19, Cell E1 contains a SUM function, which totals rows whether they are visible or not. Cell E2 contains a SUBTOTAL function. As you use the autofilter drop-downs to show just rows for sales of J730 by Jamie, the SUBTOTAL function updates to reflect the total of the visible rows. This makes the SUBTOTAL function a great tool for ad hoc reporting.

Figure 11.19
The SUBTOTAL function in Cell E2 ignores rows hidden as the result of a filter.

	A	B	C	D	E
1				Total:	1,050,884.39
2				Total Visible:	42,357.13
3					
4	Rep	Produ	Customer	Da	Revenu
5	JAMIE	J730	Magnificent Notebook In	11/14/2011	191.09
61	JAMIE	J730	Stunning Glass Company	4/23/2011	306.50
62	JAMIE	J730	Magnificent Notebook In	8/7/2011	141.73
72	JAMIE	J730	New Vise Company	12/11/2011	155.46
141	JAMIE	J730	Wonderful Thermostat C	10/2/2011	100.31

=SUBTOTAL(109,E5:E5090)

Using RAND and RANDBETWEEN to Generate Random Numbers and Data

In a number of situations, you might want to generate random numbers. Excel offers two functions to assist with this process: RAND and RANDBETWEEN.

Syntax:

=RAND()

The RAND function returns an evenly distributed random number greater than or equal to 0 and less than 1. A new random number is returned every time the worksheet is calculated.

=RAND() generates a random decimal between 0 and 0.99999. Whether you are a teacher trying to randomly assign the order for book report presentations, or the commissioner of a fantasy football league trying to figure out the draft sequence, =RAND() can help.

> **note**
> Although the function in Figure 11.19 uses the function number 109, the Subtotal command always ignores rows hidden as the result of a filter. =SUBTOTAL(9,E5:E5090) would return an identical result when the rows are hidden through a filter, as in this case. If you have rows hidden by the Hide command, you will want to use 109 to ignore the manually hidden rows.

If you want to use RAND to generate a random number but don't want the numbers to change every time the cell is calculated, you can enter =RAND() in the formula bar and then press F9 to change the formula to a random number.

To generate a random number greater than or equal to 0 but less than 100, you can use RAND()*100.

To generate a random sequence for a list, you select a blank column next to your data and enter =RAND() in the column. Every time you press the F9 key, the column generates a new set of random numbers. You might want to agree up front with the draft participants that you will press F9 three times to randomize the list and then convert the formulas to values. To do so, you follow these steps:

1. Enter the heading Random in Row 1 next to your data.

2. Enter =RAND() in Cell B2.

3. Move the cell pointer to Cell B2 and double-click the fill handle.

4. Turn off automatic calculation by using Formulas, Calculation Options, Manual.

5. Press the F9 key three times.

6. Choose one cell in Column B.

7. From the Data tab, click the AZ button to sort ascending. The new sequence of items in Column A is a random sequence (see Figure 11.20).

You can also use this technique to select a random subset from a data set. If your manager wants you to contact every 20th customer, you can select all the customers where =RAND() is 0.05 or less.

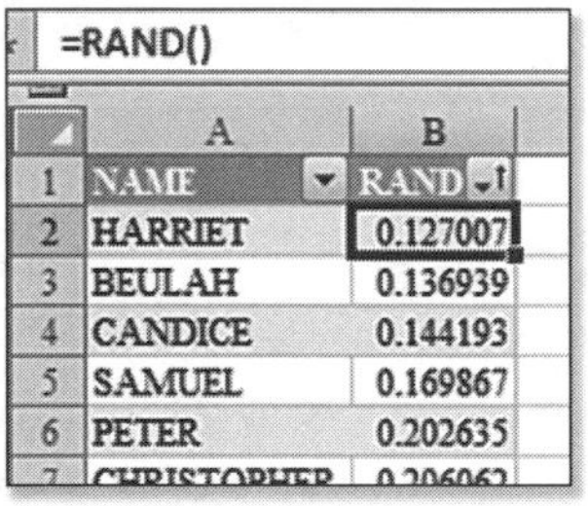

Figure 11.20
Harriet gets to draft first in this season's fantasy football league, thanks to the RAND function.

Syntax:

=RANDBETWEEN(*bottom*,*top*)

Whereas =RAND() returns a random decimal, =RANDBETWEEN generates an integer between two integers.

The RANDBETWEEN function returns a random number between the numbers you specify. A new random number is returned every time the worksheet is calculated. This function takes the following arguments:

> *bottom*—This is the smallest integer RANDBETWEEN can return.

> *top*—This is the largest integer RANDBETWEEN can return.

To generate random numbers between 50 and 59, inclusive, you use =RANDBETWEEN(50,59). RANDBETWEEN is easier to use than =RAND to achieve random integers; with =RAND, you would have to use =INT(RAND()*10)+50 to generate this same range of data.

Even though RANDBETWEEN generates integers, you can use it to generate sales prices or even letters. =RANDBETWEEN(5000,9900)/100 generates random prices between $50.00 and $99.00.

The capital letter A is also known as character 65 in the ASCII character set. B is 66, C is 67, and so on up through Z, which is character 90. You can use =CHAR(RANDBETWEEN(65,90)) to generate random capital letters.

Many of the product SKUs in this book were generated using =CHAR(RANDBETWEEN(65,90))& RANDBETWEEN(101,199).

Figure 11.21 shows many examples of RANDBETWEEN.

Figure 11.21

RAND BETWEEN can generate integers, or with a little creativity, prices or letters.

	A	B	C	D	E	F	G	H	I	J	K	L	M	N	O
							=CHAR(RANDBETWEEN(65,90))&RANDBETWEEN(101,199)								
1	55		53		F		68.16		Q151						
2	55		50		Z		91.84		A187						
3	51		56		X		67.88		Q107						
4	55		56		G		98.65		Y179						
5	58		51		M		51.14		L144						
6	53		56		U		76.52		F186						
7	53		55		X		95.42		M162						
8	58		59		Q		64.45		B106						
9	59		52		L		62.24		=CHAR(RANDBETWEEN(65,90))&RANDBETWEEN(101,199)						
10	59		52		J		=RANDBETWEEN(5000,9900)/100								
11	52		58		=CHAR(RANDBETWEEN(65,90))										
12	50		=INT(RAND()*10)+50												
13	=RANDBETWEEN(50,59)														
14															

Choosing a Random Item from a List

In Figure 11.22, you want to randomly assign employees to certain projects. The list of projects is in Column A. The list of employees is in E2:E6. As shown in Figure 11.22, the function for B2:B11 is =INDEX($E$2:$E$6,RANDBETWEEN(1,5)).

Figure 11.22

I wonder if Dilbert's pointy-haired boss assigns projects this way.

	A	B	C	D	E
		=INDEX($E$2:$E$6,RANDBETWEEN(1,5))			
1	**Project**	**Assigned To**			**Employees**
2	Project 101	ALMA			WAYNE
3	Project 102	ALMA			ALMA
4	Project 103	RUBY			YVETTE
5	Project 104	WAYNE			RUBY
6	Project 105	SARA			SARA
7	Project 106	ALMA			
8	Project 107	WAYNE			
9	Project 108	ALMA			
10	Project 109	SARA			

Syntax: =ROMAN() to Finish Movie Credits

Excel can convert numbers to Roman numerals. If you stay in the theater after a movie until the end of movie credits, you will see that the copyright date is always expressed in Roman numerals. If you are the next Steven Spielberg, you can use =ROMAN(2011) or =ROMAN(YEAR(Now())) to generate such a numeral.

Syntax:

=ROMAN(number,form)

The ROMAN function converts an Arabic numeral to Roman, as text. This function takes the following arguments:

- *number*—This is the Arabic numeral you want converted.

- *form*—This is a number that specifies the type of Roman numeral you want. The Roman numeral style ranges from Classic to Simplified, becoming more concise as the value of form increases.

 caution

In a previous book, I joked that if you had bad financial news to share with stockholders, you might try converting your financial statement to Roman numerals. However, you can use the ROMAN function only in limited circumstances. Negative numbers, 0, and numbers over 3,999 cannot be represented with the ROMAN function.

There are some arcane rules with Roman numerals. In classic Roman numbers, an I before a V is used to indicate the number 4. In classic Roman numbers, it is valid to use an I before a V or an X, but it is not valid to use an I before an L, a C, a D, or an M.

As shown in Figure 11.23, the form argument allows Excel to bend these rules progressively more:

- ROMAN(1999,0) results in MCMXCIX. The M is 1000, the CM is 900, the XC is 90, and the IX is 9; 1000 + 900 + 90 + 9 = 1999

- ROMAN(1999,1) results in MLMVLIV. The M is 1000, the LM is 950, the VL is 45, and the IV is 4; 1000 + 950 + 45 + 4 = 1999.

- ROMAN(1999,2) results in MXMIX. The M is 1000, the XM is 990, and the IX is 9; 1000 + 990 + 9 = 1999.

- ROMAN(1999,3) results in MVMIV. The M is 1000, the VM is 995, and the IV is 4; 1000 + 995 + 4 = 1999.

- ROMAN(1999,4) results in MIM. The M is 1000 and the IM is 999; 1000 + 999 = 1999.

Using ABS() to Figure Out the Magnitude of ERROR

Suppose that you work for a local TV station, and you want to prove that your forecaster is more accurate than those at the other stations in town. The forecaster at the rival station in town is horrible—some days he misses high, and other days he misses low. The rival station uses Figure 11.24 to say that his average forecast is 99% accurate. All those negative and positive errors cancel each other out in the average.

The ABS function measures the size of the error. Positive errors are reported as positive, and negative errors are reported as positive as well. You can use =ABS(A2-B2) to demonstrate that the other station's forecaster is off by 20 degrees on average.

Figure 11.23
You can create movie credit dates with Cell A3 or present bad financial news with F1:G13. Compare the various forms of Roman numerals in A7:A11.

`=ROMAN(2011)`

	A	B	C	D	E	F	G	H	I
1	NextSpielberg Productions, Inc.					VNIFORM FAVCET SVPPLY			
2	Movie Credit Assistant					INCOME STATEMENT			
3	MMXI	=ROMAN(2011)							
4	MMX	=ROMAN(YEAR(NOW()))				REVENUE	MMMCMXCIX		3999
5						COST OF GOOD SOLD	MMCCXXXIX		2239
6	MCMXCIX	=ROMAN(1999)				GROSS PROFIT	MDCCLX		1760
7	MCMXCIX	=ROMAN(1999,0)							
8	MLMVLIV	=ROMAN(1999,1)				SALES EXPENSE	DCXCIX		699
9	MXMIX	=ROMAN(1999,2)				MARKETING EXPENSE	CDXXI		421
10	MVMIV	=ROMAN(1999,3)				R&D EXPENSE	DCI		601
11	MIM	=ROMAN(1999,4)				TOTAL EXPENSES	MDCCXXI		1721
12									
13						NET INCOME	XXXIX		39
14									

Figure 11.24
ABS measures the size of an error, ignoring the sign.

`=ABS(G4-H4)`

	A	B	C	D	E	F	G	H	I
1	Weather Forecast Accuracy - Action News					Weather Forecast Accuracy Using ABS()			
2									
3	Date	Forecast	Actual	Error		Date	Forecast	Actual	Error
4	6/1/2011	87	67	20		6/1/2011	87	67	20
5	6/2/2011	52	72	-20		6/2/2011	52	72	20
6	6/3/2011	93	73	20		6/3/2011	93	73	20
7	6/4/2011	55	75	-20		6/4/2011	55	75	20
8	6/5/2011	94	74	20		6/5/2011	94	74	20
9	6/6/2011	54	74	-20		6/6/2011	54	74	20
10	6/7/2011	89	69	20		6/7/2011	89	69	20
11	6/8/2011	49	69	-20		6/8/2011	49	69	20
12	6/9/2011	93	73	20		6/9/2011	93	73	20
13	6/10/2011	48	68	-20		6/10/2011	48	68	20
14	6/11/2011	88	68	20		6/11/2011	88	68	20
15	6/12/2011	53	73	-20		6/12/2011	53	73	20
16	6/13/2011	98	78	20		6/13/2011	98	78	20
17	6/14/2011	56	76	-20		6/14/2011	56	76	20
18	6/15/2011	100	80	20		6/15/2011	100	80	20
19	6/16/2011	62	82	-20		6/16/2011	62	82	20
20	TOTAL	1171	1171	0		TOTAL	1171	1171	320
21									27.3%
22	Claim: Our forecast is 100% accurate!					Reality: The forecast averages 27% wrong			
23									

Syntax:

=ABS(*number*)

The ABS function returns the absolute value of a number—that is, the number without its sign. With this function, the argument number is the real number of which you want the absolute number.

Using PI to Calculate Cake or Pizza Pricing

How many more ingredients are in a 16-inch pizza than an 8-inch pizza? Be careful—it is not double!

The formula for the area of a circle is $\Pi \times r2$. The radius of a circle is half the diameter. The function =PI() returns the constant for PI. You use =PI()*(B7/2)^2 to calculate the number of square inches in a 16-inch pizza. As shown in Figure 11.25, the 16-inch size contains nearly four times the area of an 8-inch circle.

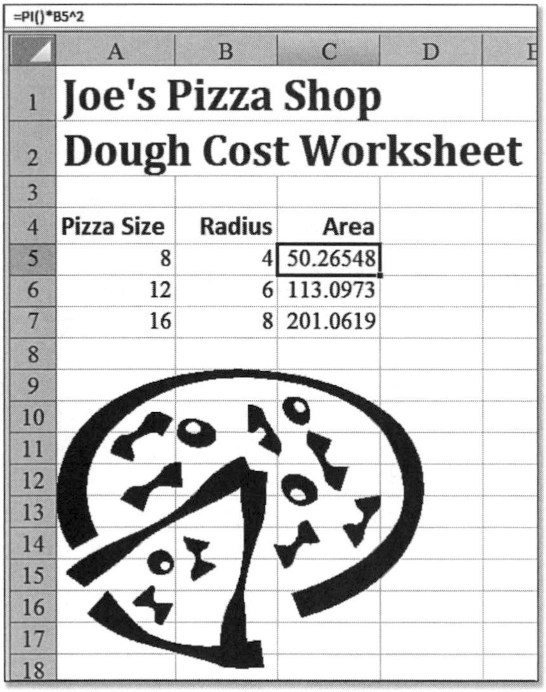

=PI()*B5^2

	A	B	C	D
1	**Joe's Pizza Shop**			
2	**Dough Cost Worksheet**			
3				
4	**Pizza Size**	**Radius**	**Area**	
5	8	4	50.26548	
6	12	6	113.0973	
7	16	8	201.0619	

Figure 11.25
Most pizza shops don't have a dedicated cost accountant.

If your company makes anything round—drink coasters, drum heads, wedding cakes, pizzas, or Frisbees—you want to use =PI() when calculating your product cost.

Syntax:

`=PI()`

The PI function returns the number 3.14159265358979, the mathematical constant, accurate to 15 digits.

Using =COMBIN to Figure Out Lottery Probability

Your office lottery pool may agree to bet $1 on the lottery each week but to double the bet when the jackpot is a higher payout than the odds against winning.

The COMBIN function can figure out the number of combinations for most lottery systems. If you have to correctly select 6 numbers out of a pool of 48 numbers, you can use `=COMBIN(48,6)` to find that there are 11.1 million combinations.

Figure 11.26 shows a variety of lottery odds.

Figure 11.26

The odds of winning the lottery in a 44-number games are twice as good as in a 50-number game.

`=COMBIN(B4,A4)`

	A	B	C	D
1	**OurCo Lottery Pool**			
2				
3	**Select**	**Out of...**	**Combinations**	
4	6	40	3,838,380	:1
5	6	44	7,059,052	:1
6	6	46	9,366,819	:1
7	6	47	10,737,573	:1
8	6	48	12,271,512	:1
9	6	50	15,890,700	:1
10				

➥ *See Chapter 14, "Using Statistical Functions," for more information about working with the* COMBIN *function.*

> **🔍 note**
>
> The COMBIN function assumes that you don't care about the sequence of the numbers chosen. If you have to worry about the sequence, you should use `=PERMUT`.

Using FACT to Calculate the Permutation of a Number

Suppose that you have seven slides in a PowerPoint presentation. Furthermore, you want to find the number of unique sequences in which the slides can be arranged; this is called the factorial of seven. You calculated this by using 7 × 6 × 5 × 4 × 3 × 2 × 1. To find the factorial of any positive integer, you use the FACT function.

Syntax:

=FACT(*number*)

The FACT function returns the factorial of a number. The factorial of a number is equal to $1 \times 2 \times 3 \times \dots \times$ number. Number is the nonnegative number of which you want the factorial. If number is not an integer, it is truncated.

By definition, FACT(0) is 1.

To figure out how many different ways you can arrange five people in a line, use =FACT(5).

There is a similar function called FACTDOUBLE. A double factorial multiplies every other number. For even numbers, this is a calculation such as FACTDOUBLE(8) = 8*6*4*2. For odd numbers, the calculation is FACTDOUBLE(9) = 9*7*5*3*1.

Various factorials are shown in Figure 11.27.

 note

It is difficult to find real-world uses for FACTDOUBLE. MathWorld.com notes some interesting uses for FACTDOUBLE (N) where N is between -1 and -2, but Excel does not calculate FACTDOUBLE for negative numbers. Fans of the poker game Texas Hold 'Em will be delighted to know that FACTDOUBLE is useful in calculating Texas Hold 'Em probabilities. For complete details, look up Poker Probabilities (Texas Hold 'Em) in Wikipedia.

=FACTDOUBLE(A11)

	A	B	C	D	E	F
1	Number	Factorial	Equivalent to		Double Factorial	Equivalent to
2	0	1			1	
3	1	1	=1		1	=1
4	2	2	=1*2		2	=2
5	3	6	=1*2*3		3	=1*3
6	4	24	=1*2*3*4		8	=2*4
7	5	120	=1*2*3*4*5		15	=1*3*5
8	6	720	=1*2*3*4*5*6		48	=2*4*6
9	7	5040	=1*2*3*4*5*6*7		105	=1*3*5*7
10	8	40320	=1*2*3*4*5*6*7*8		384	=2*4*6*8
11	9	362880	=1*2*3*4*5*6*7*8*9		945	=1*3*5*7*9
12	99	9.3E+155	=1*2*3*...*98*99		2.72539E+78	=1*3*5*...*97*99
13						

Figure 11.27
Excel calculates the FACT and FACTDOUBLE of various numbers.

Using GCD and LCM to Perform Seventh-Grade Math

My seventh-grade math teacher, Mr. Irwin, taught me about greatest common denominators and least common multiples. For example, the least common multiple of 24 and 36 is 72. The greatest common denominator of 24 and 36 is 12. I have to admit that I never saw these concepts again until my son Josh was in seventh grade. This must be permanently part of the seventh-grade curriculum.

If you are in seventh grade or you are assisting a seventh grader with his or her math lesson, you will be happy to know that Excel can calculate these values for you.

Syntax:

=GCD(*number1,number2,...*)

The GCD function returns the greatest common divisor of two or more integers. The greatest common divisor is the largest integer that divides both number1 and number2 without a remainder.

The arguments number1, number2,... are 1 to 29 values. If any value is not an integer, it is truncated. If any argument is nonnumeric, GCD returns a #VALUE! error. If any argument is less than zero, GCD returns a #NUM! error. The number 1 divides any value evenly. A prime number has only itself and 1 as even divisors.

Syntax:

=LCM(*number1,number2,...*)

The LCM function returns the least common multiple of integers. The least common multiple is the smallest positive integer that is a multiple of all integer arguments—*number1, number2,* and so on. You use LCM to add fractions with different denominators.

The arguments *number1, number2,...* are 1 to 29 values for which you want the least common multiple. If the value is not an integer, it is truncated. If any argument is nonnumeric, LCM returns a #VALUE! error. If any argument is less than one, LCM returns a #NUM! error.

Using MULTINOMIAL to Solve a Coin Problem

Although the multinomial distribution is a fairly complex mathematical concept, the following example illustrates a fun puzzle that can be solved with the function.

Syntax:

=MULTINOMIAL(*number1,number2,...*)

The MULTINOMIAL function returns the ratio of the factorial of a sum of values to the product of factorials. The arguments *number1, number2,...* are 1 to 255 values for which you want the multinomial. For example, MULTINOMIAL(a,b,c,d) is (a+b+c+d)! / a!×b! ×c! ×d!.

Suppose that you have a huge jar that contains hundreds of pennies, nickels, dimes, and quarters. You reach into the jar and pull out six coins. How many possible arrangements of the coins can there be? To picture this problem, you should sort the six types of coins from low to high. You can use three movable dividers to group the coins into denominations. In the left side of Figure 11.28, for example, you've arranged the dividers to indicate one penny, one nickel, three dimes, and one quarter. It is possible to pull out none of a particular coin. In the image on the right, you've pulled out five pennies and one dime. In this case, the dividers are adjacent for nickels and pennies. In every case, the quarter divider must always be at the bottom, so how many ways are there to arrange the other three dividers among six coins?

Someone figured out that the answer to this problem is the factorial of (Dividers + Coins) ÷ Factorial of Coins × Factorial of Dividers. In math terms, this is (3+6)! / 3! ×6!. Remarkably, Excel has a function for solving the coin problem. =MULTINOMIAL(3,6) performs the calculation (3+6)!/3! ×6!.

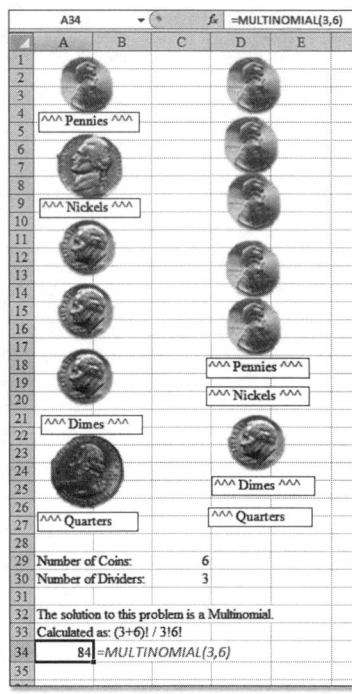

Figure 11.28
Solving this problem with MULTINOMIAL will amuse Boy Scout groups and middle school math students.

Using MOD to Find the Remainder Portion of a Division Problem

The MOD function is one of the obscure math functions that I find myself using quite frequently. Have you ever been in a group activity where everyone in the group was to count off by sixes? This is a great way to break up a group into six subgroups. It makes sure that friends who were sitting together get put into disparate groups.

Using the MOD function is a great way to perform this concept with records in a database. Perhaps for auditing, you need to check every eighth invoice. Or you need to break up a list of employees into four groups. You can solve these types of problems by using the MOD function.

Think back to when you were first learning division. If you had to divide 43 by 4, you would have written that the answer was 10 with a remainder of 3. If you divide 40 by 4, the answer is 10 with a remainder of 0.

The MOD function divides one number by another and reports back just the remainder portion of the result. You end up with an even distribution of remainders. If you convert the formulas into values and sort, your data is broken into similar-size groups.

Syntax:

`=MOD(number,divisor)`

> **note**
>
> MOD is short for modulo, the mathematical term for this operation. You would normally say that 17 modulo 3 is 2.

The MOD function returns the remainder after number is divided by divisor. The result has the same sign as divisor. This function takes the following arguments:

- *number*—This is the number for which you want to find the remainder.

- *divisor*—This is the number by which you want to divide number. If divisor is 0, MOD returns a `#DIV/0!` error.

The MOD function is good for classifying records that follow a certain order. For example, the SmartArt gallery contains 84 icons arranged with 4 icons per row. To find the column for the 38th icon, use `=MOD(38,4)`.

The example in Figure 11.29 assigns all employees to one of four groups.

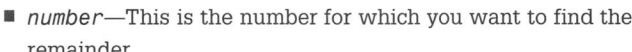

Figure 11.29
To organize these employees into four groups, use =MOD(ROW(),4). Then paste the values and sort by the remainders.

Using QUOTIENT to Isolate the Integer Portion in a Division Problem

As you just learned, the MOD function isolates the remainder portion in a division problem. The QUOTIENT function isolates the integer portion in a division problem.

If you divide 43 by 4, the answer is 10 with a remainder of 3. The QUOTIENT function returns just the whole number 10 and ignores the remainder.

This function is great for calculating full cases of products. Suppose you pay a worker for assembling products. You pay the worker for each complete case of 4 items produced. If he produces 43 items in his shift, this is 10 complete cases. `=QUOTIENT(43,4)` would provide an answer of 10.

Syntax:

=QUOTIENT(*numerator*,*denominator*)

The QUOTIENT function returns the integer portion in a division problem. You use this function when you want to discard the remainder in a division problem. This function takes the following arguments:

- *numerator*—This is the dividend.

- *denominator*—This is the divisor.

If either argument is nonnumeric, QUOTIENT returns a #VALUE! error.

Many people simulate the QUOTIENT function by using the INT function. To keep the integer portion of a division, you could use =INT(43/4). However, QUOTIENT and INT differ when the result is negative. Whereas QUOTIENT(5,-4) returns -1, INT(5/-4) actually goes down to -2. Thus, using QUOTIENT is more accurate than using INT if the results might be negative. If you are a fan of using INT to simulate the QUOTIENT, consider using TRUNC() or ISO.CEILING() instead. Figure 11.30 shows the differences between QUOTIENT, INT, TRUNC, and ISO.CEILING.

	C6		f_x	=QUOTIENT(A6,B6)	
	A	B	C	D	E	F
1	Number	Divisor	Quotient	INT(a/b)	TRUNC(a/b)	ISO.CEILING(a/b)
2	1	4	0	0	0	1
3	2	4	0	0	0	1
4	3	4	0	0	0	1
5	4	4	1	1	1	1
6	5	4	1	1	1	2
7	6	4	1	1	1	2
8	7	4	1	1	1	2
9	8	4	2	2	2	2
10	9	4	2	2	2	3
11	10	4	2	2	2	3
12	11	4	2	2	2	3
13	12	4	3	3	3	3
14	1	-4	0	-1	0	0
15	2	-4	0	-1	0	0
16	3	-4	0	-1	0	0
17	4	-4	-1	-1	-1	-1
18	5	-4	-1	-2	-1	-1
19	6	-4	-1	-2	-1	-1
20	7	-4	-1	-2	-1	-1
21	8	-4	-2	-2	-2	-2
22	9	-4	-2	-3	-2	-2
23	10	-4	-2	-3	-2	-2
24	11	-4	-2	-3	-2	-2
25	12	-4	-3	-3	-3	-3

Figure 11.30
QUOTIENT is more accurate than INT when the result is negative.

Using PRODUCT to Multiply Numbers

The PRODUCT function multiplies a range of numbers by each other. Although you could calculate =PRODUCT(2,2), the PRODUCT function is designed to multiply all numbers in a range, such as =PRODUCT(A2:A50).

Syntax:

=PRODUCT(***number1,number2,...***)

The PRODUCT function multiplies all the numbers given as arguments and returns the product. The arguments *number1, number2,...* are 1 to 255 numbers that you want to multiply. If you pass a single-cell argument that contains a text representation of a number, it is used in the multiplication. However, if one of the arguments is a multicell range, any text entry in that range is ignored.

In Figure 11.31, an array formula in B16 finds all the steps matching a particular book and multiplies the completion flags together. If 100% of the steps for a book are marked with a 1 to indicate complete, the product will also be 1. If any step is incomplete, the product will be zero. Note that the formula in B16 needs to be completed by holding down Ctrl+Shift while pressing Enter.

Figure 11.31
PRODUCT can check to see if all steps are nonzero.

{=PRODUCT(IF($A$2:$A$13=A16,$C$2:$C$13,""))}

	A	B	C	D	E	F	G
1	Book	Step	Complete				
2	In Depth	Cover	1				
3	In Depth	Text	1				
4	In Depth	Layout	0				
5	In Depth	Bar Code	0				
6	PTDC	Cover	1				
7	PTDC	Text	1				
8	PTDC	Layout	1				
9	PTDC	Bar Code	1				
10	VBA	Cover	0				
11	VBA	Text	1				
12	VBA	Layout	1				
13	VBA	Bar Code	1				
14							
15		100% Done					
16	In Depth	0	{=PRODUCT(IF($A$2:$A$13=A16,$C$2:$C$13,""))}				
17	PTDC	1					
18	VBA	0					
19							

Using SQRT and POWER to Calculate Square Roots and Exponents

Most calculators offer a square root button, so it seems natural that Excel would offer a SQRT function to do the same thing. To square a number, you multiply the number by itself, ending up with a square. For example, 5 × 5 = 25.

A square root is a number that, when multiplied by itself, leads to a square. For example, the square root of 25 is 5, and the square root of 49 is 7. Some square roots are more difficult to calculate. The square root of 8 is a number between 2 and 3—somewhere close to 2.828. You can calculate the number with =SQRT(8).

A related function is the POWER function. If you want to write the shorthand for 6 × 6 × 6 × 6 × 6, you would say "six to the fifth power," or 6^5. Excel can calculate this with =POWER(6,5).

 note

There is a specialized version of SQRT, SQRTPI. This function is handy for converting square shapes to equivalent-sized round shapes.

Syntax:

=SQRT(*number*)

The SQRT function returns a positive square root. The argument number is the number for which you want the square root. If *number* is negative, SQRT returns a *#NUM!* error.

Syntax:

=POWER(*number,power*)

The POWER function returns the result of a number raised to a power. This function takes the following arguments:

- *number*—This is the base number. It can be any real number.

- *power*—This is the exponent to which the base number is raised.

The POWER function works with all sorts of irrational numbers, such as 98.2 raised to the 3.4 power.

Figuring Out Other Roots and Powers

The SQRT function is provided because some math people expect it to be there. There are no equivalent functions to figure out other roots.

If you multiply 5 × 5 × 5 to get 125, then the third root of 125 is 5. The fourth root of 625 is 5. Even a $30 calculator offers a key to generate various roots beyond a square root. Excel does not offer a cube root function. In reality, even the POWER and the SQRT functions are not necessary.

- =6^3 is 6 raised to the third power, which is 6 x 6 x 6, or 216.

- =2^8 is 2 to the eighth power, which is 2 x 2 x 2 x 2 x 2 x 2 x 2 x 2, or 256.

For roots, you can raise a number to a fractional power:

- =256^(1/8) is the eighth root of 256. This is 2.

- =125^(1/3) is the third root of 125. This is 5.

> ➡ *To review information on how the carat operator is used to calculate powers and roots, refer back to Chapter 8, "Understanding Formulas."*

Thus, instead of using =SQRT(25), you could just as easily use =25^(1/2). However, people reading your worksheets are more likely to understand =SQRT(25) than =25^(1/2).

> ➡ *See Chapter 15, "Using Trig, Matrix, and Engineering Functions," to read more about the SQRT and SQRTPI functions.*

Using SIGN to Determine the Sign of a Number

Although the SIGN function belongs with the information functions, Microsoft groups it with the math functions. You can see it used in the MROUND function example shown previously in this chapter to prevent an error. Simply, =SIGN(*number*) reports whether *number* is negative, zero, or positive.

Syntax:

`=SIGN(number)`

SIGN determines the sign of a number. It returns 1 if the number is positive, 0 if the number is 0, and −1 if the number is negative. The argument number is any real number.

Using COUNTIF, AVERAGEIF, and SUMIF to Conditionally Count, Average, or Sum Data

The COUNTIF and SUMIF functions are young and popular. In contrast to most functions that have been around since the 1980s, these functions were added in Excel 97. The AVERAGEIF function is even newer, having been added in Excel 2007. Math purists may point out that you could perform equivalent calculations by using DSUM, or SUMPRODUCT, or even an array formula long before Microsoft added these functions. However, it is far easier to grasp doing calculations with COUNTIF, AVERAGEIF, and SUMIF.

Figure 11.32 shows a database that contains thousands of records. Your goal is to find out how many records came from each region. One way to write the formula for the east region is `=COUNTIF($C$11:$C$5011,"East")`. However, it is far more interesting to write the formula as shown in Cell B2: `=COUNTIF($C$11:$C$5011,A2)`. After this formula is entered, you can build a table of the unique regions in Column A, copy the formula down Column B, and quickly have a summary table built with the help of COUNTIF.

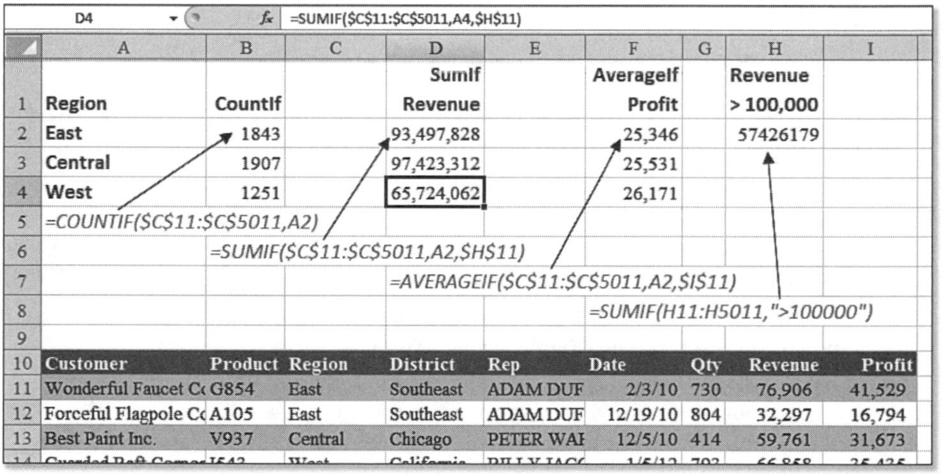

Figure 11.32
COUNTIF and SUMIF are simpler to use than DSUM, SUM-PRODUCT, or array formulas.

Syntax:

`=COUNTIF(range,criteria)`

The COUNTIF function counts the number of cells within a range that meet the given criteria. This function takes the following arguments:

- *range*—This is the range of cells from which you want to count cells.

- *criteria*—This is the criteria in the form of a number, an expression, or text that defines which cells will be counted. For example, criteria can be expressed as 32, "32", ">32", or "apples". Any criteria that contains text or a mathematical operator must be enclosed in quotes. For numeric criteria, the quotes are not required.

- You can use the wildcard characters question mark (?) and asterisk (*) in criteria. A question mark matches any single character; an asterisk matches any sequence of characters. If you want to find an actual question mark or asterisk, you need to type a tilde (~) before the character.

After you have mastered COUNTIF, it is easy to master SUMIF or AVERAGEIF. In most cases, the SUMIF function adds one new argument. Whereas COUNTIF would ask for a range of data and then the value to look for in that range, SUMIF usually needs three arguments: SUMIF asks for a range of data, the value to look for in that range, and then another range of data to be summed when a match is found.

In Figure 11.32, B11:B5011 contains the range to search. Cell A2 contains the value for which to search. When Excel finds a matching value in Column B, you want Excel to return the corresponding cell from the revenue column in H11:H5011. Most people would write =SUMIF($C$11:$C$5011,A2, $H$11:H$5011) to do this. It turns out that Excel forces the third argument to have the same shape as the first argument. If you would happen to accidentally specify H11:H4011, Excel would ignore your range and use H11:H5011 because this is the same shape as the first argument. Thus, it is sufficient to write the formula as =SUMIF($C$11:$C$5011,A2,$H$11).

Syntax:

=SUMIF(*range,criteria,sum_range*)

Syntax:

=AVERAGEIF(*range,criteria,average_range*)

The SUMIF function adds the cells specified by a given criteria. The AVERAGEIF function averages the cells specified by a given criteria. Occasionally, the range you want to search is also the range to sum. For example, perhaps your criteria is to look for rows where the revenue is greater than 100,000. In this case, because your range to add is the same as your range to search, you can leave off the third argument, as shown in Cell H2 of Figure 11.32.

The SUMIF function takes the following arguments:

- range—This is the range of cells you want evaluated.

- criteria—This is the criteria in the form of a number, an expression, or text that defines which cells will be counted.

 note

An interesting variation on the SUMIF, AVERAGEIF, and COUNTIF functions is worth mentioning. It is possible to build the criteria argument on-the-fly. To count records that are above average, you can use =COUNTIF(H11:H50 11,">"&AVERAGE(H11:H5011)).

Mastering the SUMIF and COUNTIF functions invariably leads to more questions about doing more powerful versions. If you need to sum based on more than one condition, you can use DSUM, SUMPRODUCT, or SUMIFS. The SUMIFS function is discussed in the next section.

For example, criteria can be expressed as 32, "32", ">32", or "apples".

- *sum_range*—This is the range of cells to sum. The cells in sum_range are summed only if their corresponding cells in range match the criteria. If sum_range is omitted, the cells in range are summed.

- *average_range*—If cells in the average_range are empty or contain text or TRUE/FALSE, they are ignored in the calculation of average.

> See Chapter 12, *"Using Powerful Functions: Logical, Lookup, and Database Functions," to learn more about using the* DSUM *function. To learn more about the* SUMPRODUCT *function, see Chapter 15, "Using Trig, Matrix, and Engineering Functions."*

Using Conditional Formulas with Multiple Conditions: SUMIFS(), AVERAGEIFS(), and COUNTIFS()

When someone sees how easy using SUMIF() is, they invariably want the function to do more. One of the most frequent questions at the MrExcel message board is along the lines of this: "I am using SUMIF() to get a total by region. How can I put two conditions in there to only get the total for a certain region and product?" In legacy versions of Excel, there were ways to do this, but they were difficult. You had to use either SUMPRODUCT(), DSUM(), or an array formula. There is a lot of complexity in going from a simple SUMIF() to the complex Boolean logic required to understand SUMPRODUCT().

Thankfully, Excel 2007 added plural versions of SUMIF(), COUNTIF(), and AVERAGEIF() that can handle not just two conditions, but up to 127 conditions. The three new functions add the letter S to the end of the function name (that is, SUMIFS(), COUNTIFS(), and AVERAGEIFS()), to signify that multiple IFs are being considered. With SUMIFS() and AVERAGEIFS(), you first specify the range to be summed or averaged. You then specify pairs of arguments. In each pair, you first specify the range to check and then the value to match in that range. The following sections describe these three functions.

 **tip**

The order of the arguments differs between SUMIF and SUMIFS. The ***Sum_Range*** is the first argument in SUMIFS but the third argument in SUMIF. It seems pretty common that you would be editing a SUMIF function to add additional conditions. Remember to move the *Sum_ Range* to be the first argument when you are moving from SUMIF to SUMIFS.

Syntax:

SUMIFS(sum_range,criteria_range1,criteria1[,criteria_range2, criteria2...])

The SUMIFS() function adds the cells in a range that meet multiple criteria.

Note the following in this syntax:

- *sum_range* is the range to sum.

- *criteria_range1, criteria_range2,* and so on are one or more ranges in which to evaluate the associated criteria.

- *criteria1*, *criteria2*, and so on are one or more criteria in the form of a number, an expression, a cell reference, or text that define which cells will be added. For example, they can be expressed as 32, "32", ">32", "apples", or B4.
- Each cell in *sum_range* is summed only if all the corresponding criteria specified are true for that cell.
- Cells in *sum_range* that contain TRUE evaluate to 1; cells in *sum_range* that contain FALSE evaluate to 0.
- You can use the wildcard characters question mark (?) and asterisk (*) in criteria. A question mark matches any single character; an asterisk matches any sequence of characters. If you want to find an actual question mark or asterisk, you need to type a tilde (~) before the character.
- Unlike the range and criteria arguments in SUMIF, the size and shape of each criteria_range and sum_range must be the same.

In Figure 11.33, you want to build a table that shows the total by region and product. *sum_range* is the revenue in H11:H5011. The first criteria pair consists of the regions in $C$11:$C$5011 being compared to the word East in B$1. The second criteria pair consists of the divisions in $B$11:$B$5011 being compared to G854 in $A2. The formula in B2 is =SUMIFS($H$11:$H$5011,$C$11:$C$5011,B$1,$B$11:$B$5011,$A2). You can copy this formula to B2:D6.

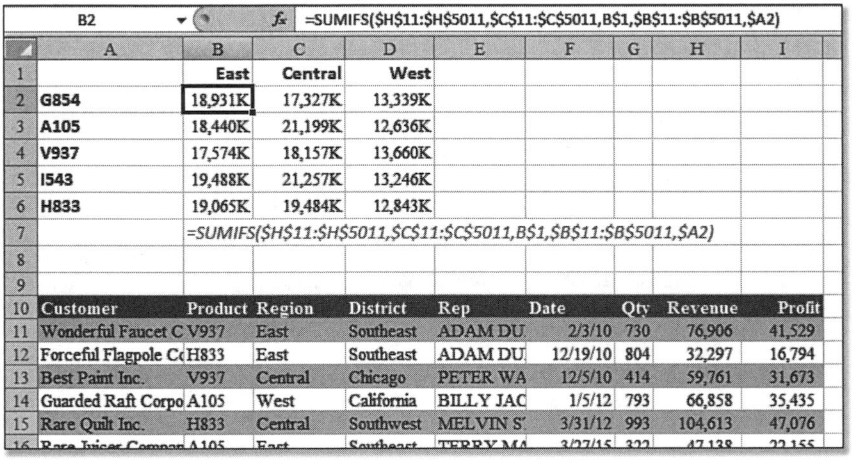

B2 | =SUMIFS($H$11:$H$5011,$C$11:$C$5011,B$1,$B$11:$B$5011,$A2)

	A	B	C	D	E	F	G	H	I
1		East	Central	West					
2	G854	18,931K	17,327K	13,339K					
3	A105	18,440K	21,199K	12,636K					
4	V937	17,574K	18,157K	13,660K					
5	I543	19,488K	21,257K	13,246K					
6	H833	19,065K	19,484K	12,843K					
7		=SUMIFS($H$11:$H$5011,$C$11:$C$5011,B$1,$B$11:$B$5011,$A2)							
8									
9									
10	Customer	Product	Region	District	Rep	Date	Qty	Revenue	Profit
11	Wonderful Faucet C	V937	East	Southeast	ADAM DU	2/3/10	730	76,906	41,529
12	Forceful Flagpole Co	H833	East	Southeast	ADAM DU	12/19/10	804	32,297	16,794
13	Best Paint Inc.	V937	Central	Chicago	PETER WA	12/5/10	414	59,761	31,673
14	Guarded Raft Corpo	A105	West	California	BILLY JAC	1/5/12	793	66,858	35,435
15	Rare Quilt Inc.	H833	Central	Southwest	MELVIN S	3/31/12	993	104,613	47,076
16	Rare Juicer Compan	A105	East	Southeast	TERRY MA	3/27/15	322	47,138	22,155

Figure 11.33 The new SUMIFS() function is used to create this summary by region and product.

Syntax:

AVERAGEIFS(*average_range*,*criteria_range1*,*criteria1*[,*criteria_range2*,*criteria2*...])

The AVERAGEIFS() function is similar to SUMIFS(). It returns the average (arithmetic mean) of all cells that meet multiple criteria. The arguments are the same as for SUMIFS().

Syntax:

COUNTIFS(*range1,criteria1[,range2, criteria2...]*)

COUNTIFS() counts the number of cells in a range that meet multiple criteria. The COUNTIFS() syntax is a bit different from the syntax of the other new functions. With COUNTIFS(), there is no need to specify *sum_range*. The arguments in COUNTIFS() consist of pairs specifying criteria. The first argument in each pair specifies a criteria region. The second argument in each pair specifies the criteria value to match.

Dates and Times in Excel

Date calculations can drive people crazy in Excel. If you gain a certain confidence with dates in Excel, you will be able to quickly resolve formatting issues that come up.

Here is why dates are a problem. First, Excel stores dates as the number of days since January 1, 1900. For example, June 30, 2011, is 40724 days after 1/1/1900. When you enter 6/30/2011 in a cell, Excel secretly converts this entry to 40724 and formats the cell to display a date instead of the value. So far, so good. The problem arises when you try to calculate something based on the date.

When you try to perform a calculation on two cells when the first cell is formatted as currency and the second cell is formatted as fixed numeric with three decimals, Excel has to decide if the new cell inherits the currency format or the fixed with three decimals format. These rules are hard to figure out. In any given instance, you might get the currency format or the fixed with three decimals format, or you might get the format previously assigned to the cell with the new formula. With numbers, a result of $80.52 or 80.521 look about the same. You can probably understand either format.

However, imagine that one of the cells is formatted as a date. Another cell contains the number 30. If you add the 30 to the date, which format does Excel use? If the cell containing the new formula happened to be previously assigned a numeric format, the answer suddenly switches from a date format to the numeric equivalent. This is frustrating. It is confusing. You start with June 30, 2011, add 30 days, and get an answer of 40754. This makes no sense to an Excel novice. It forces many people to give up on dates and start storing dates as text that look like dates. This is unfortunate because you can't easily do calculations on text cells that look like dates.

Here is a general guideline to remember: If you work with dates in the range of the years 2000 to 2020, those numeric equivalents are from 36,526 through 44,196. If you do some date math and get a strange answer in the 35,000–45,000 range, Excel probably has the right answer, but the numeric format of the answer cell is wrong. You need to select Date from the Number drop-down on the Home tab to correct the format.

The Excel method for storing dates is simple when you understand it. If you have a date cell and need to add 15 days to it, you add the number 15 to the cell. Every day is equivalent to the number 1, and every week is equivalent to the number 7. This is very simple to understand.

When you see 40359 instead of June 30, 2010, Excel calls the 40359 a *serial number*. Some of the Excel functions discussed here convert from a serial number to text that looks like a date, or vice versa.

For time, Excel adds a decimal to the serial number. There are 24 hours in a day. The serial number for 6 a.m. is 0.25. The serial number for noon is 0.5. The serial number for 6 p.m. is 0.75. The serial number for 3 p.m. on June 30, 2010, is 40359.625. To see how this works, try this out:

1. Open a blank Excel workbook.

2. In any cell, enter a number in the range of 35,000 to 45,000.

3. Add a decimal point and any random digits after the decimal.

4. Select that cell.

5. From the Home tab, select the dialog launcher in the lower-right corner of the Number group.

6. In the Date category, scroll down and select the format 3/14/01 1:30 PM. Excel displays your random number as a date and time. If the decimal portion of your number is greater than 0.5, the result will be in the p.m. portion of the day.

7. Go to another cell and enter the date you were born, using a four-digit year. (This doesn't work if you are older than 110).

8. Again select the cell and format it as a number. Excel converts to show how many days after the start of the last century you were born. This is great trivia but not necessarily useful.

The point is that Excel dates are nothing to be afraid of. You need to understand that behind the scenes, Excel is storing your dates as serial numbers and your times as decimal serial numbers. Occasionally, circumstances cause a date to be displayed as a serial number. Although this freaks some people out, it is easy to fix using the Format Cells dialog. Other times, when you want the serial number (for example, to calculate elapsed days between two dates), Excel converts the serial number to a date, indicating, for example, that an invoice is past due by "February 15 1900" days. When you get these types of non sequiturs, you can visit the Format Cells dialog.

🎙 caution

Although most Excel date issues can be resolved with formatting, you should be aware of some real date problems:

On a Macintosh, Excel dates are stored since January 1, 1904. If you are using a Mac, your serial number for a date in 2010 will be different from that on a Windows PC. Excel handles this conversion when files are moved from one platform to another.

- Excel dates cannot handle dates in the 1800s or before. This really hacks off all my friends who do genealogy. If your Great-Great-Great Uncle Silas was born on February 17, 1895, you are going to have to store that as text.

- Excel dates from January 1, 1900, through March 1, 1900, are generally wrong. See Figure 11.34 and the following sidebar for more details.

- Around Y2K, someone decided that 1930 is the dividing line for two digit years. If you enter a date with a two-digit year, the result is in the range of 1930 through 2029. If you enter 12/31/29, this will be interpreted as 2029. If you enter 1/1/30, it will be interpreted as 1930. If you need to enter a mortgage ending date of 2040, for example, be sure to use the four digit year, 6/15/2040.

Figure 11.34
A team of astronomers probably worked for hours to calculate what now takes seconds in Excel.

B17			fx	=TIME(5,48,46)					
A	B	C	D	E	F	G	H	I	J

1 **If Sisogenes Used Excel**

3 Sisogenes calculated that the trip around the sun took 365 days, 5 hours, 48 minutes, 46 seconds.

5 If you simply had a 365 day year without leap years, then the 5 hour error each year would add up.
6 In the 2055 years since Sisogenes, the calendar would be off by 497 days!
7 2055   5:48   497.72 =A7*B7

9 But, Sisogenes rounded the error off to 6 hours per year. Over time, this 11 minute 14 second error caused
10 the calendar to shift by 12 days. Pope Gregory added 11 days back to the calendar in 1582.
11 1627   0:11:14   12.69 *1582 is 1627 years after Sisogenes decided to ignore the 11 minutes*

13 Pope Gregory's astronomers figured that for every 400 years, the Julian Leap Year would
14 add 100 days, which is 3.12 days too many! They rounded this off and created a system
15 where 3 leap years out of every 400 would be skipped.
16 Years
17 400   5:48 AM   96.88 *Actual adjustment required every 400 years*
18 400   6:00 AM   100.00 *Adjustment if you had a leap year every 4 years*
19   -3.12 *Number of days to adjust every 400 years*

21 Even with the Gregorian calendar, we will gain 0.12 days every 400 years. Future civilizations
22 will have to implement a one day correction again in the year 4915.
23   8.3333333   3333.333   4915.333

Blame It on Sisogenes

The programmer who designed Lotus 1-2-3 was not a date fanatic.

Back in 45 BC, an astronomer named Sisogenes calculated that the earth took 365 days, 5 hours, 48 minutes, and 46 seconds to travel around the sun. He advised Julius Caesar that this was "close enough" to 365.25 days, and the leap year was born.

This worked through Caesar's lifetime. But those missing 11 minutes and 14 seconds began to add up. By 1582, things were out of whack by about 11 days. The spring equinox was falling on March 10 instead of March 21.

Pope Gregory mandated that the calendar jump by 11 days. In Catholic countries, they went from October 4, 1582, to October 15, 1582. Other countries, though, resisted the change. England finally added the 11 days in 1752. Russia added them in 1918. Historians note that there was rioting over the change (possibly from all the people who lost out on their birthday cake?).

To prevent further rioting, Gregory proposed that we skip three leap years out of every 400 years. This led to some arcane rules for leap years:

- Leap years happen in years divisible by 4.
- Leap years are skipped if the year is divisible by 100.
- Leap years are not skipped if the year is divisible by 400.

The date February 29, 2000, was actually an exception to an exception to an exception to an exception. But everyone thought it was just another leap year.

The problem is that there was no leap year in 1900. The programmer working on Lotus 1-2-3 in Mitch Kapor's Cambridge basement didn't know this rule and programmed a 2/29/1900 into Lotus 1-2-3.

By the late 1980s, there were millions of Lotus spreadsheets created that had dates in them. Any competitor to Lotus had to ensure that its program would come up with the exact same result as the industry-standard Lotus 1-2-3. This forced Excel, Quattro, and others to program the same error into their packages. Now, billions of spreadsheets exist with dates in them. If Microsoft ever corrects this problem, there will again be rioting in the streets.

The odds of this problem actually affecting you are slim. You would need to be calculating a date span from before February 28, 1900, to after March 1, 1900. Because Excel can handle dates going back only to January 1, 1900, only 49 possible starting dates can cause problems.

Understanding Excel Date and Time Formats

It is worthwhile to learn the various Excel custom codes for date and time formats. Figure 11.35 shows a table of how March 5 would be displayed in various numeric formats. The codes in A4:A13 show the possible codes for displaying just date, month, or year. Most people know the classic mm/dd/yyyy format, but far more formats are available. You can cause Excel to spell out the month and weekday by using codes such as dddd, mmmm d, yyyy. These are the possibilities:

	A	B	C
	B4 ▾	f_x =TEXT($A$1,A4)	
1	3/5/2011		
2			
3	**FORMAT**	**DISPLAYS AS**	**NOTE**
4	m	3	*1 or 2 digit month as needed*
5	mm	03	*Always 2 digits for month*
6	mmm	Mar	*3 letter month abbreviation*
7	mmmm	March	*Spell out the month*
8	mmmmm	M	*1st text - for JFMAMJJASOND*
9	d	5	*1 or 2 digit day as needed*
10	dd	05	*Always 2 digits for day*
11	ddd	Sat	*3 letter day abbreviation*
12	dddd	Saturday	*Spell out the weekday*
13	yy	11	*2 digits for year*
14	yyyy	2011	*4 digits for year*
15	mm/dd/yyyy	03/05/2011	
16	mmm d, yy	Mar 5, 11	
17	d-mmmm-yyyy	5-March-2011	

Figure 11.35
Any of these custom date format codes can be typed in the Custom Numeric Format box.

mm—Displays the month with two digits. Months before October are displayed with a leading zero (for example, January is 01).

m—Displays the month with one or two digits, as necessary.

mmm—Displays a three-letter abbreviation for the month (for example, Jan, Feb).

mmmm—Spells out the month (for example, January, February).

mmmmm—First letter of the month, useful for creating "JFMAMJJASOND" chart labels.

dd—Displays the day of the month with two digits. Dates earlier than the 10th of the month are displayed with a leading zero (for example, the 1st is 01).

d—Displays the day of the month with one or two digits, as needed.

ddd—Displays a three-letter abbreviation for the name of the weekday (for example, Mon, Tue).

dddd—Spells out the name of the weekday (for example, Monday, Tuesday).

yy or y—Uses two digits for the year (for example, 07).

yyyy or yyy—Uses four digits for the year (for example, 2007).

You are allowed to string together any combination of these codes with a space, comma, slash, or dash. It is valid to repeat a portion of the date format. For example, the format dddd, mmmm d, yyyy shows the day portion twice in the date and would display as Monday, March 5, 2011.

Although the date formats are mostly intuitive, several difficulties exist in the time formats. The first problem is the M code. Excel has already used M to mean month. In a time format, you cannot use M alone to mean minutes. The M code must either be preceded or followed by a colon.

There is another difficulty: When you are dealing with years, months, and days, it is often perfectly valid to mention only one of the portions of the date without the other two. It is common to hear any of these statements:

- "I was born in 1965."

- "I am going on vacation in July."

- "I will be back on the 27th."

If you have a date such as March 5, 2011, and use the proper formatting code, Excel happily tells you that this date is March or 2011 or the 5th. Technically, Excel is leaving out some really important information—the 5th of what? As humans, we can often figure out that this probably means the 5th of the next month. Thus, we aren't shocked that Excel is leaving off the fact that it is March 2011.

 tip

Custom number formats are entered in the Format Cells dialog. There are three ways to display this dialog:

1. Press Ctrl+1.

2. From the Home tab, in the Number group, select the drop-down and select More from the bottom of the drop-down.

3. Click the expand icon in the lower-right corner of the Number group on the Home tab.

When the Format Cells dialog is displayed, you select the Number tab. In the Category list, you select Custom. In the Type box, you enter your custom format. The Sample box displays the active cell with the format applied.

Imagine how strange it would be if Excel did this with regular numbers. Suppose you have the number 352. Would Excel ever offer a numeric format that would display just the tens portion of the number? If you put 352 in a cell, would Excel display 5 or 50? It would make no sense.

Excel treats time as an extension of dates and is happy to show you only a portion of the time. This can cause great confusion. To Excel, 40 hours really means 1 day and 16 hours. If you create a timesheet in Excel and format the total hours for the week as H:MM, Excel thinks that you are purposefully leaving off the day portion of the format! Excel presents 45 hours as just 21 hours because it assumes you can figure out there is 1 day from the context. But our brains don't work that way; 21 hours means 21 hours, not 1 day and 21 hours.

To overcome this problem in Excel, you use square brackets. Surrounding any time element with square brackets tells Excel to include all greater time/date elements in that one element, as in the following examples:

- 5 days and 10 hours in [H] format would be 130.

- 5 days and 10 hours in [M] format would be 7,800, to represent that many minutes.

- 5 days and 10 hours in [S] format would be 468,000, to represent that many seconds.

As shown in Figure 11.36, the time formatting codes include h, hh, s, ss, :mm, and mm:, all of which can be modified with square brackets.

	A	B	C	D	E
	B4	fx =TEXT($A$1,A4)			
1	20:05:07				
2					
3	**FORMAT**	**DISPLAYS AS**	**NOTE**		
4	h	20	*1 or 2 digit hour as needed*		
5	hh	20	*Always 2 digits for hour*		
6	h:mm	20:05	*1 or 2 digit hour as needed*		
7	hh:mm	20:05	*Always 2 digits for hour*		
8	h:mm:ss	20:05:07	*Hours, minutes, seconds in military time*		
9	h:m:s	20:5:7	*Strange looking, but a valid code*		
10	s	7	*Seconds, using 1 or 2 digits*		
11	ss	07	*Seconds, using 2 digits*		
12	h:mm AM/PM	8:05 PM	*Hours and minutes with AM or PM*		
13	[h]:mm	44:05	*Include any full days as hours*		
14	[m]	2645	*Include any hours or days as minutes*		
15	[s]	158707	*Include any days, hours or minutes as seconds*		
16	mm.ss.00	05.07.00	*Show decimal portions of seconds*		

Figure 11.36
Custom time format codes.

To display date and time, you enter the custom date format code, a space, and then the time format code.

Examples of Date and Time Functions

In all the examples in the following sections, you should use care to ensure that the resulting cell is formatted using the proper format, as discussed in the preceding section.

Using NOW and TODAY to Calculate the Current Data and Time or Current Date

There are a couple keyboard shortcuts for entering date and time. Pressing Ctrl+; enters the current date in a cell. Pressing Ctrl+: enters the current time in a cell. However, both of these hotkeys create a static value; that is, the date or time reflects the instant that you typed the hotkey, and it never changes in the future.

Excel offers two functions for calculating the current date: NOW and TODAY. These functions are excellent for figuring out the number of days until a deadline or how late an open receivable might be.

Syntax:

`=NOW() and TODAY()`

NOW returns the serial number of the current date and time. TODAY returns the serial number of the current date. The TODAY function returns today's date, without any time attached. The NOW function returns the current date and time.

Both of these functions can be made to display the current date, but there is an important distinction when you are performing calculations with the functions.

In Figure 11.37, Column A contains NOW functions, and Column C contains TODAY functions. Row 2 is formatted as a date and time. Row 3 is formatted as a date. Row 4 is formatted as numeric. Cell A3 and C3 look the same. If you need to display the date without using it in a calculation, then NOW or TODAY work fine.

 caution

It would be nice if NOW() would function like a real-time clock, constantly updating in Excel. However, the result is calculated when the file is opened, with each press of the F9 key, and when an entry is made elsewhere in the worksheet.

Row 8 calculates the number of days until a deadline approaches. Although most people would say that tomorrow is 1 day away, the formula in A8 would tend to say that the deadline is 0.6969 days away. This can be deceiving. If you are going to use the result of NOW or TODAY in a date calculation, you should use TODAY to prevent Excel from reporting fractional days. The formula in A8 is =A7-A3, formatted as numeric instead of a date.

	A2	▾	fx	=NOW()	
	A	B	C	D	
1	**NOW()**		**TODAY()**	Comment	
2	11/14/09 7:18 AM		11/14/09 12:00 AM	*Formatted as Date/Time*	
3	11/14/09		11/14/09	*Formatted as Date*	
4	40131.3045		40131.0000	*Formatted as Serial Number*	
5					
6					
7	1/15/2010		1/15/2010	*Deadline*	
8	61.6955		62.0000	*Days Until Deadline*	

Figure 11.37
NOW and TODAY can be made to look alike, but you need to choose the proper one if you are going to be using the result in a later calculation.

Using YEAR, MONTH, DAY, HOUR, MINUTE, and SECOND to Break a Date/Time Apart

If you have a column of dates in July 2011, you can easily make them all look the same by using the MMM-YY format. However, the dates in the actual cells are still different. The July 2011 records are not sorted as if they were a tie. Excel offers six functions that you can use to extract a single portion of the date: YEAR, MONTH, DAY, HOUR, MINUTE, and SECOND.

In Figure 11.38, cell A1 contains a date and time. Functions in A3 through A8 break out the date into components:

- =YEAR(date) returns the year portion as a four-digit year.
- =MONTH(date) returns the month number, from 1 through 12.
- =DAY(date) returns the day of the month, from 1 through 31.
- =HOUR(date) returns the hour, from 1 to 24.
- =MINUTE(date) returns the minute, from 1 to 60.
- =SECOND(date) returns the second, from 1 to 60.

In each case, *date* must contain a valid Excel serial number for a date. The cell containing the date serial number may be formatted as a date or as a number.

Using DATE to Calculate a Date from Year, Month, and Day

The DATE function is one of the most amazing functions in Excel. Microsoft's implementation of this function is excellent, allowing you to do amazing date calculations.

Figure 11.38
These six functions allow you to isolate any portion of a date or time.

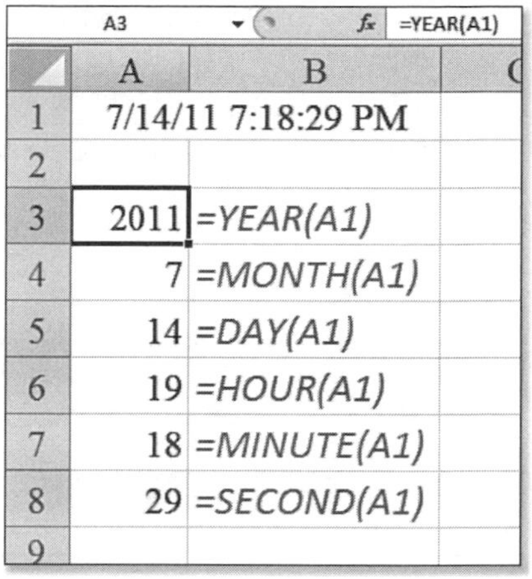

Syntax:

=DATE(*year,month,day*)

The DATE function returns the serial number that represents a particular date. This function takes the following arguments:

- *year*—This argument can be one to four digits. If *year* is between 0 and 1899 (inclusive), Excel adds that value to 1900 to calculate the year. For example, =DATE(100,1,2) returns January 2, 2000 (1900+100). If year is between 1900 and 9999 (inclusive), Excel uses that value as the year. For example, =DATE(2000,1,2) returns January 2, 2000. If *year* is less than 0 or is 10000 or greater, Excel returns a #NUM! error.

- *month*—This is a number representing the month of the year. If month is greater than 12, month adds that number of months to the first month in the year specified. For example, =DATE(1998,14,2) returns the serial number representing February 2, 1999.

- *day*—This is a number representing the day of the month. If *day* is greater than the number of days in the month specified, day adds that number of days to the first day in the month. For example, =DATE(1998,1,35) returns the serial number representing February 4, 1998. In a trivial example, =DATE(2011,3,5) returns March 5, 2011.

The true power in the DATE function occurs when one or more of the year, month, or day are calculated values. Here are some examples:

- If Cell A2 contains an invoice date and you want to calculate the day one month later, you use =DATE(Year(A2),Month(A2)+1,Day(A2)).

- To calculate the beginning of the month, you use =DATE(Year(A2),Month(A2),1).

- To calculate the end of the month, you use =DATE(Year(A2),Month(A2)+1,1)-1.

The DATE function is amazing because it enables Excel to deal perfectly with invalid dates. If your calculations for month cause it to exceed 12, this is no problem. For example, if you ask Excel to calculate =DATE(2010,16,45), Excel considers the 16th month of 2010 to be April 2011. To find the 45th day of April 2011, Excel moves ahead to May 15, 2011.

Figure 11.39 shows various results of the DATE and TIME functions.

D2		fx	=DATE(A2,B2,C2)

	A	B	C	D
1	Year	Month	Day	DATE
2	2010	16	45	5/15/2011
3	2012	1	60	2/29/2012
4	2013	1	60	3/1/2013
5	2011	3	5	3/5/2011
6				
7				
8	Hour	Minute	Second	TIME
9	1	12	23	1:12:23 AM
10	13	12	23	1:12:23 PM
11	12	72	23	1:12:23 PM
12	37	12	23	1:12:23 PM
13				

Figure 11.39
The formulas in Column D use DATE or TIME functions to calculate an Excel serial number from three arguments.

Using TIME to Calculate a Time

The TIME function is similar to the DATE function. It calculates a time serial number given a specific hour, minute, and second.

Syntax:

=TIME(hour,minute,second)

The TIME function returns the decimal number for a particular time. The decimal number returned by TIME is a value ranging from 0 to 0.99999999, representing the times from 0:00:00 (12:00:00 a.m.) to 23:59:59 (11:59:59 p.m.). This function takes the following arguments:

- *hour*—This is a number from 0 to 23, representing the hour.

- *minute*—This is a number from 0 to 59, representing the minute.

- *second*—This is a number from 0 to 59, representing the second.

As with the DATE function, Excel can handle situations in which the minute or second argument calculates to more than 60. For example, =TIME(12,72,120) evaluates to 1:14 PM.

Additional examples of TIME are shown in the bottom half of Figure 11.39 in the preceding section.

Using DATEVALUE to Convert Text Dates to Real Dates

It is easy to end up with a worksheet full of text dates. Sometimes this is due to importing data from another system. Sometimes it is caused by someone not understanding how dates work.

If your dates are in many conceivable formats, you can use the DATEVALUE function to convert the text dates to serial numbers, which can then be formatted as dates.

Syntax:

=DATEVALUE(*date_text*)

The DATEVALUE function returns the serial number of the date represented by *date_text.* You use DATEVALUE to convert a date represented by text to a serial number. The argument *date_text* is text that represents a date in an Excel date format. For example, "1/30/1998" and "30-Jan-1998" are text strings within quotation marks that represent dates. Using the default date system in Excel for Windows, date_text must represent a date from January 1, 1900, to December 31, 9999.

DATEVALUE returns a #VALUE! error if *date_text* is out of this range. If the year portion of *date_text* is omitted, DATEVALUE uses the current year from your computer's built-in clock. Time information in *date_text* is ignored.

> **⚡ caution**
>
> The DATEVALUE function must be used with text dates. If you have a column of values in which some values are text and some are actual dates, using DATEVALUE on the actual dates will cause a #VALUE error.

Any of the text values in Column A of Figure 11.40 are successfully translated to a date serial number. In this instance, Excel should have been smart enough to automatically format the resulting cells as dates. By default, the cells are formatted as numeric. This leads many people to believe that DATEVALUE doesn't work. You have to apply a date format to achieve the desired result.

Figure 11.40
The formulas in Column B use DATEVALUE to convert the text entries in Column A to date serial numbers.

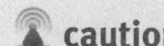

	A	B
1	TEXT	DATEVALUE
2	3/5/2011	40607
3	03/05/2011	40607
4	3/5/2011	40607
5	5-Mar-11	40607
6	Mar 5, 2011	40607
7	March 05, 2011	40607
8	03-05-2011	40607
9	3-5-2011	40607
10		

B2   *fx* =DATEVALUE(A2)

Using TIMEVALUE to Convert Text Times to Real Times

It is easy to end up with a column of text values that look like times. Similarly to DATEVALUE, you can use the TIMEVALUE function to convert these to real times.

Syntax:

=TIMEVALUE(*time_text*)

The TIMEVALUE function returns the decimal number of the time represented by a text string. The decimal number is a value ranging from 0 to 0.99999999, representing the times from 0:00:00 (12:00:00 a.m.) to 23:59:59 (11:59:59 p.m.). The argument time_text is a text string that represents a time in any one of the Microsoft Excel time formats. For example, "6:45 PM" and "18:45" are text strings within quotation marks that represent time. Date information in *time_text* is ignored.

The TIMEVALUE function is difficult to use because it is easy for a person to enter the wrong formats. In Figure 11.41, many people would interpret Cell A8 as meaning 45 minutes and 30 seconds. Excel, however, treats this as 45 hours and 30 minutes. This misinterpretation makes TIMEVALUE almost useless for a column of cells that contain a text representation of minute and seconds.

 The "Excel Troubleshooting" section later in this chapter discusses how to solve the problem of misinterpreting the TIMEVALUE function.

 caution

There are a few examples of text that DATEVALUE can not recognize. One common example is when there is no space after the comma. For example, "January 21,2011" will return an error. To solve this particular problem, use Replace to change a comma to a comma space.

 caution

There are a few examples of text that TIMEVALUE can not recognize. One common example is when there is no space before the AM or PM. For example, "11:00PM" will return an error. To solve this particular problem, use Replace to change "PM" to " PM" and to change "AM" to " AM".

Frustratingly, Excel does not automatically format the results of this function as a time. Column B shows the result as Excel presents it. Column C shows the same result after a time format has been applied.

	A	B	C
		B2 ▾ *fx* =TIMEVALUE(A2)	
1	**TEXT**	**TIMEVALUE**	**FORMATTED**
2	1:10	0.048611111	1:10:00 AM
3	1:10 AM	0.048611111	1:10:00 AM
4	1:10 PM	0.548611111	1:10:00 PM
5	13:10	0.548611111	1:10:00 PM
6	1:10:30	0.048958333	1:10:30 AM
7	1:45:30	0.073263889	1:45:30 AM
8	45:30	0.895833333	9:30:00 PM
9	0:45:30	0.031597222	12:45:30 AM
10			

Figure 11.41
The formulas in Column B use TIMEVALUE to convert the text entries in Column A to times. If there is no leading zero before entries with minutes and seconds, the formula produces an unexpected result.

Using WEEKDAY to Group Dates by Day of the Week

The WEEKDAY function would not be so intimidating if people could just agree how to number the days. This one function can give three different results.

Syntax:

=WEEKDAY(*serial_number*,*return_type*)

The WEEKDAY function returns the day of the week corresponding to a date. The day is given as an integer, ranging from 1 (Sunday) to 7 (Saturday), by default. This function takes the following arguments:

- *serial_number*—This is a sequential number that represents the date of the day you are trying to find. Dates may be entered as text strings within quotation marks (for example, "1/30/1998", "1998/01/30"), as serial numbers (for example, 35825, which represents January 30, 1998), or as results of other formulas or functions (for example, DATEVALUE("1/30/1998")).

- *return_type*—This is a number that determines the type of return value:

    - If *return_type* is 1 or omitted, WEEKDAY works like the calendar on your wall. Typically, calendars are printed with Sunday on the left and Saturday on the right. The default version of WEEKDAY numbers these columns from 1 through 7.

    - If *return_type* is 2, you are using the biblical version of WEEKDAY. In the biblical version, Sunday is the seventh day. Working backward, Monday must occupy the 1 position.

    - If *return_type* is 3, you are using the accounting version of WEEKDAY. In this version, Monday is assigned a value of 0, followed by 1 for Tuesday, and so on. This version makes it very easy to group records by week. If Cell A2 contains a date, then A2-WEEKDAY(A2,3) converts the date to the Monday that starts the week.

Figure 11.42 shows the results of WEEKDAY for all three return types.

Figure 11.42
Columns B, C, and D compare the WEEKDAY function for the three different return_type values shown in Row 3.

		B4		*fx*	=WEEKDAY($A4,B$3)		

	A	B	C	D
1		*Return_Type ----->*		
3	**Date**	**1**	**2**	**3**
4	**Sunday, April 01, 2007**	1	7	6
5	**Monday, April 02, 2007**	2	1	0
6	**Tuesday, April 03, 2007**	3	2	1
7	**Wednesday, April 04, 2007**	4	3	2
8	**Thursday, April 05, 2007**	5	4	3
9	**Friday, April 06, 2007**	6	5	4
10	**Saturday, April 07, 2007**	7	6	5
11	**Sunday, April 08, 2007**	1	7	6
12				

Using WEEKNUM to Group Dates into Weeks

WEEKNUM is a disappointing function. It is disappointing because Microsoft does not perform the function correctly. Microsoft is probably keeping the calculation consistent with some earlier spreadsheets that started doing this incorrectly. However, it would be really easy for Microsoft to add a new pair of `return_type` arguments that would calculate WEEKNUM correctly.

Syntax:

=WEEKNUM(*serial_num,return_type*)

The WEEKNUM function returns a number that indicates where the week falls numerically within a year. This function takes the following arguments:

- *serial_num*—This is a date within the week.

- *return_type*—This is a number that determines on what day the week begins. The default is 1. If return_type is 1 or omitted, the week begins on Sunday. If return_type is 2, the week begins on Monday.

Figure 11.43 shows WEEKNUM for the first eight days of each year of the next eight years. Rows 11 through 18 show WEEKNUM with a *return_type* of 1, so the week starts on Sunday.

Look at Column C. The first day of the year is a Sunday. This works; Cells C11:C17 report the first seven days as Week 1, and Cell C18 reports Sunday, January 8, 2012, as the first day of the week for Week 2.

However, look at B11:B18. In this case, the year 2011 starts on a Saturday. The first day of the year is treated as Week 1. Excel says that Week 2 starts on January 2, 2011. It is horrible to have a one-day week starting your year. It guarantees that you will have a significant Week 53 at the end of the year.

There is an ANSI standard for week numbering. This system says that your Week 1 must have at least four days. In the ANSI system, Saturday, January 1, 2011, would be called Week 0. In this system, whichever week contains January 4 is considered Week 1.

Alternative Calendar Systems and DAYS360

There are many alternative calendar systems that you might have to work with in Excel. Here are some examples:

- Manufacturers often redefine a quarter as being composed of 13 workweeks, with the first 4 weeks being called Month 1, the next 4 weeks being Month 2, and the final 5 weeks being Month 3. This is known as a 4-4-5 calendar.

- Retailers use a special retail calendar composed of 52 7-day weeks. Each week ends on a Sunday. If you compare Week 7, Day 6 of one year to Week 7, Day 6 of another year, you are assured that you are comparing a Saturday to a Saturday and can have a like comparison.

- Some accounting systems use a 360-day calendar. In this type of system, the year is divided into 12 months of 30 days. There is special handling for months with 31 days. Unfortunately, U.S. and European accounting boards disagree on the special handling, so there are two sets of rules.

Figure 11.43
Excel calculates week numbers, but they are out of sync with the rest of the world.

	A	B	C	D	E	F	G	H
	H21	▾	fx	=WEEKNUM(H1,2)				
1	Fri 1/1/10	Sat 1/1/11	Sun 1/1/12	Tue 1/1/13	Wed 1/1/14	Thu 1/1/15	Fri 1/1/16	Sun 1/1/17
2	Sat 1/2/10	Sun 1/2/11	Mon 1/2/12	Wed 1/2/13	Thu 1/2/14	Fri 1/2/15	Sat 1/2/16	Mon 1/2/17
3	Sun 1/3/10	Mon 1/3/11	Tue 1/3/12	Thu 1/3/13	Fri 1/3/14	Sat 1/3/15	Sun 1/3/16	Tue 1/3/17
4	Mon 1/4/10	Tue 1/4/11	Wed 1/4/12	Fri 1/4/13	Sat 1/4/14	Sun 1/4/15	Mon 1/4/16	Wed 1/4/17
5	Tue 1/5/10	Wed 1/5/11	Thu 1/5/12	Sat 1/5/13	Sun 1/5/14	Mon 1/5/15	Tue 1/5/16	Thu 1/5/17
6	Wed 1/6/10	Thu 1/6/11	Fri 1/6/12	Sun 1/6/13	Mon 1/6/14	Tue 1/6/15	Wed 1/6/16	Fri 1/6/17
7	Thu 1/7/10	Fri 1/7/11	Sat 1/7/12	Mon 1/7/13	Tue 1/7/14	Wed 1/7/15	Thu 1/7/16	Sat 1/7/17
8	Fri 1/8/10	Sat 1/8/11	Sun 1/8/12	Tue 1/8/13	Wed 1/8/14	Thu 1/8/15	Fri 1/8/16	Sun 1/8/17
9								
10	WEEKNUM WITH RETURN_TYPE OF 1 (Week begins on Sunday)							
11	1	1	1	1	1	1	1	1
12	1	2	1	1	1	1	1	1
13	2	2	1	1	1	1	2	1
14	2	2	1	1	1	2	2	1
15	2	2	1	1	2	2	2	1
16	2	2	1	2	2	2	2	1
17	2	2	1	2	2	2	2	1
18	2	2	2	2	2	2	2	2
19								
20	WEEKNUM WITH RETURN_TYPE OF 2 (Week begins on Monday)							
21	1	1	1	1	1	1	1	1
22	1	1	2	1	1	1	1	2
23	1	2	2	1	1	1	1	2
24	2	2	2	1	1	1	2	2
25	2	2	2	1	1	2	2	2
26	2	2	2	1	2	2	2	2
27	2	2	2	2	2	2	2	2
28	2	2	2	2	2	2	2	2
29								

Out of these three alternative calendar systems, Excel handles only the 360-day calendar. Excel provides the DAYS360 function and the YEARFRAC function to deal with the date system.

Syntax:

=DAYS360(*start_date,end_date,method*)

The DAYS360 function returns the number of days between two dates, based on a 360-day year (12 30-day months), which is used in some accounting calculations. You use this function to help compute payments if your accounting system is based on 12 30-day months. This function takes the following arguments:

- *start_date* and *end_date*—These are the two dates between which you want to know the number of days. If *start_date* occurs after *end_date*, DAYS360 returns a negative number. Dates may be entered as text strings within quotation marks (for example, "1/30/1998", "1998/01/30"), as serial numbers (for example, 35825, which represents January 30, 1998, if you're using the 1900 date system), or as results of other formulas or functions (for example, DATEVALUE("1/30/1998")).

- *method*—This is a logical value that specifies whether to use the U.S. or European method in the calculation:

- FALSE or omitted is a U.S. (National Association of Securities Dealers) method. If the starting date is the 31st of a month, it becomes equal to the 30th of the same month. If the ending date is the 31st of a month and the starting date is earlier than the 30th of a month, the ending date becomes equal to the 1st of the next month; otherwise, the ending date becomes equal to the 30th of the same month.

- TRUE is a European method. Starting dates or ending dates that occur on the 31st of a month become equal to the 30th of the same month.

Using YEARFRAC or DATEDIF to Calculate Elapsed Time

If you work in a human resources department, you might be concerned with years of service in order to calculate a certain benefit. Excel provides one function, YEARFRAC, that can calculate decimal years of service in five different ways. An old function, DATEDIF, has been hanging around since Lotus 1-2-3; it can calculate the difference between two dates in complete years, months, or days.

Syntax:

=YEARFRAC(start_date,end_date,basis)

The YEARFRAC function calculates the fraction of the year represented by the number of whole days between two dates (start_date and end_date). You use the YEARFRAC worksheet function to identify the proportion of a whole year's benefits or obligations to assign to a specific term.

This function takes the following arguments:

- *start_date*—This is a date that represents the start date. Dates may be entered as text strings within quotation marks (for example, "1/30/1998", "1998/01/30"), as serial numbers (for example, 35825, which represents January 30, 1998, if you're using the 1900 date system), or as results of other formulas or functions (for example, DATEVALUE("1/30/1998")).

- *end_date*—This is a date that represents the end date.

- *basis*—This is the type of day count basis to use. Figure 11.44 compares the five types of basis available:

  - If *basis* is 0 or omitted, Excel uses a 30/360 plan, modified for American use. In this plan, the employee earns 1/360 of a year's credit on most days. The employee earns no service on the day after any 31st of the month. In a leap year, the employee earns 2/360 of a year for showing up on March 1. In a nonleap year, the employee earns 3/360 of a year for showing up on March 1.

  - If *basis* is 1, the actual number of elapsed days is divided by the actual number of days in the year. This method works well and ensures that the year fraction ends up being 1 on the anniversary date, whether it is a leap year.

- If *basis* is 2, the actual number of elapsed days is divided by 360. If someone would show up and work for 30 years straight for one employer, this method would give that person an extra 0.43 years of credit. Sisogenes would be spinning in his grave.

- If *basis* is 3, the actual number of elapsed days is divided by 365. This works great for three out of every four years. It is slightly wrong in leap years.

- If *basis* is 4, Excel uses a 30/360 plan, modified for European use. This is similar to the default basis of 0. In this plan, the employee gets no credit for working any 31st of the month. The employee still gets triple credit for working March 1 (to make up for the 29th and 30th of February). In a leap year, March 1 is worth only double credit.

Syntax:

=DATEDIF(*start_date,end_date,unit*)

In contrast to YEARFRAC, the DATEDIF function calculates complete years, months, or days. This function calculates the number of days, months, or years between two dates. It is provided for compatibility with Lotus 1-2-3. This function takes the following arguments:

- *start_date*—This is a date that represents the first, or starting, date of the period. Dates may be entered as text strings within quotation marks (for example, "2001/1/30"), as serial numbers, or as the results of other formulas or functions (for example, DATEVALUE("2001/1/30")).

- *end_date*—This is a date that represents the last, or ending, date of the period.

- *unit*—This is the type of information you want returned. The various values for unit are shown in Table 23.6.

⚡ caution

DATEDIF has been in Excel forever, but it was only documented in Excel 2000. Why doesn't Microsoft reveal DATEDIF in help? Probably because of the strange anomaly when you try to calculate the gap from the 31st of January to the 1st of March in a nonleap year.

The "D" version of DATEDIF reports this as 29 days. This is correct.

The "M" version of DATEDIF reports this as one full month. This has to be correct, because the dates span the entire month of February.

The "MD" version of DATEDIF reports this as a negative 2 days in excess of a full month. See cell D9 in Figure 11.45. This is simply the downside of trying to express a measurement in months, when the length of a month is not constant. Negative values for the MD version of DATEDIF will happen only when the end date is March 1 or March 2.

Despite this problem, for 363 days a year, DATEDIF remains an effective way to express a date delta as a certain number of years, months, and days.

Table 11.7 Unit Values Used by the `DATEDIF` Function

Unit Value	Description
Y	The number of complete years in the period. A complete year is earned on the anniversary date of the employee's start date.
M	The number of complete months in the period. This number is incremented on the anniversary date. If the employee was hired on January 18, that person has earned one month of service on the 18th of February. If an employee is hired on January 31, then she earns credit for the month when she shows up for work on the 1st after any month with fewer than 31 days.
D	The number of days in the period. This could be figured out by simply subtracting the two dates.
MD	The number of days, ignoring months and years. You could use a combination of two `DATEDIF` functions—one using `M` and one using `MD`—to calculate days.
YM	The number of months, ignoring years. You could use a combination of two `DATEDIF` functions—one using `Y` and one using `YM`— to calculate months.
YD	The number of days, ignoring complete years.

Figure 11.44 compares the five types of *`basis`* of `YEARFRAC` with the six unit values of `DATEDIF`. Each cell uses $A$1 as the start date and that row's Column A as the end date.

J372 *fx* =DATEDIF($A$6,$A372,J$5)

	A	B	C	D	E	F	G	H	I	J	K	L	M
1	1/1/12	Basis - for YEARFRAC ---->						Unit - for DATEDIF ---->					
2		30/360	/Actual	/360	/365	30/360		Y	M	D	D^2	M^3	D^4
3		(Amer.)				(Euro)							
5	DATE	0	1	2	3	4		Y	M	D	MD	YM	YD
366	12/26/12	0.986	0.984	1.	0.986	0.986		0	11	360	25	11	360
367	12/27/12	0.989	0.986	1.003	0.989	0.989		0	11	361	26	11	361
368	12/28/12	0.992	0.989	1.006	0.992	0.992		0	11	362	27	11	362
369	12/29/12	0.994	0.992	1.008	0.995	0.994		0	11	363	28	11	363
370	12/30/12	0.997	0.995	1.011	0.997	0.997		0	11	364	29	11	364
371	12/31/12	1.	0.997	1.014	1.	0.997		0	11	365	30	11	365
372	1/1/13	1.	1.	1.017	1.003	1.		1	12	366	0	0	0
373													
374		*D^2 = days in excess of months*											
375		*M^3 = months in excess of full years*											
376		*D^4 = days in excess of full years*											
377													

Figure 11.44 If your benefits package includes information about complete months, then `YEARFRAC` with a basis value of 0 works best. Otherwise, a basis value of 1 is the most accurate.

Figure 11.45
In rare cases,
DATEDIF will report
1 month and -2
days.

	D8		▾	fx	=DATEDIF($D$3,$D$4,A8)						
	A	B	C	D	E	F	G	H	I	J	K	L
1	**Anomaly with DATEDIF...**										
2											
3			Start Date	1/31/2011							
4			End Date	3/1/2011							
5											
6	Y		Years:	0	Years (Y)						
7	YM		Months:	1	Months in Excess of Years (YM)						
8	MD		Days:	-2	Days in Excess of Months (MD)						
9	D		Days:	29	Days (D)						
10											
11	**...but it is still a cool function**										
12											
13			Start Date	2/17/1965							
14			End Date	6/30/2010							
15			Difference	45 years, 4 months, 13 days							
16	=DATEDIF(D15,D16,"Y")&" years, "&DATEDIF(D15,D16,"YM")&" months, "&DATEDIF(D15,D16,"MD")&" days"										

Using EDATE to Calculate Loan or Investment Maturity Dates

If someone invests in a 6-month CD on the 17th of the month, the maturity date is on the 17th of another month. This would be a fairly straightforward calculation if no one invested on the 31st of a month.

The maturity rules work such that if you invest on the 31st of a month, and the CD would be scheduled to mature on the 31st of June, the CD maturity actually happens on the last day of June, which is June 30.

If a CD is to mature on the 31st, 30th, or 29th day of February, the CD matures on the last day of February.

Syntax:

=EDATE(*start_date,months*)

The EDATE function returns the serial number that represents the date that is the indicated number of months before or after a specified date (that is, *start_date*). You use EDATE to calculate maturity dates or due dates that fall on the same day of the month as the date of issue. This function takes the following arguments:

- *start_date*—This is a date that represents the start date. Dates may be entered as text strings within quotation marks (for example, "1/30/1998", "1998/01/30"), as serial numbers (for example, 35825, which represents January 30, 1998, if you're using the 1900 date system), or as results of other formulas or functions (for example, DATEVALUE("1/30/1998")). If the *start_date* is not valid, EDATE returns a #NUM! error.

- *months*—This is the number of months before or after *start_date*. A positive value for months yields a future date; a negative value yields a past date. If months is not an integer, it is truncated.

Figure 11.46 shows several examples of EDATE. Note that in Column B, the function is a no-brainer. You could easily calculate it by using the DATE function. The only interesting cases occur on the 29th, 30th, and 31st of the month.

Note that EDATE can be used to back into an investment date from a maturity date. For example, the records in Rows 11 through 16 pass a negative number for the months parameter.

B4 =EDATE(B$3,$A4)

MATURITY DATES

Months	1/1/12	1/29/12	1/30/12	1/31/12
6	7/1/12	7/29/12	7/30/12	7/31/12
5	6/1/12	6/29/12	6/30/12	6/30/12
4	5/1/12	5/29/12	5/30/12	5/31/12
3	4/1/12	4/29/12	4/30/12	4/30/12
2	3/1/12	3/29/12	3/30/12	3/31/12
1	2/1/12	2/29/12	2/29/12	2/29/12
0	1/1/12	1/29/12	1/30/12	1/31/12
-1	12/1/11	12/29/11	12/30/11	12/31/11
-2	11/1/11	11/29/11	11/30/11	11/30/11
-3	10/1/11	10/29/11	10/30/11	10/31/11
-4	9/1/11	9/29/11	9/30/11	9/30/11
-5	8/1/11	8/29/11	8/30/11	8/31/11
-6	7/1/11	7/29/11	7/30/11	7/31/11

Figure 11.46
You can use EDATE to calculate the maturity date for a security.

Using EOMONTH to Calculate the End of the Month

Before Excel 2007, about 89 functions were available only in the Analysis Toolpack. Some companies had rules that you were not allowed to build spreadsheets using the functions in the Analysis Toolpack. This rule was probably created by some corporate executive who didn't know how to turn on the Analysis Toolpack!

One of my favorite puzzles at MrExcel.com came from someone who worked at such a company. How can you calculate the end of the month without using EOMONTH? This is a hard question; the end of the month is the 31st if the month number is 1, 3, 5, 7, 8, 10, or 12. It is the 30th if the month number is 4, 6, 9, or 11. If the month number is 2, then you have to look at the year to figure out if it is a leap year for 29 days or not a leap year for 28 days. The formula to solve this was horrible:

```
=DATE(YEAR(A2),MONTH(A2),CHOOSE(MONTH(A2),31,28,31,30,31,30,31,31,30,31,30,31)
    +IF(MOD(YEAR(A2),4)=0,1,0))
```

Well-known Excel guru Aladin Akyurek weighed in with the great answer and ended the entire discussion. Aladin suggested using the DATE function to move up to the first of the next month and then simply subtract one day, using this formula:

```
=DATE(YEAR(A2),MONTH(A2)+1,1)-1
```

The sheer simplicity of this is beautiful. However, the whole question becomes immaterial now that EOMONTH has been promoted to be part of the actual Excel function set.

Syntax:

`=EOMONTH(start_date,months)`

The EOMONTH function returns the serial number for the last day of the month that is the indicated number of months before or after *start_date*. You use EOMONTH to calculate maturity dates or due dates that fall on the last day of the month. This function takes the following arguments:

- *start_date*—This is a date that represents the starting date. Dates may be entered as text strings within quotation marks (for example, `"1/30/1998"`, `"1998/01/30"`), as serial numbers, or as results of other formulas or functions (for example, `DATEVALUE("1/30/1998")`). If *start_date* is not a valid date, EOMONTH returns a #NUM! error.

- *months*—This is the number of months before or after *start_date*. A positive value for months yields a future date; a negative value yields a past date. If months is not an integer, it is truncated. If *start_date* plus months yields an invalid date, EOMONTH returns a #NUM! error.

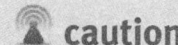

> **caution**
>
> You have to format the result of the EDATE formula to be a date to see the expected results.

`=EOMONTH(A2,0)` converts any date to the end of the month.

Using WORKDAY or NETWORKDAYS to Calculate Workdays

If you work in a service industry, allow me to apologize to you on behalf of Microsoft. If you work in retail, this section won't work for you. If you work any schedule where you don't have two consecutive days off, this won't work. The workday functions work only for those people whose work environment is a traditional Monday-through-Friday week. The new international versions of the workday functions allow for a 2-day weekend to occur on any two consecutive days of the week.

If you happen to be in a Monday-through-Friday environment, the functions WORKDAY and NETWORKDAYS are pretty cool. For example, they are great for calculating shipping days when you ship with FedEx or UPS. It takes a little work to get the holidays set up with these functions. Here's how you do it:

1. In an out-of-the-way section of a spreadsheet, enter any holidays that will fall during the work-week. This might be federal holidays, floating holidays, company holidays, and so on. The list of holidays can either be entered down a column or across a row. In the top portion of Figure 11.47, the holidays are in E2:E7 .

2. Enter a starting date in a cell, such as B1.

3. In another cell, enter the number of workdays that the project is expected to take, such as B2.

4. Enter the ending date formula as *=WORKDAY(B1,B2,E2:E7)*.

The NETWORKDAYS function takes two dates and figures out the number of workdays between them. For example, you might have a project that is due on June 17, 2011. If today is April 14, 2011, NETWORKDAYS can calculate the number of workdays until the project is due.

> **caution**
>
> You have to format the result of the EOMONTH formula to be a date to see the expected results.

Syntax:

=WORKDAY(*start_date,days,holidays*)

Syntax:

=NETWORKDAYS(*start_date,end_date,holidays*)

The NETWORKDAYS function returns the number of whole workdays between *start_date* and *end_date*. Workdays exclude weekends and any dates identified in holidays. You use NETWORKDAYS to calculate employee benefits that accrue based on the number of days worked during a specific term. This function takes the following arguments:

- *start_date*—This is a date that represents the start date. Dates may be entered as text strings within quotation marks (for example, "1/30/1998", "1998/01/30"), as serial numbers, or as results of other formulas or functions (for example, DATEVALUE("1/30/1998")).

- *end_date*—This is a date that represents the end date.

- holidays—This is an optional range of one or more dates to exclude from the working calendar, such as state and federal holidays and floating holidays. The list can be either a range of cells that contain the dates or an array constant of the serial numbers that represent the dates. If any argument is not a valid date, NETWORKDAYS returns a #NUM! error.

In Figure 11.47, the current date is entered in Cell B6. The project due date is entered in Cell B7. The holidays range is in E2:E7, as in the previous example. The formula in Cell B8 to calculate workdays is =NETWORKDAYS(B6,B7,E2:E7).

	A	B	C	D	E
	B3	▼ ● fx =WORKDAY(B1,B2,E2:E7)			
1	Start Date:	Monday, April 18, 2011			Holidays
2	# Work Days	65			1/1/2011
3	End Date:	Wednesday, July 20, 2011			5/30/2011
4		=WORKDAY(B1,B2,E2:E7)			7/4/2011
5					11/24/2011
6	Start Date:	Saturday, April 14, 2007			11/25/2011
7	End Date:	Monday, June 18, 2007			12/25/2011
8	# Work Days	46			
9		=NETWORKDAYS(B6,B7,E2:E7)			
10					

Figure 11.47
WORKDAY and NETWORKDAY can calculate the number of Monday-through-Friday days, exclusive of a range of holidays.

Excel in Practice: Converting a Holiday Range to an Array

The problem with putting the list of holidays in a range on a worksheet is that someone might accidentally overwrite or change the range of holidays.

The syntax for the workdays functions mentions that the holiday range can be converted to an array of serial numbers. To embed the holidays inside a function, you follow these steps:

1. In Figure 11.47, select cell B3.

2. In the formula bar, use the mouse to select the characters E2:E7.

3. Press the F9 key. Excel will replace the selected characters with the calculated version of those characters. In this case, the calculation is the array {40544;40693,etc.}, as shown in Figure 11.48.

4. Press Enter to accept the new formula.

5. You can now delete the holidays in column E.

Figure 11.48
You can remove the holiday cells from the worksheet after embedding the array in the formula.

	A	B	C	D	E	F	G
1	**Start Date:**	Monday, April 18, 2011			Holidays		
2	**# Work Days**	65			1/1/2011		
3	**End Date:**	=WORKDAY(B1,B2,{40544;40693;40728;40871;40872;40902})					
4		WORKDAY(start_date, days, [holidays])			7/4/2011		
5					11/24/2011		
6					11/25/2011		
7					12/25/2011		

Formula bar: =WORKDAY(B1,B2,{40544;40693;40728;40871;40872;40902})

Using International Versions of WORKDAY or NETWORKDAYS

Two new functions in Excel 2010 expand the WORKDAY and NETWORKDAYS functions for countries where the weekend is not Monday through Friday. The most common example is a weekend on Friday and Saturday which has become popular in Qatar, Bahrain, Kuwait, United Arab Emirates, and Algeria.

The international versions still require a consecutive two-day weekend.

Syntax:

=WORKDAY.INTL(*start_date,days,weekend,holidays*)

Syntax:

=NETWORKDAYS.INTL(*start_date,end_date,weekend,holidays*)

Both of these functions work as their noninternational equivalents, with the addition of having the weekend specified as two specific consecutive days of the week.

Here are the values for the weekend argument:

1—Weekend on Saturday and Sunday	11 – Sunday only
2—Weekend on Sunday and Monday	12 – Monday only
3—Weekend on Monday and Tuesday	13 – Tuesday only
4—Weekend on Tuesday and Wednesday	14 – Wednesday only
5— Weekend on Wednesday and Thursday	15 – Thursday only
6— Weekend on Thursday and Friday	16 – Friday only
7— Weekend on Friday and Saturday	17 – Saturday only

Examples of Text Functions

When they think of Excel, most people think of numbers. Excel is great at dealing with numbers, and it lets you write formulas to produce new numbers. Excel offers a whole cadre of formulas for dealing with text.

You might sometimes be frustrated because you receive data from other users, and the text is not in the format you need. Or the mainframe might send customer names in uppercase, or the employee in the next department might put a whole address into a single cell. Excel provides text functions to deal with all these situations and more.

Joining Text with the Ampersand (&) Operator

Chapter 8 mentions the ampersand (&) operator, but it is worth mentioning again here because it is the most important tool for dealing with text. The & is an operator that you use to join text.

Suppose you have a worksheet with first name in Column A and last name in Column B, as shown in Figure 11.49. You need to put these names together in a single cell. If you use the formula =A2&B2 in Cell C2, Excel smashes the names together (for example, STEVENWOODWARD). Instead, you have to join three elements. In between A2 and B2, you need to join a single space in double quotes. The formula to do this is =A2&" "&B2.

Some people prefer to use the CONCATENATE function instead of the &. This function does not perform the way that I want it to perform, and I generally avoid it, but it is described in the following section.

Syntax:

=CONCATENATE (*text1,text2,...*)

The CONCATENATE function joins several text strings into one text string. The arguments *text1*, *text2,...* are 1 to 30 text items to be joined into a single text item. The text items can be text strings, numbers, or single-cell references.

The problem with this function is that it can select only single cell references. An attempt to use =CONCATENATE(A2:B2) returns a #VALUE! error. If you have to enter =CONCATENATE(A2," ",B2),

Figure 11.49
The & character can be used to join text in cells or text enclosed in quotes.

	A	B	C
	C2	▼	fx	=A2&" "&B2
1	FIRST NAME	LAST NAME	NAME
2	STEVEN	WOODWARD	STEVEN WOODWARD
3	LINDSAY	RHODES	LINDSAY RHODES
4	VIVIAN	WALKER	VIVIAN WALKER
5	WALTER	SHAW	WALTER SHAW
6	MATTIE	PIERCE	MATTIE PIERCE
7	ELLEN	ATKINS	ELLEN ATKINS
8	MADELINE	MARTINEZ	MADELINE MARTINEZ

it is easier to use =A2&" "&B2. Further, the function can handle only 30 references. If you are joining cells with spaces in between, you will run out of terms after just 15 cells. With the &, you can join more than 30 items.

Using LOWER, UPPER, or PROPER to Convert Text Case

Three functions—LOWER, UPPER, and PROPER—convert text to or from capital letters. In Figure 11.50, the products in Column A were entered in a haphazard fashion. Some products used lowercase, and some products used uppercase. Column B uses =UPPER(A2) to make all the products a uniform uppercase.

In Cell E13, text was entered by someone who never turns off Caps Lock. You can convert this uppercase to lowercase with =LOWER(E13).

In Column E, you see a range of names in uppercase. You can use =PROPER(E2) to convert the name to proper case, which capitalizes just the first letter of each word. The PROPER function is mostly fantastic, but there are a few cells that you have to manually correct. PROPER does correctly capitalize names with apostrophes, such as O'Rasi in Cell F3. It does not, however, correctly capitalize the interior c in McCartney in Cell F4. The function is also notorious for creating company names such as Ibm, 3m, and Aep.

 note
If you want to keep the data only in Column C, you have to convert the formulas to values before deleting Columns A and B. To do this, select the data in Column C and then press Ctrl+C to copy. Then select Home, Paste, Paste Values to convert the formulas to values.

 note
It would be great if Microsoft would add a function to convert to sentence case. We can hope to find such a function in future versions of Excel.

Syntax:

=LOWER(*text*)

The LOWER function converts all uppercase letters in a text string to lowercase. The argument text is the text you want to convert to lowercase. LOWER does not change characters in text that are not letters.

	F2		▾	fx	=PROPER(E2)		
	A	B	C	D	E	F	G
1	Quantity	Product	Upper		NAME	Proper	
2	2	q754	Q754		ERIN RICHMOND	Erin Richmond	
3	1	g644	G644		JACK O'RASI	Jack O'Rasi	
4	5	G644	G644		KEITH MCCARTNEY	Keith Mccartney	
5	4	q754	Q754		ERNEST CURTIS	Ernest Curtis	
6	7	Q754	Q754		LEAH HARRISON	Leah Harrison	
7	7	d350	D350		ALLISON BRIGGS	Allison Briggs	
8	1	Q754	Q754		STEVEN CARR	Steven Carr	
9	1	g644	G644		TERRI HARDY	Terri Hardy	
10	3	G644	G644		KYLE SANCHEZ	Kyle Sanchez	
11	2	n870	N870		RYAN PITTS	Ryan Pitts	
12	3	q754	Q754				
13	4	d350	D350		MY MANAGER TYPES IN ALL CAPITALS		
14	8	q754	Q754		my manager types in all capitals		
15	5	I175	I175				
16	2	i175	I175				
17	3	i175	I175				
18							
19	C2: =UPPER(B2)						
20	E14: =LOWER(E13)						
21							

Figure 11.50
UPPER, LOWER, and PROPER can convert text to and from capital letters.

Syntax:

=PROPER(*text*)

The PROPER function capitalizes the first letter in a text string and any other letters in text that follow any character other than a letter. It converts all other letters to lowercase letters.

The argument *text* is text enclosed in quotation marks, a formula that returns text, or a reference to a cell containing the text you want to partially capitalize.

Syntax:

=UPPER(*text*)

The UPPER function converts text to uppercase. The argument *text* is the text you want converted to uppercase. text can be a reference or text string.

Using TRIM to Remove Trailing Spaces

If you frequently import data, you might be plagued with a couple of annoying situations. This section and the next one deal with those situations.

You may have trailing spaces at the end of text cells. Although "ABC" and "ABC" might look alike when viewed in Excel, they cause functions such as MATCH and VLOOKUP to fail. TRIM removes leading and trailing spaces.

In Figure 11.51, you can see a simple VLOOKUP in Column B. The formula in Cell B2 is =VLOOKUP(A2,$F$2:$G$5,2,FALSE). Even though you can clearly see that M40498 is in the lookup table, VLOOKUP returns an #N/A! error, indicating that the product ID is missing from the lookup table.

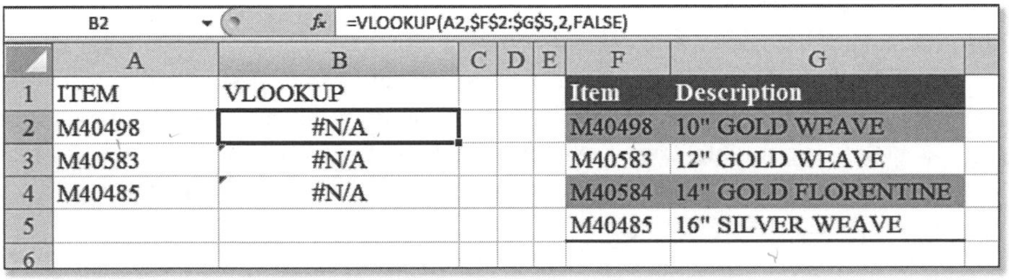

Figure 11.51
This VLOOKUP should work, but in this instance, it fails.

To diagnose and correct this problem, follow these steps:

1. Select one of the data cells in Column F. Press the F2 key to put the cell in Edit mode. A flashing insertion character appears at the end of the cell. Check to see if the flashing cursor is immediately after the last character.

2. Select one of the data cells in Column A. Press the F2 key to put the cell in Edit mode. Note whether the flashing insertion character is immediately after the last character. Figure 11.52 shows that the products in Column A have several trailing spaces after them. The products in the lookup table do not have any trailing spaces.

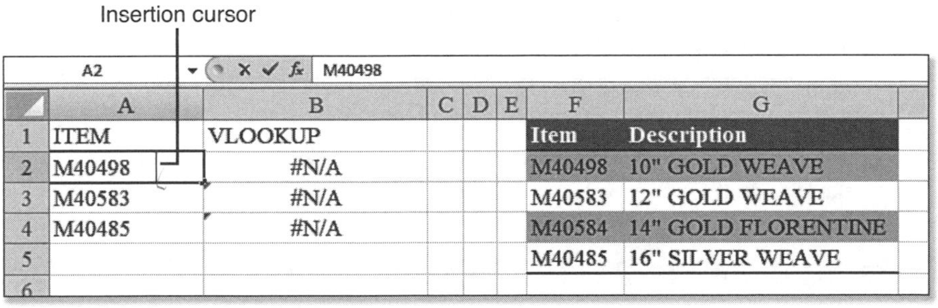

Figure 11.52
Spaces are padding the right side of the products in Column A.

Insertion cursor

3. If the problem is occurring in the values being looked up, you could modify the formula in Cell B2 to use the TRIM function. The new formula would be =VLOOKUP(TRIM(A2),$F$2:$G$5, 2,FALSE). Figure 11.53 shows how this solves the problem.

| B2 | ▼ | fx | =VLOOKUP(TRIM(A2),$F$2:$G$5,2,FALSE) |

	A	B	C	D	E	F	G
1	ITEM	VLOOKUP				Item	Description
2	M40498	10" GOLD WEAVE				M40498	10" GOLD WEAVE
3	M40583	12" GOLD WEAVE				M40583	12" GOLD WEAVE
4	M40485	16" SILVER WEAVE				M40584	14" GOLD FLORENTINE
5						M40485	16" SILVER WEAVE
6							

Figure 11.53
Using TRIM to remove leading spaces allows VLOOKUP to work.

4. If the problem is occurring in the first column of the lookup table, insert a new temporary column. Enter the function =TRIM(F2) in the temporary column. Copy this formula down to all rows of the lookup table. Copy the new formulas and select Home, Paste, Values to paste the new values. Although the old and new values look the same, the TRIM function has removed the trailing spaces, and now the products match.

Syntax:

=TRIM(*text*)

The TRIM function removes all spaces from text except for single spaces between words. You use TRIM on text that you have received from another application that may have irregular spacing. The argument *text* is the text from which you want spaces removed.

In Figure 11.54, Cell C1 contains six letters: ABC DEF. You might assume that the cell is set to be centered. However, the formula in Cell C2 appends an asterisk to each end of the value in Cell C1. This formula shows that there are several leading and trailing spaces in the value.

Using =LEN(C1) shows that the text actually contains 15 characters instead of 6 characters. The TRIM(C1) formula removes any leading spaces, any trailing spaces, and any extra interior spaces. The function still leaves one space between ABC and DEF because you want to continue to have words separated by a single space.

 note
It is not necessarily efficient to calculate, but you can solve the trailing spaces in column F by using =VLOOKUP(A2,TRIM(F$ 2:G$5),2,FALSE) if you press Ctrl+Shift+Enter to accept the formula.

The formulas in Cells C5 and C6 confirm that the leading and trailing spaces are removed and that the length of the new value is only seven characters.

Using CLEAN to Remove Nonprintable Characters from Text

Although TRIM works great, the CLEAN function no longer works as advertised. CLEAN is designed to remove nonprintable characters from text.

Besides extra spaces, another annoying problem with data from other systems is that it may contain nonprintable characters. Excel offers a function that is supposed to remove nonprintable characters, but Microsoft's definition of a nonprintable character is far too narrow. The function was clearly written before the proliferation of web queries, Oracle, and SAP.

Figure 11.54
TRIM removes leading spaces and extra interior spaces.

	A	B	C
			ABC DEF
1		Original Value:	ABC DEF
2		="*"&C1&"*"	* ABC DEF *
3		Length(C1)	15
4		TRIM(C1)	ABC DEF
5		="*"&C4&"*"	*ABC DEF*
6		LENGTH(C4)	7
7			

Syntax:

=CLEAN(*text*)

The CLEAN function removes all nonprintable characters from text. You use CLEAN on text imported from other applications that contains characters that may not print with your operating system. For example, you can use CLEAN to remove some low-level computer code that is frequently at the beginning and end of data files and cannot be printed.

The argument *text* is any worksheet information from which you want to remove nonprintable characters.

Figure 11.55 shows data in Column A with characters that I routinely find in imported data. You might expect the CLEAN function in Column B to fix all these problems. If so, you will be highly disappointed. In the first pass, CLEAN did not clean any of the bad characters. After I edited Cell A2 to use a traditional nonprintable character, Cell B2 was able to clean that one character.

To figure out exactly how CLEAN works, you need the CHAR function, which is conveniently scheduled to be discussed next. Read on for more of the CLEAN saga.

Figure 11.55
CLEAN removes a short list of nonprintable characters. Unfortunately, today's data is littered with a new crop of nonprintable characters.

	A	B	C	D
		=CLEAN(A1)		
1	M40498Š	M40498Š		
2	M40583	M40583		
3	M40585	M40585		
4	M70193Š	M70193Š		
5	M70208Š	M70208Š		
6	E91310Š	E91310Š		
7	E91131Š	E91131Š		

Using the CHAR Function to Generate Any Character

Computers have the capability to display 255 different characters in any given font. For the past 20 years, this set of 255 characters has been known as the ASCII (pronounced "ask-key") character set. My U.S. keyboard gives me the capability to type 96 of those characters. The keyboard in another country may offer several more or fewer characters, but the point is that you cannot access all 255 characters by using your keyboard.

You might have ventured into Start, All Programs, Accessories, System Tools, Character Map to find a particular character in the Wingdings character set. Also, if you have a favorite symbol, you might have memorized that you can insert the symbol by using a hotkey. For example, if you hold down Alt, type 0169 on the numeric keypad, and then release Alt, an Office program inserts the copyright symbol (©).

Syntax:

`=CHAR(number)`

The CHAR function returns the character specified by a number. You use CHAR to translate code page numbers you might get from files on other types of computers into characters.

The argument *number* is a number between 1 and 255 that specifies which character you want. The character is from the character set used by your computer.

To figure out which characters were removed by the CLEAN function (refer to the preceding section), I built a table with the numbers from 1 through 255. In Figure 11.56, Column A contains the character number. Column B has the function `=CHAR(A2)` to display that character in the Times New Roman font. Column C has a formula to reveal whether CLEAN removes that character: `=IF(LEN(CLEAN(B2))=0,"YES","NOT)`. After you copy these formulas to all 255 rows, you will learn that CLEAN removes characters numbered 1 through 31, 129, 141, 144, and 157.

To fit in one screen of cells, Figure 11.56 shows all the codes arranged on one page.

If you see a strange character in your data, you can learn the character number by using the CODE function, as described in the following section.

 **tip**

Although I know a few characters off the top of my head, I usually take a look at all characters in a set by entering `=CODE(ROW())` in Cells A1:A255. This returns Character 65 in Row 65, and so on.

Using the CODE Function to Learn the Character Number for Any Character

Each font set offers 255 different characters, numbered from 1 through 255. Old-time computer folks might know some of the popular codes off the top of their heads. For example, a capital A is 65. The capital letters run from 65 to 90, a space is 32, a lowercase letter a is 97, and the other lowercase letters run from 98 through 122.

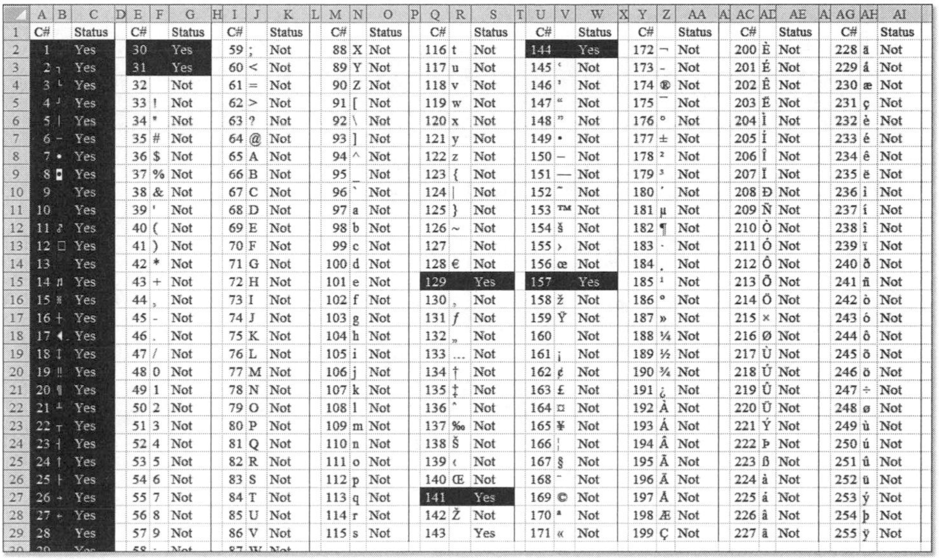

	A	B	C	E	F	G	I	J	K	M	N	O	Q	R	S	U	V	W	Y	Z	AA	AC	AD	AE	AG	AH	AI
1	C#		Status	C#		Status	C#		Status	C#		Status	C#		Status	C#		Status	C#		Status	C#		Status	C#		Status
2	1		Yes	30		Yes	59	;	Not	88	X	Not	116	t	Not	144		Yes	172	¬	Not	200	È	Not	228	ä	Not
3	2	┐	Yes	31		Yes	60	<	Not	89	Y	Not	117	u	Not	145	‘	Not	173	-	Not	201	É	Not	229	å	Not
4	3	└	Yes	32		Not	61	=	Not	90	Z	Not	118	v	Not	146	’	Not	174	®	Not	202	Ê	Not	230	æ	Not
5	4	┘	Yes	33	!	Not	62	>	Not	91	[	Not	119	w	Not	147	“	Not	175	¯	Not	203	Ë	Not	231	ç	Not
6	5	|	Yes	34	"	Not	63	?	Not	92	\	Not	120	x	Not	148	”	Not	176	°	Not	204	Ì	Not	232	è	Not
7	6	–	Yes	35	#	Not	64	@	Not	93	]	Not	121	y	Not	149	•	Not	177	±	Not	205	Í	Not	233	é	Not
8	7	•	Yes	36	$	Not	65	A	Not	94	^	Not	122	z	Not	150	–	Not	178	²	Not	206	Î	Not	234	ê	Not
9	8	◘	Yes	37	%	Not	66	B	Not	95	_	Not	123	{	Not	151	—	Not	179	³	Not	207	Ï	Not	235	ë	Not
10	9		Yes	38	&	Not	67	C	Not	96	`	Not	124	|	Not	152	˜	Not	180	´	Not	208	Ð	Not	236	ì	Not
11	10		Yes	39	'	Not	68	D	Not	97	a	Not	125	}	Not	153	™	Not	181	µ	Not	209	Ñ	Not	237	í	Not
12	11	♂	Yes	40	(	Not	69	E	Not	98	b	Not	126	~	Not	154	š	Not	182	¶	Not	210	Ò	Not	238	î	Not
13	12	□	Yes	41	)	Not	70	F	Not	99	c	Not	127		Not	155	›	Not	183	·	Not	211	Ó	Not	239	ï	Not
14	13		Yes	42	*	Not	71	G	Not	100	d	Not	128	€	Not	156	œ	Not	184	¸	Not	212	Ô	Not	240	ð	Not
15	14	♫	Yes	43	+	Not	72	H	Not	101	e	Not	129		Yes	157		Yes	185	¹	Not	213	Õ	Not	241	ñ	Not
16	15	☼	Yes	44	,	Not	73	I	Not	102	f	Not	130	‚	Not	158	ž	Not	186	º	Not	214	Ö	Not	242	ò	Not
17	16	┼	Yes	45	-	Not	74	J	Not	103	g	Not	131	ƒ	Not	159	Ÿ	Not	187	»	Not	215	×	Not	243	ó	Not
18	17	◄	Yes	46	.	Not	75	K	Not	104	h	Not	132	„	Not	160		Not	188	¼	Not	216	Ø	Not	244	ô	Not
19	18	↕	Yes	47	/	Not	76	L	Not	105	i	Not	133	…	Not	161	¡	Not	189	½	Not	217	Ù	Not	245	õ	Not
20	19	‼	Yes	48	0	Not	77	M	Not	106	j	Not	134	†	Not	162	¢	Not	190	¾	Not	218	Ú	Not	246	ö	Not
21	20	¶	Yes	49	1	Not	78	N	Not	107	k	Not	135	‡	Not	163	£	Not	191	¿	Not	219	Û	Not	247	÷	Not
22	21	┴	Yes	50	2	Not	79	O	Not	108	l	Not	136	ˆ	Not	164	¤	Not	192	À	Not	220	Ü	Not	248	ø	Not
23	22	┬	Yes	51	3	Not	80	P	Not	109	m	Not	137	‰	Not	165	¥	Not	193	Á	Not	221	Ý	Not	249	ù	Not
24	23	┤	Yes	52	4	Not	81	Q	Not	110	n	Not	138	Š	Not	166	¦	Not	194	Â	Not	222	Þ	Not	250	ú	Not
25	24	↑	Yes	53	5	Not	82	R	Not	111	o	Not	139	‹	Not	167	§	Not	195	Ã	Not	223	ß	Not	251	û	Not
26	25	├	Yes	54	6	Not	83	S	Not	112	p	Not	140	Œ	Not	168	¨	Not	196	Ä	Not	224	à	Not	252	ü	Not
27	26	→	Yes	55	7	Not	84	T	Not	113	q	Not	141		Yes	169	©	Not	197	Å	Not	225	á	Not	253	ý	Not
28	27	←	Yes	56	8	Not	85	U	Not	114	r	Not	142	Ž	Not	170	ª	Not	198	Æ	Not	226	â	Not	254	þ	Not
29	28		Yes	57	9	Not	86	V	Not	115	s	Not	143		Yes	171	«	Not	199	Ç	Not	227	ã	Not	255	ÿ	Not
30	29		Yes	58	:	Not	87	W	Not																		

Figure 11.56 This figure shows all CHAR values in the Times New Roman data set. Only the characters highlighted in black are removed by CLEAN.

In the early days of personal computers, every computer was packed with a list of the ASCII codes for each character. Today, with the character map, no one has to memorize character codes. However, in some instances, you might want to learn exactly what character you are seeing in a cell. The CODE function returns the character code for one character at a time.

Syntax:

=CODE(*text*)

The CODE function returns a numeric code for the first character in a text string. The returned code corresponds to the character set used by your computer. The argument *text* is the text for which you want the code of the first character. This is an important distinction. CODE returns the code for only the first character in a cell. =CODE("A") and =CODE("ABC") return only 65 to indicate the capital letter A.

A new problem began happening in Excel in the past few years. People started encountering values with which TRIM would not remove the spaces from the text. For example, Figure 11.57 shows a value in Column A that very clearly contains several spaces between the letters A and B.

For details using the CODE *function, see the "Syntax: MID(text,start_num,num_chars)" section later in this chapter.*

The CODE(D2) formula in Column E shows the character number for each character in the text. Things start out well enough, with a character 65 being returned for the A. They also end up okay, with a character 66 being returned for the B at the end in Row 9. However, all the middle characters are returning a character 160 instead of a typical space—character 32.

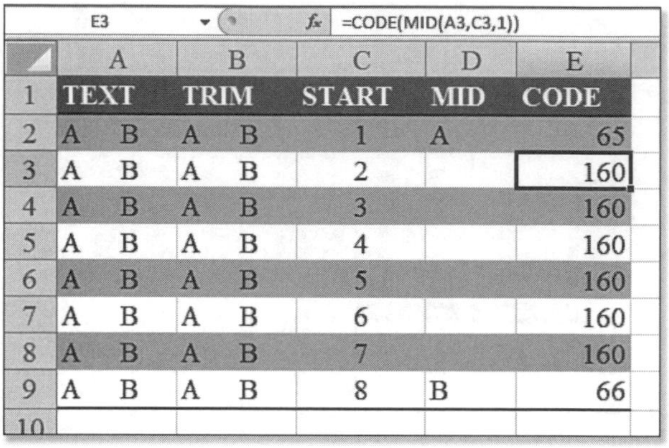

E3 | =CODE(MID(A3,C3,1))

	A	B	C	D	E
1	TEXT	TRIM	START	MID	CODE
2	A B	A B	1	A	65
3	A B	A B	2		160
4	A B	A B	3		160
5	A B	A B	4		160
6	A B	A B	5		160
7	A B	A B	6		160
8	A B	A B	7		160
9	A B	A B	8	B	66
10					

Figure 11.57
CODE is instrumental in learning why the TRIM function won't work on the data in Column A.

If you've ever created a small web page, you might have learned that browsers ignore consecutive spaces. If you really want to keep two words separated by four spaces, you need to use *Word 1   Word2*. I learned this trick somewhere on the Web and never really thought about what * * means. It turns out that it is a nonbreaking space. And, you guessed it, a nonbreaking space occupies character position 160, so it looks just like a space. Web designers use it all the time to format web pages. Consequently, it is ending up in data that people paste into Excel from the Web, and it is making it appear that TRIM does not always work.

> **note**
> Excel pros know that they can remove the extra interior spaces by using =TRIM(A2). But if you look at the formula in Cell B2, you see that TRIM is not removing the interior spaces. This requires some additional investigation, and CODE is the key to solving the problem. Because CODE can work on only the first character in a cell, formulas in Columns C and D isolate each character in the text.

Using LEFT, MID, or RIGHT to Split Text

One of the newer rules in information processing is that each field in a database should contain exactly one piece of information. Throughout the history of computers, there have been millions of examples of people trying to cram many pieces of information into a single field. Although this works great for humans, it is pretty difficult to have Excel sort a column by everything in the second half of a cell.

Column A in Figure 11.58 contains part numbers. As you might guess, the Part Number field contains two pieces of information: a three-character vendor code, a dash, and a five-digit part number.

When a customer comes in to buy a part, he probably doesn't care about the vendor. So the real question is, "Do you have anything in stock that can fix my problem?"

Excel offers three functions—LEFT, MID, and RIGHT—that allow you to isolate just the first or just the last characters, or even just the middle characters, from a column.

Figure 11.58
LEFT makes
quick work
of extract-
ing the
vendor code.
Several vari-
eties of MID
or RIGHT
extract the
part number.

	A	B	C	D	E	F	G	H	I	J
				=LEFT(A2,3)						
1	PART NUMBER	OH	OO	LEFT	MID					
2	RPM-104020	1	2	RPM	104020		Alternate choices for MID			
3	BOR-21862	1	0	BOR	21862		=MID(A2,5,100)			
4	LUK-04-158	3	1	LUK	04-158		=TRIM(MID(A2,5,100))			
5	BOR-10294E	1	0	BOR	10294E		=MID(A2,5,LEN(A2)-5)			
6	BOR-10643	3	2	BOR	10643		=RIGHT(A2,LEN(A2)-FIND("-",A2))			
7	BOR-10625B	1	2	BOR	10625B					
8	BOR-10635	1	0	BOR	10635		If the Vendor code was not always 3 letters:			
9	BOR-22816	3	1	BOR	22816		=LEFT(A2,FIND("-",A2)-1)			
10	BWW-BC42TF	0	0	BWW	BC42TF					
11	BOR-21764	0	1	BOR	21764					
12	BOR-10613A	2	0	BOR	10613A					

Syntax:

=LEFT(*text*,*num_chars*)

The LEFT function returns the first character or characters in a text string, based on the number of characters specified. This function takes the following arguments:

- *text*—This is the text string that contains the characters you want to extract.

- *num_chars*—This specifies the number of characters you want LEFT to extract. *num_chars* must be greater than or equal to zero. If *num_chars* is greater than the length of text, LEFT returns all of *text*. If num_chars is omitted, it is assumed to be 1.

Syntax:

=RIGHT(*text*,*num_chars*)

The RIGHT function returns the last character or characters in a text string, based on the number of characters specified. This function takes the following arguments:

- *text*—This is the text string that contains the characters you want to extract.

- *num_chars*—This specifies the number of characters you want RIGHT to extract. *num_chars* must be greater than or equal to zero. If num_chars is greater than the length of text, RIGHT returns all of *text*. If *num_chars* is omitted, it is assumed to be 1.

Syntax:

=MID(*text*,*start_num*,*num_chars*)

MID returns a specific number of characters from a text string, starting at the position specified, based on the number of characters specified. This function takes the following arguments:

- *text*—This is the text string that contains the characters you want to extract.

- *start_num*—This is the position of the first character you want to extract in text. The first character in text has *start_num* *1*, and so on. If *start_num* is greater than the length of text, MID returns " " (that is, empty text). If *start_num* is less than the length of text, but *start_num* plus *num_chars* exceeds the length of text, MID returns the characters up to the end of text. If *start_num* is less than 1, MID returns a #VALUE! error.

- *num_chars*—This specifies the number of characters you want MID to return from text. If *num_chars* is negative, MID returns a #VALUE! error.

In Figure 11.58, it is easy to extract the three-digit vendor code by using =LEFT(A2,3). It is a bit more difficult to extract the part number. As you scan through the values in Column A, it is clear that the vendor code is consistently three letters. With the dash in the fourth character of the text, it means that the part number starts in the fifth position. If you are using MID, you therefore use 5 as the *start_num* argument.

However, there are a few thousand part numbers in the data set. Right up front, in Cell A4, is a part number that breaks the rule. LUK-04-158 contains six characters after the dash. This might seem to be an isolated incident, but in Row 10, BWW-BC42TW also contains six characters after the dash. Because this type of thing happens in real life, two errors in the first nine records are enough to warrant a little extra attention. The four possible strategies for extracting the part number are listed in G2:G6. They are as follows:

- Ask MID to start at the fifth character and return a large enough number of characters to handle any possible length (that is, =MID(A2,5,100)).

- Ask MID to start at the fifth character but use TRIM around the whole function to prevent any trailing spaces from being included (that is, =TRIM(MID(A2,5,100))).

- Ask MID to start at the fifth character, but calculate the exact number of characters by using the LEN function (that is, =MID(A2,5,LEN(A2)-4)).

- Skip MID altogether and ask RIGHT to return all the characters after the first dash. This requires you to use the FIND function to locate the first dash—that is, =RIGHT(A2,LEN(A2)-FIND("-",A2)).

Using LEN to Find the Number of Characters in a Text Cell

It seems pretty obscure, but you will find the LEN function amazingly useful. The LEN function determines the length of characters in a cell, including any leading or trailing spaces.

Syntax:

`=LEN(text)`

The LEN function returns the number of characters in a text string. The argument text is the text whose length you want to find. Spaces count as characters.

There are instances in which LEN can be used in conjunction with LEFT, MID, or RIGHT to isolate a portion of text.

➡️ *To review information on this topic, refer back to the example in the previous section.*

LEN can also be used to find records that are longer than a certain limit. Suppose you are about to order nameplates for company employees. Each nameplate can accommodate 15 characters. In Figure 11.59, you add the LEN function next to the names and sort by the length, in descending order. Any problem names appear at the top of the list.

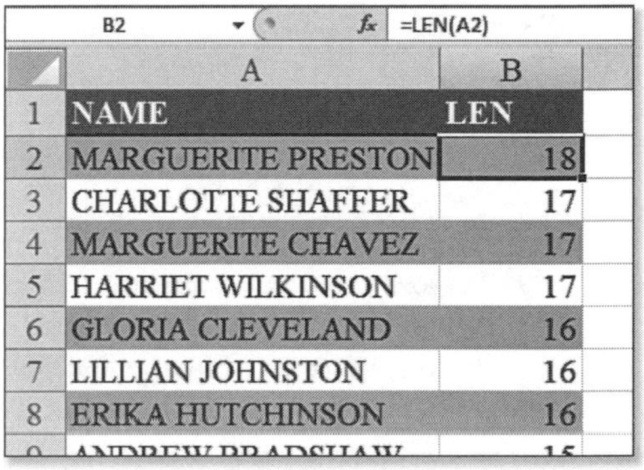

Figure 11.59
LEN identifies the number of characters in a cell.

Using SEARCH or FIND to Locate Characters in a Particular Cell

Two nearly identical functions can scan through a text cell, looking for a particular character or word. Many times, you just want to know if the word appears in the text. These functions go further than telling you if the character exists in the text; they tell you at exactly which character position the character or word is found. The character position can be useful in subsequent formulas with LEFT, RIGHT, or REPLACE.

First, let's look at an example of using FIND to determine whether a word exists in another cell. Figure 11.60 shows a database of customers. The database was created by someone who doesn't know Excel and jammed every field into a single cell.

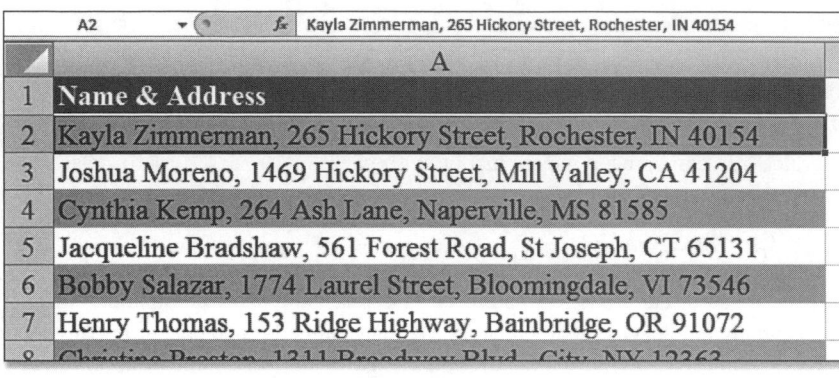

Figure 11.60
When the manager asked an employee to type this in Excel, she didn't realize that the employee had never used Excel before.

Here is how to make this work properly:

1. To find all the customers in California, in Cell B2, enter =FIND(", CA",A2). When you enter the formula, you get a #VALUE! error. This is okay. In fact, it is useful information: It tells you that CA is not found in the first record.

2. Copy the formula down to all rows.

3. Sort low to high by Column B. 98% of the records have a #VALUE! error and sort to the bottom of the list. The few California records have a valid result for the formula in Column B and sort to the top of the list, as shown in Figure 11.61.

FIND and SEARCH are similar to one another. The FIND function does not distinguish between uppercase and lowercase letters. FIND identifies CA, ca, Ca, and cA as matches for CA. If you need to find a cell with exactly AbCdEf, you need to use the SEARCH command instead of FIND. Also, SEARCH allows for wildcard characters in find_text. A question mark (?) finds a single character, and an asterisk (*) finds any number of characters.

> 🔍 **note**
>
> Like all the other data sets in this book, these names and addresses are randomly generated from lists of the most popular first name, last name, street name, and city names. Don't try to send Christmas cards to these people, because none of the addresses exist. And don't think that the ZIP codes are real; everything here is completely random.

	A	B
	B2 ▾ ⊙ 𝑓ₓ =FIND(", CA",A2)	
	A	B
1	Name & Address	California?
2	Marilyn Atkins, 1581 Twelfth Avenue, Oak Grove, CA 69942	47
3	Joshua Moreno, 1469 Hickory Street, Mill Valley, CA 41204	48
4	Kayla Zimmerman, 265 Hickory Street, Rochester, IN 40154	#VALUE!
5	Cynthia Kemp, 264 Ash Lane, Naperville, MS 81585	#VALUE!
6	Jacqueline Bradshaw, 561 Forest Road, St Joseph, CT 65131	#VALUE!
7	Bobby Salazar, 1774 Laurel Street, Bloomingdale, VI 73546	#VALUE!

Figure 11.61
You don't care where FIND found the text; you simply want to divide the list into records with valid values versus errors.

The FIND function makes it easy to find the first instance of a particular character in a cell. However, if your text values contain two instances of a character, your task is a bit more difficult. In Figure 11.62, the part numbers in Column A really contain three segments, each separated by a dash:

> **⚡ caution**
>
> The trick with this application of FIND is to look for something that is likely to be found only in California records. If you had customers in Cairo, Illinois, they would have also been found by the FIND command you just used. The theory with this sort of search is that you can quickly check through the few matching records to find false positives.

1. To find the first dash, enter =FIND("-",A2) in Column B.

2. To find the second dash, use the optional start_num parameter to the FIND function. The *start_num* parameter is a character position. You want the function to start looking after the first instance of a dash. This can be calculated as the result of the first FIND in Column B plus one. Thus, the formula in cell C2 is =FIND("-",A2,B2+1).

3. After you find the character positions of the dashes, isolate the various portions of the part number. In Column D, for the first part of the number, enter =LEFT(A2,B2-1). This basically asks for the left characters from the part number, stopping at one fewer than the first dash.

4. In Column E, for the middle part of the number, enter =MID(A2,B2+1,C2-B2-1). This asks Excel to start at the character position one after the first dash and then continue for a length that is one fewer than the first dash subtracted from the second dash.

5. In Column F, for the final part of the number, enter =RIGHT(A2,LEN(A2)-C2). This calculates the total length of the part number, subtracts the position of the second dash, and returns those right characters.

Figure 11.62
Formulaically isolating data between the first and second dashes can be done, but it helps to break each number down into small parts.

C2		f_x	=FIND("-",A2,B2+1)				
	A	B	C	D	E	F	G	H
	Part Number	**First Dash**	**Second Dash**	**First Part**	**2nd Part**	**3rd Part**		*Formulas:*
1								
2	37767-33-385568	6	9	37767	33	385568		*B2: =FIND("-",A2)*
3	632-6-43	4	6	632	6	43		*C2: =FIND("-",A2,B2+1)*
4	10-13-5656	3	6	10	13	5656		*D2: =LEFT(A2,B2-1)*
5	9-671672-119067	2	9	9	671672	119067		*E2: =MID(A2,B2+1,C2-B2-1)*
6	41-50555-51	3	9	41	50555	51		*F2: =RIGHT(A2,LEN(A2)-C2)*
7	568-536-177914	4	8	568	536	177914		
8	1506-9-25472	5	7	1506	9	25472		

Syntax:

=FIND(*find_text*,*within_text*,*start_num*)

FIND finds one text string (*find_text*) within another text string (*within_text*) and returns the number of the starting position of *find_text* from the first character of *within_text*. You can also use SEARCH to find one text string within another, but unlike SEARCH, FIND is case sensitive and doesn't allow wildcard characters.

The FIND function takes the following arguments:

- *find_text*—This is the text you want to find. If *find_text* is " " (that is, empty text), FIND matches the first character in the search string (that is, the character numbered *start_num* or 1). *find_text* cannot contain any wildcard characters.

- *within_text*—This is the text that contains the text you want to find.

- *start_num*—This specifies the character at which to start the search. The first character in *within_text* is character number 1. If you omit *start_num*, it is assumed to be 1.

Syntax:

=SEARCH(*find_text,within_text,start_num*)

SEARCH returns the number of the character at which a specific character or text string is first found, beginning with start_num. You use SEARCH to determine the location of a character or text string within another text string so that you can use the MID or REPLACE functions to change the text.

The SEARCH function takes the following arguments:

- *find_text*—This is the text you want to find. You can use the wildcard characters question mark (?) and asterisk (*) in *find_text*. A question mark matches any single character; an asterisk matches any sequence of characters. If you want to find an actual question mark or asterisk, you type a tilde (~) before the character. If you want to find a tilde, you type two tildes. If *find_text* is not found, a #VALUE! error is returned.

- *within_text*—This is the text in which you want to search for *find_text*.

- *start_num*—This is the character number in *within_text* at which you want to start searching. If *start_num* is omitted, it is assumed to be 1. If *start_num* is not greater than zero or is greater than the length of *within_text*, a #VALUE! error is returned.

> 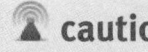 **caution**
>
> If find_text does not appear in within_text, FIND returns a #VALUE! error. If *start_num* is not greater than zero, FIND returns a #VALUE! error. If *start_num* is greater than the length of within_text, FIND returns a #VALUE! error.

Using SUBSTITUTE and REPLACE to Replace Characters

When you have the ability to find text, you might want to replace text. Excel offers two functions for this: SUBSTITUTE and REPLACE. The SUBSTITUTE function is easier to use and should be your first approach.

Syntax:

=SUBSTITUTE(*text,old_text,new_text,instance_num*)

The SUBSTITUTE function substitutes new_text for old_text in a text string. You use SUBSTITUTE when you want to replace specific text in a text string; you use REPLACE when you want to replace any text that occurs in a specific location in a text string.

The SUBSTITUTE function takes the following arguments:

- *text*—This is the text or the reference to a cell that contains text for which you want to substitute characters.

- *old_text*—This is the text you want to replace.

- *new_text*—This is the text you want to replace *old_text* with.

- *instance_num*—This specifies which occurrence of *old_text* you want to replace with *new_text*. If you specify *instance_num,* only that instance of *old_text* is replaced. Otherwise, every occurrence of *old_text* in text is changed to new_text.

For example, =SUBSTITUTE("Sales Data","Sales","Cost") would generate "Cost Data".

The SUBSTITUTE function works similarly to a traditional find and replace command. Compared to the SUBSTITUTE function, the REPLACE function is difficult enough to make even an old programmer's head spin.

Syntax:

=REPLACE(*old_text,start_num,num_chars,new_text*)

REPLACE replaces part of a text string, based on the number of characters specified, with a different text string. This function takes the following arguments:

- *old_text*—This is text in which you want to replace some characters.

- *start_num*—This is the position of the character in *old_text* that you want to replace with n*ew_text*.

- *num_chars*—This is the number of characters in *old_text* that you want *REPLACE* to replace with *new_text*.

- *new_text*—This is the text that will replace characters in *old_text*.

 tip

In order to successfully use REPLACE, you have to use functions to determine the location and number of characters to replace. In most circumstances, SUBSTITUTE is easier to use.

Using REPT to Repeat Text Multiple Times

The REPT function will repeat a character or some text a certain number of times.

Syntax:

=REPT(*text*,*number_times*)

The REPT function repeats text a given number of times. You use REPT to fill a cell with a number of instances of a text string. This function takes the following arguments:

- *text*—This is the text you want to repeat.

- *number_times*—This is a positive number that specifies the number of times to repeat text. If *number_times* is 0, REPT returns "" (that is, empty text). If *number_times* is not an integer, it is truncated. The result of the REPT function cannot be longer than 32,767 characters.

In Microsoft Word, it is easy to create a row of periods between text and a page number. In Excel, you have to resort to clever use of the REPT function to do this.

In Figure 11.63, Column A contains a page number. Column B contains a chapter title. The goal in Column C is to join enough periods between Columns B and A to make all the page numbers line up.

The number of periods to print is the total desired length, less the length of Columns A and B. The formula for Cell C2 is =B2&REPT(".",45-(LEN(A2)+LEN(B2)))&A2.

> **note**
>
> To make this work, you have to change the font in Column C to be a fixed-width font such as Courier New.

	C2		*fx* =B2&REPT(".",45-(LEN(A2)+LEN(B2)))&A2	
	A	B	C	
1	Page	Title	=B2&REPT(".",45-(LEN(A2)+LEN(B2)))&A2	
2	5	Chapter 1 - The Ribbon	Chapter 1 - The Ribbon......................5	
3	19	Chapter 2 - Quick Access Toolbar	Chapter 2 - Quick Access Toolbar...........19	
4	33	Chapter 3- The MiniBar	Chapter 3- The MiniBar.....................33	
5	47	Chapter 4 - Keyboard Shortcuts	Chapter 4 - Keyboard Shortcuts.............47	
6	105	Chapter 14 - Sorting	Chapter 14 - Sorting......................105	
7				
8		Hello Hello Hello		
9		=REPT("Hello ",3)		
10				

Figure 11.63
The REPT function can be used to calculate a certain number of repeated entries.

Using EXACT to Test Case

For the most part, Excel isn't concerned about case. To Excel, ABC and abc are the same thing. In Figure 11.64, Cells A1 and B1 contain the same letters, but the capitalization is different.

The formula in Cell C1 tests whether these values are equal. In the rules of Excel, AbC and ABC are equivalent. The formula in Cell C1 indicates that the values are equal. To some people, these two text cells may not be equivalent. If you work in a store that sells the big plastic letters that go on theater marquees, your order for 20 letter "a" figures should not be filled with an order for 20 letter "A" figures.

Excel forces you to use the EXACT function to compare these two cells to learn that they are not exactly the same.

 tip

An alternative solution is to format column A with the custom format of "@*.". This will show the text in the cell and follow it with a series of periods, enough to fill the current width of the column.

Figure 11.64
Excel usually overlooks differences in capitalization when deciding whether two values are equal. You can use EXACT to find out whether they are equal and the same case.

	A	B	C	D
1	AbC	ABC	TRUE	=A1=B1
2	AbC	ABC	FALSE	=EXACT(A2,B2)

C2   *fx* =EXACT(A2,B2)

Syntax:

=EXACT(*text1*,*text2*)

The EXACT function compares two text strings and returns TRUE if they are exactly the same and FALSE otherwise. EXACT is case sensitive but ignores formatting differences. You use EXACT to test text being entered into a document. This function takes the following arguments:

- *text1*—This is the first text string.

- *text2*—This is the second text string

Using TEXT, DOLLAR, and FIXED to Format a Number as Text

Excel is great at numbers. Put a number in a cell, and you can format it in a variety of ways. However, when you join a cell containing text with a cell containing a number or a date, Excel falls apart.

Consider Figure 11.65. Cell A11 contains a date and is formatted as a date. When you join the name in Cell B11 with the date in Cell A11, Excel automatically converts the date back to a numeric serial number. This is frustrating.

Today, the TEXT function is the most versatile solution to this problem. If you understand the basics of custom numeric formatting codes, you can easily use TEXT to format a date or a number in any conceivable format. For example, the formula in Cell C12 uses =TEXT(A12,"m/d/y") to force the date to display as a date.

The TEXT function gives you a lot of versatility. To learn the custom formatting codes for a cell, you can select the cell, display the Format Cells dialog (by pressing Ctrl+1), and select the Custom category on the Number tab. Excel shows you the codes used to create that format.

	A	B	C	D	E	F	G	H
1	1234.56	$1,234.56	=DOLLAR(A1)					
2	1234.56	$1,235	=DOLLAR(A2,0)					
3	1234.56	$1,234.56	=DOLLAR(A3,2)					
4								
5	1234.56	1,234.56	=FIXED(A5)					
6	1234.56	1,235	=FIXED(A6,0)					
7	1234.56	1235	=FIXED(A7,0,TRUE)					
8								
9	3/5/2006	Sunday, March 5, 2006						
10								
11	12/1/1989	Joe	Joe was born on 32843	=B11&" was born on "&A11				
12	12/1/1989	Joe	Joe was born on 12/1/89	=B12&" was born on "&TEXT(A12,"m/d/y")				

C12 ▾ fx =B12&" was born on "&TEXT(A12,"m/d/y")

Figure 11.65
TEXT, DOLLAR, and FIXED can be used to format a number as text.

If you don't care to learn the number formatting codes, you can use either the DOLLAR or FIXED function to return a number as text, with a few choices regarding number of decimals and whether Excel should use the thousands separator. The formulas shown in C2:C7 in Figure 11.65 return the formatted text values shown in Column B.

Syntax:

=TEXT(*value*,*format_text*)

The TEXT function converts a value to text in a specific number format. Formatting a cell with an option on the Number tab of the Format Cells dialog changes only the format, not the value. Using the TEXT function converts a value to formatted text, and the result is no longer calculated as a number.

The TEXT function takes the following arguments:

- *value*—This is a numeric value, a formula that evaluates to a numeric value, or a reference to a cell that contains a numeric value.

- *format_text*—This is a number format in text form from the Category box on the Number tab in the Format Cells dialog box. format_text cannot contain an asterisk (*) and cannot be the general number format.

Syntax:

=DOLLAR(*number*,*decimals*)

The DOLLAR function converts a number to text using currency format, with the decimals rounded to the specified place. The format used is $#,##0.00_);($#,##0.00). The major difference between formatting a cell that contains a number with the Format Cells dialog and formatting a number directly with the DOLLAR function is that DOLLAR converts its result to text. A number formatted with the

Cells command is still a number. You can continue to use numbers formatted with DOLLAR in formulas because Microsoft Excel converts numbers entered as text values to numbers when it calculates.

The DOLLAR function takes the following arguments:

- *number*—This is a number, a reference to a cell that contains a number, or a formula that evaluates to a number.

- *decimals*—This is the number of digits to the right of the decimal point. If *decimals* is negative, *number* is rounded to the left of the decimal point. If you omit *decimals*, it is assumed to be 2.

Syntax:

=FIXED(*number*,[*decimals*],[*no_commas*])

The FIXED function rounds a number to the specified number of decimals, formats the number in decimal format using a period and commas, and returns the result as text. The major difference between formatting a cell that contains a number with the Format Cells dialog and formatting a number directly with the FIXED function is that FIXED converts its result to text. A number formatted with the Format Cells dialog is still a number. This function takes the following arguments:

- *number*—This is the number you want to round and convert to text.

- *decimals*—This is the number of digits to the right of the decimal point. Numbers in Microsoft Excel can never have more than 15 significant digits, but *decimals* can be as large as 127. If *decimals* is negative, number is rounded to the left of the decimal point. If you omit *decimals*, it is assumed to be 2.

- *no commas*—This is a logical value that, if TRUE, prevents FIXED from including commas in the returned text. If *no_commas* is FALSE or omitted, the returned text includes commas as usual.

Using the T and VALUE Functions

The T and VALUE functions are left over from Lotus days.

=T("text") returns the original text. If Cell B1 contains the number 123, =T(B1) would return an empty text. Basically, T() returns the value in the cell only if it is text.

=VALUE() converts text that looks like a number or a date to the number or the date.

Using Functions for Non-English Character Sets

There are 11 more functions that have not been covered in this section. These functions deal with text in character systems where each character takes up more than 1 byte. This is true in many Asian languages.

 note

The following functions are beyond the scope of this edition: ASC, BAHTTEXT, FINDB, JIS, LEFTB, MIDB, PHONETIC, REPLACEB, RIGHTB, SEARCHB, YEN. Even so, these functions are described earlier in this chapter in Table 23.3.

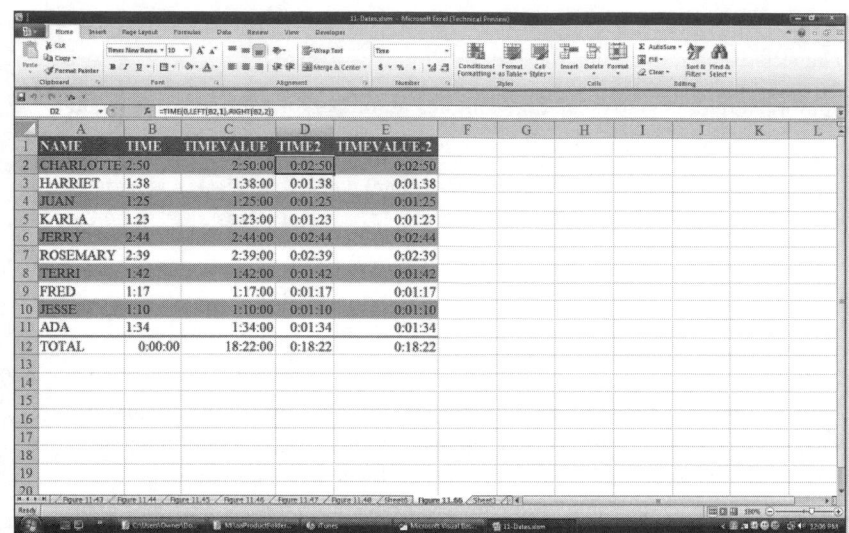

Figure 11.66
You can use the LEFT and RIGHT text functions to provide the arguments for the TIME function.

Excel Troubleshooting: Text Times Entered as M:SS Instead of H:MM:SS

In Figure 11.66, Column B contains a series of time trial results. When you total the column in Cell B12, you realize that all the times were entered as text.

The formulas in Column C use =TIMEVALUE(B2). However, a time such as 2 minutes 50 seconds is converted in the function to 2 hours 50 minutes. In this case, TIMEVALUE does not work.

There are two alternative strategies:

- One solution is to use the TIME function. In Column D, the text times are converted to real times by using the TIME function. In each case, the hours should be zero. The minutes are =LEFT(B2,1). The seconds are =RIGHT(B2,2). The formula in Cell D2 is =TIME(0,LEFT(B2,1),RIGHT(B2,2)). You copy this formula down and format the range as a time.

  The other solution is to use the concatenation operator to pad the left of Column B with 0:0. This allows the text to work in the TIMEVALUE function. The formula in Cell E2 is =TIMEVALUE("0:0"&B2). Again, you need to copy this formula down and format the range as a time.

USING POWERFUL FUNCTIONS: LOGICAL, LOOKUP, AND DATABASE FUNCTIONS

This chapter covers four groups of workhorse functions. If you process spreadsheets of medium complexity, you will turn to logical and lookup functions regularly.

- The logical functions, including the ubiquitous IF function, help make decisions.

- The information functions might be less important than they once were, now that Microsoft has added the IFERROR function, but INFO, CELL, and TYPE still come in handy.

- The lookup functions include the powerful VLOOKUP, MATCH, and INDIRECT functions. These functions are invaluable, particularly when you are doing something in Excel when it would be better to use Access. In addition, let's face it; with 1.1 million rows in Excel 2010, we will all do more things in Excel that should be done in Access.

- Finally, the database functions provide the DSUM functions. Even though these functions fell out of favor with the introduction of pivot tables, they are a powerful set of functions that are worthwhile to master.

Table 12.1 provides an alphabetical list of all Excel 2010's logical functions. Detailed examples of these functions are provided later in this chapter.

Table 12.1   Alphabetical List of Logical Functions

Function	Description
AND(*logical1*,*logical2*,...)	Returns TRUE if all its arguments are TRUE; returns FALSE if one or more arguments is FALSE.
FALSE()	Returns the logical value FALSE.
IF(*logical_test*,*value_if_true*, *value_if_false*)	Returns one value if a condition specified evaluates to TRUE and another value if it evaluates to FALSE.
IFERROR(*value*,*value_if_error*)	Returns *value_if_error* if expression is an error and the value itself if otherwise.
NOT(*logical*)	Reverses the value of its argument. You use NOT when you want to make sure a value is not equal to another particular value.
OR(*logical1*,*logical2*,...)	Returns TRUE if any argument is TRUE; returns FALSE if all arguments are FALSE.
TRUE()	Returns the logical value TRUE.

Table 12.2 provides an alphabetical list of all Excel 2010's information functions. Detailed examples of these functions are provided in the remainder of the chapter.

Table 12.2   Alphabetical List of Information Functions

Function	Description
CELL(*info_type*,*reference*)	Returns information about the formatting, location, or contents of the upper-left cell in a reference.
ERROR.TYPE(*error_val*)	Returns a number corresponding to one of the error values in Microsoft Excel or returns an #N/A error if no error exists. You can use ERROR.TYPE in an IF function to test for an error value and return a text string, such as a message, instead of the error value.
INFO(*type_text*)	Returns information about the current operating environment.
ISBLANK(*value*)	Returns TRUE if *value* refers to an empty cell.
ISERROR(*value*)	Returns TRUE if *value* refers to any error value (that is, #N/A, #VALUE!, #REF!, #DIV/0!, #NUM!, #NAME?, or #NULL!).
ISERR(*value*)	Returns TRUE if *value* refers to any error value except #N/A.
ISEVEN(*number*)	Returns TRUE if *number* is even and FALSE if number is odd.
ISLOGICAL(*value*)	Returns TRUE if *value* refers to a logical value.

Function	Description
ISNA(*value*)	Returns TRUE if *value* refers to the #N/A (value not available) error value.
ISNONTEXT(*value*)	Returns TRUE if *value* refers to any item that is not text. (Note that this function returns TRUE if *value* refers to a blank cell.)
ISNUMBER(*value*)	Returns TRUE if *value* refers to a number.
ISODD(*number*)	Returns TRUE if *number* is odd and FALSE if number is even.
ISREF(*value*)	Returns TRUE if *value* refers to a reference.
ISTEXT(*value*)	Returns TRUE if *value* refers to text.
N(*value*)	Returns a *value* converted to a number.
NA()	Returns the error value #N/A, which means "no value is available." You use NA to mark empty cells or cells that are missing information to avoid the problem of unintentionally including empty cells in your calculations. When a formula refers to a cell containing #N/A, the formula returns the #N/A error value.
TYPE(*value*)	Returns the type of *value*. You use TYPE when the behavior of another function depends on the type of value in a particular cell.

Table 12.3 provides an alphabetical list of all Excel 2010's lookup functions. Detailed examples of these functions are provided later in this chapter.

Table 12.3 Alphabetical List of Lookup Functions

Function	Description
ADDRESS(*row_num,column_num, abs_num,a1,sheet_text*)	Creates a cell address as text, given specified row and column numbers.
AREAS(*reference*)	Returns the number of areas in a reference. An area is a range of contiguous cells or a single cell.
CHOOSE(*index_num,value1, value 2, ...*)	Uses *index_num* to return a value from the list of value arguments. You use *CHOOSE* to select one of up to 254 values, based on the index number. For example, if *value1* through *value7* are the days of the week, CHOOSE returns one of the days when a number between 1 and 7 is used as *index_num*.
COLUMN(*reference*)	Returns the column number of the given reference.
COLUMNS(*array*)	Returns the number of columns in an array or a reference.

Function	Description
GETPIVOTDATA(*data_field, pivot_table,[field1],[item1],...*)	Returns data stored in a pivot table report. You can use GETPIVOTDATA to retrieve summary data from a pivot table report, if the summary data is visible in the report.
HLOOKUP(*lookup_value, table_array, row_index_num, range_lookup*)	Searches for a value in the top row of a table or an array of values and then returns a value in the same column from a row you specify in the table or array. You use HLOOKUP when your comparison values are located in a row across the top of a table of data and you want to look down a specified number of rows. You use VLOOKUP when your comparison values are located in a column to the left of the data you want to find.
HYPERLINK(*link_location, friendly_name*)	Creates a shortcut or jump that opens a document stored on a network server, an intranet, or the Internet. When you click the cell that contains the HYPERLINK function, Excel opens the file stored at *link_location*.
INDEX(*array, row_num, column_num*)	Returns the value of a specified cell or array of cells within array.
INDEX(*reference, row_num, column_num, area_num*)	Returns a reference to a specified cell or cells within *reference*.
INDIRECT(*ref_text, a1*)	Returns the reference specified by a text string. References are evaluated immediately to display their contents. You use INDIRECT when you want to change the reference to a cell within a formula without changing the formula itself.
LOOKUP(*lookup_value, lookup_vector, result_vector*)	Returns a value from either a one-row or one-column range. This vector form of LOOKUP looks in a one-row or one-column range, known as a *vector*, for a value and returns a value from the same position in a second one-row or one-column range. This function is included for compatibility with other worksheets. You should use VLOOKUP instead.
LOOKUP(*lookup_value, array*)	Returns a value from an array. The array form of LOOKUP looks in the first row or column of an array for the specified value and returns a value from the same position in the last row or column of the array. This function is included for compatibility with other spreadsheet programs. You should use VLOOKUP instead. However, unlike VLOOKUP, the LOOKUP function can process an array of lookup_values.
MATCH(*lookup_value, lookup_array, match_type*)	Returns the relative position of an item in an array that matches a specified value in a specified order. You use MATCH instead of one of the LOOKUP functions when you need the position of an item in a range instead of the item itself.

Function	Description
OFFSET(*reference, rows, cols, height, width*)	Returns a reference to a range that is a specified number of rows and columns away from a cell or range of cells. The reference that is returned can be a single cell or a range of cells. You can specify the number of rows and the number of columns to be returned.
ROW(*reference*)	Returns the row number of a reference.
ROWS(*array*)	Returns the number of rows in a reference or an array.
RTD(*progid, server, topic,[topic2],...*)	Retrieves real-time data from a program that supports COM automation. This function was new in Excel XP.
TRANSPOSE(*array*)	Returns a vertical range of cells as a horizontal range or vice versa. TRANSPOSE must be entered as an array formula in a range that has the same number of rows and columns, respectively, because array has columns and rows. You use TRANSPOSE to shift the vertical and horizontal orientation of an array on a worksheet. For example, some functions, such as LINEST, return horizontal arrays. LINEST returns a horizontal array of the slope and y-intercept for a line. Use TRANSPOSE to convert the LINEST result to a vertical array.
VLOOKUP(*lookup_value, table_array, col_index_num, range_lookup*)	Searches for a value in the leftmost column of a table and then returns a value in the same row from a column you specify in the table. You use VLOOKUP instead of HLOOKUP when your comparison values are located in a column to the left of the data you want to find.

Table 12.4 provides an alphabetical list of all of Excel 2010's database functions. Detailed examples of these functions are provided later in this chapter.

Table 12.4   Alphabetical List of Database Functions

Function	Description
DAVERAGE(*database, field, criteria*)	Averages the values in a column in a list or database that match the conditions specified.
DCOUNT(*database, field, criteria*)	Counts the cells that contain numbers in a column in a list or database that match the conditions specified.
DCOUNTA(*database, field, criteria*)	Counts all the nonblank cells in a column in a list or database that match the conditions specified.
DGET(*database, field, criteria*)	Extracts a single value from a column in a list or database that matches the conditions specified.

Function	Description
DMAX(*database, field, criteria*)	Returns the largest number in a column in a list or database that matches the conditions specified.
DMIN(*database, field, criteria*)	Returns the smallest number in a column in a list or database that matches the conditions specified.
DPRODUCT(*database, field, criteria*)	Multiplies the values in a column in a list or database that match the conditions specified.
DSTDEV(*database, field, criteria*)	Estimates the standard deviation of a population based on a sample, using the numbers in a column in a list or database that match the conditions specified.
DSTDEVP(*database, field, criteria*)	Calculates the standard deviation of a population based on the entire population, using the numbers in a column in a list or database that match the conditions specified.
DSUM(*database, field, criteria*)	Adds the numbers in a column in a list or database that match the conditions specified.
DVAR(*database, field, criteria*)	Estimates the variance of a population based on a sample, using the numbers in a column in a list or database that match the conditions specified.
DVARP(*database, field, criteria*)	Calculates the variance of a population based on the entire population, using the numbers in a column in a list or database that match the conditions specified.

Table 12.5 provides an alphabetical list of all of Excel 2010's external functions. Detailed examples of these functions are provided later in this chapter.

Table 12.5 Alphabetical List of External Functions

Function	Description
CALL(*register_id, argument1,...*)	Calls a procedure in a dynamic link library (DLL) or code resource. You use this syntax only with a previously registered code resource that uses arguments from the REGISTER function.
CALL(*file_text, resource, type_text, argument1,...*)	Calls a procedure in a DLL or code resource. You use this syntax to simultaneously register and call a code resource for the Macintosh.
CALL(*module_text, procedure, type_text, argument1,...*)	Calls a procedure in a DLL or code resource. You use this syntax to simultaneously register and call a code resource for Windows machines.

Function	Description
EUROCONVERT(*number*, *source*, *target*, *full_precision*, *triangulation_ precision*)	Converts a number to euros, converts a number from euros to a euro member currency, or converts a number from one euro member currency to another by using the euro as an intermediary (that is, triangulation). The currencies available for conversion are those of the European Union (EU) members that have adopted the euro.
REGISTER.ID(*file_text*, *resource*, *type_text*)	Returns the register ID of the specified DLL or code resource that has been previously registered. If the DLL or code resource has not been registered, this function registers the DLL or code resource and then returns the register ID for the Macintosh.
REGISTER.ID(*module_text*, *procedure*, *type_text*)	Returns the register ID of the specified DLL or code resource that has been previously registered. If the DLL or code resource has not been registered, this function registers the DLL or code re source and then returns the register ID for Windows.
SQL.REQUEST(*connection_string*, *output_ref*,*driver_prompt*, *query_text*,*col_names_logical*)	Connects with an external data source and runs a query from a worksheet. SQL.REQUEST then returns the result as an array, without the need for macro programming. If this function is not already available, you should install the Microsoft Excel ODBC add-in (XLODBC.XLA).

Examples of Logical Functions

With only seven functions, the logical function group is one of the smallest in Excel. The IF function is easy to understand, and enables you to solve a variety of problems.

Using the IF Function to Make a Decision

Many calculations in our lives are not straightforward. Suppose that a manager offers a bonus program if her team meets its goals. Or perhaps a commission plan offers a bonus if a certain profit goal is met. These types of calculations can be solved by using the IF function.

Syntax: IF(logical_test,value_if_true,value_if_false)

There are three arguments in the IF function. The first argument is any logical test that results in a TRUE or FALSE. For example, you might have logical tests such as these:

```
A2>100
B5="West"
C99<=D99
```

All logical tests involve one of the comparison operators shown in Table 12.6.

Table 12.6 Comparison Operators

Comparison Operator	Meaning	Example
=	Equal to	C1=D1
>	Greater than	A1>B1
<	Less than	A1<B1
>=	Greater than or equal to	A1>=0
<=	Less than or equal to	A1<=99
<>	Not equal to	A2<>B2

The remaining two arguments are the formula or value to use if the logical test is true and the formula or value to use if the logical test is false.

When you read an IF function, you should think of the first comma as the word *then* and the second comma as the word *otherwise*. For example, =IF(A2>10,25,0) would be read as "If A2>10, then 25; otherwise, 0."

Figure 12.1 calculates a sales commission. The commission rate is 1.5 percent of revenue. However, if the gross profit percentage is 50 percent or higher, the commission rate is 2.5 percent of revenue.

In this case, the logical test is H2>=50 percent. The formula if that test is true is 0.025*F2. Otherwise, the formula is 0.015*F2. You could build the formula as =IF(H2>=50%,0.025*F2,0.015*F2).

**note**
Mathematicians would correctly note that in both the second and third arguments of the formula =IF(H2>=50%,0.025*F2,0.015*F2), you are multiplying by F2. Therefore, you could simplify the formula by using =IF(H2>=50%,0.025,0.015)*F2.

I2			f_x	=IF(H2>=50%,0.025*F2,0.015*F2)		
	D	E	F	G	H	I	J
1	Associate	Qty	Revenue	Cost	GP%	Commission	
2	GERALD	400	15456	8400	45.7%	231.84	1.5%
3	JOSEPH	700	53928	25200	53.3%	1348.2	2.5%
4	SHELLY	100	4784	2600	45.7%	71.76	
5	JOY	1000	67680	36000	46.8%	1015.2	
6	JOY	300	20088	9300	53.7%	502.2	
7	FANNIE	500	33750	15600	52.4%	810	

Figure 12.1
In Rows 2, 4, and 5 the commission is 1.5 percent. In Rows 3 and 6 the commission is 2.5 percent.

Using the AND Function to Check for Two or More Conditions

The previous example had one simple condition: If the value in Column H was greater than or equal to 50 percent, the commission rate changed.

However, in many cases you might need to test for two or more conditions. For example, suppose that a retail store manager offers a $25 bonus for every leather jacket sold on Fridays this month. In this case, the logical test requires you to determine whether both conditions are true. You can do this with the AND function.

Syntax:

AND(*logical1,logical2,...*)

The arguments *logical1,logical2,...* are from 1 to 255 expressions that evaluate to either TRUE or FALSE. The function returns TRUE only if all arguments are TRUE.

In Figure 12.2, the function in Cell F2 checks whether Cell E2 is a jacket and whether the date in Cell D2 falls on a Friday:

=AND(E2="Jacket",WEEKDAY(D2,2)=5)

Figure 12.2
The AND function is TRUE only when every condition is met.

	A	B	C	D	E	F
	Store	Cust	Associate	Date	Item	Bonus?
1						
2	S18	C422	Jenny	4/12/2011	Handbag	FALSE
3	S5	C244	Bill	4/8/2011	Jacket	TRUE
4	S13	C668	Diana	4/25/2011	Hat	FALSE
5	S19	C825	Bill	4/12/2011	Jacket	FALSE
6	S15	C500	Bill	4/22/2011	Coaster	FALSE

Using the AND Function to Compare Two Lists

The AND function can handle up to 255 expressions. Each expression can contain a range that might contain many instances of TRUE or FALSE.

A common issue is figuring out whether two worksheets are identical. In Figure 12.3, Columns A:E contain the original worksheet. After this worksheet was passed among several co-workers, it ended back at your desk. Follow these steps to compare the two worksheets:

1. Leave three blank columns—Columns F, G, and H—to the right of your original data.

2. Copy the data range of the returned worksheet. Paste this copy, starting in Column I of the original worksheet.

3. Add the heading All Match? in Column G.

4. Add a formula in Column G to compare whether each of the cells in the original data set matches the cells in the returned data set. Add the formula =AND(A6=I6,B6=J6,C6=K6,D6=L6,E6=M6) in Cell G6 to compare all five cells in the data set.

5. Copy the formula down Column G from Cell G6 to match the number of rows in the data set.

6. In Cell G2, enter an AND formula to test whether all the formulas in Column G are TRUE. Even though this range contains more than 255 cells, it is still valid to use it as one of the

expressions in the AND function. The formula in G2 is =AND(G6:G999). This is a quick way to find out whether every row is identical without having to scroll through pages of data, looking for a single FALSE result. If Cell G2 returns TRUE, you know that the original and returned worksheets are identical. If Cell G2 returns FALSE, you know that one or more of the rows were changed.

7. Select G6:G999. From the Home tab, select Find & Select, Find. The Find and Replace dialog appears.

=AND(A6=I6,B6=J6,C6=K6,D6=L6,E6=M6)

	D	E	F	G	H	I	J	K	L	M
m - 1	Woodlawn - 1	Woodlawn - 2		All Match				Woodlawn -	oodlawn -	oodlawn - 2
0AM	10AM-11:30AM	8AM-9:30AM		FALSE				8AM-9:30A	AM-11:30	AM-9:30AM
				Match?						
k	Blue	Green		TRUE		22-Apr	Saturday	Black	Blue	Green
	N/A	N/A		TRUE		25-Apr	Tuesday	N/A	N/A	N/A
	N/A	N/A		TRUE		26-Apr	Wednesda	N/A	N/A	N/A
	N/A	N/A		TRUE		27-Apr	Thursday	N/A	N/A	N/A
h	Black	Blue		TRUE		29-Apr	Saturday	Open	Black	Blue
	N/A	N/A		FALSE		2-May	Tuesday	Red at Gra	N/A	N/A
	N/A	N/A		TRUE		3-May	Wednesda	N/A	N/A	N/A

Figure 12.3
AND can test whether a large range of logical tests are all TRUE.

---

8. In the Find and Replace dialog, type FALSE into the Find What box. You must click the Options button and change the Look In drop-down from Formulas to Values to find formulas that result in a value of FALSE.

Using OR to Check Whether Any Conditions Are Met

You might have a situation in which a certain formula is based on meeting one of several conditions. A sales manager may want to reward big orders and orders from new customers. The manager may offer a commission bonus if the order is over $50,000 or if the customer is a new customer this year.

To test whether a particular sale meets either condition, use the OR function. The OR function returns TRUE if any condition is TRUE and returns FALSE if none of the conditions are TRUE.

 **tip**

Instead of using the AND function, you can multiply the conditions. =(A6=I6)*(B6= J6)*(C6=K6)*(D6*L6)*(E6=M6) will return 1 if all the conditions are true and zero if any one of the conditions is false. Alternatively, you can type =AND(A6:E6=I6:M6) and press Ctrl+Shift+Enter to have AND evaluate the array of comparisons.

Syntax:

OR(logical1,logical2,...)

The OR function checks whether any of the arguments are TRUE. It returns a FALSE only if all the arguments are FALSE. If any argument is TRUE, the function returns TRUE.

The arguments `logical1,logical2,...` are 1 to 255 conditions that can evaluate to TRUE or FALSE.

In Figure 12.4, the logical test to see if revenue is over $50,000 is E2>50000. The logical test to see if the customer is new this year is D2=2010. The structure of this OR function is =OR(D2=2010,E2>50000).

You can use the OR function as the first argument to the IF function to produce the formula shown in Cell F2: =IF(OR(D2=2010,E2>50000),0.025*E2,0.015*E2).

Figure 12.4

OR checks whether a record meets at least one of several criteria.

	=IF(OR(D2=2010,E2>50000),0.025*E2,0.015*E2)		
C	**D**	**E**	**F**
Associate	Cust Since	Revenue	Commission
GERALD	2010	15456	386.4
JOSEPH	2006	53928	1348.2
SHELLY	2003	4784	71.76
JOY	2007	67680	1692

Nesting IF Functions

The IF function offers only two possible formulas. Either the logical test is TRUE and the first formula is used, or the logical test is FALSE and the second formula is used.

Many situations have a series of choices. For example, in a human resources department, annual merit raises may be given based on the employee's numeric rating in an annual review, in which employees are ranked on a 5-point scale. The rules for setting the raise are as follows:

- 4.5 or higher: 5 percent raise

- 4 or higher: 4.5 percent raise

- 3.25 or higher: 3 percent raise

- 2.5 or higher: 1 percent raise

- Under 2.5: no raise

You can build the IF statement by following these steps:

1. Test for the highest condition first. Excel stops testing when the first condition is met. If the first test checks to see if an employee had a rating of higher than 2.5, then anyone from 2.5 to 5 receives a 1 percent raise. In this case, you want to give a 5 percent raise to anyone with a rating of 4.5 or greater. Therefore, the formula starts out as =IF(B2>=4.5,5%,.

2. There is only one argument left in the current IF function—the argument for *value_if_false*. Instead of using a value as the third argument, start a second IF function to be used if the first test is FALSE. This IF function starts out

 caution

These IF formulas are hard to read. There is a temptation to use them for situations with very long lists of conditions. Whereas Excel 2003 prevented you from nesting more than seven levels of IF functions, Excel 2007 and later allows you to nest up to 64 IF statements. Before you start nesting that many IF statements, you should consider using VLOOKUP, which is explained later in this chapter.

IF(B2>=4,4.5%,. Combine this start of an IF function with the first IF function: =IF(B2>=4.5, 5%,IF(B2>=4,4.5%,.

3. There are still three possible raise levels and only one argument left in the second IF function. Start a third IF function to be used as the *value_if_false* argument for the second IF function: IF(B2>=3.25,3%,. At this point, if the employee did not rank above 3.25, only two possibilities are left. The employee is either 2.5 and above for a 1 percent raise, or he or she gets no raise.

4. Create the fourth IF function: IF(B2>=2.5,1%,0).

5. With the four IF functions, be careful to provide four closing parentheses at the end of the function: =IF(B2>=4.5,5%,IF(B2>=4,4.5%,IF(B2>=3.25,3%,IF(B2>=2.5,1%,0%)))) (see Figure 12.5).

=IF(B2>=4.5,5%,IF(B2>=4,4.5%,IF(B2>=3.25,3%,IF(B2>=2.5,1%,0%))))				
	A	B	C	D	E
1	EMPLOYEE	RANK	RAISE		
2	JIMMY CAMPBELL	1.6	0.00%		
3	DENNIS PENA	3.4	3.00%		
4	MARK LANCASTER	4.8	5.00%		
5	KEITH AGUIRRE	4.3	4.50%		
6	MARIAN SUAREZ	3.8	3.00%		
7	SAMUEL WOODWARD	3	1.00%		
8	PHILLIP MULLINS	2.4	0.00%		
9	JOHNNY KNOX	1.3	0.00%		
10	SEAN HAYES	2.2	0.00%		

Figure 12.5
This formula contains four nested IF functions.

Using the TRUE and FALSE Functions

There are two remaining functions in the logical group, but you should not need to use either of them. If you encounter a function with either the TRUE or FALSE function, you can replace the function with the value TRUE or FALSE. Microsoft added TRUE and FALSE to provide compatibility with other vendors' spreadsheet programs.

A formula such as =IF(OR(A2>5,B2=0),TRUE(),FALSE()) can be rewritten as =IF(OR(A2>5,B2= 0),TRUE,FALSE). If you are trying to return TRUE or FALSE, you can simply use the Boolean expression: =OR(A2>5,B2=0).

Using the NOT Function to Simplify the Use of AND and OR

In the language of Boolean logic, there are typically NAND, NOR, and XOR functions, which stand for Not And, Not Or, and Exclusive Or. To simplify matters, Excel offers the NOT function.

Syntax:

NOT(*logical*)

Quite simply, NOT reverses a logical value. TRUE becomes FALSE, and FALSE becomes TRUE when processed through a NOT function.

For example, suppose you need to find all flights landing outside of Oklahoma. You can build a massive OR statement to find every airport code in the United States. Alternatively, you can build an `OR` function to find Tulsa and Oklahoma City and then use a `NOT` function to reverse the result: `=NOT(OR(A2="Tulsa",A2="Oklahoma City"))`.

Using the `IFERROR` Function to Simplify Error Checking

The `IFERROR` function, which was introduced in Excel 2007, was added at the request of many customers. To help understand the `IFERROR` function, you need to understand how error checking was performed during the 22 years before Excel 2007 was released.

Figure 12.6 shows a typical spreadsheet that calculates a ratio of sales to hours. Even though this formula works most of the time, in occasional records, the divisor is zero, and the formula returns a `#DIV/0` error.

D2 =B2/C2

	A	B	C	D
1	Name	Sales	Hours	Sales Per Hour
2	TERRI	15	7	2.14
3	MYRTLE	13	5	2.60
4	PAUL	6	8	0.75
5	VERA	0	0	#DIV/0!
6	ALICIA	3	7	0.43
7	VICTORIA	13	4	3.25

Figure 12.6
The zero in the divisor in Row 5 causes a division-by-zero error.

The typical way to deal with this in legacy versions of Excel was to set up an `IF` function to check whether the divisor was zero: `=IF(C5=0,0,B5/C5)`. If the divisor were zero, the formula returns a zero as the result. Otherwise, the formula performs the calculation.

In legacy versions of Excel, it was typical to use this type of `IF` formula on thousands of rows of data. The formula is more complex and takes longer to calculate than the new `IFERROR` function. However, this particular formula is tame compared to some of the formulas needed to check for errors.

A common error occurs when you use the `VLOOKUP` function to retrieve a value from a lookup table. In Figure 12.7, the `VLOOKUP` function in Cell D2 asks Excel to look for the rep number S07 from Cell B2 and find the corresponding name in the lookup table of F2:G9. This works great, returning `JESSE` from the table. However, a problem arises when the sales rep is not found in the table. In Row 7, rep S09 is new and has not yet been added to the table, so Excel returns the `#N/A` result.

If you wanted to avoid `#N/A` errors, the generally accepted workaround in legacy versions of Excel was to write this horrible formula:

```
=IF(ISNA(VLOOKUP(B7,$F$2:$G$9,2,FALSE)),"New Rep", VLOOKUP(B7,$F$2:$G$9,2,FALSE))
```

D2			▾	*fx*	=IFERROR(VLOOKUP(B2,$F$2:$G$9,2,FALSE),"New Rep")		
▲	A	B	C	D	E	F	G
1	Invoice	Rep	Amount	Name		Rep	Name
2	15100	S07	128.59	JESSE		S01	GRACE
3	15101	S06	144.67	ERIN		S02	JULIE
4	15102	S05	121	JEREMY		S03	CHRISTY
5	15103	S04	169.47	THELMA		S04	THELMA
6	15104	S04	169.62	THELMA		S05	JEREMY
7	15105	S09	172.55	New Rep		S06	ERIN
8	15106	S08	112.68	MARION		S07	JESSE
9	15107	S02	145.44	JULIE		S08	MARION
10	15108	S01	101.05	GRACE			
11	15109	S05	197.68	JEREMY			

Figure 12.7
An #N/A error means that the value is not in the lookup table.

In English, this formula says to first find the rep name in the lookup table. If the rep is not found and returns the #N/A error, then use some other text, which in this case are the words New Rep. If the rep is found, then perform the lookup again and use that result.

Because VLOOKUP was one of the most time-intensive functions, it was horrible to have Excel perform every VLOOKUP twice in this formula. In a data set with 50,000 records, it could take minutes for the VLOOKUP to complete. Microsoft wisely added the new IFERROR function to handle all these error-checking situations.

Syntax:

IFERROR(*value*, *value_if_error*)

The advantage of the IFERROR function is that the calculation is evaluated only once. If the calculation results in any type of an error value such as #N/A, #VALUE!, #REF!, #DIV/0!, #NUM!, #NAME?, or #NULL!, Excel returns the alternate value. If the calculation results in any other valid value, whether it is numeric, logical, or text, Excel returns the calculated value.

The formula from the preceding section can be rewritten as =IFERROR(VLOOKUP(B7, $F$2:$G$9,2,FALSE),"New Rep") (see Figure 12.7). This calculation is easier to write and calculates much more quickly than the method required in legacy versions of Excel.

 caution

If you will be sharing your workbook with people who use legacy versions of Excel, you should avoid using IFERROR. Instead, you should test for the various error conditions as described in the next section.

Examples of Information Functions

Found under the More Function icon, the 17 information functions return eclectic information about any cell. Ten of the 17 functions are called the IS *functions* because they test for various conditions.

Using the IS Functions to Test for Errors

Figure 12.8 shows the results of the following four functions for testing error values:

- **ISERROR**—This function evaluates whether a calculation or value results in any type of error. If people using only Excel 2007 or later will use your workbooks, you should use the IFERROR function instead of ISERROR. However, if you need to share your workbook with people using legacy versions of Excel, you should use ISERROR, which is usually combined with an IF function. Here is an example: =IF(ISERROR(A2),"Unknown",A2).

- **ISERR**—This function is similar to ISERROR, except it does not report #N/A errors.

- **ISNA**—This function specifically tests whether a result returns an #N/A error.

- **ERROR.TYPE**—This function lets you know specifically what error is being returned. This function returns a value from 1 through 7 to indicate #NULL!, #DIV/0!, #VALUE!, #REF!, #NAME?, #NUM!, and #N/A, respectively. It is possible to write a lengthy formula such as the following to decode these values and provide a friendlier error message:

 note

Mathematicians in the audience may suggest that you could just as easily use =MOD(A2,2)=0 to figure out whether a number is even. However, unless you are a mathematician, it is far easier to remember =ISEVEN().

```
=IF(NOT(ISERROR(A2)),A2,CHOOSE(ERROR.TYPE(A2),"Null Value Found",
"Division by Zero","Invalid Value","Missing Reference","Undefined Name",
"Numeric Error","Value Not Available"))
```

Figure 12.8
The results of IS functions for detecting errors.

B2	▼	*fx*	=ERROR.TYPE(A2)	
	A	**B**	**C**	**D**	**E**
1	**Value**	**Error.Type**	**IsErr**	**IsError**	**IsNA**
2	#NULL!	1	TRUE	TRUE	FALSE
3	#DIV/0!	2	TRUE	TRUE	FALSE
4	#VALUE!	3	TRUE	TRUE	FALSE
5	#REF!	4	TRUE	TRUE	FALSE
6	#NAME?	5	TRUE	TRUE	FALSE
7	#NUM!	6	TRUE	TRUE	FALSE
8	#N/A	7	FALSE	TRUE	TRUE

Using IS Functions to Test for Types of Values

Figure 12.9 shows the results for the seven remaining IS functions. Each of these functions reveals if a value contains a particular type of value:

- ISBLANK—This function returns TRUE only if a cell is completely empty. A cell that contains several spaces is not considered blank. Even a cell that contains a single apostrophe and no spaces is not considered blank by the ISBLANK function. It would have been more appropriate if the folks at Lotus 1-2-3 would have called this the @IsEmpty function, but you are stuck with the bad name now that it has been in use forever.

- ISEVEN—This function indicates if a number is evenly divisible by 2. Note that Cell C8 is an empty cell, which is considered zero and reports as even. Using a date as the value in ISEVEN returns a value, but that value does not make sense. Using text or logical values in the ISEVEN function causes a #VALUE! error.

- ISODD—This function indicates whether a number is not evenly divisible by 2. An empty cell is considered zero and returns FALSE to ISODD. The same limitations listed for ISEVEN apply to ISODD. In addition, if your value contains decimal places, they are ignored by both the ISEVEN and ISODD functions. Numbers such as 1.02, 1.2, 1.5, 1.9, 1.99999999 all return TRUE for the ISODD function.

- ISLOGICAL—This function indicates if the value is either TRUE, FALSE, or an expression that results in TRUE or FALSE.

- ISTEXT—This function returns TRUE if the value contains text. This is good for finding values such as ABC in Cell A16 and for finding cells that look like numbers but are actually stored as text.

- ISNONTEXT—This returns TRUE for anything that is nontext. Numbers, logicals, dates, empty cells, and even error cells return TRUE for ISNONTEXT.

- ISNUMBER—This function returns TRUE for numeric cells and dates. Note that although the empty Cell A8 can be calculated as even in Cell C8, it returns FALSE to ISNUMBER in Cell H8.

Value	IsBlank	IsEven	IsOdd	IsLogical	IsText	IsNonText	IsNumber
1	FALSE	FALSE	TRUE	FALSE	FALSE	TRUE	TRUE
2	FALSE	TRUE	FALSE	FALSE	FALSE	TRUE	TRUE
TRUE	FALSE	#VALUE!	#VALUE!	TRUE	FALSE	TRUE	FALSE
FALSE	FALSE	#VALUE!	#VALUE!	TRUE	FALSE	TRUE	FALSE
7/1/2006	FALSE	FALSE	TRUE	FALSE	FALSE	TRUE	TRUE
ABC	FALSE	#VALUE!	#VALUE!	FALSE	TRUE	FALSE	FALSE
	TRUE	TRUE	FALSE	FALSE	FALSE	TRUE	FALSE
#N/A	FALSE	#N/A	#N/A	FALSE	FALSE	TRUE	FALSE

Figure 12.9
The results of IS functions for detecting certain types of values.

The functions in this section are nearly always used in conjunction with an IF function. For example, ZIP codes in the United States should always be five digits. This causes problems when someone keys in a ZIP code for certain eastern cities that start with a zero. For example, in Cell C6 of Figure 12.10, the proper way to key a ZIP code for Portland, Maine, is to type an apostrophe and then 04123. Most people forget the apostrophe, and Excel drops the leading zero, as shown in Cell C5.

 note

Note a very important distinction here: ISLOGICAL does not tell you whether a value is FALSE. It merely indicates that the expression results in one of the valid logical values of TRUE or FALSE.

Figure 12.10
The formula in Column D detects nontext ZIP codes and converts to text with five digits.

`=IF(ISNONTEXT(C5),RIGHT("0000"&C5,5),C5)`

	A	B	C	D
1	**City**	**ST**	**Zip Code**	**Zip Fixed**
2	Salem	OH	44460	44460
3	Uniontown	OH	44685	44685
4	Schenectady	NY	12345	12345
5	Portland	ME	4123	04123
6	Portland	ME	04123	04123
7	St Thomas	VI	801	00801
8	St Thomas	VI	00801	00801

The formula in Column D, =IF(ISNONTEXT(C5),RIGHT("0000"&C5,5),C5), fixes errant ZIP codes in Column C. If the value in Column C is nontext, the program pads the left side of the ZIP code with zeros and then takes the five right-most digits.

Another use of the IS functions is in the formulas for a conditional formatting rule. In Figure 12.11, a few cells were entered erroneously as text instead of numbers. Setting up a rule to mark any cells where the formula =ISTEXT(B2) is true reveals the cells that need to be updated.

Figure 12.11
An ISTEXT function is used in conditional formatting to mark any numbers erroneously entered as text.

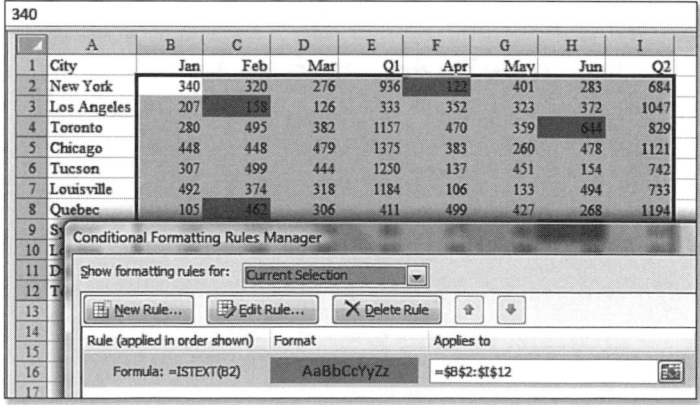

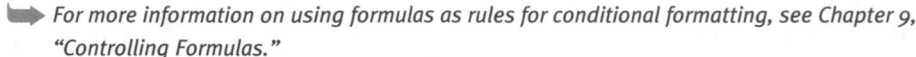 *For more information on using formulas as rules for conditional formatting, see Chapter 9, "Controlling Formulas."*

Using the ISREF Function

The ISREF function tests whether a value is a reference.

Syntax:

ISREF(*value*)

ISREF returns TRUE if the value is a valid reference. Initially, this function may seem to be useless. After all, inherently you know that A2 is a valid reference, so you would not have to use a function to test it.

The following formulas return TRUE: =ISREF(A2), =ISREF(XFD1048576), and =ISREF(A2:Z99). The following formulas return FALSE: =ISREF("A2"), =ISREF(99), and =ISREF(2+2).

ISREF is useful in one special circumstance. For example, suppose you have designed a spreadsheet with the named range "ExpenseTotal". If you are worried that someone might have deleted this particular row, you can check whether ExpenseTotal is still a valid name by using =ISREF(ExpenseTotal). Here's an example:

=IF(ISREF(ExpenseTotal),ExpenseTotal*2,"Named Range Has Been Deleted")

Using the ISREF Function to Check a Reference

The lookup function INDIRECT allows you to build a cell reference by using a formula. In Figure 12.12, the cell address in Cell D14 is built using a formula to concatenate a column letter with a row number. Cell D15 then uses the INDIRECT function to return the value stored in the cell referenced by the formula in Cell D14. As you can imagine, this process is subject to error. Someone might enter a negative number, as shown in Cell D18. Before using the INDIRECT function, you can check if the reference in Cell D14 is a valid reference by using =ISREF(INDIRECT (D14)).

Using the N Function to Add a Comment to a Formula

You can call Excel's N function a creative use for an obsolete function. Lotus 1-2-3 used to offer an N() function that converted a value as follows:

- N(any number) returned that number.
- N(a date) returned the serial number of the date.
- N(True) returned 1.
- N(False) returned 0.
- N(any error) returned the error.
- N(any text) returned 0.

Figure 12.12
Prevent problems with Indirect by checking
ISREF(INDIRECT()) first.

`=ISREF(INDIRECT(D14))`

	A	B	C	D	E	F	G
1	223	145	257	191	247		
2	401	317	170	370	395		
3	410	267	270	494	308		
4	419	123	319	473	157		
5	478	136	255	259	207		
6	480	386	268	429	205		
7	294	190	419	203	348		
8	425	293	483	285	314		
9	436	233	313	138	401		
10							
11							
12			Select a Row:	2			
13			Select a Column:	4			
14			Cell Address:	D2	=CHAR(64+D13)&D12		
15			Indirect:	370	=INDIRECT(D14)		
16			IsRef:	TRUE	=ISREF(InDirect(D14))		
17							
18			Select a Row:	-2			
19			Select a Column:	4			
20			Cell Address:	D-2	=CHAR(64+D19)&D18		
21			Indirect:	#REF!	=INDIRECT(D20)		
22			IsRef:	FALSE	=ISREF(INDIRECT(D20))		

None of these functions is terribly interesting. You can replicate just about any of them by referring to the value and changing the cell format.

An interesting unintended use of the function is that N(*any text*) always returns zero. A useful trick is to insert a comment about a long formula by adding the N function to the end of the formula. However, make sure that your comment contains text. Since N(*text*) is zero, the outcome of the function does not change. When you come back to the formula several months later, you can see the comment in the formula bar (see Figure 12.13).

Figure 12.13
Because N of text is zero, you can store a comment in the N function.

`=VLOOKUP("Tom",Z1:AA99,2,FALSE)+N(`
`"The false at the end ensures that Excel`
`will not find a close match")`

	A	B	C	D
1	Value	N(Value)		
2	5	5		123
3	15	15		
4	-15	-15		
5	2/17/2007	39130		
6	TRUE	1		
7	FALSE	0		
8	Text	0		
9	#DIV/0!	#DIV/0!		
10				

Using the NA Function to Force Charts to Not Plot Missing Data

Suppose that you are in charge of a school's annual fund drive. Each day, you mark the fundraising total on a worksheet by following these steps:

1. In Column A, you enter the results of each day's collection through 9 days of the fund drive (see Figure 12.14).

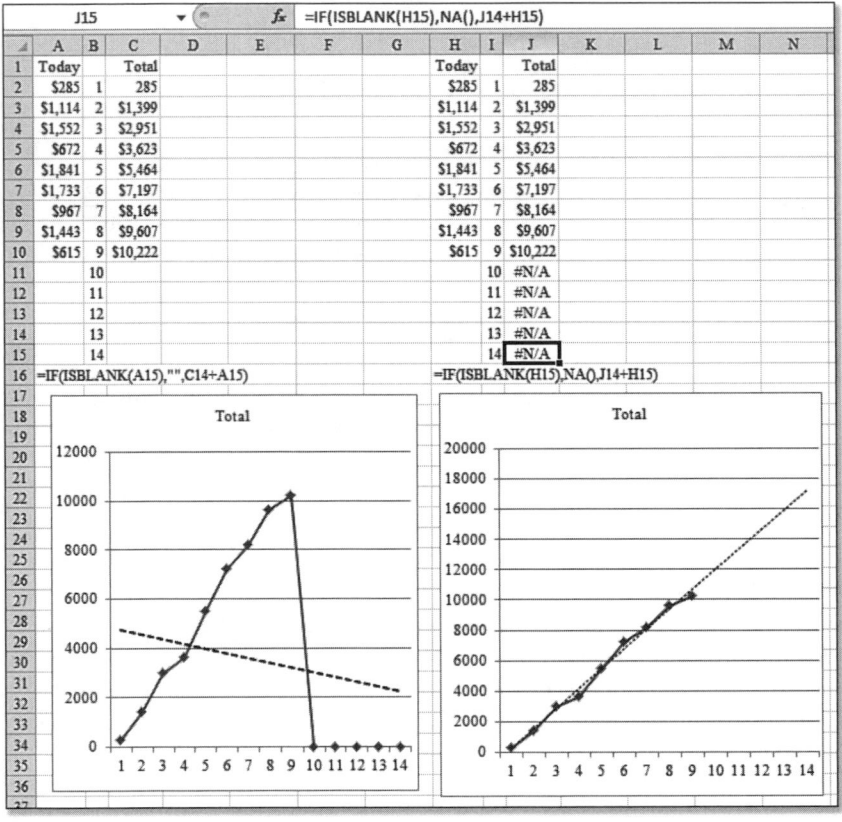

Figure 12.14
Using NA in the chart on the right allows the trendline to ignore future missing data points and project a reasonable ending result.

2. Enter a formula in Column C to keep track of the total collected throughout the fund drive.

3. To avoid making it look like the fund drive collected nothing in Days 10 through 14, enter a formula in Column C to checks whether Column A is blank. If it is, the IF function inserts a null cell in Column C. For example, the formula in Cell C15 is =IF(ISBLANK(A15)," ",A15+C14).

4. Build a line chart based on B1:C15. Add a trendline to the chart to predict future fundraising totals.

5. As shown in Columns A:C of Figure 12.14, this technique fails. Even though the totals for Days 10 through 14 are blank, Excel charts those days as zero. The linear trendline predicts that your fundraising will go down, with a projected total of just over $2,000.

6. Try the same chart again, but this time use the NA function instead of "" in the IF statement in step 3. The formula is shown in Cell H16, and the results are in Cell J15. Excel understands that NA values should not be plotted. The trendline is calculated based on only the data points available and projects a total just under $18,000.

In many cases, you are trying to avoid #N/A! errors. However, in the case of charting a calculated column, you might want to have #N/A! to produce the correct look to the chart.

Using the INFO Function to Print Information About a Computer

The remaining information functions tell you some piece of information about a particular cell or about the computer. The INFO function is left over from Lotus 1-2-3. Some of the information it provides was useful only in Lotus. However, a few of the options may be useful to display in an Excel spreadsheet.

Syntax:

=INFO(*type_text*)

The INFO function returns information about the current operating environment.

The following are valid values for the type_text argument:

- Directory—Returns the folder where the current workbook is saved. If the file is not yet saved, returns #N/A.

- NumFile—Returns the number of open files. This is not just open workbooks, but all files open on the system.

- MemAvail—Returns the available memory. This appears to be some old DOS version of the memory available. Even on a system with 128MB of RAM, the total memory reported is about 4MB, so it might be the memory assigned to the partition running Excel.

- MemUsed—Specifies the memory in use by Excel.

- TotMem—Returns the total of the previous two results.

- Origin—Returns the text "$A:" and the absolute cell address of the upper-left cell visible in the current window. The "$A:" prefix is a notation used by Lotus 1-2-3 release 3.0. You might think there could be uses for this result. For example, = INDIRECT(TRIM(MID(INFO ("Origin"),2,50))) returns the value shown in the upper-left corner of the visible window. However, note that beginning with Excel 2007, you can use the scrollbars to change the upper-left cell, and Excel does not recalculate, leaving the Origin result incorrect until you change a cell in Excel.

- OSVersion—Returns the version number of your operating system.

- Recalc—Returns either Manual or Automatic to indicate the current recalculation status. You might provide a hint to the spreadsheet reader with =IF(INFO("Recalc")="Manual","Press F9 to calculate","").

- Release—Specifies the release number of Excel. For Excel 2007, this is 12.0. You might be able to use this information in combination with IF and INDIRECT to correctly build a reference to the entire worksheet.

  System—Returns either mac or pcdos to indicate Macintosh or Windows.

Figure 12.15 shows the results of several variations of the INFO function.

	D15	▾	*fx*	=INFO(C15)				
	C	D		E	F	G	H	
5	Type_text	=INFO(Type_Text)		Comment				
6	Directory	C:\Users\Owner\Documents\		Folder where current file is stored				
7	NumFile	1		Number of workbooks open				
8	MemAvail	1048576		Available Memory				
9	MemUsed	2650220		Used Memory				
10	TotMem	3698796		Total Memory				
11	Origin	$A:$C$5		Top-left visible cell in this window				
12	OSVersion	Windows (32-bit) NT 6.00		Operating System Version				
13	Recalc	Automatic		Is Recalc turned on?				
14	Release	14.0		Version of Excel				
15	System	pcdos		Windows or Mac?				

Figure 12.15
A few of the argument values for INFO() still return useful results.

Using the CELL Function

The CELL function can tell you specific information about a specific cell, or it can tell you specific information about the last cell changed in the worksheet.

Again, some of the types of information are a bit dated. For example, the Color argument was written in the day when a cell was either black or possibly red if the value was negative. The Prefix argument is based on when cells could be left-aligned, centered, or right-aligned. Even though Excel has offered several levels of indenting for a decade, the Prefix version of the CELL function does not reveal anything about the indentation level.

Syntax:

CELL(*info_type,reference*)

To use the CELL function, you specify the type of information and optionally a cell reference. If you specify a cell reference, Excel provides information about the cell in the reference. If you leave off the reference, Excel returns information about the last cell changed in the workbook.

The argument *info_type* is a text value that specifies what type of cell information you want. The following are the possible values of *info_type* and the corresponding results:

- contents—Returns the value in the upper-left cell in reference.

- address—Returns the address of the first cell in reference, as text. As shown in Cell B5 of Figure 12.16, this is always returned in absolute reference style.

Figure 12.16
The CELL function returns information about a specific cell, in this case, Cell A1.

	A	B	C	D	E
			B4 ▾ f_x =CELL(A4,$A$1)		
1	test				
2					
3	**Info_type**	**=Cell(Info_Type,$A$1)**			
4	contents	test			
5	address	$A$1			
6	row	1			
7	col	1			
8	filename	C:\Users\Owner\Documents\[12-Cell2.xls]Specific Cell			
9	format	F1			
10	parentheses	0			
11	color	0			
12	prefix	^			
13	protect	1			
14	type	1			
15	width	13			
16					

- row—Returns the row number of the cell in reference.

- col—Returns the column number of the cell in reference.

- filename—Returns the filename as text including the full path of the file that contains *reference*. If the worksheet that contains reference has not yet been saved, empty text (" ") is returned. Interestingly, this argument now also returns the worksheet name if the workbook contains multiple worksheets.

- format—Returns the text value corresponding to the number format of the cell. Returns - at the end of the text value if the cell is formatted in color for negative values. If the cell is formatted with parentheses for positive or all values, ( ) is returned at the end of the text value. The values reported as a format reflect old Lotus 1-2-3 codes. When you format, Excel attempts to convert the current numeric format to an old-style Lotus 1-2-3 formatting code. Table 12.7 shows some examples.

- parentheses—Returns 1 if the cell is formatted with parentheses for positive or all values; otherwise, returns 0.

Table 12.7 Custom Codes in Excel and Lotus 1-2-3

Excel Format	Excel Custom	Lotus Format Code	Code
General	General	G	
Numeric, no Decimal	0		F0
Numeric, 2 Decimals	0.00	F2	
Comma, 2 Decimals	#,##0.00		,2
Currency, 2 Decimals		$#,##0.00_)	C2
Percent, 1 Decimal		0.0%	P1
Scientific Notation		0.00E+00	S2
Fractions	# ?/?		G
Date	m/d/yy D4		
Date	d-mmm-y		D1
Date	d-mmm	D2	
Date	mmm-yy		D3
Time	H:mm AM/PM	D7	

- `color`—Returns 1 if the cell is formatted in color for negative values; otherwise, returns 0.

- `prefix`—Returns the text value corresponding to the "label prefix" of the cell as follows:

  - Returns a single quotation mark (') if the cell contains left-aligned text.

  - Returns double quotation mark (") if the cell contains right-aligned text.

  - Returns a caret (^) if the cell contains centered text.

  - Returns a backslash (\) if the cell contains fill-aligned text.

  - Returns an empty text ("") if the cell contains anything else.

- `protect`—Returns 0 if the cell is not locked and 1 if the cell is locked. Remember that by default, all Excel cells start with their `locked` property set to `TRUE`. The `locked` property is taken into account only if protection is enabled. This argument for the CELL function reports a 1 even if protection is not turned on.

- `type`—Returns the text value corresponding to the type of data in the cell as follows:

  - Returns b for blank if the cell is empty.

  - Returns l for label if the cell contains a text constant.

caution

Be careful with this: It is now possible to change column widths without causing Excel to calculate. You might have to press F9 to have the result of this formula change.

- Returns v for value if the cell contains anything else.

- width—Returns the column width of the cell, rounded to an integer. Each unit of column width is equal to the width of one character in the default font size.

- reference—Is an optional cell reference. If reference is omitted, CELL returns the information about the last changed cell.

Refer back to Figure 12.16, which shows every CELL option for a specific cell: Cell A1.

For additional examples, see Excel Help for the CELL function.

Using CELL to Track the Last Cell Changed

If you leave off the second argument of the CELL function, Excel returns the information about the last cell changed in the workbook.

Follow these steps to create an interesting watch window of the last cells changed:

1. In an out-of-the-way spot, enter the formula =CELL("address").

2. Just below this formula, enter the formula =CELL("Contents").

3. Just below that formula, enter the formula =CELL("filename").

4. Select all three of these cells.

5. From the Formulas tab, select the Watch Window icon. The Watch Window dialog appears.

6. Click the Add Watch button in the Watch Window dialog.

7. Because initially, the default file widths are not wide enough to show the complete value, drag the vertical bars between the headings in the watch window so that you can see the complete Value and Formula columns. The other columns for Book, Sheet, and Cell can be made smaller.

The result, as shown in Figure 12.17, is a floating window that always reveals the last changed cell address and contents.

Figure 12.17
The watch window always shows the last cell changed and the value of that cell. Note that as in this case, the last changed cell might be on another worksheet.

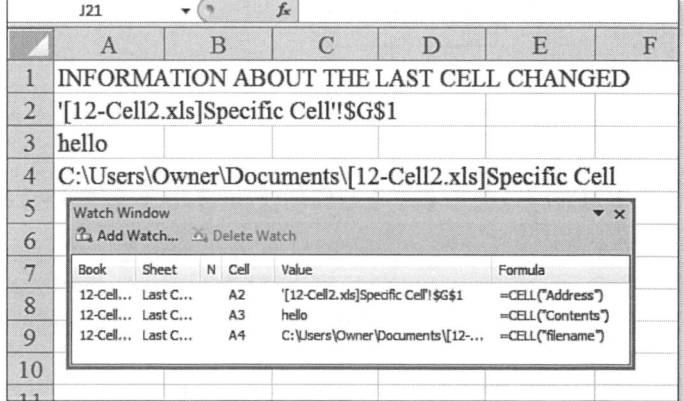

Using TYPE to Determine Type of Cell Value

The final information function is the TYPE function. You use =TYPE(*value*) to determine whether a value is a number, text, logical, an error value, or an array. Note that dates are treated as numbers.

Syntax:

=TYPE(*value*)

The TYPE function returns a numeric code that tells you about the type of value.

The TYPE function returns the following values:

- 1—For a numeric or date type
- 2—For a text type
- 4—For a logical type
- 16—For an error type
- 64—An array type

Figure 12.18 shows the results for various values in the TYPE function.

	B9	▼	*fx*	=TYPE({1,2,3})	
	A		B		C
1	**Value**		**Type(Value)**		
2	5		1		
3	-15		1		
4	2/17/2007		1		
5	TRUE		4		
6	FALSE		4		
7	Text		2		
8	#DIV/0!		16		
9			64		
10					

Figure 12.18
The TYPE function returns what type of value is specified as an argument.

Examples of Lookup and Reference Functions

The Lookup & Reference icon contains 18 functions. The all-star of this group is the venerable VLOOKUP function, which is one of the most powerful and most used functions in Excel. As database people point out, a lot of work done in Excel should probably be done in Access. The VLOOKUP function allows you to perform the equivalent of a join operation in a database.

This lookup and reference group also includes several functions that seem useless when considered alone. However, when combined, they allow for some very powerful manipulations of data. The examples in the following sections reveal details on how to use the lookup functions and how to combine them to create powerful results.

Using the CHOOSE Function for Simple Lookups

Most lookup functions require you to set up a lookup table in a range on the worksheet. However, the CHOOSE function allows you to specify up to 254 choices right in the syntax of the function. The formula that requires the lookup should be able to calculate an integer from 1 to 254 in order to use the CHOOSE function.

Syntax:

CHOOSE(*index_num,value1,value2,...*)

The CHOOSE value chooses a value from a list of values, based on an index number.

The CHOOSE function takes the following arguments:

- index_num—This specifies which value argument is selected. index_num must be a number between 1 and 254 or a formula or reference to a cell containing a number between 1 and 254:

  - If index_num is 1, CHOOSE returns value1; if it is 2, CHOOSE returns value2; and so on.

  - If index_num is a decimal, it is rounded down to the next lowest integer before being used.

  - If index_num is less than 1 or greater than the number of the last value in the list, CHOOSE returns a #VALUE! error.

- value1,value2,...—These are 1 to 254 value arguments from which CHOOSE selects a value or an action to perform based on *index_num*. The arguments can be numbers, cell references, defined names, formulas, functions, or text.

The example in Figure 12.19 shows survey data from a number of respondents. Columns B:F indicate their responses on five measures of your service. Column G calculates an average that ranges from 1 to 5. Say that you want to add words to Column H to characterize the overall rating from the respondent. The following formula is used in Cell H4:

=CHOOSE(G4,"Strongly Disagree","Disagree","Neutral","Agree","Strongly Agree")

Figure 12.19
CHOOSE is great for simple choices where the index number is between 1 and 254.

| =CHOOSE(G4,"Strongly Disagree","Disagree","Neutral","Agree","Strongly Agree") | | | | | | | | | | | |
A	B	C	D	E	F	G	H	I	J	K	L
1 **Survey Results**											
2											
3 Resp.	Q1	Q2	Q3	Q4	Q5	Avg.	Result				
4 R01	5	5	5	5	4	4.8	Agree				
5 R02	4	4	4	4	4	4	Agree				
6 R03	1	2	2	2	2	1.8	Strongly Disagree				
7 R04	5	4	4	3	4	4	Agree				
8 R05	3	3	2	2	2	2.4	Disagree				
9 R06	1	1	1	1	1	1	Strongly Disagree				

Using VLOOKUP **with** TRUE **to Find a Value Based on a Range**

VLOOKUP stands for *vertical lookup*. This function behaves differently, depending on the fourth parameter. This section describes using VLOOKUP where you need to choose a value based on a table that contains ranges.

Suppose that you have a list of students and their scores on a test. The school grading scale is based on these ranges:

- 92–100 is an A.

- 85–91 is a B.

- 70–85 is a C.

- 65–69 is a D.

- Below 65 is an F.

Follow these steps to set up a VLOOKUP for this scenario:

1. Because in this version of VLOOKUP you do not have to list every possible grade, build a table showing the scores where the grading scale changes from one grade to the next.

2. Although the published grading scale starts with the higher values, your lookup table must be sorted in ascending sequence. This requires a bit of translation as you set up the table. Although the grading scale says below 65 is an F, you need to set up the table to show that an F corresponds to any grade at 0 or above. Therefore, in Cell E2 enter 0, and in Cell F2, enter F.

3. Continue building the grading scale in successive rows of Columns E and F. Anything above a 65 is given a D. Anything above 70 is given a C. Note that this is somewhat counterintuitive because it is the opposite order that you would use if you were building a grading scale using nested IF functions.

4. Ensure that the numeric values are the leftmost column in your lookup table. In Figure 12.20, the lookup table range is E2:F6. When you use VLOOKUP, Excel searches the first column of the lookup table for the appropriate score.

5. When using this version of VLOOKUP with ranges, sort the list in ascending order. If you are not sure of the proper order, use the Sort command from the Home tab to sort the table.

6. Because the first argument in the VLOOKUP function is the student's score, in Cell C2, enter =VLOOKUP(B2,.

7. Because the next argument is the range of the lookup table, be sure to press the F4 key after typing E2:F6 to change to an absolute reference of $E$2:$F$6.

8. Ensure that the third argument specifies which column of the lookup table should be returned. Because the letter grade is in the second column of E2:F6, use 2 for the third argument.

9. Ensure that the final argument is either TRUE or simply omitted. This tells Excel that you are using the sorted range variety of lookup.

10. After you enter the formula in Cell C2, again select Cell C2 and double-click the fill handle to copy the formula down to all students.

Figure 12.20
The VLOOKUP formula in Column C finds the correct grade from the table in Columns E and F.

	C2	▼ (●	*fx*	=VLOOKUP(B2,$E$2:$F$6,2,TRUE)		
▲	A	B	C	D	E	F
1	Student	Score	Grade			
2	CECILIA ALBERT	96	A		0	F
3	KRISTEN FOREMAN	88	B		65	D
4	DOROTHY MARTINEZ	76	C		70	C
5	LUIS FISCHER	93	A		85	B
6	TERRY SKINNER	89	B		92	A
7	SHELLEY OSBORN	69	D			
8	MARVIN SCHULTZ	77	C			
9	JOE TRUJILLO	93	A			
10	WILLIAM SKINNER	93	A			

Using VLOOKUP with FALSE to Find an Exact Value

In some situations, you do not want VLOOKUP to return a value based on a close match. Instead, you want Excel to find the exact match in the lookup table.

Figure 12.21 shows a table of sales. The original table had just Columns A through C: Rep#, Date, and Sale Amount. Although a data analyst might have all the rep numbers memorized, the manager who is going to see the report prefers to have the rep names on the report.

To fill in the rep names from a lookup table, you follow these steps:

1. In Columns F and G, enter a table of rep numbers and rep names. Note that it is not important that this table be sorted by the rep number field. It is fine that the table is alphabetical.

2. Use FALSE as the fourth parameter in VLOOKUP. You need to do this because close matches are not acceptable here. If something was sold by a new rep with number R9, you do not want to give credit to the name associated with R8 just because it is a close match. Either Excel finds an exact match and returns the result, or Excel does not give you a result.

3. For Cell D2, you want Excel to use the rep number in A2, so in Cell D2, enter =VLOOKUP(A2,.

4. The lookup table is in F2:G7, so type F2:G7 and then press the F4 key to make the reference absolute. This allows you to copy the formula in step 7. After pressing F4, type a comma.

5. In the lookup table, the rep name is in Column 2 of the table, so type 2 to specify that you want to return the second column of the lookup table.

6. Finish the function with FALSE). Press Ctrl+Enter to accept the formula and keep the cursor in Cell D2.

7. Double-click the fill handle to copy the formula down to all the rows.

8. VLOOKUP is a very time-intensive calculation. Having thousands of VLOOKUP formulas significantly affects your recalculation times. In this particular case, you have successfully added rep names. It would be appropriate to convert these live formulas to their current values. Therefore, press Ctrl+C to copy. Then, from the Home tab, select Paste, Paste Values to convert the formulas to values.

9. Look through the results. If a sale was credited to a new rep who is not in the table, the name appears as #N/A. Manually fix these records, if needed.

 note

If your lookup table is arranged with the key field in Row 1, you should use HLOOKUP, which is discussed later in this chapter. If your data is vertical but the key field is not the leftmost column, you can use a combination of INDEX and MATCH, also explained later in this chapter.

	A	B	C	D	E	F	G
			fx	=VLOOKUP(A2,$F$2:$G$7,2,FALSE)			
1	Rep	Date	Sale Amt	Rep Name			
2	R5	2/17/2006	194.59	Manny		R4	Amar
3	R7	2/17/2006	117.28	Michael		R8	Jerry
4	R5	2/17/2006	112.06	Manny		R6	Linda
5	R3	2/17/2006	191.67	Marc		R5	Manny
6	R6	2/18/2006	176.63	Linda		R3	Marc
7	R3	2/18/2006	151.17	Marc		R7	Michael
8	R8	2/18/2006	173.14	Jerry			
9	R8	2/18/2006	126.85	Jerry			
10	R2	2/19/2006	127.32	#N/A			
11	R2	2/19/2006	117.03	Marc			

Figure 12.21
In this case, VLOOKUP needs to find the exact rep number from the table in Columns E and F.

To recap, the two versions of the VLOOKUP formula behave very differently. VLOOKUP with FALSE as the fourth parameter looks for an exact match, whereas VLOOKUP with TRUE as the fourth parameter looks for the closest (lower) match. In the TRUE version, the lookup table must be sorted. In the FALSE version, the table can be in any sequence. In every case, the key field must be in the left column of the lookup table.

Syntax:

VLOOKUP(*lookup_value,table_array,col_index_num,range_lookup*)

VLOOKUP searches for a value in the leftmost column of a table and then returns a value in the same row from a column you specify in the table. The VLOOKUP function takes the following arguments:

- lookup_value—This is the value to be found in the first column of the table. lookup_value can be a value, reference, or text string.

- table_array—This is the table of information in which data is looked up. You can use a reference to a range such as E2:F9 or a range name such as RepTable.

- col_index_num—This is the column number in table_array from which the matching value must be returned. A col_index_num value of 1 returns the value in the first column in table_array; a col_index_num value of 2 returns the value in the second column in table_array, and so on. If col_index_num is less than 1, VLOOKUP returns the #VALUE! error value; if col_index_num is greater than the number of columns in table_array, VLOOKUP returns the #REF! error value.

- range_lookup—This is a logical value that specifies whether VLOOKUP should find an exact match or an approximate match. If it is TRUE or omitted, an approximate match is returned. In other words, if an exact match is not found, the next largest value that is less than lookup_value is returned. If it is FALSE, VLOOKUP finds an exact match. If one is not found, the error value #N/A is returned. If VLOOKUP cannot find lookup_value and if range_lookup is TRUE, it uses the largest value that is less than or equal to lookup_value. If lookup_value is smaller than the smallest value in the first column of table_array, VLOOKUP returns an #N/A error. If VLOOKUP cannot find lookup_value, and range_lookup is FALSE, VLOOKUP returns an #N/A error.

Using VLOOKUP to Match Two Lists

If Excel is used throughout your company, you undoubtedly have many lists in Excel. People use Excel to track everything. How many times are you faced with a situation in which you have two versions of a list and you need to match them up?

In Figure 12.22, the worksheet has two simple lists. Column A shows last week's version of who was coming to an event. Column C shows this week's version of who is coming to an event. Follow these steps if you want to find out quickly if anyone is new:

1. Add the heading There? to Cell D2.

2. Because the formula in Cell D3 should look at the value in Cell C3 to see if that person is in the original list in Column A, start the formula with =VLOOKUP(C3,$A$3:$A$15,.

3. Because your only choice for the column number is to return the first column from the original list, finish the function with 1,FALSE). Then press Ctrl+Enter to accept the formula and stay in Cell D3.

4. Double-click the fill handle to copy the formula down to all rows.

For any cells where Column D contains a name, it means that the person was on the RSVP list from last week. If the result of the VLOOKUP is #N/A, you know that this person is new since the previous week.

 tip

If you study the data in Figure 12.22, you will see that three more names are in the Column C list than in the Column A list, yet four people were reported as being new this week. This means that one of the people from last week has dropped off the list. To quickly find who dropped off the list, use the formula =VLOOKUP (A3,$C$3:$C$18,1,FALSE) in B3:B15 to find that Donald Tyler has dropped off the list.

Note that you can also use MATCH to solve this problem.

	A	B	C	D
			D3 ▾ fx =VLOOKUP(C3,$A$3:$A$15,1,FALSE)	
1	RSVP's LAST WEEK		RSVP's THIS WEEK	
2				There?
3	VERONICA HAHN		ARTHUR FLETCHER	ARTHUR FLETCHER
4	ELLEN LINDSAY		BARBARA BERGER	BARBARA BERGER
5	CECILIA HARMON		CANDICE GLENN	CANDICE GLENN
6	DONALD TYLER		CECILIA HARMON	CECILIA HARMON
7	NICOLE KELLY		CHRIS PAGE	CHRIS PAGE
8	MARCIA ERICKSON		CHRISTOPHER DONOVAN	#N/A
9	BARBARA BERGER		JOANN BROOKS	#N/A
10	CHRIS PAGE		ELLEN LINDSAY	ELLEN LINDSAY
11	CANDICE GLENN		JACOB MCINTYRE	#N/A
12	STACY DUNLAP		JOHN GARRISON	JOHN GARRISON
13	ARTHUR FLETCHER		KATHLEEN RICHARD	KATHLEEN RICHARD
14	KATHLEEN RICHARD		MARCIA ERICKSON	MARCIA ERICKSON
15	JOHN GARRISON		MYRTLE MOON	#N/A
16			NICOLE KELLY	NICOLE KELLY
17			STACY DUNLAP	STACY DUNLAP
18			VERONICA HAHN	VERONICA HAHN

Figure 12.22
An #N/A error as the result of VLOOKUP tells you that the person is new to the list.

Using COLUMN to Assist with VLOOKUP When Filling a Wide Table

This section discusses some special considerations to keep in mind when you have to retrieve many columns from a table. If you think carefully about the first formula, you can copy the first formula to the entire table quickly.

Figure 12.23 shows a table of several hundred SKUs, starting in Row 21. For each SKU, the table contains the inventory of that product on hand in the 12 regional warehouses. Range A6:B13 contains a customer order for various SKUs. You want to build a table to help visualize which warehouse has most of the items in stock. If you find one warehouse that has all the inventory, you can minimize order shipping costs by shipping the entire order from that particular warehouse.

To solve this problem, follow these steps:

1. Copy the range of warehouse names from B20:M20 to C5:N5.

2. Think about the third argument in the VLOOKUP function. For the formula in Column C, you want to return the second column from the table. For the formula in Column D, you want to return the third column. If you actually enter the 2 in the formula in Column C, then after copying the formula over to D:N, you have to edit the third argument repeatedly.

3. Create a range above your table, perhaps in Row 4, that contains the numbers 2 through 13. You can then use cells in this row when building the third argument in the formula. In Cell C4, enter the function =COLUMN(B2). Because Column B is the second column, this formula returns 2.

4. Select Cell C4. Drag the fill handle to the right to copy the formula over through Column N. The Cell B2 reference is relative, resulting in the formula returning the numbers 2, 3, 4, and so on.

Figure 12.23
The COLUMN function in Row 4 ensures that you can enter the VLOOKUP formula once and copy it to the entire rectangular range.

	A	B	C	D	E	F	G	H
	C6		f_x	=VLOOKUP($B6,$A$21:$M$176,C$4,FALSE)				
1	Order Fulfillment Decision Tool							
2	Enter Customer Order in A&B, check stock in C:P							
3								
4			2	3	4	5	6	7
5	Qty	Item	WH01	WH02	WH03	WH04	WH05	WH06	W
6	2	G598	0	87	37	0	4	58
7	8	D900	0	107	3	3	0	79
8	3	N528	5	5	0	0	0	4
9	3	I301	0	5	128	25	48	0
10	4	W185	4	5	3	1	135	139
11	1	S326	4	0	3	0	45	4
12	7	H415	0	5	5	75	5	1
13	3	C252	2	26	59	0	0	134
14								
15								
16								
17								
18	Inventory By Warehouse							
19								
20	Item	WH01	WH02	WH03	WH04	WH05	WH06	WH07	W
21	F219	36	2	71	1	96	83	0
22	J645	0	3	0	0	0	85	5
23	C955	113	2	2	0	0	35	29
24	C703	4	72	0	58	6	0	110

5. In Cell C6, enter =VLOOKUP(B6. When you later copy this formula, you always want the formula to point to Column B, but you want to allow the formula to point to Rows 7, 8, and so on. If you press the F4 key three times, the reference changes to $B6. Type a comma.

6. Type A21:M176. Press F4 to change this reference to $A$21:$M$176. Type a comma.

7. For the third argument, you want to point to the number 2 in Cell C4. You always want this part of the formula to point to Row 4, and you want to allow the column letter to change as the formula is copied to the right. Press the F4 key twice to change the reference to C$4.

8. Finish the formula with ,FALSE). Press Ctrl+Enter to accept the formula and stay in Cell C4.

9. Optionally, add a conditional format to Cell C4 to highlight the cell if this formula is true: =C6>=$A6.

10. Double-click the fill handle to copy the formula to C4:C13.

11. Drag the fill handle from the corner of C13 to the right until you have filled in the formula in the range of C:N.

The result is a table that shows the current inventory for each item, by warehouse. If you added the conditional formatting in step 9, you can quickly see which warehouses can fulfill most of the order.

Although having the COLUMN function in Row 4 allows you to visually understand the example better, you can eliminate Row 4 and rewrite the formula in Cell C6 as =VLOOKUP($B6,$A$21:$M$176, COLUMN(B1),FALSE).

Syntax:

COLUMN(*reference*)

The COLUMN function returns the column number of a given reference. This function takes the argument reference, which is the cell or range of cells for which you want the column number. If reference is omitted, it is assumed to be the reference of the cell in which the COLUMN function appears.

If reference is a range of cells, and if COLUMN is entered as a horizontal array, COLUMN returns the column numbers of reference as a horizontal array. In this case, reference cannot refer to multiple areas.

Using HLOOKUP for Horizontal Lookup Tables

HLOOKUP stands for *horizontal lookup*. This function is similar to VLOOKUP.

HLOOKUP operates in two distinct manners, based on the fourth parameter. If the fourth parameter is the value FALSE, then HLOOKUP is looking for an exact match in the top row of the table. This is fine when you are looking up product codes, customer numbers, or any other discrete bits of information.

However, if the fourth parameter is the value TRUE or is omitted, HLOOKUP is treating the first row of the table as a sorted range of values. Excel looks for the closest lower value than the one you specified. This is fine when you are trying to determine in which range a value belongs.

Syntax:

HLOOKUP(*lookup_value,table_array,row_index_num,range_lookup*)

The HLOOKUP function searches for a value in the top row of a table. When the value is found, HLOOKUP returns a value from a particular row in the column. This function takes the following arguments:

- lookup_value—This is a value to be found in the first row of the table. lookup_value can be a value, a reference, or a text string.

- table_array—This is a table of information in which data is looked up. You use a reference to a range or a range name. The values in the first row of table_array can be text, numbers, or logical values. If range_lookup is TRUE, the values in the first row of table_array must be placed in ascending order such as ..., -2, -1, 0, 1, 2,...; A–Z; or FALSE, TRUE. Otherwise, HLOOKUP may not give the correct value. If range_lookup is FALSE, table_array does not need to be sorted. The search is not case-sensitive: Uppercase and lowercase text are equivalent.

- row_index_num—This is the row number in table_array from which the matching value is returned. A row_index_num of 1 returns the first row value in table_array, a row_index_num of 2 returns the second row value in table_array, and so on. If row_index_num is less than 1, HLOOKUP returns a #VALUE! error; if row_index_num is greater than the number of rows in `table_array`, HLOOKUP returns a #REF! error.

- `range_lookup`—This is a logical value that specifies whether you want HLOOKUP to find an exact match or an approximate match. If it is TRUE or omitted, an approximate match is returned. In other words, if an exact match is not found, the next largest value that is less than `lookup_value` is returned. If it is FALSE, HLOOKUP finds an exact match. If one is not found, the error #N/A is returned.

Even though you are probably familiar with sorting a list from top to bottom, most people rarely sort a list from left to right. If you are using the TRUE version of HLOOKUP, make sure that your table is sorted from left to right by the top row. To sort data from left to right, follow these steps:

1. Select your range of data. In Figure 12.24, this is G3:L8.

Figure 12.24
The table in F:L is horizontal, so you use the HLOOKUP function.

B6			*fx*	=HLOOKUP($B$2,$G$3:$L$8,3,FALSE)						
	A	B	C	D E	F	G	H	I	J	K	L
1	ADVERTISING PROMOTION CALENDAR										
2	YEAR:	2011									
3						2008	2009	2010	2011	2012	2013
4					Chinese New Year	2/7/2008	1/26/2009	2/14/2010	2/3/2011	1/23/2012	2/10/2013
5	Spring Sales Circular Planning				Easter	3/23/2008	4/12/2009	4/4/2010	4/24/2011	4/8/2012	3/31/2013
6	Easter:	4/24/2011	Sunday		4th of July	7/4/2008	7/4/2009	7/4/2010	7/4/2011	7/4/2012	7/4/2013
7	In Newspaper	4/17/2011	Sunday		Thanksgiving	11/28/2008	11/27/2009	11/26/2010	11/24/2011	11/22/2012	11/28/2013
8	Artwork due	3/24/2011	Thursday		Christmas	12/25/2008	12/25/2009	12/25/2010	12/25/2011	12/25/2012	12/25/2013
9											
10	Summer Sales Circular Planning										
11	July 4	7/4/2011	Monday								
12	In Newspaper	7/3/2011	Sunday								
13	Artwork Due	6/9/2011	Thursday								
14											
15	Black Friday Circular Planning										
16	Thanksgiving	11/24/2011	Thursday								
17	In Newspaper	11/22/2011	Tuesday								
18	Artwork Due	10/27/2011	Thursday								

2. From the Home tab, select the Sort & Filter drop-down. The Sort dialog appears.

3. In the Sort dialog, click the Options button. The Sort Options dialog appears.

4. In the Sort Options dialog, select Sort Left to Right. Click OK to close the Sort Options dialog.

5. In the Sort dialog, choose to sort by Row 3. Click OK to sort.

Figure 12.24 shows a tool used by the advertising department of a retail store. The store runs annual promotions for certain holidays. The table in F3:L8 tells the days for holidays in each of several years.

The advertising manager knows that the store wants to run a sale circular the Sunday before the holiday and that the art department needs the material 24 days before the ad is to run. By changing the year in Cell B2, the advertising manager can create a new schedule for each year. To help the advertising manager, follow these steps:

1. Ensure that the formula for each holiday starts as =HLOOKUP($B$2,. This tells Excel to use the year found in Cell B2 as the value to look up.

2. Ensure that the lookup table is in $G$3:$L$8. Excel looks through the first row of this table to find the matching year.

3. When the matching column is found, you want Excel to return the date for Easter. Although this is in Row 5 of the worksheet, it is in the third row of the table, so ensure that the third parameter for the function is 3.

4. Your years are already sorted left to right, but if you use a value of TRUE for the fourth parameter, this causes problems in the year 2014, so make the fourth parameter FALSE. Ensure that the formula in Cell B6 is =HLOOKUP($B$2,$G$3:$L$8,3,FALSE).

5. Copy this formula to Cell B11 and edit the formula to change the third parameter from 3 to 4.

Using the MATCH Function to Locate the Position of a Matching Value

At first glance, MATCH seems like a function that would rarely be useful. MATCH returns the relative position of an item in a range that matches a specified value in a specified order. You use MATCH instead of one of the lookup functions when you need the position of an item in a range instead of the item itself.

Suppose that your manager asks, "Can you tell me on which row I would find this value?" The manager wants to know the value or some piece of data on that record. However, the manager rarely wants to know that XYZ is found on the 111th relative row within the Range A99:A11432.

MATCH comes in handy in several instances. In the first instance, consider a situation in which you are using VLOOKUP to find whether an item is in a list. In this case, you do not care what value is returned. You are either interested in seeing if a valid value is returned, meaning that the entry is in the old list, or if an #N/A is returned, meaning that the entry is new. In this case, using MATCH is a slightly faster way to achieve the same result.

Another handy way to use MATCH is in conjunction with the INDEX function. MATCH has two features that make it more versatile than VLOOKUP. MATCH allows for wildcard matches. MATCH also allows for a search based on an exact match, based on the number just below the value, or based on a value greater than or equal to the lookup value. This third option is not available in the VLOOKUP or HLOOKUP functions.

Syntax:

MATCH(*lookup_value,lookup_array,match_type*)

The MATCH function returns the relative position of an item in a column of values. It is useful for determining if a certain value exists in a list.

The MATCH function takes the following arguments:

- lookup_value—This is the value you use to find the value you want in a table. lookup_value can be a value, which is a number, text, or logical value or a cell reference to a number, text, or logical value.

- lookup_array—This is a contiguous range of cells that contains possible lookup values. lookup_array can be an array or an array reference.

- match_type—This is the number -1, 0, or 1. Note that you can use TRUE instead of 1 and FALSE instead of 0. match_type specifies how Microsoft Excel matches lookup_value with values in lookup_array. If match_type is 1, MATCH finds the largest value that is less than or equal to lookup_value. lookup_array must be placed in ascending order, such as ... -2, -1, 0, 1, 2,...; A–Z; or FALSE, TRUE. If match_type is 0, MATCH finds the first value that is exactly equal to lookup_value. lookup_array can be in any order. If match_type is -1, MATCH finds the smallest value that is greater than or equal to lookup_value. lookup_array must be placed in descending order, such as TRUE, FALSE; Z–A; or ...2, 1, 0, -1, -2,.... If match_type is omitted, it is assumed to be 1.

MATCH returns the position of the matched value within lookup_array, not the value itself. For example, MATCH("b",{"a","b","c"},0) returns 2, the relative position of b within the array {"a","b","c"}.

MATCH does not distinguish between uppercase and lowercase letters when matching text values.

If MATCH is unsuccessful in finding a match, it returns an #N/A error.

If match_type is 0 and lookup_value is text, lookup_value can contain the wildcard characters asterisk (*) and question mark (?). An asterisk matches any sequence of characters; a question mark matches any single character.

Using MATCH to Compare Two Lists

You may face situations in which you have two versions of a list, and you need to match them up.

In Figure 12.25, the worksheet has two simple lists. Column A shows last week's list. Column C shows this week's version of the list. You want to find out quickly which items are new. Here's how you do it:

Figure 12.25
MATCH operates slightly more quickly than VLOOKUP and achieves the same result in this special case where you are trying to figure out whether a value is in another list.

	D3	▼	f_x =MATCH(C3,$A$3:$A$11,0)		
	A	B	C	D	
1	ENTRIES LAST WEEK		ENTRIES THIS WEEK		
2				There?	
3	PILGRIM		COLUMBIA		2
4	COLUMBIA		CONSTELLATION		8
5	MAYFLOWER		COURAGEOUS	#N/A	
6	VOLUNTEER		DEFENDER		5
7	DEFENDER		FREEDOM	#N/A	
8	RELIANCE		INTREPID		9
9	RANGER		MAYFLOWER		3
10	CONSTELLATION		PILGRIM		1
11	INTREPID		RANGER		7
12			RELIANCE		6
13			STARS AND STRIPES	#N/A	
14			VOLUNTEER		4
15			WEATHERLY	#N/A	
16			YOUNG AMERICA	#N/A	
17					

1. Add the heading There? to Cell D2.

2. Because the formula in Cell D3 looks at the value in Cell C3 to see if that value is in the original list in Column A, start the formula with =MATCH(C3,$A$3:$A$11,.

3. Because you want an exact match, use 0 as the third parameter. Finish the function with a). Press Ctrl+Enter to accept the formula and stay in Cell C3.

4. Double-click the fill handle to copy the formula down to all rows.

For any cells where Column D contains a number, it means that the entry was on the original list from last week. If the result of MATCH is #N/A, you know that this item is new since the previous week.

Using INDEX and MATCH for a Left Lookup

INDEX is another function that does not immediately seem to have many great uses. In its basic form, INDEX returns the cell from a particular row and column of a rectangular range.

As shown in Figure 12.26, using =INDEX(B5:D9,3,2) seems like a needlessly complicated way to refer to Cell C7.

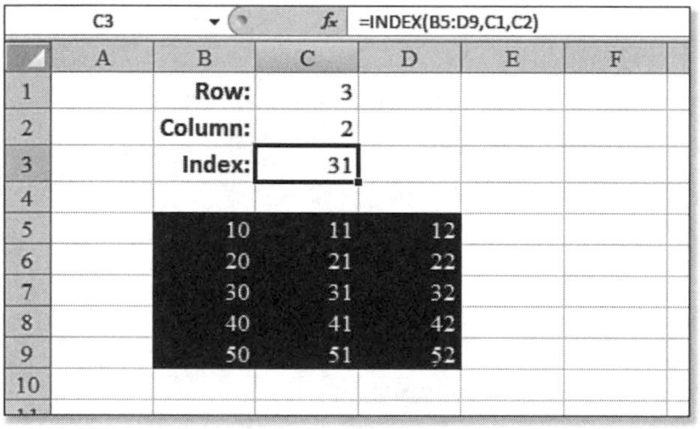

Figure 12.26
On its own, INDEX is not a particularly useful function.

However, in the previous section you learned about a function that searches through a range and tells you the position of the match within the range. Finding the position of a match is not very useful. However, finding the position of a match is very useful when used inside of the INDEX function.

In Figure 12.27, a customer number is entered in Cell A1. The customer lookup table appears in Columns F, G, and H. The main problem is that the customer table does not have the customer number on the left side.

In many cases, you would copy Column H to Column E and use Column E as the key of the table. However, the table in F:H is likely to be repopulated every day from a web query or an OLAP query. Therefore, it might become monotonous to move the data after every refresh. The solution is to use a combination of INDEX and MATCH. Here's what you do:

1. Use the formula =MATCH(B1,H2:H89,0) to search through Column H to find the row with the customer number that matches the one in Cell B1. In this case, C593 is in Row 12, which is the 11th row of the table.

2. Be sure to use exactly the same shape range as the first argument in the INDEX function: =INDEX(F2:F89,WhichRow,WhichColumn) searches through the customer names in Column F.

3. For the second parameter of the INDEX function, specify the relative row number. This information was provided by the MATCH function in step 1.

4. Ensure that the third parameter of the INDEX function is the relative column number. Because the Range F2:F89 has only one column, this is either 1 or it can simply be omitted.

5. Putting the formula together, the formula in Cell B2 is =INDEX(F2:F89,MATCH(B1,H2:H89,0),1).

Figure 12.27
This combination of INDEX and MATCH allows you to look up data that is to the left of a key field.

	B2	▾	fx	=INDEX(F2:F89,MATCH(B1,H2:H89,FALSE),1)			
	A	B	C	D	E	F	G	H
1	Cust #:	C593				Name	Address	Cust #
2	Name:	Brandy Cook				Ada Schultz	531 Hickory Circle, Bloomingd	C640
3	Address:	144 North Highway, Georgetown, MA 56702				Adam Prince	699 East Road, Rochester, WA	C686
4						Alfred Williams	1072 Ridge Circle, Vienna, NV	C814
5						Allen Gibbs	631 Spring Blvd., Middleton, N	C763
6						Arthur Steele	1165 Spring Road, Centerville,	C813
7	Match:	11	=MATCH(B1,H2:H89,0)			Benjamin Benton	1188 Poplar Highway, Middlet	C179
8	Index:	Brandy Cook	=INDEX(F2:F89,B7,1)			Benjamin Hende	969 View Lane, Franklin, VT 14	C754
9						Bernice Scott	323 Franklin Circle, Chatham, I	C499
10						Bertha Garza	1754 Walnut Lane, St Joseph,	C587

Syntax:

INDEX(*array*,*row_num*,*[column_num]*)

The INDEX function will return the value at the intersection of a particular row and column within a range.

The INDEX function takes the following arguments:

- array—This is a range of cells or an array constant. If array contains only one row or column, the corresponding row_num or column_num argument is optional. If array has more than one row and more than one column, and if only row_num or column_num is used, INDEX returns an array of the entire row or column in array.

- row_num—This selects the row in array from which to return a value. If row_num is omitted, then column_num is required.

- column_num—This selects the column in array from which to return a value. If column_num is omitted, then row_num is required.

If both the row_num and column_num arguments are used, INDEX returns the value in the cell at the intersection of row_num and column_num.

If you set `row_num` or `column_num` to 0, INDEX returns the array of values for the entire column or row, respectively. To use values returned as an array, you use the INDEX function as an array formula in a horizontal range of cells for a row and in a vertical range of cells for a column. To enter an array formula, you press Ctrl+Shift+Enter.

`row_num` and `column_num` must point to a cell within array; otherwise, INDEX returns a #REF! error.

Using MATCH and INDEX to Fill a Wide Table

The lookup functions VLOOKUP, HLOOKUP, and MATCH can be very processor-intensive when the lookup table contains hundreds of thousands of rows.

Back in Figure 12.23, Excel had to do 96 VLOOKUP functions. However, after Excel figured out the position of Item G598 in the lookup table for Cell C6, it had to go back through exactly the same steps for Cell D6, E6, F6, G6, and so on. You made Excel find exactly the same item 12 times, which is a very slow process.

If the recalculation times are taking too long, you should consider using one MATCH per row to find the relative row number and then using 12 speedy INDEX functions to fill in the values in that row. Figure 12.28 illustrates a problem where you can use this trick. In this case, the list of inventory items is 14,000 rows. Here's what you do:

1. Copy the range of warehouse names from B20:M20 to D5:O5.

2. In Cell C6, enter `=MATCH(B6,$A$21:$A$14060,0)`. This formula finds an exact match for C529. The answer 8005 means that product C529 is on the 8,005th relative row of the lookup range.

3. Copy the formula in Cell C6 to C6:C13.

4. As you build the INDEX function, be careful that the array range encompasses the same rows used in the MATCH function. Start the formula in Cell D6 as `=INDEX($B$21:$M$14060`. Make sure to press F4 to make this reference absolute.

5. Make the next argument the relative row number within the lookup range. This is the value from Column C, so use `$C6`. If you type C6 and then press the F4 key three times, Excel adds the dollar sign before the C in C6.

6. Add the final argument, the column number. For the first warehouse, this would be Column 1. However, rather than typing a 1 for the formula, use `COLUMN(A1)`. This allows you to copy the formula to the rest of the range. Finish the formula with a parenthesis. The final formula is `=INDEX($B$21:$M$14060,$C6,COLUMN(A4))`. Note that it is not important if you use `COLUMN(A1)`, `COLUMN(A4)`, or `COLUMN(A10000)`. All of those will return the number 1.

7. Optionally, add a conditional format to Cell D6 to highlight the cell if this formula evaluates to TRUE: `=D6>=$A6`.

8. Copy the formula from Cell D6 to D6:O13.

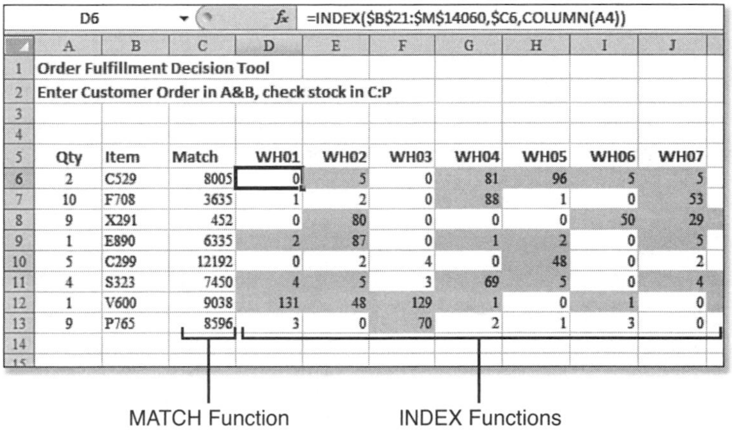

Figure 12.28
This performs eight relatively slow MATCH functions and then 96 relatively fast INDEX functions.

D6			f_x	=INDEX($B$21:$M$14060,$C6,COLUMN(A4))					
A	B	C	D	E	F	G	H	I	J
1 Order Fulfillment Decision Tool									
2 Enter Customer Order in A&B, check stock in C:P									
3									
4									
5 Qty	Item	Match	WH01	WH02	WH03	WH04	WH05	WH06	WH07
6 2	C529	8005	0	5	0	81	96	5	5
7 10	F708	3635	1	2	0	88	1	0	53
8 9	X291	452	0	80	0	0	0	50	29
9 1	E890	6335	2	87	0	1	2	0	5
10 5	C299	12192	0	2	4	0	48	0	2
11 4	S323	7450	4	5	3	69	5	0	4
12 1	V600	9038	131	48	129	1	0	1	0
13 9	P765	8596	3	0	70	2	1	3	0
14									
15									

MATCH Function   INDEX Functions

Performing Many Lookups with LOOKUP

Even Excel Help tells you to avoid the old LOOKUP function. However, LOOKUP can do one useful trick that VLOOKUP and HLOOKUP cannot do—it can process many lookups in one single array formula. LOOKUP can also deal with a lookup range that is vertical and a return range that is horizontal, or vice-versa.

The next section looks at the common use of LOOKUP and how it contrasts with VLOOKUP or HLOOKUP.

Syntax:

LOOKUP(*lookup_value, array*)

In this case, LOOKUP is acting similar to VLOOKUP or HLOOKUP. Excel examines the height and width of the array. If the array has more rows than columns, Excel assumes you are doing a VLOOKUP and looks through the first column of the array for the lookup value. If the array has more columns than rows, Excel assumes you are doing an HLOOKUP and looks through the first row of the array for the lookup value.

In this syntax of LOOKUP, Excel always returns the value from the last column or row of the array. In Figure 12.29, the formula in B2 is returning a value from Cell G3. Because the array is described as E2:G5, Excel automatically returns a value from the final column of E2:G5. Because the array is four rows and three columns, Excel assumes you want the equivalent of VLOOKUP instead of HLOOKUP. In Cell B3, the lookup array is D7:G8. Because this array is wider than it is tall, Cell B3 does the equivalent of an HLOOKUP.

In addition, LOOKUP always performs a range lookup, similar to leaving off the FALSE as the fourth parameter of VLOOKUP or HLOOKUP. For this reason, your lookup array must always be sorted.

If you do not want to return a value from the last column of the array, you can specify two vectors in the alternative form of the syntax discussed in the next section.

Syntax:

`LOOKUP(lookup_value, lookup_vector, result_vector)`

In this version of the LOOKUP function, you specify vectors that are either one row tall or one column wide. This version allows you to do a lookup similar to VLOOKUP where the result field is to the left of the key field. In Cell B4 of Figure 12.29, the result vector is to the left of the lookup vector.

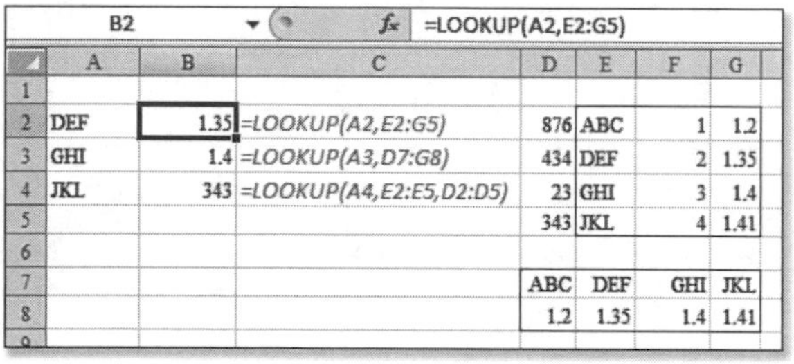

B2 =LOOKUP(A2,E2:G5)

	A	B	C	D	E	F	G
1							
2	DEF	1.35	=LOOKUP(A2,E2:G5)	876	ABC	1	1.2
3	GHI	1.4	=LOOKUP(A3,D7:G8)	434	DEF	2	1.35
4	JKL	343	=LOOKUP(A4,E2:E5,D2:D5)	23	GHI	3	1.4
5				343	JKL	4	1.41
6							
7				ABC	DEF	GHI	JKL
8				1.2	1.35	1.4	1.41

Figure 12.29
The quirky LOOKUP function decided to do a VLOOKUP or HLOOKUP depending on the shape of the lookup array.

So far, everything about LOOKUP can be accomplished using VLOOKUP, HLOOKUP, or INDEX and MATCH. However, a useful trick makes LOOKUP better than those other functions: You can ask Excel to look up many values at one time, provided that you do the following:

1. Press Ctrl+Shift+Enter to accept the formula..
2. Enclose the LOOKUP in a wrapper function such as SUM to summarize all the results from the function.

In Figure 12.30, a series of invoices appear in Rows 4 through 17. A GP% (gross profit percentage) is associated with each invoice. The sales rep will earn a bonus depending on the GP% of each invoice as shown in E6:F10. Instead of calculating a bonus for each row, you can calculate a bonus for all the rows at once. The formula in B1 of Figure 12.30 specifies an array of B4:B17 as the lookup value. This causes Excel to perform the LOOKUP 14 times, once for each value in the Range B4:B17. The formula wraps the LOOKUP results in a SUM function to add up all the bonus results. To calculate correctly, you must hold down Ctrl+Shift while pressing Enter after typing this formula.

Using Functions to Describe the Shape of a Contiguous Reference

Four functions can be used to identify the location and shape of a contiguous range:

- `COLUMN(reference)`—This returns the column number of the upper-left corner of a reference, using numbers from 1 to 16,384. If `reference` is omitted, the function returns the column number of the cell where the formula is entered.
- `ROW(reference)`—This returns the row number of the upper-left corner of the reference, using numbers from 1 to 1,045,876. If `reference` is omitted, the function returns the row number of the cell where the formula is entered.

Figure 12.30
Unlike VLOOKUP and HLOOKUP, the aging LOOKUP function can process many lookups in a single array formula.

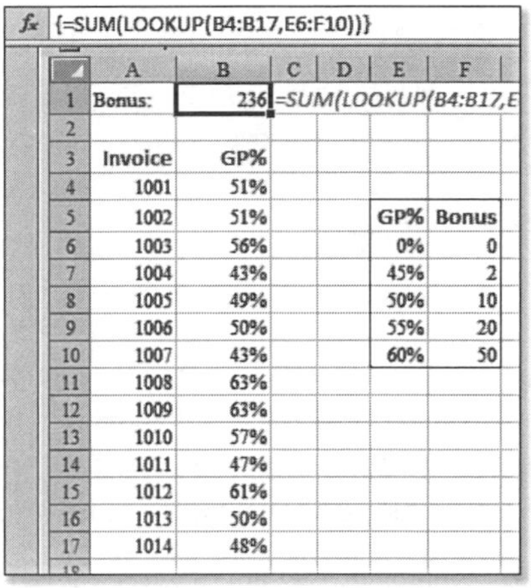

	A	B	C	D	E	F
1	Bonus:	236			=SUM(LOOKUP(B4:B17,E	
2						
3	Invoice	GP%				
4	1001	51%				
5	1002	51%			GP%	Bonus
6	1003	56%			0%	0
7	1004	43%			45%	2
8	1005	49%			50%	10
9	1006	50%			55%	20
10	1007	43%			60%	50
11	1008	63%				
12	1009	63%				
13	1010	57%				
14	1011	47%				
15	1012	61%				
16	1013	50%				
17	1014	48%				

Formula bar: {=SUM(LOOKUP(B4:B17,E6:F10))}

- COLUMNS(reference)—This returns the number of columns in a reference. In this case, reference must be a single contiguous range.

- ROWS(reference)—This returns the number of rows in a reference. Again, reference must be a single contiguous range.

Figure 12.31 displays the ROW, COLUMN, ROWS, and COLUMNS functions of a named range. The range occupies the black cells in B7:D11.

Figure 12.31
These functions describe the location and shape of a range.

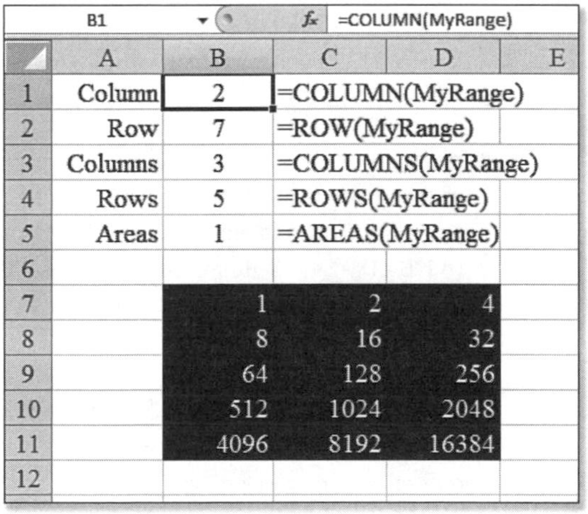

Formula bar: B1   fx   =COLUMN(MyRange)

	A	B	C	D	E
1	Column	2	=COLUMN(MyRange)		
2	Row	7	=ROW(MyRange)		
3	Columns	3	=COLUMNS(MyRange)		
4	Rows	5	=ROWS(MyRange)		
5	Areas	1	=AREAS(MyRange)		
6					
7		1	2	4	
8		8	16	32	
9		64	128	256	
10		512	1024	2048	
11		4096	8192	16384	
12					

Using AREAS and INDEX to Describe a Range with More Than One Area

All the functions listed in the preceding section fail if the `reference` describes a noncontiguous range. However, you can check for that condition by using the AREAS function.

Syntax:

AREAS(*reference*)

This function returns the number of contiguous ranges in a reference. The argument reference usually refers to a named range.

In Figure 12.32, `MyAreas` is a defined name that describes the cells in black. In Rows 1 through 4, all the traditional functions fail with #REF! errors because the reference contains more than one contiguous range.

Syntax:

INDEX(*reference,row_num,column_num,area_num*)

If you need to determine the location and shape of each contiguous range, do so one area at a time. A second syntax for the INDEX function returns a reference to one specific area of a reference. This syntax includes the following arguments:

- `reference`—Reference to one or more cell ranges. If you are entering a nonadjacent range for the reference, enclose the `reference` in parentheses. If each area in `reference` contains only one row or column, the `row_num` or `column_num` argument, respectively, is optional. For example, for a single row reference, you use INDEX(`reference,column_num`).

- `row_num`—The number of the row in `reference` from which to return a reference.

- `column_num`—The number of the column in `reference` from which to return a reference.

- `area_num`—Selects a range in `reference` from which to return the intersection of `row_num` and `column_num`. The first area selected or entered is numbered 1, the second is 2, and so on. If area_num is omitted, INDEX uses area 1. For example, if `reference` describes the Cells (A1:B4,D1:E4,G1:H4), then area_num 1 is the Range A1:B4, `area_num` 2 is the Range D1:E4, and area_num 3 is the Range G1:H4.

After `reference` and `area_num` have selected a particular range, `row_num` and `column_num` select a particular cell: `row_num` 1 is the first row in the range, `column_num` 1 is the first column, and so on. The reference returned by INDEX is the intersection of `row_num` and `column_num`.

If you set `row_num` or `column_num` to 0, INDEX returns the reference for the entire column or row, respectively.

`row_num, column_num,` and `area_num` must point to a cell within `reference`; otherwise, INDEX returns a #REF! error. If `row_num` and `column_num` are omitted, INDEX returns the area in `reference` specified by `area_num`.

Figure 12.32
To describe a reference with multiple contiguous ranges, you have to use the reference form of the INDEX function.

	A	B	C	D	E	F
	B16	▾	fx	=COLUMN(INDEX(MyAreas,,,B$15))		
1	Column	#REF!	=COLUMN(MyAreas)			
2	Row	#REF!	=ROW(MyAreas)			
3	Columns	#REF!	=COLUMNS(MyAreas)			
4	Rows	#REF!	=ROWS(MyAreas)			
5	Areas	4	=AREAS(MyAreas)			
6						
7			1	2	4	
8						
9				8	16	32
10						
11			64	128	256	
12						
13		512	1024	2048		
14						
15	Area:	1	2	3	4	
16	Column	2	3	2	1	
17	Row	7	9	11	13	
18	Columns	3	3	3	3	
19	Rows	1	1	1	1	
20	Areas	1	1	1	1	
21						

The result of the INDEX function is a reference, and it is interpreted as such by other formulas. Depending on the formula, the return value of INDEX may be used as a reference or as a value. For example, the formula CELL("width",INDEX(A1:B2,1,2)) is equivalent to CELL("width",B1). The CELL function uses the return value of INDEX as a cell reference. On the other hand, a formula such as 2*INDEX(A1:B2,1,2) translates the return value of INDEX into the number in Cell B1.

Using this version of INDEX, you can build formulas that work on one particular area in a named range. Here's how you do it:

1. In B15:E15, enter the numbers 1 through 4. These correspond to the four areas in MyAreas.

2. When you build the INDEX function, you want Excel to return a reference to the entire rows and columns of the first area of the range, so use =INDEX(MyAreas,,,1) to return such a reference.

3. Instead of using 1 for the areas argument of INDEX, use =INDEX(MyAreas,,,B$15).

4. Enter the formula =COLUMN(INDEX(MyAreas,,,B$15)) in Cell B16 to define the starting column of area 1 of MyAreas.

5. Copy the formula from step 4 to B17:B20. Edit each function to change COLUMN to ROW, COLUMNS, ROWS, and AREAS.

6. Copy B17:B20 to Columns C, D, and E.

The result, as shown in Figure 12.32, includes four sets of formulas in B16:E20 that completely describe the four areas of the named range MyAreas.

Using Numbers with OFFSET to Describe a Range

The language of Excel is numbers. There are functions that count the number of entries in a range. There are functions that can tell you the numeric position of a looked-up value. You may know that a particular value is found in Row 20, but what if you want to perform calculations on other cells in Row 20?

The OFFSET function handles this very situation. You can use OFFSET to describe a range using mostly numbers. OFFSET is flexible: It can describe a single cell, or it can describe a rectangular range.

Although INDEX can return a single cell from a rectangular range, it has limitations. If you specify C5:Z99 as the range for an INDEX function, you can select only cells below and/or to the right of C5. The OFFSET function can move up and down or left and right from the starting cell, which is C5.

Syntax:

OFFSET(*reference,rows,cols,height,width*)

The OFFSET function returns a reference to a range that is a given number of rows and columns from a given reference.

The OFFSET function takes the following arguments:

- reference—This is the reference from which you want to base the offset. reference must be a reference to a cell or range of adjacent cells; otherwise, OFFSET returns a #VALUE! error.

- rows—This is the number of rows, up or down, that you want the upper-left cell to refer to. Using 5 as the rows argument, for example, specifies that the upper-left cell in the reference is five rows below reference. Rows can be positive, which means below the starting reference, or negative, which means above the starting reference.

- cols—This is the number of columns to the left or right that you want the upper-left cell of the result to refer to. For example, using 5 as the cols argument specifies that the upper-left cell in the reference is five columns to the right of reference. cols can be positive, which means to the right of the starting reference, or negative, which means to the left of the starting reference. If rows and cols offset reference over the edge of the worksheet, OFFSET returns a #REF! error. Figure 12.33 demonstrates various combinations of rows and cols from a starting cell of Cell C5.

- height—This is the height, in number of rows that you want the returned reference to be. Height must be a positive number.

- width—This is the width, in number of columns that you want the returned reference to be. Width must be a positive number. If height or width is omitted, Excel assumes it is the same height or width as reference.

Figure 12.33
These `OFFSET` functions return a single cell that is a certain number of rows and columns away from Cell C5.

C10 fx =OFFSET($C$5,A10,B10,1,1)

	A	B	C	D	E	F
1	Examples of 1-cell ranges returned by Offset					
2						
3	1	2	4	8	16	
4	32	64	128	256	512	
5	1024	2048	4096	8192	16384	
6	32768	65536	131072	262144	524288	
7	1048576	2097152	4194304	8388608	16777216	
8						
9	Row	Column	Offset			
10	-2	0	4	=OFFSET($C$5,A10,B10,1,1)		
11	0	-2	1024			
12	0	2	16384			
13	2	0	4194304			
14	-2	-2	1			
15	2	2	16777216			
16						
17						

`OFFSET` allows you to specify a reference. It does not move any cell. It does not change the selection. It is just a numeric way to describe a reference. `OFFSET` can be used in any function that is expecting a reference argument.

Excel Help provides a trivial example of `=SUM(OFFSET(C2,1,2,3,1))`, which sums E3:E5. However, this example is silly because no one would ever write such a formula! If you were to write such a formula, you would just write `=SUM(E3:E5)` instead. The power of `OFFSET` comes when at least one of the four numeric arguments is calculated by the `COUNT` function or a lookup function.

In Figure 12.34, you can use `COUNT(A5:A99)` to count how many entries are in Column A. If you assume that there are no blanks in the range of data, you can use the `COUNT` result as the `height` argument in `OFFSET` to describe the range of numbers. Here's what you do:

1. There is nothing magic about the reference, so write it as `=OFFSET(A5,`.
2. Do not move the starting position any rows or columns from Cell A5. The starting position is A5, so you always use 0 and 0 for rows and columns. Therefore, the formula is now `=OFFSET(A5,0,0,`.
3. If you want to include only the number of entries in the list, use `COUNT(A5:A999)` as the height of the range. The formula is now `=OFFSET(A5,0,0,COUNT(A5:A999),`.
4. The width is one column, so make the function `=OFFSET(A5,0,0,COUNT(A5:A999),1)`.
5. Use your `OFFSET` function anywhere that you would normally specify a reference. You can use `=SUM(OFFSET(A5,0,0,COUNT(A5:A999),1))` or specify that formula as the series in a chart. This creates a dynamic chart that grows or shrinks as the number of entries changes.

A3	▼	fx	=SUM(OFFSET(A5,0,0,COUNT(A5:A999),1))

	A	B	C	D	E	F	G	H	I	J	K	
1	Example of Dynamic Range Generated by Offset											
2	=SUM(OFFSET(A5,0,0,COUNT(A5:A999),1))											
3	3		15		31		63		255		1023	
4												
5	1		1		1		1		1		1	
6	2		2		2		2		2		2	
7			4		4		4		4		4	
8			8		8		8		8		8	
9					16		16		16		16	
10							32		32		32	
11									64		64	
12									128		128	
13											256	
14											512	
15												

Figure 12.34
Every argument except height is hard-coded in these functions. The height argument comes from a COUNT function to allow the range to expand as more entries are added.

For a more complex example of OFFSET, examine Figure 12.35, which shows several yearly tables starting in Cell C8. Each month of the table contains from one to five entries. The person using this spreadsheet will select a year and a month from Cells E1 and E2. The goal is to find information about the entries for that particular month and year. Here's how you do it:

1. Have the formula in Cell I1 find the starting row for the particular year, using the MATCH function shown in Cell J1.

2. Have the formula in Cell I2 find the column for the chosen month, using the MATCH function shown in Cell J2.

3. Build the OFFSET function to describe the range for that month and year. You know that it starts in the row in I1 and the column in I2. If you make the reference Cell A1, then Row 15 is 14 rows below A1. Therefore, use =OFFSET(A1,I1-1,.

4. The starting column is in Cell I2. Column 8 is seven columns to the right of A1. Therefore, you now use =OFFSET(A1,I1-1,I2-1.

5. The structure of the worksheet allows for up to five entries per month, arranged down a row. Thus, height is 5 and width is 1. Use the following formula to describe the possible range for the month: =OFFSET(A1,I1-1,I2-1,5,1). This is good enough to use for MIN, MAX, SUM, and so on.

6. To chart the data, figure out the exact height. Use the =COUNT(OFFSET(A1,I1-1,I2-1,5,1)) formula in Cell I3 to count the number of entries for the month.

7. Use the formula =OFFSET(A1,I1-1,I2-1,I3,1) to describe the exact month. Add additional formulas in I4:I6 to figure out the minimum, maximum, and sum of those cells.

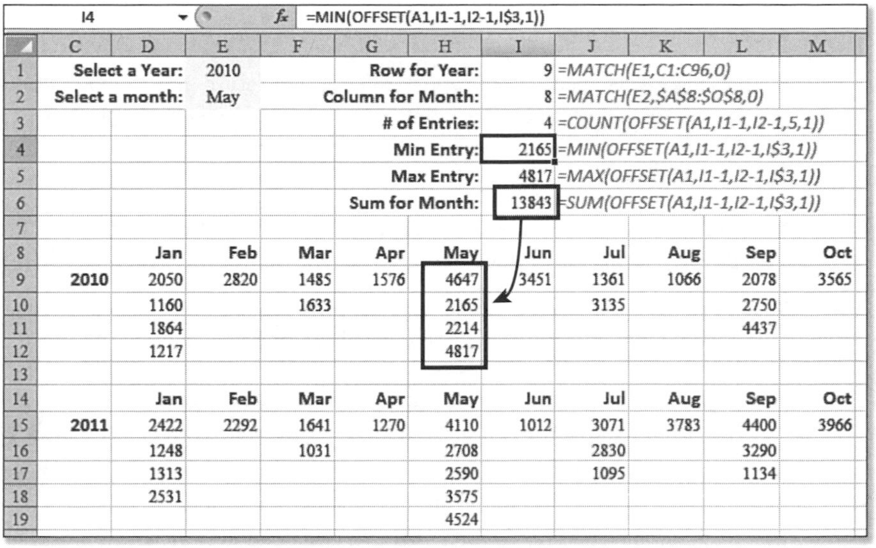
I4 =MIN(OFFSET(A1,I1-1,I2-1,I$3,1))

	C	D	E	F	G	H	I	J	K	L	M
1		Select a Year:	2010			Row for Year:	9	=MATCH(E1,C1:C96,0)			
2		Select a month:	May			Column for Month:	8	=MATCH(E2,$A$8:$O$8,0)			
3						# of Entries:	4	=COUNT(OFFSET(A1,I1-1,I2-1,5,1))			
4						Min Entry:	2165	=MIN(OFFSET(A1,I1-1,I2-1,I$3,1))			
5						Max Entry:	4817	=MAX(OFFSET(A1,I1-1,I2-1,I$3,1))			
6						Sum for Month:	13843	=SUM(OFFSET(A1,I1-1,I2-1,I$3,1))			
7											
8		Jan	Feb	Mar	Apr	May	Jun	Jul	Aug	Sep	Oct
9	2010	2050	2820	1485	1576	4647	3451	1361	1066	2078	3565
10		1160		1633		2165		3135		2750	
11		1864				2214				4437	
12		1217				4817					
13											
14		Jan	Feb	Mar	Apr	May	Jun	Jul	Aug	Sep	Oct
15	2011	2422	2292	1641	1270	4110	1012	3071	3783	4400	3966
16		1248		1031		2708		2830		3290	
17		1313				2590		1095		1134	
18		2531				3575					
19						4524					

Figure 12.35
Even with a poorly designed database spreadsheet, various combinations of OFFSET can locate and total cells for a specific month.

The OFFSET function initially seems intimidating, especially in light of the example you just walked through. Remember that for useful results from OFFSET, you usually replace one or more of the final four arguments with a calculation.

Using ADDRESS to Find the Address for Any Cell

If someone asks you for the cell address for the cell in Row 5, Column 5, you could probably come up with E5 quickly. What if someone asks you for the cell address of the cell in Row 26, Column 26? This is Z26. Again, you should come up with this if you know there are 26 letters in the alphabet.

If someone asks you to calculate the address of Row 2 and Column 30, you have to divide 30 by 26 to learn that the result is 1 with a remainder of 4. This could lead you to conclude the cell address is the first letter of the alphabet—A—and the fourth letter of the alphabet—D—to come up with AD2.

This type of calculation becomes far more complex with 16,384 columns. For example, how would you calculate the address for Row 2 of Column 14123?

Fortunately, Excel provides the ADDRESS function to convert any intersection of row and column number to an address. =ADDRESS(2,14123) returns the text of $TWE$2.

Syntax:

ADDRESS(*row_num*,*column_num*,*abs_num*,*a1*,*sheet_text*)

The default version of ADDRESS returns the cell address as an absolute address with both dollar signs. There are optional parameters to control this behavior:

- **row_num**—This is the row number to use in the cell reference.

- **column_num**—This is the column number to use in the cell reference.

- **abs_num**—This specifies the type of reference to return. If it is 1 or omitted, the returned address has both dollar signs and is absolute. If it is 2, the row is held absolute, but the column is relative. If it is 3, the row is relative and the column is absolute. If it is 4, the address is relative, with no dollar signs.

- **a1**—This is a logical value that specifies the A1 or R1C1 reference style. If a1 is TRUE or omitted, ADDRESS returns an A1-style reference; if it is FALSE, ADDRESS returns an R1C1-style reference.

- **sheet_text**—This is text that specifies the name of the worksheet to be used as the external reference. If sheet_text is omitted, no sheet name is used.

Figure 12.36 shows eight ways to describe one cell, depending on the various combinations of absolute and A1 arguments.

The sheet_text argument is interesting. It is difficult to remember the arcane rules for when to use apostrophes and where the exclamation point needs to go in an address. If you specify sheet_text as the name of a worksheet or use the style [book_name]SheetName, Excel builds the proper reference. Cell B11 in Figure 12.36 shows the result from an ADDRESS function that builds a reference to another workbook.

 tip

To find the value of a cell described by ADDRESS, use the INDIRECT function.

	A	B	C	D	E	F	G
	Row	Column	Abs	A1 vs R1C1	Result		
1	Row	Column	Abs	A1 vs R1C1	Result		
2	123	28	1	TRUE	$AB$123		
3	123	28	2	TRUE	AB$123		
4	123	28	3	TRUE	$AB123		
5	123	28	4	TRUE	AB123		
6	123	28	1	FALSE	R123C28		
7	123	28	2	FALSE	R123C[28]		
8	123	28	3	FALSE	R[123]C28		
9	123	28	4	FALSE	R[123]C[28]		
10							
11		=ADDRESS(1,1,4,TRUE,"[C:\JanIncome.xls]Income Statement")					
12		'[C:\JanIncome.xls]Income Statement'!A1					
13							

E2 ▾ *f_x* =ADDRESS(A2,B2,C2,D2)

Figure 12.36
ADDRESS can return a cell address in A1 or R1C1 style.

Using INDIRECT to Build and Evaluate Cell References On-the-Fly

The INDIRECT function is deceivingly powerful. Consider this trivial example: In Cell A1, enter the text B2. In Cell B2, enter a number. In cell C3, enter the formula, =INDIRECT(A1). Excel will return the number that you entered in cell B2 in cell C3. The INDIRECT function looks in cell A1 and expects to find something that is a valid cell or range reference. It then looks in that address to return the answer for the function.

The reference text can be any text that you can string together using various text functions. This allows you to create complex references that dynamically point to other sheets or to other open workbooks.

The reference text can also be a range name. You could have a validation list box where someone selects a value from a list. If you have predefined a named range that corresponds to each possible entry on the list, INDIRECT can point to the various named ranges on-the-fly.

When you use traditional formulas, even absolute formulas, there is a chance that someone might insert rows or columns that will move the reference. If you need a formula to always point to Cell J10, no matter how someone rearranges the worksheet, you can use =INDIRECT("J10") to handle this.

Syntax:

INDIRECT(*ref_text,a1*)

The INDIRECT function returns the reference specified by a text string.

The INDIRECT function takes the following arguments:

- ref_text—This is a reference to a cell that contains an A1-style reference, an R1C1-style refer-ence, a name defined as a reference, or a reference to a cell as a text string. If ref_text is not a valid cell reference, INDIRECT returns a #REF! error. If ref_text refers to an external workbook, the other workbook must be open. If the source workbook is not open, INDIRECT returns a #REF! error.

- a1—This is a logical value that specifies what type of reference is contained in the cell ref_text. If a1 is TRUE or omitted, ref_text is interpreted as an A1-style reference. If a1 is FALSE, ref_text is interpreted as an R1C1-style reference.

Figure 12.37 is a monthly worksheet in a workbook that has 12 similar sheets. In each worksheet, the data headings are in Row 6, and the invoices appear for some number of rows, starting in Row 7. Each worksheet has a total for the month in Cell D2.

Figure 12.37
You can add a year-to-date formula to all sheets.

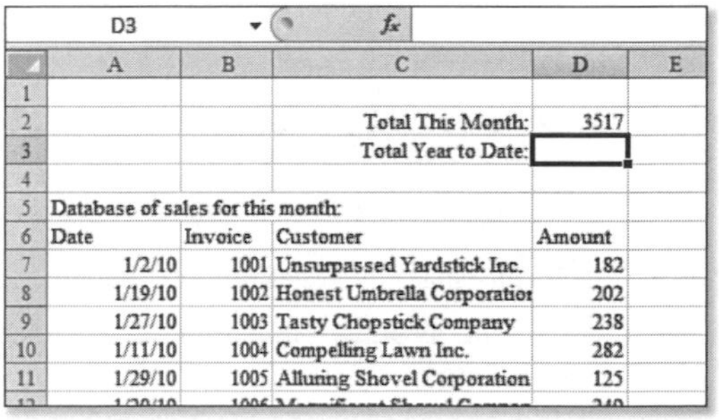

In this example, you want to add a year-to-date total in Cell D3 on each worksheet. This is fairly difficult to do without VBA. Many VBA books include a user-defined function to describe the previous sheet in a workbook. However, this function will fail if you send the workbook to someone who disables macros or her computer. Instead, you can solve this problem with clever use of text functions and the INDIRECT function. To do so, follow these steps:

1. Select the Jan worksheet.

2. Shift+click the Dec worksheet to put all 12 sheets in Group mode.

3. In Cell A1, enter the formula =A7. This adds the first date as a title for the worksheet.

4. Format Cell A1 with the custom format mmmm, yyyy. This causes the date to appear as January, 2010.

5. Right-click the Jan tab name and select Ungroup Sheets.

6. Enter =D2 as the year-to-date formula in Cell D3 of the Jan tab.

7. On the Feb worksheet, build a text formula that returns the name of the previous month. The quest becomes how to build a formula that looks like =Jan!D3.

8. Jan is a three-letter abbreviation for any date in the month of January. Therefore, enter a January date in a cell and format the cell with the custom number format mmm, so that the result is the word Jan.

9. The TEXT function takes a number or date and displays it using a specific custom number format, so on the February sheet, use =TEXT(A1,"mmm"), which results in the value Feb. This is close. If you can find a way to get the name of the previous month, the problem will be solved.

10. The value in Cell A1 is a live date. You can use date math to calculate a different date, such as the date one month earlier. Use the DATE(year,month,day) function to return a date in the previous month. For the year parameter, use YEAR(A1). For the month parameter, use MONTH(A1)-1. For the day parameter, use DAY(A1). The formula =DATE(YEAR(A1),MONTH(A1)-1,1) returns a date that is the first of the previous month.

11. Combining steps 9 and 10 into a single formula, use =TEXT(DATE(YEAR(A1),MONTH(A1)-1,1),"MMM") to return the value of Jan on the Feb worksheet, Feb on the March worksheet, and so on.

12. Use the generic formula =TEXT(DATE(YEAR(A1),MONTH(A1)-1,1),"MMM")&"!D3" to build the reference.

13. Select the Feb worksheet. Shift+click the Dec worksheet to place these 11 worksheets in Group mode. In Cell D3, enter this formula: =INDIRECT(TEXT(DATE(YEAR(A1),MONTH(A1)-1,1),"mmm")&"!D3")+D2.

14. Right-click any sheet tab and select Ungroup to take the workbook out of Group mode.

The result, as shown in Figure 12.38, is a formula on the last 11 worksheets that automatically pulls the year-to-date total from the previous worksheet and adds it to the current worksheet total.

Figure 12.38
Cell D4 dynamically builds a text formula to reference the previous sheet, and then INDIRECT evaluates the formula.

=INDIRECT(TEXT(DATE(YEAR(A1),MONTH(A1)-1,1),"mmm")&"!D3")+D2					
	A	B	C	D	E	F
1	October, 2010					
2			Total This Month:	3614		
3			Total Year to Date:	34772		
4						
5	Database of sales for this month:					
6	Date	Invoice	Customer	Amount		
7	10/7/10	1001	Stunning Shoe Corporation	239		
8	10/9/10	1002	Forceful Lawn Corporation	161		
9	10/8/10	1003	Vibrant Flagpole Corporation	169		
10	10/4/10	1004	Rare Saddle Corporation	225		
11	10/13/10	1005	Tremendous Xylophone Inc.	110		
12	10/29/10	1006	Real Electronics Traders	297		
13	10/15/10	1007	Tasty Chopstick Company	140		

Using the HYPERLINK Function to Quickly Add Hyperlinks

Excel enables you to add a hyperlink by using the Excel interface. On the Insert tab, select the Hyperlink icon. Next, you specify text to appear in the cell and the underlying address. Building links in this way is easy, but it is tedious to build them one at a time. If you have hundreds of links to add, you can add them quickly by using the HYPERLINK function.

Syntax:

HYPERLINK(*link_location,friendly_name*)

The HYPERLINK function creates a shortcut that opens a document stored on your hard drive, a network server, or on the Internet.

The HYPERLINK function takes the following arguments:

- link_location—This is the URL address on the Internet. It could also be a path, filename, and location in another file. For example, you could link to "[C:\files\Jan2007.xls]!Sheet1!A15". Note that link_location can be a text string enclosed in quotes or a cell that contains the link.

- friendly_name—This is the underlined text or numeric value that is displayed in the cell. friendly_name is displayed in blue and is underlined. If friendly_name is omitted, the cell displays the link_location value as the jump text. friendly_name can be a value, a text string, a name, or a cell that contains the jump text or value. If friendly_name returns an error (for example, #VALUE!), the cell displays the error instead of the jumptext.

Figure 12.39 shows a list of web pages in Column A. Column B contains the titles of those web pages. To quickly build a table of

 note

Note that Excel does not check whether the link location is valid at the time you created the link. If the link is not valid when someone clicks it, the person encounters an error.

 tip

It is difficult to select a cell that contains a HYPERLINK function. If you click the cell, Excel attempts to follow the hyperlink. Instead, you should click a cell near the cell and then use the arrow keys to move into the cell.

hyperlinks, you use =HYPERLINK(A2,B2) in Cell C2 and copy the formula down the column. After the hyperlinks are created, you can copy Column C and use Paste Values on Column C. You are then free to delete Columns A and B.

	A	B	C	D	E	F	G
1	Web Page	Title	Hyperlink				
2	http://www.mrexcel.com/tip035.shtml	5 Tips to Eliminate Redundant Data	5 Tips to Eliminate Redundant Data				
3	http://www.mrexcel.com/tip048.shtml	Absolute Reference Uses	Absolute Reference Uses				
4	http://www.mrexcel.com/td0132.html	Add a Certain Number to All Numbe	Add a Certain Number to All Numbers in a Range U				
5	http://www.mrexcel.com/td0072.html	Add a percentage to all cells in a ran	Add a percentage to all cells in a range				
6	http://www.mrexcel.com/tip067.shtml	Add a Trendline with 3 clicks	Add a Trendline with 3 clicks				
7	http://www.mrexcel.com/tip062.shtml	Add Median to Pivot Tables with Di	Add Median to Pivot Tables with DigDB's One-Ste				
8	http://www.mrexcel.com/td0028.html	Add Row while copying and manipu	Add Row while copying and manipulating data				
9	http://www.mrexcel.com/tip055.shtml	Add the Path to your Worksheet Fo	Add the Path to your Worksheet Footer when Print				
10	http://www.mrexcel.com/td0019.html	Add today's entries to the next empt	Add today's entries to the next empty row on a mas				
11	http://www.mrexcel.com/td0066.html	Adding every other cell in a column	Adding every other cell in a column with =SUM(M(				
12	http://www.mrexcel.com/tip015.shtml	Advanced Pivot Table Tips	Advanced Pivot Table Tips				
13	http://www.mrexcel.com/tip083.shtml	Array-CSE Entering using Condition	Array-CSE Entering using Conditional Sum Wizard				

Figure 12.39
The formulas in Column C allow you to create hundreds of hyperlinks in seconds.

Using the TRANSPOSE Function to Formulaically Turn Data

With many people using Excel in a company, there are bound to be different usage styles from person to person. Some people build their worksheets horizontally, and other people build their worksheets vertically. For example, in Figure 12.40, the monthly totals stretch horizontally across Row 80. However, for some reason, you need these figures to be arranged going vertically down from Cell B84.

The typical method is to copy C80:N80 and then use Home, Paste, Transpose. This copies a snapshot of the totals in Row 80 to a column of data.

This is fine if you only need a snapshot of the totals. However, what if you want to see the totals continually updated in Column B? Excel provides the TRANSPOSE function for such situations.

	A	B	C	D	E	F	G	H
1			Jan	Feb	Mar	Apr	May	Jun
80		Total	98592	87432	66091	83809	89668	77451
81								
82								
83		Sales						
84	Jan							
85	Feb							
86	Mar							
87	Apr							
88	May							
89	Jun							
90	Jul							
91	Aug							

Figure 12.40
Turning C80:N80 into a vertical range is called transposing the data.

Because the function returns several answers, you need to use special care when entering the formula. Here's how:

1. Note that C80:N80 contains 12 cells.

2. Select an identical number of cells starting in B84. Select B84:B95.

3. Even though you have 12 cells selected, type the formula =TRANSPOSE(C80:N80) as if you had only one cell selected.

4. To tell Excel that this is a special type of formula called an array formula, hold down Ctrl+Shift while you press Enter.

Excel shows the formula surrounded by curly braces in the formula bar. This is one single formula entered in 12 cells. Therefore, you cannot delete or change one cell in the range. If you want to change the formula, you need to delete all 12 cells in B84:B95 in a single command.

Figure 12.41 shows a TRANSPOSE function that occupies 12 cells.

Figure 12.41
One TRANSPOSE function occupies 12 cells, from B84:B95.

	A	B	C	D	E	F	G	H	I	J	K	L	M	N
			B84			f_x	{=TRANSPOSE(C80:N80)}							
1			Jan	Feb	Mar	Apr	May	Jun	Jul	Aug	Sep	Oct	Nov	Dec
80		Total	98592	87432	66091	83809	89668	77451	90330	91691	90209	63349	71840	82001
81														
82														
83		Sales												
84	Jan	98592												
85	Feb	87432												
86	Mar	66091												
87	Apr	83809												
88	May	89668												
89	Jun	77451												
90	Jul	90330												
91	Aug	91691												
92	Sep	90209												
93	Oct	63349												
94	Nov	71840												
95	Dec	82001												
96														

Syntax:

TRANSPOSE(array)

The TRANSPOSE function transposes a vertical range into a horizontal array, or vice versa.

The argument array is an array or a range of cells on a worksheet that you want to transpose. The transposition of an array is accomplished by using the first row of the array as the first column of the new array, the second row of the array as the second column of the new array, and so on.

 note

You can also use TRANSPOSE to turn a vertical range into a horizontal range.

Using the RTD Function and COM Add-ins to Retrieve Real-Time Data

Third-party applications are available to send streaming real-time data to an Excel spreadsheet. They became very popular with stock day traders back in the late 1990s. If you have one of these COM add-ins installed on your system, you can set up a formula to retrieve real-time data from the COM add-in by using the RTD function. If you have such a COM add-in installed, the vendor of the add-in should provide sample workbooks with RTD functions already in place.

Syntax:

RTD(*progid*,*server*,*topic1*,*[topic2]*,...)

The RTD function returns real-time data from a program that supports COM automation.

The RTD function takes the following arguments:

- progid—This is the name of the Program ID of a registered COM automation add-in that has been installed on the local computer. You need to enclose the name in quotation marks.

- server—This is name of the server where the add-in should be run. If there is no server and the program is run locally, leave this argument blank.

- topic1, topic2,...—These are 1 to 28 parameters that together represent a unique piece of real-time data.

Using GETPIVOTDATA to Retrieve One Cell from a Pivot Table

You might turn to this book to find out how to use most of the functions. However, for the GETPIVOTDATA function, you are likely to turn to this book to find out why the function is being automatically generated for them.

Suppose that you have a pivot table on a worksheet. You should click outside the pivot table. Next, you type an equal sign and then with the mouse, click one of the cells in the data area of the pivot table. Although you might expect this to generate a formula such as =E9, instead, Excel puts in the formula =GETPIVOTDATA("Sales",$B$5,"Customer","Astonishing Glass Company","Region","West"), as shown in Figure 12.42.

This function is annoying. As you copy the formula down to more rows, the function keeps retrieving sales to Astonishing Glass in the West region. By default, Excel is generating this function instead of a simple formula such as =E9. This happens whether you use the mouse or the arrow keys to specify the cell in the formula.

To avoid this behavior, you can type the entire formula by manually typing it on the keyboard. Typing =E9 in a cell forces Excel to create a relative reference to Cell E9. You are then free to copy the formula to other cells.

There is also a way to turn off this behavior permanently:

1. Select a cell inside an active pivot table.

Figure 12.42
Excel inserts this strange
function in the worksheet.

| fx | =GETPIVOTDATA("Sales",$B$5,"Customer","Astonishing Glass Company","Region","West") |

	C	D	E	F	G	H	I
	Region ▾						
	▾ **East**	**Central**	**West**	**Grand Total**			
	0	170	0	170			
	289	0	0	289			
ıy	0	0	314	314		314	
	190	0	0	190			
	0	246	0	246			
	0	307	0	307			
ı	0	0	249	249			

2. The Pivot Table Tools tabs appears. Select the Options tab. From the PivotTable group, select the Options drop-down and then select the Generate GetPivotData icon (see Figure 12.43). The behavior turns off.

Figure 12.43
You can disable the GETPIVOTDATA function option.

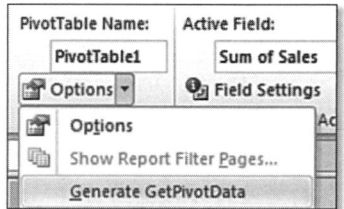

3. Enter formulas by using the mouse, arrow keys, or keyboard without generating the GETPIVOTDATA function.

Microsoft made GETPIVOTDATA the default behavior because the function is pretty cool. Now that you have learned how to turn off the behavior, you might want to understand exactly how it works in case you ever need to use the function.

Syntax:

GETPIVOTDATA(data_field,pivot_table,field1,item1,field2,item2,...)

The GETPIVOTDATA function returns data stored in a pivot table report. You can use GETPIVOTDATA to retrieve summary data from a pivot table report, provided that the summary data is visible in the report. This function takes the following arguments:

- data_field—This is the name, enclosed in quotation marks, for the data field that contains the data you want to retrieve.

- `pivot_table`—This is a reference to any cell, range of cells, or named range of cells in a pivot table report. This information is used to determine which pivot table report contains the data you want to retrieve.

- `field1, item1, field2, item2,...`—These are 1 to 14 pairs of field names and item names that describe the data you want to retrieve. The pairs can be in any order. Field names and names for items other than dates and numbers are enclosed in quotation marks. For OLAP pivot table reports, items can contain the source name of the dimension as well as the source name of the item.

Calculated fields or items and custom calculations are included in `GETPIVOTDATA` calculations.

If `pivot_table` is a range that includes two or more pivot table reports, data is retrieved from whichever report was created in the range most recently.

If the `field` and `item` arguments describe a single cell, the value of that cell is returned, regardless of whether it is a string, a number, an error, and so on.

If an item contains a date, the value must be expressed as a serial number or populated by using the `DATE` function so that the value is retained if the spreadsheet is opened in a different locale. For example, an item referring to the date March 5, 1999, could be entered as 36224 or `DATE(1999,3,5)`. Times can be entered as decimal values or by using the `TIME` function.

If `pivot_table` is not a range in which a pivot table report is found, `GETPIVOTDATA` returns `#REF!`. If the arguments do not describe a visible field, or if they include a page field that is not displayed, `GETPIVOTDATA` returns `#REF!`.

Examples of Database Functions

If you were a serious data analyst in the 1980s and the early 1990s, you would have been enamored with the database functions. I personally used @DSUM every hour of my work life for many years. It was one of the most powerful weapons in any spreadsheet arsenal. Combined with a data table, the `DSUM`, `DMIN`, `DMAX`, and `DAVERAGE` functions got a serious workout when users performed data analysis in a spreadsheet.

Then, in 1993, Microsoft Excel added the pivot table to the Data menu in Excel. Pivot tables changed everything. Those powerful database functions seemed tired and worn out. Since that day in 1993, I had never used DSUM again until I created the example described in the following section. As far as I knew, the database functions had been living in a cave in South Carolina.

Maybe it is like the nostalgia of finding a box of photos of an old girlfriend, but I realize that the database functions are still pretty powerful. Customers whined enough to have Microsoft add `AVERAGEIF` to the `COUNTIF` and `SUMIF` arsenal. This was unnecessary: Customers could have done this easily by setting up a small criteria range and using `DAVERAGE`.

Eleven of the 12 database functions are similar. `DSUM`, `DAVERAGE`, `DCOUNT`, `DCOUNTA`, `DMAX`, `DMIN`, `DPRODUCT`, `DSTDEV`, `DSTDEVP`, `DVAR`, and `DVARP` all perform the equivalent operation of their non-D equivalents, but they allow for complex criteria to include records that meet certain criteria.

To save you the hassle of looking up the confusing few, DCOUNT counts numeric cells, and DCOUNTA counts nonblank cells. DSTDEV and DVAR calculate the standard deviation and variance of a sample of a population. DSTDEVP and DVARP calculate the standard deviation and variance of the entire population. The 12th database function, DGET, has the same arguments, but it acts a bit differently, as explained later in this chapter.

Using DSUM to Conditionally Sum Records from a Database

There are three arguments to every database function. It is very easy to get your first DSUM working. The `criteria` argument is the one that offers vast flexibility. The following section explains the syntax for DSUM. The syntax for the other 11 database functions is identical to this.

Syntax:

DSUM(database,field,criteria)

The DSUM function will add records from one field in a data set, provided that the records meet some criteria that you specify.

The DSUM function takes the following arguments:

- database—This is the range of cells that make up the list or database, including the heading row. A *database* is a list of related data in which rows of related information are records and columns of data are fields. In Figure 12.44, the database is the 5,000 rows of data located at A23:I5024.

Figure 12.44
A simple criteria range specifies to limit DSUM to only records for Best Paint Inc. as a customer.

Criteria Range

	A	B	C	D	E	F	G	H	I
	B1		fx	=DSUM($A$23:$I$5024,H$23,$A$17:$I$18)					
1	DSUM	657,028							
2	DAVERAGE	59,730							
3	DCOUNT	11							
4	DCOUNTA	11							
5	DMAX	89,898							
6	DMIN	26,058							
7	DPRODUCT	2.048E+52							
8	DSTDEV	17,960							
9	DSTDEVP	17,124							
10	DVAR	322,545,029							
11	DVARP	293,222,753							
13									
17	Customer	Product	Region	District	Rep	Date	Qty	Revenue	Profit
18	Best Paint Inc.								
19									
23	Customer	Product	Region	District	Rep	Date	Qty	Revenue	Profit
24	Wonderful Faucet Co	G854	East	Southeast	ADAM DU	2/3/10	730	76,906	41,529
25	Forceful Flagpole Co	A105	East	Southeast	ADAM DU	12/19/10	804	32,297	16,794
26	Best Paint Inc.	V937	Central	Chicago	PETER WA	12/5/10	414	59,761	31,673
27	Guarded Raft Corpora	I542	West	California	BILLY JAC	1/5/12	702	66,858	35,425

Database

- `field`—This indicates which column is used in the function. You have three options when specifying a field:

  - You can point to the cell with the field name such as H23 for Revenue.

  - You can include the word `Revenue` as the `field` argument.

  - You can use the number 8 to indicate that `Revenue` is the eighth field in the database.

> **note**
>
> To conserve space, the remaining examples in the following sections show only the DSUM result. You can compare the various results to the $657,028 of revenue for the current example.

- `criteria`—This is the range of cells that contains the conditions specified. You can use any range for the `criteria` argument. The criteria range typically includes at least one column label and at least one cell below the column label for specifying a condition for the column. You can also use the computed criteria discussed in "Using the Miracle Version of the Criteria Range" later in this chapter. Learning how to create powerful criteria ranges allows you to unlock the powerful potential of the database functions. Several examples are provided in the following sections.

Creating a Simple Criteria Range for Database Functions

Although a criteria range needs only one field heading from the database, it is just as easy to copy the entire set of headings to a blank section of the worksheet. In Figure 12.44, for example, the headings in A17:I17, along with at least one additional row, create a criteria range.

In Figure 12.44, you see results of the 11 database functions for a simple criteria where the customer is Best Paint Inc. Each formula specifies a database of $A$23:$I$5024. The field is H23, which is the heading for Revenue. The criteria range is A17:I18. In this example, the criteria range could have easily been A17:A18, but the A17:I18 form allows you to enter future criteria without respecifying the criteria range.

Using a Blank Criteria Range to Return All Records

This is a trivial example, but if the second row of the criteria range is completely blank, the database function returns the total of all rows in the data set. As shown in Figure 12.45, this is $256 million. This is equivalent to using the SUM function.

	A	B	C	D	E	F	G	H	I
	B1	fx =DSUM($A$23:$I$5024,H23,$A$17:$I$18)							
1	DSUM	256,645,202							
13									
17	Customer	Product	Region	District	Rep	Date	Qty	Revenue	Profit
18									
19									
23	Customer	Product	Region	District	Rep	Date	Qty	Revenue	Profit
24	Wonderful Faucet Cc G854		East	Southeast	ADAM DU	2/3/10	730	76,906	41,529
25	Forceful Flagpole C A105		East	Southeast	ADAM DU	12/10/10	804	33,397	16,794

Figure 12.45
If the second row of the criteria is blank, the result reflects all rows.

Using AND to Join Criteria

Many people using SUMIF in Excel 2003 and earlier are likely to want to know how to conditionally sum based on two conditions. This is simple to do with DSUM. If two criteria are placed on the same row of the criteria range, they are joined by an AND. In Figure 12.46, forexample, the $123,275 is the sum of records where the customer is Best Paint and the product is V937.

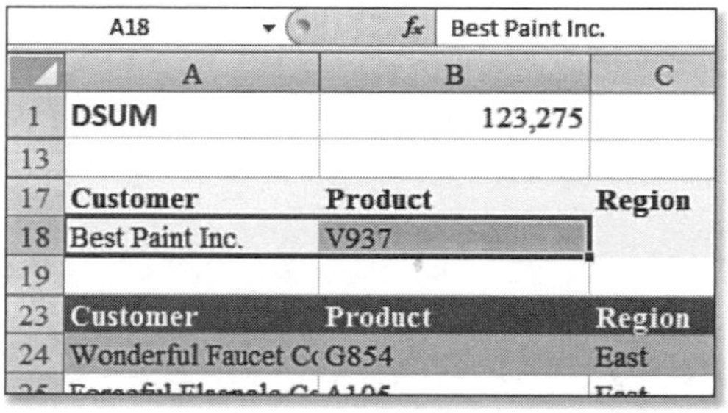

Figure 12.46
When two criterion are on the same line, they are joined by an AND function; rows must meet both criteria to be included in the DSUM.

Using OR to Join Criteria

When two criteria are placed on separate rows of the criteria range, they are joined by an OR function. In Figure 12.47, the $2.1 million represents records for either Improved Radio Traders or Best Paint.

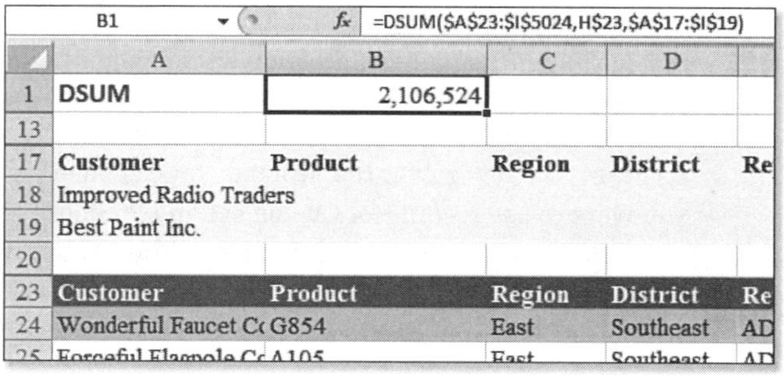

Figure 12.47
When two criteria are on different rows, they are joined by an OR function; rows can meet either criteria to be included in the DSUM.

You can use OR to join criteria from different fields. The criteria range in Figure 12.48 shows a Region value of West joined by an OR with a District value of Texas. This pulls a superset of all the West records plus just the Texas records which happen to fall in the central region.

Using Dates or Numbers as Criteria

The example in Figure 12.49 finds records with a date in 2015 and with revenue under $50,000. This data set does not contain any records from 2016, so you only need to check for items beyond 2014. The criteria in F18 for the date could have used any of these formats:

\>12/31/2014
\>=1/1/2015
\>31-Dec-2014

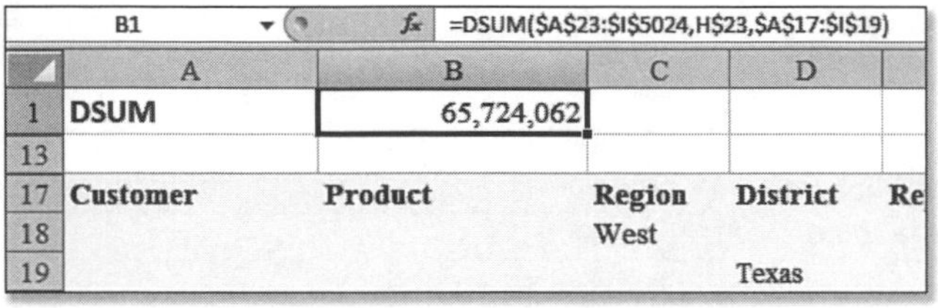

Figure 12.48
The criteria to be joined with OR can be in separate columns.

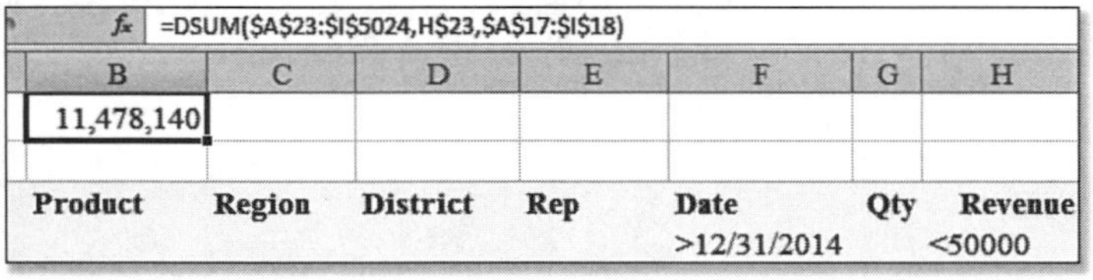

Figure 12.49
Using dates or numbers in criteria.

Using the Miracle Version of a Criteria Range

Using the criteria ranges in the preceding examples, you could easily build any complex criteria with multiple AND or OR operators.

However, this could get complex. Imagine if you wanted to pull all the records for five specific customers and five specific products. You would have to build a criteria range that is 26 rows tall. Basically, the first row is the headings for customer and product. The second row indicates that you want to see records for Customer1 and Product1. The third row indicates that you want to see records for Customer1 and Product2. The fourth row indicates that you want to see records for Customer1 and Product3. The seventh row indicates Customer2 and Product1. The 26th row indicates Customer5 and Product5.

If you need to pull the records for seven customers and seven products from five districts, your criteria range would grow to 246 rows tall and will probably never finish calculating.

There is a miraculous version of the criteria range that completely avoids this problem. Here's how it works:

- The criteria range consists of a range that is two cells tall and one or more cells wide.

- Contrary to instructions in Excel help, the top cell of the criteria range cannot contain a field heading. The top cell must be blank or contain anything which does not match the database header row. For example, you could put a heading of "Computed Criteria."

■ The second row in the criteria range can contain any formula that evaluates to TRUE or FALSE. This formula must point to cells in the first data row of the database. The formula can be as complex as you wish, with AND, OR, VLOOKUP, NOT, and MATCH; it can contain any combination of functions.

For a simple example, suppose you want to find records that match 1 of 15 customers. You copy the customers to K24:K38. In the second row of the criteria field, write the formula =NOT(ISNA(MATCH (A24,$K$24:$K$38,0))). This formula does a MATCH on the first customer in the database to see if it is in the list in K. The ISNA and NOT functions make sure that the criteria cell returns a TRUE when the customer is 1 of the 15 customers.

Very quickly and without complaint, Excel compares the 5,000 rows of your database with this complex formula, and the DSUM produces the correct value, as shown in Figure 12.50.

 To watch a video of DSUM with this criteria range, search for "Excel In Depth 12" at YouTube.

Using the DGET Function

The DGET function returns a single cell from a database. The problem is that this function is picky. If your criteria range matches zero records, DGET returns a #VALUE error. If your criteria range returns more than one row, DGET returns a #NUM! error.

To have DGET work, you need to write a criteria record that causes one and only one row to be evaluated as TRUE.

Figure 12.50

The formula version of the criteria range is rare but incredibly powerful.

	B18	▾	fx	=NOT(ISNA(MATCH(A24,$K$24:$K$38,0)))								
	A	B	C	D	E	F	G	H	I	J	K	L	M
1	DSUM	11,812,600											
15													
17													
18		TRUE											
20													
23	Customer	Product	Region	District	Rep	Date	Qty	Revenue	Profit				
24	Wonderful Faucet Cc	G854	East	Southeast	ADAM DU	2/3/10	730	76,906	41,529		Best Doorbell Company	
25	Forceful Flagpole Cc	A105	East	Southeast	ADAM DU	12/19/10	804	32,297	16,794		Cool Shoe Corporation	
26	Best Paint Inc.	V937	Central	Chicago	PETER WA	12/5/10	414	59,761	31,673		Crisp Patio Corporation	
27	Guarded Raft Corpora	I543	West	California	BILLY JAC	1/5/12	793	66,858	35,435		Easy Banister Inc.	
28	Rare Quilt Inc.	G854	Central	Southwest	MELVIN S	3/31/12	993	104,613	47,076		Enhanced Xylophone Corporation	
29	Rare Juicer Company	H833	East	Southeast	TERRY MA	3/27/15	322	47,138	22,155		Flexible Tackle Inc.	
30	Improved Radio Trad	T859	West	California	BILLY JAC	12/10/11	918	61,763	33,352		Fully Raft Corporation	
31	Different Tuner Corp	C757	Central	Midwest	EVA STEV.	3/8/15	821	47,363	22,734		Fully Yardstick Corporation	
32	Best Paint Inc.	X538	Central	Chicago	PETER WA	5/12/10	871	83,477	40,069		Ideal Aquarium Supply	
33	Fascinating Washer I	M489	East	Southeast	ADAM DU	6/14/15	563	73,950	34,017		Leading Tripod Corporation	
34	Crisp Eggbeater Corp	H833	East	Northeast	NAOMI BA	3/4/14	315	46,113	20,751		Reliable Chopstick Corporation	
35	Different Adhesive S	O913	West	California	JOHNNY F	2/23/12	547	22,334	10,497		Secure Electronics Corporation	
36	Rare Vise Inc.	O651	East	Midatlantic	BOBBIE R'	11/12/13	604	70,064	32,229		Unique Bicycle Supply	
37	Rare Oven Corporati	H957	Central	Southwest	JENNIFER	10/3/14	437	63,138	29,675		Unique Quilt Corporation	
38	Effortless Clipboard	Z819	East	Northeast	CAROLINE	8/3/13	703	55,642	27,821		Wonderful Faucet Corporation	
39	Distinctive Glass Inc	G345	Central	Midwest	WILLIE CC	11/2/12	489	21,648	11,040			

Syntax:

DGET(database,field,criteria)

The DGET function returns a single cell matching criteria from a data set.

The DGET function takes the following arguments:

- database—This is the range of cells that make up the list or database. A *database* is a list of related data in which rows of related information are records and columns of data are fields. The first row of the list contains labels for each column.

- field—This indicates which column is used in the function. Field can be given as text, with the column label enclosed between double quotation marks, such as `"Age"` or `"Yield"`, or as a number that represents the position of the column within the list (for example, 1 for the first column, 2 for the second column, and so on).

- criteria—This is the range of cells that contains the conditions you specify. You can use any range for the criteria argument, as long as it includes at least one column label and at least one cell below the column label for specifying a condition for the column.

Excel in Practice: Using DSUM with a Data Table

If you do not want to use a pivot table, you can do a crosstab analysis by using a combination of the DSUM function and the Data Table command. The Data Table command works best when a problem is set up with two variables. In the DSUM function, you might have two variables defined in the criteria range.

To set up a two-variable table using the DSUM function, follow these steps:

1. Ensure that the upper-left corner of the table is a formula that relies on at least two variables. In Figure 12.51, Cell B1 contains a DSUM that relies on the criteria ranges in A17:I18.

2. Down the left side of the table, arrange a list of values that should be substituted for one variable. In this example, the column contains a list of products that will eventually be substituted into Cell B18.

3. Across the top row of the table, arrange a list of values that should be substituted for the other variable. In this example, the row contains a list of regions that will eventually be substituted into Cell C18.

4. Select the range for the table. This selection should include the formula as the upper-left corner cell. It should also include the column and row of headings.

5. From the Data tab, select What-if Analysis, Data Table. The Data Table dialog appears, asking for twocells.

6. For the row input cell, enter the cell where the regions should be substituted. In this case, it is Cell C18 in the criteria range.

7. For the Column input cell, enter the cell where the values down the left column will be substituted. In this case, it is Cell B18 in the criteria range. The complete dialog box should look as shown in Figure 12.52.

The result is a crosstab analysis that shows the DSUM for every combination of product and region. Excel actually creates a TABLE array function to produce the answers. This is a live formula: If you change the product names or regions, the cells inside the table recalculate.

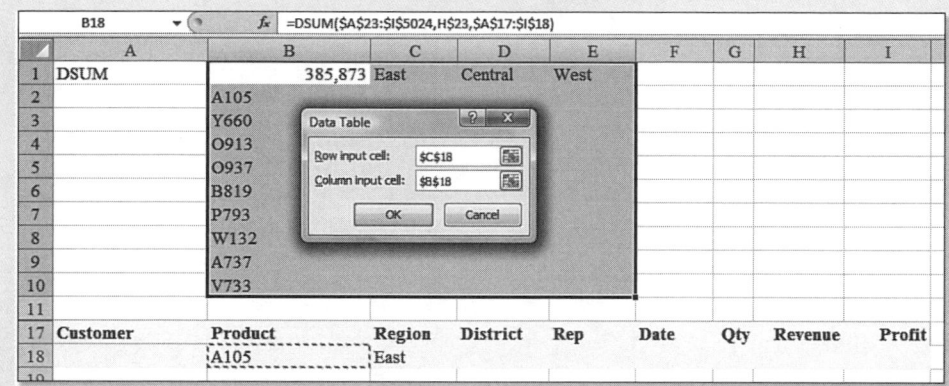

	A	B	C	D	E	F	G	H	I
	B18	▼	fx	=DSUM($A$23:$I$5024,H$23,$A$17:$I$18)					
1	DSUM		385,873	East	Central	West			
2		A105							
3		Y660							
4		O913							
5		O937							
6		B819							
7		P793							
8		W132							
9		A737							
10		V733							
11									
17	Customer	Product	Region	District	Rep	Date	Qty	Revenue	Profit
18		A105	East						

Figure 12.51
The Data Table dialog requires two cells.

	A	B	C	D	E
	C2	▼	fx	{=TABLE(C18,B18)}	
1	DSUM		385,873	East	Central	West
2		A105	385,873	601,184	259,097
3		Y660	1,152,227	1,422,736	1,111,337
4		O913	533,199	420,141	250,002
5		O937	1,562,404	1,498,932	1,146,197
6		B819	939,941	887,263	744,571
7		P793	553,087	690,740	146,925
8		W132	831,363	612,993	409,939
9		A737	1,609,888	952,950	919,978
10		V733	781,398	1,034,379	617,554
11					

Figure 12.52
The resulting table provides a crosstab analysis similar to that in a pivot table.

USING FINANCIAL FUNCTIONS

Although the bulk of Excel's financial functions are for professional financiers and investors, a few functions are useful for anyone planning to use a loan to purchase a car or house. The examples in this chapter represent a small subset of the calculations possible with Excel's financial functions.

The following financial functions use new algorithms in Excel 2010:

CUMIPMT—Cumulative interest paid on a loan

CUMPRINC—Cumulative principal paid on a loan

IPMT—Interest payment for an investment

IRR—Internal rate of return for a series of cash flows

PMT Payment for a loan

PPMT—Payment on principal for an investment

XIRR—Internal rate of return for a schedule of cash flows

The improved algorithms often affect only fringe cases of the functions. You might find that many results are the same as in previous versions of Excel. However, if the result in Excel 2010 is different, it will always be more accurate than the result from previous versions.

Table 13.1 provides an alphabetical list of all of Excel 2010's financial functions. Detailed examples of the functions are provided in the remainder of the chapter.

 note

Some of Excel's financial functions have been updated to have new algorithms in Excel 2010. Be aware that any worksheets that use these functions might produce different results than the same formula in Excel 2007.

Table 13.1 Alphabetical List of Financial Functions

Function	Description
ACCRINT (*issue, first_ interest, rate, par, fre- quency, basis*)	Returns the accrued interest for a security settlement that pays periodic interest.
ACCRINTM (*issue, maturity, rate, par, basis*)	Returns the accrued interest for a security that pays interest at maturity.
AMORDEGRC (*cost, date_ purchased, first_period, salvage, period, rate, basis*)	Returns the depreciation for each accounting period. This function is provided for the French accounting system. If an asset is purchased in the middle of the accounting period, the prorated depreciation is taken into account. The function is similar to AMORLINC, except that a depreciation coefficient is applied in the calculation, depending on the life of the assets.
AMORLINC (*cost, date_ purchased, first_period, salvage, period, rate, basis*)	Returns the depreciation for each accounting period. This function is provided for the French accounting system. If an asset is purchased in the middle of the accounting period, the prorated depreciation is taken into account.
COUPDAYBS (*settlement, maturity, frequency, basis*)	Returns the number of days from the beginning of the coupon period to the settlement date.
COUPDAYS (*settlement, maturity, frequency, basis*)	Returns the number of days in the coupon period that contains the settlement date.
COUPDAYSNC (*settlement, maturity, frequency, basis*)	Returns the number of days from the settlement date to the next coupon date.
COUPNCD (*settlement, maturity, frequency, basis*)	Returns a number that represents the next coupon date after the settlement date. To view the number as a date, you select Format, Cells and then click Date in the Category box. Then click a date format in the Type box.
COUPNUM (*settlement, matu- rity, frequency, basis*)	Returns the number of coupons payable between the settlement date and maturity date, rounded up to the nearest whole coupon.
COUPPCD (*settlement, matu- rity, frequency, basis*)	Returns a number that represents the previous coupon date before the settlement date. To view the number as a date, you select Format, Cells and then click Date in the Category box. Then click a date format in the Type box.
CUMIPMT (*rate, nper, pv, start_period, end_period, type*)	Returns the cumulative interest paid on a loan between *start_ period* and *end_period*.
CUMPRINC (*rate, nper, pv, start_period, end_period, type*)	Returns the cumulative principal paid on a loan between *start_ period* and *end_period*.
DB (*cost, salvage, life, period, month*)	Returns the depreciation of an asset for a specified period, using the fixed-declining balance method.

Function	Description
DDB (*cost, salvage, life, period, factor*)	Returns the depreciation of an asset for a specified period using the double-declining-balance method or some other specified method.
DISC (*settlement, maturity, pr, redemption, basis*)	Returns the discount rate for a security.
DOLLARDE (*fractional_dollar, fraction*)	Converts a dollar price expressed as a fraction into a dollar price expressed as a decimal number. Use DOLLARDE to convert fractional dollar numbers, such as securities prices, to decimal numbers.
DOLLARFR (*decimal_dollar, fraction*)	Converts a dollar price expressed as a decimal number into a dollar price expressed as a fraction. Use DOLLARFR to convert decimal numbers to fractional dollar numbers, such as securities prices.
DURATION (*settlement, maturity, coupon yld, frequency, basis*)	Returns the Macaulay duration for an assumed par value of $100. The duration is defined as the weighted average of the present value of the cash flows and is used as a measure of a bond price's response to changes in yield.
EFFECT (*nominal_rate, npery*)	Returns the effective annual interest rate, given the nominal annual interest rate and the number of compounding periods per year.
FV (*rate, nper, pmt, pv, type*)	Returns the future value of an investment, based on periodic, constant payments and a constant interest rate.
FVSCHEDULE (*principal, schedule*)	Returns the future value of an initial principal after applying a series of compound interest rates. Use FVSCHEDULE to calculate future value of an investment with a variable or adjustable rate.
INTRATE (*settlement, maturity, redemption, basis*)	Returns the interest rate for a fully investment invested security.
IPMT (*rate, per, nper, pv, fv, type*)	Returns the interest payment for a given period for an investment, based on periodic, constant payments and a constant interest rate. For a more complete description of the arguments in IPMT and for more information about annuity functions, see PV.
IRR (*values, guess*)	Returns the internal rate of return for a series of cash flows represented by the numbers in values. These cash flows do not have to be even, as they would be for an annuity. However, the cash flows must occur at regular intervals, such as monthly or annually. The internal rate of return is the interest rate received for an investment consisting of payments (negative values) and income (positive values) that occur at regular periods.
ISPMT (*rate, per, nper, pv*)	Calculates the interest paid during a specific period of an investment. This function is provided for compatibility with Lotus 1-2-3.

Function	Description
MDURATION (*settlement, maturity, yld, frequency, basis*)	Returns the modified duration for a security with coupon an assumed par value of $100.
MIRR (*values, finance_ rate, reinvest_rate*)	Returns the modified internal rate of return for a series of periodic cash flows. MIRR considers both the cost of the investment and the interest received on reinvestment of cash.
NOMINAL (*effect_rate, npery*)	Returns the nominal annual interest rate, given the effective rate and the number of compounding periods per year.
NPER (*rate, pmt, pv, fv, type*)	Returns the number of periods for an investment, based on periodic, constant payments and a constant interest rate.
NPV (*rate, value1, value2,...*)	Calculates the net present value of an investment by using a discount rate and a series of future payments (negative values) and income (positive values).
ODDFPRICE (*settlement, maturity, issue, first_ coupon, rate, yld, redemption, frequency, basis*)	Returns the price per $100 face value of a security having an odd (short or long) first period.
ODDFYIELD (*settlement, maturity, issue, first_ coupon, rate, pr, redemption, frequency, basis*)	Returns the yield of a security that has an odd (short or long) first period.
ODDLPRICE (*settlement, maturity, last_interest, rate, yld, redemption, frequency, basis*)	Returns the price per $100 face value of a security having an odd (short or long) last coupon period.
ODDLYIELD (*settlement, maturity, last_interest, rate, pr, redemption, frequency, basis*)	Returns the yield of a security that has an odd (short or long) last period.
PMT (*rate, nper, pv, fv, type*)	Calculates the payment for a loan based on constant payments and a constant interest rate.
PPMT (*rate, per, nper, pv, fv, type*)	Returns the payment on the principal for a given period for an investment based on periodic, constant payments and a constant interest rate.
PRICE (*settlement, maturity, rate, yld, redemption, frequency, basis*)	Returns the price per $100 face value of a security that pays periodic interest.
PRICEDISC (*settlement, maturity, redemption, basis*)	Returns the price per $100 face value of a discount discounted security.

Function	Description
PRICEMAT (settlement, maturity, rate, yld, basis)	Returns the price per $100 face value of a issue security that pays interest at maturity.
PV (rate, nper, pmt, fv, type)	Returns the present value of an investment. The present value is the total amount that a series of future payments is worth now. For example, when you borrow money, the loan amount is the present value to the lender.
RATE (nper, pmt, pv, fv, type, guess)	Returns the interest rate per period of an annuity. RATE is calculated by iteration and can have zero or more solutions. If the successive results of RATE do not converge to within 0.0000001 after 20 iterations, RATE returns a NUM! error.
RECEIVED (settlement, maturity, investment, discount, basis)	Returns the amount received at maturity for a fully invested security.
SLN (cost, salvage, life)	Returns the straight-line depreciation of an asset for one period.
SYD (cost, salvage, life, per)	Returns the sum-of-years'-digits depreciation of an asset for a specified period.
TBILLEQ (settlement, maturity, discount)	Returns the bond-equivalent yield for a Treasury bill (T-bill).
TBILLPRICE (settlement, maturity, discount)	Returns the price per $100 face value for a T-bill.
TBILLYIELD (settlement, maturity, pr)	Returns the yield for a T-bill.
VDB (cost, salvage, life, start_period, end_period, factor, no_switch)	Returns the depreciation of an asset for any specified period, including partial periods, using the double-declining-balance method or some other specified method. VDB stands for variable declining balance.
XIRR (values, dates, guess)	Returns the internal rate of return for a schedule of cash flows that is not necessarily periodic. To calculate the internal rate of return for a series of periodic cash flows, use the IRR function.
XNPV (rate, values, dates)	Returns the net present value for a schedule of cash flows that is not necessarily periodic. To calculate the net present value for a series of cash flows that is periodic, use the NPV function.
YIELD (settlement, maturity, rate, pr, redemption, frequency, basis)	Returns the yield on a security that pays periodic interest. You use YIELD to calculate bond yield.
YIELDDISC (settlement, maturity, pr, redemption, basis)	Returns the annual yield for a discounted security.
YIELDMAT (settlement, maturity, issue, rate, pr, basis)	Returns the annual yield of a security that pays interest at maturity.

Examples of Common Household Loan and Investment Functions

Although Excel is popular with banking and investment professionals, it is handy for just about anyone who deals with financial transactions. This first section of this chapter applies to anyone who is planning to buy a car or a house. With a little preplanning with Excel, you can build simple worksheets that allow you to calculate various monthly payments for various loan amounts.

You need to keep in mind two universal rules when dealing with all financial functions:

- Make sure your time units are consistent. If you calculate a monthly loan payment, the interest rate argument should be expressed as a monthly figure. Most interest rates are quoted as an annual figure, such as 5.5%. To convert, divide 5.5% by 12.

- When money changes hands, consider the direction in which money flows. In any transaction, some cash flows toward you (positive), and some cash flows away from you (negative). If you try to enter all terms as positive, you end up with a result that is not meaningful. For example, suppose you want a car loan where the bank gives $20,000 at the beginning and then gives you another $377 per month. NPER(5% /12,377,20000) would come up with an incorrect result for your problem because one of the cash flows needs to be negative. If you consider the loan from the point of view of the customer, the formula would be NPER(5% /12,-377,20000). If you consider the loan from the point of view of the bank, the formula would be NPER(5% /12,377,-20000).

Using PMT to Calculate the Monthly Payment on an Automobile Loan

Buying a car is one of the most exciting purchases. Whether the car is brand new or just new to you, nothing attracts attention in your neighborhood like a new car pulling into the driveway.

Before shopping for a car, you should take a 5-minute spin through Excel to calculate potential car payments. Knowing the price that will get you to the desired car payment will allow you to haggle with the sales rep from a position of knowledge.

Syntax:

PMT(*rate*,*nper*,*pv*,*fv*,*type*)

The PMT function calculates the payment for a loan based on constant payments and a constant interest rate. This function takes the following arguments:

- *rate* — This is the interest rate for the loan. Note that interest rate is often expressed as an annual rate. If you calculate a monthly payment, you have to divide that rate by 12.

- *nper* — This is the term, or the total number of payments for the loan.

- *pv* — This is the present value, or the loan amount; it is also known as the principal.

- *fv* — This is an optional future value, or a cash balance you want to attain after the last payment is made. For a car payment calculation, this should be 0. If *fv* is omitted, it is assumed to be 0; that is, the future value of a loan is zero.

- *type* – This is the number 0 or 1 and indicates when payments are due. The default value of 0 assumes that the first payment is due after a month has elapsed. If you have to make the first payment on the day the loan is issued, you should set this value to 1.

 To watch a video of calculating loan payments, search for "Excel In Depth 13" at YouTube

> **note**
> The payment returned by PMT includes principal and interest but not taxes, insurance, escrow, or fees sometimes associated with loans.

For a reality check, try multiplying the calculated payment by nper. This way, you can calculate the total of all payments over the life of the loan. In Figure 13.1, you see that a $29,000 car actually costs $32,835.95 in principal and interest.

Figure 13.1
PMT calculates a monthly loan payment.

	B5	▾		*fx*	=PMT(B2/12,B3,B1)		
	A	B	C	D	E	F	G
1	**Loan Amount**	-29000	*Negative, as the money is leaving the bank*				
2	**Rate**	5%	*Annual rate; divide by 12 in the function*				
3	**Term**	60	*Months*				
4							
5	**PMT**	$547.27	*=PMT(B2/12,B3,B1)*				
6							
7	**Total Paid**	$32,835.95					
8		=B3*B5					
9							

Using RATE to Determine an Interest Rate

The PMT function is useful when you are considering a new loan. If you are analyze a loan that you have been paying for a while, you might know the monthly payment but forget the interest rate. The RATE function can help you determine the rate.

Syntax:

RATE(*nper*,*pmt*,*pv*,*fv*,*type*,*guess*)

The RATE function returns the interest rate per period of an annuity. RATE is calculated by iteration and can have zero or more solutions. If the successive results of RATE do not converge to within 0.0000001 after 20 iterations, RATE returns a #NUM! error. This function takes the following arguments:

- *nper* – This is the total number of payment periods in an annuity.

> **caution**
> The algorithm behind the PMT function is new and more accurate in Excel 2010. Although this will not affect basic loan payment calculations like the one shown here, be aware that Excel 2007 and Excel 2010 might produce different results for some uses of PMT.

- *pmt*—This is the payment made each period and cannot change over the life of the annuity. Typically, pmt includes principal and interest but no other fees or taxes. If pmt is omitted, you must include the fv argument.
- *pv*—This is the present value—the total amount that a series of future payments is worth now.
- *fv*—This is the future value, or a cash balance you want to attain after the last payment is made. If fv is omitted, it is assumed to be `0`, which means the future value of a loan is zero.
- *type*—This is the number `0` or `1` to indicate when payments are due. The default value of `0` assumes that payments are due at the end of the period. A value of `1` means the payments are due at beginning of each period.
- *guess*—This is your guess for what the rate will be. If you omit guess, the rate is assumed to be `10%`. If `RATE` does not converge, you can try different values for guess. `RATE` usually converges if guess is between `0` and `1`.

Make sure you are consistent about the units you use for specifying guess and nper. If you make monthly payments on a 4-year loan at 12% annual interest, you use 12% / 12 for guess and 4 × 12 for nper. If you make annual payments on the same loan, you use 12% for guess and 4 for nper.

Figure 13.2 shows how to calculate an interest rate.

B6 | =RATE(B1, B2, B3)*12

	A	B	C	D	E
1	**Term**	60	*Months of the loan*		
2	**Payment**	377	*Monthly payment*		
3	**Loan Amount**	-20000	*Amount of the loan*		
4					
5	**Annual rate of the loan with the above terms**				
6	**Rate**	**4.95%**	*=RATE(B1, B2, B3)*12*		
7					

Figure 13.2
Given the other terms for a loan, back into the interest rate with RATE.

Using PV to Figure Out How Much House You Can Afford

If you are looking for a monthly house payment of $1,500 with a 15-year loan at 6% annual interest rate, you can back into the loan amount by using the PV function.

Syntax:

`PV(rate,nper,pmt,fv,type)`

The PV function returns the present value of an investment. The present value is the total amount that a series of future payments is worth now. For example, when you borrow money, the loan amount is the present value to the lender. This function takes the following arguments:

- *rate*—This is the interest rate per period. For example, if you obtain an automobile loan at a 10% annual interest rate and make monthly payments, your interest rate per month is 10%/12, or 0.008333. Therefore, you would enter 10% / 12, or 0.8333%, or 0.00833, into the formula as rate.

- *nper*—This is the total number of payment periods in an annuity. For example, if you get a 4-year car loan and make monthly payments, your loan has 4 × 12 (or 48) periods. You would enter 48 into the formula for nper.

- *pmt*—This is the payment made each period and cannot change over the life of the annuity. Typically, pmt includes principal and interest but no other fees or taxes. For example, the monthly payments on a $10,000, 4-year car loan at 12% are $263.33. You would enter -263.33 into the formula for pmt. If pmt is omitted, you must include the fv argument.

- *fv*—This is the future value, or a cash balance you want to attain after the last payment is made. If fv is omitted, it is assumed to be 0, which means the future value of a loan is zero. For example, if you want to save $50,000 to pay for a special project in 18 years, then $50,000 is the future value. You could then make a conservative guess at an interest rate and determine how much you must save each month. If fv is omitted, you must include the pmt argument.

- *type*—This is the number 0 or 1 to indicate when payments are due. The default value of 0 assumes that payments are due at the end of the period. A value of 1 means the payments are due at beginning of each period.

In Figure 13.3, Cell B5 calculates the loan principal amount that would result in the desired payment, including principal and interest. You also need to budget for monthly insurance, taxes, and fees that might be a part of your monthly payment to the bank.

Figure 13.3
Use PV to calculate how much you can borrow to meet a monthly payment budget.

	A	B	C	D	E	F	G
			B5	▾	fx =PV(B2/12,B3,B1)		
1	**Desired Payment**	-1500	*Negative, as it is money leaving your wallet*				
2	**Rate**	6%	*Annual rate; divide by 12 in the function*				
3	**Term**	180	*Months; =15*12*				
4							
5	**PV**	$177,755.27	*=PV(B2/12,B3,B1)*				
6							
7	*Don't forget that taxes, insurance, and escrow will be added to the*						
8	*desired payment in B1*						

Using NPER to Estimate How Long a Nest Egg Will Last

NPER stands for number of periods. If you have a 401k retirement account and are trying to calculate how long you can withdraw fixed monthly payments from the account, use NPER.

Syntax:

NPER(*rate, pmt, pv, fv, type*)

The NPER function returns the number of periods for an investment, based on periodic, constant payments and a constant interest rate. This function takes the following arguments:

- *rate*—This is the interest rate per period.

- *pmt*—This is the payment made each period; it cannot change over the life of the annuity. Typically, pmt contains principal and interest but no other fees or taxes.

- *pv*—This is the present value, or the lump-sum amount that a series of future payments is worth right now.

- *fv*—This is the future value, or a cash balance you want to attain after the last payment is made. If *fv* is omitted, it is assumed to be 0, which means the future value of a loan is zero. If you want to leave an inheritance to your kids, you use that amount as the *FV*.

- *type*—This is the number 0 or 1 to indicate when payments are due. The default value of 0 assumes that payments are due at the end of the period. A value of 1 means the payments are due at beginning of each period.

In Figure 13.4, the NPER function in Cell B5 estimates how many months you can withdraw the amount in Cell B2. Note that the monthly withdrawal is negative from the point of view of the retirement account.

B5	▼	*fx*	=NPER(B3/12,B2,B1)		
	A		B	C	D
1	**Nest Egg Today**		457124	*Value of retirement account*	
2	**Monthly Withdrawal**		-2800	*Desired monthly withdrawal*	
3	**Interest Rate**		3.5%	*Assumed interest rate*	
4					
5	**Months**		222.01	*=NPER(B3/12,B2,B1)*	
6	Years		18.5	*=B5/12*	

Figure 13.4
Use NPER to figure out how long an annuity can pay out before it ends in a zero balance.

Using FV to Estimate the Future Value of a Regular Savings Plan

The future value calculation assumes that you will make regular monthly payments to a savings plan every month. It also assumes that the interest rate does not change throughout the life of the savings plan. If you are young, it is likely that you can save more as your income grows later. However, using the savings calculator in Figure 13.5 helps you to realize the value of regular savings.

Figure 13.5
You can estimate the future value of a regular savings plan.

	B8 ▾ (●	fx =FV(B5/12,B3,-B4,-B6)		
	A	B	C	D
1	**Age Now**	25		
2	**Retirement Age**	65		
3	**Number of Months**	480	=(B2-B1)*12	
4	**Monthly Savings**	125		
5	**Interest Rate**	6%		
6	**Savings Balance Now**	542		
7				
8	**Future Value**	**$254,875.28**	=FV(B5/12,B3,-B4,-B6)	
9				

Syntax:

FV(*rate*,*nper*,*pmt*,*pv*,*type*)

The FV function returns the future value of an investment, based on periodic, constant payments and a constant interest rate. This function takes the following arguments:

- *rate*—This is the interest rate per period.

- *nper*—This is the total number of payment periods in an annuity.

- *pmt*—This is the payment made each period; it cannot change over the life of the annuity. Typically, pmt contains principal and interest but no other fees or taxes. If pmt is omitted, you must include the pv argument.

- *pv*—This is the present value, or the lump-sum amount that a series of future payments is worth right now. If pv is omitted, it is assumed to be 0, and you must include the pmt argument.

- *type*—This is the number 0 or 1 to indicate when payments are due. The default value of 0 assumes that payments are due at the end of the period. A value of 1 means the payments are due at beginning of each period.

For all the arguments, the cash you pay out, such as deposits to savings, is represented by negative numbers; the cash you receive, such as dividend checks, is represented by positive numbers.

Figure 13.5 shows how to use FV for a simple savings calculator. The formula in Cell B8 assumes that you continue making the deposit each month from Cell B4 until you retire and that interest rates remain constant. If you already have some amount in savings, you enter that in Cell B6.

 note

Note that the FV formula uses a negative version of Cells B4 and B6. This occurs because these are amounts that leave your wallet and go to the bank or mutual fund.

Examples of Functions for Financial Professionals

Whereas a typical consumer is interested in the amount of his or her monthly car payment, a loan maker is interested in the month-by-month breakdown of principal and interest. Excel offers a complete cadre of functions to do these calculations.

Using PPMT to Calculate the Principal Payment for Any Month

After a bank writes a car loan, the consumer makes monthly payments. To calculate the principal portion of the payment for any period in the loan, you use PPMT. Of course, you can use a range of these formulas—one for each month—to build an amortization table.

Syntax:

PPMT(*rate,per,nper,pv,fv,type*)

The PPMT function returns the payment on the principal for a given period for an investment, based on periodic, constant payments and a constant interest rate. This function takes the following arguments:

- *rate*—This is the interest rate per period.

- *per*—This specifies for which period the principal payment will be returned. It must be in the range 1 to *nper*.

- *nper*—This is the total number of payment periods in an annuity.

- *pv*—This is the present value—the total amount that a series of future payments is worth now.

- *fv*—This is the future value, or a cash balance you want to attain after the last payment is made. If *fv* is omitted, it is assumed to be 0, which means the future value of a loan is zero.

- *type*—This is the number 0 or 1 to indicate when payments are due. The default value of 0 assumes that payments are due at the end of the period. A value of 1 means the payments are due at beginning of each period.

In Figure 13.6, Cell B9 calculates the principal payment for Period 1. The per argument comes from the month number in Column A. Copying the formula down for all months produces an amortization table.

Figure 13.6
Similar PPMT functions in B9:B56 calculate the monthly principal portion of the loan payment.

	B9	▾	*fx*	=PPMT($B$2/12,A9,$B$3,$B$1)	
	A	B	C	D	E
1	**Loan Amt**	-22000			
2	**Rate**	5%			
3	**Term**	48			
4	**PMT**	506.64446			
5	**A9:**	*=ROW(1:1)*			
6	**B9:**	*=PPMT($B$2/12,A9,$B$3,$B$1)*			
7	**C9:**	*=IPMT($B$2/12,A9,$B$3,$B$1)*			
8	**Month**	**Principal**	**Interest**		
9	1	**$414.98**	$91.67		
10	2	$416.71	$89.94		
11	3	$418.44	$88.20		
12	4	$420.19	$86.46		

Using IPMT to Calculate the Interest Portion of a Loan Payment for Any Month

Whereas the PPMT function calculates the principal payment for any month of a loan, the IPMT function calculates the interest portion of the payment. The results of IPMT are shown in Column C of Figure 13.6.

Syntax:

IPMT(*rate,per,nper,pv,fv,type*)

The IPMT function returns the interest payment for a given period for an investment, based on periodic, constant payments and a constant interest rate. This function takes the following arguments:

- *rate*—This is the interest rate per period.

- *per*—This is the period for which you want to find the interest and must be in the range 1 to *nper*.

- *nper*—This is the total number of payment periods in an annuity.

note

In this example, the interest component could be calculated with either PMT–PPMT or using the IPMT function. IPMT is discussed in the next section.

 tip

To generate the column of numbers starting in A9, enter the formula =ROW(1:1) in Cell A9. When you copy this formula down, the 1:1 reference will change to 2:2, 3:3, and so on. This is a fast way to generate a column of sequential numbers using a single formula. Alternatively, use =ROW(A1) for the same result.

- *pv*—This is the present value, or the lump-sum amount that a series of future payments is worth right now.

- *fv*—This is the future value, or a cash balance you want to attain after the last payment is made.

- *type*—This is the number 0 or 1 to indicate when payments are due. The default value of 0 assumes that payments are due at the end of the period. A value of 1 means the payments are due at beginning of each period.

The IPMT function is similar to the PPMT function. Combined, they can create a simple amortization table (refer to Figure 13.6).

Using CUMIPMT to Calculate Total Interest Payments During a Time Frame

The CUMIPMT function is great for figuring out your yearly tax deduction for your mortgage interest. After specifying the typical components of a loan such as the rate, term, and amount, you need to specify that you want to calculate the interest for particular periods, such as Periods 6 through 18.

Syntax:

CUMIPMT(*rate,nper,pv,start_period,end_period,type*)

The CUMIPMT function returns the cumulative interest paid on a loan between *start_period* and *end_period*. This function takes the following arguments:

- *rate*—This is the interest rate.

- *nper*—This is the total number of payment periods.

- *pv*—This is the present value.

- *start_period*—This is the first period in the calculation. Payment periods are numbered beginning with 1.

- *end_period*—This is the last period in the calculation.

- *type*—This is the number 0 or 1 to indicate when payments are due. The default value of 0 assumes that payments are due at the end of the period. A value of 1 means the payments are due at beginning of each period.

The *nper, start_period, end_period,* and *type* arguments are truncated to integers. If rate is less than or equal to 0, nper is less than or equal to 0, or pv is less than or equal to 0, CUMIPMT returns a #NUM! error. If *start_period* is less than 1, *end_period* is less than 1, or *start_period*

note

You may encounter an old worksheet that uses ISPMT, which is the Lotus 1-2-3 version of IPMT. For details on ISPMT, see Excel Help. For new worksheets, you should use IPMT instead of ISPMT.

caution

The algorithm behind the IPMT function is new and more accurate in Excel 2010. Be aware that Excel 2007 and Excel 2010 might produce different results for some uses of IPMT.

caution

The algorithm behind the CUMIPMT function is new and more accurate in Excel 2010. Be aware that Excel 2007 and Excel 2010 might produce different results for some uses of CUMIPMT.

is greater than *end_period,* CUMIPMT returns a #NUM! error. If *type* is any number other than 0 or 1, CUMIPMT returns a #NUM! error.

Figure 13.7 calculates the total interest paid during each year of the loan. The mildly difficult portion of the sample spreadsheet is that the number of months in the first year will likely be less than 12. Cell D12 uses =13-MONTH(B5). Cell C13 uses =D12+1. Cell D13 uses =C12+11 to calculate the last period for each year.

Column F of this spreadsheet uses CUMPRINC, which is discussed in the next section.

Figure 13.7
Use Column E to plan your tax deductions by year.

E12	▾	*f*ₓ	=CUMIPMT($B$2/12,$B$3,$B$1,$C12,$D12,0)			
	A	B	C	D	E	F	G
1	**Mortage Amt.**	225,000					
2	**Rate**	6%					
3	**Term**	180					
4	**PMT**	-1,898.68	*Not necessary for the calculation, here FYI*			
5	**First Payment**	Aug-05	*Cell D12 uses this in =13-MONTH(B5)*			
6							
7		**E12:**	=CUMIPMT($B$2/12,$B$3,$B$1,$C12,$D12,0)			
8		**F12:**	=CUMPRINC($B$2/12,$B$3,$B$1,$C12,$D12,0)			
9			**Payment Numbers**			
11		**Year**	**From**	**Through**	**Interest**	**Principal**	
12		2005	1	5	**-5,586.12**	-3,907.27	
13		2006	6	17	-12,999.39	-9,784.74	
14		2007	18	29	-12,395.89	-10,388.24	
15		2008	30	41	-11,755.17	-11,028.97	
16		2009	42	53	-11,074.92	-11,709.21	

Using CUMPRINC to Calculate Total Principal Paid in Any Range of Periods

The corollary to CUMIPMT is a function to calculate the total principal paid during any range of periods of a loan: CUMPRINC.

Syntax:

CUMPRINC(*rate,nper,pv,start_period,end_period,type*)

The CUMPRINC function returns the cumulative principal paid on a loan between *start_period* and *end_period*. This function takes the following arguments:

- *rate*—This is the interest rate.

- *nper*—This is the total number of payment periods.

- *pv*—This is the present value.

- *start_period*—This is the first period in the calculation. Payment periods are numbered beginning with 1.

- *end_period*—This is the last period in the calculation.

- *type*—This is the number 0 or 1 to indicate when payments are due. The default value of 0 assumes that payments are due at the end of the period. A value of 1 means the payments are due at beginning of each period.

The *nper, start_period, end_period,* and *type* arguments are truncated to integers. If rate is less than or equal to 0, nper is less than or equal to 0, or pv is less than or equal to 0, CUMPRINC returns a #NUM! error. If *start_period* is less than 1, *end_period* is less than 1, or *start_period* is greater than *end_period*, CUMPRINC returns a #NUM! error. If type is any number other than 0 or 1, CUMPRINC returns a #NUM! error.

Figure 13.7 shows an example of CUMPRINC.

>  **caution**
>
> The algorithm behind the CUMPRINC function is new and more accurate in Excel 2010. Be aware that Excel 2007 and Excel 2010 might produce different results for some uses of CUMPRINC.

Using EFFECT to Calculate the Effect of Compounding Period on Interest Rates

Does it really matter if your bank compounds interest daily, monthly, or quarterly? If the numbers are big enough, it can matter. The EFFECT function converts an interest rate to an effective rate, depending on how frequently the bank compounds the interest.

Syntax:

EFFECT(*nominal_rate,npery*)

The EFFECT function returns the effective annual interest rate, given the nominal annual interest rate and the number of compounding periods per year. This function takes the following arguments:

- *nominal_rate*—This is the nominal interest rate.

- *npery*—This is the number of compounding periods per year. npery is truncated to an integer.

If either argument is nonnumeric, EFFECT returns a #VALUE! error. If *nominal_rate* is less than or equal to 0 or if npery is less than 1, EFFECT returns a #NUM! error.

In Figure 13.8, the nominal interest rate is 6%. If the bank compounds interest once per year, the effective interest rate is still 6%, as shown in Cell A5. If interest is compounded monthly, the effective rate increases to 6.17%. Row 9 compares the monthly mortgage payment at the various effective rates. Daily compounding adds about $23 per month to a typical mortgage payment.

Figure 13.8
Row 5 shows the effective interest rates for various compounding periods. Row 9 shows the monthly payment difference.

	D5	▼ (	fx	=EFFECT($B$1,D4)	
	A	B	C	D	E
1	**Interest Rate**	6%			
2					
3	*Compounding Periods ----->*				
4	**1**	**4**	**12**	**365**	
5	**0.06**	**0.061364**	**0.061678**	**0.061831**	
6				*=EFFECT($B$1,D4)*	
7					
8	*Mortgage Payment on 200K loan, 30 years*				
9	$1,199.10	$1,216.69	$1,220.76	$1,222.75	
10					

Using NOMINAL to Convert the Effective Interest Rate to a Nominal Rate

If you need to compare two investments, one quoting a nominal rate and one quoting an effective rate, you can convert the effective rate to a nominal rate by using NOMINAL.

Syntax:

NOMINAL(*effect_rate,npery*)

The NOMINAL function returns the nominal annual interest rate, given the effective rate and the number of compounding periods per year. This function takes the following arguments:

- *effect_rate*—This is the effective interest rate.

- *npery*—This is the number of compounding periods per year.

The npery argument is truncated to an integer. If either argument is nonnumeric, NOMINAL returns a #VALUE! error. If effect_rate is less than or equal to 0 or if *npery* is less than 1, NOMINAL returns a #NUM! error.

Examples of Depreciation Functions

When a company buys a large asset such as a piece of machinery, accounting rules specify how the asset should be expensed each year. This is called *depreciation*. Excel offers four common methods for calculating depreciation: straight-line, declining-balance, double-declining-balance, and sum-of-years'-digits methods.

The following terms are common to all the depreciation methods:

- **Cost**—This is the initial cost of the asset. For example, the machinery might cost $120,000.

- **Useful life**—This is how long you expect to use the asset. If you think the machinery will be used for 10 years before being replaced, the life is 10 years.

- **Salvage value**—This is the value of the asset at the end of the useful life. Perhaps after 10 years, you can sell the machine to a scrap dealer for $1,000 or to a trade school for $5,000. This is the salvage value.

Figure 13.9 compares the four depreciation methods.

	D6		f_x =DDB($B$1,$B$2,$B$3,A6)		
	A	B	C	D	E
1	Cost	120000			
2	Salvage Value	20000			
3	Useful Life	10	years		
4					
5	Year	Straight Line	Declining Balance	Double Declining	Sum of Years Digits
6	1	$10,000.00	$19,680.00	$24,000.00	$18,181.82
7	2	$10,000.00	$16,452.48	$19,200.00	$16,363.64
8	3	$10,000.00	$13,754.27	$15,360.00	$14,545.45
9	4	$10,000.00	$11,498.57	$12,288.00	$12,727.27
10	5	$10,000.00	$9,612.81	$9,830.40	$10,909.09
11	6	$10,000.00	$8,036.31	$7,864.32	$9,090.91
12	7	$10,000.00	$6,718.35	$6,291.46	$7,272.73
13	8	$10,000.00	$5,616.54	$5,033.16	$5,454.55
14	9	$10,000.00	$4,695.43	$132.66	$3,636.36
15	10	$10,000.00	$3,925.38	$0.00	$1,818.18
16					
17	**B6:** =SLN($B$1,$B$2,$B$3)				
18	**C6:** =DB($B$1,$B$2,$B$3,A6)				
19	**D6:** =DDB($B$1,$B$2,$B$3,A6)				
20	**E6:** =SYD($B$1,$B$2,$B$3,A6)				
21					

Figure 13.9
Columns B through E compare four methods of depreciation.

Using SLN to Calculate Straight-Line Depreciation

The straight-line method is the simplest depreciation method. Using this method, the value of the asset is depreciated evenly over the asset's useful life. At the end of the useful life, the item is depreciated on the company's books to the salvage value level.

Syntax:

SLN(*cost,salvage,life*)

The SLN function returns the straight-line depreciation of an asset for one period. This function takes the following arguments:

- *cost*—This is the initial cost of the asset.

- *salvage* – This is the asset's value at the end of the depreciation period. Sometimes this is called the salvage value of the asset.

- *life*—This is the number of periods over which the asset is being depreciated. Sometimes this is called the useful life of the asset.

Using DB to Calculate Declining-Balance Depreciation

In the declining-balance method, depreciation happens at a constant rate. The advantage of this method is that more depreciation happens in the earlier years, providing a better tax benefit in early years.

 note

See Excel Help for this function for details on special handling of Year 1 and the last year, as well as the algebra behind the rate formula.

Let's look at a simple example. Suppose that a $100,000 asset is depreciated 20% in Year 1. This results in a $20,000 depreciation expense. After Year 1, the asset would be have a value of $80,000 on the books. In Year 2, the remaining balance of $80,000 is multiplied by the same 20% rate to yield a depreciation of $16,000. The depreciation in Year 3 is 20% of the remaining $64,000, or $12,800.

The trick to this method is figuring out the correct percentage to use for each year. This involves fractional exponents and a little algebra. If you use the DB function, however, you do not have to worry about any of that. Excel calculates this rate, rounded to three decimal places, as the first step in the process. This rounding to three decimal places causes the calculation to be off by a few dollars at the end of the useful life.

Syntax:

DB(*cost,salvage,life,period,month*)

The DB function returns the depreciation of an asset for a specified period, using the fixed-declining-balance method. This function takes the following arguments:

- *cost*—This is the initial cost of the asset.

- *salvage*—This is the value at the end of the depreciation period. Sometimes this is called the salvage value of the asset.

- *life*—This is the number of periods over which the asset is being depreciated. Sometimes this is called the useful life of the asset.

- *period*—This is the period for which you want to calculate the depreciation. *period* must use the same units as *life*.

- *month*—This is the number of months in the first year. If month is omitted, it is assumed to be 12.

Using DDB to Calculate Double-Declining-Balance Depreciation

The double-declining-balance method is an aggressive (and legal) method for calculating depreciation. Suppose you purchased a computer. In the first year, the item might be state-of-the-art. By Year 2, it is worth far less because technology would have passed the computer by.

The name of this method reflects the fact that the depreciation rate is double the normal rate but also that the depreciation rate is applied to the declining balance of the asset's value.

If the asset is depreciated over 5 years, the normal straight-line rate would be 20%. In the double-declining-balance method, you get to use 40% in each year. For example, the first year, depreciation on a $100,000 asset would be 40%. But in Year 2, the 40% is multiplied by the remaining asset value of $60,000. This method generates much higher depreciation in the first few years of the asset life than the other methods.

Although the name of this method contains the world *double*, Microsoft covered the possibility of other multipliers. There is a 150DB method that multiplies the rate by 1.5 instead of 2. To calculate 150DB, you use 1.5 as the fifth argument. If no fifth argument is supplied, the fifth argument is assumed to be 2, resulting in DDB.

 note

In many depreciation systems, you are allowed to switch from double-declining-balance to the straight-line method when the straight-line method produces a higher depreciation. To do this, use the VDB function, which is described later in this chapter.

Syntax:

DDB(*cost,salvage,life,period,factor*)

The DDB function returns the depreciation of an asset for a specified period using the double-declining-balance method or some other specified method. This function takes the following arguments:

- *cost*—This is the initial cost of the asset.

- *salvage*—This is the value at the end of the depreciation period.

- *life* – This is the number of periods over which the asset is being depreciated.

- *period*—This is the period for which you want to calculate the depreciation. The *period* must use the same units as life.

- *factor*—This is the rate at which the balance declines. If *factor* is omitted, it is assumed to be 2, which is the double-declining-balance method.

To allow DDB to work, you need to abandon the method at some point and switch to a straight-line method for the remaining asset value. If you attempt to use DDB for the entire life of the asset, you will not write off enough of the value.

tip

Keep in mind that all five of the arguments listed previously must be positive numbers.

Figure 13.10 illustrates how DDB fails to accumulate $500,000 of depreciation. You might want to use the newer VDB method, which automatically switches for you. Column D in Figure 13.10 shows this method.

Figure 13.10
The DDB method fails to accumulate enough depreciation.

	D12	▼	f_x	=VDB($B$1,$B$2,$B$3,$A12-1,$A12,2,FALSE)	
	A	B	C	D	E	F
1	Cost	500000	*Note that saying False to NoSwitch is a*		
2	Salvage Value	0	*double negative. You are saying that you*		
3	Useful Life	10	*do want to switch to SLN...*		
4						
5	Year	Straight Line	Double Declining	VDB NoSwitch= FALSE	VDB NoSwitch= TRUE	
6	1	$50,000.00	$100,000.00	$100,000.00	$100,000.00	
7	2	$50,000.00	$80,000.00	$80,000.00	$80,000.00	
8	3	$50,000.00	$64,000.00	$64,000.00	$64,000.00	
9	4	$50,000.00	$51,200.00	$51,200.00	$51,200.00	
10	5	$50,000.00	$40,960.00	$40,960.00	$40,960.00	
11	6	$50,000.00	$32,768.00	$32,768.00	$32,768.00	
12	7	$50,000.00	$26,214.40	$32,768.00	$26,214.40	
13	8	$50,000.00	$20,971.52	$32,768.00	$20,971.52	
14	9	$50,000.00	$16,777.22	$32,768.00	$16,777.22	
15	10	$50,000.00	$13,421.77	$32,768.00	$13,421.77	
16	TOTAL	$500,000.00	$446,312.91	$500,000.00	$446,312.91	
17						
18	**B6:**	*=DDB($B$1,$B$2,$B$3,A6)*			
19	**C6:**	*=VDB($B$1,$B$2,$B$3,$A6-1,$A6,2,FALSE)*			
20	**C6 Alt:**	*=VDB($B$1,$B$2,$B$3,$A6-1,$A6)*			
21	**D6:**	*=VDB($B$1,$B$2,$B$3,$A6-1,$A6,2,FALSE)*			
22	**E6:**	*=VDB($B$1,$B$2,$B$3,$A6-1,$A6,2,TRUE)*			

To overcome this problem with DDB, you can use the VDB method. The VDB function is a far more powerful function. Using VDB to calculate a double-declining-balance problem correctly is somewhat like using a sledgehammer to push in a thumbtack. VDB is covered in detail later in this chapter, but you can follow these steps to solve the current problem:

1. Change the function name from DDB to VDB.

2. Because both DDB and VDB take the same first three arguments—*cost, salvage,* and *life*—leave those three arguments alone.

3. Change period number in DDB to start period and end period for VDB. Cell C6 specifies A6 as the period number. Change this argument to A6-1,A6. This is a bit strange because you are asking VDB to calculate the depreciation from the end of Year 0 to the end of Year 1.

4. Determine whether the DDB function is done. *Factor*, which is usually left off the function, is assumed to be 2. If DDB has no fifth argument, then VDB does not need a fifth argument.

5. To allow VDB to switch to the straight-line method, ensure that the sixth argument is FALSE. The name of this argument is no_switch. By specifying FALSE, you are invoking a double negative to ask VDB to switch to the straight-line method when appropriate. Because FALSE is the default, you can often leave off the fifth and sixth arguments with VDB.

➡ *Complete details on the more powerful uses of VDB are provided later in this chapter.*

Using SYD to Calculate Sum-of-Years'-Digits Depreciation

The sum-of-years'-digits method is another accelerated depreciation system. It ensures that the value of the asset drops more in the earlier years of the asset's life than in later years.

Suppose you have an asset with a useful life of seven years. You need to add all the years from seven to one: 7 + 6 + 5 + 4 + 3 + 2 + 1 = 28. In the first year, you can write off 7 / 28 of the value. In the next year, you can write off 6 / 28. In successive years, you can write off 5 / 28, 4 / 28, 3 / 28, 2 / 28, and 1 / 28 of the depreciable value.

Syntax:

SYD(*cost,salvage,life,per*)

The SYD function returns the sum-of-years'-digits depreciation of an asset for a specified period. This function takes the following arguments:

- *cost*—This is the initial cost of the asset.

- *salvage*—This is the value at the end of the depreciation period. Sometimes this is called the salvage value of the asset.

- *life*—This is the number of periods over which the asset is being depreciated. Sometimes this is called the useful life of the asset.

- *per*—This is the period and must use the same units as *life*.

Using VDB to Calculate Depreciation for Any Period

As mentioned in the discussion of the DDB function, the VDB function is newer and far more powerful than the other depreciation functions.

It is interesting for tax purposes to know the annual depreciation amounts. However, if you work for a public company, you have to report depreciation at least quarterly. Figure 13.11 shows an example that calculates the exact depreciation to be booked each quarter.

Syntax:

VDB(*cost,salvage,life,start_period,end_period,factor,no_switch*)

The VDB function returns the depreciation of an asset for any specified period, including partial periods, using the double-declining-balance method or some other specified method. VDB stands for *variable declining balance*.

The VDB function takes the following arguments:

- *cost*—This is the initial cost of the asset.

- *salvage*—This is the value at the end of the depreciation period.

- *life*—This is the number of periods over which the asset is being depreciated. To calculate depreciation for periods smaller than a year, multiply the number of years by 12, or even 365.

Figure 13.11
VDB allows you to calculate depreciation for each month or quarter.

	A	B	C	D	E	F
	C7	▾	f_x =VDB($B$1,$B$2,$B$3*365,$A7-$B$4,$B7-$B$4,2,FALSE)			
1	Cost	50000				
2	Salvage Value	5000				
3	Useful Life	7				
4	Start Date	5/1/2007				
5						
6	Start Date	End Date	VDB			
7	5/1/2007	6/30/2007	$2,294.92			
8	7/1/2007	9/30/2007	$3,278.63			
9	10/1/2007	12/31/2007	$3,050.74			
10	1/1/2008	3/31/2008	$2,808.57			
11	4/1/2008	6/30/2008	$2,615.40			
12	7/1/2008	9/30/2008	$2,461.61			
13						
14	**A7:**	=B4				
15	**B7:**	=VDB($B$1,$B$2,$B$3*365,$A7-$B$4,$B7-$B$4,2,FALSE)				
16	**A8:**	=B7+1				
17	**B8:**	=EOMONTH(A8,2)				

- *start_period*—This is the starting period for which you want to calculate the depreciation. *start_period* must use the same units as *life*.

- *end_period*—This is the ending period for which you want to calculate the depreciation. *end_period* must use the same units as *life*.

- *factor*—This is the rate at which the balance declines. If *factor* is omitted, it is assumed to be 2, which is the double-declining-balance method. You change *factor* if you do not want to use the double-declining-balance method.

- *no_switch*—This is a logical value that specifies whether to switch to straight-line depreciation when depreciation is greater than with the declining-balance calculation. If this is FALSE or omitted, Excel switches to the straight-line method when it becomes more beneficial to do so. If this value is TRUE, Excel holds on to the DDB method until the end of *life*.

 tip

Keep in mind that all the arguments listed previously, except no_switch, must be positive numbers.

To set up a schedule that shows depreciation for each quarter, you follow these steps:

1. Enter the cost, salvage value, and useful life at the top of the worksheet.

2. Enter the date on which the equipment is placed in service in Cell B4.

3. Enter dates for the first quarter in Cells A7 and B7. The value in Cell A7 is the date the unit is placed in service. Manually figure out the last date of the quarter for Cell B7.

4. Ensure that the formula for Columns A and B in each subsequent row is the same. In Cell A8, enter =B7+1. In Cell B8, enter is =EOMONTH(A8,2). The EOMONTH function reports the end of the month that falls two months after what is shown in Cell A8. Copy these formulas down as far as necessary.

5. To build the VDB function, use the normal values for cost and salvage value. Instead of 7 for life, use 7 × 365 to have the function calculate a daily depreciation rate.

6. For *start_period*, use the date in Column A minus the date in service.

7. For *end_period*, use the date in Column B minus the date in service.

8. If you are using the double-declining-balance method, omit the fifth and sixth arguments.

9. Copy the VDB function down to all your rows.

The table shown in Figure 13.11 shows the depreciation to be booked each quarter for this particular piece of machinery.

Functions for Investment Analysis

The invention of the computer spreadsheet in 1979 enabled the rapid growth of the mergers and acquisitions business in the 1980s. Business plans can be modeled in Excel, with the resulting series of net income values discounted to determine the current value of a business. Excel offers a wide array of functions that can be used to analyze a business investment.

> **note**
>
> If you happen to work for a French-owned company, keep in mind special considerations when calculating depreciation. Read the Help topics for AMORDEGRC and AMORLINC to understand these methods that have been added to Excel to accommodate the French accounting rules.

Using the NPV Function to Determine Net Present Value

Suppose that you have a pile of cash. You have the opportunity to invest that cash in a long-term CD that earns 2% interest. You also have the opportunity to use that cash to buy a business. The 2% is called the *hurdle rate*. If the business cannot return more than the 2% hurdle rate, you should probably look for another business.

You have analyzed the business plan and projected that the business will generate a certain series of net income over each of the next five years. You can analyze the net present value of the investment by using the NPV function.

Syntax:

NPV(*rate,value1,value2,...*)

The NPV function calculates the net present value of an investment by using a discount rate and a series of future payments (negative values) and income (positive values). This function takes the following arguments:

- *rate*—This is the rate of discount over the length of one period.

- *value1,value2,...*—These are 1 to 254 arguments representing the payments and income. Instead, you can refer to a range of values. *value1, value2,...* must be equally spaced in time and occur at the end of each period. The function uses the order of *value1, value2,...* to interpret the order of cash flows. You need to be sure to enter your payment and income values in the correct sequence.

The NPV investment begins one period before the date of the value1 cash flow and ends with the last cash flow in the list.

Arguments of *value1, value2,...* are cash flows at the end of Year 1, Year 2, and so on.

In this example, if you buy a business for $50,000, this amount should not be entered as a value in the function. Instead, you should subtract the $50,000 from the result of NPV.

NPV is similar to the PV function. The primary difference between PV and NPV is that PV allows cash flows to begin either at the end or at the beginning of the period. Unlike the variable NPV cash flow values, PV cash flows must be constant throughout the investment.

NPV is also related to the IRR function. IRR is the rate for which NPV equals zero: NPV(IRR(...), ...) = 0.

In Figure 13.12, the business will cost $50,000. The business will lose $5,000 in Year 1 and then generate $61,000 over the next 4 years. Based on these cash flows, NPV is positive, which means that the investment will do better than a CD at 2% interest.

Figure 13.12
NPV can analyze a periodic series of cash flows.

	B9	▾	*fx*	=NPV(B1,B3:B7)+B2	
	A		B	C	D
1	**Discount Rate**		2%		
2	**Cost of Business:**		-50,000		
3	**Return from year 1:**		-5,000		
4	**Return from year 2:**		5,000		
5	**Return from year 3:**		12,000		
6	**Return from year 4:**		19,000		
7	**Return from year 5:**		25,000		
8					
9	**NPV**		**1,408**		
10					
11	*B9: =NPV(B1,B3:B7)+B2*				
12					
13	**Internal Rates of Return:**				
14	**After 2 years:**		-72.98%	*=IRR(B$2:B4,-0.5)*	
15	**After 3 years:**		-35.93%	*=IRR(B$2:B5,0.01)*	
16	**After 4 years:**		-11.97%	*=IRR(B$2:B6)*	
17	**After 5 years:**		2.66%	*=IRR(B$2:B7)*	

🔍 note

NPV requires the cash flows to occur at a regular rate. If you instead have a series of projected cash flows on varying dates, you should use XNPV instead. See the section "Using XNPV to Calculate the Net Present Value When the Payments Are Not Periodic," later in this chapter.

Using IRR to Calculate the Return of a Series of Cash Flows

In the previous section, you used the NPV function to determine whether a business investment met or did not meet a certain desired rate of return. In Figure 13.12, NPV is positive, indicating that the business was able to beat a 2% return after five years. If you want to figure out the internal rate of return, use the IRR function.

One critical difference exists between IRR and NPV: In the NPV function, the initial investment in the business is **not** included in the list of arguments. In the IRR function, the initial investment in the business needs to be included as the first cash flow. Because this is money paid for the business, it should be negative.

Syntax:

IRR(*values*,*guess*)

The IRR function returns the internal rate of return for a series of cash flows, represented by the numbers in *values*. These cash flows do not have to be even, as they would be for an annuity. However, the cash flows must occur at regular intervals, such as monthly or annually. The internal rate of return is the interest rate received for an investment, consisting of payments (negative values) and income (positive values) that occur at regular periods.

The IRR function takes the following arguments:

- *values*—This is an array or a reference to cells that contain numbers for which you want to calculate the internal rate of return. *values* must contain at least one positive value and one negative value to calculate the internal rate of return. IRR uses the order of *values* to interpret the order of cash flows. You need to be sure to enter your payment and income values in the sequence you want. If an array or a reference argument contains text, logical values, or empty cells, those values are ignored.

- *guess*—This is a number that you guess is close to the result of IRR. Microsoft Excel uses an iterative technique for calculating IRR. Starting with *guess*, IRR cycles through the calculation until the result is accurate within 0.00001%. If IRR cannot find a result that works after 20 tries, a #NUM! error is returned. In most cases, you do not need to provide guess for the IRR calculation. If *guess* is omitted, it is assumed to be 0.1, which is 10%. If IRR gives a #NUM! error, or if the result is not close to what you expected, you can try again with a different value for guess.

IRR is closely related to NPV, the net present value function. The rate of return calculated by IRR is the interest rate corresponding to a net present value of zero. The following formula demonstrates how NPV and IRR are related: Enter = NPV(IRR(B1:B6),B1:B6) in a cell, which equals 3.60E-08. Within the accuracy of the IRR calculation, the value 3.60E-08 is effectively zero.

note

IRR fails to take into account that the money earned in Year 1 could start generating interest if invested in a CD. To calculate a rate of return including the reinvestment of profits, use MIRR, which is described in the following section.

caution

The algorithm behind the IRR function is new and more accurate in Excel 2010. Be aware that Excel 2007 and Excel 2010 might produce different results for some uses of IRR.

In Figure 13.12, the formula in Cell B17 shows that the business investment would generate a rate of return of 2.7% if analyzed over a 5-year period. The arguments for this function include the initial $50,000 investment in the business as well as the net incomes from the next 5 years.

Similar formulas in Cells B14 and B15 return a #NUM! error. The formulas were edited to add a *guess* value. Based on the –12% return through 4 years, *guess* for three years was –10%.

Using MIRR to Calculate Internal Rate of Return, Including Interest Rates

MIRR calculates a modified internal rate of return. This function assumes that cash flows from the business are reinvested at some interest rate. It also offers an argument to specify the initial interest rate of the business loan used to purchase the business.

Syntax:

MIRR(*values,finance_rate,reinvest_rate*)

The MIRR function returns the modified internal rate of return for a series of periodic cash flows. MIRR considers both the cost of the investment and the interest received on reinvestment of cash. This function takes the following arguments:

- *values*—This is an array or a reference to cells that contain numbers. These numbers represent a series of payments (negative values) and income (positive values) occurring at regular periods. *values* must contain at least one positive value and one negative value to calculate the modified internal rate of return. Otherwise, MIRR returns a #DIV/0! error. If an array or a reference argument contains text, logical values, or empty cells, those values are ignored; however, cells with the value 0 are included.

- *finance_rate*—This is the interest rate you pay on the money used in the cash flows.

- *reinvest_rate*—This is the interest rate you receive on the cash flows as you reinvest them.

MIRR uses the order of values to interpret the order of cash flows. You need to be sure to enter your payment and income values in the sequence you want and with the correct signs. In other words, enter positive values for cash received and negative values for cash paid.

In Figure 13.13, you are analyzing a business that was started 5 years ago with a $120,000 loan. The business has generated profits of $17,000, $34,000, $38,000, $5,000, and $32,000. The original loan had an interest rate of 5%, and the profits were reinvested at 2.25%. The MIRR in Cell B10 is 1.9%. For comparison, the IRR of the same cash flows would be only 1.64%.

Using XNPV to Calculate the Net Present Value When the Payments Are Not Periodic

The previous examples assume that everything happens on the last day of each year. In reality, the business purchase date and the business sales date might occur on other days. In such a case, you use XNPV.

B10	▼ (	*f*x	=MIRR(B1:B6,B7,B8)		
	A		B	C	
1	Cost of Business:		($120,000)		
2	Return first year		17,000		
3	Return second year		34,000		
4	Return third year		38,000		
5	Return fourth year		5,000		
6	Return fifth year		32,000		
7	Int. rate for $120K Loan		5.00%		
8	Int. rate for reinvested profits		2.25%		
9					
10	MIRR		1.9%	=MIRR(B1:B6,B7,B8)	

Figure 13.13
You can determine a modified rate of return, figuring in a financing rate and the interest rate for reinvested profits.

Syntax:

XNPV(*rate*,*values*,*dates*)

The XNPV function returns the net present value for a schedule of cash flows that is not necessarily periodic. To calculate the net present value for a series of cash flows that is periodic, you use the NPV function. The XNPV function takes the following arguments:

- *rate*—This is the discount rate to apply to the cash flows.

- *values*—This is a series of cash flows that corresponds to a schedule of payments in dates. The first payment is optional and corresponds to a cost or payment that occurs at the beginning of the investment. If the first value is a cost or payment, it must be a negative value. All succeeding payments are discounted based on a 365-day year. The series of values must contain at least one positive value and one negative value.

- *dates*—This is a schedule of payment dates that corresponds to the cash flow payments. The first payment date indicates the beginning of the schedule of payments. All other dates must be later than this date, but they may occur in any order. Only dates are considered; any times appended to the dates are truncated.

If any argument is nonnumeric, XNPV returns a #VALUE! error. If any number in dates is not a valid date, XNPV returns a #NUM! error. If any number in dates precedes the starting date, XNPV returns a #NUM! error. If *values* and *dates* contain different numbers of values, XNPV returns a #NUM! error.

In Figure 13.14, the company was purchased on March 15, 2001. The company posted no net profit in 2002. The company was sold in February 2006. The *XNPV* function in Row 9 shows that this deal clearly beat the 4% hurdle rate.

Figure 13.14
XNPV takes
into account
a series of
cash flows
on a series
of dates. The
dates do not
have to have
identical
periods, as in
NPV.

	B9		f_x =XNPV(B1,B2:B7,A2:A7)			
	A	B	C	D	E
1	**Discount Rate**	4%			
2	3/15/2001	-50,000	*Buy the business*		
3	12/31/2001	-5,000	*Loss in year 1*		
4	12/31/2003	5,000	*profit in year 3*		
5	12/31/2004	12,000	*more profit in year 4*		
6	12/31/2005	19,000	*profit in year 5*		
7	2/17/2006	242,000	*sell the business*		
8					
9	**XNPV**	**175,154**	*=XNPV(B1,B2:B7,A2:A7)*		
10					
11	**XIRR**	**40.71%**	*=XIRR(B2:B7,A2:A7)*		

Using XIRR to Calculate a Return Rate When Cash Flow Dates Are Not Periodic

As in the XNPV example, you can calculate an internal rate of return for a business deal where the dates do not necessarily fall on the last day of the year. To do so, use XIRR, as shown in the example at the bottom of Figure 13.14.

Syntax:

XIRR(*values,dates,guess*)

The XIRR function returns the internal rate of return for a schedule of cash flows that is not necessarily periodic. To calculate the internal rate of return for a series of periodic cash flows, use the IRR function. This function takes the following arguments:

- *values*—This is a series of cash flows that corresponds to a schedule of payments in *dates*. The first payment is optional and corresponds to a cost or payment that occurs at the beginning of the investment. If the first value is a cost or payment, it must be a negative value. All succeeding payments are discounted based on a 365-day year. The series of values must contain at least one positive and one negative value.

- *dates*—This is a schedule of payment dates that corresponds to the cash flow payments. The first payment date indicates the beginning of the schedule of payments. All other dates must be later than this date, but they may occur in any order.

- *guess*—This is a number that you guess is close to the result of XIRR.

Numbers in `dates` are truncated to integers. `XIRR` expects at least one positive cash flow and one negative cash flow; otherwise, *XIRR* returns a #NUM! error. If any number in `dates` is not a valid date, XIRR returns a #NUM! error. If any number in *dates* precedes the starting date, XIRR returns a #NUM! error. If *values* and *dates* contain different numbers of values, XIRR returns a #NUM! error. In most cases, you do not need to provide *guess* for the XIRR calculation. If it is omitted, *guess* is assumed to be 0.1, which is 10%.

> **⚑ caution**
>
> The algorithm behind the XIRR function is new and more accurate in Excel 2010. Be aware that Excel 2007 and Excel 2010 might produce different results for some uses of XIRR.

XIRR is closely related to XNPV, the net present value function. The rate of return calculated by XIRR is the interest rate corresponding to XNPV = 0.

Examples of Functions for Bond Investors

A bond is an I.O.U. in which you lend an amount to the issuer. The issuer pays you periodic interest payments and at the maturity date of the bond returns your money. Various governments issue many bonds. Bond maturities can extend anywhere from 1 day to 30 years. Many concepts and terms apply to the bond functions.

For the following discussion, let's assume that a city issues a 30-year municipal bond. The bond is issued on July 1, 2011. The bond's maturity date is June 30, 2040. The city agrees to pay 5% interest semiannually.

Here is what makes bonds interesting: They can be bought and sold after the issue date. Suppose that 14 months have gone past. Interest rates have now risen. The bond is going to keep paying 5% interest for the next 30 years. If interest rates have moved above 5%, a potential buyer of the bond will not want to pay $1,000 for the bond. Instead, the buyer might pay $950. Thus, there is a price paid for the bond, and there is a value of the bond at maturity.

Many bond functions ask for these arguments:

- *settlement*—This is the day that the buyer purchases the bond. It might be the issue date but is usually after the issue date. In the preceding example, the settlement date is September 1, 2011.

- *maturity*—This is the day that the issuer will pay the face value of the bond. In the preceding example, the maturity date is June 30, 2040.

- *rate*—This is the published coupon rate for the bond. In the preceding example, it is 5%.

- *pr*—This is the price that the current buyer paid for the bond. If the bond was purchased on the issue date, the price matches the face value of the bond. If it was purchased on a later date, the price is higher or lower than the face value, depending on whether interest rates go up or down. For example, if interest rates go up, bond prices go down. If interest rates go down, bond prices go up. The pr is expressed as the price per $100 of face value. If you buy a $1,000 face-value bond for $950, the price is $95 per $100, so you enter 95 for the *price* argument.

- *redemption*—This is the value of the bond on the maturity date. It is the amount the issuer will pay back to the holder of the bond. The price is expressed as the price per $100 of face value. If you buy a $1,000 face-value bond that will pay $1,000 at maturity, you enter 100 for the *redemp-tion* argument.

- *frequency*—This is the number of interest payments per year. For semiannual interest payments, enter 2. For quarterly payments, enter 4. For annual payments, enter 1. In Excel, these are the only three *frequency* values allowed.

- *basis*—This is a code used to identify the number of days in a year. The values are the same as those available in the YEARFRAC function. For most U.S. bonds, basis is 0 to indicate a 30/360 NASD calendar. For European bonds, consult Excel Help for the YIELD function.

> ➡ *For more information on basis, see the* YEARFRAC *discussion in Chapter 11, "Using Everyday Functions: Math, Date and Time, and Text Functions."*

Using YIELD to Calculate a Bond's Yield

A $1,000 bond might promise to pay 5% interest. However, if you buy the bond on the secondary market for $95, the actual yield will not be 5%. As you are trying to compare various investments, comparing the yield is one way to decide between multiple investment opportunities. To do this, you can use Excel's YIELD function.

Syntax:

YIELD(*settlement,maturity,rate,pr,redemption,frequency,basis*)

The YIELD function returns the yield on a security that pays periodic interest. You use YIELD to calculate bond yield. This function takes the following arguments:

- *settlement*—This is the security's settlement date. The security settlement date is the date after the issue date when the security is traded to the buyer. Dates may be entered as the following:

    Text strings within quotation marks, such as "1/30/1998" and "1998/01/30"

    Serial numbers such as 39156, which represents March 15, 2010

    Results of other formulas or functions, such as DATE(2010,3,15)

- *maturity*—This is the security's maturity date. The maturity date is the date when the security expires.

- *rate*—This is the security's annual coupon rate.

- *pr*—This is the security's price per $100 face value.

- *redemption*—This is the security's redemption value per $100 face value.

- *frequency*—This is the number of coupon payments per year. For annual payments, *frequency* is 1; for semiannual, *frequency* is 2; and for quarterly, *frequency* is 4.

- *basis*—This is the type of day count basis to use. It defaults to 0, which is appropriate for U.S. bonds.

The *settlement*, *maturity*, *frequency*, and *basis* arguments are truncated to integers. If *settlement* or *maturity* is not a valid date, YIELD returns a #NUM! error. If *rate* is less than 0, YIELD returns a #NUM! error. If *pr* is less than or equal to 0 or if *redemption* is less than or equal to 0, YIELD returns a #NUM! error. If *frequency* is any number other than 1, 2, or 4, YIELD returns a #NUM! error. If *basis* is less than 0 or if *basis* is greater than 4, YIELD returns a #NUM! error. If *settlement* is greater than or equal to *maturity*, YIELD returns a #NUM! error.

Figure 13.15 shows an example of YIELD.

B9	▼	*fx* =YIELD(B1,B2,B3,B4,B5,B6,B7)		
	A	B	C	D
1	**Settlement date**	1-Sep-11	1-Sep-11	1-Sep-11
2	**Maturity date**	30-Jun-40	30-Jun-40	30-Jun-40
3	**Percent coupon**	5.00%	5.00%	5.00%
4	**Price**	$95	$93	$105
5	**Redemption value**	$100	$100	$100
6	**Frequency**	2	2	2
7	**30/360 basis**	0	0	0
8				
9	**Yield**	5.34%	5.49%	4.68%
10				

Figure 13.15
Use YIELD to calculate the yield rate for a bond. In these examples, the price in Row 4 changes.

Using PRICE to Back into a Bond Price

If you know the yield for a bond, you can use PRICE to calculate the price per $100 of face value.

Syntax:

PRICE(*settlement,maturity,rate,yld,redemption,frequency,basis*)

The PRICE function returns the price per $100 face value of a security that pays periodic interest. This function takes the following arguments:

- *settlement*—This is the security's settlement date, which is the date on which you purchased the bond.

- *maturity*—This is the security's maturity date, which is the date when the security expires.

- *rate*—This is the security's annual coupon rate.

- *yld*—This is the security's annual yield.

- *redemption*—This is the security's redemption value per $100 face value.

- *frequency*—This is the number of coupon payments per year. For example, use 2 for semiannual.

- *basis*—This is the type of day count basis to use. For example, use 0 for U.S. bonds.

The *settlement*, *maturity*, *frequency*, and *basis* arguments are truncated to integers. If *settlement* or *maturity* is not a valid date, PRICE returns a #NUM! error. If *yld* is less than 0 or if *rate* is less than 0, PRICE returns a #NUM! error. If *redemption* is less than or equal to 0, PRICE returns a #NUM! error. If *frequency* is any number other than 1, 2, or 4, PRICE returns a #NUM! error. If *basis* is less than 0 or if *basis* is greater than 4, PRICE returns a #NUM! error. If *settlement* is greater than or equal to *maturity*, PRICE returns a #NUM! error.

In Figure 13.16, the yield for the bond exceeds the coupon rate. This indicates that the price will be less than $100.

Figure 13.16
If you know the yield, you can back into the price by using the PRICE function.

	A	B
1	Settlement date	1-Sep-11
2	Maturity date	30-Jun-40
3	Percent coupon	5.00%
4	Percent Yield	5.34%
5	Redemption value	$100
6	Frequency	2
7	30/360 basis	0
8		
9	Price	$ 95.02
10		

B9   *fx* =PRICE(B1,B2,B3,B4,B5,B6,B7)

When a bond is sold on the secondary market, it is often sold in between interest payments. Each interest payment date is called a coupon date. You analyze days until the next coupon date by using the COUP functions.

A whole series of COUP functions analyze the coupon period. The functions can tell you the previous coupon date, the next coupon date, how many days since the previous coupon date, and how many days until the next coupon date:

- COUPDAYS—This returns the number of days in this coupon period.

- COUPDAYBS—This returns the number of days from the beginning of the coupon period until the settlement date. The BS in the function name stands for from beginning to settlement.

- COUPDAYSNC—This returns the number of days from the settlement until the next coupon date. NC stands for next coupon.

- COUPPCD—This returns the date of the previous coupon date.

- COUPNCD—This returns the date of the next coupon date.

- COUPNUM—This returns the number of coupon dates left until maturity.

All the COUP functions require the same four arguments: *settlement*, *maturity*, *frequency*, and *basis*. For an explanation of these arguments, see the sections on YIELD and PRICE.

Figure 13.17 shows these coupon functions for a particular security.

Figure 13.17
You can analyze what portion of a coupon period has gone past at the settlement date for the bond.

	A	B	C
	B5 ▾ _fx_ =COUPDAYS(B$1,B$2,B$3)		
1	Settlement date	15-Jan-11	
2	Maturity date	30-Jun-40	
3	Frequency	4	
4			
5	# days in this coupon period	90	=COUPDAYS(B$1,B$2,B$3)
6	# days from beginning to settlement	15	=COUPDAYBS(B$1,B$2,B$3)
7	# days from settlement to next coupon	75	=COUPDAYSNC(B$1,B$2,B$3)
8	Previous coupon date	12/31/10	=COUPPCD(B$1,B$2,B$3)
9	Next coupon date	3/31/11	=COUPNCD(B$1,B$2,B$3)
10	Number of coupon dates remaining	118	=COUPNUM(B$1,B$2,B$3)

Using RECEIVED to Calculate Total Cash Generated from a Bond Investment

When you buy a bond, your settlement date is probably between two coupon dates. Unless you are buying the bond on the issue date, you receive less than the complete number of interest payments. To calculate the total future cash flows from a bond from the day you buy it until the maturity date, you use the RECEIVED function.

Syntax:

RECEIVED(*settlement,maturity,investment,discount,basis*)

The RECEIVED function returns the amount received at maturity for a fully invested security. This function takes the following arguments:

- *settlement*—This is the security's settlement date, which is the date on which you purchased the security.

- *maturity*—This is the security's maturity date, which is the date when the security expires.

- *investment*—This is the amount invested in the security.

- *discount*—This is the security's discount rate.

- *basis*—This is the type of day count basis to use. For example, use 0 for U.S. bonds.

The *settlement*, *maturity*, and *basis* arguments are truncated to integers. If *settlement* or *maturity* is not a valid date, RECEIVED returns a #NUM! error. If investment is less than or equal to 0 or if discount is less than or equal to 0, RECEIVED returns a #NUM! error. If *basis* is less than 0 or if *basis* is greater than or equal to 4, RECEIVED returns a #NUM! error. If settlement is greater than or equal to *maturity*, RECEIVED returns a #NUM! error.

In Figure 13.18, Columns B, C, and D show the total received for a bond purchased on various dates. The function takes into account the days to the next coupon date.

Figure 13.18
In the 15 days between Cells B1 and C1, you lose $2.37 in interest.

	A	B	C	D
	B7		f_x =RECEIVED(B1,B2,B3,B4,B5)	
1	**Settlement Date**	1-Mar-10	15-Mar-10	18-Jul-10
2	**Maturity Date**	15-Jun-18	15-Jun-18	15-Jun-18
3	**Investment**	1,000	1,000	1,000
4	**Discount Rate**	3.25%	3.25%	3.25%
5	**Actual/360 basis**	0	0	0
6				
7	**RECEIVED**	$1,368.72	$1,366.35	$1,345.93
8				

Using INTRATE to Back into the Coupon Interest Rate

If you have a fully invested bond and know what it will pay on maturity, you can use Excel's INTRATE function to back into the interest rate.

Syntax:

INTRATE(*settlement*,maturity,investment,redemption,basis)

The INTRATE function returns the interest rate for a fully invested security. This function takes the following arguments:

- *settlement*—This is the security's settlement date.

- *maturity*—This is the security's maturity date.

- *investment*—This is the amount invested in the security.

- *redemption*—This is the amount to be received at maturity.

- *basis*—This is the type of day count basis to use. You use 0 for U.S. bonds.

The *settlement*, *maturity*, and *basis* arguments are truncated to integers. If *settlement* or *maturity* is not a valid date, INTRATE returns a #NUM! error. If *investment* is less than or equal to 0 or if *redemption* is less than or equal to 0, INTRATE returns a #NUM! error. If *basis* is less than 0 or if *basis* is greater than 4, INTRATE returns a #NUM! error. If *settlement* is greater than or equal to *maturity*, INTRATE returns a #NUM! error.

INTRATE calculates (Redemption value – Investment) / Investment and multiplies this by (Number of days in year / Days from *settlement* to maturity).

In Figure 13.19, Excel uses INTRATE to back into the interest rate that the bond is paying.

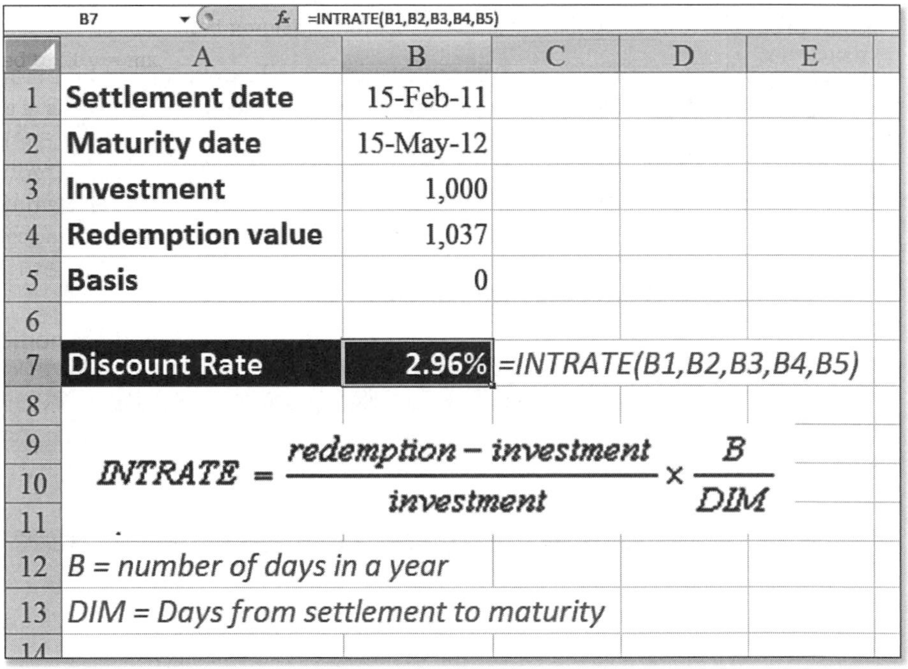

Figure 13.19
The INTRATE function can be used to derive the underlying interest rate for the bond.

	A	B	C	D	E
		B7 fx =INTRATE(B1,B2,B3,B4,B5)			
1	**Settlement date**	15-Feb-11			
2	**Maturity date**	15-May-12			
3	**Investment**	1,000			
4	**Redemption value**	1,037			
5	**Basis**	0			
6					
7	**Discount Rate**	2.96%	=INTRATE(B1,B2,B3,B4,B5)		
8					
9					
10	$INTRATE = \dfrac{redemption - investment}{investment} \times \dfrac{B}{DIM}$				
11					
12	*B = number of days in a year*				
13	*DIM = Days from settlement to maturity*				
14					

Using DISC to Back into the Discount Rate

If you have a security and know the price, you can back into the discount rate by using DISC.

Syntax:

DISC(*settlement,maturity,pr,redemption,basis*)

The DISC function returns the discount rate for a security. It takes the following arguments:

- *settlement*—This is the security's settlement date.

- *maturity*—This is the security's maturity date. The maturity date is the date when the security expires.

- *pr*—This is the security's price per $100 face value.

- *redemption*—This is the security's redemption value per $100 face value.

- *basis*—This is the day count basis. You use 0 for U.S. bonds.

The *settlement*, *maturity*, and *basis* arguments are truncated to integers. If *settlement* or *maturity* is not a valid date, DISC returns a #NUM! error. If *pr* is less than or equal to 0, or if *redemption* is less than or equal to 0, DISC returns a #NUM! error. If *basis* is less than 0 or if *basis* is greater than 4, DISC returns a #NUM! error. If settlement is greater than or equal to *maturity*, DISC returns a #NUM! error.

DISC calculates (Redemption value – Par value) / Par value and multiplies this by (Number of days in year / Days from settlement to *maturity*).

In Figure 13.20, Excel uses DISC to back into the discount rate.

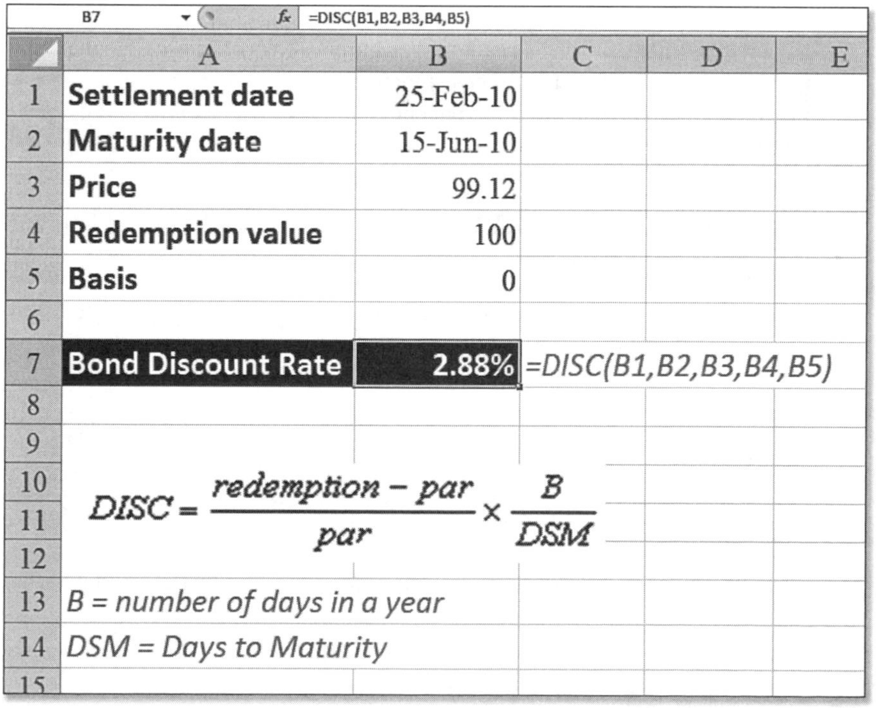

Figure 13.20
The DISC function can be used to derive the underlying discount rate for a bond.

	A	B	C	D	E
	B7 ▾ f_x =DISC(B1,B2,B3,B4,B5)				
1	**Settlement date**	25-Feb-10			
2	**Maturity date**	15-Jun-10			
3	**Price**	99.12			
4	**Redemption value**	100			
5	**Basis**	0			
6					
7	**Bond Discount Rate**	2.88%	=DISC(B1,B2,B3,B4,B5)		
8					
9					
10					
11	$DISC = \dfrac{redemption - par}{par} \times \dfrac{B}{DSM}$				
12					
13	*B = number of days in a year*				
14	*DSM = Days to Maturity*				
15					

Handling Bonds with an Odd Number of Days in the First or Last Period

Excel provides four functions—ODDFPRICE, ODDFYIELD, ODDLPRICE, and ODDLYIELD—to handle the special case in which a bond has a short or long first or last period. This period has more or fewer days than all the other periods and is called an *odd period*.

➡️ *For an explanation of the arguments to these functions, see the information on the PRICE and YIELD functions earlier in this chapter.*

Syntax:

ODDFPRICE(*settlement,maturity,issue,first_coupon,rate,yld,redemption,frequency,b asis*) and ODDFYIELD (*settlement,maturity,issue,first_coupon,rate,pr,redemption,f requency,basis*)

The ODDF functions handle cases in which the first period has an odd number of days. These are ODDFPRICE and ODDFYIELD. Each function has the extra argument *first_coupon*, which specifies the date for the odd first period.

Syntax:

ODDLPRICE(*settlement,maturity,last_interest,rate,yld,redemption,frequency,basis*) and ODDLYIELD (*settlement,maturity,last_interest,rate,pr,redemption,frequency, basis*)

The ODDL functions handle cases in which the last period has an odd number of days. These are ODDLPRICE and ODDLYIELD. These functions have the extra argument *last_interest*, which is the date of the final interest payment before maturity. Using this date, Excel can determine the length of the time for the last period.

Using PRICEMAT and YIELDMAT to Calculate Price and Yield for Zero-Coupon Bonds

A zero-coupon bond does not pay interest on the coupon dates. All interest is paid at maturity. Excel provides PRICEMAT and YIELDMAT to calculate price and yield for these securities. Figure 13.21 illustrates both of these functions.

Syntax:

PRICEMAT(*settlement_date,maturity_date,issue_date,rate_at_date_of_issue,annual_ yield,day_basis*)

The PRICEMAT function returns the price per $100 face value of a security that pays interest at maturity.

Figure 13.21
YIELDMAT and PRICEMAT calculate bonds for which the interest is not paid until maturity.

	A	B	C	D	E	F
1	Settlement date	15-Feb-11				
2	Maturity date	13-Apr-11				
3	Issue date	11-Nov-10				
4	Percent semiannual coupon	4.10%				
5	Percent yield	4.10%				
6	30/360 basis	0				
7						
8	PRICEMAT	99.992975	=PRICEMAT(B1,B2,B3,B4,B5,B6)			
9						
10	Settlement date	15-Feb-11				
11	Maturity date	13-Apr-11				
12	Issue date	11-Nov-10				
13	Percent semiannual coupon	4.10%				
14	Price	100.0123				
15	30/360 basis	0				
16						
17	YIELDMAT	3.98%	=YIELDMAT(B10,B11,B12,B13,B14,B15)			

B8   *fx* =PRICEMAT(B1,B2,B3,B4,B5,B6)

Syntax:

YIELDMAT(*settlement_date,maturity_date,issue_date,rate_at_date_of_issue,price_per_$100_of_face_value,day_basis*)

The YIELDMAT function returns the annual yield of a security that pays interest at maturity.

Using PRICEDISC and YIELDDISC to Calculate Discount Bonds

Excel provides PRICEDISC and YIELDDISC for calculating discounted bonds. Figure 13.22 illustrates these functions.

Syntax:

PRICEDISC(*settlement_date,maturity_date,discount_rate,redemption_value_per_$100,day_basis*)

The PRICEDISC function returns the price per $100 face value of a discounted security.

B8	▼	fx	=PRICEDISC(B2,B3,B4,B5,B6)	

	A	B	C
1	**Description**	**Data**	
2	**Settlement date**	16-Feb-11	
3	**Maturity date**	1-Mar-11	
4	**Percent discount rate**	3.25%	
5	**Redemption value**	$100	
6	**Day Basis**	0	
7			
8	**Bond Price**	99.864583	=PRICEDISC(B2,B3,B4,B5,B6)
9			
10	**Settlement date**	16-Feb-11	
11	**Maturity date**	1-Mar-11	
12	**Price**	99.864583	
13	**Redemption value**	$100	
14	**Actual/360 basis**	0	
15			
16	**YIELDDISC**	3.25%	=YIELDDISC(B10,B11,B12,B13,B14)

Figure 13.22
YIELDDISC and PRICEDISC calculate discounted bonds.

Syntax:

```
YIELDDISC(settlement_date,maturity_date,price_per_$100_face_value,redemption_
value_per_$100_of_face_value,day_basis)
```

The YIELDDISC function returns the annual yield for a discounted security.

Calculating T-Bills

Treasury bills, which are also referred to as T-bills, are a popular short-term investment. Backed by the U.S. government, T-bills are considered one of the safest investments, although they offer a slightly lower interest rate than other types of investments.

The Federal Reserve uses a strange method for advertising the yield on T-bills: The Fed compares the total interest to the final value paid on maturity. This is backward from every other bond yield.

For example, suppose that you pay $98.70 for a T-bill that will pay $100 on maturity 13 weeks later. The Fed expresses the yield by comparing the $1.30 in interest to the $100 final value. Every other bond yield compares the $1.30 in interest to the $98.70 invested.

The Excel TBILL functions allow you to compare T-bills and regular bonds. Figure 13.23 illustrates the three T-bill functions.

Figure 13.23
TBILLEQ and the other TBILL functions deal with the irregularities of T-bill investing.

	B5	▾	⊙	*fx*	=TBILLEQ(B1,B2,B3)	
	A		B		C	
1	Settlement date		31-Mar-11			
2	Maturity date		1-Jun-11			
3	Percent discount rate		2.375%			
4						
5	Bond Equivalent Yield		2.418%		=TBILLEQ(B1,B2,B3)	
6						
7	Settlement date		31-Mar-11			
8	Maturity date		1-Jun-11			
9	Percent discount rate		2.375%			
10						
11	T-Bill Price		99.590972		=TBILLPRICE(B7,B8,B9)	
12						
13	Settlement date		31-Mar-11			
14	Maturity date		1-Jun-11			
15	Price per $100 face value		99.42			
16						
17	T-Bill Yield		3.39%		=TBILLYIELD(B13,B14,B15)	
18						

Syntax:

TBILLEQ(*settlement_date,maturity_date,discount_rate*)

The TBILLEQ function returns the bond-equivalent yield for a T-bill.

Syntax:

TBILLPRICE(*settlement_date,maturity_date,discount_rate*)

The TBILLPRICE function returns the price per $100 face value for a T-bill.

Syntax:

TBILLYIELD(*settlement_date,maturity_date,price_per_$100_face_value*)

The TBILLYIELD function returns the yield for a T-bill.

Using ACCRINT or ACCINTM to Calculate Accrued Interest

If you are the original buyer of a bond and you buy that bond after the issue date, the bond will have earned some accrued interest during that gap. As the original buyer of the bond, you generally pay this interest back to the issuer when you take possession of the bond. This basically simplifies accounting for the issuer, which can issue identical payments at the next coupon date without having to worry about dozens of different settlement dates.

The ACCRINT function calculates this accrued interest.

Syntax:

ACCRINT(*issue,first_interest,settlement,rate,par,frequency,basis*)

The ACCRINT function returns the accrued interest for a security that pays periodic interest. This function takes the following arguments:

- *issue*—This is the security's issue date.

- *first_interest*—This is the security's first interest date.

- *settlement*—This is the security's settlement date. The security settlement date is the date after the issue date when the security is traded to the buyer. The ACCRINT function calculates the interest that would have been earned between the issue date and the settlement date.

- *rate*—This is the security's annual coupon rate.

- *par*—This is the security's par value. If you omit par, ACCRINT uses $1,000.

- *frequency*—This is the number of coupon payments per year.

- *basis*—This is the type of day count basis to use. You use 0 for U.S. bonds

If *issue* is greater than or equal to *settlement*, ACCRINT returns a #NUM! error.

Figure 13.24 demonstrates how the accrued interest changes when the gap between the issue date and settlement date extends.

> **note**
>
> The ACCRINTM function calculates accrued interest for zero-coupon bonds, as shown in Row 18 in Figure 13.24.

Using DURATION to Understand Price Volatility

Duration is a measurement, in years, of how long it takes for the price of a bond to be repaid by its cash flows. This measurement is not relevant for zero-coupon bonds because with a zero coupon bond, the duration is simultaneous with the maturity date.

Suppose that you have a 20-year bond with a 9% yield that pays interest twice a year. It might take about 6 years of interest payments before you earn back the original purchase price of the bond.

Duration is constantly changing. Immediately after a coupon date, the duration goes up slightly because the interest payment is no longer counted as a future cash flow. However, over the life

Figure 13.24
As the original buyer of the bond, you owe the accrued interest to the issuer.

	A	B	C	D	E	F
		B9	▼	f_x =ACCRINT(B1,B2,B3,B4,B5,B6,B7)		
1	Issue date	1-Apr-11	1-Apr-11	1-Apr-11	1-Apr-11	1-Apr-11
2	First interest date	31-Aug-11	31-Aug-11	31-Aug-11	31-Aug-11	31-Aug-11
3	Settlement date	1-Jun-11	7-Apr-11	14-Apr-11	1-May-11	15-May-11
4	Coupon rate	3.00%	3.00%	3.00%	3.00%	3.00%
5	Par value	1,000	1,000	1,000	1,000	1,000
6	Frequency	2	2	2	2	2
7	30/360 basis	0	0	0	0	0
8						
9	Accrued Interest	5.00	0.50	1.08	2.50	3.67
10		=ACCRINT(B1,B2,B3,B4,B5,B6,B7)				
11						
12	Issue date	1-Apr-11				
13	Maturity date	15-Jun-11				
14	Percent coupon	3.00%				
15	Par value	$1,000				
16	30/360 basis	0				
17						
18	Accrued Interest	6.16667	=ACCRINTM(B12,B13,B14,B15,B16)			

of the bond, the duration gets progressively shorter, until the duration date corresponds with the maturity date. Duration is important because the higher the duration, the higher the price volatility for the security.

When Excel calculates a duration, using the DURATION function, it uses the method designed by Frederick Macaulay in the 1930s. This method multiplies the present value of each cash flow by the time it is received. Those values are summed and divided by the total price for the security.

Excel also has a modified duration function, MDURATION. This function calculates the duration if the yield would increase by 1 percentage point. In Figure 13.25, the duration for the 5% yield is 6.879 years. The MDURATION return is 6.712 years. This is the duration if the yield would change from 5 to 6%. The difference between the duration and modified duration is an indicator of a bond price's volatility.

Syntax:

DURATION(*settlement_date,maturity_date,coupon_rate,yield_rate,frequency,basis*)

The DURATION function returns the Macaulay duration for an assumed par value of $100. Duration is defined as the weighted average of the present value of the cash flows and is used as a measure of a bond price's response to changes in yield.

	A	B	C
B8	f_x =DURATION(B1,B2,B3,B4,B5,B6)		
1	Settlement date	1-Jan-11	
2	Maturity date	1-Jan-19	
3	Percent coupon	4.00%	
4	Percent yield	5.00%	
5	Frequency	2	
6	Actual basis	1	
7			
8	DURATION	6.879	
9	MDURATION	6.712	
10			

Figure 13.25
DURATION indicates how many years it will take to earn back the security's purchase price. MDURATION shows the change in duration if the yield were to increase by 1%.

Syntax:

MDURATION(*settlement_date,maturity_date,coupon_rate,yield_rate,frequency,basis*)

The MDURATION function returns the modified duration for a security with an assumed par value of $100.

Examples of Miscellaneous Financial Functions

Excel offers a few other financial functions that may be useful if you are dealing with ancient historical data. On April 9, 2001, all U.S. stock markets were forced to start trading securities in dollars and cents instead of dollars and fractions. The United States was the last nation using the fractional system, which was an eighteenth-century system.

In the fractional system, a stock price may have been reported in the newspaper as 5 5/8, which is roughly equivalent to $5.63. However, a common system in brokerage houses was to record this as 5.5, with the .5 indicating 5/8. In an alternative system, prices were recorded in 16ths, with, for example, 1.03 meaning 3/16.

Using DOLLARDE to Convert to Decimals

If you encounter an old worksheet that uses fractional prices, you can convert them to decimals by using DOLLARDE. You must specify the price in the nomenclature of the system and specify whether the number after the decimal point is in 8ths, 16ths, or 32nds.

Syntax:

DOLLARDE(*fractional_dollar,fraction*)

The DOLLARDE function converts a dollar price expressed as a fraction into a dollar price expressed as a decimal number. You use DOLLARDE to convert fractional dollar numbers, such as securities prices, to decimal numbers.

- *fractional_dollar*—This is a number expressed as a fraction.

- *fraction*—This is the integer to use in the denominator of the fraction.

Syntax:

DOLLARFR(decimal_dollar,fraction)

The DOLLARFR function converts a dollar price expressed as a decimal number into a dollar price expressed as a fraction.

Using FVSCHEDULE to Calculate the Future Value for a Variable Scheduled Interest Rate

The FV function discussed at the beginning of this chapter assumes a constant interest rate. If you have a loan agreement that specifies a variable interest rate for future years, you can calculate the future value based on the scheduled interest rate. To do so, you use the FVSCHEDULE function.

Syntax:

FVSCHEDULE(principal,schedule)

The FVSCHEDULE function returns the future value of an initial principal after applying a series of compound interest rates. Use FVSCHEDULE to calculate the future value of an investment with a variable or adjustable rate. This function takes the following arguments:

- *principal*—This is the present value.

- *schedule*—This is an array of interest rates to apply.

The values in *schedule* can be numbers or blank cells; any other value produces a #VALUE! error for FVSCHEDULE. Blank cells are assumed to be zeros, which means no interest.

Figure 13.26 shows three examples of variable interest rates.

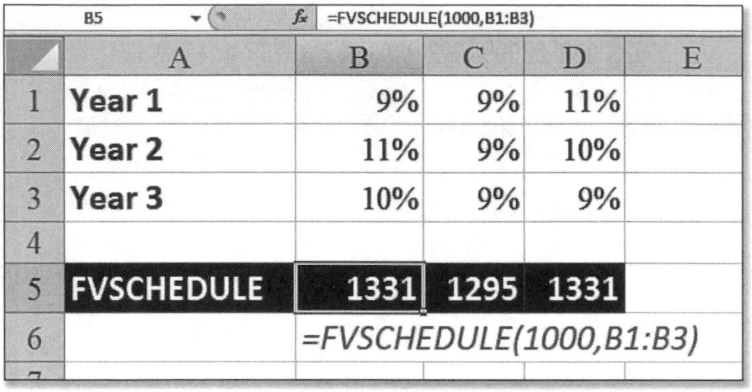

B5	▼	fx	=FVSCHEDULE(1000,B1:B3)			
	A	B	C	D	E
1	**Year 1**	9%	9%	11%	
2	**Year 2**	11%	9%	10%	
3	**Year 3**	10%	9%	9%	
4					
5	**FVSCHEDULE**	1331	1295	1331	
6		*=FVSCHEDULE(1000,B1:B3)*			
7					

Figure 13.26
Calculating a future value for a series of scheduled future interest rates by using FVSCHEDULE.

14

USING STATISTICAL FUNCTIONS

Statistics in Excel fall into three broad categories:

- **Descriptive statistics that describe a data set**—These include measures of central tendency and dispersion.

- **Regression tools**—These allow you to predict future values based on past values.

- **Inferential statistics**—This type of statistic allows you to predict the likelihood of an event happening, based on a sample of a population.

Table 14.1 provides an alphabetical list of all the Excel 2010 statistical functions. Detailed examples of the functions are provided in the remainder of the chapter.

Table 14.1 Alphabetical List of Statistical Functions

Function	Description
AVEDEV(*number1*,*number2*,...)	Returns the average of the absolute deviations of data points from their mean. AVEDEV is a measure of the variability in a data set.
AVERAGE(*number1*,*number2*,...)	Returns the average (arithmetic mean) of the arguments.
AVERAGEA(*value1*,*value2*,...)	Calculates the average (arithmetic mean) of the values in the list of arguments. In addition to numbers, text and logical values, such as TRUE and FALSE, are included in the calculation.

Function	Description
BETA.DIST(*x,alpha,beta,A,B*)	Returns the cumulative beta probability density function. The cumulative beta probability density function is commonly used to study variation in the percentage of something across samples, such as the fraction of the day people spend watching television.
BETA.INV(*probability,alpha,beta,A,B*)	Returns the inverse of the cumulative beta probability density function. That is, if probability is equal to BETADIST(*x,...*), then BETA.INV(*probability,...*) is equal to *x*. The cumulative beta distribution can be used in project planning to model probable completion times, given an expected completion time and variability.
BINOM.DIST(*number_s,trials, probability_s,cumulative*)	Returns the individual term binomial distribution probability. You use BINOM.DIST in problems with a fixed number of tests or trials, when the outcomes of any trial are only success or failure, when trials are independent, and when the probability of success is constant throughout the experiment. For example, BINOM.DIST can calculate the probability that two of the next three babies born will be male.
BINOM.INV(*trials,probability_s, alpha*)	Returns the smallest value for which the cumulative binomial distribution is greater than or equal to a criterion value. You use this function for quality assurance applications. For example, you can use BINOM.INV to determine the greatest number of defective parts that are allowed to come off an assembly line run without having to reject the entire lot.
CHISQ.DIST(*x,degrees_freedom*)	Returns the one-tailed probability of the chi-squared distribution. The chi-squared distribution is associated with a chi-squared test. You use the chi-squared test to compare observed and expected values. For example, in a genetic experiment, you might hypothesize that the next generation of plants will exhibit a certain set of colors. By comparing the observed results with the expected ones, you can decide whether your original hypothesis is valid.

Function	Description
CHISQ.DIST.RT(*x*,*degrees_freedom*)	Returns the right-tailed probability of the chi-squared distribution.
CHISQ.INV(*probability*,*degrees_freedom*)	Returns the inverse of the one-tailed probability of the chi-squared distribution. If probability is equal to CHISQ.DIST(*x*,...), then CHISQ.INV(*probability*,...) is *x*. You use this function to compare observed results with expected ones to decide whether your original hypothesis is valid.
CHISQ.INV.RT(*probability*, *degrees_freedom*)	Returns the inverse of the right-tailed probability of the chi-squared distribution.
CHISQ.TEST(*actual_range*,*expected_range*)	Returns the test for independence. CHISQ.TEST returns the value from the chi-squared distribution for the statistic and the appropriate degrees of freedom. You can use chi-squared tests to determine whether hypothesized results are verified by an experiment.
CONFIDENCE.NORM(*alpha*, *standard_dev*,*size*)	Returns the confidence interval for a population mean. The confidence interval is a range on either side of a sample mean. For example, if you order a product through the mail, you can determine, with a particular level of confidence, the earliest and latest the product will arrive. Uses standard normal distribution. Renamed from *CONFIDENCE* in 2010.
CONFIDENCE.T(*alpha*,*standard_dev*,*size*)	Returns the confidence interval based on the student's t distribution.
CORREL(*array1*,*array2*)	Returns the correlation coefficient of the *array1* and *array2* cell ranges. You use the correlation coefficient to determine the relationship between two properties. For example, you can examine the relationship between a location's average temperature and the use of air conditioners.
COVARIANCE.P(*array1*,*array2*)	Returns covariance, the average of the products of deviations for each data point pair. You use covariance to determine the relationship between two data sets. For example, you can examine whether greater income accompanies greater levels of education. Based on a population.

Function	Description
COVARIANCE.S(*array1*,*array2*)	Returns covariance, the average of the products of deviations for each data point pair. You use covariance to determine the relationship between two data sets. For example, you can examine whether greater income accompanies greater levels of education. Based on a sample.
DEVSQ(*number1*,*number2*,...)	Returns the sum of squares of deviations of data points from their sample mean.
EXPON.DIST(*x*,*lambda*,*cumulative*)	Returns the exponential distribution. You use EXPON.DIST to model the time between events, such as how long a bank's automated teller machine takes to deliver cash. For example, you can use EXPON.DIST to determine the probability that the process takes, at most, 1 minute.
F.DIST(*x*,*degrees_freedom1*, *degrees_ freedom2*)	Returns the *F* probability distribution. You can use this function to determine whether two data sets have different degrees of diversity. For example, you can examine test scores given to men and women entering high school and determine whether the variability in the females is different from that found in the males.
F.DIST.RT(*x*,*degrees_ freedom1*,*degrees_freedom2*)	Returns the right-tailed *F* probability distribution.
F.INV(*probability*,*degrees_ freedom1*,*degrees_freedom2*)	Returns the inverse of the F probability distribution. If *probability* is equal to F.DIST(*x*,...), then F.INV(*probability*,...) is equal to *x*.
F.INV.RT(*probability*,*degrees_ freedom1*,*degrees_freedom2*)	Returns the inverse of the right-tailed F probability distribution.
F.TEST(*array1*,*array2*)	Returns the result of an *F*-test. An *F*-test returns the one-tailed probability that the variances in *array1* and *array2* are not significantly different. You use this function to determine whether two samples have different variances. For example, given test scores from public and private schools, you can test whether those schools have different levels of diversity.

Function	Description
FISHER(*x*)	Returns the Fisher transformation at *x*. This transformation produces a function that is approximately normally distributed rather than skewed. You use this function to perform hypothesis testing on the correlation coefficient.
FISHERINV(*y*)	Returns the inverse of the Fisher transformation. You use this transformation when analyzing correlations between ranges or arrays of data. If y is equal to FISHER(x), then FISHERINV(y) is equal to *x*.
FORECAST(*x,known_y's,known_x's*)	Calculates, or predicts, a future value by using existing values. The predicted value is a y value for a given x value. The known values are existing x values and y values, and the new value is predicted by using linear regression. You can use this function to predict future sales, inventory requirements, or consumer trends.
FREQUENCY(*data_array,bins_array*)	Calculates how often values occur within a range of values and returns a vertical array of numbers. For example, you can use FREQUENCY to count the number of test scores that fall within ranges of scores. Because FREQUENCY returns an array, it must be entered as an array formula.
GAMMA.DIST(*x,alpha,beta,cumulative*)	Returns the gamma distribution. You can use this function to study variables that may have a skewed distribution. The gamma distribution is commonly used in queuing analysis.
GAMMA.INV(*probability,alpha,beta*)	Returns the inverse of the gamma cumulative distribution. If *probability* is equal to GAMMA.DIST(*x,...*), then GAMMA.INV(*probability,...*) is equal to *x*.
GAMMALN(*x*)	Returns the natural logarithm of the gamma function.
GEOMEAN(*number1,number2,...*)	Returns the geometric mean of an array or a range of positive data. For example, you can use GEOMEAN to calculate average growth rate given compound interest with variable rates.

Function	Description
GROWTH(*known_y's,known_x's, new_x's,const*)	Calculates predicted exponential growth by using existing data. GROWTH returns the y values for a series of new x values that you specify by using existing x values and y values. You can also use the GROWTH worksheet function to fit an exponential curve to existing x values and y values.
HARMEAN(*number1,number2,...*)	Returns the harmonic mean of a data set. The harmonic mean is the reciprocal of the arithmetic mean of reciprocals.
HYPGEOM.DIST(*sample_s,number_ sample,population_s,number_popu- lation*)	Returns the hypergeometric distribution. HYPGEOM.DIST returns the probability of a given number of sample successes, given the sample size, population successes, and population size. You use HYPGEOM.DIST for problems with a finite population, where each observation is either a success or a failure, and where each subset of a given size is chosen with equal likelihood.
INTERCEPT(*known_y's,known_x's*)	Calculates the point at which a line will intersect the y-axis by using existing x values and y values. The intercept point is based on a best-fit regression line plotted through the known x values and known y values. You use the intercept when you want to determine the value of the dependent variable when the independent variable is 0. For example, you can use the INTERCEPT function to predict a metal's electrical resistance at 0 degrees Celsius when your data points were taken at room temperature and higher.
KURT(*number1,number2,...*)	Returns the kurtosis of a data set. Kurtosis characterizes the relative peakedness or flatness of a distribution compared with the normal distribution. Positive kurtosis indicates a relatively peaked distribution. Negative kurtosis indicates a relatively flat distribution.
LARGE(*array,k*)	Returns the *k*th largest value in a data set. You can use this function to select a value based on its relative standing. For example, you can use LARGE to return a highest, runner-up, or third-place score.

Function	Description
LINEST(*known_y's,known_x's, const,stats*)	Calculates the statistics for a line by using the least-squares method to calculate a straight line that best fits the data and returns an array that describes the line. Because this function returns an array of values, it must be entered as an array formula.
LOGEST(*known_y's,known_x's, const,stats*)	In regression analysis, calculates an exponential curve that fits the data and returns an array of values that describes the curve. Because this function returns an array of values, it must be entered as an array formula.
LOGNORM.DIST(*x,mean,standard_dev*)	Returns the cumulative lognormal distribution of *x*, where LN(*x*) is normally distributed with the parameters mean and *standard_dev*. You use this function to analyze data that has been logarithmically transformed.
LOGNORM.INV(*probability,mean, standard_dev*)	Returns the inverse of the lognormal cumulative distribution function of *x*, where LN(*x*) is normally distributed with the parameters mean and *standard_dev*. If *probability* is equal to LOGNORM.DIST(*x*,...), LOGNORM.INV(*probability*,...) is equal to *x*.
MAX(*number1,number2,...*)	Returns the largest value in a set of values.
MAXA(*value1,value2,...*)	Returns the largest value in a list of arguments. Text and logical values such as TRUE and FALSE are compared, as are numbers.
MEDIAN(*number1,number2,...*)	Returns the median of the given numbers. The median is the number in the middle of a set of numbers; that is, half the numbers have values that are greater than the median and half have values that are less.
MIN(*number1,number2,...*)	Returns the smallest number in a set of values.
MINA(*value1,value2,...*)	Returns the smallest value in a list of arguments. Text and logical values such as TRUE and FALSE are compared, as are numbers.

Function	Description
MODE.MULT(*number1,number2,...*)	Returns a vertical array of the most frequently occurring, or repetitive, value in an array or a range of data. MODE.MULT is new in Excel 2010 and handles the specific case when there are two or more values that are tied for the most frequently occurring value. Whereas MODE.SNGL returns only the first mode value, MODE.MULT returns all the mode values.
MODE.SNGL(*number1,number2,...*)	Returns the most frequently occurring, or repetitive, value in an array or a range of data. Like MEDIAN, MODE.SNGL is a location measure. MODE.SNGL is renamed from MODE in Excel 2010. If there are two values that are tied for the most frequently occurring value, only the first one will be returned by MODE. SNGL. If you need to return all of the tied values, use the new MODE.MULT.
NEGBINOM.DIST(*number_f,number_s, probability_s*)	Returns the negative binomial distribution. NEGBINOM.DIST returns the probability that there will be *number_f* failures before the *number_s*th success, when the constant probability of a success is *probability_s*. This function is similar to the binomial distribution function, except that the number of successes is fixed, and the number of trials is variable. As with the binomial distribution function, trials are assumed to be independent.
NORM.DIST(*x,mean,standard_dev, cumulative*)	Returns the normal cumulative distribution for the specified mean and standard deviation. This function has a very wide range of applications in statistics, including hypothesis testing.
NORM.INV(*probability*,mean, *standard_dev*)	Returns the inverse of the normal cumulative distribution for the specified mean and standard deviation.
NORM.S.DIST(*z*)	Returns the standard normal cumulative distribution function. The distribution has a mean of zero and a standard deviation of one. You use this function in place of a table of standard normal curve areas.

Function	Description
NORM.S.INV(*probability*)	Returns the inverse of the standard normal cumulative distribution. The distribution has a mean of zero and a standard deviation of one.
PEARSON(*array1,array2*)	Returns the Pearson product–moment correlation coefficient, *r*, a dimensionless index that ranges from –1.0 to 1.0, inclusive, and reflects the extent of a linear relationship between two data sets.
PERCENTILE.EXC(*array,k*)	Returns the kth percentile of values in a range. You can use this function to establish a threshold of acceptance. For example, you can decide to examine candidates who score above the 90th percentile. PERCENTILE.EXC is renamed in Excel 2010 and assumes the percentile is between 0 and 1 exclusive.
PERCENTILE.INC(*array,k*)	Returns the *k*th percentile of values in a range. PERCENTILE.INC is new in Excel 2010 and assumes the percentile is between 0 and 1 inclusive.
PERCENTRANK.EXC(*array,x, significance*)	Returns the rank of a value in a data set as a percentage of the data set. This function can be used to evaluate the relative standing of a value within a data set. PERCENTRANK.EXC is renamed from PERCENTRANK. It assumes the percentile is between 0 and 1 exclusive.
PERCENTRANK. INC(*array,x,significance*)	Returns the rank of a value in a data set as a percentage of the data set. This function can be used to evaluate the relative standing of a value within a data set. For example, you can use PERCENTRANK.INC to evaluate the standing of an aptitude test score among all scores for the test. PERCENTRANK.INC is new in Excel 2010. It assumes percentiles from 0 to 1 inclusive.
PERMUT(*number,number_chosen*)	Returns the number of permutations for a given number of objects that can be selected from number objects. A permutation is any set or subset of objects or events where internal order is significant. Permutations are different from combinations, for which the internal order is not significant. You use this function for lottery-style probability calculations.

Function	Description
POISSON.DIST(*x,mean,cumulative*)	Returns the Poisson distribution. A common application of the Poisson distribution is predicting the number of events over a specific time, such as the number of cars arriving at a toll plaza in one minute.
PROB(*x_range,prob_range,lower_limit,upper_limit*)	Returns the probability that values in a range are between two limits. If *upper_limit* is not supplied, returns the probability that values in *x_range* are equal to *lower_limit*.
QUARTILE.EXC(*array,quart*)	Returns the quartile of a data set. Quartiles are often used in sales and survey data to divide populations into groups. For example, you can use QUARTILE.EXC to find the top 25% of incomes in a population. This function is renamed from QUARTILE in Excel 2010. It assumes percentiles run from 0 to 1 exclusive.
QUARTILE.INC(*array,quart*)	Returns the quartile of a data set. Quartiles are often used in sales and survey data to divide populations into groups. This function is new in Excel 2010 and assumes percentiles run from 0 to 1 inclusive.
RANK.AVG(*number,ref,order*)	Returns the rank of a number in a list of numbers. The rank of a number is its size relative to other values in a list. (If you were to sort the list, the rank of the number would be its position.) When two or more items are tied, RANK.AVG will average their ranks.
RANK.EQ(*number,ref,order*)	Returns the rank of a number in a list of numbers. When two or more items are tied, RANK.EQ will assign the lower rank to all items in the tie. Renamed from RANK in Excel 2010.
RSQ(*known_y's,known_x's*)	Returns the square of the Pearson product–moment correlation coefficient through data points in *known_y's* and *known_x's*. The r-squared value can be interpreted as the proportion of the variance in y attributable to the variance in *x*.

Function	Description
SKEW(*number1,number2,...*)	Returns the skewness of a distribution. Skewness characterizes the degree of asymmetry of a distribution around its mean. Positive skewness indicates a distribution with an asymmetric tail extending toward more positive values. Negative skewness indicates a distribution with an asymmetric tail extending toward more negative values.
SLOPE(*known_y's,known_x's*)	Returns the slope of the linear regression line through data points in *known_y's* and *known_x's*. The slope is the vertical distance divided by the horizontal distance between any two points on the line, which is the rate of change along the regression line.
SMALL(*array,k*)	Returns the *k*th smallest value in a data set. You use this function to return values with a particular relative standing in a data set.
STANDARDIZE(*x,mean,standard_dev*)	Returns a normalized value from a distribution characterized by mean and *standard_ dev*.
STDEV.P(*number1,number2,...*)	Calculates standard deviation based on the entire population given as arguments. The standard deviation is a measure of how widely values are dispersed from the average value (that is, the mean).
STDEV.S(*number1,number2,...*)	Estimates standard deviation based on a sample. The standard deviation is a measure of how widely values are dispersed from the average value (that is, the mean).
STDEVA(*value1,value2,...*)	Estimates standard deviation based on a sample. The standard deviation is a measure of how widely values are dispersed from the average value (that is, the mean). Text and logical values such as TRUE and FALSE are included in the calculation.
STDEVPA(*value1,value2,...*)	Calculates standard deviation based on the entire population given as arguments, including text and logical values. The standard deviation is a measure of how widely values are dispersed from the average value (that is, the mean).

Function	Description
STEYX(*known_y's*,*known_x's*)	Returns the standard error of the predicted y value for each x in the regression. The standard error is a measure of the amount of error in the prediction of y for an individual x.
SUMSQ(*number1,number2, ...*)	Returns the sum of the squares of the arguments.
SUMX2MY2(*array_x,array_y*)	Returns the sum of the difference of squares of corresponding values in two arrays.
SUMX2PY2(*array_x,array_y*)	Returns the sum of the sum of squares of corresponding values in two arrays. The sum of the sum of squares is a common term in many statistical calculations.
SUMXMY2(*array_x,array_y*)	Returns the sum of squares of differences of corresponding values in two arrays.
T.DIST(*x,degrees_freedom,tails*)	Returns the percentage points (that is, probability) for the Student t-distribution where a numeric value (x) is a calculated value of t for which percentage points are to be computed. The t-distribution is used in the hypothesis testing of small sample data sets. You use this function in place of a table of critical values for the t-distribution.
T.DIST.2T(*x,degrees_freedom*)	Returns the two-tailed probability for the Student t-distribution. New in Excel 2010.
T.DIST.RT(*x,degrees_freedom*)	Returns the right-tailed probability) for the Student t-distribution. New in Excel 2010.
T.INV(*probability, degrees_freedom*)	Returns the t-value of the Student's t-distribution as a function of the probability and the degrees of freedom.
T.INV.2T(*probability, degrees_freedom*)	Returns the right-tailed t-value of the Student's t-distribution as a function of the probability and the degrees of freedom.
T.TEST(*array1,array2,tails,type*)	Returns the probability associated with a Student's t-test. You use T.TEST to determine whether two samples are likely to have come from the same two underlying populations that have the same mean.

Function	Description
TREND(*known_y's,known_x's,new_x's, const*)	Returns values along a linear trend. Fits a straight line (using the method of least squares) to the arrays *known_y's* and *known_x's*. Returns the y values along that line for the array of new_x's that you specify.
TRIMMEAN(*array,percent*)	Returns the mean of the interior of a data set. TRIMMEAN calculates the mean taken by excluding a percentage of data points from the top and bottom tails of a data set. You can use this function when you want to exclude outlying data from your analysis.
VAR.P(*number1,number2,...*)	Calculates variance based on the entire population.
VAR.S(*number1,number2,...*)	Estimates variance based on a sample.
VARA(*value1,value2,...*)	Estimates variance based on a sample. In addition to numbers, text and logical values such as TRUE and FALSE are included in the calculation.
VARPA(*value1,value2,...*)	Calculates variance based on the entire population. In addition to numbers, text and logical values such as TRUE and FALSE are included in the calculation.
WEIBULL.DIST.DIST(*x,alpha,beta, cumulative*)	Returns the Weibull distribution. You use this distribution in reliability analysis, such as to calculate a device's mean time to failure.
Z.TEST(*array,x,sigma*)	Returns the two-tailed *p* value of a z-test. The z-test generates a standard score for *x* with respect to the data set, *array*, and returns the two-tailed probability for the normal distribution. You can use this function to assess the likelihood that a particular observation is drawn from a particular population.

Examples of Functions for Descriptive Statistics

Descriptive statistics help describe a population of data. What is the largest? The smallest? The average? Are data points grouped to the left of the average or to the right of the average? How wide is the range of expected values? Do many members of the population have values in the middle, or are they evenly spread throughout the range? All these are measures of descriptive statistics.

Many situations in a business environment involve finding basic information about a data set, such as the largest or smallest values or the rank within a data set.

Using MIN or MAX to Find the Smallest or Largest Numeric Value

If you have a large data set and want to find the smallest or largest value in a column, rather than sort the data set, you can use a function to find the value. To find the smallest numeric value, you use MIN. To find the largest numeric value, you use MAX.

Figure 14.1 shows a list of open receivables, by customer, for 59 customers. Even though the function references says that you can find the MIN for only 255 numbers, a single rectangular reference counts as one of the 255 arguments for the function. To find the smallest value in the range, you use =MIN(B2:B360). To find the largest value in the range, you use =MAX(B2:B360).

	B63	▼	ƒx	=MIN(B2:B60)		
	A		B	C	D	
1	Customer		A/R			
57	Secure Shingle Inc.		10,535.76			
58	Paramount Scooter Corporation		10,014.60			
59	Unsurpassed Sprayer Inc.		10,069.74			
60	Secure Necktie Inc.		8,800.63			
61	Total		493,005.80			
62						
63	Min		3,572.80	=MIN(B2:B60)		
64	Max		13,560.43	=MAX(B2:B60)		
65	Average		8,356.03	=AVERAGE(B2:B60)		
66	Median		8,343.71	=MEDIAN(B2:B60)		

Figure 14.1
You use MIN and MAX to find the smallest or largest receivables.

Syntax:

=MIN(*number1*,*number2*,...)

The MIN function returns the smallest number in a set of values. The arguments *number1*, *number2*,... are 1 to 255 numbers for which you want to find the minimum value. You can specify arguments that are numbers, empty cells, logical values, or text representations of numbers. Arguments that are error values or text that cannot be translated into numbers cause errors. If an argument is an array or a reference, only numbers in that array or reference are used. Empty cells, logical values, or text in the array or reference are ignored. If logical values and text should not be ignored, you should use MINA instead. If the arguments contain no numbers, MIN returns 0.

Syntax:

=MAX(*number1*,*number2*,...)

The MAX function returns the largest value in a set of values. The arguments *number1*, *number2*,... are 1 to 255 numbers for which you want to find the maximum value. The remaining rules are similar to those for MIN, described in the preceding section.

If you read the descriptions for MINA and MAXA, you might think that the functions can be used to find the smallest text value in a range. However, here is the Excel Help description for MAXA:

- MAXA(*value1*,*value2*) returns the largest value in a list of arguments. Text and logical values such as TRUE and FALSE are compared as well as numbers.

The problem, however, is that text values are treated as the number 0 in the compare. It is a struggle to imagine a scenario where this would be mildly useful. If you have a series of positive numbers and want to know if any of them are text, you can use =MINA(A1:A99). If the result is 0, then you know that there is a text value in the range.

Similarly, if you have a range of negative numbers in A1:A99, you could use =MAXA(A1:A99). If any of the values are text, the result will return 0 instead of a negative number.

MINA and MAXA could be used to evaluate a series of TRUE/FALSE values. FALSE values are treated as 0. TRUE values are treated as 1.

Using LARGE to Find the Top N Values in a List of Values

The MAX function discussed in the preceding section finds the single largest value in a list. Sometimes it is interesting to find the top 10 values in a list. Say that with a list of customer receivables, someone in accounts receivable may want to call the top 10 receivables in an attempt to collect the accounts. The LARGE function can find the first, second, third, and so on largest values in a list.

Syntax:

=LARGE(*array*,*k*)

The LARGE function returns the kth largest value in a data set. You can use this function to select a value based on its relative standing. For example, you can use LARGE to return a highest, runner-up, or third-place score. This function takes the following arguments:

- *array*—This is the array or range of data for which you want to determine the *k*th largest value. If *array* is empty, LARGE returns a #NUM! error.

- k—This is the position (from the largest) in the array or cell range of data to return. If k is less than or equal to 0 or if k is greater than the number of data points, LARGE returns a #NUM! error.

Follow these steps to build a table of the five largest customer receivables:

1. Make the second argument of the function the numbers 1 through 5. Starting from the data set shown in Figure 14.1, insert a new Column A to hold the values 1 through 5.

2. In A66:A70, enter the numbers 1 through 5, as shown in Figure 14.2.

3. In the column letters above the grid, grab the line between Columns A and B. Drag to the left to make this column narrower. It should be just wide enough to display the numbers in Column A.

4. In Column C, Row 66, enter =LARGE(. Use the mouse or arrow keys to highlight the range of data. After highlighting the data, press the F4 key to add dollar signs to the reference. This allows you to copy the reference to the next several rows while always pointing at the same range.

5. For the second argument, point to the 1 in Cell A66. Leave this reference as relative (that is, no dollar signs) so that it will change to A67, A68, and so on when copied. The first formula in Cell C66 indicates that the largest value is 13,560.43. So far, you've done a lot of work just to find out the same thing that the MAX function could have told you. However, the power comes in the next step.

6. Select Cell C66. Click the fill handle and drag down to Cell C70. You now have a list of the top five open receivables.

7. At this point, you know the amounts of the top receivables, but this immediately brings up the question of which customers have those receivables. Using lookup functions discussed in Chapter 12, "Using Powerful Functions: Logical, Lookup, and Database Functions," you can retrieve the name associated with each receivable amount. Note that this method assumes that no two customers in the top five have exactly the same receivable.

8. Enter the following intermediate formula in Cell B66: `=MATCH(C66,$C$2:$C$60,0)`. This formula tells Excel to take the receivable value in Cell C66 and to find it in the list of open receivables. The `MATCH` function returns the row number within C2:C60 that has the matching value. For example, `13,560.43` is found in Cell C9. This is the eighth row in the range of C2:C60, so `MATCH` returns the number 8.

9. The largest receivable in the eighth row of a range is not useful to a person trying to collect accounts receivables, so to return the name, ask for the eighth value in the range of B2:B66. You can use the `INDEX` function to do this. `=INDEX($B$2:$B$66,8)` returns the customer with the largest receivable.

10. Combine the formulas from step 8 and step 9 into a single formula in Cell B66: `=INDEX($B$2:$B$60,MATCH(C66,$C$2:$C$60,0))`.

11. Copy the formula in Cell B66 down through Cell B70.

As shown in Figure 14.2, the result is a table in A66:A70 that shows the five largest customers. After receiving checks today, you can update the receivable amounts in C2:C60. If Best Raft sent in a check for $10,000, the formulas would automatically move Magnificent Electronics up to the fourth position and move the sixth customer up to the fifth spot.

Rather than adding the numbers 1 through 5 in A66:A70, you could use the ROW() function to return the values of 1 to 5. In cell C66, use `=LARGE($C$2:$C$60,ROW(A1))`. Because the row number of cell A1 is 1, the row function will return a 1 as the second argument to the `LARGE` function. This method has the advantage that as you drag the formula down, it will switch to ROW(A2) for 2, ROW(A3) for 3, and so on.

	A	B	C	D	E	F
		C66	▾	*fx* =LARGE($C$2:$C$60,A66)		
1		Customer	A/R			
58		Paramount Scooter Corporation	10,014.60			
59		Unsurpassed Sprayer Inc.	10,069.74			
60		Secure Necktie Inc.	8,800.63			
61		Total	493,005.80			
62						
63		Largest	13,560.43	*=MAX(C2:C60)*		
64						
65		Largest Receivables				
66	1	Fully Toothpick Company	13,560.43	*=LARGE($C$2:$C$60,A66)*		
67	2	Savory Calculator Company	12,493.41			
68	3	Inventive Clipboard Corporation	11,604.13			
69	4	Best Raft Company	11,582.61			
70	5	Magnificent Electronics Partners	11,087.71			
71						
72		*B66: =INDEX($B$2:$B$60,MATCH(C66,$C$2:$C$60,0))*				
73						

Figure 14.2
The `LARGE` function in Column C allows this dynamic table to be built to show the five largest problems.

Using SMALL to Sequence a List in Date Sequence

The MIN function finds the smallest value in a data set. The SMALL function can find the kth smallest value. This can be great for finding not just the smallest value but the second-smallest, third-smallest, and so on. If *n* is the number of data points in an array, SMALL(*array*, *1*) equals the smallest value, and SMALL(*array*,*n*) equals the largest value.

Syntax:

=SMALL(*array*,*k*)

The SMALL function returns the kth smallest value in a data set. You use this function to return values with a particular relative standing in a data set. *array* is an array or a range of numeric data for which you want to determine the *k*th smallest value. If *array* is empty, SMALL returns a #NUM! error. *k* is the position (from the smallest) in the array or range of data to return. If *k* is less than or equal to 0 or if *k* exceeds the number of data points, SMALL returns a #NUM! error.

In Figure 14.3, range A2:B19 contains a list of book titles and their publication dates. To find the earliest dates for the books, you use =SMALL().

This example contains a twist that makes the formula easier than in the example for LARGE. In the initial formula in Cell D2, the argument for k was generated using ROW(A1). This function returns the number 1. As the formula is copied from Cell D2 down to the remaining rows, the reference changes to ROW(A2) and so on. This allows each row in Column D to show a successively larger value from *array*.

The formula in Cell D2 is =SMALL($B$2:$B$19,ROW(A1)). After you have found the year in Column D, the formula in Cell E2 to return the title is =INDEX($A$2:$A$19,MATCH(D2,$B$2:$B$19,0)).

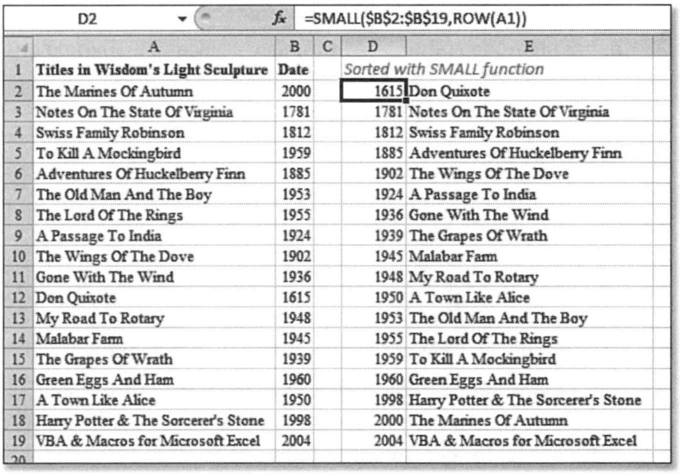

D2 =SMALL($B$2:$B$19,ROW(A1))

	A	B	C	D	E
1	Titles in Wisdom's Light Sculpture	Date		Sorted with SMALL function	
2	The Marines Of Autumn	2000		1615	Don Quixote
3	Notes On The State Of Virginia	1781		1781	Notes On The State Of Virginia
4	Swiss Family Robinson	1812		1812	Swiss Family Robinson
5	To Kill A Mockingbird	1959		1885	Adventures Of Huckelberry Finn
6	Adventures Of Huckelberry Finn	1885		1902	The Wings Of The Dove
7	The Old Man And The Boy	1953		1924	A Passage To India
8	The Lord Of The Rings	1955		1936	Gone With The Wind
9	A Passage To India	1924		1939	The Grapes Of Wrath
10	The Wings Of The Dove	1902		1945	Malabar Farm
11	Gone With The Wind	1936		1948	My Road To Rotary
12	Don Quixote	1615		1950	A Town Like Alice
13	My Road To Rotary	1948		1953	The Old Man And The Boy
14	Malabar Farm	1945		1955	The Lord Of The Rings
15	The Grapes Of Wrath	1939		1959	To Kill A Mockingbird
16	Green Eggs And Ham	1960		1960	Green Eggs And Ham
17	A Town Like Alice	1950		1998	Harry Potter & The Sorcerer's Stone
18	Harry Potter & The Sorcerer's Stone	1998		2000	The Marines Of Autumn
19	VBA & Macros for Microsoft Excel	2004		2004	VBA & Macros for Microsoft Excel
20					

Figure 14.3
The SMALL function in Column D finds the earliest years in the list.

Using MEDIAN, MODE.SNGL, MODE.MULT, and AVERAGE to Find the Central Tendency of a Data Set

You can use three popular measures when trying to find the middle scores in a range:

1. **Mean**—The mean of a data set is the mathematical average. It is calculated by adding all the values in the range and dividing by the number of values in the set. To calculate a mean in Excel, use the AVERAGE function.

2. **Median**—The median of a data set is the value in the middle when the set is arranged from high to low. In the data set, half the values are higher than the median and half the numbers are lower than the median. To calculate a median in Excel, use the MEDIAN function.

3. **Mode**—The mode of a data set is the value that happens most often. To calculate a mode in Excel 2010, use the MODE.SNGL or MODE.MULT functions.

Syntax:

=AVERAGE(*number1,number2,...*)

The AVERAGE function returns the average (that is, arithmetic mean) of the arguments. The arguments *number1, number2,...* are 1 to 255 numeric arguments for which you want the average. The arguments must be either numbers or names, arrays, or references that contain numbers. If an array or a reference argument contains text, logical values, or empty cells, those values are ignored; however, cells containing the value 0 are included.

If you have a range of True/False values and you want to see what percentage of people answered True, you can use =AVERAGEA() of the range. The AVERAGEA function will treat True values as 1 and False values as zero.

 caution

When averaging cells, keep in mind the difference between empty cells and those that contain the value 0. This can be particularly troubling if you have cleared the Show a Zero in Cells That Have a Zero Value check box. You find this setting by selecting File, Options, Advanced, Display Options for This Worksheet.

Syntax:

=MEDIAN(*number1,number2,...*)

The MEDIAN function returns the median of the given numbers. The median is the number in the middle of a set of numbers; that is, half the numbers have values that are greater than the median and half have values that are less. If there is an even number of numbers in the set, MEDIAN calculates the average of the two numbers in the middle.

The arguments *number1, number2,...* are 1 to 255 numbers for which you want the median. The arguments should be either numbers or names, arrays, or references that contain numbers. Microsoft Excel examines all the numbers in each reference or array argument. If an array or a reference argument contains text, logical values, or empty cells, those values are ignored; however, cells that contain the value 0 are included.

Syntax:

`=MODE.SNGL(number1,number2,...)`

The `MODE.SNGL` function returns the most frequently occurring, or repetitive, value in an array or a range of data. Like `MEDIAN`, `MODE.SNGL` is a location measure. In a set of values, the mode is the most frequently occurring value; the median is the middle value; and the mean is the average value. No single measure of central tendency provides a complete picture of the data. Suppose data is clustered in three areas, half around a single low value, and half around two large values. Both AVERAGE and MEDIAN may return a value in the relatively empty middle, and `MODE.SNGL` may return the dominant low value.

The arguments *number1, number2, ...* are 1 to 255 arguments for which you want to calculate the mode. You can also use a single array or a reference to an array instead of arguments separated by commas. The arguments should be numbers, names, arrays, or references that contain numbers. If an array or reference argument contains text, logical values, or empty cells, those values are ignored; however, cells that contain the value 0 are included. If the data set contains no duplicate data points, MODE returns a #N/A error.

 **note**

MODE.SNGL is a new function name introduced in Excel 2010. For backward compatibility, use the MODE function.

It is possible to have multiple values that tie as the mode. In the `MODE.SNGL` calculation, when two values tie as the mode, only the first mode value appears as the result. In Figure 14.4, the `MODE.SNGL` in E4 is reported as 88, even though both 88 and 82 appear most frequently in the data set. Microsoft added `MODE.MULT` to Excel 2010 to handle the situation where multiple values tie as the mode.

Figure 14.4 shows examples of AVERAGE, MEAN, and `MODE.SNGL`. Cell E2 calculates the arithmetic mean of the test scores in Column B: 81.4444. The median in Cell E3 is higher: 82.5. This means that half the students scored above 82.5 and half scored below 82.5. The mode in Cell E4 as reported by `MODE.SNGL` is 88. A formula in E5 indicates that 82 is also tied as a mode. This is because 82 and 88 each appeared three times in the data set.

The range in Figure 14.4 demonstrates two anomalies with the median and mode. In this case, there are an even number of entries—18. It is impossible to figure out a median in this case, so Excel takes the average of the two values in the middle—82 and 83—to produce 82.5. This is the only situation in which the median is not a value from the table.

There are also two modes in the table. Both 88 and 82 appear three times. `MODE.SNGL` reports 88 as the mode because it encounters the 88 in B8 before it encounters the 82 in B9. This is rather arbitrary and the `MODE.SNGL` would change if the data were sorted in ascending sequence.

Read on to see how `MODE.MULT` can report all the mode values.

	E6		▼	⦿	*fx*	=IF(COUNT(MODE.MULT(B2:B19))>2,INDEX(MODE.MULT(B2:B19),3),"")											

⊿	A	B	C	D	E	F	G	H	I	J	K	L	M	N	O	P	Q
1	STUDENT	SCORE															
2	ALFRED	84		Mean	81.4444	=AVERAGE(B2:B19)											
3	BRADLEY	75		Median	82.5	=MEDIAN(B2:B19)											
4	CARLOS	83		Mode	88	=MODE.SNGL(B2:B19)											
5	CHARLOTTE	91		Mode (Tie)	82	=IF(COUNT(MODE.MULT(B2:B19))>1,INDEX(MODE.MULT(B2:B19),2),"")											
6	CLARA	73		Mode (Tie)		=IF(COUNT(MODE.MULT(B2:B19))>2,INDEX(MODE.MULT(B2:B19),3),"")											
7	CLARENCE	83															
8	DENNIS	88															
9	EVA	82															
10	JUSTIN	88															
11	LOLA	79															
12	LUIS	87															
13	LYNN	82															
14	NORMAN	88															
15	REGINA	61															
16	RYAN	86															
17	SHELLEY	82															
18	VICTOR	78															
19	WHITNEY	76															
20																	

Figure 14.4
AVERAGE, MEDIAN, and MODE.SNGL all describe the central tendencies of a data set.

Syntax:

=MODE.MULT(*number1,number2,...*)

The MODE.MULT function returns a vertical array of the most frequently occurring, or repetitive, value in an array or a range of data.

MODE.MULT has been added to Excel 2010 to specifically address the situations where two or more values tie as the mode. The MODE.MULT function will return a vertical array of values as the answer.

Because MODE.MULT can return multiple values, you might think that you should enter the function in several cells and use Ctrl+Shift+Enter to enter the formula. While this works, the unpredictability of the number of values returned by MODE.MULT makes this a dicey proposition.

In Figure 14.5, you will see four different cases with MODE.MULT.

- In column B, five values each occur twice, creating a five-way tie for the MODE. Select cells C3:C7, type =MODE.MULT(B3:B12) and hold down Ctrl+Shift while pressing Enter. This enters one formula in those five cells. This works out great; five values are returned and they fill the five cells where the formula is entered.

- The first case has been copied to columns E:F. Cell E12 is changed from 5 to 6. This creates a four-way tie for the MODE. MULT. Because the formula is entered in five cells, you get the four-way tie as the first four cells and then #N/A as the fifth cell. This makes sense. There are a number of ways to deal with the #N/A value.

caution

MODE.MULT is a new function in Excel 2010. There is no equivalent function in Excel 2007 and earlier. If this workbook is opened in legacy versions of Excel, the cell will calculate as a #NAME? error.

- In column H, all 10 values appear exactly once. Excel help warns that if no value appears two or more times, the answer for mode will be #N/A. The results are all #N/A because there is officially no mode.
- In Column K, the "normal" case of having one mode causes all sorts of problems. Because MODE.MULT returns a one-cell answer, the array formula assumes that you must want to expand that one-cell answer over the entire range where the formula is entered, so you get five 1s as the answer.

Figure 14.5
MODE.MULT is challenging to use.

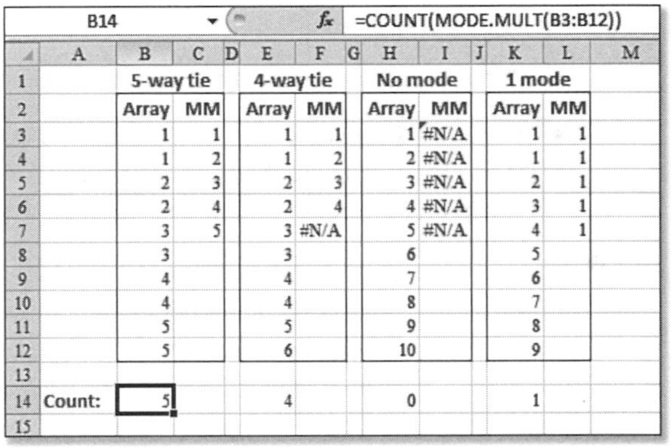
B14 =COUNT(MODE.MULT(B3:B12))

	A	B	C	D	E	F	G	H	I	J	K	L	M
1		5-way tie			4-way tie			No mode			1 mode		
2		Array	MM		Array	MM		Array	MM		Array	MM	
3		1	1		1	1		1	#N/A		1	1	
4		1	2		1	2		2	#N/A		1	1	
5		2	3		2	3		3	#N/A		2	1	
6		2	4		2	4		4	#N/A		3	1	
7		3	5		3	#N/A		5	#N/A		4	1	
8		3			3			6			5		
9		4			4			7			6		
10		4			4			8			7		
11		5			5			9			8		
12		5			6			10			9		
13													
14	Count:	5			4			0			1		
15													

In row 14 of Figure 14.5, a nonarray formula counts how many results the MODE.MULT function will return. Using =COUNT(MODE.MULT(B3:B12)) is probably the best way to go.

To return the first mode, you can use

```
=MODE.SNGL(range)
```

To see if there is a two-way tie, use

```
=IF(COUNT(MODE.MULT(range))>1,INDEX(MODE.MULT(range),2),"")
```

To see if there is a three-way tie, use

```
=IF(COUNT(MODE.MULT(range))>2,INDEX(MODE.MULT(range),3),"")
```

You can continue this pattern for as many possible modes as you might expect. In an N-row data set, there might be as many as N/2 possible modes!

Using TRIMMEAN to Exclude Outliers from the Mean

Sometimes a data set includes a few outliers that radically skew the average. For example, suppose you have a list of gross margin percentages. Most percentages fall in the 45% to 50% range, but there was one deal where for customer satisfaction reasons, the product was given away at a loss. This one data point would skew the average unusually low.

The TRIMMEAN function takes the mean of data points but excludes the n% highest and lowest values. You have to use some care in expressing the n%.

Syntax:

=TRIMMEAN(array,percent)

The TRIMMEAN function returns the mean of the interior of a data set. TRIMMEAN calculates the mean taken by excluding a percentage of data points from the top and bottom tails of a data set. You can use this function when you want to exclude outlying data from your analysis. This function takes the following arguments:

- *array*—This is the array or range of values to trim and average.

- *percent*—This is the fractional number of data points to exclude from the calculation. For example, if *percent* is 0.2, 4 points are trimmed from a data set of 20 points (that is, 20 × 0.2): 2 from the top and 2 from the bottom of the set.

If percent is less than 0 or *percent* is greater than 1, TRIMMEAN returns a #NUM! error. TRIMMEAN rounds the number of excluded data points down to the nearest multiple of 2. If *percent* equals 0.1, 10% of 30 data points equals 3 points. For symmetry, TRIMMEAN excludes a single value from the top and bottom of the data set.

Using GEOMEAN to Calculate Average Growth Rate

Suppose that your 401(k) plan is invested in a stock market index fund. The stock market goes up 5%, 40%, and 15% in three successive years. Taking the average of these numbers might lead someone to believe that the average increase was 20% per year. This is not correct. The growth rates are all multiplied together to find an ending value of your investment. To find the average growth rate, you need to find a number that, when multiplied together three times, yields the same result as 105% × 140% × 115%. You can calculate this by using GEOMEAN.

To find the geometric mean of 10 numbers, you multiply the 10 numbers together and raise the sum to the 1/10 power. Excel lets you do this quickly with GEOMEAN.

Syntax:

=GEOMEAN(*number1, number2,...*)

The GEOMEAN function returns the geometric mean of an array or a range of positive data. For example, you can use GEOMEAN to calculate average growth rate, given compound interest with variable rates.

The arguments *number1,number2,...* are 1 to 255 arguments for which you want to calculate the mean. You can also use a single array or a reference to an array instead of arguments separated by commas.

 caution
The arguments must be either numbers or names, arrays, or references that contain numbers. If an array or a reference argument contains text, logical values, or empty cells, those values are ignored. However, cells that contain the value 0 are included. If any data point is less than or equal to 0, GEOMEAN returns a #NUM! error.

Using HARMEAN **to Find Average Speeds**

The typical averaging function fails when you are measuring speeds over a period of time. Suppose that your exercise regimen is 5 minutes of walking at 2 mph, 25 minutes of running at 5 mph, and then 10 minutes of jogging at 3 mph. If you took the average of (2, 5, 5, 5, 5, 5, 3, 3), you would assume that you averaged 4.125 miles per hour.

The actual calculation for average speed would be to take the reciprocals of each speed, average those values, and then take the reciprocal of the result. In the exercise example, you would average $(^1/_2, \, ^1/_5, \, ^1/_5, \, ^1/_5, \, ^1/_5, \, ^1/_5, \, ^1/_3, \, ^1/_3)$ to obtain $^{13}/_{48}$. The you would take the reciprocal, $^{48}/_{13}$ to find the actual average speed of 3.69 mph.

Syntax:

=HARMEAN(*number1,number2,...*)

The HARMEAN function returns the harmonic mean of a data set. The harmonic mean is the reciprocal of the arithmetic mean of reciprocals. The arguments *number1,number2,...* are 1 to 255 arguments for which you want to calculate the mean. You can also use a single array or a reference to an array instead of arguments separated by commas.

The arguments must be either numbers or names, arrays, or references that contain numbers. If an array or a reference argument contains text, logical values, or empty cells, those values are ignored; however, cells that contain the value 0 are included. If any data point is less than or equal to 0, HARMEAN returns a #NUM! error. The harmonic mean is always less than the geometric mean, which is always less than the arithmetic mean.

Using AVERAGEIF **or** AVERAGEIFS

1. Excel 2007 included two new conditional calculation functions: AVERAGEIF and AVERAGEIFS. These functions find the mean of records that match one or more criteria.

Syntax:

AVERAGEIF(*range,criteria,average_range*)

AVERAGEIF returns the arithmetic mean of all the cells in a range that meet a given criteria.

- *Range*—One or more cells to average, including numbers or names, arrays, or references that contain numbers.

- *Criteria*—The criteria in the form of a number, expression, cell reference, or text that defines which cells are averaged. For example, criteria can be expressed as 32, "32", ">32", "apples", or B4.

- *Average_range*—The actual set of cells to average. If omitted, range is used.

Syntax:

AVERAGEIFS(*average_range,criteria_range1, criteria1,criteria_range2,criteria2...*)

AVERAGEIF returns the arithmetic mean of all cells that meet multiple criteria.

- *Average_range*—One or more cells to average, including numbers or names, arrays, or references that contain numbers.

- *Criteria_range1, criteria_range2, ...*—1 to 127 ranges in which to evaluate the associated criteria.

- *Criteria1, criteria2, ...*—1 to 127 criteria in the form of a number, expression, cell reference, or text that defines which cells will be averaged. For example, criteria can be expressed as 32, "32", ">32", "apples", or B4.

 note

Excel gurus have been complaining about an anomaly with the RANK function. Apparently, a bunch of scientists have also been complaining about RANK. Microsoft fixed the RANK function in Excel 2010. But they listened to the complaints of the scientists instead of the gurus. So, now there are two rank functions and neither one is going to make the Excel pros happy.

Using RANK to Calculate the Position Within a List

At times you need to determine the order of values, but you are not allowed to sort the data. The RANK function helps with this task.

Suppose five bowlers scored 187, 185, 185, 170, and 160. The traditional way to rank the players is that two players would have a rank of 2, and the next player would have a rank of 4. No one would be ranked number 3. Although this is technically correct, it can cause problems if you have lookup values expecting to find a person ranked number 3. The example at the end of this section explains how to overcome such a situation. The clever Excellers who hoped to use RANK to sort a list using formulas really want RANK to return one of every rank.

In Excel 2010, Microsoft renamed the old RANK as RANK.EQ. It added a new rank called RANK.AVG. In the same situation with the five bowlers, both of the scores of 185 would get a rank of 2.5. A rank of 2.5 is the average of the ranks of 2 and 3.

Syntax:

```
=RANK.EQ(number,ref,order)
=RANK.AVG(number,ref,order)
```

Neither RANK.EQ nor RANK.AVG will calculate in Excel 2007 or earlier. In legacy versions of Excel, use the RANK function to calculate RANK.EQ. There was no equivalent of RANK.AVG in legacy versions of Excel.

The RANK functions returns the rank of a number in a list of numbers. The rank of a number is its size relative to other values in a list. If you were to sort the list, the rank of the number would be its position. This function takes the following arguments:

- *number*—This is the number whose rank you want to find.

- *ref*—This is an array of, or a reference to, a list of numbers. Nonnumeric values in ref are ignored.

- *order*—This is a number that specifies how to rank number. For a value of 0 or if this argument is omitted, Excel ranks *number* as if *ref* were a list sorted in descending order. If *order* is any nonzero value, Excel ranks number as if ref were a list sorted in ascending order.

RANK.EQ gives duplicate numbers the same lower rank. However, the presence of duplicate numbers affects the ranks of subsequent numbers. For example, in a list of integers, if the number 10 appears twice and has a rank of 5, then 11 would have a rank of 7 (No number would have a rank of 6.)

RANK.AVG gives duplicate numbers the same rank by averaging the ranks of the next two positions. In the same example, if the number 10 appears twice and would hold the #5 and #6 positions, both of the 10s would receive an average rank of 5.5.

In Figure 14.6, Column B contains a list of scores. The formula for Cell C2 is =RANK. EQ(B2,$B$2:$B$13). Notice that the third argument is omitted, so the highest score will be ranked as number 1. Also notice that the second argument is marked as absolute so that the formula can be copied, and it will always point to the same ref range.

Figure 14.6
In this case, RANK.EQ and RANK. AVG return different values when a tie occurs.

	D2			fx	=RANK.AVG(B2,$B$2:$B$13)			
	A	B	C	D	E	F	G	H
1	NAME	COMPLETED	RANK.EQ	RANK.AVG				
2	YOLANDA HILL	83	9	9	C2: =RANK.EQ(B2,$B$2:$B$13)			
3	LEE DOUGLAS	80	10	10	D2: =RANK.AVG(B2,$B$2:$B$13)			
4	GREGORY BOWEN	135	2	2				
5	LOUIS MOLINA	85	8	8				
6	ANDREW HALL	88	7	7				
7	RANDY TRUJILLO	117	4	4				
8	MARTHA PHELPS	70	11	11.5				
9	CRAIG VAUGHAN	70	11	11.5				
10	SHARON COMPTON	146	1	1				
11	DOUGLAS BYERS	104	5	5				
12	LAURIE MEYER	133	3	3				
13	SONIA TRUJILLO	93	6	6				
14								

Column D uses the new RANK.AVG to rank the scores. Note the differences in rows 8 & 9. The tied values both receive a lower rank of 11 with RANK.EQ and a value of 11.5 with RANK.AVG.

If you need the lowest value to be ranked as number 1, add a third argument of 1 to indicate that the lowest number is the best. For example: =RANK(B2,$B$2:$B$8,1).

A common Excel trick is to use the ranking function combined with VLOOKUP or MATCH to sort a range with a formula. You might assign ranks and then use VLOOKUP to find the people who are ranked first, second, and third.

The VLOOKUP function certainly is not expecting two people to be ranked at #2 as RANK.EQ would do. It definitely would never expect the duplicate 2.5 values that RANK.AVG would return. The generally accepted solution is to use RANK.EQ and then add a COUNTIF function that checks to see how many rows above this row have the identical value.

In Figure 14.7, examine the formula in Cell C8. COUNTIF asks how many times the value in Cell B8 was found in B$2:B7. This final reference is an interesting reference. It tells Excel to count always from Row 2 down to the row above the current row. It is easier to build this formula in the final cell of the column and then copy it upward.

	C1	▾	*fx*	RANK						
⊿	A	B	C	D	E	F	G	H	I
1	RUNNER	TIME	RANK						
2	JO BOYLE	17:15	1	=RANK.EQ(B2,$B$2:$B$8,1)					
3	YVETTE ALVARADO	18:42	6	=RANK.EQ(B3,$B$2:$B$8,1)+COUNTIF(B$2:B2,B3)					
4	JEFFERY SWEENEY	17:32	4	=RANK.EQ(B4,$B$2:$B$8,1)+COUNTIF(B$2:B3,B4)					
5	LAURA MANN	18:50	7						
6	CYNTHIA GRIFFIN	17:17	2						
7	VERA RASMUSSEN	17:17	3						
8	ELLEN WIGGINS	17:59	5	=RANK.EQ(B8,$B$2:$B$8,1)+COUNTIF(B$2:B7,B8)					
9									
10	Top 3 finishers								
11		1 JO BOYLE		=INDEX($A$2:$A$8,MATCH(A11,$C$2:$C$8,FALSE))					
12		2 CYNTHIA GRIFFIN							
13		3 VERA RASMUSSEN							

Figure 14.7
You use a COUNTIF to break ties.

More Than You Ever Wanted to Know About the Controversy of Percentiles and Quartiles

A huge argument is raging over the best way to calculate percentiles and quartiles. Suppose that you have 11 scores. You ask Excel to tell you the score at the 15th percentile. Typically, Excel assigns the smallest value to the 0th percentile and the largest value to the 100th percentile. Because there are 10 steps between the smallest and largest value, the 10th percentile will be the second-smallest number, and the 20th percentile will be the third-smallest number. What number is at the 15th percentile? How about at the 17th percentile? Excel divides the gap between the second and third values into 10 equal parts and uses that interpolation to calculate the number at the 11th percentile and so on.

In 1996, two scholars named Hyndman and Fan published a paper detailing 12 different methods for calculating percentiles and quartiles. Legacy versions of Excel used method #7, which was defined by Gumbull. Other software such as MiniTab and SPSS used method #6, which was defined by Weibull. People who care a lot about Percentiles and Quartiles will talk about "Hyndman and Fan Method # X."

- If you want to read all the details, check out http://www.daheiser.info/excel/notes/ NOTE%20N.pdf for a comparison of the methods.

In Excel 2010, the Hyndman and Fan method #7 is still available as QUARTILE.INC, PERCENTILE. INC and PERCENTRANK.INC. Excel 2010 introduces support for Hyndman and Fan method #6 as QUARTILE.EXC, PERCENTILE.EXC, and PERCENTRANK.EXC.

Here is what you have to know about the controversy: With a data set of 100 numbers or more, the difference between .EXC and .INC versions will be small—less than one-half of one percent. However, in small data sets of n=4 to n=7, the values at the first quartile can swing by 40%. For example, in the data set of {10,22,33,40}, Weibull calculates the first quartile at 13 and Gumbull calculates the first quartile at 19. The delta between 19 and 13 is 6, which is 46% of 13.

Also, in the .EXC version, there is no 0th percentile and no 100th percentile. The .EXC stands for percentiles from 0% to 100% exclusive. The .INC stands for percentiles from 0% to 100% inclusive.

Using QUARTILE.INC to Break a Data Set into Quarters

Use QUARTILE.INC to divide populations into groups.

> **note**
> MIN, MEDIAN, and MAX return the same value as QUARTILE.INC when quart is equal to 0, 2, and 4, respectively.

Syntax:

```
=QUARTILE.INC(array,quart)
=QUARTILE.EXC(array,quart)
```

The old QUARTILE function is included in Excel for compatibility only. QUARTILE.INC is the renamed version of QUARTILE. The QUARTILE.INC function returns the quartile of a data set. Quartiles are often used in sales and survey data to divide populations into groups. For example, you can use QUARTILE.INC to find the top 25% of incomes in a population. These functions take the following arguments:

- *array*—This is the array or cell range of numeric values for which you want the quartile value. If array is empty, QUARTILE returns a #NUM! error.

- *quart*—This indicates which value to return. You use 0 for the minimum value, 1 for the first quartile (25th percentile), 2 for the median value (50th percentile), 3 for the third quartile (75th percentile), and 4 for the maximum value. If *quart* is not an integer, it is truncated. If *quart* is less than 0 or if *quart* is greater than 4, QUARTILE returns a #NUM! error.

In Figure 14.8, the formulas in B20:C23 break out the limits for each quartile. The formula in Cell B20 is =QUARTILE.INC($B$2:$B$17,0) to find the minimum value. The formula in Cells C20 and B21 is =QUARTILE.INC($B$2:$B$17,1) to define the end of the first quartile and the start of the second quartile.

After the QUARTILE.INC functions build the table in B20:C23, the VLOOKUP function returns the text in C2:C17. The formula in Cell C2 is =VLOOKUP(B2,$B$20:$D$23,3,TRUE).

Using PERCENTILE.INC to Calculate Percentile

The QUARTILE.INC function is fine if you are trying to find every record that is in the top 25% of a range. Sometimes, however, you need to find some other percentile. For example, all employees ranked above the 81st percentile may be eligible for a bonus this year. You can use the PERCENTILE.INC function to determine the threshold for any percentile.

B20 =QUARTILE.INC($B$2:$B$17,0)

	A	B	C	D	E
1	Customer	Revenue	Where		
2	Distinctive Marble Supply	600	First Quartile		
3	First-Rate Marble Inc.	70000	Fourth Quartile		
4	New Toothpick Inc.	100	First Quartile		
5	Refined Marble Inc.	100000	Fourth Quartile		
6	Powerful Shingle Corporation	6000	Second Quartile		
7	Bright Linen Inc.	600	First Quartile		
8	Stunning Vise Inc.	40000	Fourth Quartile		
9	Trendy Shovel Inc.	10000	Third Quartile		
10	Trouble-Free Toothpick Company	10000	Third Quartile		
11	Unique Tuner Corporation	90000	Fourth Quartile		
12	Tasty Chopstick Corporation	1000	Second Quartile		
13	Astonishing Bottle Corporation	40000	Fourth Quartile		
14	Easy Quilt Company	10000	Third Quartile		
15	Easy Furnace Supply	300	First Quartile		
16	Agile Freezer Corporation	3000	Second Quartile		
17	Wonderful Luggage Inc.	7000	Second Quartile		
18					
19		From	Thru		
20	First Quartile	100	900	First Quartile	
21	Second Quartile	900	8500	Second Quartile	
22	Third Quartile	8500	40000	Third Quartile	
23	Fourth Quartile	40000	100000	Fourth Quartile	
24					

Figure 14.8
The QUARTILE.INC function can break up a data set into four equal pieces.

Syntax:

```
=PERCENTILE.INC(array,k)
=PERCENTILE.EXC(array,k)
```

The Excel 2007 PERCENTILE function is included in Excel 2010 for compatibility with older versions. In Excel 2010, the PERCENTILE.INC function is equivalent to PERCENTILE. The new PERCENTILE.EXC function debuts in Excel 2010.

The PERCENTILE.INC function returns the kth percentile of values in a range. You can use this function to establish a threshold of acceptance. For example, you can decide to examine candidates who score above the 90th percentile. This function takes the following arguments:

- *array*—This is the array or range of data that defines relative standing. If array is empty, PERCENTILE.INC returns a #NUM! error.
- *k*—This is the percentile value in the range 0...1, inclusive. If k is nonnumeric, PERCENTILE.INC returns a #VALUE! error. If *k* is less than 0 or if *k* is greater than 1, PERCENTILE.INC returns a #NUM! error. If *k* is not a multiple of 1 / (n – 1), PERCENTILE.INC interpolates to determine the value at the *k*th percentile.

In Figure 14.9, 33 employees are in Column A. Their ratings on an annual review are shown in Column B. The formula in Cell F3, =PERCENTILE.INC(B2:B34,F2), calculates the level of the 81st percentile. After you determine the particular percentile, you can mark all the qualifying employees by using the formula =B2>=$F$3 in cells C2:C33.

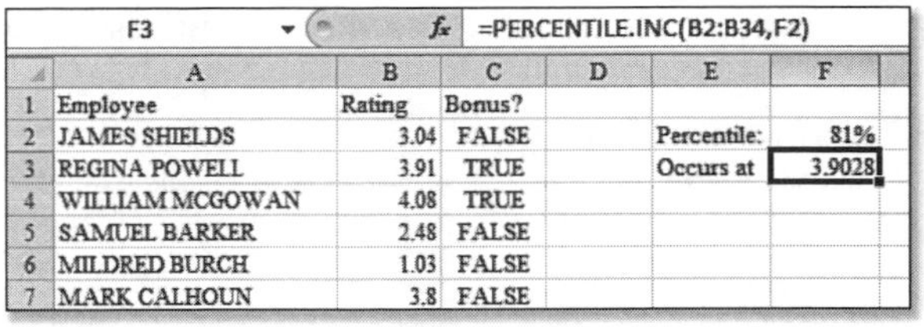

Figure 14.9
Unlike QUARTILE.INC, the PERCENTILE.INC function can determine the breaking point for any particular percentile.

	A	B	C	D	E	F
		F3	▼	fx	=PERCENTILE.INC(B2:B34,F2)	
1	Employee	Rating	Bonus?			
2	JAMES SHIELDS	3.04	FALSE		Percentile:	81%
3	REGINA POWELL	3.91	TRUE		Occurs at	3.9028
4	WILLIAM MCGOWAN	4.08	TRUE			
5	SAMUEL BARKER	2.48	FALSE			
6	MILDRED BURCH	1.03	FALSE			
7	MARK CALHOUN	3.8	FALSE			

Using PERCENTRANK.INC to Assign a Percentile to Every Record

Suppose you have a database of students in a graduating class. Each student has a certain grade point average. To determine each student's standing in the class, you use the PERCENTRANK.INC function.

Syntax:

=PERCENTRANK.INC(*array,x,significance*)
=PERCENTRANK.EXC(*array,x,significance*)

The Excel 2007 PERCENTRANK function is being replaced by PERCENTRANK.INC. Excel 2010 debuts the new PERCENTRANK.EXC function.

The PERCENTRANK.INC function returns the rank of a value in a data set as a percentage of the data set. This function can be used to evaluate the relative standing of a value within a data set. For example, you can use PERCENTRANK.INC to evaluate the standing of an aptitude test score among all scores for the test. This function takes the following arguments:

- *array*—This is the array or range of data with numeric values that defines relative standing. If *array* is empty, PERCENTRANK.INC returns a #NUM! error.

- *x*—This is the value for which you want to know the rank. If *x* does not match one of the values in *array*, PERCENTRANK.INC interpolates to return the correct percentage rank.

- *significance*—This is an optional value that identifies the number of significant digits for the returned percentage value. If it is omitted, PERCENTRANK.INC uses three digits (that is, 0.xxx). If *significance* is less than 1, PERCENTRANK.INC returns a #NUM! error.

This function is slightly different from RANK, so use caution. Typically, RANK and other functions would ask for x as the first argument and array as the second argument. If you use this function and everyone is assigned to the 100% level, you might have reversed the arguments. The Excel Help is a bit misleading with regard to significance. The Help topic indicates that a significance of 3 generates a value accurate to 0.xxx%. In fact, a significance of 3 returns xx.x%.

In Figure 14.10, the students' GPAs are in B3:B302. The rank for the first student is =PERCENTRANK. INC($B$3:$B$302,B2,3). Note that PERCENTRANK.INC always starts with the lowest score at the lowest percentile.

D302			f_x =PERCENTRANK.EXC($B$3:$B$302,B302,3)						
	A	B	C	D	E F	G	H	I	J
1			PERCENTRANK						
2	Student	GPA	.INC	.EXC					
3	TRAVIS COMPTON	4.00	99.6%	99.3%	C3: =PERCENTRANK.INC($B$3:$B$302,B3,3)				
4	VICTOR REID	4.00	99.6%	99.3%	D3: =PERCENTRANK.EXC($B$3:$B$302,B3,3)				
5	ERIN COLE	3.99	98.6%	98.3%					
6	CANDICE MATTHEWS	3.99	98.6%	98.3%					
7	KEITH RATLIFF	3.99	98.6%	98.3%	Significance				
8	RONALD GAMBLE	3.98	98.3%	98.0%	1	0.9			
9	PHILLIP BLEVINS	3.97	97.9%	97.6%	2	0.99			
10	JANICE LEWIS	3.96	97.6%	97.3%	3	0.996			
11	JAMIE TURNER	3.95	97.3%	97.0%	4	0.9966			
12	MAXINE HENDRIX	3.93	96.9%	96.6%	5	0.99665			
13	LYNN POTTS	3.92	96.6%	96.3%					
298	ANDREW NOEL	1.83	1.3%	1.6%					
299	RYAN BRADLEY	1.82	0.6%	0.9%					
300	KRISTINE DAY	1.82	0.6%	0.9%					
301	TIFFANY BOOTH	1.81	0.3%	0.6%					
302	CHRISTOPHER MOON	1.80	0.0%	0.3%					
303									

Figure 14.10
The PERCENTRANK.INC function assigns percentile values to an array of values.

The table in F7:G12 shows the actual behavior of the *significance* argument. The values in Column G show the PERCENTRANK.INC of Cell B2 to the significance in Column F. You can see that the student ranked at the 99.6th percentile is in the 90th percentile when the significance is 1. A significance of 1 would assign 30 records to be at the 90th percentile.

Figure 14.10 also shows the difference between PERCENTRANK.INC and PERCENTRANK.EXC. Although Christopher Moon is at the 0.0th percentile in cell C302 using PERCENTRANK.INC, the .EXC version never assigns a value to the 0.0 percentile. Cell D302 shows a percentile of 0.3% for the lowest score in a 300 row data set.

Using AVEDEV, DEVSQ, VAR.S, and STDEV.S to Calculate Dispersion

Functions such as AVERAGE tell you about the center of a range of data. Seeing the center is not always the entire picture. The other key element of descriptive statistics is dispersion. If you have a population, the average height might be x. If you look at dispersion, you can find out if every member of the population is tightly grouped around the average or if there is wide variability.

Here are several measures of dispersion:

- Average deviation is calculated by measuring the absolute difference of each data point from the mean and then averaging these values. Suppose the values in a population are 12, 14, 16, 18, and 20. The mean is 16. Average deviation adds up 4, 2, 0, 2, and 4 and divides the total by 5 to yield 2.4. Excel offers AVEDEV to calculate this.

- Average deviation is not perfect. Suppose you have another population of 11, 15, 16, 17, and 21. Again, the mean is 16. The average deviation averages 5, 1, 0, 1, and 5 to yield an average deviation of 2.4. If you want to measure how far from the mean the points range, you can add up the squares of each deviation. In this case, the square of 5 is 25, and it indicates more dispersion than the square of 4. Excel offers DEVSQ to calculate the squares of each deviation.

- Variance is a common measurement of dispersion. It averages the square deviations to come up with the variance of a data set. Here is the one odd thing about variance: Suppose you have 20 measurements, and they represent the entire population (for example, the 20 fish in an aquarium). In this case, you divide DEVSQ by 20 to calculate the variance. You use VAR.P in Excel to do this. However, if your 20 values are a random sample, then variance is calculated by dividing DEVSQ by 20 − 1, or 19. You use VAR.S in Excel to calculate this.

- The measurement for variance is a square, right? You took all the deviations, squared them, and then averaged (or nearly averaged) them. The final popular measure of dispersion is calculated by taking the square root of the variance. This number is called standard deviation. Excel offers two functions for standard deviation. You use STDEV.P if your data set represents the entire population, and you use STDEV.S if your data set represents only a sample of the population.

Theories About Standard Deviation

There are many theories about standard deviation. One general rule states that 95% of a population will be located within two standard deviations of the mean. If you extend your range to within three standard deviations of the mean, that range should encompass 99.7% of the population.

Figure 14.11 shows the lengths of fish. Column A contains the lengths of all 20 fish in one particular tank at a science museum. Column E contains the lengths of 20 random fish observed while snorkeling at a coral reef. Both groups have a mean value of 18.58 inches, as shown in Cells C4 and G4.

Figure 14.11
Although the averages are the same, the dispersion measurements paint a different picture of these populations.

The fish in the museum tank have an average deviation of 1.45 inches from the mean. Cells C6, C8, and C10 walk through the calculation of squares of deviation, variance, and standard deviation. The theory about standard deviation says that of the fish in the tank, 95% will occur between 15.08 inches and 22.07 inches.

The fish at the coral reef have an average deviation of 6.7 inches from the mean. Cells G6, G7, and G9 walk through the calculation of squares of deviation, variance, and standard deviation. The theory about standard deviation says that of the fish at the coral reef, 95% will be between 0.78 inches and 36.37 inches long.

Comparing these two results helps you to picture the likely populations of both locations. Although both have the same mean size, the variety of fish (that is, the measure of dispersion) at the coral reef is much higher than that at the aquarium.

Syntax:

=AVEDEV(*number1*,*number2*,...)

The AVEDEV function returns the average of the absolute deviations of data points from their mean. AVEDEV is a measure of the variability in a data set. AVEDEV is influenced by the unit of measurement in the input data.

Syntax:

=DEVSQ(*number1*,*number2*,...)

The DEVSQ function returns the sum of squares of deviations of data points from their sample mean.

Syntax:

=VAR.S(*number1*,*number2*,...)

The VAR.S function estimates variance based on a sample.

Syntax:

=VAR.P(*number1*,*number2*,...)

The VAR.P function calculates variance based on the entire population.

> **caution**
>
> Logical values (TRUE/FALSE) are ignored in the STDDEV.S and STDDEV.P calculations. For some statistics, you need to figure out how many people answered TRUE to a question. In order to count TRUE values as 1 and FALSE values as 0, you use VARA, VARPA, STDEVA, and STDEVPA versions of those four functions.

Syntax:

=STDEV.S(*number1*,*number2*,...)

The STDEV.S function estimates standard deviation based on a sample. The standard deviation is a measure of how widely values are dispersed from the average value (that is, the mean). The standard deviation is calculated using the "nonbiased" or "n – 1" method.

Syntax:

=STDEV.p(*number1*,*number2*,...)

The STDEV.P function calculates standard deviation based on the entire population, given as arguments. The standard deviation is a measure of how widely values are dispersed from the average value (that is, the mean). STDEV.P assumes that its arguments are the entire population. If your data represents a sample of the population, you can compute the standard deviation by using STDEV.S. For large sample sizes, STDEV.S and STDEV.P return approximately equal values. The standard deviation is calculated using the "biased" or "n" method.

In legacy versions of Excel, VAR.S was simply known as VAR. VAR.P was known as VARP. STDEV.S was STDEV. STDEV.P was STDEVP. If you are going to be sharing your workbook with people using legacy versions of Excel, use the old names instead of the new names.

The arguments *number1, number2, . . .* are 1 to 255 arguments for which you want the average of the absolute deviations. You can also use a single array or a reference to an array instead of arguments separated by commas. The arguments must be either numbers or names, arrays, or references that contain numbers. If an array or a reference argument contains text, logical values, or empty cells, those values are ignored; however, cells that contain the value 0 are included.

Examples of Functions for Regression and Forecasting

Regression analysis allows you to predict the future, based on past events. Suppose you have observed total sales for the past several years. Regression analysis finds a line that best fits the past data points. You can then use the description of that line to predict results for the future data points.

Regression works by finding a line that can best be drawn through existing data points. In real-life data, the data points aren't arranged exactly in a line. Any line that the computer draws will have errors at any data point. Regression finds the line that minimizes the errors at each data point.

Consider the error in a regression line. The actual data point in Year 1 might be higher than the regression line by 2. In Year 2, the data might be lower by 1, and in Year 3 it might be lower by 1. If you added up these three errors, you would have an error of 0. This is a bad method. If you used this method to judge a line with errors of +400, −300, −100, it would also add up to an error of 0.

Instead, the regression engine sums the square of each error. In this case, the first line would have an error of $2^2 + -1^2 + -1^2$ or $4 + 1 + 1$, or 6. The second line would have an error of $400^2 + -300^2 + -100^2$ or $160,000 + 90,000 + 10,000$, or 260,000. With this method, the error for the first line is clearly better than the error for the second line. This method is called the least-squares method.

You might wonder why regression doesn't add the absolute value of each error. Ideally, the errors around the regression line should be narrow. A line with errors of −4, +4, −4, +4 would result in a sum of squares of 64. A line with errors of −7, 1, 7, −1 would result in a sum of squares of 100. The sum of squares method would deem the earlier line to be better, whereas using absolute values would call them equal.

Considerations When Using Regression Analysis

You need to consider one question before doing regression analysis: Is the data series growing linearly or exponentially? Sales for a company might grow linearly. The number of bacteria cells in a Petri dish might grow exponentially. You use LINEST and TREND to predict sales that are growing linearly. You use LOGEST and GROWTH to predict bacteria that are growing exponentially.

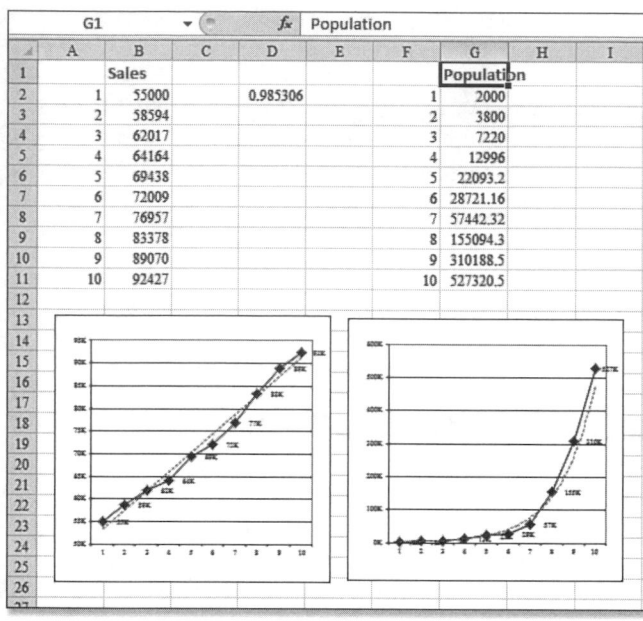

Figure 14.12
These two data sets can be accurately predicted using regression.

In Figure 14.12, the chart on the left shows sales over time. These sales are growing linearly and could probably be predicted fairly well by a straight line. The dotted line in the chart is the straight-line regression for the data set. Although each data point is either above or below the regression line, the error at any given data point is fairly small.

The chart on the right shows an exponential growth curve. In this chart, the dotted line shows the regression line plotted using LOGEST. Again, although the dotted line does not correlate exactly with the actual data points, it is fairly close.

Here is the problem: Regression always finds a line to fit your data set. In Figure 14.13, no apparent correlation exists between sales and time. Each year, the sales fluctuate wildly up or down. If you asked Excel to use regression, it would gladly predict the dotted line shown in the graph. The problem is that this line has no predictive ability. If you base your future sales on this line, you will get results that will vary greatly from the prediction.

Part of the results of regression analysis are statistics that tell how well the regression line fits the actual data. You should always check statistics such as r-squared or the standard error to see if the past data shows a relationship between the variables. The r-squared value is a value between 0 and 1. The closer that r-squared is to 1, the better the regression line. The r-squared for the left chart in Figure 14.12 is 0.985. The r-squared for the chart in Figure 14.13 is 0.000001, indicating that no correlation exists.

When you have data like the data in Figure 14.13, it does not mean that you cannot use regression analysis. It means that you need to think about the data to see if other factors could help describe the data. Suppose that the data represents sales of squares of roofing shingles in Florida. If you add data to the chart that describes the number of category 3+ hurricanes making landfall each year,

Figure 14.13
This data set has no correlation to time. LINEST happily predicts a line, but it is severely wrong most of the time.

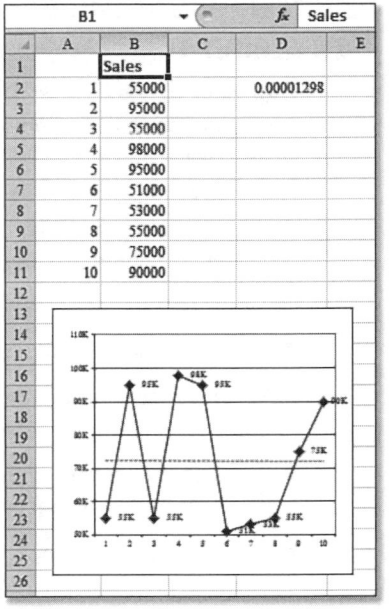

the sales numbers begin to make sense. The *r*-squared for predicting sales based on year is nearly 0. The *r*-squared for predicting sales based on hurricanes is 0.987. Because an *r*-squared of 1 means almost perfect correlation, you could base prediction of sales on a forecast of hurricanes.

Regression Function Arguments

For all the following regression functions, the arguments list generally includes these two arguments (for brevity, they are described here once):

- *known_y's*—This is an array or a cell range of numeric dependent data points. This is the range of data that you want to predict. It might be the actual sales for the past several years or the population of bacteria for the past several hours.

- *known_x's*—This is the set of independent data points. These are the values that you think will lead to a prediction of the y values. For a simple time series, this might be a list of year numbers. It might be a list of other independent data points, such as the number of hurricanes making landfall each year.

The arguments must be numbers or names, arrays, or references that contain numbers. If an array or a reference argument contains text, logical values, or empty cells, those values are ignored; however, cells that contain the value 0 are included. If *known_y's* and *known_x's* are empty or have a different number of data points, the function returns a #N/A error.

Functions for Simple Straight-Line Regression: SLOPE and INTERCEPT

With many things in Excel, there is a right way to do something. However, sometimes the powers-that-be decide that the right way is too difficult for Excel customers, so they offer alternative, easier ways to solve problems.

The LINEST function is powerful, and using it is the right way to calculate straight-line regression. However, because the LINEST function returns an array of values, it seemed too difficult, so Microsoft also offers the SLOPE and INTERCEPT functions to retrieve the key results from LINEST.

In mathematical terms, a line is described as $y = mx + b$:

- **y**—This is the value you are trying to predict. It could be sales for a given year.

- **b**—This is called the y-intercept. This is the base level of sales that you can count on year after year.

- **m**—This is the slope of the line. If your sales are going up by 1,000 per year, the slope is 1,000. If your sales are going up by 100,000 per year, the slope is 100,000.

- **x**—This is a point along the x-axis. In a problem where you are measuring sales over a span of several years, you can assign year numbers 1, 2, 3, and so on to each year. x then corresponds to a year number.

If you have a series of year numbers and sales for each year, you need to calculate both the SLOPE and INTERCEPT to describe the line.

Syntax:

```
=SLOPE(known_y's,known_x's)
```

The SLOPE function returns the slope of the linear regression line through data points in *known_y's* and *known_x's*. The slope is the vertical distance divided by the horizontal distance between any two points on the line; in other words, it is the rate of change along the regression line.

Syntax:

```
=INTERCEPT(known_y's,known_x's)
```

The INTERCEPT function calculates the point at which a line intersects the y-axis by using existing x values and y values. The intercept point is based on a best-fit regression line plotted through the known x values and known y values. You use the intercept when you want to determine the value of the dependent variable when the independent variable is 0.

In Figure 14.14, the sales in B2:B11 are the dependent variables. In the language of Excel, these are the *known_y's*. You are predicting that sales are increasing linearly over time. The year numbers in A2:A11 are the independent variables. In the language of Excel, these are the *known_x's*.

The formula in Cell E2 calculates the intercept for the line by using =INTERCEPT(B2:B11,A2:A11). The answer of 49,041 means that the model predicts that your sales in a hypothetical Year 0 would have been 49,041.

Figure 14.14
Using the SLOPE and INTERCEPT functions is a simple way to calculate a linear regression line.

	E8			f_x	=$E$2+$E$3*D8		
	A	B	C	D	E	F	G	H
1	Year	Sales						
2	1	55000		Intercept:	49,041	=INTERCEPT(B2:B11,A2:A11)		
3	2	58594		Slope:	4,230	=SLOPE(B2:B11,A2:A11)		
4	3	62017						
5	4	64164						
6	5	69438		Prediction:				
7	6	72009		Year	Sales			
8	7	76957		11	95,570	=$E$2+$E$3*D8		
9	8	83378		12	99,800			
10	9	89070		13	104,029			
11	10	92427		14	108,259			
12				15	112,489			
13								

The formula in Cell E3 calculates the slope of the line by using =SLOPE(B2:B11,A2:A11). The answer of 4,230 means that the model predicts that your sales are increasing by about 4,230 each year.

When you have the slope and y-intercept, you can build a new table to predict future sales. You enter year numbers 11 through 15 in D8:D12. The formula in Cell E8 needs to multiply the year number by the slope and add the intercept. That formula is =$E$2+$E$3*D8.

The values in Cells E8 through E12 are one prediction of future sales. This assumes that the past trends continue to work over the next 5 years.

Using LINEST to Calculate Straight-Line Regression with Complete Statistics

Although SLOPE and INTERCEPT would do the job, the more powerful function is LINEST. Here is the difficulty: LINEST returns both the slope and the intercept. In addition, it returns a whole series of statistics. Anytime a function returns several values, you must enter the function by using Ctrl+Shift+Enter. You should also select a large enough range in advance before entering the formula. Figuring out the size of the range in advance is difficult because it varies, depending on the shape of the independent variables and also if you ask for statistics.

However, LINEST is far more powerful than SLOPE and INTERCEPT. Additional arguments available in LINEST are not available in the easier functions.

Syntax:

=LINEST(*known_y's*,*known_x's*,const,stats)

The LINEST function calculates the statistics for a line by using the least-squares method to calculate a straight line that best fits the data, and it returns an array that describes the line. Because this function returns an array of values, it must be entered as an array formula with Ctrl+Shift+Enter. The equation for the line is y = mx + b or y = m1x1 + m2x2 + ... + b (if there are multiple ranges of x values) where the dependent y value is a function of

 note

Note that y, x, and m can be vectors. The array that LINEST returns is backward from what you would expect. The slope for the last independent variable appears first: {mn,mn-1,...,m1,b}. LINEST can also return additional regression statistics.

the independent x values. The m values are coefficients corresponding to each x value, and b is a constant value.

The LINEST function takes the following arguments:

- *known_y's*—This is the set of y values you already know in the relationship y = mx + b. If the array *known_y's* is in a single column, each column of *known_x's* is interpreted as a separate variable. If the array *known_y's* is in a single row, each row of *known_x's* is interpreted as a separate variable.

- *known_x's*—This is an optional set of x values that you may already know in the relationship y = mx + b. The array *known_x's* can include one or more sets of variables. If only one variable is used, *known_y's* and *known_x's* can be ranges of any shape, as long as they have equal dimensions. If more than one variable is used, *known_y's* must be a vector (that is, a range with a height of one row or a width of one column). If *known_x's* is omitted, it is assumed to be the array {1,2,3,...} that is the same size as *known_y's*.

- const—This is a logical value that specifies whether to force the constant b to equal 0. If const is TRUE or omitted, b is calculated normally. If const is FALSE, b is set equal to 0, and the m values are adjusted to fit y = mx.

- stats—This is a logical value that specifies whether to return additional regression statistics. If stats is TRUE, LINEST returns the additional regression statistics, so the returned array is {mn,mn-1,...,m1,b;sen,sen1,...,se1,seb;r2,sey;F,df;ssreg,ssresid}. If stats is FALSE or omitted, LINEST returns only the m coefficients and the constant b. If you specify TRUE for stats, the additional regression statistics shown in Table 14.2 are possible return values.

Table 14.2 Additional Regression Statistics for LINEST

Statistic	Description
se1,se2,...,sen	The standard errors for the coefficients m1,m2,...,mn.
Seb	The standard error for the constant b (seb = #N/A when const is FALSE).
r2	The coefficient of determination. You compare estimated and actual y values and ranges in value from 0 to 1. If it is 1, there is a perfect correlation in the sample—that is, no difference exists between the estimated y value and the actual y value. At the other extreme, if the coefficient of determination is 0, the regression equation is not helpful in predicting a y value.
Sey	The standard error for the y estimate.
F	The F statistic, or the F observed value. You use the F statistic to determine whether the observed relationship between the dependent and independent variables occurs by chance.
df	The degrees of freedom. You use the degrees of freedom to help you find F critical values in a statistical table. You compare the values you find in the table to the F statistic returned by LINEST to determine a confidence level for the model.

Statistic	Description
ssreg	The regression sum of squares.
ssresid	The residual sum of squares.

Figure 14.16, later in this chapter, shows a visual map of the statistics being returned.

The accuracy of the line calculated by LINEST depends on the degree of scatter in the data. The more linear the data, the more accurate the LINEST model. LINEST uses the method of least squares for determining the best fit for the data.

The line- and curve-fitting functions LINEST and LOGEST can calculate the best straight line or exponential curve that fits the data. However, you have to decide which of the two results best fits the data. You can calculate TREND(*known_y's,known_x's*) for a straight line or GROWTH(*known_y's, known_x's*) for an exponential curve. These functions, without the *known_x's* argument, return an array of y values predicted along that line or curve at your actual data points. You can then compare the predicted values with the actual values. You might want to chart them both for a visual comparison.

In regression analysis, Microsoft Excel calculates for each point the squared difference between the y value estimated for that point and its actual y value. The sum of these squared differences is called the residual sum of squares. Microsoft Excel then calculates the sum of the squared differences between the actual y values and the average of the y values, which is called the total sum of squares (that is Regression sum of squares + Residual sum of squares). The smaller the residual sum of squares compared with the total sum of squares, the larger the value of the coefficient of determination, r-squared, which is an indicator of how well the equation resulting from the regression analysis explains the relationship among the variables.

Case Study: Application of Regression Analysis

Suppose that you rent a snow-cone cart at a local amusement park. You create a table showing total snow cones sold for each day of last summer. In Figure 14.15, Column E shows the total snow cones sold by day. As you can see, the sales rise and fall sharply from day to day.

Figure 14.15
The results of the LINEST function in G4:J8 are seemingly meaningless.

The previous manager of the cart had noticed certain trends in the data. Sales were better on the weekends than on weekdays. Sales were horrible when it rained. Sales improved as the weather became hotter in July and August.

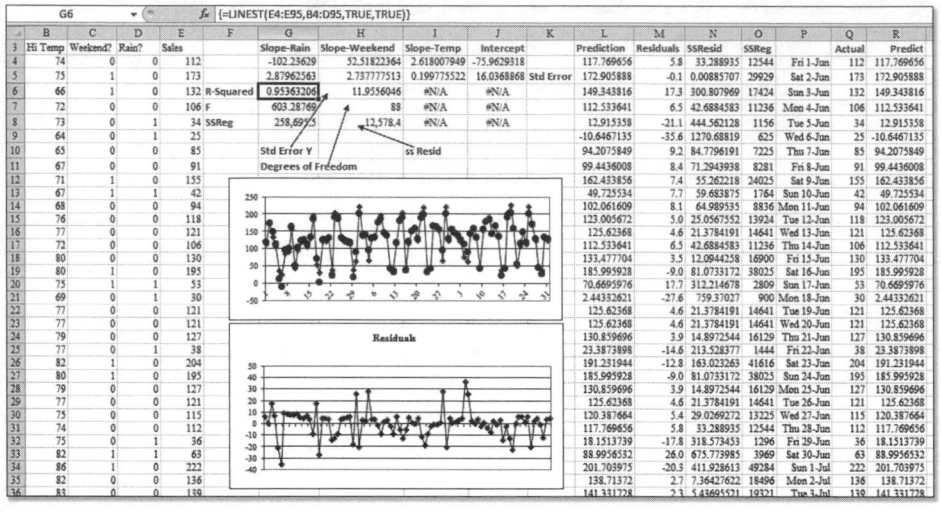

Columns B:D in Figure 14.15 contain data related to temperature, weekends, and rain. Note that in Column C, the weekend data is binary data—either 0 or 1. In Column D, the manager could have kept information about the amount of rainfall each day but instead kept this as binary data as well. If the day was predominantly rainy, the manager recorded a 1 to indicate a rainout. If the day had just a spot of rain, the manager recorded it as a nonrainy day.

To perform regression on this data, follow these steps:

1. Total the number of independent variables and add one. This is the number of columns the results of the regression will occupy. In the snow cone cart example, that is four columns.

2. Figure out how may rows the result of the regression will occupy. Because you plan to ask for statistics in the snow cone example, this is five rows.

3. Off to the side of the data, select a range that is four columns wide by five columns tall. This size is determined by the results of the first two steps.

4. Start to type the formula, =LINEST(.

5. For the *known_y's*, use the sales data in Column E; this is E4:E95.

6. For the *known_x's*, use the values for temperature, weekend, and rain. This is B4:D95. Note that the dates in Column A are not being used as an independent variable. The amusement park is an established park, and there is nothing to indicate that attendance rises over the course of the season.

7. Use TRUE for the next argument, which asks whether the intercept should be forced to be 0. This is not a requirement in the current situation. You want to allow the intercept to be calculated normally.

8. Use 1 or TRUE for the *stats* argument.

9. Although you have now typed the complete formula, =LINEST(E4:E95,B4:D95,TRUE,TRUE), do not press the Enter key. This is one formula that returns many results. You have to tell Excel to interpret the formula as an array formula. To do this, hold down Ctrl+Shift while pressing Enter. The function returns a seemingly meaningless range of numbers, as shown in Figure 14.15.

10. Start labeling the regression results in the upper-right corner. The value in the upper-right corner is the y-intercept. This is equivalent to the result of the INTERCEPT function.

11. Working in the top row from right to left, look at the slopes of the independent variables. These appear backward from how you originally specified them. Your independent variables were temperature, weekend, and rain. The slope for the last independent variable is in the top-left corner of the results. In Figure 14.16, Cell G4 is the slope associated with rain. Cell H4 is the slope associated with weekend. Cell H5 is the slope associated with temperature.

12. Take a look at these numbers for a second to see if they make sense. The intercept says you are going to sell −75 snow cones each day. This initially seems wrong. However, the value in Column I says that you will sell 2.6 snow cones for every degree of temperature. Because the lowest minimum high temperature for the summer would be about 60 degrees, the result suggests that you would sell a minimum of (60 × 2.6), or about 156 snow cones, due to temperature. Adding the −75 and 156 gets you to a minimum of 80 snow cones on a sunny day. Cell H4 suggests that you would sell about 52 extra snow cones on a weekend. Cell G4 suggests that you would sell 102 fewer snow cones on a rainy day.

13. Fill in the rest of the labels for statistics. The second row of the results shows the standard error for the number above it. The first column of the third row returns the all-important r-squared value. If this value is close to 1, your model is doing a good job of predicting the data. The value of 0.95 shows that this model is fairly good. Row 3, Column 2 shows the standard error of Y. It is normal to have #N/A in any additional columns of Row 3. Row 4 contains the F statistic and degrees of freedom. Row 5 contains the sum of squares of the regression and the residual sum of squares. This is the number that Excel is trying to minimize when it fits the line using least squares.

14. In Column L, build a formula to predict sales with the results of the regression. This formula would be Intercept + Slope temp × Temp + Slope weekend × Weekend + Slope rain × Rain. The formula in Cell L4 is therefore =$J$4+$I$4*B4+$H$4*C4+$G$4*D4.

15. To visually compare the data, plot the actuals in Column E and the prediction in Column L on a chart. The chart in rows 12:22 shows that the prediction is tracking fairly well with the actual. There was a cold, rainy weekday near the beginning where the model predicted −10 sales versus an actual of 25.

16. For another interesting test, calculate the residual or error for each day. The data in Column M is the difference between L & E. Plot this data. You should see many small positive and negative values. (Notice that the scale of this chart is smaller than the original chart.) The values should swing from positive to negative frequently. The amount of scatter should not vary over time. You should not see many clusters of points that are either positive or negative. The chart in rows 24:34 shows that there are many positive residuals early in the summer, and fewer later in the summer. This might mean that the model is less successful at lower June temperatures than at higher August temperatures. Perhaps only real snow-cone fans buy the product at temperatures of 60 to 80. Above 80 degrees, more people might buy the product.

Troubleshooting LINEST

Remember that LINEST returns an array of values. In addition, you need to select a large enough range before entering the function, and you need to use Ctrl+Shift+Enter to enter the formula.

If you forget to use Ctrl+Shift+Enter, Excel returns just the top-left cell from the resultset. In the data set in Figure 14.15, this would be the slope for the final independent variable (-102.236). If you enter LINEST and receive just one value, you should follow these steps:

1. Select a range starting with the LINEST formula in the upper-left corner. The range should be five rows tall. It should be at least two columns wide for models with one *known_x* column. Add additional columns for additional *known_x* series.

2. Press the F2 key to edit the current LINEST formula.

3. Hold down Ctrl+Shift+Enter to reenter the formula as an array.

Alternatively, you can use the INDEX function to pluck one particular value out of the LINEST function. For example, if you wanted to retrieve the F statistic from Row 4, Column 1, you could use =INDEX(LINEST(E4:E95,B4:D95,TRUE,TRUE),4,1).

In the simpler situation when you have only one independent x variable, you can obtain the slope and y-intercept values directly by using the following formula for slope:

INDEX(LINEST(*known_y's,known_x's*),1)

Use the following formula for the y-intercept:

INDEX(LINEST(*known_y's,known_x's*),2)

Using FORECAST to Calculate Prediction for Any One Data Point

When you understand straight-line regression, you can use the FORECAST function to return a prediction for any point in the future.

Syntax:

=FORECAST(x,*known_y's,known_x's*)

The FORECAST function calculates, or predicts, a future value by using existing values. The predicted value is a y value for a given x value. The known values are existing x values and y values, and the new value is predicted by using linear regression. You can use this function to predict future sales, inventory requirements, or consumer trends.

The FORECAST function takes the following arguments:

- *x*—This is the data point for which you want to predict a value. If x is nonnumeric, FORECAST returns a #VALUE! error.

- *known_y's*—This is the dependent array or range of data.

- *known_x's*—This is the independent array or range of data.

 note

Note that FORECAST works only for straight-line regression. It also does not offer the capability to force the intercept to be 0. If you need this capability, you have to use LINEST and then build a prediction formula as in step 14 of the previous section or the TREND function as discussed in the next section.

If *known_y's* and *known_x's* are empty or contain a different number of data points, FORECAST returns an #N/A error. If the variance of *known_x's* equals 0, then FORECAST returns a #DIV/0! error.

Figure 14.17 shows actual sales data for the past decade. Years are in Column A, and sales are in Column C. The sales data in C2:C12 is the range of *known_y's*. The years in A2:A12 is the range of *known_x's*.

To predict sales for future periods, follow these steps:

1. Enter future years in A13:A217.
2. In Column B, enter Actual or Forecast for each row so that the person reading the table understands that the new values are a forecast.
3. To predict sales for 2011, enter this formula in Cell C13: =FORECAST(A13,$C$2:$C$12,$A$2:$A$12).
4. Copy the formula from Cell C13 down to C14:C17.

Figure 14.17
You use the FORECAST function to find the data point for one future time period.

C13 | =FORECAST(A13,$C$2:$C$12,$A$2:$A$12)

	A	B	C	D	E	F	G	H	I
1	Year	Type	Sales						
2	2000	Actual	5500						
3	2001	Actual	6500						
4	2002	Actual	7800						
5	2003	Actual	9000						
6	2004	Actual	11500						
7	2005	Actual	10600						
8	2006	Actual	10000						
9	2007	Actual	8600						
10	2008	Actual	10200						
11	2009	Actual	10500						
12	2010	Actual	10900						
13	2011	Forecast	11803.64	=FORECAST(A13,$C$2:$C$12,$A$2:$A$12)					
14	2012	Forecast	12239.09						
15	2013	Forecast	12674.55						
16	2014	Forecast	13110						
17	2015	Forecast	13545.45						

Using TREND to Calculate Many Future Data Points at Once

The TREND function is another array function. This means that it can return many values from a single formula. If you think about the previous use of FORECAST in Figure 14.17, you realize that Excel really had to perform the linear regression multiple times—once for each of the cells in C13:C17. It would be better if you could perform the regression once and have Excel calculate all the values from that regression. The TREND function helps you do this.

Syntax:

=TREND(*known_y's*,*known_x's*,new_x's,const)

The TREND function returns values along a linear trend. It fits a straight line (using the least-squares method) to the arrays *known_y's* and *known_x's*. It returns the y values along that line for the array of new_x's that you specify.

The TREND function takes the following arguments:

- *known_y's*—This is the set of y values you already know in the relationship y = mx + b. If the array *known_y's* is in a single column, each column of *known_x's* is interpreted as a separate variable. If the array *known_y's* is in a single row, each row of *known_x's* is interpreted as a separate variable.

- *known_x's*—This is an optional set of x values that you may already know in the relationship y = mx + b. The array *known_x's* can include one or more sets of variables. If only one variable is used, *known_y's* and *known_x's* can be ranges of any shape, as long as they have equal dimensions. If more than one variable is used, *known_y's* must be a vector (that is, a range with a height of one row or a width of one column). If *known_x's* is omitted, it is assumed to be the array {1,2,3,...} that is the same size as *known_y's*.

- new_x's—These are new x values for which you want TREND to return corresponding y values. new_x's must include a column (or row) for each independent variable, just as *known_x's* does. So, if *known_y's* is in a single column, *known_x's* and new_x's must have the same number of columns. If *known_y's* is in a single row, *known_x's* and new_x's must have the same number of rows. If you omit new_x's, it is assumed to be the same as *known_x's*. If you omit both *known_x's* and new_x's, they are assumed to be the array {1,2,3,...} that is the same size as *known_y's*.

- const—This is a logical value that specifies whether to force the constant b to equal 0. If const is TRUE or omitted, b is calculated normally. If *const* is FALSE, b is set equal to 0, and the m values are adjusted so that y = mx.

Case Study: Forecasting Using Regression Analysis

Suppose that you are responsible for forecasting the material needs for a company that supplies roofing material. You have historical trends of usage by year. You've included past hurricane and recession data because those events caused extraordinary demand. Your job is to predict how much roofing material you will sell, assuming that there are no hurricanes, but how much you might want to have lined up in case there are one, two, or three hurricanes. Here's what you do:

1. As in the worksheet shown in Figure 14.18, enter the actual data in A4:D23. Make the sales in Column D the *known_y's*.

2. Make the years, recession and hurricane data in Columns A:C the *known_x's*.

3. Enter a new table in A26:C33. You want to find the forecasted requirements for 2010 and 2011 for the possibility that there are zero, one, two, or three hurricanes. The year, recession, and hurricane columns must be in the same format as the *known_x's* in step 2.

4. Keep in mind that because the TREND function is an array function, it can return several answers from one formula. Select the range D26:D33. With that range selected, start to type the formula =TREND(.

5. Enter D5:D23 for *known_y's*, which are past sales. Enter A5:C23 for *known_x's*. The new x values are the data in A26:C33.

6. Ensure that your formula is now =TREND(D5:D23,A5:C23,A26:C33). To finish the formula, hold down Ctrl+Shift while pressing Enter.

Figure 14.18
The TREND function is an array formula that can do one regression and return many future data points.

	A	B	C	D	E	F	G	H
	D26		▼	*fx* {=TREND(D5:D23,A5:C23,A26:C33)}				
1	Demand for Roofing Materials in Florida							
3	Actual Demand							
4	Year	Recession	Hurricanes	Sales				
5	1991	1	0	51000				
6	1992	0	1	81650				
7	1993	0	0	61800				
8	1994	0	0	63050				
9	1995	0	0	67900				
10	1996	0	0	72750				
11	1997	0	0	78400				
12	1998	0	0	85850				
13	1999	0	0	92700				
14	2000	0	0	96900				
15	2001	1	0	95000				
16	2002	0	0	107100				
17	2003	0	0	107800				
18	2004	0	2	168450				
19	2005	0	2	170000				
20	2006	0	0	108000				
21	2007	0	0	109000				
22	2008	1	0	104030				
23	2009	2	0	92000				
25	Forecast Demand							
26	2010	1	0	115,347				
27	2010	1	1	145,043				
28	2010	1	2	174,739				
29	2010	1	3	204,435				
30	2011	0	0	131,424				
31	2011	0	1	161,119				
32	2011	0	2	190,815				
33	2011	0	3	220,511				
34								

The result is shown in D26:D33. The TREND function predicts that you will need a base level of 115,000 in 2010 with no hurricanes. With two hurricanes in 2010, demand would rise to 174,000.

Using LOGEST to Perform Exponential Regression

Some patterns in business follow a linear regression. However, other items are not linear at all. If you are a scientist monitoring the growth of bacteria in a Petri dish, you will see exponential growth in the generations.

If you try to fit an exponential growth to a straight line, you have a large error. If the *r*-squared from linear regression is too low, you can try using exponential regression to see if the pattern of data matches exponential regression better. For exponential regression, you use the LOGEST function, which is similar to the LINEST function.

Syntax:

=LOGEST(*known_y's*,*known_x's*,*const*,*stats*)

In regression analysis, the LOGEST function calculates an exponential curve that fits the data and returns an array of values that describes the curve. Because this function returns an array of values, it must be entered as an array formula. The equation for the curve is y = b*m^x or y = (b*(m1^x1)*(m2^x2)*_) (if there are multiple x values), where the dependent y value is a function of the independent x values. The m values are bases that correspond to each exponent x value, and b is a constant value.

The LOGEST function takes the following arguments:

- *known_y's*—This is the set of y values you already know in the relationship y = b × m^x. If the array *known_y's* is in a single column, each column of *known_x's* is interpreted as a separate variable. If the array *known_y's* is in a single row, each row of *known_x's* is interpreted as a separate variable.

- *known_x's*—This is an optional set of x values you may already know in the relationship y = b × m^x. The array *known_x's* can include one or more sets of variables. If only one variable is used, *known_y's* and *known_x's* can be ranges of any shape, as long as they have equal dimensions. If more than one variable is used, *known_y's* must be a range of cells with a height of one row or a width of one column (which is also known as a vector). If *known_x's* is omitted, it is assumed to be the array {1,2,3,...} that is the same size as *known_y's*.

- *const*—This is a logical value that specifies whether to force the constant b to equal 1. If *const* is TRUE or omitted, b is calculated normally. If *const* is FALSE, b is set equal to 1, and the m values are fitted to y = m^x.

- *stats*—This is a logical value that specifies whether to return additional regression statistics. If stats is TRUE, LOGEST returns the additional regression statistics (refer to Figure 14.16), so the returned array is {mn,mn-1,...,m1,b;sen,sen-1,...,se1,seb;r2,sey; F,df;ssreg,ssresid}. If stats is FALSE or omitted, LOGEST returns only the m coefficients and the constant b.

The more a plot of data resembles an exponential curve, the better the calculated line fits the data. Like LINEST, LOGEST returns an array of values that describes a relationship among the values, but LINEST fits a straight line to the data; LOGEST fits an exponential curve.

Performing an Exponential Regression

Figure 14.19 shows an estimated population in Column B and the generation in Column A. To perform an exponential regression, follow these steps:

1. Because there is one independent variable, the results from the regression occupy two columns, so find a blank range of the spreadsheet and select a range that is two columns wide by five rows tall, such as E2:F6.

2. Enter the beginning of the formula: =LOGEST(. Enter the *known_y's* as B2:B9 and the *known_x's* as A2:A9. Leave the *const* value blank. Specify TRUE for statistics. The formula should be =LOGEST(B2:B9,A2:A9,,TRUE).

3. Do not press Enter for the formula. Instead, hold down Ctrl+Shift while pressing Enter to tell Excel to interpret the result as an array formula and to return a table of values from LOGEST.

4. Add some labels to help interpret the statistics. The labels shown in Column D and G are examples.

5. To use the results of the regression in a prediction calculation, enter a different formula than with LINEST. The formula is Intercept × Slope^X. In Figure 14.19, to predict population values for a given generation in Cell I2, use =$F$2*$E$2^I2. Alternatively, you can use the GROWTH function, discussed in the next section.

Figure 14.19
When data is growing at an exponential rate, you use LOGEST to perform a regression analysis.

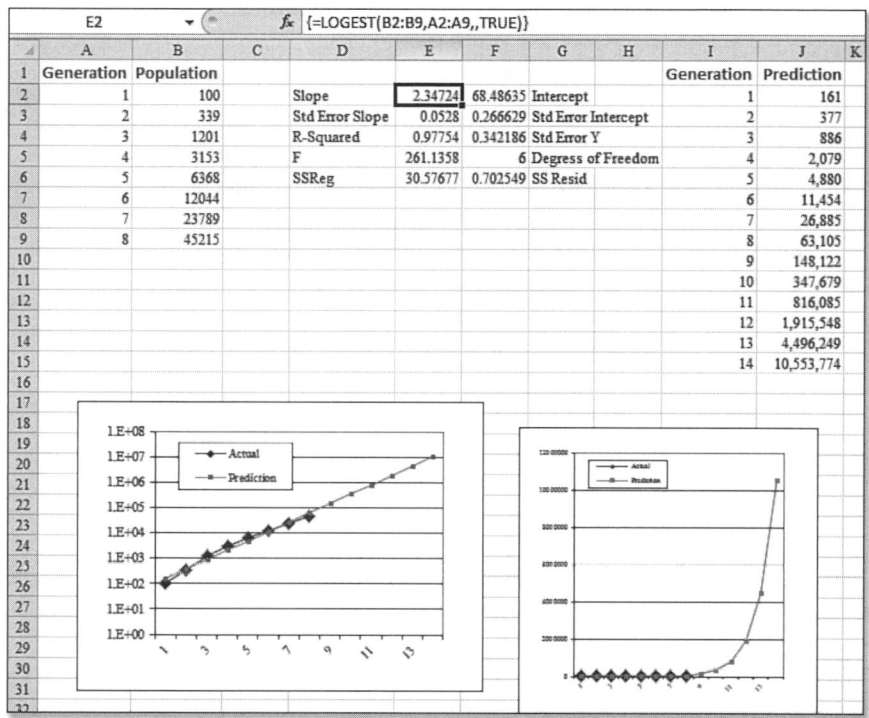

Using GROWTH to Predict Many Data Points from an Exponential Regression

As the TREND function is able to extrapolate points from a linear regression, the GROWTH function is able to extrapolate points from an exponential regression.

Syntax:

=GROWTH(*known_y's,known_x's,new_x's,const*)

The GROWTH function calculates predicted exponential growth by using existing data. GROWTH returns the y values for a series of new x values that you specify by using existing x values and y values. You can also use the GROWTH worksheet function to fit an exponential curve to existing x values and y values. This function takes the following arguments:

- *known_y's*—This is the set of y values you already know in the relationship $y = b \times m^\wedge x$. If the array *known_y's* is in a single column, each column of *known_x's* is interpreted as a separate variable. If the array *known_y's* is in a single row, each row of *known_x's* is interpreted as a separate variable. If any of the numbers in *known_y's* is 0 or negative, GROWTH returns a #NUM! error.

- *known_x's*—This is an optional set of x values that you may already know in the relationship $y = b \times m^\wedge x$. The array *known_x's* can include one or more sets of variables. If only one variable is used, *known_y's* and *known_x's* can be ranges of any shape, as long as they have equal dimensions. If more than one variable is used, *known_y's* must be a vector (that is, a range with a height of one row or a width of one column). If *known_x's* is omitted, it is assumed to be the array {1,2,3,...} that is the same size as *known_y's*.

- *new_x's*—These are new x values for which you want GROWTH to return corresponding y values. *new_x's* must include a column (or row) for each independent variable, just as *known_x's* does. So, if *known_y's* is in a single column, *known_x's* and *new_x's* must have the same number of columns. If *known_y's* is in a single row, *known_x's* and *new_x's* must have the same number of rows. If *new_x's* is omitted, it is assumed to be the same as *known_x's*. If both *known_x's* and *new_x's* are omitted, they are assumed to be the array {1,2,3,...} that is the same size as *known_y's*.

> **🅦 tip**
>
> When you have formulas that return arrays, you must enter them as array formulas after selecting the correct number of cells. To specify an array formula, you hold down Ctrl+Shift while pressing Enter.

- *const*—This is a logical value that specifies whether to force the constant b to equal 1. If *const* is TRUE or omitted, b is calculated normally. If *const* is FALSE, b is set equal to 1, and the m values are adjusted so that $y = m^\wedge x$.

In Figure 14.20, the original data is the population for the first 10 generations in A2:B11.

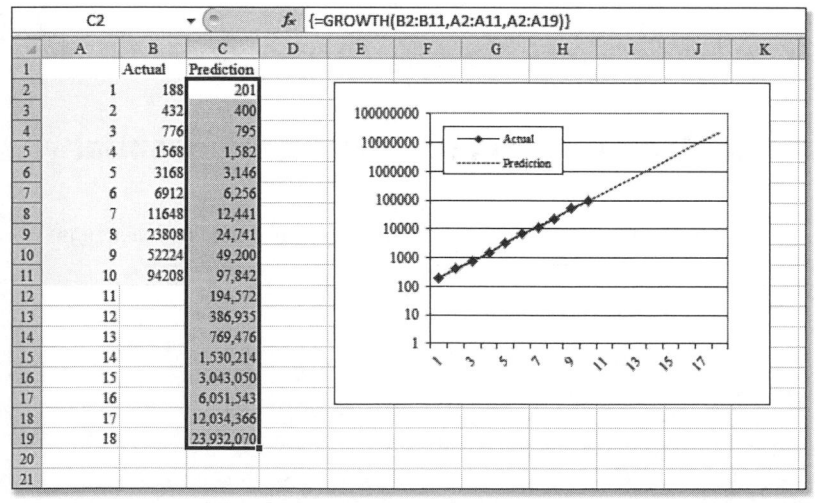

Figure 14.20
GROWTH performs an exponential regression and extrapolates the results in one step.

Exponential Regression Used to Predict Future Generations

It would be interesting to run an exponential regression and see the prediction for future generations but also for the known generations. This would allow you to see how well the prediction tracks with current values. To do this, follow these steps:

1. Add new generation numbers in A12:A19. The GROWTH function will use these numbers and return an array of values.

2. Select the entire range C2:C19 for the results before entering the formula.

3. Put the *known_y's* in B2:B11. The *known_x's* are in A2:A11. Put the new_x's in A2:A19. The formula is =GROWTH(B2:B11,A 2:A11,A2:A19).

4. After typing the formula, hold down Ctrl+Shift while pressing Enter. This should cause the formula to return values in each cell in C2:C19.

5. To visualize the original data and the prediction, plot A1:C19 on a line chart. Numbers at the end of the progression (24 million) make the scale of the chart so large that you cannot see the detail of the first 12 generations.

6. Right-click the numbers along the y-axis and select Format Axis. On the Scale tab, select Logarithmic Scale. The resulting chart allows you to examine both the smaller and larger numbers in the chart.

 note

I am somewhat jealous that Microsoft has named an obscure function after fellow Excel consultant Chip Pearson. I am lobbying Microsoft for the inclusion of a JELEN function, possibly used to measure the degree of laid-backness caused by the gel in your shoe insoles. Seriously, Chip Pearson's website is one of the best established sources of articles on the web about Excel. To peruse the articles, visit www.cpearson.com.

Using PEARSON to Determine Whether a Linear Relationship Exists

Remember that Excel blindly fits a regression line to any data set. The fact that Excel returns a regression line does not mean that you should use it to make any predictions. The initial question to ask yourself is, Does a linear relationship exist in this data?

The Pearson product–moment correlation coefficient, named after Karl Pearson, returns a value from −1.0 to +1.0. The calculation could make your head spin, but the important thing to know is that a PEARSON value closer to 1 or −1 means that a linear relationship exists. A value of 0 indicates no correlation between the independent and dependent variables.

Syntax:

=PEARSON(*array1*,*array2*)

The PEARSON function returns the Pearson product–moment correlation coefficient, r, a dimensionless index that ranges from −1.0 to 1.0, inclusive, and reflects the extent of a linear relationship between two data sets.

The PEARSON function takes the following arguments:

- *array1*—This is a set of independent values.

- *array2*—This is a set of dependent values.

The arguments must be either numbers or names, array constants, or references that contain numbers. If an array or a reference argument contains text, logical values, or empty cells, those values are ignored; however, cells that contain the value 0 are included. If *array1* and *array2* are empty or have a different number of data points, PEARSON returns an #N/A error.

The result of PEARSON is also sometimes known as r. Multiplying PEARSON by itself leads to the more famous r-squared test.

Using RSQ to Determine the Strength of a Linear Relationship

r-squared is a popular measure of how well a regression line explains the variability in the y values. It is popular because the values range from 0 to 1. Numbers close to 1 mean that the regression line does a great job of predicting the values. Numbers close to 0 mean that the regression result can't predict the values at all.

r-squared is the statistic in the third row, first column of a LINEST function. It is also the square of the PEARSON function. You could use =INDEX(LINEST(),3,1) or =PEARSON()^2. But instead, Excel provides the easy-to-remember RSQ function.

Syntax:

=RSQ(*known_y's*,*known_x's*)

The RSQ function returns the square of the Pearson product–moment correlation coefficient through data points in *known_y's* and *known_x's*. The r-squared value can be interpreted as the proportion of the variance in y that is attributable to the variance in x.

> ➥ *For more information on the Pearson coefficient, see the section on the* PEARSON *function, earlier in this chapter.*

The RSQ function takes the following arguments:

- *known_y's*—This is an array or a range of data points.

- *known_x's*—This is an array or a range of data points.

The arguments must be either numbers or names, arrays, or references that contain numbers. If an array or a reference argument contains text, logical values, or empty cells, those values are ignored; however, cells that contain the value 0 are included. If *known_y's* and *known_x's* are empty or have a different number of data points, RSQ returns an #N/A error.

Figure 14.21 shows four data sets and their associated r-squared values:

- The chart in the top-left corner has an *r*-squared near 0. There is little predictive ability in this regression line. In fact, the regression line is practically a horizontal line drawn through the mean of the data points.

Figure 14.21
As r-squared approaches 1.0, the predictive ability of the regression line improves.

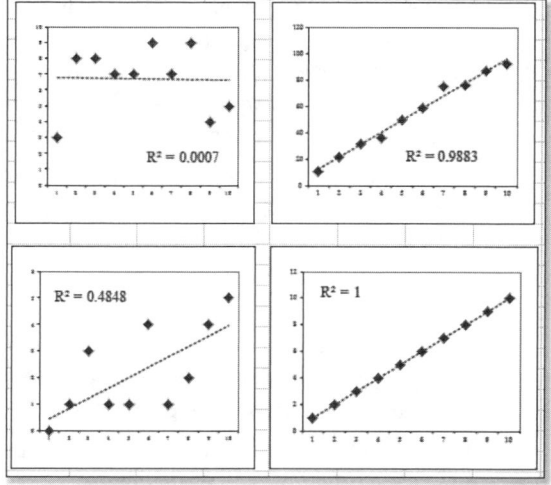

- The chart in the lower-left corner has an *r*-squared of 0.48. There is a lot of variability in the dots, but they do seem to trend up. There are huge relative errors on certain data points (for example, the value of y = 1 when x = 7).

- The chart in the upper-right corner shows a nearly perfect correlation. The *r*-squared is appropriately high, at 0.988. This means that most of the variability in y is explained by x. There are some tiny minor variations above or below the line, but the regression is doing a great job.

- The final chart, in the lower right, illustrates a perfect correlation and an *r*-squared of 1.0. Every occurrence of y falls exactly on the regression line.

Using STEYX to Calculate Standard Regression Error

Standard error is a measure of the quality of a regression line. In rough terms, the standard error is the size of an error that you might encounter for any particular point on the line. Smaller errors are better, and larger errors are worse. Standard error can also be used to calculate a confidence interval for any point.

Syntax:

=STEYX(*known_y's*,*known_x's*)

The STEYX function returns the standard error of the predicted y value for each x in the regression. The standard error is a measure of the amount of error in the prediction of y for an individual x.

The STEYX function takes the following arguments:

- *known_y's*—This is an array or a range of dependent data points.

- *known_x's*—This is an array or a range of independent data points.

The arguments must be either numbers or names, arrays, or references that contain numbers. If an array or a reference argument contains text, logical values, or empty cells, those values are ignored; however, cells that contain the value 0 are included. If *known_y's* and *known_x's* are empty or have a different number of data points, STEYX returns an #N/A error.

> **note**
>
> COVARIANCE.P is the new name for the old COVAR function. COVAR is included in Excel 2010 for backward compatibility.

To calculate standard error, you square all the residuals and add them together. Then you divide by the number of points, excluding the starting and ending points. Finally, you take the square root of that result to calculate standard error.

In general, a lower standard error is better than a higher one. A standard error of 2,000 when you are trying to predict the price of a $30,000 car isn't too bad. A standard error of 2,000 when you are trying to predict the price of a $3 jar of pickles is horrible. You need to compare the standard error to the size of the value you are predicting.

In Figure 14.22, two regressions attempt to predict the price of a car based on either mileage or age. The standard error for the mileage method is a little less than the standard error for the age method.

G6			f_x	=STEYX(D5:D48,B5:B48)

	B	C	D	E	F	G	H
1	Used Land Rover Discovery for Sale						
2	Within 50 miles of 44685						
3							
4	Age	Mileage	Price				
5	3	35846	29995			Age	Mileage
6	2	28000	29250		Std Error	3673.4856	3259.68
7	3	21495	28890				
8	2	34357	25980				
9	4	35571	24900				
10	3	30583	23990				

Figure 14.22
Standard error is another measure of the quality of a regression line.

Using COVARIANCE.P to Determine Whether Two Variables Vary Together

Covariance is a measure of how greatly two variables vary together. If the value is 0, the variables do not appear to be related. For positive values, covariance indicates that as x increases, y also increases. For negative values, covariance indicates that as x increases, y decreases.

Syntax:

```
=COVARIANCE.P(array1,array2)
=COVARIANCE.S(array1,array2)
```

The COVARIANCE.P function returns covariance, the average of the products of deviations for each data point pair. You use covariance to determine the relationship between two data sets. For example, you can examine whether greater income accompanies greater levels of education. COVARIANCE.P assumes that the arrays represent an entire population. If the arrays are a sample of the population, use the new COVARIANCE.S function.

The `COVARIANCE.P` and `COVARIANCE.S` functions take the following arguments:

- *array1*—This is the first cell range of integers.

- *array2*—This is the second cell range of integers.

The arguments must be either numbers or names, arrays, or references that contain numbers. If an array or a reference argument contains text, logical values, or empty cells, those values are ignored; however, cells that contain the value 0 are included. If *array1* and *array2* have different numbers of data points, `COVARIANCE.P` returns an #N/A error. If either *array1* or *array2* is empty, `COVARIANCE.P` returns a #DIV/0! error.

Covariances can become incredibly large. The unit of measurement is on the order of x times y. For a dimensionless measurement of correlation, you use `CORREL` instead of `COVARIANCE.P`.

In Figure 14.23, the `CORREL` function measures the covariance between mileage and price. As mileage increases, price decreases.

Using CORREL to Calculate Positive or Negative Correlation

Instead of using covariance, you can calculate a correlation coefficient for two arrays. Let's use the mileage and price comparison from Figure 14.23. The two values would have a strong positive correlation if price went up as mileage went up. A perfect positive correlation would result in a correlation coefficient of 1.0.

Figure 14.23
`COVARARIANCE.P` shows that price and mileage are inversely correlated.

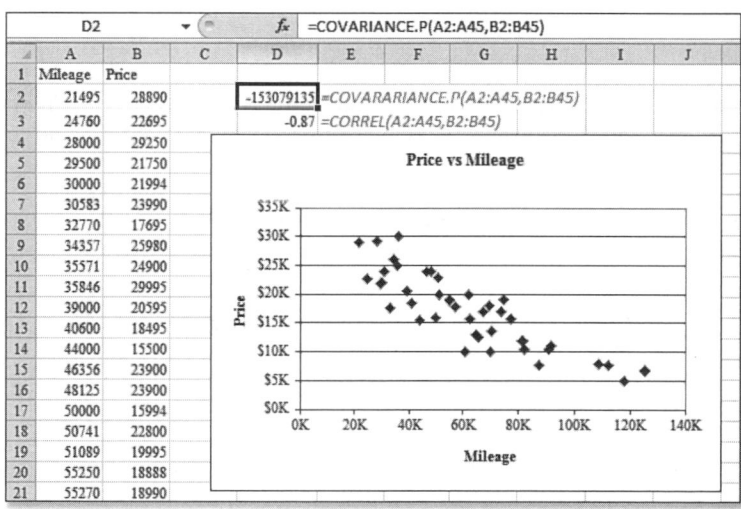

It is also possible (as in the mileage–price comparison case) for values to have an inverse correlation. As mileage increases, the price tends to decrease. If mileage were the only factor in the price of a car, the correlation coefficient would be –1.0 to indicate a perfect inverse correlation.

A correlation coefficient of 0 indicates that there is no correlation between the values.

Syntax:

=CORREL(*array1*,*array2*)

The CORREL function returns the correlation coefficient of the *array1* and *array2* cell ranges. You use the correlation coefficient to determine the relationship between two properties. For example, you can examine the relationship between a location's average temperature and the use of air conditioners.

The CORREL function takes the following arguments:

- *array1*—This is a cell range of values.

- *array2*—This is a second cell range of values.

The arguments must be numbers or names, arrays, or references that contain numbers. If an array or reference argument contains text, logical values, or empty cells, those values are ignored; however, cells that contain the value 0 are included. If *array1* and *array2* have a different number of data points, CORREL returns an #N/A error. If either *array1* or *array2* is empty, or if s (the standard deviation) of their values equals 0, CORREL returns a #DIV/0! error.

In Figure 14.24, price and mileage have a correlation coefficient of -0.87. This indicates a fairly strong inverse correlation. As mileage increases, price decreases. The bottom-left chart shows two series with no correlation at all; the correlation coefficient is very close to 0. The bottom-right chart shows two series with perfect positive correlation of 1.0.

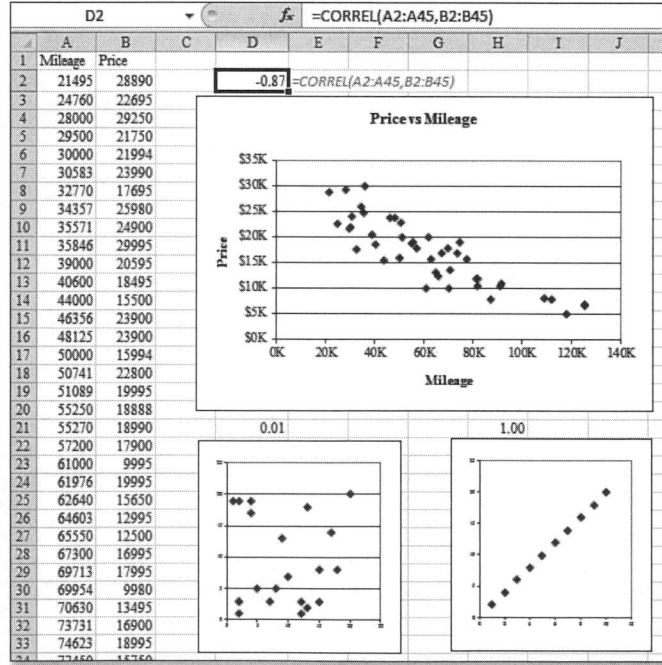

Figure 14.24
The CORREL function returns values from −1.0 to 1.0. Values near 0 indicate no correlation.

Using FISHER to Perform Hypothesis Testing on Correlations

The Pearson value does not have a normal distribution. The graph of expected r values skews heavily toward 1. A statistician named Fisher found a formula that would transform the skewed r value into a normal distribution. You use the FISHER function to convert an r value. To take a FISHER value and return it to an r value, you use FISHERINV.

Syntax:

=FISHER(*x*)

The FISHER function returns the Fisher transformation at x. This transformation produces a function that is approximately normally distributed rather than skewed. You use this function to perform hypothesis testing on the correlation coefficient.

The argument x is a numeric value for which you want the transformation. If x is nonnumeric, FISHER returns a #VALUE! error. If x is less than or equal to –1 or if x is greater than or equal to 1, FISHER returns a #NUM! error.

Syntax:

=FISHERINV(*y*)

The FISHERINV function returns the inverse of the Fisher transformation. You use this transformation when analyzing correlations between ranges or arrays of data. If y is equal to FISHER(*x*), then FISHERINV(y) is equal to x.

The argument y is the value for which you want to perform the inverse of the transformation. If y is nonnumeric, FISHERINV returns a #VALUE! error.

Using SKEW and KURTOSIS

Two final statistics are used to describe a population:

- **Skew**—Skew is an indicator of symmetry. Actually, it is a measure of lack of symmetry. A skew value of 0 indicates that the population is perfectly symmetrical around the mean. Negative values indicate that the data is skewed to the left of the mean. Positive values indicate that the data is skewed to the right of the mean. You can use Excel's SKEW function to calculate skew.

- **Kurtosis**—Kurtosis indicates whether the distribution contains a spiky peak or is relatively flat. This measure compares a population to the standard normal distribution. If the kurtosis is less than 0, the population is flatter than the normal distribution. If the kurtosis is greater than 0, the population is spikier than the normal distribution. You use Excel's KURT function to calculate kurtosis.

In Figure 14.25, there are two populations. The population in Column A contains one large spike of 19 data points at 2.36 inches and a single data point at 60.25 inches. You can think of this as a tank with 1 shark and 19 goldfish. The average size is 5.25 inches. The tail of the distribution is a very long tail to the right of the 5.25 inches mean, indicating a positive skew. The 19 goldfish cause a very spiky data point, causing a high kurtosis.

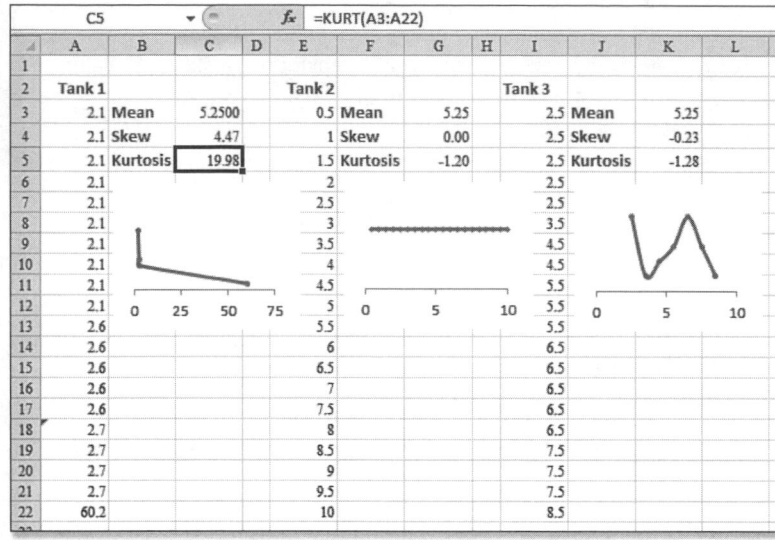

Figure 14.25
Skew and kurtosis return information about the symmetry and spikiness of a data set.

In Column E, the data points are uniformly distributed around the mean. The data is perfectly symmetrical, leading to a skew of 0.00. No data point has more than one member, causing the data to be extremely flat, with a negative kurtosis.

Syntax:

=SKEW(*number1*,*number2*, . . .)

The SKEW function returns the skewness of a distribution. Skewness characterizes the degree of asymmetry of a distribution around its mean. Positive skewness indicates a distribution with an asymmetric tail extending toward more positive values. Negative skewness indicates a distribution with an asymmetric tail extending toward more negative values.

The arguments *number1*,*number2*... are 1 to 255 arguments for which you want to calculate skewness. You can also use a single array or a reference to an array instead of arguments separated by commas. The arguments must be either numbers or names, arrays, or references that contain numbers. If an array or a reference argument contains text, logical values, or empty cells, those values are ignored; however, cells that contain the value 0 are included. If there are fewer than three data points, or if the sample standard deviation is 0, SKEW returns a #DIV/0! error.

Syntax:

=KURT(*number1*,*number2*, . . .)

The KURT function returns the kurtosis of a data set. Kurtosis characterizes the relative peakedness or flatness of a distribution compared with the normal distribution. Positive kurtosis indicates a relatively peaked distribution. Negative kurtosis indicates a relatively flat distribution.

The arguments *number1,number2, . . .* are 1 to 255 arguments for which you want to calculate kurtosis. You can also use a single array or a reference to an array instead of arguments separated by commas. The arguments must be either numbers or names, arrays, or references that contain numbers. If an array or a reference argument contains text, logical values, or empty cells, those values are ignored; however, cells that contain the value 0 are included. If there are fewer than four data points, or if the standard deviation of the sample equals zero, KURT returns a #DIV/0! error.

Examples of Functions for Inferential Statistics

Inferential statistics is the powerful side of statistics. With descriptive statistics, you can describe a data set. Describing a data set might allow you to understand the data set better. With regression, you use past trends to predict future results. With inferential statistics, you extrapolate information about a sample of the population to make predictions about the entire population.

Understanding the Language of Inferential Statistics

Excel 2010 offers functions for 14 different types of probability distributions. Each distribution predicts a different shape of the population. You'll read about the various distributions in the following sections, but for now, consider the distribution in Figure 14.26.

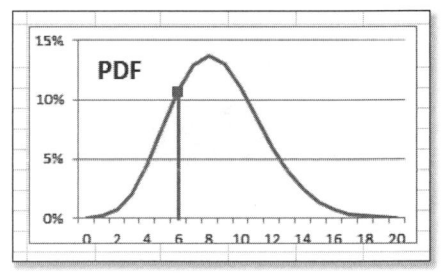

Figure 14.26
The Point Density Function describes the probability that a member of a population has one specific value.

If you are asked to predict the likelihood that a member of a population has a value of 6, you can look at Figure 14.26 and see that the probability is just over 10%. This value is called the Point Density Function, or PDF.

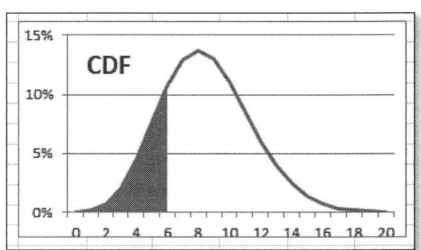

Figure 14.27
The Cumulative Density Function describes the probability that a member of a population is less than one specific value.

A different question would be to estimate what percentage of the population has a value of 6 or less? This is known as the Cumulative Density Function (CDF). Figure 14.27 graphs the CDF. To calculate the CDF without Excel, you would have to use a little calculus to integrate from 0 to 6 over the distribution function. Thankfully, with Excel, you do not have use calculus!

All 14 distribution functions in Excel calculate both the PDF and CDF. Look for an argument in each function called Cumulative. If you specify True for Cumulative, you are getting the CDF from Figure 14.27. If you specify False, you are getting the PDF function from Figure 14.26.

When you see a function that includes .DIST, this function is used to calculate either the PDF or the CDF, depending on whether you specify Cumulative = False or Cumulative = True.

Here is a simple math quiz: If the .DIST function predicts that there is a 30% chance the value is 6 or less, what is the prediction that the value is more than 6? Although you would have needed Calculus to figure out the 30% answer, after you know the 30% answer, you don't even need a calculator to know that the probability of the answer being more than 6 is 70%.

If the area in Figure 14.27 is 30%, the area in Figure 14.28 is going to be 100% - 30%, or 70%. That is called the right-tailed CDF. You can calculate the right-tailed CDF by subtracting the left-tailed CDF from 100%. But, for a matter of convenience, Excel offers .RT versions of Chi-Squared, F, and T distributions.

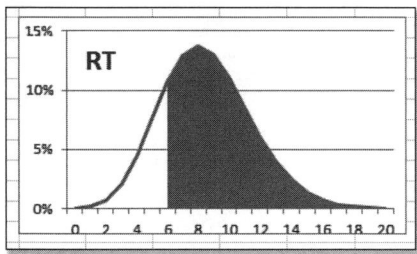

Figure 14.28
Three distributions in Excel include a function to calculate the right-tailed CDF.

Some distributions are symmetric around a mean. With these distributions, you might ask about the probability of a member of the population being with x% of the mean. The opposite question is to find the probability that a member will fall outside of that area. This is known as a two-tailed CDF and is shown in the bottom chart in Figure 14.29. Excel offers a 2T version of the Student's T distribution.

The real-life applications of inferential statistics usually involve a different type of question. The manager of a bank wants to make sure that the staffing levels allow there to be no wait 80% of the time. Whereas the DIST function can tell you the probability for a certain value, the INV function does the opposite. It tells you the value at a certain probability. The INV functions are always cumulative.

Of the 14 types of distributions, 9 of them offer an inverse function.

To recap, when you see an inferential statistics function in Excel, it will start with the name of the distribution and be followed by one or more suffixes:

- `.DIST` indicates that you can calculate the PDF or CDF.

- `.RT` indicates it will calculate the right-tailed CDF.

Figure 14.29
The area shown in the lower chart is a two-tailed CDF. T.DIST.2T is
the only function to calculate two-tailed probability.

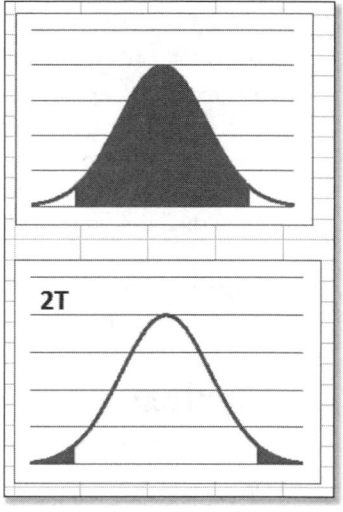

- .2T indicates it will calculate the two-tailed CDF.

- .INV indicates that it will find the value at which the CDF meets a certain probability.

Figure 14.30 shows a matrix of the distribution functions in Excel 2010.

Figure 14.30
Functions for inferential statistics in
Excel 2010.

Excel 2010 Statistical Functions

Distribution	PDF/CDF	Right-tailed CDF	Inverse left-tail CDF	Inverse right-tailed
Beta	BETA.DIST		BETA.INV	
Binomial	BINOM.DIST		BINOM.INV	
Chi-squared	CHISQ.DIST	CHISQ.DIST.RT	CHISQ.INV	CHISQ.INV.RT
Exponential	EXPON.DIST			
F	F.DIST	F.DIST.RT	F.INV	F.INV.RT
Gamma	GAMMA.DIST		GAMMA.INV	
Hypergeometric	HYPGEOM.DIST			
Logonormal	LOGNORM.DIST		LOGNORM.INV	
Negative Binomial	NEGBINOM.DIST			
Normal	NORM.DIST		NORM.INV	
Standard Normal	NORM.S.DIST		NORM.S.INV	
Poisson	POISSON.DIST			
Student's t	T.DIST	T.DIST.RT	T.INV	
Student's t (2 tailed)		T.DIST.2T		T.INV.2T
Weibull	WEIBULL.DIST			

All functions have been renamed. Items in yellow are additions to Excel 2010.

Using BINOM.DIST to Determine Probability

A binomial test is a situation in which there are only two possible outcomes: Either an event happens or it does not happen.

For example, suppose you have determined that on several nights of the week, someone has been sneaking in and eating leftovers from the department fridge. You don't know if it is the night security guard or the cleaning crew or even just Charley, who works later than everyone else. After tracking this behavior for a month, you determine that food has been missing 27% of the time. How many days next week will food be missing? The BINOM.DIST function can answer this question.

caution

100% of the function names in Figure 14.30 are new in Excel 2010. None of those function names are backward compatible with Excel 2007 or earlier.

Syntax:

=BINOM.DIST(*number_s,trials, probability_s,cumulative*)

The BINOM.DIST function returns the individual term binomial distribution probability. You use BINOM.DIST in problems with a fixed number of tests or trials, when the outcomes of any trial are only success or failure, when trials are independent, and when the probability of success is constant throughout the experiment. For example, BINOM.DIST can calculate the probability that two of the next three babies born will be male.

The BINOM.DIST function takes the following arguments:

- *number_s*—This is the number of successes in trials.

- *trials*—This is the number of independent trials.

- *probability_s*—This is the probability of success on each trial.

- *cumulative*—This is a logical value that determines the form of the function. If cumulative is TRUE, then BINOM.DIST returns the cumulative distribution function, which is the *probability* that there are at most number_s successes; if cumulative is FALSE, BINOM.DIST returns the probability mass function, which is the probability that there are number_s successes.

tip

The BINOM.DIST always calculates the probability starting from the left side of the curve. If you wanted to calculate the probability of three or more successes next week, you would have to use one minus the probability of two or fewer successes, as shown in Cell B22.

number_s and *trials* are truncated to integers. If number_s, trials, or *probability_s* is non-numeric, BINOM.DIST returns a #VALUE! error. If number_s is less than 0 or number_s is greater than trials, BINOMDIST returns a #NUM! error. If *probability_s* is less than 0 or *probability_s* is greater than 1, BINOM.DIST returns a #NUM! error.

In Figure 14.31, range B5:B10 calculates the probability that food will be missing x days next week. In each case, trials is 5 because there are five workdays next week. The *probability_s* is 0.27.

Cell B15 calculates the cumulative probability that 0 or 1 successes will be encountered next week.

Figure 14.31
For tests that are either TRUE or
FALSE, the BINOM.DIST function can
calculate the probability of events.

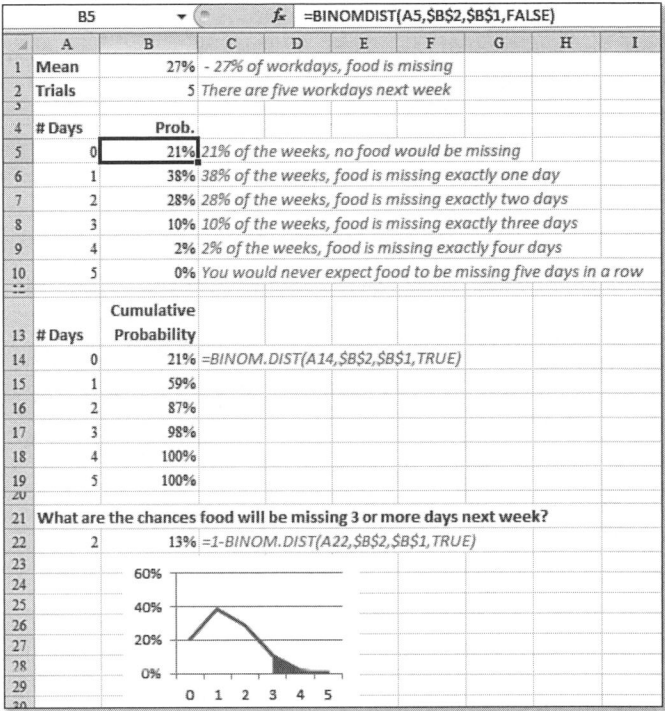

	A	B	C	D	E	F	G	H	I
	B5	▼	f_x =BINOMDIST(A5,$B$2,$B$1,FALSE)						
1	Mean	27%	- 27% of workdays, food is missing						
2	Trials	5	There are five workdays next week						
3									
4	# Days	Prob.							
5	0	21%	21% of the weeks, no food would be missing						
6	1	38%	38% of the weeks, food is missing exactly one day						
7	2	28%	28% of the weeks, food is missing exactly two days						
8	3	10%	10% of the weeks, food is missing exactly three days						
9	4	2%	2% of the weeks, food is missing exactly four days						
10	5	0%	You would never expect food to be missing five days in a row						
13	# Days	Cumulative Probability							
14	0	21%	=BINOM.DIST(A14,$B$2,$B$1,TRUE)						
15	1	59%							
16	2	87%							
17	3	98%							
18	4	100%							
19	5	100%							
21	What are the chances food will be missing 3 or more days next week?								
22	2	13%	=1-BINOM.DIST(A22,$B$2,$B$1,TRUE)						

Using BINOM.INV to Cover Most of the Possible Binomial Events

Many tests are binomial, as described in the preceding section. Suppose you are exhibiting at a trade show. You expect 2,000 attendees at the trade show. Based on data from past trade shows, you predict that there is a 17% chance that an attendee will visit your booth and take a catalog. Your goal is to have enough catalogs so that you will be 95% sure to have enough catalogs for everyone. You can use the BINOM.INV function to predict how many catalogs you need.

 note

BINOM.DIST is a new name in Excel 2010. For compatibility with legacy versions of Excel, use BINOMDIST instead.

Syntax:

=BINOM.INV(trials,probability_s,alpha)

The BINOM.INV function returns the smallest value for which the cumulative binomial distribution is greater than or equal to a criterion value. You use this function for quality assurance applications. For example, you can use BINOM.INV to determine the greatest number of defective parts you can allow to come off an assembly line run without needing to reject the entire lot.

The BINOM.INV function takes the following arguments:

- *trials*—This is the number of Bernoulli trials.

- *probability_s*—This is the probability of a success on each trial.

- *alpha*—This is the criterion value.

If any argument is nonnumeric, BINOM.INV returns a #VALUE! error. If trials is not an integer, it is truncated. If trials is less than 0, BINOM.INV returns a #NUM! error. If *probability_s* is less than 0 or if *probability_s* is greater than 1, BINOM.INV returns a #NUM! error. If alpha is less than 0 or if alpha is greater than 1, BINOM.INV returns a #NUM! error.

In the trade show example, the number of trials is 2,000: Each attendee has a chance of picking up a catalog. The *probability_s* is 17%, and *alpha* is 0.95, although it would be interesting to see how many catalogs could be required at each level. Using this information, you follow these steps to determine how many catalogs you need:

1. Build a range with different values for alpha in Column A.

2. End the formula =BINOM.INV($B$2,$B$1,A8) in Cell B8.

3. Copy the formula from Cell B8 to the other cells in Column B.

As shown in Figure 14.32, you need to have 368 catalogs for the trade show.

 **note**

In legacy versions of Excel, BINOM.INV was called CRITBINOM.

	B5		▼	f_x	=BINOM.INV($B$2,$B$1,A5)		
	A	B	C	D	E	F	G	H
1	Mean	17%	- *percent chance of any one attendee taking a catalog*					
2	Trials	2000	*Number of attendees expected*					
3								
4	Confidenc	# catalogs						
5	70%	349	=BINOM.INV($B$2,$B$1,A5)					
6	80%	354						
7	90%	362						
8	95%	368						
9	99%	380						
10								

Figure 14.32
Based on response rates at last year's trade show, you can use BINOM.INV to predict how many catalogs to print.

Using NEGBINOM.DIST to Calculate Probability

It is a fact that LeBron James has a career free-throw percentage of 0.741. What are the odds that James would miss three free throws before he makes one free throw? You can use Excel's NEGBINOM.DIST function to figure this out.

Syntax:

=NEGBINOM.DIST(*number_f*,number_s,probability_s)

The NEGBINOM.DIST function returns the negative binomial distribution. It returns the probability that there will be *number_f* failures before the *number_s*th success, when the constant probability of a success is *probability_s*.

This function is similar to the binomial distribution function, except that the number of successes is fixed, and the number of trials is variable. As with the binomial distribution function, trials are assumed to be independent. For example, you need to find 10 people who have excellent reflexes, and you know the probability that a candidate has these qualifications is 0.3. NEGBINOM.DIST calculates the probability that you will interview a certain number of unqualified candidates before finding all 10 qualified candidates.

The NEGBINOM.DIST function takes the following arguments:

- *number_f*—This is the number of failures.

- *number_s*—This is the threshold number of successes.

- *probability_s*—This is the probability of a success.

 **note**

In Excel 2007, this function was called NEGBINOMDIST.

number_f and number_s are truncated to integers. If any argument is nonnumeric, NEGBINOM. DIST returns a #VALUE! error. If *probability_s* is less than 0 or if probability is greater than 1, NEGBINOM.DIST returns a #NUM! error. If (*number_f* + number_s – 1) is less than or equal to 0, NEGBINOM.DIST returns a #NUM! error.

To solve the LeBron James problem, you use =NEGBINOM.DIST(3,1,0.741,0). The answer is a 1.28% probability.

Using POISSON.DIST to Predict a Number of Discrete Events Over Time

Suppose you have to predict the number of discrete events that will happen over a certain period of time. This might be the number of customers who walk into a bank in an hour. It might be the number of lightning strikes on the John Hancock Building in a year. (It can also be discrete events that occur in a certain distance or area or any other measurement.)

Unlike the binomial distribution, in which an event either happens or does not happen, the Poisson distribution can be zero, one, two, three, and so on events in the period. The nature of the Poisson distribution is that before the third customer can walk into the bank, the second customer has to walk into the bank. In theory, if you had a run on the bank, the upper limit would be the number of total account holders, but in practice, there is probably some logical upper limit to how many customers walk in, such as the number that walk in during a Friday payday lunch hour.

If you measure the average number of customers per hour over the several weeks, you can use this number to predict the likelihood that a particular number of customers will enter the bank in any hour by using the POISSON.DIST function.

Syntax:

=POISSON.DIST(*x,mean,cumulative*)

The POISSON.DIST function returns the Poisson distribution. A common application of the Poisson distribution is predicting the number of events over a specific time, such as the number of cars arriving at a toll plaza in one minute. This function takes the following arguments:

- *x*—This is the number of events.

- *mean*—This is the expected numeric value.

- *cumulative*—This is a logical value that determines the form of the probability distribution returned.

If *x* is not an integer, it is truncated. If x or mean is nonnumeric, POISSON.DIST returns a #VALUE! error. If x is less than or equal to U, POISSON.DIST returns a #NUM! error. If mean is less than or equal to 0, POISSON.DIST returns a #NUM! error. If cumulative is TRUE, POISSON.DIST returns the cumulative Poisson probability that the number of random events occurring will be between 0 and x, inclusive; if cumulative is FALSE, it returns the Poisson probability mass function that the number of events occurring will be exactly *x*.

 **note**

In Excel 2007, this function was called POISSON.

To solve the bank customer example, follow these steps:

1. Calculate the mean number of customers entering the bank per hour over several weeks. Enter this in Cell B1 of the worksheet.

2. In A4:A24, enter the numbers from 0 to 20.

3. In Column B, calculate the probability that exactly *n* customers will enter the bank. In Cell B4, enter the formula =POISSON.DIST($A4,$B$1,FALSE).

4. In Column C, calculate the probability that 0 to n customers will enter the bank. In Cell C4, enter the formula =POISSON.DIST($A4,$B$1,TRUE).

In Figure 14.33, you can see that 84% of the time, your number of customers is expected to be between 0 and 11 customers per hour. If you staff up to handle 11 customers per hour, you should be covered 85% of the time.

Using FREQUENCY to Categorize Continuous Data

The past few examples count whole numbers. It would be fairly difficult to have 0.3 persons walk into a bank. The outcome from the Poisson distribution would therefore have to be a whole number.

Other measurements are continuous. The speed of a car passing a checkpoint is an example. Depending on the accuracy of the radar unit, a car could be determined to be going 55.1, 55.2, 55.3, 55.4 and so on miles per hour. It would not make sense to try to predict how many cars will be going exactly 55.0123 miles per hour. If you did, you would be lucky to have a height of 2 for any point along the continuous scale. Typically, the prediction question would be, What percentage of cars are likely to be going between 65 and 70 miles per hour?

When you are working with a continuous range of measurements, the normal procedure is to group the measurements into ranges. Statisticians call each range a *bin*.

Figure 14.33
You can figure the number of customers per hour by using POISSON.DIST.

	B4	▼ (●	f_x	=POISSON($A4,$B$1,FALSE)		
▲	A	B	C	D	E	F	G
1	Mean	8.5	Average number of customers per hour at the bank			
2						
3		Individual Probability	CDF			
4	0	0.02%	0.02%			
5	1	0.17%	0.19%			
6	2	0.74%	0.93%			
7	3	2.08%	3.01%			
8	4	4.43%	7.44%			
9	5	7.52%	14.96%			
10	6	10.66%	25.62%			
11	7	12.94%	38.56%			
12	8	13.75%	52.31%			
13	9	12.99%	65.30%			
14	10	11.04%	76.34%			
15	11	8.53%	84.87%			
16	12	6.04%	90.91%			
17	13	3.95%	94.86%			
18	14	2.40%	97.26%			
19	15	1.36%	98.62%			
20	16	0.72%	99.34%			
21	17	0.36%	99.70%			
22	18	0.17%	99.87%			
23	19	0.08%	99.95%			
24	20	0.03%	99.98%			
25						

In Figure 14.34, the left chart shows the frequency curve for the speed of 2,000 cars passing a highway checkpoint. The recording unit measured speeds to the accuracy of 0.1 mile. The curve is incredibly noisy, with intense variation from point to point.

Figure 14.34
With continuous variables, you can group the observed values into bins to see the underlying distribution curve emerge.

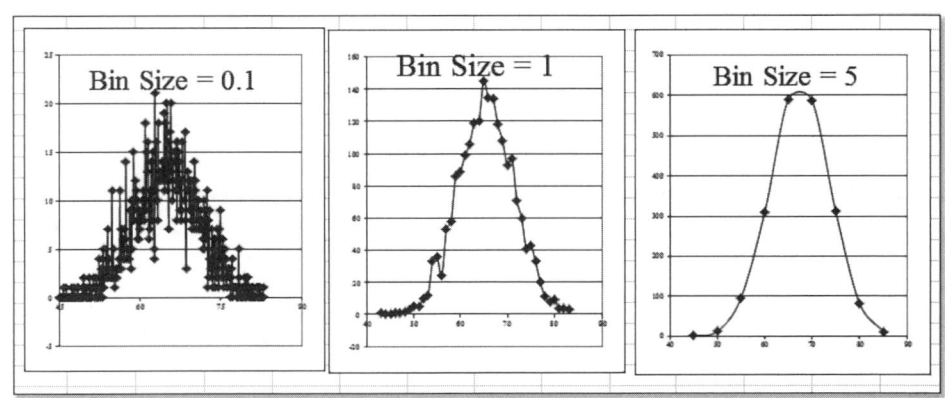

The middle chart shows the frequency curve after the data has been fit into bins of 1 mph each. There is still some noise in the distribution. For some reason, fewer people happened to be going 56 mph.

The right chart shows the frequency curve after the data has been fit into bins of 5 mph each. This curve is very smooth and shows that the data points seem to follow the normal bell curve.

The process of grouping data into bins is handled with another array function: the FREQUENCY function.

Syntax:

=FREQUENCY(*data_array*,*bins_array*)

The FREQUENCY function calculates how often values occur within a range of values, and it returns a vertical array of numbers. For example, you can use FREQUENCY to count the number of test scores that fall within ranges of scores. Because FREQUENCY returns an array, it must be entered as an array formula.

The FREQUENCY function takes the following arguments:

- *data_array*—This is an array of or a reference to a set of values for which you want to count frequencies. If data_array contains no values, FREQUENCY returns an array of zeros.

- *bins_array*—This is an array of or a reference to intervals into which you want to group the values in *data_array*. If *bins_array* contains no values, FREQUENCY returns the number of elements in *data_array*.

You enter FREQUENCY as an array formula after you select a range of adjacent cells into which you want the returned distribution to appear.

The number of elements in the returned array is one more than the number of elements in *bins_array*. The extra element in the returned array returns the count of any values above the highest interval. For example, when counting three ranges of values (intervals) that are entered into three cells, you need to be sure to enter FREQUENCY into four cells for the results. The extra cell returns the number of values in *data_array* that are greater than the third interval value. FREQUENCY ignores blank cells and text.

To use the FREQUENCY function, follow these steps:

1. Figure out the expected range of values in the original data set. You can do this by sorting the data set or by using the MIN and MAX functions.

2. Decide on your bin sizes. Each bin should be roughly the same size. Use enough bins to get an accurate picture but not so many bins that the data becomes spiky and noisy. In Figure 14.35, the goal was bins of 5 mph each.

3. Enter the bins. This process is a bit tricky. If you want a bin for 40–45 mph, enter the number 45. For the bin of 45–50 mph, enter the number 50. In C2–C10, the numbers represent bins starting with 40–45 and ending with 80–85.

4. Select the range where the values will be returned. (The FREQUENCY function returns several values at once.) In Figure 14.35, select Cells D2:D11. Notice that this selection is one cell larger than your range of bins. The function returns one extra value in case there are any speeds faster than your top bin speed.

Figure 14.35
The tedious process of grouping values into ranges is handled easily with the FREQUENCY function.

	A	B	C	D	E	F	G
1	Speed			Frequency			
2	43.0		45	1			
3	45.8		50	12			
4	46.3		55	96			
5	47.4		60	310			
6	47.8		65	589			
7	48.3		70	588			
8	48.4		75	312			
9	48.5		80	81			
10	49.3		85	11			
11	49.5			0			
12	49.5						

D2 ▾ fx {=FREQUENCY(A2:A2001,C2:C10)}

5. With D2:D11 selected, type the formula =FREQUENCY(A2:A2001,C2:C10). Do not press Enter at the end. You have to tell Excel to evaluate the formula as an array formula, so hold down Ctrl+Shift and then press Enter. Excel automatically groups the 2,000 individual data points into the 10 bins. You can then chart or analyze this range.

▶ *To see a demo of using* FREQUENCY, *search for "Excel In Depth 14" at YouTube.*

Using NORM.DIST to Calculate the Probability in a Normal Distribution

In Figure 14.36, the observed speeds along a highway seem to be following a normal distribution. A normal distribution is sometimes referred to as a *bell curve*. When you have a normal distribution, the curve can be described mathematically using only the average and standard deviation of the data.

Figure 14.36
If your data is normally distributed, you can predict the future by using NORM.DIST.

	A	B	C	D	E	F	G	H	I	J
1	Speed		Mean		65.0	=AVERAGE(A2:A2001)				
2	43.0		Std Dev		5.979512	=STDEV.S(A2:A2001)				
3	45.8									
4	46.3		Probability car going 75 or less:			95.3%	=NORM.DIST(75,$D$1,$D$2,TRUE)			
5	47.4		Probability car going 65 or less:			50.2%	=NORM.DIST(65,$D$1,$D$2,TRUE)			
6	47.8	Probability car going between 65 and 75:				45.1%	=F4-F5			
7	48.3									
8	48.4									

C2 ▾ fx Std Dev

The NORM.DIST function has a strange twist: It always returns the probability that a car will be going less than or equal to a value x. If you want to know the probability that the next car will be traveling between 65 and 75 mph, you have to figure out the cumulative probability of the car going less than 75 miles per hour and then subtract the cumulative probability of the car going less than 65 miles per hour. This requires two calls to the NORM.DIST function.

Syntax:

```
=NORM.DIST(x,mean,standard_dev,cumulative)
```

The NORM.DIST function returns the normal cumulative distribution for the specified mean and standard deviation. This function has a very wide range of applications in statistics, including hypothesis testing. This function takes the following arguments:

- *x*—This is the value for which you want the distribution.

- *mean*—This is the arithmetic mean of the distribution.

- *standard_dev*—This is the standard deviation of the distribution.

- *cumulative*—This is a logical value that determines the form of the function. If cumulative is TRUE, NORM.DIST returns the cumulative distribution function; if cumulative is FALSE, NORM.DIST returns the probability mass function.

If mean or *standard_dev* is nonnumeric, NORM.DIST returns a #VALUE! error. If *standard_dev* is less than or equal to 0, NORM.DIST returns a #NUM! error. If mean is 0 and *standard_dev* is 1, NORM.DIST returns the standard normal distribution.

In Figure 14.36, the range of observed values is in A2:A2001. Formulas in Cells D1 and D2 calculate the average and standard deviation of the data set. The goal is to find the probability of any car going between 65 and 75 mph. The formula in Cell F4 is =NORM.DIST(75,$D$1,$D$2,TRUE); it predicts the likelihood of a car going 75 mph or less at 95.3%. The formula in Cell F5 is =NORM.DIST(65,$D$1,$D$2,TRUE). This predicts the probability of a car going 65 mph or less at 50.2%.

note
In Excel 2007, this function was called NORMDIST.

You can back into the probability that the car will be going between 65 and 75 mph by subtracting 50.2% from 95.3%. The answer to your problem is 45.1% that the next car passing the checkpoint will be going between 65 and 75 mph.

Using NORM.INV to Calculate the Value for a Certain Probability

In the preceding section, you used NORM.DIST to find the probability that a car was going less than 75 mph. Sometimes, you might want to find the speed associated with a certain probability. For example, say you need to design a billboard that can be read by 80% of the drivers. If you know the mean and standard deviation of the speeds on the highway, you can use the NORM.INV function to ask Excel to tell you that 80% of the drivers will be driving at X miles per hour or less.

Syntax:

```
=NORM.INV(probability,mean,standard_dev)
```

The NORM.INV function returns the inverse of the normal cumulative distribution for the specified mean and standard deviation. This function takes the following arguments:

- *probability*—This is a probability corresponding to the normal distribution.

- *mean*—This is the arithmetic mean of the distribution.

- *standard_dev*—This is the standard deviation of the distribution.

If any argument is nonnumeric, NORM.INV returns a #VALUE! error. If probability is less than 0 or if probability is greater than 1, NORM.INV returns a #NUM! error. If *standard_dev* is less than or equal to 0, NORM.INV returns a #NUM! error.

NORM.INV uses an iterative technique for calculating the function. Given a probability value, NORM.INV iterates until the result is accurate to within $\pm 3 \times 10^{-7}$. If NORM.INV does not converge after 100 iterations, the function returns an #N/A error.

In Figure 14.37, a sample of speeds is listed in Column A. The formulas in Cells D2 and D3 calculate the mean and standard deviation. If you assume that the speeds follow a normal distribution, then 80% of the cars will be traveling 70 mph or less along this stretch of highway. The formula in Cell E6 is =NORM.INV(D6,D$1,D$2).

Figure 14.37
Rather than use Goal Seek with the NORM.DIST function, you can let Excel handle the iterations to back into an answer using NORM.INV.

	E6		▼	f_x	=NORM.INV(D6,D$1,D$2)		
	A	B	C	D	E	F	G	H
1	Speed		Mean	65.0	=AVERAGE(A2:A2001)		
2	43.0		Std Dev	5.978017	=STDEV.P(A2:A2001)		
3	45.8						
4	46.3						
5	47.4		Probability	Speed			
6	47.8		80%	70.00	=NORM.INV(D9,D1,D2)		
7	48.3		85%	71.16			
8	48.4		90%	72.63			
9	48.5		95%	74.80			

Using NORM.S.DIST to Calculate Probability

Before the days of spreadsheets, most statistics textbooks had tables of probabilities. In such a textbook, the basic problem states, for example, that the mean is 57.1 and the standard deviation is 8.2. To calculate the probability that a member of the population would have a value of 64 or less, your first step is to calculate a z value. z is simply the number of standard deviations away from the mean. In this case, 64 is 6.9 units above the mean. The standard deviation is 8.2. Your z score is 6.9 / 8.2, or 0.841. Thus, you need to find the probability that any value is at 0.841 standard deviations above the mean or less. You then turn to a large appendix in the back of the textbook that lists many different z scores and the probability associated with each one. The table would look somewhat like Figure 14.38.

note

In Excel 2007, NORM.INV was NORMINV.

Depending on the accuracy of the table, you could find the probability associated with the z score. In Figure 14.38, you would go down the left column to the 0.8 row and across the table to the 0.04 column to find a value of 0.7995. This means that there is a 0.7995 probability that any random member will be at 0.84 standard deviations above the mean or below it.

The NORM.S.DIST function makes this table obsolete. (In fact, I created the table in the figure by using NORM.S.DIST). Although the typical statistics textbook would show the approximate probability for z = 0.84 as 0.7995, Excel can now calculate the exact probability for z = 0.841 as 0.7998.

C16 =NORM.S.DIST(B16,1)

	A	B	C	D	E	F	G	H	I	J	K
1											
2		Second Digit of Z ---->									
3	z	0.00	0.01	0.02	0.03	0.04	0.05	0.06	0.07	0.08	0.09
4	0.0	0.5000	0.5040	0.5080	0.5120	0.5160	0.5199	0.5239	0.5279	0.5319	0.5359
5	0.1	0.5398	0.5438	0.5478	0.5517	0.5557	0.5596	0.5636	0.5675	0.5714	0.5753
6	0.2	0.5793	0.5832	0.5871	0.5910	0.5948	0.5987	0.6026	0.6064	0.6103	0.6141
7	0.3	0.6179	0.6217	0.6255	0.6293	0.6331	0.6368	0.6406	0.6443	0.6480	0.6517
8	0.4	0.6554	0.6591	0.6628	0.6664	0.6700	0.6736	0.6772	0.6808	0.6844	0.6879
9	0.5	0.6915	0.6950	0.6985	0.7019	0.7054	0.7088	0.7123	0.7157	0.7190	0.7224
10	0.6	0.7257	0.7291	0.7324	0.7357	0.7389	0.7422	0.7454	0.7486	0.7517	0.7549
11	0.7	0.7580	0.7611	0.7642	0.7673	0.7704	0.7734	0.7764	0.7794	0.7823	0.7852
12	0.8	0.7881	0.7910	0.7939	0.7967	0.7995	0.8023	0.8051	0.8078	0.8106	0.8133
13	0.9	0.8159	0.8186	0.8212	0.8238	0.8264	0.8289	0.8315	0.8340	0.8365	0.8389
14	1	0.8413	0.8438	0.8461	0.8485	0.8508	0.8531	0.8554	0.8577	0.8599	0.8621
15											
16		0.840	0.7995	=NORM.S.DIST(B16,1)							
17		0.841	0.7998	=NORM.S.DIST(B17,1)							

Figure 14.38
The NORM.S.DIST formula in Cell C17 makes tables of probabilities in statistics textbooks (like the one displayed in A2:K14) obsolete.

Syntax:

=NORM.S.DIST(*z,cumulative*)

The NORM.S.DIST function returns the standard normal distribution function. The distribution has a mean of 0 and a standard deviation of 1. You use this function in place of a table of standard normal curve areas.

The argument z is the value for which you want the distribution. If z is nonnumeric, NORM.S.DIST returns a #VALUE! error.

Changes to NORM.S.DIST Function in Excel 2010

In Excel 2007, the NORMSDIST function was always cumulative. In the process of rewriting the function for Excel 2010, Microsoft added the cumulative argument. If you use True or 1 for this argument, NORM.S.DIST calculates the cumulative distribution function just as NORMSDIST would have done. With Excel 2010, if you choose False or 0 for the cumulative function, NORM.S.DIST will return the amount from the mean to the specific point. An example might make this clear. To find out how many items appear at the mean, the cumulative NORM.S.DIST will report 50%. To find how many items are .26 above the mean, the cumulative function will report 60% of the items. If you ask for the noncumulative function, you will find only the amount from the mean to the z score of 0.26, which would be 10%.

Using NORM.S.INV to Calculate a z Score for a Given Probability

To calculate a z score for a given probability, you use the NORM.S.INV function. In Figure 14.39, the z score for 15% is –1.036. This means that in a normally distributed population, 15% of the population exists at the value of the mean minus 1.036 standard deviations.

Figure 14.39
You can back into a z score from a probability by using NORM.S.INV. You can then take the z score multiplied by a standard deviation to figure out the distance that your value lies from the mean.

	A	B	C	D
1	Probability	Z-Score		
2	1%	-2.326	=NORM.S.INV(A2)	
3	5%	-1.645		
4	15%	-1.036		
5	25%	-0.674		
6	50%	0.000		
7	75%	0.674		
8	85%	1.036		
9	95%	1.645		
10	99%	2.326		

Syntax:

=NORM.S.INV(*probability*)

The NORM.S.INV function returns the inverse of the standard normal cumulative distribution. The distribution has a mean of 0 and a standard deviation of 1.

The argument probability is a probability that corresponds to the normal distribution. If probability is nonnumeric, NORMSINV returns a #VALUE! error. If probability is less than 0 or if probability is greater than 1, NORM.S.INV returns a #NUM! error.

NORM.S.INV uses an iterative technique for calculating the function. Given a probability value, NORM.S.INV iterates until the result is accurate to within $\pm 3 \times 10^{-7}$. If NORM.S.INV does not converge after 100 iterations, the function returns an #N/A error.

The z score refers to a number of standard deviations away from the mean. If the z score is negative, the value lies to the left of the mean. if the z score is positive, the value lies to the right of the mean.

Using STANDARDIZE to Calculate the Distance from the Mean

To calculate the distance from a mean, use the STANDARDIZE function. This function returns the positive or negative distance from the mean, expressed as the number of standard deviations.

Syntax:

=STANDARDIZE(*x,mean,standard_dev*)

The STANDARDIZE function returns a normalized value from a distribution characterized by mean and *standard_dev*. This function takes the following arguments:

- *x*—This is the value you want to normalize.

- *mean*—This is the arithmetic mean of the distribution.

- *standard_dev*—This is the standard deviation of the distribution.

If *standard_dev* is less than or equal to 0, STANDARDIZE returns a #NUM! error. In Figure 14.40, a population has a mean of 65 and a standard deviation of 5. The normalized value of 75 is 2, indicating that 75 is 2 standard deviations away from the mean of 65.

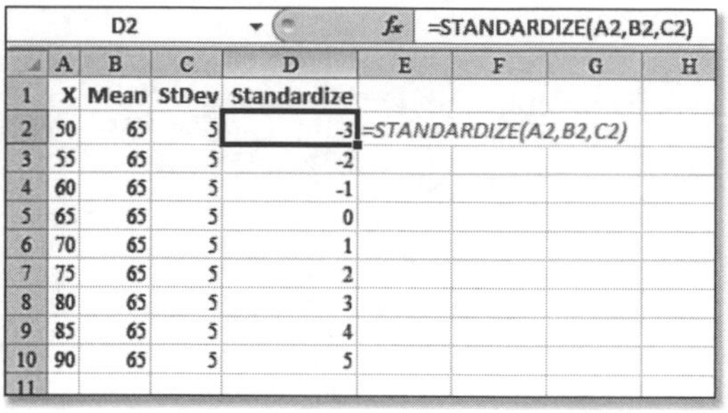
D2 =STANDARDIZE(A2,B2,C2)

	A	B	C	D	E	F	G	H
1	X	Mean	StDev	Standardize				
2	50	65	5	-3	=STANDARDIZE(A2,B2,C2)			
3	55	65	5	-2				
4	60	65	5	-1				
5	65	65	5	0				
6	70	65	5	1				
7	75	65	5	2				
8	80	65	5	3				
9	85	65	5	4				
10	90	65	5	5				
11								

Figure 14.40
`STANDARDIZE` does the basic math to calculate the distance from the mean, expressed as a number of standard deviations.

Using Student's t-Distribution for Small Sample Sizes

All the previous examples using a normal distribution assume that the sample size is 30 or more. If you are using a small sample size—even as small as three members—you should use the Student's *t*-distribution.

An important concept in the Student's *t*-distribution is the degrees of freedom. If you know the mean of the sample but not the standard deviation of the population, the degrees of freedom is the sample size minus 1. When the degrees of freedom is 29 or above, the Student's *t*-distribution is nearly identical with the normal distribution. However, as the degrees of freedom drops, the distribution becomes flatter and wider.

Changes to `TDIST` Function in Excel 2010

Microsoft added several functions to Excel 2010. In legacy versions of Excel, the `TDIST` function required three arguments: x, degrees of freedom, and # of tails. In Excel 2010, Microsoft moved the # of tails to the function name.

In Excel 2007, the two-tailed `TDIST` function

```
=TDIST(2.5,10,2)
```

This is now equivalent to Excel 2010's `T.DIST.2T` function:

```
=T.DIST.2T(2.5,10)
```

In Excel 2007, the one-tailed `TDIST` function

```
=TDIST(2.5,10,1)
```

This is now equivalent to the `T.DIST.RT` function:

```
=T.DIST.RT(2.5,10)
```

Excel 2010 offers a new `T.DIST` function with arguments for x, degrees of freedom, and cumulative.

Syntax:

```
=T.DIST(x,degrees_freedom,cumulative)
=T.DIST.2T(x,degrees_freedom)
=T.DIST.RT(x,degrees_freedom)
```

The T.DIST.2T function returns the percentage points (that is, probability) for the Student's t-distribution, where a numeric value (x) is a calculated value of t for which the percentage points are to be computed. The t-distribution is used in the hypothesis testing of small sample data sets. You use this function in place of a table of critical values for the t-distribution.

The T.DIST.2T function takes the following arguments:

- x—This is the numeric value at which to evaluate the distribution.

- *degrees_freedom*—This is an integer that indicates the number of degrees of freedom.

If any argument is nonnumeric, T.DIST returns a #VALUE! error. If *degrees_freedom* is less than 1, T.DIST returns a #NUM! error. The *degrees_freedom* argument are truncated to integers.

Syntax:

```
=T.INV.2T(probability,degrees_freedom)
```

The T.INV.2T function returns the t-value of the Student's t-distribution as a function of the probability and the degrees of freedom. This function takes the following arguments:

- probability—This is the probability associated with the two-tailed Student's *t*-distribution.

- *degrees_freedom*—This is the number of degrees of freedom to characterize the distribution.

If either argument is nonnumeric, T.INV.2T returns a #VALUE! error. If probability is less than 0 or if probability is greater than 1, T.INV.2T returns a #NUM! error. If *degrees_freedom* is not an integer, it is truncated. If *degrees_freedom* is less than 1, T.INV.2T returns a #NUM! error. T.INV.2T is calculated as T.INV.2T = p(t<X), where X is a random variable that follows the t-distribution.

T.INV.2T uses an iterative technique for calculating the function. Given a probability value, T.INV.2T iterates until the result is accurate to within $\pm 3 \times 10^{-7}$. If T.INV.2T does not converge after 100 iterations, the function returns an #N/A error.

 note

Excel 2010's T.INV.2T is equivalent to TINV in legacy versions of Excel. The Excel 2010 function T.INV is a new function to provide the inverse of the cumulative T.DIST function.

Syntax:

```
=T.TEST(array1,array2,tails,type)
```

Excel can also calculate the t-test to predict whether two samples come from populations with the same mean. For this, you use the T.TEST function. The T.TEST function returns the probability associated with a Student's t-test. You use T.TEST to determine whether two samples are likely to have come from the same two underlying populations that have the same mean.

The T.TEST function takes the following arguments:

- *array1*—This is the first data set.
- *array2*—This is the second data set.
- tails—This specifies the number of distribution tails. If tails is 1, TTEST uses the one-tailed distribution. If tails is 2, TTEST uses the two-tailed distribution.
- type—This is the kind of *t*-test to perform. See Table 14.3 for more information.

Table 14.3 Types of *t*-Tests Available with the T.TEST Function

If Type Equals	This Test Is Performed
1	Paired
2	Two-sample equal variance (homoscedastic)
3	Two-sample unequal variance (heteroscedastic)

If *array1* and *array2* have a different number of data points, and if type is 1 (paired), T.TEST returns an #N/A error. The tails and type arguments are truncated to integers. If tails or type is non-numeric, T.TEST returns a #VALUE! error. If tails is any value other than 1 or 2, T.TEST returns a #NUM! error.

In Figure 14.41, the means of the two samples are different: 11.15 versus 13.5. However, in Cell F2, T.TEST returns 0.1577. Because this is greater than the typical alpha of 0.05, the difference in means may not be statistically significant. It is possible that these two samples were taken from the same population.

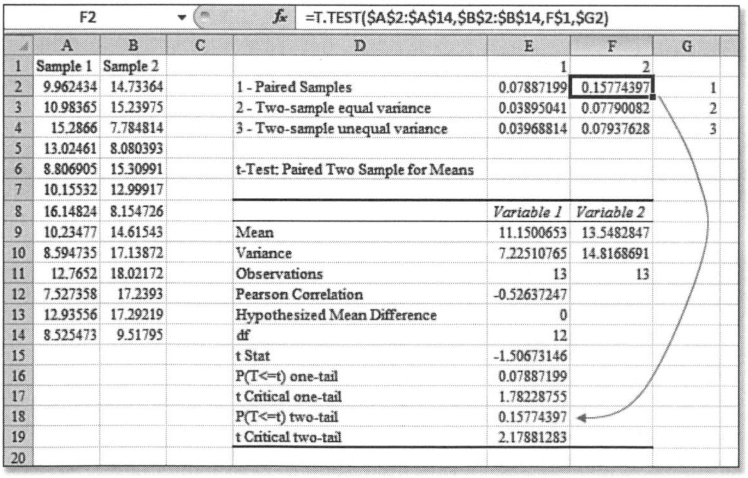

F2 =T.TEST($A$2:$A$14,$B$2:$B$14,F$1,$G2)

	A	B	C	D	E	F	G
1	Sample 1	Sample 2			1	2	
2	9.962434	14.73364		1 - Paired Samples	0.07887199	0.15774397	1
3	10.98365	15.23975		2 - Two-sample equal variance	0.03895041	0.07790082	2
4	15.2866	7.784814		3 - Two-sample unequal variance	0.03968814	0.07937628	3
5	13.02461	8.080393					
6	8.806905	15.30991		t-Test: Paired Two Sample for Means			
7	10.15532	12.99917					
8	16.14824	8.154726			*Variable 1*	*Variable 2*	
9	10.23477	14.61543		Mean	11.1500653	13.5482847	
10	8.594735	17.13872		Variance	7.22510765	14.8168691	
11	12.7652	18.02172		Observations	13	13	
12	7.527358	17.2393		Pearson Correlation	-0.52637247		
13	12.93556	17.29219		Hypothesized Mean Difference	0		
14	8.525473	9.51795		df	12		
15				t Stat	-1.50673146		
16				P(T<=t) one-tail	0.07887199		
17				t Critical one-tail	1.78228755		
18				P(T<=t) two-tail	0.15774397		
19				t Critical two-tail	2.17881283		
20							

Figure 14.41
T.TEST provides a formulaic equivalent to the key result from the Analysis ToolPak's T-Test feature.

Using CHISQ.TEST to Perform Goodness-of-Fit Testing

A chi-squared test compares expected frequencies with observed frequencies. The CHISQ.TEST function performs the chi-square test for independence.

CHISQ.INV.RT is used to find the critical chi value for a certain probability and degrees of freedom. CHISQ.DIST.RT is used to determine the probability for a chi value and certain degrees of freedom.

 **note**

The Excel 2010 T.TEST function is equivalent to TTEST in legacy versions of Excel.

Syntax:

=CHISQ.TEST(*actual_range,expected_range*)

The CHISQ.TEST function returns the test for independence. CHISQ.TEST returns the value from the chi-squared distribution for the statistic and the appropriate degrees of freedom. You can use chi-squared tests to determine whether hypothesized results are verified by an experiment.

The CHISQ.TEST function takes the following arguments:

- *actual_range*—This is the range of data that contains observations to test against expected values.

- *expected_range*—This is the range of data that contains the ratio of the product of row totals and column totals to the grand total.

If actual_range and expected_range have different numbers of data points, CHISQ.TEST returns an #N/A error.

The chi-squared test first calculates a chi-squared statistic and then sums the differences of actual values from the expected values. CHISQ.TEST returns the probability for a chi-squared statistic and degrees of freedom, df, where df = (r - 1) (c - 1).

Syntax:

=CHISQ.DIST.RT(*x,degrees_freedom*)

The CHISQ.DIST.RT function returns the one-tailed probability of the chi-squared distribution. The chi-squared distribution is associated with a chi-squared test. You use the chi-squared test to compare observed and expected values. For example, a genetic experiment might hypothesize that the next generation of plants will exhibit a certain set of colors. By comparing the observed results with the expected ones, you can decide whether your original hypothesis is valid.

The CHISQ.DIST.RT function takes the following arguments:

- *x*—This is the value at which you want to evaluate the distribution.

- *degrees_freedom*—This is the number of degrees of freedom.

If either argument is nonnumeric, CHISQ.DIST.RT returns a #VALUE! error. If x is negative, CHISQ.DIST.RT returns a #NUM! error. If *degrees_freedom* is not an integer, it is truncated. If *degrees_freedom* is less than 1 or if *degrees_freedom* is greater than or equal to 10^10, CHISQ.DIST.RT returns a #NUM! error.

Syntax:

=CHISQ.INV.RT(*probability,degrees_freedom*)

The CHISQ.INV.RT function returns the inverse of the one-tailed probability of the chi-squared distribution. If probability equals CHISQ.DIST.RT(x,...), CHISQ.INV.RT(probability,...) equals *x*. You use the CHISQ.INV.RT function to compare observed results with expected ones to decide whether your original hypothesis is valid.

The CHISQ.INV.RT function takes the following arguments:

- *probability*—This is a probability associated with the chi-squared distribution.
- *degrees_freedom*—This is the number of degrees of freedom.

If either argument is nonnumeric, CHISQ.INV.RT returns a #VALUE! error. If probability is less than 0 or probability is greater than 1, CHISQ.INV.RT returns a #NUM! error. If *degrees_freedom* is not an integer, it is truncated. If *degrees_freedom* is less than 1 or if *degrees_freedom* is greater than or equal to 10^10, CHISQ.INV.RT returns a #NUM! error.

CHISQ.INV.RT uses an iterative technique for calculating the function. Given a probability value, CHISQ.INV.RT iterates until the result is accurate to within ±3 × 10^–7. If CHISQ.INV does not converge after 100 iterations, the function returns an #N/A error.

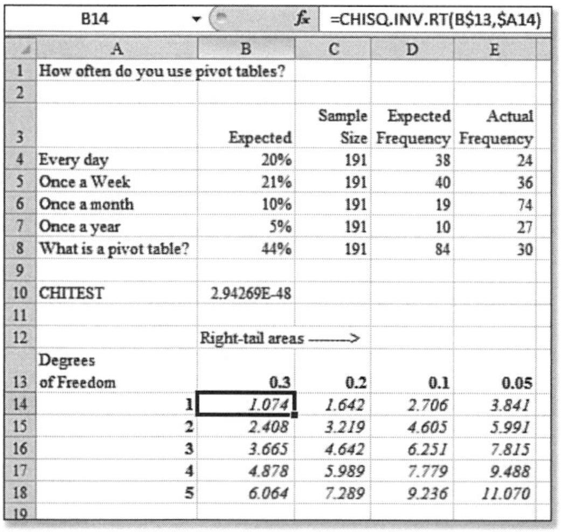

B14 =CHISQ.INV.RT(B$13,$A14)

	A	B	C	D	E
1	How often do you use pivot tables?				
2					
3		Expected	Sample Size	Expected Frequency	Actual Frequency
4	Every day	20%	191	38	24
5	Once a Week	21%	191	40	36
6	Once a month	10%	191	19	74
7	Once a year	5%	191	10	27
8	What is a pivot table?	44%	191	84	30
9					
10	CHITEST	2.94269E-48			
11					
12		Right-tail areas ------->			
13	Degrees of Freedom	0.3	0.2	0.1	0.05
14	1	1.074	1.642	2.706	3.841
15	2	2.408	3.219	4.605	5.991
16	3	3.665	4.642	6.251	7.815
17	4	4.878	5.989	7.779	9.488
18	5	6.064	7.289	9.236	11.070
19					

Figure 14.42
You can calculate chi-squared testing with CHISQ.TEST.

The Sum of Squares Functions

Excel offers four functions with confusingly similar names. The hardest part of using these functions is figuring out which function does what. The first three functions require two identically sized arrays, named x and y. These are Excel's four sum of squares functions:

- SumX2MY2—For each pair of x and y, Excel calculates $x^2 - y^2$ and then sums these values. In this case, the M in the function name indicates *minus*.

- SumX2PY2—For each pair of x and y, Excel calculates $x^2 + y^2$ and then sums these values. In this case, the P in the function name indicates *plus*.

- SumXMY2—For each pair of x and y, Excel calculates $(x - y)^2$ and then sums these values. Again, the M indicates *minus*, and the lack of a 2 after the X indicates that it is the difference that is squared.

- SumSQ—Returns the sum of the squares of the arguments.

In Figure 14.43, the x array is in A2:A5, and the y array is in B2:B5. The formulas in D2:D5 calculate x – y for each pair. The formulas in E2:E5 square that difference for each pair. The formula in Cell E6 totals the sum of the squares. You could replace the five formulas in Column E with a single formula in Cell D6: =SUMSQ(D2:D5). Alternatively, you could replace all the formulas in Columns D and E with a single use of SumXMY2 in Cell B9.

Sum of the Sum of the Squares

Some statistical processes ask you to calculate the sum of the sum of the squares. However, a casual survey of several mathematicians could not find one concrete example of when this would be useful. In fact, the formula for SUMX2PY2(A2:A5,B2:B5) is mathematically equivalent to SUMSQ(A2:B5). Further, the formula for SUMX2MY2(A2:A5,B2:B5) is the same as SUMSQ(A2:A5) - SUMSQ(B2:B5). My theory on this is that some early spreadsheets included these functions in an effort to claim that they had more functions than a competitor did. All future spreadsheets have included the functions just because some other competitor included them.

Syntax:

=SUMSQ(*number1,number2,...*)

The SUMSQ function returns the sum of the squares of the arguments. The arguments *number1,number2,...* are 1 to 255 arguments for which you want the sum of the squares. You can also use a single array or a reference to an array instead of arguments separated by commas.

Syntax:

=SUMXMY2(*array_x,array_y*)

The SUMXMY2 function returns the sum of squares of differences of corresponding values in two arrays. It takes the following arguments:

- *array_x*—This is the first array or range of values.

- *array_y*—This is the second array or range of values.

The arguments should be either numbers or names, arrays, or references that contain numbers. If an array or reference argument contains text, logical values, or empty cells, those values are ignored;

	D6		▼	●	*fx*	=SUMSQ(D2:D5)	
◢	A	B	C	D	E	F	
1	x	y			x-y	(x-y)^2	
2	1	2		-1	1		
3	2	4		-2	4		
4	3	6		-3	9		
5	4	8		-4	16		
6			SumSQ:	30	30		
7				=SUMSQ(D2:D5)			
8							
9	SumXMY2		30	=SUMXMY2(A2:A5,B2:B5)			
10							

Figure 14.43
Without doing any regression, you use SUMXMY2 to calculate the sum of the squares of the difference of two arrays.

however, cells that contain the value 0 are included. If array_x and array_y have a different number of values, SUMXMY2 returns an #N/A error.

Syntax:

=SUMX2MY2(*array_x,array_y*)

The SUMX2MY2 function returns the sum of the difference of squares of corresponding values in two arrays. This function takes the following arguments:

- *array_x*—This is the first array or range of values.

- *array_y*—This is the second array or range of values.

The arguments should be either numbers or names, arrays, or references that contain numbers. If an array or a reference argument contains text, logical values, or empty cells, those values are ignored; however, cells that contain the value 0 are included. If *array_x* and *array_y* have a different number of values, SUMX2MY2 returns an #N/A error.

Syntax:

=SUMX2PY2(*array_x,array_y*)

The SUMX2PY2 function returns the sum of the sum of squares of corresponding values in two arrays. The sum of the sum of squares is a common term in many statistical calculations. This function takes the following arguments:

- *array_x*—This is the first array or range of values.

- *array_y*—This is the second array or range of values.

> **note**
> I will go out on a limb and propose that none of the 500 million people using Excel actually use SUMX2PY2.

The arguments should be either numbers or names, arrays, or references that contain numbers. If an array or reference argument contains text, logical values, or empty cells, those values are ignored; however, cells that contain the value 0 are included. If *array_x* and *array_y* have a different number of values, SUMX2PY2 returns an #N/A error.

Figure 14.44
Microsoft won't say that these two functions are useful in statistics. I don't think they are useful anywhere.

	B9			f_x	=SUMX2PY2(A2:A5,B2:B5)	
	A	B	C	D	E	F	G
1	x	y		(x^2+y^2)	(x^2-y^2)		
2	1	2		5	-3		
3	2	4		20	-12		
4	3	6		45	-27		
5	4	8		80	-48		
6			Total	150	-90		
7							
8							
9	SumX2pY2	150	=SUMX2PY2(A2:A5,B2:B5)				
10	SumX2mY2	-90	=SUMX2MY2(A2:A5,B2:B5)				
11							
12	SumSQ	150	=SUMSQ(A2:B5)				
13	SumSQ	-90	=SUMSQ(A2:A5)-SUMSQ(B2:B5)				

In Figure 14.44, the one SUMX2PY2 formula in Cell B9 is much simpler than the five formulas in Column D, but if you really wanted to do this calculation, you could use SUMSQ, as shown in Cell B12.

Figure 14.45
The LOGNORM.DIST and LOGNORM.INV functions can make sense of a population where the natural logarithm of the population is normally distributed.

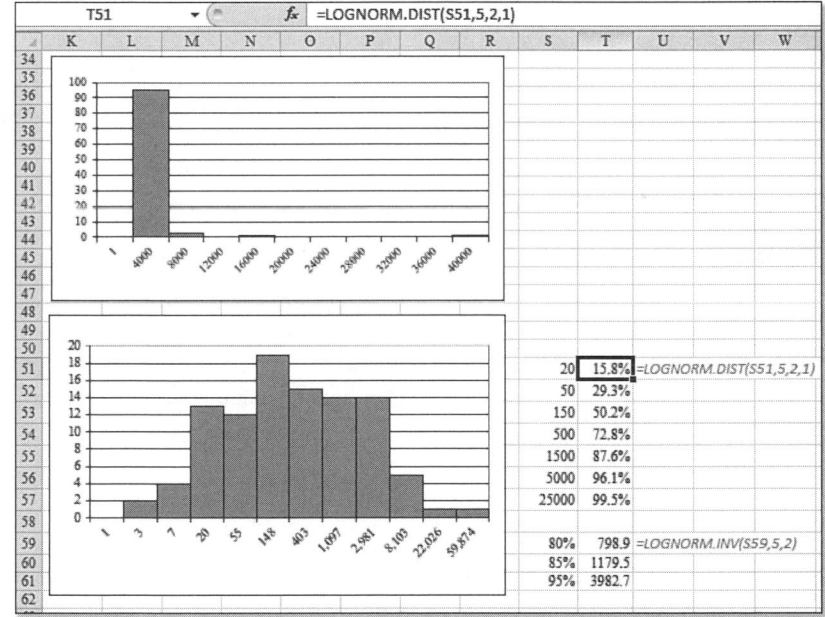

Testing Probability on Logarithmic Distributions

In the life sciences, a number of populations have logarithmic distributions. In the population shown in Figure 14.45, the values in the sample range from under 2 to over 38,000. The data clearly does not follow a normal distribution.

However, if you took the natural logarithm of each data point, the LN(x) of the members does follow a normal distribution. The mean of the natural logarithms is 5, with a standard deviation of 2.

Populations where the natural logarithm is normally distributed are called *lognormal distributions*. An example of a population with a lognormal distribution is the length of time that bacteria live in a disinfectant.

In the example where the mean of the natural logarithm values is 5 and the standard deviation is 2, take a look at what this really means: You use EXP(5) to see that the mean of 5 translates to 148. You would expect 65% of the population to be within 1 standard deviation of the mean. This range from EXP(3) to EXP(7) is from 20 to 1,096. The range for two standard deviations from the mean is EXP(1) and EXP(9), or 2.7 and 8,103.

Given a lognormal distribution where the mean of the natural logarithm of the population is 5 and the standard deviation is 2, you can predict what percentage of the population will be at a number x or below by using LOGNORM.DIST. To find the value of x associated with a certain probability, you use LOGNORM.INV.

Syntax:

=LOGNORM.DIST(*x,mean,standard_dev,cumulative*)

> **note**
>
> LOGNORM.INV in Excel 2010 is equivalent to LOGINV in Excel 2007.

The LOGNORM.DIST function returns the cumulative lognormal distribution of x, where the natural logarithm is normally distributed with the parameters mean and *standard_dev*. You use this function to analyze data that has been logarithmically transformed. This function takes the following arguments:

- *x*—This is the value at which to evaluate the function.

- *mean*—This is the mean of the natural logarithm.

- *standard_dev*—This is the standard deviation of the natural logarithm.

- *cumulative*—Use 1 or True to calculate the CDF. Use 0 or False to calculate the PDF.

If any argument is nonnumeric, LOGNORM.DIST returns a #VALUE! error. If x is less than or equal to 0 or if *standard_dev* is less than or equal to 0, LOGNORM.DIST returns a #NUM! error.

Syntax:

=LOGNORM.INV(probability,mean,*standard_dev*)

The LOGNORM.INV function returns the inverse of the lognormal cumulative distribution function of x, where the natural logarithm is normally distributed with the parameters mean and *standard_dev*. If probability is equal to LOGNORM.DIST(x,...), LOGNORM.INV(probability,...) is equal to x. You use the lognormal distribution to analyze logarithmically transformed data.

The LOGNORM.INV function takes the following arguments:

- *probability*—This is a probability associated with the lognormal distribution.

- *mean*—This is the mean of the natural logarithm.

- *standard_dev*—This is the standard deviation of the natural logarithm.

If any argument is nonnumeric, LOGNORM.INV returns a #VALUE! error. If probability is less than 0 or if probability is greater than 1, LOGNORM.INV returns a #NUM! error. If *standard_dev* is less than or equal to 0, LOGNORM.INV returns a #NUM! error.

In Figure 14.45, the population varies from 1.7 to 38,577, but the LOGNORM.DIST function predicts that 72.8% of the population is under 500, 87.6% is under 1,500, and 96.1% is under 5,000.

In Cell T61, the LOGNORM.INV function reveals that 95% of the population should be under 3,983.

 note

In Excel 2007, the NORMDIST function always calculated the CDF. When you switch to the LOGNORM.DIST function, you need to add a fourth argument of 1 or True to calculate the equivalent function.

Using GAMMA.DIST and GAMMA.INV to Analyze Queuing Times

Earlier in this chapter, we discussed how to use a Poisson distribution to analyze how many customers might walk into a bank during any given hour. However, if the time between customers is relevant, you need to use the gamma distribution. The gamma distribution is described by two variables—alpha and beta. For a gamma distribution described by alpha and beta, you can find the probability that a value of x or less will occur with GAMMA.DIST. To find the value of x for a certain probability, you use GAMMA.INV. The other remaining gamma-related function is GAMMALN.

Syntax:

=GAMMA.DIST(x,alpha,beta,cumulative)

The GAMMA.DIST function returns the gamma distribution. You can use this function to study variables that may have a skewed distribution. The gamma distribution is commonly used in queuing analysis. This function takes the following arguments:

- *x*—This is the value at which you want to evaluate the distribution.

- *alpha*—This is a parameter to the distribution.

- *beta*—This is a parameter to the distribution.

- *cumulative*—This is a logical value that determines the form of the function. If cumulative is TRUE, GAMMA.DIST returns the cumulative distribution function; if *cumulative* is FALSE, GAMMA.DIST returns the probability mass function.

If beta is 1, GAMMA.DIST returns the standard gamma distribution. If *x, alpha,* or *beta* is nonnumeric, GAMMA.DIST returns a #VALUE! error. If *x* is less than 0, GAMMA.DIST returns a #NUM! error. If alpha is less than or equal to 0 or if beta is less than or equal to 0, GAMMA.DIST returns a #NUM! error. When alpha is a positive integer, GAMMA.DIST is also known as the Erlang distribution.

Syntax:

=GAMMA.INV(*probability,alpha,beta*)

The GAMMA.INV function returns the inverse of the gamma cumulative distribution. If probability is equal to GAMMA.DIST(x,...), then GAMMA.INV(probability,...) is equal to *x*. You can use this function to study a variable whose distribution may be skewed. This function takes the following arguments:

- *probability*—This is the probability associated with the gamma distribution.

- *alpha*—This is a parameter to the distribution.

- *beta*—This is a parameter to the distribution. If *beta* is 1, GAMMA.INV returns the standard gamma distribution.

>  **note**
>
> The Excel 2010 function GAMMA.DIST is equivalent to the Excel 2007 GAMMADIST function.

If any argument is nonnumeric, GAMMA.INV returns a #VALUE! error. If *probability* is less than 0 or *probability* is greater than 1, GAMMA.INV returns a #NUM! error. If *alpha* is less than or equal to 0 or if *beta* is less than or equal to 0, GAMMA.INV returns the #NUM! error. If *beta* is less than or equal to 0, GAMMA.INV returns a #NUM! error.

GAMMA.INV uses an iterative technique to do its calculation. Given a probability value, GAMMA.INV iterates until the result is accurate to within $\pm 3 \times 10^{-7}$. If GAMMA.INV does not converge after 100 iterations, the function returns an #N/A error.

Syntax:

=GAMMALN(*x*)

The GAMMALN function returns the natural logarithm of the gamma function, $\Gamma(x)$. The argument x is the value for which you want to calculate GAMMALN.

If *x* is nonnumeric, GAMMALN returns a #VALUE! error. If *x* is less than or equal to 0, GAMMALN returns a #NUM! error. The number *e* raised to the GAMMALN(*i*) power, where i is an integer, returns the same result as (i − 1)!.

> **note**
>
> BETA.DIST in Excel 2010 is similar to BETADIST in legacy versions of Excel. BETADIST always calculated the CDF. To switch from BETADIST to BETA.DIST, add a 1 as the third argument to indicate that the function should be cumulative.

Calculating Probability of Beta Distributions

A beta distribution is used to describe the variability of the percentage of something across samples, such as the percentage of the day people spend sleeping.

A beta distribution curve is described by two parameters, alpha and beta. For any given distribution, you can predict the likelihood that a value will be less than or equal to x by using BETA.DIST. To find the value of x associated with a certain probability, you use BETA.INV.

Syntax:

=BETA.DIST(*x,alpha,beta,cumulative,A,B*)

The BETA.DIST function returns the cumulative beta probability density function. The cumulative beta probability density function is commonly used to study variation in the percentage of something across samples, such as the fraction of the day people spend watching television. This function takes the following arguments:

- *x*—This is the value between a and b at which to evaluate the function.

- *alpha*—This is a parameter to the distribution.

- *beta*—This is a parameter to the distribution.

- *cumulative*—True or 1 for the CDF, False or 0 for the PDF.

- *a*—This is an optional lower bound to the interval of x.

- *b*—This is an optional upper bound to the interval of x.

If any argument is nonnumeric, BETA.DIST returns a #VALUE! error. If *alpha* is less than or equal to 0 or *beta* is less than or equal to 0, BETA.DIST returns a #NUM! error. If *x* is less than *a*, *x* is greater than *b*, or a equals *b*, BETA.DIST returns a #NUM! error. If you omit values for a and b, BETA.DIST uses the standard cumulative beta distribution, so that a equals 0 and b equals 1.

Syntax:

=BETA.INV(probability,alpha,beta,A,B)

The BETA.INV function returns the inverse of the cumulative beta probability density function. That is, if probability is equal to BETADIST(x,...), then BETA.INV(*probability,...*) is equal to *x*. The cumulative beta distribution can be used in project planning to model probable completion times, given an expected completion time and variability.

The BETA.INV function takes the following arguments:

- *probability*—This is a probability associated with the beta distribution.

- *alpha*—This is a parameter to the distribution.

- *beta*—This is a parameter to the distribution.

- *a*—This is an optional lower bound to the interval of x.

- *b*—This is an optional upper bound to the interval of x.

If any argument is nonnumeric, BETA.INV returns a #VALUE! error. If *alpha* is less than or equal to 0 or if *beta* is less than or equal to 0, BETA.INV returns a #NUM! error. If *probability* is less than or equal to 0 or *probability* is greater than 1, BETA.INV returns a #NUM! error. If you omit values for a and b, BETA.INV uses the standard cumulative beta distribution, so that a equals 0 and b equals 1.

BETA.INV uses an iterative technique for calculating the function. Given a probability value, BETA.INV iterates until the result is accurate to within $\pm 3 \times 10 - 7$. If BETA.INV does not converge after 100 iterations, the funcion returns an #N/A error.

Using F.TEST to Measure Differences in Variability

There are three functions for measuring variability among two populations. Suppose you need to compare test results from males and test results from females. To determine whether one population has more variability than the other, you use F.TEST. The F.DIST function determines the probability that a value will be less than or equal to X. The F.INV function returns the X value associated with a certain probability.

Syntax:

=F.TEST(*array1*,*array2*)

The F.TEST function returns the result of an F-test. An F-test returns the one-tailed probability that the variances in *array1* and *array2* are not significantly different. You use this function to determine whether two samples have different variances. For example, given test scores from public and private schools, you can test whether these schools have different levels of diversity.

The F.TEST function takes the following arguments:

- *array1*—This is the first array or range of data.

- *array2*—This is the second array or range of data.

The arguments must be numbers or names, arrays, or references that contain numbers. If an array or a reference argument contains text, logical values, or empty cells, those values are ignored. However, cells that contain the value 0 are included. If the number of data points in *array1* or *array2* is less than 2, or if the variance of *array1* or *array2* is 0, F.TEST returns a #DIV/0! error.

Syntax:

=F.DIST.RT(*x*,*degrees_freedom1*,*degrees_freedom2*)

The F.DIST.RT function returns the F probability distribution. You can use this function to determine whether two data sets have different degrees of diversity. For example, you can examine test scores given to men and women entering high school and determine whether the variability in the females is different from that found in the males.

The F.DIST.RT function takes the following arguments:

- *x*—This is the value at which to evaluate the function.

- *degrees_freedom1*—This is the numerator degrees of freedom.

- *degrees_freedom2*—This is the denominator degrees of freedom.

If any argument is nonnumeric, F.DIST.RT returns a #VALUE! error. If x is negative, F.DIST.RT returns a #NUM! error. If *degrees_freedom1* or *degrees_freedom2* is not an integer, it is truncated. If *degrees_freedom1* is less than 1 or *degrees_freedom1* is greater than or equal to 10^10, F.DIST.RT returns a #NUM! error. If *degrees_freedom2* is less than 1 or *degrees_freedom2* is greater than or equal to 10^10, F.DIST.RT returns a #NUM! error. F.DIST.RT is calculated as F.DIST.RT=P(F<x), where F is a random variable that has an F distribution.

Syntax:

=F.INV.RT(*probability, degrees_freedom1,degrees_freedom2*)

The F.INV.RT function returns the inverse of the F probability distribution. If probability is equal to F.DIST.RT(*x,...*), then F.INV.RT(*probability,...*) is equal to x. The F distribution can be used in an F-test that compares the degree of variability in two data sets. For example, you can analyze income distributions in the United States and Canada to determine whether the two countries have a similar degree of diversity.

This function takes the following arguments:

- *probability*—This is a probability associated with the *F* cumulative distribution.

- *degrees_freedom1*—This is the numerator degrees of freedom.

- *degrees_freedom2*—This is the denominator degrees of freedom.

 note

F.INV.RT is the Excel 2010 equivalent of FINV in legacy versions of Excel. The new Excel 2010 function of F.INV returns the inverse of the F distribution.

If any argument is nonnumeric, F.INV.RT returns a #VALUE! error. If *probability* is less than 0 or *probability* is greater than 1, F.INV.RT returns a #NUM! error. If *degrees_freedom1* or *degrees_freedom2* is not an integer, it is truncated. If *degrees_freedom1* is less than 1 or *degrees_freedom1* is greater than or equal to 10^10, F.INV.RT returns a #NUM! error. If *degrees_freedom2* is less than 1 or *degrees_freedom2* is greater than or equal to 10^10, F.INV.RT returns a #NUM! error.

F.INV.RT can be used to return critical values from the F distribution. For example, the output of an ANOVA calculation often includes data for the F statistic, F probability, and F critical value at the 0.05 significance level. To return the critical value of F, you use the significance level as the probability argument to F.INV.RT.

F.INV.RT uses an iterative technique for calculating the function. Given a probability value, F.INV.RT iterates until the result is accurate to within ± 3 × 10^-7. If F.INV.RT does not converge after 100 iterations, the function returns an #N/A error.

 note

HYPGEOM.DIST in Excel 2010 is similar to HYPGEOMDIST in legacy versions of Excel. To convert to HYPGEOMDIST, add a 1 as the cumulative argument for HYPGEOMDIST.

Other Distributions: Exponential, Hypergeometric, and Weibull

A few remaining probability distributions are available in Excel: exponential, hypergeometric, and Weibull.

Syntax:

=EXPON.DIST(*x,lambda,cumulative*)

 note

EXPON.DIST in Excel 2010 is equivalent to the EXPONDIST in legacy versions of Excel.

The EXPON.DIST function returns the exponential distribution. You use EXPON.DIST to model the time between events, such as how long a bank's automated teller machine takes to deliver cash. For example, you can use EXPON.DIST to determine the probability that the process takes, at most, one minute.

The EXPON.DIST function takes the following arguments:

- *x*—This is the value of the function.

- *lambda*—This is the parameter value.

- *cumulative*—This is a logical value that indicates which form of the exponential function to provide. If *cumulative* is TRUE, EXPON.DIST returns the cumulative distribution function; if *cumulative* is FALSE, EXPON.DIST returns the probability density function.

If *x* or *lambda* is nonnumeric, EXPON.DIST returns a #VALUE! error. If *x* is less than 0, EXPON.DIST returns a #NUM! error. If *lambda* is less than or equal to 0, EXPON.DIST returns a #NUM! error.

Syntax:

=HYPGEOM.DIST(*sample_s,number_sample,population_s,number_population,cumulative*)

The HYPGEOM.DIST function returns the hypergeometric distribution. HYPGEOM.DIST returns the probability of a given number of sample successes, given the sample size, population successes, and population size. You use HYPGEOM.DIST for a problem that has a finite population, where each observation is either a success or a failure, and where each subset of a given size is chosen with equal likelihood.

The HYPGEOM.DIST function takes the following arguments:

- *sample_s*—This is the number of successes in the sample.

- *number_sample*—This is the size of the sample.

- *population_s*—This is the number of successes in the population.

- *number_population*—This is the population size.

- *cumulative*—1 or True for CDF. False or 0 for PDF.

All arguments are truncated to integers. If any argument is nonnumeric, HYPGEOM.DIST returns a #VALUE! error. If *sample_s* is less than 0 or *sample_s* is greater than the lesser of *number_sample* or *population_s*, HYPGEOM.DIST returns a #NUM! error. If *sample_s* is less than the larger of 0 or (*number_sample - number_population + population_s*), HYPGEOM.DIST returns a #NUM! error. If *number_sample* is less than 0 or *number_sample* is greater than *number_population*, HYPGEOM.DIST returns a #NUM! error. If *population_s* is less than 0 or *population_s* is greater than *number_population*, HYPGEOM.DIST returns a #NUM! error. If *number_population* is less than 0, HYPGEOM.DIST returns a #NUM! error. HYPGEOM.DIST is used in sampling without replacement from a finite population.

Syntax:

=WEIBULL.DIST(*x,alpha,beta,cumulative*)

The WEIBULL.DIST function returns the Weibull distribution. You use this distribution in reliability analysis, such as for calculating a device's mean time to failure. This function takes the following arguments:

- *x*—This is the value at which to evaluate the function.

- *alpha*—This is a parameter to the distribution.

- *beta*—This is a parameter to the distribution.

- *cumulative*—This determines the form of the function.

> **note**
>
> In Excel 2010, WEIBULL.DIST is equivalent to WEIBULL in legacy versions of Excel.

If *x, alpha,* or *beta* is nonnumeric, WEIBULL.DIST returns a #VALUE! error. If *x* is less than 0, WEIBULL.DIST returns a #NUM! error. If *alpha* is less than or equal to *0* or if *beta* is less than or equal to 0, WEIBULL.DIST returns a #NUM! error.

Using PROB to Calculate Probability for a Population That Fits No Distribution Curve

In some cases, you might have a data set that does not appear to follow any standard probability distribution curve. However, you may have sufficient past data to figure the probability of each outcome. In such a case, you can build a table of the possible outcomes and the probability of each outcome. You use the PROB function to figure out the chances that a value X will fall between an upper and a lower limit.

Syntax:

=PROB(*x_range,prob_range,lower_limit,upper_limit*)

The PROB function returns the probability that values in a range are between two limits. If *upper_limit* is not supplied, PROB returns the probability that values in *x_range* are equal to *lower_limit*. This function takes the following arguments:

- *x_range*—This is the range of numeric values of *x* with which there are associated probabilities.

- prob_range—This is a set of probabilities associated with values in *x_range*.

- *lower_limit*—This is the lower bound on the value for which you want a probability.

- *upper_limit*—This is the optional upper bound on the value for which you want a probability.

If any value in *prob_range* is less than or equal to 0, or if any value in *prob_range* is greater than 1, PROB returns a #NUM! error. If the sum of the values in *prob_range* is greater than 1, PROB returns a #NUM! error. If *upper_limit* is omitted, PROB returns the probability of being equal to *lower_limit*. If *x_range* and *prob_range* contain a different number of data points, PROB returns an #N/A error.

In Figure 14.46, the table in A2:B9 shows the probability of achieving a particular score on a seven-point quiz. The range of possible scores in A2:A9 is used as the first argument. The range of probabilities in B2:B9 is used as the second argument. Various formulas in Column G find the probability of any given test falling between two values.

	F3		▼	(		fx	=PROB($A$2:$A$9,$B$2:$B$9,D3,E3)			
⊿	A	B	C	D	E	F	G	H	I	J
1	Result	Probability								
2	0	0.50%		Between	and	Probability				
3	1	1%		0	2	3.0%	=PROB($A$2:$A$9,$B$2:$B$9,D3,E3)			
4	2	1.50%		0	3	6.0%				
5	3	3%		3	5	33.0%				
6	4	12%		4	5	30.0%				
7	5	18%		6	7	64.0%				
8	6	52%								
9	7	12%								
10										

Figure 14.46
This may not fall into any known distribution curve, but the *PROB* function can calculate probabilities, nonetheless.

Using Z.TEST, CONFIDENCE.NORM, and CONFIDENCE.T to Calculate Confidence Intervals

Confidence testing is one of the most confusing topics in statistics. Suppose that you have a very large population, such as the 500 million people who use Microsoft Excel. You would like to find out how many minutes per month people use pivot tables. It would be difficult to survey the 500 million people.

Instead, you find a way to survey 30 people. The mean of those 30 answers is 155 minutes per month. Think about the standard deviation of the entire population. There has to be wide variability because more than half the people using Excel never use pivot tables, and their answer would be zero. Somehow, you miraculously figure out that the standard deviation of the entire population is 220.

You can use the CONFIDENCE.NORM function to ask for the 90% confidence interval about this statistic. The formula =CONFIDENCE(0.10,220,30) returns a confidence interval of 66. This means that for any sample of 30 people using Excel, the mean of that sample will be within 66 of the true population mean 90% of the time.

In Figure 14.47, a confidence interval is drawn around the sample mean of 11 samples. The 90% confidence level is saying that in 90% of the samples, the confidence level drawn on the chart will include the true mean of the population.

Although the data in Figure 14.47 is fictitious, the actual mean of that entire population is 78. Of the 11 series drawn on the chart, 10 of the 11 happen to encompass the true mean of 78. Note, however, that the first sample mean of 156 is the one that does not include the true mean.

 caution

It is tempting to interpret the CONFIDENCE.NORM result to say that 90% of the population is within the error bars. This is wrong. Reread the last paragraph: If you use the sample mean plus or minus the confidence interval, you will include the true mean 9 out of 10 times.

Syntax:

=CONFIDENCE.NORM(*alpha,standard_dev,size*)

The CONFIDENCE.NORM function returns the confidence interval for a population mean. The confidence interval is a range on either side of a sample mean. For example, if you order a product through the mail, you can determine, with a particular level of confidence, the earliest and latest the product will arrive. This function takes the following arguments:

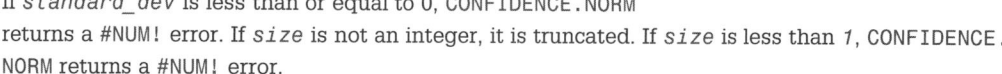

	A	B	C	D	E	F	G	H	I	J	K	L
							Sample					
1	Minutes	RAND				Low	Mean	High				
2	20	6.795E-05		Sample 1	1	88.899	155.03	221.17	1			
3	0	8.298E-05		Sample 2	2	-24.201	41.933	108.07	31			
4	0	0.0002435		Sample 3	3	61.599	127.73	193.87	61			
5	466	0.0004857		Sample 4	4	0.6652	66.8	132.93	91			
6	0	0.0013722		Sample 5	5	-41.301	24.833	90.968	121			
7	32	0.0020556		Sample 6	6	-20.368	45.767	111.9	151			
8	735	0.0026099		Sample 7	7	58.899	125.03	191.17	181			
9	0	0.0026742		Sample 8	8	-24.235	41.9	108.03	211			
10	974	0.0039359		Sample 9	9	-30.368	35.767	101.9	241			
11	334	0.0051067		Sample 10	10	-23.635	42.5	108.63	271			
12	0	0.0057		Sample 11	11	-27.235	38.9	105.03	301			
13	1070	0.0057162										
14	0	0.0060438		Std Deviation			220.22					
15	36	0.0060831										
16	58	0.0060835		Confidence			66.135					
17	56	0.0063463										
18	0	0.0064758										
19	20	0.0070511										
20	16	0.0072707										
21	0	0.0077129										
22	577	0.0077883										
23	0	0.0080734										
24	28	0.0080954										
25	55	0.0085526										
26	0	0.0087284										
27	24	0.009117										
28	59	0.0095646										
29	33	0.0098762										
30	58	0.01004										
31	0	0.0101687										
32	0	0.0102148										
33	296	0.0102271										

G16 =CONFIDENCE.NORM(0.1,G14,30)

Figure 14.47
The CONFIDENCE.NORM function does not give me a lot of confidence that I can predict the activities of 500 million people using Excel based on a survey of 10 people.

- *alpha*—This is the significance level used to compute the confidence level. The confidence level equals 100 × (1 – *alpha*)% or, in other words, an alpha of 0.05 indicates a 95% confidence level.

- *standard_dev*—This is the population standard deviation for the data range and is assumed to be known.

- *size*—This is the sample size.

If any argument is nonnumeric, CONFIDENCE.NORM returns a #VALUE! error. If *alpha* is less than or equal to *0* or *alpha* greater than or equal to *1*, CONFIDENCE.NORM returns a #NUM! error. If *standard_dev* is less than or equal to 0, CONFIDENCE.NORM returns a #NUM! error. If *size* is not an integer, it is truncated. If *size* is less than *1*, CONFIDENCE.NORM returns a #NUM! error.

 note

The Excel 2010 function Z.TEST is equivalent to the ZTEST function in legacy versions of Excel.

Using Z.TEST to Accept or Reject a Hypothesis

You use the Z.TEST function for hypothesis testing. Suppose that I make a claim that you will be more confident using pivot tables after attending one of my Power Excel seminars. One month after one of my seminars, I randomly select 30 students from the class and ask them how many minutes during the month they used pivot tables. The sample mean comes back at 156 minutes. This mean is higher than most sample means. But is it high enough to be statistically valid? Could I have achieved a sample mean of 156 just randomly?

Syntax:

=Z.TEST(*array,x,sigma*)

The Z.TEST function returns the two-tailed *p* value of a *z*-test. The *z*-test generates a standard score for *x* with respect to the data set, array, and returns the two-tailed probability for the normal distribution. You can use this function to assess the likelihood that a particular observation is drawn from a particular population. This function takes the following arguments:

- *array*—This is the array or range of data against which to test x.

- *x*—This is the value to test.

- *sigma*—This is the population (known) standard deviation. If this argument is omitted, the sample standard deviation is used.

If *array* is empty, Z.TEST returns an #N/A error.

 caution

A slight problem with the confidence interval function is that the CONFIDENCE.NORM function expects that you know with certainty the standard deviation of the entire population. In real life, if you don't know the mean of the 500 million people using Excel, how would you ever calculate the standard deviation? In reality, when you don't know the population standard deviation, you often substitute the sample standard deviation, but this causes you to have to use the t distribution instead of CONFIDENCE.NORM. Microsoft added CONFIDENCE.T to Excel 2010 to handle this situation.

Using PERMUT to Calculate the Number of Possible Arrangements

Suppose your company has 40 products in its catalog. You must choose four items to be featured in an upcoming SkyMall issue. The sequence in which the products appear in the ad is relevant. You would like to test the possible ads with a test audience. How many different possible ads could you generate? You use the PERMUT function to solve this problem.

Syntax:

=PERMUT(*number,number_chosen*)

The PERMUT function returns the number of permutations for a given number of objects that can be selected from number objects. A permutation is any set or subset of objects or events in which internal order is significant. Permutations are different from combinations, for which the internal order is not significant. You use this function for lottery-style probability calculations.

The PERMUT function takes the following arguments:

- *number*—This is an integer that describes the number of objects.

- *number_chosen*—This is an integer that describes the number of objects in each permutation.

Both arguments are truncated to integers. If *number* or *number_chosen* is nonnumeric, PERMUT returns a #VALUE! error. If number is less than or equal to 0 or if *number_chosen* is less than 0, PERMUT returns a #NUM! error. If *number* is less than *number_chosen*, PERMUT returns a #NUM! error.

The formula to solve the SkyMall problem is =PERMUT(40,4). The result is that there are 2,193,360 possible permutations of products to appear in a one-page ad in the catalog. That is a lot of possibilities!

Using the Analysis ToolPak to Perform Statistical Analysis

The functions discussed in this chapter are wonderful for doing statistical analysis. If you can use a function to perform some analysis, the function offers a live result. You can change some assumptions, and the results automatically update.

However, many statisticians instead rely on the data tools available in the Analysis ToolPak. The Analysis ToolPak can provide beautiful snapshot-type reports that analyze a data set. Although these reports provide more information than a typical function, they have the downside that they do not automatically recalculate. If you change one of the assumptions in the data set, you will have to rerun the analysis.

Excel offers many options for performing statistical analysis. Using functions in Excel provides real-time, live results of the data.

On the other hand, some of the tools, such as Regression, provide additional statistics that run circles around the equivalent functions in Excel. In this case, it would be advantageous to use the Analysis ToolPak.

Remember, however, that when you use the Data Analysis tools from the Analysis ToolPak, they create static snapshots of the results. If you change the underlying data, you have to rerun the analysis.

 note

The Data Analysis tools in the Analysis ToolPak vary greatly. Some of them are poorly implemented and provide such narrow functionality that it is usually better to use your own functions rather than those tools.

Installing the Analysis ToolPak in Excel 2010

In legacy versions of Excel, many people would install the Analysis ToolPak because they needed it to enable the 89 functions it contained. When you enabled the Analysis ToolPak to access the additional functions, Excel silently added a new Data Analysis item to the Tools menu.

However, in Excel 2010, those 89 functions are already part of the core Excel product. Thus, it is much less likely that you already have the Analysis ToolPak installed. To install it, follow these steps:

1. Select File, Options.

2. From the left list, select Add-Ins. You see a long list of active and inactive add-ins.

3. From the bottom of the window, select the Manage drop-down box and then select Excel Add-ins. Click Go. You are taken back to the Excel 2003 Add-Ins dialog.

4. In the Add-Ins dialog, select the Analysis ToolPak check box. Click OK.

If this process is successful, you get a new Analysis group on the Data tab. The group has a single button called Data Analysis, as shown in Figure 14.48. Note that this item is rather finicky. You must click Data Analysis to invoke the Data Analysis dialog box.

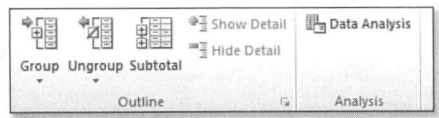

Figure 14.48
After you successfully install the Analysis ToolPak, a new group on the Data tab offers access to the Data Analysis dialog box.

Generating Random Numbers Based on Various Distributions

Whereas the RAND and RANDBETWEEN functions generate random numbers, the Random Number Generation choice in the Data Analysis dialog box allows you to create more sophisticated random number populations. Here's how you use it:

1. Make sure the Analysis ToolPak is installed.

2. From the Data tab, select Data Analysis.

3. Scroll down and select Random Number Generation and click OK. The Random Number Generation dialog appears (see Figure 14.49).

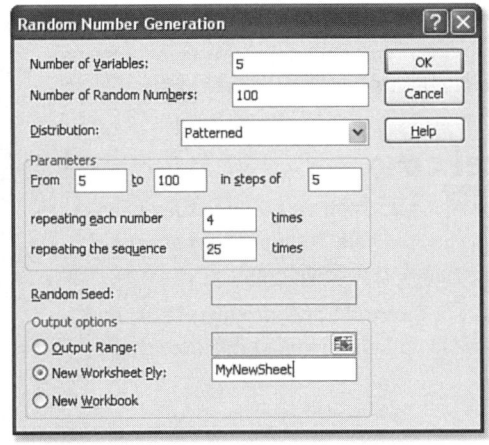

Figure 14.49
You can generate random numbers by using the Random Number Generation dialog.

4. In the Random Number Generation dialog, choose the number of columns that you would like to fill with random numbers. If you want three columns of random numbers, enter 3 in the Number of Variables text box.

5. Choose the number of rows that you would like to fill with random numbers. If you want 100 rows of random numbers, fill in 100 in the Number of Random Numbers text box.

6. Select one of the seven options in the Distribution drop-down. The questions in the Parameters frame change for each distribution option:

- For a uniform distribution, you choose upper and lower limits in the Parameters frame. This functionality is similar to using the RAND worksheet function.

- For a normal distribution, you choose a mean and standard deviation. This functionality is very cool and is not available through the normal Excel functions.

 **note**

There is nothing random about a patterned distribution method. You are simply creating numbers that follow a certain pattern.

- For a Bernoulli distribution, you choose a probability of success on each trial. Bernoulli random variables have a value of 0 or 1. If you want to model LeBron James's ability to make free throws, you use a Bernoulli distribution with a probability of success of 79.4%

- For a binomial distribution, you specify a p value and the number of trials. For example, you can generate number-of-trials Bernoulli random variables, the sum of which is a binomial random variable.

- For a Poisson distribution, you specify a value, *lambda*, that is equal to 1 / Mean. Poisson distributions are often used to characterize the number of events that occur per unit of time (for example, the average rate at which cars arrive at a toll plaza).

- For a patterned distribution, you specify five parameters. You specify a lower and upper limit in steps of a certain value. You can also specify that each number repeats n times and that the whole sequence repeats y times.

- For a discrete distribution, you specify a range of values and their probabilities. In this case, you might have a list of 40 products in A2:A41 and then their probabilities of being selected in B2:B41. Note that the sum of the values in the probability column must add to 100%.

7. In the Random Seed text box, enter any numeric seed. This concept is a little bizarre. In a computer, random numbers are not really random. Scientists call them *pseudo-random*. If you leave the Random Seed text box, Excel uses some strange number (perhaps the number of seconds since 1900 or perhaps the free memory in the stack) as a seed. This ensures that you get different random numbers every time. However, if you enter your own seed, such as 123, and then come back a month later with the same seed, Excel generates exactly the same list of random numbers.

8. For the output range, you can choose an output range, a new worksheet, or a new workbook. For some unknown reason, this dialog box refers to a new worksheet as New Worksheet Ply.

Generating a Histogram

Consider a set of 100 observations. If the possible values are from a continuous series, it is likely that you won't have any two values that are exactly the same. The chart of this data will show a lot of noise, as shown in Figure 14.50.

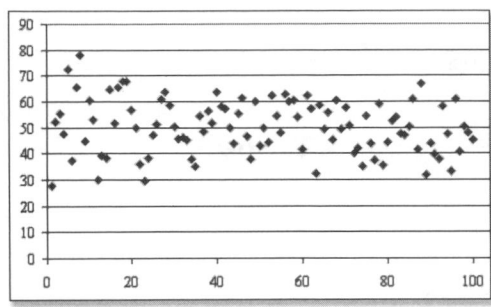

Figure 14.50
Plotting the individual points of a sample does not tell you a lot about the sample.

Statisticians instead prefer to group those values into similar categories. Perhaps logical categories for this data set are 24–34, 35–44, 45–54, and so on. The technical term for these groups is *bins*.

The Histogram tool takes a set of observations and groups them into bins, similarly to the way that the FREQUENCY function normally does. However, the histogram function goes further, offering the cumulative percentage of each bin, and then it re-sorts the bins into a Pareto analysis. Excel also offers to create a chart based on the output.

To use the Histogram tool, follow these steps:

1. Make sure the Analysis ToolPak is installed.

2. Think about some groupings for your data and enter these in a new column in the worksheet. The first bin should be less than the minimum value in your data set. If your bin range contains 25, 35, 45, the first bin will include from 25 up through values just less than 35.

3. From the Data tab, select Data Analysis. Then select Histogram and click OK. The Histogram dialog appears.

4. In the Histogram dialog, specify the range that contains your observations as the input range. This range does not need to be sorted. You may include a one-cell heading as part of the range. If you do, you must also include a one-cell heading for the bin range and also check the Labels option in step 6.

5. Specify your range from step 2 as the bin range.

6. If your input and bin ranges contain one-cell headings, select the Labels check box.

7. For the output, specify the upper-left corner of a blank spot on the current worksheet, or specify a new worksheet or a new workbook.

8. Select the Pareto check box. Excel produces the histogram and then produces a second histogram. In the second histogram, the most popular bin is sorted to the top of the list.

9. Select the Cumulative check box. Excel reports the cumulative percentage accounted for by values from the bottom of the list through the current bin.

10. Select the Chart Output check box to ask for a chart. Note that this default chart is fairly plain looking and needs some customization to be acceptable.

11. Click OK to create the histogram.

Figure 14.51 shows the Histogram dialog box, along with the results of the histogram.

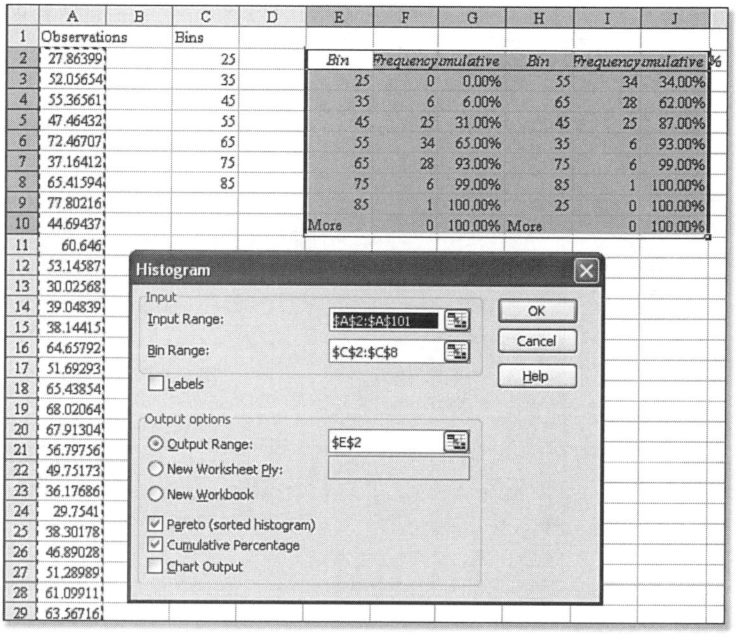

Figure 14.51
Using input area of Column A and the bins in Column C, Excel produces a histogram in E:J. This is significantly easier than using the FREQUENCY array formula.

Generating Descriptive Statistics of a Population

Excel provides a large number of functions to describe data sets. Earlier in this chapter, you learned about functions to calculate the mean, median, mode, skew, and so on of your data. By using the Data Analysis tools, you can generate all these statistics in a single command. To do so, follow these steps:

1. Make sure the Analysis ToolPak is installed.

2. From the Data tab, select Data Analysis. Then select Descriptive Statistics and click OK. The Descriptive Statistics dialog appears.

3. In the Descriptive Statistics dialog, choose the input range for your data set.

4. If the range in step 3 contains a heading in the first row, select the Labels check box.

5. Set the output as a new range, a new worksheet, or a new workbook.

6. Select Summary Statistics. Excel provides values for mean, standard error (of the mean), median, mode, standard deviation, variance, kurtosis, skewness, range, minimum, maximum, sum, count, largest (#), smallest (#), and confidence level.

7. Select the Confidence Level for Mean check box and specify the confidence level you want to use. For example, a confidence level of 95% calculates the confidence level of the mean at a significance of 5%.

8. If you would like row(s) in the output for the kth largest and/or smallest values, select the appropriate check boxes and fill in the value for k. For example, if you ask for the kth largest with a value of 3, Excel report the third-largest value in the data set.

9. Click OK. Results similar to those shown in Figure 14.52 are generated.

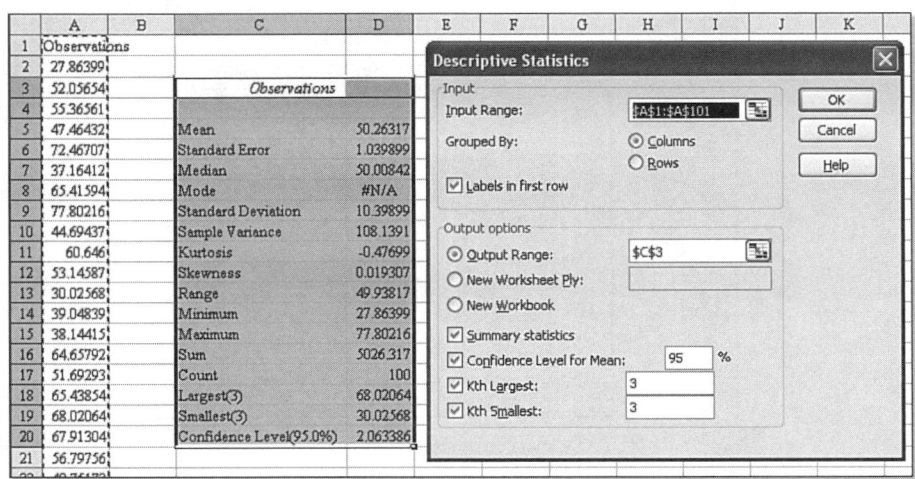

Figure 14.52
Excel can generate every descriptive statistic for a data set with a single command. The output range in C3:D20 is generated from the dialog box shown.

Ranking Results

The Excel RANK function has an inherent problem when two results in the data set are tied. Whereas the RANK.AVG function provides a workaround for this problem, the Rank and Percentile feature cannot overcome this limitation. If you are worried about the possibility of a tie in your data set, you should use the RANK.AVG function instead of this command.

To assign a rank and percentage to a data set, follow these steps:

1. Make sure the Analysis ToolPak is installed. Then scroll down and select Rank and Percentile and click OK. The Rank and Percentile dialog appears.

2. From the Data tab, select Data Analysis.

3. In the Rank and Percentile dialog, choose the input range for your data set. The input range may contain a single-cell heading at the top of the data, but it may not contain any other nonnumeric data. In Figure 14.53, it would be nice if Excel could accept the names associated with each data point, but it cannot. You have to add them back later.

4. If your input range has a heading in the first row, select the Labels in First Row check box.

5. Choose an output range for the data set. Excel returns the statistics shown in D1:G16 in Figure 14.53. Notice that the scores have been sorted in high-to-low sequence. In Column D, Excel refers to each cell as being at Point 1, Point 2, Point 3, and so on.

In Figure 14.53, Column H was added after the fact, using the formula =INDEX($A$2:$A$16,D2). Cell D2 contains the point number for this row. Basically, this function asks for the third value in A2:A16.

Notice that Carla and Jessica are in a tie for second place. No one in this data set is ranked third because of this tie. If you used the RANK function as described earlier in this chapter, you could break the ties by using a COUNTIF function.

Figure 14.53
The rank and percentile function will sort the data and calculate a rank and a percentile function. It cannot resolve ties, however.

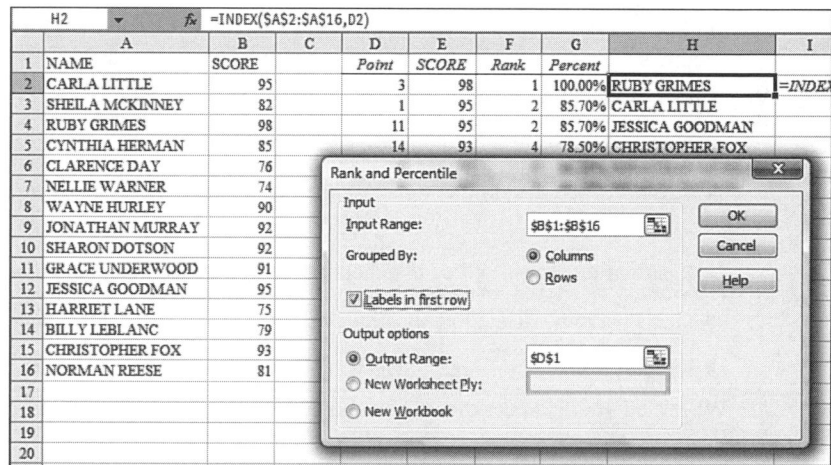

Using Regression to Predict Future Results

The Regression tool available in the Analysis ToolPak runs circles around the LINEST function in Excel. As described previously, LINEST returns a bizarre unlabeled set of results for a regression. The Regression tool, on the other hand, provides a myriad of well-labeled statistics, analysis, and charts as the output.

To perform a regression analysis using the Regression tool, you follow these steps:

1. Make sure the Analysis ToolPak is installed.

2. Ensure that your data includes one independent variable, such as sales per day. It can also contain one or more dependent variables—items that might explain the variability in sales. (In this example, dependent variables include outside temperature, if it rained, and if it was a weekend.)

3. From the Data tab, select Data Analysis. Then scroll down, select Regression, and click OK. The Regression dialog appears.

4. In the Regression dialog, the Input Y range must be a single column of data. In this example, it is the range containing sales for each day. Be sure to include a cell at the top of the column that describes the data.

5. In the Input X Range text box, use a range that is the same height as the Y range. The X range can contain one column for each independent variable. In this example, the X range contains columns for temperature, rain, and weekend. For best results, include a cell at the top of each column, with the name of the variable.

6. If your ranges in steps 4 and 5 include headings, select the Labels check box.

7. If you want to force the y-intercept to be 0, select the Constant Is Zero check box.

8. The Confidence Level box is interesting. The program always gives statistics for a 95% confidence level. If you enter a different percentage in this box, you get two confidence levels: one for the default 95%, and one for the other value you enter.

9. Specify the output range as the top-left cell of a range. In this example, the regression output occupies from G2 to O119, so make sure that you have a really large area set aside for the results.

10. Fill in the remaining options in the Regression dialog to add sections to the report:

   ■ **Residuals**—Select this to include residuals in the residuals output table.

   ■ **Standardized Residuals**—Select this to include standardized residuals in the residuals output table.

   ■ **Residual Plots**—Select this to generate a chart for each independent variable versus the residual.

   ■ **Line Fit Plots**—Select this to generate a chart for predicted values versus the observed values.

   ■ **Normal Probability Plots**—Select this to generate a chart that plots normal probability.

   When you are done, the dialog box should look roughly as shown in Figure 14.54.

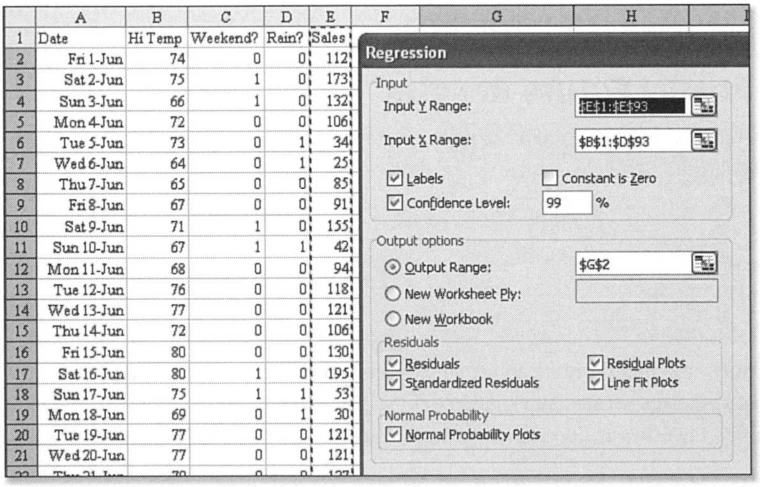

Figure 14.54
The hardest part of specifying a regression is remembering that the y range is the value you are trying to predict.

After you run the regression, Excel provides the following sections of the report (see Figure 14.55):

■ Regression statistics such as *r*-squared are provided in the top section.

■ An ANOVA analysis is provided.

■ The actual regression results are provided in Column 2 of the third section. In this example, the prediction for sales comes from H18:H21. The formula would be that sales for any day will be −75 + 2.6 × High temperature + 52 if it is a weekend. If it is raining, you subtract 102 from this prediction. Remaining columns in this section return the standard error, *t* statistic, *p* value, and confidence limits for each variable.

■ The next section goes far beyond the LINEST function. Excel uses the regression results to predict sales for each day in the data set. The predicted sales are in Column 2 of the data set which is column H in the figure. The comparison of predicted sales to actual sales is shown in the Residuals column.

■ Finally, Excel provides a probability table. The table explains that on the worst 12.5% of days, you might sell $44 or less.

Figure 14.55
The regression report from the Analysis ToolPak is fantastic. It provides a more comprehensive view than the LINEST function.

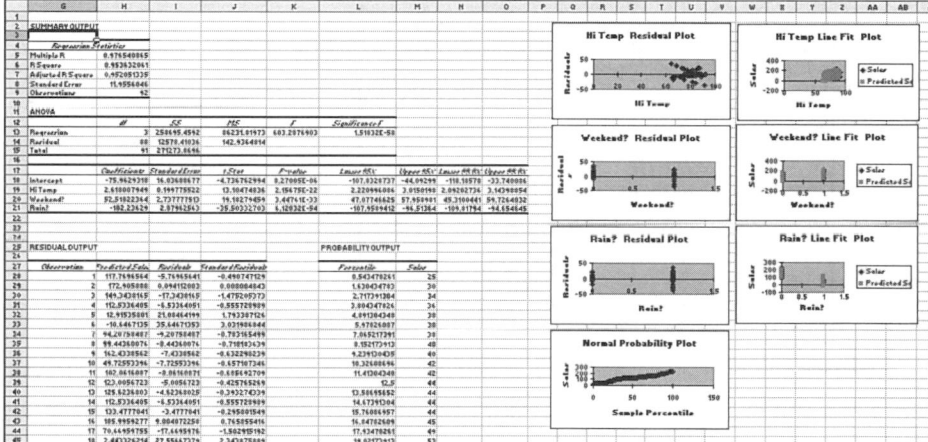

Using a Moving Average to Forecast Sales

The Moving Average command in the Data Analysis tools is disappointing. The technique of using a moving average to produce future forecasts is based on the concept that variability in the month-to-month actuals is lessened if you always average three months.

After choosing Data Analysis, Moving Average, you can specify an input range that contains one column of sales data. The interval value of 3 produces a three-month moving average.

After you use the Moving Average command, Excel adds one column with a series of simple =AVERAGE() formulas. Each formula averages the sales from the previous month, this month, and the next month. In theory, you would then use this column as input to the forecasting methods to produce a future forecast.

In Figure 14.56, Column C is the new moving average column. Column D is the standard error column. This command is really a lot of hassle when you could easily add your own =AVERAGE formula in Column C.

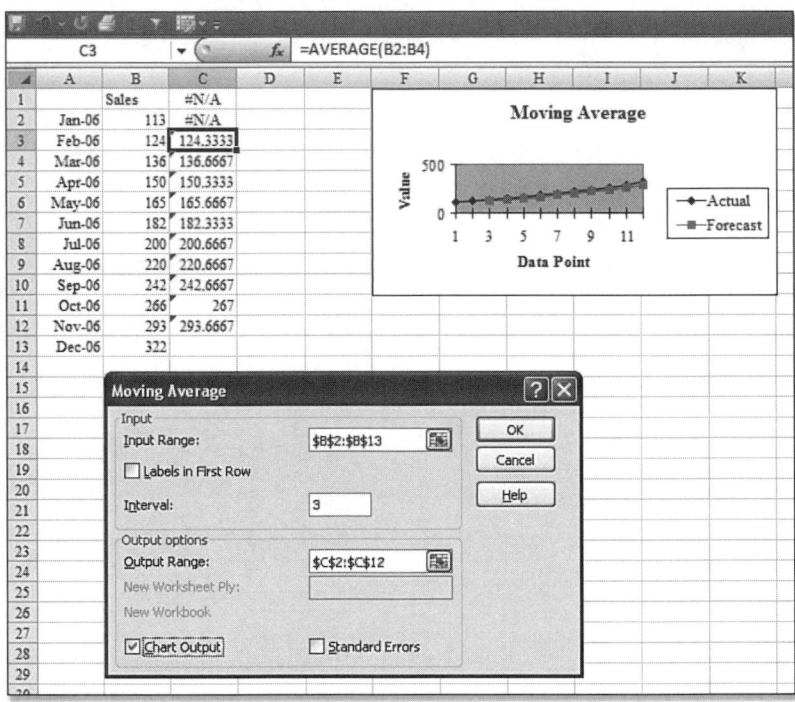

Figure 14.56
The Moving Average feature of the Data Analysis tools is a long route to adding a simple formula.

Using Exponential Smoothing to Forecast Sales

The Exponential Smoothing feature in the Data Analysis tools allows you to set up a forecasting formula that uses exponential smoothing.

This method of forecasting requires only two points: the forecast for the previous month and the actual for the current month. The forecast for the next month is created by adding together 75% of the most recent actuals and 25% of the prior forecast.

In this example, the 25% is called a *damping factor*. You can assign any damping factor that you want, but values in the 20% to 30% range are recommended.

To set up an exponential smoothing forecast, follow these steps:

1. Make sure the Analysis ToolPak is installed.

2. Ensure that your data includes one column of sales data, such as sales per month.

3. From the Data tab, select Data Analysis. Then select Exponential Smoothing and click OK. The Exponential Smoothing dialog appears.

4. In the Exponential Smoothing dialog, the Input range should be your single column of sales data. If you include a heading cell, select the Labels check box.

5. Ensure that the damping factor is between 0.20 and 0.30. With a damping factor of 0.30, the current forecast is based 70% on the most recent actuals and 30% on all the past forecasts.

6. Limit the output range to a cell on the current worksheet. Ideally, this range starts in the same row as your input range, in an adjacent column.

7. To create a chart comparing forecast and actuals, select the Chart Output check box.

8. Select the Standard Errors check box. The output contains a second column with a standard error calculation. This calculation analyzes the current period and last three periods. In Row 5, enter the standard error formula =SQRT(SUMXMY2(B3:B5,C2:C4)/3). This formula subtracts the forecast from the actual for the last three months, squares the differences, adds them, divides to find an average, and then takes the square root of the average.

9. Click OK to produce the analysis.

Figure 14.57 shows the Exponential Smoothing dialog and the subsequent results of the analysis.

Figure 14.57
Exponential smoothing provides a forecast that is heavily weighted toward recent actuals.

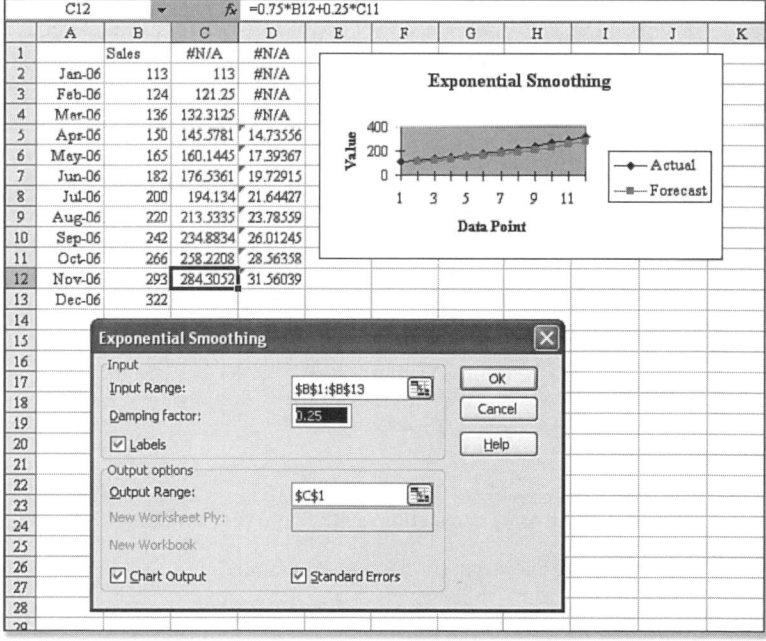

Because the standard error column must analyze four months of forecasts and actuals, the first three data points in the standard error column are always #N/A!.

Using Correlation or Covariance to Calculate the Relationship Between Many Variables

 **note**

A bug prevents Excel from entering the label Sales Forecast in the top row of the output. You have to manually change the headings Excel generates.

Both covariance and correlation are measures of the extent to which two measurement variables vary together. I prefer the correlation coefficient because it is independent of the units involved.

Say that you are comparing height in inches or centimeters to weight in pounds or kilograms. The correlation coefficient returns a value from 1 to –1. Correlation coefficient values close to 0 indicate little or no correlation between the measures. A value close to 1 indicates a strong positive correlation: As one variable increases, the other is likely to increase. A value close to –1 indicates a strong negative correlation: The value of one variable is likely to decrease as the value of the other variable increases.

You could calculate these values manually by using the CORREL or PEARSON functions in Excel, but the Data Analysis version is particularly well suited to data sets that have many measurements for each member of a population. In this case, the Correlation tool generates a correlation coefficient for every possible combination of the measurement statistics.

Figure 14.58 shows a database of body statistics for a sample of 125 people. For each person, the clinician measured 13 key measurements, such as height, weight, and so on. It would be interesting to see if height is a good predictor of weight or if some other measurement is appropriate.

	B2		▼		*fx*	160.5	
	A	B	C	D	E	F	G
1	ID	Weight	Age	Height	Abdomen	Ankle	Biceps	C
2	101	160.5	29	71.5	84.7	21.7	30.3
3	102	198.25	54	72.25	100	22	35.9
4	103	158.5	47	72.5	86.9	22.6	26.2
5	104	188	35	69.75	96.4	23.1	36.1
6	105	203.25	50	67.25	108.3	24.9	34.3
7	106	177.25	46	70.25	95.6	22.5	29.1
8	107	205.25	44	29.75	104.5	23.9	33.8
9	108	217.25	48	70.25	111.2	25	36.7
10	109	177.25	43	69.5	98.8	22.2	30.3

Figure 14.58
In a collection of key measurement stats for 125 members of a population, which measurements are most related?

To build a matrix of correlation coefficients (or covariances), you follow these steps:

1. Make sure the Analysis ToolPak is installed.

2. Ensure that your data includes several columns of measurements for a population. Each row should represent another member of the population. Try to avoid missing values. If one measurement is missing for a population member, that member is thrown out of the entire calculation.

3. From the Data tab, select Data Analysis. Then select Correlation (or Covariance) and click OK. The Correlation dialog appears.

4. In the Correlation dialog, ensure that the input range includes your row of headings and all the measurements. If you have an ID field, do not include it in the input range.

5. If your data has labels as the first row or column of the input range, select the Labels check box.

6. Select the upper-left corner of the output range. If your input range has n columns, the size of the output range will be $(n + 1) \times (n + 1)$.

7. Click OK to create the correlation matrix.

Figure 14.59 shows the Correlation dialog box and the resulting correlation matrix. In this particular example, height and weight have a weak correlation coefficient of 0.21. You can compare this to the correlation coefficient for hip and weight, which has a positive correlation of 0.93.

The covariance feature works the same as the correlation feature, except the output table is not scaled to provide answers between −1 and 1.

Figure 14.59
The correlation coefficient matrix produces results from −1 to 1. Values further away from o indicate a strong correlation between the measurement variables.

	Weight	Age	Height	Abdomen	Ankle	Biceps	Chest	Forearm	Hip	Knee	Neck	Thigh	Wrist
Weight	1												
Age	-0.04385	1											
Height	0.212495	-0.10121	1										
Abdomen	0.875	0.199683	0.017032	1									
Ankle	0.551508	-0.09416	0.178332	0.389644	1								
Biceps	0.783243	-0.0635	0.138199	0.665566	0.430837	1							
Chest	0.894235	0.093076	0.093197	0.906529	0.434664	0.724031	1						
Forearm	0.696212	-0.11284	0.214936	0.542617	0.392694	0.71767	0.668817	1					
Hip	0.932978	-0.08046	0.03459	0.869817	0.488254	0.720737	0.831917	0.582675	1				
Knee	0.846664	-0.0283	0.116215	0.747254	0.529144	0.69455	0.730452	0.631785	0.819955	1			
Neck	0.811978	0.084627	0.223508	0.723415	0.416404	0.690761	0.762351	0.667752	0.708693	0.65764	1		
Thigh	0.85348	-0.22601	-0.02171	0.766655	0.443509	0.753886	0.749784	0.636531	0.894339	0.803796	0.686064	1	
Wrist	0.725927	0.196743	0.305715	0.603123	0.485761	0.625066	0.653793	0.718965	0.595863	0.632301	0.749882	0.531882	1

Correlation

Input
Input Range: $B$1:$N$126
Grouped By: ⊙ Columns ○ Rows
☑ Labels In first row

Output options
⊙ Output Range: $P$1
○ New Worksheet Ply:
○ New Workbook

OK
Cancel
Help

Using Sampling to Create Random Samples

Earlier in this chapter, in the section on the RAND function, you learned about a way to collect a random sample. You can also allow the Data Analysis tools to produce a random sample for you.

The Random Sampling feature offers two interesting ways to collect a sample. Excel can either randomly select n members of the population, or you can specify that Excel should select every kth member of the population.

You follow these steps to select a random sample:

1. Make sure the Analysis ToolPak is installed.

2. Ensure that your data is completely numeric. This feature works best on a single column of data, so ensure that you are selecting just a single column. If you have multiple columns of data, Excel randomly selects cells from the entire range; for example, the random sample might include Cells B2, A5, C7, D10, B2. Ensure that you do not include column headings if your data spans multiple columns.

> **tip**
> In step 4, do not include labels if your population spans multiple columns.

3. From the Data tab, select Data Analysis. Then scroll down, select Sampling, and click OK. The Sampling dialog appears.

4. In the Sampling dialog, ensure that the input range includes your data range. If your data includes a single column, and you have headings in the first cell, select the Labels check box.

5. For random sampling, ask for a specific number of samples. The other option is to specify periodic sampling, which provides every *n*th value in the data set.

6. Specify the top-left cell of the output range and click OK.

In Figure 14.60, Excel has produced a random sample of 10 from a rectangular range of data.

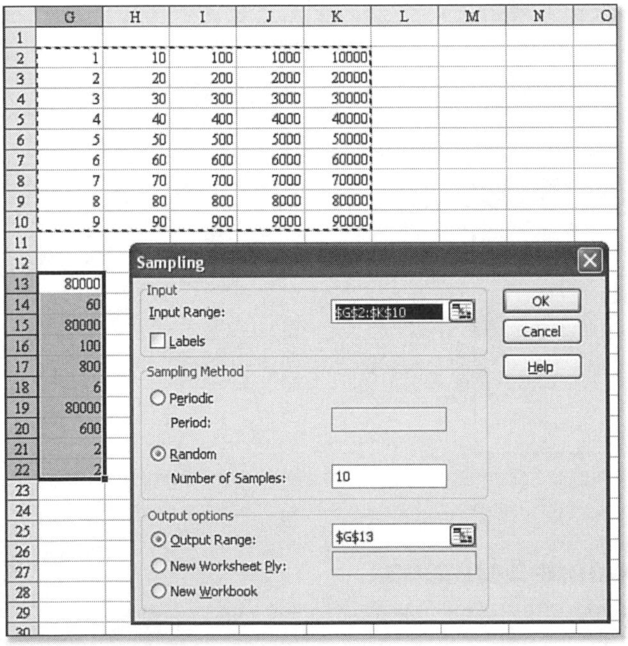

Figure 14.60
A random sample from the Sampling dialog might include duplicates.

> The Random Sampling feature allows for duplicates within the same sample. If you need to make sure that any given sample contains no duplicates, you should use the RAND function instead.
>
> If you ask for a periodic sample, Excel traverses each column from left to right. Selecting every fourth value from G2:K10 in Figure 14.60 would select 4, 8 from the first column, and then 30, 70 from the second column. From 70, Excel would skip the next three values of 80, 90, and 100, and it would return 200 as the next periodic member of the sample.

Using ANOVA to Perform Analysis of Variance Testing

ANOVA stands for analysis of variance. The Data Analysis tools offer three forms of ANOVA testing:

- **Single-factor ANOVA**—This is for measuring variance for two or more samples with a single variable. For example, suppose that you have 18 farm fields. All are planted with the same variety of wheat. Six are treated with Nutrient A, six are treated with Nutrient B, and six are treated with Nutrient C. Single-variable ANOVA would analyze whether the variances in the populations were random or due to the fertilizers.

- **Two-factor ANOVA without replication**—This is for use when your data can be classified along two different dimensions. For example, suppose that half of the farm fields are downwind from an interstate highway that is heavily traveled by diesel trucks. You could analyze the variance caused by the fertilizer versus the variance caused by the carbon monoxide from the highway.

- **Two-factor ANOVA with replication**—If you have enough samples so that every combination of {fertilizer, highway} has multiple samples, you can perform two-factor ANOVA with replication. Otherwise, you use two-factor ANOVA without replication.

Follow these steps to perform a one-way ANOVA test:

1. If your data is set up as records with data for each field, arrange the data in columns for each variable. In Figure 14.61, this means taking the data from Column B and arranging it in three columns, E, F, and G, with a heading above each column.

2. Choose a null hypothesis. For example, your null hypothesis might be that all the nutrients produce a similar mean. If you can reject the null hypothesis, then your hypothesis is that the selection nutrient has an impact on yield.

3. Choose a significance level, alpha, of 0.05. If the statistics from the ANOVA output show a p value greater than the alpha, you can reject the null hypothesis and assume that the nutrient has an impact on yield.

4. Make sure the Analysis ToolPak is installed.

5. From the Data tab, select Data Analysis. Then select ANOVA: Single Factor and click OK. The ANOVA: Single Factor dialog appears.

6. In the ANOVA: Single Factor dialog, ensure that the input range includes your columns of means.

	A	B	C	D	E	F	G	H
3	Field #	Yield	Nutrient		Nutrient --->			
4	1	27.6	B		A		B	C
5	2	25.1	A			25.1	27.6	27.3
6	3	28.2	B			29.1	28.2	31
7	4	29.4	B			26.3	29.4	25.8
8	5	29.1	A			25.7	25.9	30.2
9	6	27.3	C			29.7	29.9	29.4
10	7	25.9	B			29.2	27.3	30.6
11	8	31	C					
12	9	26.3	A		Anova: Single Factor			
13	10	29.9	B					
14	11	25.7	A		SUMMARY			
15	12	25.8	C		Groups	Count	Sum	Average	Variance
16	13	27.3	B		A	6	165.1	27.51667	4.145667
17	14	29.7	A		B	6	168.3	28.05	2.131
18	15	29.2	A		C	6	174.3	29.05	4.255
19	16	30.2	C					
20	17	29.4	C					
21	18	30.6	C		ANOVA			
22					Source of Variation	SS	df	MS	F	P-value	F crit
23					Between Groups	7.271111	2	3.635556	1.035607	0.379054	3.68232
24					Within Groups	52.65833	15	3.510556
25								
26					Total	59.92944	17

Anova: Single Factor dialog:

Input
Input Range: $E$4:$G$10
Grouped By: ⦿ Columns / ◯ Rows
☑ Labels in first row
Alpha: 0.05

Output options
⦿ Output Range: $E$12
◯ New Worksheet Ply:
◯ New Workbook

Figure 14.61
The difference in the sample means is statistically significant.

7. If your input range includes a heading above each column, select the Labels in First Row check box.

8. In the Alpha box, enter the level at which you want to evaluate critical values for the F statistic. The alpha level is a significance level related to the probability of having a type I error (that is, rejecting a true hypothesis).

9. Select the top-left corner for the output range.

10. Click OK to produce the result.

In Figure 14.61, the important statistic is the *p* value in Cell J23. Because this number is larger than alpha, you can reject the null hypothesis and assume that the nutrients had an impact on the yield.

Follow these steps to perform a two-way ANOVA test with replication:

1. Arrange your data so that one dimension is spread across the columns. (This can be tricky.)

2. Ensure that you have equal numbers of samples along the second dimension. In Figure 14.62, there were three rows of yields from fields downwind from a highway. These rows must be arranged together. For convenience, have a row label in Cell G7 to identify this block of data.

3. Because you had three rows of sample yields for fields adjacent to highways, you also have to find three rows of sample yields for fields away from highways. This block of three rows must immediately follow the other data.

4. Make sure the Analysis ToolPak is installed.

5. From the Data tab, select Data Analysis. Then select ANOVA: Two-Factor with Replication and click OK. The ANOVA: Two-Factor with Replication dialog appears.

tip

Again, for convenience, in step 3 make sure there is a heading in the first column and first row of this block to identify the value along the second dimension.

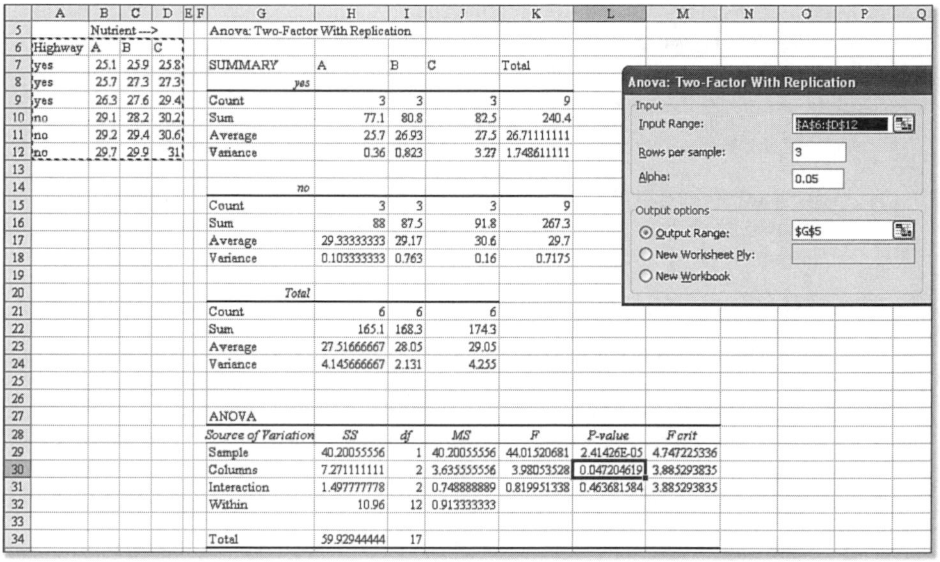

Figure 14.62
Setting up
the input
range in
equal size
rows is
the key to
success-
ful use of
Two-Factor
ANOVA
analysis.

6. In the ANOVA: Two-Factor with Replication dialog, ensure that the input range includes sample values as well as an additional row above to identify the first-dimension variables and an additional column to the left to identify the second-dimension variable.

7. In the Rows per Sample text box, enter the number of rows in each block of data. In this present example, there are three rows of yields for highway fields and three rows for nonhighway fields, so enter 3.

8. In the Alpha box, enter the level at which you want to evaluate critical values for the F statistic. The alpha level is a significance level related to the probability of having a type I error (that is, rejecting a true hypothesis).

9. For the output range, select the top-left corner of a large blank area. The ANOVA results will take up 30 rows by 7 columns.

10. Click OK to perform the analysis.

Evaluating the Results

In the results from this analysis, watch for the values in italic in the first column of the output range. The first block of data in the output range describes the first block of three rows in the input range, with a value of "yes" to the highway question.

The final block of the analysis shows the p values for each dimension and the two dimensions combined. In this particular analysis, it appears that much of the variability is due to highway proximity and does not necessarily have that much to do with the nutrients. The p value of 0.047 for the columns is not enough to reject the null hypothesis that the variability due to nutrients could be random.

In some cases, you may have two factors for the ANOVA testing, but you may not have multiple samples for every combination of {dimension1, dimension2}. In this case, you can run two-factor ANOVA testing without replication. The results from this test contain less analysis than do the results from the test with replication. In this test, Excel does not predict if factors beyond the two dimensions are causing variability.

To perform a two-factor ANOVA without replication, follow these steps:

1. Arrange your data in a crosstab fashion. Have values from Dimension 1 going across the top row of the data. Have values from Dimension 2 going down the left column of the data. Enter the sample value in each intersection.

2. Make sure the Analysis ToolPak is installed.

3. From the Data tab, select Data Analysis. Then select ANOVA: Two-Factor Without Replication and click OK. The ANOVA: Two-Factor Without Replication dialog appears.

4. In the ANOVA: Two-Factor Without Replication dialog, ensure that the input range includes sample values, as well as an additional row above to identify the first-dimension variables and an additional column to the left to identify the second-dimension variables.

5. Select the Labels check box so Excel can get the headings for the Dimension 1 and Dimension 2 values from the worksheet.

6. In the Alpha box, enter the level at which you want to evaluate critical values for the F statistic. The alpha level is a significance level related to the probability of having a type I error (that is, rejecting a true hypothesis).

7. Click OK to run the analysis.

Excel analyzes the variance based on the rows and columns, as shown in Figure 14.63.

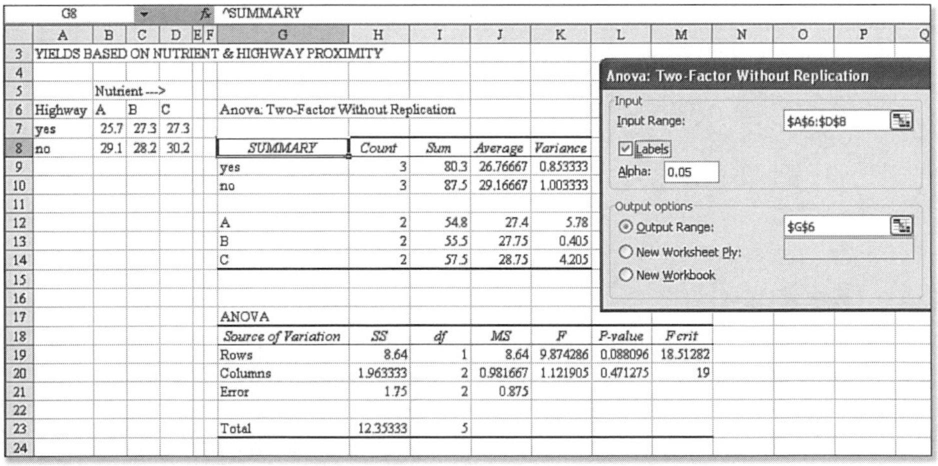

Figure 14.63
In this particular sample, the column drives variability more than the rows.

Using the *F*-Test to Measure Variability Between Methods

If you want to compare two methods, it is helpful to know if the variances in the two methods are roughly the same. The *F*-test was designed by statistician R. A. Fisher. (The *F* here stands for Fisher and nothing intuitive.) The *F*-test compares two variances, V1 / V2, to produce an *F* statistic. Values close to 1 indicate that the variances are similar.

To run an *F*-test, follow these steps:

1. Set up two ranges with samples from each population. These samples do not have to have the same number of members.

2. Make sure the Analysis ToolPak is installed.

3. From the Data tab, select Data Analysis. Then select F-Test Two-Sample for Variances. The F-Test Two Sample for Variances dialog appears.

4. In the F-Test Two Sample for Variances dialog, choose the range for both of your sample ranges.

5. In the Alpha box, enter the level at which you want to evaluate critical values for the F statistic. The alpha level is a significance level related to the probability of having a type I error (that is, rejecting a true hypothesis).

6. Select the top-left cell of an output range.

7. Click OK to produce the analysis.

The F-Test tool provides the result of a test of the null hypothesis that these two samples come from distributions with equal variances against the alternative that the variances are not equal in the underlying distributions.

The F-Test tool calculates the value of an *F* statistic. A value of *F* close to 1 provides evidence that the underlying population variances are equal.

There is a tricky element to the output table. If the *F* value is less than 1, you need to look to the next row, which has the label "P(F <= f) one-tail." It gives the probability of observing a value of the *F* statistic less than f when population variances are equal. The next row, labeled "F Critical one-tail," gives the critical value less than 1 for the chosen significance level, alpha.

If the *F* statistic is greater than 1, the meanings of these rows are reversed. The row labeled "P(F <= f) one-tail" gives the probability of observing a value of the *F* statistic greater than f when population variances are equal, and "F Critical one-tail" gives the critical value greater than 1 for alpha.

In Figure 14.64, the *F* statistic of 0.88 is less than 1. This means that the null hypothesis is that the variances are unequal. The F critical value is 0.35, meaning that you can reject the null hypothesis.

	G4		▼		ƒx	∧Variable 2		
	A	B	C	D	E	F	G	H
1	27		47					
2	52		72		F-Test Two-Sample for Variances			
3	55		75					
4	47		67			Variable 1	Variable 2	
5	72		92		Mean	50.61538462	72.88888889	
6	37		57		Variance	236.2564103	266.8611111	
7	65		85		Observations	13	9	
8	77		97		df	12	8	
9	44		64		F	0.885315996		
10	60				P(F<=f) one-tail	0.409718146		
11	53				F Critical one-tail	0.351053934		
12	30							
13	39							

F-Test Two-Sample for Variances

Input

Variable 1 Range: $A$1:$A$13

Variable 2 Range: $C$1:$C$9

☐ Labels

Alpha: 0.05

Output options

⦿ Output Range: $E$2

○ New Worksheet Ply:

○ New Workbook

OK Cancel Help

Figure 14.64
The *F*-test indicates whether two populations have an equal variance.

Performing a *z*-Test to Determine Whether Two Samples Have Equal Means

You use the Z-Test tool to test the null hypothesis that there is no difference between two population means against either one-sided or two-sided alternative hypotheses. z-tests are appropriate when the sample sizes are greater than 30. For sample sizes smaller than 30, you use t-tests, as described in the following section.

To run a z-test, follow these steps:

1. Set up two ranges with data from each sample. Calculate the standard deviation of each population.

2. Make sure the Analysis ToolPak is installed.

3. From the Data tab, select Data Analysis. Then scroll down and select z-Test: Two-Sample for Means. The z-Test: Two Sample for Means dialog appears.

4. For Variable 1 Range, select the range of data for your first sample.

5. For Variable 2 Range, select the range of data for your second sample.

6. For Hypothesized Mean Difference, if you have a reason to believe that there is a shift from one population to the other caused by an external event, note it here. For example, if you measured

tip
In step 4, if you choose a heading cell in this range, be sure to also choose a heading cell in step 5.

note
If variances are not known, the worksheet function Z.TEST should be used instead.

the height of every kid in the classroom, and the next day you measured the height of every kid while they were standing on a 6-inch bench, the 6 inches would be an explainable shift in the means.

7. For the variances, enter the standard deviations for both populations. As mentioned previously, if you don't know these, you should use the Z.TEST worksheet function instead of this tool.

8. In the Alpha box, enter the confidence level for the test. This value must be in the range 0...1. The alpha level is a significance level related to the probability of having a type I error (that is, rejecting a true hypothesis).

9. Select the top-left cell of an output range.

10. Click OK to produce the analysis.

The results of a z-test are shown in Figure 14.65.

When analyzing the results, you should be careful to understand the output:

- "P(Z <= z) one-tail" is really $P(Z >= ABS(z))$, the probability of a z value further from 0 in the same direction as the observed z value when there is no difference between the population means.

- "P(Z <= z) two-tail" is really $P(Z >= ABS(z) \text{ or } Z <= -ABS(z))$, the probability of a z value further from 0 in either direction than the observed z value when there is no difference between the population means. The two-tailed result is just the one-tailed result multiplied by 2.

Performing Student's t-Testing to Test Population Means

The two-sample T-Test tool tests for equality of the population means underlying each sample. There are three varieties of this test, based on assumptions:

- **t-Test: Paired Two Sample for Means**—If the two samples came from the same population, one before a treatment and one after the treatment, you use this test.

- **t-Test: Two-Sample Assuming Equal Variances**—If you believe that the variances of each population are equal, you use this test.

- **t-Test: Two Sample Assuming Unequal Variances**—If you believe that the variances of the two populations are unequal, you use this test.

All three varieties produce a *t* statistic. The *t* statistic can be negative or nonnegative. Under the assumption of equal underlying population means, if *t* is less than 0, "P(T <= t) one-tail" gives the probability that a value of the *t* statistic would be observed that is more negative than *t*. If *t* is greater than or equal to 0, "P(T <= t) one-tail" gives the probability that a value of the *t* statistic would be observed that is more positive than *t*. "t Critical one-tail" gives the cutoff value so that the probability of observing a value of the *t* statistic greater than or equal to "t Critical one-tail" is alpha.

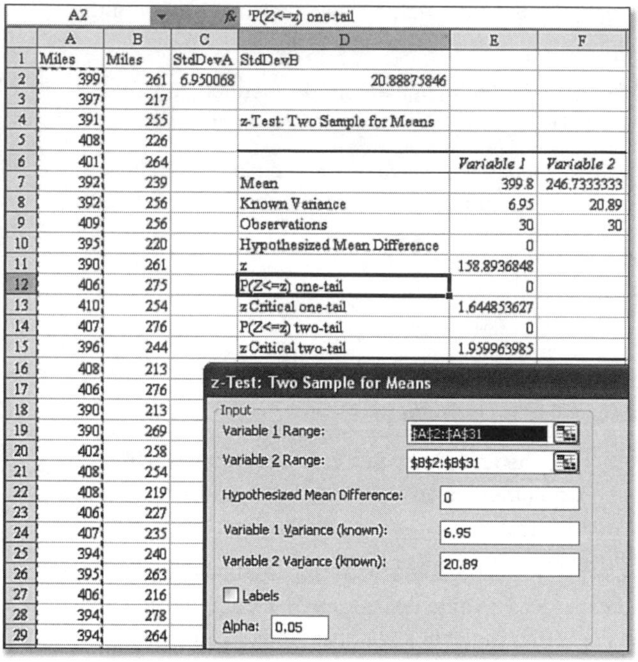

Figure 14.65
This z-test indicates that the samples came from different populations.

"P(T <= t) two-tail" gives the probability that a value of the t statistic would be observed that is larger in absolute value than t. "P Critical two-tail" gives the cutoff value so that the probability of an observed t statistic larger in absolute value than "P Critical two-tail" is alpha.

To perform a t-test, follow these steps:

1. Set up two ranges with data from each sample.

2. Make sure the Analysis ToolPak is installed.

3. From the Data tab, select Data Analysis. Then scroll down and select t-Test: Two-Sample Assuming Equal Variance. The t-Test dialog appears.

4. For Variable 1 Range, select the range of data for your first sample.

5. For Variable 2 Range, select the range of data for your second sample.

6. For Hypothesized Mean Difference, if you have a reason to believe that there is a shift from one population to the other caused by an external event, note it here.

7. In the Alpha box, enter the confidence level for the test. This value must be in the range 0...1. The alpha level is a significance level related to the probability of having a type I error (that is, rejecting a true hypothesis).

8. Select the top-left cell of an output range.

9. Click OK to produce the analysis.

The results of a *t*-test are shown in Figure 14.66.

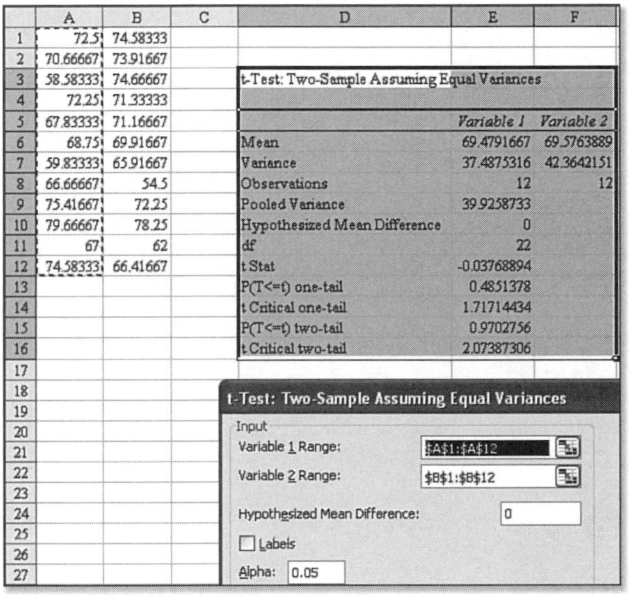

Figure 14.66
Based on a *t* statistic close to 0, you cannot assume that these came from different populations.

Using Functions Versus the Analysis ToolPak Tools

Excel offers many options for performing statistical analysis. Using functions in Excel provides real-time, live results of the data.

The Data Analysis tools in the Analysis ToolPak vary greatly. Some of them are poorly implemented and provide such narrow functionality that it is usually better to use your own functions rather than those tools.

On the other hand, some of the tools, such as Regression, provide additional statistics that run circles around the equivalent functions in Excel. In this case, it would be advantageous to use the Analysis ToolPak.

Remember, however, that when you use the Data Analysis tools from the Analysis ToolPak, they create static snapshots of the results. If you change the underlying data, you have to rerun the analysis.**Table 14.1** Continued**Table 14.1** Continued**Table 14.1** Continued**Table 14.1** Continued**Table 14.1** Continued**Table 14.1** Continued**Table 14.1** Continued**Table 14.1** Continued**Table 14.1** Continued**Table 14.1** Continued**Table 14.1** Continued

15

USING TRIG, MATRIX, AND ENGINEERING FUNCTIONS

Scientists, mathematicians, and engineers, as well as high school mathematics students, will get the broadest use out of the functions in this chapter. Even though many of the trigonometry functions might seem intimidating, this chapter includes practical household examples for many of the functions. Anyone who has to lean a ladder against a house can find a use for the trig functions.

The imaginary number functions might be useful only to electrical engineers, but any business analyst can make use of the techniques for solving linear equations.

Table 15.1 provides an alphabetical list of all of Excel 2010's trig functions. Detailed examples of the functions are provided later in the chapter.

Table 15.1 Alphabetical List of Trig Functions

Function	Description
ACOS(*number*)	Returns the arccosine of a number. The arccosine is the angle whose cosine is number. The returned angle is given in radians in the Range 0 to π.
ACOSH(*number*)	Returns the inverse hyperbolic cosine of a number. number must be greater than or equal to 1. The inverse hyperbolic cosine is the value whose hyperbolic cosine is *number*, so ACOSH(COSH(*number*)) equals number.
ASIN(*number*)	Returns the arcsine of a number. The arcsine is the angle whose sine is number. The returned angle is given in radians in the Range –π / 2 to π/ 2.

Function	Description
ASINH(*number*)	Returns the inverse hyperbolic sine of a number. The inverse hyperbolic sine is the value whose hyperbolic sine is number, so ASINH(SINH(*number*)) equals *number*.
ATAN(*number*)	Returns the arctangent of a number. The arctangent is the angle whose tangent is *number*. The returned angle is given in radians in the Range $-\pi/2$ to $\pi/2$.
ATAN2(*x_num,y_num*)	Returns the arctangent of the specified x- and y-coordinates. The arctangent is the angle from the x-axis to a line containing the origin (0, 0) and a point with coordinates (*x_num, y_num*). The angle is given in radians between $-\pi$ and ϖ, excluding $-\pi$.
ATANH(*number*)	Returns the inverse hyperbolic tangent of a number. number must be between -1 and 1 (excluding -1 and 1). The inverse hyperbolic tangent is the value whose hyperbolic tangent is number, so ATANH(TANH(*number*)) equals *number*.
COS(*number*)	Returns the cosine of the given angle.
COSH(*number*)	Returns the hyperbolic cosine of a number.
DEGREES(*angle*)	Converts radians into degrees.
LN(*number*)	Returns the natural logarithm of number. Natural logarithms are based on the constant e such as 2.71828182845904).
LOG(*number,base*)	Returns the logarithm of *number* to the specified base.
LOG10(*number*)	Returns the base-10 logarithm of *number*.
RADIANS(*angle*)	Converts degrees to radians.
SIN(*number*)	Returns the sine of the given angle.
SINH(*number*)	Returns the hyperbolic sine of *number*.
TAN(*number*)	Returns the tangent of the given angle.
TANH(*number*)	Returns the hyperbolic tangent of *number*.

Table 15.2 provides an alphabetical list of all Excel 2010's matrix functions. Detailed examples of the functions are provided later in the chapter.

Table 15.2 Alphabetical List of Matrix Functions

Function	Description
MDETERM(*array*)	Returns the matrix determinant of an array.
MINVERSE(*array*)	Returns the inverse matrix for the matrix stored in an array.

Function	Description
MMULT(array1,array2)	Returns the matrix product of two arrays. The result is an array with the same number of rows as array1 and the same number of columns as array2.
SERIESSUM(x,n,m, coefficients)	Returns the sum of a power series based on the formula $SERIES(x,n,m,a) \approx a_1 x^n + a_2 x^{(n+m)} + a_3 x^{(n+2m)} + \ldots + a_i x^{(n+(i-1)m)}$
SUMPRODUCT(array1,array2, array3,...)	Multiplies corresponding components in the given arrays and returns the sum of those products.

Table 15.3 provides an alphabetical list of all Excel 2010's engineering functions. Detailed examples of the functions are provided later in the chapter.

Table 15.3 Alphabetical List of Engineering Functions

Function	Description
BESSELI(x,n)	Returns the modified Bessel function, which is equivalent to the BESSELJ function evaluated for purely imaginary arguments.
BESSELJ(x,n)	Returns the Bessel function of the first kind.
BESSELK(x,n)	Returns the modified Bessel function of the second kind, which is equivalent to the BESSELY functions evaluated for purely imaginary arguments.
BESSELY(x,n)	Returns the Bessel function of the second kind. This is the most commonly used form of the Bessel functions. This function provides solutions of the Bessel differential equation and are infinite at x=0. This function is sometimes called the Neumann function.
BIN2DEC(number)	Converts a binary number to decimal.
BIN2HEX(number,places)	Converts a binary number to hexadecimal.
BIN2OCT(number,places)	Converts a binary number to octal.
COMPLEX(real_num,i_num,suffix)	Converts real and imaginary coefficients into a complex number in the form $x + yi$ or $x + yj$.
CONVERT(number,from_unit,to_unit)	Converts a number from one measurement system to another. For example, CONVERT can translate a table of distances in miles to a table of distances in kilometers.
DEC2BIN(number,places)	Converts a decimal number to binary.
DEC2HEX(number,places)	Converts a decimal number to hexadecimal.

Function	Description
DEC2OCT(*number*,*places*)	Converts a decimal number to octal.
DELTA(*number1*,*number2*)	Tests whether two values are equal. Returns 1 if number1 = number2; returns 0 otherwise. You use this function to filter a set of values. For example, by summing several DELTA functions, you can calculate the count of equal pairs. This function is also known as the Kronecker Delta function.
ERF(*lower_limit*, *upper_limit*)	Returns the ERROR function integrated between *lower_limit* and *upper_limit*.
ERFC(x)	Returns the complementary ERF function integrated between x and infinity.
GESTEP(*number*,*step*)	Returns 1 if *number* is greater than or equal to *step*; otherwise returns 0. You use this function to filter a set of values. For example, by summing several GESTEP functions, you can calculate the count of values that exceed a threshold.
HEX2BIN(*number*,*places*)	Converts a hexadecimal number to binary.
HEX2DEC(*number*)	Converts a hexadecimal number to decimal.
HEX2OCT(*number*,*places*)	Converts a hexadecimal number to octal.
IMABS(*inumber*)	Returns the absolute value (modulus) of a complex number in x + yi or x + yj text format.
IMAGINARY(*inumber*)	Returns the imaginary coefficient of a complex number in x + yi or x + yj text format.
IMARGUMENT(*inumber*)	Returns the argument θ (theta), an angle expressed in radians.
IMCONJUGATE(*inumber*)	Returns the complex conjugate of a complex number in x + yi or x + yj text format.
IMCOS(*inumber*)	Returns the cosine of a complex number in x + yi or x + yj text format.
IMDIV(*inumber1*,*inumber2*)	Returns the quotient of two complex numbers in x + yi or x + yj text format.
IMEXP(*inumber*)	Returns the exponential of a complex number in x + yi or x + yj text format.
IMLN(*inumber*)	Returns the natural logarithm of a complex number in x + yi or x + yj text format.
IMLOG10(*inumber*)	Returns the common logarithm (base-10) of a complex number in x + yi or x + yj text format.
IMLOG2(*inumber*)	Returns the base-2 logarithm of a complex number in x + yi or x + yj text format.

Function	Description
IMPOWER(*inumber,number*)	Returns a complex number in x + *yi* or x + *yj* text format raised to a power.
IMPRODUCT(*inumber1, inumber2,...*)	Returns the product of 2 to 255 complex numbers in x + *yi* or x + *yj* text format.
IMREAL(*inumber*)	Returns the real coefficient of a complex number in x + *yi* or x + *yj* text format.
IMSIN(*inumber*)	Returns the sine of a complex number in x + *yi* or x + *yj* text format.
IMSQRT(*inumber*)	Returns the square root of a complex number in x + *yi* or x + *yj* text format.
IMSUB(*inumber1,inumber2*)	Returns the difference of two complex numbers in x + I or x + *yj* text format.
IMSUM(*inumber1, inumber2,...*)	Returns the sum of two or more complex numbers in x + *yi* or x + yj text format.
OCT2BIN(*number,places*)	Converts an octal number to binary.
OCT2DEC(*number*)	Converts an octal number to decimal.
OCT2HEX(*number,places*)	Converts an octal number to hexadecimal.

A Brief Review of Trigonometry Basics

There are numerous real-life situations for which trigonometry can be used. In case trigonometry is just a distant nightmare for you, the following sections review some of the basics.

Radians Versus Degrees

Nonmathemeticians discuss angles in terms of *degrees*. Most corners of a room are at a 90-degree angle. Mathematicians discuss angles in a different measurement called *radians*.

Although a circle is composed of 360 degrees, it is also composed of about 6.28 radians. Each radian is equal to about 57.3 degrees. The exact relationship of degrees to radians requires you to use the mathematical constant pi (π), which is about 3.14159. There are two π radians in a circle.

Because the trig functions were written with mathematicians in mind, they always expect the arguments to be expressed in radians.

The formula to convert degrees to radians is to multiply the degrees by PI() and divide by 180. To use this method, you need to write formulas as shown in Cell C16 of Figure 15.1. Fortunately, Excel provides the functions RADIANS and DEGREES to convert from one measurement to another.

B2		f_x	=RADIANS(A2)	
	A	B	C	D	E
1	**Degrees**	**Radians**			
2	30	0.523599	=RADIANS(A2)		
3	45	0.785398			
4	60	1.047198			
5	90	1.570796			
6	120	2.094395			
7	135	2.356194			
8	150	2.617994			
9	180	3.141593			
10					
11	**Radians**	**Degrees**			
12	1.570796	90	=DEGREES(A12)		
13	1.047198	60			
14	0.785398	45			
15					
16		0.866025	=SIN(60*PI()/180)		
17		0.866025	=SIN(RADIANS(60))		

Figure 15.1
The trig functions in Excel expect degrees to be in radians. These two functions convert back and forth from radians to degrees.

Syntax:

DEGREES(*angle*)

The DEGREES function converts radians into degrees. The argument *angle* is the angle, in radians, that you want to convert.

Syntax:

RADIANS(*angle*)

The RADIANS function converts degrees to radians. The argument *angle* is an angle, in degrees, that you want to convert.

In Figure 15.1, B2:B9 converts degrees to radians. The range B12:B14 converts radians back to degrees. The formulas in Rows 16 and 17 contrast using PI() / 180 with the RADIANS function.

Pythagoras and Right Triangles

Trigonometry relies on triangles. Figure 15.2 shows a right triangle, which is a triangle that has one 90-degree angle. In a right triangle, the side opposite the right angle is known as the *hypotenuse*. In a right triangle, the square of the hypotenuse is equal to the sum of the squares of the two other sides. This is frequently expressed as c^2 = a^2 + b^2.

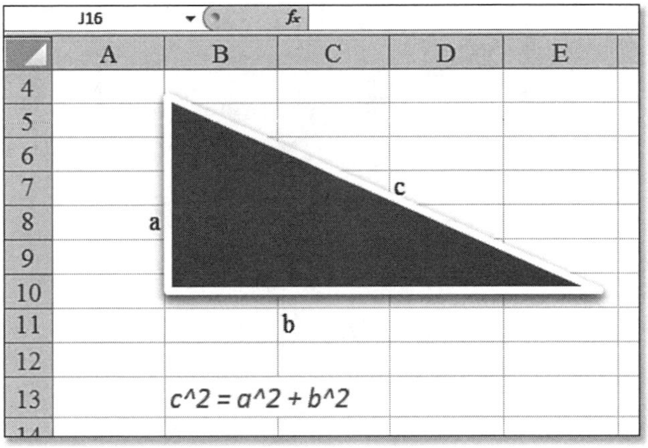

Figure 15.2
The Pythagorean theorem allows you to figure out the length of one leg of a right triangle if you know the length of the other two legs.

If you know that the two shorter legs of a right triangle measure 3 feet and 4 feet, then you know the following:

c^2 = 3^2 + 4^2

c^2 = 9 + 16

c^2 = 25

c = SQRT(25)

c = 5

Although this formula was discovered a thousand years before Pythagoras was alive, he certainly popularized this formula, which is known as the *Pythagorean theorem*.

One Side Plus One Angle = Trigonometry

There are three classic functions in trigonometry: sine, cosine, and tangent. These functions describe the ratio of two sides of a triangle when you know the angles of the triangle.

Consider Figure 15.3. One angle is a right angle, which is 90 degrees. If you can figure out one of the other angles and the length of one leg of the triangle, you can figure out the length of all three sides of the triangle by using Excel.

In Figure 15.3, one angle is marked Θ (theta). The side across from Θ is known as the opposite side. The side that is not the hypotenuse and is part of the angle Θ is the *adjacent* side. Three classic functions describe the ratio of any two sides:

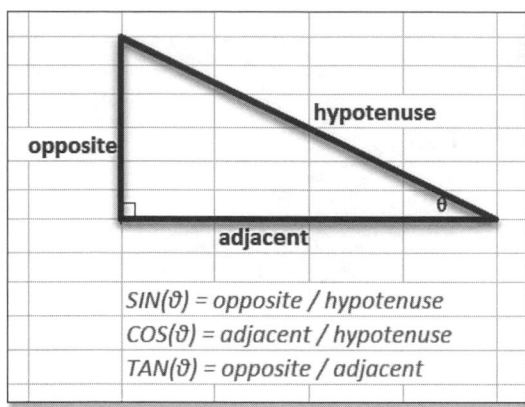

Figure 15.3
If you know one angle and the length of one side of a right triangle, you can calculate all the sides of the triangle by using trigonometry.

Table 15.4   Guide to Trig Functions

SIN(Θ)	= Opposite / Hypotenuse
COS(Θ)	= Adjacent / Hypotenuse
TAN(Θ)	= Opposite / Adjacent

Excel offers three trig functions that allow you to find various angles or lengths of a right triangle when you know various combinations of the other angles and/or sides. The examples in this section provide some real-world examples of using trigonometry.

Using TAN to Find the Height of a Tall Building from the Ground

Suppose you want to measure the height of a tall building from the ground. The tangent function can find the height of a right triangle if you know the length of the base and the angle to the top of the triangle. To calculate the height of a building, follow these steps:

1. Starting from the building, measure out 35 feet along level ground. Sight to the top of the building and determine the angle from that point on the ground to the top of the building such as 69 degrees. The 35-feet figure is the length of the adjacent side of the triangle. You want to solve for the opposite side of the triangle. The TAN function describes the ratio of the opposite side to the adjacent side.

2. In a cell in Excel, enter =TAN(RADIANS(69)). This tells you that the ratio of the height of the building to the 35 feet is 2.605.

3. Because 2.605 = Opposite / Adjacent, plug in 35 for the adjacent side, to get 2.605 = Opposite / 35.

4. To solve this equation, multiply both sides by 35. The answer, as shown in Cell E8 in Figure 15.4, is that the building is more than 91 feet tall.

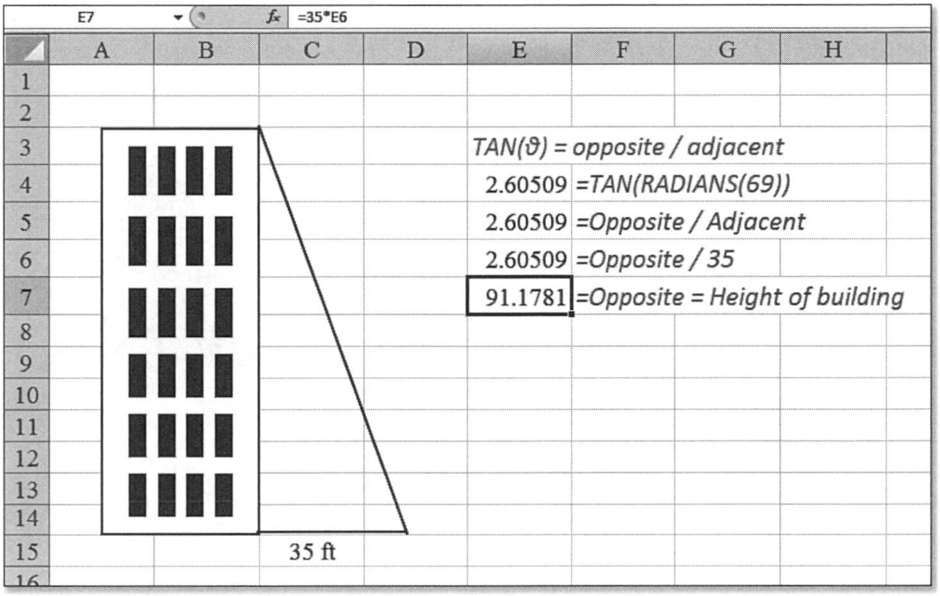

Figure 15.4
You can use the TAN function to find the height of this building.

Syntax:

TAN(*number*)

The TAN function returns the tangent of the given angle. The argument *number* is the angle, in radians, for which you want the tangent. If your argument is in degrees, you convert it to radians by using RADIANS(*degrees*) or multiply it by PI() / 180.

Using SIN to Find the Height of a Kite in a Tree

Suppose your children are flying a kite. They have let out all 150 feet of string. The kite is caught at the top of a faraway tree, as shown in Figure 15.5.

To find the height of this tree, follow these steps:

1. Sight the angle from the end of the string to the top of the tree. It measures 29 degrees.

2. Refer to Table 15.4 earlier in this chapter. Because you know the hypotenuse and want to find the opposite side, use the SIN function.

3. In a cell in Excel, enter =SIN(RADIANS(29)). The result is 0.484.

4. Because the sine is the ratio of the opposite side to the hypotenuse, create the formula 0.484 = Opposite / 150.

5. To solve for the opposite side, multiply both sides of the equation by 150. You find that the tree is over 72 feet tall.

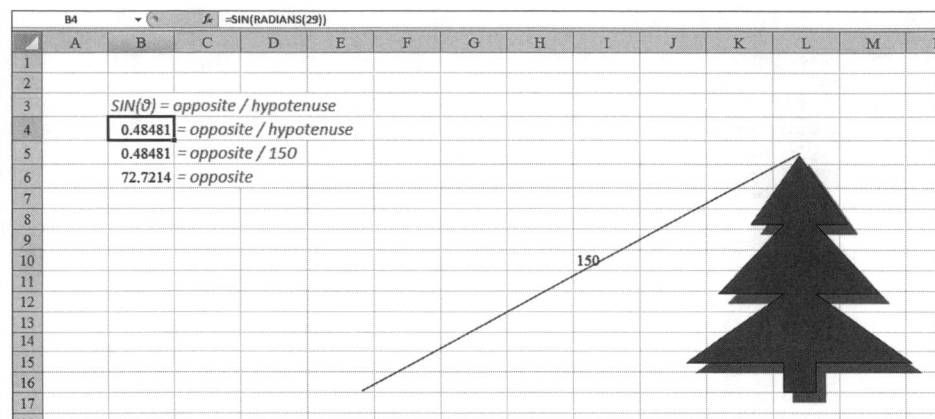

Figure 15.5
The SIN function can find the height of this tree when you know the length of the string.

6. Assess your tree-climbing skills. If you do not currently work for Davey Tree Experts, perhaps you should decide to buy the kids a new kite.

Syntax:

SIN(*number*)

The SIN function returns the sine of the given angle. The argument *number* is the angle, in radians, for which you want the sine. If your argument is in degrees, you multiply it by PI() / 180 to convert it to radians.

Using COS to Figure Out a Ladder's Length

Every year, my wife, Mary Ellen, hires Kevin the landscaper to hang a huge holiday wreath on the second story of our house. The holidays come and go, and I find that Kevin is wintering in Florida. The ladder that I own is not long enough to reach the wreath. Much to the humor of my neighbors, I stand next to the house, with my too-short ladder, and assess the situation. Figure 15.6 shows that I am 10 feet from the house, and the angle to the wreath hanger is 55 degrees. How long of a ladder do I need to borrow from the neighbors?

Table 15.4, which was included earlier in this chapter, shows that the COS function determines the relationship between the adjacent side and the hypotenuse. To find the length of the ladder, follow these steps:

1. In Excel, enter =COS(RADIANS(55)). The result is 0.574.

2. Create the equation Adjacent / Hypotenuse = 0.574.

3. Divide both sides of the equation by 10. This tells you that the 1 / Hypotenuse is 17.43.

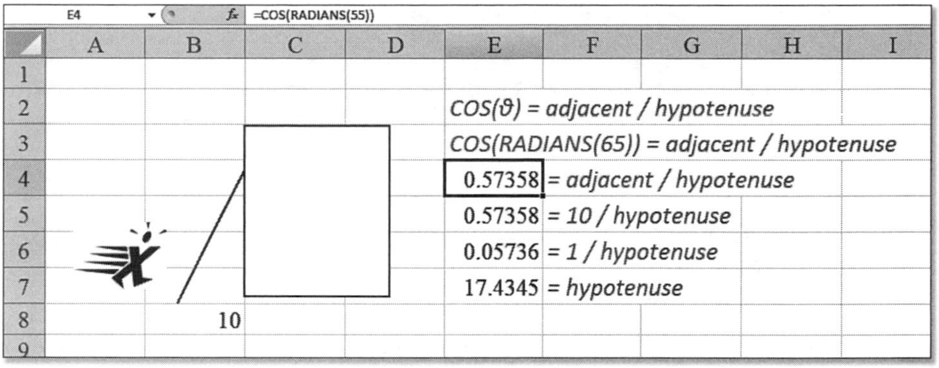

Figure 15.6
The COS function can find the length of the ladder needed to reach the objective.

	E4	▾	⊙	f_x	=COS(RADIANS(55))				
	A	B	C	D	E	F	G	H	I
1									
2					$COS(\vartheta)$ = adjacent / hypotenuse				
3					$COS(RADIANS(65))$ = adjacent / hypotenuse				
4					0.57358	= adjacent / hypotenuse			
5					0.57358	= 10 / hypotenuse			
6					0.05736	= 1 / hypotenuse			
7					17.4345	= hypotenuse			
8		10							
9									

4. Divide both sides of the equation into 1. The result tells you that the hypotenuse is almost 17.5 feet.

It looks like I had better visit Dick, the neighbor with the 18-foot ladder.

Syntax:

COS(*number*)

The COS function returns the cosine of the given angle. The argument number is the angle, in radians, for which you want the cosine. If the angle is in degrees, you multiply it by PI() / 180 to convert it to radians.

Excel in Practice: Measuring the Distance Across a Canyon

Have you ever seen a pair of surveyors working in your neighborhood? One of the pair is holding a tall pole, and the other person is looking through a sighting device. The surveyor can use trigonometry to measure distances or the angle of decline of a piece of land.

To try your surveying skills, you can measure the distance across a canyon. You start by standing on one side of the canyon with a sighting tool. Have your friend stand on the other side of the canyon, holding a 6-foot pole. The angle from the sighting device to the bottom of the 6-foot pole will be ridiculously small, but measurable. You find that the angle comes out to 0.006 degrees. If you know the height of the opposite side is 6 feet and the angle is 0.006 degrees, you can find the distance across that portion of the canyon by using trigonometry.

Table 15.4 defines the tangent as the length of Opposite / Adjacent. Now that you have this information, you can follow these steps to find the distance across the canyon:

1. To convert 0.006 degrees to a tangent, use =TAN(RADIANS(0.006)). The result, 0.000105, is 6 / Adjacent.

2. Multiply both sides of the equation by Adjacent. Divide both sides of the equation by 0.000105.

3. In Cell F16 in Figure 15.7, the formula =6/0.000105 indicates that the canyon is 57,142 feet across.

4. In Cell F17, divide F16 by 5,280 to find that the canyon is 10.82 miles across at that point. Even if you are Evil Knievel, you probably do not want to attempt to jump across in your rocket-powered motorcycle.

Figure 15.7

You can calculate distances across a lake or canyon by using trigonometry.

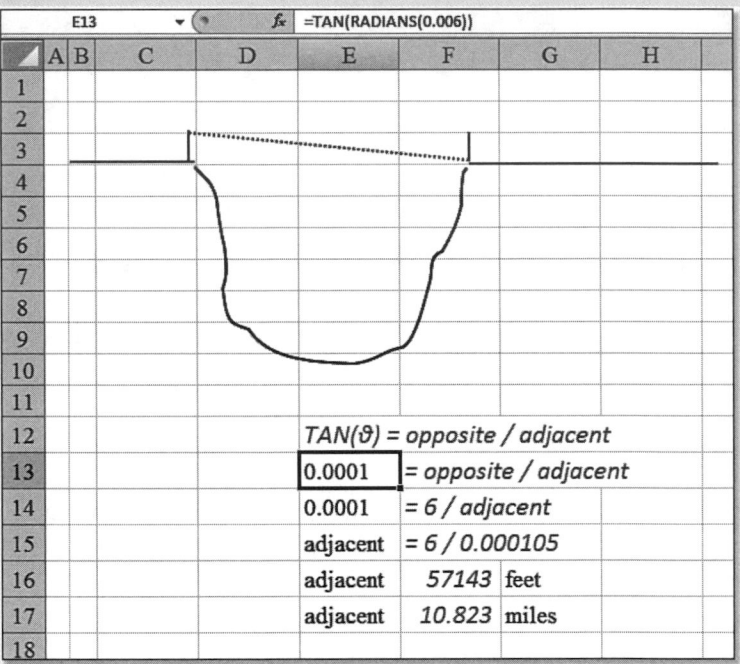

| E13 | ▼ | fx | =TAN(RADIANS(0.006)) |

	A	B	C	D	E	F	G	H
1								
2								
3								
4								
5								
6								
7								
8								
9								
10								
11								
12					*TAN(ϑ) = opposite / adjacent*			
13					0.0001	*= opposite / adjacent*		
14					0.0001	*= 6 / adjacent*		
15					adjacent	*= 6 / 0.000105*		
16					adjacent	*57143*	feet	
17					adjacent	*10.823*	miles	
18								

Using the ARC Functions to Find the Measure of an Angle

If you know the lengths of two sides of a right triangle, you can determine the angles of the triangle by using trigonometry.

The ARC function converts a sine value to an angle, in radians. Suppose that you know the opposite side of a triangle has a length of 3 and the hypotenuse has a length of 5. The sine value is Opposite / Hypotenuse, or 0.6. You use =ASIN(0.6) to convert the sine back to the measure of the angle.

 note

The result of ASIN(0.6) produces the size of the angle, in radians. To convert from radians to degrees, you use =DEGREES(ASIN(0.6)).

Excel provides functions to reverse all three of the basic trig functions. You use ACOS to reverse COS, ASIN to reverse SIN, and ATAN to reverse TAN.

Figure 15.8 demonstrates how to use ACOS, ASIN, and ATAN to find the angle size of a right triangle. Keep in mind that the three angles in a triangle always add up to 180. Because you know that the right angle is 90 degrees, and Figure 15.8 calculates the second angle as 37 degrees, the third angle must be 53 degrees.

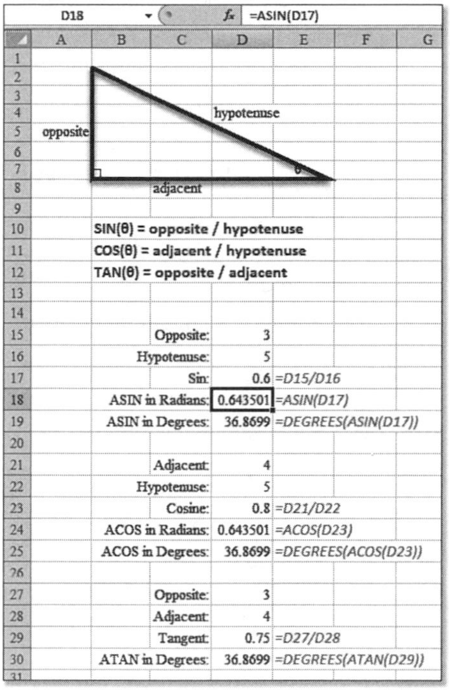

Figure 15.8
The ARC functions find an angle from the ratio of two sides of the triangle.

Syntax:

ACOS(*number*)

The ACOS function returns the arccosine of a number. The arccosine is the angle whose cosine is *number*. The returned angle is given in radians, in the Range 0 to π. The argument number is the cosine of the angle you want and must be from –1 to 1. If you want to convert the result from radians to degrees, multiply it by 180 / PI() or use the DEGREES function.

Syntax:

ASIN(*number*)

The ASIN function returns the arcsine of a number. The arcsine is the angle whose sine is *number*. The returned angle is given in radians, in the Range –π / 2 to π /2. The argument *number* is the sine of the angle you want and must be from –1 to 1. To express the arcsine in degrees, multiply the result by 180 / PI().

Syntax:

ATAN(*number*)

The ATAN function returns the arctangent of a number. The arctangent is the angle whose tangent is *number*. The returned angle is given in radians, in the Range $-\pi / 2$ to $\pi / 2$. The argument *number* is the tangent of the angle you want. To express the arctangent in degrees, you multiply the result by 180 / PI().

Using ATAN2 to Calculate Angles in a Circle

Figure 15.9 shows a unit circle. This is a circle with a radius of 1, plotted on a Cartesian grid. The point on the right side of the circle has a value of x = 1 and y = 0. This is defined as the *angle at zero degrees*.

The point at the top of the circle has a value of y = 1 and x = 0. This is defined as the *angle at 90 degrees*.

Given the coordinates of any two points on the circle, or of any two points anywhere, you can calculate the angle by using the ATAN2 function.

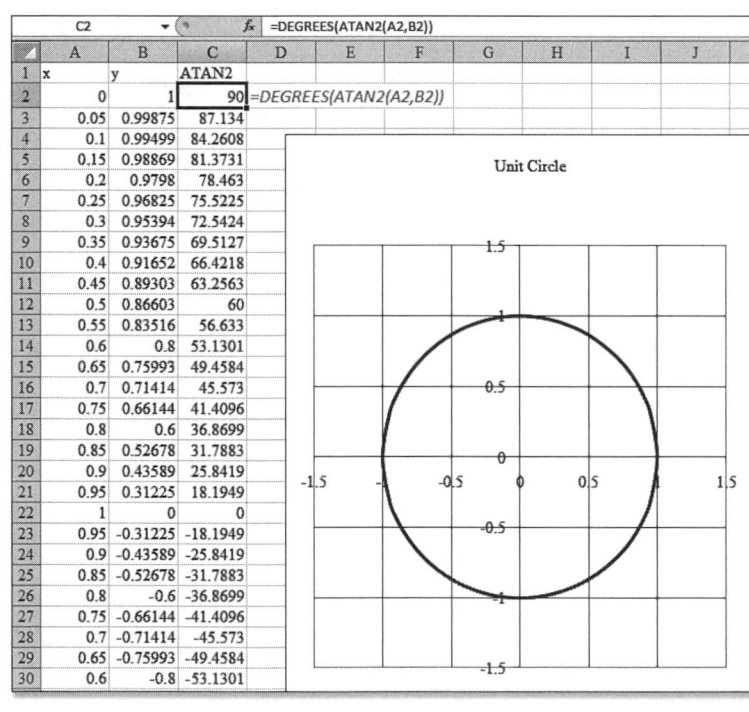

Figure 15.9
You use ATAN2 to find the angle from the x-axis to any point in Cartesian coordinates.

Syntax:

ATAN2(*x_num*,*y_num*)

The ATAN2 function returns the arctangent of the specified x- and y-coordinates. The arctangent is the angle from the x-axis to a line containing the origin (0, 0) and a point with coordinates (*x_num*, *y_num*). The angle is given in radians, between –π and π, excluding –π. A positive result represents a counterclockwise angle from the x-axis; a negative result represents a clockwise angle.

This function takes the following arguments:

- *x_num*—This is the x-coordinate of the point.

- *y_num*—This is the y-coordinate of the point.

ATAN2(*a*,*b*) equals ATAN(*b*/*a*), except that a can equal 0 in ATAN2.

If both *x_num* and *y_num* are 0, ATAN2 returns a #DIV/0! error. To express the arctangent in degrees, you multiply the result by 180 / PI() or use the DEGREES function.

The formulas in Column C of Figure 15.9 find the ATAN2 of the points in Columns A and B. The result must be converted to degrees by using =DEGREES(ATAN2(A2,B2)).

Emulating Gravity Using Hyperbolic Trigonometry Functions

You can apply the trigonometry functions shown so far in this chapter to solve problems in your environment. The hyperbolic trigonometry functions, which we examine next, are far more complex. As shown in Figure 15.10, the hyperbolic cosine function, COSH, is effective at graphing the arc of a rope hung between two points.

According to MathWorld.com, other uses for hyperbolic trigonometry include the following:

- Calculating the gravitational potential of a cylinder

- Calculating the rapidity of special relativity

- Calculating the profile of a laminar jet

- Calculating the Schwarzschild metric, using external isotropic Kruskal coordinates

- Emulating a uniform gravity field by a uniform acceleration, in general relativity

- These are complex tasks and I won't fill you in on the details here. However, if you need to calculate the profile of a laminar jet, head to MathWorld.com for details.

Excel offers the hyperbolic functions SINH, COSH, and TANH, as well as the reverse functions ASINH, ACOSH, and ATANH.

Syntax:

SINH(*number*)

The SINH function returns the hyperbolic sine of a number. The argument number is any real number.

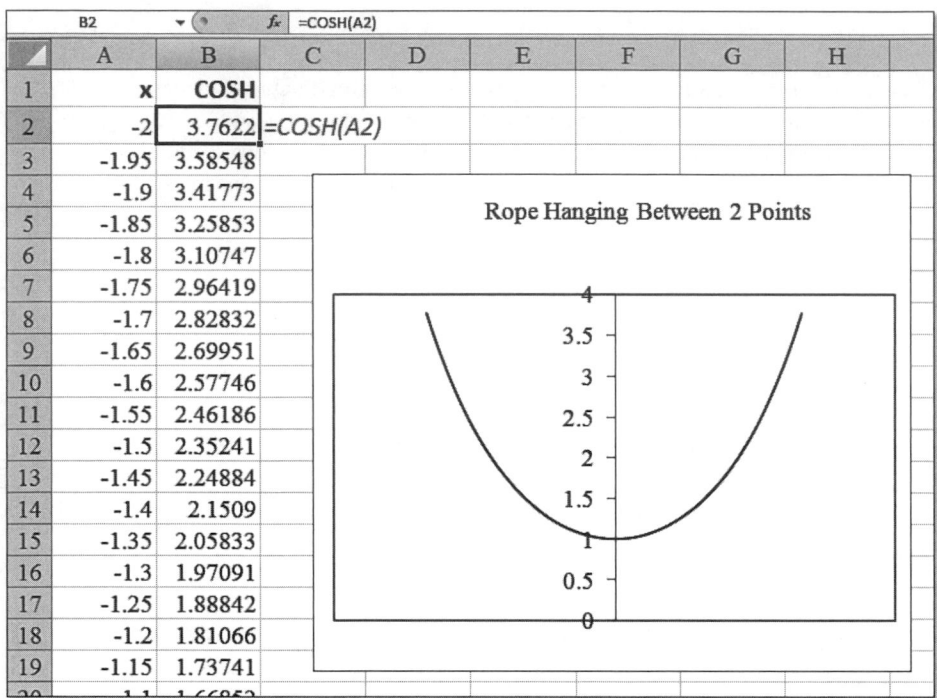

Figure 15.10
This shape
defined by
COSH is also
known as a
catenary.

Syntax:

COSH(*number*)

The COSH function returns the hyperbolic cosine of a number. The argument *number* is any real number for which you want to find the hyperbolic cosine.

In Figure 15.10, the COSH function is used in Column B to calculate the path of a rope hanging between two points.

Syntax:

TANH(*number*)

The TANH function returns the hyperbolic tangent of a number. The argument *number* is any real number.

Syntax:

ASINH(*number*)

The ASINH function returns the inverse hyperbolic sine of a number. The inverse hyperbolic sine is the value whose hyperbolic sine is number, so ASINH(SINH(*number*)) equals *number*. The argument number is any real number.

Syntax:

ACOSH(*number*)

The ACOSH function returns the inverse hyperbolic cosine of a number. *number* must be greater than or equal to 1. The inverse hyperbolic cosine is the value whose hyperbolic cosine is number, so ACOSH(COSH(*number*)) equals *number*. The argument *number* is any real number equal to or greater than 1.

Syntax:

ATANH(*number*)

The ATANH function returns the inverse hyperbolic tangent of a number. *number* must be between −1 and 1, excluding −1 and 1. The inverse hyperbolic tangent is the value whose hyperbolic tangent is number, so ATANH(TANH(*number*)) equals number. The argument *number* is any real number between 1 and −1.

Examples of Logarithm Functions

If you have read many of my books, you know that I used to have a day job involving forecasting and operations planning. I was constantly battling with the sales force to provide accurate sales forecasts. At the end of each month, we produced a chart to show the forecasted demand and the actual demand. If the forecast and actual were within 15 percent of each other, this was considered a tolerable error, and no discussion was necessary. However, for any points outside the 15 percent tolerance, a team would figure out why we missed the forecast and how to prevent a similar miss in future months.

The initial charts looked horrible. There were 20 products being forecasted, and the monthly demand fell by anywhere from 50 units a month to 10,000 units a month. There were only a few products above the 5,000-unit level, but those few products made it impossible to see any detail for the 17 smaller products, as shown in Figure 15.11.

Rather than produce several different charts, our solution involved giving the y-axis of the chart a logarithmic scale.

Common Logarithms on a Base-10 Scale

In a logarithmic scale, the distance from 1 to 10 on the scale is the same as the distance from 10 to 100 and the same as the distance from 100 to 1,000 and the same as the distance from 1,000 to 10,000. Each gridline basically appears at 10^1, 10^2, 10^3, 10^4, and so on.

The resulting chart allows you to see detail for the items selling 100 units as well as the items selling 8,000 units. Figure 15.12 shows the result of converting the chart in Figure 15.11 to a chart with a logarithmic y-axis.

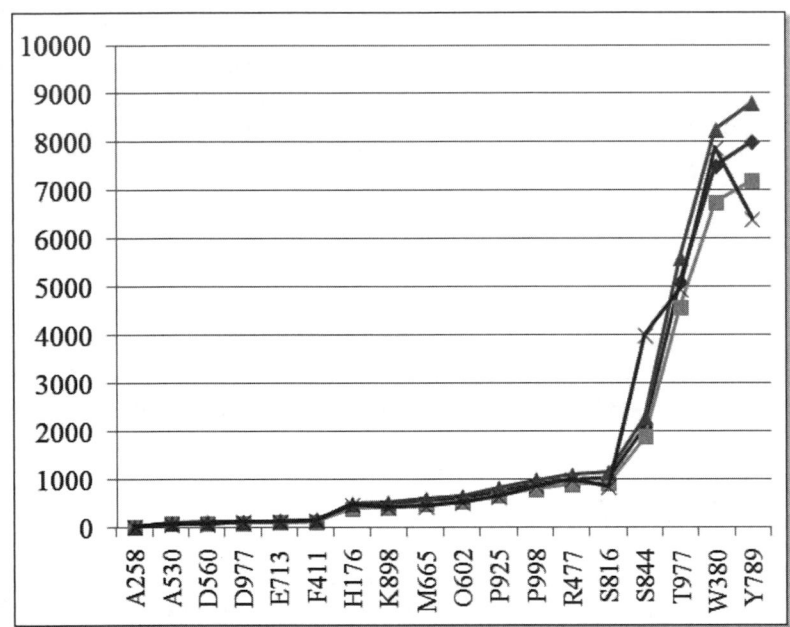

Figure 15.11
No one can make out any detail for the smaller values on this chart. The scale of the two or three large products ruins the view of the smaller products.

Basically, a logarithm raises a number—the base—to a certain power. In the case of the chart in Figure 15.12, each plot on the chart is located at a certain power of 10. In Figure 15.13, Columns B:E show the original numbers for the table. Columns G:J show the base-10 logarithm for the number.

10^1 is 10. 10^2 is 100. The number in Cell B3 is 98. This logarithm is going to be between 1 and 2, and probably much closer to 2. The formula in Cell G3 reveals that if 10 is raised to the 1.99126th power, you get 98.

As another example, 10^2 is 100, and 10^3 is 1,000. Cell B17 contains 5,100. The logarithm for 5,100 is somewhere between 2 and 3. The formula in Cell G17, =LOG10(B17), shows that 10^3.707 results in 5,100.

Excel offers four functions for dealing with logarithms. LOG10 calculates the logarithms based on raising 10 to a certain power. LOG can calculate the logarithm for any base. LN and EXP deal with a special logarithm.

Figure 15.12
You can
change
the y-axis
to show a
logarithmic
scale, and
the detail of
the smaller
quantities
becomes
clear.

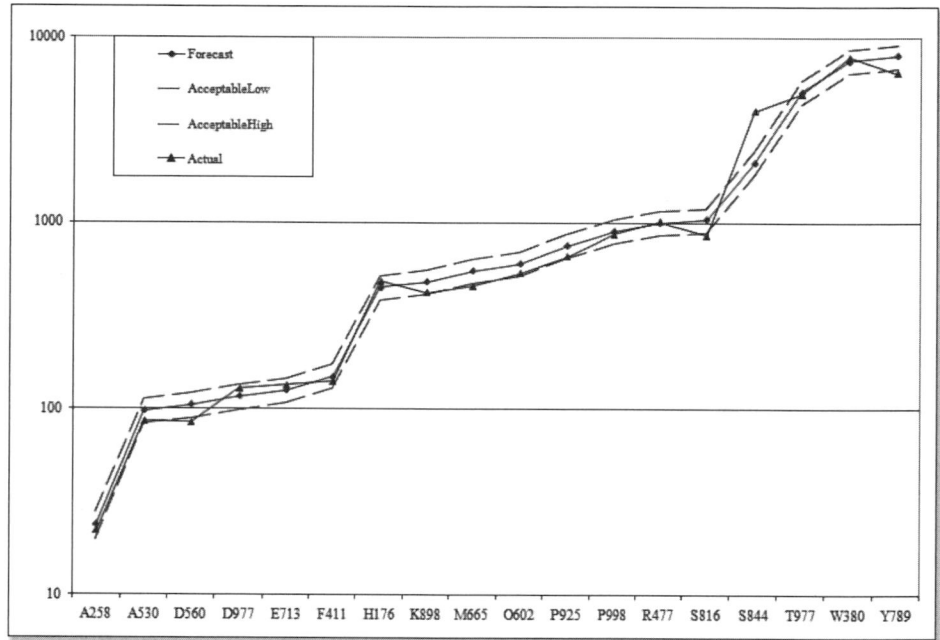

Figure 15.13
The table in G:J
is the base-10
logarithm of the
numbers in B:E.

G2			f_x =LOG10(B2)						

	A	B	C	D	E	F	G	H	I	J
			Acceptable	Acceptable						
1	Product	Forecast	Low	High	Actual		LOG10	LOG10	LOG10	LOG10
2	A258	24	20	28	22		1.38021	1.30103	1.44716	1.34242
3	A530	98	83	113	86		1.99123	1.91908	2.05308	1.9345
4	D560	105	89	121	85		2.02119	1.94939	2.08279	1.92942
5	D977	117	99	135	129		2.06819	1.99564	2.13033	2.11059
6	E713	126	107	145	135		2.10037	2.02938	2.16137	2.13033
7	F411	150	128	173	141		2.17609	2.10721	2.23805	2.14922
8	H176	450	383	518	486		2.65321	2.5832	2.71433	2.68664
9	K898	480	408	552	422		2.68124	2.61066	2.74194	2.62531
10	M665	550	468	633	457		2.74036	2.67025	2.8014	2.65992
11	O602	600	510	690	534		2.77815	2.70757	2.83885	2.72754
12	P925	750	638	863	660		2.87506	2.80482	2.93601	2.81954
13	P998	900	765	1035	864		2.95424	2.88366	3.01494	2.93651
14	R477	1000	850	1150	1010		3	2.92942	3.0607	3.00432
15	S816	1040	884	1196	853		3.01703	2.94645	3.07773	2.93095
16	S844	2100	1785	2415	3995		3.32222	3.25164	3.38292	3.60152
17	T977	5100	4335	5865	4947		3.70757	3.63699	3.76827	3.69434
18	W380	7500	6375	8625	7875		3.87506	3.80448	3.93576	3.89625
19	Y789	8000	6800	9200	6400		3.90309	3.83251	3.96379	3.80618
20										

Syntax:

LOG10(*number*)

The LOG10 function returns the base-10 logarithm of a number. The argument *number* is the positive real number for which you want the base-10 logarithm.

Using LOG to Calculate Logarithms for Any Base

Excel makes it simple to calculate the logarithm for any base, using the LOG function. Cell B2 of Figure 15.14 contains the formula =LOG(A2,2) to express the number in Column A as a base-2 logarithm. Cell E2 contains the formula =LOG(D2,2) to express the number in Column E as a base-5 logarithm.

	K2	▾	fx	=LOG($J$1,J2)								
	A	B	C	D	E	F	G	H	I	J	K	L
1	Number	LOG(A2,2)		Number	Log(D2,5)		Number	LOG(G2,12)		123456	=LOG($J$1,J2)	
2	2	1		5	1		12	1		2	16.9136	
3	4	2		25	2		144	2		3	10.6713	
4	8	3		125	3		1728	3		4	8.45682	
5	16	4		625	4		20736	4		5	7.28431	
6	32	5		3125	5		248832	5		6	6.54309	
7	64	6		15625	6					7	6.02476	
8	128	7		15630	6.0002					8	5.63788	
9	256	8		1250	4.43068					9	5.33566	
10	512	9		15630	6.0002					10	5.09151	
11	1024	10		3750	5.11328					11	4.88914	
12	2048	11		15750	6.00495					12	4.71794	
13	4096	12										
14	2080	11.02237										
15												

Figure 15.14
The LOG function can calculate a logarithm with any base.

Syntax:

LOG(*number*,*base*)

The LOG function returns the logarithm of a number to the specified base. It takes the following arguments:

- *number*—This is the positive real number for which you want the logarithm.
- *base*—This is the base of the logarithm. If base is omitted, it is assumed to be 10.

Little TwelveToes

Here is a simple test to see if you attended the same Saturday morning school that I did. Fill in this phrase: "Conjunction Junction, _____ _____ _____?"

If you instinctively sang, "What's My Function?" then you are a fellow alumnus of the school of Tom Yohe and David McCall. From 1973 until 1985, ABC snuck in educational cartoons in the middle of its other Saturday morning fare. Known collectively as *School House Rock*, these segments taught children multiplication tables, grammar, science facts, and American history.

Perhaps the most ambitious segment was the "Multiplication Rock" segment, about an alien planet where everyone had 12 toes. In this system, there are new digits after 9: "dek, el, do. In addition, his 12—do—is written 1-0. Get it?" This little 60-second cartoon and jingle introduced a generation of children to the concept of a base-12 numbering system in a way that made perfect sense.

Column H of Figure 15.14 uses =LOG(x,12) to express logarithms in a base-12 system.

Using LN and EXP to Calculate Natural Logarithms

Only two logarithms are used frequently in science. The first is the base-10 logarithm that was discussed previously. The second is a natural logarithm where numbers are expressed as a power of the number e. e is a special number. You can calculate e by adding up all the numbers in the series of 1 + [1 / (1!)] + [1 / (2!)] + [1 / (3!)] + [1 / (4!)] + [1(5!)] + [1 / (7!)] + [1(8!)] + [1 / (9!)] + [1 / (10!)] + ...

Luckily, 10! is 3.7 million, so 1 / (10!) is a very small number: 0.000000275573. After about 1 / (17!), the numbers are small enough that they are beyond Excel's 15-digit precision.

This infinite series converges toward a number around 2.718281. This number is known as the *transcendental number,* which is abbreviated as e. Logarithms for base e are known as natural logarithms. You can calculate e in Excel by using a range such as the one shown in A4:C22 in Figure 15.15, or you can use =EXP(1), as shown in Cell C24.

Natural logarithms are very popular in science because anything with a constant rate of growth follows a curve described by natural logarithms. Radioactive isotopes, for example, decay along a curve described by natural logarithms.

Whereas common logarithms with base 10 are called *logs*, natural logarithms with base e are written as *ln*, which is often pronounced *lon*. You calculate natural logarithms by using the LN function.

Syntax:

LN(*number*)

The LN function returns the natural logarithm of a number. Natural logarithms are based on the constant e, which is 2.71828182845904. The argument *number* is the positive real number for which you want a natural logarithm.

C24	▼ (●	fx	=EXP(1)

	A	B	C
1	e = 1 + (1/1!) + (1/2!) + (1/3!) + (1/4!) + (1/5!) + ...		
2			
3	x	FACT(x)	1/Fact(x)
4	0	1	1.00000000000000000000
5	1	1	1.00000000000000000000
6	2	2	0.50000000000000000000
7	3	6	0.16666666666666700000
8	4	24	0.04166666666666670000
9	5	120	0.00833333333333333000
10	6	720	0.00138888888888889000
11	7	5040	0.00019841269841269800
12	8	40320	0.00002480158730158730
13	9	362880	0.00000275573192239859
14	10	3628800	0.00000027557319223986
15	11	39916800	0.00000002505210838544
16	12	479001600	0.00000000208767569879
17	13	6227020800	0.00000000016059043837
18	14	87178291200	0.00000000001147074560
19	15	1,307,674,368,000	0.00000000000076471637
20	16	20,922,789,888,000	0.00000000000004779477
21	17	355,687,428,096,000	0.00000000000000281146
22		Total:	2.71828182845905000000
23			
24		=EXP(1):	2.718281828
25			

Figure 15.15
The calculation of e is fairly complex, as shown in A4:C22. Instead, you can use =EXP(1).

With common logarithms, you can convert the logarithm back to the original number by using =10^x. However, it is fairly difficult to write 2.71828182845904^x. Therefore, Excel provides the function EXP to raise e to any power.

Syntax:

EXP(number)

The EXP function returns e raised to the power of number. The constant e equals 2.71828182845904, the base of the natural logarithm. The argument number is the exponent applied to the base e.

To calculate powers of other bases, you use the exponentiation operator (^). EXP is the inverse of LN, the natural logarithm of number.

To convert the logarithms in Column B in Figure 15.16, use EXP(B2), as shown in Column C.

Multiplying and Dividing by Adding and Subtracting

Think about the problem 3^4 x 3^7. In this problem, both of the base numbers are the same. The result is 3^(7+4), or 3^11.

Similarly, if you want to divide 7^21 by 7^5, you can find the solution by subtracting: 7^(21 − 5), or 7^16.

In Figure 15.16, E2:H9 walks through a long-winding way of multiplying using only LN and addition. To multiply 4.215 × 7.643, you take the LN of each number in Cells F4 and F5. You can then add these numbers in Cell F6. The formula in Cell G6 uses EXP to find the actual answer of 32.21525. Now, I realize that this all seems ridiculous because if you are doing this, you obviously have Excel and can just do the multiplication directly, as shown in Cell G8. However, this is an interesting property of logarithms.

Figure 15.16
To reverse the LN function, you use EXP.

	A	B	C	D	E	F	G	H
			G6		f_x =EXP(F6)			
1		x	LN(x)	EXP(b)				
2		2	0.69315	2	Question: What is 4.215 * 7.643?			
3		4	1.38629	4	**Number**	LN		
4		5	1.60944	5	4.215	1.43865	=LN(E4)	
5		8	2.07944	8	7.643	2.03379	=LN(E5)	
6		9	2.19722	9	Total	3.47244	32.2152	=EXP(F6)
7		10	2.30259	10				
8		13	2.56495	13	4.215	7.643	32.2152	=F8*E8
9		14	2.63906	14				
10		19	2.94444	19	Question: What is 27.453 / 4.873?			
11					**Number**	LN		
12			9		27.453	3.31248	=LN(E12)	
13			2.19722	=LOG(B12,EXP(1))	4.873	1.58371	=LN(E13)	
14			2.19722	=LN(B12)	**Difference**	1.72877	=F12-F13	
15				9 =EXP(1)^B14	EXP(F14)	5.6337	=EXP(F14)	
16								
17						27.453		
18						4.873		
19					Check	5.6337	=F17/F18	
20								

The decay of radioactive isotopes follows a natural logarithmic curve. The basic formula is as follows:

Number of atoms after time T = Original number of atoms × e^(T × *Constant*).

For Radium 226, the constant is −0.000436. The table in Figure 15.17 shows how to raise e to a certain power by using a table of years. You can see that about half the original sample will have decayed after 1,500 years!

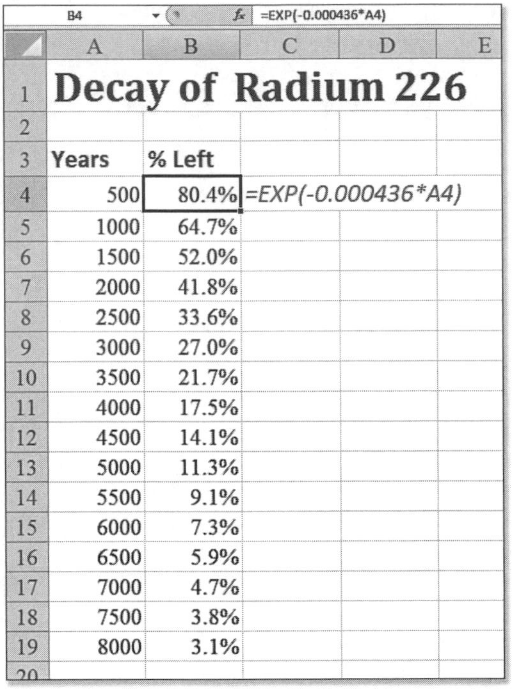

B4 =EXP(-0.000436*A4)

	A	B	C	D	E
1	Decay of Radium 226				
2					
3	Years	% Left			
4	500	80.4%	=EXP(-0.000436*A4)		
5	1000	64.7%			
6	1500	52.0%			
7	2000	41.8%			
8	2500	33.6%			
9	3000	27.0%			
10	3500	21.7%			
11	4000	17.5%			
12	4500	14.1%			
13	5000	11.3%			
14	5500	9.1%			
15	6000	7.3%			
16	6500	5.9%			
17	7000	4.7%			
18	7500	3.8%			
19	8000	3.1%			
20					

Figure 15.17
For constant growth or decay problems, you can use `EXP` to raise e to a power.

Working with Imaginary Numbers

Multiply the number 2 by itself: `=2^2` is 4. The square root of 4 is 2. Multiply the number –2 by itself: `=-2^2` is also 4. Excel says `=SQRT(4)` is 2, but clearly it can also be –2 as well.

So, what is the square root of –4? There is no real number that produces –4 when multiplied by itself. Excel says that `=SQRT(-4)` is `#NUM!`.

To deal with theoretical numbers where the square root is a negative number, mathematicians invented the concept of the imaginary number, i. This number is the square root of –1. At first, no one was sure if this were relevant, so these numbers were given the name *imaginary numbers*. Since their invention, imaginary numbers have been discovered to have real-world applications. They are used extensively in the physics of electrical circuits. The name *imaginary* continues to stick.

In the parlance of imaginary numbers, the square root of –4 is 2i.

Often, the answer to a problem appears as an expression such as $a + b \times i$. In this case, a and b are both real numbers. This expression is a complex number. You can plot complex numbers on a coordinate graph, plotting *a* along the *x*-axis and *b* along the *y*-axis, and then do trigonometry with imaginary numbers.

Excel offers nine functions that deal with imaginary, or complex, numbers: COMPLEX, IMREAL, IMAGINARY, IMSUM, IMPRODUCT, IMDIV, IMABS, IMARGUMENT, and IMCONJUGATE.

Using COMPLEX to Convert *a* and *b* into a Complex Number

It is hard to deal with complex numbers in Excel because they are basically text. Think about how you can store 5 + 2*i* in a cell; it will be difficult to do.

You can create a large range of complex numbers in the form *a* + *bi* if you have ranges of values for *a* and *b*. In Figure 15.18, pairs of *a* and *b* values are stored in the first two columns of a worksheet. The COMPLEX function in Column C converts these numbers to complex numbers.

Figure 15.18

The COMPLEX function builds text results in Column C. The eight IM functions can do math on these text values.

	C2			*fx* =COMPLEX(A2,B2)	
	A	B	C	D	E
1	**a**	**b**	**Complex**		
2	15	15	15+15i	=COMPLEX(A2,B2)	
3	5	10	5+10i		
4	9	15	9+15i		
5	18	5	18+5i		
6	15	13	15+13i		
7	3	7	3+7i		
8	10	6	10+6i		
9	3	15	3+15i		
10	5	17	5+17i		
11	6	4	6+4i		
12	2	12	2+12i		
13	3	6	3+6i		
14					

Syntax:

COMPLEX(*real_num*, *i_num*, *suffix*)

The COMPLEX function converts real and imaginary coefficients into a complex number in the form x + y*i* or x + y*j*. This function takes the following arguments:

- *real_num*—This is the real coefficient of the complex number.

- *i_num*—This is the imaginary coefficient of the complex number.

 note

All complex number functions accept i and j in the suffix. However, they will not accept either I or J. Using uppercase results in a #VALUE! error. All functions that accept two or more complex numbers require that all suffixes match.

- *suffix*—This is the suffix for the imaginary component of the complex number. If omitted, the suffix is assumed to be i.

If *real_num* is nonnumeric, COMPLEX returns a #VALUE! error. If *i_num* is nonnumeric, COMPLEX returns a #VALUE! error. If *suffix* is neither i nor j, COMPLEX returns a #VALUE! error.

Using IMREAL and IMAGINARY to Break Apart Complex Numbers

Complex numbers are in the form *a* + *bi*, where *i* is the imaginary square root of −1. Excel stores all complex numbers as text. If you use any of the IM functions to generate new complex numbers, you can extract the numbers a and b by using IMREAL and IMAGINARY.

In Figure 15.19, Column A contains a range of complex numbers. The formulas in Column B extract the real number portion of the complex number. The formulas in Column C extract the value that is multiplied by i in the complex number.

	A	B	C	D	E
	C2			*fx*	=IMAGINARY(A2)
1	**a+bi**	**a**	**b**		
2	14-10i	14	-10	*B2:*	*=IMREAL(A2)*
3	2-2i	2	-2	*C2:*	*=IMAGINARY(A2)*
4	7-13i	7	-13		
5	8+13i	8	13		
6	10+15i	10	15		
7	13-18i	13	-18		
8	11+19i	11	19		
9	13-13i	13	-13		
10	11-10i	11	-10		
11	8-8i	8	-8		
12					

Figure 15.19
IMREAL and IMAGINARY break a complex number expression in the form *a* + *bi* into the numbers for a and b.

Syntax:

IMREAL(*inumber*)

The IMREAL function returns the real coefficient of a complex number in *x* + *yi* or *x* + *yj* text format. The argument *inumber* is a complex number for which you want the real coefficient.

If *inumber* is not in the form *x* + *yi* or *x* + *yj*, IMREAL returns a #NUM! error.

Syntax:

IMAGINARY(*inumber*)

The IMAGINARY function returns the imaginary coefficient of a complex number in *x + yi* or *x + yj* text format. The argument *inumber* is a complex number for which you want the imaginary coefficient.

If inumber is not in the form *x + yi* or *x + yj*, IMAGINARY returns a #NUM! error.

Using IMSUM to Add Complex Numbers

Figure 15.20 shows two columns of complex numbers. A complex number is in the form *a + bi*. Both *a* and *b* are real numbers. The letter *i* is the imaginary square root of −1.

Note that all of the "numbers" stored in Columns A and B are stored as text.

Figure 15.20
Even though all the complex numbers in Columns A and B are text, the IMSUM function adds them with ease.

	C2		f_x	=IMSUM(A2,B2)	
	A	B	C	D	E
1			**IMSUM**		
2	13+15i	11+9i	24+24i	=IMSUM(A2,B2)	
3	14+19i	10+18i	24+37i		
4	17+4i	19+14i	36+18i		
5	18+17i	7+7i	25+24i		
6	19-20i	5-9i	24-29i		
7	6+3i	8+9i	14+12i		
8	6+9i	4+19i	10+28i		
9	5+2i	15+11i	20+13i		
10	20+16i	5+12i	25+28i		
11	15+11i	6-12i	21-i		
12	6+12i	19+16i	25+28i		
13	3+11i	6+8i	9+19i		
14	3+18i	15+3i	18+21i		
15	12+6i	15+17i	27+23i		
16	20-13i	9+11i	29-2i		
17		Total:	331+243i	=IMSUM(C2:C16)	

To add (*a + bi*) + (*c + di*), you use the formula (*a + b*) + (*c + d*) *i*. You use IMSUM to calculate this.

Syntax:

IMSUM(*inumber1*,*inumber2*,...)

The IMSUM function returns the sum of two or more complex numbers in $x + yi$ or $x + yj$ text format. The arguments *inumber1,inumber2,...* are 1 to 255 complex numbers to add.

If any argument is not in the form $x + yi$ or $x + yj$, IMSUM returns a #NUM! error.

Using IMSUB, IMPRODUCT, and IMDIV to Perform Basic Math on Complex Numbers

As with the IMSUM function, similar rules exist for subtracting, multiplying, and dividing complex numbers. These are numbers stored as text in the form a + bi, where the constant i is an imaginary number representing the square root of −1. These are the rules for the IMSUB, IMPRODUCT, and IMDIV functions:

- To subtract complex numbers, you use IMSUB. The formula for $(a + bi) - (c + di)$ is $(a - c) + (b - d)\, i$.

- To multiply complex numbers, you use IMPRODUCT. The formula for $(a + bi) \times (c + di)$ is $(ac - bd) + (ad + bc)\, i$.

- To divide complex numbers, you use IMDIV. The formula for $(a + bi) / (c + di)$ is $[(ac + bd) + (bc - ad)\, i] / (c\char`\^2 + d\char`\^2)$.

Figure 15.21 shows the results of the basic math functions for complex numbers.

Syntax:

IMSUB(*inumber1,inumber2*)

The IMSUB function returns the difference between two complex numbers in $x + yi$ or $x + yj$ text format. This function takes the following arguments:

- inumber1—This is the complex number from which to subtract *inumber2*.

- inumber2—This is the complex number to subtract from *inumber1*.

If either number is not in the form $x + yi$ or $x + yj$, IMSUB returns a #NUM! error.

Syntax:

IMPRODUCT(*inumber1,inumber2,...*)

The IMPRODUCT function returns the product of 2 to 255 complex numbers in $x + yi$ or $x + yj$ text format. The arguments *inumber1, inumber2,...* are 1 to 255 complex numbers to multiply.

If *inumber1* or *inumber2* is not in the form $x + yi$ or $x + yj$, IMPRODUCT returns a #NUM! error.

Syntax:

IMDIV(inumber1,inumber2)

The IMDIV function returns the quotient of two complex numbers in $x + yi$ or $x + yj$ text format. This function takes the following arguments:

- *inumber1*—This is the complex numerator or dividend.

- *inumber2*—This is the complex denominator or divisor.

If *inumber1* or *inumber2* is not in the form *x + yi* or *x + yj*, IMDIV returns a #NUM! error.

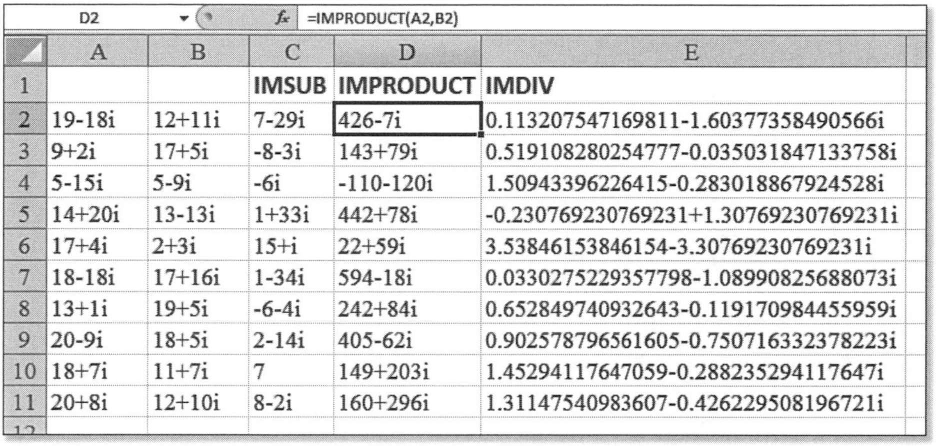

Figure 15.21
You can perform basic math with complex numbers.

D2			*fx* =IMPRODUCT(A2,B2)	
	A	B	C	D	E
1			IMSUB	IMPRODUCT	IMDIV
2	19-18i	12+11i	7-29i	426-7i	0.113207547169811-1.60377358490566i
3	9+2i	17+5i	-8-3i	143+79i	0.519108280254777-0.0350318471337758i
4	5-15i	5-9i	-6i	-110-120i	1.50943396226415-0.283018867924528i
5	14+20i	13-13i	1+33i	442+78i	-0.230769230769231+1.30769230769231i
6	17+4i	2+3i	15+i	22+59i	3.53846153846154-3.30769230769231i
7	18-18i	17+16i	1-34i	594-18i	0.0330275229357798-1.08990825688073i
8	13+1i	19+5i	-6-4i	242+84i	0.652849740932643-0.119170984455959i
9	20-9i	18+5i	2-14i	405-62i	0.902578796561605-0.750716332378223i
10	18+7i	11+7i	7	149+203i	1.45294117647059-0.288235294117647i
11	20+8i	12+10i	8-2i	160+296i	1.31147540983607-0.4262295081967211i
12					

Using IMABS to Find the Distance from the Origin to a Complex Number

A complex number is in the form *a + bi*, where i is an imaginary number representing the square root of −1. To plot complex numbers on a Cartesian grid, you use *a* for the *x-axis* and *b* for the *y-axis*.

The IMABS function calculates the distance from the (0, 0) origin in the grid. If you have a complex number in the form *a + bi*, the formula for an absolute value is =SQRT(a^2+b^2). This results in a real number.

Syntax:

IMABS(*inumber*)

The IMABS function returns the absolute value, or modulus, of a complex number in *x + yi* or *x + yj* text format. The argument *inumber* is a complex number for which you want the absolute value.

If *inumber* is not in the form *x + yi* or *x + yj*, IMABS returns a #NUM! error.

Figure 15.22 shows IMABS functions for several complex numbers. Note that the result of IMABS(a+bi) is equal to IMABS(b+ai).

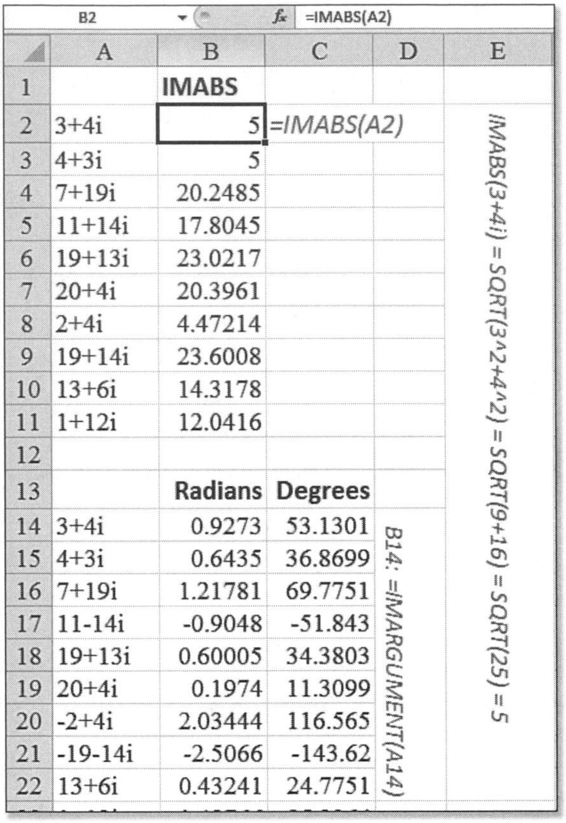

B2	▾ (●	*f*ₓ	=IMABS(A2)	
	A	B	C	D	E
1		**IMABS**			
2	3+4i	5	=IMABS(A2)		
3	4+3i	5			
4	7+19i	20.2485			
5	11+14i	17.8045			
6	19+13i	23.0217			
7	20+4i	20.3961			
8	2+4i	4.47214			
9	19+14i	23.6008			
10	13+6i	14.3178			
11	1+12i	12.0416			
12					
13		**Radians**	**Degrees**		
14	3+4i	0.9273	53.1301		
15	4+3i	0.6435	36.8699		
16	7+19i	1.21781	69.7751		
17	11-14i	-0.9048	-51.843		
18	19+13i	0.60005	34.3803		
19	20+4i	0.1974	11.3099		
20	-2+4i	2.03444	116.565		
21	-19-14i	-2.5066	-143.62		
22	13+6i	0.43241	24.7751		

IMABS(3+4i) = SQRT(3^2+4^2) = SQRT(9+16) = SQRT(25) = 5

B14: =IMARGUMENT(A14)

Figure 15.22
Taking the absolute value of a complex number results in a real number.

Using IMARGUMENT to Calculate the Angle to a Complex Number

A complex number is in the form *a* + *bi*, where i is an imaginary number representing the square root of −1. To plot complex numbers on a Cartesian grid, you use *a* for the x-axis and *b* for the y-axis.

The angle to a complex number assumes that the x-axis is 0 and rotates counter-clockwise. To find the angle, in radians, to any complex number plotted on a grid, you use IMARGUMENT.

B14:B23 in Figure 15.22 shows the angle for several complex numbers.

Syntax:

IMARGUMENT(inumber)

The IMARGUMENT function returns the angle (Θ) for an imaginary number. *inumber* is a complex number for which you want to calculate theta.

If *inumber* is not in the form x + yi or x + yj, IMARGUMENT returns a #NUM! error.

Using IMCONJUGATE to Reverse the Sign of an Imaginary Component

A complex number is in the form $a + bi$, where i is an imaginary number representing the square root of -1. To plot complex numbers on a Cartesian grid, you use a for the x-axis and b for the y-axis.

The IMCONJUGATE function creates a mirror image of a point, flipped across the x-axis. Put another way, the function changes the sign of the imaginary component. For example, $10 + 3i$ becomes $10 - 3i$, and $10 - 3i$ becomes $10 + 3i$.

Syntax:

IMCONJUGATE(inumber)

The IMCONJUGATE function returns the complex conjugate of a complex number in $x + yi$ or $x + yj$ text format. The argument inumber is a complex number for which you want the conjugate.

If inumber is not in the form $x + yi$ or $x + yj$, IMCONJUGATE returns a #NUM! error.

Figure 15.23 shows the results of several IMCONJUGATE formulas.

Figure 15.23
You can reverse the sign of the imaginary component of a complex number with IMCONJUGATE.

	B2		f_x	=IMCONJUGATE(A2)	
	A	B	C	D	
1		**IMCONJUGATE**			
2	17+7i	17-7i	=IMCONJUGATE(A2)		
3	14+3i	14-3i			
4	13+15i	13-15i			
5	9-16i	9+16i			
6	20-9i	20+9i			
7	17+2i	17-2i			
8	1+5i	1-5i			
9	2+1i	2-i			
10	20-6i	20+6i			
11	14+7i	14-7i			
12					

Calculating Powers, Logarithms, and Trigonometry Functions with Complex Numbers

The remaining eight IM functions calculate powers, exponents, logs, and trig functions from complex numbers:

- IMSQRT—Calculates the square root of a complex number.
- IMPOWER—Raises a complex number to a certain power.

- IMLOG10—Calculates the base-10 logarithm or common logarithm of a complex number.

- IMLOG2—Calculates the base-2 logarithm of a complex number.

- IMEXP—Raises the constant e to a complex number.

> ➡ *For more information about the* IMEXP *function, see "Using* LN *and* EXP *to Calculate Natural Logarithms" covered earlier in this chapter.*

- IMLN—Calculates the natural log of a complex number.

- IMSIN—Calculates the sine of a complex number.

- IMCOS—Calculates the cosine of a complex number.

Figure 15.24 shows the results of these functions for a complex number.

	B2 ▾ f_x =IMSQRT(B1)	
	A	B
1		**10+3i**
2	IMSQRT(B1)	3.19689744196702+0.469204917339189i
3	IMPOWER(B1,3)	730+873i
4	IMLOG10(B1)	1.01871324897031+0.126578077554948i
5	IMLOG2(B1)	3.38409216238846+0.420483272026613i
6	IMEXP(B1)	-21806.035863485+3108.375030493511i
7	IMLN(B1)	2.34567394111457+0.291456794477867i
8	IMSIN(B1)	-5.47702066300171-8.40571363343848i
9	IMCOS(B1)	-8.44748854502214+5.44993544667603i
10	IMARGUMENT(B1)	0.291456794
11		

Figure 15.24
These functions calculate powers, logs, and trig functions, using text-based complex numbers.

Solving Simultaneous Linear Equations with Matrix Functions

The Solver add-in can be used to solve simultaneous equations. However, Excel also offers three matrix functions that you can use to solve these equations. Although the math involved is beyond the scope of this book, the steps to produce an answer are fairly straightforward.

The following is a problem taken from a math textbook in the Han Dynasty. The solution can be derived by using matrix functions in Excel.

There are three types of grain. Three bundles of the first, two of the second, and one of the third make 39 bushels. Two of the first, three of the second, and one of the third make 34 bushels. One of the first, two of the second, and three of the third make 26 bushels. How many bushels are in the bundles of each type of grain? To solve this problem, follow these steps:

1. Convert the problem's words into algebraic equations. Assuming that the first type of grain is a, the second is b, and the third is c, you have these three equations: $3a + 2b + 1c = 39$ $2a + 3b + 1c = 34$ $1a + 2b + 3c = 26$

2. In Excel, set up three columns with headings a, b, and c. In the three rows below these columns, enter the coefficients from each equation. For example, the first row contains 3, 2, and 1. The second row contains 2, 3, and 1. The third row contains 1, 2, and 3. In Figure 15.25, the Range C5:E7 contains the matrix of coefficients.

3. In another range, enter a matrix of the answers for each equation. This range should be one column wide by three rows tall. The cells should contain 39, 34, and 26. In Figure 15.25, this range is in G5:G7.

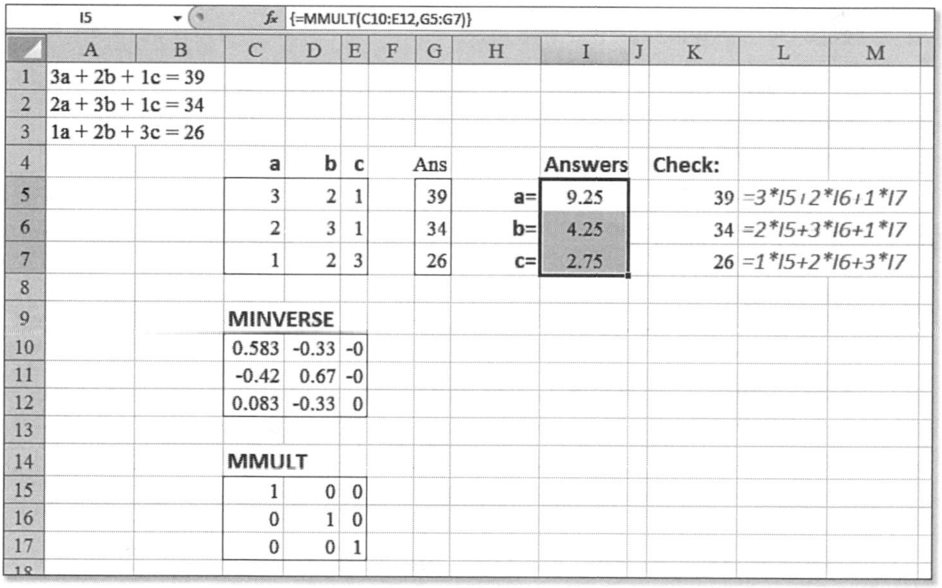

Figure 15.25
Amazingly, Excel can solve simultaneous equations by using a pair of matrix functions.

4. Select a new range that is the same size as the range in step 2. This range will hold an intermediate step with the inverse matrix. In the new range, type the formula =MINVERSE(C5:E7). Do not press Enter. Instead, hold down Ctrl+Shift while you press Enter. This key combination tells Excel to calculate an array and enter the results in all the selected cells (see Range C10:E12 in Figure 15.25). The inverse of an array is an array that, when multiplied by the original array, produces a new array with ones along the diagonal and zeros everywhere else. In Figure 15.25, the Range C15:E17 contains the array formula =MMULT(C5:E7,C10:E12). The result of the MMULT operation is indeed a matrix with a one along the diagonal and zeros everywhere else,

as shown in Figure 15.25. Array formulas are special multi-cell formulas that are entered using Ctrl+Shift+Enter.

5. Select a range that is three cells high and one column wide. In this column, enter a MMULT function that multiplies the MINVERSE array from step 4 by the answers in step 3. In Figure 15.25, the formula in I5:I7 is =MMULT(C10:E12,G5:G7). Again, you must select all three cells before entering this formula. Next, you must hold down Ctrl+Shift+Enter to enter the formula. The results in Cells I5, I6, and I7 stand for the values of a, b, and c, respectively.

6. To make sure that everything worked, set up test formulas in Column K. For example, the test formula in K5 checks to see if 3a+2b+c equals 39.

This entire process is fairly amazing. All the formulas are live formulas. If you change one of the input variables in any of the ranges, all the matrix functions instantly recalculate to solve the three simultaneous equations.

Syntax:

MINVERSE(*array*)

The MINVERSE function returns the inverse matrix for the matrix stored in an array. The argument *array* is a numeric array with an equal number of rows and columns. The *array* can be given as a cell range such as A1:C3. It can also be given as an array constant such as {1,2,3;4,5,6;7,8,9}. Finally, it can be given as a name for either of these.

Formulas that return arrays must be entered as array formulas. To indicate that a formula is an array formula, type the formula, then hold down Ctrl and Shift while pressing Enter.

Inverse matrices, like determinants, are generally used for solving systems of mathematical equations that involve several variables. The product of a matrix and its inverse is the identity matrix—the square array in which the diagonal values equal 1 and all other values equal 0.

As an example of how a two-row, two-column matrix is calculated, suppose that the Range A1:B2 contains the letters a, b, c, and d, which represent any four numbers. Table 15.5 shows the inverse of the matrix A1:B2.

 tip

An array can be entered in curly braces and is called an array constant. Each comma in the array constant indicates that Excel should move to the next column in the current row. Each semi-colon indicates that Excel should move to the next row. To picture the actual shape of {1,2,3;4,5,6;7,8,9}, picture the value 1 in A1, 2 in B1, 3 in C1, 4 in A2, and so on down to 9 in C3.

 note

If any cells in array are empty or contain text, MINVERSE returns a #VALUE! error. MINVERSE also returns a #VALUE! error if array does not have an equal number of rows and columns.

Table 15.5 Inverse of the Matrix Shown in A1:B2 (see Figure 15.26)

	Column A	Column B
Row 1	d/(a*d-b*c)	b/(b*c-a*d)
Row 2	c/(b*c-a*d)	a/(a*d-b*c)

Figure 15.26
Range A6:B7 contains the MINVERSE of the original array. When you multiply an array and its MINVERSE array, the resulting array in A10:B11 contains 1s along the diagonal.

A6	▼		f_x {=MINVERSE(A2:B3)}		
	A	B	C	D	E	F

	A	B	C	D	E	F
1	ARRAY:				ARRAY:	
2	1	2			a	b
3	3	4			c	d
4						
5	MINVERSE				MINVERSE	
6	-2	1			d/(a*d-b*c)	b/(b*c-a*d)
7	1.5	-0.5			c/(b*c-a*d)	a/(a*d-b*c)
8						
9	MMULT					
10	1	0				
11	0	1				

MINVERSE is calculated to an accuracy of approximately 16 digits, which may lead to a small numeric error when the cancellation is not complete. Thus, when you use MMULT on this array with the original array, you might find 0.00000000000001 instead of 0 in some cells.

Some square matrices cannot be inverted and return a #NUM! error with MINVERSE. The determinant for a noninvertible matrix is 0.

The MMULT function multiplies two arrays. The basic logic is that the top-left cell of the resulting array is the sum of multiplying the first row of Array 1 by the first column of Array 2. Figure 15.27 shows the rest of the rules for a 2 × 2 matrix.

Syntax:

MMULT(array1,array2)

The MMULT function returns the matrix product of two arrays. The result is an array with the same number of rows as *array1* and the same number of columns as *array2*.

The arguments *array1* and *array2* are the arrays you want to multiply. The number of columns in *array1* must be the same as the number of rows in *array2*, and both arrays must contain only numbers. *array1* and *array2* can be given as cell ranges, array constants, or references. If any cells are empty or contain text, or if the number of columns in *array1* is different from the number of rows in *array2*, MMULT returns a #VALUE! error.

In Figure 15.27, A2:B3 contains Array A. A6:B7 contains Array B. The result of the MMULT formula, Array M, is in A10:B11. The rules for the calculation of each cell in M are shown in D2:D5. The actual formulas are shown in D10:D13.

	A	B	C	D	E	F	G	
	A10	▼		f_x {=MMULT(A2:B3,A6:B7)}				
1	**ARRAY A**							
2	1	2		M(1,1) = A(1,1)*B(1,1) + A(1,2)*B(2,1)				
3	3	4		M(1,2) = A(1,1)*B(1,2) + A(1,2)*B(2,2)				
4				M(2,1) = A(2,1)*B(1,1) + A(2,2)*B(2,1)				
5	**ARRAY B**			M(2,2) = A(2,1)*B(1,2) + A(2,2)*B(2,2)				
6	5	6						
7	7	8						
8								
9	**MMULT**							
10	19	22		A10 = 1*5 + 2*7 = 19				
11	43	50		B10 = 1*6 + 2*8 = 22				
12				A11 = 3*5 + 4 * 7 = 43				
13				B11 = 3*6 + 4*8 = 50				
14								

Figure 15.27
The MMULT function performs matrix multiplication.

Using MDETERM to Determine Whether a Simultaneous Equation Has a Solution

If your matrix of simultaneous equations is square, Excel can calculate a determinant of the array by using MDETERM. The determinant returns a single number, which means this function does not need to be entered as an array. If the determinant of an array is nonzero, the simultaneous equation has a solution.

Figure 15.28 shows the calculation for the determinant of a 2 × 2 matrix.

Syntax:

MDETERM(*array*)

The MDETERM function returns the matrix determinant of an array. The argument *array* is a numeric array with an equal number of rows and columns. The *array* can be given as a cell range such as A1:C3; an array constant such as {1,2,3;4,5,6;7,8,9}; or a name to either of these. If any cells in *array* are empty or contain text, MDETERM returns a #VALUE! error. MDETERM also returns #VALUE! if *array* does not have an equal number of rows and columns.

The matrix determinant is a number derived from the values in *array*. For a three-row, three-column array, A1:C3, the determinant is defined as follows:

MDETERM(A1:C3) = A1*(B2*C3-B3*C2) + A2*(B3*C1-B1*C3) + A3*(B1*C2-B2*C1)

Matrix determinants are generally used for solving systems of mathematical equations that involve several variables.

MDETERM is calculated with an accuracy of approximately 16 digits, which may lead to a small numeric error when the calculation is not complete. For example, the determinant of a singular matrix may differ from zero by $1E - 16$.

Figure 15.28 shows a MDETERM calculation for a 2×2 array.

Figure 15.28

MDETERM returns the determinant of any square array. Determinants that are nonzero indicate that the simultaneous equations have a solution.

	A	B	C	D	E	F	G
1	**ARRAY A**						
2	1	2		-2			
3	3	4					
4							
5	a	b		*MDETERM = ad - bc*			
6	c	d		*MDETERM = 1*4 = 2*3 = 4-6 = -2*			
7							

D2 · *fx* =MDETERM(A2:B3)

Using SERIESSUM to Approximate a Function with a Power Series

There are situations in mathematics in which a value can be approximated by summing many factors in a series. If the series gets progressively smaller such as 1/2, 1/3, 1/4, 1/5, 1/6, 1/7, the numbers eventually become smaller than Excel's 15-digit significance limit. This is referred to as a *power series*. In a power series, the exponent of each term is progressively changed. An example of a power series is $=a_1x^1 + a_2x^3 + a_3x^5 + a_4x^7 + a_5x^9$.

Figure 15.29 shows a long, complex calculation. The coefficients in Column D are found by dividing factorials of even number digits into the number 1 and then multiplying every other value by −1. The value of x is 60 degrees, or PI() / 3. The exponents shown in Column E increase from 0 to 16 by 2s. In Column F, you raise X to the power in Column E. In Column G, you multiply Column D by Column F. Finally, you add up all the values in Column G to arrive at 0.5, which is a really good approximation of the cosine of 60 degrees.

This example is rather trivial because Excel offers a COS function. However, other functions use a power series to approximate a function. For example, one SERIESSUM function in B17 replaces all the calculations in Columns E, F, and G. The function needs the list of coefficients in Column D. In fact, the number of coefficients tells Excel how far to extend the series.

Syntax:

SERIESSUM(*x,n,m,coefficients*)

The SERIESSUM function returns the sum of a power series. Many functions can be approximated by a power series expansion. This function takes the following arguments:

- *x*—The input value to the power series.

B16			f_x =SERIESSUM(B1,E4,E5,D4:D12)					
	A	B	C	D	E	F	G
1	X:	1.047198	=PI()/3				
2							
3	Even #s	Pos/Neg	1/A!	B*C	Exp	X^E	D*F
4	0	1	1.000E+00	1.000E+00	0	1	1.000E+00
5	2	-1	5.000E-01	-5.000E-01	2	1.09662	-5.483E-01
6	4	1	4.167E-02	4.167E-02	4	1.20258	5.011E-02
7	6	-1	1.389E-03	-1.389E-03	6	1.31878	-1.832E-03
8	8	1	2.480E-05	2.480E-05	8	1.4462	3.587E-05
9	10	-1	2.756E-07	-2.756E-07	10	1.58594	-4.370E-07
10	12	1	2.088E-09	2.088E-09	12	1.73918	3.631E-09
11	14	-1	1.147E-11	-1.147E-11	14	1.90722	-2.188E-11
12	16	1	4.779E-14	4.779E-14	16	2.0915	9.996E-14
13							0.50
14							
15	=SeriesSum(x,n,m,a,a,a,a,a) = a1x^n + a2x^(n+m) + a3x^(n+2m)...						
16		0.5	=SERIESSUM(B1,E4,E5,D4:D12)				

Figure 15.29
The SERIESSUM function can calculate a power series, given a value X, a pattern for the exponents, and a list of coefficients.

- *n*—The initial power to which you want to raise x.

- *m*—The step by which to increase n for each term in the series.

- *coefficients*—A set of coefficients by which each successive power of x is multiplied. The number of values in *coefficients* determines the number of terms in the power series. For example, if there are three values in *coefficients*, there will be three terms in the power series.

If any argument is nonnumeric, SERIESSUM returns a #VALUE! error.

Using SQRTPI to Find the Square Root of a Number Multiplied by Pi

The SQRTPI function multiplies a number by π and then takes the square root of the result. In the previous editon of this book, I was at a loss to explain a use for this function. The difficulty in finding uses for SQRTPI and DOUBLEFACT became a running joke in my Power Excel seminars. Finally, someone from Custom Metalcraft in Springfield, Missouri, pointed out that SQRTPI is used when you need to figure out what size of a square tank is equivalent to a certain size round tank.

As a general example, Figure 15.30 shows how to use SQRTPI to find that a pizza that is 10.6" square contains the same area as a 12" round pizza.

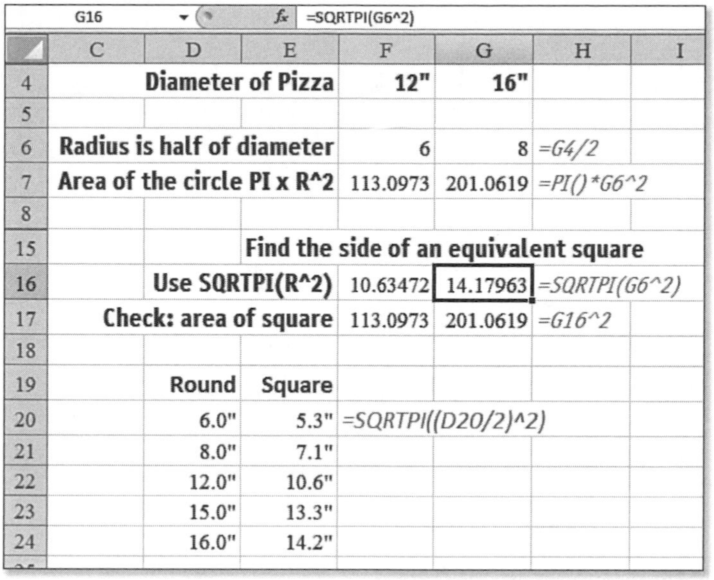

Figure 15.30
SQRTPI is useful for converting round areas to square areas.

	C	D	E	F	G	H	I
			G16	fx =SQRTPI(G6^2)			
4		**Diameter of Pizza**		**12"**	**16"**		
5							
6		**Radius is half of diameter**		6	8	=G4/2	
7		**Area of the circle PI x R^2**		113.0973	201.0619	=PI()*G6^2	
8							
15			**Find the side of an equivalent square**				
16		**Use SQRTPI(R^2)**		10.63472	14.17963	=SQRTPI(G6^2)	
17		**Check: area of square**		113.0973	201.0619	=G16^2	
18							
19		**Round**	**Square**				
20		6.0"	5.3"	=SQRTPI((D20/2)^2)			
21		8.0"	7.1"				
22		12.0"	10.6"				
23		15.0"	13.3"				
24		16.0"	14.2"				

Syntax:

SQRTPI(*number*)

The SQRTPI function returns the square root of π. The argument *number* is the number by which π is multiplied. If *number* is less than 0, SQRTPI returns a #NUM! error.

=SQRTPI(5) calculates 5*PI() as 15.7 and then takes the square root of 15.7, to return 3.96.

Using SUMPRODUCT to Sum Based on Multiple Conditions

The use of SUMPRODUCT is dropping dramatically since Excel 2007. Until this point, SUMPRODUCT was one of the favorite methods for solving a particular limitation with SUMIF. However, since Microsoft added the SUMIFS function to Excel 2007, there is less need for SUMPRODUCT.

In case you need to share your workbooks with people using legacy versions of Excel, you can work through this example to solve the problem of conditionally summing a range based on two conditions. Suppose you are starting with the data in Column A:C of Figure 15.31. This simple data set has fields for region, product, and sales.

The SUMIF command can add all the sales that occurred in the east:

=SUMIF(A2:A17,"East",C2:C17). However, there is no way to use SUMIF to find the sum of all records that are in the east and for Product A. Using SUMPRODUCT to solve this problem requires you to think about a couple virtual arrays. These arrays are entered as intermediate steps in Figure 15.31 so you can picture them:

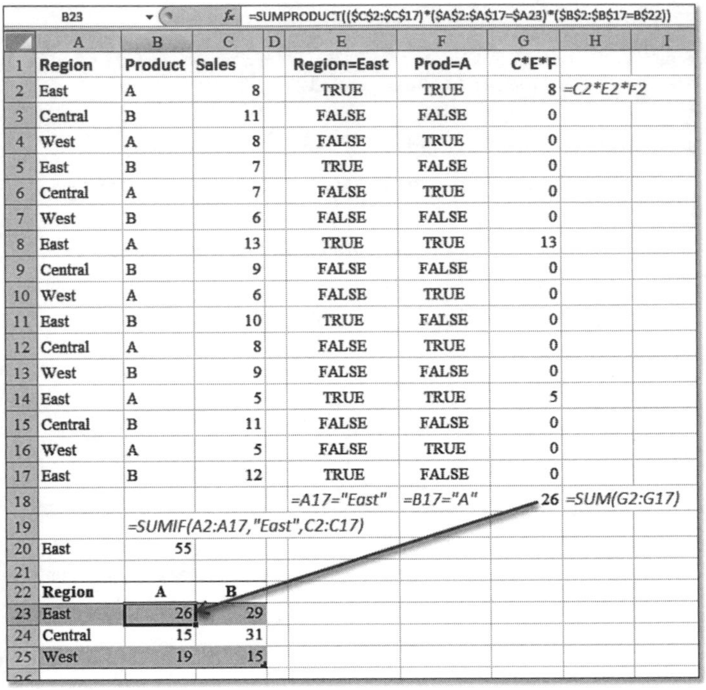

B23 =SUMPRODUCT(($C$2:$C$17)*($A$2:$A$17=$A23)*($B$2:$B$17=B$22))

	A	B	C	D	E	F	G	H	I
1	Region	Product	Sales		Region=East	Prod=A	C*E*F		
2	East	A	8		TRUE	TRUE	8	=C2*E2*F2	
3	Central	B	11		FALSE	FALSE	0		
4	West	A	8		FALSE	TRUE	0		
5	East	B	7		TRUE	FALSE	0		
6	Central	A	7		FALSE	TRUE	0		
7	West	B	6		FALSE	FALSE	0		
8	East	A	13		TRUE	TRUE	13		
9	Central	B	9		FALSE	FALSE	0		
10	West	A	6		FALSE	TRUE	0		
11	East	B	10		TRUE	FALSE	0		
12	Central	A	8		FALSE	TRUE	0		
13	West	B	9		FALSE	FALSE	0		
14	East	A	5		TRUE	TRUE	5		
15	Central	B	11		FALSE	FALSE	0		
16	West	A	5		FALSE	TRUE	0		
17	East	B	12		TRUE	FALSE	0		
18					=A17="East"	=B17="A"	26	=SUM(G2:G17)	
19		=SUMIF(A2:A17,"East",C2:C17)							
20	East	55							
21									
22	Region	A	B						
23	East	26	29						
24	Central	15	31						
25	West	19	15						

Figure 15.31
The rather long and winding calculations in E2:G18 answer how many units meet two conditions. A single formula in B23 replaces all these steps.

- In Column E, the formula tests whether the cell in Column A is equal to East.
- In Column F, the formula tests whether the cell in Column B is equal to A.
- Column G contains an interesting formula. Cell G2 multiplies the sales in Cell C2 by the TRUE/FALSE value in Cell E2 and then multiplies that by the TRUE/FALSE value in Cell G2. In Excel's treatment of TRUE/FALSE values, a TRUE is calculated as a 1, and a FALSE is calculated as a 0. Thus, in Cell G2, the 8 × TRUE × TRUE is like multiplying 8 × 1 × 1, which results in 8.
- If either cell in Column E or Column F is FALSE, Excel treats the value as a zero. Because zero times anything is zero, the result in Column G shows up as zero if the corresponding value in either Column E or Column F is FALSE.
- In Cell G18, a SUM function totals the products from Column G to answer how many sales of Product A were made in the east.

The SUMPRODUCT function does all the steps from Columns E, F, and G in a single function, as shown in Cell B23 in Figure 15.31.

There is a strange problem when using SUMPRODUCT to multiply arrays that contain TRUE or FALSE. Although Boolean logic says that TRUE × TRUE is TRUE, the SUMPRODUCT function can not do this operation. Thus, you have to change the array of TRUE/FALSE values to an array of 0's and 1's. There are three generally accepted ways of doing this.

Method 1 replaces the commas indicated in the syntax with asterisks. This forces the TRUE values in the arrays to become 1's and the FALSE values to become 0.

`=SUMPRODUCT(($C$2:$C$17)*($A$2:$A$17=$A$23)*($B$2:$B$17=$B$22))`

Method 2 surrounds the TRUE/FALSE arrays with the N() function.

`=SUMPRODUCT($C$2:$C$17,N($A$2:$A$17=$A$23),N($B$2:$B$17=$B$22))`

Method 3 uses a double negative before each TRUE/FALSE array to change the TRUE/FALSE values to 1/0.

`=SUMPRODUCT($C$2:$C$17,--($A$2:$A$17=$A$23),--($B$2:$B$17=$B$22))`

Syntax:

`SUMPRODUCT(array1,array2,array3,...)`

The SUMPRODUCT function multiplies corresponding components in the given arrays and returns the sum of those products. The arguments *array1, array2, array3,...* are 2 to 255 arrays whose components you want to multiply and then add together.

The *array* arguments must have the same dimensions. If they do not, SUMPRODUCT returns a #VALUE! error. SUMPRODUCT treats array entries that are not numeric as if they were zeros.

To solve a problem that has multiple conditions, you need to create three virtual arrays in the function arguments. Here's how you do it:

1. Make the first array the sales in C2:C17.

2. Make the second array a test to see if A is equal to East. This will be (A2:A17="East").

3. Make the third array a test to see if B is equal to A. This will be (B2:B17="A").

4. Multiply these three arrays to get the formula =SUMPRODUCT((C2:C17)*(A2:A17="East")* (B2:B17="A")). This provides a result of 26, just as in the previous example.

5. Make the function from step 4 more generic. In Figure 15.31, a summary table in A19:C22 has the headings East, Central, West, A, and B. The formula in B20 is =SUMPRODUCT(($C$2:$C$17)* ($A$2:$A$17=$A20)*($B$2:$B$17=B$19)). This formula adds dollar signs so that the formula can be copied. It also replaces "East" with $A20 and "A" with B$19.

6. Copy this formula to the rest of the table. You now have an efficient conditional total that sums records based on two criteria.

Examples of Engineering Functions

There are not many true engineering functions in Excel. You will notice that in this book, most of the IM functions are reclassified into the previous section on imaginary numbers. All the BIN2, DEC2, HEX2, and OCT2 functions are, at best, interesting to software engineers.

The CONVERT function is interesting to everyone and is truly the one engineering function that could have been included in Chapter 11, "Using Everyday Functions: Math, Date and Time, and Text Functions."

Therefore, there are just a handful of true engineering functions: The various BESSEL functions, ERF, DELTA, and the GESTEP functions are of use exclusively to engineers.

Converting from Decimal to Hexadecimal and Back

A long time ago, I held a summer internship writing COBOL programs for a company. Whenever one of my programs crashed in the middle of the night, I was supposed to read a hexadecimal printout of the computer memory to figure out what went wrong.

In the hexadecimal numbering system, there are 16 digits. In order, the digits are 0, 1, 2, 3, 4, 5, 6, 7, 8, 9, A, B, C, D, E, and F. The number that you know as 10 is written as A in hexadecimal. The number 15 is written as F in hexadecimal. After F comes the hexadecimal number 10, which is equivalent to 16 in decimal.

Hexadecimal numbers can get rather large. For example, the hex number C2 means $12 \times 16 + 2$. Keep in mind that C is equivalent to a decimal 12. The hex number 1111 means $1 \times 16^3 + 1 \times 16^2 + 1 \times 16 + 1$, or 4,369.

Hexadecimal calculators exist that let you add a number such as A52B with C2D4 to come up with the answer 167FF.

In Excel, you can convert numbers in the base-10 system to hexadecimal by using DEC2HEX. Similarly, you can convert hex numbers to a base-10 numbering system by using HEX2DEC.

Syntax:

DEC2HEX(*number,places*)

The DEC2HEX function converts a decimal number to hexadecimal. This function takes the following arguments:

- *number*—This is the decimal integer you want to convert. If *number* is negative, the *places* argument is ignored, and DEC2HEX returns a 10-character, which is 40-bit hexadecimal number in which the most significant bit is the sign bit. The remaining 39 bits are magnitude bits. Negative numbers are represented using two's-complement notation.

- *places*—This is the number of characters to use. If *places* is omitted, DEC2HEX uses the minimum number of characters necessary. places is useful for padding the return value with leading 0s.

If *number* is less than −549,755,813,888 or greater than 549,755,813,887, DEC2HEX returns a #NUM! error. If *number* is nonnumeric, DEC2HEX returns a #VALUE! error. If DEC2HEX requires more than places characters, it returns a #NUM! error.

If *places* is not an integer, it is truncated. If *places* is nonnumeric, DEC2HEX returns a #VALUE! error. If places is negative, DEC2HEX returns a #NUM! error.

Syntax:

HEX2DEC(*number*)

The HEX2DEC function converts a hexadecimal number to decimal. The argument *number* is the hexadecimal number you want to convert. *number* cannot contain more than 10 characters, which is 40 bits. The most significant bit of *number* is the sign bit. The remaining 39 bits are magnitude bits. Negative numbers are represented using two's-complement notation.

If *number* is not a valid hexadecimal number, HEX2DEC returns a #NUM! error.

Figure 15.32 shows a conversion from decimal to hexadecimal and back. Note that Cell B2 uses the places argument to specify that leading zeros should be added to generate a number that is 4 digits long.

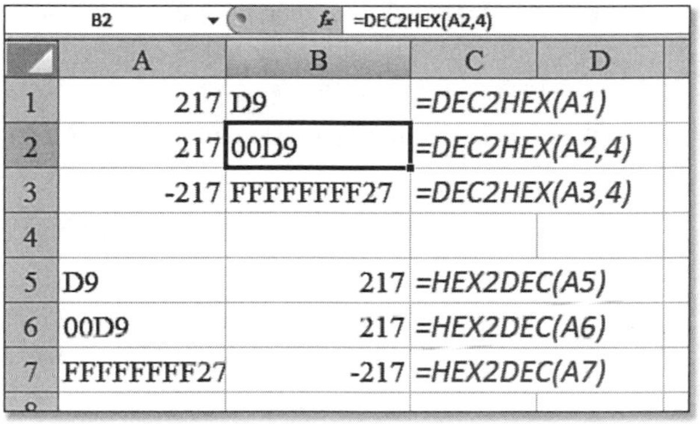

Figure 15.32
Converting from decimal to hexadecimal and back.

	A	B	C	D
	B2	▼	*fx* =DEC2HEX(A2,4)	
1	217	D9	=DEC2HEX(A1)	
2	217	00D9	=DEC2HEX(A2,4)	
3	-217	FFFFFFFF27	=DEC2HEX(A3,4)	
4				
5	D9	217	=HEX2DEC(A5)	
6	00D9	217	=HEX2DEC(A6)	
7	FFFFFFFF27	-217	=HEX2DEC(A7)	

Converting from Decimal to Octal and Back

The octal numbering system is a base-8 numbering system. In this system, there are only eight digits, from 0 through 7. The decimal number 8 is represented in octal as 10.

Each numeric place in an octal number represents an additional power of 8. The octal number 1111 represents $1 \times 8^3 + 1 \times 8^2 + 1^8 + 1$, or $512 + 64 + 8 + 1$, or 585 in decimal.

You use DEC2OCT to convert from decimal to octal and OCT2DEC to convert from octal to decimal.

Syntax:

DEC2OCT(*number*,*places*)

The DEC2OCT function converts a decimal number to octal. This function takes the following arguments:

- *number*—This is the decimal integer you want to convert. If *number* is negative, *places* is ignored, and DEC2OCT returns a 10-character, which is 30-bit octal number in which the most significant bit is the sign bit. The remaining 29 bits are magnitude bits. Negative numbers are represented using two's-complement notation.

- *places*—This is the number of characters to use. If *places* is omitted, DEC2OCT uses the minimum number of characters necessary. places is useful for padding the return value with leading 0s.

If number is less than −536,870,912 or greater than 536,870,911, DEC2OCT returns a #NUM! error. If number is nonnumeric, DEC2OCT returns a #VALUE! error. If DEC2OCT requires more than places characters, it returns a #NUM! error. If places is not an integer, it is truncated. If places is nonnumeric, DEC2OCT returns a #VALUE! error. If places is negative, DEC2OCT returns a #NUM! error.

Syntax:

OCT2DEC(*number*)

The OCT2DEC function converts an octal number to decimal. The argument *number* is the octal number you want to convert. *number* cannot contain more than 10 octal characters, which is 30 bits. The most significant bit of *number* is the sign bit. The remaining 29 bits are magnitude bits. Negative numbers are represented using two's-complement notation.

If *number* is not a valid octal number, OCT2DEC returns a #NUM! error.

Converting from Decimal to Binary and Back

Although hexadecimal and octal numbering systems are seldom encountered anymore, many people still encounter binary number systems. Binary number systems are the language of computers because every circuit has a state of either 1, which means electricity is present, or 0, which means electricity is not present. Thus, the binary number system has only 2 digits, 0 and 1:

- The rightmost digit in a binary number means 0 or 1.

- The next rightmost digit represents 2^1, or 2.

- The next digit represents 2^2, or 4.

- The next digit represents 2^3, or 8.

- The next digit represents 2^4, or 16.

- The next digit represents 2^5, or 32.

- The next digit represents 2^6, or 64.

For example, the binary number 1010101 means 64 + 16 + 4 + 1, or 85 in decimal. You use DEC2BIN to convert from decimal to binary and BIN2DEC to convert from binary to decimal. Note that DEC2BIN works only with the numbers 512 and lower.

Syntax:

DEC2BIN(*number,places*)

The DEC2BIN function converts a decimal number to binary. This function takes the following arguments:

- *number*—This is the decimal integer you want to convert. If *number* is negative, places is ignored, and DEC2BIN returns a 10-character, which is 10-bit binary number in which the most significant bit is the sign bit. The remaining 9 bits are magnitude bits. Negative numbers are represented using two's-complement notation.

- *places*— This is the number of characters to use. If *places* is omitted, DEC2BIN uses the minimum number of characters necessary. *places* is useful for padding the return value with leading 0s.

If *number* is less than –512 or greater than 511, DEC2BIN returns a #NUM! error. If *number* is nonnumeric, DEC2BIN returns a #VALUE! error. If DEC2BIN requires more than *places* characters, it returns the #NUM! error. If *places* is not an integer, it is truncated. If *places* is nonnumeric, DEC2BIN returns a #VALUE! error. If *places* is negative, DEC2BIN returns a #NUM! error.

Syntax:

BIN2DEC(*number*)

The BIN2DEC function converts a binary number to decimal. The argument *number* is the binary number you want to convert. *number* cannot contain more than 10 characters, which is 10 bits. The most significant bit of number is the sign bit. The remaining 9 bits are magnitude bits. Negative numbers are represented using two's-complement notation.

If *number* is not a valid binary number, or if *number* contains more than 10 characters, which is 10 bits, BIN2DEC returns a #NUM! error.

The formulas in Figure 15.33 convert from decimal to binary and from binary to decimal.

	A	B	C	D
		B2 ▼ *fx* =DEC2BIN(A2,9)		
1	255	11111111	=DEC2BIN(A1)	
2	511	111111111	=DEC2BIN(A2,8)	
3	-512	1000000000	=DEC2BIN(A3)	
4				
5	101010101	341	=BIN2DEC(A5)	
6	1100	12	=BIN2DEC(A6)	
7	11111	31	=BIN2DEC(A7)	
8	1000000000	-512	=BIN2DEC(A7)	

Figure 15.33
Converting from decimal to binary and back.

Explaining the Two's Complement for Negative Numbers

In all the previous examples, the hex, octal, and binary numbers look bizarre for negative numbers. This is a special notation called *two's complement*. In Excel, we have to agree that a negative number occupies 10 characters. For example, Cell A1 in Figure 15.34 contains the number five in binary.

	A1	▾ (	fₓ	'00 0000 0101				
◢	A	B	C	D	E	F	G	H
1	00 0000 0101	*Original Number in Binary (5)*						
2	11 1111 1010	*Switch 0 and 1 to move to Ones complement*						
3	11 1111 1011	*Add 1 to convert to two's complement (-5)*						
4								
5	00 0000 0000	*Zero in Binary*						
6	11 1111 1111	*Switch 0 and 1 to move to Ones complement*						
7	00 0000 0000	*Add 1 to convert to two's complement (ignoring the overflow digit)*						
8								
9	00 0000 0001	*One in binary*						
10	11 1111 1110	*Ones complement*						
11	11 1111 1111	*Add one to create one's complement*						
12								
13	11 1111 1011	*-5 in two's complement*						
14	00 0000 0100	*Switch 0 and 1*						
15	00 0000 0101	*Add 1 to produce positive five in binary*						
16								

Figure 15.34
Negative numbers in two's complement are initially unnerving, until you understand the steps for converting them.

If the leftmost bit is a 1, then the number is assumed to be negative, and Excel assumes that the number is in two's-complement notation. There are two simple steps to convert a positive number to a negative number in two's complement:

1. Change every 0 to a 1 and every 1 to a 0. This produces a number in one's complement, as shown in Cell A2 in Figure 15.34.

2. Add 1 to the result from step 1 to convert to two's complement, as shown in Cell A3 in Figure 15.34.

Converting from negative to positive in two's complement follows exactly the same method. Cell A13 in Figure 15.34 contains −5 in two's complement. In Cell A14, you switch all the 0s and 1s. In Cell A15, you add 1 to produce the original result in binary.

🔍 **note**

The leftmost bit is always set to a 1 for a negative number. This prevents Excel from representing 512 in binary. The binary representation of 512—1000000000— has a 1 in the leftmost digit, which means no numbers over 511 can be represented in binary in Excel.

Converting from Binary to Hex to Octal and Back

Excel offers six additional functions that can convert directly from octal to hexadecimal to binary. The major limitation of these functions is that Excel can represent as binary only numbers up to 511 in decimal. This is a significant limitation; anything larger than 1FF in hex or larger than 777 in octal returns an error if you try to convert it to binary.

These are the additional conversion functions:

- BIN2HEX(*number*,*places*)—Converts a binary number to hexadecimal.

- BIN2OCT(*number*,*places*)— Converts a binary number to octal.

- HEX2BIN(*number*,*places*)—Converts a hexadecimal number to binary.

- HEX2OCT(*number*,*places*)—Converts a hexadecimal number to octal.

- OCT2BIN(*number*,*places*)—Converts an octal number to binary.

- OCT2HEX(*number*,*places*)—Converts an octal number to hexadecimal.

Figure 15.35 demonstrates these conversion functions.

Figure 15.35
You can convert between hex, octal, and binary by using these six functions.

	A	B	C	D	E
1	511	**Decimal**		D2	**Hex**
2	777	**DEC2OCT**		322	**HEX2OCT**
3	111111111	**DEC2BIN**		11010010	**HEX2BIN**
4	1FF	**DEC2HEX**		210	**HEX2DEC**
5					
6	331	**Octal**		1010011	**Binary**
7	11011001	**OCT2BIN**		123	**BIN2OCT**
8	D9	**OCT2HEX**		53	**BIN2HEX**
9	217	**OCT2DEC**		83	**BIN2DEC**
10					

A2   *fx* =DEC2OCT(A$1)

Using CONVERT to Convert English to Metric

The CONVERT function is an incredibly versatile function. It can convert measures in the following areas:

- Weight and mass

- Distance

- Time

- Pressure

- Force

- Energy

- Power

- Magnetism

- Temperature

- Liquid measure

Syntax:

CONVERT(*number,from_unit,to_unit*)

The CONVERT function converts a number from one measurement system to another. For example, CONVERT can translate a table of distances in miles to a table of distances in kilometers. This function takes the following arguments:

- *number*—This is the value in *from_units* to convert.

- *from_unit*—This is the units for number.

- *to_unit*— This is the units for the result.

> To see a video demo about CONVERT, *search for "Excel In Depth 15" at YouTube.*

Tables 15.6 through 15.15 list the text values that CONVERT accepts for *from_unit* and *to_unit*, which can be summarized as follows:

- If the input data types are incorrect, CONVERT returns a #VALUE! error. If the unit does not exist, CONVERT returns an #N/A error.

- If the unit does not support an abbreviated unit prefix, CONVERT returns an #N/A error.

- If the units are in different groups, CONVERT returns an #N/A error.

- The unit abbreviations to use in CONVERT are case-sensitive.

Table 15.6 shows conversions possible for weights.

Table 15.6 Units of Weight and Mass

Unit of Weight	Abbreviation to Use in CONVERT
Gram	g
Slug	sg
Pound mass	1bm
Atomic unit	u
Ounce mass	ozm
Exagram	Eg

Unit of Weight	Abbreviation to Use in CONVERT
Petagram	Pg
Teragram	Tg
Gigagram	Gg
Megagram	Mg
Kilogram	kg
Hectogram	hg
Dekaogram	eg
Decigram	dg
Centigram	cg
Milligram	mg
Microgram	ug
Nanogram	ng
Pictogram	pg
Femtogram	Fg
Attogram	Ag

Figure 15.36 shows a conversion of weights and masses.

Table 15.7 shows conversion units for distance.

Table 15.7 Units of Distance

Unit of Distance	Abbreviation to Use in CONVERT
Statute mile	mi
Nautical mile	Nmi
Inch	in
Foot	ft
Yard	yd
Angstrom	ang
Pica (1/72 in.)	Pica
Meter	M

Unit of Distance	Abbreviation to Use in CONVERT
Exameter	Em
Petameter	Pm
Terameter	Tm
Gigameter	Gm
Megameter	Mm
Kilometer	Km
Hectometer	Hm
Dekaometer	Em
Decimeter	Dm
Centimeter	Cm
Millimeter	Mm
Micrometer	Um
Nanometer	Nm

E28			f_x	=CONVERT(1,"sg","u")			
	A	B	C	D	E	F	G	H

				Gram	Slug	Pound Mass	Atomic Unit	Ounce Mass
3				TO---->				
4								
5				g	sg	lbm	u	ozm
6	FROM	Gram	g	1	6.85218E-05	0.002205	6.02E+23	0.035274
7		Slug	sg	14593.9	1	32.17405	8.79E+27	514.7848
8		Pound Mass	lbm	453.5924	0.03108095	1	2.73E+26	16
9		Atomic Unit	u	1.66E-24	1.13783E-28	3.66E-27	1	5.86E-26
10		Ounce Mass	ozm	28.34952	0.001942559	0.0625	1.71E+25	1
11		exagram	Eg	1E+18	6.85218E+13	2.2E+15	6.02E+41	3.53E+16
12		petagram	Pg	1E+15	68521765857	2.2E+12	6.02E+38	3.53E+13
13		teragram	Tg	1E+12	68521765.86	2.2E+09	6.02E+35	3.53E+10
14		gigagram	Gg	1E+09	68521.76586	2204623	6.02E+32	35273962
15		megagram	Mg	1000000	68.52176586	2204.623	6.02E+29	35273.96
16		kilogram	kg	1000	0.068521766	2.204623	6.02E+26	35.27396
17		hectogram	hg	100	0.006852177	0.220462	6.02E+25	3.527396
18		dekaogram	eg	10	0.000685218	0.022046	6.02E+24	0.35274
19		decigram	dg	0.1	6.85218E-06	0.00022	6.02E+22	0.003527
20		centigram	cg	0.01	6.85218E-07	2.2E-05	6.02E+21	0.000353
21		milligram	mg	0.001	6.85218E-08	2.2E-06	6.02E+20	3.53E-05
22		microgram	ug	0.000001	6.85218E-11	2.2E-09	6.02E+17	3.53E-08
23		nanogram	ng	1E-09	6.85218E-14	2.2E-12	6.02E+14	3.53E-11
24		picogram	pg	1E-12	6.85218E-17	2.2E-15	6.02E+11	3.53E-14
25		femtogram	fg	1E-15	6.85218E-20	2.2E-18	6.02E+08	3.53E-17
26		attogram	ag	1E-18	6.85218E-23	2.2E-21	602217	3.53E-20
27								
28		Atomic Units in a slug?		8.7887E+27				

Figure 15.36
This table converts between the mass units in the left column and the various units along the top row.

Figure 15.37 shows a conversion of distances. Table 15.8 shows conversion abbreviations for measures of time.

Table 15.8 Units of Time

Unit of Time	Abbreviation to Use in CONVERT
Year	yr
Day	day
Hour	hr
Minute	mn
Second	sec

D31 =CONVERT(1,"mi","Pica")

	A	B	C	D	E	F	G	H	I	J	K
3		Distances		TO---->							
4				Statute mile	Nautical mile	Inch	Foot	Yard	Angstrom	Pica (1/72 in.)	Meter
5				mi	Nmi	in	ft	yd	ang	Pica	m
6	FROM	Statute mile	mi	1	0.8689762	63360	5280	1760	1.60934E+13	4561920	1609.344
7		Nautical mile	Nmi	1.150779	1	72913.386	6076.1155	2025.372	1.852E+13	5249763.78	1852
8		Inch	in	1.58E-05	1.371E-05	1	0.0833333	0.027778	254000000	72	0.0254
9		Foot	ft	0.000189	0.0001646	12	1	0.333333	3048000000	864	0.3048
10		Yard	yd	0.000568	0.0004937	36	3	1	9144000000	2592	0.9144
11		Angstrom	ang	6.21E-14	5.4E-14	3.937E-09	3.281E-10	1.09E-10	1	2.83465E-07	1E-10
12		Pica (1/72 in.)	Pica	2.19E-07	1.905E-07	0.0138889	0.0011574	0.000386	3527777.778	1	0.00035278
13		Meter	m	0.000621	0.00054	39.370079	3.2808399	1.093613	10000000000	2834.645669	1
14		exameter	Em	6.21E+14	5.4E+14	3.937E+19	3.281E+18	1.09E+18	1E+28	2.83465E+21	1E+18
15		petameter	Pm	6.21E+11	5.4E+11	3.937E+16	3.281E+15	1.09E+15	1E+25	2.83465E+18	1E+15
16		terameter	Tm	6.21E+08	539956803	3.937E+13	3.281E+12	1.09E+12	1E+22	2.83465E+15	1E+12
17		gigameter	Gm	621371.2	539956.8	3.937E+10	3.281E+09	1.09E+09	1E+19	2.83465E+12	1000000000
18		megameter	Mm	621.3712	539.9568	39370079	3280839.9	1093613	1E+16	2834645669	1000000
19		kilometer	km	0.621371	0.5399568	39370.079	3280.8399	1093.613	1E+13	2834645.669	1000
20		hectometer	hm	0.062137	0.0539957	3937.0079	328.08399	109.3613	1E+12	283464.5669	100
21		dekaometer	em	0.006214	0.0053996	393.70079	32.808399	10.93613	1E+11	28346.45669	10
22		decimeter	dm	6.21E-05	5.4E-05	3.9370079	0.328084	0.109361	1000000000	283.4645669	0.1
23		centimeter	cm	6.21E-06	5.4E-06	0.3937008	0.0328084	0.010936	100000000	28.34645669	0.01
24		millimeter	mm	6.21E-07	5.4E-07	0.0393701	0.0032808	0.001094	10000000	2.834645669	0.001
25		micrometer	um	6.21E-10	5.4E-10	3.937E-05	3.281E-06	1.09E-06	10000	0.002834646	0.000001
26		nanometer	nm	6.21E-13	5.4E-13	3.937E-08	3.281E-09	1.09E-09	10	2.83465E-06	1E-09
27		picometer	pm	6.21E-16	5.4E-16	3.937E-11	3.281E-12	1.09E-12	0.01	2.83465E-09	1E-12
28		femtometer	fm	6.21E-19	5.4E-19	3.937E-14	3.281E-15	1.09E-15	0.00001	2.83465E-12	1E-15
29		attometer	am	6.21E-22	5.4E-22	3.937E-17	3.281E-18	1.09E-18	0.00000001	2.83465E-15	1E-18
30											
31		Picas in a mile?		4561920							

Figure 15.37
This table converts between the distance units in the left column and the various units along the top row.

Figure 15.38 shows a conversion of times.

Table 15.9 shows conversion values for units of pressure.

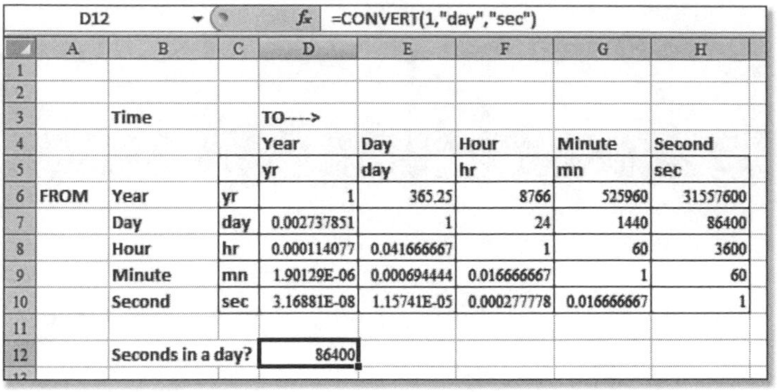

D12 =CONVERT(1,"day","sec")

	A	B	C	D	E	F	G	H
1								
2								
3		Time		TO---->				
4				Year	Day	Hour	Minute	Second
5				yr	day	hr	mn	sec
6	FROM	Year	yr	1	365.25	8766	525960	31557600
7		Day	day	0.002737851	1	24	1440	86400
8		Hour	hr	0.000114077	0.041666667	1	60	3600
9		Minute	mn	1.90129E-06	0.000694444	0.016666667	1	60
10		Second	sec	3.16881E-08	1.15741E-05	0.000277778	0.016666667	1
11								
12		Seconds in a day?		86400				

Figure 15.38
This table converts between the time units in the left column and the various units along the top row.

Table 15.9 Units of Pressure

Unit of Pressure	Abbreviation to Use in CONVERT
Pascal	Pa
Atmosphere	atm
mm of Mercury	mmHg
Exaatmosphere	Eatm
Petaatmosphere	Patm
Teraatmosphere	Tatm
Gigaatmosphere	Gatm
Megaatmosphere	Matm
Kiloatmosphere	katm
Hectoatmosphere	hatm
Dekaoatmosphere	eatm
Deciatmosphere	datm
Centiatmosphere	catm
Milliatmosphere	matm
Microatmosphere	uatm
Nanoatmosphere	natm
Picoatmosphere	patm
Femtoatmosphere	fatm
Attoatmosphere	aatm

Figure 15.39 shows a conversion of pressures.

Figure 15.39
This table converts between the pressure units in the left column and the various units along the top row.

			D7	▼	f_x =CONVERT(1,$C7,D$5)

	A	B	C	D	E	F
3		Pressure		TO---->		
4				Pascal	Atmosphere	mm of Mercury
5				Pa	atm	mmHg
6	FROM	Pascal	Pa	1	9.86923E-06	0.007500617
7		Atmosphere	atm	101325	1	760
8		mm of Mercury	mmHg	133.3223684	0.001315789	1
9		exaatmosphere	Eatm	1.01325E+23	1E+18	7.6E+20
10		petaatmosphere	Patm	1.01325E+20	1E+15	7.6E+17
11		teraatmosphere	Tatm	1.01325E+17	1E+12	7.6E+14
12		gigaatmosphere	Gatm	1.01325E+14	1000000000	7.6E+11
13		megaatmosphere	Matm	1.01325E+11	1000000	760000000
14		kiloatmosphere	katm	101325000	1000	760000
15		hectoatmosphere	hatm	10132500	100	76000
16		dekaoatmosphere	eatm	1013250	10	7600
17		deciatmosphere	datm	10132.5	0.1	76
18		centiatmosphere	catm	1013.25	0.01	7.6
19		milliatmosphere	matm	101.325	0.001	0.76
20		microatmosphere	uatm	0.101325	0.000001	0.00076
21		nanoatmosphere	natm	0.000101325	0.000000001	0.00000076
22		picoatmosphere	patm	1.01325E-07	1E-12	7.6E-10
23		femtoatmosphere	fatm	1.01325E-10	1E-15	7.6E-13
24		attoatmosphere	aatm	1.01325E-13	1E-18	7.6E-16
25						

Table 15.10 shows conversion values for units of force.

Table 15.10 Units of Force

Unit of Force	Abbreviation to Use in CONVERT
Newton	N
Dyne	dyn
Pound force	lbf
Exanewton	EN
Petanewton	PN
Teranewton	TN
Giganewton	GN
Meganewton	MN
Kilonewton	kN

Unit of Force	Abbreviation to Use in CONVERT
Hectonewton	hN
Dekaonewton	eN
Decinewton	dN
Centinewton	cN
Millinewton	mN
Micronewton	uN
Nanonewton	nN
Piconewton	pN
Femtonewton	fN
Attonewton	aN
Exadyne	Edyn
Petadyne	Pdyn
Teradyne	Tdyn
Gigadyne	Gdyn
Megadyne	Mdyn
Kilodyne	kdyn
Hectodyne	hdyn
Dekaodyne	edyn
Decidyne	ddyn
Centidyne	cdyn
Millidyne	mdyn
Microdyne	udyn
Nanodyne	ndyn
Picodyne	pdyn
Femtodyne	fdyn
Attodyne	adyn

Figure 15.40 shows a conversion of forces.

Table 15.11 shows conversions available for energy.

Figure 15.40
This table converts between the force units in the left column and the various units along the top row.

D7 | f_x =CONVERT(1,$C7,D$5)

	A	B	C	D	E	F
3		Force		TO--->		
4				Newton	Dyne	Pound force
5				N	dyn	lbf
6	FROM	Newton	N	1	100000	0.2248089
7		Dyne	dyn	0.00001	1	2.248E-06
8		Pound force	lbf	4.4482216	444822.16	1
9		exanewton	EN	1E+18	1E+23	2.248E+17
10		petanewton	PN	1E+15	1E+20	2.248E+14
11		teranewton	TN	1E+12	1E+17	2.248E+11
12		giganewton	GN	1E+09	1E+14	224808943
13		meganewton	MN	1000000	1E+11	224808.94
14		kilonewton	kN	1000	100000000	224.80894
15		hectonewton	hN	100	10000000	22.480894
16		dekaonewton	eN	10	1000000	2.2480894
17		decinewton	dN	0.1	10000	0.0224809
18		centinewton	cN	0.01	1000	0.0022481
19		millinewton	mN	0.001	100	0.0002248
20		micronewton	uN	0.000001	0.1	2.248E-07
21		nanonewton	nN	1E-09	0.0001	2.248E-10
22		piconewton	pN	1E-12	0.0000001	2.248E-13
23		femtonewton	fN	1E-15	1E-10	2.248E-16
24		attonewton	aN	1E-18	1E-13	2.248E-19
25		exadyne	Edyn	1E+13	1E+18	2.248E+12
26		petadyne	Pdyn	1E+10	1E+15	2.248E+09
27		teradyne	Tdyn	10000000	1E+12	2248089.4
28		gigadyne	Gdyn	10000	1E+09	2248.0894
29		megadyne	Mdyn	10	1000000	2.2480894
30		kilodyne	kdyn	0.01	1000	0.0022481
31		hectodyne	hdyn	0.001	100	0.0002248
32		dekaodyne	edyn	0.0001	10	2.248E-05
33		decidyne	ddyn	0.000001	0.1	2.248E-07
34		centidyne	cdyn	0.0000001	0.01	2.248E-08
35		millidyne	mdyn	1E-08	0.001	2.248E-09
36		microdyne	udyn	1E-11	0.000001	2.248E-12
37		nanodyne	ndyn	1E-14	1E-09	2.248E-15
38		picodyne	pdyn	1E-17	1E-12	2.248E-18
39		femtodyne	fdyn	1E-20	1E-15	2.248E-21
40		attodyne	adyn	1E-23	1E-18	2.248E-24

Table 15.11 Units of Energy*

Unit of Energy	Abbreviation to Use in CONVERT
Joule	J
Erg	e
Thermodynamic calorie	c
IT calorie	cal
Electron volt	eV
Horsepower-hour	HPh
Watt-hour	Wh
Foot-pound	flb
BTU	BTU
Exajoule	EJ

Unit of Energy	Abbreviation to Use in CONVERT
Petajoule	PJ
Terajoule	TJ
Gigajoule	GJ
Megajoule	MJ
Kilojoule	kJ
Hectojoule	hJ
Dekaojoule	eJ
Decijoule	dJ
Centijoule	cJ
Millijoule	mJ
Microjoule	uJ
Nanojoule	nJ
Picojoule	pJ
Femtojoule	fJ
Attojoule	aJ

*This table shows the complete metric prefixes for joules. Similar metric prefixes can also be applied to ergs, thermodynamic calories, IT calories, electron volts, and Watt-hours. This adds 80 additional measurements available in the CONVERT function for Energy.Figure 15.41 shows a conversion of energies.

Table 15.12 shows conversions available for power.

Table 15.12   Units of Power

Unit of Power	Abbreviation to Use in CONVERT
Horsepower	HP
Watt	W
Exawatt	EW
Petawatt	PW
Terawatt	TW
Gigawatt	GW

Unit of Power	Abbreviation to Use in CONVERT
Megawatt	MW
Kilowatt	kW
Hectowatt	hW
Dekaowatt	eW
Deciwatt	dW
Centiwatt	cW
Milliwatt	mW
Microwatt	uW
Nanowatt	nW
Picowatt	pW
Femtowatt	fW
Attowatt	aW

Figure 15.41
This table converts between the energy units in the left column and the various units along the top row.

	A	B	C	D	E	F	G	H	I	J	K	L
						Thermodynamic		Electron	Horsepower-	Watt-	Foot-	
4				Joule	Erg	calorie	IT calorie	volt	hour	hour	pound	BTU
5				J	e	c	cal	eV	HPh	Wh	flb	BTU
6	FROM	Joule	J	1	10000000	0.239005736	0.2388459	6.24E+18	3.72506E-07	0.000278	0.737562	0.000948
7		Erg	e	0.0000001	1	2.39006E-08	2.3885E-08	6.24E+11	3.72306E-14	2.78E-11	7.38E-08	9.48E-11
8		Thermodynamic calorie	c	4.184	41840000	1	0.99933123	2.61E+19	1.55857E-06	0.001162	3.08596	0.003966
9		IT calorie	cal	4.1868	41868000	1.000669216	1	2.61E+19	1.5596lE-06	0.001163	3.088025	0.003968
10		Electron volt	eV	1.60219E-19	1.60219E-12	3.82933E-20	3.8268E-20	1	5.96826E-26	4.45E-23	1.18E-19	1.52E-22
11		Horsepower-hou	HPh	2684519.538	2.68452E+13	641615.5683	641186.476	1.68E+25	1	745.6999	1980000	2544.434
12		Watt-hour	Wh	3600	36000000000	860.4206501	859.845228	2.25E+22	0.001341022	1	2655.224	3.412142
13		Foot-pound	flb	1.355817948	13558179.48	0.324048267	0.32383155	8.46E+18	5.05051E-07	0.000377	1	0.001285
14		BTU	BTU	1055.055853	10550558526	252.1644007	251.995761	6.59E+21	0.000393015	0.293071	778.1693	1
15		kilojoule	kJ	1000	10000000000	239.0057361	238.845897	6.24E+21	0.000372506	0.277778	737.5621	0.947817
16		kiloerg	ke	0.0001	1000	2.39006E-05	2.3885E-05	6.24E+14	3.72506E-11	2.78E-08	7.38E-05	9.48E-08
17		kilocalorie (Ther	kc	4184	41840000000	1000	999.331231	2.61E+22	0.001558566	1.162222	3085.96	3.965667
18		kilocalorie (IT)	kcal	4186.8	41868000000	1000.669216	1000	2.61E+22	0.001559609	1.163	3088.025	3.968321
19		kiloelecton volt	keV	1.60219E-16	1.60219E-09	3.82933E-17	3.8268E-17	1000	5.96826E-23	4.45E-20	1.18E-16	1.52E-19
20		kilowatt-hour	kWh	3600000	3.6E+13	860420.6501	859845.228	2.25E+25	1.34102209	1000	2655224	3412.142
21		exajoule	EJ	1E+18	1E+25	2.39006E+17	2.3885E+17	6.24E+36	3.72506E+11	2.78E+14	7.38E+17	9.48E+14
22		petajoule	PJ	1E+15	1E+22	2.39006E+14	2.3885E+14	6.24E+33	372506136	2.78E+11	7.38E+14	9.48E+11
23		terajoule	TJ	1E+12	1E+19	2.39006E+11	2.3885E+11	6.24E+30	372506.136	2.78E+08	7.38E+11	9.48E+08
24		gigajoule	GJ	1000000000	1E+16	239005736.1	238845897	6.24E+27	372.506136	277777.8	7.38E+08	947817.1
25		megajoule	MJ	1000000	1E+13	239005.7361	238845.897	6.24E+24	0.372506136	277.7778	737562.1	947.8171
26		kilojoule	kJ	1000	10000000000	239.0057361	238.845897	6.24E+21	0.000372506	0.277778	737.5621	0.947817
27		hectojoule	hJ	100	1000000000	23.90057361	23.8845897	6.24E+20	3.72506E-05	0.027778	73.75621	0.094782
28		dekaojoule	eJ	10	100000000	2.390057361	2.38845897	6.24E+19	3.72506E-06	0.002778	7.375621	0.009478
29		decijoule	dJ	0.1	1000000	0.023900574	0.02388459	6.24E+17	3.72506E-08	2.78E-05	0.073756	9.48E-05
30		centijoule	cJ	0.01	100000	0.002390057	0.00238846	6.24E+16	3.72506E-09	2.78E-06	0.007376	9.48E-06
31		millijoule	mJ	0.001	10000	0.000239006	0.00023885	6.24E+15	3.72506E-10	2.78E-07	0.000738	9.48E-07
32		microjoule	uJ	0.000001	10	2.39006E-07	2.3885E-07	6.24E+12	3.72506E-13	2.78E-10	7.38E-07	9.48E-10
33		nanojoule	nJ	0.000000001	0.01	2.39006E-10	2.3885E-10	6.24E+09	3.72506E-16	2.78E-13	7.38E-10	9.48E-13
34		picojoule	pJ	1E-12	0.00001	2.39006E-13	2.3885E-13	6241457	3.72506E-19	2.78E-16	7.38E-13	9.48E-16
35		femtojoule	fJ	1E-15	0.00000001	2.39006E-16	2.3885E-16	6241.457	3.72506E-22	2.78E-19	7.38E-16	9.48E-19
36		attojoule	aJ	1E-18	1E-11	2.39006E-19	2.3885E-19	6.241457	3.72506E-25	2.78E-22	7.38E-19	9.48E-22
37		The metric prefixes also apply to e, c, cal, eV, Wh										

E6 ▾ (fx =CONVERT(1,Cb,E5)

Figure 15.42 shows a conversion of powers.

	A	B	C	D	E
3		Power		TO---->	
4				Horsepower	Watt
5				HP	W
6	FROM	Horsepower	HP	1	745.6998716
7		Watt	W	0.001341022	1
8		exawatt	EW	1.34102E+15	1E+18
9		petawatt	PW	1.34102E+12	1E+15
10		terawatt	TW	1341022090	1E+12
11		gigawatt	GW	1341022.09	1000000000
12		megawatt	MW	1341.02209	1000000
13		kilowatt	kW	1.34102209	1000
14		hectowatt	hW	0.134102209	100
15		dekaowatt	eW	0.013410221	10
16		deciwatt	dW	0.000134102	0.1
17		centiwatt	cW	1.34102E-05	0.01
18		milliwatt	mW	1.34102E-06	0.001
19		microwatt	uW	1.34102E-09	0.000001
20		nanowatt	nW	1.34102E-12	0.000000001
21		picowatt	pW	1.34102E-15	1E-12
22		femtowatt	fW	1.34102E-18	1E-15
23		attowatt	aW	1.34102E-21	1E-18

D6 f_x =CONVERT(1,$C6,D$5)

Figure 15.42
This table converts between the power units in the left column and the various units along the top row.

Table 15.13 shows conversions available for units of magnetism.

Table 15.13 Units of Magnetism

Unit of Magnetism	Abbreviation to Use in CONVERT
Tesla	T
Gauss	Ga
Exatesla	ET
Petatesla	PT
Teratesla	TT
Gigatesla	GT
Megatesla	MT
Kilotesla	kT
Hectotesla	hT
Dekaotesla	eT

Unit of Magnetism	Abbreviation to Use in CONVERT
Decitesla	dT
Centitesla	cT
Millitesla	mT
Microtesla	uT
Nanotesla	nT
Picotesla	pT
Femtotesla	fT
Attotesla	aT
Exagauss	Ega
Petagauss	Pga
Teragauss	Tga
Gigagauss	Gga
Megagauss	Mga
Kilogauss	kga
Hectogauss	hga
Dekaogauss	ega
Decigauss	dga
Centigauss	cga
Milligauss	mga
Microgauss	uga
Nanogauss	nga
Picogauss	pga
Femtogauss	fga
Attogauss	aga

Figure 15.43 shows a conversion of magnetisms.

Table 15.14 shows conversion factors available for temperature systems.

	E6		f_x	=CONVERT(1,$C6,E$5)	

	A	B	C	D	E
4				Tesla	Gauss
5				T	ga
6	FROM	Tesla	T	1	10000
7		Gauss	ga	0.0001	1
8		exatesla	ET	1E+18	1E+22
9		petatesla	PT	1E+15	1E+19
10		teratesla	TT	1E+12	1E+16
11		gigatesla	GT	1000000000	1E+13
12		megatesla	MT	1000000	1000000000
13		kilotesla	kT	1000	10000000
14		hectotesla	hT	100	1000000
15		dekaotesla	eT	10	100000
16		decitesla	dT	0.1	1000
17		centitesla	cT	0.01	100
18		millitesla	mT	0.001	10
19		microtesla	uT	0.000001	0.01
20		nanotesla	nT	0.000000001	0.00001
21		picotesla	pT	1E-12	0.00000001
22		femtotesla	fT	1E-15	1E-11
23		attotesla	aT	1E-18	1E-14
24		exagauss	Ega	1E+14	1E+18
25		petagauss	Pga	1E+11	1E+15
26		teragauss	Tga	100000000	1E+12
27		gigagauss	Gga	100000	1000000000
28		megagauss	Mga	100	1000000
29		kilogauss	kga	0.1	1000
30		hectogauss	hga	0.01	100
31		dekaogauss	ega	0.001	10
32		decigauss	dga	0.00001	0.1
33		centigauss	cga	0.000001	0.01
34		milligauss	mga	0.0000001	0.001
35		microgauss	uga	1E-10	0.000001
36		nanogauss	nga	1E-13	0.000000001
37		picogauss	pga	1E-16	1E-12
38		femtogauss	fga	1E-19	1E-15
39		attogauss	aga	1E-22	1E-18

Figure 15.43
This table converts between the magnetism units in the left column and the various units along the top row.

Table 15.14   Units of Temperature

Unit of Temperature	Abbreviation to Use in CONVERT
Degree Celsius	C
Degree Fahrenheit	F
Degree Kelvin	K

Figure 15.44 shows a conversion of temperature systems.

	D6		f_x	=CONVERT(1,$C6,D$5)	

	A	B	C	D	E	F
3		Temperature		TO---->		
4				Degree Celsius	Degree Fahrenheit	Degree Kelvin
5				C	F	K
6	FROM	Degree Celsius	C	1	33.8	274.15
7		Degree Fahrenheit	F	-17.2222	1	255.9277778
8		Degree Kelvin	K	-272.15	-457.87	1

Figure 15.44
This table converts between the temperature scales in the left column and the various scales along the top row.

Table 15.15 shows conversion units available for liquid measurements.

Table 15.15   Units of Liquid Measure

Unit of Liquid Measure	Abbreviation to Use in CONVERT
Teaspoon	tsp
Tablespoon	tbs
Fluid ounce	oz
Cup	cup
U.S. pint	pt
U.K. pint	uk_pt
Quart	qt
Gallon	gal
Liter	l
Exaliter	El
Petaliter	Pl
Teraliter	Tl
Gigaliter	Gl
Megaliter	Ml
Kiloliter	kl
Hectoliter	hl
Dekaoliter	el
Deciliter	dl
Centiliter	cl
Milliliter	ml
Microliter	ul
Nanoliter	nl
Picoliter	pl
Femtoliter	fl
Attoliter	al

Figure 15.45 shows a conversion of liquid measures.

	F11		▼ (•	*fx*	=CONVERT(1,$C11,F$5)							
	A	B	C	D	E	F	G	H	I	J	K	L
					Table	Fluid		U.S.	U.K.			
4				Teaspoon	spoon	ounce	Cup	pint	pint	Quart	Gallon	Liter
5				tsp	tbs	oz	cup	pt	uk_pt	qt	gal	l
6	FROM	Teaspoon	tsp	1	0.3333	0.1667	0.021	0.01	0.0087	0.0052	0.0013	0.0049
7		Tablespoon	tbs	3	1	0.5	0.063	0.031	0.026	0.0156	0.00391	0.0148
8		Fluid ounce	oz	6	2	1	0.125	0.063	0.052	0.0313	0.00781	0.0296
9		Cup	cup	48	16	8	1	0.5	0.4163	0.25	0.0625	0.2366
10		U.S. pint	pt	96	32	16	2	1	0.8327	0.5	0.125	0.4732
11		U.K. pint	uk_pt	115.291193	38.43	19.215	2.402	1.201	1	0.6005	0.15012	0.5683
12		Quart	qt	192	64	32	4	2	1.6653	1	0.25	0.9464
13		Gallon	gal	768	256	128	16	8	6.6614	4	1	3.7854
14		Liter	l	202.884136	67.628	33.814	4.227	2.113	1.7598	1.0567	0.26417	1
15		exaliter	El	2.0288E+20	7E+19	3E+19	4E+18	2E+18	2E+18	1E+18	2.6E+17	1E+18
16		petaliter	Pl	2.0288E+17	7E+16	3E+16	4E+15	2E+15	2E+15	1E+15	2.6E+14	1E+15
17		teraliter	Tl	2.0288E+14	7E+13	3E+13	4E+12	2E+12	2E+12	1E+12	2.6E+11	1E+12
18		gigaliter	Gl	2.0288E+11	7E+10	3E+10	4E+09	2E+09	2E+09	1E+09	2.6E+08	1E+09
19		megaliter	Ml	202884136	7E+07	3E+07	4E+06	2E+06	2E+06	1E+06	264172	1E+06
20		kiloliter	kl	202884.136	67628	33814	4227	2113	1759.8	1056.7	264.172	1000
21		hectoliter	hl	20288.4136	6762.8	3381.4	422.7	211.3	175.98	105.67	26.4172	100
22		dekaoliter	el	2028.84136	676.28	338.14	42.27	21.13	17.598	10.567	2.64172	10
23		deciliter	dl	20.2884136	6.7628	3.3814	0.423	0.211	0.176	0.1057	0.02642	0.1
24		centiliter	cl	2.02884136	0.6763	0.3381	0.042	0.021	0.0176	0.0106	0.00264	0.01
25		milliliter	ml	0.20288414	0.0676	0.0338	0.004	0.002	0.0018	0.0011	0.00026	0.001
26		microliter	ul	0.00020288	7E-05	3E-05	4E-06	2E-06	2E-06	1E-06	2.6E-07	1E-06
27		nanoliter	nl	2.0288E-07	7E-08	3E-08	4E-09	2E-09	2E-09	1E-09	2.6E-10	1E-09
28		picoliter	pl	2.0288E-10	7E-11	3E-11	4E-12	2E-12	2E-12	1E-12	2.6E-13	1E-12
29		femtoliter	fl	2.0288E-13	7E-14	3E-14	4E-15	2E-15	2E-15	1E-15	2.6E-16	1E-15
30		attoliter	al	2.0288E-16	7E-17	3E-17	4E-18	2E-18	2E-18	1E-18	2.6E-19	1E-18

Figure 15.45
A pint in the U.K. contains 19.2 fluid ounces.

Using DELTA or GESTEP to Filter a Set of Values

The functions DELTA and GESTEP are left over from a long-ago era. In the SUMPRODUCT function, you can see that Excel can now evaluate TRUE*100 as 100 and FALSE*100 as 0. In early spreadsheet programs, you needed to convert TRUE to 1 and FALSE to 0 explicitly. These two functions explicitly return 1 when a condition is true and 0 when a condition is false, allowing you to multiply the original number by the function in order to get conditional sums.

DELTA tests whether two values are equal. GESTEP tests whether a value is greater than or equal to a threshold value.

Syntax:

DELTA(number1,number2)

The DELTA function tests whether two values are equal. It returns 1 if number1 equals number2; it returns 0 otherwise. You use this function to filter a set of values. For example, by summing several DELTA functions, you can calculate the count of equal pairs. This function is also known as the Kronecker Delta function. This function takes the following arguments:

- *number1*—This is the first number.

- *number2*—This is the second number. If omitted, number2 is assumed to be 0.

If either *number1* or *number2* is nonnumeric, DELTA returns a #VALUE! error.

Figure 15.46 shows a list of students and their test scores in Columns A and B. A large matrix of DELTA functions in C:W counts how many students achieved each score. Excel has many newer, better functions, such as COUNTIF, that can also achieve this result.

Figure 15.46
The DELTA functions in C2:W24 check whether the score in Column B is the same as the score in Row 1. Totals in Row 25 complete the analysis.

	C2			fx		=DELTA($B2,C$1)																	
	A	B	C	D	E	F	G	H	I	J	K	L	M	N	O	P	Q	R	S	T	U	V	W
1	STUDENT	SCORE	80	81	82	83	84	85	86	87	88	89	90	91	92	93	94	95	96	97	98	99	100
2	RAYMOND	81	0	1	0	0	0	0	0	0	0	0	0	0	0	0	0	0	0	0	0	0	0
3	SEAN	100	0	0	0	0	0	0	0	0	0	0	0	0	0	0	0	0	0	0	0	0	1
4	ERIN	100	0	0	0	0	0	0	0	0	0	0	0	0	0	0	0	0	0	0	0	0	1
5	JACK	90	0	0	0	0	0	0	0	0	0	0	1	0	0	0	0	0	0	0	0	0	0
6	BRYAN	90	0	0	0	0	0	0	0	0	0	0	1	0	0	0	0	0	0	0	0	0	0
7	RANDY	85	0	0	0	0	0	1	0	0	0	0	0	0	0	0	0	0	0	0	0	0	0
8	HOWARD	92	0	0	0	0	0	0	0	0	0	0	0	0	1	0	0	0	0	0	0	0	0
9	TERESA	90	0	0	0	0	0	0	0	0	0	0	1	0	0	0	0	0	0	0	0	0	0
10	ELLA	89	0	0	0	0	0	0	0	0	0	1	0	0	0	0	0	0	0	0	0	0	0
11	BETTY	83	0	0	0	1	0	0	0	0	0	0	0	0	0	0	0	0	0	0	0	0	0
12	LUZ	89	0	0	0	0	0	0	0	0	0	1	0	0	0	0	0	0	0	0	0	0	0
13	ALICIA	97	0	0	0	0	0	0	0	0	0	0	0	0	0	0	0	0	0	1	0	0	0
14	CHARLENE	100	0	0	0	0	0	0	0	0	0	0	0	0	0	0	0	0	0	0	0	0	1
15	VICTORIA	83	0	0	0	1	0	0	0	0	0	0	0	0	0	0	0	0	0	0	0	0	0
16	LAUREN	87	0	0	0	0	0	0	0	1	0	0	0	0	0	0	0	0	0	0	0	0	0
17	TRACEY	97	0	0	0	0	0	0	0	0	0	0	0	0	0	0	0	0	0	1	0	0	0
18	KYLE	83	0	0	0	1	0	0	0	0	0	0	0	0	0	0	0	0	0	0	0	0	0
19	WILMA	100	0	0	0	0	0	0	0	0	0	0	0	0	0	0	0	0	0	0	0	0	1
20	MARCIA	89	0	0	0	0	0	0	0	0	0	1	0	0	0	0	0	0	0	0	0	0	0
21	WILLIE	98	0	0	0	0	0	0	0	0	0	0	0	0	0	0	0	0	0	0	1	0	0
22	EUGENE	83	0	0	0	1	0	0	0	0	0	0	0	0	0	0	0	0	0	0	0	0	0
23	LEAH	90	0	0	0	0	0	0	0	0	0	0	1	0	0	0	0	0	0	0	0	0	0
24	LORI	86	0	0	0	0	0	0	1	0	0	0	0	0	0	0	0	0	0	0	0	0	0
25		Total	0	1	0	4	0	1	1	1	0	3	4	0	1	0	0	0	0	2	1	0	4

Syntax:

GESTEP(*number,step*)

The GESTEP function returns 1 if *number* is greater than or equal to *step*; it returns 0 otherwise. You can use this function to filter a set of values. For example, by summing several GESTEP functions, you can calculate the count of values that exceed a threshold. This function takes the following arguments:

- *number*—This is the value to test against step.

- *step*—This is the threshold value. If you omit a value for *step*, GESTEP uses 0.

If any argument is nonnumeric, GESTEP returns a #VALUE! error.

Using ERF and ERFC to Calculate the Error Function and Its Complement

An error function is designed to make it easier to represent integrals in the form $x^n \times e^{(-ax^2)} dx$. All such integrals can be written in terms of the integral $e^{(-u^2)} du$. If you integrate this from 0 to infinity, it converges to SQRT(PI)/2. The ERF function, then, is defined so that ERF converges to 1 at infinity.

The ERF function is ERF(x) = 2/SQRT(PI()) times the integral of $e^{(-u^2)}du$ integrated from 0 to x. The result of ERF is a value between 0 and 1.

Contrary to what Excel Help says, there are two syntax options available in Excel for ERF:

- ERF(*x*)—The common use of ERF is with a single argument. In this case, the function returns the ERF function. In the preceding formula, the integral is evaluated from 0 to x. For example, ERF(0.1) is 0.112463.

note

Although ERF is defined for negative values, Excel does not calculate ERF for less than 0. If you need to do this, you have to turn to more comprehensive calculation engines, such as Mathematica.

- ERF(*lower_limit,upper_limit*)—The second syntax for ERF provides a lower and an upper limit. In this case, Excel integrates from x to y.

The ERFC function provides the complement to ERF. In all cases, ERFC(x) is equal to 1-ERF(x).

Figure 15.47 charts the ERF and ERFC functions.

	A	B	C	D	E	F	G	H
		ERF	**ERFC**					
1								
2	0	0	1		0.8427	=ERF(1)		
3	0.05	0.056371978	0.94363		0.99532	=ERF(2)		
4	0.1	0.112462916	0.88754		0.15262	=ERF(1,2)		
5	0.15	0.167995971	0.832					
6	0.2	0.222702589	0.7773					
7	0.25	0.27632639	0.72367					
8	0.3	0.328626759	0.67137					
9	0.35	0.379382054	0.62062					
10	0.4	0.428392355	0.57161					
11	0.45	0.47548172	0.52452					
12	0.5	0.520499878	0.4795					
13	0.55	0.563323366	0.43668					
14	0.6	0.603856091	0.39614					
15	0.65	0.642029327	0.35797					
16	0.7	0.677801194	0.3222					
17	0.75	0.711155634	0.28884					
18	0.8	0.742100965	0.2579					
19	0.85	0.770668058	0.22933					
20	0.9	0.796908212	0.20309					
21	0.95	0.820890807	0.17911					

Cell B3, formula bar: =ERF(A3)

Figure 15.47
ERF converges very close to 1 for values of 3 or above. ERFC is 1 – *ERF*.

Syntax:

ERF(*x*)

In this first syntax, the ERF function returns the error function for x.

Syntax:

ERF(*lower_limit,upper_limit*)

In this second syntax, the ERF function returns the error function integrated between lower_limit and upper_limit. This function takes the following arguments:

- *lower_limit*—This is the lower bound for integrating ERF.

- *upper_limit*—This is the upper bound for integrating ERF. If any argument is nonnumeric, ERF returns a #VALUE! error. If any argument is negative, ERF returns a #NUM! error.

Syntax:

ERFC(*x*)

The ERFC function returns the complementary ERF function integrated between x and infinity. The argument *x* is the lower bound for integrating ERF. If *x* is nonnumeric, ERFC returns a #VALUE! error. If *x* is negative, ERFC returns a #NUM! error.

Calculating the BESSEL Functions

The BESSEL function is useful in many physics applications that involve solving classical partial differential equations in cylindrical coordinates. Excel offers four versions of the BESSEL function:

- BESSELJ—This solves the BESSEL function of the first kind. You use this function to solve BESSEL differential equations that are nonsingular at the origin.

- BESSELY—This solves the BESSEL functions of the second kind. You use this function to solve BESSEL differential equations that are singular at the origin. The BESSEL functions of the second kind are sometimes called Weber or Neumann functions.

- BESSELI—This solves the modified BESSEL differential equation. It is closely related to BESSELJ.

- BESSELK—This solves the modified BESSEL function of the second kind. This function is also known as the Basset function, Macdonald functions, or BESSEL functions of the third kind.

Each Bessel function takes two required arguments:

- x—This is the value at which to evaluate the function.

- n—This is the order of the BESSEL function. If n is not an integer, it is truncated.

If *x* is nonnumeric, BESSELI returns a #VALUE! error. If *n* is nonnumeric, BESSELI returns a #VALUE! error. If *n* is less than 0, BESSELI returns a #NUM! error.

Figure 15.48 shows the BESSELJ and BESSELY functions for orders of n from 0 through 4.

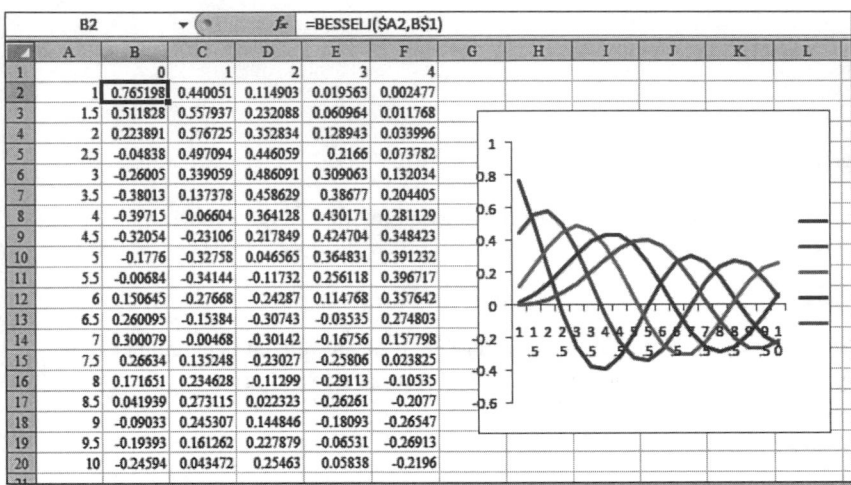

Figure 15.48
This chart shows the BESSELJ and BESSELY functions.

Using the Analysis Toolpack to Perform Fast Fourier Transforms (FFTs)

Many of the engineering functions have been promoted from the Analysis Toolpack to the regular version of Excel. However, one feature is left orphaned in the Analysis Toolpack. If you need to perform Fourier analysis, you should install the Analysis Toolpack.

> See the "Installing the Analysis Toolpack in Excel 2010" section in Chapter 14, "Using Statistical Functions".

Fourier transforms are used to evaluate the output of an analog-to-digital conversion (ADC). To perform a Fourier Transform, follow these steps:

1. Import your ADC data into Excel. The ADC record should contain a specific number of records that are powers of 2, up to 4,096 such as 2, 4, 8, 16, 32, 64, 128, 256, 512, 1,024, 2,048, or 4,096.

2. Make sure the Analysis Toolpack is installed.

3. From the Data tab, select Data Analysis.

4. Select Fourier Analysis and click OK. The Fourier Analysis dialog appears.

5. In the Fourier Analysis dialog, select your ADC data as the input range. If your input range includes a heading, select the Labels in First Row check box. In this case, your data must be $(n\wedge2) + 1$ records long.

6. Select the top-left cell of the output range.

7. Leave the Inverse check box clear. This check box is used to convert FFT numbers in imaginary format back to the ADC format.

8. Click OK to perform the transformation.

In Figure 15.49, the original data is in Column A, and the transformed data is in Column C.

Figure 15.49
The Fourier
analysis tool
can convert
ADC data
to complex
Fourier num-
bers.

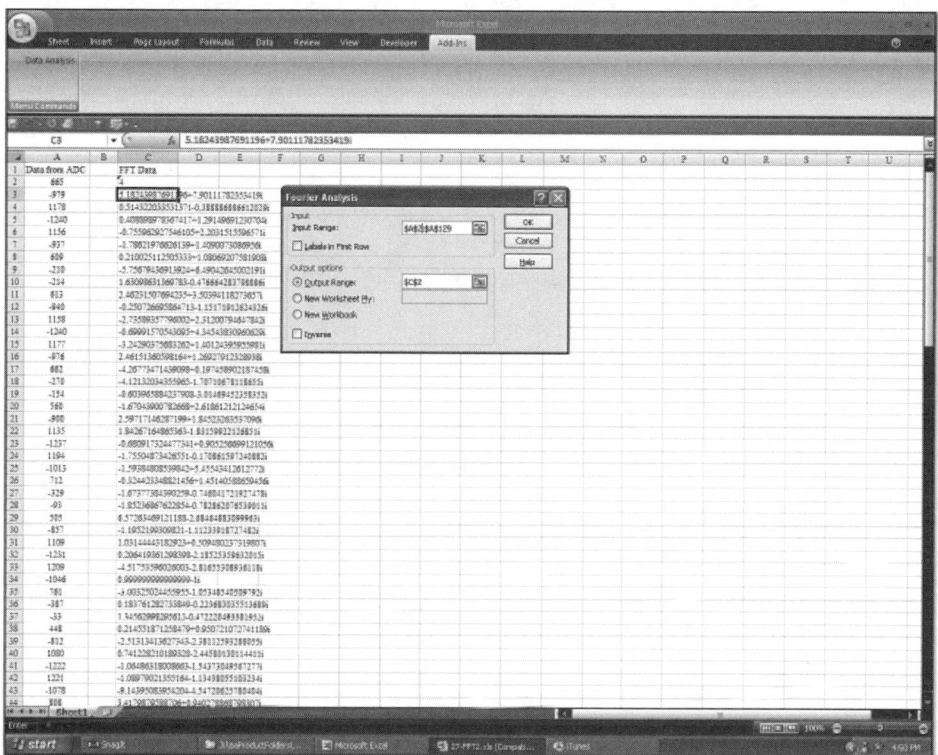

Excel Troubleshooting: Sharing Workbooks with Legacy Versions

A total of 89 functions that are part of the core set of functions in Excel 2010 were not included in the core functions in legacy versions of Excel.

Legacy versions of Excel were shipped with an add-in called the Analysis Toolpack. Hard-core Excel users such as scientists, engineers, and finance professionals often rely on the Analysis Toolpack. If you share your Excel 2010 workbook with a person who only occasionally uses Excel, it is possible that he or she has not enabled the Analysis Toolpack.

On a computer that does not have the Analysis Toolpack enabled, any reference to the following functions will automatically return the NAME error:

```
ACCRINT, ACCRINTM, AMORDEGRC, AMORLINC, BESSELI, BESSELJ, BESSELK, BESSELY,
BIN2DEC, BIN2HEX, BIN2OCT, COMPLEX, CONVERT, COUPDAYBS, COUPDAYS, COUPDAYSNC,
COUPNCD, COUPNUM, COUPPCD, CUMIPMT, CUMPRINC, DEC2BIN, DEC2HEX, DEC2OCT,
```

```
DELTA, DISC, DOLLARDE, DOLLARFR, DURATION, EDATE, EFFECT, EOMONTH, ERF, ERFC,
FACTDOUBLE, FVSCHEDULE, GCD, GESTEP, HEX2BIN, HEX2DEC, HEX2OCT, IMABS,
IMAGINARY, IMARGUMENT, IMCONJUGATE, IMCOS, IMDIV, IMEXP, IMLN, IMLOG10,
IMLOG2, IMPOWER, IMREAL, IMSIN, IMSQRT, IMSUB, INTRATE, ISEVEN, ISODD, LCM,
MDURATION, MROUND, MULTINOMIAL, NETWORKDAYS, NOMINAL, OCT2BIN, OCT2DEC,
OCT2HEX, ODDFPRICE, ODDFYIELD, ODDLPRICE, ODDLYIELD, PRICE, PRICEMAT,
QUOTIENT, RANDBETWEEN, RECEIVED, SERIESSUM, SQRTPI, TBILLEQ, TBILLPRICE,
TBILLYIELD, WEEKNUM, WORKDAY, XIRR, XNPV, YEARFRAC, YIELD, YIELDDISC, and
YIELDMAT.
```

If you are sharing workbooks that use these functions with people using legacy versions of Excel, be sure to remind them that they need to visit Tools, Add-Ins to make sure that the Analysis Toolpack option is selected before they open your workbooks.

CONNECTING WORKSHEETS, WORKBOOKS, AND EXTERNAL DATA

In Chapters 10, "Understanding Formulas," and 11, "Using Everyday Functions: Math, Date and Time, and Text Functions," you learned how to set up formulas that calculate based on values within one worksheet. You can also easily connect a worksheet to several other worksheets or connect various workbooks. Excel 2010 offers easier-than-ever ways to connect a worksheet to data from the Web, data from text files, or data from databases such as Access.

In this chapter, you learn how to do the following:

- Connect two worksheets
- Connect two workbooks
- Manage links between workbooks
- Connect to Web data
- Connect to text data
- Connect to Access data
- Manage connections

Connecting Two Worksheets

Although Excel 2010 offers 17 billion cells on every worksheet, it is fairly common to separate any model onto several worksheets. You might choose to have one worksheet for each month in a year or to have one worksheet for each functional area of a business. For example, Figure 16.1 shows a workbook with worksheets for revenue and expenses. Because different departments might be responsible for the functional areas, it makes sense to separate them into different worksheets. Eventually, though, you will want to pull information from the various worksheets into a single summary worksheet.

16-LinkingWorksheetsA.xlsm:2							
	A	B	C	D	E	F	G	H
1		Actual	Actual	Actual	Actual	Actual	Budget	
2		2007	2008	2009	2010	2011	2012	
3	Hardware	1754	2017	2320	2668	3068	3528	
4	Software	264	304	350	403	463	532	
5	Service	246	283	325	374	430	495	
6	Total Revenue	4271	4612	5004	5455	5972	6567	
7								

Summary / **Revenue** / Expense Summary /

	A	B	C	D	E	F	G
1		Actual	Actual	Actual	Actual	Actual	Budget
2		2007	2008	2009	2010	2011	2012
3	COGS	842	968	1114	1281	1473	1693
4	Selling Expense	513	553	600	655	717	788
5	Marketing Expense	257	277	300	328	359	394
6	R&D - Hardware	125	125	125	125	125	125
7	R&D - Software	75	75	75	75	75	75
8	Total Expenses	3819	4006	4223	4474	4760	5087

Summary / Revenue / **Expense Summary** /

Figure 16.1
Different functional areas need to work on budgets for revenue and expenses, so revenue and expenses are kept on separate worksheets.

Excel in Practice: Seeing Two Worksheets of the Same Workbook Side by Side.

The workbook in Figure 16.1 illustrates a useful trick—seeing two worksheets of the same workbook side by side. Using new tricks, such as the alternative drag-and-drop menu, enables you to see both the target and source worksheet side by side.

Follow these steps to see two worksheets of the same workbook side by side.

1. Open the first worksheet that you want to view.

2. On the View tab, click New Window. If your workbook is in full-screen mode, it appears that nothing happened. However, when you look in the title bar, you will see your workbook title has ":2" after the title.

3. On the View tab, click Arrange All, and then click either Vertical or Horizontal. The arrangement in Figure 16.1 is horizontal, whereas the arrangement in Figure 16.2 is vertical.

4. In the second window, click the second worksheet tab that you want to view. You can now see both worksheets of the same workbook side by side.

To return to a single window, click the Close Window icon, which is the white "X" in the top-right corner of window 2. Note that this is different from the red "X" in the top-right corner of the Excel application.

 **note**

Note that you have not created a second workbook. Instead, you have created a second camera looking at a different section of the same workbook. Any changes that you make in the left window appear in the second window.

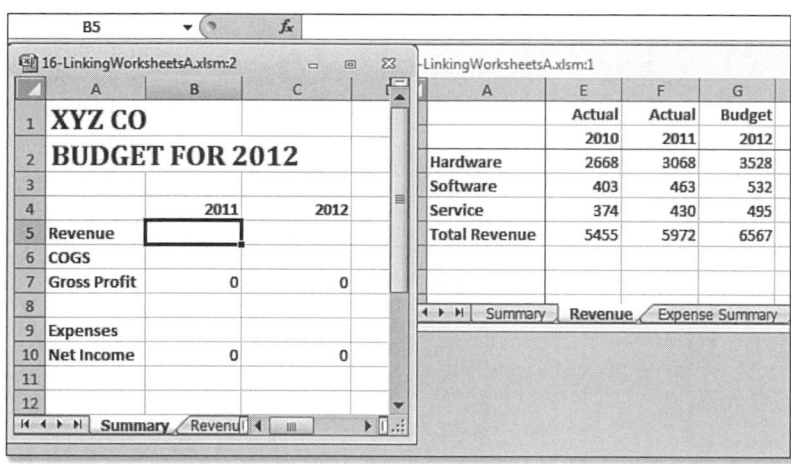

Figure 16.2
Set up a link to get information from the Revenue tab to appear on the Summary tab.

As shown in Figure 16.2, the goal is to have the values from Cells F6:G6 on the Revenue tab carry forward to Cells B5:C5 on the Summary tab. There are four ways to achieve this goal:

1. Type a formula such as =Revenue!F6 in Cell B5.

2. Build the formula using the mouse.

3. Right-drag Cells F6:G6 on the Revenue tab to the proper location on the Summary tab and then select Link Here.

4. Copy Cells F5:G6 on the Revenue tab. Paste to Cells B5:C6 and then use the paste options flyout menu to Link Here. This is the newest method and is discussed in the next section.

Creating Links Using Paste Options Menu

Follow these steps to set up a link using the new Paste Options flyout menu:

1. Select the cells that have the figures that you want to copy. For this example, select Cells F6:G6 on the Revenue tab.

2. Press Ctrl+C to copy those cells.

3. Select the cells where the link should appear. For this example, select B5:C6 on the Summary tab.

4. Press Ctrl+v to paste. As shown in Figure 16.3, the formula from the source cells is pasted in the target cells, giving the wrong answer, but do not panic. In addition, note that a new Paste Options menu appears near the pasted cell.

5. Press Ctrl to open the Paste Options menu. Select the Chain icon in the bottom row of the flyout menu. Alternatively, you can press N to Paste Link (see Figure 16.3).

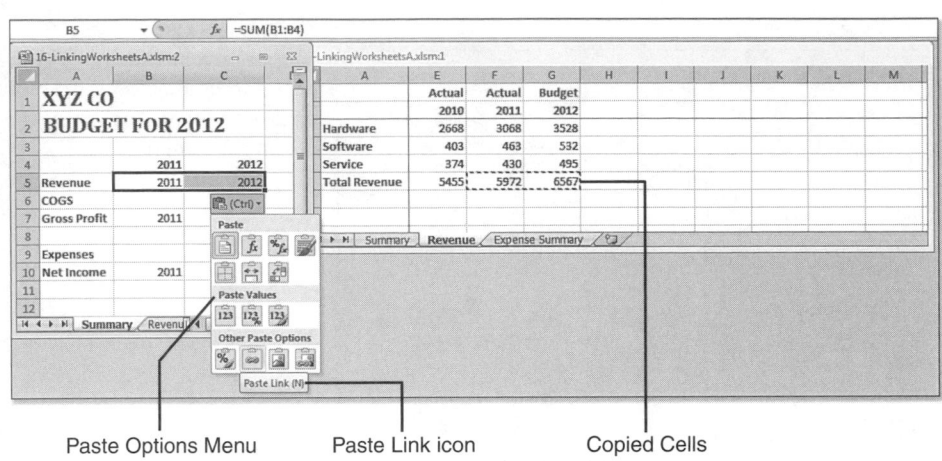

Figure 16.3
Copy the source cells to the target range.

Paste Options Menu   Paste Link icon   Copied Cells

Excel changes the formula from Figure 16.3 to have the correct syntax to point to Cells F6 on the Revenue tab (see Figure 16.4). Note that if data changes on the Revenue worksheet, the new results appear on the Summary worksheet. In Figure 16.4, the hardware budget changed from 3528 to 3590, and the resulting change appears on the Summary worksheet.

Correct Formula

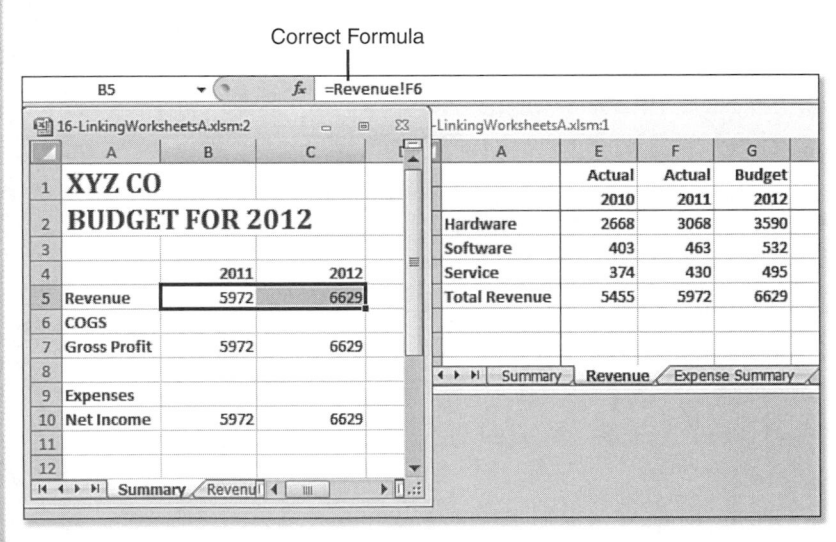

Figure 16.4
After choosing Paste Link, the formula is correct.

 To see a video demo of this technique, search for "Excel In Depth 16" at YouTube.

Creating Links Using Right-Drag Menu

If you are adept with the mouse, there is an easier way to create links. This is particularly true if you have the two worksheets arranged side by side, which was presented previously in the Excel in Practice section.

This method uses the Alternate Drag-and-Drop menu. This amazing menu, which has been hiding in Excel for several versions, offers a fast way to copy cells, link cells, change formulas to values, and more.

The Alternate Drag-and-Drop menu appears anytime that you right-click the border of a selection, right-drag to a new location, and then release the mouse button.

In Figure 16.5, on the Expense Summary tab, select Cells F3:G3. Hover over the edge of the selection rectangle until you see the four-headed arrow. Right-click and begin to drag to the other window.

Figure 16.5
Right-click and
drag the source
cells.

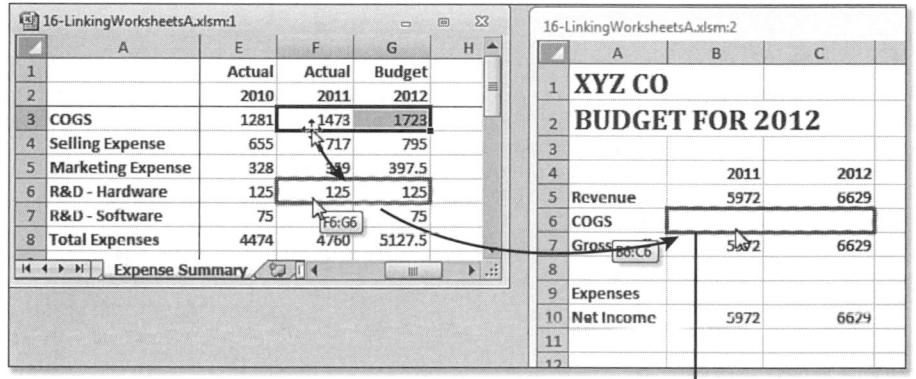

Right-Drag to New Location

When you have arrived at the new location, release the right-mouse button and select Link Here, as shown in Figure 16.6.

Excel builds a formula in the target location that has the proper syntax to link to the source cells.

Note that because the worksheet name contains a space, Excel wraps the sheet name in apostrophes: =' Expense   ' !F3 (see Figure 16.7).

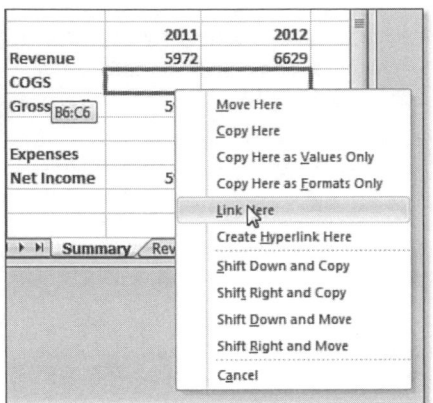

Figure 16.6
Release the mouse button to access this menu.

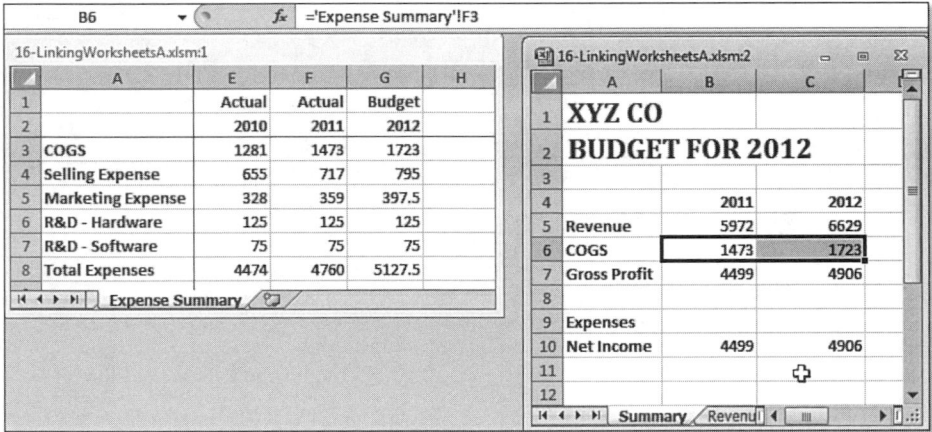

Figure 16.7
Excel builds the proper formula.

Building a Link by Using the Mouse

Another method is to build a formula by pointing to the correct cell with the mouse. Start in a target cell such as Cell B9 on the Summary tab (see Figure 16.8).

Instead of trying to remember the exact syntax, you can point to the correct cell. Type the equal sign and then click the desired worksheet tab. Using the mouse, click a cell to get the value from that cell. Excel builds the formula =`'Expense Summary'!F8` in the formula bar (see Figure 16.8). Excel waits for you to either press the Enter key to accept the formula or press another operator key to add other cells to the formula.

When you press the Enter key to accept the formula, Excel jumps back to the starting worksheet. The desired figure is carried through to the worksheet.

 note

The formula that Excel builds is a relative formula. You can copy B9 to B10 to retrieve the 2012 budget.

Figure 16.8
Type an equal sign; then click the source cell.

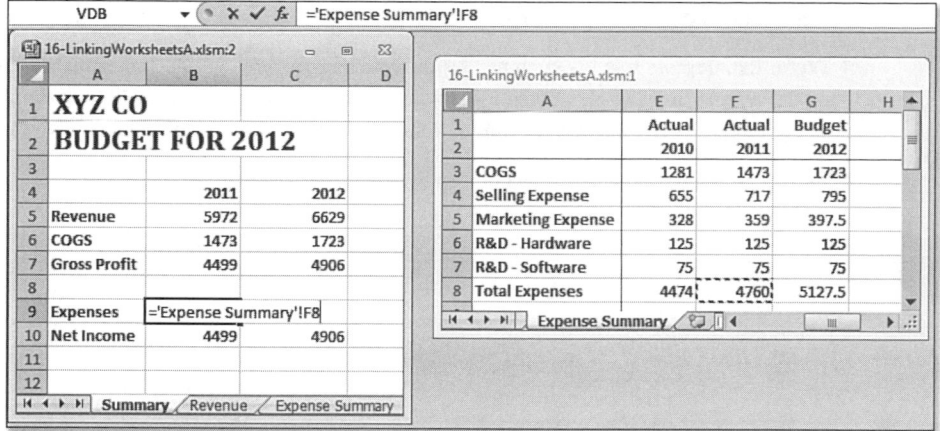

Links to External Workbooks Default to Absolute References

You can use any of the four methods described previously for building links to other worksheets when you want to build links to external workbooks. It is easiest if you open both workbooks.

Note that if you use any of the methods illustrated previously, Excel will default to adding dollar signs into the external reference. The dollar signs create an absolute reference that make it more difficult to copy.

Here is an example. When you use the mouse method described in Figure 16.8 to link to worksheet in the same workbook, the cell reference will be something like F8. If you use the same method to link to a worksheet in a different workbook, the cell reference created by Excel will automatically be $F$8. The dollar signs make this an absolute reference which will be difficult to copy. If you need to copy this formula to other cells, you should press the F4 key three times to change from an absolute reference to a relative reference.

Building a Formula by Typing

You can always build the links by typing the formula. This is the least popular method, because you need to understand an array of syntax rules. Keep in mind that these syntax rules change depending on whether the worksheet name contains a space, whether the link is external, and whether the linked workbook is open or closed.

Here are the syntax rules:

- For an internal link where the worksheet name does not contain a space, use =SheetName!CellAddress. For example, =Result!B3.

- When the worksheet name contains a space or certain special characters, Excel automatically adds apostrophes around the workbook name and sheet name. An example is ='Result Sheet'!B3.

- For an external link, the name of the workbook is wrapped in square brackets and appears before the sheet name. For example: =[LinkToMe.xlsm]Sheet1!B3.

- If the workbook name or sheet name contains a space, add an apostrophe before the opening square bracket and after the sheet name. For example, =`'[My File.xls]Income Statement'!B3`.

- When Excel refers to a file such as [RegionTotals.xlsm], you can assume that the file is currently open. When you close the linked file, Excel updates the formula in the linking workbook to include the complete pathname. For example, =`SUM('C:\[Region Totals.xlsm]Quota'!$B$2:$E$2)`.

- Figure 16.9 illustrates examples of various formulas:

Link Syntax		
Type	Spaces?	Formula
Internal	No	=Result!B3
Internal	Yes	='Result Sheet'!B3
External	No	=[16LinkToMe.xlsm]Sheet1!$B$3
External	Yes	='[16-Link To Me.xlsm]Sheet3'!$B$4
External Closed	No	='C:\Users\Owner\Documents\[16Closed.xlsm]Sheet1'!$B$3
External Closed	No	='C:\Users\Owner\Documents\[16Closed.xlsm]Sheet 2'!$B$3

Figure 16.9
Syntax for various types of links.

Creating Links to Unsaved Workbooks

You can build a formula that links to a source workbook where the source workbook has not been saved. This formula might point to Book1 or Book3 or a workbook such as that. When you attempt to save the target workbook, Excel presents a dialog that asks, "Is It OK to Save with References to Unsaved Documents?" In general, you should cancel the save, switch to the unsaved source workbook, and then select File, Save As to save the file with a permanent name. Then you can come back to save the linking workbook.

Using the Links Tab on the Trust Center

By default, Excel applies security settings that frustrate your attempts to pull values from closed workbooks. Consider the following scenario using two workbooks labeled Workbook A and Workbook B:

1. Establish a link from Workbook A to Workbook B.

2. Save and close Workbook A.

3. Make changes to Workbook B. Save and close Workbook B.

4. On a future day, open Workbook B.

5. Open Workbook A.

In this case, the new values in Workbook B automatically flow through to Workbook A.

However, if you attempt to later open Workbook A before opening Workbook B, you see the following message below the Ribbon and above the formula bar: Security Warning. Automatic Update of Links Has Been Disabled. (see Figure 16.10). Select Enable Content to allow the links to update.

Figure 16.10
The link message initially appears in the Info bar.

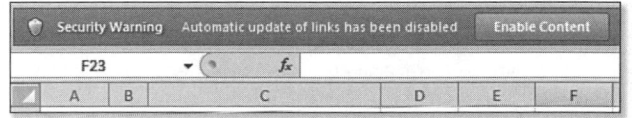

This behavior is different from legacy versions of Excel. In those versions, you had to answer the link question before you could work in the workbook. Now, you can click around the workbook and examine the links before you click Enable Content.

After you enable the content the first time, Excel marks the document as a trusted document. The next time you open the workbook, Excel displays a message similar to the one in Excel 2003, as shown in Figure 16.11.

Figure 16.11
Later, the Excel 2003 style link question appears.

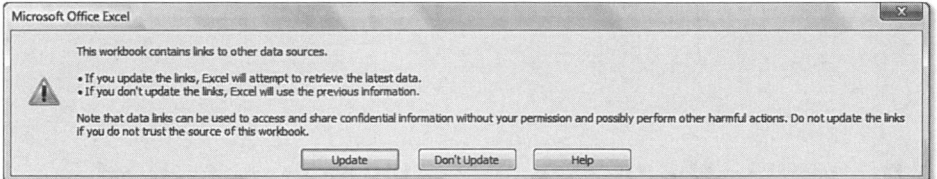

Opening Workbooks with Links to Closed Workbooks

Suppose that you have saved and closed the linking workbook. You update numbers in the linked workbook. You save and close the linked workbook. Later, when you open the linking workbook, Excel asks if you want to update the links to the other workbook. If you created both workbooks and you have possession of both workbooks, it is fine to allow the workbooks to update.

Dealing with Missing Linked Workbooks

If you received a linking workbook via email and do not have access to the linked workbooks, Excel alerts you that the workbook contains one or more links that cannot be updated. In this case, you should click Continue in the dialog box, as shown in Figure 16.12.

Figure 16.12
This message means that the linked workbook cannot be found. It shows up most often when someone mails you only the linking workbook.

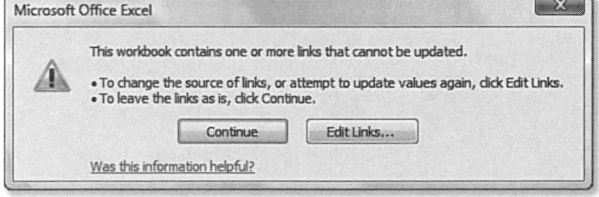

You also get this message if the linked workbook were renamed, moved, or deleted. In that case, you should click the Edit Links button to display the Edit Links dialog (see Figure 16.13). Then you should click the Change Source button to tell Excel that the linked workbook has a new name or location. Alternatively, you might need to click the Break Link button to change all linked formulas to their current values.

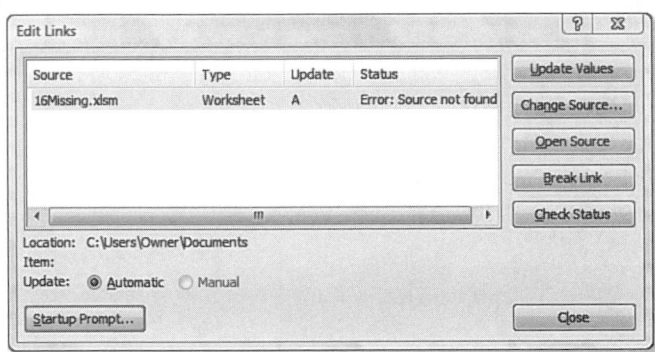

Figure 16.13
Manage or change links by using this dialog.

Preventing the Update Links Dialog from Appearing

Suppose that you need to send a linking workbook to a co-worker. You want your co-worker to see the current values of the linking formulas without having the linked workbook. In this case, you want the co-worker to click Continue in Figure 16.12. However, some newer Excel customers think that every warning box is a disaster, so you might prefer to suppress that box for your co-worker. To do so, follow these steps:

1. On the Data tab, in the Manage Connections group, select Edit Links to Files.

2. In the lower-left corner of the dialog that appears, click the Startup Prompt button. The Startup Prompt dialog appears.

3. Select Don't Display the Alert and Don't Update Automatic Links (see Figure 16.14).

After emailing the workbook to your co-worker, you need to redisplay the Startup Prompt dialog and change it back so that you will get the updated links.

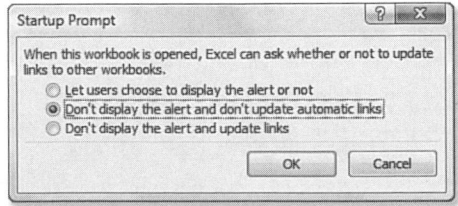

Figure 16.14
You can prevent others from seeing the Update Links message.

Connecting to Data on a Web Page

Many web pages comprise many tables of data. Anytime you see columns of numbers or columns of data, it is likely that you see the results of a table. Usually, the only things not in a table are paragraphs of body copy. In addition, it is not usually necessary to update this information on a daily basis. Excel 2010 makes it even easier than past versions of Excel to link your Excel worksheet to a table on any web page.

Setting Up a Connection to a Web Page

To set up a connection between a worksheet and a web page, follow these steps:

1. Find a section of the worksheet that has several blank rows and blank columns. Depending on the size of the selected sections of the web page, you can return many rows or columns of data.

2. On the Data tab, from the Get External Data group, select From Web. Excel opens the New Web Query dialog. This dialog looks remarkably like a mini web browser, and it even opens to your default home page from Internet Explorer. However, as shown in Figure 16.15, the rendered web page includes several yellow boxes with black arrows. These arrows indicate the tops of various tables on the page.

Figure 16.15
Notice the arrows indicating available tables on the web page.

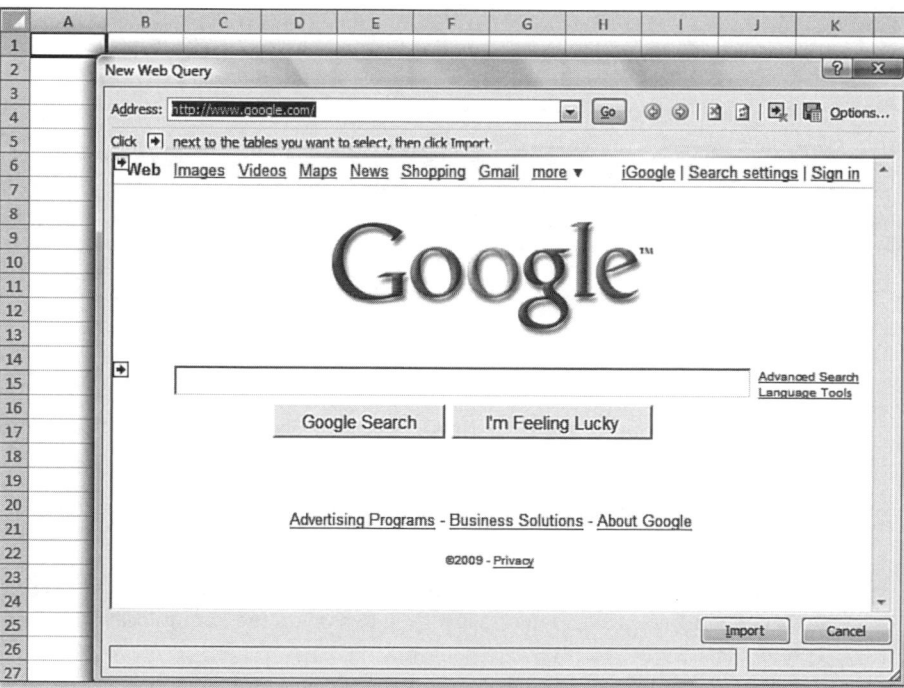

3. Using the search bar or the address bar, navigate to the selected web page. For example, to retrieve stock quotes, you might use http://finance.yahoo.com.

4. If the web page has a form, enter any values needed by the form. In this example, enter your desired ticker symbols into the Yahoo Get Quotes box and then press Go. The resulting web page will probably have many tables. The Yahoo quotes page has at least 14 tables, many of which are tables that display advertisements.

5. Hover the mouse over various yellow and black arrows. Excel highlights the entire range of each table.

6. When you find the table that contains the information you want, click that arrow. The arrow changes to a green check mark, as shown in Figure 16.16.

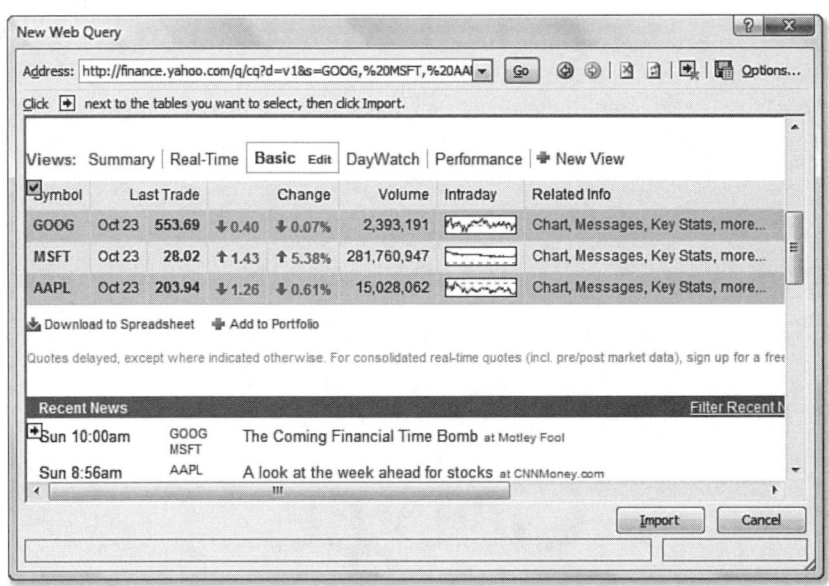

Figure 16.16
Select the table that contains the data for the worksheet.

7. In the upper-right corner of the New Web Query dialog, click the Options button. The Web Query Options dialog appears (see Figure 16.17).

8. Select whether the data from the web page should be retrieved as text only or have full HTML formatting in the results. Then click OK.

9. Click the Import button in the lower-right corner of the New Web Query dialog. Excel displays the Import Data dialog, which allows you to confirm the output location for the data from the web query (see Figure 16.18).

10. If desired, click the Properties button to set up automatic refreshing of the web data. The Connection Properties dialog appears (see Figure 16.19).

Figure 16.17
Most of the time, you want unformatted text.

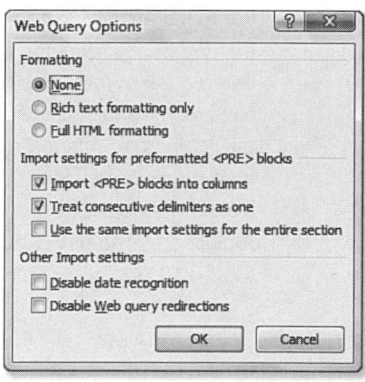

Figure 16.18
Confirm where the data should be returned.

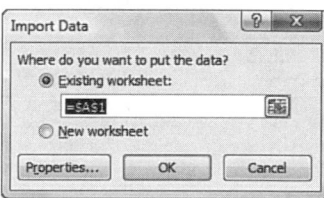

Figure 16.19
Control the refresh rate for the web query on this dialog.

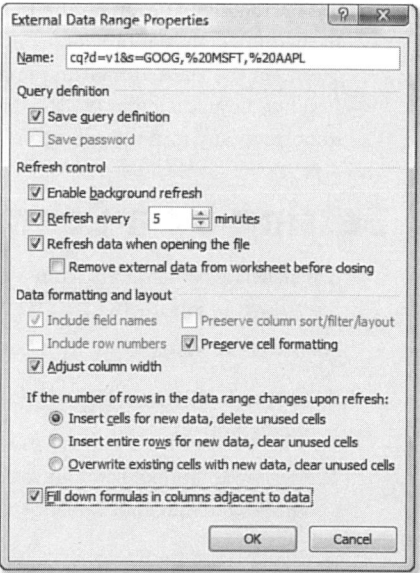

11. Use the Connection Properties dialog to set refresh options. For example, you can have the web query refreshed every so many minutes, and you can also have the web data refreshed when a file opens. This way, you can retrieve new data each day when you open the file. When you are done selecting options on this dialog, click OK. You briefly see a bit of web query code appear in the worksheet at your destination location. If your Internet connection is working, this is soon replaced by the data from the web page, as shown in Figure 16.20.

note

In Figure 16.20 all the Get External Data options in the Ribbon are disabled. This happens when your cell pointer is located in external data. To set up a new web query on the same worksheet, move the cell pointer to a cell outside the retrieved data. For example, Cell A6 would be safe in the worksheet shown in Figure 16.20.

	A	B	C	D	E	F	G	H
1	Symbol	Last Trade		Change		Volume	Intraday	Related Info
2	GOOG	23-Oct	553.69	Down 0.40	Down 0.07%	2,393,191		Chart, Messages, Key Stats, more...
3	MSFT	23-Oct	28.02	Up 1.43	Up 5.38%	281,760,947		Chart, Messages, Key Stats, more...
4	AAPL	23-Oct	203.94	Down 1.26	Down 0.61%	15,028,062		Chart, Messages, Key Stats, more...

Figure 16.20
The results of the web query are imported to your workbook.

Managing Properties for Web Queries

After you retriev a web query, you can select a single cell in the query and select Properties from the Connections group on the Data tab. The External Data Range Properties dialog appears, similar to the dialog shown previously in Figure 16.19. This dialog box includes additional properties for the query. In the Data Formatting and Layout section, you can choose options to preserve cell formatting and adjust column widths. Most important, you can specify that if the query returns more rows tomorrow, any formulas adjacent to the web query should be expanded.

Setting Up a Connection to a Text File

It is possible to load data from a text file into Excel using the connection group. Consider the text file shown in Figure 16.21.

Follow these steps to set up a connection:

1. On the Data tab, select the From Text icon in the Get External Data group. The Import Text File dialog appears.

2. Browse to and select your text file. Excel launches the familiar Text Import Wizard—Step 1 of 3, where you can specify that the text is either delimited or fixed width.

3. Select Delimited, as shown in Figure 16.22, and then click Next.

4. In step 2 of the wizard, change the Excel default tab character between fields to a comma, as shown in Figure 16.23.

Figure 16.21
Connect to a simple text file using Excel.

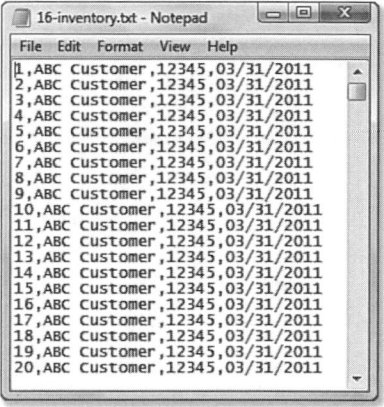

Figure 16.22
You navigate through the Text Import Wizard to set up a connection to a text file.

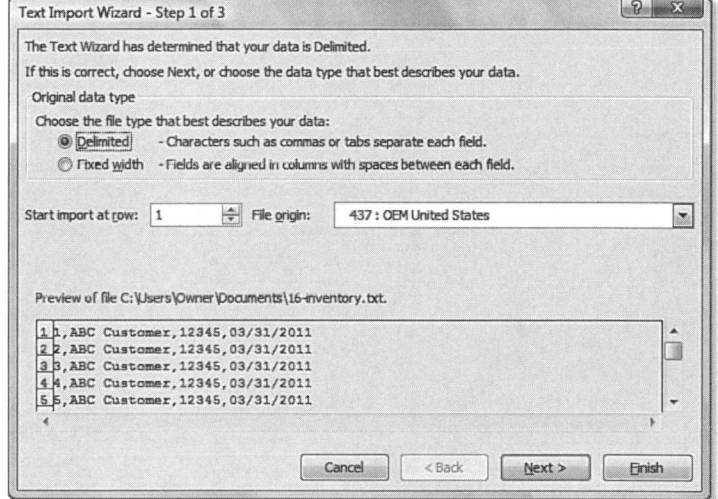

5. In step 3, specify the field type for each field and whether certain fields should be skipped.

6. If you have a column of numbers where a leading zero needs to be preserved (for example, the ZIP code of Fort Kent, Maine, needs to stay as 04743 instead of being converted to 4743), select Text as the field type for the ZIP code field.

7. Click the Advanced button to specify the characters used for thousands and decimal separators (see Figure 16.24). You can also specify that the minus appears after the number.

 note

Delimited text is text in which each column is separated by a character such as a comma or a tab. Fixed-width data is where each field is neatly lined up when viewed in a monospace font such as Courier New.

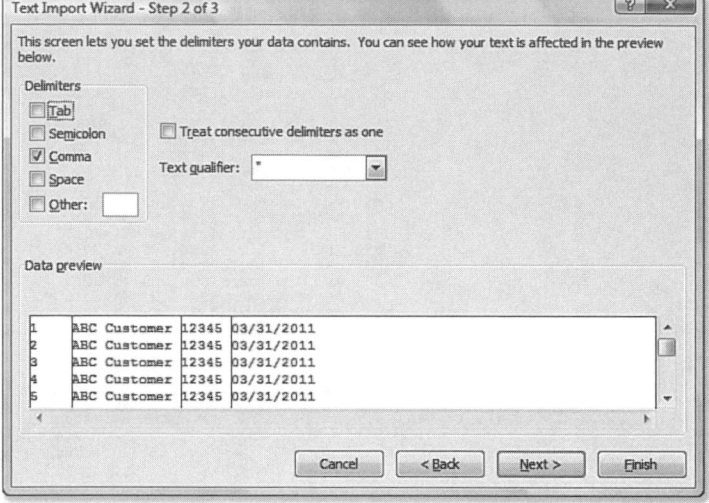

Figure 16.23
You specify the delimiter character in step 2.

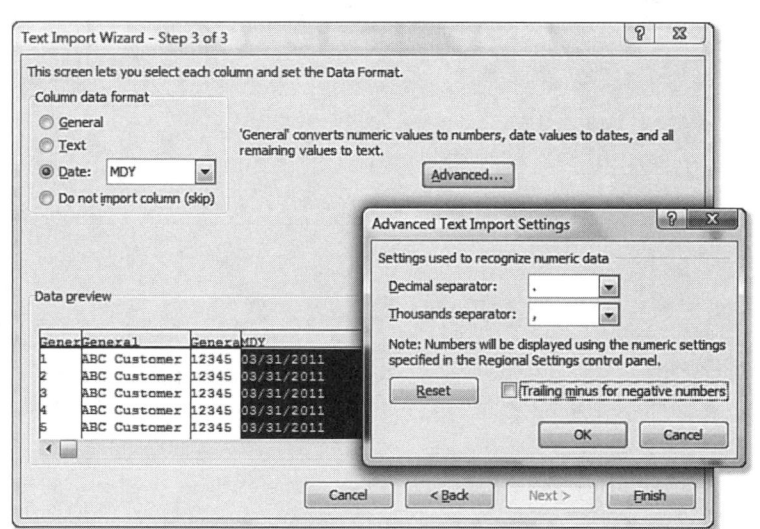

Figure 16.24
You select field types in step 3.

8. Click Finish. The Import Data dialog appears.

9. Specify a starting cell for the data, as shown in Figure 16.25.

10. Click the Properties button. The Properties dialog appears.

11. Determine whether to have Excel ask you for the filename each day or if you should use the same filename each day. If your IT department puts out an inventory.txt file every day, you will always want to connect to inventory.txt. Instead, your IT department might export inv070217.txt today and inv070218.txt tomorrow. In that case, you want Excel to ask you for a filename during every refresh. Excel defaults to Prompt for File Name on Refresh, as shown in Figure 16.26. If your filename will be the same and in the same folder every day, clear this default setting.

note

You may occasionally encounter files with a delimiter such as a pipe (|) or some other character. You can specify such a delimiter by selecting the Other check box and then specifying the character.

Figure 16.25
In addition to specifying a starting cell, click the Properties button.

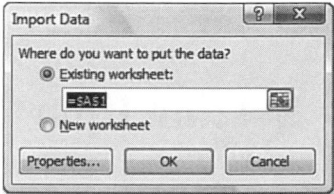

Figure 16.26
By default, Excel asks you for the filename during every refresh from a text connection. Turn this off if your file will be in a consistent location with the same name.

Prompt for Filename on Refresh

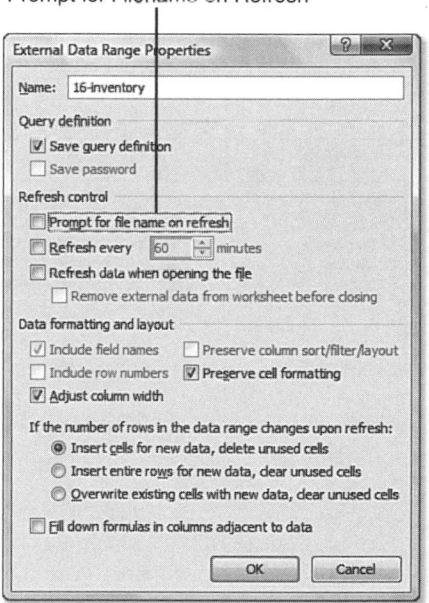

12. Accept the location for the import. Excel brings in all the records from the text file.

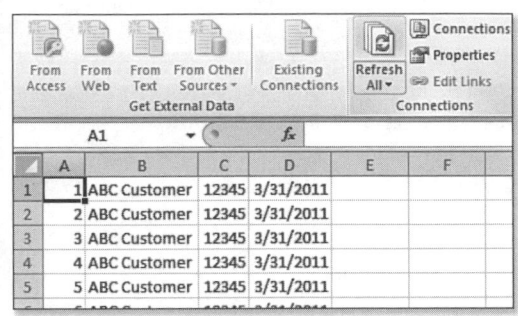

Figure 16.27
Click Refresh to reload the current text file.

Setting Up a Connection to an Access Database

Although Excel 2010 can handle 1.1 million rows, you might encounter larger data sets that need to be stored in Access. You can connect to these larger data sets. You can create a connection to any table in an Access database by following these steps:

1. On the Data tab, in the Get External Data group, select From Access.

2. Browse to select the .mdb file to which you want to link. You are then given an opportunity to choose any one table or query from the database. Each query is listed in the Type column as VIEW, as shown in Figure 16.28.

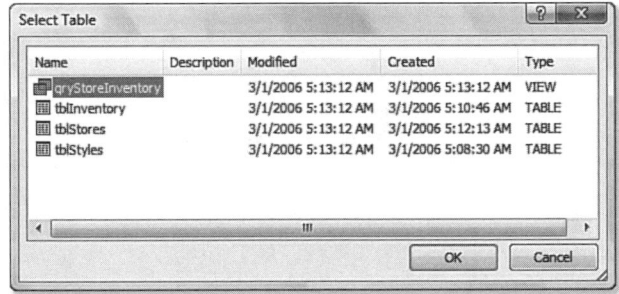

Figure 16.28
Using an Access connection, you can import a table or a predefined query.

3. Choose whether your data should be imported as a table or used in a pivot table. With the Access connection, there is an additional option, as shown in Figure 16.29. You can have the table imported to a regular table or have the data used as the data source for a pivot table report. When the Access data is delivered to Excel, it is automatically set up as an Excel table with default formatting, as shown in Figure 16.30.

 **note**

Note that if you select a query in Access, a delay might occur as the query is calculated. Excel displays a Getting Data message in the table while the calculation is in process.

Figure 16.29
Access connections can be returned as a table or used as the source in a pivot table report.

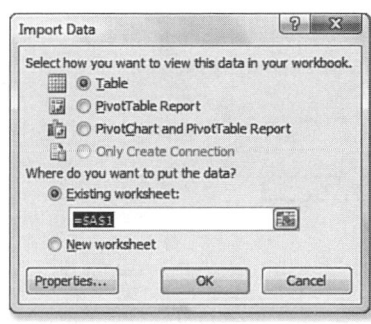

Figure 16.30
By default, Excel treats the data with Excel 2010's table formatting and features.

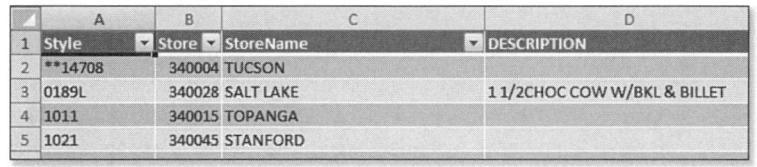

⬤➤ *To learn more about pivot tables, see Chapter 23, "Summarizing Data with Pivot Tables."*

Setting Up SQL Server, XML, OLE DB, and ODBC Connections

Although Excel 2010 offers icons for Access, web, and text connections, you can connect to a variety of other data sources. You access all these sources by clicking the From Other Sources icon on the Data tab. When you choose this option, you are presented with five choices, as shown in Figure 16.31.

SQL Server is Microsoft's structured query language database. Typically, when applications get too big to run smoothly in Microsoft Access, they will be migrated to the more robust SQL Server platform. Because SQL Server is a Microsoft product, connecting to SQL Server is a straightforward process. To connect, you need the Server name, a userid, and a password.

Analysis Services is Microsoft's cube functionality, currently marketed as SQL Server Analysis Services. A cube database represents data along three or more dimensions. To connect, you need the Server name, a userid, and a password.

XML stands for Extensible Markup Language. This is a simple text file that includes both data and tags used to identify the data. An example illustrating a connection to XML data is shown in the next section.

OLE DB stands for Object Linking and Embedding for Databases. This is a Microsoft interface written in the COM environment that allows Windows-based applications to access a variety of database types. Consult your database administrator for required settings to connect through OLE-DB.

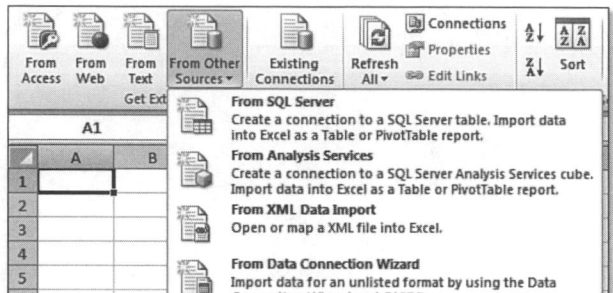

Figure 16.31
Excel can connect to SQL Server, Analysis Services, XML, OLE DB data sources, or ODBC through Microsoft Query.

Microsoft Query is an older technology that uses Open Database Connectivity (ODBC). If your company has implemented a non-Microsoft platform, ODBC is the interface that allows other programs such as Excel to connect to the database. Typically, the administrator of the system will be able to provide you with a connect string that you will use to access the other system's data. Microsoft Query also provides a method for Excel to build SQL queries against Access databases.

➡ *For an example, see "Connecting Using Microsoft Query" later in this chapter.*

Connecting to XML Data

In the future, you will find more and more data sets based on XML. In reality, XML is like a CSV (comma-separated value) file on steroids. You can create or edit XML files by using Notepad. The difference between a CSV file and an XML file is that each field in XML contains a field identifier. This allows you to intelligently import only certain fields into a spreadsheet. Figure 16.32 shows a simple XML file that has two records.

Figure 16.32
In this XML file seen in Notepad, note that each field starts and ends with <fieldname> and </fieldname> tags.

In addition to the actual XML file, it is possible to have a definition document known as an XSD file or a database schema. You may also have one or more XSL files that are used to transform the data. But as long as you have at least one XML file, Excel will be happy to infer a schema, as shown in Figure 16.33.

Figure 16.33
Without a schema file, Excel is limited to importing the data as a table. Fortunately, Excel creates a schema file for you.

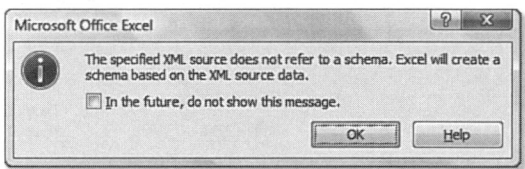

As you can see in Figure 16.34, the data is then imported as an Excel table. This is pretty basic functionality. By using a trick in the VBA Editor, however, you can retrieve the schema and save it to allow Excel to do more XML tricks.

Figure 16.34
The data from Figure 16.32 after being imported to Excel.

	A	B	C	D	E	F	G	H
1	Customer	Address	City	State	Zip	ItemSKU	Quantity	UnitPrice
2	ABC Co	123 Main	Salem	OH	44460	12345	100	10.5
3	YXZ Co	234 State	Akron	OH	44313	23456	10	20.5

After Excel has imported the data, you can retrieve the schema by using the VBA Editor. To do so, follow these steps:

1. Press Alt+F11 or click the VBA Editor icon on the Developer tab. The VBA Editor appears.

2. In the VBA Editor, press Ctrl+G to display the Immediate pane.

3. In the Immediate pane, type this line:
   print activeworkbook.XmlMaps(1).Schemas(1).XML
   Then press Enter. Excel responds by printing the entire schema for the XML file, as shown in Figure 16.35.

Figure 16.35
Excel replies with the Schema.

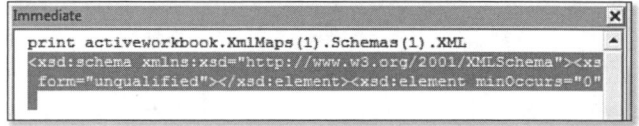

4. Copy this text into a blank Notepad file and save as test.xsd in the same directory as the XML file.

Figure 16.36 shows the complete schema in Notepad, with WordWrap turned on.

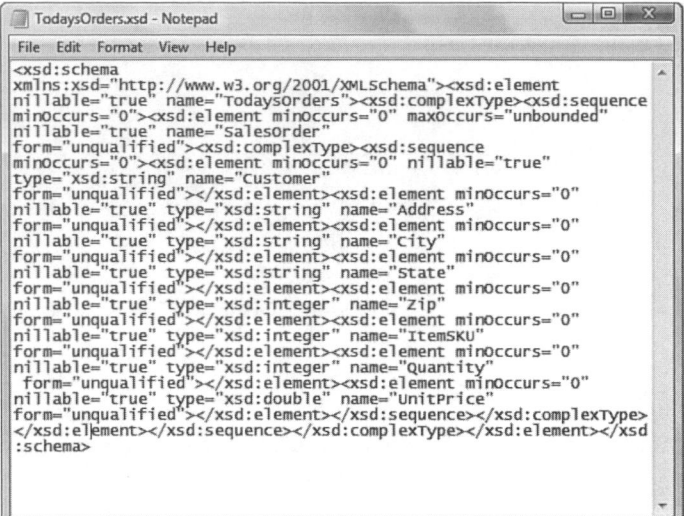

Figure 16.36
Save the schema to enable additional XML features in Excel.

Connecting Using Microsoft Query

The From Access icon on the Data tab allows you to retrieve all fields from any Access table or predefined query. At times, you might want to join Access tables, filter records, or select only a subset of fields from a query. Excel 2010 offers the old Microsoft Query product for building such connections.

To build a new query against a table in an Access database, follow these steps:

1. In Excel 2010, select Data, Get External Data, From Other Sources, From Microsoft Query. The Choose Data Source dialog appears.

2. Select MS Access Database, as shown in Figure 16.37. Click OK. The Select Database dialog appears.

 note

The Choose Data Source dialog differentiates between Access and Access 2010 databases. If your data is in an Access 2010 database, select MS Access 12.0 Databases instead.

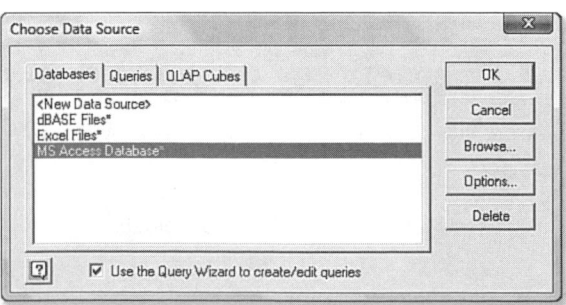

Figure 16.37
Select MS Access Database in the Choose Data Source dialog.

3. In the Select Database dialog, select the Access database, as shown in Figure 16.38. The Query Wizard dialog appears.

4. Choose to include particular fields from any table or query in the database. You Choose fields on the left side of the dialog and click the > button to move them to the right side of the dialog, as shown in Figure 16.39.

 **note**

Even though Office 2010 was supposed to be a complete rewrite, it is apparent that the Windows 3.1–style dialog box shown in Figure 16.38 has not been updated in many years.

Figure 16.38
Select the Access database.

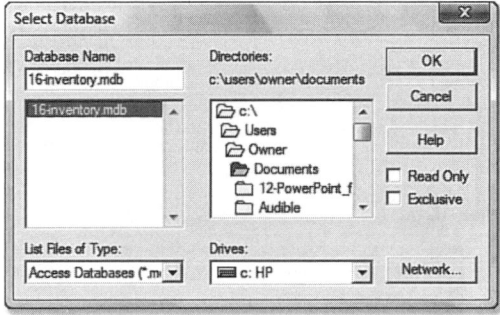

Figure 16.39
Select fields to be included in the query.

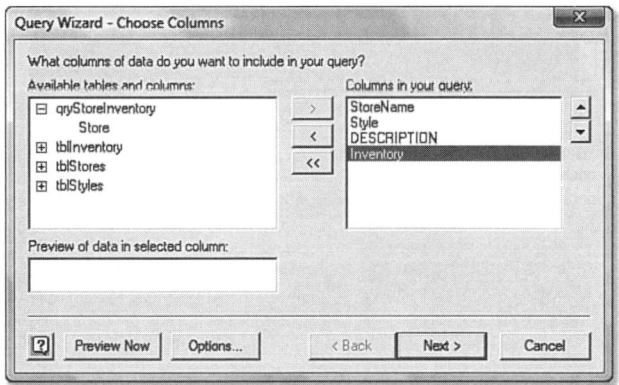

5. In the next step of the Query Wizard, set up filters for the query. In Figure 16.40, the filter is defined as only items where the inventory is greater than five.

6. In the next step of the Query Wizard, specify up to three sort fields for the query, as shown in Figure 16.41.

7. In the final step of the Query Wizard, specify that you want to return the data to Microsoft Office Excel, as shown in Figure 16.42. You are presented with an Import dialog that is similar to the one shown earlier.

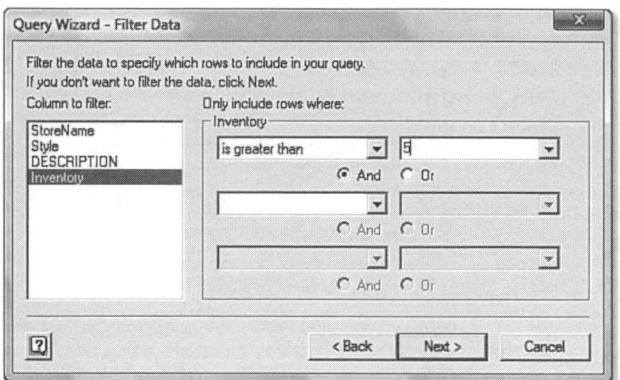

Figure 16.40
Define filters for the query.

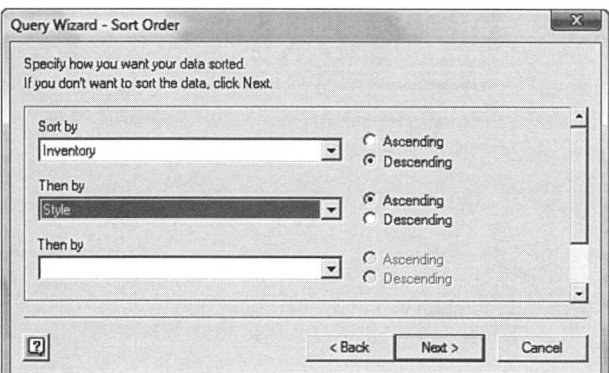

Figure 16.41
Specify sort criteria.

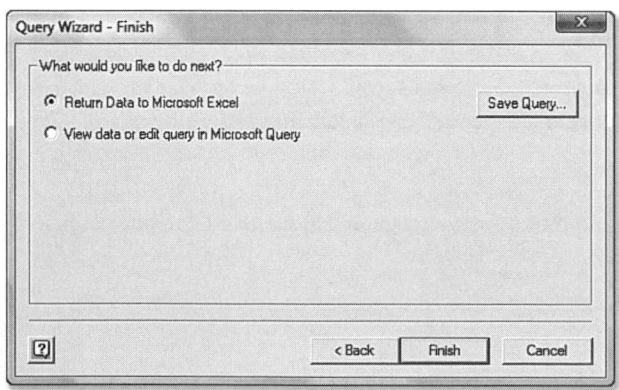

Figure 16.42
Return the data to Excel.

Contrast the current example with the previous example in "Setting Up a Connection to an Access Database." Although the previous example and this example use the same query from Access, the Microsoft Query option enables you to retrieve only the records with more than five items in inventory. The overhead involved in returning few records causes the query to run significantly faster. As shown in Figure 16.43, the data is returned in a sorted manner.

	A	B	C
1	StoreName	Style	DESCRIPTION
2	WELLINGTON	D28016	
3	ST LOUIS	D28016	
4	SOUTH WINDSOR	30090	1 1/8 BLK/PNT CROCO REVRSBLE
5	IRVINE SPECTRUM	D28016	
6	WOODFIELD	D28016	
7	KING OF PRUSSIA	D28016	

Figure 16.43
The final results from the MS Query connection.

Managing Connections

The Data tab includes a group called Manage Connections. As shown in Figure 16.44, this group includes an option to refresh all connections. Although the icon says Refresh All, a drop-down enables you to choose to refresh only the current query or to view properties for a connection.

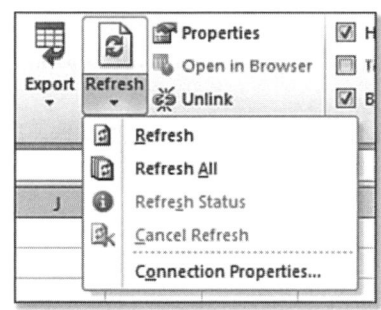

Figure 16.44
You have one-click access to refreshing all connections.

Clicking the Connections icon brings up a summary of all the web, text, Access, or ODBC connections in your workbook. This is a fantastic improvement in Excel 2010. As shown in Figure 16.45, you can click any connection in the top and then follow the hyperlink Click Here to See Where the Selected Connections Are Used to jump to the worksheet range that houses the results of the connection.

Although this new dialog is nearly a one-stop source for all external links, you might be disappointed to learn that links to other workbooks are not included here. You have to select Edit Links to Files from the Manage Connections group to display the Edit Links dialog, where you can check the status of any workbook links as well as maintain the link location, break the links, or adjust the startup prompt. (see Figure 16.46)

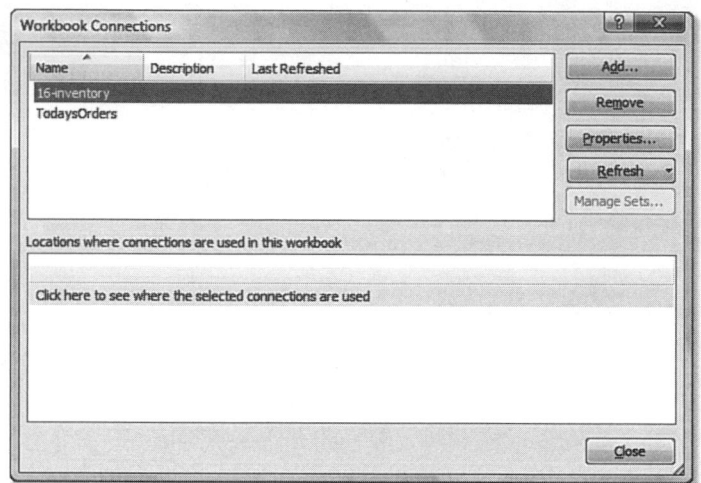

Figure 16.45
The new Workbook Connections dialog provides one stop to see all connections in the workbook.

Excel offers fantastic connections. Although users have been able to link to Access databases for several versions, Excel 2010's improved support for SQL Server, XML, ODBC, text, web, and Access data is unparalleled. The following Excel in Practice sidebar talks about setting up a connection to one of the newest data stores: an Excel 2010 workbook with half a million records.

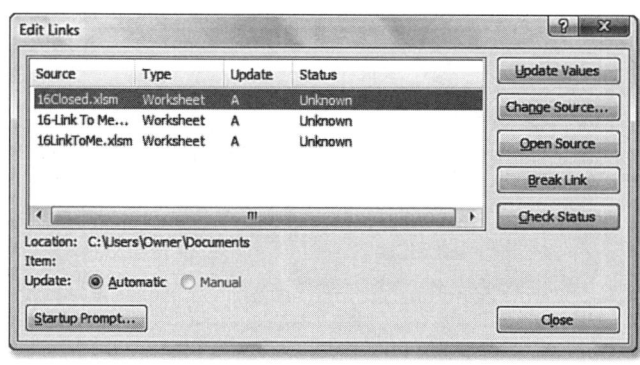

Figure 16.46
Use Edit Links to manage formula links between workbooks.

Excel in Practice: Defining a Connection to a Separate Closed Workbook

Although you can write formulas that link to external closed workbooks, those formulas cannot reference more than 10,000 cells. This is a serious limitation now that you can have more than a million rows in the external worksheet.

Instead of using simple linking via a formula, you can treat the other Excel file as a database file and connect to it using the Connection Manager! This technique allows you to run queries against millions of cells in the external workbook.

For example, Figure 16.47 shows an Excel worksheet with more than 1 million records. Link formulas will not be able to access more than 2 percent of the rows in this workbook. Using a connection overcomes this limitation.

Figure 16.47
With 12 columns, this worksheet contains 12 million cells.

	STORE #	STYLE	CLASS	SUB-CLASS	DESCRIPTION	ON H
1046873	340123	J37842	8	27	SIL/STN/MOP BLU	
1046874	340123	J37852	8	27	SIL/MOP BLUE BE	
1046875	340123	J37872	8	27	SIL/STN SPOT OF	
1046876	340123	J47652	8	26	SIL/GB/RES BAY C	
1046877	340123	J47661	8	26	SIL/GP IVY MEDA	
1046878	340123	J47722	8	26	SIL/MOP BLUE BE	
1046879	340123	J47742	8	26	SIL/STN/PRL SPO	
1046880	340123	J47872	8	26	SIL/GP/STN JUST	
1046881	340123	T32898	4	12	BRK SPOT OF ROS	
1046882	340123	T32936	4	12	NAVY BORA BOR	

To create a connection to the external workbook, follow these steps:

1. From a blank workbook, select Data, Get External Data, From Other Sources, From Microsoft Query. In the Choose Data Source dialog that appears, select Excel Files.

2. In the Select Workbook dialog, select the Excel file and click OK. If you receive a message that the data source contains no visible tables, perform steps 3 and 4. Otherwise, continue with step 5.

3. Click Options in the Query Wizard - Choose Columns dialog.

4. Choose System Tables from the Options dialog and click OK.

5. In the next three Query Wizard dialogs, select your fields, the filter, and the sort.

6. In the final step, choose the option to view the query in Microsoft Query. The Microsoft Query dialog appears.

7. In the Microsoft Query dialog, select View, Query Properties. The Query Properties dialog appears (see Figure 16.48).

8. Select the Group Records check box and click OK. This will tell the query to return a summary data set, totaling numeric fields for each unique combination of key fields. You specify which fields to group and sum in the next two steps.

9. Select the Sum of Quantity heading in the lower half of the screen. Click the Sigma button in the toolbar to toggle through Sum, Min, Max, and Normal. Select Sum, as shown in Figure 16.49.

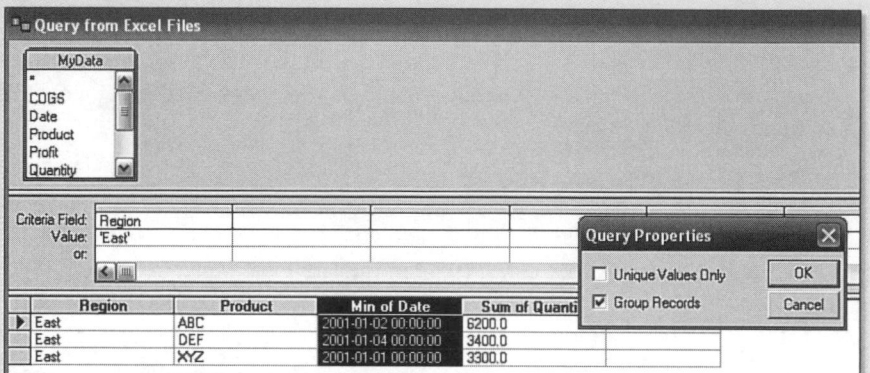

Figure 16.48
Grouping records will return one record per Region and Product.

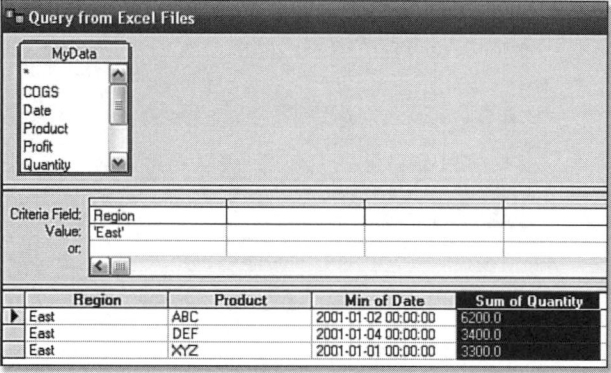

Figure 16.49
Select a sum property for each column.

10. Select File, Return Data to Microsoft Excel, as shown in Figure 16.50.

You now have a refreshable data connection to an external Excel workbook that has 1,000,000 records. The result is shown in Figure 16.51.

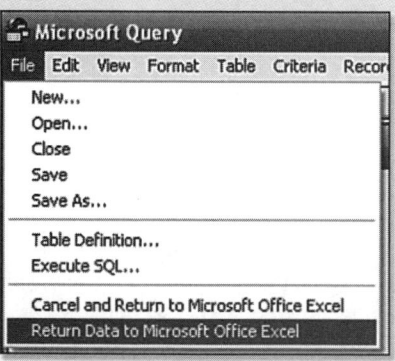

Figure 16.50
Close Microsoft Query and return the data.

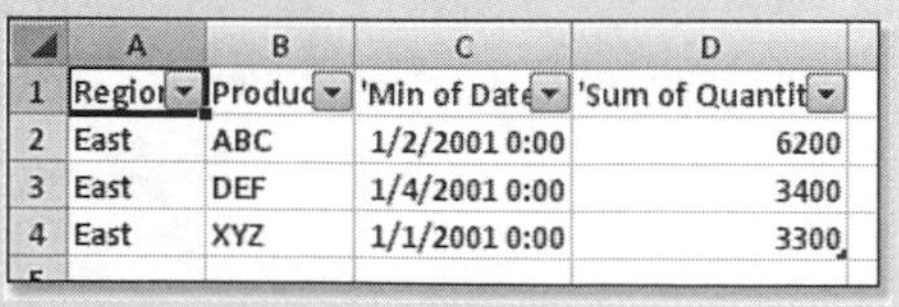

Figure 16.51
This is a three-line summary from the 750,000-record external workbook.

USING SUPER FORMULAS IN EXCEL

Excel offers an amazing variety of formulas. This chapter covers some of the
unorthodox formulas that you can build in Excel. In this chapter, you learn about
the following:

- Using a formula to add the same cell across many sheets

- Using a formula to reference the previous sheet

- Editing multiple formulas into one

- Assigning a formula to a name

- Letting data determine the cell reference to use with the INDIRECT function

- Using a dynamic range with an offset

- Transposing relative column references to rows

- Using Row() or Column() to return an array of numbers

- Replacing thousands of formulas with one Ctrl+Shift+Enter (CSE) formula

- Using one formula to return a whole range of answers

- Doing conditional sums based on two or more conditions

Using 3D Formulas to Spear Through Many Worksheets

It is common to have a workbook composed of identical worksheets for each
month or quarter of the year. Every worksheet needs to have the same arrangement of rows.

If you want to total a particular cell across all the worksheets, you might try to
write a formula with one term for each sheet—for example, =Sheet1!A1+Sheet
2!A1+Sheet3!A1.... However, Excel supports a special type of

formula that will spear through several worksheets to add a particular cell from each worksheet. The syntax of the formula is =SUM(Sheet1:Sheetn!A1).

As shown in Figure 17.1, Net Revenue is in Row 4 on the January worksheet and is in the same row on the December worksheet. You cannot see this in Figure 17.1, but the arrangement of rows is identical on every worksheet.

When creating a worksheet, you might be tempted to write a formula such as =Jan!B4+Feb!B4+Mar!B4+Apr!B4, but doing so would be rather tedious.

Instead, you can write a formula that totals Cell B4 from each worksheet, Jan through Dec. The syntax of the formula is =SUM(Jan:Dec!B4). After you enter this formula in Cell B, you can easily copy it to all the other relevant cells in the worksheet, as shown in Figure 17.2.

 To see a demo of adding a 3D references, search for "Excel In Depth 17" at YouTube.

 tip

Sometimes you might need to sum a cell on all sheets that have a common naming convention. Perhaps you have worksheet names such as CostQ1, ExpensesQ1, CostQ2, ExpensesQ2, CostQ3, ExpensesQ3, CostQ4, ExpensesQ4. To sum cell B4 on all of the cost sheets, type =SUM('Cost*'!B4). Remarkably, Excel will convert this shorthand to a formula that points to each of the cost sheets: =SUM(CostQ1!B4,CostQ2!B4, CostQ3!B4,CostQ4!B4). A tip of the cap to Microsoft MVP Bob Umlas for this cool trick.

Referring to the Previous Worksheet

When you have an arrangement of several sequential worksheets, you might want to keep a running total. This total would be calculated as the total on this sheet plus the running total from the previous sheet.

It is somewhat difficult to build a formula that will always point to the previous sheet. Many try this wrong approach: Build a formula on Sheet2 that points to Sheet1. When you make copies of Sheet2, to Sheet3, Sheet4, and so on, the formula continues to always point back to Sheet1. This is rarely what you want.

The solution involves a tiny user-defined function that can be written in Excel's macro editor.

This specific example shows you how to build a general purpose function that will return a value from a previous worksheet. This function can work in any situation.

Figure 17.3 shows a formula that returns the value from the previous month. On the Feb worksheet, this would refer to =Jan!B4. You could easily copy this formula to other cells within the Feb worksheet. However, if you copy the formula to Mar or Apr, the formula still points to the Jan worksheet, which is not what you want.

Excel offers a very cool solution to this problem. The solution requires a few lines of VBA macro code. Don't be afraid. I will get you there and back without any problems. Here's what you do:

1. Press Alt+F11 to launch the VBA editor.

2. In the VBA editor, select Insert, Module.

3. Type these lines into the blank module:

Figure 17.1
The 12 workbooks, Jan through Dec, contain an identical arrangement of rows and columns.

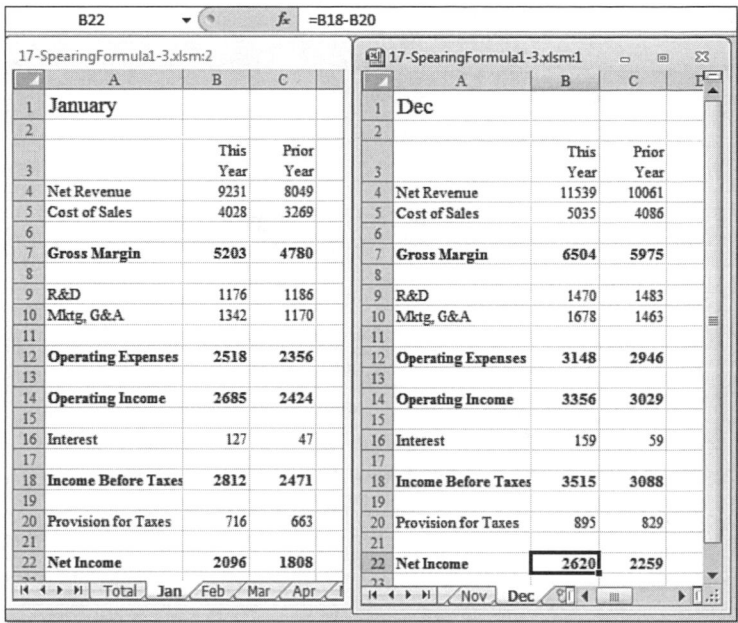

Figure 17.2
This formula spears through 12 worksheets to total Cell B4 from each worksheet from Jan through Dec.

	A	B	C	D	E
1	Total Year				
2					
3		This Year	Prior Year		
4	Net Revenue	119727	104394		
5	Cost of Sales	49911	40508		
6					
7	Gross Margin	69816	63886		
8					
9	R&D	15253	15383		
10	Mktg, G&A	17406	15176		
11					
12	Operating Expenses	32659	30559		
13					
14	Operating Income	37157	33327		
15					
16	Interest	1648	610		
17					
18	Income Before Taxes	38805	33937		
19					
20	Provision for Taxes	9286	8599		
21					
22	Net Income	29519	25338		

B4 =SUM(Jan:Dec!B4)

```
Function PrevSheet(ByVal cl As Range)
    Application.Volatile
    On Error Resume Next
    PrevSheet = Sheets(cl.Parent.Index - 1).Range(cl.Address)
End Function
```

	A	B	C	D	E
	E4	▼	f_x =Jan!B4		
1	**February**				
2					
3		This Year	Prior Year		Prior Month
4	Net Revenue	9416	8210		9231
5	Cost of Sales	4109	3335		
6					
7	Gross Margin	5307	4875		
8					
9	R&D	1200	1210		
10	Mktg, G&A	1369	1193		
11					
12	Operating Expenses	2569	2403		
13					
14	Operating Income	2738	2472		
15					
16	Interest	130	48		
17					
18	Income Before Taxes	2868	2520		
19					
20	Provision for Taxes	730	676		
21					
22	Net Income	2138	1844		

Figure 17.3
You need to rewrite this formula for each of the 11 other months.

Your screen should look similar to Figure 17.4.

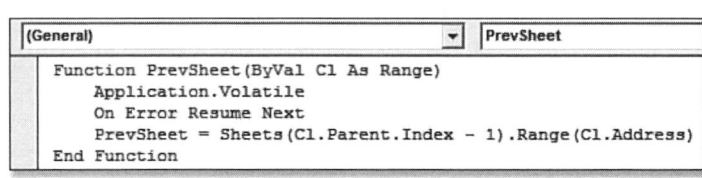

Figure 17.4
The VBA editor screen should look like this.

4. Select File, Close And Return to Microsoft Excel to return to Excel.

To realize the power of this function, you can put the workbook in Group mode and enter the function in 11 worksheets at once:

1. Select the Feb worksheet.

2. Hold down the Shift key while clicking the Dec worksheet tab. This highlights all 11 worksheets. Although you see the Feb worksheet, anything you do will also happen to all 11 selected worksheets.

3. In Cell E4, enter =PrevSheet(B4). Press Enter to accept the formula. The Feb worksheet picks up the value from Jan, but each additional worksheet picks up the value from the previous sheet, as shown in Figure 17.5.

5. With the worksheets still in Group mode, copy Cell B4 from the Feb worksheet to Cells B5, B7, and so on.

6. Right-click any sheet tab and select ungroup.

 tip

To examine worksheets from the same workbook, select View, Window, New Window to create a second window of the workbook. Then select View, Window, Arrange, Vertical, OK to arrange the windows vertically. You now have two views of the same workbook, and you can change the right pane to be a different worksheet. The screenshot in Figure 17.5 reflects four new window commands before the windows are arranged vertically.

Figure 17.5
One formula using the custom function PrevSheet solves the prior month problem seamlessly across all the worksheets.

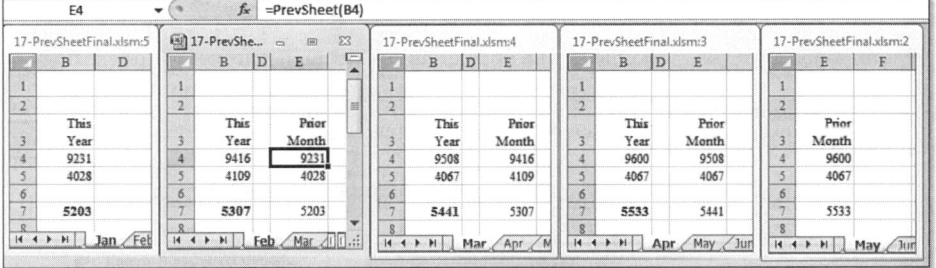

Combining Multiple Formulas into One Formula

With more than 410 functions available in Excel, it is possible to perform just about any calculation. Many times, however, it is easier to break the task down into many subformulas as you try to solve the problem.

For example, fellow Excel MVP and guru Bob Umlas taught me that I could use the Substitute function to locate the last space in a word. This is handy for finding the last word in a sentence or name. However, unlike Bob, I always need to build this formula over the course of several columns. It takes me seven columns to do a trick that Bob can do in one. Figure 17.6 shows all the formulas used to replicate the trick.

After you have puzzled out a complicated set of interrelated functions to achieve a result, you can begin consolidating the formulas into one monster formula.

There is an easier way to combine many formulas into one formula. In general, follow these steps:

Figure 17.6
It takes me seven formulas to isolate the last name.

1. Examine the final formula. It will reference cells that contain one or more subformulas. Let's say that one of the subformulas is a cell such as ZZ123.

2. Move the cell pointer to the subformula in ZZ123.

3. Press F2 to put the formula in edit mode.

4. With the mouse, highlight the formula in the formula bar, but do not highlight the equal sign in the subformula.

5. Press Ctrl+C to copy this portion of the subformula to the Clipboard.

6. Go back to the final formula. Press F2 to put the formula in edit mode.

7. In the formula bar, using the mouse, highlight the characters that point to the subformula. In this case, it is cell ZZ123.

8. Press Ctrl+V to paste the subformula in place of the ZZ123 reference.

9. Press Enter to accept this intermediate formula.

10. If there are additional references to a cell with a subformula in the final formula, repeat steps 1–10 for the next reference.

I realize this may be difficult to follow in the abstract. If you would like to follow along with a real example, follow these steps:

1. In Cell H2, the formula has a reference to Cell G2, as shown in Figure 17.7.

2. Move the cell pointer to G2.

3. In the formula bar, click and drag with the mouse to select all the characters in this formula except the equal sign, as shown in Figure 17.8.

4. Press Ctrl+C to copy the selected characters to the Clipboard.

Figure 17.7
The goal is to replace G2 in this formula.

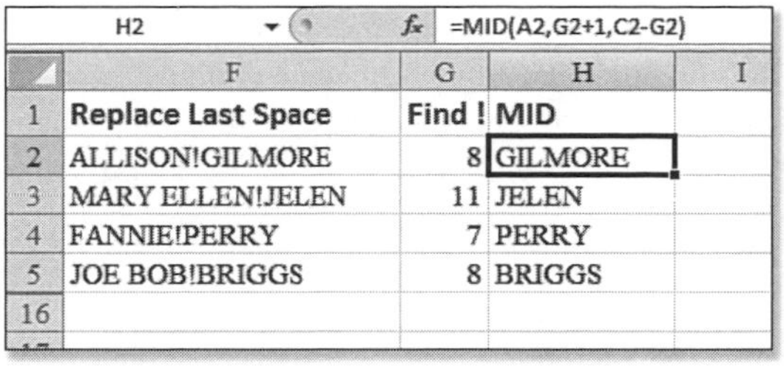

	H2			fx	=MID(A2,G2+1,C2-G2)	
	F		G	H		I
1	Replace Last Space		Find !	MID		
2	ALLISON!GILMORE		8	GILMORE		
3	MARY ELLEN!JELEN		11	JELEN		
4	FANNIE!PERRY		7	PERRY		
5	JOE BOB!BRIGGS		8	BRIGGS		
16						

Figure 17.8
Copying characters from the formula bar is different from copying a cell.

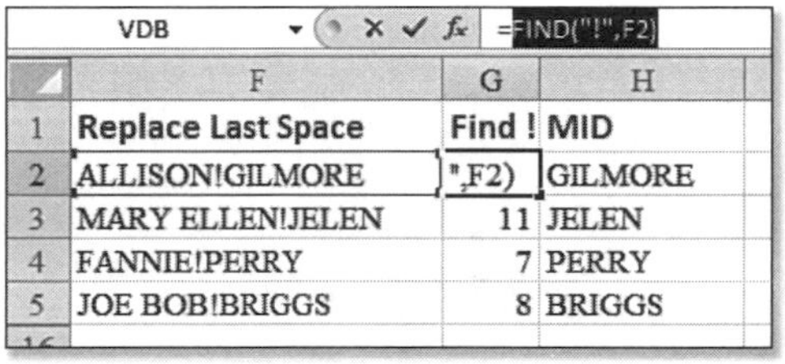

	VDB		× ✓ fx	=FIND("!",F2)	
	F		G	H	
1	Replace Last Space		Find !	MID	
2	ALLISON!GILMORE		",F2)	GILMORE	
3	MARY ELLEN!JELEN		11	JELEN	
4	FANNIE!PERRY		7	PERRY	
5	JOE BOB!BRIGGS		8	BRIGGS	

5. Press Esc to exit edit mode.

6. Move the cell pointer back to Cell H2 and highlight the characters G2 in the formula bar, as shown in Figure 17.9.

Figure 17.9
With the formula from Cell G2 on the Clipboard, you select G2 in the final formula.

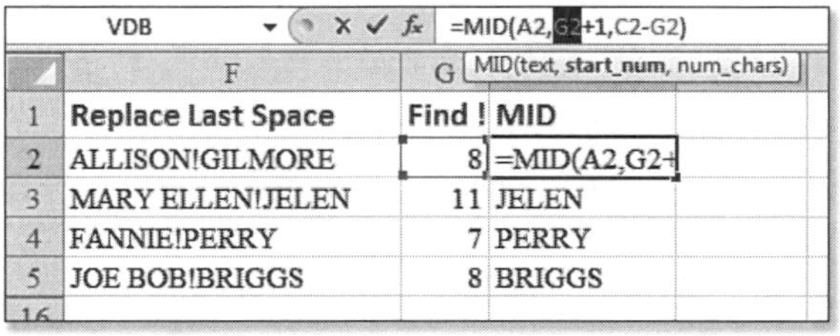

	VDB		× ✓ fx	=MID(A2,G2+1,C2-G2)	
	F		G	MID(text, **start_num**, num_chars)	
1	Replace Last Space		Find !	MID	
2	ALLISON!GILMORE		8	=MID(A2,G2+	
3	MARY ELLEN!JELEN		11	JELEN	
4	FANNIE!PERRY		7	PERRY	
5	JOE BOB!BRIGGS		8	BRIGGS	
16					

7. Press Ctrl+V to replace G2 with the formula from Cell G2, as shown in Figure 17.10.

8. Repeat this process to replace the other G2 and C2 in the Cell H2 formula. note that pasting the formula from Cell G2 introduces references to Cell F2.

9. Continue to replace any reference to a column other than Column A. After doing several copy and paste operations in the formula bar, you eventually end up with one monster formula.

VDB	▼ ⓧ ✗ ✓ ƒx	=MID(A2,FIND("!",F2)+1,C2-G2)

	F	G	MID(text, **start_num**, num_chars)
1	**Replace Last Space**	**Find !**	**MID**
2	ALLISON!GILMORE	8	ND("!",F2)+1,
3	MARY ELLEN!JELEN	11	JELEN
4	FANNIE!PERRY	7	PERRY
5	JOE BOB!BRIGGS	8	BRIGGS
16			

Figure 17.10
You can press Ctrl+V to paste the characters from the Cell G2 formula instead of the reference to Cell G2.

10. Delete Columns B through G. People will be impressed with how you were able to write such an amazing formula (see Figure 17.11). In fact, someone might even say to you, "Wow! You are as smart as Bob Umlas!"

B2	▼ ⓢ	ƒx	=MID(A2,FIND("!",SUBSTITUTE(A2," ", "!",LEN(A2)-LEN(SUBSTITUTE(A2," ","")))))+1,LEN(A2)-FIND("!",SUBSTITUTE(A2," ","!",LEN(A2)-LEN(SUBSTITUTE(A2," ",""))))

	A	B	C	D	E	F	
1	NAME	LAST NAME					
2	ALLISON GILMORE	GILMORE					
3	MARY ELLEN JELEN	JELEN					
4	FANNIE PERRY	PERRY					
5	JOE BOB BRIGGS	BRIGGS					
6	JOSEPH HOWE	HOWE					

Figure 17.11
After several iterations of replacing references in the formula, you end up with one monster formula to replace the six subformulas.

Calculating a Cell Reference in the Formula by Using the INDIRECT Function

Usually a formula points to a particular cell or range of cells. Sometimes, though, you want a formula to point to a different cell as the result of a calculation. You can do this by using the INDIRECT function.

In general, this process involves writing a text-based formula that evaluates to a cell address. Although your particular situation will certainly be different, here are some examples of formulas that evaluate to a cell address:

- =CHAR(64+COLUMN(B275)&ROW(ZZ999)—Evaluates to B999.

- ="Sheet"&ROW(A1)&"!C2"—Evaluates to Sheet1!C2 in the current row, but to Sheet2!C2 when copied down one row, and to Sheet3!C2 when copied down to a third row.

- =CHAR(65+MONTH(ROW(A1)))&"19"—Evaluates to cell B19 in January, C19 in February, and so on.

note
Excel gurus will point out another benefit of the INDIRECT function. If you have a formula such as =SUM(A1:A10), and you insert a new Row 5, the formula normally expands to =SUM(A1:A11). However, at times you might want to sum only the first 10 records on the sheet. In this case, you can use the formula =SUM(INDIRECT("A1:A10")) to always point to Rows 1 through 10, no matter what rows are inserted or deleted.

After you have a formula that evaluates to text that looks like a cell reference, you can use that formula as the argument to the INDIRECT() function. Excel returns the value in the cell indicated by the text formula.

One concrete example: If cell Z99 contains the value 1, the formula of =INDIRECT("Z99") will return a value of 1. A more practical concrete example follows.

Suppose that in Figure 17.12, you would like to build a table to copy the current-month totals from each worksheet to a summary table on the Total worksheet. Without the INDIRECT function, you would have to separately enter 12 different formulas in Row 4—one for each month (for example, =Jan!$B4 for January, =Feb!$B4 for February, and so on).

Figure 17.12
The first of 12 different formulas required in E4:P4.

E4					*fx*	=Jan!B4	
	A	B	C	D	E	F	
1	**Total Year**						
2							
3		This Year	Prior Year		Jan	Feb	
4	Net Revenue	119727	104394		9231		
5	Cost of Sales	49911	40508				
6							
7	Gross Margin	69816	63886				
8							
9	R&D	15253	15383				
10	Mktg, G&A	17406	15176				
11							
12	Operating Expenses	32659	30559				

You can solve this problem with a single formula that you can copy to the entire total worksheet. Follow these steps:

1. You want to design a text formula in Cell E4 to point to the correct sheet and cell.

2. The worksheet has month headings in Row 3, so you can start to build a formula as =E$3&"!". note that the $ before the 3 ensures that as the formula is copied to lower rows in the summary table; it will always point to the month heading in Row 3.

3. The next trick is finding a function that will return the address of Column B for Row 3. To do this, you can use the versatile function called CELL. The CELL function can return many bits of information about a reference, including the address of the cell. For example, =CELL("address",$B4) returns the text $B$4.

4. Figure 17.13 shows the intermediate result of entering =E$3&"!B"&ROW()) into the table.

The last step is to wrap the INDIRECT function around the formula in Cell E4. This tells Excel to evaluate the function inside INDIRECT to learn that Excel should return the value from Cell B4 on the Jan worksheet.

 caution

There is an important limitation with INDIRECT functions. If you build an INDIRECT function that points to an external workbook, the formula works only when the external workbook is open. For a VBA workaround, type "Harlan Grove PULL" into your favorite search engine.

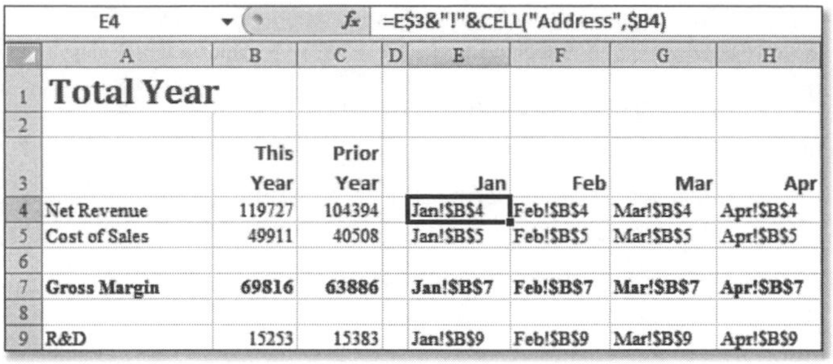
E4 =E$3&"!"&CELL("Address",$B4)

	A	B	C	D	E	F	G	H
1	Total Year							
2								
3		This Year	Prior Year		Jan	Feb	Mar	Apr
4	Net Revenue	119727	104394		Jan!$B$4	Feb!$B$4	Mar!$B$4	Apr!$B$4
5	Cost of Sales	49911	40508		Jan!$B$5	Feb!$B$5	Mar!$B$5	Apr!$B$5
6								
7	**Gross Margin**	**69816**	**63886**		**Jan!$B$7**	**Feb!$B$7**	**Mar!$B$7**	**Apr!$B$7**
8								
9	R&D	15253	15383		Jan!$B$9	Feb!$B$9	Mar!$B$9	Apr!$B$9

Figure 17.13
All the formulas in E4:P22 are identical, but they return the reference to the cell from which the result should be copied.

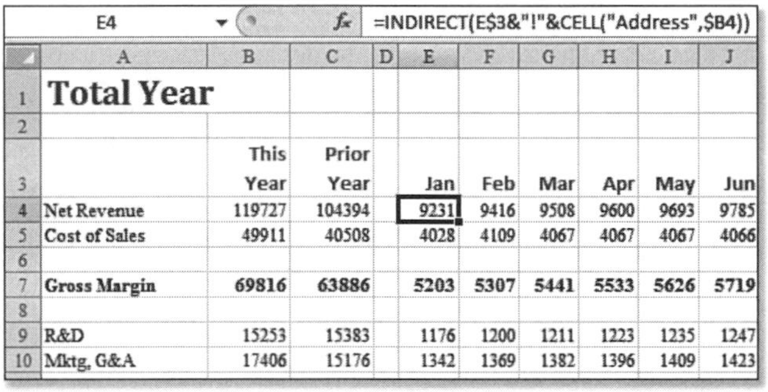
E4 =INDIRECT(E$3&"!"&CELL("Address",$B4))

	A	B	C	D	E	F	G	H	I	J
1	Total Year									
2										
3		This Year	Prior Year		Jan	Feb	Mar	Apr	May	Jun
4	Net Revenue	119727	104394		9231	9416	9508	9600	9693	9785
5	Cost of Sales	49911	40508		4028	4109	4067	4067	4067	4066
6										
7	**Gross Margin**	**69816**	**63886**		**5203**	**5307**	**5441**	**5533**	**5626**	**5719**
8										
9	R&D	15253	15383		1176	1200	1211	1223	1235	1247
10	Mktg, G&A	17406	15176		1342	1369	1382	1396	1409	1423

Figure 17.14
You can wrap the formulas in the `INDIRECT` function to allow one formula to fill the entire table.

The whole trick to being efficient in Excel is being able to write one formula that can be copied to an entire range. Rather than going through the tedium of entering 12 different formulas in Row 4, you can use the `INDIRECT` function to enter just one formula everywhere in the range (see Figure 17.14).

Using Offset to Refer to a Range That Dynamically Resizes

When you first read the Help topic on the `OFFSET` function, you might wonder about the point of such a function. The `OFFSET` function allows you to describe a range by specifying five parameters:

- Any cell from which to start.
- The number of rows to move from the original cell to get to the upper-left corner of the reference. Positive numbers move down the worksheet, and negative number move up the spreadsheet.
- The number of columns to move from the original cell to get to the upper-left corner of the reference. Positive numbers move to the right from the original cell, and negative numbers move to the left.
- The number of rows in the reference.
- The number of columns in the reference.

It would be difficult to imagine why you would ever use =OFFSET(A1,2,3,4,5) to refer to the range D3:H6. However, when you consider that these arguments can be functions that calculate the size of a range, it starts to make sense.

Suppose that you start entering invoice amounts in Cell B2 and proceed down Column B. To write a sum formula that can expand to include any number of entries in Column B, you could count the number of numeric entries in Column B by using =COUNT(B:B). If you then use the COUNT function as the fourth argument in the OFFSET function, you have set up a dynamic formula that will always expand as new items are entered, as shown in Figure 17.15.

Figure 17.15
The OFFSET function allows you to describe a rectangular range that starts a calculated number of rows and columns from a starting point.

	E1			f_x	=SUM(OFFSET(B2,0,0,COUNT(B:B),1))		
	A	B	C	D	E	F	G
1	Invoice	Amount		Total:	$2,527		
2	1010	$101					
3	1011	$150					
4	1012	$199					
5	1013	$166					
6	1014	$131					
7	1015	$121					
8	1016	$113					

Assigning a Formula to a Name

When you set up a named range, the Names box shows that the name has a value like =Sheet1!A1. Because this value contains an equal sign, you know that this value is a formula.

It is possible to assign a complex formula to a name. Suppose that you have a workbook with 100 worksheets, with 20 columns of X and Y data in each worksheet, as shown in Figure 17.16. You want to continually update a transformation formula used on all the X and Y points. Every time the formula changes, you have to copy the new formula to all 20 columns on the 20 worksheets.

Figure 17.16
Every time the formula changes, you must copy it to 400 nonadjacent columns.

	C2			f_x	=COS(A2)/SIN(B2)			
	A	B	C	D	E	F	G	H
1	X	Y	Formula		X	Y	Formula	
2	0.639523	0.477897	1.744636		0.811692	0.239272	2.904152	
3	0.966707	0.194101	2.944834		0.621389	0.706054	1.253122	
4	0.238926	0.150594	6.47619		0.850939	0.36347	1.854406	
5	0.703421	0.129919	5.886595		0.372584	0.791509	1.309208	
6	0.509818	0.155577	5.633007		0.253356	0.77192	1.387899	
7	0.131213	0.607468	1.736897		0.549832	0.92877	1.064589	
8	0.852168	0.691925	1.031867		0.205876	0.027312	35.84466	
9	0.354155	0.572903	1.730281		0.887501	0.149772	4.231213	

The technique involves writing a relative formula that will carry out the same transformation as your original formula. Assign this formula to a name. In each of the cells, use =NamedFormula instead of the formula.

The advantage is that you can now edit the formula in the Edit Name box and the new formula will be used throughout the workbook.

The following specific examples walk through the steps for one particular formula.

You can use an R1C1 version of the INDIRECT function to create a formula to take the cosine of a cell two cells to the left of the formula cell and divide it by the sine of the cell to the left of the formula cell. To do so, you follow these steps:

1. To take the cosine of a cell two cells to the left of the current cell, use =COS(INDIRECT("RC[-2]",False)).

2. To take the sin of the cell to the left of the formula cell, use =SIN(INDIRECT("RC[-1]",False)).

3. Use Formulas, Named Cells, Name Manager to open the Name Manager dialog box.

4. Use the Name Manager dialog to assign the formula =COS(INDIRECT("rc[-2]",FALSE))/SIN(INDIRECT("rc[-1]",FALSE)) to a name such as MyFormula, as shown in Figure 17.17.

Figure 17.17
You can assign a name to a formula.

5. In each worksheet, replace the current formula with =MyFormula, as shown in Figure 17.18.

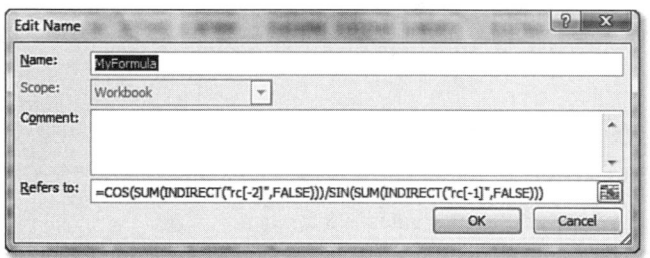

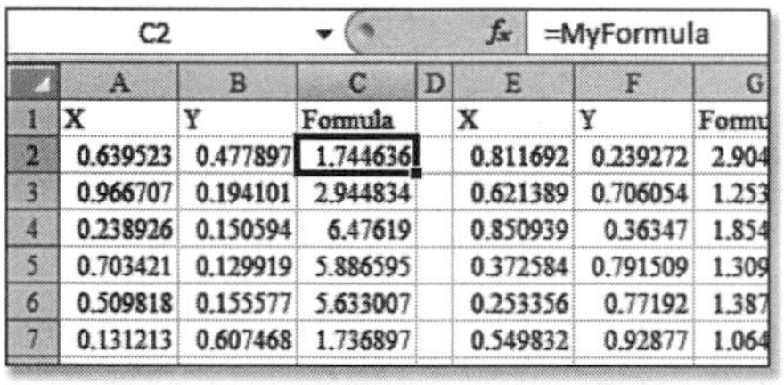

Figure 17.18
One last time, you copy the formula name to all 400 nonadjacent columns.

6. Change the formula in the Edit Name dialog box and have the new calculation carried out in all 400 nonadjacent columns.

➡️ *For a complete discussion of R1C1 style references, see "Using R1C1 Style Formulas," in Chapter 27, "Automating Repetitive Functions Using VBA Macros."*

Turning a Range of Formulas on Its Side

The Transpose option in the Paste Options dialog is great for changing values that span across several columns into values that go down a column. Here's an example:

1. In Figure 17.19, you select B1:M1 and then press Ctrl+C.

2. Select the top-left cell where the range should be copied. In this example, select cell A7.

3. Right-click. In the Paste Options section, select Transpose, as shown in Figure 17.19. The month names now go down the row.

However, there is no good way to copy the calculation for profit from Row 4 to the new table. You normally have to enter 12 different formulas in the range B7:B17, as shown in Figure 17.20.

Figure 17.19
Use the Transpose option to turn B1:M1 on its side.

	A	B	C	D	E	F	G	H	I	J	K	L	M
1		Jan	Feb	Mar	Apr	May	Jun	Jul	Aug	Sep	Oct	Nov	Dec
2	Sales	1000	1090	1123	1213	1286	1350	1485	1530	1668	1701	1735	1891
3	Cost	530	545	618	631	694	689	728	796	867	833	850	927
4	Profit	470	545	505	582	592	661	757	734	801	868	885	964
5													
6													
7	Jan												
8	Feb												
9	Mar												
10	Apr												
11	May												
12	Jun												
13	Jul												
14	Aug												
15	Sep												
16	Oct												
17	Nov												
18	Dec												

A7 | fx

Paste Options:

Figure 17.20
Transposing with a formula requires a different formula in each cell.

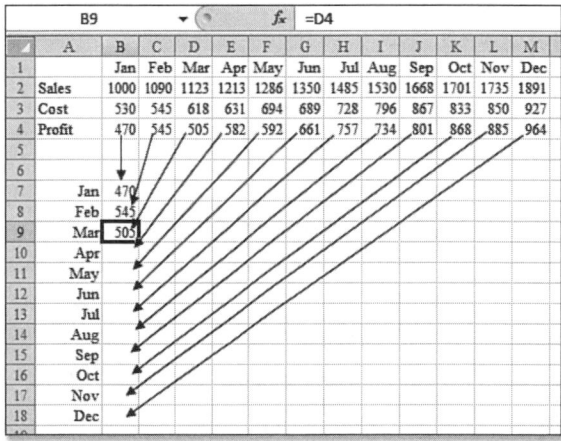

B9 | fx | =D4

But there are two ways to easily enter a single formula that will turn those results on their side.

First, you can use the OFFSET function you learned about earlier in this chapter. You can set up an OFFSET function that points to $A$4 and offsets by an additional column as you copy the formula down the rows. Try it:

1. In Cell B7, enter =ROW(A1). The result is the number 1.

2. Copy the formula from Cell B7 down to B7:B18. The result returns a string of integers from 1 through 12.

3. Use the formula =ROW(A1) as the third argument in the OFFSET function. A formula of =OFFSET($A$4,0,ROW(A1)) will achieve the perfect result, as shown in Figure 17.21.

B7		▼		f_x	=OFFSET($A$4,0,ROW(A1))								
◢	A	B	C	D	E	F	G	H	I	J	K	L	M
1		Jan	Feb	Mar	Apr	May	Jun	Jul	Aug	Sep	Oct	Nov	Dec
2	Sales	1000	1090	1123	1213	1286	1350	1485	1530	1668	1701	1735	1891
3	Cost	530	545	618	631	694	689	728	796	867	833	850	927
4	Profit	470	545	505	582	592	661	757	734	801	868	885	964
5													
6													
7	Jan	470											
8	Feb	545											
9	Mar	505											
10	Apr	582											
11	May	592											
12	Jun	661											
13	Jul	757											
14	Aug	734											
15	Sep	801											
16	Oct	868											
17	Nov	885											
18	Dec	964											
19													

Figure 17.21
You can use the ROW(A1) trick as the Column Offset parameter in the OFFSET function to turn a range on its side.

One danger exists with just about every method described in this chapter: They produce results that the average person does not understand. So if you want to end up with straightforward formulas in B7:B18, you can use the following method:

1. Enter a formula such as =B4 in Cell B5.

2. Copy the first formula across Row 5 for each month.

3. Highlight the formulas in B5:M5.

4. Use Home, Editing, Find & Select, Replace to display the Find and Replace dialog. In the Find What box, enter an equal sign. In the Replace With box, enter an exclamation point. Click Replace All to change every occurrence of = to !. This converts the formulas to text, as shown in row 5 of Figure 17.22.

5. Copy the range and highlight a new cell (in this example, Cell B7).

6. Right-click and select Transpose. Because the cells are all text, they transpose perfectly, as shown in B7:B18 of Figure 17.22.

Figure 17.22
Converting the formulas to text allows them to be transposed.

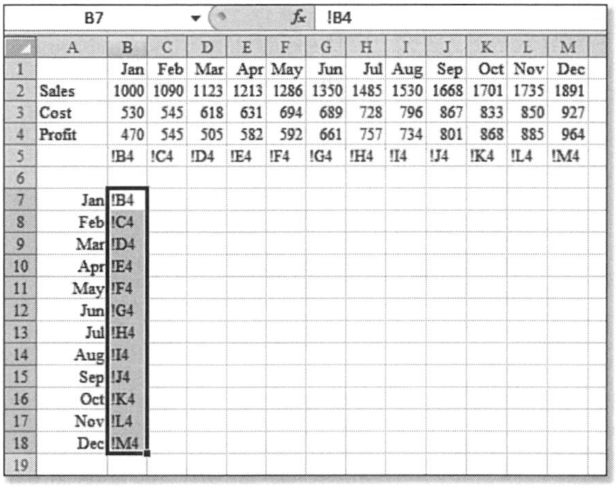

7. Use Ctrl+H or Home, Editing, Find & Select, Replace to display the Find and Replace dialog. Type an exclamation point in Find What and an equal sign in Replace With. Click Replace All to change every ! back to =. It now looks as if you actually typed all 12 formulas individually.

Replacing Multiple Formulas with One Array Formula

A wildly powerful type of formula exists that most Excel users have never experienced. This formula can do thousands of calculations in a single formula.

The formula is known as an array formula. You must use Ctrl+Shift+Enter when entering an array formula to tell Excel to evaluate the formula as an array.

Here is an example of the power of an array formula.

It is not easy to sum, count, or average based on multiple conditions using SUMIFS, COUNTIFS, or AVERAGEIFS. However, what if you need to calculate a standard deviation on records that match multiple conditions? An array formula can solve this problem.

A simple formula such as =STDEV.P(A1:A10) calculates a standard deviation, as shown in cell A12 of Figure 17.23. In this particular example, some outliers are causing the standard deviation to be large.

Suppose that you want to calculate a standard deviation after throwing out the smallest and largest value in the data.

As shown in Figure 17.24, you could perform this calculation by adding many new formulas to the worksheet:

- Add a formula in D2 to calculate the minimum value in the data.

- Add a formula in D3 to calculate the minimum value in the data.

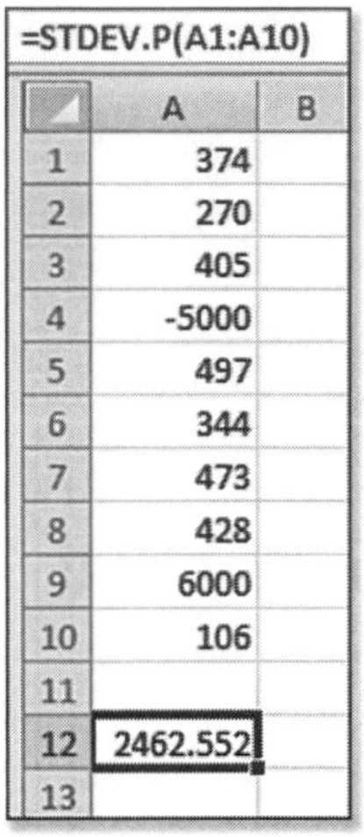

=STDEV.P(A1:A10)

	A	B
1	374	
2	270	
3	405	
4	-5000	
5	497	
6	344	
7	473	
8	428	
9	6000	
10	106	
11		
12	2462.552	
13		

Figure 17.23
The goal is to build a model to calculate standard deviation of all but the largest and smallest values.

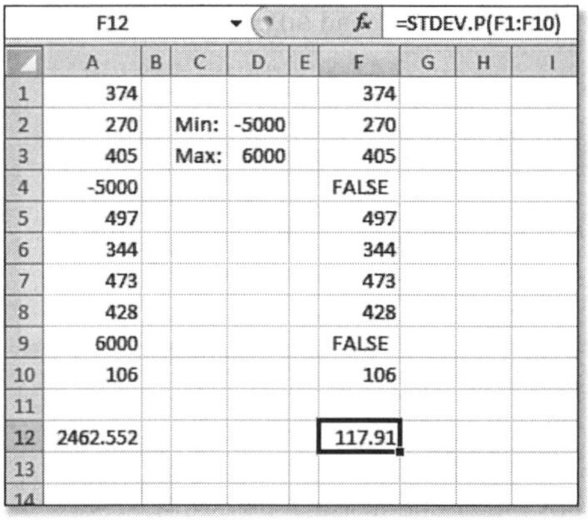

F12 =STDEV.P(F1:F10)

	A	B	C	D	E	F	G	H	I
1	374					374			
2	270		Min:	-5000		270			
3	405		Max:	6000		405			
4	-5000					FALSE			
5	497					497			
6	344					344			
7	473					473			
8	428					428			
9	6000					FALSE			
10	106					106			
11									
12	2462.552					117.91			
13									
14									

Figure 17.24
Thirteen formulas are required for this 10-row data set. If you had 1 million rows, you would need 1,000,003 formula cells.

- Then, for every row in the data set, add a new formula that compares the data point to the minimum and maximum values. If the data point is between the minimum or maximum value, bring the original number to column F. Otherwise, use the value FALSE. The standard deviation calculation will ignore cells that contain FALSE.
- Finally, add a formula in F12 to calculate the standard deviation of the new column.

Another approach is to replace the IF functions with SMALL functions. By asking for the smallest second through ninth values, you are removing the smallest and largest values from the data set (see Figure 17.25):

- Enter the numbers 2 through 9 in C2:C9. These cells could contain constants, or they could contain a formula such as =ROW(A2).

- Enter =SMALL(A$1:A$10,C2) in cell D2 and copy down to D9.

- Enter a STDEV.P function in D12.

Figure 17.25
A series of SMALL functions will eliminate the outliers.

	D2		▾		f_x	=SMALL($A$1:$A$10,C2)
	A	B	C	D	E	F	G	H
1	374		Item					
2	270		2	106				
3	405		3	270				
4	-5000		4	344				
5	497		5	374				
6	344		6	405				
7	473		7	428				
8	428		8	473				
9	6000		9	497				
10	106							
11								
12	2462.552			117.91				

Setting Up an Array Formula

Both of the preceding approaches require many formulas. You can use an array formula to solve the problem with a single formula.

The SMALL function has two arguments. The first argument is usually a range containing many values. The second argument is usually a single number.

Imagine if there were a way to ask the SMALL function to return items 2 through 9 at one time. With this small data set, you could type:

=SMALL(A1:A10,{2,3,4,5,6,7,8,9})

This approach would not work if your data set contains hundreds or thousands of data points.

Instead of typing the position numbers 2 through 9, you could ask for ROW(A2:A9). This function will return an array of {2;3;4;5;6;7;8;9}.

Using SMALL(A1:A10,ROW(A2:A9)) will return an array of the second through ninth smallest values in A1:A10.

A single cell cannot hold an array of nine values, so you want to wrap the formula in the STDEV.P function.

The formula =STDEV.P(SMALL(A1:A10,ROW(A2:A9))) is known as an array formula. To make the array formula work, you must hold down Ctrl+Shift while pressing Enter. When you press Ctrl+Shift+Enter, Excel evaluates the formula as an array. It displays the formula in the formula bar surrounded by curly braces.

 tip

Because a single array formula can replace thousands of intermediate formulas, I call these Super Excel formulas. At MrExcel.com, I have many examples of formulas that I call CSE formulas. The CSE acronym stands for Create Super Excel and also stands for the keystokes that must be held down after typing the formula: Ctrl+Shift+Enter.

Understanding an Array Formula

The Evaluate Formula tool on the Formulas tab helps you to visualize how an array formula is being calculated. In Figure 17.26, a single array formula is shown in cell A12.

The underlined portion of the formula in the Evaluate Formula dialog shows the portion of the formula that will be solved next. In this example, Excel will solve ROW(A2:A9) first.

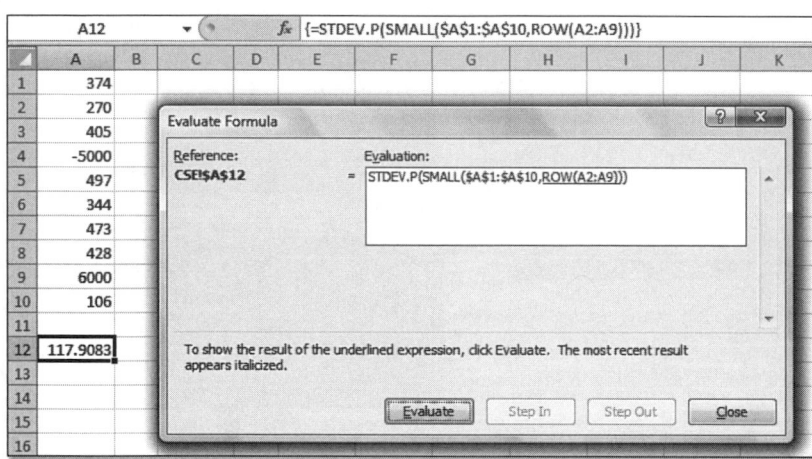

Figure 17.26
Excel starts evaluating the formula by solving ROW(A2:A9).

Click Evaluate. You will see that the ROW(A2:A9) is changed to {2;3;4;5;6;7;8;9}. Click Evaluate to have Excel calculate the SMALL function. The result is an array of {106;270;344;374; 405;428;473;497}. Click Evaluate to have Excel calculate the STDEV.P of that array. The result is 117.9082688.

Contrast this result to a nonarray formula. Edit the formula in A12 and press Enter instead of Ctrl+Shift+Enter. The result changes to a zero. Using Evaluate Formula, you can see that the ROW(A2:A9) function returns a single value of 2. The SMALL function then returns a single value of 106. The Standard Deviation of a single number is always zero.

> **note**
> Pressing Ctrl+Shift+Enter allows Excel to return many intermediate values even though the function may be expecting only a single value. Excel stores all these results in memory and essentially is calculating the function repeatedly for each element in the array.

Coercing a Range of Dates Using an Array Formula

Suppose that you want to find out how many Wednesdays occurred between two dates. Enter the starting and ending date in cells in an Excel worksheet, as shown in Figure 17.27.

To start, the WEEKDAY function will return a number from 1 to 7 corresponding to the day of the week. =WEEKDAY(C1) will return the number 4 if the day is a Wednesday.

To check to see if a particular day is a Wednesday, use the IF function:

```
=IF(WEEKDAY(C1)=4,1,0)
```

Using that formula, you could build a table showing all dates from the beginning date to the ending date as rows. The second column would use the IF/WEEKDAY function to test if each date is a Wednesday. Sum that column to count the Wednesdays in the range. However, this table will contain hundreds of rows for every year in the data range.

Instead, use ROW(INDIRECT(C1&":"&C2)) to build an array in memory of all the dates. Although cell C1 is displaying 6/30/2010, it actually contains the number 40359. Similarly, cell C2 contains the number 40801. Concatenating C1 with a colon and C2 builds a text string of "40359:40801". This text is a valid reference, pointing to all the rows from 40359 to 40801. Asking for the ROW of that reference will return an array with the numbers 40359 to 40801.

To build the array formula, replace "C1" in the original IF/WEEKDAY function with the ROW/INDIRECT functions:

```
=IF(WEEKDAY(ROW(INDIRECT(C1&":"&C2)))=4,1,0)
```

That formula will return a series of zeroes and ones. Because you want to add up the ones in the resulting array, wrap the formula in a SUM function:

```
=SUM(IF(WEEKDAY(ROW(INDIRECT(C1&":"&C2)))=4,1,0))
```

Type that formula and press Ctrl+Shift+Enter. Excel will calculate hundreds of intermediate results and show the answer in a single cell.

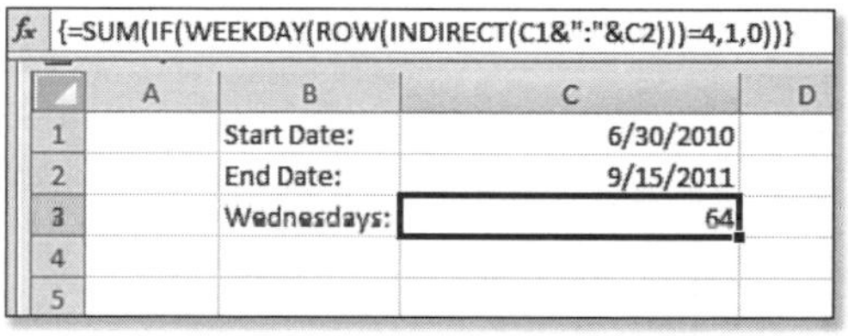

Figure 17.27
This single array formula replaces hundreds of intermediate calculations.

	A	B	C	D
1		Start Date:	6/30/2010	
2		End Date:	9/15/2011	
3		Wednesdays:	64	
4				
5				

f_x {=SUM(IF(WEEKDAY(ROW(INDIRECT(C1&":"&C2)))=4,1,0))}

Excel in Practice: Copying Array Formulas

There is a difficulty when copying array formulas. In Figure 17.28, the array formula in D5 needs to be copied to D5:J35.

Normally, you would copy Cell D5 and then paste to Cells D5:J35. With array formulas, this leads to an error. If you attempt to do this copy, you are told that you cannot move or change part of an array. The solution is to do the copy in two pieces:

1. Copy Cell D5 to D6:D35.
2. Copy D5:D35 and paste it to E5:J35.

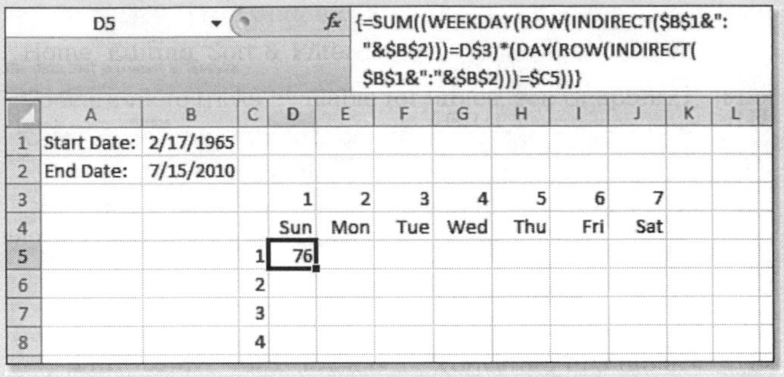

| | D5 | ▾ (| *fx* | {=SUM((WEEKDAY(ROW(INDIRECT($B$1&":"&$B$2)))=D$3)*(DAY(ROW(INDIRECT($B$1&":"&$B$2)))=$C5))} |

	A	B	C	D	E	F	G	H	I	J	K	L
1	Start Date:	2/17/1965										
2	End Date:	7/15/2010										
3				1	2	3	4	5	6	7		
4				Sun	Mon	Tue	Wed	Thu	Fri	Sat		
5			1	76								
6			2									
7			3									
8			4									

Figure 17.28
You want to copy this formula to the rest of the summary table.

USING NAMES IN EXCEL

Long before Microsoft introduced tables and formulas like =[@Revenue]-[@Cost], spreadsheets have offered the ability to assign a name to a cell, range of cells, or formula. The theory is that using a name for a range would be easier to understand when used in a formula. =SUM(MyExpenses) would make formulas more self-documenting than =SUM(Sheet5!AB2:AB99). In Excel 2010, you use the Name Manager interface to assign and use names effectively.

Use the Name Box to Define a Name for a Cell

There are a variety of uses for names in a workbook. A name can be applied to any cell or range. Names are also useful for the following:

- Making formulas easier to understand

- Quick navigation

- Forcing a formula reference to remain absolute, without having to use the dollar sign

- Improving Solver's report results

- Storing a value that will be used repeatedly, but that might occasionally need to change such as a sales tax rate

- Storing formulas

- Defining a dynamic range

There are various ways to name a cell. The easiest way to define a name for a cell is to use the Name box. To do so, select any cell in your worksheet. To

 note

Excel 2010 offers the new Table functionality, which is described in Chapter 19, "Fabulous Table Intelligence." Although the Table feature allows you to create formulas using column names, the individual column names and table name are not considered named ranges.

the left of the formula bar is a box with the address of that cell. This box is known as the *Name* box (see Figure 18.1). The quick way to assign a name is to click inside the Name box and type a name, such as Revenue.

When you press Enter, Excel centers the name in the Name box, which indicates that the name has been assigned. This is your only indication that the name is valid and has been accepted.

The following are some basic rules for valid names:

- Names can be up to 255 characters long.

- Names cannot contain spaces. However, you can use an underscore or a period in a name. For example, the names Gross_Profit and Gross.Profit are valid.

- Names cannot look like cell addresses.

- Names cannot contain operator characters such as these: +-*/()^&<>=%.

- Names cannot contain special characters such as !"#$',;:@[]{}`|~.

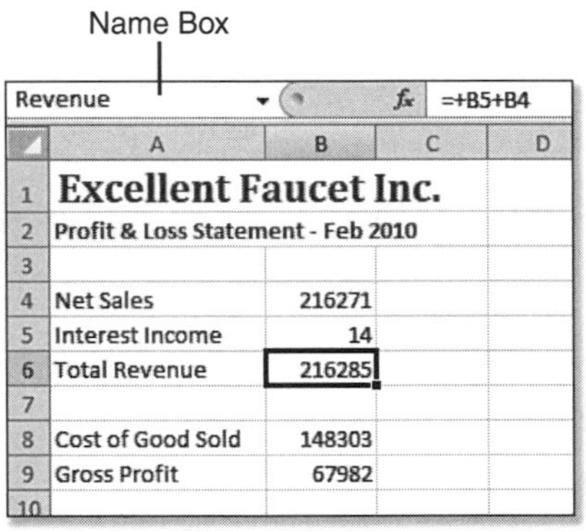

Name Box

Figure 18.1
The Name box is to the left of the formula bar.

Table 18.1 provides some examples of valid and invalid names.

Table 18.1   Examples of Valid and Invalid Names

Valid Names	Invalid Names (why)
SalesTax	Sales Tax (includes a space)
Sales_Tax	XFD123 (valid cell address)
Sales.Tax	Tax2010 (valid cell address)
SalesTax2010	MyResults! (invalid special character)

Naming a Cell by Using the Name Dialog

The Formulas tab contains a group called Defined Names. The following example introduces the Name dialog:

1. Select a cell that you would like to name. Click the Define Name icon from the Formulas tab. The New Name dialog box appears. In Figure 18.2, Cell B8 is being assigned a name.

2. The New Name box uses IntelliSense to propose a name. Notice that in this particular example, Excel's IntelliSense was able to ascertain that this cell contains the text Cost of Good Sold. Because that is not a valid name, Excel instead proposed naming the cell Cost_of_Good_Sold. You can either keep that name or override it with a name that you prefer. In this case, override that name with the name COGS.

As you can see in Figure 18.3, the name was applied because the Name box now shows COGS instead of B8.

Figure 18.2
Choose a cell to be named and then select Define Name from the Formulas tab.

Figure 18.3
After you assign a name, the Name box reflects the new name.

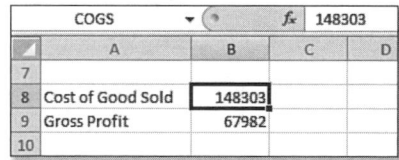

Using the Name Box for Quick Navigation

One advantage of using names is that you can use the drop-down in the Name box to jump to any named cell. This includes cells that might be in distant sections of the worksheet or even on other sheets in the workbook.

If you plan to use the Name box for navigation, assign a name to the upper-left corner of each section of your workbook. The Name box drop-down will then provide a minitable of contents, and people can use the Name box to jump to any section of the workbook.

To illustrate this concept, follow these steps:

1. Click the New Sheet icon (next to the right-most sheet tab) to add a new sheet to the workbook.

2. On the new sheet, go to a distant cell. Give that cell a name, such as SectionTwo. Return to the original sheet in the workbook.

3. Click the Name box's drop-down arrow to access a list of all names in the workbook, as shown in Figure 18.4.

4. Choose a name from the list to navigate quickly to that cell, even if it is on another worksheet.

As you can see, named ranges are a great tool for quickly navigating a workbook. Note that names are presented in the Name box alphabetically. If you want the names to appear sequentially, you can add names such as Section1, Section2, Section3, and so on. You can also prefix the section names with letters such as A-Income, B-Costs, C-Expense, D-Tax, E-Income. Then, you can jump to a section by choosing it from the alphabetical list in the Name box. When used in this way, names in Excel are almost like bookmarks in Word.

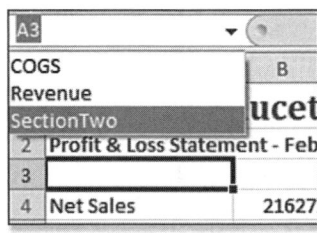

Figure 18.4
The Name Box drop-down contains a list of all names in the workbook.

Using Scope to Allow Duplicate Names in a Workbook

Ideally, you should keep the names unique throughout a workbook. Although it is technically legal to add a name such as SectionOne to both Sheet1 and Sheet2, it is not a good idea. When you define the name on the first sheet, it is defined as a name with workbook-level scope. This means that you can easily navigate to SectionOne from any sheet in the workbook. If you attempt to set up the same name on a second worksheet, that name will have to be set up with worksheet-level scope. Names with worksheet-level scope override the workbook-level scope only on the sheets on which they

are defined. For example, suppose you have a workbook with Sheet1, Sheet2, Sheet3, Sheet4, and Sheet5:

- On Sheet2, you use the Name box to assign the name SectionOne to Cell N16.

- On Sheet3, you use the New Name dialog to assign the name SectionOne to Cell A1. In the New Name dialog, you need to change the Scope setting from Workbook to Sheet3, as shown in Figure 18.5

> 🔍 **note**
>
> The names Print_Area and Print_ Titles are common worksheet-level names. These names are assigned by Excel after you set certain print settings.

Figure 18.5
Change the scope of the duplicate name to apply only on Sheet3.

Scope

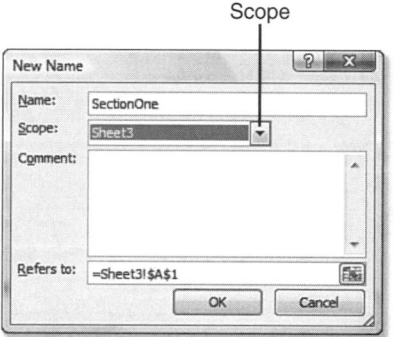

- If you are on Sheet3 and use the Name box to navigate to SectionOne, you will jump to Cell A1 on Sheet3.

- If you are on any other sheet in the workbook and use the Name box to navigate to SectionOne, you will jump to Cell N16 on Sheet2.

You can see that this can be confusing. In general, you should stick with unique names that can have workbook-level scope. You should switch to using duplicate names with worksheet-level scope only when you have many nearly identical sheets in a workbook.

Inadvertently Creating Worksheet-Level Scope

It is easy to set up worksheet-level scope accidentally. Suppose that you set up a worksheet for January. You assign five workbook-level names on the worksheet. Next, you make a copy of this worksheet for February. All the names continue to exist on the February worksheet, but they have their scope set to only the February worksheet.

To avoid this problem, make copies of the worksheets before assigning names.

Using Named Ranges to Simplify Formulas

As introduced at the start of this chapter, the original reason for having named ranges was to simplify formulas. In theory, it is easier to understand a formula such as =(Revenue-Cost)/Revenue.

Be sure to define the names before entering formulas that refer to those cells. When you create a formula using the mouse or arrow key methods, Excel will automatically use the names in the formula.

In the following example, the worksheet in Figure 18.6 has a name of "Revenue" assigned to A6 and a name of "Cost" assigned to A8. Rather than typing =A6-A8 in Cell A9, follow these steps to have Excel create a formula using names.

1. Select the cell where the formula should go. In this example, it is Cell A9.

2. Type =.

3. Using the mouse, click the first cell in your formula. In this case, it is Cell A6.

4. Type -.

5. Using the mouse, click the next cell in your formula. In this case, it is Cell A8.

6. Press Enter.

7. Move the cell pointer back to the formula cell and look in the formula bar. You can see that Excel has built the formula =Revenues-COGS, as shown in Figure 18.6. In theory, this formula is self-documenting and easier to understand than =C6-C8.

You can also type a formula that uses names directly in a cell. For example, Figure 18.7 shows =Revenue*1.1 entered in Cell E6. When you press Enter, Excel recognizes this formula and multiplies Cell A6 by 1.1.

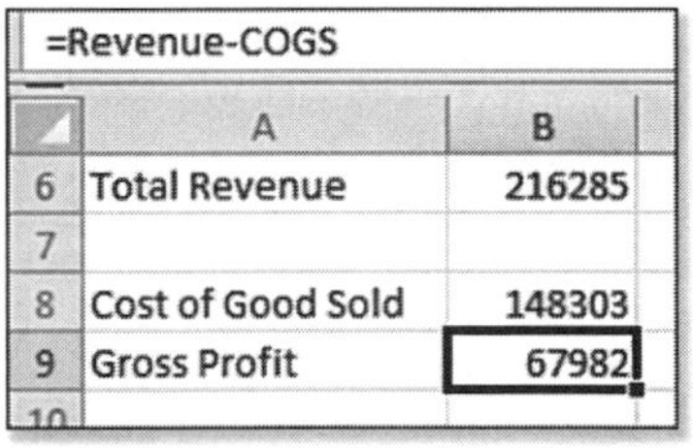

Figure 18.6
New formulas created after names have been assigned reflect the cell names in the formula.

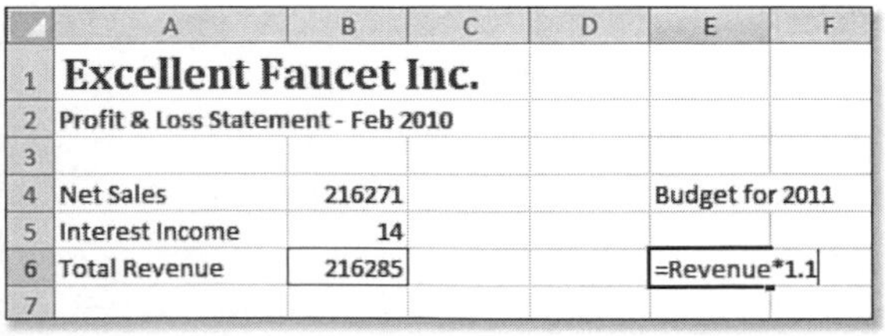

Figure 18.7
You can type formulas to reference existing cell names.

However, a problem crops up when one of the cells in the formula contains a name—especially if that name is defined strictly for navigational purposes. In this case, Excel creates an absolute reference to that cell. When you copy a formula that contains a name, the copied formula always points to the name. This can lead to unhappy results.

Here is an example to show how easily this can happen.

Figure 18.8 shows Cell A2 named SectionThree so that the name can be used as a bookmark.

Figure 18.8
Cell A2 is named Section Three to aid navigation.

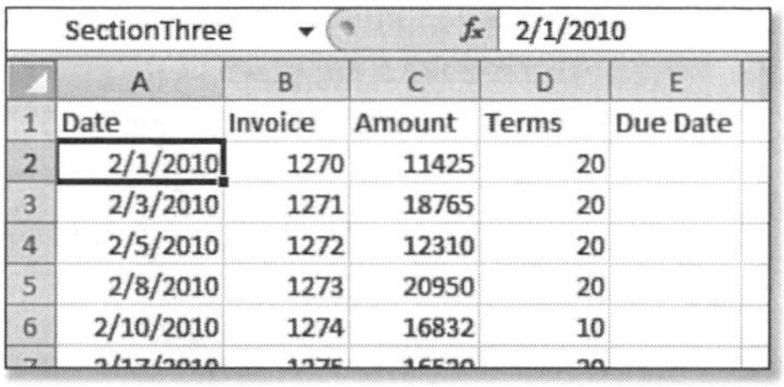

	A	B	C	D	E
1	Date	Invoice	Amount	Terms	Due Date
2	2/1/2010	1270	11425	20	
3	2/3/2010	1271	18765	20	
4	2/5/2010	1272	12310	20	
5	2/8/2010	1273	20950	20	
6	2/10/2010	1274	16832	10	

In Cell E2 you enter a formula to calculate a due date. Using the mouse method, you type =, touch Cell A2 with the mouse, type +, and then touch Cell D2 with the mouse. Instead of entering the formula =A2+D2, you end up with the formula =SectionThree+D2.

Select Cell E2 and double-click the fill handle to copy the formula down to all rows. Examine the formula in Cell E5. As shown in Figure 18.9, although Cell D2 was correctly changed to Cell D5 in the copied formula, this cell and all the remaining cells in Column E are incorrectly pointing to Cell A2 because it was previously defined as a named range.

Figure 18.9
When you copy this formula, every cell points at Cell A2 because that cell previously had a defined name.

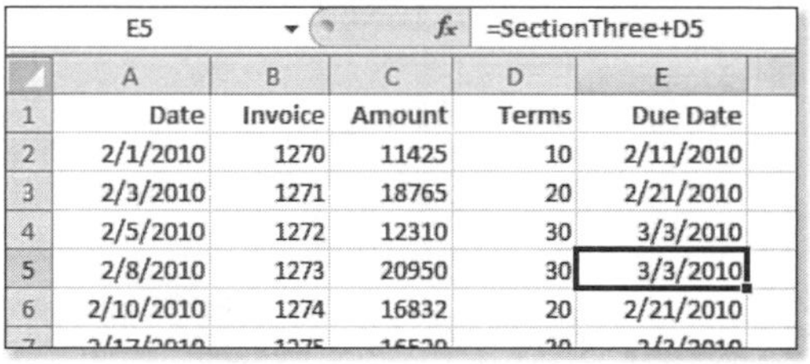

	A	B	C	D	E
1	Date	Invoice	Amount	Terms	Due Date
2	2/1/2010	1270	11425	10	2/11/2010
3	2/3/2010	1271	18765	20	2/21/2010
4	2/5/2010	1272	12310	30	3/3/2010
5	2/8/2010	1273	20950	30	3/3/2010
6	2/10/2010	1274	16832	20	2/21/2010

To overcome this problem, use care when entering the original formula: Type =, type A2+, and then touch Cell D2. This overrides Excel's default behavior of automatically converting relative reference names to preexisting range names.

Retroactively Applying Names to Formulas

When you learn the trick that was discussed in the "Using Named Ranges to Simplify Formulas" section, you might start naming all the input cells in your workbook, hoping that all the preexisting formulas will take on the new names. Unfortunately, this does not work automatically.

In Figure 18.10, the formula in Cell B16 was entered first. Later, Cells B9 and B14 were given the names GrossProfit and TotalExpenses, respectively. However, the preexisting formula in B16 continues to reflect the cell addresses instead of the names.

To make the names become part of existing formulas, you have to use the Apply command. To do this, follow these steps:

1. On the Formulas tab, select the drop-down next to Define Name and select Apply Names. The Apply Names dialog appears, as shown in Figure 18.10.

2. Choose as many names as you want in the Apply Names box. In this example, you should choose at least GrossProfit and TotalExpenses and then click OK. Any existing formulas that point to these named cells change to include the cell names in the formula, as shown in Figure 18.11.

 tip
If you recently defined the names, those names will be preselected when you open the Apply Names dialog.

 To watch a video of retroactively applying names to formulas, search for "Excel In Depth 18" at YouTube.

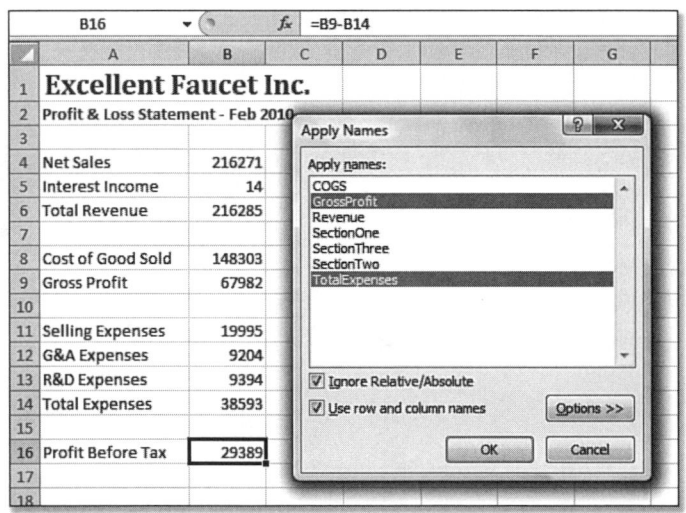

Figure 18.10
The legacy formula in Cell B16 does not reflect the new named ranges. Use Name a Range, Apply to display this dialog.

	A	B	C	D
9	Gross Profit	67982		
10				
11	Selling Expenses	19995		
12	G&A Expenses	9204		
13	R&D Expenses	9394		
14	Total Expenses	38593		
15				
16	Profit Before Tax	=GrossProfit-TotalExpenses		
17				

Figure 18.11
After you apply names, existing formulas are rewritten.

Using Names to Refer to Multiple-Cell Ranges

It is possible to define a name that refers to a larger range of cells. For example, you can select C11:C13 in Figure 18.12 and type a name such as Expenses into the Name box.

If you later select Expenses from the Name box, your cursor moves to Cell C11, and the entire range is selected. Having a name apply to a range allows formulas such as =Sum(Expenses).

Figure 18.12
A name can refer to a rectangular range.

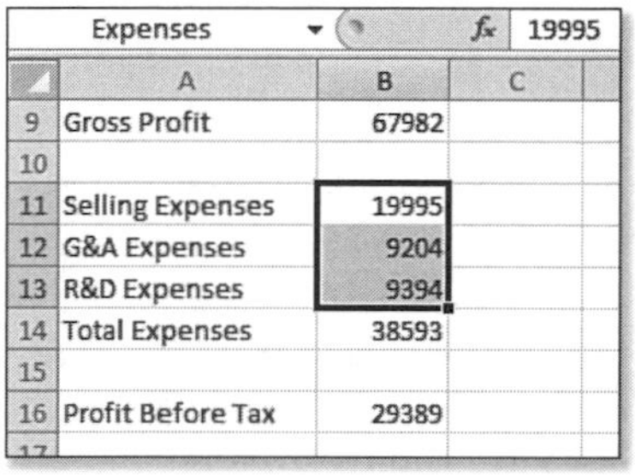

Expenses		f_x	19995

	A	B	C
9	Gross Profit	67982	
10			
11	Selling Expenses	19995	
12	G&A Expenses	9204	
13	R&D Expenses	9394	
14	Total Expenses	38593	
15			
16	Profit Before Tax	29389	

Dealing with Invalid Legacy Naming

To prevent confusion, a valid cell address may not be used as a name. In legacy versions of Excel, this eliminated names from A1 through IV65536.

Excel 2010 has columns named A through Z, AA through ZZ, and AAA through XFD. The same rule applied to Excel 2010 now invalidates names that start with IW through ZZ and AAA through XFD.

You can think of many three-letter names such as Tax2007 and ROI5 that might have been common in Excel 2003. Although those are perfectly legal in Excel 2003, they are no longer valid in Excel 2010 because they duplicate existing cell addresses in Excel2010.

Figure 18.13 shows an Excel 2003 workbook that contains names such as Tax2004, Tax2005, and so on.

Figure 18.13
In Excel 2003, a range named Tax2004 for Cell B4 was perfectly legal because with only 256 columns, there was not a column called Tax.

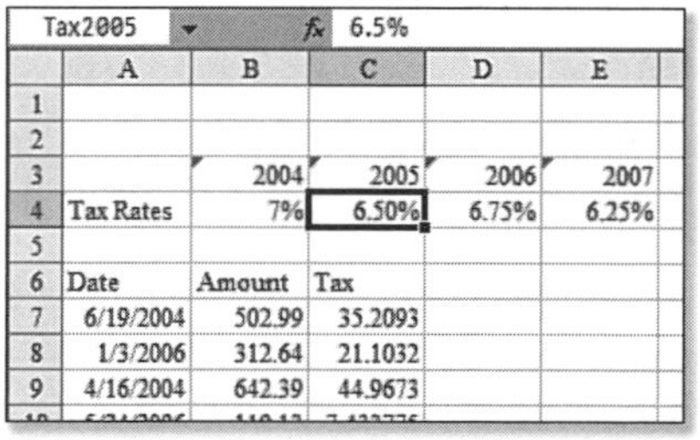

Tax2005		f_x	6.5%	

	A	B	C	D	E
1					
2					
3			2004	2005	2006	2007
4	Tax Rates	7%	6.50%	6.75%	6.25%
5					
6	Date	Amount	Tax		
7	6/19/2004	502.99	35.2093		
8	1/3/2006	312.64	21.1032		
9	4/16/2004	642.39	44.9673		

You can open this workbook in Excel 2010. The workbook initially opens in Compatibility mode, with columns only through IV. When you attempt to save the file as an Excel 2010 workbook, Excel warns you of the first named range that must be changed. In Figure 18.14, Tax2004 is being changed to _Tax2004.

Excel attempts to warn you about every existing name that must be changed. You can either click OK to each message or skip them by clicking OK to All. Note that after the Save As, the workbook is still in Compatibility mode. Close the workbook and then reopen it to see the new names.

Excel does a great job of updating the names and the formulas that use invalid names. Figure 18.15 shows the Excel 2003 worksheet after it is converted to Excel 2010. Each name now has an underscore at the beginning.

caution

Excel is not able to update some formulas. It would be efficient to rewrite the formula in Figure 18.13 as =B7*INDIRECT("TAX"&YEAR(A7)). During the conversion of names from TAX2004 to _TAX2004, Excel will not update your formula to refer to "_TAX". Formulas such as these will fail after the conversion. You will have to edit the formula manually.

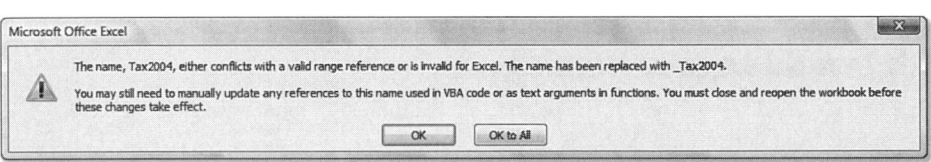

Figure 18.14
When you try to save the Excel 2003 workbook as an Excel 2010 file, the established names must be changed.

Underscore Added

Figure 18.15
Excel correctly updated these references.

Adding Many Names at Once from Existing Labels and Headings

With Excel 2010 you can add many names in a single command, particularly if the names exist as labels or headings adjacent to the cells.

Suppose you have a worksheet with a series of labels in Column A and values in Column B. One example is shown in Figure 18.16. To do a wholesale assignment of names to the cells in Column B, follow these steps:

1. Select the range of labels and the cells to which they refer. In this example, this would be A4:B16.

2. Select Formulas, Names, Create from Selection. Excel displays the Create Names from Selected Range dialog.

3. Because the row labels are in the left column of the selected range, select Left Column and then click OK, as shown in Figure 18.16.

Figure 18.16
When you make this selection, Excel uses the text values in the left column to assign names to all the nonblank cells in Column B of this range.

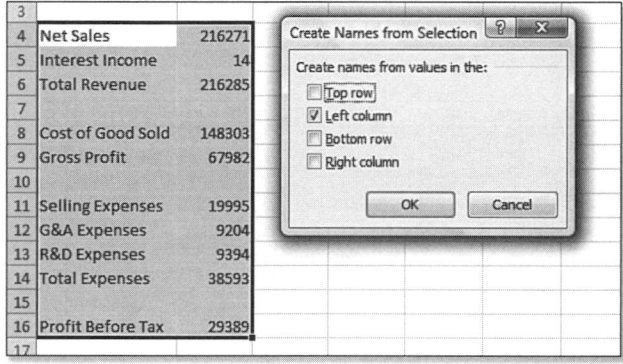

Excel does a fairly good job of assigning the names. Spaces are replaced with underscores to make the names valid. Figure 18.17 shows the names created as a result of this command. In this example, Cell B4 is assigned the name Net_Sales. Cell C8 is assigned the name Cost_of_Good_Sold. In Row 12, where the label contains an ampersand (&), Excel replaces the ampersand with an underscore, to form the name G_A_Expenses. Although this is not as meaningful as it could be if you wrote the name yourself, it is still pretty good.

Figure 18.17
Excel replaces spaces and ampersands with underscores when creating names from a selection.

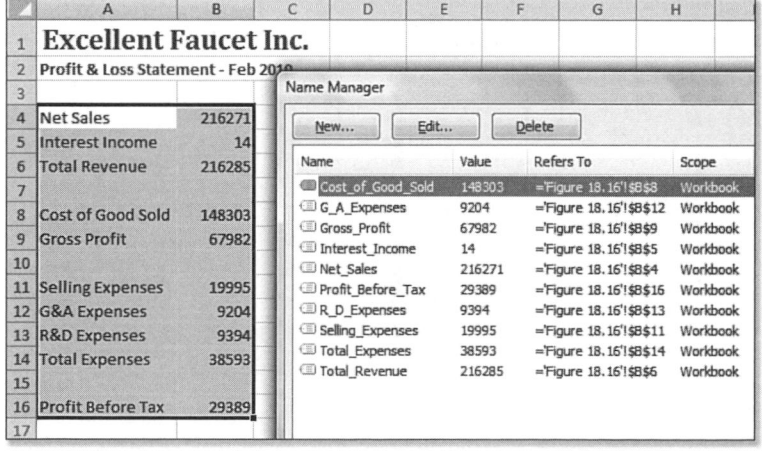

In Excel 2010, you can apply names by using both the row labels and column headings at the same time. In Figure 18.18, the selections in the Create Names from Selected Ranges dialog mean that six new names will be added to the workbook. For example, Jan will refer to B2:B4.

The Create Names from Selected Range dialog is so flexible that it will even let you select all four options at once. If you select all the check boxes in the Create Names from Selected Range dialog and then click OK, 12 new names will be added to the workbook (see Figure 18.18).

caution

If Cell A12 were G & A Expenses, Excel would replace every space and ampersand with an underscore, creating the name G___A_Expenses.

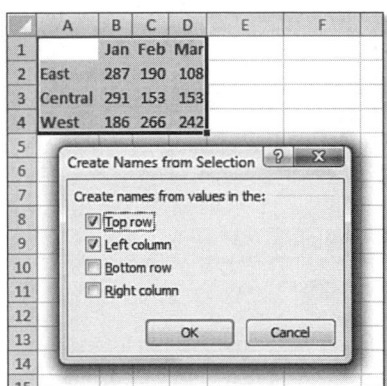

Figure 18.18
In Excel 2010, you can create names based on the row labels and column headers at the same time.

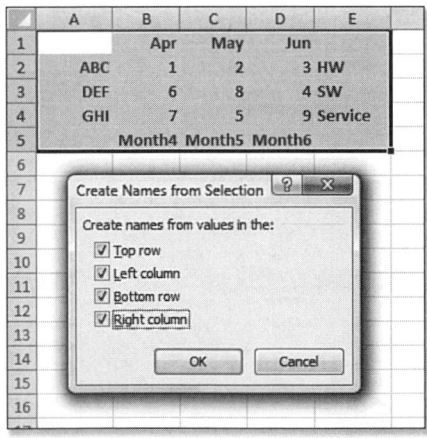

Figure 18.19
You can create names based on labels on all four edges of a range. However, it is difficult to imagine a scenario in which you would want to do this.

In this example, the name Jun will refer to D2:D4. The name Month6 will also refer to D2:D4. If you select Month6 from the drop-down, Excel selects D2:D4, as shown in Figure 18.20. However, the name in the Name box reflects Jun because that is the first name, alphabetically, that applies to that range.

Figure 18.20
D2:D4 is called both Jun and Month6.

Managing Names

Excel 2007 was a great improvement over legacy Excel versions in terms of managing names. Whereas older versions of Excel used the Insert Names dialog to manage names, Excel 2007 offered the Name Manager dialog, shown in Figure 18.21. To open this dialog, click the Name Manager icon on the Formulas tab.

The Name Manager dialog shows the five fields for each name. Initially, certain columns may not be wide enough to show all the text in each column. You can resize the entire dialog by using the triangle in the lower-right corner. You can also resize columns by dragging the vertical bars between the column headings.

Listed below are the columns in the Name Manager dialog:

- **Name**—Shows the current name.

- **Value**—Shows the current value. If the Name column refers to a rectangular range, each value in the range is shown in the Value column.

- **Refers To**—Shows the formula defined for the name. This might be a reference to a cell address, a constant value, or a formula.

- **Scope**—Indicates whether the name applies to the whole workbook or just to a certain worksheet.

- **Comment**—Shows any comments you might have typed when you originally defined a name.

Working with the Name Manager dialog is straightforward:

- To create a new name, click the New Name button.

- To delete a name, highlight the name and click Delete Name. However, this should be done with caution. If the name is being used, all the formulas that point to that name change to #NAME? errors.

- To view the cells represented by a certain name, select the name from the Name column of the dialog and then click at the end of the Refers To box. Excel shows you the section of the worksheet behind the dialog.

- To reassign a name to a different set of cells, choose the name from the Name column of the dialog and then click in the Refers To box. On the worksheet, point to the new location for the name. After you select a new location, click the check box to accept the new location. Click the x button to revert to the original location.

- If you click a name from the Name column of the dialog and then click Edit Name, you have an opportunity to add or change the comment to the name or to change the scope.

- When you modify an existing name in the Name column of the dialog, any formulas that specifically reference that name are updated to point to the new cell.

Filtering the Name Manager Dialog

In the upper-right corner of the Name Manager dialog is a button labeled Filter that can be clicked to access many powerful options. If you have defined names that have scope only to a worksheet, you can select Names Scoped to Worksheet to limit the Name Manager dialog to only those names, as shown in Figure 18.22.

Figure 18.22
The Filter button allows you to narrow the scope to certain names.

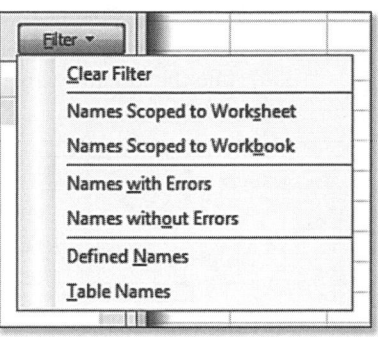

Following are the options in the Filter drop-down:

- **Clear Filter**—Restores the list to the complete list.

- **Names Scoped to Worksheet**—Shows all worksheet-level names for the active worksheet and other worksheets.

- **Names Scoped to Workbook**—Shows all the global names that are scoped to a workbook.

- **Names with Errors**—Finds all names where the value is a cell error. Often, stray names left behind after copying a worksheet to a new workbook have #REF! errors. You can use the Names with Errors filter to find those names.

- **Names Without Errors**—Hides any invalid names.

- **Defined Names**—Specifies the names defined using the techniques described in this chapter. This option removes names defined as a result of creating pivot tables or formatting ranges as tables.

- **Table Names**—Shows only the values of table names. When you define a range as a table, the entire table is given a name such as Table1.

Using a Name to Simplify an Absolute Reference

A common scenario is when a formula such as VLOOKUP is used in a data set to look up data on another worksheet. You might enter a VLOOKUP formula in Cell B2 and copy it to hundreds of records. The formula in Cell B2 might be =VLOOKUP(A2,'Lookup Table'!A2:B25,2,False). As you copy this formula to Row 3, the reference in the second argument will incorrectly change to 'Lookup Table'!A3:B26. When you need the reference to always point to A2:B25, you can add dollar signs to the reference: $A$2:$B$25.

If you will be frequently adding VLOOKUP formulas that will point to 'Lookup Table'!$A$2:$B$25, it can get tedious to continually use the syntax. After all, it is a confusing mix of dollar signs, apostrophes, and exclamation points.

To simplify the VLOOKUP formula, give A2:B25 a name such as ItemLookup. Then, the formula simply becomes =VLOOKUP(A2,ItemLookup,2,False). As you copy the formula down, it continues to point to A2:B25 on the Lookup Table worksheet. Figure 18.23 compares the formula without a name in B2 and the formula with a name in B3.

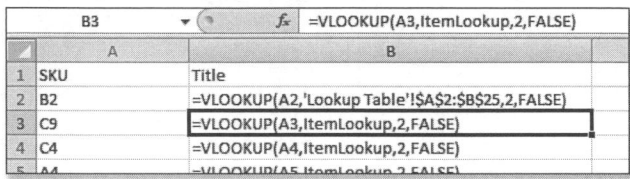

Figure 18.23
The formula in B3 is easier to type because it uses a named range for the lookup table.

Using a Name to Hold a Value

So far, all the names defined in this chapter have referred to a cell or a range of cells. It is possible to assign a constant value to a name by using the New Name dialog. You might do this to hold a value that could possibly change, but would likely rarely change, such as a sales tax rate.

To use a name to hold a value, follow these steps:

1. Either click the Name a Range icon or the Name Manager icon and then click Add Names. Both icons are located in the Defined Names group on the Formulas tab. The New Name dialog appears.

2. In the Name field of the New Name dialog, type a name such as Sales_Tax.

3. In the Refers To box, remove any existing cell reference and type the new value (=6.5%, as shown in Figure 18.24).

4. Write formulas that refer to the new name such as Sales_Tax. The formula might be something like =C2*Sales_Tax. In Figure 18.25, the range has been defined as a table. Thus, the formula of =[@MerchAmt]*Sales_Tax uses both a table name in square brackets and the defined name Sales_Tax.

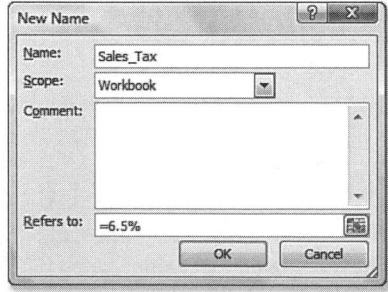

Figure 18.24
In the New Name dialog, you can assign a constant value to a name.

Figure 18.25
MerchAmt, in square brackets, is a field name in the table. Sales_Tax is a defined name.

	C2			f_x	=[@MerchAmt]*Sales_Tax	
	A	B		C	D	E
1	Invoice	MerchAmt		Sales Tax		
2	1901		159.8	10.387		
3	1902		59.85	3.89025		
4	1903		39.9	2.5935		
5	1904		79.9	5.1935		
6	1905		79.8	5.187		
7	1906		79.9	5.1935		

Figure 18.26
With defined names and table column names floating around, ambiguous formulas like this can turn up.

	E2			f_x	=[@Total]/(1+Sales_Tax)-([@Total]-[@[Sales Tax]])	
	A	B	C	D	E	F
1	Invoice	MerchAmt	Sales Tax	Total	Rounding Error	
2	1901	159.8	10.387	170.19	-0.000183099	
3	1902	59.85	3.89025	63.74	1.52582E-05	
4	1903	39.9	2.5935	42.49	0.000213615	
5	1904	79.9	5.1935	85.09	0.000213615	
6	1905	79.8	5.187	84.99	-0.000183099	
7	1906	79.9	5.1935	85.09	0.000213615	

The advantage of using a name to refer to a constant is that if your tax rate changes, you can edit the value defined in the name, and all the formulas in the workbook will recalculate. To edit an existing name, click the Name Manager, click the name, and then select Edit Name.

> **caution**
> Use care when viewing potentially ambiguous references such as Sales_Tax and [@ Sales Tax] as shown in Figure 18.26. Remember, the name in square brackets is a table name assigned automatically by Excel.

Assigning a Formula to a Name

Although names are traditionally used to refer to cells or constant values, an interesting use is to use a name to refer to a formula.

Notice the Refers To box in Figure 18.27. Although the value in this figure is a standard name that refers to a single cell, the Refers To box contains = at the beginning, which means this named range is actually a formula.

As described in the following sections, assigning a formula to a name can be useful in a variety of situations.

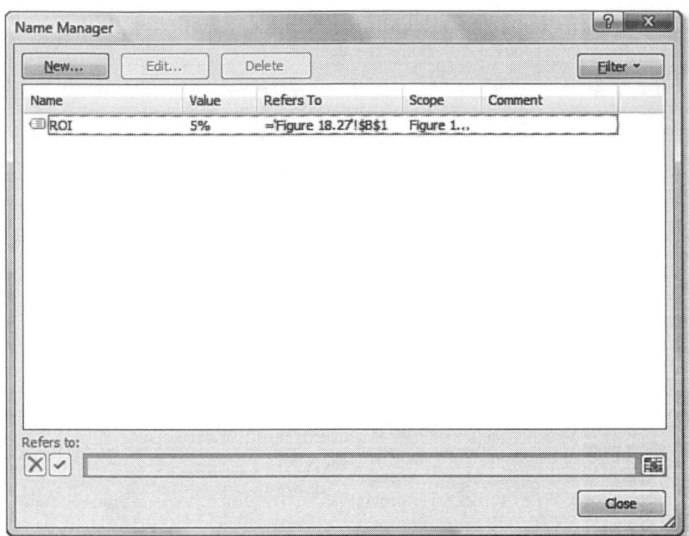

Figure 18.27
Even a simple named range can be a formula assigned to a name.

Using Basic Named Formulas

A named formula allows you to replace a complicated formula with an easy to remember name. In this basic case, the formula does not contain cell references.

For example, suppose you have discovered a fairly complex formula that would be difficult to remember, such as the formula shown in Figure 18.28.

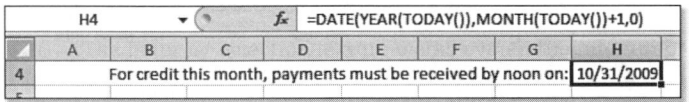

Figure 18.28
You can assign a complicated formula to a simpler name.

In this case, you could assign the formula =Date(Year(Today()),Month(Today())+1,0) to a name such as MonthEnd, as shown in Figure 18.29

You could then use =MonthEnd in any cell to calculate the end of the current month.

Using Dynamic Named Formulas

An interesting example of a named formula is a reference that dynamically expands as more data is filled down a column.

Suppose that you have a list of valid sales reps on a hidden RepList to be used as the list for a data validation drop-down. The list might extend from A1:A9 today, but as new sales reps are hired, the list may expand to A10, A11, A12, and so on.

Figure 18.29
After a formula has been assigned to a name, you can use it as you would a constant.

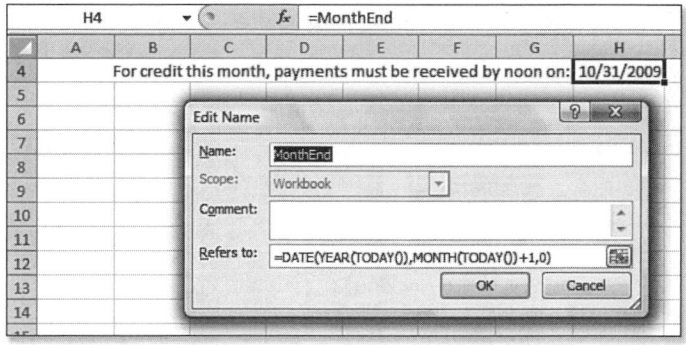

The OFFSET() function has a parameter that specifies that a range should extend for X rows. If you use COUNTA to return the number of rows, you can create a formula to dynamically expand or contract as cells are filled in or deleted. In theory, you would set up a formula to point to this range: =OFFSET(RepList!A1,0,0,COUNTA(RepList!A:A),0). However, absolute references should be used in the definition. In Figure 18.30, for example, the formula assigned to RepList is =OFFSET(Rep List!$A$1,0,0,COUNTA(RepList!$A:$A),1).

Figure 18.30
This formula can expand to include the number of entries in Column A.

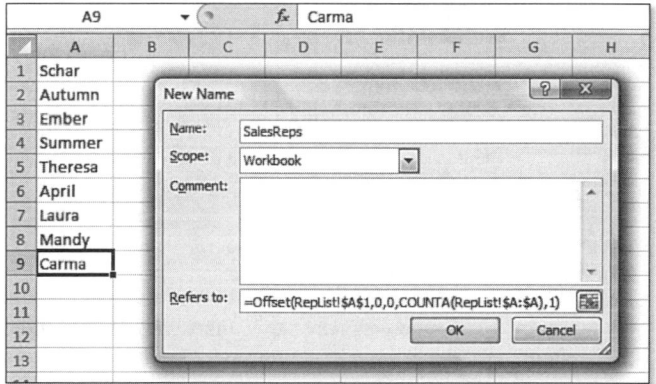

The name automatically expands as new entries are added. To make use of this name in an in-cell drop-down, follow these steps:

1. Select Data, Data Validation.

2. Change the Allow drop-down to List.

3. In the source box, type =SalesReps.

4. Leave the In-cell drop-down box selected.

The completed dialog box is shown in Figure 18.31.

Initially, the cell with validation offers a drop-down that lists the nine current reps, as shown in Figure 18.32.

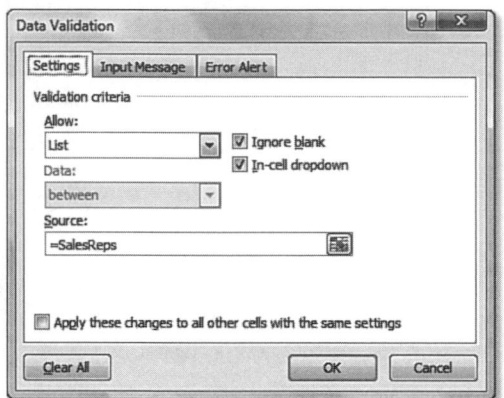

Figure 18.31
You can set up data validation to use a dynamic name.

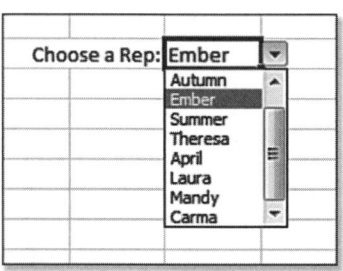

Figure 18.32
The result of adding data validation to a cell.

When the list on RepList is edited, the drop-down is automatically updated. For example, in Figure 18.33, you can see that Jeanette replaced Mandy, and two new reps were added. The window on the left shows the new list on RepList, and the window on the right shows the current drop-down list.

You can use a similar technique to make a chart series expand as new months are added.

➡️ *For details on charting, see Chapter 32, "Using Excel Charts."*

Using a Named Formula to Point to the Cell Above

In the example shown in Figure 18.33, it was important to make sure that all references were absolute. Although it seems strange, it is possible to make use of a relative reference in a named formula. However, this should be done only if you understand one slightly buggy gotcha and two cautions if you use VBA or share the workbook with someone using Excel 97.

Figure 18.33
As the list on RepList changes, the dynamic formula expands to include the new cells in the list.

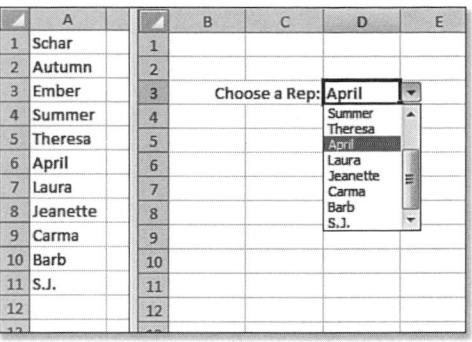

- The gotcha happens in workbooks with multiple worksheets. A relative formula will work fine on the original worksheet, but incorrectly when used on another worksheet. A workaround that starts the reference with an ! solves this problem.

- The first caution is that this method fails if you are using VBA macros and the macro causes the worksheet to calculate.

- The second caution is that this method will crash Excel if the workbook is opened in Excel 97.

In Figure 18.34, the cell pointer is on the Relative worksheet in Cell A3. The name AboveMe is being defined as pointing to Cell A2. However, in the Refers To box, press F4 three times to remove all the dollar signs from the reference.

Figure 18.34
Defining a relative reference in a named formula.

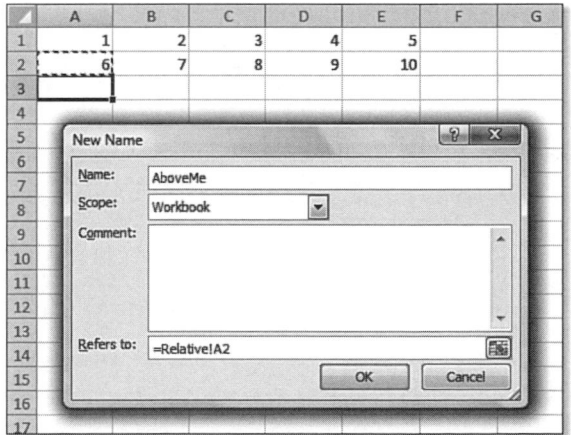

This relative formula initially appears to work perfectly. Cells A3:E3 in Figure 18.35 all contain the formula =AboveMe+2.

	E3			ƒx	=+AboveMe+2	
	A	B	C	D	E	
1	1	2	3	4	5	
2	6	7	8	9	10	
3	8	9	10	11	12	
4						

Figure 18.35
In this example, the relative reference in the named formula is working fine.

However, if you go to Sheet2 and enter the formula =AboveMe+2 in Cells A3:E3, the formula returns the value from Row 2, but from the Relative sheet instead of the current worksheet. Figure 18.36 shows the answer 8 when you would expect 103.

	A3			ƒx	=AboveMe+2	
	A	B	C	D	E	F
1	101	102	103	104	105	
2	101	102	103	104	105	
3	8	9	10	11	12	
4						
5						

Figure 18.36
The relative reference in the named formula fails on another sheet.

The solution is to edit the name. To do so, remove the reference to Sheet1, leaving a definition of =!A2, as shown in Figure 18.37.

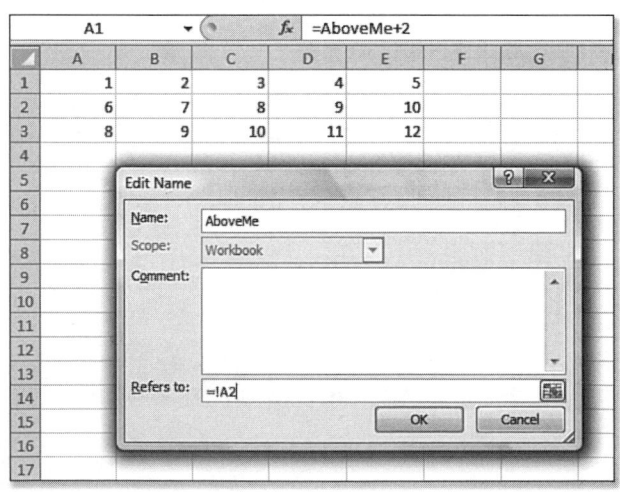

Figure 18.37
Edit the formula to point to =!A2.

Now, when you close the Name Manager dialog, the formulas work as expected, as shown in Figure 18.38.

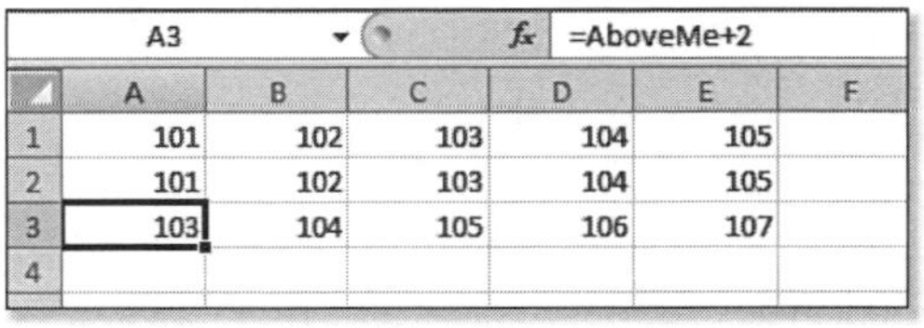

Figure 18.38
The relative reference of =!A2 now works as expected.

	A	B	C	D	E	F
1	101	102	103	104	105	
2	101	102	103	104	105	
3	103	104	105	106	107	
4						

A3   *fx* =AboveMe+2

FABULOUS TABLE INTELLIGENCE

A fundamental use of Excel is for analyzing two-dimensional tables of data. Most worksheets contain headings at the top and then rows of data. Most Excel customers spend a lot of time working with tables of data. Microsoft recognized this and added intelligent tables beginning with Excel 2007. If you explicitly tell Excel 2010 that you are working on a table of data, it displays a custom Table tab that has a number of amazing features.

Excel's intelligent tables enable you to do the following:

- Automatically add AutoFilter drop-downs to the headings in a table.

- Have one-click access to banded rows, banded columns, and other autoformats.

- Toggle a total row on or off.

- Have one-click access to removing duplicates.

- Automatically copy new formulas to all cells in a column.

- Automatically extend a table when new data is typed below or to the right of the table. This feature also affects any charts, formulas, or pivot tables that pointed to the table, causing them to expand as well.

- Extend conditional formatting to new rows in the table.

- Automatically freeze panes to show the heading row as you scroll off the page.

- Automatically set up range names for an entire table and each column within the table.

Tables were introduced in Excel 2007. Minor refinements to the table formula syntax has occurred in Excel 2010 with the @ replacing the ThisRow syntax. Otherwise, Excel 2010 tables are similar to what you encountered in Excel 2007.

If you are upgrading from Excel 2003, the table functionality is dramatically improved from the List functionality introduced in Excel 2003.

Defining Suitable Data for Excel Tables

Many Excel spreadsheets contain data that is suitable for Excel tables. For the purpose of this chapter, a table is a range of Excel data. Each row in the range is one record of data. For example, each row might describe an invoice, a customer, or an inventory item. Each column in the table creates another field for each row. Fields might include invoice number, customer name, and total sales. A table usually includes headings in the first row.

The simple range in Figure 19.1 makes a suitable table because each row in this range is a record, and each column is a field.

	A	B	C	D	E
1					
2	Region	Customer	Revenue	Cost	
3	East	Leading Camera Traders	65073	31235	
4	Central	Magnificent Sandal Company	23345	12840	
5	West	Special Edger Corporation	98274	51102	
6	East	Cool Scooter Company	20619	10310	
7	Central	Hip Calculator Corporation	71626	34380	
8	West	Different Radio Inc.	45541	20949	
9	East	Matchless Clipboard Company	45521	24126	

Figure 19.1
This makes an ideal table in Excel.

Defining a Table

You can define a table in Excel 2010 in four ways:

- Choose a cell in the data set and then select Insert, Tables, Table.

- Select a cell in the data set and then select Home, Styles, Format as Table. Choose a Style and then press OK.

- Select a cell in the data set and press Ctrl+T.

- Select a cell in the data set and press Ctrl+L.

When you use any of these methods, Excel uses IntelliSense to determine the edge of the table. Excel looks for a completely blank row and a completely blank column to define the edges of the table.

Excel shows the suspected table range in the Create Table dialog, as shown in Figure 19.2. You need to verify that this range is correct. If your table has headers, leave the My Table Has Headers check box selected and press OK.

As shown in Figure 19.3, Excel adds a default table format to your range. The headings gain autofilter drop-downs. A Ribbon tab called Table Tools—Design is displayed. Excel assigns a name similar to Table1 to the table.

Figure 19.2
Excel's IntelliSense guesses the extent of the table.

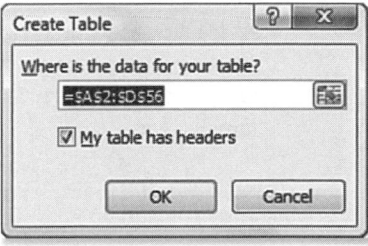

Figure 19.3
The table has an interesting autoformat, but there are many more features.

	A	B	C	D
2	Region ⏷	Customer ⏷	Revenue ⏷	Cost ⏷
3	East	Leading Camera Traders	65073	31235
4	Central	Magnificent Sandal Company	23345	12840
5	West	Special Edger Corporation	98274	51102
6	East	Cool Scooter Company	20619	10310
7	Central	Hip Calculator Corporation	71626	34380

Keeping Headers in View

Notice that in Figure 19.3, the headings appear in Row 2 of the worksheet. As you scroll through the table, you can eventually scroll to the point where Row 2 is no longer visible in the window. At this point, Excel moves the headings from Row 2 and shows them where column names A, B, C, D normally display. Figure 19.4 shows the headings as column names.

Figure 19.4
When you do not use the Freeze Panes command, Excel automatically moves the heading values up to the column names when you scroll the headings off the window.

Headings Replace Column Letters!

	Region ⏷	Customer ⏷	Revenue ⏷	Cost ⏷
8	West	Different Radio Inc.	45541	20949
9	East	Matchless Clipboard Company	45521	24126
10	Central	Top-Notch Kiln Inc.	62009	29144
11	West	Alluring Belt Partners	19846	9725
12	East	Fascinating Edger Inc.	94488	45354
13	Central	Guaranteed Bicycle Supply	40088	18841

These heading names stay as column names as long as each factor listed here is true:

- The cell pointer is inside the range of the table.

- The header row is not visible in the window.

- At least one row of the table is visible in the window. If you leave the cell pointer in the table and then use a scrollbar to scroll the table out of view, the column names revert to column letters.

When any of the preceding conditions is no longer true, the headings disappear from the column name area.

Although Microsoft introduced this feature in Excel 2007, it made one significant improvement in Excel 2010. The Filter drop-downs are now available after the headers move up to become the column labels.

 caution

For several versions, Excel has offered a feature called Custom Views. If any worksheet in your workbook contains a table, then Custom Views will be grayed out for the entire workbook. Since not many people use Custom Views, this is not entirely a bad thing. However, if you use Custom Views, it can be a horrible limitation.

Freezing Worksheet Panes

Excel 2010's automatic heading visibility feature is very cool. With legacy versions of Excel, many did not know there was a way to freeze panes. Whether you knew about that feature, it is a positive feature 90 percent of the time, although it is not perfect.

For example, it is a bit annoying that the headings disappear when you select a cell outside the table. It seems logical that if you can see part of a table in the window, Excel should keep the headings up as part of the column names. In addition, the cell pointer can be a distraction in a data set. For example, if you are showing your manager something on the screen, you might have a tendency to click outside the table so that the manager does not think you are trying to show one particular cell.

Another annoying issue is that the automatic heading visibility feature does not work with labels in the left column. For example, in Figure 19.5, a wide table has labels in Column A. After you select First Column, Excel properly formats Column A. However, if you scroll over to see the month of December, Excel does not make the Column A values stay visible as they normally do with row numbers.

The old-style Freeze Panes command is still available and is even a bit easier to use in Excel 2010.

In legacy versions of Excel, you had to put the cell pointer in the first cell that should not be frozen before invoking the Freeze Panes command. However, beginning with Excel 2007, Microsoft added two commands that allow you to freeze the first row or the first column from anywhere. Here's how you freeze the first row:

1. Make sure the row that you want to stay at the top of the window is the first visible row in the window.

2. From the Window group of the View tab, select Freeze Panes. The drop-down that appears is shown in Figure 19.6.

3. Select Freeze Top Row.

Figure 19.5
The automatic heading visibility feature does not work for the first column.

	A	B	C	
1	Name	Jan	Feb	Mar
2	A	48	19	
3	B	82	82	
4	C	20	14	
5	D	90	56	
6	E	64	70	
7	F	64	39	
8	G	78	18	
9	H	16	28	
10	I	21	26	
11	J	67	75	
12	K	60	22	
13	L	69	53	

You can now scroll anywhere on the worksheet and always see the first row.

It is annoying, but the Freeze First Column resets the Freeze First Row icon, and vice versa. If you need to freeze both the first column and first row, you have to use the Freeze Panes command as described in the following sections.

Figure 19.6
Excel 2010 offers two commands to the Freeze Panes area.

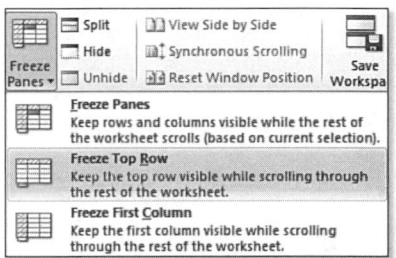

Clearing Freeze Panes

To turn off the Freeze Panes option, select the Freeze Panes icon again in the View tab. Now the first option in the drop-down is to Unfreeze Panes. Select this option to unlock the view, which enables you to scroll anywhere in the window.

Using the Old Version of Freeze Panes for Absolute Control

At times, you might want several rows or columns to remain visible. Just as in legacy versions of Excel, you can do this when you understand how Freeze Panes works.

Consider the worksheet in Figure 19.7. Suppose you always want to see the data in Columns A:D at the left side of the window. Several rows of title information don't necessarily need to be visible at the top of the worksheet as you scroll, but it would be good to see Rows 5 and 6 at the top of the window as you scroll.

	A	B	C	D	E	F	G	H	I
1	**XYZ COMPANY**								
2	**SALES REPORT**								
3	**QUARTER 1, 2011**								
4									
5						Product Line A			Product Line B
6	Country	Region	District	Sales Rep	Sales	Profit	GP%	Sales	Profit
7	USA	East	Northeast	Bauer	9680	4743	49.0%	4132	1694
8	USA	East	Northeast	Walker	6406	2819	44.0%	6544	2748
9	USA	East	Northeast	Strong	4916	2163	44.0%	20694	9105
10	USA	East	Northeast	Mosley	10103	4142	41.0%	14380	5752
11	USA	East	Northeast	Wilkins	22590	10391	46.0%	13835	6918
12	USA	East	Northeast	Walters	3731	1679	45.0%	1420	611

Figure 19.7
This worksheet is too complex for the Freeze Top Row command to work as desired.

You can set up the headings to stay visible by following these steps:

1. Click the arrow at the bottom of the vertical scrollbar four times to make Row 5 the first row visible in the window.

2. Select the first cell that will not be frozen in the window. Everything visible in the window above and to the left of this cell will be frozen. In Figure 19.8, this would be Cell E7. It is critical that you select this cell before moving on to step 3.

E7				f_x	9680

	A	B	C	D	E	F
5						Product Line A
6	Country	Region	District	Sales Rep	Sales	Profit
7	USA	East	Northeast	Bauer	9680	4743
8	USA	East	Northeast	Walker	6406	2819
9	USA	East	Northeast	Strong	4916	2163

Figure 19.8
Select the first cell that will not be frozen.

3. From the Window group of the View tab, select the Freeze Panes drop-down, and then select Freeze Panes again.

The result is that you can scroll down and right. Even when you are at Column V, Row 62, you can still see the headings in Rows 5:6 and the values in Columns A:D, as shown in Figure 19.9.

The key to using the Freeze Panes command is that you must place the cell pointer before using the command. The command freezes everything that was above and to the left of the cell pointer location when the command was invoked.

To freeze only Columns A:B and no rows, you would invoke the command from Row 1 of Column C. However, because there is nothing above the cell pointer, no rows are frozen.

Figure 19.9
After you use the
original Freeze
Panes command,
you can have mul-
tiple rows and col-
umns frozen at the
top and left of the
worksheet.

	A	B	C	D	Q	R	S	T	U	V
5						Product Line E			Total	
6	Country	Region	District	Sales Rep	Sales	Profit	GP%	Sales	Profit	GP%
52	USA	West	Southern CA	Jacobs	12195	6098	50.0%	50096	23583	47.1%
53	USA	West	Southern CA	Christian	15485	6813	44.0%	71579	30468	42.6%
54	USA	West	Southern CA	Robertson	13196	5410	41.0%	83251	36824	44.2%
55	USA	West	Southern CA	Duke	6066	3033	50.0%	66755	31176	46.7%
56	USA	West	Southern CA	Wilkins	6179	3028	49.0%	50730	23575	46.5%
57	USA	West	Southern CA	Harvey	7569	3557	47.0%	28716	13223	46.0%
58	USA	West	Southern CA	Ballard	5361	2412	45.0%	42453	18869	44.4%
59	USA	West	Northern CA	Gamble	7906	3241	41.0%	65368	28317	43.3%
60	USA	West	Northern CA	Jacobson	20216	9299	46.0%	97511	43316	44.4%
61	USA	West	Northern CA	Ortiz	18270	7491	41.0%	89676	39172	43.7%
62	USA	West	Northern CA	Welch	9244	3698	40.0%	45533	19588	43.0%
63										

Adding a Total Row to a Table

There is a Totals Row check box in the Table Styles Options group of the Table Tools Design tab.
When you select this box, Excel automatically adds a total to the bottom of your table.

By default, Excel adds the word Total to the first column of the table and adds a formula to the
right-most column of the table to sum the column.

Figure 19.10 shows the default total row for a table. A drop-down appears when you select a cell in
the total row. To add a sum formula to Column C, select the cell for Column C in the total row. When
a drop-down arrow appears, select Sum from the list.

In Figure 19.10, instead of using the SUM formula, Excel uses the SUBTOTAL function, with a first
argument of 109. The SUBTOTAL function is similar to the SUM function, with two exceptions. First,
the function ignores other SUBTOTAL functions in the range. Second, with a first argument in the
101–109 range, Excel ignores any values that are hidden including rows that are hidden by the autofilter drop-downs.

The total cost in Figure 19.10 is $1.54 million. In Figure 19.11, the Region column is filtered to only
the Central region. Because the SUBTOTAL function ignores hidden rows, the total cost automatically
updates to show $493,756.

Toggling Totals

When you use tables, you can toggle the total row on and off. Use the Total Row check box in the
Table Tools Design tab to turn the totals on or off. In most cases, Excel remembers when you have
customized the totals to provide totals for the last two columns. However, you might find that if you
add new columns to a table, you need to add these totals to the new columns using the drop-down
in the total row.

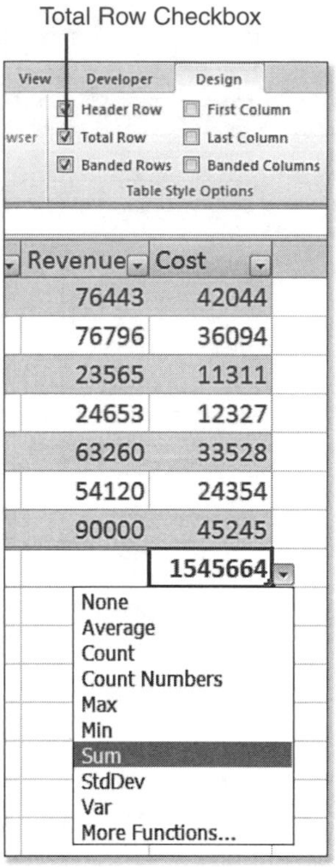

Total Row Checkbox

Figure 19.10
Clicking the Total Row check box in the ribbon adds a default total row. Use the drop-downs to change the function or add totals to other columns.

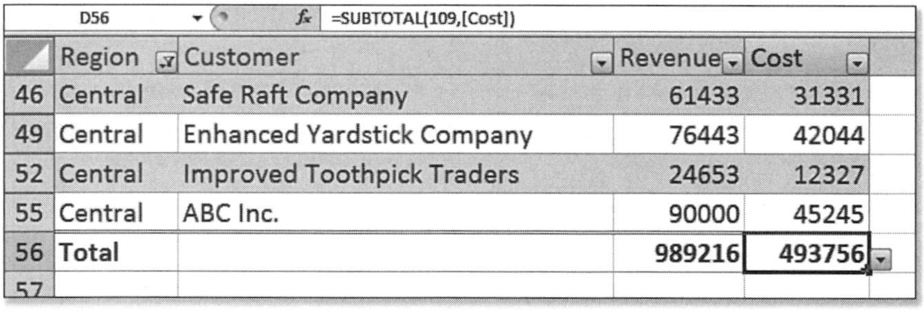

Figure 19.11
Choose a region from the filter drop-down, and the SUBTOTALS function reflects the total of the visible rows.

Expanding a Table

A common feature of tables is that they tend to grow and expand. Every day, you might add new records to a table or paste new records to the bottom of a table, or you might add a new column with a new calculation.

Excel can automatically expand a table, or you can choose to expand a table manually. When you expand a table, any references to the table automatically expand.

Adding Rows to a Table Automatically

The easiest way to add rows to a table is from the last row of the table. If you are in the last column of the last row and press the Tab key, Excel adds a new row to the table and moves the cell pointer to the first column in the new row. This behavior is similar to existing functionality in tables in Microsoft Word.

However, the simplest way to add a new row to a table is to click in the blank row under the table and type new data. As soon as you enter something in a cell just below the table, Excel expands the table formatting to include the new row. Excel also displays an AutoCorrect lightning bolt icon. If you do not want Excel to expand the table automatically, you can use the drop-down next to this icon to undo the table AutoExpansion, as shown in Figure 19.12.

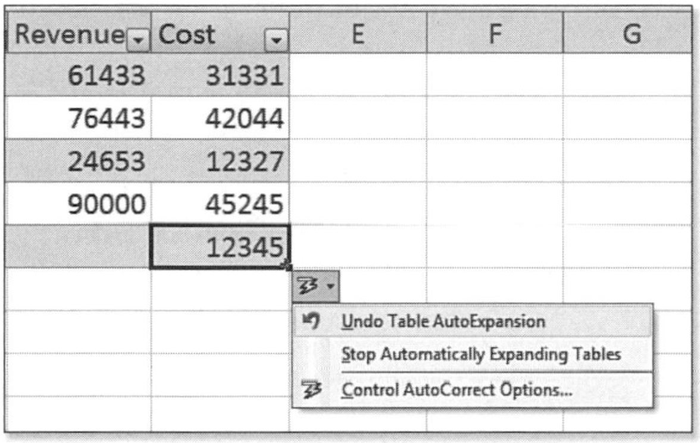

Revenue	Cost	E	F	G
61433	31331			
76443	42044			
24653	12327			
90000	45245			
	12345			

⟲ Undo Table AutoExpansion
Stop Automatically Expanding Tables
ℬ Control AutoCorrect Options...

Figure 19.12
If you type a new value below the table, Excel automatically extends the table to include the new row.

Manually Resizing a Table

The bottom-right cell of a table contains a small angle bracket in the lower-right corner of the cell. You can use this angle bracket to extend the table manually.

When you click the angle bracket, you can either drag down to add more rows or drag right to add more columns to the table.

You can also select Table Tools, Design, Properties, Resize Table. The Resize Table dialog appears, allowing you to specify the new range for the table. However, a few limitations exist; for example, you cannot change the header row during this process.

Adding New Columns to a Table

To add a new column to a table, go to the blank cell to the right of the last header and type a new header for the column. Excel automatically extends the table by another column and copies any table formatting to the new column. The AutoCorrect lightning bolt icon appears. If you do not want the new column to be part of the table, use the drop-down next to the AutoCorrect icon to undo the table AutoExpansion.

Adding New Formulas to Tables

Way back in Excel 97, Microsoft added something called Natural Language Formulas to Excel. Beginning with Excel 2007, those old formulas are officially depreciated. Even so, the newer style table formulas are reminiscent of those formulas.

In Figure 19.13, a new column has been added to the table, with the heading Profit. To add a formula to that column, follow these steps.

1. Select Cell E3.

2. Type an equal sign.

3. Using either the mouse or the arrow keys, select the first revenue cell in C3. Note that the formula is unlike any formula that you have seen before. It starts out with =[@Revenue], as shown in Figure 19.13.

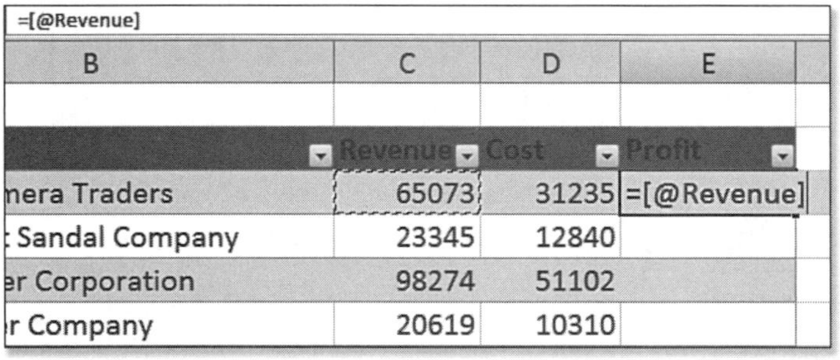

Figure 19.13
When you start entering a formula in a table, Excel uses table nomenclature for the formula references.

4. Type a minus sign.

5. Click Cell D3 for Cost. The formula now reads =[@Revenue]-[@Cost], as shown in Figure 19.14.

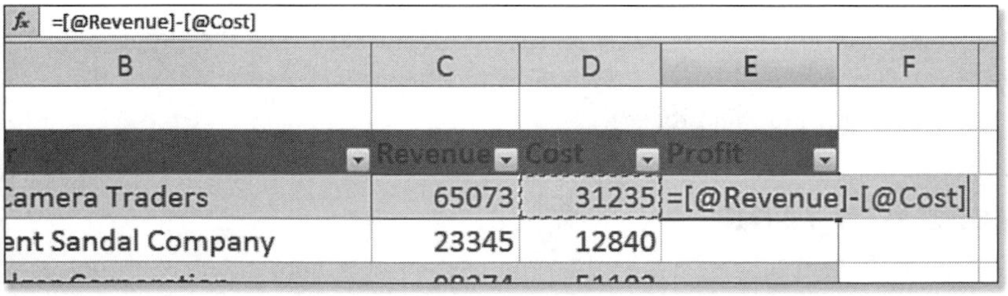

Figure 19.14
Without adding any named ranges, the formula =[@Revenue]-[@Cost] is easier to understand than D3–C3.

6. An amazing thing happens when you press the Enter key to accept the formula: Excel automatically copies the formula to all rows in the table, as shown in Figure 19.15.

In legacy versions of Excel, after adding a formula to a new column, you had to double-click the fill handle to copy the formula down to all rows of the table. This functionality saves you time.

If you do not want to have the formula copied to all rows, you can undo the behavior by selecting the AutoCorrect icon and then choosing the appropriate option.

 To see a demo of adding formulas to a table, search for "Excel In Depth 19" at YouTube.

Figure 19.15
The new formula is copied to all rows of the table automatically.

Profit	
235	33838
340	10505
102	47172
310	10309
380	37246
949	24592
126	21395
144	32865

↩ Undo Calculated Column
■ Stop Automatically Creating Calculated Columns
Control AutoCorrect Options...

Stopping the Automatic Copying of Formulas

At some point, you might have a column in a table and not want Excel to use the same formula everywhere in that column. Excel 2010 calls this a *calculated column exception*. Because any formula that you enter in the column is copied automatically to the entire column, you need to use special care to set up a calculated column exception.

> **tip**
> When you set up a single-cell column exception, Excel stops automatically copying formulas in that column.

Suppose that you already have a formula in a column and want to change to a different formula in just one cell. In this case, follow these steps:

1. Enter the different formula in the one cell. Excel automatically copies the formula to the entire column.

2. Immediately click the Undo button in the Quick Access toolbar.

Excel marks this cell with a green triangle. If you hover your mouse over the green triangle, Excel tells you, "This cell is inconsistent with the column formula."

There are other ways to set up a first column exception:

- Type data other than a formula in a calculated column cell.

- Delete a single formula from one or more cells in the calculated column.

- Move or delete a cell on another worksheet area that is referenced by one of the rows in the calculated column. This changes the formula in that one cell, creating a column exception. Excel then stops copying the calculation in that column.

Formatting the Results of a New Formula

The automatic copying of formulas includes one minor annoyance. In legacy versions of Excel, you would add a new column by following these steps:

1. Type the heading.

2. Type the first formula.

3. Format the first formula.

4. Double-click the fill handle to copy the formula.

Now that Excel is essentially performing the last step for you, there is no chance to format the first cell before it is copied. In Figure 19.16, the calculation for gross profit percentage was copied before the cell could be formatted as a percentage.

This requires a small change in your usual process. You can try formatting Cell F3 before entering the formula. However, this is a bit tricky since you do not have a number in that cell to use to check that you clicked Increase Decimal the proper number of times. Since it is common for people to confuse the Increase Decimal and Decrease Decimal icons, hover over the icon to see the tool tip before clicking the icon three times.

Profit	▼	GP%	▼	
	33838	0.520001		
	10505	0.449989	☞	
	47172	0.480005		
	10309	0.499976		
	37246	0.520007		
	24592	0.539997		
	21205	0.470003		

Figure 19.16
Excel copies a formula to all rows before you have a chance to format the new column.

Selecting Only the Data in the Column

You can use several new options when selecting data in a table. If you are going to format a table, you probably just want to format the numbers in the table and not the headings. Excel includes distinct methods for selecting the data portion of a column or selecting the entire table column with headings and totals.

Selecting by Right-Clicking

One way to select the data in a column is to right-click a cell in the table. From the context menu, choose the Select option. The flyout menu offers three choices, as shown in Figure 19.17:

- **Table Column Data**—Choose this option to select just the data rows of that column. This skips the heading row and the total row.

- **Entire Table Column**—Choose this option to include the heading for the column and the cell in the total row.

- **Table Row**—Choose this option to select an entire row of a table.

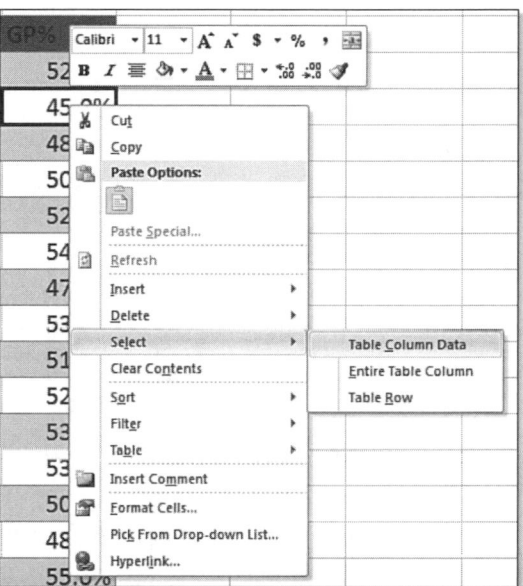

Figure 19.17
Right-click to select the data in the column.

Selecting by Using Shortcuts

You can also use the tried and true Excel shortcuts to select rows or columns. Keep in mind that these shortcut keys are modified when you are in a table:

- Press Shift+spacebar once to select an entire row in a table.

- Press Shift+spacebar a second time to select the entire worksheet row.

- Press Ctrl+spacebar once to select the table data in the current column of the table. This excludes the total row and the heading row. Figure 19.18 shows the selection after pressing Ctrl+spacebar once from Cell C6.

Figure 19.18
Press Ctrl+spacebar once to select the data portion of the current column.

Press Ctrl+spacebar again to expand the selection to include the heading and total cell for that column, as shown in Figure 19.19.

Press Ctrl+spacebar a third time to select the entire worksheet column.

Figure 19.19
Press Ctrl+spacebar a second time to expand the selection to include the heading and total cells.

Selecting by Using the Arrow Mouse Pointers

Beginning with Excel 2007, an arrow mouse pointer was added that could be used to select table rows and table columns. However, it is a bit tricky to use this mouse pointer. The following figures provide some examples for using the mouse pointer effectively:

- In Figure 19.20, the mouse is hovering over the box containing the Column A column letter. Make sure the mouse pointer does not extend below the bottom edge of the Column A heading box. You are in the correct place when the background behind the letter A turns a dark gray. With your mouse in this position, click to select all of Column A. You can click here any number of times to select the entire column.

- In Figure 19.21, the mouse is moved down slightly so that it is partially above Cell A1, which is the first row of the table. The first click here selects A2:A8. The second click here selects A1:A9. Alternating clicks toggle between A2:A8 (the table data without headers and totals) and A1:A9 (the complete table column).

Figure 19.20
The traditional select column mouse pointer causes the column letter to be highlighted.

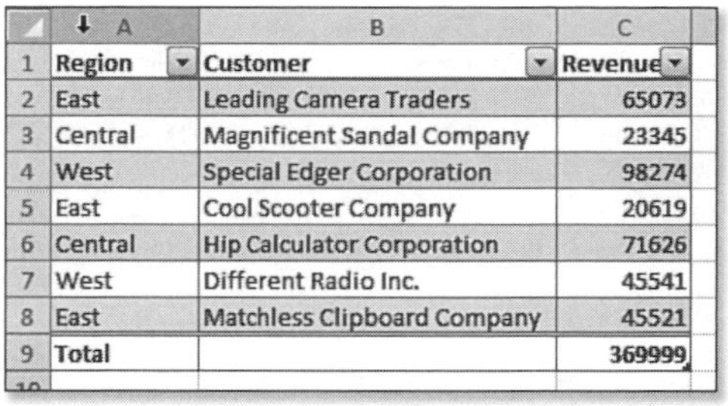

	A	B	C
1	Region ▾	Customer ▾	Revenue ▾
2	East	Leading Camera Traders	65073
3	Central	Magnificent Sandal Company	23345
4	West	Special Edger Corporation	98274
5	East	Cool Scooter Company	20619
6	Central	Hip Calculator Corporation	71626
7	West	Different Radio Inc.	45541
8	East	Matchless Clipboard Company	45521
9	Total		369999

Figure 19.21
Move just a bit into the table header and the new (but identically appearing) mouse pointer takes over.

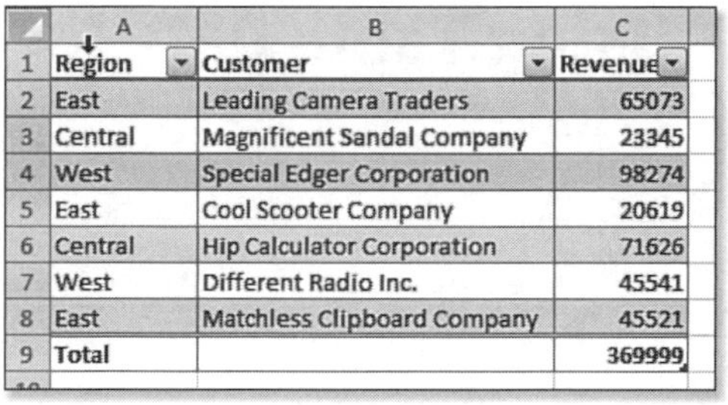

	A	B	C
1	Region ▾	Customer ▾	Revenue ▾
2	East	Leading Camera Traders	65073
3	Central	Magnificent Sandal Company	23345
4	West	Special Edger Corporation	98274
5	East	Cool Scooter Company	20619
6	Central	Hip Calculator Corporation	71626
7	West	Different Radio Inc.	45541
8	East	Matchless Clipboard Company	45521
9	Total		369999

- In Figure 19.22, the mouse is hovering over the top-left corner of Cell A1. The first click here selects A2:C8 (the table without headings and totals). The next click selects A1:A9 (the entire table). Additional clicks toggle between these two selections.

Figure 19.22
Move to the corner of the table to get the table selection mouse pointer.

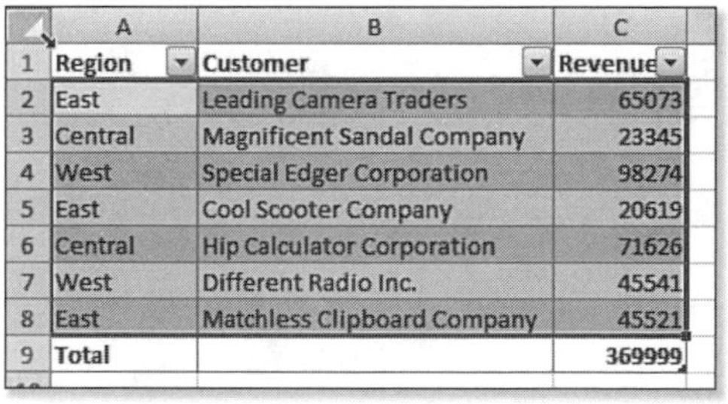

	A	B	C
1	Region ▾	Customer ▾	Revenue ▾
2	East	Leading Camera Traders	65073
3	Central	Magnificent Sandal Company	23345
4	West	Special Edger Corporation	98274
5	East	Cool Scooter Company	20619
6	Central	Hip Calculator Corporation	71626
7	West	Different Radio Inc.	45541
8	East	Matchless Clipboard Company	45521
9	Total		369999

- In Figure 19.23, the mouse is hovering near the left edge of Cell A2. Clicking here any number of times selects the entire table row (Cells A2:C2).

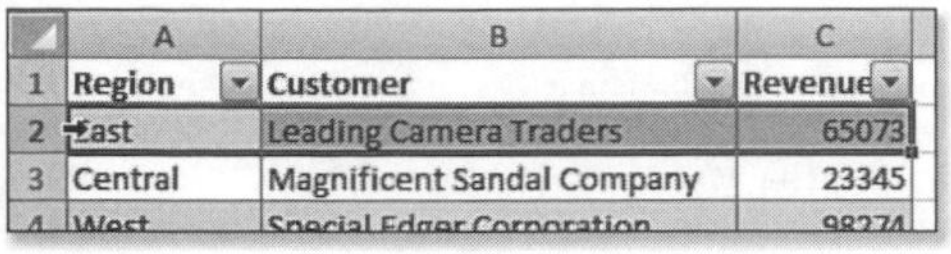

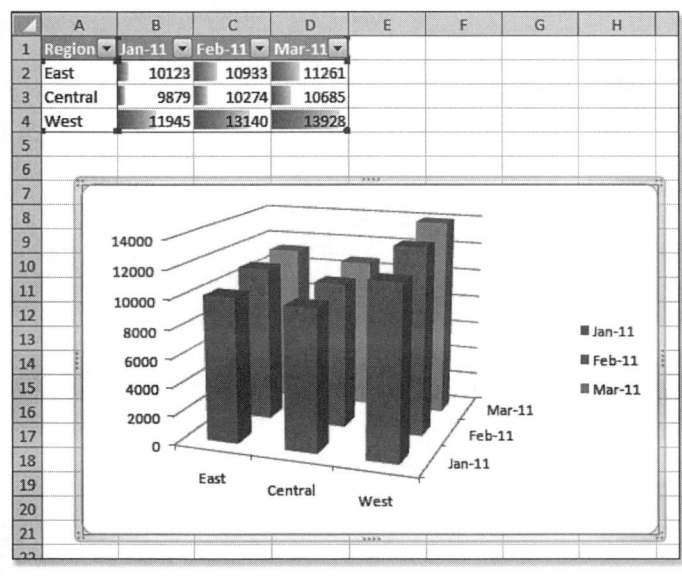

Figure 19.23
At the left edge of a table row, the table row selection pointer appears.

If you are a heavy-duty user of Excel, you will likely use these new table selection methods. The new conditional formatting options such as data bars and color scales require you to select the data in a column without the total row. Mastering the various selection methods will greatly enhance your ability to work with the new formatting.

Using Table Data for Charts to Ensure Stickiness

When you define a range as a table and expand the table, any references to the table also expand. If you routinely re-create new charts every month when you receive new data, you will love this feature.

Before creating a chart, make a table out of the underlying data. For example, in Figure 19.24, the chart is based on the table in A1:D4. Currently, the chart has 3 months' worth of data.

Figure 19.24
This chart is based on the table in A1:D4.

If you type a heading for the new month in Cell E1, immediately the chart redraws to include data for April. After you fill in the data for the new month, you will not have to ever re-create a chart. Instead, the new data is added to the chart, preserving the old formatting, as shown in Figure 19.25.

Figure 19.25
Add new data to the table and the chart automatically expands.

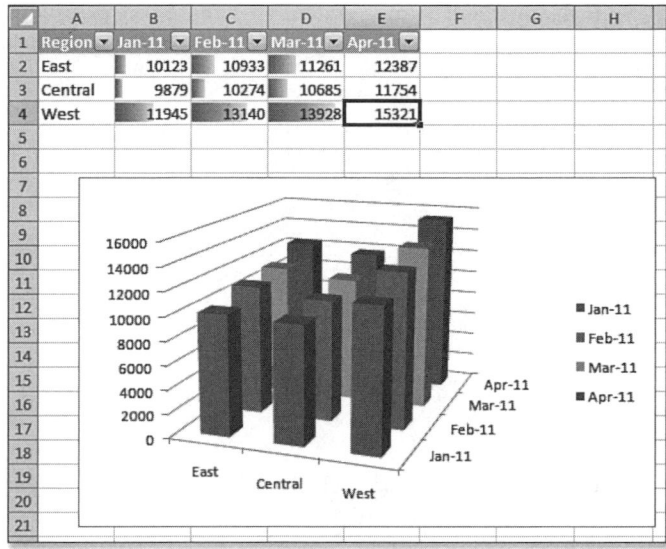

Replacing Named Ranges with Table References

A benefit of using tables is that Excel understands a new reference style for formulas that point to data in a table. A new name is created automatically when a table is defined. The name includes the name of the table, such as `Table1`, and the name of the column.

The biggest benefit of this referencing style is that the ranges that the names refer to are expanded automatically when the table expands. This referencing style eliminates many chances for errors that exist when using named ranges.

Referencing an Entire Table from Outside the Table

When a table is defined, it becomes easier to reference the table from outside the table. Figure 19.26 shows a sales rep look up table. Because this is the first table in the workbook, Excel has assigned the name `Table1` to this table.

Figure 19.27 shows an invoice register located on another sheet in the workbook. Like many main-frame reports, this one includes the sales rep number, without the name and region information. To add a VLOOKUP function to Figure 19.27 that references Table1, follow these steps:

1. Start to type a VLOOKUP formula in Column D. When you get to the second argument, type the letter T, and the AutoComplete list scrolls down to the T entries. Among the function names is an entry for `Table1`, as shown in Figure 19.27.

2. Select Table1 from the list and press Tab.

3. Finish the formula so that it is =VLOOKUP($B2,Table1,COLUMN(B2),False).

Table Name

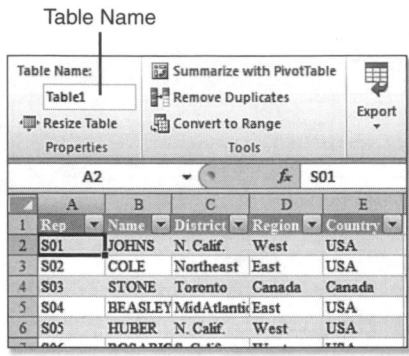

Figure 19.27
Even though there are no defined names in the workbook, Excel understands the Table1 nomenclature.

4. Copy the formula to the rest of the range. Like chart references, table references are sticky. In Figure 19.28, there are a couple records for a new sales rep, S26, who is not yet in the original table.

5. Go back to the original table and add a new row with S26 data. Notice that all the formulas that reference Table1 automatically recalculate to include the new rows.

Referencing Table Columns from Outside a Table

To reference an entire column from outside a table, use the syntax TableName[ColumnName]. When you do this, Excel's AutoComplete feature provides a list of column names. After you type **Table2[**, the AutoComplete list shows all the columns in the table, plus additional keywords. See the following section, "Using Structured References to Refer to Tables in Formulas" for more information about keywords. The AutoComplete list is shown in Figure 19.29.

Figure 19.28
When you add the missing reps to Table1, the references to Table1 also expand.

▲	A	B	C	D	E	F
1	Invoice	Rep	Amount	Name	District	Region
2	1010	S17	147	FORBES	Detroit	Central
3	1011	S14	128	BROCK	MidAtlan	East
4	1012	S22	158	STEVENS	S. Calif.	West
5	1013	S15	172	BARRY	Southeast	East
6	1014	S22	144	STEVENS	S. Calif.	West
7	1015	S12	148	WEBER	Quebec	Canada
8	1016	S10	152	BARR	Southeast	East
9	1017	S13	163	GREEN	Chicago	Central
10	1018	S13	145	GREEN	Chicago	Central
11	1019	S23	173	CRUZ	Northeast	East
12	1020	S26	138	#N/A	#N/A	#N/A
13	1021	S19	138	MASON	N. Calif.	West
14	1022	S26	138	#N/A	#N/A	#N/A

#N/A Errors

Figure 19.29
Excel offers AutoComplete entries from which you can choose the column name when entering a formula.

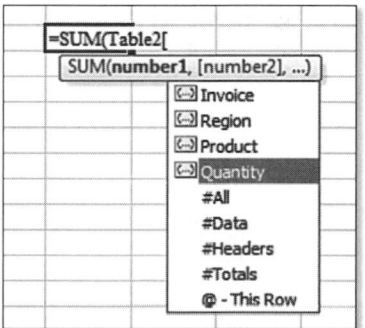

References to a table column do not include the header or total row. Although this behavior is usually desired, there might be instances when you use an INDEX or OFFSET function that you expect Excel to include the heading as Row 1 in the function.

The formula in Figure 19.30 uses three references to a table to find the sales for a particular product and a particular region. The nomenclature Quantity, Product, and Region is easier to understand than cell addresses such as D2:D87. This is the complete formula in Cell G3:

```
=SUMIFS(Table2[Quantity],Table2[Product],$F3,Table2[Region],G$2)
```

Table references are valid on any worksheet in the workbook. If you want to refer to a table that is seven worksheets away, you can still use the Table2 nomenclature, without prefixing the worksheet name.

					=SUMIFS(Table2[Quantity],Table2[Product],$F3,Table2[Region],G$2)						
B	**C**	**D**	**E**	**F**	**G**	**H**	**I**	**J**	**K**	**L**	**M**
Region	Product	Quantity									
Americas	M465	50		Product	Americas	EMEA	Asia				
Asia	H952	30		M465	=SUMIFS(Table2[Quantity],Table2[Product],$F3,Table2[Region],G$2)						
Americas	S864	10		H952	570	500	450				
Americas	H803	30		S864	410	500	450				
Asia	H952	20		H803	480	380	460				
EMEA	S864	50		U300	340	340	610				
EMEA	H803	50									

Figure 19.30
This formula is a fairly complex conditional sum that relies on three columns from the table.

Using Structured References to Refer to Tables in Formulas

Microsoft has created a fairly comprehensive way to refer to various parts of tables. You have seen some of the table nomenclature syntax in the previous two sections. The following are complete details for writing formulas that refer to tables:

- The reference to a table starts with the table name. If you are creating the formula within the table itself, you can omit the table name.

- If no further qualifiers are entered, the table name refers to the data rows of the table. This excludes the headings and total rows.

- Further qualifiers should be enclosed in square brackets. If you are using one qualifier, only one set of square brackets is needed. You may specify `TableName[Qualifier]` or `TableName[[Qualifier]]`.

- If you are specifying multiple qualifiers, each qualifier must be surrounded by square brackets. The qualifiers must be separated by commas. The complete set of qualifiers must be surrounded by square brackets. The syntax follows this pattern: TableName[[Qualifier1],[Qualifier2], [Qualifier3]].

- For a table with a header row, each column heading is automatically added to the list of qualifiers.

- For a table without a header row, the list of qualifiers includes `Column1`, `Column2`, and so on.

- Every table also has these qualifiers: `#All`, `#Data`, `#Headers`, `#Totals`, and `@` which means `This Row`.

- The @ qualifier must be used in conjunction with another qualifier.

 note

In Excel 2007, the @ qualifier was actually spelled out as #ThisRow. Formulas originally created in Excel 2007 as =Table1[[#ThisRow], [Revenue]] will appear in Excel 2010 as =Table1[@Revenue].

This system allows you to select a variety of references without having to use cell references. To get the total of sales from `Table1`, you can either use `=SUM(Table1[Sales])` or `=Table1[[#Total],[Sales]]`. The second syntax returns a `#REF!` error if someone turns off the Totals Row check box in the Table Tools Design tab.

Figure 19.31 shows various structured references.

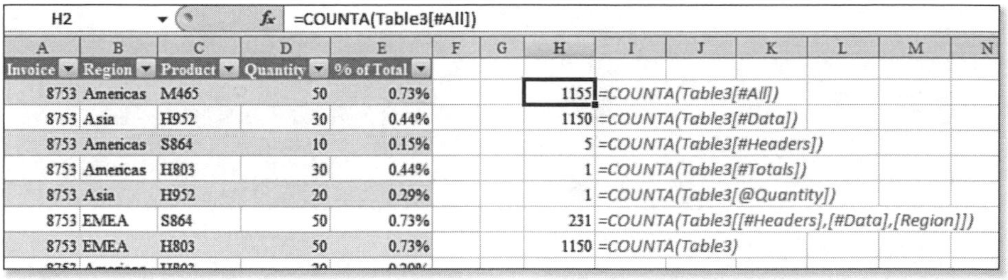

Figure 19.31
Structured references are shown in Column I.

	A	B	C	D	E	F	G	H	I	J	K	L	M	N
	Invoice	Region	Product	Quantity	% of Total									
	8753	Americas	M465	50	0.73%			1155	=COUNTA(Table3[#All])					
	8753	Asia	H952	30	0.44%			1150	=COUNTA(Table3[#Data])					
	8753	Americas	S864	10	0.15%			5	=COUNTA(Table3[#Headers])					
	8753	Americas	H803	30	0.44%			1	=COUNTA(Table3[#Totals])					
	8753	Asia	H952	20	0.29%			1	=COUNTA(Table3[@Quantity])					
	8753	EMEA	S864	50	0.73%			231	=COUNTA(Table3[[#Headers],[#Data],[Region]])					
	8753	EMEA	H803	50	0.73%			1150	=COUNTA(Table3)					
	8753	Americas	H803	30	0.20%									

H2 fx =COUNTA(Table3[#All])

Creating Banded Rows and Columns with Table Styles

In legacy versions of Excel, creating banded rows or columns required creative conditional formatting or tedious manual work. However, creating banded rows or columns in a table is relatively straightforward in Excel 2010.

The fourth group on the Table Tools Design tab is Table Style Options. This group includes check boxes for Banded Rows and Banded Columns. These check boxes work only if the selected table style includes rules for banded columns and/or banded rows. If you have selected the plain white table style, turning on or off banded rows and columns will have no effect.

Figure 19.32 shows five tables. The first table contains banded rows. The second table has banded columns. The third table leaves banded rows and columns off, but the first column, last column, header row, and total row are checked. The top table in Column H contains both banded rows and banded columns. The last table contains a custom format to change the banding from one stripe to two stripes. The next section provides details on how to customize the table style.

Customizing a Table Style: Creating Double-Height Banded Rows

At the bottom of the Table Styles gallery is a New Table Style button. It is recommended that you not use this button! It can be rather intimidating to set up a completely new style. It is often easier to start with an existing style and modify it. To do this, right-click a style and select Duplicate, as shown in Figure 19.33.

After you select Duplicate, Excel displays the Modify Table Quick Style dialog box. Excel assigns a new name to the style, adding a 2 to the existing style name. You can rename the style if you like.

To create double-height banded rows, follow these steps:

1. Select First Row Stripe from the Table Element list. A Stripe Size drop-down appears.

2. Select 2 from the Stripe Size drop-down.

3. Select Second Row Stripe from the Table Element list. A Stripe Size drop-down appears.

4. Select 2 from the Stripe Size drop-down (see Figure 19.34).

	A	B	C	D	E	F	G	H	I	J	K	L	M
1	Name	Q1	Q2	Q3	Q4	Total		Name	Q1	Q2	Q3	Q4	Total
2	Andy	629K	3,188K	2,925K	1,534K	8,275K		Andy	629K	3,188K	2,925K	1,534K	8,275K
3	Charley	2,644K	2,067K	779K	651K	6,141K		Charley	2,644K	2,067K	779K	651K	6,141K
4	Danielle	3,120K	923K	1,773K	2,058K	7,874K		Danielle	3,120K	923K	1,773K	2,058K	7,874K
5	Francine	2,020K	676K	613K	486K	3,794K		Francine	2,020K	676K	613K	486K	3,794K
6	Helen	3,070K	3,491K	353K	3,140K	10,054K		Helen	3,070K	3,491K	353K	3,140K	10,054K
7	Isabel	698K	922K	1,253K	731K	3,604K		Isabel	698K	922K	1,253K	731K	3,604K
8	Total	12,181K	11,266K	7,696K	8,600K	39,743K		Total	12,181K	11,266K	7,696K	8,600K	39,743K
9													
10	Name	Q1	Q2	Q3	Q4	Total							
11	Andy	629K	3,188K	2,925K	1,534K	8,275K		Name	Q1	Q2	Q3	Q4	Total
12	Charley	2,644K	2,067K	779K	651K	6,141K		Andy	629K	3,188K	2,925K	1,534K	8,275K
13	Danielle	3,120K	923K	1,773K	2,058K	7,874K		Charley	2,644K	2,067K	779K	651K	6,141K
14	Francine	2,020K	676K	613K	486K	3,794K		Danielle	3,120K	923K	1,773K	2,058K	7,874K
15	Helen	3,070K	3,491K	353K	3,140K	10,054K		Francine	2,020K	676K	613K	486K	3,794K
16	Isabel	698K	922K	1,253K	731K	3,604K		Helen	3,070K	3,491K	353K	3,140K	10,054K
17	Total	12,181K	11,266K	7,696K	8,600K	39,743K		Isabel	698K	922K	1,253K	731K	3,604K
18								Julio	6,542K	5,421K	542K	125K	12,631K
19								Karen	452K	785K	672K	436K	2,345K
20	Name	Q1	Q2	Q3	Q4	Total		Larry	1,237K	945K	1,099K	888K	4,168K
21	Andy	629K	3,188K	2,925K	1,534K	8,275K		Total	20,412K	18,418K	10,008K	10,048K	58,886K
22	Charley	2,644K	2,067K	779K	651K	6,141K							
23	Danielle	3,120K	923K	1,773K	2,058K	7,874K							
24	Francine	2,020K	676K	613K	486K	3,794K							
25	Helen	3,070K	3,491K	353K	3,140K	10,054K							
26	Isabel	698K	922K	1,253K	731K	3,604K							
27	Total	12,181K	11,266K	7,696K	8,600K	39,743K							

Figure 19.32
These tables exhibit various combinations of the table style options. The fifth table requires a customization of the table style.

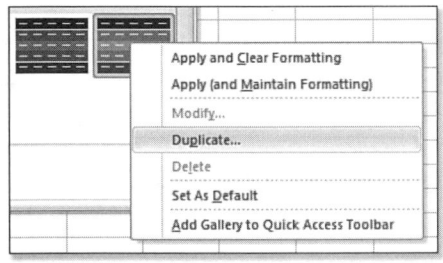

Figure 19.33
Instead of using New Table Quick Style, you can duplicate an existing style.

5. If you would like the modified theme to be the default style for all new tables created in this document, select the Set as Default Table Quick Style for This Document check box in the lower-left corner of the dialog.

6. Click OK, and your custom style is saved to a new Custom section at the top of the Table Styles drop-down.

Figure 19.34
For double-height row banding, change the stripe size.

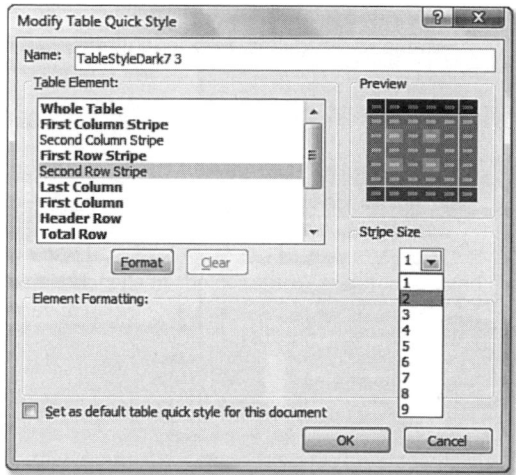

Creating Banded Rows Outside a Table

You might find some of the table behavior annoying. For example, you might want banded columns, but you do not want to use a full-fledged table. In this case, you can temporarily create a table, apply a banded row format to the table, and then convert it back to a range to have a banded row format on the range. Here's how you do it:

1. Select a cell in the range to be formatted.

2. Press Ctrl+T to make the range a table.

3. If your default table style does not include banded rows, choose a new table style from the Table Styles gallery on the Table Tools Design tab.

4. In the Table Tools Design tab, select Tools, Convert to Range. This removes the table properties but keeps the table formatting.

Dealing with the AutoFilter Drop-Downs

A common spreadsheet style rule says that you should right-align the headings above numeric columns. If you regularly follow this convention, you will certainly be annoyed with the default choice that all tables are automatically created with the autofilter drop-downs applied.

In Figure 19.35, the first range contains data with the Q1 headings in the first row. If you apply a table to a range, the autofilter drop-downs completely cover the headings, making the table useless, as shown in Rows 9:15.

One option, shown in Row 17, is to begin centering your headings instead of right justifying them.

The final option, shown in Row 25, is to keep the table, but turn off the autofilter for the table. Unfortunately, this option does not appear on the Table Tools Design tab. Instead, you need to go to Home, Editing, Sort & Filter, Filter to toggle away the drop-downs.

To learn more tricks available for tables, see Chapter 21, "Removing Duplicates and Filtering," and Chapter 20, "Sorting Data."

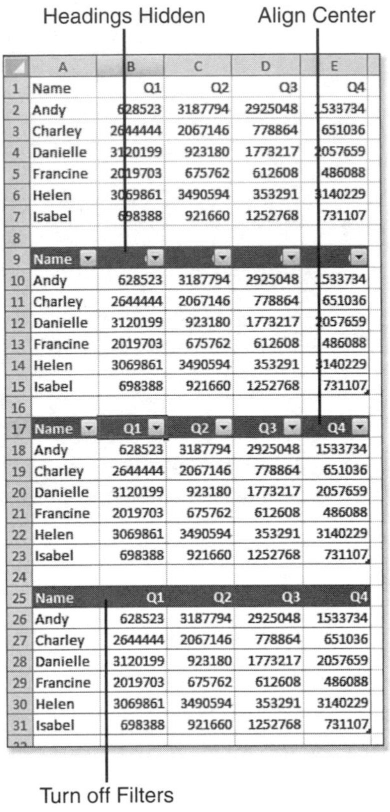

Headings Hidden   Align Center

	A	B	C	D	E
1	Name	Q1	Q2	Q3	Q4
2	Andy	628523	3187794	2925048	1533734
3	Charley	2644444	2067146	778864	651036
4	Danielle	3120199	923180	1773217	2057659
5	Francine	2019703	675762	612608	486088
6	Helen	3069861	3490594	353291	3140229
7	Isabel	698388	921660	1252768	731107
8					
9	Name				
10	Andy	628523	3187794	2925048	1533734
11	Charley	2644444	2067146	778864	651036
12	Danielle	3120199	923180	1773217	2057659
13	Francine	2019703	675762	612608	486088
14	Helen	3069861	3490594	353291	3140229
15	Isabel	698388	921660	1252768	731107
16					
17	Name	Q1	Q2	Q3	Q4
18	Andy	628523	3187794	2925048	1533734
19	Charley	2644444	2067146	778864	651036
20	Danielle	3120199	923180	1773217	2057659
21	Francine	2019703	675762	612608	486088
22	Helen	3069861	3490594	353291	3140229
23	Isabel	698388	921660	1252768	731107
24					
25	Name	Q1	Q2	Q3	Q4
26	Andy	628523	3187794	2925048	1533734
27	Charley	2644444	2067146	778864	651036
28	Danielle	3120199	923180	1773217	2057659
29	Francine	2019703	675762	612608	486088
30	Helen	3069861	3490594	353291	3140229
31	Isabel	698388	921660	1252768	731107

Turn off Filters

Figure 19.35
The headings in Row 1 become unusable when the range is converted to a table.

SORTING DATA

Sorting data is one of the key capabilities of a spreadsheet program such as Excel. With a click of the mouse, you can rearrange data so that it is presented in an alphabetical sequence or in a sequence with the largest numbers at the top or bottom of a list of data.

One of the considerations when sorting is what happens when there are ties in the column on which the sort is based. If you have a database of product sales and sort the data by the product field, it is likely you will have many rows with identical products. In that case, you can specify a secondary sort criteria. You might want to have Excel sort the records so that the sales date is to be used to sequence records when there is a tie in the product field. In this case, you might say you want to sort by sales date within product. Excel simplifies this task.

In legacy versions of Excel, only three key fields could be handled in a sort. You could specify that you wanted to sort by date within product within region. However, in a large company it is likely you would sell the same product on the same date in the same region. With only three sort levels, ties would still occur in the data.

With the powerful sorting capabilities in Excel 2010, you are not limited to three sorting levels. Options are available to do case-sensitive sorting. In addition, you can sort data by color. This sounds like a silly feature, but it is handy for finding all the cells marked in red or to bring together the results of conditional formatting. Methods used in legacy versions of Excel to sort by a custom list and sort from left to right are still available in Excel 2010, and now they are a bit more accessible.

Introducing the Sort Dialog

Sorting in Excel 2010 is handled with the Sort dialog or using the AZ or ZA buttons on the Data tab. In all, there are five entry points for sorting:

1. Select the Home tab and then select Editing, Sort & Filter, Sort.

2. Right-click any cell and choose Sort.

3. Select Sort from any autofilter drop-down.

4. Select the Data tab and then select Sort & Filter, AZ or Sort & Filter, ZA.

5. Open the Sort dialog box by selecting Sort & Filter, Sort on the Data tab.

The Sort dialog in Excel 2010 offers up to 64 different sorting levels. If you get into sorting by color, you often have to specify several rules for one column, so the theoretical number of columns you can sort by is probably fewer than 64. However, compared to the limit of three sort levels in legacy versions, this is a fantastic improvement.

For example, to sort a data set by the values in four columns, follow these steps:

1. Ensure that each column has a one-row heading above the data.

2. Select a cell within the data.

3. Select the Home tab and then select Editing, Sort & Filter, Custom Sort. Alternatively, you can select the Data tab and then select Sort & Filter, Sort. The Sort dialog appears.

4. If your data is not in a defined table, make sure that the My Data Has Headers check box is selected.

5. In the Sort By drop-down, select the Major Sort field. If you want to sort by region and then customer with region, for example, select the Region field as the First Sort field.

6. To sort by values, leave the Sort On drop-down set to Values.

7. In the Order drop-down, choose either A to Z or Z to A. If your column contains dates, this drop-down offers Oldest to Newest and Newest to Oldest. If your column contains mostly numbers, this drop-down offers Smallest to Largest and Largest to Smallest.

8. Click the Add Level button.

9. Repeat steps 5 through 8 for each additional sort field.

10. Review your sort choices, which should look similar to the ones shown in Figure 20.1. If you see that one of the fields was added in the wrong order, you can select that field and use the up-arrow or down-arrow button at the top of the Sort dialog to reorder the fields in the sort.

11. When you are ready to perform the sort, click OK.

If you have multiple records with identical values in all four fields, the sort retains the previous sequence for the tied records. If you ever have to sort by more than 64 columns, this feature allows you to sort by the minor columns first and then by the major columns.

Figure 20.1
Performing a four-field sort based on values.

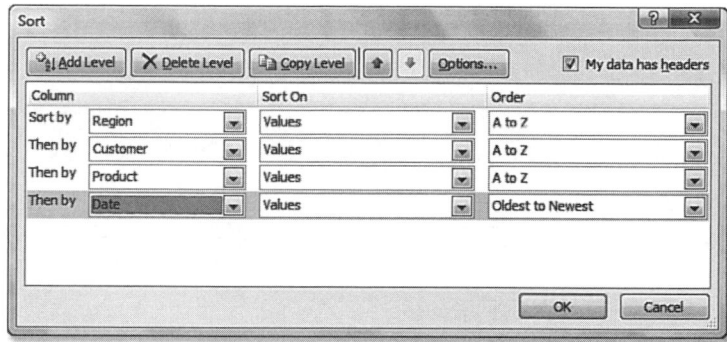

Using Specialized Sorting

Although the process shown in Figure 20.1 is the typical use for sorting, specialized options also are available.

In certain cases, you might want to sort by color, case, a custom sequence, or even data in a left-to-right fashion.

Excel 2010 offers methods to solve all these needs.

Sorting by Color or Icon

Excel can sort data by fill color, font color, or icon sets. This also works with color applied through conditional formatting or color that you applied by using the cell format icons.

Because color is subjective, there is not a default color sequence. If one column contains 17 colors, you need to set up 17 rules in the Sort dialog just to sort by that one column.

To sort by color, follow these steps:

1. Select a cell within your data.

2. Select the Home tab and then select Editing, Sort & Filter, Custom Sort. Alternatively, you can select the Data tab and then select Sort & Filter, Sort. The Sort dialog appears.

3. Select the desired field from the Sort By drop-down.

4. Change the Sort On drop-down to Cell Color.

5. In the Order drop-down, choose the color that should appear first.

6. In the final drop-down, select On Top.

7. To specify the next color, click the Copy Level button at the top of the Sort dialog.

8. Choose the next color in the Order drop-down for the copied rule.

9. Repeat steps 7 and 8 for each additional color. The Sort dialog should look as shown in Figure 20.2.

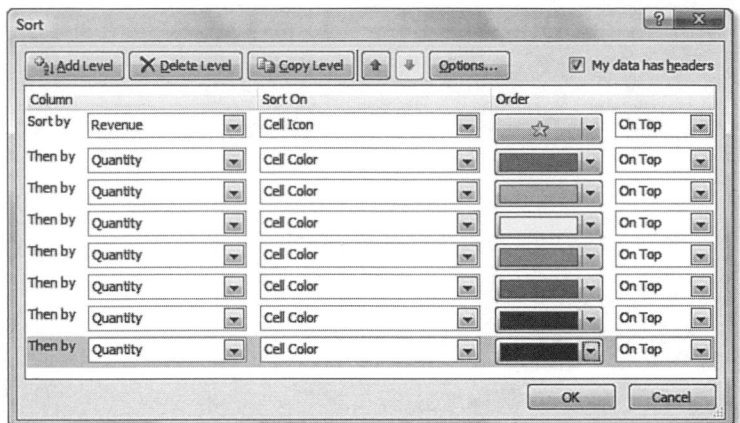

Figure 20.2
When you sort by color, explicitly specify the order of the colors.

10. If you want to specify that values in another column should be used to break ties in the color column, select the Add Level button and specify the additional columns.

11. Click OK to sort the data.

Factoring Case into a Sort

Typically, an Excel sort ignores the case of the text. Values that are lowercase, uppercase, or any combination of the two are treated equally in a sort. For example, in Figure 20.3, all the values in A2:A9 would be considered a tie.

In Excel 2010, a case-sensitive sort sorts lowercase values before uppercase values. For example, abc will sort before ABC. Similarly, ABc will sort before ABC.

If you want Excel to consider case when sorting, follow these steps:

1. On the Sort dialog, select the Options button.

2. Select a cell within your data.

3. Select the Data tab and then select Sort & Filter, Sort. Alternatively, select the Home tab and then select Editing, Sort & Filter, Custom Sort. The Sort dialog appears.

4. Choose the column from the Sort By drop-down.

5. Click the Options button. The Sort Options dialog appears.

6. Select the Case Sensitive check box, as shown in Figure 20.3.

7. Click OK to close the Sort Options dialog.

8. Click OK to sort.

Figure 20.3
Use Sort Options when you need Excel to factor uppercase and lowercase into a sort.

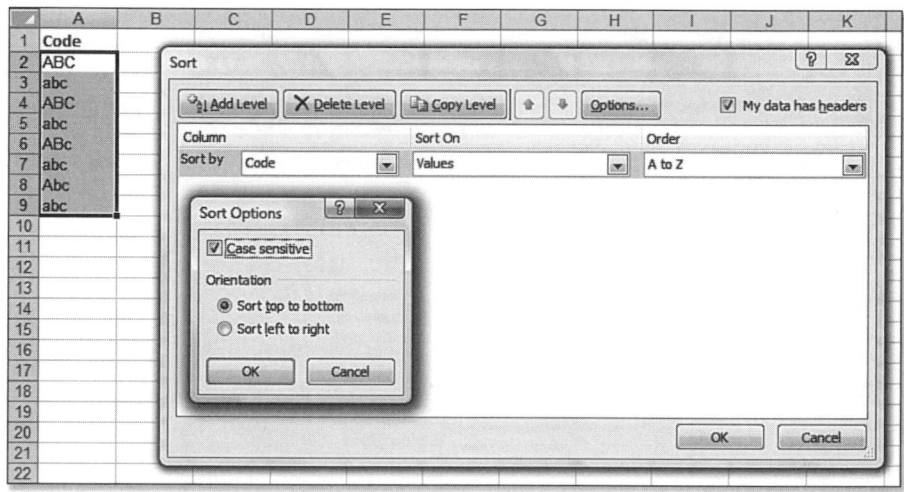

Reordering Columns with a Left-to-Right Sort

If you receive a data set from a colleague and the columns are in the wrong sequence, you could cut and paste them into the right sequence, or you could fix them all in one pass by using a left-to-right sort. To do this, follow these steps:

1. Insert a new blank row above the headings.

2. In the new row, type numbers corresponding to the correct sequence of the columns.

3. Make sure that one cell in the range is selected.

4. Select the Data tab and then select Sort & Filter, Sort. Alternatively, you can select the Home tab and then select Editing, Sort & Filter, Custom Sort. The Sort dialog appears.

5. Click the Options button. The Sort Options dialog appears.

6. Select Sort Left to Right. Click OK to close the Sort Options dialog.

7. The Sort By drop-down now contains a list of row numbers. Choose the first row. The remaining drop-downs should already include Values and A to Z, as shown in Figure 20.4.

8. Click OK to perform the sort.

9. Delete your temporary extra row at the top of the data set. The columns are then resequenced into the desired order.

Figure 20.4
Add an extra row to specify the correct sequence of the columns and then sort from left to right.

Sorting into a Unique Sequence by Using Custom Lists

Sometimes, company tradition dictates that regions or products should be presented in an order that is not alphabetic. For example, the sequence East, Central, West makes more sense geographically than the alphabetic sequence Central, East, West.

It is possible to set up a custom list to tell Excel that the region sequence is East, Central, West. You can then sort your data based on this sequence. You need to set up the custom list only once per computer. Follow these steps to do so.

1. Go to a blank section of any worksheet. Type the correct sequence for the values in a column.

2. Select this range.

3. Select File, Options. The Options dialog appears.

4. Click the Advanced Group. Scroll down to the Display section and then select Edit Custom Lists. The Custom Lists dialog appears.

5. In the Custom Lists dialog, the bottom section shows the range of cells you selected in step 2 (see Figure 20.5). If it is correct, click the Import button. Your new list, with the correct sequence, is added to the default custom lists.

6. Click OK to close the Custom Lists dialog. Click OK to close the Options dialog.

7. Clear your temporary data range from step 1.

 **tip**
Excel does not change the original column widths. Select all cells with Ctrl+a. Use Home, Format, AutoFit Column Width to resize all of the columns.

After you set up a custom list, it is available for more than just custom sorting. For example, the custom list can be used when dragging the fill handle in order to extend a list. Here are the steps to use the new custom list with the fill handle:

1. Type East into a cell and then select the cell.

2. Drag the square dot from the lower-right corner to the right. Excel automatically types additional values from your custom list.

To use the list with custom sorting, follow these steps:

1. Select one cell in your data.

2. Select the Data tab and then select Sort & Filter, Sort. Alternatively, you can select the Home tab and then select Editing, Sort & Filter, Custom Sort. The Sort dialog appears.

3. In the Sort By drop-down, choose the region with the custom sort sequence.

4. From the Order drop-down, select Custom List. You should now be back in the Custom Lists dialog shown in Figure 20.5.

Figure 20.5
By preselecting the range with your correct list sequence, you only have to click Import and OK in this dialog.

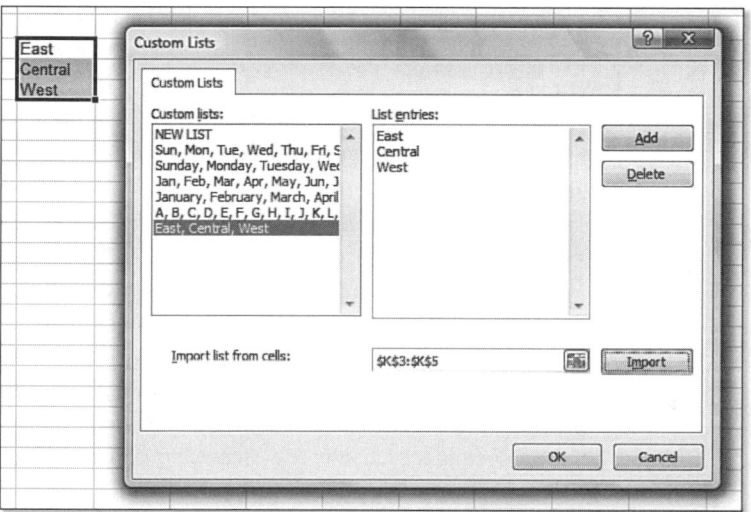

5. Click your custom list and then click OK. The Sort dialog shows that the order is based on your custom list (see Figure 20.6).

Figure 20.6
Excel indicates that the Region field will be sorted into East, Central, West sequence.

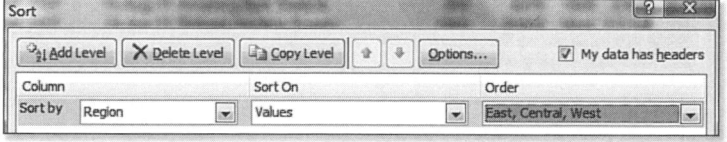

6. Click OK to sort into the custom sequence.

 To watch a video of custom sorting, search for "Excel In Depth 20" at YouTube.

One-Click Sorting

All the examples discussed so far in this chapter have used the Sort dialog box, which is required for left-to-right sorting, custom sorting, and case-sensitive sorting. It also makes color sorting easier. You can accomplish all other sorts by using the AZ buttons on the various tabs.

It is important to select a single cell in the column to be sorted. When you select a single cell, Excel extends the selection to encompass the entire current region. If you select two cells or even the whole column, Excel warns you that it is about to sort part of your data and ignore the adjacent data. This is rarely what you want.

The one-click sorting options are found on the Home and Data tabs. On the Home tab, they are in the Sort & Filter drop-down. On the Data tab, they are clearly visible as AZ and ZA buttons.

You can also find sorting options by right-clicking a cell in the column you want to sort and selecting Sort. As shown in Figure 20.7, options in this menu allow you to sort in ascending or descending order. You can also put the cell color, font color, or icon on top.

Additional quick-sorting options are located in the autofilter drop-downs. You can use these options to sort in ascending order, descending order, and by color. For tips on setting up the autofilter drop-downs, see Chapter 21, "Removing Duplicates and Filtering."

> **note**
>
> Whereas legacy versions of Excel used the phrase Sort Ascending, Excel 2010 uses one of several phrases including Sort A to Z, Sort Oldest to Newest, and Sort Smallest to Largest. Each of these phrases is equivalent to Sort Ascending. Excel selects which phrase to use based on whether the selected column contains mostly text, dates, or numbers.

> **note**
>
> In legacy versions of Excel, you could not combine a custom list sort with other custom list sorts. However, when using Excel 2010, you can sort every column by additional custom lists. You can also optionally add additional columns to the sort.

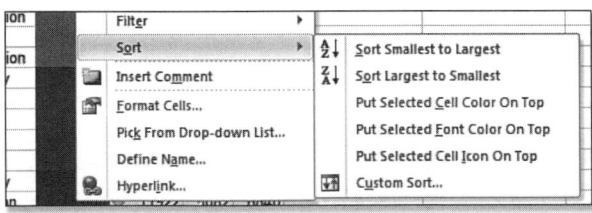

Figure 20.7
By using the context menu, you can do rudimentary quick sorts by color.

Sorting by Several Columns Using One-Click Sorting

Even though the AZ button sorts by one column at a time, you can also sort a list by several columns by using the AZ button.

Remember that when Excel encounters a tie in the Sort column, the previous order remains intact. Because of this rule, you can perform quick sorts in reverse order. For example, if you want to sort by product within region, follow these steps:

1. Select one cell in the Product column.

2. Click the AZ button in the Data tab.

3. Select one cell in the Region column.

4. Click the AZ button in the Data tab.

Sorting Randomly

Suppose that you have a list of students, and you need to select the sequence in which they should present their science projects. Rather than always allowing Amber and Andy to go first, you can sort the class into a random sequence. To do so, follow these steps:

1. Add a new column to the right of your list. Give the column a heading, such as Sequence or Random.

2. In the first data cell of the new column, type =RAND( ) and then press Ctrl+Enter. The formula calculates a random decimal value between 0 and 1.

3. Double-click the fill handle in the lower-right corner of this cell to copy the formula to all rows of your data.

4. Select the heading in the new column.

5. From the Data tab, select Sort & Filter, AZ. The list is sorted into a random sequence.

6. Delete the data in the temporary new column.

 note

When you perform a random sort, it is important to note that the data is sorted into a new sequence. However, the numbers in the =RAND column do not appear to be in sequence. This is because the random numbers are recalculated after the sort is completed.

Excel Troubleshooting: Fixing Sort Problems

If it appears that a sort did not work correctly, check this list of troubleshooting tips:

■ If the headers were sorted into the data, it usually means that one or more columns had a blank heading. Every column should have a nonblank heading. If you want the heading to appear blank, use an underscore in a white font to fool Excel. If you cannot insert a heading, you will have to use the Sort Dialog.

Unhide rows and columns before sorting. Hidden rows are not resequenced in a sort.

■ Use only one row for headings. If you need the headings to appear as if they are taking up several rows, put the headings in one row and wrap the text. To have control over where the text wraps, type the first line, press Alt+Enter, and then type the second line.

- Data in a column should be a similar type. For example, if you have a column of ZIP codes, you might have numeric cells for ZIP codes of 10001 through 99999 and text cells for ZIP codes of 00001 through 09999. Because text cells are sorted sequentially after numeric cells, sorting the ZIP codes in this case will appear not to work. To fix this problem, convert the entire column to one data type to achieve the expected results.

- If your data has volatile formulas or formulas that point to cells outside the sort range, Excel calculates the range after sorting. If your sort sequence is based on this column, Excel accurately sorts the data, based on the information before the recalculation. If the values change after calculation, it will appear that the sort did not work. For an example, see Figure 20.8.

- If your data must have blank columns or rows, follow the steps in the sidebar "Excel in Practice: Sorting with Blank Columns."

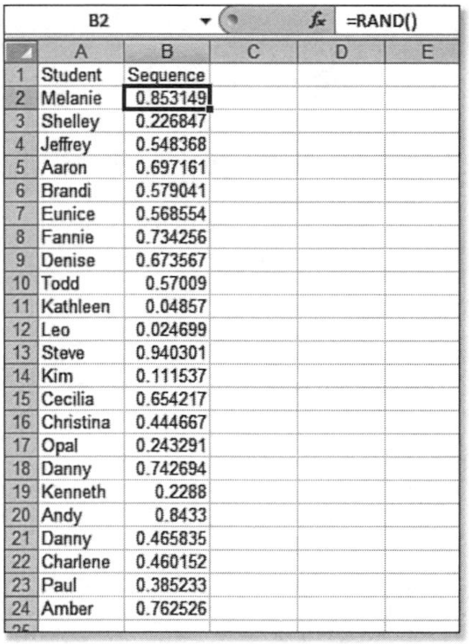

	A	B	C	D	E
1	Student	Sequence			
2	Melanie	0.853149			
3	Shelley	0.226847			
4	Jeffrey	0.548368			
5	Aaron	0.697161			
6	Brandi	0.579041			
7	Eunice	0.568554			
8	Fannie	0.734256			
9	Denise	0.673567			
10	Todd	0.57009			
11	Kathleen	0.04857			
12	Leo	0.024699			
13	Steve	0.940301			
14	Kim	0.111537			
15	Cecilia	0.654217			
16	Christina	0.444667			
17	Opal	0.243291			
18	Danny	0.742694			
19	Kenneth	0.2288			
20	Andy	0.8433			
21	Danny	0.465835			
22	Charlene	0.460152			
23	Paul	0.385233			
24	Amber	0.762526			

B2 f_x =RAND()

Figure 20.8
After you randomly sort, the RAND( ) function recalculates, giving the appearance that the sort did not work.

Excel in Practice: Sorting with Blank Columns

In a perfect world, you will never have data sets with completely blank columns. However, this is not always possible. I have worked for managers who demanded a blank column between each data column in order to have a small break between the bottom cell borders in the headings. In addition, QuickBooks is notorious for exporting data to Excel with blank columns between data columns.

You cannot successfully sort a data set that contains blank columns by using the quick-sort buttons. Therefore, you need to follow these steps to sort the data by using the Sort dialog:

1. Examine the data. Even if there are multiple rows of headings, include only the last row of headings, directly above your data row.

2. Select a range that includes all columns and the one heading row.

3. From the Data tab, click the Sort button. The Sort dialog appears.

4. In the Sort dialog, select the My Data Has Headers check box.

5. As shown in Figure 20.9, the Sort By column contains a mix of column headings and place-holders for blank headings such as (Column F). Choose the proper heading from the drop-down. Click OK, and the entire data set is properly sorted.

Figure 20.9
To sort data with blank columns, you must first preselect the entire range to be sorted.

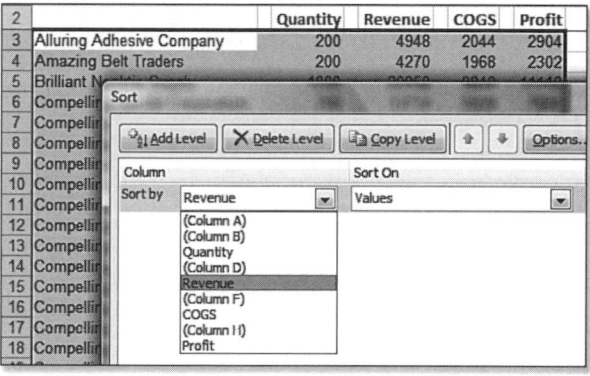

REMOVING DUPLICATES AND FILTERING

Autofiltering has been in Excel for a decade, but it received a makeover in Excel 2007. The autofilter drop-downs allow you to multiselect values and offer smart filters. The elusive Filter by Selection feature allows you to invoke filters even faster than before.

The Advanced Filter command continues to be available and is as complicated as ever. The hope is that with the excellent improvements to autofiltering and the addition of duplicate handling, you will never have to turn to Advanced Filter. In legacy versions of Excel, I almost always had to resort to using Advanced Filter to find a list of unique values. However, the Remove Duplicates command allows you to find unique values with a couple mouse clicks.

Duplicate data is a common problem in Excel. Beginning with Excel 2007, Microsoft provided tools to make finding and eliminating duplicates easier.

Filtering Records

Microsoft added powerful new features to the Filter command in Excel 2007. This feature was formerly called AutoFilter, but it has been renamed simply as a Filter since Excel 2007. Filtering works on any range of data with headings in the first row of the range. It works with ranges that have been defined as tables as well as regular ranges.

The following are some Excel filtering features:

- Multiselection is available in the filter drop-down. Use the regular filter if you want to select rows that meet one of two values or rows for all but one particular value.

- You can filter by color or icon set.

- You can filter text columns based on cells that begin with a value, end with a value, or contain a value.

- You can filter number columns based on cells that are greater than, less than, or between values. You can choose Top 10, Above Average, or Below Average.

- You can filter date values by year or month. You can filter to conceptual values such as this month, last quarter, or year to date.

- You can filter by selection. Rather than choosing from the filter drop-down, you can select any value and use Filter by Selection to filter the data to that value.

The various features work great when one column contains values of the same type. For example, Excel expects that if you have dates in a column, all the cells except the header will be dates. Excel offers special text, number, or date formats based on what it sees in the column. These special formats are mutually exclusive. If you have a column with a mix of dates, numbers, and text, Excel offers only the special filtering type for the value type that occurs most frequently in the column. If you happen to have exactly 150 values with text, 150 values with numbers, and 150 values with dates, Excel offers the text filters. With a tie between dates and values, Excel offers the value filters.

Using a Filter

The icon to turn on the filter drop-downs toggles the feature on and off. To turn on the feature, click the icon once. To turn off the feature, click the icon again.

You need to select one cell in your data range before clicking the filter. You should have no blank rows or blank columns in the range to be filtered.

You can turn on the filter drop-downs by using any of these methods:

- From the Home tab, select Editing, Sort & Filter, Filter.

- From the Data tab, select Sort & Filter, Filter.

- Apply a table format to a range.

- Right-click any cell, select Filter, and then select one of the options under Filter. In addition to performing the filter, this will turn on the filter feature if it were not previously turned on.

- Choose any value, and then select the AutoFilter icon from the Quick Access Toolbar. The Filter by Selection feature has been in Excel since Excel 2003, but the icon has never been included in the standard user interface. In addition, this icon has always been mislabeled in the Customize dialog. See "Filtering by Selection - Easy Way" later in this chapter for more information.

When the filter is turned on, a drop-down arrow is added to each heading in the range.

Figure 21.1 shows the menu available for one drop-down. This particular column includes text values, so the special filter flyout menu includes various special text filters.

Figure 21.1
The filter drop-down now features a multiselect list, as well as new special filters.

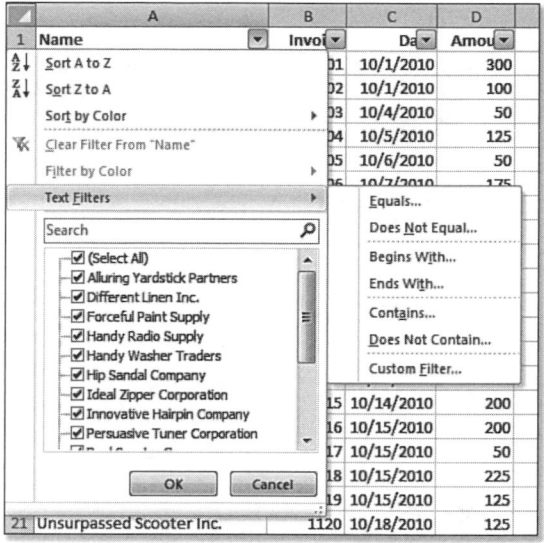

Selecting One or Multiple Items from the Filter Drop-Down

In legacy versions of Excel, the filter drop-down included a simple list of items in the column, and you selected one of the values. The multiselect nature of filters included since Excel 2007 offers far more power, but you have to exercise special care in using the drop-down.

Follow these steps to select a single item:

1. When you initially select the drop-down, all the check boxes that appear in the column are selected, as shown in Figure 21.1.

2. To select a single value, click Select All. This clears all the items in the list, as shown in Figure 21.2.

3. Click the value on which you want to filter, as shown in Figure 21.3.

4. Click OK at the bottom of the drop-down to apply the filter.

The process you use to filter to multiple values is similar. First click Select All to clear the check boxes for all items. You can then select the items that should be included in the filter.

The multiselection ability is a vast improvement for filtering that can be completed in four clicks. Even though the old autofilter in legacy versions of Excel required only two clicks, the improvements are worth this hassle. For example, when you need to select everything except one certain value, you select the drop-down, clear the undesired value, and click OK.

Select All

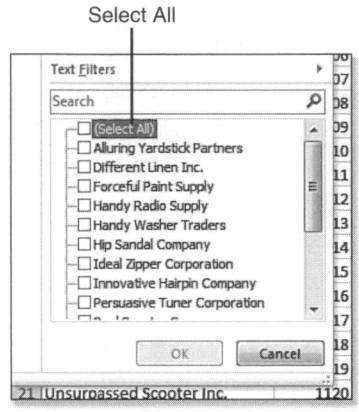

Figure 21.2
Click Select All to clear the check boxes for all items.

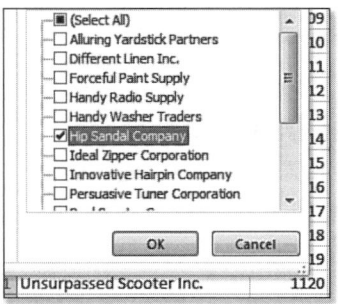

Figure 21.3
When the check boxes have been cleared, select the one value of interest and click OK.

Identifying Columns With Filters

Listed below are the visual clues in Excel 2010 you can use to identify columns in which a filter has been applied to a data set:

- The row numbers in the range appear in blue to indicate that the rows have a filter applied.

- The message area of the status bar in the lower-left corner of the screen shows a message similar to "6 of 34 records found."

- The drop-down for the filtered column changes from a simple drop-down arrow to a Filter icon, as shown in Figure 21.4.

 tip

With more than 1 million rows in Excel, you have the possibility for a long list of items in the Filter list. In fact, the number of items that can be listed in the list increased from 1,000 to 10,000 starting in Excel 2007. Using the scrollbar to navigate through a list of 10,000 items will be inexact. However, there is a fast way to jump to a certain section of the list. Click any name in the list to activate the list. Then, type the first letter of your selection. Excel instantly jumps to the first item that starts with this letter. You can then use PgDn or PgUp to move quickly through the items that start with that letter.

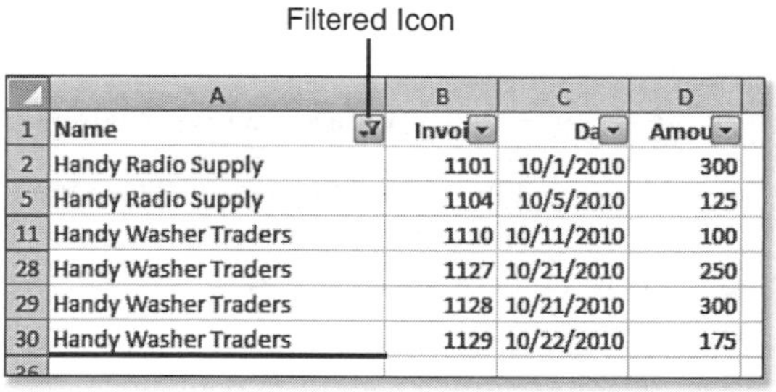

Filtered Icon

Figure 21.4
After you apply a filter to Column A, the icon on the filter drop-down changes.

Combining Filters

Filters are additive, which means that after you place a filter on a column, you can apply a filter to another column to show even fewer rows. Two filters can be applied to the same column, such as when you want to select all the West region cells that are red.

Clearing Filters

After a filter has been applied, you have several options for clearing the filter:

- From the filter drop-down, select Clear Filter from Column. This leaves filters on in other columns.

- From the filter drop-down, choose a different filter.

- From the Data tab, select Sort & Filter, Clear. This clears selected filters from any column but leaves the drop-downs in place, so you can continue to select other filters.

- Select the Filter icon from the Data tab or the Home tab to clear all filters and turn off the filter feature.

Refreshing Filters

Keep in mind that when data in a range changes, the filters do not update automatically. This can happen when you add new rows or edit data. It can also happen if your data range has formulas that point to lookup tables in other parts of the workbook.

In such a case, you need to have Excel calculate the filter again. Excel calls this feature *Reapply*. There are several ways you can reapply a filter:

- On the Data tab select the Sort & Filter group and then click Reapply.

- On the Home tab, select Editing Group, Sort & Filter, Reapply.

- Right-click a cell and then select Filter, Reapply.

Resizing the Filter Drop-Down

The filter drop-down always starts fairly small. If you have a long list of items, you might want the drop-down to be larger. To do this, hover your mouse over the three dots in the lower-right corner of the drop-down menu. When the mouse pointer changes to a two-headed diagonal arrow, click and drag down or to the right.

Filtering by Selection—Hard Way

You can filter without using the filter drop-downs. Microsoft Access has offered a Filter by Selection icon in the toolbar for more than a decade. Excel includes this functionality, but it is hidden where most people will never find it.

To access the Filter by Selection feature, right-click any cell and then select Filter from the context menu. You then have an opportunity to filter based on the cell's value, color, font color, or icon, as shown in Figure 21.5.

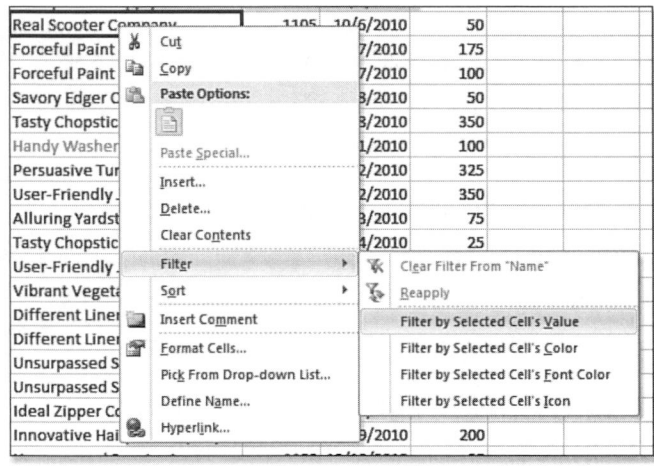

Figure 21.5
Although it is hidden, the Filter by Selection command provides a quick way to see all the other rows that match a single cell.

The Filter by Selection feature works even if the filter drop-downs have not been activated previously. Using this feature turns on the filter drop-downs for the data set.

It would be helpful if you could use this feature to multiselect values, such as if you selected a cell that said East and then Ctrl+clicked on a cell for West. You might think that filtering by selection would filter to both East and West, but that does not work in Excel 2010.

Filtering by Selection—Easy Way

The fast way to Filter by Selection is to add the AutoFilter icon to the Quick Access Toolbar.

To get one-click access to Filter by Selection, follow these steps:

1. Right-click the Quick Access Toolbar and select Customize Quick Access Toolbar.

2. In the Choose Commands From drop-down, select Commands Not in the Ribbon.

3. In the left list box, browse to and select AutoFilter as shown in Figure 21.6. Click the Add button.

4. Click OK to close the Excel Options dialog.

Figure 21.6
The icon labeled "AutoFilter" actually is Filter by Selection.

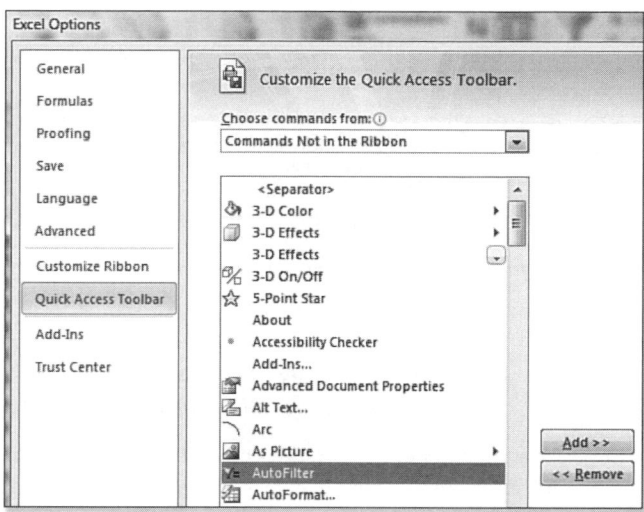

Filter by Selection is additive, which means you can choose another value in another column and click the AutoFilter icon to filter the data set further.

In Figure 21.7, the data set is filtered to show Central region invoices for the Clothing & Textiles market. This was accomplished in four mouse clicks: Select Cell C20. Click the AutoFilter icon. Select Central in Cell B20. Click the AutoFilter icon.

 To watch a video of Filter by Selection in action, search for "Excel In Depth 21" at YouTube.

Filtering by Color or Icon

Cell colors are more prevalent in Excel 2010 than in legacy versions, given the greatly improved conditional formatting tools. However, the Filter by Color feature also works with cells to which you have manually applied fill color.

Imagine that you are tracking numerous projects in Excel. You manually highlight certain projects in red if you are missing key elements of the project information. You can use Filter by Color to show only the rows that have red fill.

Filter by Color works for the cell color, font color, or the icon in the cell.

 note

You might wonder why this icon is mislabeled as AutoFilter instead of something more obvious, such as Filter by Selection. In legacy versions of Excel, the AutoFilter icon toggled the filter drop-downs. However, Microsoft decided to improve this icon by adding logic to Filter by Selection when the active cell was on a value in a data set. It isn't clear if this was a rogue feature added by a developer or just a feature that no one cared to document. In any case, no one bothered to change the label on the icon from AutoFilter to Filter by Selection. Even though the AutoFilter command was renamed to Filter beginning in Excel 2007, this rogue feature continues to have the incorrect label of AutoFilter.

 tip

Keep in mind that icons are available only from conditional formatting.

Filter by Selection on QAT

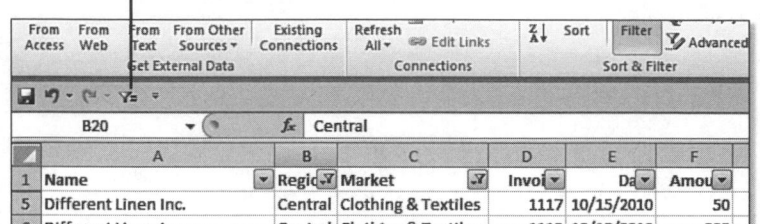

Figure 21.7
Filter by Selection is used twice to filter based on Column C and then Column B.

➡️ *For more information on icon sets, see the "Setting Up an Icon Set" section in Chapter 31, "Using Data Visualizations and Conditional Formatting."*

As shown in Figure 21.8, the Filter by Color flyout menu offers to filter based on fill color, font color, or icon. Note that the sections of the flyout menu appear only if you have used color or icons in the range. If all your cells contain black text, Filter by Font Color will not appear in the flyout menu. If your range contains all black text on white background, without icons, the Filter by Color menu will be disabled.

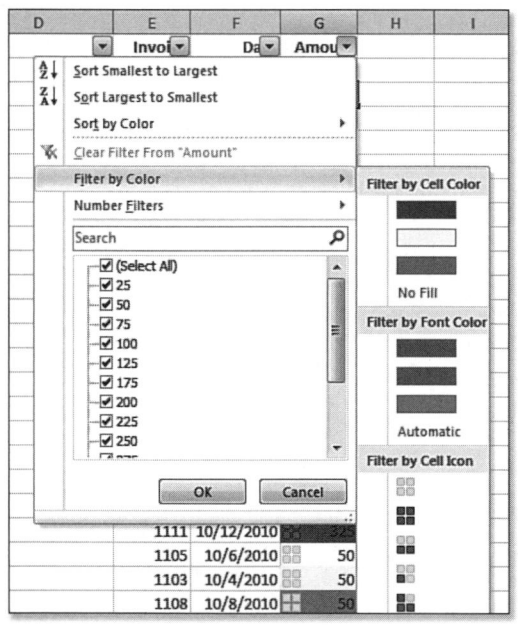

Figure 21.8
The Filter by Color flyout menu offers to filter by icon, cell color, or font color.

Handling Date Filters

The default method for filtering a column of dates changed dramatically after Excel 2003. In legacy versions of Excel, the drop-down list contained a list of the dates in the column. However, after Excel 2007, Excel automatically groups the dates into hierarchical groups.

In Figure 21.9, the underlying data contains daily dates. However, the default drop-down shows options for the years found in the data set.

Click the plus sign that is next to any year to expand the list to show months within the year, as shown in Figure 21.10. You can then click the plus sign next to a month to see the days within the month.

 tip

You can turn off the hierarchical grouping of dates in the filter drop-down. To do so, click the File menu and choose Options. In the Options dialog, choose the Advanced category. Scroll down to the section for Display for This Workbook. Next, select a workbook and then clear the check box for Group Dates in the AutoFilter Menu.

Figure 21.9
Excel automatically groups dates up to years in the filter drop-down.

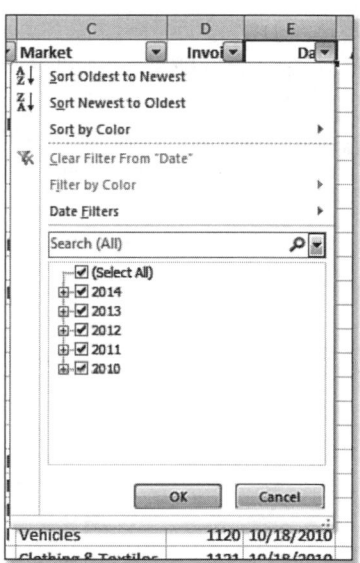

Figure 21.10
Expand the hierarchical view to see months within the years.

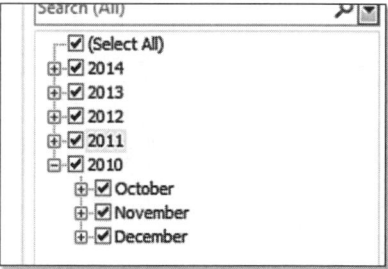

Using Special Filters for Dates, Text, and Numbers

Excel examines the data in a column to determine whether it contains mostly text, dates, or numeric values. Depending on which data type appears most often, Excel offers special filters designed for that data type.

For columns that contain mostly text, Excel offers the filters Begins With, Ends With, Contains, Does Not Contain, Equals, and Does Not Equal. You are allowed to use wildcard characters in these filters. For example, you can use an asterisk (*) for any number of characters or a question mark (?) to represent a single character.

For columns with mostly numeric values, the special filters include Top 10, Above Average, Below Average, Between, Less Than, Greater Than, Does Not Equal, and Equals. For the Top 10 filter, you can specify the top or bottom values. You can also specify whether the results are based on the top 10 items or the top 10 percent of items. Finally, you can change the number 10 to any number. Thus, you can use this filter to show the bottom 20 percent or the top three items.

For columns with mostly dates, the special filters include Before, After, or Between a particular day, week, month, quarter, or year. The special filters also include Year to Date or All Dates in a particular period, as shown in Figure 21.11.

All the special filters offer a pathway to the Custom AutoFilter dialog. This filter allows you to combine two conditions by using an AND or OR clause. This feature solves your problems some of the time, but there are still complex conditions that require you to resort to using the advanced filter.

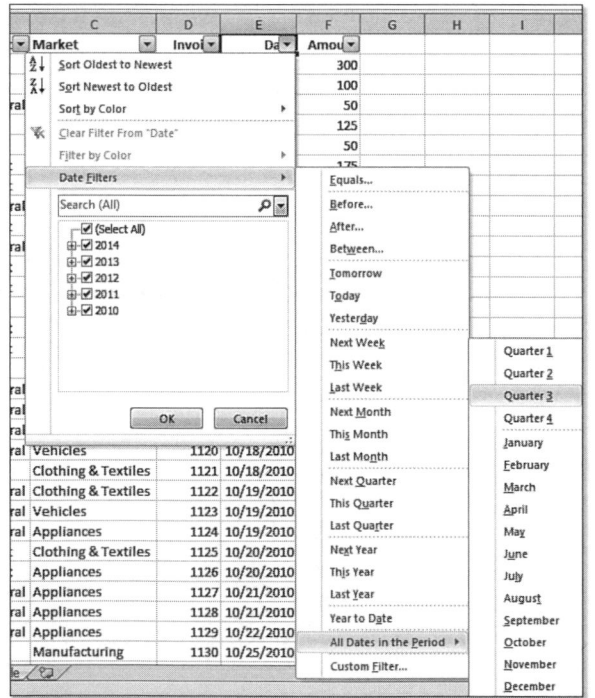

Figure 21.11
Excel offers a myriad of date filters.

The Custom AutoFilter dialog was nominally improved in Excel 2007. For example, a calendar control was added that can be used to select dates when you are filtering a date column. You can use the dialog shown in Figure 21.12 to select dates that are within a certain range of dates.

Figure 21.12
The custom filters allow you to build simple combinations of two conditions for filtering.

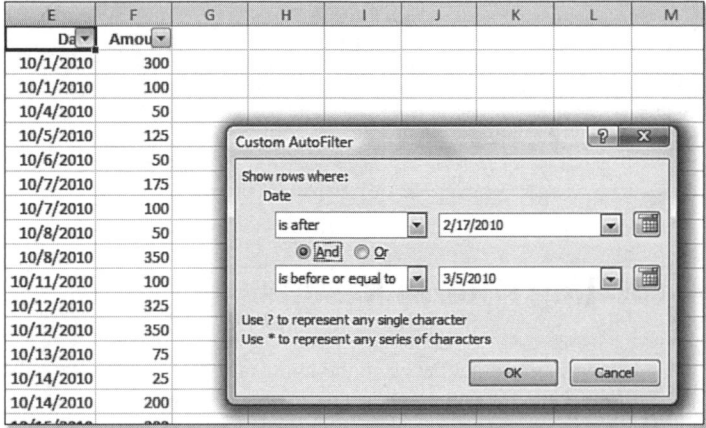

Sorting Filtered Results

The Filter drop-down provides choices to sort a column. Note that if you apply a filter and then sort the results, the sort commands apply only to the visible rows. In Figure 21.13, a Top 10 filter shows the 10 largest invoices in a data set. Note that you can see Rows 221, 591, 1081, and so on.

Figure 21.13
After applying the Top 10 filter to Column F, Excel shows the top 10 values, but they are unsorted.

	Name	Region	Market	Invoi	Date	Amou
221	Vibrant Vegetable Inc.	East	Natural Materials	1320	4/1/2011	96200
591	User-Friendly Juicer Company	West	Appliances	1690	1/31/2012	95350
1081	User-Friendly Juicer Company	West	Appliances	2180	3/6/2013	99025
1221	Alluring Yardstick Partners	East	Manufacturing	2320	7/1/2013	97375
1311	Different Linen Inc.	Central	Clothing & Textiles	2410	9/13/2013	99225
1391	Alluring Yardstick Partners	East	Manufacturing	2490	11/18/2013	96375
1421	User-Friendly Juicer Company	West	Appliances	2520	12/11/2013	96025
1451	Innovative Hairpin Company	Central	Clothing & Textiles	2550	1/7/2014	97200
1701	Alluring Yardstick Partners	East	Manufacturing	2800	7/29/2014	98325
1751	Vibrant Vegetable Inc.	East	Natural Materials	2850	9/12/2014	99200

If you use the Sort Largest to Smallest selection in the drop-down in Cell F1, Excel sorts the 10 visible rows and leaves the hidden rows in their original location. In Figure 21.14, you can still see Rows 221, 591, 1081, and so on, but the $99225 from F1311 moves to Row 221.

	A	B	C	D	E	F	G
1	Name	Regio	Market	Invoi	Da	Amou	Note Old R
221	Different Linen Inc.	Central	Clothing & Textiles	2410	9/13/2013	99225	1311
591	Vibrant Vegetable Inc.	East	Natural Materials	2850	9/12/2014	99200	1751
1081	User-Friendly Juicer Company	West	Appliances	2180	3/6/2013	99025	1081
1221	Alluring Yardstick Partners	East	Manufacturing	2800	7/29/2014	98325	1701
1311	Alluring Yardstick Partners	East	Manufacturing	2320	7/1/2013	97375	1221
1391	Innovative Hairpin Company	Central	Clothing & Textiles	2550	1/7/2014	97200	1451
1421	Alluring Yardstick Partners	East	Manufacturing	2490	11/18/2013	96375	1391
1451	Vibrant Vegetable Inc.	East	Natural Materials	1320	4/1/2011	96200	221
1701	User-Friendly Juicer Company	West	Appliances	2520	12/11/2013	96025	1421
1751	User-Friendly Juicer Company	West	Appliances	1690	1/31/2012	95350	591
1975							

Figure 21.14
Use the sort command in the Filter drop-down. Excel sorts the 10 visible rows, leaving all the hidden rows in their original unsorted location.

Totaling Filtered Results

After you have applied a filter, you might want to sum the visible cells in a column. This task is straightforward in Excel 2010. Select the first visible blank cell below the column and click the AutoSum button. Instead of inserting a SUM function, Excel inserts a SUBTOTAL function. The =SUBTOTAL(9,F2:F999) function sums the visible rows from a data set that has been filtered. You can edit the first argument in the SUBTOTAL function to find the count, average, minimum, and maximum, as well as other calculations on the visible rows.

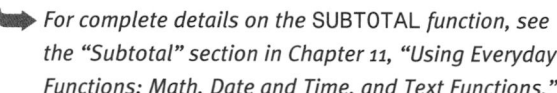 *For complete details on the* SUBTOTAL *function, see the "Subtotal" section in Chapter 11, "Using Everyday Functions: Math, Date and Time, and Text Functions."*

Formatting and Copying Filtered Results

When you apply a filter, some rows are hidden and other rows are visible. The rows hidden by the filter are different from rows hidden with the Hide Rows command. Rows that are hidden using Hide Rows will often be included when you copy or format a range that contains those rows. When you have manually hidden rows, you must use Alt+; to narrow your selection to only the visible rows. It is not necessary to use Alt+; when the rows have been hidden by the Filter command.

You can use this behavior to format or copy rows matching a criteria. If you want to highlight all rows matching a criteria by changing the background color of the cell, follow these steps:

1. Select one cell in the unfiltered data set that matches the proper criteria.

2. Click the Filter by Selection icon in the Quick Access Toolbar.

3. Select the first visible cell below the headings.

> ⚠ **caution**
>
> When you get beyond the 11 basic functions offered in the SUBTOTAL command, it becomes incredibly difficult to have formulas operate on the visible results of a filter. One option is to copy the filtered records to another section of the worksheet. For an example of how you can simulate the COUNTIF function on the visible rows of a filtered data set, see episode #946 of the Learn Excel from MrExcel podcast. To see this podcast, search for "Learn Excel 946" at YouTube.

4. Press Ctrl+Shift+Down Arrow and then Ctrl+Shift+Right Arrow to select all the cells below the heading.

5. Format the cells as desired.

6. Select Data, Filter to remove the filter and show all rows. You will find that only the rows that were visible during the filter have the new formatting.

Using the Advanced Filter Command

The Advanced Filter command is still present in Excel 2010. Microsoft should give this feature a new name because it is remarkably powerful and does much more than filtering. However, the Advanced Filter command is admittedly one of the more confusing commands in Excel. This is particularly true because you can use the Advanced Filter in eight ways, and each method requires slightly different steps.

The eight ways to use the Advanced Filter are derived by multiplying 2 x 2 x 2. There are three options in the Advanced Filter Dialog, and depending on your choices for those three options, you can have possible combinations.

1. You can choose to either Filter in Place or Copy to a New Location.

2. You can choose to filter with a criteria range or without any criteria.

3. You can choose to return all matching values or only the unique values.

In reality, there are more than eight ways to use Advanced Filter. If you choose to copy records to a new location, you can either copy all the input columns in order or specify a subset of columns and/or a new sequence of columns.

You can build a simple filter for one column. You can combine any number of filters for multiple columns. You can build incredibly complex filters, using any formula imaginable. Alternatively, you can use no criteria at all. Using no criteria is common when you are using Advanced Filter to extract unique values or when you want to use Advanced Filter to reorder the sequence of columns.

 tip

You can only copy filtered results to the active sheet, not to a new sheet. However, if you start on a blank sheet, you can specify that you want to filter data from another sheet and pull that data to the active sheet.

To use Advanced Filter on a data set, follow these steps:

1. If you are using criteria, copy one or more headings from your data set to a blank section of the worksheet. Under each heading, list the value(s) that you want to be included.

2. If you are using an output range and want to reorder the columns or include a subset of the columns, copy the headings into the appropriate order in a blank section of the worksheet. If you want all the original columns in their original sequence, the output range can be any blank cell.

3. Select a cell in your data range.

4. Select Data, Sort & Filter, Advanced.

5. Verify that the list range contains your original data set.

6. If you are using criteria, enter the criteria range.

7. If you want to copy the matching records to a new location, select Copy to Another Location. This enables the reference box for Copy to. Fill in the output range.

8. If you want the output range to contain only unique values, click Unique Records Only. If your output range contained a single field, a list of the values in that field is displayed that match the criteria. If your output range contains two or more fields, every unique combination of those two or more fields is displayed.

9. Click OK to perform the filter.

Troubleshooting Excel: Advanced Filter Criteria

Even though it is not obvious from the instructions for using Advanced Filter, you can build advanced filter criteria that can ask for a range of values. For example, if you are using an advanced filter, it is unlikely you will want to filter to the customer with exactly $7,553 in sales. However, you might want to filter to invoices that are over $5,000 in sales. To set up this criteria, type Sales into Cell K1. In Cell K2, type the text >5000. When you issue the Advanced Filter, Excel returns all invoices in excess of $5,000.

In Figure 21.15, the Advanced Filter operation extracts all east region sales in the Vehicles market. Three columns from the matching records will be copied to Columns L:N.

Figure 21.15
Advanced Filter is a powerful tool that can do much more than filter.

Excel in Practice: Using Formulas for Advanced Filter Criteria

Sometimes you might need to filter based on criteria that are too complex for any of Excel's built-in rules. For example, suppose that you want to create an advanced filter to find all records where one of 30 customers bought one of 20 products. The necessary criteria range would cover 601 rows and would take hours to build.

There is one obscure syntax of advanced filter criteria that allows you to filter to anything for which you can build a TRUE/FALSE formula. Use the following specifics to set up a filter that contains formulas:

1. This criteria range is two cells tall by one column wide.

2. The top cell is blank.

3. The second cell contains a formula that should have relative references pointing to the first data row of the input range.

4. The formula should evaluate to TRUE or FALSE. For example, to select all the West records where the invoice is above average for the West, use this:

   `=AND(B2="West",F2>AVERAGEIF($B$2:$B$1874,"West",$F$2:$F$1874))`

When Excel sees that the first row of the criteria range is blank, it takes the formula in the second cell and applies it to all rows in the range. Any rows that would evaluate to TRUE are returned in the filter.

Using Remove Duplicates to Find Unique Values

By its nature, transactional data has a lot of detail. You end up with transactional data in Excel because it is often the easiest to obtain. As you start to analyze transactional data, you often want to find the number of customers, number of products, or number of something in the data set.

For example, transactional data can tell you that there were 34 invoices issued last month, but that doesn't mean there were 34 customers. Some of those customers might have made repeat purchases. In this case, 20 customers could account for 34 invoices.

To find the number of unique customers, you need a way to eliminate the duplicate records in a data set. In legacy versions of Excel, this usually meant using Advanced Filter, some IF functions, or possibly a pivot table. However, there is a Remove Duplicates data tool in Excel 2010 that makes it easier to remove duplicates.

The first thing to realize is that the Remove Duplicates tool is destructive because it really removes the duplicate records. If you want to keep the original transactional data intact, you should either make a copy of the customer column in a blank section of the workbook or make a backup copy of the workbook.

To find the unique values in a data set, follow these steps:

1. Copy the data set to a blank section of the worksheet. Make sure to leave a blank column between your real data and the copy of the data.

2. Select a single cell within the data set.

3. On the Data tab, in the Data Tools group, select Remove Duplicates. Excel expands the selection to include the entire range. In the Remove Duplicates dialog, Excel predicts if your data has headers. This dialog also shows a list of all the fields in the data set.

4. Because you are interested in a unique list of customers, click the Unselect All button to clear all check boxes, and then select the Customer field, as shown in Figure 21.16.

5. Click OK to perform the action. Excel tells you how many duplicate values were found and removed. It also tells you how many unique values remain.

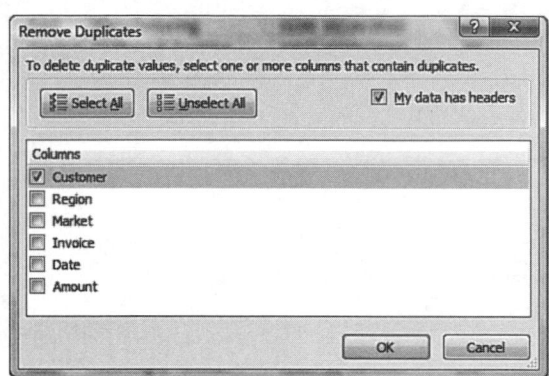

Figure 21.16
Choose which columns should be considered when analyzing duplicates.

Removing Duplicates Based on Several Columns

In the previous set of steps, you analyzed only a single column when looking for duplicates. However, sometimes you need to find each unique combination of two fields, such as a list of each unique combination of region and market. In this case, follow these steps:

1. Copy the data set to a blank section of the worksheet. Make sure to leave a blank column between your real data and the copy of the data.

2. Select a single cell within the data set.

3. On the Data tab, in the Data Tools group, select Remove Duplicates.

4. In the Remove Duplicates dialog, leave the check boxes for both of the fields selected.

5. Click OK to remove the duplicate values.

In this case, the result is a list of all unique combinations of market and customer.

 tip

Remember that the Remove Duplicates command is destructive. For this reason, sometimes you might want to find the duplicates and choose which version to remove. In that case, you Select Home, Conditional Formatting, Highlight Cell Rules, Duplicate Values.

Other times, you might want to send a copy of the unique values to a new location. In this case, use the Advanced Filter command discussed earlier in this chapter.

Finally, you might want to remove duplicates, but add up the sales for all the removed records and then add them to the Customer field. Although this can be achieved with pivot tables, it can also be achieved using the Consolidate feature, which is discussed in the next section.

Handling Duplicates Other Ways

The Remove Duplicates command is also available in Table Tools, Design tab. For example, you can use this option to remove duplicates from a table that you have defined as a range.

Combining Duplicates and Adding Values

In Figure 21.17, each customer appears one or more times in the list with a sales, cost, and profit values. In addition to finding a unique list of customers, you would like to know the total sales and profit for each customer. You can use a pivot table to find the total sales for each customer. Alternatively, you can use the data tools to consolidate the table down to one record per customer.

Figure 21.17
Start at a blank section of the workbook before invoking the Consolidate feature.

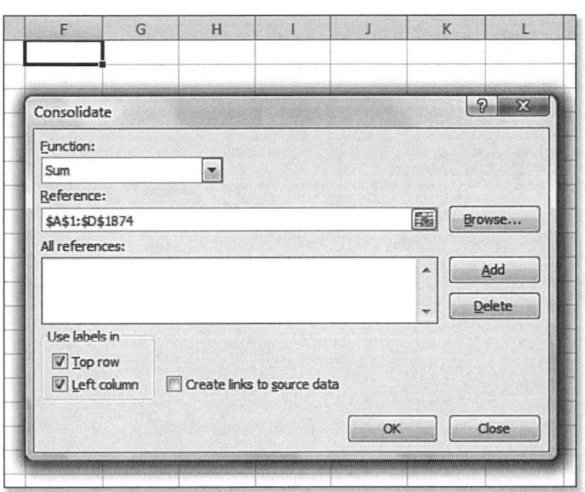

To use the Consolidate feature to total sales from all the records for that customer, follow these steps:

1. Instead of preselecting the data, move the cell pointer to a blank section of the worksheet.

2. Select Data, Data Tools, Consolidate. The Consolidate dialog box appears.

3. In the Consolidate dialog box, enter the reference to your data in the Reference box. The data will be combined based on the field in the left column of the range. If you had multiple lists of customers, you could click the Add button and enter additional ranges.

4. Make sure to select the Top Row and Left Column check boxes in the Use Labels in section.

5. Click OK.

Excel creates a new table. Each customer appears in the table just once. The sales associated with all the records of the customer appear in the new total, as shown in Figure 21.18.

	A	B	C	D	E	F	G	H	I
1	Customer	Sales	COGS	Profit			Sales	COGS	Profit
2	Handy Radio Supply	300	151.8	148.2		Handy Radio Supply	532675	263796.6	268878.4
3	Ideal Zipper Corporation	100	49.3	50.7		Ideal Zipper Corporation	946850	470308.7	476541.3
4	Savory Edger Corporation	50	22.25	27.75		Savory Edger Corporation	1228675	629414.6	599260.5
5	Handy Radio Supply	125	55.125	69.875		Real Scooter Company	2750	1376.4	1373.6
6	Real Scooter Company	50	26.35	23.65		Forceful Paint Supply	658125	334804.7	323320.3
7	Forceful Paint Supply	175	92.575	82.425		Tasty Chopstick Traders	702625	337767.2	364857.9
8	Forceful Paint Supply	100	55.9	44.1		Handy Washer Traders	1124375	559745.1	564629.9
9	Savory Edger Corporation	50	27.95	22.05		Persuasive Tuner Corporation	17875	8945.95	8929.05
10	Tasty Chopstick Traders	350	166.95	183.05		User-Friendly Juicer Company	1265625	647611.6	618013.4
11	Handy Washer Traders	21100	9368.4	11731.6		Alluring Yardstick Partners	1233625	620172.9	613452.2
12	Persuasive Tuner Corporation	325	176.8	148.2		Vibrant Vegetable Inc.	620000	319127.8	300872.2
13	User-Friendly Juicer Company	350	193.2	156.8		Different Linen Inc.	609125	309001.4	300123.6
14	Alluring Yardstick Partners	75	40.5	34.5		Unsurpassed Scooter Inc.	648125	307050.8	341074.2
15	Tasty Chopstick Traders	25	13.475	11.525		Innovative Hairpin Company	755000	367083.2	387916.8
16	User-Friendly Juicer Company	200	109.4	90.6		Hip Sandal Company	33000	16735.3	16264.7
17	Vibrant Vegetable Inc.	200	93	107		Trustworthy Glass Supply	17875	8984.95	8890.05
18	Different Linen Inc.	50	24.05	25.95					

Figure 21.18
Excel consolidates all data by customer.

Two annoyances remain with this command. First, the heading for the leftmost column is never filled in. Second, the command leaves the results in the same sequence in which they originally appeared. In this example, you will probably want to add the heading to Cell F2 and also sort the data.

22

USING AUTOMATIC SUBTOTALS

The subtotal command was added way back in Excel 97. Not enough people realize that the command is in Excel, and those who have tried it often don't realize how powerful the command truly is. I used to have a regular gig as the Excel guy on Leo Laporte's "Call for Help" television show. During one appearance, I showed people how to use the Subtotal command. I figured it was probably the most boring 6 minutes of television in the history of the world. That one show generated more fan email than any others. People wrote to say that they have been spending 2 hours every day adding subtotals manually and used the trick from the show to reduce the task to a minute.

Adding Automatic Subtotals

When you have a database of detailed data, you might want to add subtotals to each group of records. If your data has one field that identifies the groups, you can use the Subtotals command to quickly add the subtotals. Figure 22.1 shows a data set that is suitable for this.

Follow these steps to add subtotals to a data set:

1. Sort the data set by your group field. Select one cell in that column and then select Data, Sort & Filter, AZ.

2. Select one cell in your data set.

3. Select Data, Outline, Subtotal. Excel displays the Subtotal dialog box.

4. In the Subtotal dialog, change the At Each Change In drop-down to reflect your group field.

5. Ensure that Use Function is set to Sum.

6. For each field that you want totaled, select the field in the Add Subtotal To list, as shown in Figure 22.2.

	A	B	C	D	E	F	G	H
1	Region	Product	Date	Customer	Quantity	Revenue	COGS	Profit
2	East	XYZ	1/1/2011	Functional Eggb	1000	22810	10220	12590
3	Central	DEF	1/2/2011	Vivid Edger Co	100	2257	984	1273
4	East	DEF	1/4/2011	Powerful Edger	800	18552	7872	10680
5	East	XYZ	1/4/2011	Trendy Noteboo	400	9152	4088	5064
6	East	DEF	1/7/2011	Tremendous Th	1000	21730	9840	11890
7	East	ABC	1/7/2011	Improved Vegeta	400	8456	3388	5068

Figure 22.1
After sorting, you can quickly add subtotals to this data set.

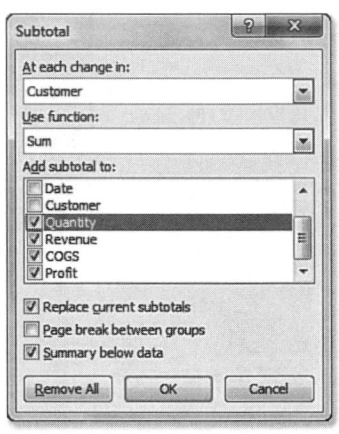

Figure 22.2
You specify the fields to be totaled in the Subtotal dialog.

7. If you want a page break after each group, select Page Break Between Groups.

8. Click OK to add subtotals. Excel adds a subtotal between each group, as shown in Figure 22.3.

	A	B	C	D	E	F
1	Region	Product	Date	Customer	Quantity	Revenue
73	East	ABC	10/21/2012	Crisp Opener Partners	900	18576
74	East	XYZ	12/8/2012	Crisp Opener Partners	900	18756
75	East	XYZ	12/27/2012	Crisp Opener Partners	700	15225
76				Crisp Opener Partners Total	18700	406326
77	East	XYZ	2/16/2011	Distinctive Oven Co	800	16936
78	East	ABC	5/13/2011	Distinctive Oven Co	500	9635
79	West	XYZ	7/9/2011	Distinctive Oven Co	1000	24130
80	Central	DEF	4/24/2012	Distinctive Oven Co	1000	20950
81				Distinctive Oven Co Total	3300	71651
82	Central	DEF	2/26/2011	Easy Sandal Co	900	20610
83	East	ABC	3/15/2011	Easy Sandal Co	400	8116

Figure 22.3
Excel inserts extra rows between groups and adds subtotals.

At the very bottom of the data set, Excel has added a Grand Total row. This row is smart enough to ignore all the other subtotal rows in the data set (see Figure 22.4).

Adding hundreds of subtotal rows is amazing in and of itself. However, the subtotals command offers so much more. You can go on to show only the subtotals, show the largest groups at the top, or copy the subtotals.

Figure 22.4
At the bottom of the data set, Excel
inserted a Grand Total row.

	A	B	C	D	E	F
1	Region	Product	Date	Customer	Quantity	Revenue
584	East	DEF	11/12/2012	Wonderful Kettle Corp	700	14784
585	Central	ABC	11/14/2012	Wonderful Kettle Corp	500	8970
586	West	ABC	11/19/2012	Wonderful Kettle Corp	400	6880
587	East	DEF	11/29/2012	Wonderful Kettle Corp	800	19280
588	West	XYZ	12/19/2012	Wonderful Kettle Corp	800	18560
589	Central	XYZ	12/24/2012	Wonderful Kettle Corp	200	4690
590	West	DEF	12/26/2012	Wonderful Kettle Corp	700	14560
591				Wonderful Kettle Corp Total	40400	869454
592				Grand Total	313900	6707812

Working with the Subtotals

Take a close look at the left side of the worksheet in Figure 22.3. You'll see three new buttons to the left of column A labeled 1, 2, and 3. Those buttons are called Group and Outline buttons and were added automatically by the Subtotals command. They are the key to further analysis of the subtotals.

Showing a One-Page Summary with Only the Subtotals

The 1, 2, and 3 buttons to the left of column A are Group and Outline buttons. They are added automatically when you invoke the Subtotals command.

Click the #2 button. Excel hides all the detail rows, leaving only the customer subtotals and the Grand Total row.

After setting the print area, you would have a one-page summary of the 500+ rows of data (see Figure 22.5).

If you click the #1 Group and Outline button, Excel hides everything except for the Grand Total. If you click the #3 button, Excel brings the detail rows back.

Sorting the Collapsed Subtotal View So the Largest Customers Are on Top

In Figure 22.5, you have the customers in alphabetical sequence. Your manager is probably going to want to see the largest customers at the top of the report.

Think about this request, though. In row 591, the subtotal for Wonderful Kettle is the largest customer in the group, adding up data in rows 526 through 590. If you try to sort descending, and the data in row 591 comes up to row 2, that formula that looks at 64 rows of data will certainly evaluate to a #REF! error.

	A	B	C	D	E	F	G	H
1	Region	Product	Date	Customer	Quantity	Revenue	COGS	Profit
6				Agile Calculator Inc. Total	2400	51240	22824	28416
47				Cool Bottle Co Total	23100	498937	219978	278959
76				Crisp Opener Partners Total	18700	406326	178585	227741
81				Distinctive Oven Co Total	3300	71651	32471	39180
86				Easy Sandal Co Total	2600	54048	23780	30268
135				Excellent Doghouse Corp To	29100	613514	275105	338409
140				Exclusive Washer Corp Total	2000	39250	18614	20636
145				Fine Shingle Supply Total	2700	57516	26765	30751
212				Flexible Aerobic Co Total	33400	704359	311381	392978
269				Functional Eggbeater Co Tot	28900	622794	274978	347816
322				Guaranteed Paint Co Total	26600	568851	252522	316329
383				Improved Vegetable Inc. Tot	35700	750163	334614	415549
388				Inventive Door Inc. Total	1400	31369	13730	17639
393				Magnificent Shingle Corp To	2600	55251	24632	30619
438				Matchless Hardware Traders	19700	427349	189331	238018
443				Mouthwatering Bicycle Corp	2000	46717	19961	26756
448				New Faucet Co Total	3000	62744	28644	34100
453				Powerful Edger Supply Total	1900	42316	18764	23552
458				Rare Door Inc. Total	1400	31021	13745	17276
463				Savory Opener Inc. Total	2800	60299	27049	33250
468				Special Luggage Inc. Total	2300	50030	21612	28418
473				Supreme Clipboard Inc. Tota	3300	72680	31946	40734
478				Sure Linen Corp Total	1700	34710	16423	18287
483				Tremendous Thermostat Par	2700	59881	25913	33968
488				Trendy Notebook Corp Total	1600	34364	15576	18788
525				Vivid Edger Co Total	18600	390978	177281	213697
591				Wonderful Kettle Corp Total	40400	869454	382170	487284
592				Grand Total	313900	6707812	2978394	3729418

Figure 22.5
Click the #2 Group and Outline button to show a summary report.

Amazingly, though, you can easily sort data when it is in the collapsed #2 view. Follow these steps:

1. Add subtotals as indicated previously in this chapter.

2. Collapse the subtotals by clicking the #2 Group and Outline button.

3. Select one single cell in your revenue column.

4. Sort descending by clicking the ZA button on the Data tab.

The result is shown in Figure 22.6. The total for Wonderful Kettle comes flying to the top of the data set, but it does not come to Row 2. Instead, the total comes to Row 67. The total for the second largest customer is in Row 128.

Figure 22.7 shows the #3 view of Figure 22.6. You can see that Excel sorted groups of records when the data was collapsed. All the detail rows for Wonderful Kettle came along with the subtotal in Row 67.

Figure 22.6
Amazingly, you can sort data when it is collapsed.

	A	B	C	D	E	F	G	H
F67				fx	=SUBTOTAL(9,F2:F66)			
1	Region	Product	Date	Customer	Quantity	Revenue	COGS	Profit
67				Wonderful Kettle Corp Total	40400	869454	382170	487284
128				Improved Vegetable Inc. Tot	35700	750163	334614	415549
195				Flexible Aerobic Co Total	33400	704359	311381	392978
252				Functional Eggbeater Co Tot	28900	622794	274978	347816
301				Excellent Doghouse Corp To	29100	613514	275105	338409
354				Guaranteed Paint Co Total	26600	568851	252522	316329
395				Cool Bottle Co Total	23100	498937	219978	278959
440				Matchless Hardware Traders	19700	427349	189331	238018
469				Crisp Opener Partners Total	18700	406326	178585	227741
506				Vivid Edger Co Total	18600	390978	177281	213697
511				Supreme Clipboard Inc. Tota	3300	72680	31946	40734
516				Distinctive Oven Co Total	3300	71651	32471	39180
521				New Faucet Co Total	3000	62744	28644	34100
526				Savory Opener Inc. Total	2800	60299	27049	33250
531				Tremendous Thermostat Par	2700	59881	25913	33968
536				Fine Shingle Supply Total	2700	57516	26765	30751
541				Magnificent Shingle Corp To	2600	55251	24632	30619
546				Easy Sandal Co Total	2600	54048	23780	30268
551				Agile Calculator Inc. Total	2400	51240	22824	28416
556				Special Luggage Inc. Total	2300	50030	21612	28418
561				Mouthwatering Bicycle Corp	2000	46717	19961	26756
566				Powerful Edger Supply Total	1900	42316	18764	23552
571				Exclusive Washer Corp Total	2000	39250	18614	20636
576				Sure Linen Corp Total	1700	34710	16423	18287
581				Trendy Notebook Corp Total	1600	34364	15576	18788
586				Inventive Door Inc. Total	1400	31369	13730	17639
591				Rare Door Inc. Total	1400	31021	13745	17276
592				Grand Total	313900	6707812	2978394	3729418

Figure 22.7
Excel brings all the collapsed detail rows along with the subtotal row during a sort.

	C	D	E	F	G	H
1	Date	Customer	Quantity	Revenue	COGS	Profit
62	11/19/2012	Wonderful Kettle Corp	400	6880	3388	3492
63	11/29/2012	Wonderful Kettle Corp	800	19280	7872	11408
64	12/19/2012	Wonderful Kettle Corp	800	18560	8176	10384
65	12/24/2012	Wonderful Kettle Corp	200	4690	2044	2646
66	12/26/2012	Wonderful Kettle Corp	700	14560	6888	7672
67		Wonderful Kettle Corp Total	40400	869454	382170	487284
68	1/7/2011	Improved Vegetable Inc.	400	8456	3388	5068
69	1/9/2011	Improved Vegetable Inc.	800	16416	6776	9640

Copying Only the Subtotal Rows

A problem occurs when you try to copy the collapsed subtotal rows from Figure 22.7. If you select D1:H592, Copy, and then Paste to a new worksheet, you will discover that Excel copied all the hidden rows as well. Worse, the pasted data no longer has the group and outline symbols, so there is no way to collapse the data again (see Figure 22.8).

	A	B	C
1	Customer	Quantity	Revenue
2	Wonderful Kettle Corp	900	21438
3	Wonderful Kettle Corp	300	6714
4	Wonderful Kettle Corp	300	5532
5	Wonderful Kettle Corp	1000	20250
6	Wonderful Kettle Corp	500	10385
7	Wonderful Kettle Corp	1000	23810
8	Wonderful Kettle Corp	500	11525
9	Wonderful Kettle Corp	1000	25140
10	Wonderful Kettle Corp	400	8708

Figure 22.8
Try to copy the collapsed subtotals and Excel brings all the details rows along, too.

The key to this task is to use a trick called Go To Special, Visible Cells Only. Excel still makes it hard to find this command.

Follow these steps:

1. Add subtotals to a data set as described previously.

2. Collapse to the subtotal only view by clicking the #2 Group and Outline button.

3. Select the entire range of collapsed subtotals.

4. Open the Find and Select drop-down from the right side of the Home tab. Select the Go To Special command. Excel displays the Go To Special dialog, as shown in Figure 22.9. This dialog allows you to narrow a selection down to only certain types of elements within your selection. This is a powerful dialog box.

 tip

You can replace steps 4 and 5 with a single keystroke. Hold down the Alt key while pressing the semicolon key. It turns out that Alt+; is the equivalent of selecting Home, Find & Select, Go To Special, Visible Cells Only, OK.

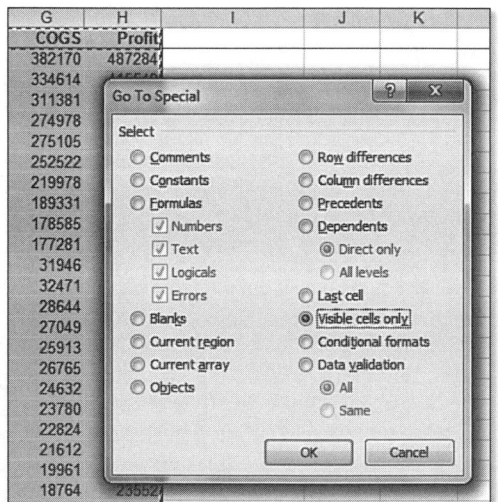

Figure 22.9
The Go To Special dialog allows you to reduce your selection to items meeting a certain criteria.

5. In the Go to Special dialog, select Visible Cells Only. Click OK. Excel will deselect all the hidden rows.

6. Click Ctrl+C to copy those rows. As you can see in Figure 22.10, Excel has selected each visible row separately.

Figure 22.10
Excel copies only the visible rows.

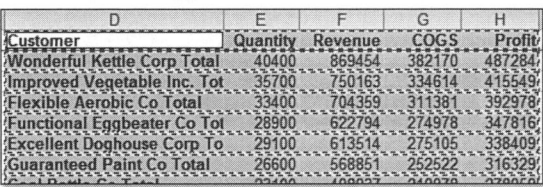

7. Select a blank section of the workbook. Use Ctrl+V to paste only the subtotals. As shown in Figure 22.11, the subtotals formulas are converted to values. This is the only thing that would make sense.

Figure 22.11
After pasting, you have static values instead of formulas.

Customer	Quantity	Revenue	COGS	Profit
Wonderful Kettle Corp Total	40400	869454	382170	487284
Improved Vegetable Inc. Total	35700	750163	334614	415549
Flexible Aerobic Co Total	33400	704359	311381	392978
Functional Eggbeater Co Total	28900	622794	274978	347816
Excellent Doghouse Corp Total	29100	613514	275105	338409

 To see a demo of copying the subtotal rows, search for "Excel In Depth 22" at YouTube.

Formatting the Subtotal Rows

When the subtotal command adds subtotals, it inserts a new row for each subtotal. Excel copies your key field to the new row and appends the word "Total" after the key field. This text in the key field column is bolded.

The other subtotal columns get a formula that uses the SUBTOTAL function. Strangely, the cells containing the formulas in each subtotal row are not bolded.

When I am doing my Power Excel seminars, a common question is how to bold the subtotal rows.

Many people try selecting E67:H592 and pressing Ctrl+B, as shown in Figure 22.12. Although it looks like it worked in Figure 22.12, this actually fails.

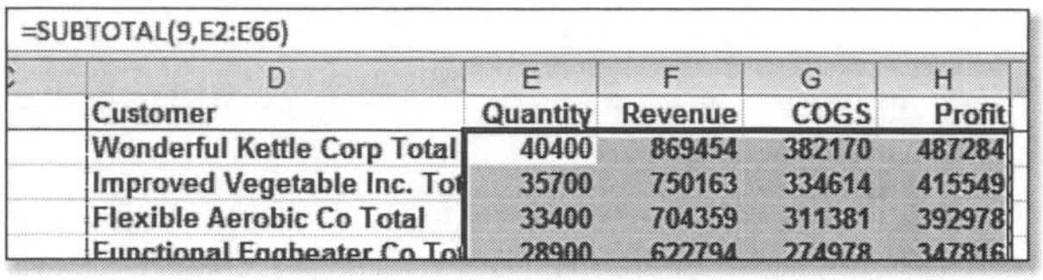

Figure 22.12
Try formatting the subtotal rows in collapsed view...

The problem becomes apparent when you go back to the #3 view to see the detail rows. The detail rows up through Row 66 are fine. The problem is that all the detail rows from Row 68 through the end of the data set have been bolded (see Figure 22.13). For some reason, Microsoft formats the rows hidden as the result of the subtotal command.

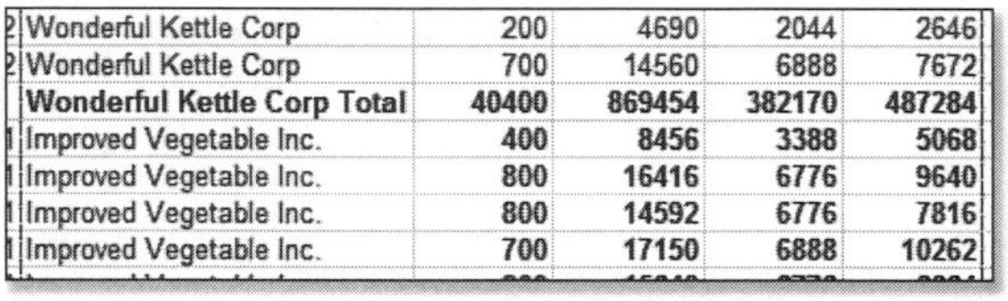

Figure 22.13
...and the hidden detail rows are formatted as well.

At this point, many people press Undo twice and start the process of manually formatting each individual subtotal row. There is, of course, an easier way. Follow these steps to format the subtotal rows:

1. Add subtotals to a data set as described previously.

2. Click the #2 Group and Outline button to collapse the data set to show only the subtotals.

3. Select from the first subtotal row down to the grand total row. In the current data set, select from D67 through H592.

4. Hold down Alt and press semicolon. Excel selects on the visible rows, which in this case are only the subtotal rows.

5. Apply any formatting desired. In Figure 22.14, the cells are showing a mix of Cell Styles, Heading 4, and a light red background from the Fill drop-down.

6. Click the #3 Group and Outline button to show all the detail rows.

Step 4 in this process is the key step. Using Alt+; selects only the visible rows in the collapsed subtotal view.

Figure 22.14
Format only the subtotal rows.

Customer	Quantity	Revenue	COGS	Profit
Easy Sandal Co	900	20610	8856	11754
Easy Sandal Co	400	8116	3388	4728
Easy Sandal Co	300	7032	3066	3966
Easy Sandal Co	1000	18290	8470	9820
Easy Sandal Co Total	2600	54048	23780	30268
Agile Calculator Inc.	800	18072	8176	9896
Agile Calculator Inc.	600	14004	5904	8100
Agile Calculator Inc.	200	4060	1968	2092
Agile Calculator Inc.	800	15104	6776	8328
Agile Calculator Inc. Total	2400	51240	22824	28416
Special Luggage Inc.	800	19344	7872	11472
Special Luggage Inc.	500	10760	4920	5840
Special Luggage Inc.	200	4614	2044	2570
Special Luggage Inc.	800	15312	6776	8536
Special Luggage Inc. Total	2300	50030	21612	28418
Mouthwatering Bicycle Corp	800	19520	7872	11648

Removing Subtotals

After you add subtotals and copy those subtotal rows to another worksheet, you might want to remove the subtotals from the original data set. Follow these steps to remove the subtotals:

1. Select one cell in the subtotaled data set.

2. Go back to the Subtotals command on the Data tab of the Ribbon.

3. In the lower-left corner of the Subtotals dialog box, click the button for Remove All.

The subtotal rows will be removed.

Using Specialty Subtotal Techniques

Over the years, the MrExcel podcast has covered a number of unusual questions about subtotals. The next section goes through the techniques for two of the more useful subtotal situations.

Summing Some Columns While Counting Another Column

It is easy for Excel to sum the numeric columns with the subtotal command. Sometimes, your manager will want to see a count of how many sales were made to a particular customer.

Microsoft has a solution to this problem that yields an ugly result. Using Microsoft's solution, you add totals to the numeric columns first. Then, you go back to the subtotals dialog, specify to Count a text column, and clear the check box for Replace Current Subtotals (see Figure 22.15).

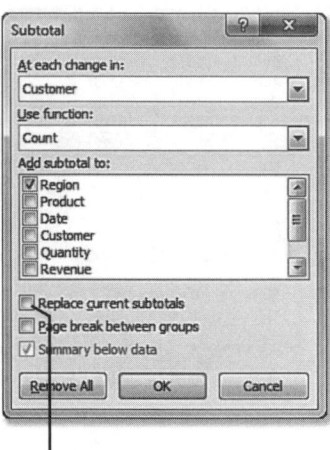

Replace Current Subtotals

The result shown in Figure 22.16 is that the Count occurs on one row, and the totals appear on another row. This creates a horrible looking summary view because every customer appears twice.

	A	B	C	D	E	F	G	H
1	Region	Product	Date	Customer	Quantity	Revenue	COGS	Profit
510	East	ABC	10/6/2012	Vivid Edger Co	700	13195	5929	7266
511	East	XYZ	10/17/2012	Vivid Edger Co	900	19161	9198	9963
512	Central	XYZ	10/30/2012	Vivid Edger Co	100	2092	1022	1070
513	East	XYZ	12/1/2012	Vivid Edger Co	600	13290	6132	7158
514	East	DEF	12/12/2012	Vivid Edger Co	500	10295	4920	5375
515	36			Vivid Edger Co Count				
516				Vivid Edger Co Total	18600	390978	177281	213697
517	East	ABC	1/21/2011	Supreme Clipboard Inc.	800	14440	6776	7664
518	Central	DEF	6/18/2011	Supreme Clipboard Inc.	1000	22140	9840	12300
519	East	XYZ	11/19/2011	Supreme Clipboard Inc.	1000	24420	10220	14200
520	West	XYZ	12/26/2012	Supreme Clipboard Inc.	500	11680	5110	6570
521	4			Supreme Clipboard Inc. Count				
522				Supreme Clipboard Inc. Total	3300	72680	31946	40734
523	East	XYZ	2/16/2011	Distinctive Oven Co	800	16936	8176	8760

Figure 22.16
If you count one field and sum the others, you get two summary rows per customer.

Here is a workaround that produces a suitable-looking summary report. Follow these steps:

1. Add subtotals to a data set. In the subtotal dialog box, choose to sum all the numeric columns. Also, choose to sum one text column. The result is that the subtotals added to the text column are all zero.

2. Examine the formula in the subtotal row of one of the text columns. The formula will be something like =SUBTOTAL(9,A479:A514). Compare this to the formula in the formula bar of Figure 22.16. That formula is =SUBTOTAL(3,A479:A514). The difference between summing and counting in the SUBTOTAL function is that the initial argument is a 3 instead of a 9.

3. Select your entire text column.

4. Use Home, Find & Select, Replace. In the Find and Replace dialog, choose to replace every (9, with a (3, as shown in Figure 22.17. Click Replace All.

Figure 22.17
Edit the formulas in column A to convert from Sum to CountA.

The result shown in Figure 22.18 is a count in column A and sums in the numeric columns. You have only one total line per customer.

Figure 22.18
The result is a count in column A and sums elsewhere.

	A	B	C	D	E	F	G	H
1	Region	Product	Date	Customer	Quantity	Revenue	COGS	Profit
67	65			Wonderful Kettle Corp Total	40400	869454	382170	487284
128	60			Improved Vegetable Inc. Tot	35700	750163	334614	415549
195	66			Flexible Aerobic Co Total	33400	704359	311381	392978
252	56			Functional Eggbeater Co Tot	28900	622794	274978	347816
301	48			Excellent Doghouse Corp To	29100	613514	275105	338409
354	52			Guaranteed Paint Co Total	26600	568851	252522	316329
395	40			Cool Bottle Co Total	23100	498937	219978	278959
440	44			Matchless Hardware Traders	19700	427349	189331	238018
469	28			Crisp Opener Partners Total	18700	406326	178585	227741
506	36			Vivid Edger Co Total	18600	390978	177281	213697

A195 · =SUBTOTAL(3,A129:A194)

Adding a Blank Row After Each Subtotal

This seems like it should be an easy request. But the problem is that the Insert Rows command adds a blank row *above* the selected cells.

After answering this question a dozen times in my Power Excel seminars, I think that I have the shortest possible set of steps when using subtotals.

This technique makes use of the Go To Special dialog twice; once to select the visible cells and once to select the nonblank cells.

Follow these steps to add a blank row after each subtotal.

1. Add Subtotals as described previously.

2. Click the #2 Group and Outline button to show only the subtotal rows.

3. Move out to the right of the data set and select a range in the first blank column to the right of your data. The range should extend from the first subtotal row down to the last subtotal row, not including the Grand Total.

4. Type Alt+; to select only the visible cells in that column.

5. Type 1 and press Ctrl+Enter to enter the number 1 next to each subtotal row, as shown in Figure 22.19.

G	H	I
COGS	**Profit**	
382170	487284	1
334614	415549	1
311381	392978	1
274978	347816	1
275105	338409	1
252522	316329	1
219978	278959	1
189331	238018	1
178585	227741	1

Figure 22.19
Ctrl+Enter adds 1s on each row in the selection.

6. Click the #3 Group and Outline button to show all the detail rows. Provided you successfully performed step 4, the 1s should appear only on the subtotal rows (see Figure 22.20).

D	E	F	G	H	I
Customer	**Quantity**	**Revenue**	**COGS**	**Profit**	
Agile Calculator Inc.	600	14004	5904	8100	
Agile Calculator Inc.	200	4060	1968	2092	
Agile Calculator Inc.	800	15104	6776	8328	
Agile Calculator Inc. Total	2400	51240	22824	28416	1
Special Luggage Inc.	800	19344	7872	11472	
Special Luggage Inc.	500	10760	4920	5840	
Special Luggage Inc.	200	4614	2044	2570	
Special Luggage Inc.	800	15312	6776	8536	
Special Luggage Inc. Total	2300	50030	21612	28418	1
Mouthwatering Bicycle Corp	800	19520	7872	11648	
Mouthwatering Bicycle Corp	100	1810	847	972	

Figure 22.20
Only the subtotal rows have 1s.

7. Select the first cell containing a 1 in the new column.

8. Select Home, Insert, Insert Cells, Shift Cells Down, OK (see Figure 22.21). This moves the 1s to the first row of each group.

9. Select the entire new column by clicking the column letter.

10. Select Home, Find & Select, Go To Special. In the Go To Special dialog, select Constants and click OK. This will select only the 1s in the column. You have now effectively selected one cell in the first row of each group of customers.

Figure 22.21
Shift the 1s down one row with Insert Cells.

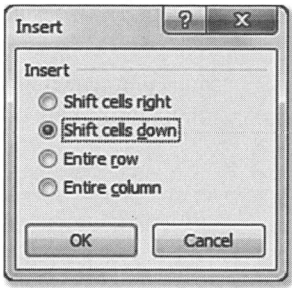

11. From the menu, select Home, Insert, Insert Sheet Rows. Go ahead and scroll through your data. You will see that you have now added a blank row after every subtotal row (see Figure 22.22)!

12. Select the new column and press the Delete key to clear the 1s from that column.

Figure 22.22
Insert rows and you have added a blank row before every 1, which happens to be after every subtotal row.

D	E	F	G	H	I
Customer	Quantity	Revenue	COGS	Profit	
New Faucet Co Total	3000	62744	28644	34100	
Savory Opener Inc.	700	12474	5929	6545	1
Savory Opener Inc.	800	20408	8176	12232	
Savory Opener Inc.	900	17757	8856	8901	
Savory Opener Inc.	400	9660	4088	5572	
Savory Opener Inc. Total	2800	60299	27049	33250	
Tremendous Thermostat Partne	1000	21730	9840	11890	1
Tremendous Thermostat Partne	200	4754	1968	2786	
Tremendous Thermostat Partne	700	12853	5929	7924	

Add Subtotals by Two Fields

Suppose you would like to add subtotals by region and product. You will add the subtotals twice. In the second subtotal command, make sure you clear the Replace Current Subtotals check box.

Make sure that your data is sorted properly. You can either use the Sort dialog to sort by Region and then by Product, or you can follow these steps, which require only four clicks.

1. Select one cell in the product column.

2. Click the AZ button on the Data tab.

3. Select one cell in the Region column.

4. Click the AZ button on the Data tab.

Because the sort in step 4 keeps ties in the previous sequence, this set of steps effectively sorts by product within region.

It is important that you add subtotals to the outer group first. Use the instructions earlier in this chapter to add totals to the Region field.

Run the Subtotals command again. This time, specify Each Change In Product. Clear the Replace Current Subtotals check box.

You will now have four Group and Outline buttons. If you press the #3 button, you will see product totals and region totals, as shown in Figure 22.23. Note that Excel supports a maximum of eight group and outline buttons, so you could add up to six levels of subtotals.

	A	B	C	D	E	F
1	**Region**	**Product**	**Date**	**Customer**	**Quantity**	**Revenue**
76		ABC Total			40200	766469
137		DEF Total			34900	776996
205		XYZ Total			36200	832414
206	Central Total				111300	2375879
277		ABC Total			36500	703255
354		DEF Total			40300	891799
418		XYZ Total			39600	897949
419	East Total				116400	2493003
479		ABC Total			33300	631646
522		DEF Total			22600	494919
575		XYZ Total			30300	712365
576	West Total				86200	1838930
577	Grand Total				313900	6707812

Figure 22.23
Two sets of subtotals mean four Group and Outline buttons.

USING PIVOT TABLES TO ANALYZE DATA

A pivot table enables you to summarize thousands or millions of records of data to a one-page summary in just a few clicks.

Pivot tables were introduced in Excel 95 and have been evolving ever since. Excel 2007 simplified the pivot table interface and added new filters. Excel 2010 offers new calculations, visual filters called slicers, and the capability to mash up million-row data sets using PowerPivot.

Suppose you have 400,000 records of transactional data. It is easy for some people to figure out that this represents $x million. But to learn some things about the data, you need to do some more analysis to spot trends in the data. A pivot table lets you analyze trends in data without having to worry about formulas. Your focus is more on finding trends than on worrying about writing formulas in Excel.

By using a pivot table, it is possible to create a number of views of your data, including the following:

- Breakdown of sales by product

- Sales by month, this year versus last year

- Percentage of sales by customer

- Customers who bought xyz in the east

- Sales by product by month

- Top five customers with products

Of course, these are just examples. You can use pivot tables to slice and dice your data in almost any imaginable way.

The following features are new in pivot tables in Excel 2010:

■ Slicers are a new type of visual filter.

> *Read about slicers in Chapter 24, "Using Slicers and Filtering a Pivot Table."*

■ It is easier to show a values field as a percentage, with a new drop-down added to the Options tab. New calculations such as % of Parent item and Rank have been added to the list.

■ When you have multiple fields in the row area, you can finally fill in the blank cells in the outer row field by repeating all labels.

■ If your pivot table is based on OLAP data or PowerPivot data, a new feature called Named Sets will allow you to create asymmetric pivot tables, where you show actuals for last year and forecast for this year.

> *Read about named sets in Chapter 25, "Mashing Up Data with PowerPivot."*

■ A new PowerPivot add-in enables you to create pivot tables from multiple tables on multiple worksheets. PowerPivot is not constrained by the 1,048,576 row limit in Excel. PowerPivot introduces a new powerful DAX formula language that allows for interesting calculated columns such as Fiscal Year to Date Sales as a percentage of prior Fiscal Year to Date sales.

> *Read more about PowerPivot in Chapter 25, "Mashing Up Data with PowerPivot."*

If you upgrade from Excel 2003, you also notice the following features introduced in Excel 2007:

■ You no longer drag fields directly to drop zones on the report. Instead, you drag fields to four drop zones in the pivot table field list. Two of the drop zones have been renamed; the Page area is now called Report Filter. The Data area is now called Values.

■ A new set of filters can be applied to fields in the row or column areas. These filters have some date intelligence, so you can set up a conceptual filter such as dates in the current month, next quarter, or last week.

■ A new layout joins the old Outline and Tabular layouts. When you have two or more fields in the row area of the pivot table, this Compact Layout will jam those fields into a single column. Although it makes for a great presentation, data analysts realize that it violates the rule of mixing two fields in a single column.

■ The pivot table toolbar is replaced with two new tabs on the Ribbon.

■ The red exclamation icon that was used to refresh pivot tables has been replaced by a large icon that actually says Refresh. This will make the Refresh feature far more discoverable. Truly refreshing.

■ Fifty-four useful autoformats replace the 14 hideous table formats from Excel 2003. You can design your own formats and choose which format should be the default for future pivot tables.

Creating Your First Pivot Table

Pivot tables are best created from transactional data—that is, raw data files directly from your company's IS department.

To create the best pivot tables, make sure your data follows these rules:

- Make sure each column has a one-cell heading. Keep the headings unique; don't use the same heading for two columns. If you need your headings to appear on two rows, type the first word, press Alt+Enter, and then type the second word.

- If a column should contain numeric data, don't allow blank cells in the column. Use zeros instead of blanks.

- Do not use blank rows or blank columns.

- If totals are embedded in your report, remove them.

- The workbook should not be in Compatibility mode. Many new pivot table features from Excel 2007 and Excel 2010 will be disabled if the workbook is in Compatibility mode.

- If you add new data to the bottom of your data set each month, you should strongly consider converting your data set to a table using Ctrl+T. Pivot tables created from tables automatically pick up new rows pasted to the bottom of the table after a refresh.

- If your data has months spread across many columns, go back to the source software program to see if a different view of the data is available.

When you have your data in the correct format, creating and changing a pivot table is easy.

Suppose that your manager has asked you to summarize some data to show revenue by region and product. To create a pivot table to do this, follow these steps:

1. Select one cell in your data.

2. From the Insert tab, click the PivotTable icon.

3. Excel displays the Create PivotTable dialog, as shown in Figure 23.1. In the top portion of the dialog, confirm that Excel's IntelliSense chose the right range for your data. If your data is formatted as a table, the table name appears here. Otherwise, you see a range address such as A1:H300. In the lower portion of the dialog, you can choose to create your pivot table on a new worksheet or in a blank portion of the existing worksheet.

Figure 23.2 shows the start of a pivot table. Because you no longer drag fields to the report, the graphic shown in columns A:C is a placeholder to indicate where the pivot table will appear after you choose some fields. The PivotTable Field List has a list of fields from your original data set at the top and four drop zones at the bottom. To build your report, you add fields to the drop zones at the bottom.

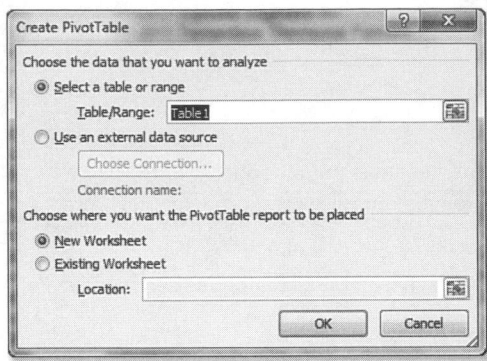

Figure 23.1
Most of the time, you can click OK to get through this dialog.

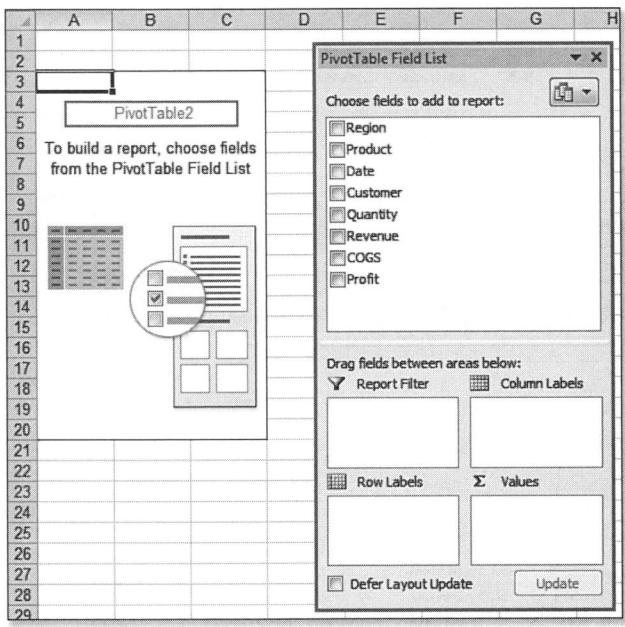

Figure 23.2
A blank pivot table and the redesigned PivotTable Field List.

> **note**
>
> The field list is generally docked to the right side of the Excel window. The figures in this book show the field list as undocked. To undock the field list, drag the title bar away from the edge of the window. It is hard to redock the field list. You have to grab the left side of the title bar and drag the field list more than 50% off the right side of the screen.

You are now just three clicks away from the answer you need. In the top of the PivotTable Field List, select the fields for Region, then Product, and then Revenue check boxes. Because the Region and Product fields contain text, they are automatically moved to the row area. Because Revenue is numeric, it is automatically moved to the Values area. Figure 23.3 shows your first pivot table.

Dealing with the Compact Layout

Figure 23.3
It takes six clicks to summarize the original data set into this table.

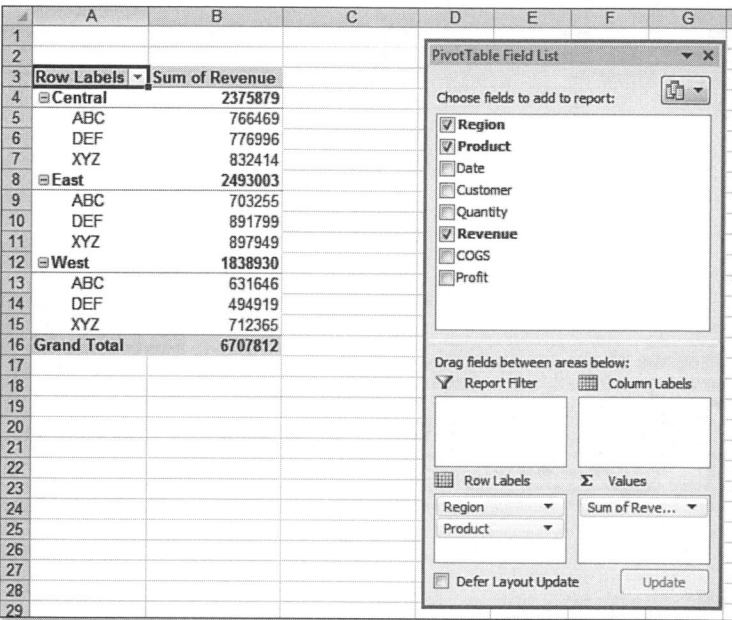

If you've been using pivot tables for many versions of Excel, you have to wonder about the bizarre layout of the pivot table in Figure 23.3. The totals appear at the top of each group instead of at the bottom. Two fields, Region and Product, are appearing in column A. Collapse buttons appear next to the regions.

This is a new layout called Compact view. It is beautiful if you plan to present your pivot table in an interactive touch-screen kiosk complete with slicers. If you plan to reuse the results of the pivot table, the compact layout is horrible. Here is how to go back to the tabular layout.

1. Make sure that the active cell is inside the pivot table.

2. Go to the Design tab in the Ribbon. Open the Report Layout drop-down. Select Show in Tabular Form. As shown in Figure 23.4, the totals move back to the bottom of each region. Product moves to column B.

3. Try out a new Excel 2010 feature. Open the Report Layout drop-down and select Repeat All Item Labels. This eliminates the blanks in column A of the pivot table, as shown in Figure 23.5. This is a feature that has been badly needed in Excel for 15 years.

	A	B	C
1			
2			
3	Region ▾	Product ▾	Sum of Revenue
4	⊟Central	ABC	766469
5		DEF	776996
6		XYZ	832414
7	Central Total		2375879
8	⊟East	ABC	703255
9		DEF	891799
10		XYZ	897949
11	East Total		2493003
12	⊟West	ABC	631646
13		DEF	494919
14		XYZ	712365
15	West Total		1838930
16	Grand Total		6707812
17			

Figure 23.4
Use the Design tab to return to a normal pivot table layout.

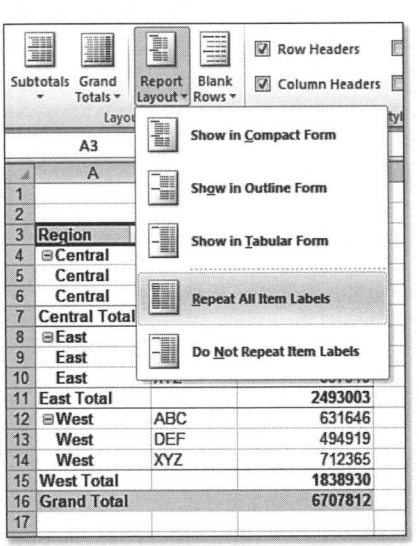

Figure 23.5
Repeat All Item Labels fills in the blanks in the outer row fields.

Rearranging a Pivot Table

The drop zone sections of the PivotTable Field List Box are as follows:

- **Report Filter**—You use this section to limit the report to only certain criteria. This section is analogous to the PageField section in the old pivot table model. It is virtually replaced by the new slicer feature.

  ➡ *Read about filtering pivot tables in Chapter 24, "Using Slicers and Filtering a Pivot Table."*

- **Row Labels**—This section is for fields that appear on the left side of the table. By default, all text fields move here when you select the check boxes in the top of the field list.

- **Column Labels**—This section is for fields that stretch along the top rows of columns of your table. Old database geeks refer to this as a crosstab report.

- **Values**—This section is for all the numeric fields that are summarized in the table. By default, most fields are automatically summed, but you can change the default calculation to an average, minimum, maximum, or other calculations.

To rearrange a pivot table, you drag fields from one drop zone to another. For example, drag the Region field from the Row Labels drop zone to the Column Labels drop zone. You now have a report showing regions across the top and products down the side (see Figure 23.6).

Figure 23.6
Move the Region heading to the Column Labels drop zone to change the report.

3	Sum of Revenue	Region			
4	Product	Central	East	West	Grand Total
5	ABC	766469	703255	631646	2101370
6	DEF	776996	891799	494919	2163714
7	XYZ	832414	897949	712365	2442728
8	Grand Total	2375879	2493003	1838930	6707812

Drag fields between areas below:

Report Filter | Column Labels — Region

Row Labels — Product | Σ Values — Sum of Reve...

Rearranging fields in the drop zones might also involve moving a field within the same drop zone. Here is an example.

1. Select the Customer field check box in the top of the pivot table field list. Customer moves to the last field in the Row Labels drop zone. This creates a great report for a product manager, as it shows each product and a list of customers who bought that product, as shown in Figure 23.7.

Figure 23.7
With Customer as the second row field, you have a product report.

	A	B	C	D	E	F
3	Sum of Revenue		Region			
4	Product	Customer	Central	East	West	Grand Total
5	⊟ABC	Agile Calculator Inc.			15104	15104
6	ABC	Cool Bottle Co	37600	75912	28900	142412
7	ABC	Crisp Opener Partners	24003	89960		113963
8	ABC	Distinctive Oven Co		9635		9635
9	ABC	Easy Sandal Co		8116	18290	26406
10	ABC	Excellent Doghouse Corp	80366	69991	53165	203522
11	ABC	Exclusive Washer Corp			17250	17250
12	ABC	Fine Shingle Supply		5532		5532
13	ABC	Flexible Aerobic Co	136774	60556	96808	294138
14	ABC	Functional Eggbeater Co	90995	27550	73083	191628
15	ABC	Guaranteed Paint Co	77683	61660	38039	177382
16	ABC	Improved Vegetable Inc.	124738	69040	87189	280967
17	ABC	Inventive Door Inc.			4158	4158
18	ABC	Magnificent Shingle Corp		17840		17840
19	ABC	Matchless Hardware Traders	29644	39273	30627	99544
20	ABC	Mouthwatering Bicycle Corp		1819		1819
21	ABC	New Faucet Co			17190	17190
22	ABC	Powerful Edger Supply			3552	3552
23	ABC	Rare Door Inc.			5859	5859

☑ Region
☑ Product
☐ Date
☑ Customer
☐ Quantity
☑ Revenue
☐ COGS
☐ Profit

Drag fields betw
Report Filt

Row Labels
Product
Customer

☐ Defer Layou

2. Drag the Product field in the Row Labels drop zone and move it below the Customer Field. This creates a customer-centric report, where the first customer appears, followed by a list of products that the customer purchased (see Figure 23.8).

⊿	A	B	C
1			
2			
3	Sum of Revenue		Region ▼
4	Customer ▼	Product ▼	Central	Ea
5	⊟Agile Calculator Inc.	ABC	
6	Agile Calculator Inc.	DEF	4060
7	Agile Calculator Inc.	XYZ	
8	Agile Calculator Inc. Total		4060
9	⊟Cool Bottle Co	ABC	37600
10	Cool Bottle Co	DEF	84778
11	Cool Bottle Co	XYZ	28932
12	Cool Bottle Co Total		151310
13	⊟Crisp Opener Partners	ABC	24003
14	Crisp Opener Partners	DEF	85317

☐COGS
☐Profit

Drag fields betwee
▼ Report Filter

▦ Row Labels
Customer
Product

Figure 23.8
Move Product to the second row field and you have a report that focuses on each customer.

Finishing Touches: Numeric Formatting and Removing Blanks

After you arrange your data in the report, you want to consider formatting the numeric fields. For example, in Figure 23.8, it would be helpful if the numbers were formatted with commas as thousands separators. Also, consider changing the words Sum of Revenue to something less awkward, like Total Revenue or even Revenue.

Follow these steps to apply a numeric format to the Revenue field:

1. Select one cell that contains a revenue amount. If you look on the Options tab, youl see a box that reports the Active Field. By choosing a cell with Revenue, the Active Field box indicates that Sum of Revenue is the active field.

2. Click the Field Settings icon in the Active Field group of the Options tab. Excel displays the Value Field Settings dialog.

3. The label for this field appears in the Custom Name box at the top of the dialog. Change Sum of Revenue by typing a space and then the word Revenue. Note that the space is critical. You cannot use just the word Revenue without a space as this would create a duplicate field name.

4. Click the Number Format button in the bottom of the Value Field Settings dialog. Excel displays the familiar Number tab of the Format Cells dialog.

5. Select the Number category. Select 0 decimal places. Add a thousands separator. Click OK to close the Format Cells dialog. Click OK to close the Value Field Settings dialog.

 caution
Avoid the temptation to format cells B5:F113 using the formatting commands on the Home tab. This will format the current pivot table, but as you continue to add fields to the pivot table later, the shape of the pivot table will change and the Home tab formatting will not stick. When you go through the process previously described, the Revenue field will continue to have the correct format.

Figure 23.9 shows the new number format applied to the pivot table, along with the Field Settings icon and the Value Field Settings dialog.

Figure 23.9
Access the Number Format button by using the Field Settings icon.

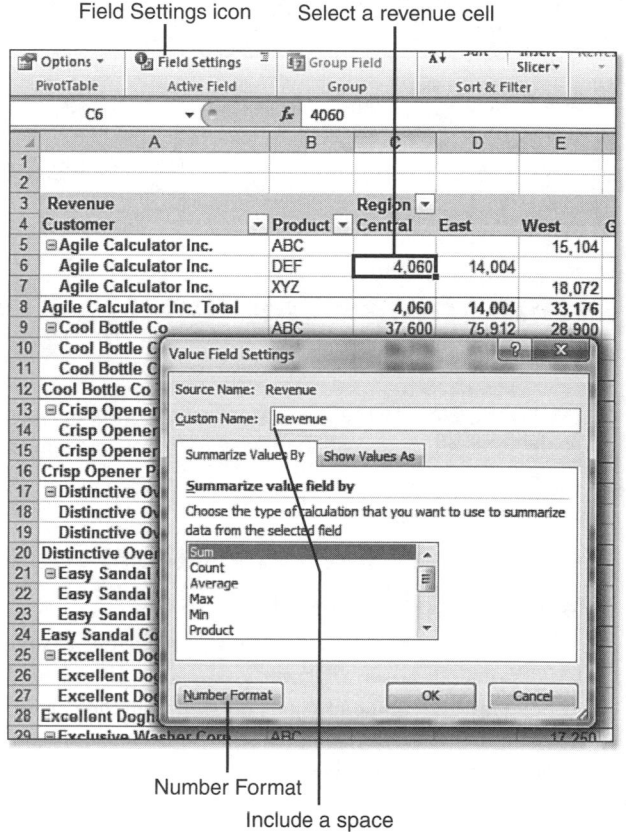

Notice the blank cells in the values area of the pivot table. For example, the blank cell in C5 of the pivot table means that there are no records in the data set where Agile Calculator bought product ABC in the Central region. You would probably rather have zeros in those cells instead of blanks. You will perform the following steps so often, you will wonder why Microsoft did not make this the default choice:

1. Select any one cell inside the pivot table.

2. On the Options tab, select the Options icon on the left side of the Ribbon.

3. On the Layout & Format tab of the PivotTable Options dialog, type a zero next to For Empty Cells Show.

4. Click OK. Excel will fill in the empty cells with zeros.

The final pivot table is shown in Figure 23.10.

Revenue Customer	Product	Region Central	East	West	Grand Total
⊟Agile Calculator Inc.	ABC	0	0	15,104	15,104
Agile Calculator Inc.	DEF	4,060	14,004	0	18,064
Agile Calculator Inc.	XYZ	0	0	18,072	18,072
Agile Calculator Inc. Total		4,060	14,004	33,176	51,240
⊟Cool Bottle Co	ABC	37,600	75,912	28,900	142,412
Cool Bottle Co	DEF	84,778	51,445	46,532	182,755
Cool Bottle Co	XYZ	28,932	72,625	72,213	173,770
Cool Bottle Co Total		151,310	199,982	147,645	498,937
⊟Crisp Opener Partners	ABC	24,003	89,960	0	113,963

Figure 23.10
This pivot table shows sales by region and product for each customer.

Four Things You Have to Know When Using Pivot Tables

Pivot tables are the greatest invention in spreadsheets. But you have to understand these four issues, presented in order of importance.

Your Pivot Table Is in Manual Calculation Mode Until You Click Refresh!

Most people are shocked to learn that changes to underlying data do not appear in a pivot table. After all, you change a cell in Excel, and all the formulas derived from the cell automatically change. You would think that the same should hold true for pivot tables, but it does not.

> ### 📡 caution
> Pivot tables are fast because the data from the worksheet is loaded into a special cache in memory. If you build a pivot table and then change the underlying data, you must click the Refresh icon in the Options tab to have the change appear in the pivot table (see Figure 23.11).

Figure 23.11
If you don't click this button, changes to the underlying data set will not appear in the pivot table.

One Blank Cell in a Value Column Causes Excel to Count Instead of Sum

Suppose your data set has thousands of rows of data. For any reason, if one of the revenue cells happens to be blank, this completely confuses Excel. There can be 999,999 cells with numbers and 1 blank cell, but Excel no longer realizes that the Revenue column is a numeric column. When you add Revenue to the pivot table, Excel decides to count the number of rows instead of summing the revenue. To correct the problem, you have two choices:

- Delete the pivot table, fill the blanks in the original data with zeros, and re-create the pivot table.

- Select one cell that contains Count of Revenue. Select the Field Settings icon. Change from Count to Sum in that dialog.

If You Click Outside of the Pivot Table, All the Pivot Table Tools Disappear

If your field list disappeared and the Options and Design tabs are missing, it is likely that you clicked outside of the pivot table.

I've had the argument with Microsoft that because nothing is on the worksheet other than the pivot table, that I am still looking at the pivot table even though I clicked outside of the pivot table. I continue to lose this argument. If the field list disappears and the tabs are gone, click back inside of your pivot table.

You Cannot Change, Move a Part of, or Insert Cells in a Pivot Table

Many times, pivot tables get you very close to the final report you want, and you just want to insert a row or move one bit of the table. You cannot do this. If you try, you will be greeted with the ubiquitous message that you cannot change a pivot table. This is a fair limitation. After all, Excel needs to figure out how to redraw the table when you move something in the field list.

The solution is to copy the entire pivot table and then use Paste Values to convert the report to regular Excel data. You can either put this on a new worksheet or paste the entire table back over itself. If you go to a new worksheet, you can continue to modify the original pivot table. If you paste values over the original worksheet, the pivot table converts to a range, and you cannot pivot it further.

Calculating and Roll-Ups with Pivot Tables

Pivot tables offer many more calculation options than those shown so far in this chapter. One of the most amazing features of pivot tables built from regular data is the capability to roll daily dates up to months, quarters, and years.

Grouping Daily Dates to Months and Years

Good pivot tables start with good transactional data. Invariably, that transactional data is stored with daily dates instead of monthly summaries. It is easy to roll a pivot table up to months, quarters, and years.

To produce a summary by month, quarter, and year, follow these steps:

1. Build a pivot table with daily dates going down the row field.

2. Select either the Date heading or one of the cells containing a date.

3. From the Options tab, select Group Field.

4. In the Group Field dialog box, select Months, Quarters, and Years, as shown in Figure 23.12.

Choose a date cell   Group Field icon

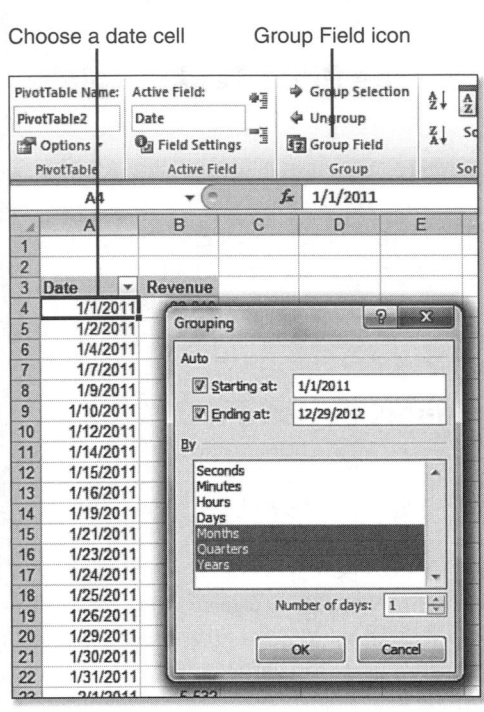

Figure 23.12
Roll daily dates up to months.

5. Click OK. The resulting field has years, then quarters, and then months as row labels. Because of a strange bug, the year and quarter fields do not have subtotals (see Figure 23.13).

6. The cell pointer should be on the first year cell. Select the Field Settings button in the Options tab. Select Automatic and click OK.

7. Move the cell pointer to the first quarter cell. Select Field Settings and click Automatic. Click OK.

You now have a pivot table that provides totals by month, quarter, and year. Notice that your pivot table field list includes three fields related to dates; the years and quarters field are virtual fields. The original Date field includes the months. This was a brilliant design decision on Microsoft's part.

Take the Years field and drag it to the Column Labels drop zone in the PivotTable Field List. You now have a report comparing year-over-year sales (see Figure 23.14).

 To see a demo of rolling daily dates up to years and months, search for "Excel In Depth 23" at YouTube.

Figure 23.13
After grouping, the outer row fields don't have subtotals.

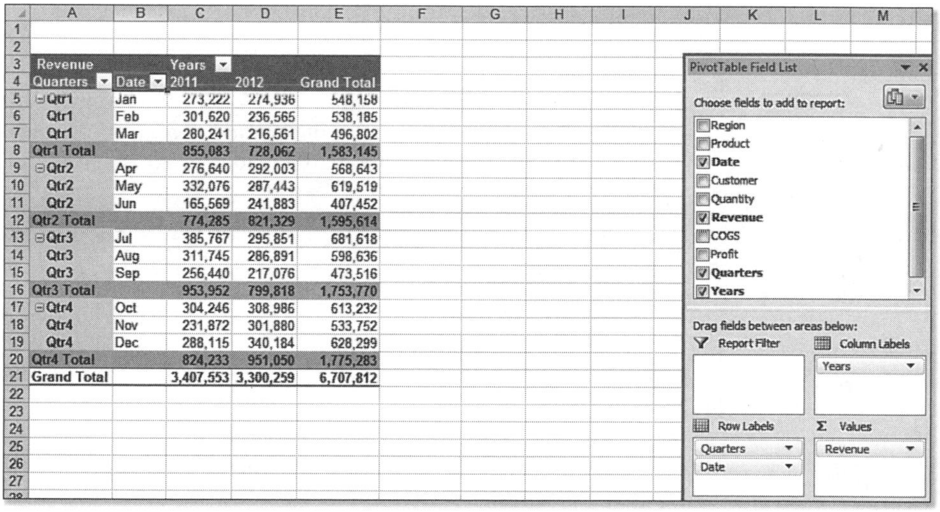

	A	B	C	D
1				
2				
3	**Years** ▼	**Quarter** ▼	**Date** ▼	**Revenue**
4	⊟2011	⊟Qtr1	Jan	273,222
5	2011	Qtr1	Feb	301,620
6	2011	Qtr1	Mar	280,241
7	2011	⊟Qtr2	Apr	276,640
8	2011	Qtr2	May	332,076
9	2011	Qtr2	Jun	165,569
10	2011	⊟Qtr3	Jul	385,767
11	2011	Qtr3	Aug	311,745
12	2011	Qtr3	Sep	256,440
13	2011	⊟Qtr4	Oct	304,246
14	2011	Qtr4	Nov	231,872
15	2011	Qtr4	Dec	288,115
16	⊟2012	⊟Qtr1	Jan	274,936
17	2012	Qtr1	Feb	236,565
18	2012	Qtr1	Mar	216,561
19	2012	⊟Qtr2	Apr	292,003
20	2012	Qtr2	May	287,443
21	2012	Qtr2	Jun	241,883
22	2012	⊟Qtr3	Jul	295,851
23	2012	Qtr3	Aug	286,891
24	2012	Qtr3	Sep	217,076
25	2012	⊟Qtr4	Oct	308,986
26	2012	Qtr4	Nov	301,880
27	2012	Qtr4	Dec	340,184
28	**Grand Total**			**6,707,812**

Figure 23.14
Move the virtual year field to the column fields and you have a year-over-year comparison.

	A	B	C	D	E
1					
2					
3	Revenue		Years ▼		
4	Quarters ▼	Date ▼	2011	2012	Grand Total
5	⊟Qtr1	Jan	273,222	274,936	548,158
6	Qtr1	Feb	301,620	236,565	538,185
7	Qtr1	Mar	280,241	216,561	496,802
8	Qtr1 Total		855,083	728,062	1,583,145
9	⊟Qtr2	Apr	276,640	292,003	568,643
10	Qtr2	May	332,076	287,443	619,519
11	Qtr2	Jun	165,569	241,883	407,452
12	Qtr2 Total		774,285	821,329	1,595,614
13	⊟Qtr3	Jul	385,767	295,851	681,618
14	Qtr3	Aug	311,745	286,891	598,636
15	Qtr3	Sep	256,440	217,076	473,516
16	Qtr3 Total		953,952	799,818	1,753,770
17	⊟Qtr4	Oct	304,246	308,986	613,232
18	Qtr4	Nov	231,872	301,880	533,752
19	Qtr4	Dec	288,115	340,184	628,299
20	Qtr4 Total		824,233	951,050	1,775,283
21	Grand Total		3,407,553	3,300,259	6,707,812

PivotTable Field List

Choose fields to add to report:
- ☐ Region
- ☐ Product
- ☑ Date
- ☐ Customer
- ☐ Quantity
- ☑ Revenue
- ☐ COGS
- ☐ Profit
- ☑ Quarters
- ☑ Years

Drag fields between areas below:

▼ Report Filter	▦ Column Labels
	Years ▼

▦ Row Labels	Σ Values
Quarters ▼	Revenue ▼
Date ▼	

Adding Calculations Outside the Pivot Table

In Figure 23.14, you would probably rather show a % of Growth instead of the Grand Total column in column F. After you grouped the dates in the pivot table, you are prevented from adding a calculated item inside the pivot table, so you have to turn back to regular Excel to provide the % Growth column.

However, it is not simple Excel to create that column. In particular, step 2 will trip most people up. Follow these steps:

1. Select cells E3:E21. Copy those cells. Use Paste, Paste Special, Formats to copy the table formatting to cell F3.

2. In cell F5, type =D5/C5-1. You really have to type this formula! Do not touch the mouse or the arrow keys while you are building the formula, or you will be stung by the GetPivotData bug.

3. Format cell F5 as percentage with one decimal place.

4. Copy cell F5.

5. Select F5:F21. Open the Paste drop-down and select the Formulas & Number Formatting icon. (It is the icon with % and fx symbols; see Figure 23.15.)

6. Move the cell pointer back to column E so that you are inside the pivot table and have access to the pivot table tabs.

7. Click the Options icon on the Options tab. Go to the Totals & Filters tab of the PivotTable Options dialog. Clear the Show Grand Total for Rows check box. Click OK.

8. Delete the now-empty column E.

	E5			f_x	=D5/C5-1	
	A	B	C	D	E	
1						
2						
3	Revenue		Years			
4	Quarters	Date	2011	2012	% Growth	
5	Qtr1	Jan	273,222	274,936	0.6%	
6	Qtr1	Feb	301,620	236,565	-21.6%	
7	Qtr1	Mar	280,241	216,561	-22.7%	
8	Qtr1 Total		855,083	728,062	-14.9%	
9	Qtr2	Apr	276,640	292,003	5.6%	
10	Qtr2	May	332,076	287,443	-13.4%	
11	Qtr2	Jun	165,569	241,883	46.1%	
12	Qtr2 Total		774,285	821,329	6.1%	
13	Qtr3	Jul	385,767	295,851	-23.3%	
14	Qtr3	Aug	311,745	286,891	-8.0%	
15	Qtr3	Sep	256,440	217,076	-15.4%	
16	Qtr3 Total		953,952	799,818	-16.2%	
17	Qtr4	Oct	304,246	308,986	1.6%	
18	Qtr4	Nov	231,872	301,880	30.2%	
19	Qtr4	Dec	288,115	340,184	18.1%	
20	Qtr4 Total		824,233	951,050	15.4%	
21	Grand Total		3,407,553	3,300,259	-3.1%	

Figure 23.15
The % Growth column is a regular formula outside the pivot table, formatted to look like it is part of the pivot table.

Showing Percentage of Total

Excel 2010 adds several new calculations and did a great job of bringing the old calculations to the forefront by adding the Show Values As drop-down to the Pivot Table Options tab.

To see some of the new calculations, use the following steps to build a pivot table with two fields in the row area and no fields in the column area:

1. This will sound counterintuitive, but drag the revenue field to the Values drop zone three times. You will be comparing the different ways to show the Revenue field.

2. Leave the first Revenue column in the pivot table alone.

3. Move the cell pointer to the second Revenue column in the pivot table. From the Show Values As drop-down, select % of Column Total.

4. Move the cell pointer to the third Revenue column. From the Show Values As drop-down, select % of Parent Row Total. This is one of the new calculations in Excel 2010.

5. Type new headings for the three columns: something like Revenue (with a leading space), then % of Total, and % of Parent.

Figure 23.16 shows the results of the pivot table. Pay careful attention to the differences between column J and column K. In Column J, the % of Column total shows the percentage of the Grand Total row. The 8.02% for January means that January is 8.02% of the total in the pivot table. In column K, the % of Parent Row is a new and clever calculation. The 31.95% for January means that January is 31.95% of Quarter 1. The 25.09% for Qtr 1 means that this quarter is 25.09% of the total for the year. This calculation has been driving people crazy for the last several versions of Excel and it is great to see it added in Excel 2010.

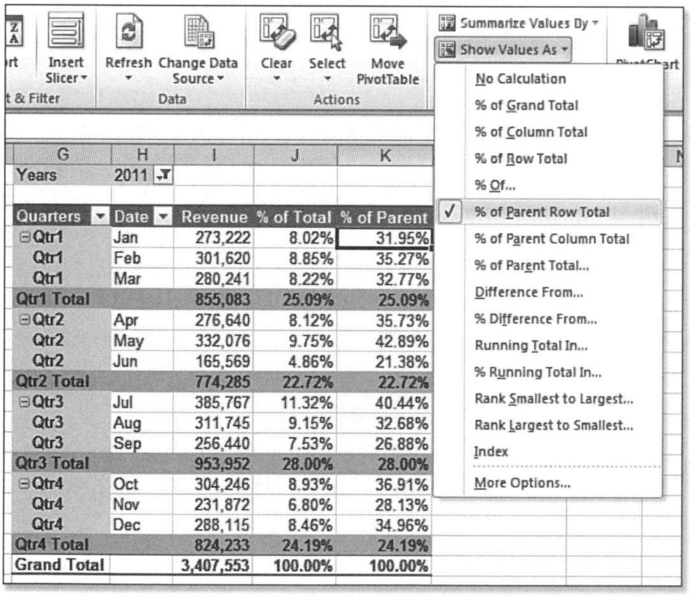

Figure 23.16
% of Parent is a new calculation in Excel 2010 pivot tables.

Showing Running Totals and Rank

Other options in the Show Values As drop-down include running totals and a ranking. These work best when there is only one field in the row area.

Use the following steps to build a pivot table with one field in the row area and no fields in the column area:

1. Drag the Revenue field to the Values area five times.

2. Leave the first Revenue column showing a Normal calculation.

3. Go to the second column with Revenue. From the Show Values As drop-down, select Running Total In. This time, Excel asks one additional question; specify that you are looking for Running Totals in the Date field. Change the heading of this field to be YTD.

4. Go to the third Revenue column. From the Show Values As drop-down, select % Running Total In. Again, select Date. Change the heading to % YTD.

5. Go to the fourth Revenue column. From the Show Values As drop-down, select Rank Largest to Smallest. Select Date. Change the heading to Rank.

6. Go to the fifth Revenue column. From the Show Values As drop-down, select % Of.

7. In the Show Values As dialog that appears, select Date as the Base Field. Select (previous) as the Base Item. Click OK.

8. Change the heading to % Change from Previous Month.

Figure 23.17 shows the resulting pivot table.

- Column I shows a running total within the months field. This is essentially a year-to-date calculation.

- Column J shows the % of the yearly revenue that was achieved by the end of each month.

- Column K shows the rank of each month. July was the best sales month. June was the worst sales month.

- Column L shows the % Change from the previous month. The 304,246 sold in October is 118.64% of the $256,440 sold in September.

The Show Values As drop-down is a useful improvement to Excel 2010. Many of those calculations were previously buried where most people would never find them.

Using a Formula to Add a Field to a Pivot Table

The previous examples took an existing field and used the Show Values As drop-down to change how the data is presented in the pivot table. In this example, you learn how to add a brand new calculated field to the pivot table.

Figure 23.17
Rank and % of YTD are new in Excel 2010.

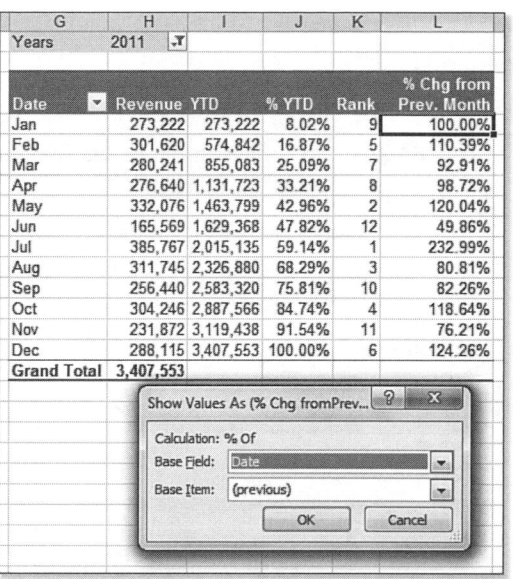

In Figure 23.18, the pivot table is showing Quantity, Revenue, COGS, and Profit for each customer in the data set. You would like to add two new columns: for Gross Profit Percent and Average Price Per Unit.

Figure 23.18
Add new calculations that compare two columns in the pivot table.

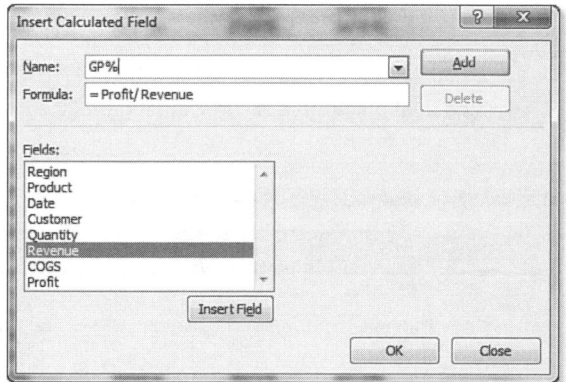

Follow these steps to add a calculated field:

1. Select one of the numeric cells in the pivot table.

2. From the Options tab, open the Fields, Items & Sets drop-down. Select Calculated Field. Excel displays the Insert Calculated Field dialog. The default field name of Field 1 and the default formula of =0 appear in the dialog.

3. Type a new name such as GP%.

4. The Formula field starts out as an equal sign, a space, and then a zero. You have to click in this field and backspace to remove the zero.

5. Build the formula by double-clicking Profit, typing a slash, and then double-clicking Revenue. The dialog box should look like Figure 23.19. Click OK.

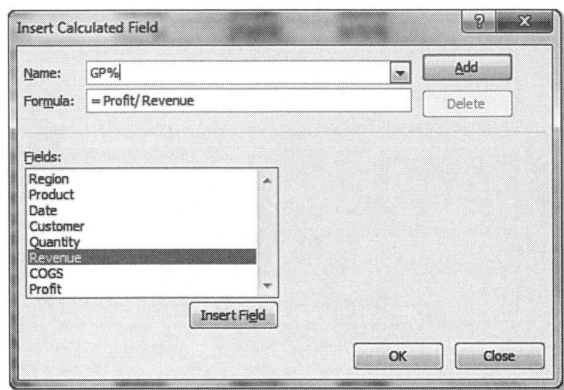

Figure 23.19
Build a calculated Field.

6. Repeat steps 1 and 2. The calculation for Average Price is Revenue / Quantity. Click OK.

7. The headings for calculated fields always appear strange. Change Sum of % to GP% with a leading space. Change Sum of AvgPrice to Avg. Price

8. Change the numeric format of the calculated fields.

The final pivot table is shown in Figure 23.20.

Customer	Qty	Revenue	COGS	Profit	GP%	Avg Price
Agile Calculator Inc.	2,400	51,240	22,824	28,416	55.5%	21.35
Cool Bottle Co	23,100	498,937	219,978	278,959	55.9%	21.60
Crisp Opener Partners	18,700	406,326	178,585	227,741	56.0%	21.73
Distinctive Oven Co	3,300	71,651	32,471	39,180	54.7%	21.71
Easy Sandal Co	2,600	54,048	23,780	30,268	56.0%	20.79
Excellent Doghouse Corp	29,100	613,514	275,105	338,409	55.2%	21.08
Exclusive Washer Corp	2,000	39,250	18,614	20,636	52.6%	19.63
Fine Shingle Supply	2,700	57,516	26,765	30,751	53.5%	21.30
Flexible Aerobic Co	33,400	704,359	311,381	392,978	55.8%	21.09
Functional Eggbeater Co	28,900	622,794	274,978	347,816	55.8%	21.55

Figure 23.20
This pivot table includes four value fields plus two calculated fields.

Formatting a Pivot Table

Excel offers a PivotTable Styles gallery on the Design tab. Instead, if you try to format individual cells in a pivot table, you will experience frustration. After you rearrange the pivot table, your manual formatting will be lost.

Using the PivotTable Styles

The PivotTable Styles gallery on the Design tab contains 73 built-in styles for a pivot table. These styles differ significantly from the hideous built-in styles available in Excel 2003. Whereas the AutoFormat styles in Excel 2003 would actually change the shape of a pivot table, the formatting styles in Excel 2010 apply a style to the table, without changing the structure.

The 73 styles are further modified by using the four check boxes for Banded Rows, Banded Columns, Row Headers, and Column Headers. That makes 577 styles. Multiply that by the 20 color themes on the Page Layout tab, and you have 11,521 different styles. Multiply by the three report layouts, two options for blank rows, Grand Totals On or Off for Rows or Columns, Subtotals Above or Below, and you have more than half a million styles available for your pivot table. And, unlike the formats in Excel 2003, all of these styles look good!

You can also build new styles. For example, if you would like the banded rows to be two rows tall, you can design a style for that.

To format a pivot table, select Banded Rows, Row Headers, and Column Headers from the Design tab of the Ribbon. Then open the Styles gallery. Figure 23.21 shows some of the choices available in the gallery.

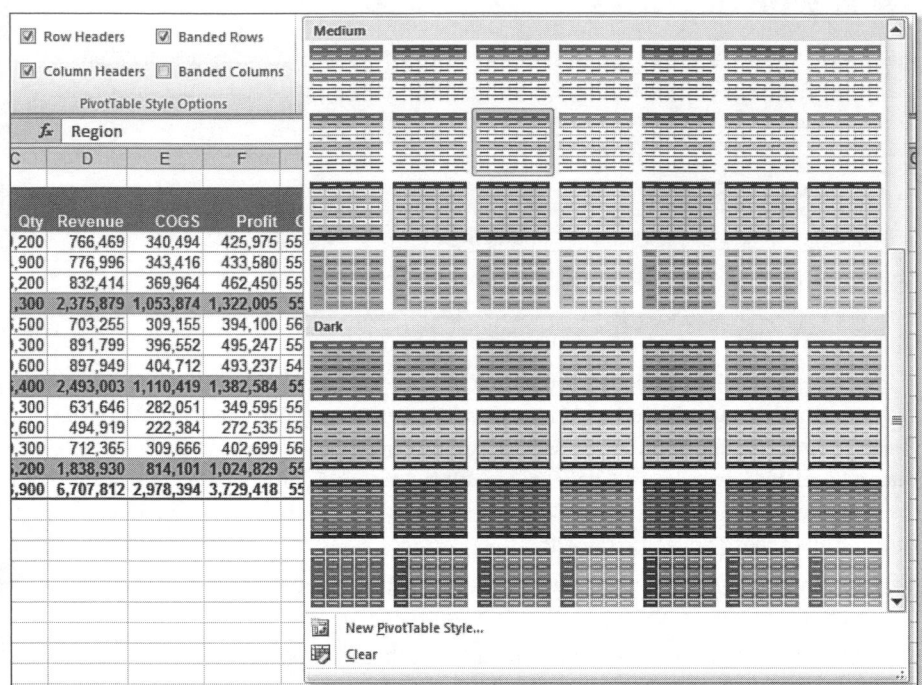

Figure 23.21
Select a style from the gallery on the Design tab.

Finding More Information on Pivot Tables

Chapter 24 covers slicers and other ways to filter a pivot table.

Chapter 25 covers the new PowerPivot add-in.

For more information on pivot tables, check out my other books on pivot tables:

- *Pivot Table Data Crunching* (QUE, ISBN 978-0-789-74313-8), coauthored with Mike Alexander
- *PowerPivot for the Excel Data Analyst* (QUE ISBN 978-0-789-74315-2)

USING SLICERS AND FILTERING A PIVOT TABLE

Pivot table filters have been quietly evolving over the past several versions of Excel. Back in Excel 2003, you were able to select multiple items in the row labels filter. In Excel 2007, you could select multiple items in the page filter. Finally, in Excel 2010, you see the vision of where this work was leading. Excel 2010 pivot tables introduce a new visual filter called a *slicer*. Slicers allow you to perform ad-hoc analysis by choosing various items from various fields in the pivot table.

Filtering Using the Row Label Filter

Figure 24.1 shows a pivot table with two row fields. Drop-downs in cells A3 & B3 lead to the row filter menus.

Figure 24.1
Drop-downs in A3 & B3 lead to filters for Customer and Date.

	A	B	C	
2				
3	Customer ▼	Date ▼	Qty	R
4	⊟Agile Calculator Inc.	8/31/2011	800	
5	Agile Calculator Inc.	4/13/2012	600	
6	Agile Calculator Inc.	6/24/2012	200	
7	Agile Calculator Inc.	11/4/2012	800	
8	Agile Calculator Inc. Total		2,400	
9	⊟Cool Bottle Co	1/14/2011	100	
10	Cool Bottle Co	3/21/2011	300	

Figure 24.2 shows the Filter menu for the Customer field. This drop-down contains four separate filter mechanisms:

- The Label Filters flyout menu appears for fields that contain text values. You can use this flyout to select customer names that contain certain words, begin with, end with, or fall between certain letters.

- The Value Filters flyout menu allows you to filter the customers based on values in the pivot table. If you want only orders over $20,000, or if you want to see the Top 10 customers, use the Values Filter flyout.

- The Search box is new in Excel 2010 and is similar to using the Label Filters, but faster.

- The check boxes allow you to exclude individual customers, or if you select Select All, you can clear or select all customers.

Search Box   Value Filters

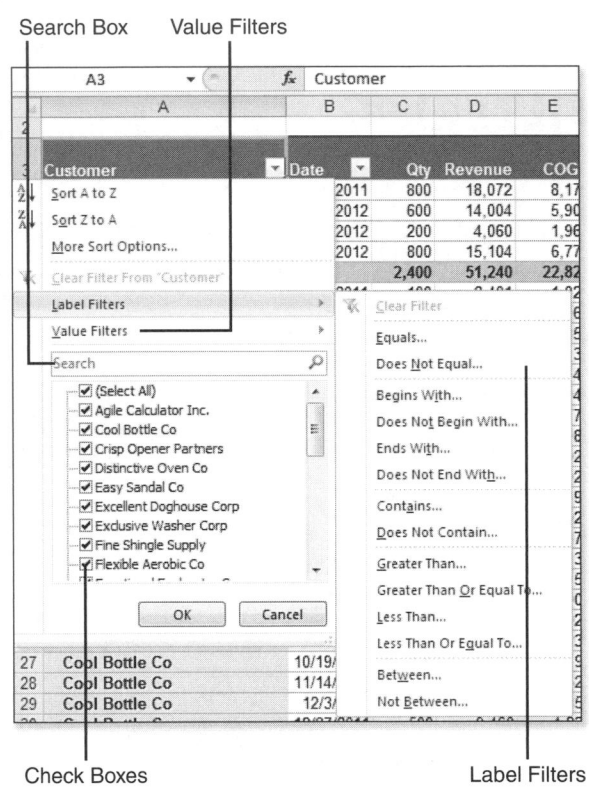

Check Boxes   Label Filters

Figure 24.2
Four separate filter mechanisms exist in this drop-down menu.

Figure 24.3 shows the detail of the Value Filter flyout. All these filters except Top 10 were new in Excel 2007.

When you access the filter drop-down for a field that contains 100% dates, the Labels filter flyout is replaced by a Date Filters flyout, as shown in Figure 24.4. This flyout offers conceptual filters, such as Last Month, Next Quarter, or This Year. The All Dates in Period choice leads to a second flyout where you can choose based on month or quarter.

Figure 24.3
Detail of the Value Filter flyout.

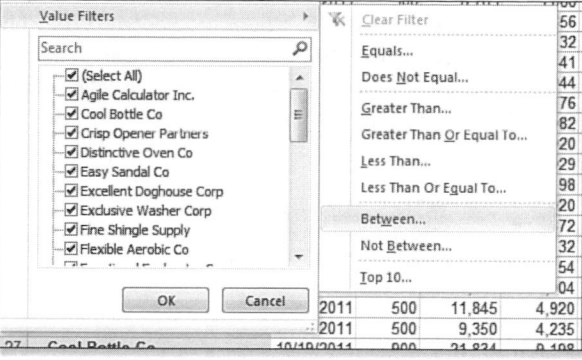

Figure 24.4
The Date Filter flyouts appear when your field contains all date values.

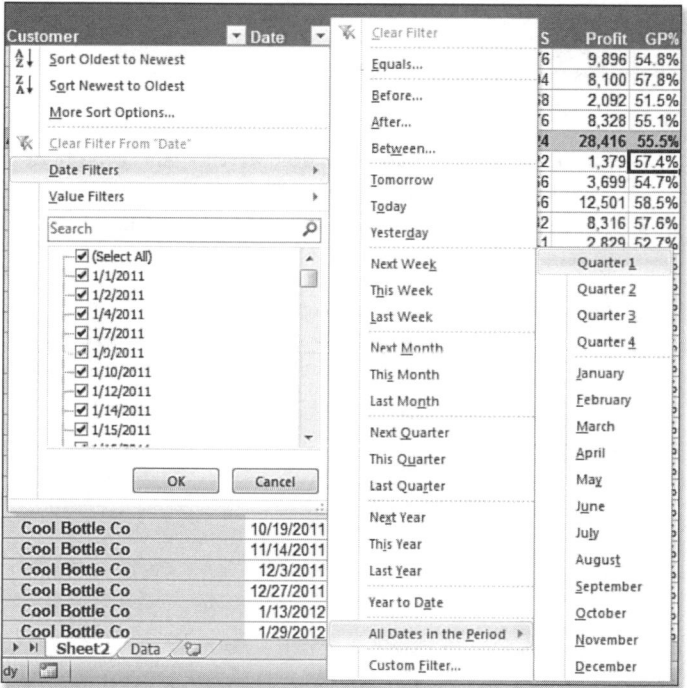

Filtering Using the Search Box

The search box is new in Excel 2010 and works amazingly well. The search box lets you filter to labels that include a certain word. The power of the search box is when you go back to the search box a second time to search for another word. You can add the results of the second search to the results from the first search.

Here is an example:

1. Open the Customer filter drop-down. Type **Shingle** into the search box. Pause for a moment and Excel shows the customers who contain shingle in their name. By default, a special check box called (Select All Search Results) is selected (see Figure 24.5). Click OK to filter the pivot table to the shingle customers.

Figure 24.5
The first time you use search, it seems like an easier version of Label Contains.

2. Open the Customer filter drop-down again. Type **Door** into the search box. Pause for a moment. The door customers appear. This time, you want to select the check box called Add Current Selection to Filter (see Figure 24.6). Click OK.

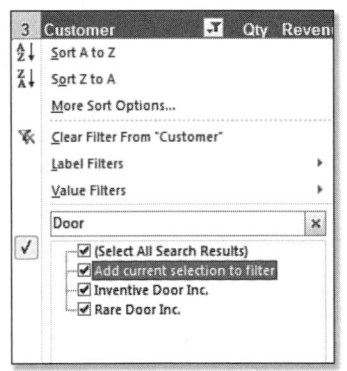

Figure 24.6
The second time you use search, the capability to add these results to the previous makes the search box powerful.

3. Repeat step 2 looking for customers with Faucet in their name. Select Add Current Selection to Filter. Click OK.

The result shown in Figure 24.7 is a union of the customers returned by all three searches.

Figure 24.7
This pivot table contains all customers from three searches.

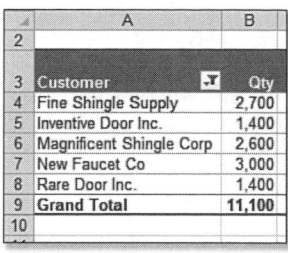

	A	B
2		
3	Customer	Qty
4	Fine Shingle Supply	2,700
5	Inventive Door Inc.	1,400
6	Magnificent Shingle Corp	2,600
7	New Faucet Co	3,000
8	Rare Door Inc.	1,400
9	**Grand Total**	**11,100**
10		

Clearing a Filter

To clear all filters in the pivot table, use the Clear icon in the Sort & Filter group of the Data tab.

To clear filters from one field in the pivot table, open the filter drop-down for that field and select Clear field From "Field".

Filtering Using the Check Boxes

The Customer drop-down includes a list of all the customers in the database. If you needed to exclude a few specific customers, you could clear their check boxes in the filter list.

The (Select All) item restores any cleared boxes. If all the boxes are already selected, clicking (Select All) clears all the boxes.

Because it is easier to select 3 customers than to clear 27, if you need to remove most of the items from the list of customers, you can follow these steps:

1. If any customers are cleared, select (Select All) to reselect all customers.

2. Select (Select All) to clear all customers.

3. Select the particular customers you want to view, as shown in Figure 24.8.

Filtering Using the Label Filter Flyout

All of the Label Filter choices shown previously in Figure 24.2 lead to the same dialog box. Suppose that you are interested in finding all customers whose names end in Corp.

1. Open the Customer filter drop-down.

2. Open the Label Filters flyout.

3. Select Ends With. Excel displays the Label Filter dialog.

4. Type **Corp**, as shown in Figure 24.9. Click OK. The pivot table is filtered to customers whose names end with "Corp".

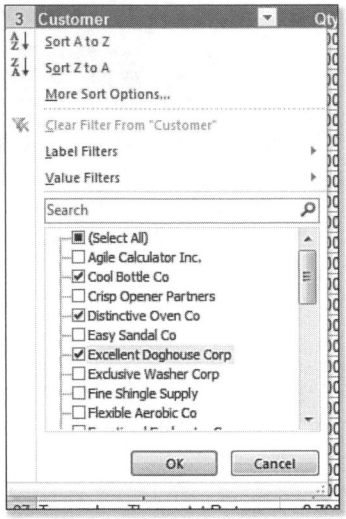

Figure 24.8
Select (Select All) to clear all customers and then select the few desired customers.

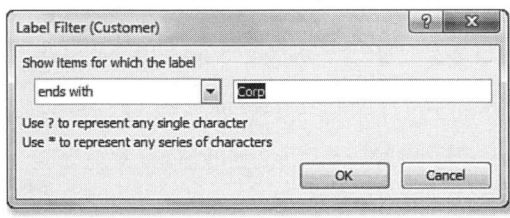

Figure 24.9
Look for customer names matching a pattern.

If you open the first drop-down in the Label Filter dialog, you will see the following choices:

- equals

- does not equal

- is greater than

- is greater than or equal to

- is less than

- is less than or equal to

- begins with

- does not begin with

- ends with

- does not end with

- contains

- does not contain

- is between

- is not between

As noted in the dialog box, you can use the wildcards * and ?. Whereas * represents any character(s), the ? represents one single character.

Filtering Using the Date Filters

When a field in the original data set contains only values formatted as dates, Excel offers the Date Filters flyout shown previously in Figure 24.4.

Many of the date filters contain conceptual filters. If you filter a pivot table to "Yesterday" and then refresh the data set a week later, the dates returned by the filter will change.

The list of conceptual filters feels like it was borrowed from QuickBooks, but it is not quite as complete as those from Quickbooks. It would be nice to have choices such as Last 30 Days, Month to Date, and so on.

The penultimate choice in the first flyout is All Dates in the Period, which leads to a second flyout. Choosing January or Quarter 1 is great when you have dates from several years and you want to compare January from each year.

As shown in Figure 24.10, the last choice in the first flyout is Custom Filter. You can use this filter to build a custom date range. Change the first drop-down to Is Between. Then use the date icons to choose your selected dates.

Figure 24.10
The Custom Filter in a date field offers to let you build any range of dates.

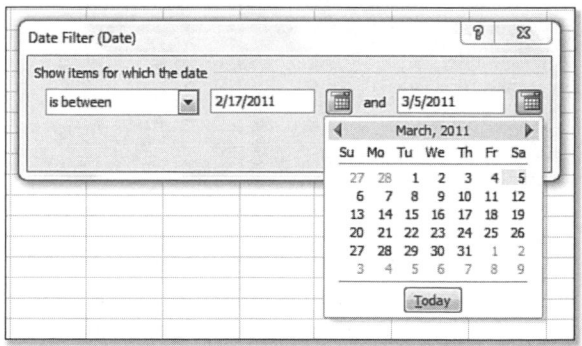

Filtering Using Value Filters

The Value Filters are fairly powerful in Excel 2010. You can choose to filter the customers based on other values in the pivot table.

Suppose you want to see all the customers who had revenue greater than $100,000. You could apply this filter to the customer field using the Value Filters flyout. Follow these steps:

1. Open the Customer Field drop-down.

2. Select the Values Filter flyout.

3. Select Great Than or Equal To. Excel displays the Value Filter dialog.

4. Open the first drop-down and choose the appropriate numeric field. Although the dialog defaults to the first numeric field in the pivot table, you can choose any of the fields in the Values area, including calculated fields such as GP%, as shown in Figure 24.11

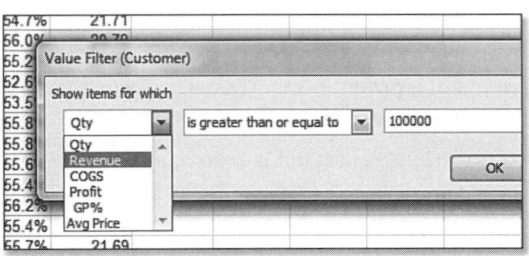

Figure 24.11
Filter the customer field based on Revenue.

5. Fill in **100000** as the third field in the dialog. Click OK. Only customers with revenue greater than $100,000 will be shown in the pivot table (see Figure 24.12).

	A	B	C	D	E
2					
3	Customer	Qty	Revenue	COGS	Profit
4	Excellent Doghouse Corp	29,100	613,514	275,105	338,409
5	Flexible Aerobic Co	33,400	704,359	311,381	392,978
6	Functional Eggbeater Co	28,900	622,794	274,978	347,816
7	Guaranteed Paint Co	26,600	568,851	252,522	316,329
8	Improved Vegetable Inc.	35,700	750,163	334,614	415,549
9	Wonderful Kettle Corp	40,400	869,454	382,170	487,284
10	Grand Total	194,100	4,129,135	1,830,770	2,298,365

Figure 24.12
The pivot table shows only items with revenue greater than $100,000.

Figure 24.13 illustrates this concept further. When the Date field is added as a new row field, the pivot table continues to show daily sales for Excellent Doghouse, even though those daily sales are not above $100,000. All of the day's sales for Excellent Doghouse make it into the filter because the total sales for the customer exceed the $100,000 limit. When you move Customer to the second row field, the filter starts working on the sales for that customer for that day. Because no customers bought $100,000 in one day, no customers appear as the result of the filter.

 note

The Value Field operates at a total level. When you ask for customers with revenue greater than $100,000, the filter is applied at the total customer level. The filter does not work by looking for individual records in the original data set where the revenue is greater than the threshold.

Figure 24.13
Adding new inner row fields does not change the Value filter for Customer.

	A	B	C	D
2				
3	Customer ⊽	Date ⊽	Qty	Revenue
4	⊟Excellent Doghouse C	1/16/2011	600	11,628
5	Excellent Doghouse C	1/25/2011	1,000	20,770
6	Excellent Doghouse C	2/8/2011	100	1,817
7	Excellent Doghouse C	2/14/2011	700	13,867
8	Excellent Doghouse C	3/13/2011	1,000	24,430
9	Excellent Doghouse C	3/16/2011	900	18,783

Here is another example. Figure 24.14 is filtered to show only days with sales over $30K. January 7, 2011 makes it into the report because of the two sales that day.

Figure 24.14
Apply a filter to the outer row field.

	A	B	C	D
2				
3	Date ⊽	Customer ⊽	Qty	Revenue
4	⊟1/7/2011	Improved Vegetable Inc.	400	8,456
5	1/7/2011	Tremendous Thermostat Partners	1,000	21,730
6	1/7/2011 Total		1,400	30,186
7	⊟2/20/2011	Flexible Aerobic Co	600	11,124
8	2/20/2011	Functional Eggbeater Co	300	5,700
9	2/20/2011	Wonderful Kettle Corp	1,000	23,810
10	2/20/2011 Total		1,900	40,634
11	⊟2/26/2011	Easy Sandal Co	900	20,610
12	2/26/2011	Functional Eggbeater Co	600	13,206

If you then apply a filter to customer asking to only see customers where the daily sales for that customer is greater than $20,000, the January 7 record for Improved Vegetable Inc. will be hidden. January 7 continues to be shown in the pivot table because the unfiltered total for January 7. would have been above the $30K limit (see Figure 24.15).

Figure 24.15
Further filter by an inner row field. The inner filter does not change which values are selected by the outer filter.

	A	B	C	D
2				
3	Date ⊽	Customer ⊽	Qty	Revenue
4	⊟1/7/2011	Tremendous Thermostat Partners	1,000	21,730
5	1/7/2011 Total		1,000	21,730
6	⊟2/20/2011	Wonderful Kettle Corp	1,000	23,810
7	2/20/2011 Total		1,000	23,810
8	⊟2/26/2011	Easy Sandal Co	900	20,610
9	2/26/2011	Wonderful Kettle Corp	1,000	25,140

Filtering to the Top 10

The problem with the value filter is that you have to commit to a threshold value. At the beginning of a year, you might have no customers who have purchased at the $100,000 level yet.

Pivot tables offer a feature called Top 10. Despite the name, the filter is not just for finding the top 10 values. You can use the filter to find top or bottom items. You can specify 5, 10, 7, or any number of items.

The Top 10 Filter has some new features since Excel 2003.

To start the filter, open the Customer filter drop-down. Open the Values filter flyout and select Top 10. Excel displays the Top 10 Filter dialog.

In Figure 24.16, the report has been filtered to show the top 5 customers based on revenue.

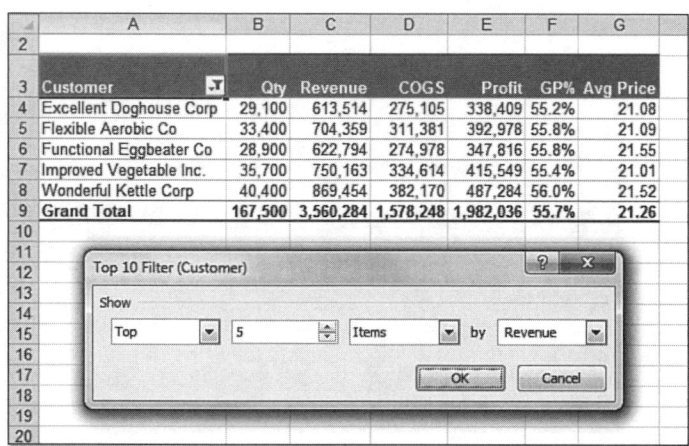

Figure 24.16
Filter to the top 5 customers based on revenue.

- The first drop-down in the dialog offers a choice between Top and Bottom.

- The second field is a spin button and a text box. You can use the spin button to change from 5 to 10. If you need to get to 1,000,000, you should type that value into the text box instead of trying to hit the spin button 999,990 times.

- The next field is a drop-down with choices of Items, Percent, and the new choice of Sum. These three choices are discussed in the next sections.

- The final drop-down offers all of the numeric fields in the values area of the pivot table.

The Items/Percent/Sum drop-down offers a lot of flexibility.

If you select Percent, the pivot table shows you enough customers so that you see n% of the value field. For example, in Figure 24.17, the pivot table shows enough customers to represent the top 80% of profit.

If you choose Sum, you can specify a large number as the second field in the dialog. In Figure 24.18, you are looking for the smallest customers, up to about $500,000 in sales.

Figure 24.17
Filter to 80% of the revenue based on Profit.

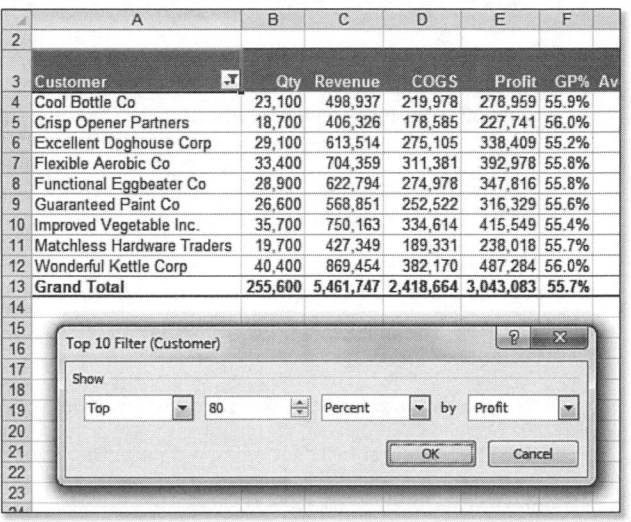

Figure 24.18
Find the bottom $500K of customers based on revenue.

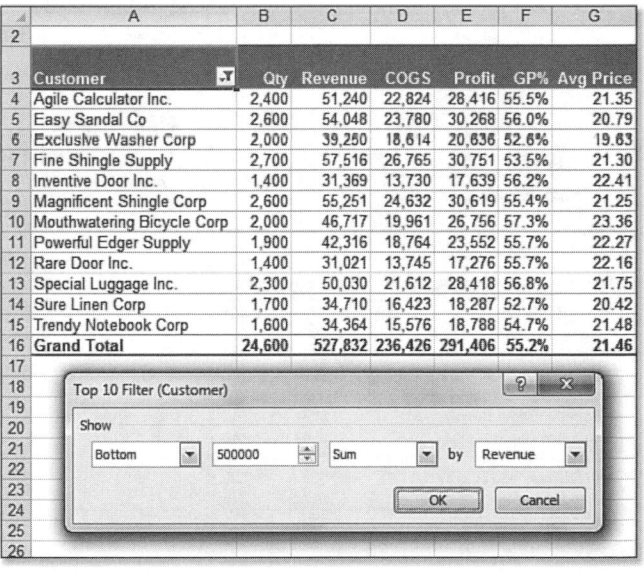

Filtering Using Report Filter Fields

Those who are familiar with pivot tables in legacy versions of Excel know the Report Filter as the Page Field area of the layout. Although the new field filtering tools described in the preceding sections offer far more powerful filtering, you can use the Report Filter drop zone to add filter cells to a pivot table to do basic ad hoc analysis.

To add filter drop-downs to the top of the pivot table, you drag the fields to the Report Filter drop zone in the pivot table field list.

The Date Filters in the Report Filter of the Pivot Field are not as intelligent as a date field in the regular Filter. The pivot table filter drop-down will offer hundreds of daily dates without the month and year hierarchies. Before adding a date field to the Report Filter, follow these steps to create your own hierarchy:

1. Add the date field temporarily to the row field area of the pivot table.

2. Select the first cell containing a date in the pivot table.

3. In the Options tab, click Group.

4. In the Grouping dialog box, select Days, Months, Quarters, and Years. Click OK.

5. Move the Date, Months, Quarters, and Years fields to the Report Filter drop zone.

In Figure 24.19, six fields have been added to the Report Filter area. If you need to see a report of East region customers who purchased in January 2011, you would select from the drop-downs in B1, B3, and B5.

	A	B	C
1	Region	East	
2	Product	(All)	
3	Years	2011	
4	Quarters	(All)	
5	Months	Jan	
6	Date	(All)	
7			
8	Customer	Qty	Revenue
9	Cool Bottle Co	100	2,401
10	Excellent Doghouse Corp	600	11,628
11	Functional Eggbeater Co	1,000	22,810
12	Improved Vegetable Inc.	1,900	41,246
13	Matchless Hardware Traders	1,000	20,734
14	Powerful Edger Supply	800	18,552
15	Supreme Clipboard Inc.	800	14,440
16	Tremendous Thermostat Partners	1,000	21,730
17	Trendy Notebook Corp	800	16,288
18	Vivid Edger Co	500	9,345
19	Wonderful Kettle Corp	300	6,714
20	Grand Total	8,800	185,888

Figure 24.19
Fields in the Report Filter area allow for interesting ad hoc reporting.

Arranging the Filters

When you have many fields in the Report Filter area, you might want to arrange those filters. The vertical arrangement in Figure 24.19 means that seven rows of your screen will be taken up with noncustomer data.

Select one cell in your pivot table, and click the Options icon in the left side of the Options tab.

In the PivotTable Options dialog box, the Layout & Format tab offers two settings that affect the arrangement of the Report Filter. In Figure 24.20, the Display Fields in Report Filter Area is set to Over, Then Down. The Report Filter Fields Per Row is set to 2. This creates a 3x2 arrangement of the six filter fields.

Figure 24.20
Use the Options dialog to rearrange the Report Filter fields.

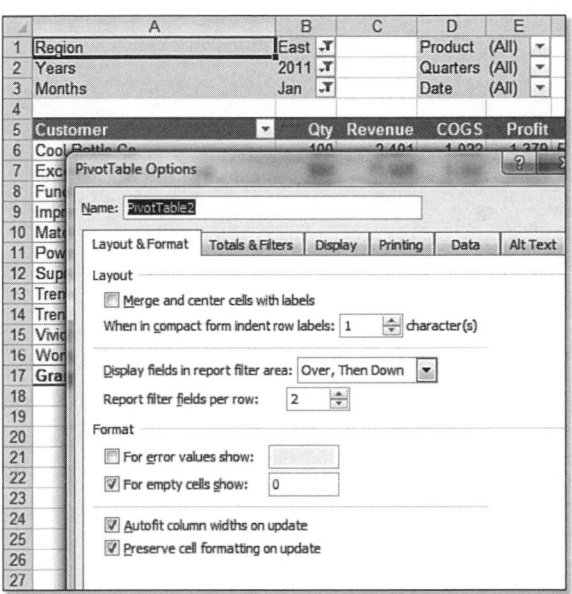

Selecting Multiple Items

Excel 2007 introduced the capability to choose multiple items from a Report Filter field.

Figure 24.21 shows the initial state of the Region filter.

To enable the capability to select multiple items, select Select Multiple Items in the bottom of the drop-down. Check boxes appear, and you can select multiple items from the list. Figure 24.22 shows a selection for Central and West.

 caution

It feels like the Select Multiple Items feature wasn't quite done in Excel 2007. When you choose multiple items from the list and close the drop-down, the filter shows the not-very-useful heading of (Multiple Items), as shown in Figure 24.23. When you print this report, no one will have any idea what items are actually selected in the filter. When you see the slicers described in the next section, you will understand that the Select Multiple Items was an intermediate solution added to make slicers possible.

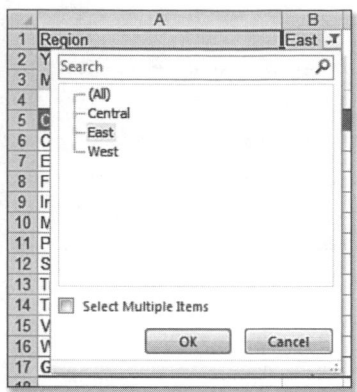

Figure 24.21
Initially, the filter allows you to select one item or (All).

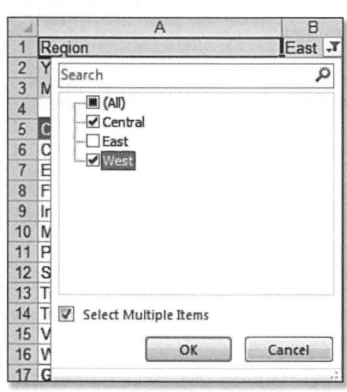

Figure 24.22
You can now select multiple items from the filter drop-down.

	A	B	C	D	E
1	Region	(Multiple Items) .T		Product	(All) ▼
2	Years	2011 .T		Quarters	(All) ▼
3	Months	Jan .T		Date	(All) ▼
4					
5	**Customer** ▼	**Qty**	**Revenue**	**COGS**	**Profit**
6	Excellent Doghouse Corp	1,000	20,770	8,470	12,300 5
7	Improved Vegetable Inc.	1,600	31,008	13,552	17,456 5
8	Matchless Hardware Traders	300	6,267	2,541	3,726 5
9	Powerful Edger Supply	200	3,552	1,694	1,858 5
10	Vivid Edger Co	200	4,299	1,968	2,331 5
11	Wonderful Kettle Corp	900	21,438	9,198	12,240 5
12	**Grand Total**	**4,200**	**87,334**	**37,423**	**49,911 5**

Figure 24.23
Regions are filtered to (Multiple Items). Is this the worst title ever?

Filtering Using Slicers

Slicers are visual filters that are new in Excel 2010. They solve the problem of selecting Multiple Items, as shown in Figure 24.23. Although slicers take up much more space than the equivalent Report Filters, the slicer arrangement invites people to start running ad hoc analyses by clicking the slicers.

Adding Slicers

Before you add slicers, insert some extra rows above your pivot table, insert some extra columns to the left of your pivot table, or do both. Slicers take up a lot of room.

To add default slicers, follow these steps:

1. Select one cell in your pivot table.

2. On the Options tab, select the Insert Slicer icon. Excel shows the Insert Slicers dialog.

3. Choose any fields that would make suitable filter fields. In Figure 24.24, five fields are selected. Note that the Date field would still offer 500 daily dates, far too many for an effective slicer. So, this field is not included. Click OK.

tip

To clear all the filters and return them to the (All) selection, click the Clear icon in the Sort & Filter section of the Data tab.

Figure 24.24
Choose all fields that are suitable for visual filters.

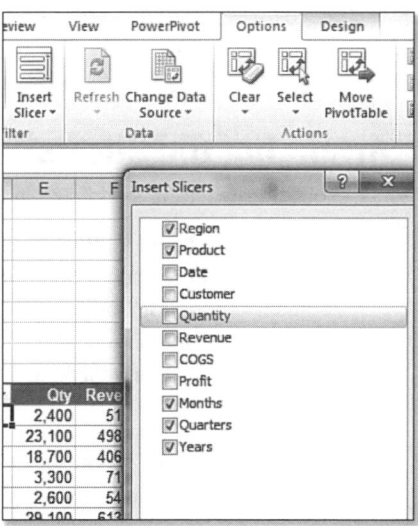

Excel adds five ugly default filters, tiled in the center of your screen (see Figure 24.25).

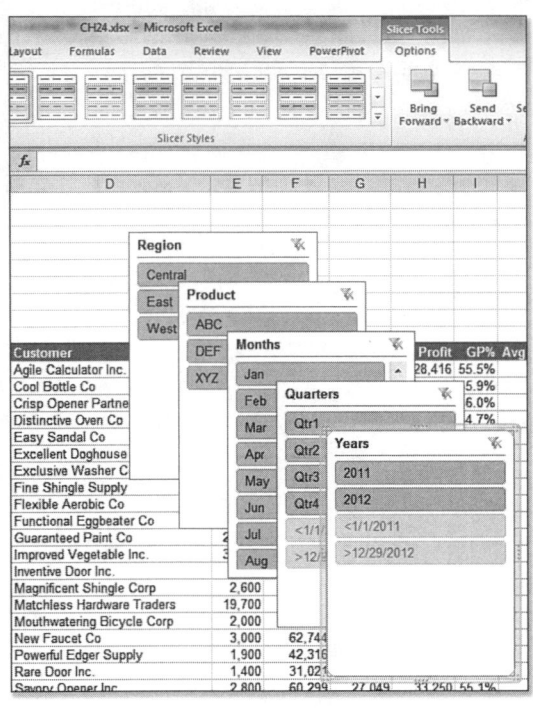

Figure 24.25
Excel tiles a bunch of one-column slicers.

Arranging the Slicers

You can reposition and resize the slicers. Choose a logical arrangement for the slicers.

Following are some examples:

The Year slicer is wider than it needs to be. There are also two "silly" items in the slicer that are a remnant of the grouping operation. By making the Year slicer shorter, those extra items are hidden out of view at the bottom of the list. This does force a scrollbar to appear, so the slicer can't be quite as narrow as you might like. Still, the slicer neatly fits in A1:B6, as shown in Figure 24.26.

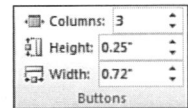

Figure 24.26
The Slicer Tools Options tab allows you to control the number of columns in a slicer.

The Quarter field can be resized and stacked below the year slicer in columns A & B. Again, by making the slicer shorter, the extra < and > items are hidden from view.

Months are composed of a dozen short entries. These work well as a horizontal slicer, often arranged in four rows of three columns. To create that arrangement, click the slicer and use the Columns spin button in the Slicer Tools Options tab to specify three columns (see Figure 24.26). After you adjust the number of columns, make the slicer wider to fit all the buttons.

Region and Product work well as single-row slicers. Increase the number of columns for each to 3 and resize the slicers to fit the values.

 To see a demo of formatting slicers, search for "Excel In Depth 24" at YouTube.

Formatting the Slicers

A gallery on the Slicer Tools Options offers 14 slicers color themes. Click each slicer and choose a different color scheme for each slicer.

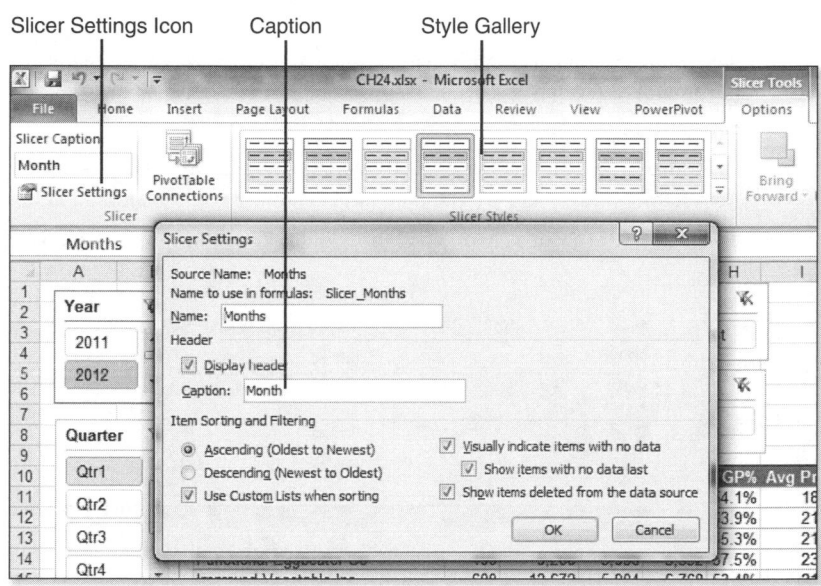

Figure 24.27
Tools for formatting a slicer.

You can also control the caption that appears at the top of each slicer. Choose a slicer. Click the Slicer Settings icon on the left side of the Slicer Tools Options tab. You can adjust the caption in the Slicer Settings dialog.

Figure 24.28 shows the slicers after resizing and formatting.

Using the Slicers

To select a single item from a slicer, choose that item.

To multiselect from a single slicer, hold down the Ctrl key while selecting the multiple items. To select adjacent items, click on the first item and drag to the last item to be selected.

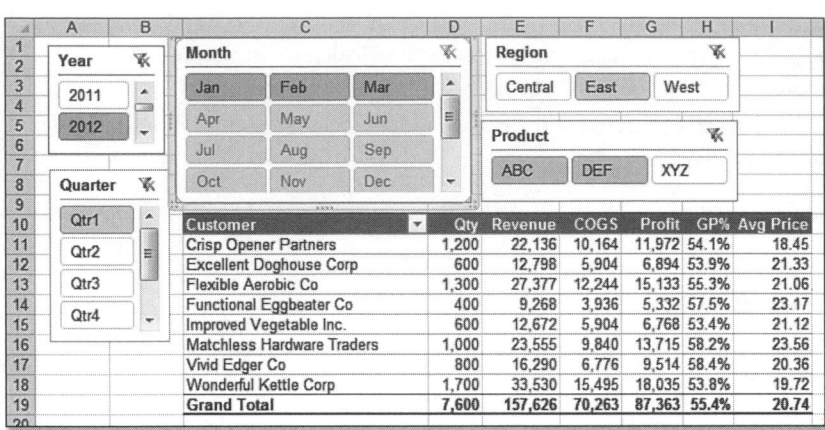

Figure 24.28
Slicers provide a visual indication of what is included in the report.

Selections in one slicer might cause items in other slicers to gray out. In this case, those items move to the end of the list. This gives you a visual indication that the item is not available based on the current filters.

In Figure 24.29, the Customer slicer has not been filtered. On the basis of choosing ABC Product, East Region, 2012, and Q1-Q2, only nine customers had records matching those other filters.

To clear a filter from a slicer, click the Funnel-X icon in the top right of the slicer.

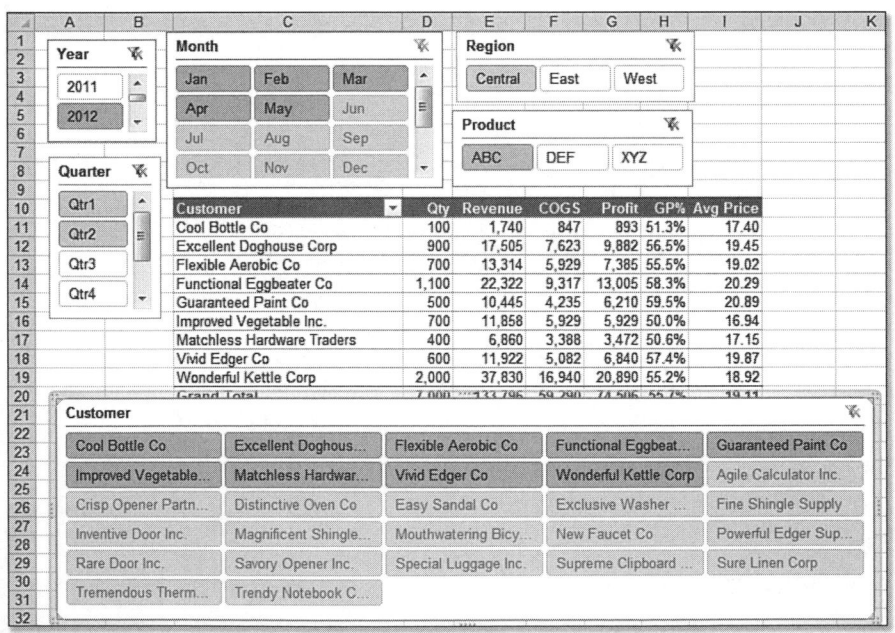

Figure 24.29
Filters applied to Year, Region, Product, and Quarter limit the list of customers active in the Customer slicer to nine.

Filtering Oddities

The next sections discuss a few additional features available for filtering pivot tables.

AutoFiltering a Pivot Table

I was doing a Power Excel seminar in Philadelphia when someone in the audience asked if you can AutoFilter a pivot table. The answer is no; the Filter field is grayed out when you are inside a pivot table.

There is a surprising bug.

If you put the cell pointer to the right of the last heading of a data set and click the Filter icon, Excel turns on the AutoFilter drop-downs.

There is a guy at Microsoft who is in charge of graying out the AutoFilter icon when you are in a pivot table. That guy forgot about that magic cell to the right of the headings. If you put the cell pointer in cell J10, Microsoft forgets to gray out the Filter icon. In Figure 24.30, the AutoFilter icons are added to the pivot table.

Figure 24.30
Although this works, the AutoFilters are not recalculated after a Refresh.

Applying Row Label Filters to Fields Not in the Pivot Table Report

You can apply a filter to a field that does not appear in the pivot table.

Go to the top of the Pivot Table Field List and hover over any field. A drop-down appears on that field, as shown in Figure 24.31. Open the drop-down and you can apply a filter to the field, even though it is not in the current report.

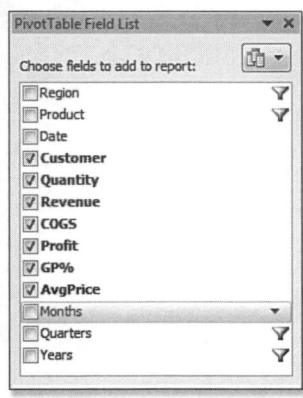

Figure 24.31
Hover over a field in the top of the pivot table field list to reveal a secret drop-down.

Replicating a Pivot Table for Every Customer

This technique makes many copies of the pivot table, with a different Report Filter value in each copy. If your pivot table contains at least one Report Filter field, select the Options drop-down from the Options tab. Select Show Report Filter Pages from the drop-down menu as shown in Figure 24.32. Confirm which field should be used. Excel adds worksheets to your workbook. Each worksheet contains the original pivot table, with a different value chosen for the selected filter field.

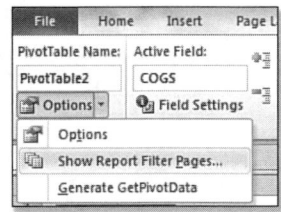

Figure 24.32
Replicate your pivot table for every value in a Report Filter field.

Sorting a Pivot Table

In all the pivot tables so far in this chapter, the customers are presented in alphabetical sequence. In each case, the report would be more interesting if it were presented sorted by revenue instead of by customer name.

 caution

Slicers are not copied to the other pivot tables when you use this technique.

The Customer drop-down offers choices to sort a field in ascending or descending order, as shown in Figure 24.33. However, you can find more powerful options by selecting More Sort Options from this drop-down.

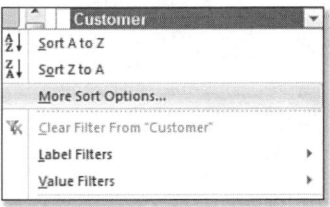

Figure 24.33
Use More Sort Options.

When you choose More Sort Options from the Customer drop-down, the Sort dialog appears. This dialog initially offers to sort in ascending order, based on customer. If you choose Descending and then use the drop-down, you can choose to sort the report based on sum of revenue. This produces the report shown in Figure 24.34.

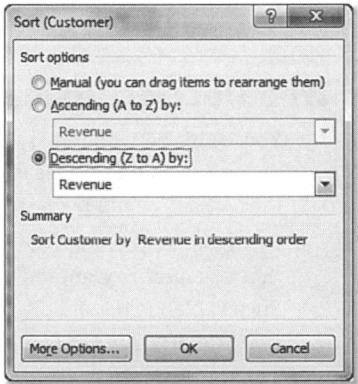

Figure 24.34
Sort descending based on revenue.

One more sorting option is available in Excel 2010.

Suppose that you have a pivot table showing revenue with quarters going across the columns and customers down the rows. If you want to sort the report by Q4 revenue, Excel 2010 allows this.

1. Open the Customer filter drop-down.

2. Select More Sort Options.

3. Select Descending by Revenue.

4. Click More Options.

5. In the More Sort Options dialog, specify that you want to sort by Value in Select Column. Click the column containing Q4 (see Figure 24.35).

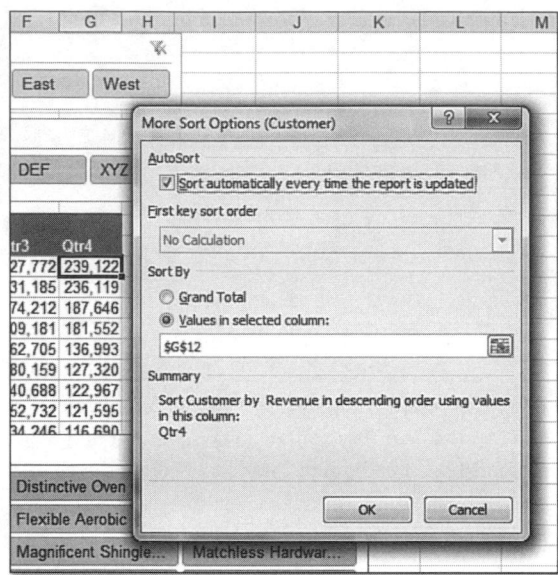

Figure 24.35
Excel offers to sort by one specific column.

Why Not Sort Using the Data Tab?

You might be wondering why you should go to the hassle of using the Sort and More Sort Options dialogs. Wouldn't it be easier to select Cell G11 and use the Sort Descending button on the Data tab? Yes. It would be easier to sort by clicking this button for this one view of the pivot table.

However, as you continue to pivot the table into other configurations, Excel does not remember that you always want the data sorted into this particular sort. If you use the sort options in the PivotTable Field List box, you are telling Excel to always sort this pivot table in a certain way. Any sort property you set here will remain in effect as you add and remove fields.

MASHING UP DATA WITH POWERPIVOT

PowerPivot is a free add-in for Excel 2010 brought to you by the SQL Server Analysis Services team at Microsoft. One of the themes for the 2010 release of Office was to improve Excel as a Business Intelligence tool. PowerPivot makes it possible to do jaw-dropping analyses in Excel.

Benefits and Drawbacks to PowerPivot

There are some pluses to PowerPivot but also a few minuses. But first, let's start with the mega-pluses, the things that will make you love PowerPivot.

Mega-Benefits of PowerPivot

Following are five mega-benefits to using PowerPivot. Any one of these benefits are enough to make me upgrade to Excel 2010.

- **Process far more than a million rows of data**—I've seen demos with 100 million rows. If you have data sets that extend beyond row 1048576, you can now sort, filter, scroll, and pivot those data sets in PowerPivot.

- **Create pivot tables from multiple tables, without writing a VLOOKUP**— You no longer have to write processor-intensive VLOOKUP formulas to join data from two worksheets before creating a pivot table. PowerPivot takes your various Excel tables and mashes them together without you having to code VLOOKUPs.

- **Mash-up data from disparate sources**—The PowerPivot window can import text, Access, RSS, SQL Server, and Excel data and present it in a single pivot table.

- **Get access to Sets**—Microsoft added a cool Set feature to Excel 2010 pivot tables that allows asymmetric reporting. One problem: It works only with OLAP pivot tables, not regular Excel data. The good news: Take your regular data through PowerPivot and you've just created an OLAP pivot table. I am sure that the heads of the Excel team will spin when I say it, but just having access to Sets is enough to make me run every future pivot table through PowerPivot!

- **Do calculations that make Excel's Calculated Fields look like they were designed by someone in kindergarten**—Microsoft introduced a new formula language in PowerPivot called DAX. DAX stands for Data Analysis Expressions. DAX is composed of 117 functions that let you to do two types of calculations. There are 81 typical Excel functions that you can use to add a calculated column to a table in the PowerPoint window. Then you can use 54 functions to create a new measure in the pivot table. These 54 functions add incredible power to pivot tables. Some examples:

- COUNTROWS(DISTINCT()) finally lets you count the number of distinct rows.

- CALCULATE(Expression,Filter1, Filter2,...FilterN) is like SUMIFS but for any expression. (Think MAXIFS and more.)

- There are 34 time intelligence functions that let you compare TOTALYTD sales versus a PARALLELPERIOD.

Moderate Benefits of PowerPivot

The following benefits are nice, but not jaw-dropping amazing:

- **Compression**—Excel workbooks with PowerPivot data are smaller than workbooks that use traditional PivotCache pivot tables. The data is still stored inside the .xlsx workbook file, but the PowerPivot team came up with better ways to compress the data.

- **Join two pivot tables with a single set of slicers**—You can have one set of slicers that control two separate PowerPivot tables.

- **Slicer Autolayout**—Slicers created in regular Excel are always one column and always start at the same size. Slicers created in PowerPivot attempt to use some IntelliSense to be sized appropriately. It is not foolproof, but at least you can see that the PowerPivot team is trying to be thoughtful about your slicers.

- **PivotCharts without PivotTables**—Well, not really. But it looks like it. PowerPivot can automatically build a chart on your presentation worksheet and then tuck the linked pivot table away on another worksheet.

Why Is This Free?

Up until Excel 2010, what was the greatest innovation in spreadsheets? Your answer will depend on the type of work that you have to do, but some possible answers might be the following:

- **Pivot Tables**—When Pito Salas brought the pivot table concept to Lotus 1-2-3, it meant that you never had to do @DSUM and /Data Table 2 anymore.

- **VLOOKUP**—Join data from two tables. It is what allows people to do things in Excel that should be done in Access.

- **IF / SUMIFS / AGGREGATE**—These functions allow various conditional calculations.

- **1048576 Rows in Excel 2007**—For me, this feature meant that I would never have to open Microsoft Access again.

A new add-in for Excel 2010 is as good as all four of those innovations wrapped into one. You can now do analysis of massive data sets, even data 100 times larger than Excel 2007. You can join tables without writing a VLOOKUP. You have aggregation and time series functions that have been lacking in Excel. You have the capability to do all this in a pivot table. It is not an exaggeration to say that PowerPivot is the best spreadsheet improvement to come out of Microsoft since pivot tables debuted in 1993.

Why then is this free?

Because 500 million people use Excel. That is a massive market of people. I should know—I make a living selling books to that market. If you can somehow sell something to one hundredth of one percent of that market, you have a bestseller on your hands.

The SQL Server Analysis Services team give the client side version of PowerPivot to 500 million people because they figure that some small tiny percentage of those people will upgrade to the server version of PowerPivot. To get a server version, you buy SharePoint and SQL Server and other expensive technologies. By empowering Excel pros with these amazing tools, they figure that they might double their existing customer base of SQL Server customers.

 **note**

In this book, I do not cover the server version of PowerPivot, but I mention some benefits of the server version.

Benefits of the Server Version of PowerPivot

If you get your IT folks to install PowerPivot Server, you get these additional benefits:

- **Automatic Refresh**—In the client side, you have to open PowerPivot every day and click Refresh to have PowerPivot read the updated data sources. With the server version, this can automatically happen overnight.

- **Publish to Report Gallery**—With the server version, you can publish your PowerPivot pivot tables to a SharePoint server. Someone without Excel can open your workbook in a web page and use the slicers to filter the data. Those people will have a nice gallery of report thumbnails from which to choose. The people in IT will get to monitor which reports are actually used and by whom.

Drawbacks to Using PowerPivot

As you start using PowerPivot, you might run into a few annoyances.

- **No Grouping**—PowerPivot cannot use the Group feature of pivot tables. I use this feature a lot to roll daily dates up to months, quarters, and years. You can work around this by using the DAX language to define year, quarter, and month columns, but it is not as simple as using the Group feature.

- **You lose Undo**—PowerPivot is an add-in. Traditionally, when you run a macro or some external code, the Undo stack is cleared. Thus, anytime you deal with PowerPivot, you lose the ability to Undo anything before you go in to PowerPivot.

- **No VBA**—You can automate regular pivot tables with VBA. You cannot use VBA to control PowerPivot.

- **No Drilldown**—Usually, you can double-click a cell in a pivot table and see the rows that make up that cell. This feature is not in the first version of PowerPivot.

- **Excel 2010 only**—PowerPivot works only with Excel 2010. You cannot use it with Excel 2007. You cannot use it with files stored in compatibility mode.

Installing PowerPivot

The main trick here is to get the PowerPivot add-in that matches your version of Office. Office 2010 ships in 32-bit and 64-bit versions. If you have a new computer running 64-bit Windows, it is possible that you have 32-bit or 64-bit office.

Go to the File menu in Excel 2010 and select Help. The right side of the Backstage view shows a version number. If the version number ends with (64-bit), you need the 64-bit version of the add-in.

After installing the add-in, you should see a PowerPivot tab on the Excel 2010 Ribbon, as shown in Figure 25.1.

note

If you plan to deal with millions of records, you want to go with the 64-bit versions of Office and PowerPivot. You are still constrained to a 2GB file size limit, but because PowerPivot can compress data, you can fit 10 times that amount of data in a PowerPivot file. The 64-bit version of Office can make use of memory sizes beyond the 4GB limit in 32-bit Windows.

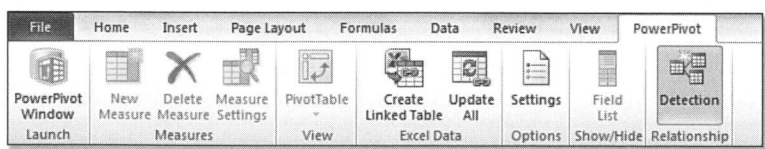

Figure 25.1
After successful installation, you have a PowerPivot tab in the Ribbon.

Case Study: Building a PowerPivot Report

This case study walks you through your first PowerPivot data mash-up. In this example, you create a report that merges a 1.8 million row CSV file with a store identifying data in Excel.

Your main table is a 1.8 million record CSV file called demo.txt. This file is shown in Notepad in Figure 25.2. It is important that you have column headings in row 1 of the CSV file. The point-of-sale vendor who provides this data usually had a "Run on mm/dd/yyyy" row at the top of the file, a blank row, and then headings in row 3.

 note

This will not work for PowerPivot. You need to get rid of those extraneous rows at the top of the data set.

Import a Text File

To import the 1.8 million row file into PowerPivot, follow these steps.

1. Select the PowerPivot tab in Excel 2010.

2. Select the PowerPivot Window icon. A new PowerPivot application window appears. PowerPivot offers two Ribbon tabs; Home and Design. The Home tab is shown in Figure 25.3.

Figure 25.2
This 1.8 million row file is too big for Excel.

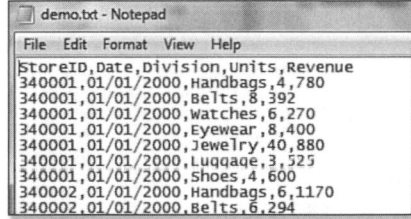

Figure 25.3
The Home tab of the PowerPivot application.

3. You want to import your main table first. This is the large CSV file shown in Figure 25.2. From the Get External Data group, select From Text. PowerPivot shows the Table Import Wizard.

4. Select a Friendly Connection Name, such as Sales History. Click the Browse button and locate your text file. PowerPivot does not default to see the first row as column headers, so the data preview offers five unfriendly column names of F1, F2, F3, and so on (see Figure 25.4).

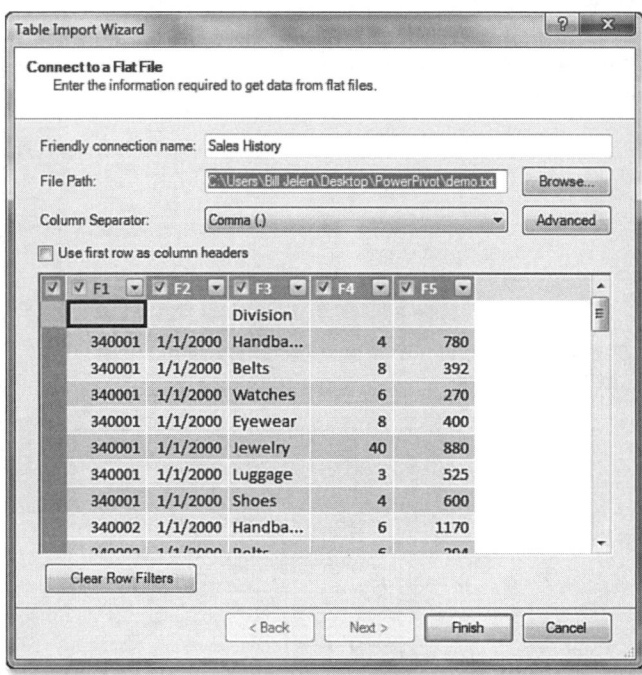

Figure 25.4
Initially, the headers are not recognized.

5. Verify that your delimiter is a comma. The drop-down offers standard delimiters, such as comma, semicolon, vertical bar, and so on.

6. Select the check box for Use First Row as Column Headers. The preview now shows the real column names.

7. If there are any columns that you don't need to import, clear them. The entire file is going to be read into memory. If you have extraneous columns, particularly columns with long text values, you can save memory by clearing them. Figure 25.5 shows the data preview with Units cleared.

8. Note that there are filter drop-downs for each field. You can sort and filter this 1.8 million row data set here, although it will be slower than in a few steps from now. If you open a filter field, you can choose to exclude certain values from the import.

9. Click Finish, and PowerPivot begins loading the file into memory. The wizard shows how many rows have been fetched so far (see Figure 25.6).

Figure 25.5
Choose which columns to import.

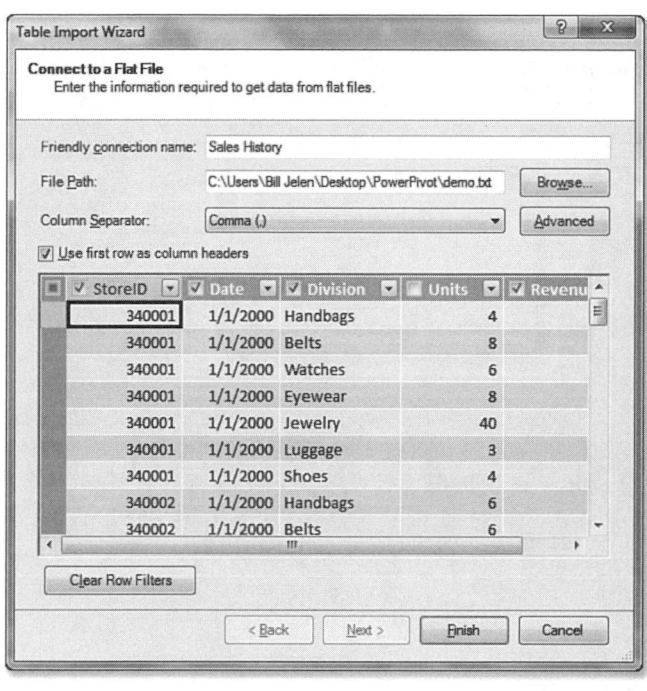

Figure 25.6
In less than a minute, PowerPivot is up to
1.5 million rows.

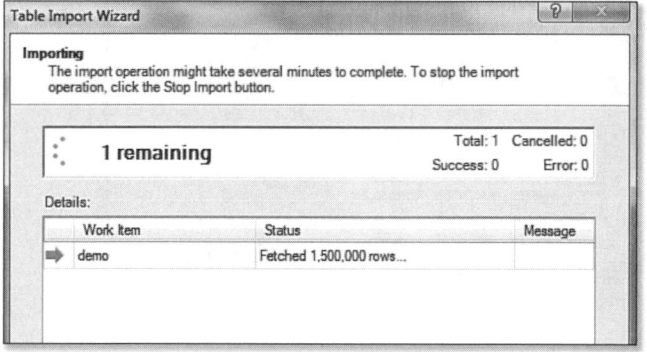

10. When the file is imported, the wizard confirms how many rows have been imported, as shown in Figure 25.7. Click Close to return to the PowerPivot window.

11. The 1.8 million row data set is shown in the PowerPivot window. Go ahead. Grab the vertical scrollbar and scroll through the records. You can also Sort, change the number format, or filter (see Figure 25.8).

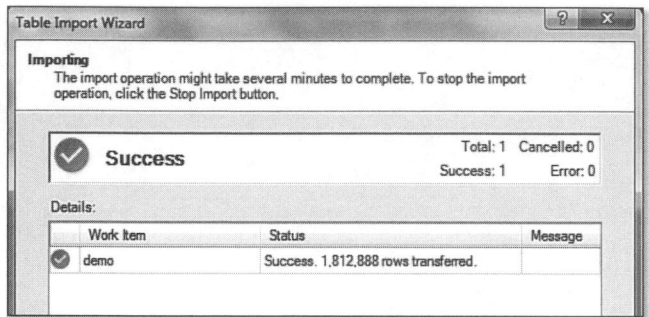

Figure 25.7
Success.

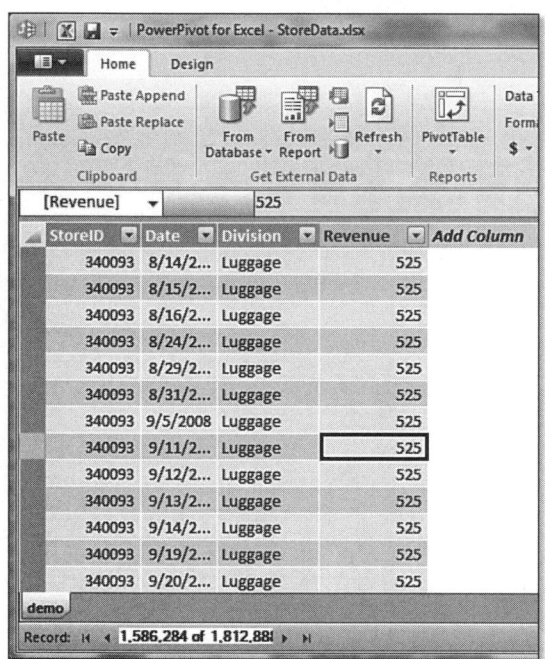

Figure 25.8
1.8 Million records are in a grid that feels a lot like Excel.

The Filters in PowerPivot are not as powerful as the new filters introduced in Excel 2007. In particular, the date columns do not show a hierarchical filter where you can choose a year or month.

If you right-click a column, a menu appears where you can rename, freeze, copy, hide, and unhide the columns (see Figure 25.9).

The bottom line is that you have 1.8 million records you can sort, filter, and later, pivot. This is going to be cool.

 note

Note that although this feels like Excel, it is not Excel. You cannot edit an individual cell. If you add a calculation in what amounts to cell E1, that calculation will automatically get copied to all rows. If you format the revenue in one cell, all the cells in that column will get formatted.

You can change column widths by dragging the border between the column names just like in Excel.

Figure 25.9
Right-click a column to rename it.

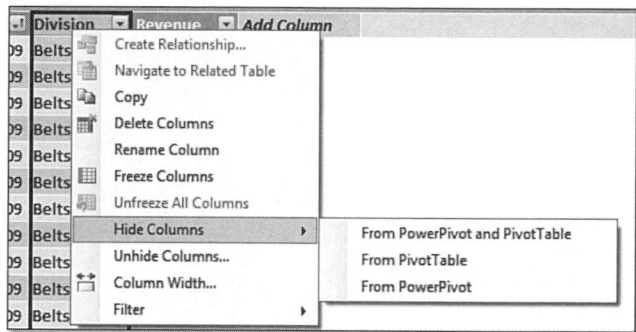

Add Excel Data by Copying and Pasting

The file imported previously has only StoreID as a field. It does not have the store name or location. But you probably have a small Excel file that maps StoreID to the store name and other relevant data. You can add this data as a new tab in PowerPivot. Follow these steps:

1. Open this workbook in Excel.

2. Select the data with Ctrl+*.

3. Copy it with Ctrl+C.

4. Click the PowerPivot tab. On the left side of the Ribbon is an icon to return to PowerPivot (see Figure 25.10).

⊿	A	B	C	D
1	StoreID	Selling SF	Mall Developer	Store Name
2	340001	603	Westfield	Main Place Mall
3	340002	654	Westfield	Sherman Oaks Fashion Squa
4	340003	998	Simon Property Group	Brea Mall
5	340004	858	General Growth Properties	Park Place
6	340005	746	Westfield	Galleria at Roseville
7	340006	1633	Simon Property Group	Mission Viejo Mall
8	340007	725	Irvine Retail Group	Corona Del Mar Plaza
9	340008	535	Westfield	San Francisco Center
10	340009	1190	The Macerich Company	Kierland Commons

Figure 25.10
Copy Excel data.

5. Click the PowerPivot window icon. PowerPivot returns and you see your 1.8 million row data set.

6. Click the Paste icon on the left side of the PowerPivot Home tab. You will see a Paste Preview window.

7. Give the new table a better name than "Table": perhaps StoreInfo (see Figure 25.11). Click OK.

You now see the store information in a new StoreInfo tab. Notice that there are now two worksheet tabs in PowerPivot, as shown in Figure 25.12.

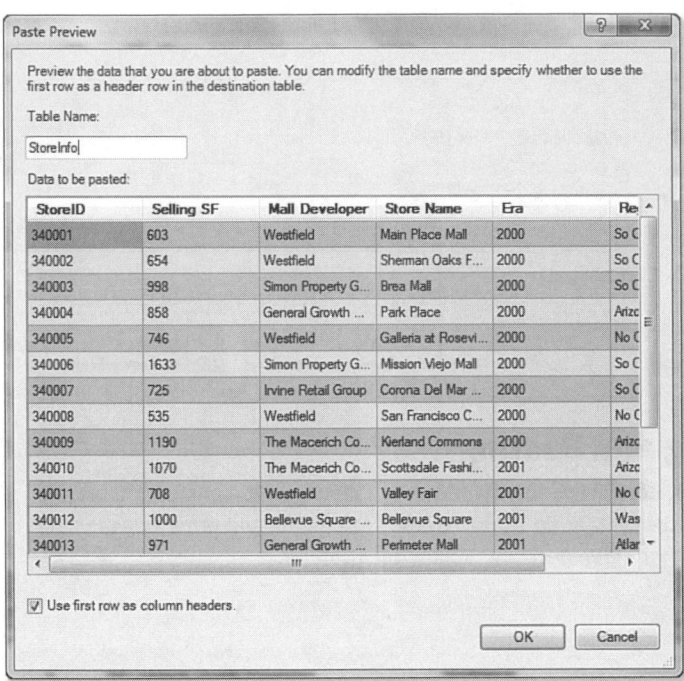

Figure 25.11
Give the pasted table a name.

Figure 25.12
You now have two unrelated tables in the PowerPivot window.

Add Excel Data by Linking

In the previous example, you added the StoreInfo table by using Copy and Paste. This creates two copies of the data. One is stored in an Excel worksheet somewhere, and the other is stored in the PowerPivot window. If the original worksheet changes, those changes will not make it through to PowerPivot. An alternative is to link the data from Excel to PowerPivot.

To link to Excel data, that data must be converted to the Table Format introduced in Excel 2007.

1. If you start with an Excel worksheet, make sure that you have single-row headings at the top, no blank rows or blank columns.

2. Select one cell in the worksheet and press Ctrl+T. Excel asks you to confirm the extent of your table and if your data has headers (see Figure 25.13).

Figure 25.13
Convert your regular Excel data to a Table.

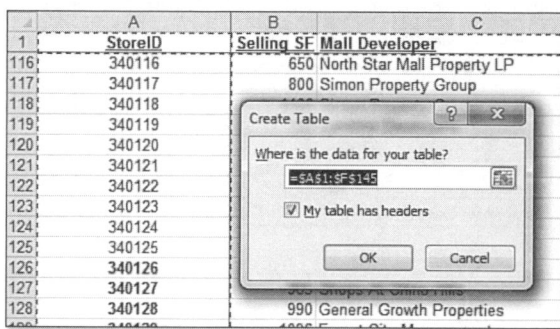

3. The table gets a default format. You can use the Table Tools Design tab to change that format if the dark blue banded rows are too much for you.

4. Go to the Table Tools Design tab. On the left side of the Ribbon, you see that this table is called Table1. Type a new name, such as StoreInfo.

5. On the PowerPivot tab, select Create Linked Table, as shown in Figure 25.14.

The table appears in the PowerPivot window.

Figure 25.14
Use the Create Linked Table to get this data into PowerPivot.

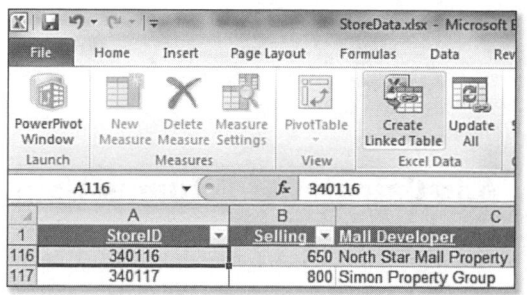

Define Relationships

Normally, in regular Excel you would be creating VLOOKUPs to match the two tables. It is far easier in PowerPivot. Follow these steps:

1. You link from one column in your main table to a column in another table. To simplify the relationship process, navigate to your main table and select a cell in the column from which you will link.

2. Click the Design tab in the PowerPivot Ribbon.

3. Select Create Relationship. The Create Relationship dialog appears. By default, the selected table and column appear in the first two fields, as shown in Figure 25.15.

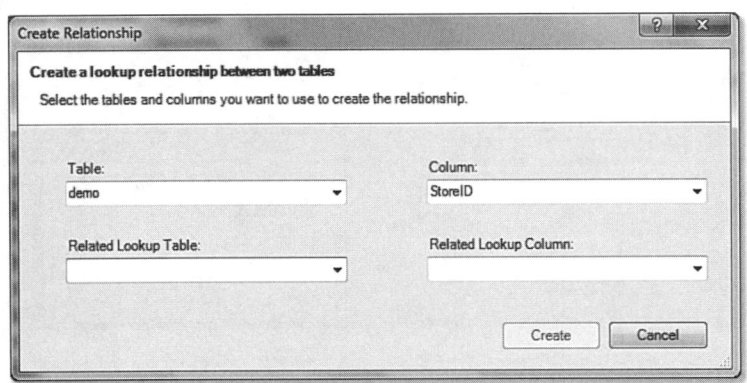

Figure 25.15
Define a relationship between tables. By selecting the key column before starting, two of the four fields are populated.

4. If you skipped step 1 and the correct table is not shown in the Table drop-down, select Demo from the Table drop-down.

5. If you did not select the correct column in step 1, open the Column drop-down. Select StoreID.

6. Open the Related Lookup table drop-down. Select StoreInfo.

7. Because the column names match, PowerPivot automatically changes the Related Lookup Column to read StoreID, as shown in Figure 25.16.

8. Click Create. You've now created a relationship between the two tables.

 To see a demo of defining relationships in PowerPivot, search for "Excel In Depth 25" at YouTube.

Add Calculated Columns Using DAX

One downside to pivot tables created from PowerPivot data is that they cannot automatically group daily data up to years. Before building the pivot table, let's use the DAX formula language to add a new calculated column to the Demo table.

Figure 25.16
This simple dialog replaces the VLOOKUP.

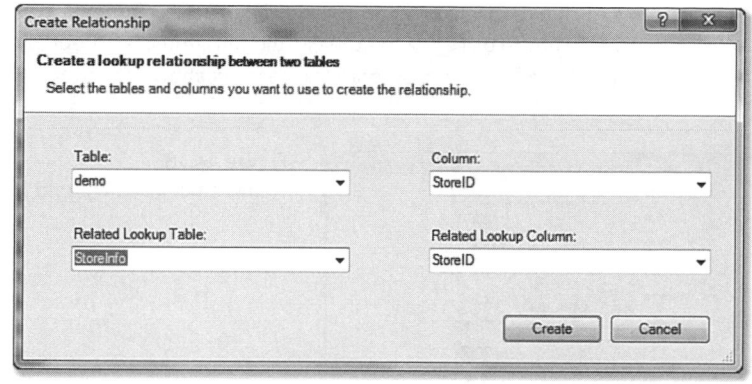

Follow these steps to add a Year field to the Demo table:

1. Click the Demo worksheet tab at the bottom of the PowerPivot Window.

2. The column to the right of Revenue has a heading of Add Column. Click in the first cell of this blank column.

3. Click the fx icon to the left of the formula bar. The Insert Function dialog appears with categories for All, Date & Time, Math & Trig, Statistical, Text, Logical, and Filter. Select Date & Time from the drop-down. You instantly notice that this is not the same list of functions in Excel. Five of the first six functions that appear in the window are exotic and new (see Figure 25.17).

Figure 25.17
DAX offers a different list of functions than Excel does.

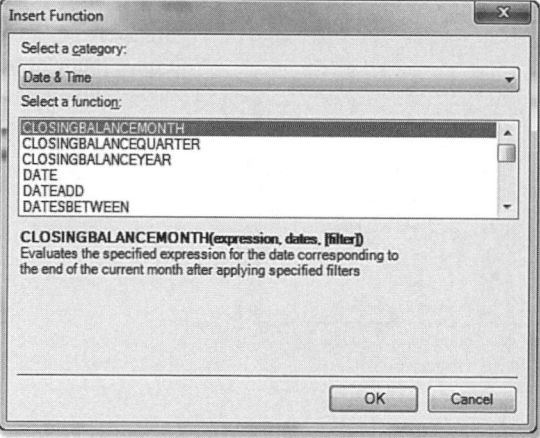

4. Luckily, some familiar old functions are in the list as well. Scroll down and select the YEAR function. Click the first date in the Date column. PowerPivot proposes a formula of =year(demo[Date]. Type the closing parentheses and press Enter. Excel fills in the column with the year associated with the date, as shown in Figure 25.18.

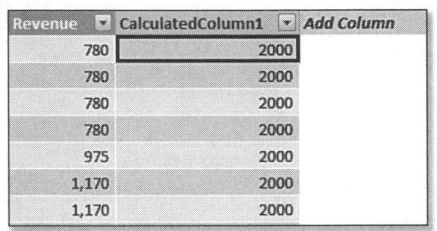

Figure 25.18
A new calculated column is added. You want to rename this.

5. Right-click the column and select Rename Column. Type a name, such as Year.

There are many more columns that you might think of adding, but let's move on to using the pivot table.

Build a Pivot Table

One of the advantages of PowerPivot is that multiple tables can share the same data and slicers. Open the PivotTable drop-down on the Home tab of the PowerPivot Ribbon. As shown in Figure 25.19, you have choices for a single pivot table, a single chart, a chart and a table, two charts, and so on.

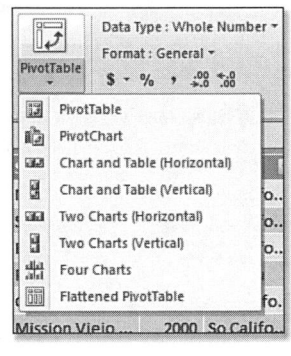

Figure 25.19
You have many options beyond a single table or chart.

 To learn how to deal with two or more pivot charts, see the "Combination Layouts" section later in this chapter.

- The PowerPivot Field List (see Figure 25.21) is a third variation of the pivot table field list. It is actually a new entry in the Task pane.

- Both tables are available in the top of the Field List. The main table is expanded to show the field names, but you can expand the other table and add those fields to this pivot table.

- Two new sections in the drop zones offer vertical or horizontal slicers.

- Because you are in a pivot table, the PivotTable Tools tabs are available.

Figure 25.20
Select the location for the pivot table.

Figure 25.21
The PowerPivot field list is different from the regular pivot table field list.

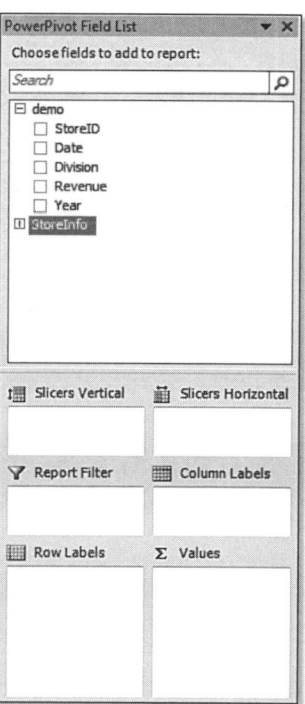

3. Select Revenue from the PowerPivot Field List. Expand the StoreInfo table. Select Region from the StoreInfo table. Excel builds a pivot table showing sales by region (see Figure 25.22). At this point, you have a pivot table from 1.8 million rows of data with a virtual link to a lookup table.

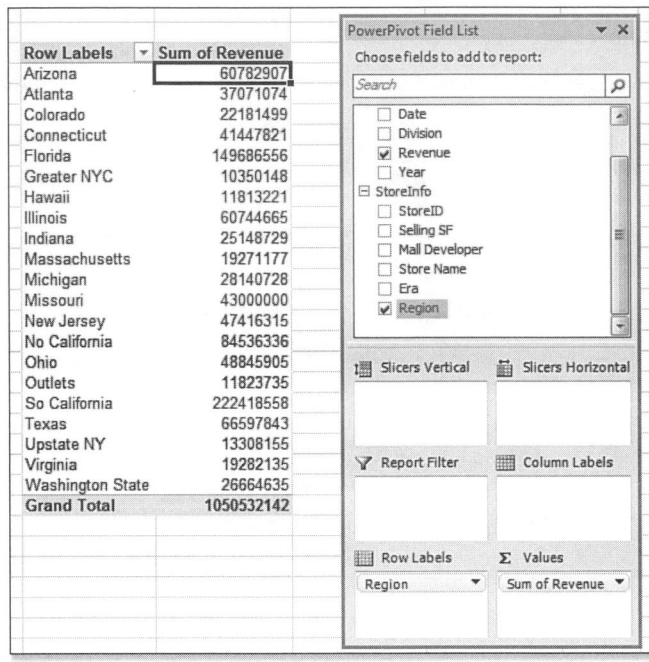

Figure 25.22
This pivot table summarizes 1.8 million rows and data from two tables.

At this point, you might want to go to the PivotTable Tools tabs to further format the pivot table. You could apply a currency format and rename the Sum of Revenue field. Choose a format with banded rows, and so on.

To show off some more features of the PowerPivot pivot table, let's add some slicer functionality.

Slicers in PowerPivot

Slicers are new in Excel 2010. The slicers in PowerPivot are slightly different from slicers in regular Excel.

First, notice that the PowerPivot Field List offers boxes for Slicers Vertical and Slicers Horizontal. Vertical slicers will be placed to the left of your pivot table. They are great for long lists that might need a scrollbar. Horizontal slicers will go above your pivot table.

Drag the Year field to the Slicers Horizontal drop zone. The years appear in a small slicer surrounded by a big box, as shown in Figure 25.23. Your first reaction will be to make that big box smaller, but don't.

Figure 25.23
Microsoft
draws a big
box around a
small slicer.

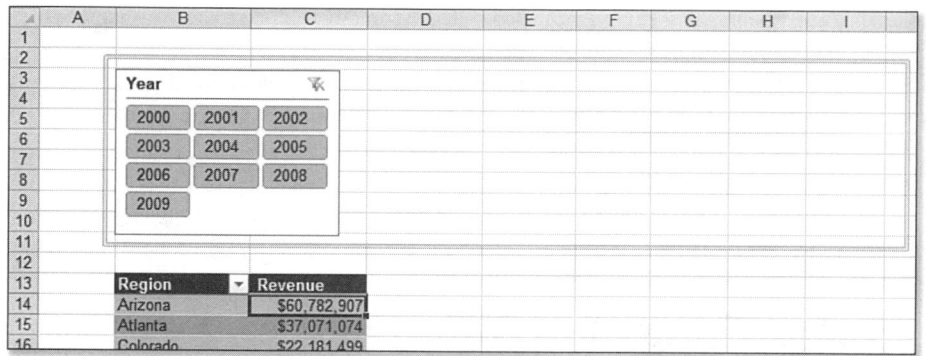

1. That big box is the slicer parent control. It is actually a drawing object that defines the boundary for all the horizontal slicers. If you make the slicer parent control box small, there won't be room for additional slicers.

2. Add Division and Era to the Slicers Horizontal.

3. All of a sudden the box around the three slicers looks almost the right size. It is as if Microsoft knew that you were going to add two more slicers!

4. Add Mall Developer to the vertical slicer. Because it has a long list of relatively long names, it fits well as the only vertical slicer.

5. Slicers work the same as they do in regular Excel pivot tables. Click one item to select it. Ctrl+click additional items to select them as well.

Figure 25.24 shows the default slicers after applying a few filters.

Figure 25.24
Microsoft
chooses the
number of col-
umns for each
slicer.

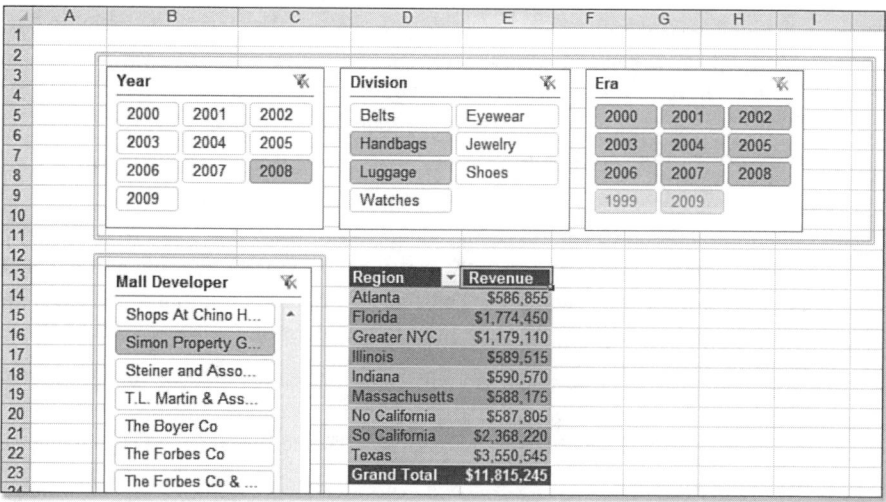

You will probably like the PowerPivot slicers better than regular Excel slicers. The PowerPivot spec calls for some IntelliSense to choose how many columns might work for each slicer. The fact that the PowerPivot takes a guess at arranging the slicers means that you might not have to adjust the slicers. In regular Excel, you will find yourself always adjusting the slicers.

 tip

To format the slicers, you have to click the slicer, not the bounding box.

The slicer parent control box disappears after you click outside of the pivot table. It comes back when the PowerPivot Field List displays. You can resize that box if you want the slicers to take up more or less room. Click the box once and resizing handles appear.

Some Things Are Different

If you have spent your whole Excel life building pivot tables out of regular Excel data, you are going to find some annoyances with these PowerPivot pivot tables. Many of these issues are not because of PowerPivot. They are because any PowerPivot pivot table automatically is an OLAP pivot table. This means that it behaves like an OLAP pivot table.

Some items to note:

- Days of the week do not automatically sort into the proper sequence. You have to choose More Sort Options, Ascending, More Options…. Uncheck the AutoSort box. Open the First Key Sort Order dropdown and choose Sunday, Monday, Tuesday.

- There is a trick in regular Excel pivot tables that you can do instead of dragging field names to the right place. You can go to a cell that contains the word Friday and type Monday there. When you press Enter, the Monday data will move to that new column. This does not work in PowerPivot pivot tables!

- Decide between Compact, Tabular, and Outline layouts before you drag fields to the correct location. Otherwise, everything snaps back to the original sequence.

- The PowerPivot Field List looks like the regular Field List, but a lot of functionality is missing. You cannot access filters by hovering over fields in the top of the field list. You cannot rearrange the field list. If you add multiple fields to the Values drop zone, you cannot access the Values field to move it to a new position. The good news is that the real PivotTable Field List is available. Turn it back on using PivotTable Tools Options, Field List. You can then move the Values field to the proper location.

- When you enter a formula in the Excel interface, you can point to a cell to include that cell in the formula. You can do this using the mouse or the arrow keys. Apparently, the PowerPivot team is made up of mouse people, because they support building a formula using the mouse in PowerPivot. Old-time Lotus 1-2-3 customers who build their formulas using arrow keys will be disappointed to find that the arrow key method doesn't work.

- You can use two types of refresh with these pivot tables. If you go to the PowerPivot tab and Update All, new data will be read from the data sources. This does not automatically refresh the pivot tables. You then have to go to the PivotTable Tools Options tab to click Refresh.

Certainly the Customer Experience Improvement Program data shows that everyone immediately goes from one Refresh to the other Refresh in quick succession. I would complain loudly that these are two separate steps, but remember that we are dealing with two different products here, so I can live with it.

Two Kinds of DAX Calculations

You've already seen an example where you used a DAX function to add a calculated column to a table in the PowerPivot window. There are 81 functions that are mostly copied straight from Excel for doing these types of calculations. The RELATED function can also be used in a calculated column to grab a value from a different table.

DAX can also be used to create new measures in the pivot table. These functions do not calculate a single cell value. They are all aggregate functions that calculate a value for the filtered rows behind any cell in the pivot table. There are 54 new DAX functions to enable these calculations. The real power is in these functions.

DAX Calculations for Calculated Columns

You've already seen one example of a calculated column. The functions are remarkably similar to the same function in Excel and mostly won't require a lot of explanation.

In the Date & Time category are 17 functions. The first 16 are identical to Excel's function. The rarely documented DATEDIF function in Excel is now renamed as YEARFRAC and is rewritten to actually work.

- DATE(<year>, <month>, <day>)
- DATEVALUE(date_text)
- DAY(<date>)
- EDATE(<start_date>, <months>)
- EOMONTH(<start_date>, <months>)
- HOUR(<datetime>)
- MINUTE(<datetime>)
- MONTH(<datetime>)
- NOW()
- SECOND(<time>)
- TIME(hour, minute, second)
- TIMEVALUE(time_text)
- TODAY()

- WEEKDAY(<date>, <return_type>)

- WEEKNUM(<date>, <return_type>)

- YEAR(<date>)

- YEARFRAC(<start_date>, <end_date>, <basis>)

In the Information category are six functions from Excel:

- ISBLANK(<value>)

- ISERROR(<value>)

- ISLOGICAL(<value>)

- ISNONTEXT(<value>)

- ISNUMBER(<value>)

- ISTEXT(<value>)

In the Logical Functions are seven Excel functions. Don't be concerned that SUMIFS is not in this list. See a discussion on CALCULATE later.

- ISBLANK(<value>)

- ISERROR(<value>)

- ISLOGICAL(<value>)

- ISNONTEXT(<value>)

- ISNUMBER(<value>)

- ISTEXT(<value>)

Math and Trig offer 22 familiar functions:

- ABS(<number>)

- CEILING(<number>, <significance>)

- EXP(<number>)

- FACT(<number>)

- FLOOR(<number>, <significance>)

- INT(<number>)

- LN(<number>)

- LOG(<number>,<base>)

- LOG10(<number>)

- MOD(<number>, <divisor>)
- MROUND(<number>, <multiple>)
- PI()
- POWER(<number>, <power>)
- QUOTIENT(<numerator>, <denominator>)
- RAND()
- RANDBETWEEN(<bottom>,<top>)
- ROUND(<number>, <num_digits>)
- ROUNDDOWN(<number>, <num_digits>)
- ROUNDUP(<number>, <num_digits>)
- SIGN(<number>)
- SQRT(<number>)
- TRUNC(<number>,<num_digits>)

In the Statistical category are 10 functions:

- AVERAGE(<column>)
- AVERAGEA(<column>)
- COUNT(<column>)
- COUNTA(<column>)
- COUNTBLANK(<column>)
- MAX(<column>)
- MAXA(<column>)
- MIN(<column>)
- MINA(<column>)
- SUM(<column>)

There are some items to note in the Text category.

First, you will have to start using CONCATENTATE or the & operator to build concatentations in PowerPivot. Because PowerPivot cannot join two tables based on two fields in each table, you will find that you are using CONCATENATE frequently to join fields together.

Second, the Excel TEXT function has been renamed to FORMAT. It still works the same. Apparently, the PowerPivot team wanted a more descriptive explanation of what TEXT actually does.

- CODE(<text>)

- CONCATENATE(<text1>, <text2>,...)

- EXACT(<text1>,<text2>)

- FIND(<find_text, within_text, start_num)

- FIXED(<number>, <decimals>, <no_commas>)

- FORMAT(<value>, <format_string>)

- LEFT(<text>, <num_chars>)

- LEN(<text>)

- LOWER(<text>)

- MID(<text>, <start_num>, <num_chars>)

- REPLACE(<old_text>, <start_num>, <num_chars>, <new_text>)

- REPT(<text>, <num_times>)

- RIGHT(<text>, <num_chars>)

- SEARCH(<search_text>, <within_text>, [start_num])

- SUBSTITUTE(<text>, <old_text>, <new_text>, <instance_num>)

- TRIM(<text>)

- UPPER (<text>)

- VALUE(<text>)

Most of the items in the Filter and Value Functions category are used for creating new measures. Two items are of use in calculated columns.

First, DAX introduces the BLANK() function. Because some of the aggregation functions can base a calculation on either the ALLNONBLANKROW or FIRSTNONBLANK, you can use the BLANK() function in an IF() function to exclude certain rows from measure calculations.

Second, you have the RELATED() function, which is described next.

Using RELATED() to Base a Column Calculation on Another Table

The next several examples make use of a sample file called Ch10WeatherMashup.xlsx. This file started out with a generic sales by day by store data set. A company sells products both in a mall location and at an airport. The two stores are less than 10 miles apart but might show different sales trends.

I used a web query and a macro to download weather data for the 3 years of daily dates. Several examples in the DAX Measure calculation mash up the sales and weather data to look for trends.

While preparing this workbook, I used DAX to create some calculated columns:

- WeekdayName uses =FORMAT(Sales[Date], "dddd") to convert the date to the day of the week. I was disappointed that PowerPivot pivot tables would not respect the custom list when presenting weekdays, so I added a new WeekdayID column.

- WeekdayID uses =WEEKDAY(Sales[Date],2). The "2" argument matches the same function in Excel. "2" numbers the days starting with 1 for Monday through 7 for Sunday. The Weekday table is a 7-row table that maps 1 to "1-Mon" and so on. This way, the day names would sort correctly.

- LocationDays is =CONCATENATE(Sales[Location],Sales[Date]). You see this used later when calculating the distinct number of store days.

Next, I wanted to calculate sales per store associate. The two locations have different scheduling requirements. The airport location usually operates with one associate, but staffs up to two on the busy travel days of Sunday, Monday, and Friday. The mall location staffs up on Friday and Saturday. To calculate the number of staff on a given day, you need to concatenate Location and Weekday. The formula for LocationWeek is =Concatenate(Sales[Location],Sales[WeekdayName]). Note that calculated columns have no problem referring to other calculated columns.

A relationship links this column to the Staffing table.

You might think that because PowerPivot understands the relationship between the Sales table and the Staffing table, you could write a formula such as =Sales[Net Sales]/Staffing[Staff Level], as shown in Figure 25.25. Unfortunately, this evaluates to an error.

The problem is that the calculation is trying to divide this row's sales of 2202 by all 14 values in the Staffing table.

The solution is to use the Related function. Rewrite the formula as =Sales[Net Sales]/Related(Staffing[StaffLevel]). The related function tells DAX that you don't want to divide 2202 by all 14 values in the table but only by the one value that is related to AirportSunday.

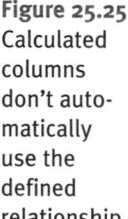
Figure 25.25
Calculated
columns
don't auto-
matically
use the
defined
relationship.

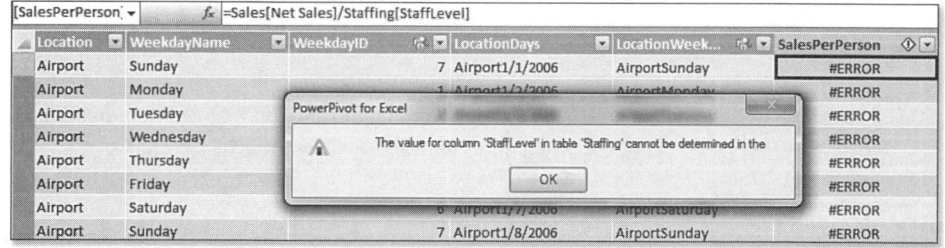

Figure 25.26 shows the result. In the first row, the airport location had two people staffing the store. Thus, the sales per person is half of the 2202. On Tuesday, only one person staffs the store, so SalesPerPerson is the same as Net Sales.

[SalesPerPerson] f_x =Sales[Net Sales]/Related(Staffing[StaffLevel])

D...	Net Sales	Location	WeekdayN...	We...	LocationDays	LocationWe...	SalesPerPerson
1/1/2006	2202	Airport	Sunday	7	Airport1/1/2006	AirportSunday	1101
1/2/2006	2896	Airport	Monday	1	Airport1/2/2006	AirportMonday	1448
1/3/2006	2659	Airport	Tuesday	2	Airport1/3/2006	AirportTuesday	2659
1/4/2006	3389	Airport	Wednesday	3	Airport1/4/2006	AirportWednesday	3389
1/5/2006	2219	Airport	Thursday	4	Airport1/5/2006	AirportThursday	2219
1/6/2006	3265	Airport	Friday	5	Airport1/6/2006	AirportFriday	1632.5

Figure 25.26
The Related function is like a 1-argument VLOOKUP.

Using these calculated columns and relationships, you can create some interesting pivot tables.

Figure 25.27 shows an analysis of sales by weekday at the two locations. You can see in cell I10 that sales peak at the Mall on Saturday. At the airport, you would think that sales would peak on Friday when business travelers need a gift on their way back home. Instead, they peak on Sunday when business travelers are purchasing new items for their upcoming business meetings.

		Day							
Values	Location	1 - Mon	2 - Tue	3 - Wed	4 - Thu	5 - Fri	6 - Sat	7 - Sun	Grand Total
Net Sales									
	Airport	402,729	368,299	369,055	383,688	402,217	416,262	448,157	2,790,407
	Mall	450,320	437,546	456,181	432,157	553,421	800,635	413,661	3,543,921
% of Sales									
	Airport	14%	13%	13%	14%	14%	15%	16%	100%
	Mall	13%	12%	13%	12%	16%	23%	12%	100%

Figure 25.27
Sales at the airport location peak on Sunday.

The percentages in rows 9 and 10 of Figure 25.27 work out okay because over 3 years, there are roughly the same number of Mondays as Fridays in the data set.

As you continue to do other analyses, the results are not as meaningful. In Figure 25.28, a report of sales by the amount of rain shows that most sales happened on sunny days. But this could just be telling you that it is sunny a lot more in Florida than rainy.

Net Sales	Location		
Rain	Airport	Mall	Grand Total
0-None	1,743,909	2,268,816	4,012,725
1-Trace	726,746	947,691	1,674,437
2-Moderate Rain	171,848	186,903	358,751
3-Heavy Rain	67,751	53,320	121,071
4-Rainforest Rain	55,389	57,110	112,499
5-Hurricane Rain	24,764	30,081	54,845
Grand Total	2,790,407	3,543,921	6,334,328

Figure 25.28
Do people hit the mall more often on sunny days? You cannot tell from this report.

The answer is to use DAX to create new measures that calculate sales per store per day.

Using DAX to Create New Measures

A Measure is the OLAP term for a Calculated Field.

But DAX Measures can run circles around Calculated Fields.

Before you dive in, you need to remember one mantra: "Filter first, then calculate." To understand this mantra, consider cell C15 in Figure 25.29.

Figure 25.29
How many filters are on cell C15?

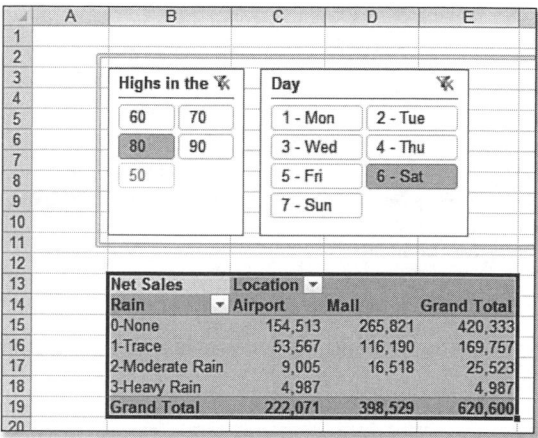

Think about how many filters are applied to cell C15. Would you say two? I think that the answer is four.

Everyone would agree that cell C15 is filtered to show only records that fell on a Saturday with high temperatures in the 80s. That is two filters.

In addition, the row and column fields are really filters as well. For cell C15, you want only records with sales at the airport location. You also only want days where there was no rain. That is two additional filters for cell C15.

As you start to think about DAX measures, remember that to figure out the measure for a particular cell in the pivot table, they first filter and then calculate the result using the DAX formula.

Count Distinct Using DAX

DAX lets you count how many distinct values meet the filter.

Wait, that is so good; I am going to repeat it.

DAX lets you count how many distinct values meet the filter! Do you understand the gravity of that statement? People who create advanced pivot tables always get tripped up because pivot tables cannot come up with a distinct count of something.

In Chapter 27, *"Automating Repetitive Functions Using VBA Macros,"* I offer a ridiculous formula =1/COUNTIFS(...) to try to replicate the Count Distinct. DAX will now let you count how many distinct values meet the filter.

To create a new Measure in DAX, use the New Measure icon in the PowerPivot tab. It seems confusing, so I will point out that this is not a tab in the PowerPivot window; it is the PowerPivot tab on the Excel Ribbon. To be clear, click the New Measure icon shown in Figure 25.30.

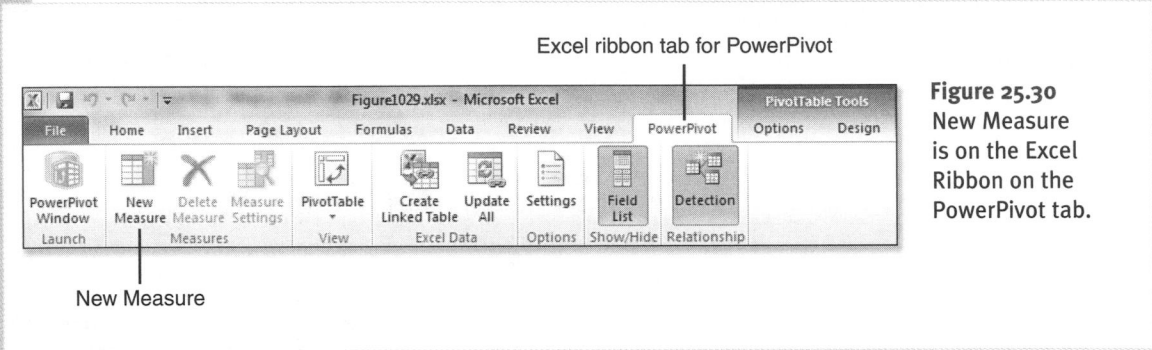

Excel ribbon tab for PowerPivot

New Measure

Figure 25.30
New Measure is on the Excel Ribbon on the PowerPivot tab.

When you click New Measure, you get the Measure Settings dialog, as shown in Figure 25.31.

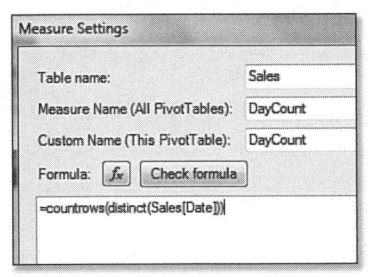

Figure 25.31
Edit measures in this dialog.

1. The Table Name should be the base table where your main numerical data is located. Change the first drop-down from Weather to Sales.

2. For the Measure Name, use a name such as DayCount.

3. Use the same name for Custom Name.

Measures are always aggregate functions, not cell-level functions. Thus, you must use an aggregate function such as SUM or COUNTROWS.

The magic function here is Distinct(Sales[Date]). For any cell in the pivot table, the distinct function returns a list of the distinct values for the rows that match the filter. Note that distinct must be used on a column in the home table. It cannot be applied to a value in a linked table. It is affected by filters applied to linked tables, but you must be using a value in the home table.

1. Distinct returns a one column table with a list of the distinct values. To count how many items there are, use =CountRows(Distinct(Sales[Date])).

2. After typing the formula, click the Check Formula button to make sure that your syntax is correct (see Figure 25.32).

Figure 25.32
Build a formula and then check the syntax.

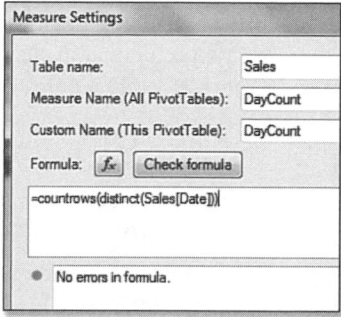

Think of DayCount as an intermediate result to illustrate the concept of using Distinct. You could then define a measure of Net Sales divided by DayCount. However, you could also skip DayCount altogether and build Sales Per Day with a single formula:

=SUM(Sales[Net Sales])/COUNTROWS(Distinct(Sales[Date]))

Figure 25.33 shows Sales Per Day based on the amount of rain and the location.

Figure 25.33
Both locations do better on sunny days.

Sales Per Day	Location		
Rain	Airport	Mall	Grand Total
0-None	2,845	5,008	6,329
1-Trace	2,550	4,175	5,638
2-Moderate Rain	2,322	3,398	4,659
3-Heavy Rain	2,053	2,962	3,669
4-Rainforest Rain	1,910	3,006	3,879
5-Hurricane Rain	1,905	2,735	3,428
Grand Total	2,665	4,526	5,833

You might have thought that sales would pick up in the airport on rainy days because of rain delays. Apparently, people are too stressed out to shop when their flights are delayed.

The airport location was open for all of the 3 years. The mall location opened late in 2006, so there are fewer days for the mall location. The airport is open on Christmas, but the mall is not. Thus, there are many days where only one store was open.

Column I shows total sales of both stores. The DayCount in column J counts a day when either one store or the other was open. Thus, both stores did sell $6.3 million over the course of the data set. But because both stores were not open for the entire period, the calculation of $6.3 million divided by 1086 days is wrong.

The solution is to count the distinct number of a concatenated column of location and date. The Location Days column is a calculated column in the PowerPivot window. To see it, turn back to Figure 25.25. In Figure 25.35, two new measures appear:

```
LocationDayCount =CountRows(Distinct(Sales
[LocationDays]))
```

```
Sales Per Store Per Day =Sum(Sales[Net Sales])/
CountRows(Distinct(Sales[LocationDays]))
```

Although these new measures produce the same results for the Airport or Mall Sales Per Day; the improvement is that the final column in K shows the true average sales per store per day.

 caution

Something is wrong with the totals in Figure 25.33. The Grand Total row for the airport is accurate; there were really an average of $2,665 in sales per day at the airport. But if the airport is averaging $2,665 a day and the mall is averaging $4,526 a day, how can the Grand Total column be showing $5,833?

Luckily, you have the intermediate DayCount column available. Figure 25.34 shows a test report showing sales, days, and sales per day.

B	C	D	E	F	G	H	I	J	K
	Location ⯆ **Values**								
									Total # **Total Sales**
	Airport			**Mall**			**Total Sales**	**Days**	**Per Day**
			Sales Per			Sales Per			
Rain ⯆	**Sales**	**# Days**	**Day**	**Sales**	**# Days**	**Day**			
0-None	1,743,909	613	2,845	2,268,816	453	5,008	4,012,725	634	6,329
1-Trace	726,746	285	2,550	947,691	227	4,175	1,674,437	297	5,638
2-Moderate Rain	171,848	74	2,322	186,903	55	3,398	358,751	77	4,659
3-Heavy Rain	67,751	33	2,053	53,320	18	2,962	121,071	33	3,669
4-Rainforest Rain	55,389	29	1,910	57,110	19	3,006	112,499	29	3,879
5-Hurricane Rain	24,764	13	1,905	30,081	11	2,735	54,845	16	3,428
Grand Total	2,790,407	1047	2,665	3,543,921	783	4,526	6,334,328	1086	5,833

Figure 25.34
Something is wrong in J12.

B	C	D	E	F	G	H	I	J	K
	Location ⯆ **Values**								
								Total Location	Total Sales Per
	Airport			**Mall**			**Total Sales**	**DayCount**	**Store Per Day**
		Location	Sales Per		Location	Sales Per			
Rain ⯆	**Sales**	**DayCount**	**Store Per Day**	**Sales**	**DayCount**	**Store Per Day**			
0-None	1,743,909	613	2,845	2,268,816	453	5,008	4,012,725	1066	3,764
1-Trace	726,746	285	2,550	947,691	227	4,175	1,674,437	512	3,270
2-Moderate Rain	171,848	74	2,322	186,903	55	3,398	358,751	129	2,781
3-Heavy Rain	67,751	33	2,053	53,320	18	2,962	121,071	51	2,374
4-Rainforest Rain	55,389	29	1,910	57,110	19	3,006	112,499	48	2,344
5-Hurricane Rain	24,764	13	1,905	30,081	11	2,735	54,845	24	2,285
Grand Total	2,790,407	1047	2,665	3,543,921	783	4,526	6,334,328	1830	3,461

Figure 25.35
This calculation works better.

When "Filter, Then Calculate" Doesn't Work in DAX Measures

Suppose that you create a DAX Measure for SUM(Sls[Sales]). By definition, all filters are taken into account before PowerPivot starts calculating. To get the 851 in cell D6 in Figure 25.36, the program will filter the data to where Rep=Bill, Date = 6/2/2011. The remaining rows are added to get the 851.

Figure 25.36
Excel applies a filter to calculate the 851.

	A	B	C	D	E
1					
2					
3		Sum of Sales	Rep ▼		
4		Date ▼	Amber	Bill	Chris
5		6/1/2011	1083	346	49
6		6/2/2011	1094	851	429
7		6/3/2011	1444	765	1028
8		6/4/2011	954	659	851
9		6/5/2011	900	1304	578
10		6/6/2011	533	1201	526

In essence, without the DAX calculation specifying any filters, the result for cell D6 in the pivot table is automatically going to sum up the rows shown by the arrows in Figure 25.37.

Figure 25.37
The answer in Figure 25.36 adds up all the arrow rows.

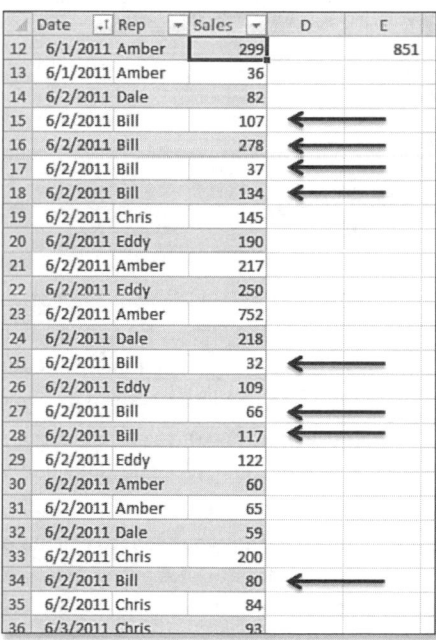

	Date ▼	Rep ▼	Sales ▼	D	E
12	6/1/2011	Amber	299		851
13	6/1/2011	Amber	36		
14	6/2/2011	Dale	82		
15	6/2/2011	Bill	107	←	
16	6/2/2011	Bill	278	←	
17	6/2/2011	Bill	37	←	
18	6/2/2011	Bill	134	←	
19	6/2/2011	Chris	145		
20	6/2/2011	Eddy	190		
21	6/2/2011	Amber	217		
22	6/2/2011	Eddy	250		
23	6/2/2011	Amber	752		
24	6/2/2011	Dale	218		
25	6/2/2011	Bill	32	←	
26	6/2/2011	Eddy	109		
27	6/2/2011	Bill	66	←	
28	6/2/2011	Bill	117	←	
29	6/2/2011	Eddy	122		
30	6/2/2011	Amber	60		
31	6/2/2011	Amber	65		
32	6/2/2011	Dale	59		
33	6/2/2011	Chris	200		
34	6/2/2011	Bill	80	←	
35	6/2/2011	Chris	84		
36	6/3/2011	Chris	93		

Incidentally, the formula in E12 of Figure 25.37 is =SUMIFS(Sls[Sales],Sls[Rep], "Bill",Sls [Date],DATE(2011,6,2)) and also returns 851. The DAX formula of =SUM(Sls[Sales]) is a bit shorter, isn't it?

You should appreciate that for most calculations, you never have to specify a filter.

This assumption leads to trouble, though, when you need part of your formula to look at all rows, not just the filtered rows.

Suppose that you want to see how the sales compared to the total sales for the month. You need to calculate a fraction. The numerator of the fraction is going to be SUM(Sls[Sales]). The denominator of the fraction needs to be all the records in the sales table. That is going to be tougher.

In DAX, you don't use SUMIFS; you use Calculate. Calculate asks for an expression and then one or more filters. For those filters, you use a special function called ALL. If you ask for Calculate (Sum(Sls[Sales]),ALL(Sls)), the filter is almost an "anti-Filter." Rather than further limiting the calculation, ALL says that you want it to look not just at Bill's sales for 6/2/2011 but all the sales in the table.

In Figure 25.38, a new measure calculates % of Grand Total sales by using =SUM(Sls[Sales])/ Calculate(Sum(Sls[Sales]),All(Sls)). The % of Grand Total for cell F7 says that Bill's $851 in sales on June 2 represents 0.9% of the grand total sales.

Rep	Values			
Amber		Bill		Cl
Date	Sum of Sales	% of Grand Total	Sum of Sales	% of Grand Total	Su
6/1/2011	1083	1.1%	346	0.4%
6/2/2011	1094	1.1%	851	0.9%
6/3/2011	1444	1.5%	765	0.8%
6/4/2011	954	1.0%	659	0.7%
6/5/2011	900	0.9%	1304	1.3%
6/6/2011	533	0.5%	1201	1.2%
6/7/2011	1184	1.2%	976	1.0%

Figure 25.38
The denominator of these calculations is always the tough part.

The past example might seem trivial, because you could replace that calculation with Show Values As, % of the Total. But don't skip over understanding the ALL(Sls) syntax. After you understand that syntax, you can replace the first argument in Calculate with Max, Min, Average, or any function. So Calculate becomes like SUMIFS, AVERAGEIFS, MINIFS, MAXIFS, and so on.

Early on in the days of the PowerPivot beta, many people blogged an example or two that calculated the % of the total using Calculate and All. I don't think that this is the most powerful use of calculated measures.

Suppose that you want to calculate how Bill's $851 sale on June 2 compared to all sales on June 2. The numerator of the DAX Measure will be =Sum(Sls[Sales]). Again, the denominator is going to be the hard part.

For the denominator, you want to say, "Look at all the sales that match today, but don't pay any attention to the sales rep filter. Give me all sales reps."

If you asked for ALL(Sls), the calculation would throw out all the filters.

This time, you need to ask for `AllExcept(Sls,Sls[Date])`. I can't even count if this is a quadruple or a quintuple negative, but I can tell you that it takes some time to wrap your head around this. You might think of it like this: "DAX is already going to be filtering by date and sales rep. Go ahead and throw out all the filters except for the Date filter. Keep filtering by date."

In Figure 25.39, the DAX Measure calculates =SUM(Sls[Sales])/Calculate(Sum(Sls[Sales])),AllExcept(Sls,Sls[Date])). This calculation shows you the percentage of each day's sales achieved by a certain rep.

Figure 25.39
AllExcept says to ignore all filters except the Date filter.

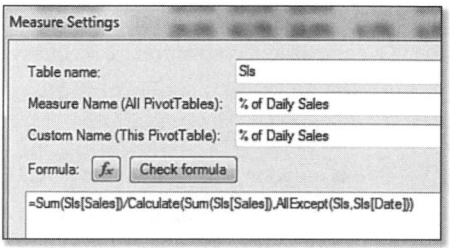

You can also override the filters by specifying other filters in the Calculate function. The actual syntax of the Calculate function is: `Calculate(Expresion,[filter 1], [filter 2], [filter 3], [filter 4], ...)`. Just like SUMIFS in Excel 2010, you can keep adding additional filters.

=Calculate(Sls[Sales],Sls[Rep]="Amber") will get all Amber sales for this row. If Amber is the sales star in the store, perhaps someone would want to show everyone's sales as a percentage of Amber's Sales.

=SUM(Sls[Sales])/ Calculate(Sls[Sales],Sls[Rep]="Amber") shows sales as a percentage of Amber's total sales for that day. See the report in Figure 25.40. I wonder if the store manager posted this report if Chris would call home on the 16th to say, "Guess what! I sold 259.2% of that suck-up Amber.

Figure 25.40
Show all values as a % of Amber is not one of the built-in selections.

	B	C	F	H	I	K	
3		Rep ▼					
4		Amber	Bill		Chris		D
5	Date ▼	Sum of Sales	Sum of Sales	% of Amber	Sum of Sales	% of Amber	S
15	6/10/2011	1105	201	18.2%	436	39.5%	
16	6/11/2011	2495	1197	48.0%	702	28.1%	
17	6/12/2011	1113	435	39.1%	29	2.6%	
18	6/13/2011	1845	1572	85.2%	1550	84.0%	
19	6/14/2011	1667	520	31.2%	534	32.0%	
20	6/15/2011	1951	186	9.5%	736	37.7%	
21	6/16/2011	441	773	175.3%	1143	259.2%	
22	6/17/2011	556	1157	208.1%	478	86.0%	

Mix In Those Amazing Time Intelligence Functions

Remember that you can apply many filters in the Calculate function. As you saw in the previous example, you could filter to show total sales for the rep named Amber. You can also filter to all dates that match a certain date function.

There are 34 Time Intelligence functions. Suppose that you want to calculate a running MTD total. You can use the Calculate function and specify a filter of `DatesMTD(Sls[Date])`. That's the complete filter. You don't need to say, "This row's date falls within the MTDDates compared to the current date in the report." You just have to say `DatesMTD(Sls[Date])`.

In pseudo code: "I want a formula that will add up all the sales for dates that fall in the MTD period compared to the current row but only for reps that match the current column."

Add up all the sales is `=Calculate(Sum(sls[Sales])`.

For dates that are MTD is `DatesMTD(Sls[Date])`.

But only for reps that match is `AllExcept(Sls,Sls[Rep])`.

The complete formula in Figure 25.41 is `=Calculate(Sum(sls[Sales]), DatesMTD(Sls[Date]) ,AllExcept(Sls,Sls[Rep]))`.

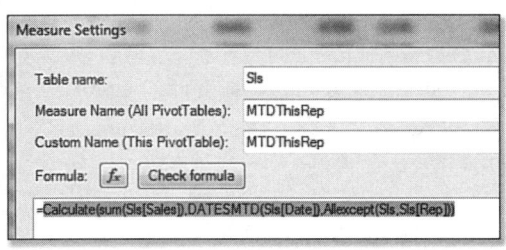

Figure 25.41
MTD Sales for each rep.

Notice that Dale did not work on June 4 and thus gets no calculation for MTD Sales on that date. If you use pivot tables a lot, you understand that empty cells usually show up as blank, and you generally change the pivot table options to have empty cells show up as 0. The same thing is happening here. Because there was no data for Dale for June 4, none of the MDX measures gets calculated for that cell. The solution would be to go back to the original data and add in a zero-sale record for every person for every day.

If you download the sample files for this book and look at Ch10DAXMeasures.xlsx, you see other calculated measures in the field list.

Note that a measure can refer to another measure. To get to This Rep's Percentage of MTD Sales versus all MTD Sales, I first built MTDThisRep as shown previously. I then built MTD

 tip

The filtering techniques such as `All()` and `AllExcept()` work well in the home table. If you need to have a calculation ignore or respect a filter in a linked table, your results may vary. It is always best to have the filter fields in the home table. One workaround is to use the `=Related()` function in the PowerPivot window to bring a copy of the field from the linked table into the home table.

All Reps using =Calculate(Sum(Sls[Sales]),DatesMTD(Sls[Date]),All(Sls)). When it came time to create the formula to divide those two, it was easiest to simply build the formula as =Sls[MTDThisRep]/Sls[MTD All Reps]), as shown in Figure 25.42.

Figure 25.42
You can use previously defined measures to simplify the calculation for another measure.

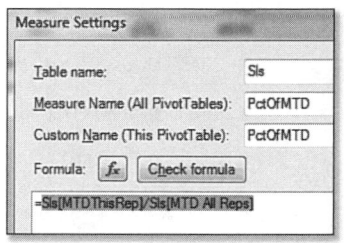

The following is a complete list of Time Intelligence Functions.

- CLOSINGBALANCEMONTH(<expression>,<dates>,<filter>)

- CLOSINGBALANCEQUARTER(<expression>,<dates>,<filter>)

- CLOSINGBALANCEYEAR(<expression>,<dates>,<filter>)

- DATEADD(<date_column>,<number_of_intervals>,<interval>)

- DATESBETWEEN(<column>,<start_date>,<end_date>

- DATESINPERIOD(<date_column>,<start_date>,<number_of_intervals>,<intervals>)

- DATESMTD(<date_column>)

- DATESQTD (<date_column>)

- DATESYTD (<date_column> [,<YE_date>])

- ENDOFMONTH(<date_column>)

- ENDOFQUARTER(<date_column>)

- ENDOFYEAR(<date_column>)

- FIRSTDATE (<datecolumn>)

- LASTDATE (<datecolumn>)

- LASTNONBLANK (<datecolumn>,<expression>)

- NEXTDAY(<date_column>)

- NEXTMONTH(<date_column>)

- NEXTQUARTER (<date_column>)

- NEXTYEAR(<date_column>[,<YE_date>])

- OPENINGBALANCEMONTH(<expression>,<dates>,<filter>)

- OPENINGBALANCEQUARTER(<expression>,<dates>,<filter>)

- OPENINGBALANCEYEAR(<expression>,<dates>,<filter>)

- PARALLELPERIOD(<date_column>,<number_of_intervals>,<intervals>)

- PREVIOUSDAY(<date_column>)

- PREVIOUSMONTH(<date_column>)

- PREVIOUSQUARTER(<date_column>)

- PREVIOUSYEAR(<date_column>)

- SAMEPERIODLASTYEAR(<dates>)

- STARTOFMONTH (<date_column>)

- STARTOFQUARTER (<date_column>)

- STARTOFYEAR(<date_column>[,<YE_date>])

- TotalMTD(<expression>,<dates>,<filter>)

- TotalQTD(<expression>,<dates>,<filter>)

- TotalYTD(<expression>,<dates>,<filter>)

Check out the optional Year Ending date parameter in DatesYTD and other arguments; yes, you can finally deal with fiscal years other than those ending on December 31!

For completeness, these are the remaining functions supported by DAX:

- BLANK()

- RELATED(<column>)

- ALL(<table_or_column>)

- DISTINCT(<column>)

- EARLIER(<column>, <number>)

- EARLIEST(<table_or_column>)

- VALUES(<column>)

- ALLEXCEPT(<table>,column1,<column2>,...)

- CALCULATE(<expression>,<filter1>,<filter2>...)

- CALCULATETABLE(<expression>, <filter1>, <filter2>,...)

- FILTER(<table>,<filter>)

- RELATEDTABLE(<table>)

- ALLNONBLANKROW(<column>)

- FIRSTNONBLANK(<column>,<expression>)

- AVERAGEX(<table>, <expression>)

- COUNTAX(<table>, <expression>)

- COUNTROWS(<table>)

- COUNTX(<table>, <expression>)

- MAXX(<table>, <expression>)

- MINX(<table>, < expression>)

- SUMX(<table>, <expression>)

Other Notes

The topic of PowerPivot deserves a whole book. (In fact, you can find my whole book on the subject: *PowerPivot for the Excel Data Analyst*, published by QUE.)

The next section cover a few miscellaneous topics that didn't make it elsewhere in this chapter.

Combination Layouts

The PivotTable drop-down in the PowerPivot Window offers eight choices.

The first choice is a single pivot table and has been used throughout this chapter.

The last choice is a flattened pivot table. That is a pivot table that starts in Outline layout instead of Compact layout. The Repeat All Row Labels feature is turned on. If you plan to convert the pivot table to values to reuse it, choosing a flattened pivot table can save you a few clicks along the way.

The other six layouts include pivot charts. I don't get this. PivotCharts look great in Microsoft demos, but no one actually uses them. I can see why Microsoft had to put them here, because it will give them something to demo, but I cannot figure out why Microsoft gives you six different versions. If one PivotChart is bad, why would anyone ever want four of them?

But, assume you are actually trying to do this and you found this section in the index.

When you choose a combination of multiple elements, you have multiple outlines on the worksheet. In Figure 25.43, the pivot table on the right is the active table. You can tell because the cell pointer is inside the outline for that pivot table. Any changes that you make to the PowerPivot Field list affect that pivot table first.

When you are ready to work on another element in the combination, click that element. The Field List resets to blank, and you can design that element. All elements share the same slicers.

Note that for each chart on your layout, Microsoft inserted a new worksheet to hold the actual pivot table for the chart.

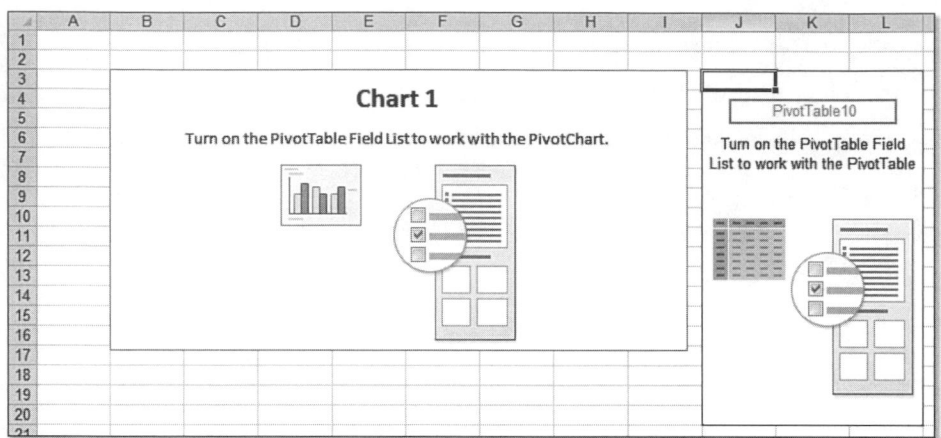

Figure 25.43
A combination report offers one or more pivot tables or charts.

Report Formatting

I am excited about PowerPivot. It lets people who cannot do VLOOKUPs mash up data and do reports that have never been imagined before. However, every Microsoft blog is busy showing the same layout for PowerPivot demos.

Because you've probably seen 1,000 of them, let's talk about how to replicate those layouts shown in the blogs and press:

1. Insert a new worksheet to hold the workbook.

2. Create a combo of two or four pivot charts. Choose a location rather than letting them default. Choose a spot on row 5 of the new workbook.

3. Add as many slicers as possible to the top and left of the chart.

4. Build the charts.

5. Make row 1 very tall—perhaps 270 to 300 points tall. Use Insert, Screenshot to add an interesting graphic to row 1.

6. Add an interesting graphic below the charts to balance the graphic on top of the charts.

7. Go to File, Options, Advanced, Display Options for This Worksheet. Clear the Gridlines check box. If you want to go all out, scroll up and remove the scrollbars, sheet tabs, and formula bars.

8. Minimize the Ribbon.

9. Add a fill color behind the whole worksheet.

10. While the pivot table is active, click the bounding box around each slicer. Right-click the border. Select Properties. Select Move and Size with cells.

11. Click away from the pivot table. See the result in Figure 25.44.

Figure 25.44
This dashboard tracks how many publications have shown this style of dashboard generated by PowerPivot.

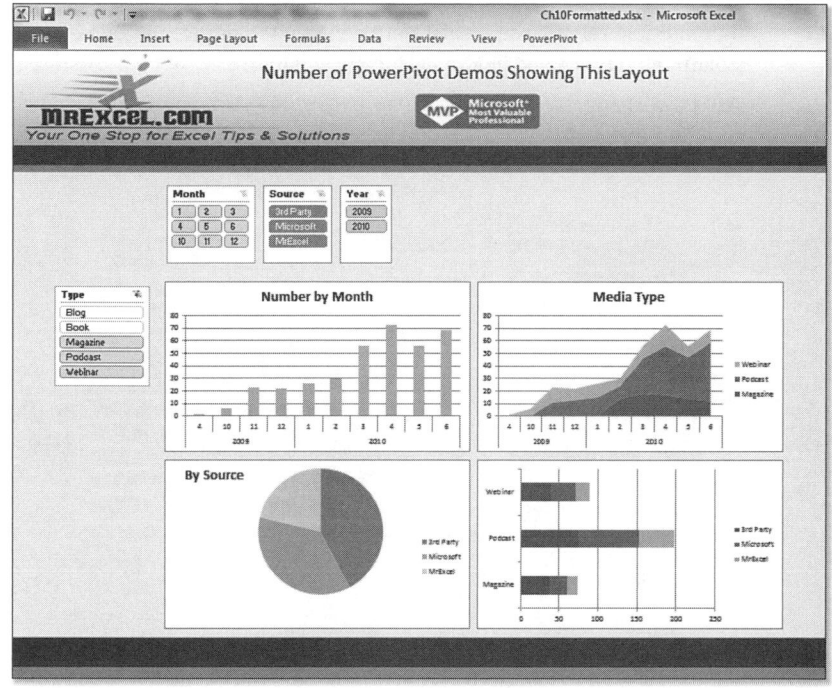

If your layout contains an actual pivot table, consider converting the pivot table to formulas. You can then insert extra rows between the pivot table rows, adding color, and so on.

Refreshing PowerPivot Versus Refreshing Pivot Table

Suppose that your underlying data changes. If it is stored in an Excel linked table, you would go to the PowerPivot tab in the Excel Ribbon and click Refresh All. If it is stored in an External Data Source, you would go to the PowerPivot window and select the Refresh button. If the data were pasted to PowerPivot, you can Paste Append new data or do a Paste Replace.

This does not refresh the pivot table! When you return to Excel, you have to remember to go to the PivotTable Tools Options tab and select Refresh.

Getting Your Data into PowerPivot with SQL Server

Data coming from SQL Server already has a lot of relationships defined. Find the main Fact table, select that table, and then click the button for Select Related Tables. PowerPivot reads the database schema and brings in all the tables with relationships predefined. It is, of course, then possible to add in additional Excel or text data to mash up with the SQL Server data.

Other Issues

Can multiple relationships exist between two tables? No. If you need two relationships, import the lookup table twice and link to each copy separately.

Will PowerPivot ever be available for Excel 2007? No. PowerPivot relies on a number of features added to Excel 2010.

USING WHAT-IF, SCENARIO MANAGER, GOAL SEEK, AND SOLVER

When Dan Bricklin invented VisiCalc in 1979, he was trying to come up with a tool that would let him quickly recalculate his MBA school case studies. Three decades later, spreadsheets are still used for the same functionality.

Newer spreadsheet tools such as Goal Seek and Solver allow you to back directly into the assumptions that lead to a solution. This chapter discusses some of Excel 2010's features that are helpful when you try to find a specific answer.

Using What-If

After you have set up a model in Excel, you can make copies of the model side by side and then change the various input variables to test their impact on the final result. Because this type of analysis answers the question of what happens if a change is made, it is known generically as *what-if changes*.

What-if analyses are the least formal method in this chapter. You copy the input variables and formulas multiple times. You can then vary the input variables until you reach a suitable solution.

For example, Figure 26.1 shows a worksheet to calculate the monthly payment on a car purchase. Cells E1, E2, and E3 are the known values: the price, term, and interest rate. Cell E4 calculates the monthly payment using the =PMT() function.

Cells E1:E4 are a self-contained minimodel. You can copy these cells several times over and perform what-if analysis on the car payment model.

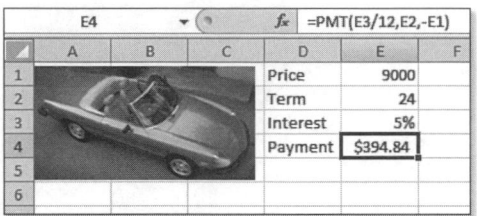

Figure 26.1
You may not like the answer in Cell E4, but Excel makes the answer easy to find.

Figure 26.2 shows a basic what-if worksheet that you can use to plug in different numbers manually. Columns F and G show the effects of changing the number of months. Columns H:J factor in a lower interest rate. Columns K:M show the effects of finding a lower price. Based on a number of options, Column N starts to hone in on a scenario to get to the $225 target payment: Use 42 months, 5% interest, and a price of $8750.

f_x	=PMT(N3/12,N2,-N1)										
D	E	F	G	H	I	J	K	L	M	N	O
Price	9000	9000	9000	9000	9000	9000	8500	8500	8500	8700	
Term	36	42	48	36	42	48	36	42	48	42	
Interest	5.0%	5.0%	5.0%	4.5%	4.5%	4.5%	5.0%	5.0%	5.0%	5.0%	
Payment	$270	$234	$207	$268	$232	$205	$255	$221	$196	$226	

Figure 26.2
By making multiple copies of the table, you can create a What-If model.

There is nothing magic about this type of what-if analyses. There are no Ribbon commands involved. You copy the model and plug in a few different numbers. This is how most Excel worksheets use what-if analyses. The remaining topics in this chapter cover the format What-If commands on the Ribbon.

Creating a Two-Variable What-If Table

The analysis in Figure 26.2 is fairly ad hoc in that it basically enables you to try various combinations until you find one that is close to your target payment. If you have two variables to manipulate, you can use Excel's fairly powerful Data Table command. To use a data table, follow these steps:

1. Enter a formula in the upper-left corner of the table. This formula should point to at least two variable cells.

2. Along the left column of the table, enter various values for one of the input values. These values will be substituted in a cell known as the Column Input Cell.

3. Along the top row of the table, enter various values for the other input variable. These values will be substituted in a cell that Excel calls the Row Input Cell.

4. Select the entire table.

5. From the Data tab, select Data Tools, What-If Analysis, Data Table.

6. In the Data Table dialog box, enter a row input cell and a column input cell.

7. Click OK to complete the table.

You can use the Data Table command to negotiate the price and term of the loan by following these steps:

1. Use the formula in Cell E4 as the formula in the top-left corner of your table.

2. From E5:E21, fill in various possible values for purchase price.

3. From F4:K4, fill in various possible values for the term of the loan.

4. Select the entire table, E4:K17, as shown in Figure 26.3.

Figure 26.3
Preparing for
a two-variable
what-if analysis.

	A	B	C	D	E	F	G	H	I	J	K
		E4			f_x	=PMT(E3/12,E2,-E1)					
1				Price	9000						
2				Term	24						
3				Interest	5%						
4				Payment	$394.84	24	30	36	42	48	54
5					5000						
6					5250						
7					5500						
8					5750						
9					6000						
10					6250						
11					6500						
12					6750						
13					7000						
14					7250						
15					7500						
16					7750						
17					8000						
18					8250						
19					8500						
20					8750						
21					9000						

5. Select Data Table from the Data tab to display the Data Table dialog box, as shown in Figure 26.4. The dialog box asks you for a row input cell and a column input cell. The Row Input Cell field offers to take each value from the top row of the table and plug it into a particular cell.

6. Because the values in F4:K4 are loan terms, specify E2 for the row input cell.

7. Similarly, the Column Input Field offers to take each value from the left column and replace that value in a particular cell. Because these cells contain vehicle prices, select E1 as the column input cell.

8. Click OK. Excel fills in the intersection of each row and column with the monthly payment, based on the price in the left column combined with the loan term in the top row. Figure 26.5 shows the resulting table.

Replace the top row in the Row Input Cell

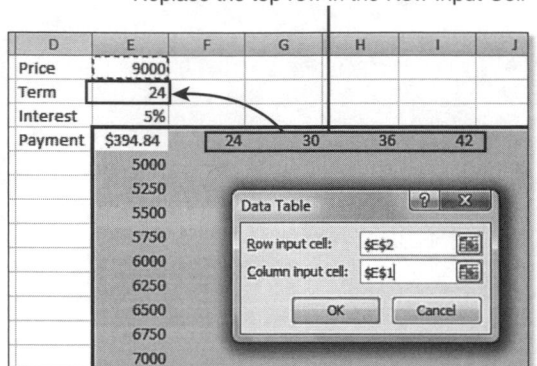

Figure 26.4
Setting up the Table dialog.

Figure 26.5
Excel performs 102 what-if analyses in one command.

9. Select just the interior of the table. You can see that Excel represents the table with the TABLE ( ) array function. Figure 26.6 shows the table after applying a color scale.

 For more information on data visualizations, see the "Creating Heat Maps with Color Scales" section in Chapter 31, "Using Data Visualizations and Conditional Formatting."

note

Note that the values calculated in the table are live formula values. If you change the numbers along the edge of the table, the TABLE ( ) array formula recalculates new loan payment amounts.

Figure 26.6
The values in the table are calculated by
a single TABLE ( ) array formula.

	D	E	F	G	H	I	J	K
	Price	9000						
	Term	24						
	Interest	5%						
	Payment	$394.84	24	30	36	42	48	54
		5000	219.3569	177.6468	149.8545	130.0152	115.1465	103.5915
		5250	230.3248	186.5292	157.3472	136.5159	120.9038	108.7711
		5500	241.2926	195.4115	164.8399	143.0167	126.6611	113.9507
		5750	252.2605	204.2938	172.3327	149.5174	132.4184	119.1302
		6000	263.2283	213.1762	179.8254	156.0182	138.1758	124.3098
		6250	274.1962	222.0585	187.3181	162.519	143.9331	129.4894
		6500	285.164	230.9409	194.8108	169.0197	149.6904	134.669
		6750	296.1319	239.8232	202.3036	175.5205	155.4477	139.8485
		7000	307.0997	248.7056	209.7963	182.0212	161.2051	145.0281
		7250	318.0676	257.5879	217.289	188.522	166.9624	150.2077
		7500	329.0354	266.4702	224.7817	195.0227	172.7197	155.3873
		7750	340.0033	275.3526	232.2745	201.5235	178.477	160.5668
		8000	350.9711	284.2349	239.7672	208.0243	184.2343	165.7464
		8250	361.939	293.1173	247.2599	214.525	189.9917	170.926
		8500	372.9068	301.9996	254.7526	221.0258	195.749	176.1056
		8750	383.8747	310.8819	262.2453	227.5265	201.5063	181.2851
		9000	394.8425	319.7643	269.7381	234.0273	207.2636	186.4647

Using Scenario Manager

The Data Table command is great for models with two variables that can change. However, sometimes you have models with far more variables that can change. In such a case, you should use the Scenario Manager, which allows you to create multiple scenarios, each changing up to 32 variables.

With up to 32 variables changing, it is best to use named ranges for all the input variables before you define your first scenario. One of the results of the Scenario Manager is a summary report. Using named ranges for all the input cells makes the report easier to understand.

➡ *To learn how to use named ranges to your advantage, see the "Using Named Ranges to Simplify Formulas" section in Chapter 18, "Using Names in Excel."*

Generally, Scenario Manager allows you to set up named scenarios such as Best Case, Worst Case, and Most Likely. In each scenario you can specify values for up to 32 variables. You would then have a model that calculates results based on the 32 input variables. For example, you might have a business plan that projects sales for the next 120 months using growth rates in the input variable section of the spreadsheet. The important distinction is that although you may only have 32 input variables, you might base millions of formulas on these 32 input variables.

Use the Scenario Manager dialog box to switch to a different set of input variables. The worksheet can be calculated using Best Case and Worst Case scenarios. For a specific example, Figure 26.7

shows a sales forecasting model. All the highlighted cells are variables that can change. The model calculates a total forecast in Cell B16 and a ratio in Cell B18. To set up and use scenarios, follow these steps:

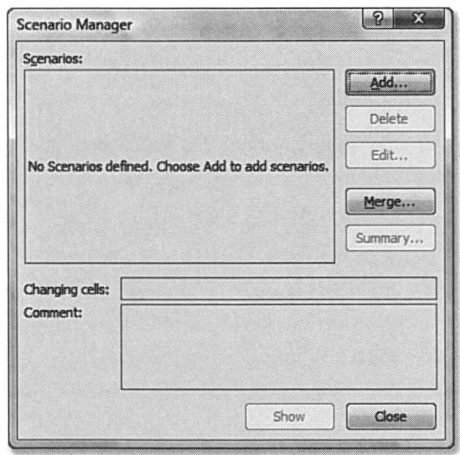

OurCoConversionPct		f_x	=+B16/B17		
	A	B	C	D	E
1	Sales Forecasting Model				
2		Total	2006	2007	2008
3	Existing Market Size	400,000,000	400,000,000	400,000,000	400,000,000
4	% Upgrading		7%	24%	9%
5	Total Upgraders		28,000,000	96,000,000	36,000,000
6	% Upgraders buying book		15%	12%	2%
7	Upgrade Books		4,200,000	11,520,000	720,000
8	Market Growth	1%	4,000,000	4,000,000	4,000,000
9	% New Buying Book		15%	15%	15%
10	Growth Books		600,000	600,000	600,000
11	Total Books		4,800,000	12,120,000	1,320,000
12	OurCo Market Share	12%			
13	Competitor A	10%			
14	Competitor B	11%			
15	All Others	67%			
16	OurCo Book Sales	2,188,800	576,000	1,454,400	158,400
17	Office Sales	172,000,000	32,000,000	100,000,000	40,000,000
18	Conversion Rate	1.3%			
19					

Figure 26.7
This forecast model is based on nine variable cells.

1. Select Data, Data Tools, What-If Analysis, Scenario Manager to display the Scenario Manager dialog. Initially, the Scenario Manager indicates that no scenarios are defined, as shown in Figure 26.8.

Figure 26.8
The Scenario Manager dialog before you add the first scenario.

2. Click the Add button to add the first scenario. The Edit Scenario dialog appears.

3. In the Edit Scenario dialog, enter a name for this scenario. Choose which cells will be changing. Because the variable

> **note**
>
> It is best to add one scenario that represents your starting assumptions. Otherwise, those numbers will be lost.

cells are not adjacent, select the first contiguous range and then Ctrl+click to add additional ranges, as shown in Figure 26.9.

The Scenario Values dialog box appears, which can be used to edit the values for each starting cell (see Figure 26.10). Note that if you had previously named your input cells, the cell names will appear in this dialog instead of addresses.

4. Edit any values in the Scenario Values dialog. If you have additional scenarios to add, click the Add button. When you are done assigning scenarios, click OK.

 tip

It is a little annoying that the Scenario Values dialog can show only five values at a time. If your model contains the maximum of 32 values that can change, you need to scroll several times to see all the values in this dialog.

Figure 26.9
Ctrl+click to select all the changing cells.

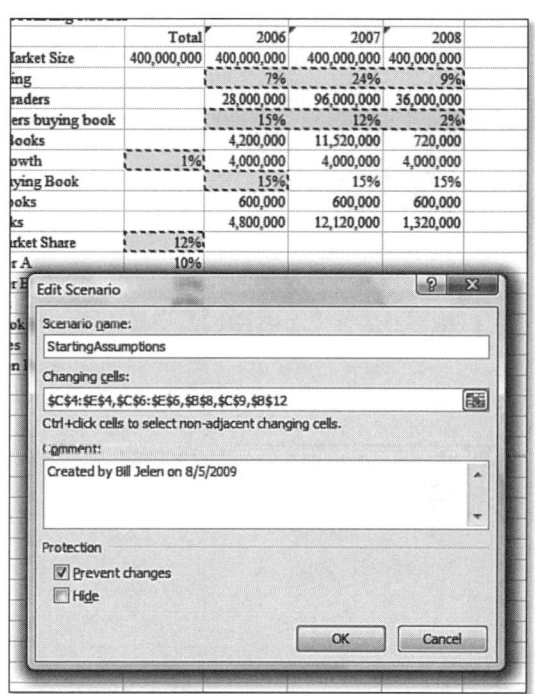

Figure 26.10
Use the Scenario Values dialog to edit values for a scenario.

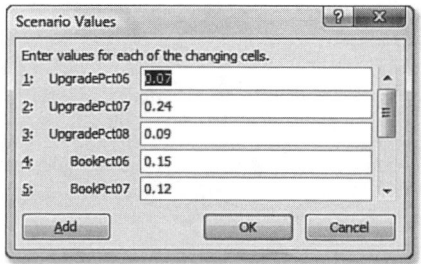

5. Try switching between scenarios in the Scenario Manager by either double-clicking a scenario or clicking the scenario and clicking Show, as shown in Figure 26.11. If you are going to add a new scenario similar to one existing scenario, show that scenario before clicking Add.

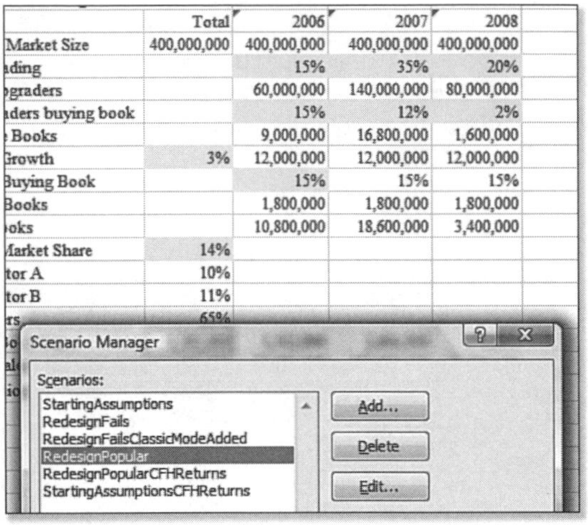

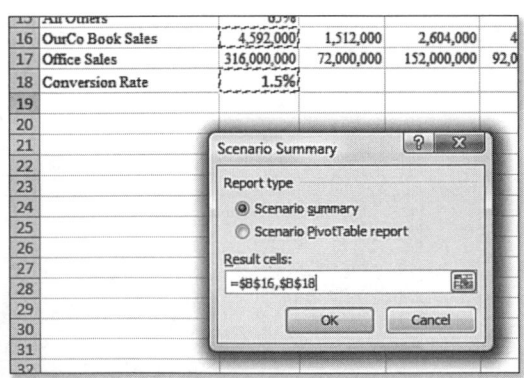

Figure 26.11
The new scenario is shown behind the dialog box after you double-click a scenario name.

Creating a Scenario Summary Report

One powerful feature of Excel scenarios is the capability to create a Scenario Summary report. When you click the Summary button on the Scenario Manager dialog, Excel allows you to choose either a scenario summary report or a pivot table report. In either case, you should select one or more cells that represent the results of the model. For example, Figure 26.12 shows OurCo Book Sales and Conversion Rate selected.

After specifying the results cells, the Scenario Summary report is added on a new worksheet in the workbook. This is a useful report that has a number of valuable features.

Figure 26.12
Hold down Ctrl to select more than one result cell.

After the initial creation, the summary is as shown in Figure 26.13. Notice the group and outline buttons along both the rows and the columns of the report. The plus sign next to Cell A3 indicates that the comments in Row 4 are currently hidden.

Figure 26.13
The default Scenario Summary report.

	Scenario Summary	Starting Assumptions	Redesign Fails	RedesignFails ClassicModeAdded	Redesign Popular	RedesignPopular CFHReturns	StartingAssumptions CFHReturns
Changing Cells:							
UpgradePct06	7%	5%	5%	15%	15%	7%
UpgradePct07	24%	4%	2%	35%	35%	24%
UpgradePct08	9%	2%	48%	20%	20%	9%
BookPct06	15%	15%	8%	15%	15%	15%
BookPct07	12%	8%	2%	12%	12%	12%
BookPct08	2%	2%	2%	2%	2%	2%
MktGrowth	1%	1%	1%	3%	3%	1%
BookPctNew	15%	1%	8%	15%	15%	15%
OurCoShare	12%	8%	12%	14%	17%	15%
Result Cells:							
OurCoSalesForecas	2,188,800	360,000	787,200	4,592,000	5,576,000	2,736,000
OurCoConversionP	1.3%	0.7%	0.3%	1.5%	1.8%	1.6%

Notes: Current Values column represents values of changing cells at time Scenario Summary Report was created. Changing cells for each scenario are highlighted in gray.

You can use word wrapping in a summary report. For example, Figure 26.14 shows that word wrapping was used to make the headings in Row 3 appear on two lines and that the column widths were adjusted. You will probably always have to make these adjustments to make your summary reports look better.

 tip

To force word wrapping in the middle of a cell, position your cursor at the break point and press Alt+Enter.

Scenario Summary

	Starting Assumptions	Redesign Fails	RedesignFails ClassicModeAdded	Redesign Popular	RedesignPopular CFHReturns	StartingAssumptions CFHReturns
Changing Cells:						
UpgradePct06	7%	5%	5%	15%	15%	7%
UpgradePct07	24%	4%	2%	35%	35%	24%
UpgradePct08	9%	2%	48%	20%	20%	9%
BookPct06	15%	15%	8%	15%	15%	15%
BookPct07	12%	8%	2%	12%	12%	12%
BookPct08	2%	2%	2%	2%	2%	2%
MktGrowth	1%	1%	1%	3%	3%	1%
BookPctNew	15%	1%	8%	15%	15%	15%
OurCoShare	12%	8%	12%	14%	17%	15%
Result Cells:						
OurCoSalesForecas	2,188,800	360,000	787,200	4,592,000	5,576,000	2,736,000
OurCoConversionP	1.3%	0.7%	0.3%	1.5%	1.8%	1.6%

Notes: Current Values column represents values of changing cells at time Scenario Summary Report was created. Changing cells for each scenario are highlighted in gray.

Figure 26.14
Word wrapping and column widths can be adjusted.

If you click the minus sign next to Row 5, you can hide the assumption cells and just show the results, as shown in Figure 26.15.

As you create each scenario, the Scenario Manager adds a comment with your name and the date and time. You can also add your own comments. You can reveal the comments in the report by clicking the plus sign next to Row 3 (see Figure 26.16).

> **caution**
> The Scenario Summary report is a snapshot in time. If you later change scenarios or add new scenarios, you have to re-create and reformat the Scenario Summary report.

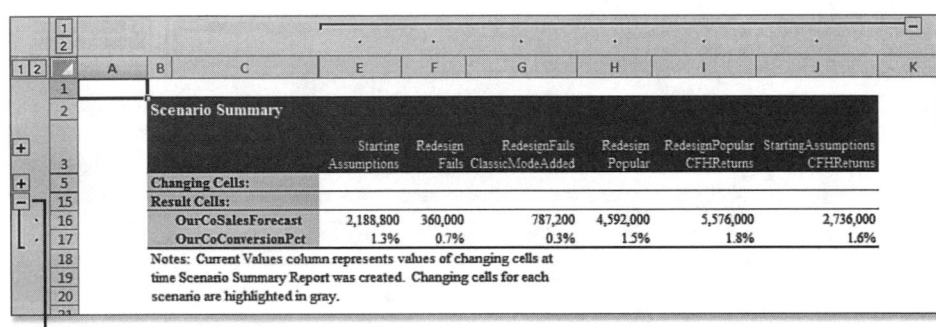

Use second collapse button

Figure 26.15
To make the table easier to read, you can show just the results.

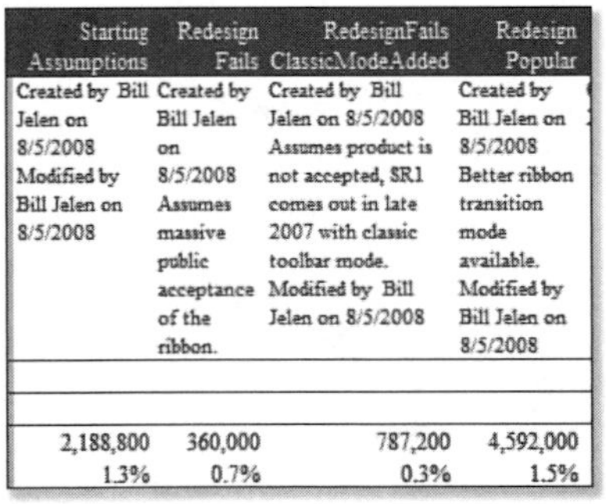

Figure 26.16
You can display comments in a report.

Adding Multiple Scenarios

You might want to share a workbook with others and have them add their own scenarios to get opinions from people in other areas of your company, such as sales, marketing, engineering, and manufacturing. To do this, follow these steps:

1. Save the workbook with just the starting scenario.

2. Route the workbook to each person. In a hidden field, Excel keeps track of who adds each scenario.

3. When you get the routed workbook back, open both the original workbook and the routed workbook.

4. Display the Scenario Manager in the original workbook.

5. Click the Merge button to display the Merge Scenarios dialog, as shown in Figure 26.17.

Figure 26.17
Merged scenarios from a workbook routed to others.

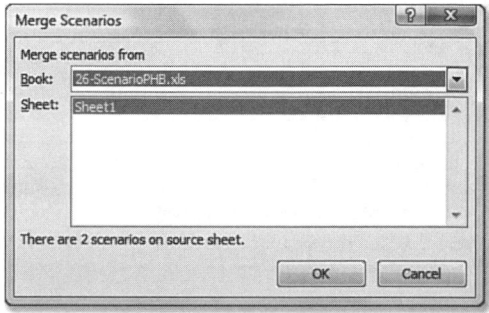

6. In the Book drop-down, select the name of the routed workbook. In Figure 26.17, the dialog shows that two scenarios are available on Sheet 1.

7. Excel usually encounters identically named scenarios in the merge process. It differentiates any scenarios with identical names by adding a date or name to the incoming scenarios, as shown in Figure 26.18. If these scenarios are truly identical to the scenario that you originally sent out, delete those scenarios.

Figure 26.18
Merged scenarios are added to the bottom of the list.

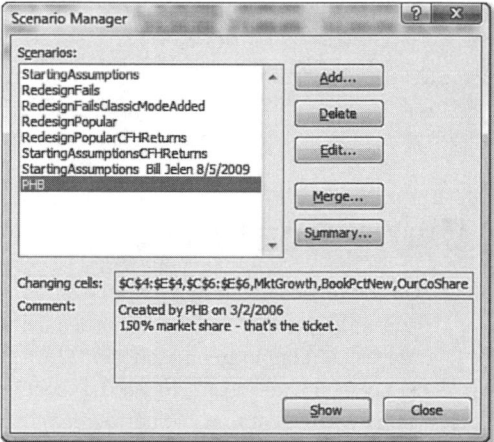

8. In the Scenario Manager, click Summary. The Scenario Summary dialog appears.

9. In the Scenario Summary dialog, click Scenario PivotTable report. The initial pivot table appears, as shown in Figure 26.19.

	A	B	C
1	$C$4:$E$4,$C$6:$E$6,MktGrowth,	(All) ⏷	
2			
3	Row Labels ⏷	OurCoSalesForecast	OurCoConversionPct
4	PHB	79200000	0.084615385
5	RedesignFails	360000	0.0072
6	RedesignFailsClassicModeAdded	787200	0.003393103
7	RedesignPopular	4592000	0.014531646
8	RedesignPopularCFHReturns	6560000	0.020759494
9	StartingAssumptions	2188800	0.012725581
10	StartingAssumptions Bill Jelen 8/5/2009	2188800	0.012725581
11	StartingAssumptionsCFHReturns	2736000	0.015906977
12			

Figure 26.19
The default pivot table shows scenarios from all people on the routing list.

10. Drag the field from the Report Filter area to be the first Row Labels field. You can now see scenarios grouped by author. As shown in Figure 26.20, although this is an interesting view, there is not a good way to see the assumptions that each author used to arrive at his or her results.

3	Row Labels ⏷	OurCoSalesForecast	OurCoConversionPct
4	⊟ Bill Jelen	19412800	0.087242382
5	RedesignFails	360000	0.0072
6	RedesignFailsClassicModeAdded	787200	0.003393103
7	RedesignPopular	4592000	0.014531646
8	RedesignPopularCFHReturns	6560000	0.020759494
9	StartingAssumptions	2188800	0.012725581
10	StartingAssumptions Bill Jelen 8/5/2009	2188800	0.012725581
11	StartingAssumptionsCFHReturns	2736000	0.015906977
12	⊟ PHB	79200000	0.084615385
13	PHB	79200000	0.084615385

Figure 26.20
Move the field from the Report Filter to the first row label to compare scenarios by person.

Using Goal Seek

On the television show *The Price Is Right*, one of the games is the Hi-Lo game. A contestant tries to guess the price of an item, and the host tells the player that the actual price is higher or lower. The process of honing in on a price of $1.67 might involve guesses of $2, $1, $1.50, $1.75, $1.63, $1.69, $1.66, $1.68, and $1.67. Using the techniques described so far in this chapter, you might play this game with Excel to try to narrow in on an answer.

You might have an Excel worksheet set up that calculates a final value using several input variables. To solve the formula in reverse, you need to find input variables that generate a certain answer. One difficult option is to determine if another Excel function reverses the calculation. For example, =ARCSIN() performs the opposite of =SIN(). Another difficult option is to use algebra to attempt to solve for one of the input variables. However, most people simply play the Hi-Lo game, successively plugging in higher and lower answers to the input cell until they narrow in to an input variable that produces the desired result.

If you play the Hi-Lo game, consider using the Goal Seek command. In effect, this command plays the Hi-Lo game at hyperspeed, arriving at an answer within a second.

Consider the car payment example at the beginning of the chapter. You want to find a price that yields a $225 monthly payment. You might find the =PV( ) function that can solve this. However, most people plug in successively higher or lower values for the price in Cell E1 (see Figure 26.21).

Excel has an option called Goal Seek that allows you to hone in quickly on a value. To use Goal Seek, follow these steps:

1. Select the answer cell. In this example, it would be the payment in Cell E4.

2. From the Data Tools group of the Data tab, select the What If Analysis drop-down and then select Goal Seek. The Goal Seek dialog appears, as shown in Figure 26.21.

Figure 26.21
Goal Seek lets you find one value by changing one other cell.

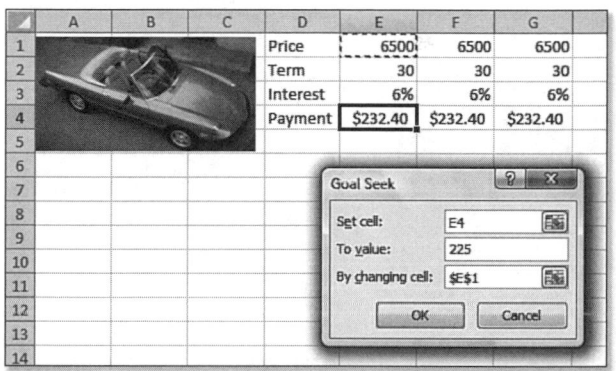

3. In the Goal Seek dialog, indicate that you want to set the answer cell to a particular value by changing a particular input cell. In this example, set Cell E4 to the value of $225 by changing Cell E1. Excel begins trying to hone in on a value. When Excel gets to within a penny of the value, the Goal Seek Status dialog appears, as shown in Figure 26.22. This dialog reports that it was trying to reach a target value of $225 and reached that value. Behind the dialog, the worksheet shows the proposed price of $6293.053 in the worksheet.

4. Either accept this value by clicking OK or revert to the original value by clicking Cancel.

    To watch a video of Goal Seek in action, search for "Excel In Depth 26" at YouTube.

Goal Seek works well for quick calculations, such as the two additional Goal Seek operations that were done in Figure 26.23. One operation set Cell F4 to $225 by changing the term in Cell F2. The next operation set Cell G4 to $225 by changing the interest rate in Cell G3.

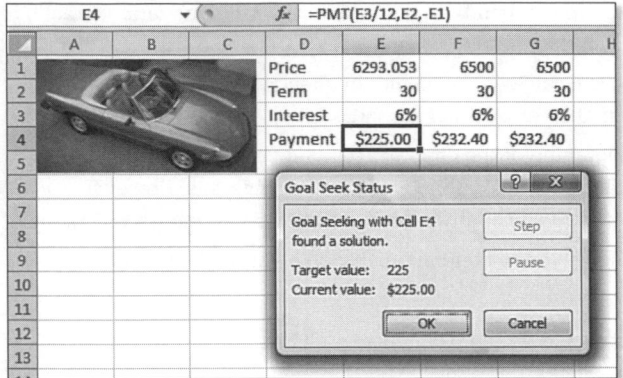

Figure 26.22
Choose to accept the proposed solution or revert to the previous numbers.

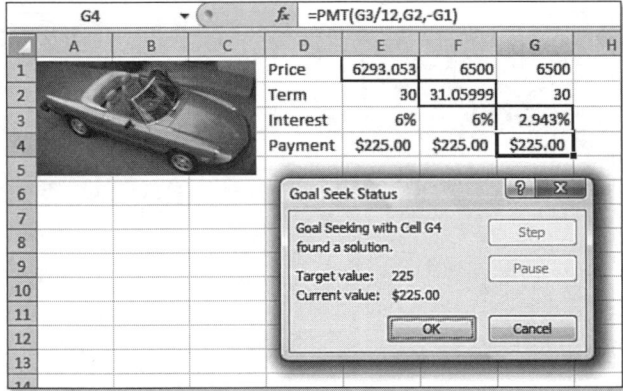

Figure 26.23
Three different Goal Seek commands find how to yield a $225 payment by changing either the price, term, or rate.

Is It Cheating to Use Brute Force to Think Less?

Most of the time when you could use Goal Seek, there is a brainier solution. If you have a complex series of formulas set up using just the +, -, *, /, and ^ operators, you could almost certainly get out a pencil and do the algebra required to derive the formula you need.

In the preceding text, Figure 26.23 shows how you can use Goal Seek to figure out how to achieve a certain monthly payment by changing three different cells. Besides Goal Seek, Excel provides the NPER() function, which can correctly find the term for a given price, interest, and payment. For example, you can use the NPER() function in Cell G11 to calculate a more exact version than Goal Seek is able to discover (see Figure 26.24). Similarly, in Cell E11 you can use =PV(E9/E12,E8,-E10) to discover the present value (that is, the vehicle price) of a loan. In Cell I11 you can use =RATE(I9,-I10,18)*12 to discover the rate needed to generate a monthly payment of $225 for a certain price and term.

Excel might have to go through 100 iterations of a lightning-fast Hi-Lo-type game to find the solution. However, the solution is usually found within a second or two. This is definitely faster than using paper and pencil to do the algebra or pulling out this book to learn about the NPER() function.

If you are a loan officer at a bank, it might be worthwhile for you to learn how to use the NPER() function. However, if you are using this worksheet once every four years to figure out your next car purchase, it is perfectly fine to let Excel sweat through the brute-force calculations with Goal Seek.

By the way, on the day I wrote this chapter, I purchased the 1981 Alfa Romeo Spider shown in Figure 26.23!

Figure 26.24
Goal Seek prevents you from having to learn functions such as NPER().

f_x	=NPER(G9/12,-G10,G8)					
D	E	F	G	H	I
Price	6293.05294		6500		6500
Term	30		31.05999		30
Interest	6%		6%		2.943%
Payment	$225.00		$225.00		$225.00
Term	30	Price	6500	Price	6500
Interest	6%	Interest	6%	Term	30
Payment	$225.00	Payment	$225.00	Payment	$225.00
Price	$6,293.05	Term	31.05999	Rate	2.943%

Troubleshooting Tip: When Goal Seek Won't Work

Some problems are not well suited to using Goal Seek. Goal Seek needs a clear mathematical relationship between the starting and ending cells. For example, the model in Figure 26.25 is set up to choose from among 20 different package plans. Each package offers a different number of tickets, meals, and vouchers. Cell E1 chooses a particular plan, and Cell E2 uses the INDEX() function to calculate the number of tickets associated with the plan. Because there is no mathematical sequence to the number of tickets in each plan, Goal Seek will have little chance of succeeding in this situation.

Suppose that you want to set the Total value in Cell E4 equal to 6950. A quick scan through the list of plans shows that Plan G offers 10 tickets, which would be worth exactly $6,950. However, Excel will not be able to figure this out using Goal Seek.

The following steps illustrate how you can watch the Goal Seek process in slow motion to see if Excel is getting closer:

1. Start Goal Seek. An answer is not immediately found.

2. Click the Pause button on the Goal Seek Status dialog. The Pause button changes to a Continue button. As shown in Figure 26.26, Excel is on its 80th attempt at finding a value. In this pass, Excel is trying 18.24 in Cell E1. This is producing a value of 13205 instead of the desired value of 6950.

	E2		▼	●		f_x =INDEX(B7:B26,ROUND(E1,0))		
	A	B	C	D	E	F	G	H
1				Plan	19			
2				Tickets	2			
3				Value	695			
4				Total	1390			
5								
6	Plans:	Tickets	Meals	Vouchers				
7	A	4	15	6				
8	B	12	4	9				
9	C	13	11	1				
10	D	5	18	2				
11	E	6	11	8				
12	F	20	1	4				
13	G	10	6	9				
14	H	7	14	4				
15	I	8	7	10				
16	J	15	2	8				
17	K	16	6	3				
18	L	11	0	14				
19	M	18	0	7				
20	N	17	5	3				
21	O	3	15	7				
22	P	9	8	8				
23	Q	14	8	3				
24	R	19	0	6				
25	S	2	1	22				
26	T	1	8	16				
27								

Figure 26.25
Because there is no mathematical order to the number of tickets offered in each plan, Goal Seek has little chance of finding a solution in this case.

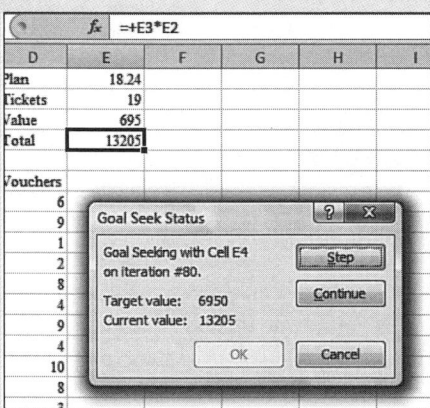

	f_x =+E3*E2				
D	E	F	G	H	I
Plan	18.24				
Tickets	19				
Value	695				
Total	13205				
Vouchers					
	6				
	9				
	1				
	2				
	8				
	4				
	9				
	4				
	10				
	8				

Goal Seek Status

Goal Seeking with Cell E4
on iteration #80.

Target value: 6950
Current value: 13205

Step
Continue
OK
Cancel

Figure 26.26
After pausing, you can examine how Excel is trying to solve the problem.

3. Click the Step button to proceed to the next guess. On the 84th iteration, Excel tries a plan of 5.5299E+10, which produces a #REF! error. Excel successively tries higher and higher values. Eventually, after 100 iterations, Excel gives up and reports that it cannot find a solution, as shown in Figure 26.27.

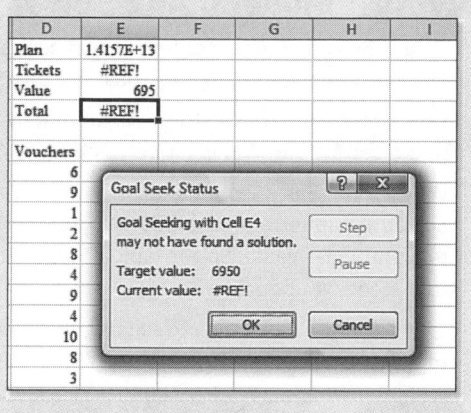

Figure 26.27
Goal Seek gives up after 100 iterations.

Using Solver

It is possible to design problems that are far too complex for Goal Seek. These problems may have dozens of independent variables and various constraints. In such a case, you can use the Excel Solver add-in.

Using Solver is a bit tricky. With Solver, you specify a range of cells that can be changed. You are allowed to specify certain constraints on the solution. Next, you can indicate that you want one particular formula cell to either be maximized, minimized, or set to a particular value.

The Solver add-in, which is free with Excel, was written by Frontline Systems. Solver cannot solve some complex modeling systems. In such cases, you can purchase a premium version of Solver that can handle up to 2,000 input variables. To learn more about the premium version of Solver, visit Frontline Systems, at www.Solver.com.

Installing Solver

To install Solver, follow these steps:

1. Click the File menu, and then click Options. The Options dialog appears.

2. Select Add-Ins from the menu on the left of the Options dialog.

3. At the bottom of the Add-Ins page that appears, select Excel Add-ins from the Manage dropdown. The Add-Ins dialog appears.

4. Click Go.

5. In the Add-Ins dialog, make sure that Solver is checked.

Solving a Model Using Solver

To use Solver, your worksheet should contain one or more input variables. The worksheet should also contain one or more formulas that result in a solution within a single cell.

For each input variable, there might be certain constraints. For example, you might want to assume that a certain variable must be positive or that it should be in a certain range of values.

When using Solver, you identify the input range, the output cell, and the constraints. You can ask Solver to minimize or maximize the input cell. Alternatively, you can ask Solver to set the output cell to a particular value. Solver rapidly loops through many input variables, trying to find a combination that meets your goal.

This might be easier to understand with a concrete example. Figure 26.28 shows a worksheet used to model production of widgets. Cell B23 indicates that each worker in your factory can make five widgets per hour. Workers who work evenings, nights, or weekends are paid a shift differential. You can choose to keep your factory running for anywhere from five shifts a week (Monday through Friday, first shift) up to 21 shifts per week. You can sell as many widgets as you can produce, provided that the overall cost is less than $2 per widget. You have a skilled workforce of 100 workers available for first shift, 82 workers for second shift, and 75 workers for third shift. How many shifts should the plant be open to maximize production? Solver runs circles around Goal Seek in situations that deal with multiple constraints. To use Solver to find the answer, follow these steps:

D22			f_x	=SUM(D13:D21)			
	A	B	C	D	E	F	
1	Manufacturing Plant Productivity						
2							
3	Day Shift M-F	5					
4	Evening Shift M-F	5					
5	Night Shift M-F	5					
6	Day Shift Saturday	1					
7	Evening Shift Sat	1					
8	Night Shift Sat	1					
9	Day Shift Sun	1					
10	Evening Shift Sun	1					
11	Night Shift Sun	1					
12	Labor Cost Per Shift		Workers Avail per Shift	Total Widgets	Total Cost		
13	Day Shift M-F	7.85	100	20000	36400		
14	Evening Shift M-F	8.24	82	16400	32027.2		
15	Night Shift M-F	8.64	75	15000	30920		
16	Day Shift Saturday	11.775	80	3200	8536		
17	Evening Shift Sat	12.36	72	2880	8119.36		
18	Night Shift Sat	12.96	65	2600	7739.2		
19	Day Shift Sun	15.7	50	2000	7280		
20	Evening Shift Sun	16.48	36	1440	5746.24		
21	Night Shift Sun	17.28	30	1200	5147.2	Per Widget	
22	Overhead per shift	1000	Total	64720	141915.2	2.192756	
23	Widgets Per Worker Per Shift	40					

Figure 26.28
A worksheet to model widget production.

1. Note that Cells B3 through B11 define how many shifts the factory will be open. All the remaining cells in the model calculate the total number of widgets produced and the average cost per widget.

2. As with Goal Seek, start by telling Solver that you want to set a target cell equal to a maximum, minimum, or certain value by changing other cells. For example, the Solver Parameters dialog shown in Figure 26.29 indicates that the goal is to maximize widget production by altering the number of shifts.

Figure 26.29
Maximizing widget production.

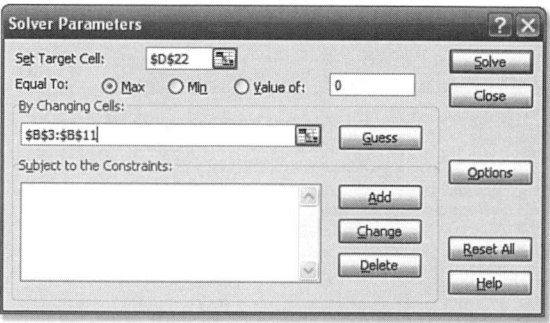

3. Enter the first constraint, which is that the market will bear only a manufacturing cost of $2 per widget. To specify this constraint, click the Add button in the Solver Parameters dialog.

4. Next, tell Solver that the manufacturing cost must be less than or equal to $2 per widget, as shown in Figure 26.30.

Figure 26.30
Building the cost constraint.

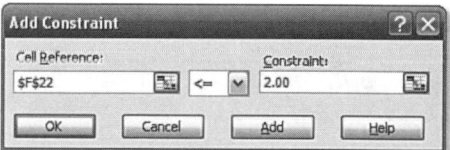

5. Tell Solver that there cannot be a negative number of shifts. To do so, you need to add a constraint to indicate for each shift that the shift count must be greater than or equal to zero, as shown in Figure 26.31.

Figure 26.31
Solver must be told that it cannot have negative numbers of shifts.

	A	B	C	D	E	F	G	H
1	Manufacturing Plant Productivity							
2								
3	Day Shift M-F	5						
4	Evening Shift M-F	5						
5	Night Shift M-F	5						
6	Day Shift Saturday	1						
7	Evening Shift Sat	1						
8	Night Shift Sat	1						
9	Day Shift Sun	1						
10	Evening Shift Sun	1						
11	Night Shift Sun	1						

Add Constraint

Cell Reference:
$B$3:$B$11   >=   0

6. Specify that Cells B3:B5 must be less than or equal to five because you can have only five of each shift during the week.

7. In this model, it is not valid to work 0.32 shifts; only integer values can be used in a given range. Therefore, select the value int for the comparison operator to tell Solver that a certain range can accept only integers (see Figure 26.32).

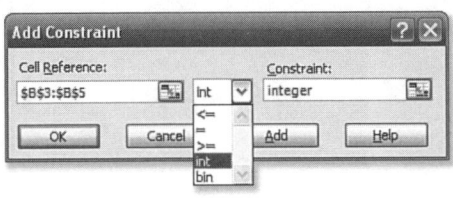

Figure 26.32
Use the integer constraint to prevent fractional answers.

8. In this case, the Saturday and Sunday shifts are a special case: The company is either open or not, which means the only two possible values for each cell are 0 or 1. This is a special constraint called a *binary constraint*. Select the bin value in the comparison operator to specify that Cells B6 through B11 are limited to binary values.

9. After you have entered all the constraints, click OK to return to the Solver Parameters dialog.

10. Click the Options button on the Solver Parameters dialog to open the Solver Options dialog. By default, Solver works for no more than 100 seconds, as shown in Figure 26.33. This is designed to prevent Solver from trying to find a solution for a long time.

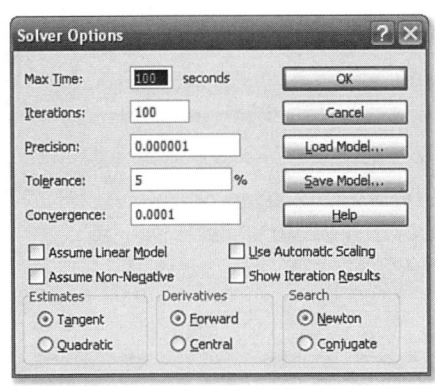

Figure 26.33
Use the Solver Options dialog to fine-tune the processes used.

11. When you have entered all the constraints and parameters, click OK to close the Solver Options dialog and return to the Solver Parameters dialog.

12. Click the Solve button on the Solver Parameters dialog. Solver begins to iterate through possible solutions. If Solver finds a result, it reports success, as shown in Figure 26.34.

Figure 26.34
Solver reports
success.

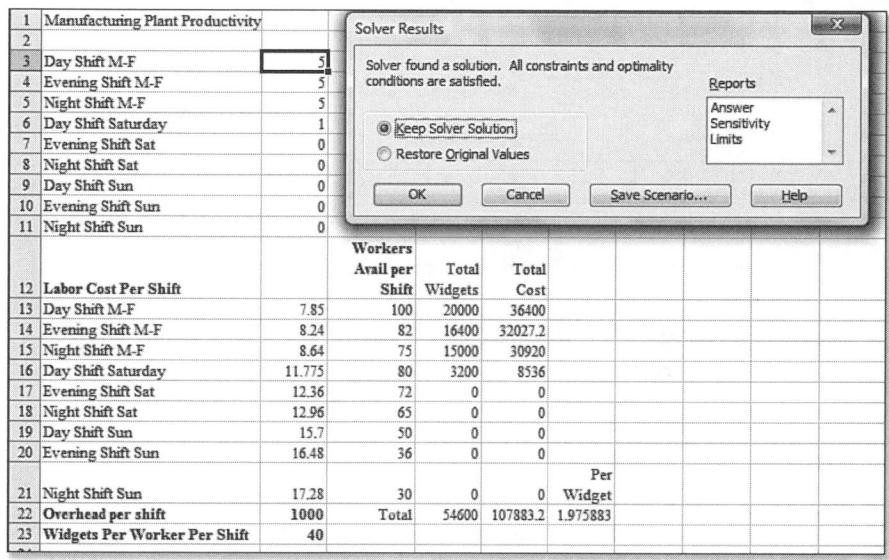

13. In the Solver Results dialog, select the Answer Report to have Excel provide a new worksheet that compares the original and final values. As shown in Figure 26.35, the answer report is added as a new worksheet. In the answer report, Solver tells you that you can produce 54,600 widgets by operating five of each shift during the week and one Saturday shift. The remaining shifts are not cost-effective to keep the cost per widget in Cell F22 under $2. With this current solution, the cost per widget is $1.97.

You can save each Solver solution as a scenario. All these scenarios later show up in the Scenario Manager.

	A	B	C	D	E	F	G
6		Target Cell (Max)					
7		Cell	Name	Original Value	Final Value		
			Total Total				
8		$D$22	Widgets	57480	54600		
9							
10							
11		Adjustable Cells					
12		Cell	Name	Original Value	Final Value		
13		$B$3	Day Shift M-F	5	5		
14		$B$4	Evening Shift M-F	5	5		
15		$B$5	Night Shift M-F	5	5		
16		$B$6	Day Shift Saturday	1	1		
17		$B$7	Evening Shift Sat	1	0		
18		$B$8	Night Shift Sat	0	0		
19		$B$9	Day Shift Sun	0	0		
20		$B$10	Evening Shift Sun	0	0		
21		$B$11	Night Shift Sun	0	0		
22							
23							
24		Constraints					
25		Cell	Name	Cell Value	Formula	Status	Slack
			Total Per				
26		$F$22	Widget	1.975882784	$F$22<=2	Not Binding	0.024117216
27		$B$3	Day Shift M-F	5	$B$3<=5	Binding	0
28		$B$4	Evening Shift M-F	5	$B$4<=5	Binding	0

Figure 26.35
The evening shift workers will be losing some Saturday overtime because of Solver.

Excel in Practice: Emergency Room Staffing

During flu season, the hospital emergency room (ER) has an overflow of patients. Here is a line of questioning about the problem.

What is the basic flow when a patient is taken to the ER?

The patient is assessed by a nurse. The resident sees the patient. The resident then consults with an attending physician about the plans.

What is the total amount time the resident spends with each patient?

Fifteen minutes with the patient, plus 5 minutes of paperwork.

How long does the attending physician spend per patient?

Five minutes with the patient, plus 5 minutes of consultation with the resident.

How long does the nurse spend per patient?

About 30 minutes.

How long is the typical patient in the ER?

One hour.

How many treatment rooms does the ER have?

Twenty rooms.

What is the current staffing per shift?

Two attending physicians, known as "attendings," 10 nurses, and six residents.

Given all this information, you need to build a Solver model to find a way to get more patients through the ER. To do so, here is how the model works:

- Cells B2 through B4 of the model contain the current staffing levels for residents, attendings, and nurses. These will be the input cells for Solver.

- Cell B5 contains a critical constraint: There are 20 treatment rooms. Therefore, no matter how many people you staff, there cannot be more than 20 patients seen at once.

- Cells B6 through B10 state how many minutes each resource will spend with the patient. These values are fixed in the model. You are not trying to make the doctors spend less time with the patients.

- As shown in Figure 26.36, Cell B12 calculates how many minutes of nursing time are available in an 8-hour shift. The formula calculates Cell B2 × 8 hours × 60 minutes per hour. Similar formulas in Cells B13:B15 calculate how many minutes of each other resource are available per shift.

- In cell B17, if a nurse spends 30 minutes per patient, and the 10 nurses have 4,800 minutes available per shift, it means that 10 nurses could potentially serve 160 patients in one shift. The formula in Cell B17 is B12/B7. Similar formulas in cells B18 through B20 calculate the process capacity for residents, attendings, and the rooms.

- Cell B21 takes the minimum of Cells B17:B20. If a bottleneck occurs because of staffing, it will slow down all the other areas. At this point, the model is trying to solve two problems: It is trying to maximize the number of patients seen while trying to make sure that there is not extra staff standing around. On the one hand, you want to maximize throughput, and on the other hand, you want to minimize cost. The model takes a radical turn here, to come down to one number to represent both of these goals.

- Cell B22 estimates some amount of revenue per patient.

- Cell B23 calculates the total revenue.

- Cells B24 through B26 express the cost per resource per shift. Nursing costs $23 per hour, so you multiply that by 8 hours per shift and by the number of nurses in Cell B2.

- Cell B27 calculates the total of the labor cost.

- Cell B28 calculates a hypothetical profit figure by subtracting labor cost from revenue. Even if these numbers aren't exact, the model can ask Solver to maximize profit. The act of maximizing profit will seek to get the most patients through subject to constraints and also keep the staff to a minimum.

After converting all those words to formulas, you can have Solver try to find the optimal staffing. To do so, follow these steps:

1. Start Solver.

2. Ask Solver to produce the maximum value in Cell B28 by changing the staffing levels in B2:B4. There are certain constraints. For example, you cannot have half a doctor cover a shift, so Cells B2:B4 must be integers and must be greater than zero. (See Figure 26.37.)

In a few seconds, Solver proposes a solution. The answer report suggests that you should increase staffing by adding 1 resident and 2 attendings, as shown in Figure 26.38.

The answer report does not indicate any impact on patients. However, if you examine the new answers in the original sheet, as shown in Figure 26.39, you see that the patient throughput has gone from 96 to 160. The model is suggesting that the attendings, and to a lesser degree, the residents, are the bottleneck in the process. Unless you build a new wing, you cannot increase from the 20 existing treatment rooms. However, by adding staff, you can increase throughput in the existing rooms.

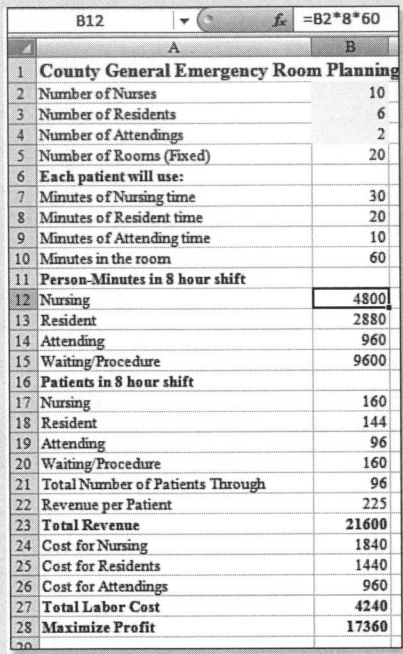

Figure 26.36
This formula in Cell B12 calculates the number of available nursing minutes per shift.

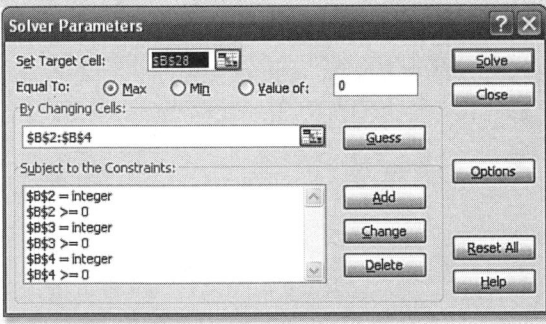

Figure 26.37
Asking Solver to maximize profit while adjusting staffing levels.

Figure 26.38
The answer report shows the optimal staffing level.

6	Target Cell (Max)			
7	Cell	Name	Original Value	Final Value
8	$B$28	Maximize Profit	17360	30560
9				
10				
11	Adjustable Cells			
12	Cell	Name	Original Value	Final Value
13	$B$2	Number of Nurses	10	10
14	$B$3	Number of Residents	6	7
15	$B$4	Number of Attendings	2	4
16				
17				
18	Constraints			

19	Cell	Name	Cell Value	Formula	Status	Slack
20	$B$2	Number of Nurses	10	$B$2>=0	Not Binding	10
21	$B$3	Number of Residents	7	$B$3>=0	Not Binding	7
22	$B$4	Number of Attendings	4	$B$4>=0	Not Binding	4
23	$B$2	Number of Nurses	10	$B$2=integer	Binding	0
24	$B$3	Number of Residents	7	$B$3=integer	Binding	0
25	$B$4	Number of Attendings	4	$B$4=integer	Binding	0

Figure 26.39
Patient throughput increases from 96 to 160 in the new model.

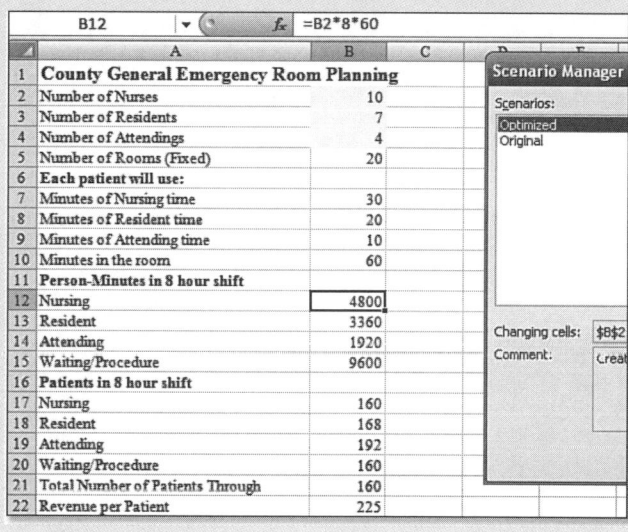

	B12	f_x =B2*8*60		
	A	B	C	
1	**County General Emergency Room Planning**			
2	Number of Nurses	10		
3	Number of Residents	7		
4	Number of Attendings	4		
5	Number of Rooms (Fixed)	20		
6	**Each patient will use:**			
7	Minutes of Nursing time	30		
8	Minutes of Resident time	20		
9	Minutes of Attending time	10		
10	Minutes in the room	60		
11	**Person-Minutes in 8 hour shift**			
12	Nursing	4800		
13	Resident	3360		
14	Attending	1920		
15	Waiting/Procedure	9600		
16	**Patients in 8 hour shift**			
17	Nursing	160		
18	Resident	168		
19	Attending	192		
20	Waiting/Procedure	160		
21	Total Number of Patients Through	160		
22	Revenue per Patient	225		

Scenario Manager

Scenarios:

Optimized
Original

Changing cells: $B$2
Comment: Creat

27

AUTOMATING REPETITIVE FUNCTIONS USING VBA MACROS

Every copy of Excel shipped since 1995 has included the powerful Visual Basic for Applications (VBA) lurking behind the grid. With VBA, you can do anything that you can do in the regular interface, and you can do it much faster. VBA shines when you have many repetitive tasks to undertake.

Learning to use macros is a good news/bad news proposition. The good news is that Microsoft Office provides a macro recorder that can write a macro as you work. The bad news is that it is not easy to record a macro that works consistently with any data set. To unleash the power of macros, you need to understand how to edit recorded macro code. You can then record a macro that is close to what you want and edit that macro to create something that runs the way you want it to work.

Checking Security Settings Before Using Macros

On March 26, 1999, a hacker named Kwyjibo launched the Melissa virus. This particular virus used VBA macros in Word to propagate itself. Microsoft took a lot of heat because macros could run without the knowledge of the person running the computer. In response, Microsoft has made it more difficult to run macros in subsequent versions of Excel. At one point, there was some concern that Microsoft would remove support for VBA macros, but Microsoft has committed to supporting VBA macros for another 10 to 15 years.

Before you can use macros, you have to take some positive steps to affirm that you want to record or run a macro.

> **Triple Word Score**
>
> The original Melissa virus macro spread via email as a Word document. The document would arrive with the message subject "Here is the document that you asked for." When a user opened the document in Word, the virus would attach itself to the Normal.dot file and attempt to email itself to others in the user's address book. This propagation method is what attracted the attention.
>
> The point of the Melissa virus was to check the system clock every time the user opened a document. If the user happened to open the document when the minute, day, and month all matched, the virus would perform its dirty work. Therefore, for example, if you opened the document on October 10 at 8:10 a.m. or perhaps on June 6 at 6:06 p.m., the virus would kick in. Assuming an 8-hour workday, there are 96 minutes throughout the year when opening the Word document would trigger the virus. That works out to about a 7 in 1,000 chance that a user who opened the email attachment would be struck by the virus.
>
> In a tip of the hat to the old board game Scrabble, the hacker had an insidious plan. If the user opened the document at the moment when the month, day, and minute matched on the system clock, the program would insert the following text in the Word document: "Twenty-two points, plus triple-word-score, plus fifty points for using all my letters. Game's over. I'm outta here."
>
> Thanks to this silly virus, VBA programmers now have to jump through hoops to use macros.

Enabling VBA Security

To enable VBA security, follow these steps:

1. Select File, Excel Options to open the Excel Options dialog.

2. Select the Customize Ribbon category. In the right-side list box, select the Developer tab check box.

3. Click OK to exit the Excel Settings dialog. You now have a Developer tab on the Ribbon.

4. On the Developer tab, click Macro Security in the Code group. The Security dialog appears.

5. In the Security dialog, change the Macro Settings to Disable All Macros with Notification. With this setting, Excel alerts you whenever you open a workbook that has macros attached.

6. When you open a document and get the warning that the document has macros attached, if this is a document that you wrote and you expect macros to be there, click Enable Content to enable the macros.

Recording a Macro

Before you start recording a macro, you need to think about how to break the task into easily repeatable steps. The macro recorder is great at recording navigation done using arrow keys. Therefore, you want to use only the keyboard for navigation while using the macro recorder.

Plan your macro before recording it by thinking through the steps you need to perform. If you need to fix many items in a worksheet, you might want to select the first item first. This way, the macro can perform an action on cells relative to the original selection.

To record a macro, follow these steps:

1. On the Developer tab, select Record Macro.

2. In the Record Macro dialog box, type a name for the macro. The name cannot contain spaces. For example, instead of using `Macro Name`, you need to use `MacroName`.

3. Choose whether you want to store the macro in the current workbook, a new workbook, or a special Personal Macro Workbook. The personal macro workbook is a special workbook designed to hold general-purpose macros that might apply to any workbook. If you are unsure, select to store the recorded macro in the current workbook.

4. Assign a shortcut key for the macro. Ctrl+J is a safe key because nothing is currently assigned to Ctrl+J. This shortcut key allows you to run the macro again.

5. Click OK to close the Record Macro dialog.

6. Turn on relative recording by clicking the Use Relative References icon in the Code group of the Developer tab. Relative recording records the action of moving a certain numbers of cells from the active cell.

7. Perform the actions you want to store in the macro.

8. Click the red Stop Recording button on the left side of the status bar.

9. Save the workbook before testing the macro.

10. Test the macro playback by typing the shortcut key assigned in step 4.

> **caution**
>
> The alternative is an absolute recording. This method is extremely literal. The action of moving down three cells from A1 is recorded as "Select Cell A4." That action is extremely limited—it would work only when the macro is played back with the active cell in A1.

Case Study: Macro for Formatting for a Mail Merge

Suppose that your co-worker has some names and addresses in Excel and she needs to do a mail merge in Word. Instead of teaching her how to do a mail merge, you offer to do the mail merge for her. In theory, this should take you a couple minutes. However, when the list of names arrives in the Excel worksheet, you realize the data is in the wrong format. In the Excel worksheet, the names are going down Column A, as shown in Figure 27.1.

To complete a mail merge successfully, the Excel worksheet should have fields for name, street address, and city+state+zip code, as shown in Figure 27.2.

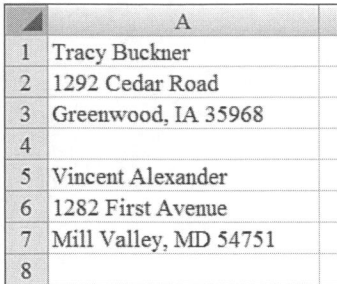

	A
1	Tracy Buckner
2	1292 Cedar Road
3	Greenwood, IA 35968
4	
5	Vincent Alexander
6	1282 First Avenue
7	Mill Valley, MD 54751
8	
9	Pearl Guzman

Figure 27.1
A simple task such as doing a mail merge is incredibly difficult when the data is in the wrong format.

J26

	A	B	C	D	E
1	Tracy Buckner	1292 Cedar Road	Greenwood, IA 35968		
2	Vincent Alexander	1282 First Avenue	Mill Valley, MD 54751		
3	Pearl Guzman	1919 Washington Avenue	Midway, TX 65197		
4	Matthew Rodgers	1825 Jackson Blvd.	Greenwood, AZ 75420		
5	Nancy Roach	1144 Davis Lane	Riverside, NY 89224		
6	Jeannette Ross	454 Hill Highway	Centerville, WA 82020		

Figure 27.2
The goal is to produce data with fields in columns.

Before you start recording a macro, you need to think about how to break the task into easily repeatable steps. The macro recorder is great at recording navigation done using arrow keys. Therefore, ideally, you want to use only the keyboard for navigation while using the macro recorder.

It would be good to record a macro that can fix one name in the list. Assume that you start with the cell pointer on a person's name at the beginning of the macro, as shown in Figure 27.3. The macro would need to perform these steps to fix one record and end up on the name of the second person in the list:

	A
1	Tracy Buckner
2	1292 Cedar Road
3	Greenwood, IA 35968
4	
5	Vincent Alexander
6	1282 First Avenue
7	Mill Valley, MD 54751

Figure 27.3
You start with a name selected.

1. Press the down-arrow key to move to the address cell.

2. Press Ctrl+X to cut the address.

3. Press the up-arrow key and then the right-arrow key to move next to the name.

4. Press Ctrl+V to paste the address, as shown in Figure 27.4.

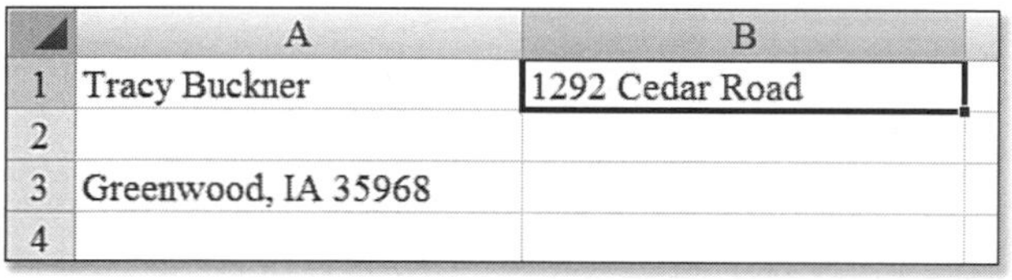

	A	B
1	Tracy Buckner	1292 Cedar Road
2		
3	Greenwood, IA 35968	
4		

Figure 27.4
You cut and paste the address.

5. Press the left-arrow key once and the down-arrow key twice to move to the cell for city, state, and ZIP code.

6. Press Ctrl+X to cut the city, as shown in Figure 27.5.

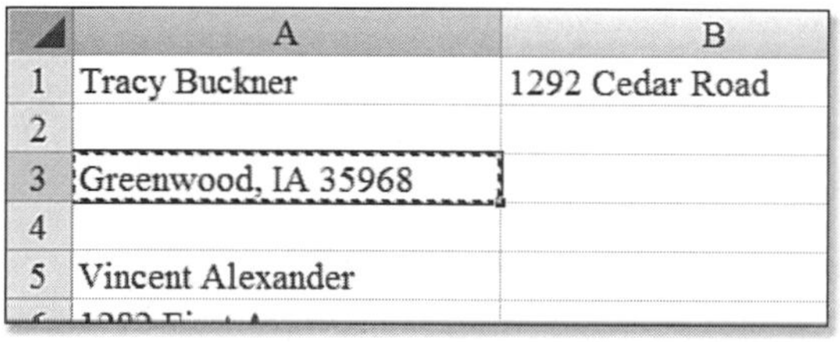

	A	B
1	Tracy Buckner	1292 Cedar Road
2		
3	Greenwood, IA 35968	
4		
5	Vincent Alexander	

Figure 27.5
Cut the city.

7. Press the up-arrow key twice and the right-arrow key twice to move to the right of the street cell.

8. Press Ctrl+V to paste the city.

9. Press the left-arrow key twice and the down-arrow key once to move to the now blank row just below the name.

10. Hold down the Shift key while pressing the down-arrow key twice to select the three blank rows, as shown in Figure 27.6.

11. Press Ctrl+- to invoke the delete command. Press R+Enter to delete the row.

When you run a macro that goes through these steps, Excel deletes the three blank rows, but the selection now contains the three cells that encompass the next record, as shown in Figure 27.7. Ideally, the macro should end with only the name selected. Therefore, the macro now needs to press the up-arrow key and the down-arrow key. Moving the cell pointer up a cell and then back to the name causes only a single cell to be selected, as shown in Figure 27.8.

	A	B	C
1	Tracy Buckner	1292 Cedar Road	Greenwo
2			
3			
4			
5	Vincent Alexander		
6	1282 First Avenue		
7	Mill Valley, MD 54751		
8			

Figure 27.6
Select three blank rows prior to deleting.

	A	B
1	Tracy Buckner	1292 Cedar Road
2	Vincent Alexander	
3	1282 First Avenue	
4	Mill Valley, MD 54751	
5		
6	Pearl Guzman	

Figure 27.7
You need only one cell selected instead of three.

	A
1	Tracy Buckner
2	Vincent Alexander
3	1282 First Avenue
4	Mill Valley, MD 54751

Figure 27.8
Finish the macro with the cell pointer on the next name.

If the macro correctly performs all these steps, the first name and address are properly formatted. The blank rows left between the first and second names are deleted.

By making sure that the macro starts on a name and ends up on the next name, you allow the macro to be run repeatedly. If you assign this macro to the keyboard shortcut Ctrl+J, you can then hold down Ctrl+J and quickly fix records, one after the other.

How Not to Record a Macro: The Default State of the Macro Recorder

The default state of the macro recorder is a stupid state. If you recorded the preceding steps in the macro recorder, the macro recorder would take your actions literally. The English pseudocode for recording these steps would say this:

1. Move to Cell A2.

2. Cut Cell A2 and paste to Cell B1.

3. Move to Cell A3.

4. Cut Cell A3 and paste to Cell C1.

5. Delete Rows 2 through 4.

6. Select Cell A2.

This macro works, but it works for only one record. After you recorded this macro, your worksheet looks like the one shown in Figure 27.9.

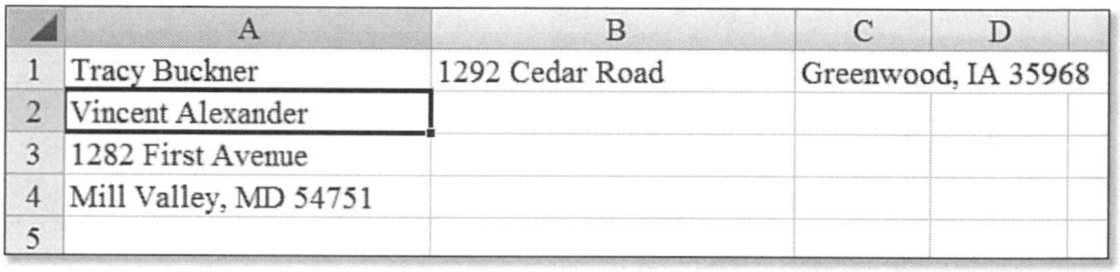

Figure 27.9
After recording the macro in default mode, the first record is fixed, and you might think you are ready to run the macro to fix the second record.

	A	B	C	D
1	Tracy Buckner	1292 Cedar Road	Greenwood, IA 35968	
2	Vincent Alexander			
3	1282 First Avenue			
4	Mill Valley, MD 54751			
5				

When the default macro runs, it moves the name Vincent Alexander from Cell A2 and pastes it on top of the address in Cell B1. It then takes the address in Cell A3 and pastes it on top of the city in Cell C1. It then deletes Rows 2, 3, and 4, removing the city and state. As shown in Figure 27.10, the macro provides the wrong result.

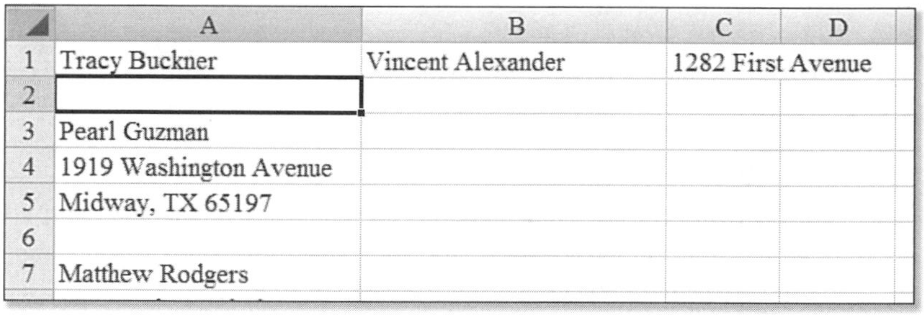

Figure 27.10
When the default macro runs, it ruins two records.

	A	B	C	D
1	Tracy Buckner	Vincent Alexander	1282 First Avenue	
2				
3	Pearl Guzman			
4	1919 Washington Avenue			
5	Midway, TX 65197			
6				
7	Matthew Rodgers			

If you blindly ran this macro 100 times to convert 100 addresses, the macro would happily "eat" all 100 records, leaving you with just one record (and not even a correct record), as shown in Figure 27.11.

To overcome this problem, use relative references as discussed in the next section.

▲	A	B
1	Tracy Buckner	Rosemount, NY 93801
2		
3		

Figure 27.11
If you run the default macro 100 times, it destroys your entire data set. Fortunately, a different mode is available for recording relative macros, as described in the next section.

Relative References in Macro Recording

There is an icon in the Code group on the Developer tab on the ribbon called Use Relative References. The key to recording useful macros is to be judicious in turning on and off the relative recording setting. If you performed the steps described in the preceding section in relative recording mode, Excel would write code that does this:

1. Move down one cell.

2. Cut that cell.

3. Move up and over one cell and paste.

4. Move left and down two cells.

5. Cut that cell.

6. Move up and over two cells and paste.

7. Move left two cells, move down one cell, and delete three rows.

8. Move up and down one cell to select a single cell.

These steps are far more generic than those recorded using the default state of the macro recorder. These steps work for any record, provided that you started the macro with the cell pointer on the first cell that contains a name.

For this example, you need to record the entire macro with relative recording turned on.

Starting the Macro Recorder

At this point, you have rehearsed the steps needed for a macro that puts data records into a format that is usable for a mail merge. After you make sure that the cell pointer is starting on the name in Cell A1, you are ready to turn on the macro recorder.

You should not be nervous, but you need to perform the steps correctly. If you move the cell pointer in the wrong direction, the macro recorder happily records that for you and plays it back. It is annoying to watch the macro recorder play back your mistakes 100 times a day for the next 5 years. Therefore, follow these steps to create the macro correctly:

1. On the Developer tab, click the Record Macro icon from the Code group. The Record Macro dialog appears.

2. Excel suggests giving this macro the unimaginative name Macro1. Use any name you want, up to 64 characters and without spaces. For this example, name the macro FixOneRecord.Choose a shortcut key for the macro. The shortcut key is important. Because you have to run this macro once for each record in the present example, you might choose something like Ctrl+A, which is easy to press.

4. Make a selection from the Store Macro In drop-down. You have the option of storing the macro in this workbook, in a new workbook, or in the personal macro workbook. If this is a general-purpose macro that you will use everyday on every file, it makes sense to store the macro in the personal macro workbook. However, because this macro will be used just to solve a current problem, store it in the current workbook.

5. Fill in a description if you think you will be using this macro long enough to forget what it does. When you are done making selections on the Record Macro dialog (see Figure 27.12), click OK. The Record Macro icon changes to a Stop Recording icon.

6. Click the Use Relative References icon in the Developer tab. The icon is highlighted.

7. Press the down-arrow key to move to the address cell.

8. Press Ctrl+X to cut the address.

9. Press the up-arrow key and then the right-arrow key to move next to the name.

 **note**

Keep in mind that assigning a macro to Ctrl+A overwrites the usual action of that keystroke (selecting all cells). If you are writing a macro that will be used all day, every day, you should use a shortcut key that is not assigned to any existing short-cuts such as Ctrl+J. Although most of the letter keys are already assigned to a shortcut, you can always used the shifted shortcut keys. To assign a macro to Ctrl+Shift+A, type Shift+A into the shortcut field.

Figure 27.12
After making the needed selections, click OK to begin recording.

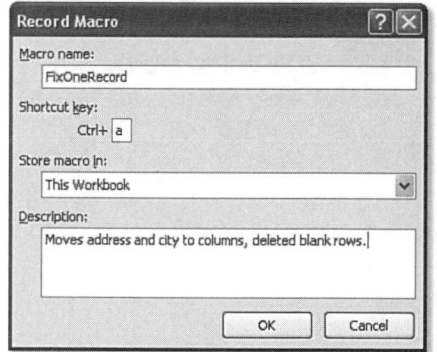

10. Press Ctrl+V to paste the address.

11. Press the left-arrow key once and the down-arrow key twice to move to the cell for city, state, and ZIP code.

12. Press Ctrl+X to cut the city.

13. Press the up-arrow key twice and the right-arrow key twice to move to the right of the street cell.

14. Press Ctrl+V to paste the city.

15. Press the left-arrow key twice and the down-arrow key once to move to the now blank row just below the name.

16. Hold down the Shift key while pressing the down-arrow key twice to select the three blank rows.

17. Press Ctrl+- to invoke the delete command. Press R then Enter to delete the row.

18. Press the up-arrow key and the down-arrow key. Moving the cell pointer up a cell and then back to the name causes only a single cell to be selected.

19. When you are done, click the Stop Recording button.

This macro will successfully fix any record in the database, provided the cell pointer is on the cell containing the name when you run the macro. Try playing back the macro by pressing Ctrl+A to fix one record. To fix all records, hold down Ctrl+A until all records are fixed.

 To watch a video of recording a macro with relative references, search for "Excel In Depth 27" at YouTube.

Running a Macro

To run a macro, follow these steps:

1. Click the green triangle on the Code group of the Developer tab. The Macro dialog appears, as shown in Figure 27.13.

Figure 27.13
Playing back a macro by using the Macro dialog.

2. Select your macro and click the Run button. The macro fixes the first record.

3. Press Ctrl+A to run the FixOneRecord macro. As shown in Figure 27.14, the second record is fixed.

Figure 27.14
Results of a successful macro.

▲	A	B	C	D	E
1	Tracy Buckner	1292 Cedar Road	Greenwood, IA 35968		
2	Vincent Alexander	1282 First Avenue	Mill Valley, MD 54751		
3	Pearl Guzman				
4	1919 Washington Avenue				
5	Midway, TX 65197				

4. Hold down Ctrl+A to repeatedly run the macro. In a matter of seconds, all 100 names are in a format ready to use in a mail merge.

This example represents an ideal use of a one-time macro. The process of fixing the data someone gave involved mindless repetition. If there had just been four records, you could have mindlessly fixed the records. However, because there were 100 records in this example, it made sense to record a macro and then run the macro repeatedly to solve the problem. You recorded the entire macro in relative mode, and you did not have to edit the macro. You probably run into a few situations a week where a quick one-time-use macro would make your job easier.

 caution

When you run a macro, there is no undo. Therefore, you should save a file before running a new macro on it. It is easy to have accidentally recorded the macro in default mode instead of relative mode. You need to save the macro so that you can easily go back to the current state in case something does not work right.

Everyday-Use Macro Example: Formatting an Invoice Register

The macro recorder does not solve all tasks perfectly, however. Many times, you need to record a macro and then edit the recorded code to make the macro a bit more general. This example demonstrates how to do that.

In this example, a system writes out a file every day. This file contains a list of invoices generated on the previous day. The file predictably contains six columns—NAME, DATE, INVOICE, REVENUE, SALES TAX, and TOTAL—as shown in Figure 27.15. The file also looks horrible: The columns are the wrong width, there is no title, and there is not a total row at the bottom. You would like a macro that would open this file, make the columns wider, add a total row, add a title, make the headings bold, and save the file with a new name. The following sections describe how to create this macro.

Using the End Key to Handle a Variable Number of Rows

One of the inherent problems with this example is that your file will have a different number of rows every day. If you record a macro for this today to add totals in Row 16, it will not work tomorrow, when you might have 22 invoices. The solution is to use the End key to navigate to the last row of your data.

You use the End key to move to the edge of a contiguous range of data. In Figure 27.15, if you press the End key and then the down-arrow key, you would move to Cell A15. If you press the End key and then the up-arrow key, you move back to Cell A1. You can press the End key followed by the right-arrow key to move to Cell F1.

◢	A	B	C	D	E	F
1	NAME	DATE	INVOICE	REVENUE	SALES TAX	TOTAL
2	TERRI D(	2/17/2007	10217	252.11	15.13	267.24
3	ELSIE H(	2/17/2007	10218	68.67	4.12	72.79
4	HAROLD	2/17/2007	10219	111.4	6.68	118.08
5	SHAWN (	2/17/2007	10220	151.47	9.09	160.56
6	KRISTIN	2/17/2007	10221	131.71	7.9	139.61
7	DAVID A	2/17/2007	10222	221.62	13.3	234.92
8	ROSA PR	2/17/2007	10223	225.02	13.5	238.52
9	NORA SH	2/17/2007	10224	261.84	15.71	277.55
10	CRAIG B]	2/17/2007	10225	195.08	11.7	206.78
11	BILLIE C]	2/17/2007	10226	72.31	4.34	76.65
12	ADAM W	2/17/2007	10227	168.12	10.09	178.21
13	ANDREW	2/17/2007	10228	79.54	4.77	84.31
14	BRANDI	2/17/2007	10229	258.73	15.52	274.25
15	LAURIE F	2/17/2007	10230	248.44	14.91	263.35

Figure 27.15
Create a macro to format this file every day.

You can also use the End key to jump over an abyss of empty cells. If you are currently at the edge of a range—for example, Cell F1—and press End followed by the right-arrow key, Excel jumps over all the blank cells and stops either at the next nonblank cell in Row 1 or at the right edge of the worksheet, Cell XFD1.

You might be tempted to start in Cell A1, press End, press the down-arrow key, and then press the down-arrow key again to move to the first blank row in the data. However, that is the wrong thing to do. This data file is coming from another system. Undoubtedly, one day, a cashier will find a way to enter an order without a customer name. She will happen upon the accidental keystroke combination that causes the cash register to allow an order without a customer name. On that day, the End+down-arrow key combination will stop at the wrong row and add totals in the middle of your data set. To prevent this problem, you should go through these steps to record the macro:

1. Open the file.

2. Turn on absolute recording.

3. Press the F5 key to display the GoTo dialog.

4. Go to Cell A1048576 (the last cell in the worksheet).

5. Turn on relative recording.

6. Press End+up-arrow to move to the last row that contains data.

7. Press the down-arrow key to move to the blank row.

8. Type the word `Total`.

9. Move right three cells.

10. Type a formula of `=SUM(D$2:D15)`. Press Ctrl+Enter to stay in the current cell. Be sure to include a single dollar sign to lock the start of the range to Row 2. Do not use the AutoSum icon to add this formula!

11. Press Ctrl+C to Copy. Press the right-arrow. Hold down Shift while pressing the right arrow again. Press Ctrl+V to paste.

12. Select all cells.

13. Select Home, Format, AutoFit Column Width.

14. Turn on absolute recording.

15. Select Row 1.

16. Press Ctrl+B to apply bold.

17. Insert two rows using your favorite method. One method is `Alt+I+R` twice..

18. Move to Cell A1.

19. Enter the formula `="Invoices for "&TEXT(B4,"mmmm d, yyyy")`.

20. Use Save As to save the file with a new name to reflect today's date.

21. Click the Stop Recording button.

Before recording this macro, you need to open a blank Excel workbook and save it with the name MacroToImportInvoices.xlsm.

In this macro example, you use a mix of relative and absolute recording to produce a macro that handles any number of rows of data. The macro will be somewhat useful, with two annoying limitations:

- If you saved the file as 2011-Feb-17Invoices.xls, the macro will attempt to overwrite that file everyday.

- The macro will always want to open the same file. This is great if your cash register system always produces a file with the same name in the same folder. However, you might want the option to browse for a different file each day.

Both of these changes require you to edit the recorded macro, as described in the next section.

Editing a Macro

To edit a macro, follow these steps:

1. Go to the Developer tab, and in the Code group, click the Macros button. The Macro dialog appears.

2. In the Macro dialog, select your macro and click Edit (see Figure 27.16). The Visual Basic Editor (VBE) is launched.

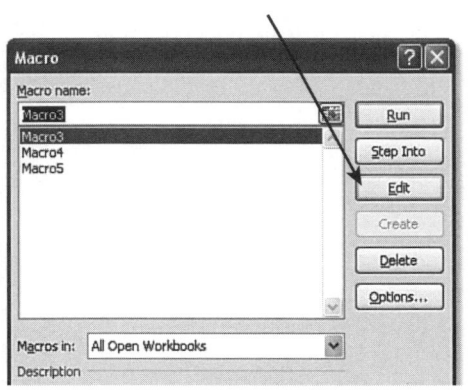

Figure 27.16
Launching the VBE through the Macro dialog is an easy way to make sure you find the proper code.

A number of panes are available in the VBE, but it is common to have three particular panes displayed, as shown in Figure 27.17:

- **Code pane**—The actual lines of the macro code are in the Code pane, which is usually on the right side of the screen.

- **Project Explorer pane**—This pane, which is in the upper left, shows every open workbook. Within the workbooks, you can see objects for each worksheet, an object for this workbook, and one or more code modules. If you cannot see the Project pane, you press Ctrl+R or select View, Project Explorer to open it.

- **Properties pane**—This pane, in the lower left, is useful if you design custom dialog boxes. You can Press F4 to display the Properties pane.

Figure 27.17
The VBE allows editing
of recorded macro code.

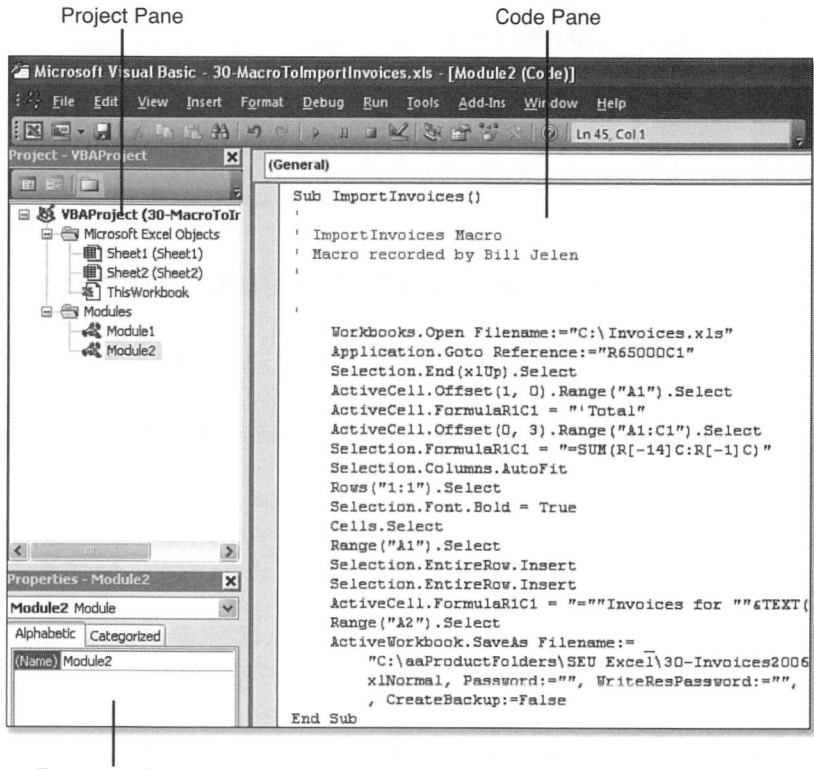

Project Pane

Code Pane

Properties Pane

Understanding VBA Code—An Analogy

In the 1980s and early 1990s, many people going through school were exposed to an introductory class in a programming language called BASIC. Although Excel macros are written in Visual Basic for Applications, the fact that both languages contain the word *basic* does not mean that BASIC and VBA are the same or even similar. BASIC is a procedural language. VBA is an object-oriented language. In VBA, the focus is on objects. This can make VBA confusing to someone who has learned to program in BASIC.

The syntax of VBA consists of objects, methods, collections, arguments, and properties. If you have never programmed in an object-oriented language, these terms, and the VBA code itself, might seem foreign to you. The following sections compare these five elements to parts of speech:

- An object is similar to a noun.

- A method is similar to a verb.

- A collection is similar to a plural noun.

- An argument is similar to an adverb.

- A property is similar to an adjective.

Each of the following sections describes the similarity between the VBA element and a part of speech. These sections also describe how to recognize the various elements when you examine VBA Code.

Comparing Object.Method to Nouns and Verbs

As an object-oriented language, the objects in VBA are of primary importance. Think of an object as any noun in Excel. Examples of objects are a cell, a row, a column, a worksheet, and a workbook.

A method is any action that you can perform on an object. This is similar to a verb. You can add a worksheet. You can delete a row. You can clear a cell. In Excel VBA, words like "Add," "Delete," and "Clear," are methods.

Objects and methods are joined by a period, although in VBA, people pronounce the period as a dot. The object is first, followed by a dot, followed by the method. For example, object.method, which is pronounced "object-dot-method," indicates that the method performs on the object. This is confusing because it is backward from how English is spoken. If everyone spoke VBA instead of English, we would use sentences such as "car.drive" and "dinner.eat." When you see a period in VBA, it usually means that the word after the period is acting upon the word to the left of the period.

Comparing Collections to Plural Nouns

In an Excel workbook, there is not a single cell but a collection of many cells. Many workbooks contain several worksheets. Anytime you have multiple instances of a certain object, VBA refers to this as a collection.

The "s" at the end of an object may seem subtle, but it indicates you are dealing with a collection instead of a single object. Although ThisWorkbook refers to a single workbook, Workbooks refers to a collection of all the open workbooks. This is an important distinction to understand.

There are two main ways to refer to a single worksheet in a collection of worksheets:

- By its number such as Worksheets(1)

- By its name such as Worksheets("Jan")

Comparing Parameters to Adverbs

When you invoke a command such as the Save As command, a dialog box pops up, and you have the opportunity to specify several options that change how the command is carried out. If the Save As command is a method, then the options for it are parameters. Just as an adverb modifies a verb, a parameter modifies a method.

Most of the time, parameters are recorded by using the syntax `ParameterName:=ParameterValue`.

One of the reasons that recorded code gets to be so long is that the macro recorder makes note of every option on the dialog box, whether you select it.

Consider this line of code for SaveAs:

```
ActiveWorkbook.SaveAs Filename:="C:\Something.xls", _
FileFormat:=xlOpenXMLWorkbookMacroEnabled, _
CreateBackup:=False
```

In this recorded macro for SaveAs, the recorder noted parameter values for Filename, FileFormat, and CreateBackup. Figure 27.18 shows the Save As dialog box. Filename and FileFormat are evident on the form. However, where are the rest of the options?

Figure 27.18
It seems like the macro recorder is making up options that are not on the dialog box.

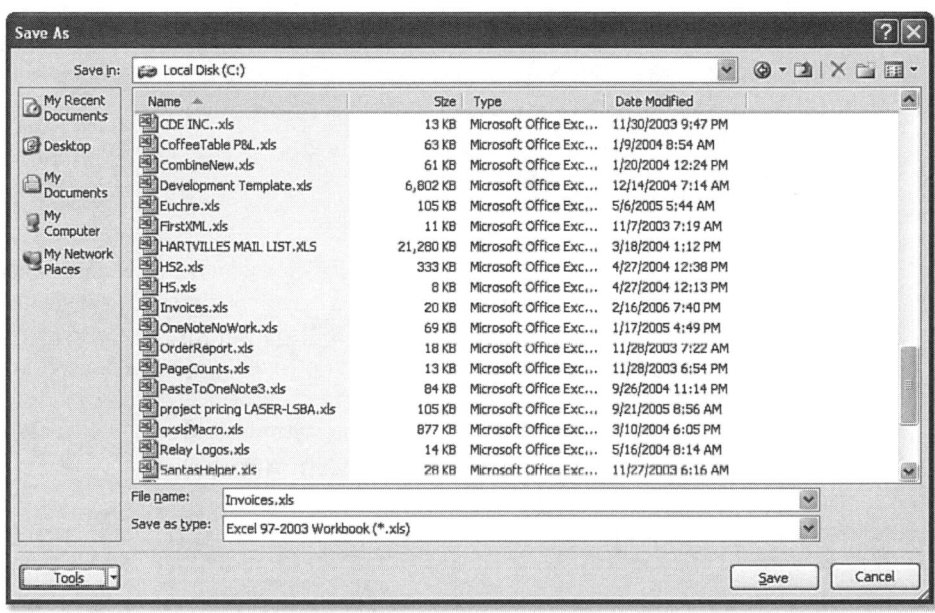

In the bottom corner of the dialog is a Tools drop-down. If you select Tools, General Options, you see a dialog box with four additional options, as shown in Figure 27.19. Even though you did not touch this Save Options dialog, Excel recorded the values in it for you.

Figure 27.19
Even though you did not touch the Save Options dialog box, the macro recorder recorded the values from it.

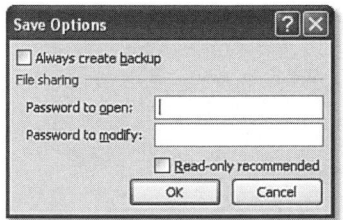

Parameters have some potentially confusing aspects. Most of the time, there is a space following the method and then a list of one or more `ParameterName:=ParameterValue` constructs, separated by a comma and a space. However, there are a couple exceptions:

- If the result of the method is acted upon by another method, the list of parameters is enclosed in parentheses, and there is no space after the method name. One example is when you add a shape to a worksheet and then Excel selects the shape. The code to insert the shape would uses the AddShape method and five named parameters:

```
ActiveSheet.Shapes.AddShape Type:=msoShapeRectangle, _
    Left:=60, Top:=120, _
    Width:=100, Height:=100
```

- The macro recorder will record the process of adding the shape and then selecting the shape. Because the .Select method is acting upon the result of the .AddShape method, you see the parameters for the AddShape method surrounded by parentheses:

```
ActiveSheet.Shapes.AddShape(Type:=msoShapeRectangle, _
    Left:=60, Top:=120, _
    Width:=100, Height:=100).Select
```

- When you use the parameter name, you can specify the parameters in any sequence you like. The Help topic for the method reveals the official default order for the parameters. If you specify the parameters in the exact sequence specified in Help, you are allowed to leave off the parameter names. However, this is a poor coding practice. Even if you have memorized the default order for the parameters, you cannot assume that everyone else reading your code will know the default order. The problem is that sometimes the macro recorder will record code in this style. For example, here is a line of code that was recorded when I added `WordArt` to a worksheet:

```
ActiveSheet.Shapes.AddTextEffect(msoTextEffect2, "Test", _
"Arial Black", 36#, msoFalse, msoFalse, 323.25, 142.5). _
Select
```

- It would be difficult to figure out this line of code without looking at the help topic. To access Help, click anywhere in the method of `AddTextEffect` and then press the F1 key. The help topic reveals that the correct parameter order is the one shown in Figure 27.20.

> **note**
>
> Keep in mind that parameters are like adverbs. They generally appear with a `Parameter Name:=Parameter Value` construct. However, there are times when the macro recorder lists the parameter values in their default order, without the parameter names or the :=.

Figure 27.20
The Help topic for each method helps decode the default order of the parameters.

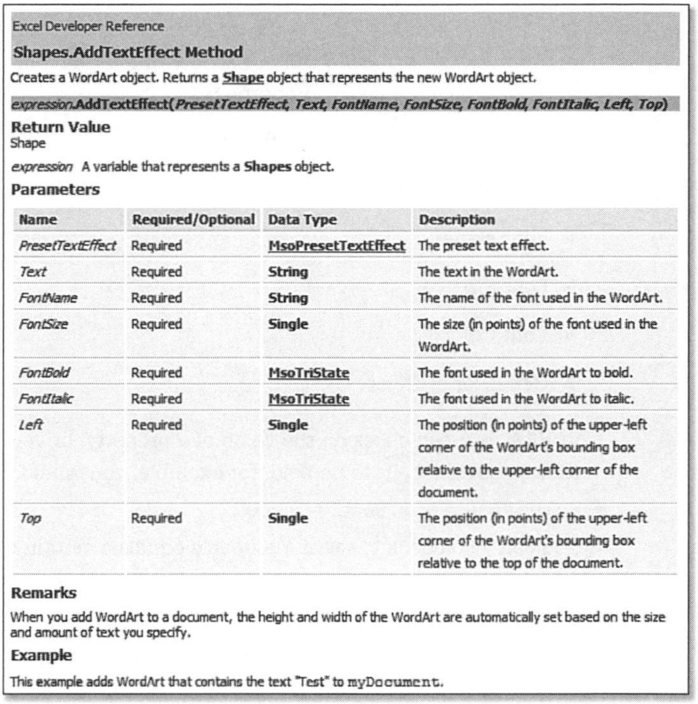

Excel Developer Reference

Shapes.AddTextEffect Method

Creates a WordArt object. Returns a **Shape** object that represents the new WordArt object.

expression.**AddTextEffect(*PresetTextEffect, Text, FontName, FontSize, FontBold, FontItalic, Left, Top*)**

Return Value

Shape

expression A variable that represents a **Shapes** object.

Parameters

Name	Required/Optional	Data Type	Description
PresetTextEffect	Required	**MsoPresetTextEffect**	The preset text effect.
Text	Required	**String**	The text in the WordArt.
FontName	Required	**String**	The name of the font used in the WordArt.
FontSize	Required	**Single**	The size (in points) of the font used in the WordArt.
FontBold	Required	**MsoTriState**	The font used in the WordArt to bold.
FontItalic	Required	**MsoTriState**	The font used in the WordArt to italic.
Left	Required	**Single**	The position (in points) of the upper-left corner of the WordArt's bounding box relative to the upper-left corner of the document.
Top	Required	**Single**	The position (in points) of the upper-left corner of the WordArt's bounding box relative to the top of the document.

Remarks

When you add WordArt to a document, the height and width of the WordArt are automatically set based on the size and amount of text you specify.

Example

This example adds WordArt that contains the text "Test" to `myDocument`.

Accessing VBA Help

If you will be recording and editing macros, you need to have the VBA Help file installed on the computer. Frustratingly, it is not installed by default. If VBA Help is not installed on your machine, it is worth your time to find the installation disc and reinstall Excel with the VBA Help option selected.

When VBA Help is installed, you can click any object, method, argument, or parameter in VBA and press the F1 key to display a complete description of the item. The Help topic lists the valid properties associated with the object and the valid methods that can be used on the object. Often, the Help topic will include an example as well. To use the code in the example, you can highlight the code, press Ctrl+C to copy, and then paste this code directly into the Code pane of the Visual Basic Editor (also known as the VBE).

Comparing Adjectives

The final construct in VBA is the adjective used to describe an object. In VBA, adjectives are called *properties*. Think about a cell in Excel with a formula in it. The cell has many properties. These are some of the most popular properties:

- Value (the value shown in the cell)

- Formula (the formula used to calculate Value)

- Font Name

- Font Size

- Font Color

- Cell Interior Color

In VBA, you can check on the value of a property, or you can set the property to a new value. To change several cells to be bold, for example, you would change their Bold property to true:

```
Selection.Font.Bold = True
```

You can also check to see if a property equals a certain value.

```
If Selection.Value = 100 then Selection.Font.Bold = True
```

Properties are generally used with the dot construct, and they are almost always followed by =, as contrasted with the := used with parameters. For example, PropertyName = value.

Using the Analogy While Examining Recorded Code

When you understand that a period generally separates an object from a method or a property, you can start to make sense of the recorded code.

For example, the following line performs the Open method:

```
Workbooks.Open Filename:="C:\Invoices.xls"
```

In this example, the Filename parameter is shown with := after the parameter name. This first line in the following example performs the Select method on one particular member of the Rows collection:

The advantage of this method is that the macro will run even faster than before.

```
Rows("1:1").Select
Selection.Font.Bold = True
```

The second line then sets the Bold property of the Font property of the selection to true. Using these two lines of code is equivalent to selecting Row 1 and clicking the Bold icon. You notice that one property such as Font can have subproperties such as Bold and Italic.

 tip

In the Excel user interface, you generally have to select a cell before you can change something in it. In a macro, there is no need to select something first. For example, you can replace the two lines in the preceding example with this single line of code: Rows("1:1").Font.Bold = True

Using Simple Variables and Object Variables

The macro recorder never records a variable, but you can add variables to a macro when you edit the code. Suppose that you need to do a number of operations to the row where the totals will be located. Instead of repeatedly going to the last row in the spreadsheet and pressing End+up-arrow, you can assign the row number to a variable:

```
FinalRow = Range("A1048576").End(xlup).Row
TotalRow = FinalRow + 1
```

The words `FinalRow` and `TotalRow` are variables that each hold a single value. If you have data in Rows 2 through 25 today, `FinalRow` will hold the value 25, and `TotalRow` will hold the value of 26. This allows you to use efficient code such as the following:

```
Range("A" & TotalRow).Value = "Total"
Range("C" & TotalRow).Formula = "=SUM(C2:C"& TotalRow & ")"
Range("D" & TotalRow).Formula = "=SUM(D2:D"& TotalRow & ")"
Range("E" & TotalRow).Formula = "=SUM(E2:E"& TotalRow & ")"
```

VBA also offers a powerful variable called an *object variable*. An object variable can be used to represent any object such as a worksheet, chart, or cell. Whereas a simple variable holds one value, an object variable holds values for every property associated with the object.

Object variables are declared using the Dim statement and then assigned using the Set statement:

```
Dim WSD as worksheet
Set WSD = Worksheets("Sheet1")
```

Using object variables offers the following advantages:

- It is easier to refer to WSD than to `ActiveWorkbook.Worksheets("Sheet1")`.

- If you define the object variable with a `DIM` statement at the beginning of the macro, as you type new lines of code, the VBE's AutoComplete feature shows a list of valid methods and properties for the object, as shown in Figure 27.21.

Figure 27.21
Object variables hold many properties instead of a single value.

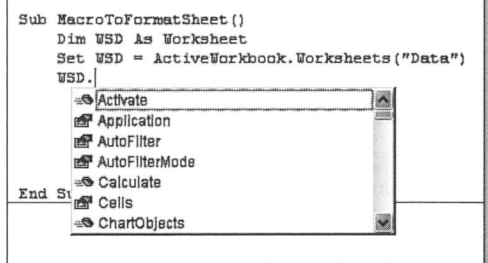

Using R1C1-Style Formulas

If you are a history buff of technology, you might know that VisiCalc was the first spreadsheet program for PCs. When Dan Bricklin and Bob Frankston invented VisiCalc, they used the A1 style for naming cells. In those early days, VisiCalc had competitors such as SuperCalc and a Microsoft program called MultiPlan. This early Microsoft spreadsheet used the notation of R1C1 to refer to Cell A1. The cell that we know today as E17 would have been called R17C5, for Row 17, Column 5.

In 1985, Microsoft launched Excel version 1.0 for the Macintosh. Excel originally continued to use the R1C1 style of notation. During the next 10 years, Excel and Lotus 1-2-3 were locked in a bitter battle for market share. Lotus was the early leader, and it had adopted the A1 notation style familiar to VisiCalc customers. To capture more market share, Microsoft allowed Excel to use either A1-style notation or R1C1-style notation. Even today, in Excel 2010, you can turn on R1C1 style notation by selecting Office Button, Excel Options, Formulas, R1C1 Reference Style. Hardly anyone uses R1C1 reference style; however, the macro recorder always records formulas in R1C1 style.

Figure 27.22 shows the familiar formula =SUM(D$2:D15). When entered in Cell D16, this formula adds up everything from Row 2 to the row just above the current cell.

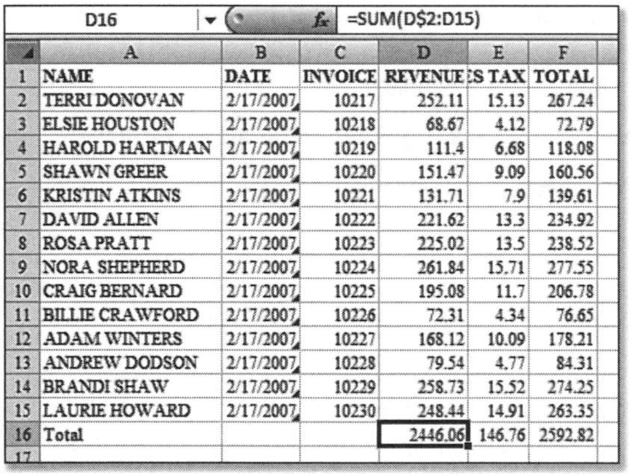

Figure 27.22
This familiar formula is in A1-style notation.

If you now turn on R1C1 style in this worksheet, the formula changes to =SUM(R2C:R[-1]C), as shown in Figure 27.23.

In R1C1 notation, the reference RC refers to the current cell. You can modify RC by adding a particular row number or column number. For example, R2C refers to the cell in Row 2 of the current column. RC1 refers to the cell in this row that is in Column 1.

If you put a row number or column number in square brackets, it refers to a relative number of cells from the current cell. If you have a formula in Cell D16 and use the reference R[1]C[-2], you are referring to the cell one row below D16 and two columns to the left of D16, which would be cell B17.

You are probably wondering why the macro recorder uses this arcane notation style when recording formulas. It turns out that this style is fantastic for formulas. For example, notice that every formula in Column F of the worksheet is a little different (see Figure 27.24). When you copy F2 to F3, Excel changes the references of E2 and D2 to be E3 and D3.

Figure 27.23
The formula in R1C1 notation would be confusing to most spreadsheet users.

R16C4	▼	fx	=SUM(R2C:R[-1]C)		
	1	2	3	4	5	6
1	NAME	DATE	INVOICE	REVENUE	S TAX	TOTAL
2	TERRI DONOVAN	2/17/2007	10217	252.11	15.13	267.24
3	ELSIE HOUSTON	2/17/2007	10218	68.67	4.12	72.79
4	HAROLD HARTMAN	2/17/2007	10219	111.4	6.68	118.08
5	SHAWN GREER	2/17/2007	10220	151.47	9.09	160.56
6	KRISTIN ATKINS	2/17/2007	10221	131.71	7.9	139.61
7	DAVID ALLEN	2/17/2007	10222	221.62	13.3	234.92
8	ROSA PRATT	2/17/2007	10223	225.02	13.5	238.52
9	NORA SHEPHERD	2/17/2007	10224	261.84	15.71	277.55
10	CRAIG BERNARD	2/17/2007	10225	195.08	11.7	206.78
11	BILLIE CRAWFORD	2/17/2007	10226	72.31	4.34	76.65
12	ADAM WINTERS	2/17/2007	10227	168.12	10.09	178.21
13	ANDREW DODSON	2/17/2007	10228	79.54	4.77	84.31
14	BRANDI SHAW	2/17/2007	10229	258.73	15.52	274.25
15	LAURIE HOWARD	2/17/2007	10230	248.44	14.91	263.35
16	Total			2446.06	146.76	2592.82
17						

Figure 27.24
In A1 style, every formula in F2:F15 is different.

D	E	F
REVENUE	SALES TAX	TOTAL
252.11	=ROUND(0.06*D2,2)	=+E2+D2
68.67	=ROUND(0.06*D3,2)	=+E3+D3
111.4	=ROUND(0.06*D4,2)	=+E4+D4
151.47	=ROUND(0.06*D5,2)	=+E5+D5
131.71	=ROUND(0.06*D6,2)	=+E6+D6
221.62	=ROUND(0.06*D7,2)	=+E7+D7
225.02	=ROUND(0.06*D8,2)	=+E8+D8
261.84	=ROUND(0.06*D9,2)	=+E9+D9
195.08	=ROUND(0.06*D10,2)	=+E10+D10
72.31	=ROUND(0.06*D11,2)	=+E11+D11
168.12	=ROUND(0.06*D12,2)	=+E12+D12
79.54	=ROUND(0.06*D13,2)	=+E13+D13
258.73	=ROUND(0.06*D14,2)	=+E14+D14
248.44	=ROUND(0.06*D15,2)	=+E15+D15
=SUM(D$2:D15)	=SUM(E2:E15)	=SUM(F2:F15)

Now look at these same formulas in R1C1 style, as shown in Figure 27.25. Every formula in that range is identical. This makes sense because the formula is saying, "Add the sales tax one cell to the left of me to the merchandise amount that is two cells to the left of me."

If you were forced to use A1-style formulas in a macro, you might try to enter the formula in Cell F2 and then copy the formula from F2 to the remaining cells:

```
Range("F2").Formula = "=D2+E2"
Range("F2").Copy Destination:=Range("F3:F15")
```

Instead, you can enter all the formulas in one line of code when using R1C1 style formulas:

```
Range("F2:F15").FormulaR1C1 = "=RC[-2]+RC[-1]"
```

 tip

While the macro recorder always records formulas in R1C1 style, you are allowed to write the macros using regular formulas. Change the FormulaR1C1 property to Formula. The following two lines of code are equivalent:

```
Range("F2:F15").FormulaR1C1 = _
    "=RC[-2]+RC[-1]"
Range("F2:F15").Formula = _
    "=D2-E2"
```

4	5	6
REVENUE	SALES TAX	TOTAL
252.11	=ROUND(0.06*RC[-1],2)	=+RC[-1]+RC[-2]
68.67	=ROUND(0.06*RC[-1],2)	=+RC[-1]+RC[-2]
111.4	=ROUND(0.06*RC[-1],2)	=+RC[-1]+RC[-2]
151.47	=ROUND(0.06*RC[-1],2)	=+RC[-1]+RC[-2]
131.71	=ROUND(0.06*RC[-1],2)	=+RC[-1]+RC[-2]
221.62	=ROUND(0.06*RC[-1],2)	=+RC[-1]+RC[-2]
225.02	=ROUND(0.06*RC[-1],2)	=+RC[-1]+RC[-2]
261.84	=ROUND(0.06*RC[-1],2)	=+RC[-1]+RC[-2]
195.08	=ROUND(0.06*RC[-1],2)	=+RC[-1]+RC[-2]
72.31	=ROUND(0.06*RC[-1],2)	=+RC[-1]+RC[-2]
168.12	=ROUND(0.06*RC[-1],2)	=+RC[-1]+RC[-2]
79.54	=ROUND(0.06*RC[-1],2)	=+RC[-1]+RC[-2]
258.73	=ROUND(0.06*RC[-1],2)	=+RC[-1]+RC[-2]
248.44	=ROUND(0.06*RC[-1],2)	=+RC[-1]+RC[-2]
=SUM(R2C:R[-1]C)	=SUM(R[-14]C:R[-1]C)	=SUM(R[-14]C:R[

Figure 27.25
In R1C1 style, every formula in F2:F15 is identical.

If you are not yet convinced to learn how to use R1C1-style formulas, the final straw is that you have to use R1C1-style formulas when setting up conditional formatting in VBA.

Fixing Calculation Errors in Macros

Probably the most important reason to understand R1C1 formulas is to make sure that the macro recorder recorded the proper formula. This is important because the macro recorder does not do a good job of recording the intent of the AutoSum button. If your data set has numbers in D2:D15 today, pressing AutoSum from Cell D16 will record the following line of macro code:

```
Selection.FormulaR1C1 = "=SUM(R[-14]C:R[-1]C)"
```

This formula adds a range from 14 rows above the selection to the cell just above the selection. This works only on days when you have exactly 14 rows of data. This is one of the most annoying bugs in a macro.

It is annoying because this type of logic error will not cause an actual error. If you run this macro on the invoice file you receive tomorrow that contains 20 invoices, the macro will happily total only the last 14 invoices instead of all 20. This means that you could distribute this report with a wrong total for several days before someone realizes that something is amiss.

However, this formula can be corrected. You know that you have headings in Row 1 and the first invoice will appear in Row 2. You need the macro to sum from Row 2 to the row just above the current cell. Therefore, you need to change the formula to this:

```
Selection.FormulaR1C1 = "=SUM(R2C:R[-1]C)"
```

Customizing the Everyday-Use Macro Example: GETOPENFILENAME and GETSAVEASFILENAME

The everyday-use macro you recorded earlier in this chapter for formatting an invoice register is hard-coded to always open the same file and always save with the same filename. To make the macro more general, you can allow the person running the macro to browse for the file each morning and to specify a new filename during the Save As. Excel offers a straightforward way to display the File Open or File Save As dialog. Here is the code you need to use:

```
FileToOpen = Application.GetOpenFileName( _
    FileFilter:="Excel Files,*.xl*", _
    Title:="Select Today's Invoice File")
```

Note that this code displays the File Open dialog and allows a file to be selected. When you click Open, the dialog assigns the filename to the variable. It does not actually open the file. You then need to open the file specified in the variable:

```
Workbooks.Open Filename:=FileToOpen
```

When you want to ask for the filename to use in saving the file, use this code:

```
NewFileName = Application.GetSaveAsFilename( _
    Title:="Select File Name for Today")
ActiveWorkbook.SaveAs Filename:=NewFileName, _
    FileFormat:=xlOpenXMLWorkbookMacroEnabled
```

The following macro is the final macro to use each day:

```
Sub ImportInvoicesFixed()
' ImportInvoices Macro
' With Changes
    FileToOpen = Application.GetOpenFileName( _
        FileFilter:= _
        "Excel files (*.xls;*.xlsb;*.xlsx;*.xlsm)" & _
        ",*.xls;*.xlsb;*.xlsx;*.xlsb)", _
        Title:="Select Today's Invoice File")
    Workbooks.Open Filename:=FileToOpen
    Application.Goto Reference:="R1048576C1"
    Selection.End(xlUp).Select
    ActiveCell.Offset(1, 0).Range("A1").Select
    ActiveCell.FormulaR1C1 = "'Total"
    ActiveCell.Offset(0, 3).Range("A1:C1").Select
    Selection.FormulaR1C1 = "=SUM(R2C:R[-1]C)"
    Selection.Columns.AutoFit
    Rows("1:1").Select
    Selection.Font.Bold = True
    Cells.Select
    Range("A1").Select
    Selection.EntireRow.Insert
    Selection.EntireRow.Insert
    ActiveCell.FormulaR1C1 = _
        "=""Invoices for ""&TEXT(R[3]C[1],""mmmm d, yyyy"")"
    Range("A2").Select
    NewFileName = Application.GetSaveAsFilename( _
        Title:="Select File Name for Today")
    ActiveWorkbook.SaveAs Filename:=NewFileName, _
        FileFormat:=xlOpenXMLWorkbookMacroEnabled
End Sub
```

Of the 19 lines in the macro, you added two lines and corrected two lines. This is typical because between 10 percent and 20 percent of a recorded macro generally needs to be adjusted.

From-Scratch Macro Example: Loops, Flow Control, and Referring to Ranges

Suppose you work for a company that sells printers and scanners to commercial accounts. When you sell a piece of hardware, you also try to sell a service plan for that hardware. Customers in your state are taxed. Your accounting software provides a daily download that looks like Columns A:D in Figure 27.26.

	A	B	C	D
1	Invoice	Customer	Product	Revenue
2	1010	Supreme Toothpick Company	Printer	262
3	1010	Supreme Toothpick Company	Scanner	454
4	1010	Supreme Toothpick Company	Service Plan	107
5	1010	Supreme Toothpick Company	Sales Tax	49.38
6	1011	Fashionable Necktie Company	Printer	127
7	1011	Fashionable Necktie Company	Scanner	994
8	1011	Fashionable Necktie Company	Sales Tax	67.26
9	1012	Top-Notch Juicer Inc.	Printer	985
10	1012	Top-Notch Juicer Inc.	Service Plan	148
11	1012	Top-Notch Juicer Inc.	Sales Tax	67.98
12	1013	Unusual Aquarium Traders	Printer	290
13	1013	Unusual Aquarium Traders	Scanner	655
14	1013	Unusual Aquarium Traders	Sales Tax	56.7

Figure 27.26
Your accounting software groups all hardware, service, and tax amounts into a single column.

You want to create a macro that examines each row in the data set and carries out a different action, based on the value in Column D. You will probably want to write this a macro from scratch. The following sections describe how to do this.

Finding the Last Row with Data

The recorded macro examples discussed earlier in this chapter suggested going to the last cell in Column A and then typing End followed by the up arrow to find the last row with data in Column A.

In legacy versions of Excel, this would be accomplished with this code:

```
FinalRow = Range("A65536").End(xlUp).Row
```

This command became more complicated in Excel 2007.

The solution is to use Rows.Count, which is shorthand for Application.Rows.Count. This solution returns the total number of rows available in the current worksheet. Note that this property returns 65,536 in Excel 2003 and 1048576 in Excel 2010.

> **tip**
>
> If you are not sure if your code is running in Excel 2003 or Excel 2007, you might need to start at A1084576 instead of A65536. Even if you are sure it is running in Excel 2007 or Excel 2010, there is the chance that someone will open an old .xls file in Compatibility mode, which means Excel 2010 will not have more than 65,536 rows.

The following line of code finds the last row in Column A with a nonblank value:

```
FinalRow = Cells(Rows.Count, 1).End(xlUp).Row
```

Looping Through All Rows

The loop most commonly used in VBA is a For-Next loop. This is identical to the loop that you might have learned about in a BASIC class.

In this example, the loop starts with a For statement. You specify that on each pass through the loop, a certain variable will change from a low value to a high value. This simple macro will run through the loop 10 times. On the first pass through the loop, the variable x will be equal to 1. The two lines inside the loop will assign the value 1 to Cells A1 and B1. When the macro encounters the Next x line, it will return to the start of the loop, increment x by 1, and run through the loop again. The next time through the loop, the value of x will be 2. Cell A2 will be assigned the number 2, and cell B2 will show 4, which is the square of 2. Eventually, x will be equal to 10. At the Next x line, the macro will allow the loop to finish. The following is the code for this macro:

```
Sub WriteSquares()
    For x = 1 To 10
        Range("A" & x).Value = x
        Range("B" & x).Value = x * x
    Next x
End Sub
```

After you run this macro, you have a simple table that shows the numbers 1 through 10 and their squares, as shown in Figure 27.27

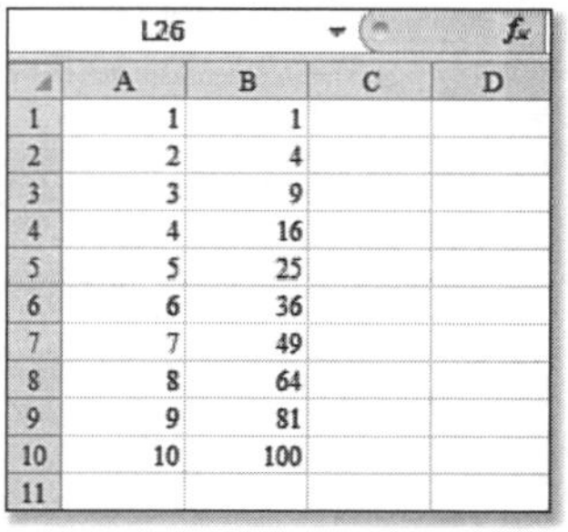

Figure 27.27
This simple loop fills in 10 rows.

	A	B	C	D
1	1	1		
2	2	4		
3	3	9		
4	4	16		
5	5	25		
6	6	36		
7	7	49		
8	8	64		
9	9	81		
10	10	100		
11				

After a loop is written, it can be adjusted easily. For example, if you want a table showing all the squares from 1 to 100, you can adjust the For x = 1 to 10 line to be For x = 1 to 100.

There is an optional clause in the For statement called the step value. If no step value is shown, the program moves through the loop by incrementing the variable by one each time through the loop. If you wanted to check only the even-numbered rows, you could change the loop to be For x = 2 to 100 in Step 2.

If you are going to be optionally deleting rows from a range of data, it is important to start at the bottom and proceed to the top of the range. You would use –1 as the step value:

```
For x = 100 to 1 step –1
```

Referring to Ranges

The macro recorder uses the Range property to refer to a particular range. You might see the macro recorder refer to ranges such as Range("B3") or Range("W1:Z100").

The loop code shown in the preceding section emulates this style of referring to ranges. On the third time through the loop, this line of code would refer to Cell B3:

```
Range("B" & x).value = x * x
```

However, how would you handle looping through each column? If you wanted to continue using the Range property, you need to jump through some hoops to figure out the letter that is associated with Column 5:

```
For y = 1 to 26
    ThisCol = Char(64+y)
    Range(ThisCol & 1).value = ThisCol
Next y
```

This method works fine if you are using only 26 or fewer columns. However, if you need to loop through all the columns out to Column XFD, you will spend all day trying to write the logic to assign the column label WMJ to Column 15896.

The solution is to use the Cells property instead of the Range property. Cells require that you specify a numeric row number and a numeric column number. For example, Cell B3 is specified as follows:

```
Cells(3, 2)
```

If you need to refer to a rectangular range, you can use the Resize property. Resize requires you to specify the number of rows and the number of columns. For example, to refer to W1:Z100 use this:

```
Cells(1, 23).Resize(100, 4)
```

It is difficult to figure out that this refers to W1:Z100, but it allows you to loop through rows or columns.

You can use the following code to make every other column bold:

```
For y = 1 to 100 step 2
    Cells(1, y).Resize(200, 1).Font.Bold = True
Next y
```

Combining a Loop with FinalRow

Earlier in this chapter, you learned how to use the End key to find the final row in a data set. After finding the final row in the data set and assigning it to a variable, you can specify that the loop should run through FinalRow:

```
FinalRow = Cells(1048576, 1).End(xlUp).row
For x = 2 to FinalRow
    ' Perform some action
Next x
```

Making Decisions by Using Flow Control

Flow control is the ability to make decisions within a macro. The following sections describe two commonly used flow control constructs:

`If - End if` and `Select Case`.

Using the `If - End if` Construct

Say you need a macro to delete any records that say Sales Tax. You could accomplish this with a simple `If - End if` construct:`If Cells(x, 4).Value = "Sales Tax" Then`

```
    Rows(x).Delete
End If
```

This construct always starts with the word `If`, followed by a logical test, followed by the word `Then`. Every line between the first line and the `End If` line is executed only if the logical test is `true`.

Now suppose that you want to enhance the macro so that any other amounts that contain service plan revenue are moved to Column F. To do this, you use the `ElseIf` line to enter a second condition and block of lines to be used in that condition:

```
If Cells(x, 4).Value = "Sales Tax" Then
    Cells(x, 1).EntireRow.Delete
ElseIf Cells(x, 4).Value = "Service Plan" Then
    Cells(x, 5).Cut Destination:=Cells(x, 6)
End If
```

You could continue adding `ElseIf` statements to handle other situations. Eventually, just before the `End If`, you could add an `Else` block to handle any other condition that you have not thought about.

Using the `Select Case` Construct

If you reach a point where you have many `ElseIf` statements all testing the same value, it might make sense to switch to a `Select Case` construct. For example, suppose you want to loop through all the records to examine the product in Column C. If Column C contains a printer, you want to move the amount in Column D to a new Column E. Scanner revenue should go to a new Column F. Service plans go to a new Column H. Sales tax goes to a new Column I. You should also handle the situation when something is sold that contains none of those products. In that case, you would move the revenue to a new Column G.

The construct begins with `Select Case` and then the value to check. The construct ends with `End Select`, which is similar to `End If`.

Each subblock of code starts with the word `Case` and one or more possible values. If you needed to check for `Printer` or `Printers`, you would enclose each in quotes and separate them with a comma.

After checking for all the possible values you can think of, you might add a `Case Else` subblock to handle any other stray values that might be entered in Column C.

The following code checks to see what product is in Column C. Depending on the product, the program copies the revenue from Column D to a specific column.

```
Select Case Cells(x, 3).Value
    Case "Printer", "Printers"
        Cells(x, 4).Copy Destination:=Cells(x, 5)
    Case "Scanner", "Scanners"
        Cells(x, 4).Copy Destination:=Cells(x, 6)
    Case "Service Plan"
        Cells(x, 4).Copy Destination:=Cells(x, 8)
    Case "Sales Tax"
        Cells(x, 4).Copy Destination:=Cells(x, 9)
    Case Else
        ' Something unexpected was sold
        Cells(x, 4).Copy Destination:=Cells(x, 7)
End Select
```

Putting Together the From-Scratch Example: Testing Each Record in a Loop

Using the building blocks described in the preceding sections, you can now write the code for a macro that finds the last row, loops through the records, and copies the total revenue to the appropriate column. Now you need to add new headings for the additional columns, as shown in Figure 27.28.

D	E	F	G	H	I
Revenue	Printer	Scanner	Accessory	Service	Tax
262					
454					
107					
49.38					
127					
994					
67.26					

Figure 27.28
Adding new headings before running the macro.

The macro should use the `End` property to locate the final row and prefill Columns E through I with zeros. Next, it should loop from Row 2 down to the final row. For each record, the revenue column should be moved to one of the columns. At the end of the loop, the program alerts you that the program is complete, using a `MsgBox` command. The following is the complete code of this macro:

```
Sub MoveRevenue2()
    FinalRow = Cells(Rows.Count, 1).End(xlUp).Row
    Range("E2", Cells(FinalRow, 9)).Value = 0
    For x = 2 To FinalRow
        Select Case Cells(x, 3).Value
            Case "Printer", "Printers"
```

```
                Cells(x, 4).Copy Destination:=Cells(x, 5)
            Case "Scanner", "Scanners"
                Cells(x, 4).Copy Destination:=Cells(x, 6)
            Case "Service Plan"
                Cells(x, 4).Copy Destination:=Cells(x, 8)
            Case "Sales Tax"
                Cells(x, 4).Copy Destination:=Cells(x, 9)
            Case Else
                ' Something unexpected was sold
                Cells(x, 4).Copy Destination:=Cells(x, 7)
        End Select
    Next x
    MsgBox "Macro complete"
End Sub
```

Figure 27.29
After running the macro, you have a breakout of revenue by product.

▲	1	2	3	4	5	6	7	8	9
1	Invoice	Customer	Product	Revenue	Printer	Scanner	Accessory	Service	Tax
2	1010	Supreme Toothpick Company	Printer	262	262	0	0	0	0
3	1010	Supreme Toothpick Company	Scanner	454	0	454	0	0	0
4	1010	Supreme Toothpick Company	Service Plan	107	0	0	0	107	0
5	1010	Supreme Toothpick Company	Sales Tax	49.38	0	0	0	0	49.38
6	1011	Fashionable Necktie Company	Printer	127	127	0	0	0	0
7	1011	Fashionable Necktie Company	Scanner	994	0	994	0	0	0
8	1011	Fashionable Necktie Company	Sales Tax	67.26	0	0	0	0	67.26
9	1012	Top Notch Injector Inc	Printer	985	985	0	0	0	0

After you run this macro, you see that the revenue amounts have been copied to the appropriate columns, as shown in Figure 27.29.

A Special Case: Deleting Some Records

If a loop is conditionally deleting records, you will run into trouble if it is a typical For-Next loop. Suppose you want to delete all the sales tax records, as follows:

```
Sub ThisWontWork()
    FinalRow = Cells(Rows.Count, 1).End(xlUp).Row
    For x = 2 To FinalRow
        If Cells(x, 3).Value = "Sales Tax" Then
            Cells(x, 1).EntireRow.Delete
        Else
            Cells(x, 5).Value = "Checked"
        End If
    Next x
End Sub
```

Consider the data in Figure 27.30.

The first time through the loop, x is equal to 2. Cell C2 does not contain sales tax, so Cell E2 has the word checked. A similar result

tip

An alternative syntax of the Range property is to specify the top-left and bottom-right cells in the range, separated by a comma. In the macro described here, for example, you know you want to fill from Cell E2 to the last row in Column I. You can describe this range as follows:Range("E2", Cells(FinalRow, 9))

This syntax is sometimes simpler than using Cells() and Resize().

occurs for Rows 3 and 4. The fourth time through the loop, Cell C5 contains sales tax. The macro deletes the tax in Row 5. However, Excel then moves the old Row 6 up to Row 5, as shown in Figure 27.31. The next time through the loop, the program inspects Row 6, and the data that is now in Row 5 will never be checked.

The macro succeeds in deleting tax. However, several rows were not checked, and several extra blank rows at the bottom were checked needlessly, as shown in Figure 27.32.

Figure 27.30
A forward-running loop encounters problems.

	A	B	C	D
1	Invoice	Customer	Product	Revenue
2	1010	Supreme Toothpick Company	Printer	262
3	1010	Supreme Toothpick Company	Scanner	454
4	1010	Supreme Toothpick Company	Service Plan	107
5	1010	Supreme Toothpick Company	Sales Tax	49.38
6	1011	Fashionable Necktie Company	Printer	127

A31 ▾ *fx* 1018

C6 ▾ *fx* Scanner

	A	B	C	D	E
1	Invoice	Customer	Product	Revenue	
2	1010	Supreme Toothpick Company	Printer	262	Checked
3	1010	Supreme Toothpick Company	Scanner	454	Checked
4	1010	Supreme Toothpick Company	Service Plan	107	Checked
5	1011	Fashionable Necktie Company	Printer	127	
6	1011	Fashionable Necktie Company	Scanner	994	

Figure 27.31
The old Row 6 data moves up to occupy the deleted Row 5. This row will never be checked.

C	D	E
Product	Revenue	
Printer	262	Checked
Scanner	454	Checked
Service Plan	107	Checked
Printer	127	
Scanner	994	Checked
Printer	985	
Service Plan	148	Checked
Printer	290	
Scanner	655	Checked
Printer	250	
Scanner	679	Checked
Service Plan	139	Checked
Printer	800	
Scanner	154	Checked
Printer	320	
Service Plan	48	Checked
Printer	715	
Scanner	596	Checked
Service Plan	197	Checked
Printer	374	
Scanner	740	Checked
Printer	125	
Scanner	851	Checked
Service Plan	146	Checked
		Checked
		Checked
		Checked

Figure 27.32
Several rows were not checked in this loop.

The solution is to have the loop run backward. You need to start at the final row and proceed up through the sheet to Row 2. When the macro deletes tax in Row 31, it can then proceed to checking Row 30, knowing that nothing has been destroyed (yet) in Row 30 and above.

To reverse the flow of the loop, you have to tell the loop to start at the final row, but you also have to tell the loop to use a step value of -1. The start of the loop would use this line of code:

```
For x = FinalRow to 2 Step -1
```

The macro you need here represents a fairly common task: looping through all the records to do something conditionally to each record.

The following macro correctly deletes all the sales tax records:

```
Sub DeleteTaxOK()
    FinalRow = Cells(Rows.Count, 1).End(xlUp).Row
    For x = FinalRow To 2 Step -1
        If Cells(x, 3).Value = "Sales Tax" Then
            Cells(x, 1).EntireRow.Delete
        Else
            Cells(x, 5).Value = "Checked"
        End If
    Next x
End Sub
```

> **note**
>
> It is common to indent each line of code with four spaces. Any lines of code inside an If-EndIf block or inside a For-Next loop are indented an additional four spaces. If you have typed a line of code that is indented eight spaces and then press Enter at the end of the line of code, the VBE automatically indents the next line to eight spaces. Each press of the Tab key indents by an additional four spaces. Pressing Shift+Tab removes four spaces of indentation. While four is the default number of spaces for a tab, you can change this to any number of spaces using Tools, Options in the Visual Basic Editor.

For the example described here, the macro recorder would be almost no help. You would have to write this simple macro from scratch. However, it is a powerful macro that can simplify tasks when you have hundreds of thousands of rows of data.

Combination Macro Example: Creating a Report for Each Customer

Many real-life scenarios require you to use a combination of recorded code and code written from scratch. For example, Figure 27.33 shows a data set with all your invoices for the year. In this case, suppose you would like to produce a workbook for each customer that you can mail to the customer.

One way to handle this task would be to use an advanced filter to get a list of all unique customers in Column A. You would then loop through these customers, applying an AutoFilter to the data set to see only the customers that match the selected customer. After the data set is filtered, you can select the visible cells only and copy them to a new workbook. Then you can save the workbook with the name of the customer and then return to the original workbook.

You can start by creating a blank procedure with comments to spell out the steps in the preceding paragraphs. Then you add code for the loop and other simple tasks such as copying the selection to a new workbook. Whenever you encounter a step for which you have never written code, you can leave a comment with question marks. This allows you to go back and record parts of the process to finish the macro.

▲	A	B	C	D	E	F
1	Customer	Invoice	Date	Purchases	Paid	Open Balance
2	Hip Lawn Corporation	1001	1/4/11	8846	8846	0
3	Vivid Chopstick Traders	1002	1/4/11	1688	1688	0
4	Unusual Doorbell Company	1003	1/4/11	8415	8415	0
5	Excellent Utensil Corporation	1004	1/4/11	2619	2619	0
6	Hip Lawn Corporation	1005	1/5/11	11476	11476	0
7	Fascinating Oven Supply	1006	1/5/11	4958	0	4958
8	Savory Glass Inc.	1007	1/5/11	11243	11243	0
9	Superior Bobsled Corporation	1008	1/5/11	4419	4419	0
10	Hip Lawn Corporation	1009	1/5/11	12562	12562	0
11	Savory Glass Inc.	1010	1/5/11	7409	7409	0
12	Fascinating Oven Supply	1011	1/6/11	8141	0	8141
13	Steadfast Meter Inc.	1012	1/6/11	2744	2744	0
14	Hip Lawn Corporation	1013	1/6/11	4876	4876	0

Figure 27.33
The goal is to provide a subset of this data to each customer.

Your first pass at a well-commented macro might look like this:

```
Sub ProduceReportForEachCustomer()
    ' Define object variables for new workbook
    ' Suffix of N means New
    Dim WBN As Workbook
    Dim WSN As Worksheet
    ' Define object variables for the current workbook
    ' Suffix of O means Old
    Dim WBO As Workbook
    Dim WSO As Worksheet
    Set WBO = ActiveWorkbook
    Set WSO = ActiveSheet
    ' Find the FinalRow in today's dataset
    FinalRow = Cells(Rows.Count, 1).End(xlUp).Row

    ' Use an Advanced filter to copy unique customers
    ' from column A to column H
    ' ???

    'Find the final customer in column H
    FinalCust = Cells(Rows.Count, 8).End(xlUp).Row
    ' Loop through each customer
    For x = 2 To FinalCust
        ' Turn on the AutoFilter for this customer
        ' ???

        ' Create a new workbook
        Set WBN = Workbooks.Add
        Set WSN = WBN.Worksheets(1)

        ' In the original workbook, select visible cells
        ' ???
```

```
        ' Copy the selection to the new workbook
        Selection.Copy Destination:=WSN.Cells(3, 1)


        ' AutoFit columns in the new workbook
        WSN.Columns.AutoFit


        ' Add a title to the new workbook
        WSN.Range("A1").Value = _
            "Recap of Purchases for " & WSN.Cells(4, 1).Value


        ' Save the new book
        WBN.SaveAs Filename:="C:\" & WSN.Cells(4, 1).Value & ".xlsx"
        WBN.Close SaveChanges:=False


        'Return to the original workbook
        WBO.Activate
        WSN.Select
    Next x

End Sub
```

The following sections describe that to create this macro, you need to figure out how to code the advanced filter to copy a unique list of customers to Column H. You then need to figure out how to apply a filter to Column A. Finally, you need to figure out how to select only the visible cells from the filter.

Using the Advanced Filter for Unique Records

You need to figure out how to use an advanced filter to finish the following section of code.

```
' Find the FinalRow in today's dataset
FinalRow = Cells(Rows.Count, 1).End(xlUp).Row

' Use an Advanced filter to copy unique customers
' from column A to column H
' ???
```

To use an advanced filter on this section of code, follow these steps:

1. Turn on the macro recorder.

2. On the Data tab, in the Sort & Filter group, click the Advanced icon to open the Advanced Filter dialog.

3. Select the option Copy to Another Location.

4. Adjust the list range to refer only to Column A. The copy-to range will be Cell H1.

5. Check the Unique Records Only box.

6. When the dialog looks as shown in Figure 27.34, click OK. The result is a new range of data in Column H, with each customer listed just once, as shown in Figure 27.35.

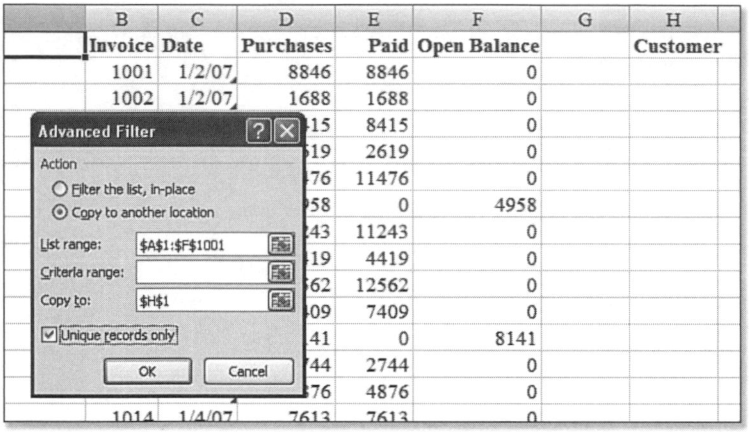

Figure 27.34
Using an advanced filter to get a unique list of customers.

Figure 27.35
The advanced filter produces a list of customers for the macro to loop through.

7. On the Developer tab, click Stop Recording.

8. Use the Macros button to select Macro1 and then select Edit.

Even though the Advanced Filter dialog is still one of the most complicated facets of Excel 2010, the recorded macro is remarkably simple:

```
Sub Macro1()
'
' Macro1 Macro
'


'
    Range("A1:A1001").AdvancedFilter Action:=xlFilterCopy, CopyToRange:=Range( _
        "H1"), Unique:=True
    Range("H1").Select
End Sub
```

In your macro, there is no reason to select Cell H1 to delete that line of code. The remaining problem is that the macro recorder hard-coded that today's data set contains 1,001 rows. You might want to generalize this to handle any number of rows. The follow code reflects these changes:

```
FinalRow = Cells(Rows.Count, 1).End(xlUp).Row
Range("A1:A" & FinalRow) .AdvancedFilter Action:=xlFilterCopy, _
    CopyToRange:=Range("H1"), Unique:=True
```

Using AutoFilter

When you have a list of customers, the macro will loop through each customer. The goal is to use an AutoFilter to display only the records for each particular customer. Next, finish this section of code as follows:

```
' Loop through each customer
For x = 2 To FinalCust
    ' Turn on the AutoFilter for this customer
    ' ???
```

 tip

Even though you have an existing Module1 with your code, Excel chooses to record the new macro into a new module. Therefore, you need to copy recorded code from Module2 and then use the Project Explorer to switch to Module1 to paste the code into your macro.

To apply an AutoFilter to this section of code, follow these steps:

1. On the Developer tab, select Record Macro.

2. On the Home tab, select the icon Sort & Filter—Filter. Drop-down arrows are turned on for each field.

3. In the drop-down in Cell A1, clear Select All and then select Hip Lawn Corporation.

4. Back on the Developer tab, stop recording the macro.

5. Use the Macros button to locate and edit Macro2 as follows:

```
Sub Macro2()
'
' Macro2 Macro
```

```
    Range("A2").Select
    Application.CutCopyMode = False
    Selection.AutoFilter
    Selection.AutoFilter Field:=1, Criteria1:="Hip Lawn Corporation"
End Sub
```

The macro recorder always does too much selecting. You rarely have to select something before you can operate on it. You can theorize that the only line of this macro that matters is the `Selection.AutoFilter` line. Because you will always be looking at the AutoFilter drop-down in Cell A1, you can replace `Selection` with `Range("A1")`. Rather than continually ask for one specific customer, you can replace the end of the line with a reference to a cell in Column H:

```
Range("A1").AutoFilter Field:=1, Criteria1:=Cells(x, 8).Value
```

Selecting Visible Cells Only

After you use the AutoFilter in the macro, you see records for only one customer. However, as you can see in Figure 27.36, the other records are still there, but they are hidden. If you copied the range to a new worksheet, all the hidden rows would come along, and you would end up with 20 copies of your entire data set.

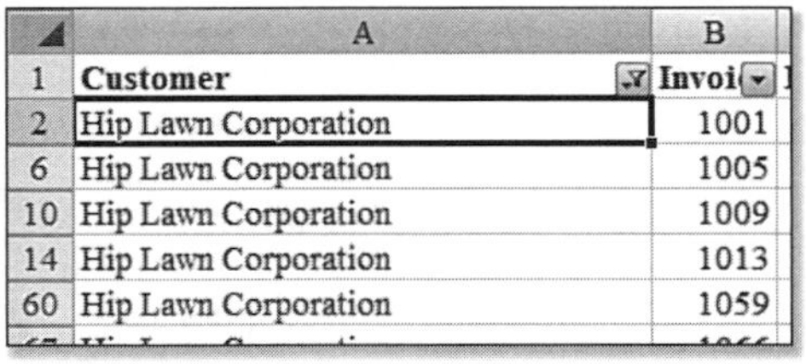

◢	A	B
1	**Customer** ▾	Invoi ▾
2	Hip Lawn Corporation	1001
6	Hip Lawn Corporation	1005
10	Hip Lawn Corporation	1009
14	Hip Lawn Corporation	1013
60	Hip Lawn Corporation	1059

Figure 27.36
If you copy this range to a new worksheet, the hidden rows copy as well.

The long way to select visible cells only is to press F5 to display the GoTo dialog. In the GoTo dialog, click the Special button and then click Visible Cells Only. However, the shortcut is to press Alt+;.

To learn how to select visible cells only in VBA, record the macro by following these steps:

1. Select the data in Columns A through F.

2. Turn on the macro recorder and press Alt+;.

3. Stop the macro recorder. You should see that the recorded macro has just one line of code:

```
Sub Macro5()

' Macro5 Macro
'
```

```
'
        Selection.SpecialCells(xlCellTypeVisible).Select
End Sub
```

In your original outline of the macro, you had contemplated selecting visible cells only and then doing the copy in another statement, like this:

```
' In the original workbook, select visible cells
' ???


' Copy the selection to the new workbook
Selection.Copy Destination:=WSN.Cells(3, 1)
            Instead, copy the visible cells in one statement:
' In the original workbook, select visible cells
WSO.Range("A1:F" & FinalRow).SpecialCells(xlCellTypeVisible).Copy _
    Destination:=WSN.Cells(3, 1)
```

Combination Macro Example: Putting It All Together

The following macro started as a bunch of comments and a skeleton of a loop:

```
Sub ProduceReportForEachCustomerFinished()
    ' Define object variables for new workbook
    Dim WBN As Workbook
    Dim WSN As Worksheet
    ' Define object variables for the current workbook
    Dim WBO As Workbook
    Dim WSO As Worksheet
    Set WBO - ActiveWorkbook
    Set WSO = ActiveSheet

    ' Find the FinalRow in today's dataset
    FinalRow = Range("A60000").End(xlUp).Row

    ' Use an Advanced filter to copy unique customers
    ' from column A to column H
    Range("A1:A" & FinalRow).AdvancedFilter Action:=xlFilterCopy, _
        CopyToRange:=Range("H1"), Unique:=True

    'Find the final customer in column H
    FinalCust = Range("H1").End(xlDown).Row

    ' Loop through each customer
    For x = 2 To FinalCust
        ' Turn on the AutoFilter for this customer
        Range("A1").AutoFilter Field:=1, Criteria1:=Cells(x, 8).Value

        ' Create a new workbook
```

```
        Set WBN = Workbooks.Add
        Set WSN = WBN.Worksheets(1)

        ' In the original workbook, select visible cells
        WSO.Range("A1:F" & FinalRow).SpecialCells(xlCellTypeVisible).Copy _
            Destination:=WSN.Cells(3, 1)

        ' AutoFit columns in the new workbook
        WSN.Columns.AutoFit

        ' Add a title to the new workbook
        WSN.Range("A1").Value = "Recap of Purchases for " & WSN.Cells(4, 1).Value

        ' Save the new book
        WBN.SaveAs Filename:="C:\" & WSN.Cells(4, 1).Value & ".xls"
        WBN.Close SaveChanges:=False

        'Return to the original workbook
        WBO.Activate
        WSO.Select
    Next x


End Sub
```

After doing three small tests with the macro recorder, you were able to fill in the sections to copy the customer records to a new workbook. After running this macro, you should have a new workbook for each customer on your hard drive, ready to be distributed via e-mail.

VBA macros open up a wide possibility of automation for Excel worksheets. Any time you are faced with a daunting, mindless task, you can turn it into a challenging exercise by trying to design a macro to do the task instead. It usually takes less time to design a macro than it does to complete the task. You should save every macro you write. Soon you will have a library of macros that handle many common tasks, and they will allow you to develop macros faster. The next time you need to perform a similar task, you can roll out the macro and perform the steps in seconds instead of hours.

MORE TIPS AND TRICKS FOR EXCEL 2010

This book is full of tips and tricks throughout the chapters. This particular chapter is a catch-all for some of the tips that did not find a home elsewhere in the book.

A few of the features discussed in this chapter, such as the Equation Editor, are new in Excel 2010. Other features, such as multithreaded calculation, digital signatures, and translations, were new to Excel 2007. Some, such as protecting a worksheet, have been around for a decade but are overlooked by most people who use Excel.

 tip

If you like the tips in this chapter, check out Learn Excel from MrExcel: 427 Excel Mysteries Solved at www.mrexcel.com/learn-excel.html. It is filled with 427 quick tips like these. You can also download four or five tips every week—absolutely free—by signing up at the website.

Speeding Up Calculation by Using Multithreaded Calculation

For the first time, Excel 2007 was written to take advantage of dual-core machines (that is, machines with two CPUs). Multithreaded calculation allows Excel to spot formulas that can be calculated concurrently and then run those formulas on multiple processors simultaneously.

The first time you calculate a spreadsheet in Excel 2010 on a dual-core machine, Excel has to examine the formula dependency table and then perform the calculation. The process of deciding which formulas can be calculated concurrently causes the first calculation to take as long as normal. The time required for the next calculation dramatically decreases. In a perfect example, a workbook with Monte Carlo simulation, the reduction is linear: A workbook calculates in half the time. In other workbooks, the reduction is significant but not linear.

To enable multithreaded calculation, follow these steps:

1. Select File, Options. The Excel Options dialog appears.

2. Select the Advanced category and scroll down to the Formulas section.

3. Select Enable Multithreaded Calculation, as shown in Figure 28.1.

4. Unless you are using XLL add-ins, select the Use All Processors setting. If you are using XLL add-ins, see the following note.

Watching the Results of a Distant Cell

Sometimes you need to keep an eye on a single result on a worksheet other than the one you're currently in. For example, you might have a workbook in which assumptions on multiple worksheets produce a final ROI. As you change the assumptions, it would be good to know the impact on ROI.

It can be time consuming to constantly switch back and forth to the results worksheet after every change. Instead, you can set up

 note

It is possible to set the calculation threads to a number higher than the number of processors. This is beneficial if your workbook is making calls to XLL user-defined functions on a server. If each function requires 15 seconds and you have a dozen such functions, Excel must wait for each function to finish before calling the next function, requiring 3 minutes to calculate. If you set the number of threads to 12, Excel could call all 12 XLL functions simultaneously, reducing calculation time to less than 30 seconds.

The option for allowing XLL functions to run on a compute cluster is new in Excel 2010. Some applications in the insurance industry have workbooks that take 2 to 3 days to calculate. Microsoft is now supporting a High Performance Computing Cluster for processing of the XLL functions. If you are interested, type "HPC XLL" into a search engine to read about case studies where people have 100 desktop computers calculating their Excel workbook.

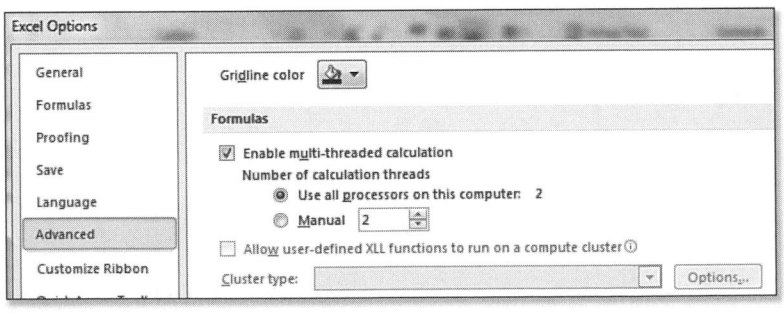

Figure 28.1
The multithreaded calculation option is buried in the Advanced category of the Excel Options dialog.

a watch to show you the current value of the distant cell(s). People developing VBA macros in Excel have had a Watch Window dialog available in VBA for more than a decade. Microsoft finally added a Watch Window dialog to Excel 2003.

To set up a watch, follow these steps:

1. Select Formulas, Formula Auditing, Watch Window to display the floating Watch Window dialog over the worksheet.

2. Click Add Watch in the Watch Window dialog.

3. In the Add Watch dialog, click the RefEdit button and then click the cells that you want to watch.

4. Click Add to add the cell(s) to the Watch Window dialog.

5. Repeat steps 2–4 as necessary.

6. Position the Watch Window dialog in an out-of-the-way location above your worksheet so that you can continue to work.

Every time you make a change to the worksheet, the Watch Window dialog shows you the current value of the watched cells, as shown in Figure 28.2.

 tip

You can double-click any entry in the Watch Window dialog to scroll to that cell.

Figure 28.2
The Watch Window dialog shows you the results of key cells that you define. These cells can be in far-off cells or on other worksheets.

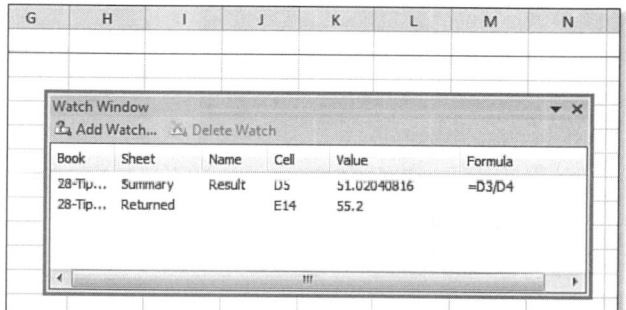

When the watch is defined, you can toggle the Watch Window dialog by using the Watch Window icon in the Formulas tab.

Opening the Same Files Every Day

In some jobs, you might have to open the same workbooks at the same time to perform a certain recurring task. For example, perhaps you spend an hour every morning recording new accounts receivable balances while processing the morning postal mail. This task might require you to open the AR.xlsm file, the Customer.xlsm file, and the BankDeposit.xlsm file. If these three files are stored in different folders, it can be slightly tedious to open each document one at a time.

After opening the files manually, you can specify that the files belong to a workspace. Then when you open that workspace, Excel opens all the documents associated with the workspace.

To set up a workspace, follow these steps:

1. Close all open workbooks.

2. Open each workbook associated with the task.

3. From the View tab, select Window, Save Workspace. The Save Workspace dialog appears.

4. Browse to a location to save the workspace. Give the workspace a name. Click Save. Note that the file is saved with an .xlw extension.

The next time you need to open those files, select File, Open and select the XLW file.

If you later rename one of the files or move one of them to a new location, you have to re-create and resave the workspace.

Comparing Documents Side by Side with Synchronous Scrolling

Suppose you have two documents that should be nearly identical. Perhaps you started with a workbook and then routed the workbook to a co-worker. You have your original workbook and the new workbook, and you want to compare them visually.

A feature introduced in Excel 2003 lets you scroll both windows at the same time. You can arrange the windows so that they are both visible. As you scroll the active document, the other document scrolls at the same rate. This can allow you to compare the documents visibly.

To compare two documents side by side in this manner, follow these steps:

1. Close all other documents.

2. Open the first workbook.

3. Open the second workbook.

4. Select View, Window, View Side by Side.

5. If you have more than two workbooks open, you have to choose just one of the other workbooks to be used for the comparison. The two workbooks appear together.

6. If the windows are split horizontally, one above the other, select View, Window, Arrange, Vertical to have the worksheets appear side by side.

7. Begin scrolling through the data using the scrollbar or the wheel on your scroll mouse.

Synchronous scrolling does not work well if someone deleted or inserted extra rows in one workbook. To solve this problem, follow these steps:

1. If one worksheet has extra rows and is out of sync with the other worksheet, click View, Window, Synchronous Scrolling to temporarily turn off this feature.

2. Use the arrow keys or scrollbar to line up the worksheets. Scroll one worksheet so that both worksheets have the same record as the top row in the window.

3. Click View, Window, Synchronous Scrolling again to turn the feature back on. You can now continue scrolling the rows below the mismatched rows.

For example, someone inserted five blank rows in the right document in Figure 28.3. To fix this problem, turn off Synchronous Scrolling, line up Row 20 on the left with Row 15 on the right, and turn scrolling back on.

Figure 28.3
Use View Side by Side with Synchronous Scrolling to visually compare two workbooks.

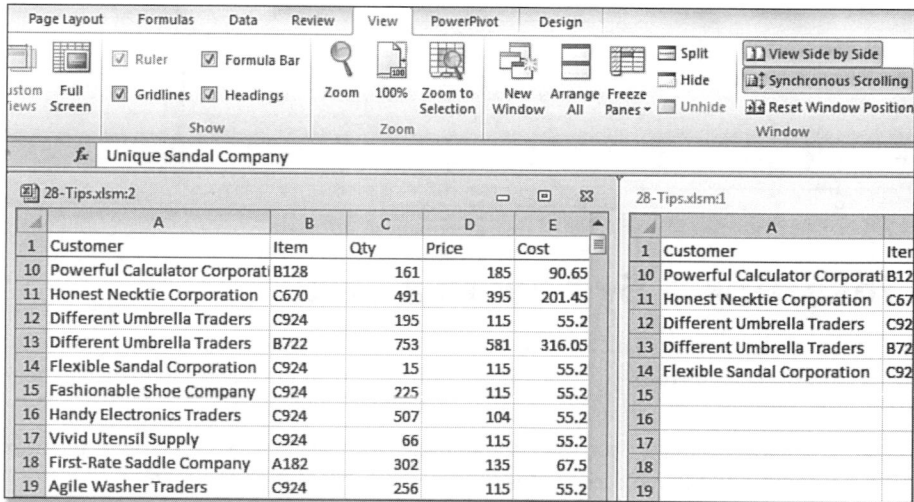

Calculating a Formula in Slow Motion

If you have a particularly complicated formula, you can watch how Excel calculates the formula in slow motion. This can help you locate any logic errors in the worksheet.

To evaluate a formula in slow motion, follow these steps:

1. Select the cell that contains the formula.

2. Select Formulas, Formula Auditing, Evaluate Formula. The Evaluate Formula dialog box appears, showing the formula. One element of the formula is underlined, indicating that this element will be calculated next.

3. To see the value of the underlined element immediately, click Evaluate.

4. If you want to see how that element is calculated, instead of clicking Evaluate, click Step In. Excel shows the formula for that element.

 tip

Watch for the underlined portion of the formula because that is the element to be calculated next. Using the Evaluate Formula dialog enables you to verify the order of operations that Excel uses.

5. Eventually, the final level is evaluated to a number. Click Step Out to return one level up the dialog.

6. Continue clicking Evaluate until you arrive at the answer shown in the cell.

Figure 28.4 shows an Evaluate Formula dialog after Evaluate was clicked a few times.

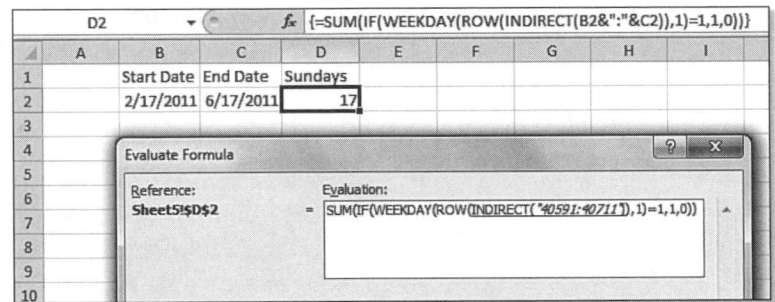

Figure 28.4
The Evaluate Formula dialog allows you to watch the formula calculation in slow motion.

Inserting a Symbol in a Cell

Obscure key combinations are available to insert many symbols. However, you do not have to learn any of them. Instead, you can use the Symbol icon on the Insert tab to display the Symbol dialog box.

In the Symbol dialog, you scroll through many subsets of the current font. When you find the desired symbol, select it and click the Insert button, as shown in Figure 28.5.

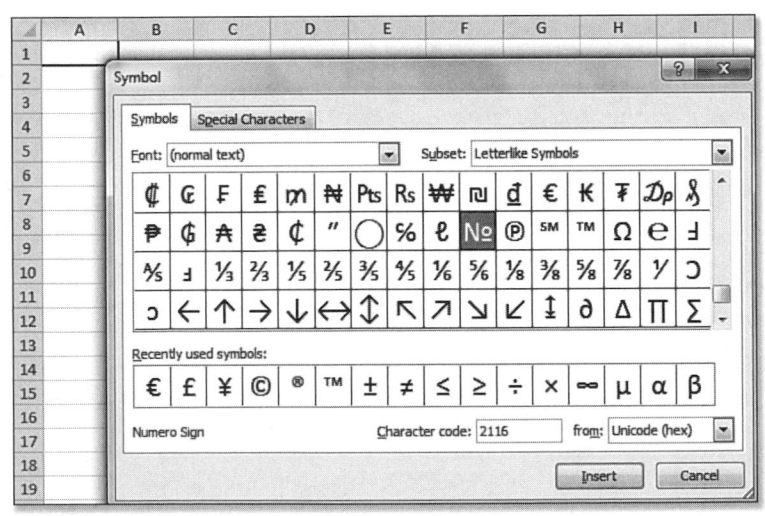

Figure 28.5
Instead of memorizing arcane key combinations, you can use Insert Symbol to add symbols to a workbook.

Edit an Equation

Microsoft Word 2007 introduced a new equation editor. This editor has been added to Excel 2010.

The Equation drop-down on the Insert tab offers nine prebuilt equations. If you happen to need one of these equations, you can select it from the drop-down (see Figure 28.6).

Figure 28.6
A few common equations are prebuilt.

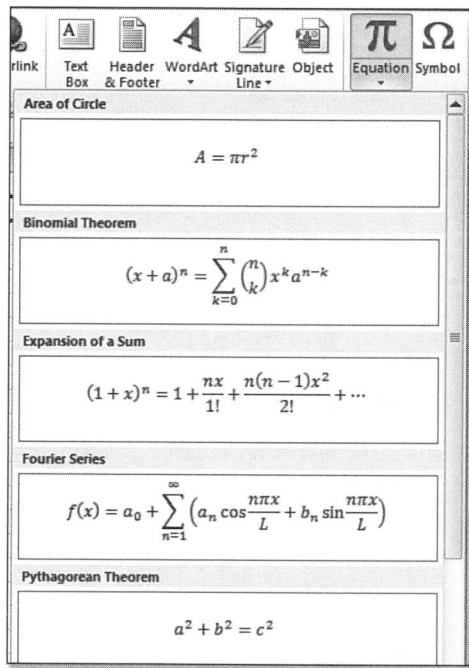

If you need to build some other equation, insert a shape in the worksheet first. While the shape is selected, use Insert, Equation, Insert New Equation. A blank equation is added to the shape.

It seems very touchy, but you have to be inside the equation to have the Equation Tools Design tab showing. From the Ribbon, you can open the various drop-downs to insert a mathematical symbol. In Figure 28.7, some symbols have three placeholders. These are tiny text boxes where you can type various values.

 To see a demo of using the Equation editor, search for Excel In Depth 28 at YouTube.

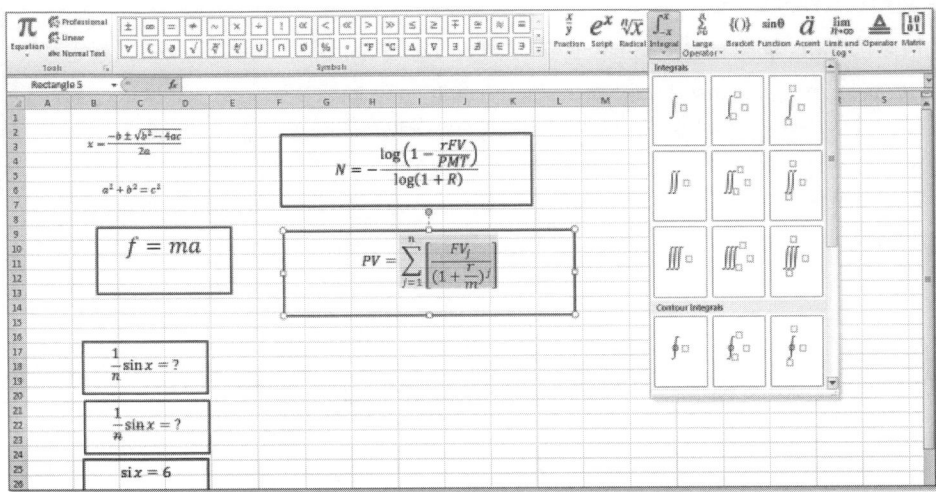

Figure 28.7
Most equations will be built using the dropdowns on the Equation Tools Design tab.

Adding a Digital Signature Line to a Workbook

You've probably encountered web pages where the authenticity of the web owner is verified with a digital certificate. Most likely, you notice this when the person's certificate has expired.

Microsoft has added a similar concept to Microsoft Excel 2010 and Microsoft Word 2010. When you attach a digital signature to a document, you are authenticating that you are really you. This process helps to prevent others from altering your work. After you sign a document, it is converted to read-only to ensure that no one changes the document after you sign it.

Digital signatures are provided by a third-party certifying authority. There is a fee for this service. To purchase a digital signature, you select Insert, Text, Signature Line, Add Signature Services. This leads to a list of approved digital certificate providers. Choose a provider and follow the steps on the provider's website to purchase and install the signature.

To add a digital signature to a file, open the file and then select Insert, Text, Digital Signature. Then right-click the signature and select Signature Setup to access the dialog box shown in Figure 28.8.

To sign a signature line, follow these steps:

1. Double-click the signature line in the document. The Sign dialog appears.

2. In the Sign dialog, do one of the following:

- Type your name in the box next to the X to add a printed version of your signature.

- Click Select Image and choose a graphics file of your signature.

- On a tablet PC, sign your name in the box by using the inking feature.

Figure 28.8
After adding a signature, right-click to access the Signature Setup dialog.

Your document is now electronically signed. This marks the document as final, as shown in Figure 28.9.

Figure 28.9
Signing a document marks it as final. If someone changes the document, the signature disappears.

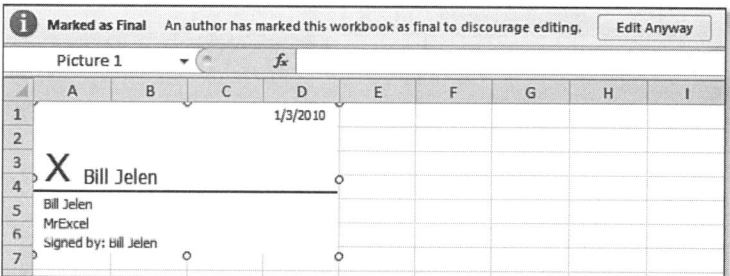

Protecting a Worksheet

If you have many formulas in a worksheet, you might want to prevent others from changing them. In a typical scenario, your worksheet might have some input variables at the top. You may want to allow those items to be changed, but you might not want your formulas to be changed.

To protect a worksheet, follow these steps:

1. Select the input cells in your worksheet. These are the cells that you want to allow someone to change.

2. Press Ctrl+1 or go to the Cells group of the Home tab and select Format, Format Cells. The Format Cells dialog appears.

3. On the Protection tab of the Format Cells dialog, clear the Locked check box, as shown in Figure 28.10. Click OK.

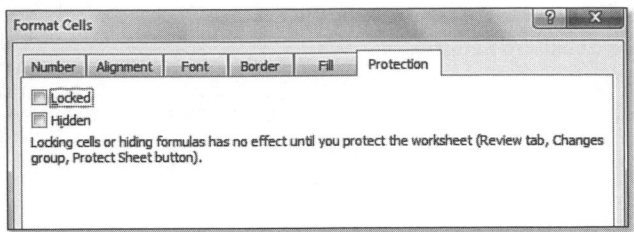

Figure 28.10
By default, all cells have their locked property set to TRUE.

4. Select Home, Cells, Protection, Protect Sheet. The Protect Sheet dialog appears, as shown in Figure 28.11.

Figure 28.11
Do not rely on this password for security, because it can easily be broken.

5. Optionally, change what is allowed to happen in the protected workbook.

6. Click OK to apply the protection.

Sharing a Workbook

Excel is not a collaborative program. Multiple people cannot access a workbook at the same time. Excel offers a Share Workbook icon under Review, Changes, Share Workbook. After you share a workbook, it becomes so limited that it is practically unusable.

Shared workbooks cannot have tables. You cannot insert blocks of cells in them. You cannot delete their worksheets. You cannot merge cells, add conditional formats, add validation, add charts, add pictures, add or change pivot tables, insert hyperlinks, use scenarios, use subtotals, write macros, or edit array formulas in shared workbooks. Basically, all but the simplest spreadsheets are unsharable.

You can find one new feature in Excel 2010 regarding sharing by selecting the Office icon and then Publish, Create Document Workspace. With the Create Document Workspace feature, you can save a workbook to a server and require others to check the file out before editing. This prevents multiple people from simultaneously editing the workbook.

Separating Text Based on a Delimiter

Depending on the source of your data, you might find that information is loaded into Excel with many fields in one cell. If the fields are separated by a character, you can separate the data into multiple columns. To do so, follow these steps:

1. Select the one-column range that contains multiple values in each cell.

2. Select Data, Data Tools, Convert Text to Column. Excel displays the Convert Text to Columns Wizard dialog.

3. In step 1 of the wizard, select Delimited and click Next.

4. In step 2 of the wizard, choose your delimiter. Excel offers check boxes for Tab, Semicolon, Comma, and Space. If your delimiter is something different, select the Other box and type the delimiter. Click Next.

5. In step 3 of the wizard, indicate whether any of your columns are dates. Click the column in the Data Preview section and then select Date in the Column Data Format section.

6. By default, Excel replaces the selected column and uses adjacent blank columns. To write the results to a different output area, enter a destination in step 3 of the wizard, as shown in Figure 28.12.

Figure 28.12
You specify field types and an output range in step 3 of the wizard.

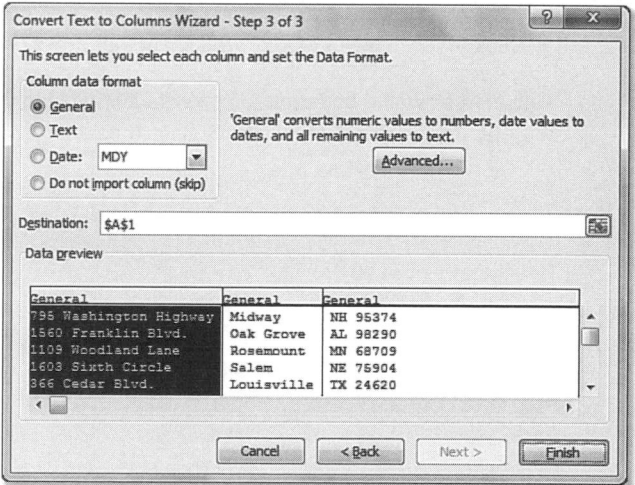

7. Click Finish to parse the column.

8. Excel does not automatically make the columns wide enough, so select the Cells section of the Home tab and then select Format, Width, AutoFit to make the output columns wide enough for the contents.

Translating Text

If you are a fan of AltaVista's Babel Fish Translation website, you can now perform a similar translation inside your Excel documents. The Babel Fish project is not a professional translator. The translations produced are often very rough and sometimes humorous.

However, if someone has sent you a document in a foreign language, you can convert the text from the foreign language to a form of broken English so that you can often get the basic meaning of the text.

Instead of using Babel Fish, the Excel 2010 translation service offers two services for most language pairs. Excel 2010 introduces the new Microsoft Translation service. You can change back to the Excel 2007 default of WorldLingo, which seems to provide a better translation.

The Excel 2010 service can translate only a single cell at a time. To use the service, follow these steps:

1. Select the cell containing text that you want to translate.

2. On the Review tab, click Translate.

3. In the Research task pane, choose a From and a To language. The Research pane shows you the translation, as shown in Figure 28.13.

4. Select the translated text by dragging over it with the mouse. Press Ctrl+C to copy the translation to the Clipboard.

5. Click in a cell in your Excel worksheet and press Ctrl+V to paste.

This feature would be far more powerful if you could translate entire blocks of cells and automatically return the translations in an adjacent column.

Figure 28.13
The translation service is not leaving me the wild one.

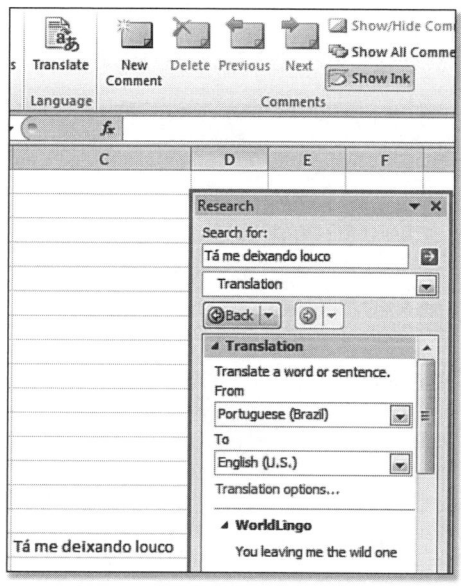

For more tips, subscribe to the free daily MrExcel iTunes podcast.
See www.mrexcel.com/podcast.shtml for details.

TOUR OF THE BEST ADD-INS
FOR EXCEL

Although Excel can do amazing things, it cannot do everything. Plenty of niche industries need more functions or more specialized operations than what is available in Excel.

Sometimes, someone recognizes a common need. After seeing dozens of questions in Excel newsgroups about converting uppercase to lowercase, for example, a developer might offer an add-in to make that task easier than the current five-step process.

Literally thousands of add-ins are available for Excel. This chapter is by no means a comprehensive list of available add-ins, but it contains some of my favorites.

Charting Utilities from Jon Peltier

Jon Peltier's website has always listed bizarre techniques for coaxing unusual charts out of Excel. Jon now offers the PTS Chart Utilities add-ins that enable you to easily make the following types of charts:

- Waterfall Charts

- Box and Whisker Charts

- Cluster Stack Charts (see Figure 29.1)

- Marimekko (Mosaic) Charts

- Dot Plot Charts

- Cascade Charts

Read more about Jon's add-in at http://peltiertech.com/Utility/.

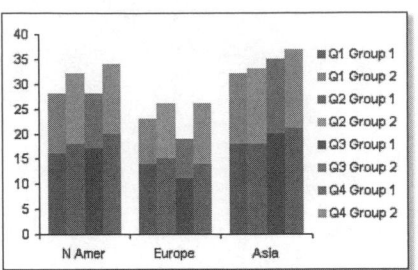

Figure 29.1
Jon Peltier simplifies the creation process for several unusual chart types.

Creating Dashboards by Using Speedometer Chart Creator

When executive dashboards became the rage, many people wanted to take the term literally and offer a series of speedometer charts on their dashboards. The circular chart shown in Figure 29.2, created using Speedometer Chart Creator from Mala Singh, has various colors around the perimeter of the speedometer. A pointer indicates today's value, and an alternate pointer shows yesterday's value, so you can see whether there has been improvement.

➡ *To purchase the speedometer chart creator, visit www.mrexcel.com/speedometer.html.*

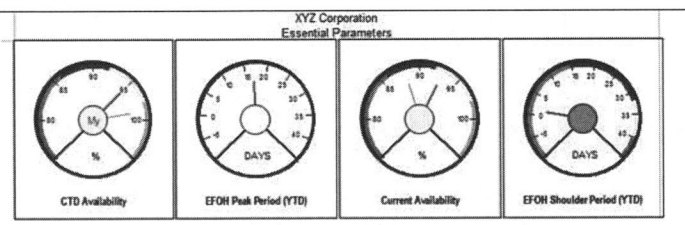

Figure 29.2
You can create dashboards by using the Speedometer Chart Creator from Mala Singh.

Add Labels to XY Charts

Adding labels to Scatter charts in Excel is a nightmare. Microsoft doesn't have an interest in fixing the problem, because any customers who need to label XY charts probably already use this free utility from Rob Bovey.

Rob's XY Chart Labeler is currently in its seventh release and is still free. It lets you specify any range to use as the labels for an XY chart, as well as control the positioning and color of the labels.

➡ *Download the chart labeler from www.appspro.com/Utilities/ChartLabeler.htm.*

Loading PDF Data to Excel by Using Able2Extract

People love sending data in PDF files. Now that Microsoft is providing a PDF creation utility, more and more documents will be emailed via PDF.

The authors of PDF documents often use PDF format to ensure that the data cannot be altered. Other times, the authors want to make sure that someone who does not have Excel can still view the data. Although these are fine ideas, getting data back out of PDF and into Excel is very difficult.

Data copied and pasted from PDF to Excel usually loses its columnar format. Able2Extract solves this problem. You simply open a PDF file in Able2Extract, and you can convert the contained data to Excel with one click. If you need absolute control, you can specify regions so that, for example, titles and headers beyond page 1 are not imported.

In some PDF files, the entire document is a scanned image of the original file. The Professional version of Able2Extract can even deal with these.

> *You can download a free trial version of Able2Extract from www.investintech.com/able2extract.html.*

Customizing the Ribbon Using CustomizeRibbon

Whereas it was extremely easy to customize the menus in Excel 2003, it is nearly impossible to do so in Excel 2007. You have to be a developer who can work with Ribbon XML to customize the ribbons.

Patrick Schmid wrote the must-have solution for any normal person who wants to customize the ribbons. His COM add-in adds a CustomizeRibbon icon to the View tab. You can then use CustomizeRibbon to add new groups to any tab or even add a new tab to the Ribbon.

> *Patrick plans to offer a limited freeware version and a more powerful version for sale. You can download or purchase Patrick's add-in from http://pschmid.net/office2007/ribboncustomizer/index.php.*

Accessing More Functions by Using MoreFunc.dll

MVP Laurent Longre offers a free Excel add-in that has 66 new functions. Although some of the functions are specialized, there are great functions of use to many people using Excel. The following are just some of the new functions:

- LastRow—This function finds the last filled row in any column.
- PageNum—This function finds the page number of any cell.
- SheetName—This function finds the name of the current sheet.
- WordCount—This function finds the number of words in text.
- NBText—This function spells out a number as text in any of 13 languages.

- `ISO.Weeknum`—This function finds the ISO-compliant week number of a day.

- `CountIf.3D`—This function is the same as `Countif` but for 3-D references.

▶ *You can download the MoreFunc.dll for free from http://xcell05.free.fr/.*

▶ *To merge all workbooks in a folder, Ron de Bruin offers many free add-ins at www.rondebruin. nl/addins.htm. One of the best is his RDBMerge add-in, which allows Excel to read all the workbooks in a folder and merge them into a single worksheet. This is great for doing budget roll-ups.*

General Purpose Utility Suites

There are many utilities that add a new suite of commands to Excel. These utilities generally fall into one of two camps. The first set focuses on tasks for formatting worksheets. They might offer a way to format every nth row in a certain color or convert a range of uppercase data to proper case, and so on. The second set is designed to simplify data analysis.

- ASAP Utilities offers a noncommercial, free version: www.asap-utilities.com/.

- JMT Utilities offers a free version: www.andrewsexceltips.net/JMT%20Full%20List.htm.

- J-Walk's Power Utility Pack: http://spreadsheetpage.com/index.php/pupv6/home.

Utilities for Data Analysis Tasks

Two other utilities focus on data analysis tasks. The tagline for DigDB offers to let you do Access with Excel. When you have to match and merge massive amounts of data in Excel, these utilities simplify the process:

- DigDB offers a suite of 40 separate Excel add-ins that simplify data analysis. Download a trial from www.digdb.com/.

- Easy-XL offers a similar integrated suite of data processing commands, including support for macro recording. Download a trial from www.easy-xl.com/.

▶ *You can also read more about the Easy-XL utility in Chapter 38, "Saving Time Using the Easy-XL Program."*

FORMATTING WORKSHEETS

Formatting adds interest and readability to documents. If you have taken time to create a spreadsheet, you should also take the time to make sure that it is eye catching and readable.

You can format documents in Excel 2010 with any of these three methods:

- **Use tables styles—Y**ou can use table styles to format a table with banded rows, accents for totals, and so on.

  ➡ *Refer back to Chapter 19, "Fabulous Table Intelligence," for more information on the use table styles method.*

- **Use cell styles—**You can use cell styles to identify titles, headings, and accent cells. The advantage of using cell styles is that you can quickly apply new themes to change the look and feel of a document.

- **Use formatting commands—**You can use traditional formatting commands to change the font, borders, fill, numeric formatting, columns widths, and row heights. The usual formatting icons are now found on the Home tab as well as in the Format Cells dialog box.

Why Format Worksheets?

You can open a blank worksheet and fill it with data without ever touching any of Excel's formatting commands. The result is functional, but not necessarily readable or eye catching.

Figure 30.1 contains an unformatted report in Excel.

	A	B	C	D	E	F	G
1	Astonishing Treadmill Inc.						
2	Sales Forecast						
3	2011						
4							
5	Line	Product	Jan	Feb	Mar	Q1	Apr
6	Consumer	A451	278.00	285.00	271.00	834.00	291.0
7		A636	357.00	334.00	387.00	1078.00	456.0
8		A686	161.00	144.00	244.00	549.00	165.0
9		B416	428.00	443.00	425.00	1296.00	448.0
10		B519	711.00	706.00	764.00	2181.00	697.0
11		D553	128.00	116.00	104.00	348.00	147.0
12		D555	376.00	405.00	378.00	1159.00	471.0
13		D801	353.00	352.00	377.00	1082.00	366.0
14		D914	296.00	274.00	279.00	849.00	394.0
15		E196	625.00	611.00	724.00	1960.00	700.0
16		E476	458.00	471.00	479.00	1408.00	484.0
17		Subtotal	4171.00	4141.00	4432.00	12744.00	4619.0
18	Profession	K121	174.00	244.00	149.00	567.00	193.0
19		K658	245.00	321.00	272.00	838.00	225.0

Figure 30.1
After typing data into a spreadsheet, you have an unformatted report.

Figure 30.2 contains exactly the same data but with formatting applied. The formatted report in Figure 30.2 is more interesting and easier to read than the unformatted one for the following reasons:

- The reader can instantly focus on the totals for each line.
- Headings are aligned with the data.
- Borders break the data into sections.
- Accent colors highlight the subtotals and totals.
- The title is prominent, in a larger font, and a headline typeface is used.
- Numeric formatting has removed the extra decimal places and added thousands separators.
- The column widths are adjusted properly.
- A short row adds a visual break between the product lines.
- Headings for each product line are rotated, merged, and centered.

The formatting applied to Figure 30.2 takes a few extra minutes, but it dramatically increases the readability of the report. Because you have taken the time to put the worksheet together, it is worth a couple of extra minutes to make the worksheet easier for the consumer to read.

Figure 30.2
Readability is improved after formatting the report.

Headings aligned with data
Bold text
Larger font size — Italic text — Numeric formatting adds commas — Borders between sections

Line	Product	Jan	Feb	Mar	Q1	Apr	May	Jun	Q2	Jul	Aug	Sep	Q3	Oct	Nov	Dec	Q4	Total
	Astonishing Treadmill Inc.																	
	Sales Forecast																	
	2011																	
Consumer	A451	278	285	271	834	291	332	294	917	254	258	259	771	273	473	302	1,048	3,570
	A636	357	334	387	1,078	456	358	381	1,195	440	376	363	1,179	340	468	344	1,152	4,604
	A686	161	144	244	549	165	225	213	603	170	140	239	549	156	256	185	597	2,298
	B416	428	443	425	1,296	448	432	425	1,305	416	403	443	1,262	429	519	580	1,528	5,391
	B519	711	706	764	2,181	697	789	766	2,252	771	714	690	2,175	718	862	686	2,266	8,874
	D553	128	116	104	348	147	194	117	458	116	153	115	384	123	307	257	687	1,877
	D555	376	405	378	1,159	471	450	391	1,312	385	374	393	1,152	479	458	400	1,337	4,960
	D801	353	352	377	1,082	366	354	456	1,176	350	336	345	1,031	372	458	371	1,201	4,490
	D914	296	274	279	849	394	315	311	1,020	362	351	374	1,087	324	377	272	973	3,929
	E196	625	611	724	1,960	700	651	623	1,974	687	626	704	2,017	643	807	607	2,057	8,008
	E476	458	471	479	1,408	484	463	480	1,427	446	485	530	1,461	456	649	622	1,727	6,023
	Subtotal	**4,171**	**4,141**	**4,432**	**12,744**	**4,619**	**4,563**	**4,457**	**13,639**	**4,397**	**4,216**	**4,455**	**13,068**	**4,313**	**5,634**	**4,626**	**14,573**	**54,024**
Professional	K121	174	244	149	567	193	259	261	713	196	273	172	641	199	271	300	770	2,691
	K658	245	321	272	838	225	235	236	696	319	240	254	813	241	345	225	811	3,158
	N713	301	368	325	994	289	329	311	929	329	299	312	940	395	405	459	1,259	4,122
	O855	720	739	715	2,174	789	737	785	2,311	698	740	714	2,152	726	835	740	2,301	8,938
	O980	222	302	218	742	220	204	234	658	320	230	231	781	252	401	357	1,010	3,191
	P450	388	412	363	1,163	405	383	409	1,197	390	407	396	1,193	379	504	408	1,291	4,844
	R737	360	342	380	1,082	355	373	380	1,108	382	343	342	1,067	453	543	372	1,368	4,625
	S484	104	175	83	362	107	81	131	319	114	85	89	288	107	228	95	430	1,399
	T676	683	733	782	2,198	713	776	711	2,200	750	751	780	2,281	779	806	833	2,418	9,097
	X388	281	283	294	858	283	280	350	913	337	306	297	940	276	377	267	920	3,631
	X862	367	451	423	1,241	373	355	359	1,087	389	385	397	1,171	348	496	369	1,213	4,712
	Z353	272	281	292	845	284	281	249	814	289	294	288	871	269	428	287	984	3,514
	Subtotal	**4,117**	**4,651**	**4,296**	**13,064**	**4,236**	**4,293**	**4,416**	**12,945**	**4,513**	**4,353**	**4,272**	**13,138**	**4,424**	**5,639**	**4,712**	**14,775**	**53,922**

Separator row
Merged, centered, and rotated headings

Using Traditional Formatting

Formatting is typically carried out in the Format Cells dialog box or using the formatting icons located on the Home tab.

In Excel 2010, Microsoft took the icons formerly on the Excel 2003 Formatting toolbar and arranged them in the Font, Alignment, and Number groups on the Home tab, as shown in Figure 30.3. Additional column- and row-formatting commands are available in the Format drop-down in the Cells group on the Home tab.

While analyzing SQM data from Microsoft Excel 2003, the Excel 2007 development team decided to promote some settings from the Format Cells dialog to the Home tab. Therefore, beginning with Excel 2007, icons for wrapping text, vertical alignment, and text rotation have been added to the icons that were on the Formatting toolbar in legacy versions of Excel.

Figure 30.3
Most icons from the former Formatting toolbar are in the Font, Alignment, and Number groups on the Home tab.

If your favorite setting is not on the Home tab, you can take one of the four entry paths to the Format Cells dialog, which provides access to additional settings, such as Shrink to Fit, Strikethrough, and more border settings:

- Press Ctrl+1, which is Ctrl and the number 1. You can press Ctrl+Shift+F to display the Font tab on the same dialog.

- Click the dialog launcher icons in the lower-right corner of the Font, Alignment, or Number groups. Each icon opens the dialog, with the focus on a different tab.

- Right-click any cell and select Format Cells.

- Select Format Cells from the Format dropdown on the Home tab.

As shown in Figure 30.4, the Format Cells dialog includes the following six tabs:

- **Number**—Gives you absolute control over numeric formatting. You can choose from 96,885 built-in formats or use the Custom category to create your own.

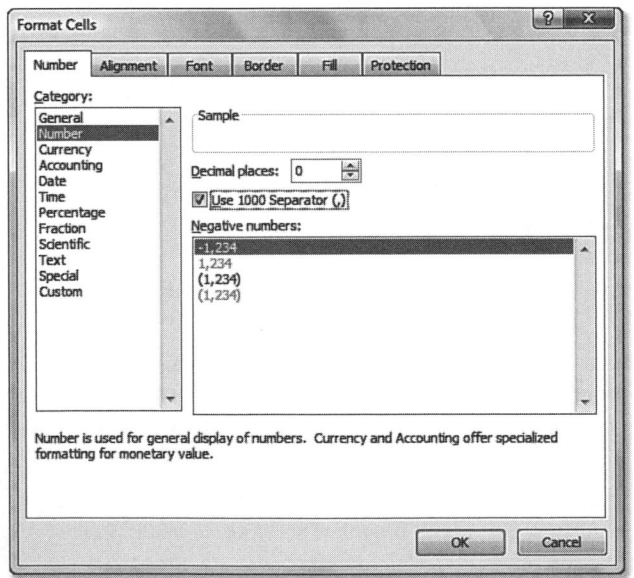

Figure 30.4
The Format Cells dialog offers complete control over cell formatting. You can visit this dialog when the icons on the ribbon do not provide enough detail.

- **Alignment**—Offers settings for horizontal alignment, vertical alignment, rotation, wrap, merge, and shrinking to fit.

- **Font**—Controls font, size, style, underline, color, strikethrough, superscript, and subscript.

- **Border**—Controls line style and color for each of the four borders and the diagonals on each cell.

- **Fill**—Offers 16 million fill colors and patterns. Beginning with Excel 2007, cell gradients are available.

- **Protection**—Used to lock or unlock certain cells.

➡️*See Chapter 37, "Excel Web App and Other Ways to Share Workbooks," for more information.*

Changing Numeric Formats by Using the Home Tab

If you ever shop for hardware at a general-purpose store, you have probably experienced how they can have almost what you need, but never exactly what you need. At this point, you probably curse your decision to stop at the general-purpose retailer and drive another mile down the road to Home Depot or Lowe's, where they always have exactly what you need.

Using the Number group on the Home tab is like shopping at a general-purpose retailer. It has many settings for numeric formatting, but often they are not exactly what you need. When this happens, you end up visiting the Number tab on the Format Cells dialog.

To start, there are three icons: currency, percentage, and comma style. The Percentage icon is useful. Unfortunately, the Currency and Comma icons apply an Accounting style to a cell, and the Accounting style is inappropriate for everyone except accountants. Furthermore, these three icons are not toggle buttons, which means that when you use one of them, there is not an icon to go back quickly to a general style, other than Undo.

The Increase and Decrease Decimal icons are useful. Each click of one of these buttons forces Excel to show one more or one fewer decimal place. If you have numbers showing two decimal places in all cells, two clicks on the Decrease Decimal icon solves the problem.

Figure 30.5 shows the Currency, Percentage, Comma, Increase Decimal, and Decrease Decimal buttons in the Number group of the Home tab.

Above the five buttons in the Number group is a new drop-down that has a dozen popular number styles. Figure 30.6 shows the styles in the drop-down. The Range A2:F12 shows these styles applied to four different numbers.

 tip

Excel uses the value in the active cell for each of the formats inside the dropdown, and no sample if the cell is blank.

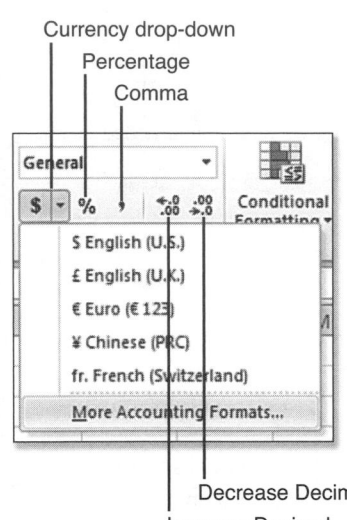

Currency drop-down
Percentage
Comma

Decrease Decimal
Increase Decimal

Figure 30.5
The Currency and Comma icons both use an Accounting style. This is wonderful for accountants, but others should resist using them.

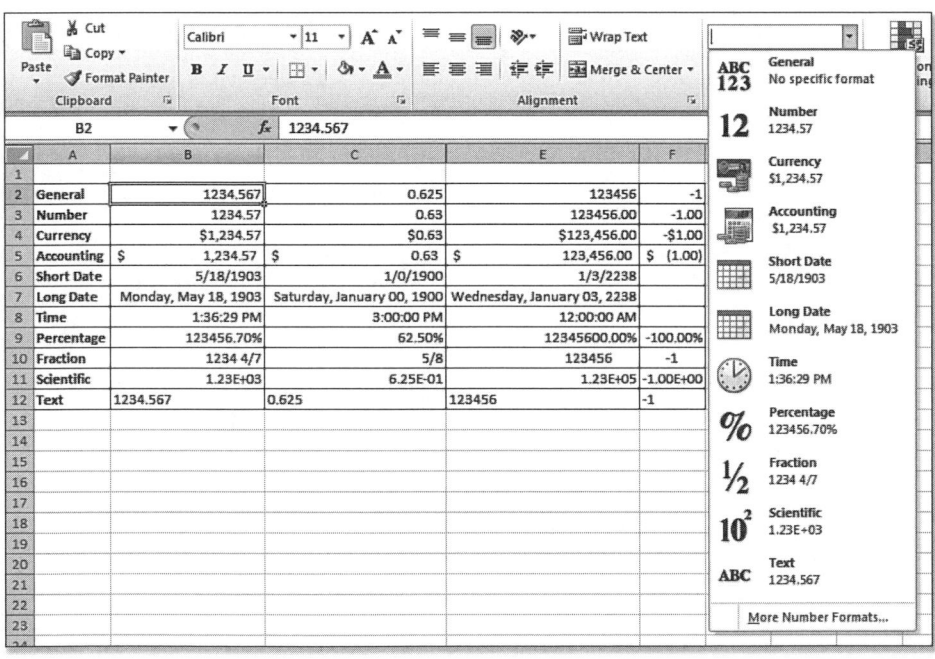

Figure 30.6
Excel 2010 offers 11 popular number styles in this drop-down.

The following list shows some comments and cautions about using the number styles from the drop-down in the Home tab.

- General Format is a number format. Decimal places are shown if needed. No thousands separator is used. A negative number is shown with a minus sign before the number.

- Number does not use a thousands separator. It forces two decimal places, even with numbers that do not need decimal places, such as in Cell E3.

- Currency is a useful format for everyone. The currency symbol is shown immediately before the number. All numbers are expressed with two decimal places. Negatives are shown with a hyphen before the number.

- Accounting is great for financial statements and annoying for everything else. Negative numbers are shown in parentheses. Currency symbols are left-aligned with the edge of the cell. Positive numbers appear one character from the right edge of the cell to allow them to line up with negative numbers.

- Percentage uses two decimal places when selected from the drop-down. This is one format for which it is actually better to use the icon on the ribbon than the Format Cells dialog.

- Fraction defaults to showing a fraction with a one-digit divisor. If you have a number such as 0.925, some Excel number formats correctly show this as 15/16. Unfortunately, the Fraction setting in this drop-down rounds it to one-digit divisors.

Changing Numeric Formats by Using Built-in Formats in the Format Cells Dialog

The Format Cells dialog offers far more number formats than the Home tab. My favorite number format can be accessed only through the Format Cells dialog. I find that I avoid the buttons in the Number group in the Home tab and go directly to the Format Cells dialog.

You can display the Format Cells dialog by clicking the dialog launcher icon in the lower-right corner of the Number group of the Home tab. When you open the Format Cells dialog this way, the Number tab is the active tab.

There are 12 categories on the left side of the Number tab. The General and Text categories each have a single setting. The Custom category allows you to use formatting codes to build any number format. The remaining nine categories each offer a collection of controls to customize the numeric format.

Using Numeric Formatting with Thousands Separators

Using numeric formatting with thousands separators is my favorite format. The thousands separators make the number easy to read. You can suppress the decimal places from the numbers. Microsoft does not offer buttons on the Home tab to select this format. The comma button is a perfect place for it, but instead, Microsoft assigns that to the accounting format.

To format cells in numeric format, follow these steps:

1. Press Ctrl+1 to display the Format Cells dialog.

2. Select the Number category from the Number tab.

3. Select the Use 1000 Separator check box.

4. Optionally, adjust the Decimal Places spin button to 0.

5. Optionally, select a method for displaying negative numbers.

Figure 30.7 shows the Number category of the Format Cells dialog.

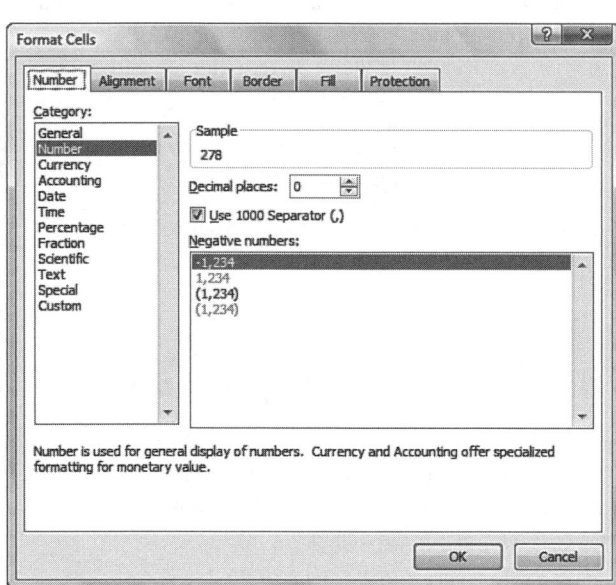

Figure 30.7
The Number category is the workhorse in Excel.

Displaying Currency

There are two categories for currency. The Currency category is identical to the Number category shown in Figure 30.7, with the addition of a currency symbol drop-down. This drop-down offers 409 different currencies from around the world.

The second category is Accounting. With this category, the currency symbol is always left-aligned in the cell. The last digit of positive numbers appears one character from the right edge of the cell so that positive and negative numbers line up. In addition, negative numbers are always shown in parentheses.

Displaying Dates and Times

The Date category offers 17 built-in formats for displaying dates, and the Time category offers nine built-in formats for displaying time. Each category has two formats that display both date and time.

The date formats vary from short dates such as 3/14 to long dates such as Wednesday, March 14, 2001. You should pay particular attention to the Date formats and the Sample box. Some formats show only the month and the day. Other formats show the month and the year. For example, the values in the Type box are for March 14, 2001. Other types such as March-01 display month-year. Types such as 14-Mar display day-month.

An interesting format near the bottom of the list is the M type. This displays month names in JFMAMJJASOND style, as shown in Figure 30.8. Readers of the *Wall Street Journal's* financial charts will instantly recognize that each month is represented by the first letter of the month in this style. This style works great when used as the labels along the x-axis of a chart.

Figure 30.8
A variety of date and time formats is available.

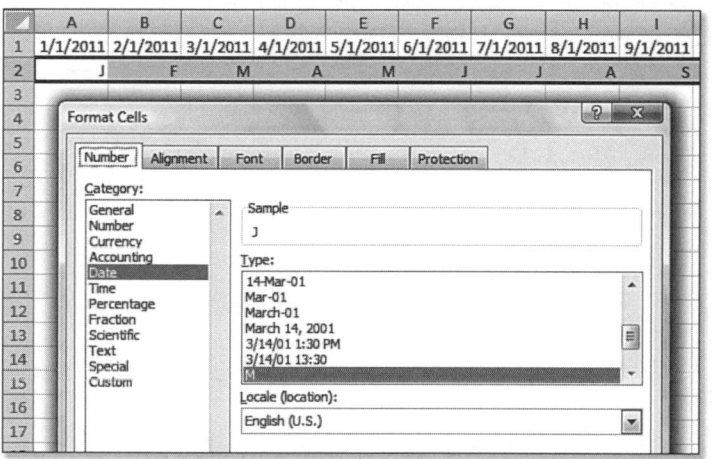

In the Time category, pay attention to an important distinction between the 1:30 PM, 13:30, and 37:30:55 types. The first type displays times from 12:00 AM through 11:59 PM. The second type displays military time. In this system, midnight is 0:00, and 11:59 PM is 23:59. Neither of these types displays hours in excess of 24 hours. If you are working on a weekly timesheet or any application where you need to display hours that total to more than 24 hours, you need to use the 37:30:55 type in the Time category. This format is one of few that displays hours in excess of 24.

Displaying Fractions

The Fractions category rounds a decimal number to the nearest fraction. Types include fractions in halves, quarters, eighths, sixteenths, tenths, and hundredths. In addition, the first three types specify that the decimal should be reduced to the nearest fraction with up to one, two, or three digits in the denominator.

Figure 30.9 shows a variety of decimals formatted with five different fractional types. In Row 14, notice that this random number can appear as 1/2, 49/92, or 473/888 when using the Up To n Digit types. Excel rounds the number to the closest fraction.

In Column E, note that if you ask Excel to show the number in eighths, Excel uses 4/8 and 2/8 instead of 1/2 or 1/4.

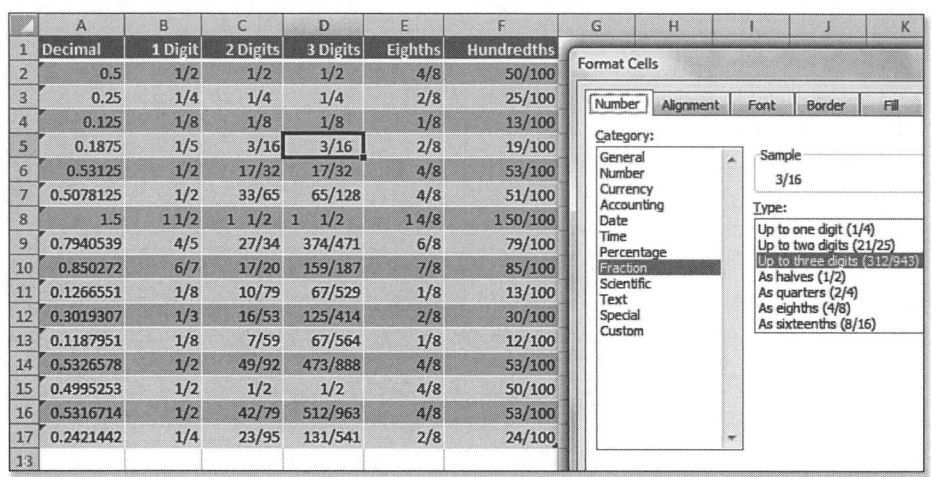

Figure 30.9
Excel can display decimals as fractions in a variety of formats.

	A	B	C	D	E	F
1	Decimal	1 Digit	2 Digits	3 Digits	Eighths	Hundredths
2	0.5	1/2	1/2	1/2	4/8	50/100
3	0.25	1/4	1/4	1/4	2/8	25/100
4	0.125	1/8	1/8	1/8	1/8	13/100
5	0.1875	1/5	3/16	3/16	2/8	19/100
6	0.53125	1/2	17/32	17/32	4/8	53/100
7	0.5078125	1/2	33/65	65/128	4/8	51/100
8	1.5	1 1/2	1 1/2	1 1/2	1 4/8	1 50/100
9	0.7940539	4/5	27/34	374/471	6/8	79/100
10	0.850272	6/7	17/20	159/187	7/8	85/100
11	0.1266551	1/8	10/79	67/529	1/8	13/100
12	0.3019307	1/3	16/53	125/414	2/8	30/100
13	0.1187951	1/8	7/59	67/564	1/8	12/100
14	0.5326578	1/2	49/92	473/888	4/8	53/100
15	0.4995253	1/2	1/2	1/2	4/8	50/100
16	0.5316714	1/2	42/79	512/963	4/8	53/100
17	0.2421442	1/4	23/95	131/541	2/8	24/100

You probably feel as if you spent too much time in junior high math learning how to reduce fractions. The good news is that the first three fraction types of number formatting in Excel eliminate the need for manually reducing fractions.

Displaying ZIP Codes, Telephone Numbers, and Social Security Numbers

Spreadsheets were invented in Cambridge, Massachusetts. However, if you enter the ZIP code for Cambridge (02138) in a cell, Excel does not display the ZIP code correctly. It truncates the leading zero, giving you a ZIP code of 2138.

To combat this problem, Excel provides four special formatting types, all of which are U.S. centric:

- The Zip Code and Zip Code + 4 styles ensure that east coast cities do not lose the leading zeros in their ZIP codes.

- The Phone Number type formats a telephone number with parentheses around the area code and a hyphen after the exchange.

 note

If you happen to live in one of the 191 countries in the world besides the United States, you will undoubtedly need other formatting for your postal codes, telephone numbers, or national ID numbers. You can create number formats such as the ones shown in the Special category as well as the other formats you might need by using the Custom category, as discussed in the next section.

- The Social Security Number type groups the digits into groups of three, two, and four numbers that are separated by hyphens.

Figure 30.10 shows cells formatted with the four types that are available in the Special category.

Figure 30.10
United States customers will appreciate the Special category in the Format Cells dialog.

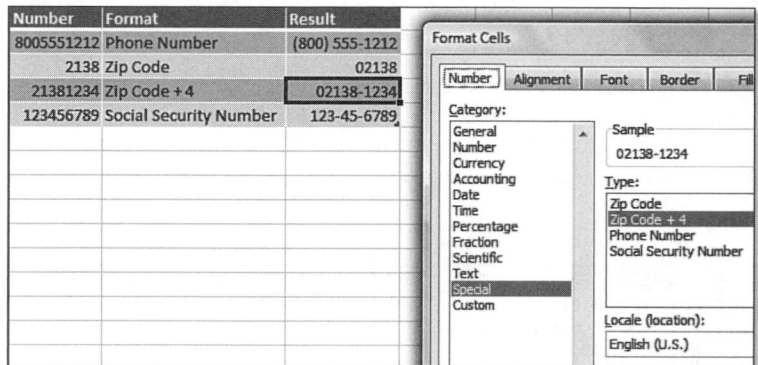

Changing Numeric Formats Using Custom Formats

Custom number formats provide incredible power and flexibility. Although you do not need to know the complete set of rules for them, you will probably find a couple custom number formats that work perfectly for you and be able to make use of them.

To use a custom number format, follow these steps:

1. Select the cells to be highlighted.

2. Display the Format Cells dialog by pressing Ctrl+1

3. Select the Number tab.

4. Select the Custom category.

5. Type the formatting codes into the Type box. Excel shows you a sample of the active cell formatted with this format in the Sample box.

6. After you make sure this format looks correct, click OK to accept it.

Using the Four Zones of a Custom Number Format

A custom number format can contain up to four different formats, each separated by a semicolon. The semicolons divide the format into up to four zones. Excel allows different formatting, depending

 tip

A good way to learn custom number formatting codes is to select a format, then click Custom to see the code for the selected format. For example, click on Fraction, then click on As Quarters (2/4).. When you click on Custom, you will learn that the custom number code is "# ?/4". Using this knowledge, you could build a new custom format code to show data in 17ths: "# ?/17".

on whether a cell contains a positive number, a negative number, a zero, or text. You need to keep in mind the following:

- Separate formatting codes for zones by using semicolons.

- If you type only one number format, it applies to all numbers.

- If you type only two formats, the first format applies to positive and zero. The second format is used for negative.

- If all four formats are used, they refer to positive, negative, zero, and text values, respectively.

In Figure 30.11, a custom number format uses all four zones. The table in Rows 11:14 shows how various numbers are displayed in this format. Notice that Cell B12 appears in red type.

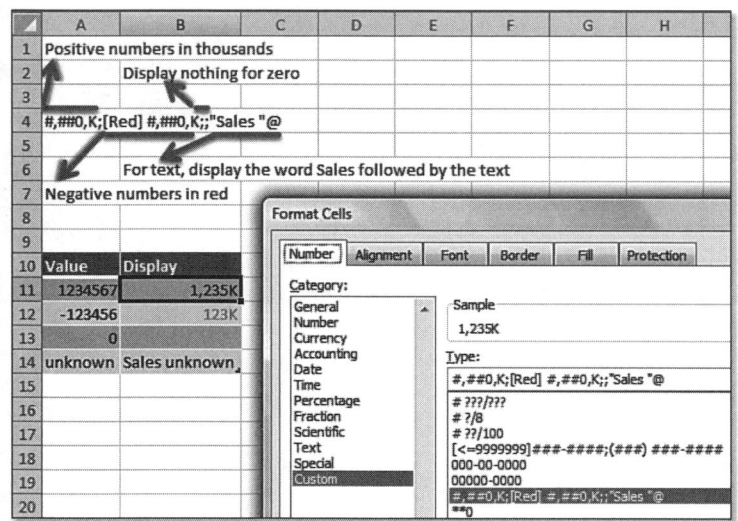

Figure 30.11
The four zones of a custom number format can cause positive, negative, zero, and text values to display differently.

Controlling Text and Spacing in a Custom Number Format

You can display a mix of text and numbers in a numeric cell. To do so, include the text in double quotation marks. For example, `"The total is "$#,##0` precedes the number with the text shown in quotes.

If you need a single character, you can omit the quotation marks and precede the character with a backslash (\). For example, the code `$#,##0,,\M` displays numbers in millions and adds an M indicator after the number.

Some characters require neither a backslash nor quotation marks. These special characters are $ - + / ( ) : ! ^ & ' ~ { } = < > and the space character.

To add a specific amount of space to a format, you enter an underscore followed by a character. Excel then includes enough space to include that particular character. One frequent use for this is to include _) at the end of a positive number to leave enough space for a closing parenthesis. The positive numbers then line up with the negative numbers shown in parentheses.

To fill the space in a cell with a repeating character, use an asterisk followed by the character. For example, the format `**0` fills the leading space in a cell with asterisks. The format `0*-` fills the trailing space in a cell with hyphens.

If you are expecting numbers but think you might occasionally have text in the cell, you can use the fourth zone of the format. You use the @ character to represent the text in the cell. For example, `0;0;0;"Unexpected entry of "@` highlights the text cells with a note. If someone types a number, they get the number. If someone types hello, they get "Unexpected entry of hello".

Controlling Decimal Places in a Custom Number Format

Use a zero as a placeholder when you want to force the place to be included. For example, `0.000` formats all numbers with three decimal places. If the number has more than three places, it will be rounded to three decimal places.

Use a pound sign (#) as a placeholder to display significant digits but not insignificant zeros. For example, `0.###` displays up to three decimal places, if needed, but can display `"1."` for a whole number.

Use a question mark to replace insignificant zeros on either size of the decimal point with enough space to represent a digit in a fixed-width font. This format was designed to allow decimal points to line up, but with proportional fonts, it may not always work.

To include a thousands separator, include a comma to the left of the decimal point. For example, `#,##0` displays a thousands separator.

To scale a number by thousands, include a comma after the numeric portion of the format. Each comma divides the number by a thousand. For example, `0,` displays numbers in thousands, and `0,,` displays numbers in millions.

Using Conditions and Color in a Custom Number Format

The condition codes available in numeric formatting predate conditional formatting by a decade. You should consider the flexible conditional formatting features for any new conditions. However, in case you encounter an old worksheet with these codes, it is valid to use colors in the format: red, blue, green, yellow, cyan, black, white, magenta, Color 1, …, Color 56. You include the color in square brackets. It should be the first element of any numeric formatting zone.

➡ *See Chapter 31, "Using Data Visualizations and Conditional Formatting" for more information about flexible conditional formatting features.*

You can include a condition in square brackets after the color but before the numeric formatting. For example, `[Red][<=100];[Color 17][>100]` displays numbers under 100 in red and other numbers in blue. The United States telephone special format uses this custom condition `[<=9999999]###-####;(###) ###-####`.

Using Dates and Times in a Custom Number Format

Although many of these settings are arcane, I still regularly use many of the date and time formats shown in Table 30.1. The various m and d codes allow flexibility in expressing dates.

Table 30.1 Date and Time Formats

To Display This	Use This Code
Months as 1–12	m
Months as 01–12	mm
Months as Jan–Dec	mmm
Months as January–December	mmmm
Months as the first letter of the month	mmmmm
Days as 1–31	d
Days as 01–31	dd
Days as Sun–Sat	ddd
Days as Sunday–Saturday	dddd
Years as 00–99	yy
Years as 1900–9999	yyyy
Hours as 0–23	h
Hours as 00–23	hh
Minutes as 0–59	m
Minutes as 00–59	mm
Seconds as 0–59	s
Seconds as 00–59	ss
Hours as 4 AM	h AM/PM
Time as 4:36 PM	h:mm AM/PM
Time as 4:36:03 P	h:mm:ss A/P
Elapsed time in hours such as 25:02	[h]:mm
Elapsed time in minutes such as 63:46	[mm]:ss
Elapsed time in seconds	[ss]
Fractions of a second	h:mm:ss.00

The custom number format m/d/yy displays the month and day numbers as one digit if possible. For example, dates formatted with this code display as 1/9/08, 1/31/08, 9/9/09, and 12/31/08.

A custom number format of mm/dd/yy always uses two digits to display the month and day. Examples are 01/09/08 and 01/31/08.

The remaining date and time codes can display months as Jan, January, or J and days as 1, 01, Fri, or Friday.

 note

Note that the letter m can be used either as a month or as a minute. If the m is preceded by an h or followed by an s, Excel assumes you are referring to minutes. Otherwise, the month is displayed instead.

Displaying Scientific Notation in Custom Number Formats

To display numbers in scientific format, you use E-, or E+ exponent codes in a zone.

If a format contains a zero (0) or pound sign (#) to the right of an exponent code, Excel displays the number in scientific format and inserts an E. The number of zeros or pound signs to the right of a code determines the number of digits in the exponent. E- or e- places a minus sign by negative exponents. E+ or e+ places a minus sign by negative exponents and a plus sign by positive exponents.

Take the following, for example:

- 1450 formatted with 0.00E+00 display as 1.45E+03
- 1450 formatted with 0.00E-00 display as 1.45E03
- 0.00145 formatted with either code display 1.45E-03

Aligning Cells

Worksheets look best when the headings above a column are aligned with the data in the column. Excel's default behavior is to left-align text and right-align values and dates.

On the left side of Figure 30.12, the month headings in Row 5 are left-aligned, and the numeric values starting in Row 6 are right-aligned. This makes the worksheet look haphazard. To solve the problem, you can right-align the headings cells. The right side of Figure 30.12 shows the headings right-aligned.

To right-align cells, select the cells and click the Right Align icon in the Alignment group of the Home tab.

 note

The Alignment tab of the Format Cells dialog offers additional alignment choices such as justified and distributed.

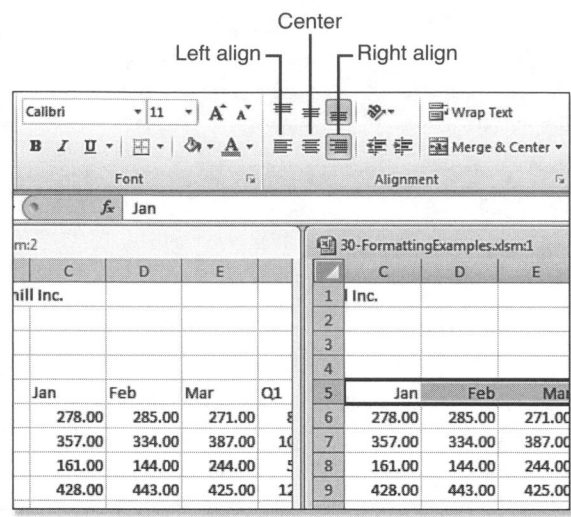

Figure 30.12
In the left side of the image, the left-aligned headings appear out of alignment with the numbers. The worksheet on the right shows the headings after the Right Align icon is clicked.

Changing Font Size

There are three icons in the Font group of the Home tab for changing font size:

- The Increase Font Size (A^) icon increases the font size in the selected cells to the next larger setting.

- The Decrease Font Size (Av) icon decreases the font size in the selected cells to the next smaller setting.

- The Font Size drop-down offers a complete list of font sizes. You can hover over any font size to see the Live Preview of that size in the selected cells of the worksheet (see Figure 30.13).

 note

If you need a font size that is not in the dropdown, you can type a new value in the dropdown. While the dropdown jumps from 12 to 14, you can click on the value and type 13.

Changing Font Typeface

Beginning with Excel 2007, changing the font typeface is vastly improved. In some legacy versions of Excel, the Font drop-down showed the font names in the style of each font. However, beginning with Excel 2007, Live Preview shows how the font will look as you hover over the font in the selected cells (see Figure 30.14). Notice that the Font name drop-down is in the Font group of the Home tab.

Figure 30.13
When you use the Font Size drop-down, Live Preview shows you the effect of an increased font before you select the font.

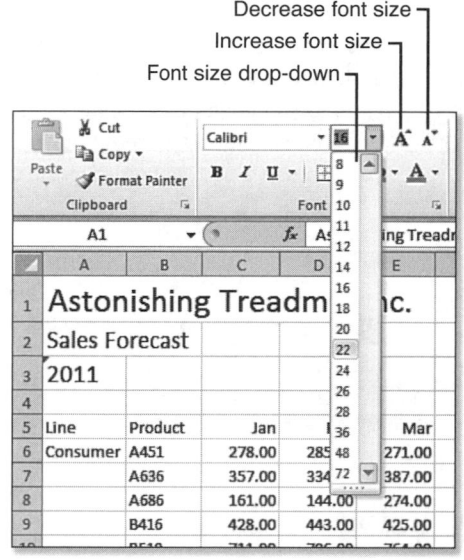

Figure 30.14
The Font drop-down in the Home tab shows the look of each font, and Live Preview shows how individual cells will look with the font applied.

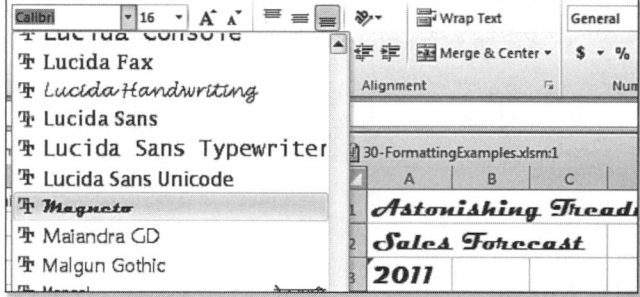

Applying Bold, Italic, and Underline

Three icons in the Font group in the Home tab allow you to change the font to apply bold, italic, and underline. Unlike the icons in the Number group, these icons behave properly, toggling the property on and off. The Bold icon is a bold letter B. The Italic icon is an italic letter I. The Underline icon is either an underlined U or a double-underlined D. The Underline icon is actually a drop-down.

 note

By using the Font tab of the Format Cells dialog, you can also apply strikethrough, superscript, and subscript.

As shown in Figure 30.15, you can select the drop-down to change from Single Underline to Double Underline.

The underline style underlines the characters in the cell. If you have a cell that contains 123, the underline is 3 characters wide. If you have a cell with 1,234,567.89, the underline is 12 characters wide. If you need an underline to extend the entire width of a cell, you can select Single Accounting Underline or Double Accounting Underline on the Font tab of the Format Cells dialog. Alternatively, you can use a bottom border in the cell.

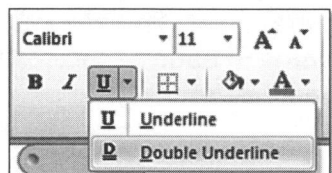

Figure 30.15
Bold, Italic, and Underline icons toggle the style on and off for the selected cells.

Using Borders

There are 1.7 billion unique combinations of borders for any four-cell range. The Borders drop-down in the Font group of the Home tab offers 13 popular border options plus five border tools, as shown in Figure 30.16.

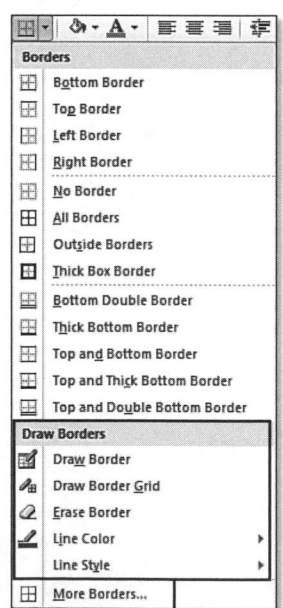

Border Drawing Tools

Figure 30.16
The Borders drop-down offers 13 of the most popular border choices and five border drawing tools. The border drawing tools might be the fastest way to create anything other than basic borders.

Excel 2007 offered only the 13 border choices before you had to use the Border tab of the Format Cells dialog to find additional choices. However, you may find that the five tools in the Draw Borders section of the drop-down are the fastest way to draw borders.

To use the Draw Borders tool, follow these steps:

 note

Note that doing either step 1 or step 2 automatically puts you in Draw Border mode. In this case, you can skip step 3.

1. If you desire a color other than black, open the Borders drop-down, hover over Line Color, and choose a color from the flyout menu.

2. If you desire a thickness other than a continuous hairline border, open the Borders drop-down, hover over Line Style, and choose a style from the flyout menu.

3. If you opted for black continuous hairline borders and skipped steps 1 and 2, open the Borders drop-down and select Draw Border. The mouse cursor changes to a pencil.

4. To draw in a single border, click one edge of a cell. In Figure 30.17, the stair-step in Rows 2 through 4 was achieved in five clicks.

   ■ Click the border between B2 and B3.

   ■ Click the border between B3 and C3.

   ■ Click the border between C3 and C4.

   ■ Click the border between C4 and D4.

   ■ Click the border between D4 and D5.

5. To draw an outline around a range, click in one corner cell and drag it down to the opposite corner. The outline around B6:D9 in Figure 30.17 was achieved by clicking in B6 and dragging to D9.

6. To draw a grid in a range, hold down the Ctrl key while dragging. The grid in B11:D14 was achieved by Ctrl+dragging from B11 to D14.

7. Drawing diagonals takes a bit of practice. Click at the top left corner of a cell and drag to the bottom right corner of the cell. As you are dragging, Excel starts to draw in a border around the whole cell. When you reach the bottom right corner, the outline changes to a diagonal. Three separate diagonal borders are shown in Row 16 of Figure 30.17.

8. If you make a mistake, use Undo or hold down Ctrl+Shift while dragging the mouse to erase borders.

9. When you are done drawing borders, press the Esc key to exit Draw Borders mode.

To watch a video of using the Border Drawing tools, search for "Excel In Depth 30" at YouTube.

Figure 30.17
After being absent from the Excel 2007 ribbon, the Draw Borders tool returns to Excel 2010.

> **note**
> The Draw Border Grid icon in the drop-down will draw a border around each individual cell in a range. This is equivalent to holding down the Ctrl key while using the Draw Border tool.

Drawing a Border Around a Range

You need to understand an important concept when applying borders to a range. Suppose you select 20 rows by 20 columns, such as cells A1:T20. If you apply a top border by using the drop-down, only the top row of Cells A1:T1 have the border. Often, this is not what you were expecting. For example, you might have wanted a border on the top of all 400 cells.

Notice that in the Format Cells dialog box, there is a representation of a 2×2 cell range. The border style drawn in the top edge of this box affects only the top edge of the range. The border style drawn in the middle horizontal line of the box affects all the horizontal borders on the inside of the selected range.

The fastest way to select all horizontal and vertical borders in the range is to click the Outline button and then the Inside button in the Presets section of the dialog.

> **caution**
> The Erase Border tool will not clear all borders in a range. By default, the tool will clear only the outline border around the entire range. This is rarely what you want. You can hold down the Ctrl key while using the Erase Border tool, or instead make a habit of preselecting the range and then choosing No Border, the fifth item in the Borders drop-down. Ctrl+Shift+Minus will also clear all borders.

Coloring Cells

Excel 2007 added the capability to use a gradient to fill a cell. This can provide an interesting look for a title cell. Gradient formatting is available only in the Format Cells dialog.

The Font group on the Home tab offers a paint bucket drop-down and an A drop-down. The paint bucket is a color chooser for the background fill of the cell. The A drop-down is a color chooser for the font color in the cell. Both drop-downs offer six shades of the 10 theme colors, 10 standard colors, and the option More Colors. The paint bucket drop-down also offers the menu choice No Fill, as shown in Figure 30.18.

Figure 30.18
The color drop-down offers theme colors, 10 standard colors, and the link
More Colors.

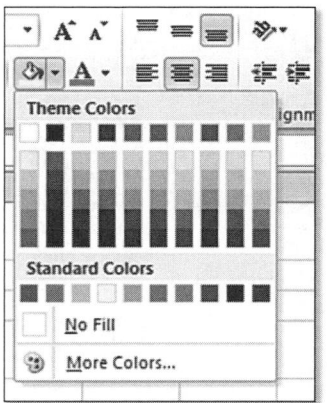

The More Colors drop-down offers the two-tabbed Colors dialog. You can either choose a color from the Standard tab or enter an RGB value on the Custom tab.

The two-color gradient in a cell was a new feature beginning with Excel 2007. To activate this feature, follow these steps:

1. Select one or more cells. If you select a range of cells, Excel repeats the gradient for each cell in the range.

2. Press Ctrl+1 to display the Format Cells dialog.

3. Select the Fill tab.

4. Click the Fill Effects button.

5. In the Color 1 and Color 2 drop-downs, choose two colors or choose one color and white.

6. In the Shading Styles section, choose a shading style.

7. In the Variants section, choose one of the three variations. A sample is shown in the Sample box.

8. Click OK to close the Fill Effects dialog.

9. Click OK to close the Format Cells dialog.

Figure 30.19 shows the Fill Effects dialog. Cell A1 contains a vertical shading, from left to right. Cell A4 shows the opposite variant of vertical shading. Cell A9 shows the from-the-center variant of the vertical shading. Cell A13 shows a diagonal-down shading style.

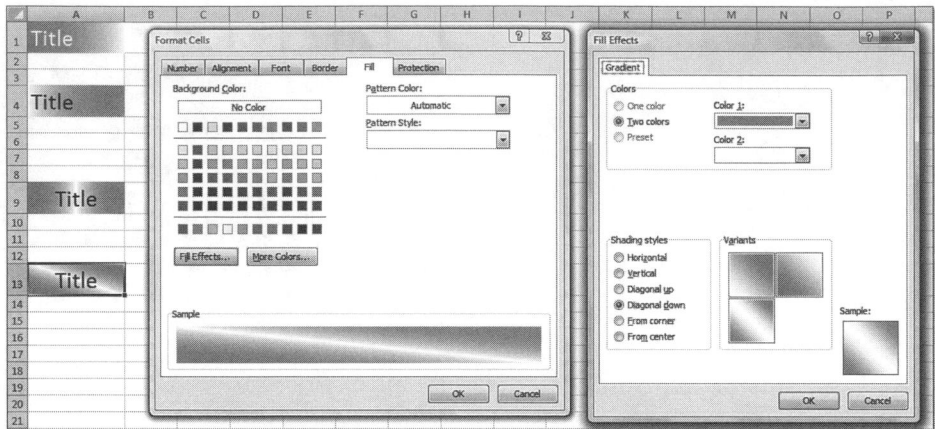

Figure 30.19
Since Excel 2007, you can add gradients as the fill within cells.

Adjusting Column Widths and Row Heights

You can adjust the width of every column in a worksheet. In many cases, narrowing the columns to reduce wasted space can allow a report to fit on one page.

There are usually three or more ways to accomplish most tasks in Excel. In most cases, I have a favorite method to do any task and use that method exclusively. However, setting column widths and row heights is a task where I actively use many methods, depending on the circumstances.

You can use the following seven methods to adjust column width. Each method applies equally well to adjusting row heights:

- **Click the border between the column headings**—As shown in Figure 30.20, you can drag to the left to make the column narrow. You can drag to the right to make the column wide. A ToolTip appears, showing the width in points and pixels. The advantage of this method is that you can drag until the column feels like it is the right width. The disadvantage is that this method fixes one column at a time.

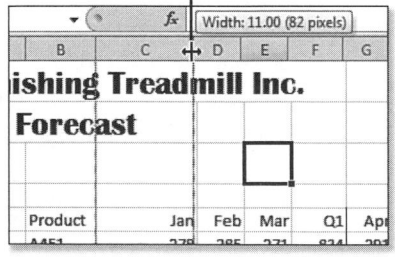

Figure 30.20
The right border between one cell letter and the next is the key to adjusting column widths.

- **Double-click the border between column headings**—Excel automatically adjusts the left column to fit the widest value in the column. The advantage of this method is that the column is exactly wide enough for the contents. The disadvantage is that a very long title in Cell A1 (for example) makes this method ineffective. You might have been planning to allow the title in Cell A1 to spill over to B1, C1, and D1. However, the double-click method makes the column wide enough for the long title. In this case, you want to use the last method in this list.

- **Select many columns and drag the border for one column**—When you do this, the width for all columns is adjusted. The advantage of this method is that you can adjust all columns at once, and they are all a uniform width.

- **Select many columns and double-click one of the borders between column letters**—When you do this, all the columns adjust to fit their widest value.

- **Use the ribbon**—Select one or more columns. From the Cells group of the Home tab, select Format, Column Width. Then enter a width in characters and click OK.

- **Apply one column's width to other columns**—If one column is a suitable width, and you want all other columns to be the same width, you should use this method. Select the column with the correct width, and then press Ctrl+C to copy. Next, select the columns to be adjusted. Select the Clipboard section of the Home tab and select Paste, Paste Special, Column Widths. Finally, click OK.

- **Autofit a column to all the data below the title rows**—If you have a long title in the first few rows and need to autofit the column to all the data below the title rows, use this method. Click the first cell in the data range; then press the End key. Next, hold down the Ctrl and Shift keys while pressing the Down Arrow key. This selects a contiguous range from the starting cell downward. Now select the Cells section of the Home tab and then select Format, AutoFit Selection. If you were a power user in Excel 2003 or before, you might remember this method as Alt+O+C+A. This legacy keyboard shortcut still works.

Using Merge and Center

In general, merged cells are bad. If you have a merged cell in the middle of a data table, you will be unable to sort the data. You will be unable to cut and paste data unless the same cells are merged. However, it is okay to use merged cells as a title to group several columns together.

In Figure 30.21, the Consumer and Professional headings correspond to the Columns B:F and G:K, respectively. It is appropriate to center each heading above its columns.

 tip

Merging cells brings some negative side-effects. Say that you had merged B100:G100. You start in cell B1, hold down the shift key, and start pressing PgDn to select cells in column B. When you reach or pass the merged cell B100, your selection size will automatically expand to be 6 columns wide, since this was the width of the merged cell. To prevent this problem, you might use Center Across Selection found in the Home tab. This will give the same look as the merged cell, without the problems caused by the merge.

▲	A	B	C	D	E	F	G	H	I
1									
2		Consumer					Professional		
3	Month	A451	A636	A686	B416	B519	K121	K658	N7
4	Jan	167	198	168	139	153	145	144	1!
5	Feb	166	132	135	150	183	170	198	1(
6	Mar	191	103	112	190	136	124	151	1(
7	Apr	125	147	175	150	190	182	154	1
8	May	121	160	147	169	170	183	147	1
9	Jun	131	166	548	179	196	165	140	1
10	Jul	182	118	144	116	172	171	158	1(
11	Aug	137	129	183	163	105	188	103	1
12	Sep	130	108	124	177	170	108	168	1(
13	Oct	146	197	180	177	143	180	152	1
14	Nov	154	153	180	158	129	110	118	1
15	Dec	107	162	151	145	158	178	180	1
16									

Figure 30.21
Because the Row 2 categories are not part of the data table and will never need to be sorted, it is okay to merge and center those cells.

To merge and center cells, follow these steps:

1. Click in the cell that contains the value that is to be centered, and then drag to select the entire range to be merged. In this example, click in Cell B2 and drag to Cell F2. The result is that B2 is the active cell, and B2:F2 is selected.

2. From the Home tab, select Alignment, Merge and Center, and then select Merge and Center again, as shown in Figure 30.22.

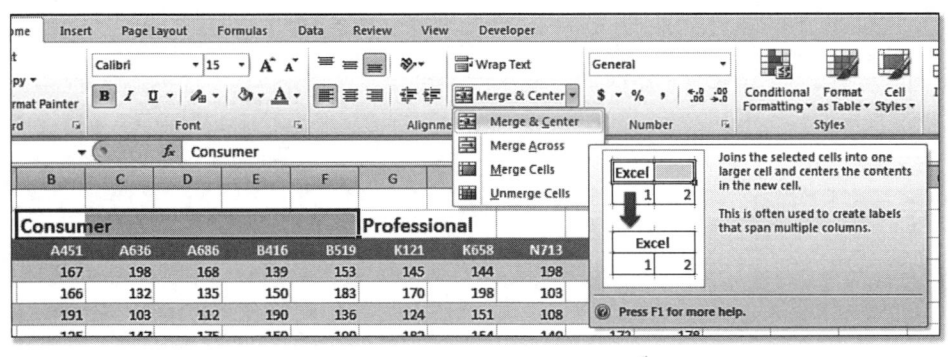

Figure 30.22
Select Merge and Center from the drop-down.

3. Repeat steps 1 and 2 for any other column headings.

4. Optionally, apply an outline border around the merged cells.

Note that after you merge the cells, the entire range becomes one cell. In Figure 30.23, the word *Consumer* is in an ultra-large Cell B2. In this worksheet, Cells C2, D2, E2, and F2 no longer exist. If you attempt to use the Go To dialog to move to Cell C2, you will be taken to Cell B2 instead.

Figure 30.23
Columns are visually grouped into product lines by the merged cells.

	A	B	C	D	E	F	G	H	I	J	K
1											
2				Consumer				Professional			
3	Month	A451	A636	A686	B416	B519	K121	K658	N713	O855	O980
4	Jan	167	198	168	139	153	145	144	198	195	168
5	Feb	166	132	135	150	183	170	198	103	195	194
6	Mar	191	103	112	190	136	124	151	108	167	182
7	Apr	125	147	175	150	190	182	154	140	173	178
8	May	121	160	147	160	170	183	147	128	196	181

Rotating Text

Vertical text is difficult to read. However, at times space considerations make it advantageous to use vertical text. In Figure 30.24, for example, the names in Row 5 are much wider than the values in the rest of the table. If you use Format, Autofit Selection, the report is too wide.

Figure 30.24
The headings are much wider than the data. Vertical text can solve the problem.

C	D	E	F	G	H
Blankenship	Cunningham	Fitzpatrick	Hamilton	Hernderson	Montgomery	R
339	258	293	316	252	304
438	332	377	408	325	392
218	166	188	203	162	196
513	389	442	477	380	460
844	640	727	786	626	756
178	135	154	166	132	160
472	358	407	439	350	423
427	324	368	397	317	383
374	283	322	348	277	335
761	578	656	709	564	683
573	434	494	533	425	513
5,137	3,897	4,428	4,782	3,810	4,605
256	194	221	238	190	229

In the Alignment tab of the Home group, an Orientation drop-down offers five variations of vertical text. Figure 30.25 compares the five available options. Although the Angle options look great, they only reduce the column width by 12 percent. Vertical Text reduces the column width by 75 percent but takes far more vertical space. The option Rotate Text Up reduces the column width by 73 percent and takes up less than half the vertical space of the Vertical Text option.

 note

After you rotate the text, select the Cells section of the Home tab and then select Format, AutoFit Selection again to narrow the columns.

If you need more control over the text orientation, you can select the Alignment option in the drop-down to display the Alignment tab of the Format Cells dialog. This tab allows rotation from 90 degrees to -90 degrees, in 1 degree increments, as shown in Figure 30.26.

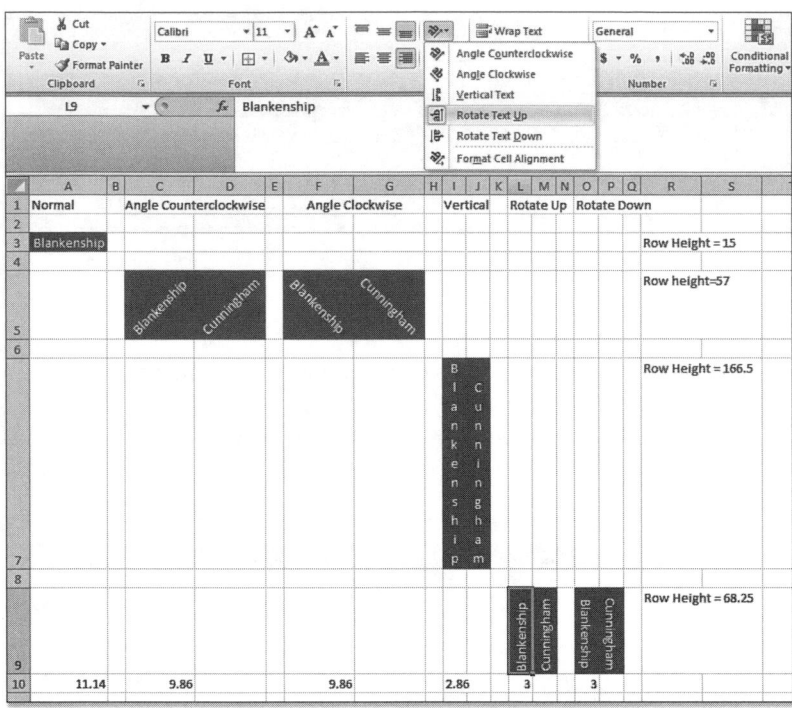

Figure 30.25
Of the five options, the Rotate Text options take up the least space.

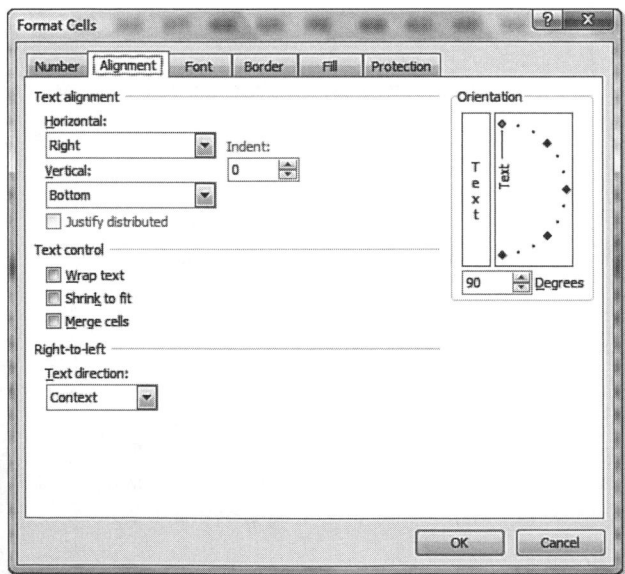

Figure 30.26
The Alignment option allows 182 different orientation settings.

Formatting with Styles

Instead of using the settings in the Font group of the Home tab, you can format a report by using the built-in cell styles. Cell styles have been popular in Word for more than a decade. They have been available in legacy versions of Excel, but because they were not given a spot on the Formatting toolbar, few people took advantage of them.

Figure 30.27 shows the styles available when you select Styles, Cell Styles in the Home tab.

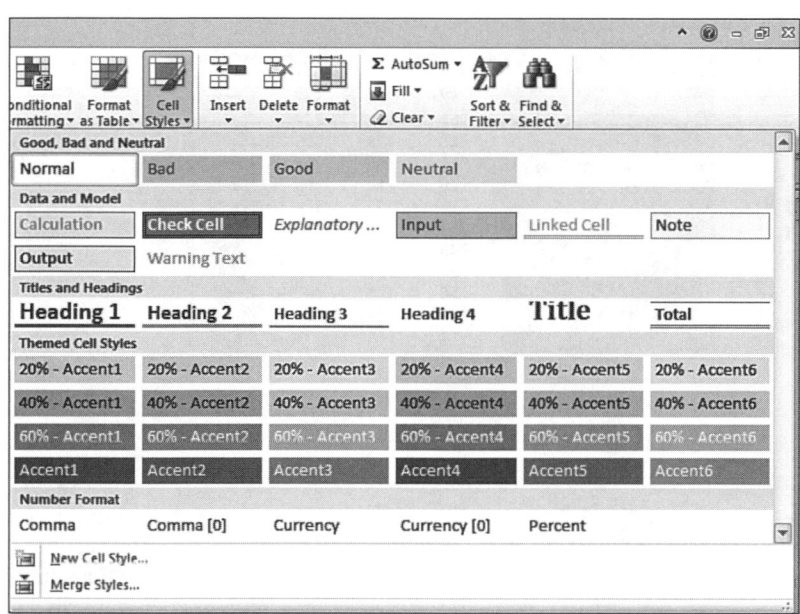

Figure 30.27
The Cell Styles gallery offers various built-in cell styles.

An advantage to using cell styles is that you can convert the look and feel of a report by choosing from the themes on the Page Layout tab. Figure 30.28 shows 1 of the 20 available themes applied to the report.

The Cell Styles gallery offers a menu item to add additional styles to a workbook. Using cell styles provides an interesting alternative to the traditional method of formatting.

 note

You might wonder why Excel 2010 suggests that calculated cells should be in orange font or why Notes should have a yellow background. I spent the first two years of working with Excel 2007 wondering why calculated cells should be orange. However, the better question is, "Why not orange?" When I receive worksheets from others who use this convention, it is easy to understand that they are using the built-in cell styles, which makes it easier to follow the logic of the worksheet. In Figure 30.29, the forecasting model was formatted using Cell Styles from the Data and Model section of the Cell Styles menu. If everyone in your company used these styles, it would be easier to spot the input cells in any model.

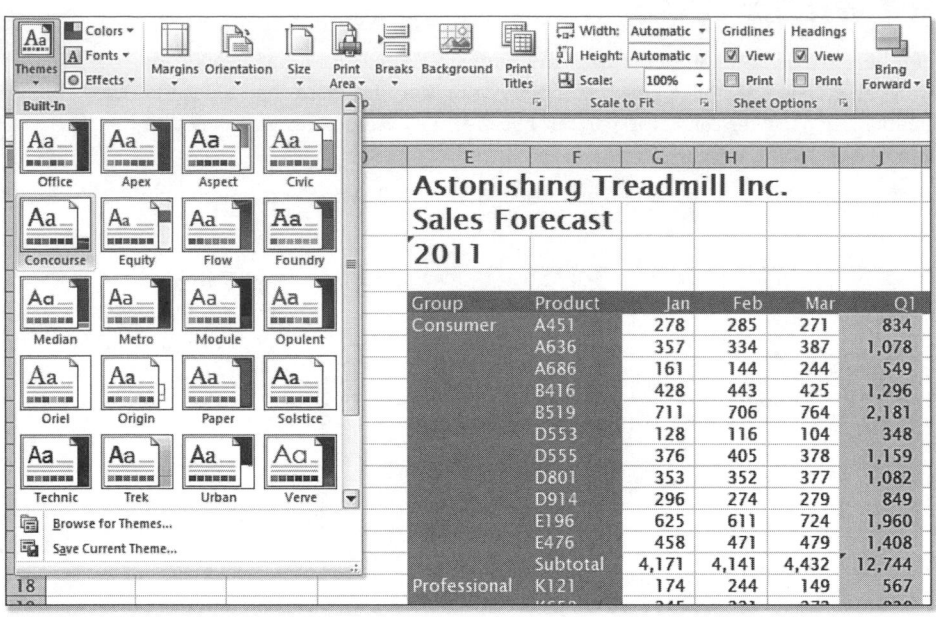

Figure 30.28
When you choose a new theme, a report formatted with cell styles takes on a new look.

Figure 30.29
Adopt the cell styles suggestions for input cells, calculated cells, and so on to make it easier to see the logic in the model.

Understanding Themes

A *theme* is a collection of colors, fonts, and effects. Office 2010 has 20 built-in themes. You can also download new themes from Office Online or design your own themes.

Themes are shared in simple XML files, which means they can be propagated throughout a company.

A theme has the following components:

- **Fonts**—A theme has two fonts: one for body text and one for titles. The fonts come into play more often in PowerPoint and Word than in Excel. However, styles in Excel also use fonts.

- **Colors**—There are 12 colors: four for text and backgrounds, six accent colors that are used in charts and table accents, and two for hyperlinks. One of the two colors for hyperlinks indicates followed hyperlinks, whereas the other color indicates hyperlinks that have not been followed. You see the 10 colors besides the hyperlink colors in the first row of the color chooser, as shown in Figure 30.30. The first four colors are for text and backgrounds. The next six colors are the accent colors. In each column, you then see various shades of these 10 colors.

- **Effects**—Each theme includes a number of object effects, such as bevel and line style.

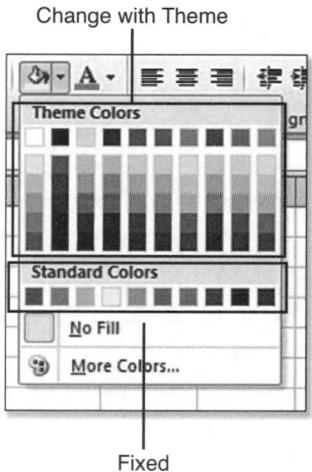

Change with Theme

Figure 30.30
The color chooser shows six shades of each of the 10 theme colors.

Fixed

Choosing a New Theme

Themes are managed on the Page Layout tab. Listed next are the four drop-downs available in the Themes group:

- **Themes**—Allows you to switch among the 20 built-in themes.

- **Colors**—Allows you to change the color scheme to use the colors from another theme.

- **Fonts**—Allows you to use the fonts from another theme.
- **Effects**—Allows you to use the effects from another theme.

Changing a theme affects charts, tables, SmartArt diagrams, and inserted objects.

To switch to another theme, follow these steps:

1. Arrange your worksheet so that you can see any themed elements, such as tables or charts, on the right side of the screen.

2. From the Page Layout tab, select the Themes drop-down from the Themes group.

3. Hover over the various themes. The worksheet updates to show the new colors, fonts, and effects.

4. When you identify a theme you like, click the theme to apply it to the workbook.

Figures 30.31 and 30.32 show the same worksheet with two different themes.

> **note**
>
> Note that you can use only one theme per workbook. If you are changing the theme on Sheet33, the same changes are made on all the other worksheets in the workbook.

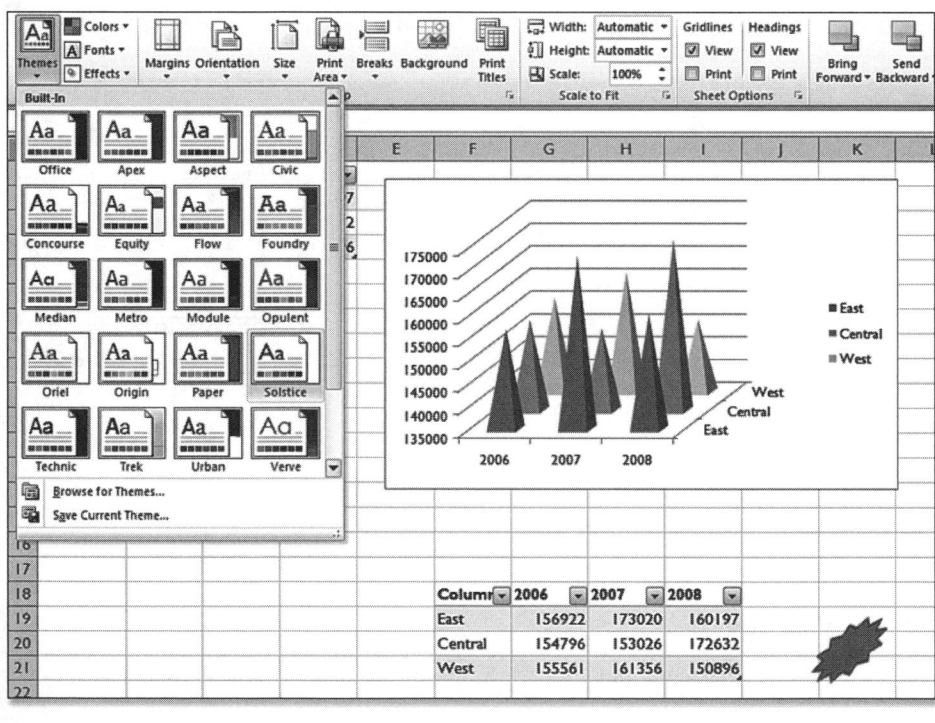

Figure 30.31
The Solstice theme features a sans-serif font and bright colors.

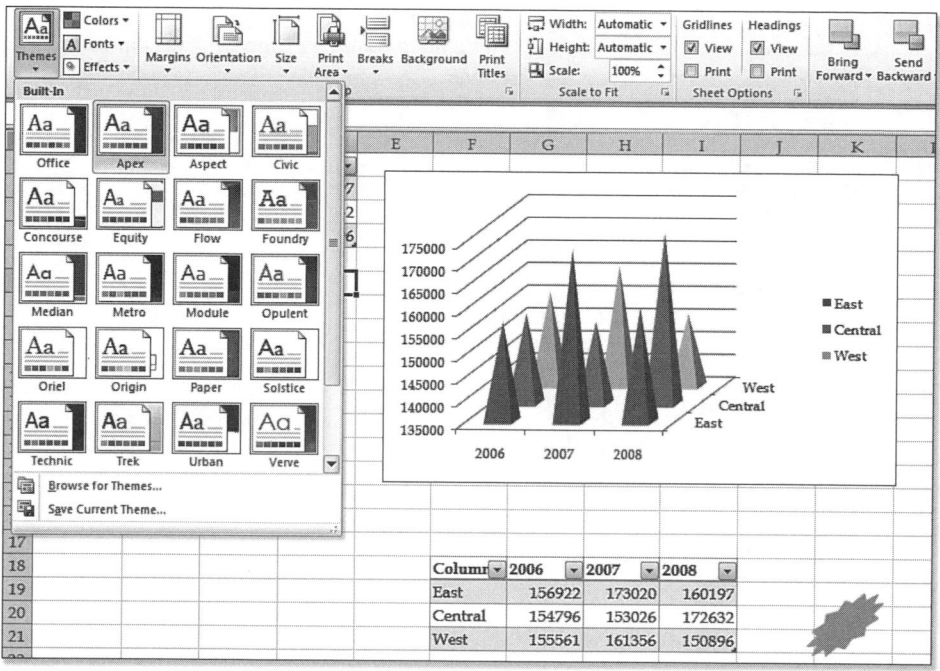

Figure 30.32 The Apex theme features a serif font, muted colors, and different effects.

If you are strictly interested in the accent colors, you can select the Colors drop-down from the Themes group to see the accent colors used in each theme. Figure 30.33 shows the options in the Colors drop-down.

Creating a New Theme

You might want to develop a special theme, which is fairly easy to do. First you need to select two fonts and six accent colors. For example, suppose you want to create a theme to match your company's color scheme. The hardest part is finding six colors to represent your company, because most company logos have two or three colors. The following sections describe how to create a new theme and suggest resources for choosing complementary colors for your company colors.

Understanding RGB Color Codes

Colors on computer monitors are described as a mix of red (R), green (G), and blue (B). Each color channel is assigned a value from 0 to 255. For example, a color of R=255, G=0, B=0 is a bright red. As you add more blue, the red shifts toward a pink or violet color. A color of R=255, G=0, B=128 is a pinkish violet color.

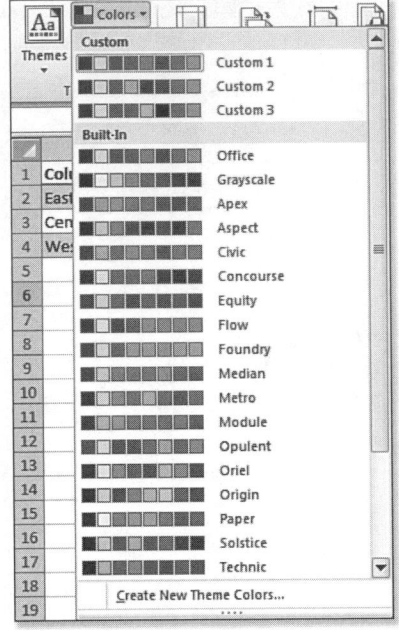

Figure 30.33
The Colors drop-down shows the accent colors for all 20 themes at once.

A color of R=0, G=0, B=0 is black. A color of R=255, G=255, B=255 is white. You can create 16.7 million different colors by using combinations of red, green, and blue.

To discover the codes for your company's color scheme, follow these steps:

1. Open your company's Home page in a browser.

2. In Internet Explorer, select View, Source. In Firefox, select View, Page Source. You now see the underlying HTML code.

3. Find the colors used in the page by searching for a pound sign (#). A web page specifies colors by using a pound sign followed by six characters such as #4F81BD.

 tip
The color chooser in Photoshop shows the RGB value for any #123456 notation.

Even though every web page uses the #123456 notation for describing colors, Microsoft Excel's theme specification needs the RGB value for the color. Fortunately, it is fairly easy to convert between the two.

Hexadecimal is a numbering system that has digits 0 through 9 and A through F. Including 0, there are 16 digits in the hexadecimal numbering system. In the decimal system, a 2-digit number can represent 10×10 different combinations. There are 100 numbers, from 00 to 99. In a hex system, a 2-digit number can represent 16×16 different numbers—that is, 256 numbers, from 0 to 255.

In the #123456 nomenclature, the # sign indicates that the number is in hexadecimal. The first two digits are the hex representation of the red value. The next two digits are the hex representation of the green value. The next two digits are the hex representation of the blue value.

Converting from Hex to Decimal

If you do not have Photoshop or another tool that converts from a hex color to an RGB value for you automatically, you can use functions in Excel to do the conversion. For example, the worksheet in Figure 30.34 converts from a hex color in Cell B1 to the RGB values in B7:B9:

- The formulas in B2:B4 use the MID function to extract each pair of numbers from the color code. The formula for Cell B2 is shown in Cell C2.

- The formulas in B7:B9 use the HEX2DEC function to convert the 2-digit hex number to decimal.

To represent the color #FF9108 in Excel, for example, use R=255, G=145, B=8.

Figure 30.34
This quick Excel worksheet can convert from a 6-digit hex color code to a decimal RGB value.

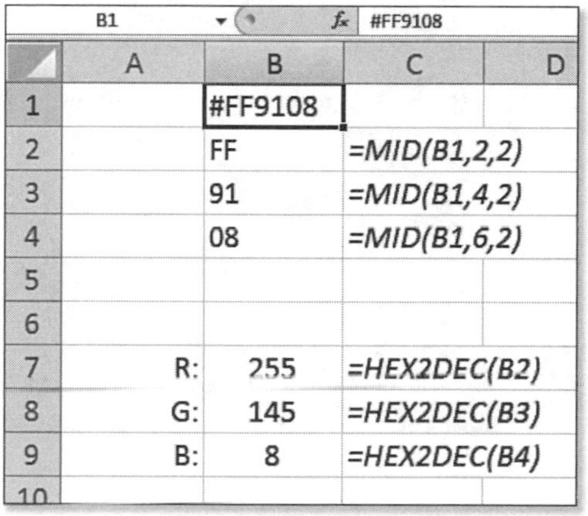

	A	B	C	D
1		#FF9108		
2		FF	=MID(B1,2,2)	
3		91	=MID(B1,4,2)	
4		08	=MID(B1,6,2)	
5				
6				
7	R:	255	=HEX2DEC(B2)	
8	G:	145	=HEX2DEC(B3)	
9	B:	8	=HEX2DEC(B4)	
10				

B1 — fx #FF9108

Finding New Colors

If you look at your company's logo and website, you can probably identify two or three colors to use in the theme. You need to come up with a total of six accent colors for a theme.

> ➡ *You can use the free Web-based tool at http://colorschemedesigner.com/ to find colors that look good together.*

To find complementary colors, follow these steps:

1. Start with a hex representation of one of your logo colors.

2. Open http://colorschemedesigner.com in a browser.

3. In the bottom, just left of center, click the RGB code.

4. In the window that pops up, enter the portion of the color code after the pound sign, such as FF9108.

5. Click each of the six icons under the color wheel on the left. The six icons represent mono, complement, triad, tetrad, analogic, and accented analogic. In the Triad view, the website shows your original color, three others, and three variations of each.

6. In the bottom navigation, select Color List. The website shows the hex color codes for all the colors shown.

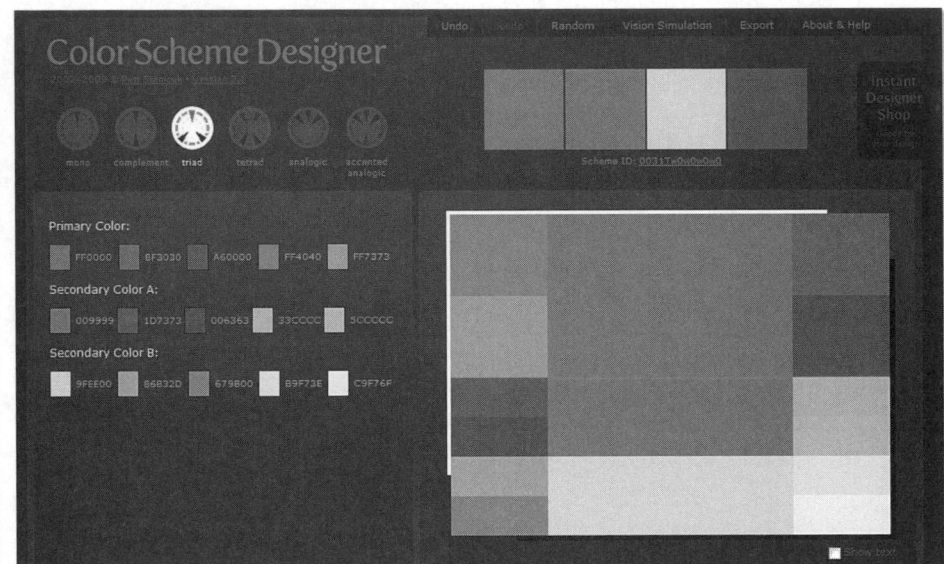

Figure 30.35
This web page suggests colors that complement your logo colors.

Specifying a Theme's Colors

To specify new theme colors, follow these steps.

1. Select Page Layout, Themes, Colors, Create New Theme Colors. The Create New Theme Colors dialog appears. Remember that a theme is composed of two text colors, two background colors, six accent colors, and two hyperlink colors. These 12 colors are shown in the Create New Theme Colors dialog (see Figure 30.36).

2. To change the first accent color, select the drop-down next to Accent 1. The color chooser appears.

3. From the bottom of the color chooser drop-down, select More Colors. The Colors dialog appears.

4. In the Custom tab of the Colors dialog, enter values for red, green, and blue, as shown in Figure 30.37. The New color block shows the color. Click OK to accept the color.

5. Repeat steps 2–4 for each of the accent colors.

Figure 30.36
The 12 colors in the current theme are shown here.

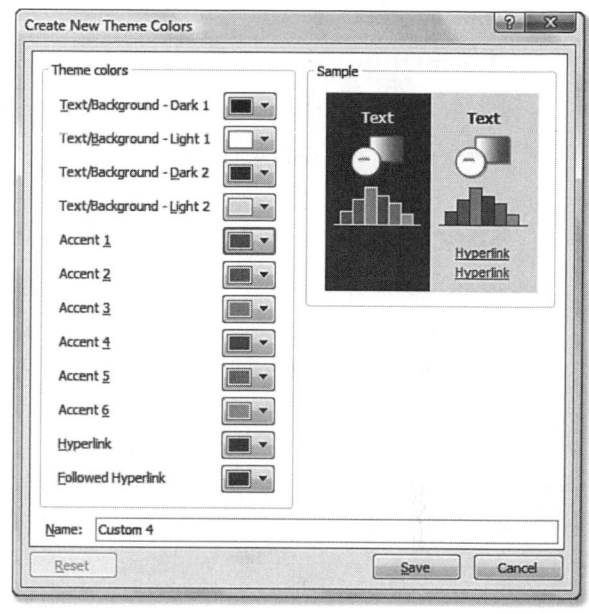

Figure 30.37
You specify the RGB values for the first color.

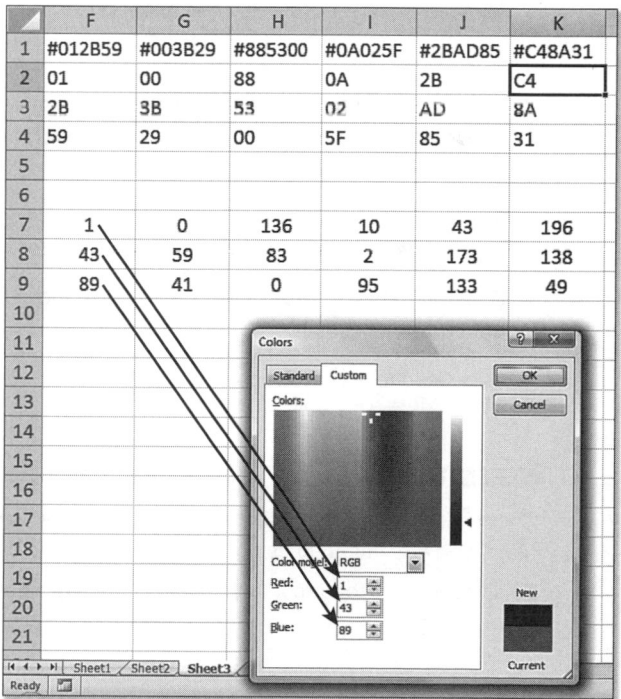

6. If you want to change the colors for Hyperlink, Followed Hyperlink, and Text, repeat steps 2–4 for any of those.

7. In the Name box, give the theme a name, such as your company name.

8. Click Preview to see the theme applied to your workbook.

9. Click Save to accept the theme.

Specifying a Theme's Fonts

To specify new theme fonts, follow these steps:

1. Select Page Layout, Themes, Fonts, Create New Theme Fonts. The Create New Theme Fonts dialog appears, as shown in Figure 30.38. Remember that a font theme contains a heading font and a body font.

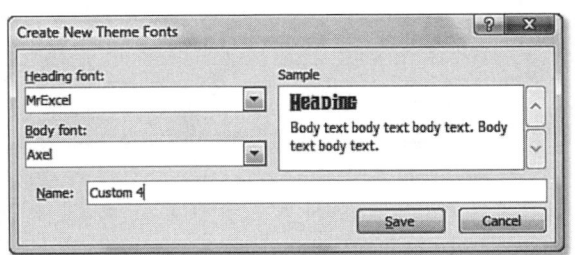

Figure 30.38
A theme is composed of two fonts.

2. Select a font from the Heading Font drop-down. If a custom font is used in your company's logo, using it might be appropriate.

3. Select a font from the Body Font drop-down. This should be a font that is easy to read. Avoid stylized fonts for body copy.

4. Give the theme a name. It is okay to reuse the same name from the color theme.

5. Click Save to accept the theme changes.

 **tip**

In June 2009, famed font designer Erik Spiekermann released the Axel font family, which he designed specifically for showing tables of numbers in Microsoft Excel.

Reusing Another Theme's Effects

There is no dialog box to choose the effects associated with a theme. Other than editing the XML by hand, you are limited to using the effects from one of the built-in themes.

To select effects for a theme, from the Page Layout select Themes, Effects, and then choose one of the existing themes.

The Effects drop-down is initially vexing. There are only subtle clues about the effects used in the theme, as shown in Figure 30.39. Each effects icon consists of a circle, an arrow, and a rectangle. These shapes give you clues about the effects in the theme.

When you insert a shape on a worksheet, six rows of Shape Styles are available in the gallery on the Drawing Tools—Format tab. These styles range from simple (Row 1) to moderate (Row 4) to intense (Row 6).

- The circle in the icon relates to simple shape styles.

- The arrow in the icon relates to moderate shape styles.

- The rectangle in the icon relates to intense shape styles.

Figure 30.39
The Effects drop-down offers subtle clues about the effects in a theme.

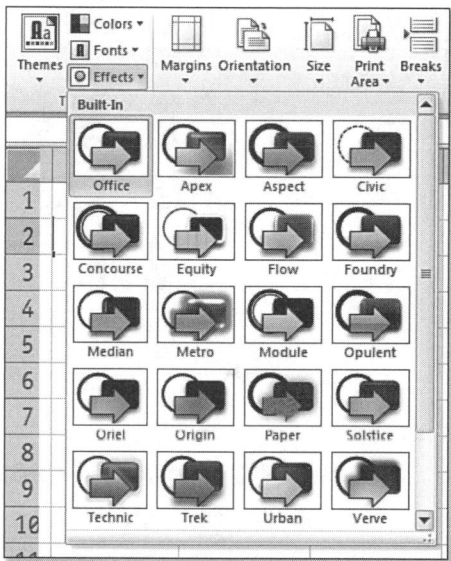

Examine the circle in the upper-left of each theme icon. Aspect, Concourse, Currency, and Opulent use a double line for the simple shape styles. Civic uses a broken line.

The effects used on the arrow indicate the shape effects used for moderate shape effects. For example, Equity uses a vertical pattern of lines in moderate styles. Currency applies a slight gradient. Trek uses more of a shadow than Technic does.

The rectangle indicates the effects applied to intense styles. Even though it is barely perceptible, there is a bit of a reflection under the rectangle in Deluxe, and a glow around the rectangle in Metro.

These effects apply to various shape styles. In Figure 30.40, a dozen pairs of rounded rectangles are shown with 12 different Theme Effects. The top shape in each pair uses a moderate shape style. The bottom shape in each pair uses an intense shape style.

 note

Figure 30.40 is a composite of 12 screenshots put together in Photoshop. There is no way to represent more than one theme in a single Excel workbook.

The 12 pairs are arranged in the same order as effects in the theme box—Office, Apex, Aspect, and Civic in the first two rows; Concourse, Currency, Deluxe, and Equity in the next two rows; and Flow, Foundry, Median, and Metro in the last two rows.

These real examples show that Apex offers a more pronounced shadow than the other themes. Equity is darker. Metro has more of a glow.

➡ *For a color version of this figure, see http://www.mrexcel.com/30fig40.jpg.*

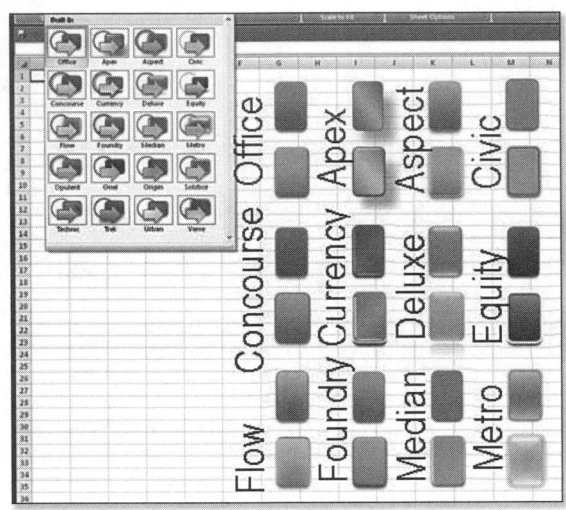

Figure 30.40
These shapes illustrate changes introduced by the Theme Effects drop-down.

Saving a Custom Theme

To reuse a theme, you must save it. To save a theme, from the Page Layout tab select Themes, Themes, Save Current Theme (see Figure 30.41).

By default, themes are stored in the Document Themes folder. In Windows XP, this folder is in `C:\ Documents and Settings\user name\Application Data\Microsoft\Templates\Document Themes\`. In Windows Vista and Windows 7, the folder is in `C:\Users\user name\AppData\ Roaming\Microsoft\Templates\Document Themes`.

Be sure to give your theme a useful name and then click Save.

Using a Theme on a New Document

When you open a new document on the same computer, the Custom theme is in the Themes drop-down on the Page Layout tab. You can use this theme on all future documents.

Sharing a Theme with Others

If you want to share a theme with others, you need to send them the `.thmx` file from the theme folder.

Figure 30.41
The option to save a theme is at the bottom of the Themes drop-down.

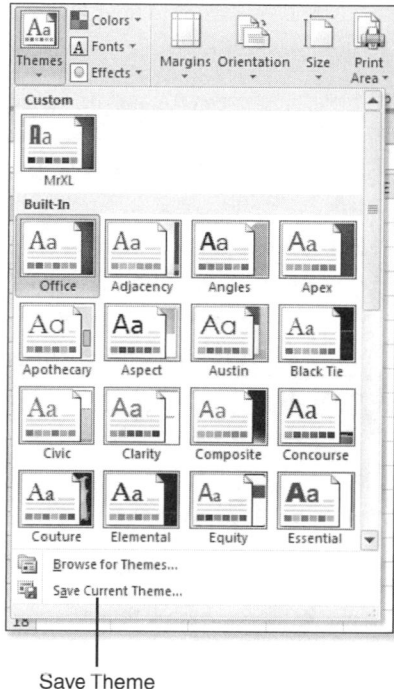

Save Theme

The people you share the theme with can either copy the .thmx file to their equivalent folder or save the .thmx file to their desktop and use the Browse for Themes option, by choosing Page Layout, Themes, Browse for Themes.

Other Formatting Techniques

Now that you have the basics for formatting cells and worksheets, the rest of this chapter provides an overview of various formatting tips and tricks. These techniques discuss how to mix formatting within a single cell, wrap text in several cells, and use cell comments.

Formatting Individual Characters

Occasionally, you might find yourself entering a short memo on a worksheet. This might occur as an introduction or as instructions to a lengthy workbook. Although Excel is not a full-featured word processor, it can do a few word processing tricks.

One trick is to highlight individual characters in a cell in order to add emphasis or to make them stand out. You can do this to any cell that does not contain a formula. In Figure 30.42, for example,

 tip

After selecting characters in the cell, move the mouse pointer to the right and up to activate a shortened version of the Mini toolbar. You can use icons on this floating toolbar to format the selected characters.

text has been typed in Column A and allowed to extend over the edge of the column into Columns A:J. One word in Row 4 is in a bold, underlined, red font.

| A7 | ▾ | (| X | ✓ | *fx* | The budget deadline is October 28. No exceptions! |

◢	A	B	C	D	E	F	G	H	I	J
1	2011 Budget Planning Process									
2										
3	Enclosed are your budget planning worksheets. Please									
4	review/edit your projections. Expenses may <u>**not**</u> increase									
5	by more than 3% this year. Any budget with expense increases									
6	in excess of 3% will be returned for rework.									
7	ons!									
8										

Figure 30.42
Formatting for individual characters in a cell can be changed by selecting those characters in the formula bar.

To format individual characters, follow these steps:

1. Display the Home tab.

2. Select the cell that contains the characters to be formatted.

3. Press the F2 key to edit the cell.

4. Using the mouse, highlight the characters in the formula bar.

5. Although most of the ribbon is grayed out, the options for font size, color, underline, bold, italic, and font name are available in the Font group of the Home tab. Apply any formatting, as desired, from this group.

6. If the changes are not visible in the formula bar, press Enter to accept the changes in order to preview them.

Changing the Default Font

Excel offers a default font setting to be used for all new workbooks. With the Excel 2010 paradigm of themes, the default font for new workbooks is initially the generic value of BODY FONT. However, this is not an actual font; instead, it refers to the main font used by the current theme.

To change your default font for all new workbooks, follow these steps:

1. The menu for changing the default font does not offer Live Preview of the fonts. Therefore, go to the Font section of the Home tab and select the Font drop-down to inspect the available fonts in their actual styles. Find the name of the font you want to use.

 note

If you like the concept of using themes to change the look and feel of a document, you should leave the default font setting as BODY FONT and change the font used in the theme.

2. From the File menu, select Excel Options. The Excel Options dialog appears.

3. Click the Popular category in the left margin.

4. In the second section, When Creating New Workbooks, select the Use This Font drop-down. Select the font name you chose in step 1.

5. Click OK to close the Excel Options dialog.

6. Close and restart Microsoft Excel for the changes to take effect.

The default font setting has an effect only in new workbooks. It does not affect workbooks previously created.

Wrapping Text in a Cell

You might have one column in a table that contains long, descriptive text. If the text contains several sentences, it would be impractical to make the column wide enough to include the longest value in the column. Excel offers the capability to wrap text on a cell-by-cell basis to solve this problem.

When you wrap text, one annoying feature of Excel becomes evident. All cells in Excel are initially set to have their cell contents aligned with the bottom of the cell. You probably do not notice this because most cells in Excel are the same height. However, when you wrap text, the cell heights double or more. When this occurs, it becomes evident that the bottom alignment looks strange. To correct this problem, follow these steps:

 note

If the rows are too tall, you will have a tendency to grab the right edge of the column and drag it outward to make the description column wider. A long-standing bug causes Excel not to resize the row heights automatically after this step. Instead, you need to select the Cells section of the Home tab and then select Format, Autofit Row Height to resize the row height after adjusting the column width.

1. Decide on a reasonable column width for the column that contains the descriptive text. If you try to wrap text in a column that is only 8 points wide, you will be lucky to fit one word per line. If you have the space, a width of at least 24 allows suitable results for the text wrapping.

2. From the Cells section of the Home tab, select Format, Column Width. Choose a width of 24 or greater.

3. Choose the cells in the column to be wrapped.

4. From the Home tab, select Alignment, Wrap Text.

5. Select all cells in the table.

6. From the Home tab, select Alignment, Top Align. The values in the other columns now align with the top of the descriptive text.

Figure 30.43 shows a table where the descriptions in Column B have had their text wrapped and all the cells are top-aligned.

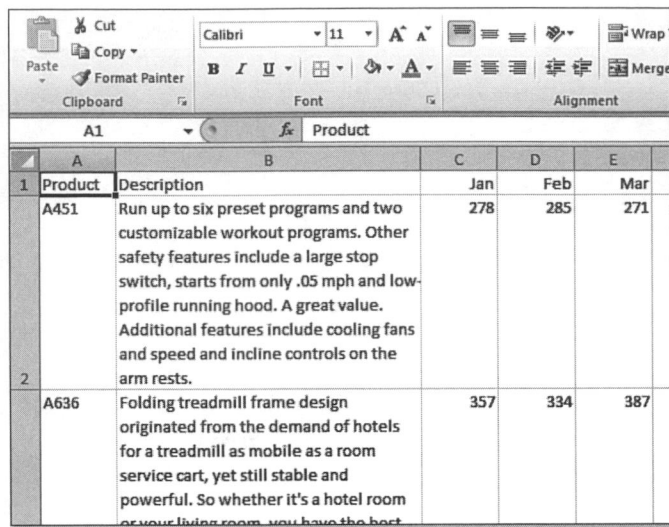

Justifying Text in a Range

When using Excel as a word processor to include a paragraph of explanatory body copy in a worksheet, you usually have to decide where to break each line manually. Otherwise, Excel offers a command that reflows the text in a paragraph to fit a certain number of columns.

For this reason, you should to do some careful preselection work before invoking the command by following these steps:

1. Ensure that your text is composed of one column of cells that contain body copy. It is fine if the sentences extend beyond one column, but the text should be arranged so that the left column contains text and the remaining columns are blank.

2. Ensure that the upper-left cell of your selection starts with the first line of text.

3. Ensure that the selection range is as wide as you want the finished text to be.

4. If your sentences currently extend beyond the desired width, Excel requires more rows in order to wrap the text. Include several extra rows in the selection rectangle. Figure 30.44 shows a suitable-sized selection range.

5. From the Home tab, select Editing, Fill, Justify. Excel flows the text so that each line is shorter than the selection range. Figure 30.45 shows the result.

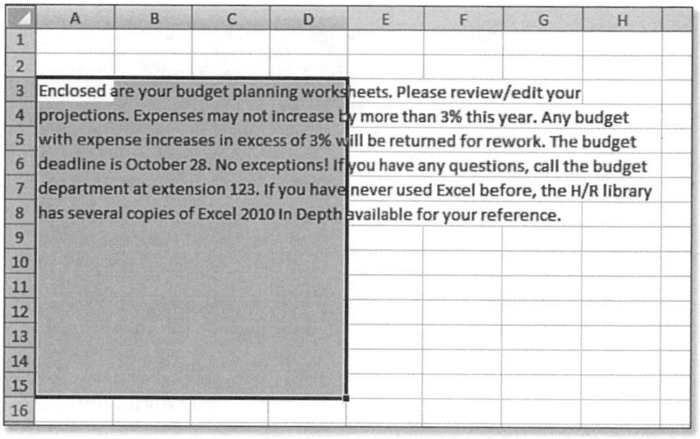

Figure 30.44
You need to select more rows than
necessary. The number of columns
selected determines the width of the
final text.

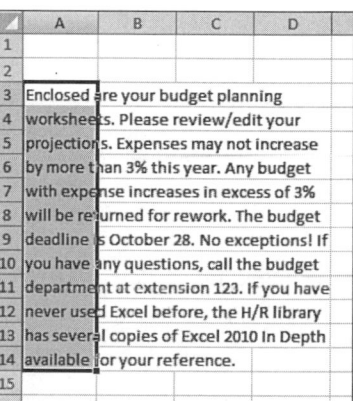

Figure 30.45
Excel flows the text to fit the width of the original selection.

Adding Cell Comments

Cell comments can contain a few sentences or paragraphs to explain a cell. Although the default is
for all comments to use a yellow sticky-note format, you can customize comments with colors, fonts,
or even pictures.

In the default case, a comment causes a red triangle to appear in a cell. If you hover over the triangle, the comment appears. Alternatively, you can request that comments be displayed all the time.
This creates an easy way to add instructions to a worksheet.

Follow these steps to insert a comment, format it, and cause it to be displayed continuously:

1. Select a cell to which you want to add a comment.

2. Select Review, Comments, New Comment or right-click the cell and select New Comment, or press Shift+F2.

3. The default comment starts with your name in bold on line 1 and the insertion point on line 2. To remove your name from the comment, backspace through your name and then press Ctrl+B to turn off the bold.

 **note**

Keep in mind that a comment can contain more than 2,000 words of body copy.

4. Type instructions to the person using the worksheet. You can make the instructions longer than the initial size of the comment.

5. After entering the text, click the resize handle in the lower-right corner of the comment. Drag to allow the comment to fit the text.

6. The selection border around the comment can be made of either diagonal lines or dots. If your selection border is diagonal lines, click the selection border to change it to dots.

7. Right-click the selection border and select Format Comment. The Format Comment dialog appears.

8. In the Format Comment dialog, change the font, alignment, colors, and so on as desired. The Transparency setting on the Colors and Lines tab allows the underlying spreadsheet to show through the comment. If you choose the Fill Color drop-down, you can select Fill Effects and insert a picture as the background in the comment.

9. Click OK to return to the comment.

10. Right-click in the cell and select Show/Hide Comments. This causes the comment to be permanently displayed on the worksheet.

11. To reposition the comment, click the comment. Drag the selection border to a new location.

Figure 30.46 shows a comment that has been formatted, resized, and set to be displayed.

	A	B	C	D	E	F	G	H	I	J
1	2011 Budget Planning Process									
2										
3	Enclosed are your budget planning worksheets. Please review/edit your									
4	projections. Expenses may not increase by more than 3% this year. Any budget									
5	with expense increases in excess of 3% will be returned for rework. The budget									
6	deadline is October 28. No exceptions! If you have any questions, call the budget									
7	department at extension 123. If you have never used Excel before, the H/R library									
8	has several copies of Excel 2010 In Depth available for your reference.									
9										
10			2011 Sales Quota:							
11										
12										
13										
14										
15										

Enter your 2011 sales quota here. This number should include your expected sales from the retail and wholesale channels.

Do not forget to factor in a company targeted growth rate of 3% for retail and 10% for wholesale channels.

Figure 30.46
Cell comments can provide instructions or tips for people who use your spreadsheet.

Copying Formats

Excel worksheets tend to have many similar sections of data. After you have taken the time to format the first section, it would be great to be able to copy the formats from one section to another section. The next sections in this chapter discuss the two methods offered in Excel 2010 for doing this: pasting formats and using the Format Painter icon.

Pasting Formats

An option on the Paste Options menu allows you to paste only the formats from the Clipboard. The rules for copying and pasting formats are as follows:

- If your original selection is one cell, you can paste the formats to as many cells as you want.

- If your original selection is one row tall and multiple cells wide, you can paste the formats to multiple rows, and the final paste area will be as wide as the original copied range.

- If your original selection is one column wide and multiple cells tall, you can paste the formats to multiple columns, and the final paste area will be as tall as the original copied range.

Follow these steps to copy formats:

1. Select a formatted section of a report. This might be one cell, one row of cells, or a rectangular range of cells.

2. Press Ctrl+C to copy the selected section to the Clipboard.

3. Select an unformatted section of your worksheet. If your selection in step 1 is a rectangular range, you can select just the top-left cell of the destination range.

4. Press Ctrl+V to paste. Press Ctrl again to open the Paste Options menu, as shown in Figure 30.47. Type R to paste only the formats. The formats from the original selection are copied to the new range. Although the amounts initially changed after pressing Ctrl+C, the original amounts are restored after pressing R.

5. If you have multiple target destinations to format, repeat step 4 as needed.

 caution

Do not attempt to use the Column Widths icon in the Paste Options menu to solve this problem. The Column Widths icon always pastes the values along with the column widths. Because you are only trying to copy formats and column widths in this example, this is not be a suitable result.

The disadvantage of using the Paste Formats method is that it does not change column widths. To copy column widths without pasting values, on the Home tab, click the Paste drop-down, and then select Paste Special, Column Widths, OK, as shown in Figure 30.48.

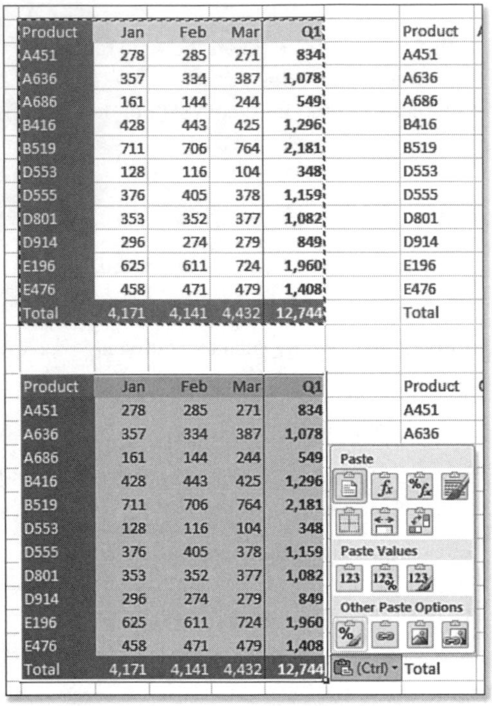

Figure 30.47
Format from the Paste Options menu copies cell formatting without affecting values or formulas.

Figure 30.48
Use Paste Special to paste column widths.

Pasting Conditional Formats

The rules changed in Excel 2010 when you paste a range with one conditional formatting onto another range with a different conditional formatting. Starting in Excel 2010, the copied conditional format will replace the existing conditional formatting. There might be times when you want to merge the existing icon set in the source range with the existing color scale in the target range. In this case, choose "All Merging Conditional Formats" from the Paste Special dialog, or the elusive icon in the second row, fourth column of the Paste Options menu. Note that this will paste formats, formulas and borders as well as merging the conditional formats."

Using the Format Painter

The Format Painter icon appears in the Clipboard group of the Home tab. The prominent location of the icon might encourage you to attempt to use this feature. The Format Painter is still tricky to use.

To copy a format from a source range to a destination range, follow these steps:

1. Select the source range. If you want to copy column widths, the source range must include complete columns.

2. Click the Format Painter icon once in the Clipboard group of the Home tab. The mouse icon changes to a plus and a paintbrush.

3. Immediately use the mouse to click and drag to select a destination range. If the source range was five columns wide, the destination range should also be five columns wide.

4. If you accidentally click somewhere else or click the wrong size range, undo and start over.

The new ToolTip for the Format Painter icon advertises a little-known feature of the Format Painter. This feature enables you to copy a format to many different ranges. To do this, follow these steps:

1. Select the source range.

2. Double-click the Format Painter icon.

3. Click a new destination range. The format is copied. Alternatively, you can drag to paint a different size range.

4. Repeat step 3 as many times as you want.

5. When you are done formatting ranges, press Esc or single-click the Format Painter icon to turn off the feature.

Copying Formats to a New Worksheet

You can use a straightforward way to make a copy of a worksheet. This method is better than creating a new worksheet and copying formats from the original sheet to the new sheet. Among its advantages are the fact that column widths and row heights are copied and page setup settings are copied.

To copy a worksheet within the current workbook, follow these steps:

1. Activate the worksheet to be copied.

2. Hold down the Ctrl key. Click the worksheet tab and drag it to a new location. A new sheet is created with a strange name, such as Sheet3 (2).

3. Right-click the sheet tab and select Rename. The cursor moves to the tab, which is now editable.

4. Type a new name and press Enter. The tab has a new name.

To copy a worksheet to a new workbook, follow these steps:

1. Activate the worksheet to be copied.

2. Right-click the sheet tab. Select Move or Copy to display the Move or Copy dialog.

3. In the To Book drop-down, select (new book).

4. Click Create a Copy.

5. Click OK. The single worksheet is copied to a new workbook.

Excel in Practice: Elbow Formatting

A slick effect for the upper-left corner of a table is to include two headings: a heading for the column labels and a heading for the row labels. Figure 30.49 shows an example. Although it may require a little trial and error, you can achieve this effect by using these steps:

1. Select the top-left cell in a table.

2. Press the spacebar four or five times.

3. Type the heading for the column labels.

4. Press Alt+Enter twice.

5. Type the heading for the row labels.

6. Press Ctrl+Enter to finish entering the cell and to keep the cell pointer in the top-left cell.

7. From the Home tab, select Font, Borders, More Borders.

8. In the Format Cells dialog, on the Border tab, click the lower-right icon in the Border section. This icon is for a diagonal that goes from the top-left to the bottom right.

9. Click OK to close the Format Cells dialog.

10. If the top word hits the diagonal line in the cell, edit the cell and add a space or two before the top word.

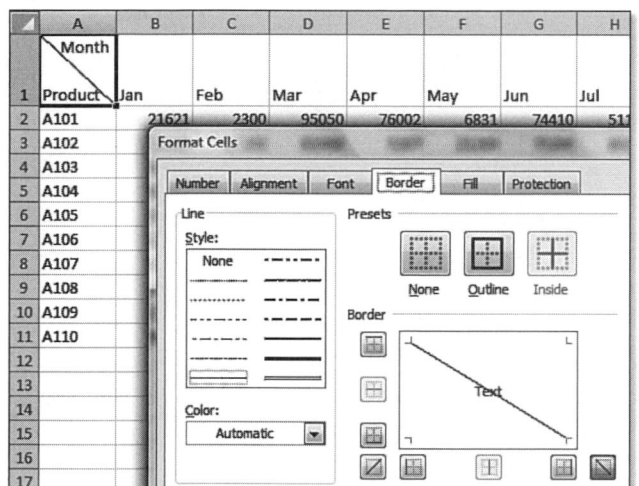

Figure 30.49
The elbow effect is used in Cell A1.

Excel Troubleshooting: Unmerging Cells in Data Pasted from the Web

Web designers use invisible tables as the underlying structure for almost every web page. In an obsessive attempt to control spacing, the author of the HTML for a page will often define that certain values should span two columns or multiple rows. Unfortunately, when you copy and paste this data from the Web to Excel, the spanning of columns or rows causes Microsoft to turn on merged cells in the data. Although merged cells are fine for headings, they should not be used in the middle of data.

To turn off merged cells in data pasted from a web page, follow these steps:

1. Select the pasted data.
2. Display the Format Cells dialog by pressing Ctrl+1.
3. Select the Alignment tab.
4. The Merge Cell icon has a square in the check box to indicate that the selection has a mixture of merged and unmerged cells. Click the box once to select the box. Click the box a second time to clear the Merge Cells check box.
5. Click OK. The merged cells are converted to individual cells. You can now sort and copy the data as usual.

USING DATA VISUALIZATIONS AND CONDITIONAL FORMATTING

Many people feel their eyes glaze over when they encounter a screen full of numbers. Fortunately, Microsoft has added terrific new data visualization features to Excel that make those screens full of numbers a little easier on the eyes.

Excel has had a weak conditional formatting feature since Excel 97. It was limited and tricky to use. Excel tipsters often showed the incredibly hard way to make conditional formatting just a bit more powerful.

Beginning with Excel 2007, Microsoft made data visualization easy to use. You are just a few clicks away from features that would have required a Ph.D. in legacy versions of Excel. The following are some of the possibilities in data visualization:

- Adding data bars (that is, tiny, in-cell bar charts) to cells based on the cell value. In Excel 2010, data bars can be negative, include an axis, and have new scaling options.

- Adding color scales to cells based on the cell value. This is often called a heat map. Whereas the old conditional formatting would allow you to apply one color if a value exceeds a certain amount, a color scale applies a range from a gradient based on how high the value is.

- Adding icon sets (think traffic lights) to cells based on the cell value. Excel 2010 adds three new icons sets.

- Adding color, bold, italic, patterns, and so on to cells based on the cell values.

- Quickly identifying cells that are above average. Quickly identifying the top n or bottom n% of cells.

- Quickly identifying duplicate values.

- Quickly identifying dates that are today or yesterday or last week.

- After you've added icons or color, sorting by color or by icon. This is a huge improvement.

The following are some of the improved conditional formatting features that were added to Excel 2007:

- A cell can meet more than one condition. If you have one rule that makes the cell bold and another rule that makes the cell red, for example, you can have some cells that are red, some that are red bold, some that are bold, and some that are normal.

- There is no longer a limit of only three rules per cell.

- You can easily manage rules. If you want to change the order in which rules are applied, it is easy to reorder the rules.

- It is now obvious that a cell's format can be based on other cell values. This was always the case in legacy versions of Excel, but most people using conditional formatting never discovered the secret. Further, a big improvement is that a formula can now refer to a cell on another worksheet in the current workbook.

Although it is easy to set up basic conditional formatting, you need to know a few tricks, which you learn later in this chapter, for creating better conditional formatting than most people will figure out on their own.

Using Data Bars to Create In-Cell Bar Charts

A data bar is a swath of color that starts at the side of a cell and extends into the cell based on the value of the cell. Small numbers get less color. The largest numbers might be 100% filled with color. This creates a visual effect that enables you to visually pick out the larger and smaller values. Figure 31.1 shows many examples of data bars.

Many new options are available in Excel 2010 data bars:

- Data bars can be solid or a gradient. In Excel 2010, the default gradient bar has a border. Tufte and others complained that the gradient in E14:E20 was misleading. The gradient is useful for helping to see the numbers behind the data bar. (Contrast the solid bar in B2 and the gradient in B8). By adding the border around the gradient, Microsoft leaves no doubt where the data bar ends, but allows the numbers to show through.

- Values of zero now actually get no data bar as shown in cell E10. Previously, the smallest value would get 4 pixels of color.

- Data bars can now be negative. Negative bars are shown in a different color and usually extend to the left of a central axis. You have three choices in where to place the zero axis. In cells B14:B20, the setting is Automatic. Because the largest positive number is further from zero than the smallest negative number, the axis appears slightly to the left of center. This allows the bar for 4.5% in B15 to appear larger than the bar for -3.3% in B17. You can also force the axis to appear in the center as in cells C14:C20. Or, in a bizarre setting, you can force the negative bars to extend in the same direction as the positive values, but with a different color. There are two philosophical ways to show the negative bars. You can assign -3.3% the most color because it is farthest from zero, or you could assign -1.3% the most color because it is the mathematically the largest of the negative numbers (-1.3% > -3.3%). Excel 2010 uses the latter method.

Figure 31.1
The data bars illustrate many of the new properties in Excel 2010 data bars.

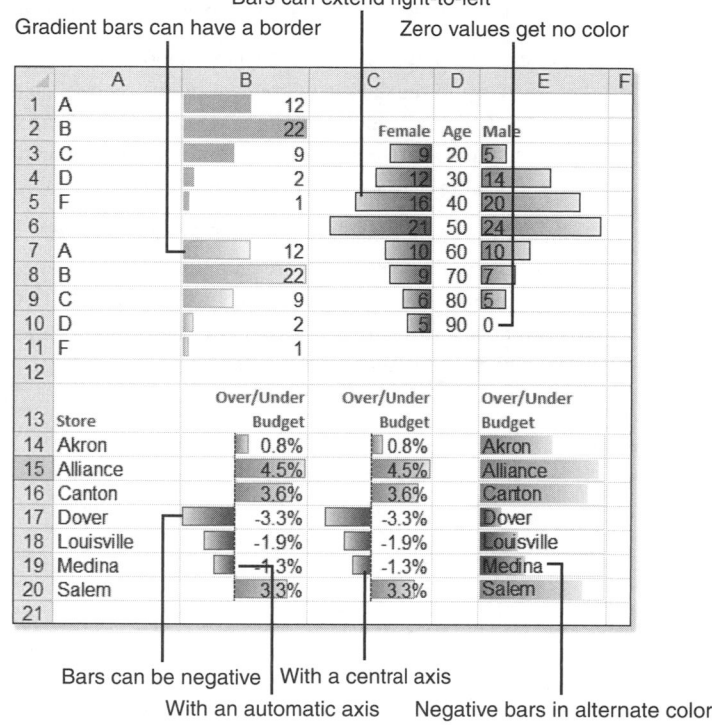

You can control the color of the positive bar, the positive bar border, the negative bar, the negative bar border, and the axis color.

Bars can now extend right-to-left, as shown in cells C3:C10. This allows comparative histograms as in C2:E10.

The following options are not new in Excel 2010, but remain from Excel 2007:

You can specify the scale of the data bars. Although the scale is initially set to automatic, you can specify that the min and/or max is set to a certain number or to the lowest value, a percentage, a percentile, or a formula.

You can choose to show only the data bar and to hide the number in the cell. This is how I managed to get words in cells E14:E20. The numbers are hidden by the conditional formatting dialog, and then a linked picture of the words is pasted over the cells. Because the data bars are on a drawing layer above the regular drawing layer, this works.

All data bars in a group have the same scale. This is unlike sparklines where the scale is allowed to change from graphic to graphic.

Creating Data Bars

Creating data bars requires just a few clicks. Follow these steps:

1. Select a range of numeric data. Do not include the total in this selection. If the data is in noncontiguous ranges, hold down the Ctrl key while selecting additional areas. This range should be numbers of similar scale. For example, you can select a column of sales data or a column of profit data.

2. From the Home tab, select Conditional Formatting, Data Bars. You see six built-in colors for the data bars: blue, green, red, orange, bright blue, and pink. The colors appear both in solid and gradient forms. Select one of them.The result is a swath of color in each cell in the selection, as shown in Figure 31.2.

 note

If you don't like the six basic colors Excel offers for data bars, you can choose any other color, as described in the next section.

 caution

In step 1, if you attempt to select a range that contains both units sold and revenue dollars, the size of the revenue numbers will overpower the units sold numbers, and no color will appear in the units sold cells.

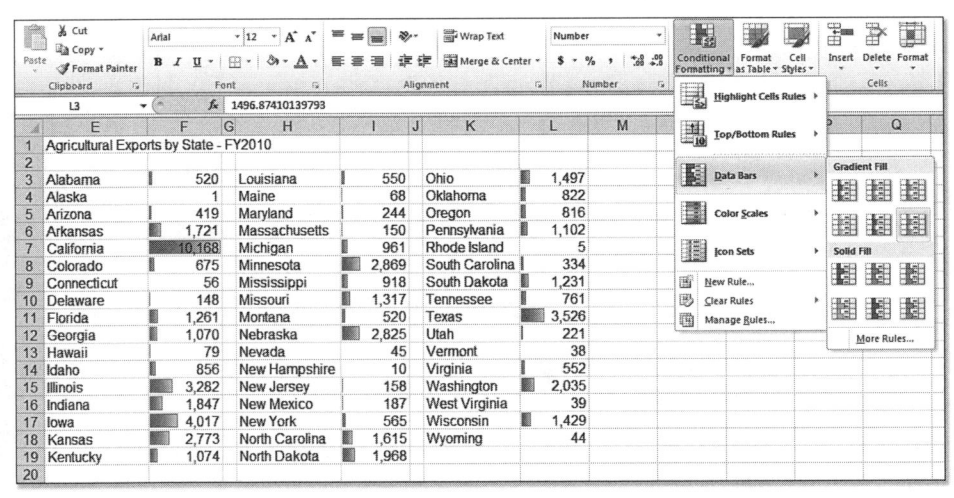

Figure 31.2
After applying a data bar, you can easily see that California is a leading exporter of agriculture products.

Customizing Data Bars

By default, Excel assigns the largest data bar to the cell with the largest value and the smallest data bar to the cell with the smallest value. You can customize this behavior by following these steps:

1. From the Conditional Formatting drop-down on the Home tab, select Manage Rules.

2. From the Show Formatting Rules drop-down, select This Worksheet. You now see a list of all rules applied to the sheet.

3. Click the Data Bar rule.

4. Click the Edit Rule button. You see the Edit Formatting Rule dialog, as shown in Figure 31.3.

Figure 31.3
You customize data bars by using the Edit Formatting Rule dialog.

A number of customizations are available in this dialog.

Select the Show Bar Only setting to hide the numbers in the cells and to show only the data bar.

- For the Minimum and Maximum values, you can choose from Automatic, Number, Percent, Percentile, Formula, or Smallest/Largest Number. If you select Automatic, Excel will choose a minimum and maximum value. You can override this by setting one value to a specific number.

- In the Bar Appearance section, you can specify gradient or solid fill for the bar. You can specify a solid border or no border. Two color chooser drop-downs allow you to change the color of the bar and the border.

- The Bar Direction drop-down allows you to select Context, Left to Right or Right to Left. The default choice of Context will

 caution
One frustrating feature with data bars is that you cannot reverse their size, using the smallest bar for the highest number and vice versa. Although in some scenarios, such as top 100 rankings, the lowest score might deserve the largest bar, there is no way to make this happen with data bars. If you need to do this, you should consider using color scales instead.

always be left to right, unless you are in an international edition of Excel where the language reading order is right-to-left..

When you choose Negative Values and Axis, you have new settings to adjust the color of the bar and the border for negative bars. You can also control if the zero axis is shown at the cell midpoint or at an automatic location based on the relative size of the negative and positive numbers. If the axis is shown, you can adjust the color as well.

Showing Data Bars for a Subset of Cells

In the data bars examples given in the previous sections, every cell in the range receives a data bar. But what if you just want some of the values (for example, the top 20% or the top 10) to have data bars? The process for making this happen isn't intuitive, but it is possible. Basically, you apply the data bar to the entire range. Then you add a new conditional format (a very boring format) to all the cells that you don't want to have data bars. For example, you might tell Excel to use a white background on all cells with values outside of the top 10.

The final important step is to manage the rules and tell Excel to stop processing more rules if the white background rule is met. This requires clever thinking. If you want to apply data bars to cells in the top 10, you first tell Excel to make all the cells in the bottom 40 look like every other cell in Excel. Turning on Stop if True (in the Conditional Formatting Rules Manager dialog) is the key to getting Excel to not apply the data bar to cells with values outside of the top 10.

Figure 31.4 shows data bars applied to only the top 10 states.

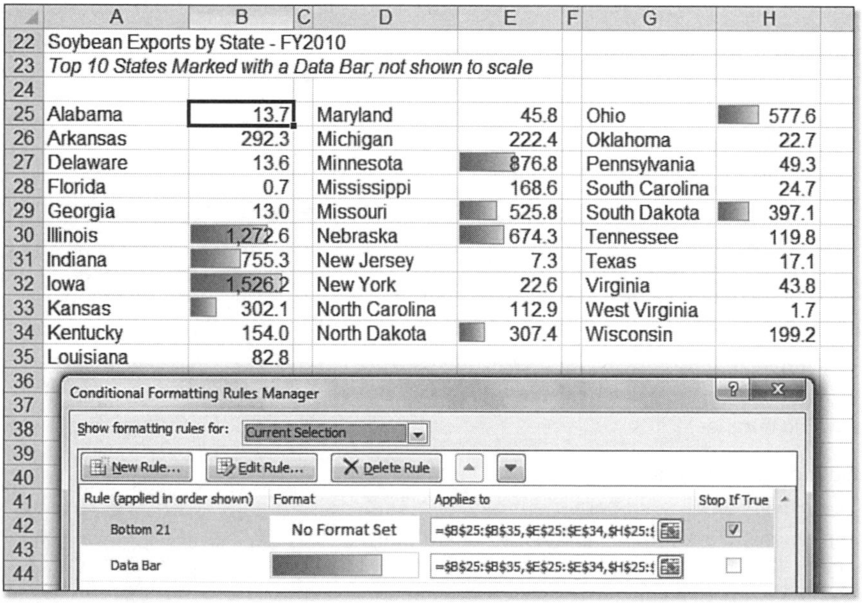

Figure 31.4
Using Stop if True after formatting the lower 21 with no special formatting allows the data bars to appear only on the top states.

Using Color Scales to Highlight Extremes

Color scales are similar to data bars. Instead of having a variable-size bar in each cell, however, color scales use gradients of two or three different colors to communicate the relative size of each cell. Here's how you apply color scales:

1. Select a range that contains numbers. Be sure not to include headings or total cells in the selection.

2. Select Conditional Formatting, Color Scales from the Home tab.

3. From the Color Scales flyout menu, select one of the 12 styles to apply the color scale to the range. (Note that this flyout menu offers subtle differences that you should pay attention to. The first six options are scales that use three colors. These are great onscreen or with color printers. The last six options are scales that use two colors. These are better with monochrome printers.)

In a two-color red-white color scale, the largest number is formatted with a dark red fill. The smallest number has a white fill. All the numbers in between receive a lighter or darker shade of pink based on their position within the range (see Figure 31.5).

Figure 31.5
Excel provides a range of shading, depending on the value. You can see that Carole's and John's receivables have been increasing throughout the year.

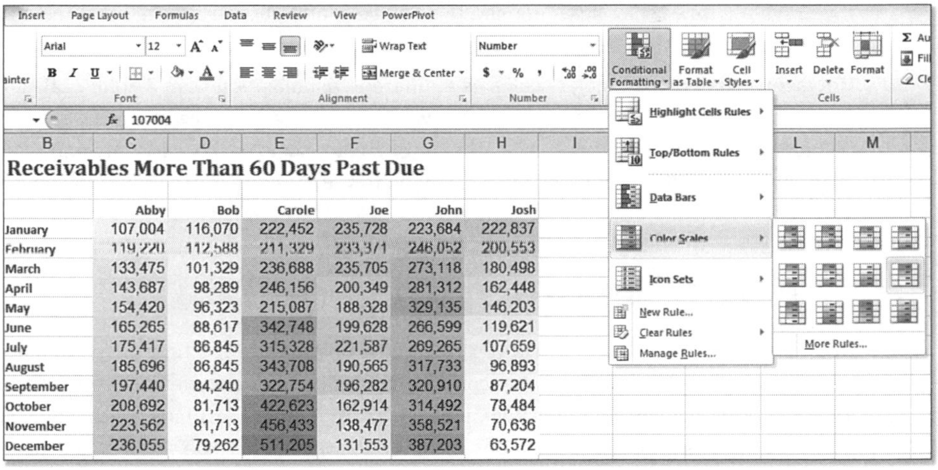

Customizing Color Scales

You are not limited to the color scales shown in the flyout menu. If you select Home, Conditional Formatting, Manage Rules, Edit Rule, you can choose any two or three colors for the color scale.

You also can choose where to assign the smallest, largest, and midpoint values (see Figure 31.6).

You should be aware of one strange situation: Normally, Excel will let you mix conditional formatting in the same range. You might apply both a color scale and an icon set.

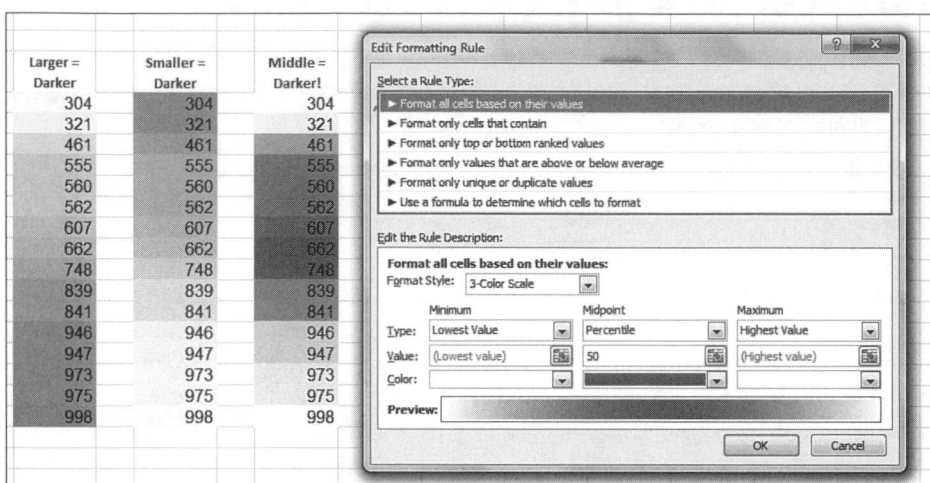

Figure 31.6
You can
choose any
colors to use
in the color
scale.

If you have a three-color scale applied to some cells and choose a different three-color scale from the flyout menu, the latter choice will overwrite the first choice.

However, Excel treats 2-color scales as a different visualization than 3-color scales. If you have a 3-color scale applied and you then try to switch it to a 2-color scale using the flyout menu, Excel will create two rules for those cells. The latter 2-color scale will be the only one to appear in Excel 2010, but you might be confused when you go to the Manage Rules dialog to see two different rules applied to the cells.

Using Icon Sets to Segregate Data

Icon sets, which were popular with expensive management reporting software in the late 1990s, have now been added to Excel. An icon set might include green, yellow, and red traffic lights or another set of icons to show positive, neutral, and negative meanings. With icon sets, Excel automatically applies an icon to a cell, based on the relative size of the value in the cell compared to other values in the range.

Excel 2010 ships with 20 icon sets that contain three, four, or five different icons. The icons are always left-aligned in the cell. Excel applies rules to add an icon to every cell in the range:

- **Three-icon sets**—For the three-icon sets, you have a choice between arrows, flags, two varieties of traffic lights, signs, stars, triangles, and two varieties of what Excel calls "3 Symbols." This last group consists of a green check mark for the good cells, a yellow exclamation point for the middle cells, and a red X for the bad cells. You can either get the symbols in a circle (that is, 3 Symbols (Circled)) or alone on a white background (that is, 3 Symbols). One version of the arrows is available in gray. All the other icon sets use red, yellow, and green.

■ **Four-icon sets**—For the four-icon sets, there are two varieties of arrows: a black-to-red circle set, a set of cell phone power bars, and a set of four traffic lights. In the traffic light option, a black light indicates an option that is even worse than the red light. The power bars icons seem to work well on both color displays and monochromatic printouts.

■ **Five-icon sets**—For the five-icon sets, there are two varieties of arrows, boxes, a five-power bar set, and an interesting set called "5 Quarters." This last set is a monochromatic circle that is completely empty for the lowest values, 25% filled, 50% filled, 75% filled, and completely filled for the highest values.

Setting Up an Icon Set

Icon sets require a bit more thought than the other data visualization offerings. Before you use icon sets, you should consider whether they will be printed in monochrome or displayed in color. Several of the 20 icon sets rely on color for differentiation and look horrible in a black-and-white report.

To set up an icon set, follow these steps:

1. Select a range of numeric data of a similar scale. Do not include the headers or total rows in this selection.

2. From the Home tab, select Conditional Formatting, Icon Sets. Select 1 of the 20 icon sets. Figure 31.7 shows the "3 Triangles" choice selected.

 **tip**

After creating several reports with icon sets, I have started to favor the cell phone power bars, which look good in both color and black and white.

Figure 31.7
You can choose from the 20 icon sets.

Moving Numbers Closer to Icons

In the top rows of Figure 31.8, the icon set has been applied to a rectangular range of data. The icons are always left-aligned. Numbers are typically right-aligned. This can be problematic. Someone might think that the icon at the left side of cell G3 is really referring to the right-aligned number in F3.

You might try centering the numbers to get the numbers closer to the icons in rows 7–9. This will drive purists crazy, because the final digit of the 100 in cell H8 doesn't line up with the final digits of cells H7 and H9.

A better solution is to use the Alignment tab of the Format Cells dialog. Select Right (Indent) for the horizontal alignment. Bump the indent figure up to move the numbers closer to the icon. In rows 12–14, the indent is set at four characters.

If you don't want to show numbers at all, you can edit the conditional formatting rule and select Show Icon Only. Rows 17 through 19 show this solution. Ironically, when the numbers are no longer displayed, you can position the icons by using the Left Align, Center Align, and Right Align icons.

The over-the-top solution in rows 22–24 involve using Show Icon Only and then pasting a linked picture of the numbers from other cells.

Figure 31.8
Changing the alignment of the numbers moves them closer to the icon.

	D	E	F	G	H
1	**Normal**	Speed	Quality	Satisfaction	Efficiency
2	Akron	◑ 85	● 95	◐ 82	◔ 89
3	Boise	● 95	◕ 76	● 95	● 100
4	Chicago	○ 67	○ 65	◕ 75	● 95
5					
6	**Centered**	Speed	Quality	Satisfaction	Efficiency
7	Akron	◑ 85	● 95	◐ 82	◔ 89
8	Boise	● 95	◕ 76	● 95	● 100
9	Chicago	○ 67	○ 65	◕ 75	● 95
10					
11	**Indented**	Speed	Quality	Satisfaction	Efficiency
12	Akron	◑ 85	● 95	◐ 82	◔ 89
13	Boise	● 95	◕ 76	● 95	● 100
14	Chicago	○ 67	○ 65	◕ 75	● 95
15					
16	**Icon Only**	Speed	Quality	Satisfaction	Efficiency
17	Akron	◑	●	◐	◔
18	Boise	●	◕	●	●
19	Chicago	○	○	◕	●
20					
21	**Tricky**	Speed	Quality	Satisfaction	Efficiency
22	Akron	◑ 85	● 95	◐ 82	◔ 89
23	Boise	● 95	◕ 76	● 95	●100
24	Chicago	○ 67	○ 65	◕ 75	● 95

Here are the steps to create rows 22 through 24:

1. Select one of the cells with the icon set formatting.

2. From the Home tab, select Conditional Formatting, Manage Rules.

3. In the Conditional Formatting Rules Manager dialog, click the Icon Set rule and then click Edit Rule.

4. In the middle of the Edit Formatting Rule dialog, select Show Icon Only. Click OK twice to close the two dialog boxes.

5. Select all the cells that contain icons and click the Align Center button on the Home tab.

6. Page down so that you are outside of the printed range. Stay in the same column. Set up a formula to point to the number in the top-left corner of the icon set range. Copy this formula down and over to be the same size as your icon set range. This will give you a range of just the numbers.

7. Format this range of numbers to be right-aligned with an indent of 1.

8. Copy this range of numbers.

9. Go back to the original set of icons and Paste, Picture Link. A picture of the original numbers will appear, behind the icons.

Using the Top/Bottom Rules

The top/bottom rules are a mix of the old- and new-style conditional formatting. They are similar to the old conditional formatting because you must select one formatting scheme to apply to all the cells that meet the rule. However, they are new because rather than specifying a particular number limit, you can ask for any of these conditions:

- **Top 10 Items**—You can ask for the top 10, top 20, or any number of items.

- **Top 10%**—If 20% of your records account for 80% of your revenue, you can highlight the top 20% or any other percentage.

- **Bottom 10 Items**—To highlight the lowest-performing records, select Bottom 10.

- **Bottom 10%**—To highlight the records in the lowest 5%, select Bottom 10%.

- **Above Average**—You can highlight the records that are above the average. As with all the other rules, the average is recalculated as the numbers in the range change.

- **Below Average**—You can highlight the records that are below the average.

Setting Up Conditional Formatting Rules

To set up any of these conditional formatting rules, follow these steps:

1. From the Home tab, select Conditional Formatting, Top/Bottom Rules, and then choose one of the six rule types shown in Figure 31.9.

2. The dialog for above/below average does not require you to select a threshold value, but for the other four rule types, Excel asks you to enter the value for N. As you change the spin button, the Live Preview feature keeps updating the selection with the appropriate number of highlighted cells.

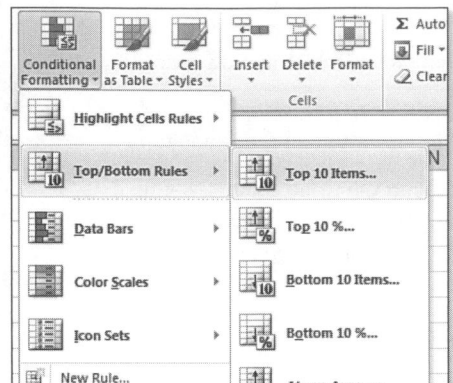

Figure 31.9
You can choose one of these six rule types.

3. The drop-down portion of the dialog initially shows Light Red Fill with Dark Red Text. When you select the drop-down, you have the six default styles shown in Figure 31.10 and the powerful Custom Format option. If one of the six styles is suitable, choose it. Otherwise, proceed to step 4.

4. If you choose Custom Format, you are taken to a special version of the Format Cells dialog box. This version has Number, Font, Border, and Fill tabs. You can choose settings on one or more of these tabs. Click OK to close the Format Cells dialog.

5. Click OK to close the dialog box for your particular rule.

Excel adds the rule to the list of rules. By default, rules added most recently are applied first.

⊿	A	B	C	D	E	F	G
1		Adam	Bill	Chris	Donna	Ed	Fred
2	January	131,369	155,769	58,421	255,092	183,467	191,526
3	February	199,094	152,907	64,380	226,175	183,736	184,273
4	March	176,510	135,689	61,378	228,949	231,998	185,963
5	April	124,482	137,682	60,432	208,101	186,445	128,692
6	May	132,782	142,384	76,085	278,058	230,828	176,436
7	June	165,798					177,299
8	July	127,024					123,445
9	August	146,890					120,453
10	September	168,492					173,064
11	October	196,041					129,799
12	November	171,187					163,686
13	December	120,209					146,684
14							
15							

Top 10 Items

Format cells that rank in the TOP:

8 [⇕] with Light Red Fill with Dark Red Text [▼]

Light Red Fill with Dark Red Text
Yellow Fill with Dark Yellow Text
Green Fill with Dark Green Text
Light Red Fill
Red Text
Red Border
Custom Format...

Figure 31.10
Six canned format styles are available for any rule. If you don't like these, you can select Custom Format.

Using the Highlight Cells Rules

The traditional conditional formatting rules appear in the Highlight Cells Rules menu item of the Conditional Formatting drop-down, along with several new rules. The traditional rules include Greater Than, Less Than, Between, and Equal To. Note that slightly obscure rules such as Greater Than or Equal To are hidden behind the More Rules option. The following are the new rules:

 note
The conceptual rules are based on the system clock, so if you open the workbook next week, the rows highlighted change, based on the system clock.

- **Text That Contains**—This rule allows you to highlight cells that contain certain text.

- **A Date Occurring**—With this rule, you can define conceptual rules such as yesterday, today, tomorrow, last week, this week, next week, last month, this month, next month, or in the last seven days.

- **Duplicate Values**—With this rule, you can highlight both records of a duplicate or highlight all the records that are not duplicated.

The options for Highlight Cell Rules are shown in Figure 31.11.

Figure 31.11
Many powerful and easy conditions are available in the Highlight Cell Rules menu.

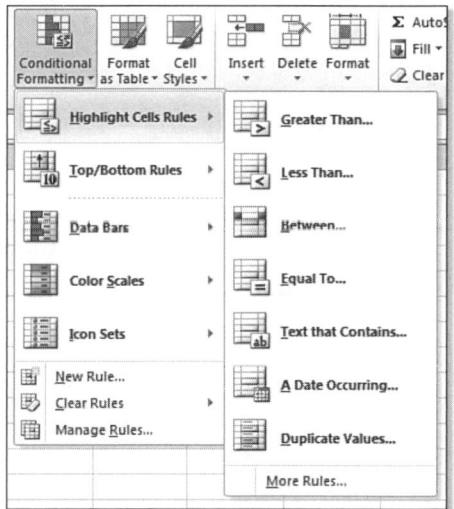

Highlighting Cells by Using Greater Than and Similar Rules

You might think that Greater Than and the similar rules for Less Than, Equal To, or Not Equal To are some of the less powerful conditional formatting rules. In fact, these are the first rules described in this chapter that you can use to base the conditional format threshold on a particular cell or cells. This allows you to build some fairly complex rules without having to resort to the formula option of conditional formatting.

To set up a rule to highlight values greater than a threshold, follow these steps:

1. Select a range of data. Unlike with the other rules, you might choose to include totals in this selection.

2. Select Home, Styles, Conditional Formatting, Highlight Cell Rules, Greater Than to display the Greater Than dialog box.

3. Enter a threshold value in the Greater Than dialog.

4. Choose one of the six formats from the With drop-down. Or choose Custom Format from the With drop-down to have complete control over the number format, font, borders, and fill.

5. Click OK to apply the format.

By way of example, let's look at several options for filling in the threshold value in the Greater Than dialog box. Figure 31.12 shows the conditional formatting rule for all cells greater than 200,000. This is a simple threshold value.

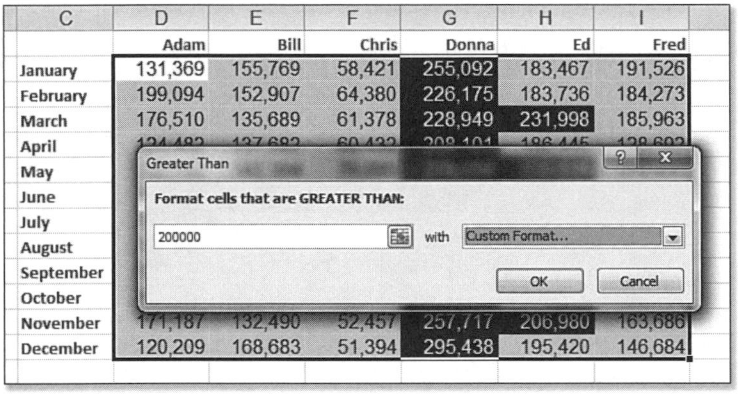

Figure 31.12
You can format all cells greater than a certain value, such as 200,000.

You can specify a cell as the threshold value. You can either use the reference icon at the right side of the box or type an equal sign and the cell reference. In Figure 31.13, the formula highlights any cell that does not exceed the quota in row 1 above the current cell using =D$1.

The formula in Figure 31.13 has to be written for the active cell. Although D4:I15 is the selected range, the name box shows that D4 is the active cell. The formula of =D$1 is compared to the active cell of D4. The threshold cell then becomes the cell in row 1 that is in the same column as each cell in the selection.

The greater-than concepts discussed here apply equally well to the Less Than, Equal to, and Between rules. If you need to access other rules, such as Less Than or Equal To, you can follow these steps:

1. Set up the rule by using Less Than.

2. From the Conditional Formatting icon, select Manage Rules.

Figure 31.13
You can format all cells greater than a certain cell. Prefix the cell reference with an equal sign.

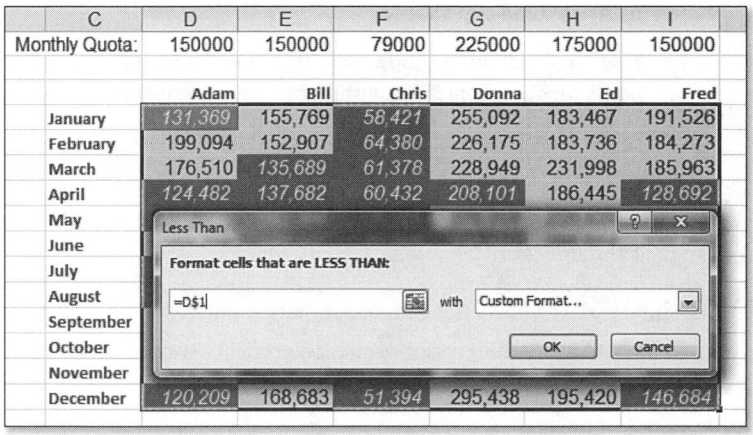

3. Select the Less Than rule and click Edit Rule.

4. Use the drop-down shown in Figure 31.14 to select Less Than or Equal To.

Figure 31.14
After using a quick format with Less Than, you can go to the Manage Rules option to access Less Than or Equal To.

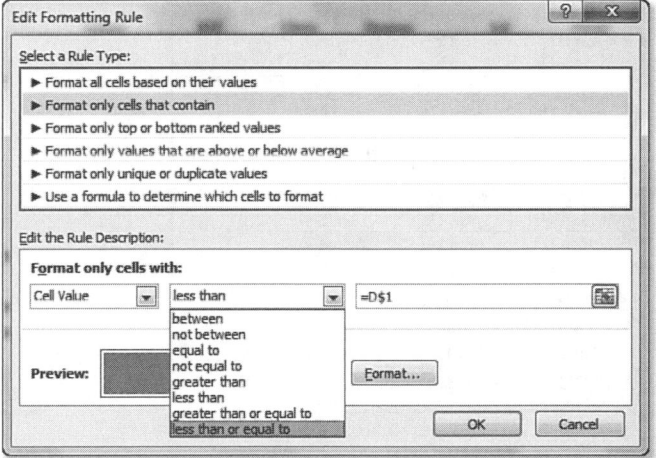

Comparing Dates by Using Conditional Formatting

The date feature was added in Excel 2007. If you are familiar with the reporting engine in Quicken or QuickBooks, the list of available dates will seem similar. A nice feature is that Excel understands the dates conceptually. If you define a feature to highlight dates from last week, the rule automatically updates based on the system clock. If you open the workbook a month from now, new dates are formatted, based on the conditional formatting.

Some of the date selections are self-explanatory, such as Yesterday, Today, and Tomorrow. Other items need some explanation:

- A week is defined as the seven days from Sunday through Saturday. Choosing This Week highlights all days from Sunday through Saturday, including the current date.

- In the Last 7 Days includes today and the six days before today.

- This Month corresponds to all days in this calendar month. Last Month is all days in the previous calendar month. For example, if today is May 1 or May 31, the period Last Month applies to April 1 through April 30.

Figure 31.15 shows the various formatting options, with a system date of January 3, 2010.

The date formatting option would be particularly good for highlighting the items in a to-do list that are due, overdue, or about to be due.

◢	A	B	C	D	E	F	G
1	Today is Sunday, Jan 3, 2010						
2	**This Week**		**Last Week**		**Next Week**		**Last 7 Days**
3	Fri 1/1		Sat 12/26		Fri 1/8		Sat 12/26
4	Sat 1/2		Sun 12/27		Sat 1/9		Sun 12/27
5	Sun 1/3		Mon 12/28		Sun 1/10		Mon 12/28
6	Mon 1/4		Tue 12/29		Mon 1/11		Tue 12/29
7	Tue 1/5		Wed 12/30		Tue 1/12		Wed 12/30
8	Wed 1/6		Thu 12/31		Wed 1/13		Thu 12/31
9	Thu 1/7		Fri 1/1		Thu 1/14		Fri 1/1
10	Fri 1/8		Sat 1/2		Fri 1/15		Sat 1/2
11	Sat 1/9		Sun 1/3		Sat 1/16		Sun 1/3
12	Sun 1/10		Mon 1/4		Sun 1/17		Mon 1/4
14	Today		Yesterday		Tomorrow		
15	Fri 1/1		Fri 1/1		Fri 1/1		
16	Sat 1/2		Sat 1/2		Sat 1/2		
17	Sun 1/3		Sun 1/3		Sun 1/3		
18	Mon 1/4		Mon 1/4		Mon 1/4		
19	Tue 1/5		Tue 1/5		Tue 1/5		
21	This Month		Last Month		Next Month		
22	Tue 11/3		Tue 11/3		Tue 11/3		
23	Thu 12/3		Thu 12/3		Thu 12/3		
24	Sun 1/3		Sun 1/3		Sun 1/3		
25	Wed 2/3		Wed 2/3		Wed 2/3		
26	Wed 3/3		Wed 3/3		Wed 3/3		
27							

Figure 31.15
In the Last 7 days is the odd option among the date formatting options.

Identifying Duplicate or Unique Values by Using Conditional Formatting

Conditional formatting claims that it can mark either duplicate or unique values in a list of values. It seems that Microsoft missed an opportunity to include a different version of unique values than the one that it included. It would be very useful if Microsoft had included an option to mark only the first occurrence of each unique item.

In Column A of Figure 31.16, Excel has marked the duplicate values. Both Adam and Bill appear twice in the list, and Excel has marked both occurrences of the values. You might be tempted to sort by color to bring the red cells to the top, but you will still have to carefully go through to delete one of each pair.

Figure 31.16
Marking duplicates or unique values with the built-in conditional formatting choices requires additional work to decide which of the duplicates to keep in order to produce a unique list.

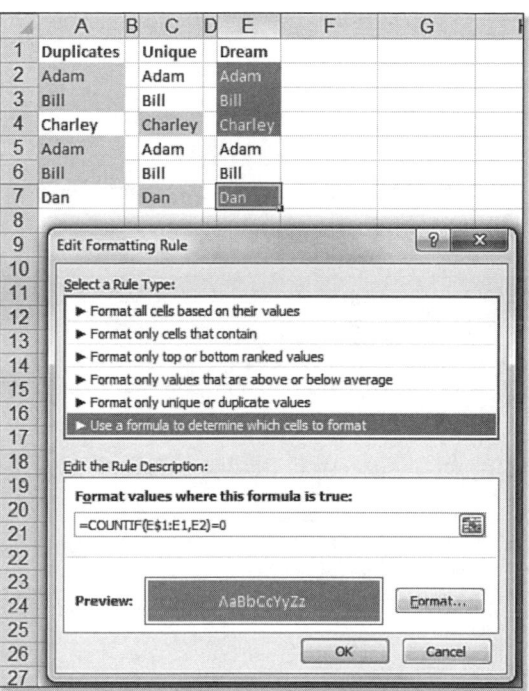

In Column C of Figure 31.16, Excel has applied a conditional format to the unique values in the list. In Excel parlance, this means that Excel marks the items that appear only once in a list. If you would keep just the marked cells as a list of the unique names in the list, you would effectively miss any name that was duplicated.

In a perfect world, this feature would have the logic to include one of each name in the conditional format. The conditional formatting in column E resorts to using the fairly complex formula of =COUNTIF(E$1:E1,E2)=0 to highlight the unique values.

➡ *See more about using formulas to mark cells, in the "Using a Formula for Rules" section later in this chapter.*

Using Conditional Formatting for Text Containing a Value

The Text That Contains formatting rule is designed to search text cells for cells that contain a certain value.

Figure 31.17 contains a column of cells. Each cell in the column contains a complete address, with street, city, state, and ZIP. It would normally be fairly difficult to find all the records for a particular state. However, this is easy to do with conditional formatting. Follow these steps:

1. Select a range of cells that contains text.

2. From the Home tab, select Conditional Formatting, Highlight Cell Rules, Text That Contains.

3. In the Refers To box, enter a comma, a space, and the state that you want to find. Note that this test is not case sensitive (for example, searching for ", pa" is the same as searching for ", PA").

4. Choose an appropriate color from the drop-down.

5. Click OK to apply the format.

As with the Find dialog box, you are allowed to use wildcard characters. You can use an asterisk (*) to indicate any number of characters and a question mark (?) to indicate a single character.

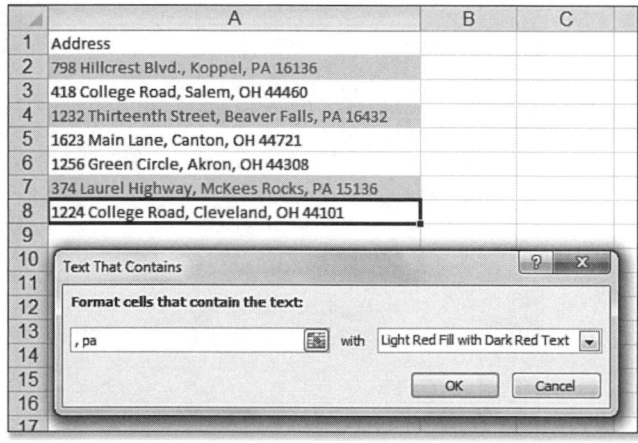

Figure 31.17
Without having to use a wildcard character, the new Text That Contains dialog allows you to mark cells based on a partial value.

Tweaking Rules with Advanced Formatting

All the formats available from icons on the Conditional Formatting group are referred to as quick formatting. According to legend, the Excel team bought a number of Excel books, and if the author spent a page trying to explain a convoluted way to format something using formulas in conditional formatting, then that option became a quick formatting icon.

Every quick formatting item has an option at the bottom called More Rules. When you click this option and get to the New Formatting Rule dialog, you find options that didn't make it as quick formatting icons.

The next section of this chapter discusses using the formula option for conditional formatting. Almost anything is possible by using the formula option, but it is harder to use than the quick formatting icons. If Excel offers a built-in, advanced option, you should certainly use it instead of trying to build a formula to do the same thing.

The lists shown in Tables 31.1 and 31.2 are organized to show all the options for specific rule types. The six rule types are in the top of the New Formatting Rule dialog. Items listed in the right column are advanced options that are available only by clicking More Rules.

Table 31.1   Options for Formatting Cells Based on Content

Option	Advanced Options Available
	Using More Rules
Cell value between x and y.	Cell value not between x and y.
Cell value equal to x.	Cell value not equal to x.
Cell value greater than x.	Cell value less than x.
Cell value greater than or equal to x.	Cell value less than or equal to x.
Specific text containing x.	Specific text not containing x.
	Specific text beginning with x.
	Specific text ending with x.
Dates occurring yesterday.	
Dates occurring today.	
Dates occurring tomorrow.	
Dates occurring in the last 7 days.	
Dates occurring last week.	
Dates occurring next week.	
Dates occurring last month.	
Dates occurring this month.	
Dates occurring next month.	
More Rules	Blanks.
	No Blanks.
	Errors.
	No Errors.

Table 31.2 Options for Formatting Values That Are Above or Below Average

Option	Advanced Options Available Using More Rules
Above the average for the selected range.	1 standard deviation above the average for the selected range.
	2 standard deviations above the average for the selected range.
	3 standard deviations above the average for the selected range.
Below the average for the selected range.	1 standard deviation below the average for the selected range.
	2 standard deviations below the average for the selected range.
	3 standard deviations below the average for the selected range.

Using a Formula for Rules

Excel has three dozen quick conditional formatting rules and twice as many advanced conditional formatting rules. What if you need to build a conditional format that is not covered in the quick or advanced rules? As long as you can build a logical formula to describe the condition, you can build your own conditional formatting rule based on a formula.

Some basic tips can help you successfully use formulas in conditional formatting rules. When you understand these rules, you can build just about any rule you can imagine.

One feature introduced in Excel 2007 is that a formula is allowed to refer to cells on another worksheet. This allows you to compare cells on one worksheet to a worksheet from a previous month or to use a VLOOKUP table on another worksheet.

Getting to the Formula Box

To set up a conditional format based on a rule, follow these steps:

1. Select a range of cells.

2. In the Style group of the Home tab, select Conditional Formatting, Add New Rule.

3. In the New Formatting Rule dialog, choose the rule type Use a Formula to Determine Which Cells to Format. You now see the New Formatting Rule dialog box.

The following sections give you some tips for building a successful formula.

Working with the Formula Box

Following are the key concepts involved in writing a successful formula:

- The formula must start with an equal sign.

- The formula must evaluate to a logical value of TRUE or FALSE. The numeric equivalents of 1 and 0 are also acceptable results.

- When you use the mouse to select a cell or cells on a worksheet, Excel inserts an absolute reference to the cell. This is rarely what you need for a successful conditional formatting rule. You can immediately press the F4 key three times to toggle away the dollar signs in the formula.

- You probably have many cells selected before starting the conditional formatting rule. You need to look at the left of the formula bar to see which cell in the selection is the active cell. If you write a relative formula, you should write the formula that will appear in the active cell. Excel applies the formula appropriately to all cells. This is a key point.

- If the dialog box is in the way of cells you need to select, you can drag the dialog box out of the way by dragging the blue title bar. If you absolutely need to get the dialog box out of the way, you can use the Collapse Dialog button at the right side of the formula box. This collapses the dialog to a tiny area. To return it to full size, you click the Expand Dialog button at the right side of the collapsed dialog.

 caution

The annoying thing about the formula box is that from Enter mode, if you use any of the navigation keys (that is, Page Down, Page Up, left arrow, right arrow, down arrow, up arrow), Excel also changes to Point mode. This can be very frustrating if you are using the left-arrow key to edit a portion of the formula.

- The formula box is one of the evil set of controls that have three possible statuses: Enter, Point, and Edit. Look in the lower-left corner of the Excel screen. The status initially says that you are in Enter mode. This means that Excel is expecting you to type characters such as the equal sign. If, instead, you use the mouse to select a cell, Excel changes to Point mode. In Point mode, the selected cell's address is added to the formula box.

- The solution to working with the formula bar is to use the F2 key. You can press the F2 key to toggle between Enter, Edit, and Point mode. Before using the Left Arrow key or Right Arrow key to move within a formula, you must press F2 until the status bar indicates that you are in Edit mode.

The following sections describe several useful conditional formatting rules. This list only scratches the surface of the possible rules you can build. It is designed to generate ideas of what you can accomplish by using conditional formatting.

Finding Cells Within Three Days of Today

The quick formatting feature offers to highlight yesterday or today or tomorrow, but what if you need to find any cells within three days of today, either plus or minus? If the active cell is B2, then use a formula of =ABS(TODAY()-B2)<4.

Finding Cells Containing Data from the Past 30 Days

The Excel quick formatting option offers to highlight this month or last month. However, highlighting this month or last month can mean a number of vastly different things. Highlighting this month on the second of the month shows a lot of the future and only one day of the past. The same rule on the 29th of the month highlights a lot of the past and only a few days of the future. It would be more predictable to write a rule that shows the past 30 days.

You create this rule similarly to the way you created the Next Seven Days rule in the preceding section. You first compare the date in the cell by using TODAY() to make sure the date in the cell is less than today. Because the active cell in Figure 31.18 is F4, you use the following formula:

```
=AND(F4<TODAY(),(TODAY()-F4)<=30)
```

To generalize this formula for other periods, such as the past 15 days or the past 45 days, you change the 30 to a different number.

 To see a demo of setting up a formula-based conditional format, search for "Excel In Depth 31" at YouTube.

Highlighting Data from Specific Days of the Week

The WEEKDAY() function converts a date to a number from 1 through 7. When used without any additional arguments, the value of WEEKDAY(date) for a Sunday is 0 and Saturday is 7.

In Figure 31.19, the active cell is H4. If you needed to highlight all the Wednesdays, you could check to see whether WEEKDAY(H4)=4. To find all the Fridays, you would check to see whether WEEKDAY(H4)=6. To find either date, you would use =OR(WEEKDAY(H4)=4,WEEKDAY(H4)=6).

To generalize this formula, you could substitute any number from 1 through 7 to highlight Sundays, Mondays, and so on.

Highlighting an Entire Row

Most conditional formatting highlights a cell based on the value in that cell. In this case, you would like to highlight the entire row for the row with the largest product sale.

In Figure 31.18, cell A2 is the active cell. You need to select the entire range of A2:G14. Your goal is to write a rule for all of those cells that will look at Column D for the same row as the cell. In this case and in any case in which you want to highlight the entire row based on one column, you use the mixed reference with a dollar sign before the column letter.

You want to see whether =$D2 is equal to the largest value in the range.

To find the largest value in Column D, you use an absolute reference to D2:D14—that is, =MAX($D$2:$D$14). The conditional formatting formula for this specific case is =$D2=MAX($D$2:$D$14).

To change this rule to highlight the smallest value in Column D, you change MAX to MIN.

To base the test on another column, change D to the other column in three places in the formula.

 note

The Excel table formatting allows you to create alternate formatting where every other two rows are formatted. To duplicate this with conditional formatting, you have to divide the row number by 4 and examine the remainder. There are four possible remainders; 0, 1, 2, and 3. You can either look for results greater than 1 or less than 2 to be formatted. To do this, you change the preceding formula to =MOD(ROW(),4)<2.

Figure 31.18
The combination of a mixed reference and the absolute reference allows you to highlight an entire row.

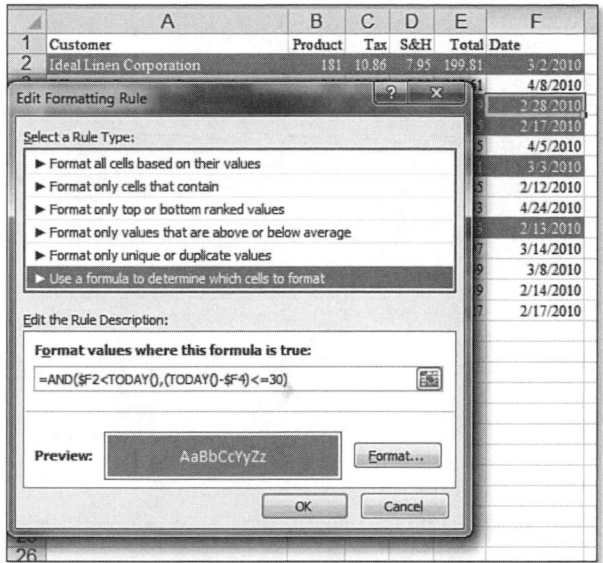

Highlighting Every Other Row Without Using a Table

You might find yourself using the Format as Table feature only to add alternating bands of color to a table. If you don't need the other table features, using a conditional format can achieve the same effect.

Do you remember when you were first learning to do division? You would express the quotient as an integer and then a remainder. For example, 9 divided by 2 is 4 with a remainder of 1, sometimes written as 4R1.

The trick to formatting every other row is to check the remainder of the row number after dividing by 2. Excel has functions that make this easy. First, =ROW() returns the row number of the given cell. Next, =MOD(ROW(),2) divides the row number by 2 and tells you the remainder. The task is then simply to highlight the rows where the remainder is equal to 1 or equal to zero.

In Figure 31.19, the active cell is A2. The formula to achieve the banding effect is
=MOD(ROW(),2)=0.

To generalize this formula for your particular data set, you could change A2 to be the active cell's address.

Combining Rules

A major improvement in conditional formatting in Excel 2010 is the ability to have multiple conditions evaluate to TRUE. In legacy versions of Excel, when a condition was met, Excel quit evaluating

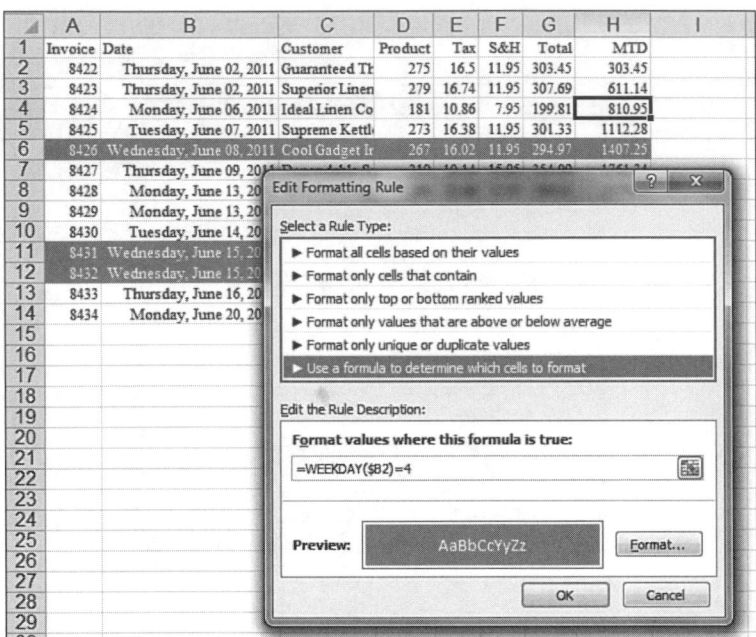

Figure 31.19
It is possible to create a row banding effect without using the Excel table formatting.

additional conditions. For each rule in Excel 2010, you can decide whether Excel should stop evaluating additional rules or whether Excel can continue evaluating rules.

For example, one rule might set the font color to blue. Another rule might set the font style to bold. Cells meeting both rules can be formatted in blue bold. Cells meeting one rule can be either blue or bold. Cells meeting neither rule will be in normal font style.

If two rules attempt to create conflicting formatting, Excel uses the first rule in the list. For example, if Rule 1 turns the font red and Rule 7 turns the font blue, the font is red.

There are 10 types of formatting that can be changed in each cell. Naturally, each type conflicts with others of the same type. Only the first rule that evaluates to TRUE can change the fill color.

Very few formatting styles conflict with each other. Only the cell fill and the color scale are mutually exclusive. Otherwise, you can have up to nine rules evaluate to TRUE for any given cell. Table 31.3 illustrates the interplay between the 10 formatting styles.

Table 31.3   Cell Formatting Styles

Style	Effect
Font color	Changes the font color for cells meeting a condition.
Font style	Applies normal, bold, italic, or bold italic to cells meeting a condition.
Underline	Adds or removes single or double underlining for cells meeting a condition.

Style	Effect
Strikethrough	Applies strikethrough for cells meeting a condition.
Number format	Changes the number format for cells meeting a condition.
Border	Alters the borders for cells meeting a condition. You might think that you could combine two rules that both affect the border. For example, you might want to make the top border blue for cells that meet Rule 1 and the right border red for cells that meet Rule 2. Even though this conceptually makes sense, Excel allows only the first true rule to change the borders.
Cell fill	Changes the cell background for cells meeting a condition. Amazingly, this works fine in combination with data bars. (The cell fill appears to the right of the data bar.) It also works fine with icon sets, and it works fine with all the preceding options. However, cell fill and color scales cannot coexist. Only the first true rule appears in the cell.
Color scale	Changes the cell background for all cells in the range, with the color being determined by the value of one cell in relation to the other cells in the range. This rule can coexist with everything but itself and the cell fill formatting.
Data bar	Adds an in-cell bar chart in each cell. This rule can coexist with any other type of rule.
Icon set	Adds an icon in the left side of the cell. This rule can coexist with any other type of rule.

Clearing Conditional Formats

You can use a number of ways to clear conditional formats. A few quick options are available from the Ribbon:

- You can highlight the entire range with conditional formatting and then use Home, Styles, Conditional Formatting, Clear, Selected Cells. This removes all conditions from the current selection.

- To clear all the conditional formats from the current worksheet, you can use Home, Styles, Conditional Formatting, Clear, Entire Sheet. This is handy if you have only one set of rules set up on the sheet. You can delete all the rules without having to select the entire range.

- If you have rules assigned to a pivot table or a table, you can select one cell in the pivot table or table. This enables new options for Home, Styles, Conditional Formatting, Clear, This Table or Home, Styles, Conditional Formatting, Clear, This PivotTable.

If you have multiple rules assigned to a range and you need to delete just a portion of those rules, you can use Home, Styles,

 note

Deleting columns or deleting rows deletes the rules associated with those columns or rows. Selecting Home, Editing, Clear, All or Home, Editing, Clear, Formats removes the rules.

Conditional Formatting, Manage Rules. In the Conditional Formatting Rules Manager dialog, you should use the top drop-down to display rules in the current selection, this worksheet, or any other worksheet. You can then highlight a specific rule and click the Delete Rule button.

Extending the Reach of Conditional Formats

In every example in this chapter, you have been advised to highlight the entire range before setting up the conditional format. It is also possible to assign a conditional format to one cell and then extend the rule to other cells. There are two ways to copy a conditional format:

- You can select a cell with the appropriate rule and then press Ctrl+C to copy it. Then you select the new range and select Home, Clipboard, Paste, Paste Special, Formats, OK to copy the conditional formatting from the one cell to the entire range.

- You can select Home, Styles, Conditional Formatting, Manage Rules. Then you select a rule. In the Applies To column you see the list of cells that have this rule. You can type a new range there or use the collapse button to make the dialog smaller so that you can highlight the new range.

When you are using conditional formats that compare one cell to the entire range, using the second method is safer to ensure that Excel understands your intention.

Special Considerations for Pivot Tables

This section talks about the special conditional formatting options that are available for pivot tables.

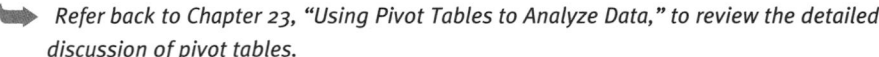 *Refer back to Chapter 23, "Using Pivot Tables to Analyze Data," to review the detailed discussion of pivot tables.*

A typical pivot table might contain two or more levels of summary data. In the pivot table in Figure 31.20, for example, Cells H4:J16 contain sales data. However, if you tried to create a data bar for this entire range, the subtotal values in rows 9 and 15 would make the data bars in the other rows look too small.

To set up a data bar for the detail items in a pivot table, follow these steps:

1. Select a detail cell in the pivot table. In Figure 31.20, a cell such as H4 will do.

2. From the Home tab, select Conditional Formatting, New Rule. The New Formatting Rule dialog appears.

3. Because your selection is inside a pivot table, you have new options at the top of the New Formatting Rule dialog:

   - **Selected Cells**—You can apply the rule to just the one cell. This is not what you want in this case.

   - **All cells showing "Sum of Sales" values**—You can apply the rule to cells including the total column, grand total row, and all the subtotal rows. Remember that the size of the grand total causes all the detail items to have data bars that are too small.

Figure 31.20
The trick to a successful conditional format in a pivot table is to apply the format only to items at the same detail level.

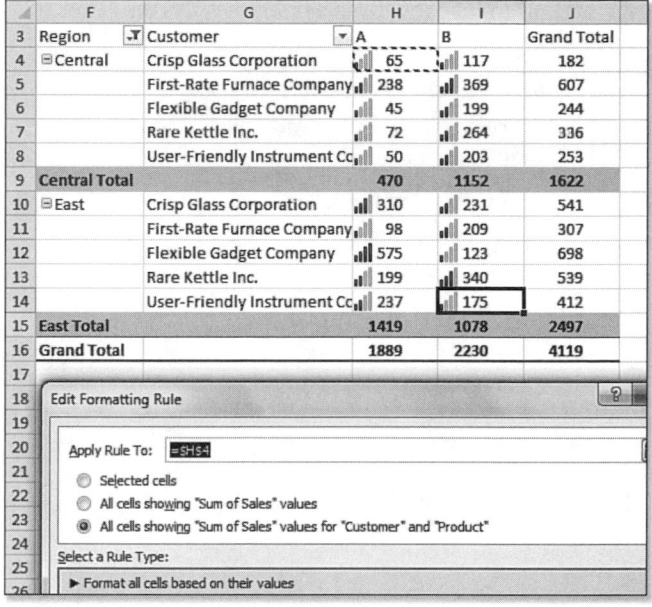

- **All cells showing "Sum of Sales" values for "Customer" and "Product"**—This is the option you use most of the time. The meaning of this option is dependent on careful selection of a detail cell in step 1. If you selected a subtotal row instead, this option would apply the data bars only to the subtotal rows.

  Your actual words in the second and third options vary, depending on the fields displayed in your pivot table. For successful pivot table formatting, select the third option.

4. Define the data bar as usual in the New Formatting Rule dialog.

Excel in Practice: Showing Data Bars in Two Colors

This obscure trick has been posted in the Microsoft Excel team blog.

It turns out that every conditional formatting rule has a formula value that determines whether the rule is shown. Microsoft exposed this rule in the user interface for some conditional formatting rules but not for the data bars. You can, however, access it in the VBA editor!

Suppose that your goal is to add a data bar to a range of cells. If the value is 90 or above, you would like the bars to be green. If the value is 89 or below, you would like the bars to be red. Here's how you accomplish this:

1. Select the range of cells to be formatted.

2. Use the conditional formatting quick options to add to the range a data bar that is red.

3. Select Conditional Formatting, Add New Rule to add a second rule that applies a green data bar. You see only the most recent rule, so all the data bars are green.

4. Note in the Name box which cell is the active cell. You will need this information in step 7.

5. Press Alt+F11 to switch to the VBA editor.

6. Press Ctrl+G to display the Immediate pane.

7. Type Selection.FormatConditions(1).Formula = "=if(A2⋯>89, TRUE, FALSE)" and then press Enter. Cell A2 should be changed to the name of the active cell from step 4.

The result is that the green bars are visible only when the value is 90 or above. In all other cases, the bars appear red.

USING EXCEL CHARTS

The charting engine in legacy versions of Excel was antique. Nothing had changed in the past 15 years. Microsoft attempted a giant step forward with the charting engine for Office 2007. However, in practice, the Office 2007 charting engine was slower and included several bugs. The charting engine in Excel 2010 includes fixes for bugs, is nearly as fast as Excel 2003, and restores some favorite features that were removed in Excel 2007. In addition, Excel 2010 adds a new type of word-sized chart called *Sparklines*. To read about these charts, see Chapter 33, "Using Sparklines."

Although Sparkline charts offer a lot of eye-candy appeal, there are still no new chart types in Excel 2010. You are limited to the same basic 73 types of charts that have been around for the past decade. Excel abandoned the four-step Chart Wizard after Excel 2003. Although this gets you a chart in two clicks instead of four steps, you still need to make a variety of choices on the Design and Layout tabs to bring the chart to fruition.

If you have been using Excel 2007, look for these features in Excel 2010:

- Two limits have been removed. You are no longer limited to 32,000 points in a 2D chart series. You are no longer limited to 256,000 points in a chart. Both of these limits have been expanded to as many points that are allowed by available memory.

- Pattern fills are back after a hiatus in Excel 2007. Pattern fills are great for charts that will be printed in black and white.

- The macro recorder works for charts again in Excel 2010.

- You can double-click any element in a chart to format it. You can also right-click and choose Format. New in Excel 2010: the right-click Mini Bar offers a drop-down that allows you to select chart elements.

- Charts render faster, scroll faster, save faster, and open faster. Excel 2007 had been rerendering the complete chart as you attempted to scroll. Excel 2010 uses a cached version of the chart to address the speed issues.

- On-chart controls return to pivot charts. This is one feature that I actually liked better in Excel 2007. Fortunately, you can turn the on-chart controls off.

Understanding the Components of a Chart

A chart graphically represents numerical data. For every chart, there is underlying data. In Excel, the data is usually in a range of a worksheet. This range is called the *Source Data*.

A simple chart has one series of data. A series might be monthly sales for the East region for each month from January through June. Typically, a series includes the following components:

- **Series Name**—This is one cell that contains the name of the series. An example might be a cell with the value "East Region."

- **Series Values**—This is a row or column of cells that contain the individual sales for each time period.

- **Category Labels**—This is a row or column of cells that contain the name for each time period. The Category Labels typically have the same size and shape as the Series Values.

You will often include multiple series on one chart. For example, you might include additional series for Central and West regions. This allows you to compare sales for the East, Central, and West regions at a glance. Each additional series requires another cell for a Series Name and cells for Series Values. There is no need to repeat the Category Labels.

As the data is translated to a chart, look for these elements.

The Category Labels appear along the Category Axis. This is typically the axis along the bottom of the chart. Mathematicians call this the *X-axis*.

Each Series is plotted with a slightly different color. A legend typically appears on the right side of the chart to identify the color for each series.

The Value Axis indicates the scale for the data points. In Figure 32.1, the scale is from 0 to 30,000.

 note

If you are a fan of visual information, I recommend that you buy every book available from Edward Tufte. Most charting books recommend his book, *The Visual Display of Quantitative Information*, as the source for ideas about how to display information graphically. I also recommend buying the complete suite: *Envisioning Information*, *Beautiful Evidence*, and *Visual Explanations: Images and Quantities, Evidence and Narrative*.

 note

Following the discussion about chart components, there are series values in B1:G4 and series labels in A2:A4. The category labels are in B1:G1. There is no need to have a label in A1 for the category labels. When Excel sees text in A1 and numbers in B1:G1, it assumes there are no category labels, and your chart rarely appears as you want.

Figure 32.1
Components of source data and a chart.

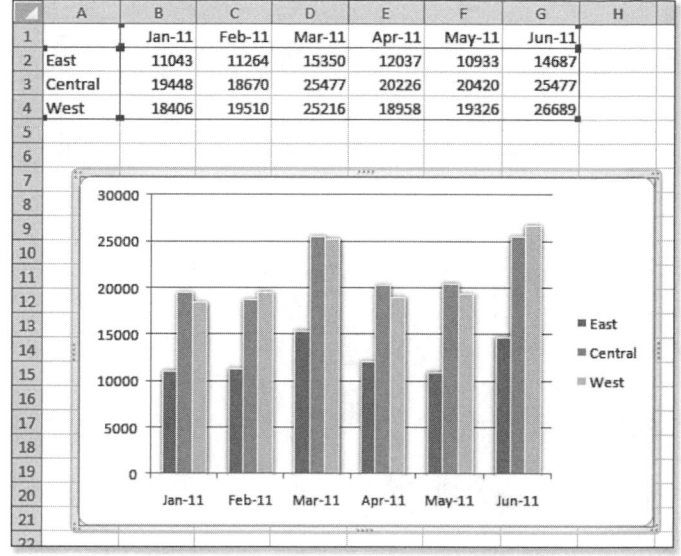

Setting Up Data for Charting

The first step in creating a chart is to set up your data. There are a number of things you should do before you start charting:

- Ensure that your chart data is in a contiguous block.

- Ensure that headings along the left column and top row identify each series.

- If either your row or column headings contain dates or numerals, take care to leave the upper-left corner of the chart range blank (see Cell A1 in Figure 32.2). Leaving this cell blank allows Excel's IntelliSense to work correctly.

If your data follows these rules, you can create charts with just a few mouse clicks. If your data does not follow these rules, you can still chart the data, but you will have to enter the address manually for each data series value, the data series label, and the category labels.

Figure 32.2
If your data has numeric or date headings, leave the upper-left corner cell blank.

	A	B	C	D	E	F	G
1		Jan-11	Feb-11	Mar-11	Apr-11	May-11	Jun-11
2	East	11043	11264	15350	12037	10933	14687
3	Central	19448	18670	25477	20226	20420	25477
4	West	18406	19510	25216	18958	19326	26689

Inserting a Chart by Choosing a Chart Type

For the most popular chart types, creating a chart in Excel 2010 takes just three clicks. Microsoft makes available 73 basic chart types from seven drop-down icons on the Insert tab.

The Charting group on the Insert tab includes seven drop-downs, as shown in Figure 32.3. The first six of these drop-downs hold the most popular charting types. The following seven drop-downs are available in the Charting group:

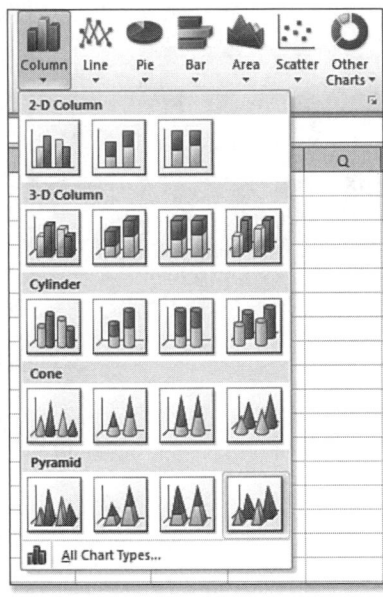

Figure 32.3
This figure displays the drop-down for Column charts.

- **Column**—This drop-down includes 2D Column, 3D Column, Cylinder, Cone, and Pyramid chart types. All column chart types feature markers that relate the vertical height to size.

- **Line**—This drop-down includes 2D Line and 3D Line chart types.

- **Pie**—This drop-down includes 2D Pie and 3D Pie chart types. A pie chart is suitable for a data set that has only one series of information.

- **Bar**—This drop-down includes 2D Bar, 3D Bar, Cylinder, Cone, and Pyramid chart types. All bar chart types feature markers that relate the horizontal width to size.

- **Area**—This drop-down includes 2D area and 3D area chart types. Area charts are similar to line charts except that the area underneath the line is filled with color.

- **Scatter**—This drop-down is used to plot data on x and y axes.

- **Other Charts**—This drop-down includes stock, surface, doughnut, bubble, and radar charts.

To create a chart using the drop-downs in the Charting group on the Insert tab, follow these steps:

1. Select your data in the worksheet. Include headings in the top row and left column.

2. From the Charts group of the Insert tab, select the drop-down for a chart type.

3. From the gallery that appears, choose a chart type. A default chart of a default size is added to the worksheet, as shown in Figure 32.4.

Figure 32.4
This is a default chart at a default size that can be customized.

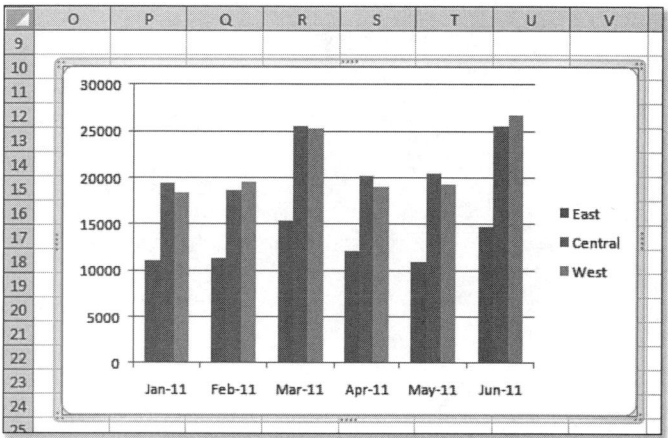

Using the Create Chart Dialog

At the bottom of each charting drop-down is the link All Chart Types. After a chart is created, you can either click All Chart Types or select Design, Change Chart Type. Clicking either button leads to the Change Chart Type dialog box that shows the 73 available chart types (see Figure 32.5).

Although there are 73 chart types, the following three basic patterns run through most chart types (see Figure 32.6)

- **Clustered**—In a clustered chart, bars from each series are plotted side-by-side. This type of chart allows you to compare each element to the next. The drawback to this type of chart is that you cannot easily tell if the sum of the data is increasing or decreasing. A clustered chart is shown in the lower-left corner of Figure 32.6. In the Change Chart Type dialog, clustered chart types show a light blue and dark blue marker next to each other.

- **Stacked**—In a stacked chart, bars from each series are plotted on top of each other. With this type of chart, it is very easy to tell if the total of all series is increasing or decreasing, but it is difficult to tell if a particular series (other than the first series) increases from month to month. A stacked chart is shown in the upper-right corner of Figure 32.6. In the Change Chart Type dialog, stacked chart types show a dark blue marker on top of a light blue marker. The markers shown are of different heights.

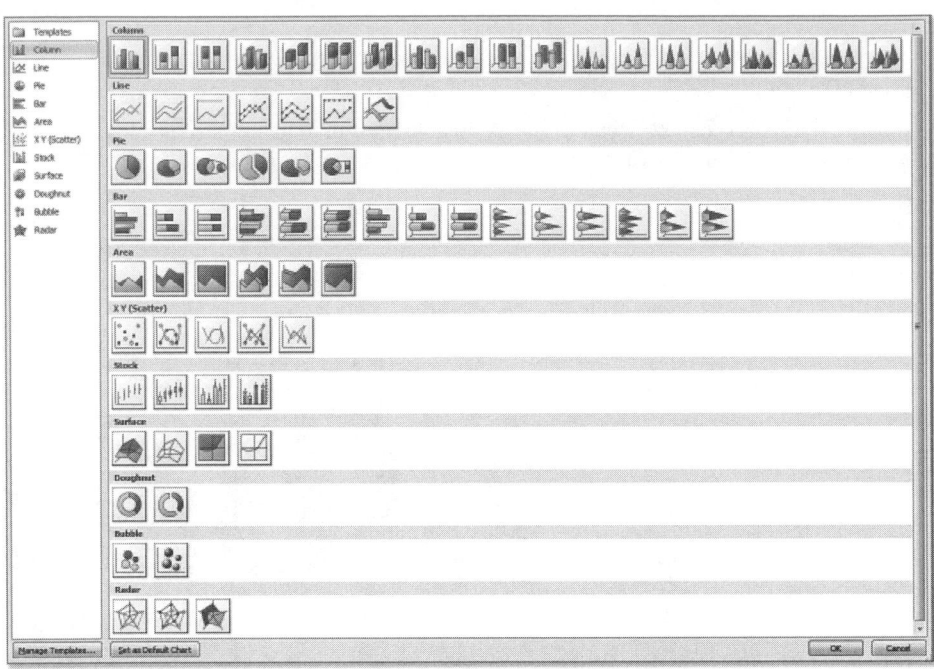

Figure 32.5
The 73 chart types seem like a dizzying array of choices.

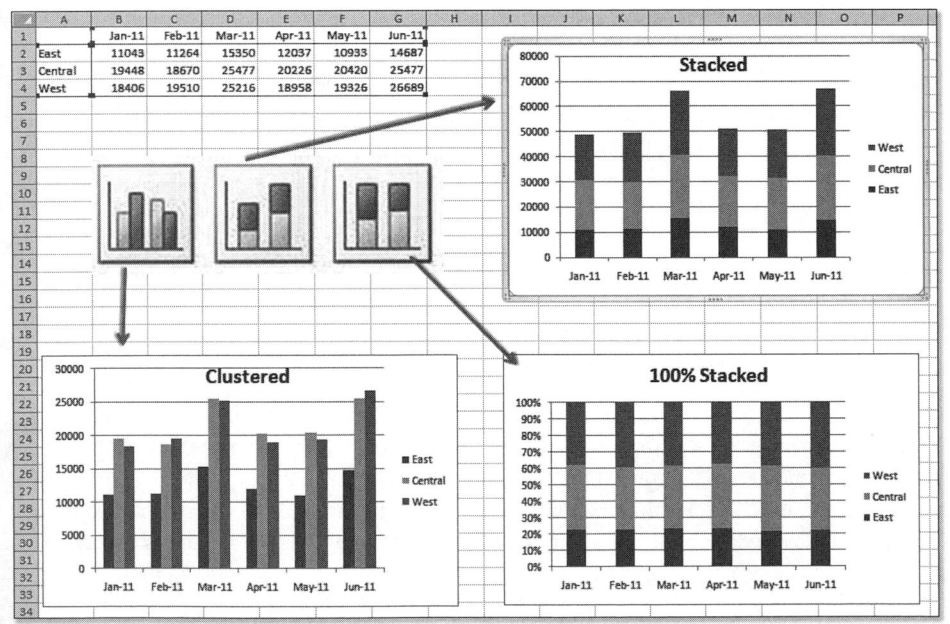

Figure 32.6
Clustered, stacked, and 100% stacked chart choices pervade most of the chart types.

■ **100% Stacked**—In a 100% stacked chart, bars from each series are plotted on top of each other, and all bars are scaled to have a height of 100%. This chart type allows you to tell which data points make up the largest percentage of each bar. A 100% stacked chart appears in the lower-right corner of Figure 32.6. In the Change Chart Type dialog, a 100% stacked type has a dark marker on top of a light marker, and the heights of the two markers are identical.

When you look through the 3D chart types, you usually see the three types described here, plus a fourth type, 3D column, where the markers for each series are placed in front of each other. This chart type has problems if some of the markers for the last series are shorter than the markers for the earlier series. The 3D column type of chart is shown in the upper-right corner of Figure 32.7. In the Change Chart Type dialog, this type of chart shows the short light-blue markers in front of the tall dark-blue markers.

Figure 32.7
If you are choosing from 3D chart types, a fourth option appears, with the markers for each series one in front of the other.

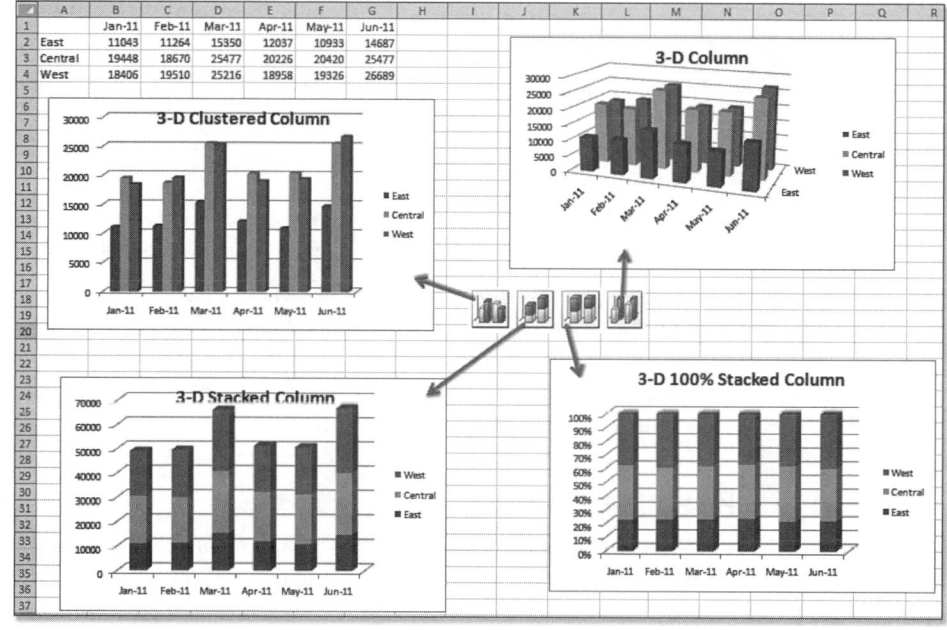

As you look through the 73 chart types in the Change Chart Type dialog, you see that the column, line, bar, and area charts have multiple groups that repeat these three or four chart styles. For the most part, the various groups switch between rectangles, cubes, cylinders, cones, pyramids, lines showing markers, and lines without markers.

Figure 32.8 shows logical chart groupings of the icons that appear in the Insert Chart dialog box.

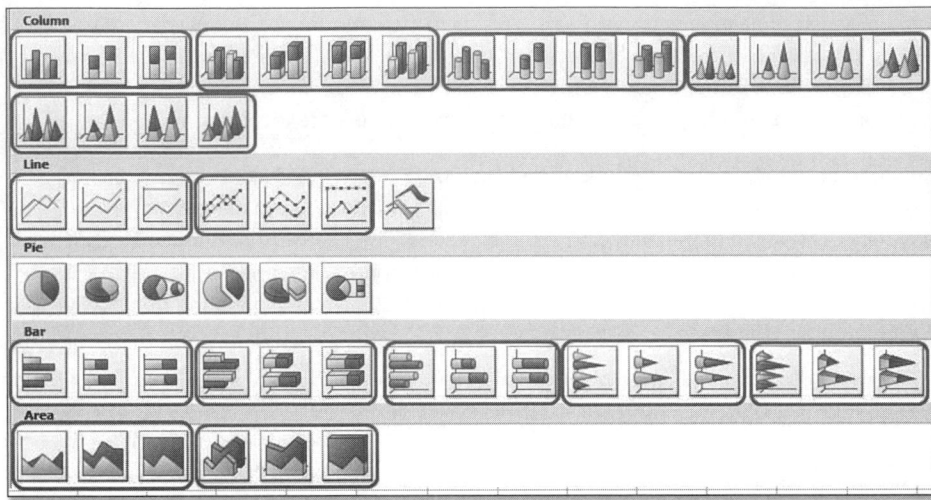

Figure 32.8
Column, line, bar, and area charts comprise several logical groups of the basic chart types.

Changing a Chart's Type

On the Design tab, the leftmost icon is the Change Chart Type icon, which you click to access the Change Chart Type dialog. You can then select from among the 73 chart types.

For some reason, Microsoft does not include the Live Preview capability in the Change Chart Type dialog. You might find yourself clicking a chart type and then clicking OK and repeating this several times until you find the right chart. (When you consider your annoyance with the lack of Live Preview on this dialog, it is amazing how quickly you have become used to the concept of Live Preview everywhere else in Excel 2010!)

Moving or Resizing a Chart

Move a chart by clicking the border of the chart and dragging to a new location. You face a subtle challenge when you want to move a chart. You may find that you initially click in the wrong place when trying to move a chart. This occurs because you are conditioned that when you hover and see a four-headed arrow, you can click and move the object.

There are many spots inside of a chart that show a four-headed arrow when you hover over them. However, the four-headed arrow might be offering to do the following:

- Move the plot area within the chart area
- Move the legend within the chart area
- Move the chart area within the chart container

For this reason, if you are trying to move the chart to a new location, you need to click whitespace somewhere outside the plot area. For example, click the whitespace between the axis values or the whitespace above the legend.

 tip

If you are unsure how to move a chart, hover the mouse above the chart and wait for a ToolTip to appear. If the ToolTip reads Chart Area, you can click and drag the entire chart.

For trouble-free moving, make sure to hover the mouse over the border of the chart object (see Figure 32.9). You can then click and drag to a new location.

Figure 32.9
Click the border of the chart object to move the chart.

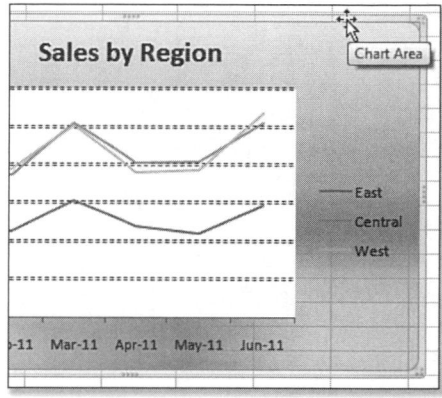

To resize a chart, click the dots in the border of the chart and drag. There are eight sets of dots in the border. If you click the dots in any of the four corners, you can resize the chart in two directions. If you click the dots in the center of each of the four edges, you can resize the chart in one direction.

Choosing a Chart Layout to Further Customize the Chart Type

As discussed previously, your first decision in creating a chart was to choose a chart type. Your next decision is to choose a chart layout.

In legacy versions of Excel, many settings for legends, data tables, titles, and so on were scattered across various steps of the Chart Wizard and other dialog boxes. Using these settings, you could produce more than 54,000 permutations of each chart type. Out of these 50,000+ options, Microsoft chose anywhere from 4 to 12 combinations and put them in the Chart Layouts gallery on the Design tab in Excel 2010. The Chart Layouts gallery should be your second stop when creating a chart.

The chart layouts vary, depending on the chart type selected. Figure 32.10 shows the 12 layouts available for a line chart.

Figure 32.11 shows the 11 chart styles available for 2D clustered columns charts. In Gerry Verschuuren's book, *Excel for Scientists and Engineers*, he spends two pages discussing the legacy steps required to make a chart that is the staple of scientific analyses— the histogram chart. Note that Microsoft now includes the histogram as Layout 8, as shown in Figure 32.11.

> **note**
>
> The charting team at Microsoft studied numerous chart examples in magazines, books, and customer spreadsheets to find popular ways of organizing charts. The canned layouts shipped with Excel 2010 reflect a consensus opinion of possible popular layouts. Remember that these are 12 (or less) choices out of thousands of possibilities. The odds are extremely slim that the exact permutation of the 50,000 possibilities that you want will be in the gallery. Instead of hoping to find the exact settings, find a layout that is close to the desired chart and then head to the Layout tab to customize the chart.

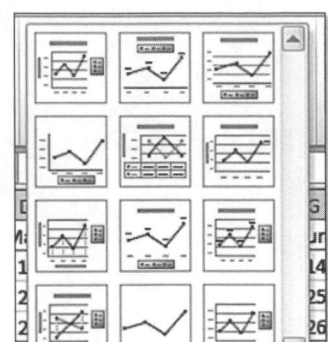

Figure 32.10
There are 12 layouts available for line charts.

Easy Histograms

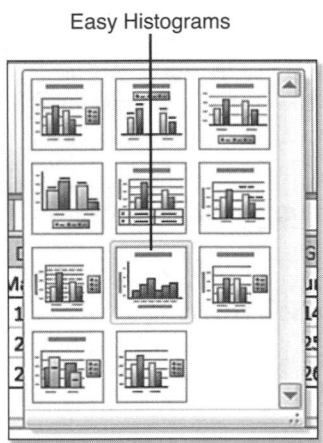

Figure 32.11
The 11 layouts for column charts are different from layouts for line charts.

As you change the chart type to each of the 73 layouts, you find that the number and organization of available chart layouts changes. Unfortunately, there is no way to add new layouts to the gallery. Instead, if you want to create a new layout, you need to use a template, which is discussed in the "Saving a Favorite Chart Style as a Template" section later in this chapter.

Customizing a Chart Using the Chart Tools Tabs

Although some chart adjustments are made on the Home or Page Layout tabs, most of the changes happen on the Design, Layout, and Format tabs. You should move through these three tabs from left to right, starting with the Design tab for major changes to the entire chart. Move to the Layout tab for adjustments to the 11 major elements of a chart. If further refinements are necessary, move to the Format tab.

Customizing a Chart by Using the Design Tab

So far in this chapter, we have covered the first two steps in creating a chart: selecting a chart type and selecting a chart layout. Next, you can customize the colors in the chart.

To customize the colors on a chart, from the Design tab open the Chart Styles gallery. There are 48 styles in this gallery, as shown in Figure 32.12. The colors and effects in this gallery will change depending on the Theme you have chosen on the Page Layout tab.

- Each theme in Office has six defined accent colors. The 48 styles represent various combinations of these six colors.

- Six styles use a mix of accent colors. Six styles are designed in grayscale for monochrome printers. Thirty-six styles use a single accent color but show it in different hues.

- The left column contains grayscale styles. The next column uses a different accent color for each series.

- The next six columns of styles offer varying hues of one accent color. Each row offers a slightly different mix of effects applied to the data points. The last row of icons has dark backgrounds that match many slide layouts in PowerPoint.

 caution

Frustratingly, Microsoft hides the Chart Tools tabs when you click outside of a chart. If you are looking for the Design, Layout, or Format tab and they are not there, click back inside your chart.

 tip

To minimize chart junk, choose a style from the top row of the gallery. Rows 2 through 6 add needless embellishments to your chart. These embellishments are dreadful when combined with themes such as Metro.

Figure 32.12
The 48 chart styles use various colors from the current theme.

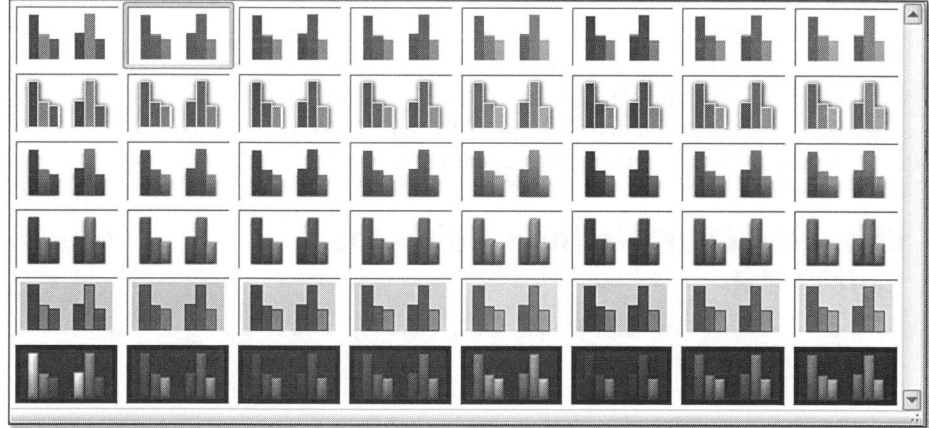

If you do not like the 48 chart styles, you can change to a new theme. On the Page Layout tab, select the Colors icon from the Themes group to see the various color themes that can be applied to the chart, as shown in Figure 32.13. The Colors drop-down shows the six fill colors for each theme. This drop-down is a good place to start if you are preparing a color presentation.

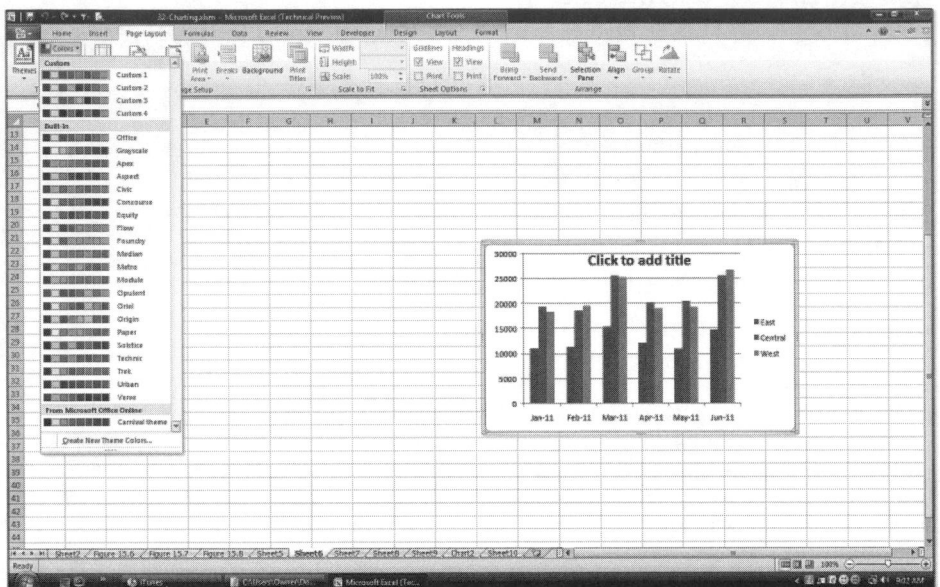

Figure 32.13
Choose new
colors from
the built-in
themes.

For a well-balanced design, it is best to note the color scheme from the Colors drop-down and then select that theme from the Themes drop-down. When you do this, you apply the matching font and effects from the theme.

With what you have learned so far, you can make millions of different chart combinations, and we have only touched on the Design tab. Two additional charting tabs—Layout and Format— allow you to control various elements of a chart. The following sections discuss how to use the options on these tabs.

Changing Chart Settings Using the Layout Tab

In the Design tab, you selected a built-in chart layout to create a certain combination of titles, legend, data labels, data table, axes, gridlines, and background. By using the Layout tab, you can customize the settings for those elements.

 note

There are 40-built in themes, each of which has an associated font theme, color theme, and effects theme. However, you can choose one theme from the font area, a different theme from the color area, and a different theme from the effects area. When combined with the 48 chart styles, approximately 10 chart layouts, and 73 chart types, you have 280 million chart variations within six clicks of the mouse.

The Layout tab offers drop-downs for 11 major elements of a chart. Drop-downs offer choices for elements such as the Chart Title, Legend, and Data Labels. Figure 32.14 shows the Chart Title drop-down as well as icons for the other drop-downs.

Each drop-down offers a few choices and a More option. In some lucky cases, the selection you want is actually in the drop-down. However, in many cases, plan to go to the More item to access the full dialog box with all the options.

Figure 32.14
The Layout tab offers easy-to-find drop-downs to control the major elements of a chart.

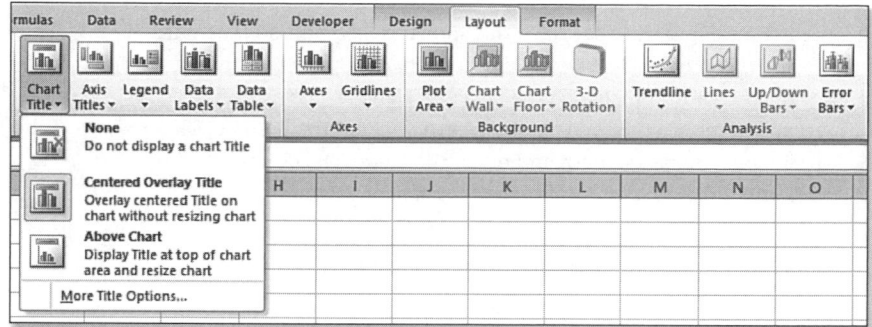

 note

Some elements offer the most popular choices in the drop-down. For example, the Chart Title drop-down shown in Figure 32.14 offers three logical choices. Either you have no title, a title above the chart, or an overlay on the chart with a title.

In other drop-downs, Microsoft seems to promote obscure options that were not previously popular but should have been. For example, the choices in the Axes drop-down are excellent and something people could rarely find before. You can save a lot of space in your axis labels by choosing thousands or millions from the menu, as shown in Figure 32.15.

In other drop-downs, the choices seem to be ones that would never be used. For example, I never use any of the settings in the Data Labels drop-down. Instead, I head to the More Data Label Options selection nearly all of the time. Selecting More takes you to the new Format dialog.

Figure 32.15
Even though these were not the most popular axis settings, Microsoft wanted to call attention to these rarely used settings.

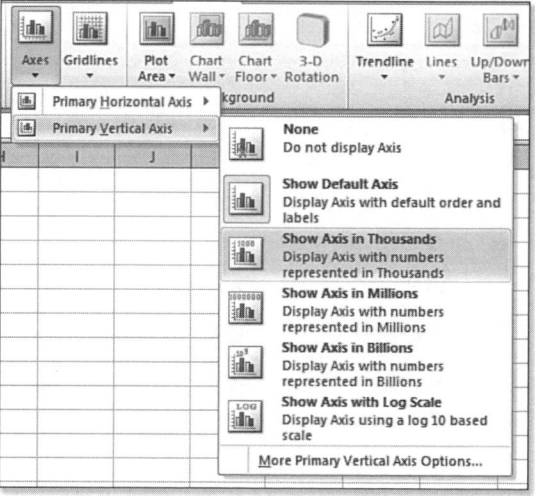

Micromanaging Using the Format Tab

Beginning with Excel 2007, the Format dialog offered a useful trick. You can select something in a chart, display the Format dialog, and then change the selected element just as before. The useful trick is that you can then reach behind the Format dialog and choose something new in the chart. The choices in the Format dialog change to reflect options for the newly selected item.

You can select an item on a chart in several ways:

- Click the item in the chart.

- Select the element from the drop-down on the left side of the Layout and Format tabs.

- Right-click the chart and use the new drop-down in the Mini Toolbar (see Figure 32.16).

 caution

Some chart elements never appear in the drop-down lists. For example, if you first select a particular series, and then perform a single-click on one column in the series, you will have successfully selected that single data point. The Selected Item might show that you have selected Series West Point June. These sub-items never appear in the drop-down list. Instead, you have to use the mouse to select items such as a single data point or a single entry in a legend.

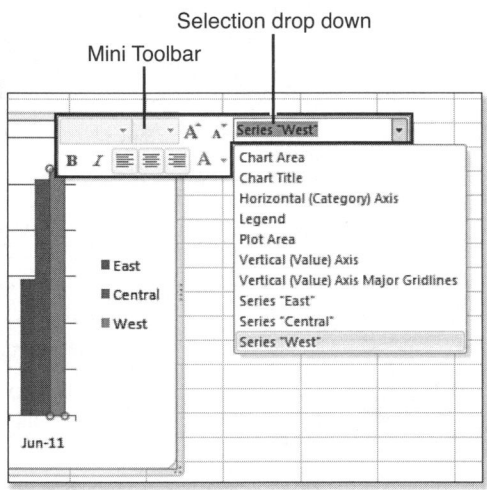

Figure 32.16
Right-click a chart to access the new element selection drop-down from the Mini Toolbar.

After an item is selected, you can format it using any of these methods:

- Choose a setting from the Format tab (see Figure 32.17).

- Double-click the item to open the Format tab.

- Right-click the item and select Format from the bottom of the context menu.

- Press Ctrl+1, which is the universal shortcut for Format Selection.

- Press the Format Selection icon on the left side of either the Layout or Format tabs.

Figure 32.17
Settings on the Format tab offer a dizzying array of choices you will never use in charts.

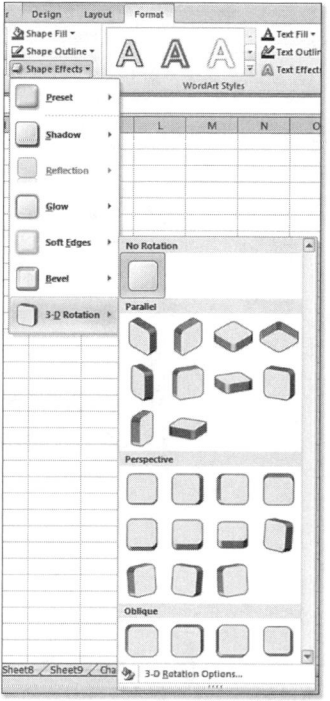

The Format dialog offers many more choices than are available in the tabs. For example, in Figure 32.18, a rectangular gradient has been applied with four color stops and a 72% transparency. You would never be able to have this much control by staying in the drop-downs on the Format tab.

Charting Tips and Tricks

Although Excel 2010 offers millions of nice-looking charts, there are still secret tips and tricks. For this reason, people who take the time to read this book will have the information they need to do what is not obvious to others. Read on to learn these tips and tricks.

Showing Numbers of Different Scale on a Chart

Suppose your data series contains numbers of vastly different scales. For example, in Figure 32.19, a sales chart shows total dollars and unit sales for one particular product line. Because sales are in the thousands and the units are less than 10, there is no chance to see the second series to right-click it, as was described in the example in the previous section.

In this case, you want the first series plotted against one axis and the second series plotted against a second axis. Each chart can have two scales, corresponding to the first and second vertical axes.

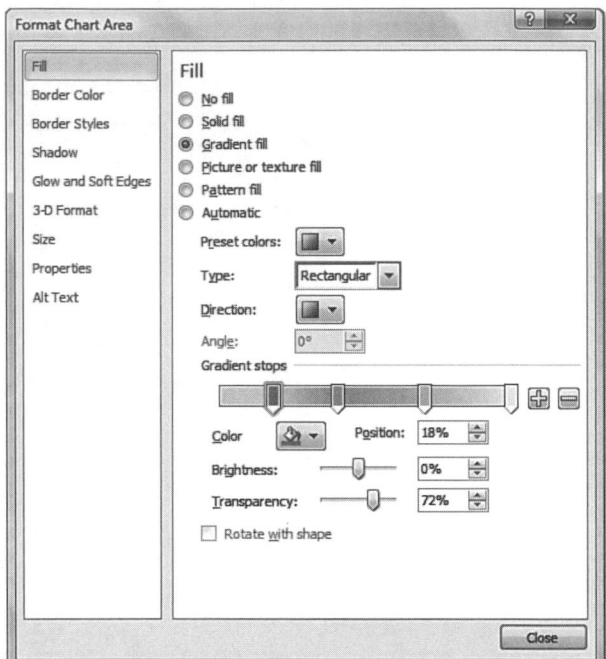

Figure 32.18
The Format tab offers far more control over the formatting of an element.

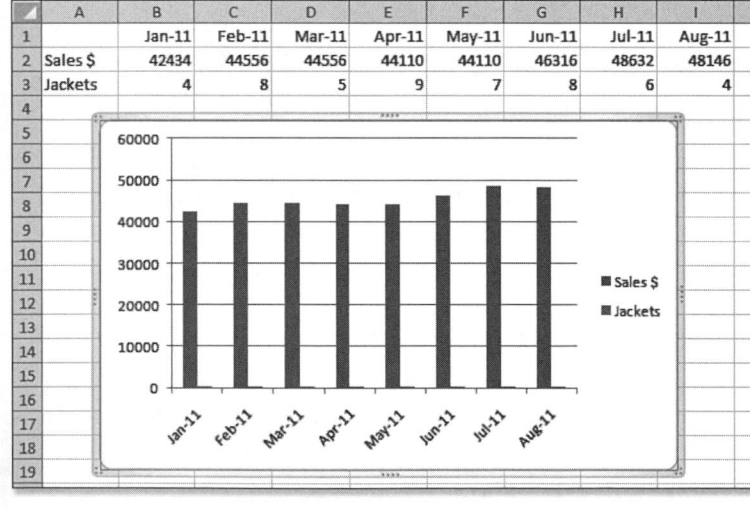

Figure 32.19
The order-of-magnitude difference between the series makes it impossible to see Series 2.

To enable the second axis, follow these steps:

1. Right-click the chart. From the Mini Toolbar that appears, open the drop-down and select the second series.

2. Press Ctrl+1 or select Format Selection from the Layout or Format tabs.

3. In the Series Options category, select Secondary Axis in the Plot Series On frame. This adds a second vertical axis with a scale suitable for the second series, as shown in Figure 32.20. Unfortunately, Microsoft plots the first and second series directly on top of each other, so you cannot always see the first series sticking up behind the second series.

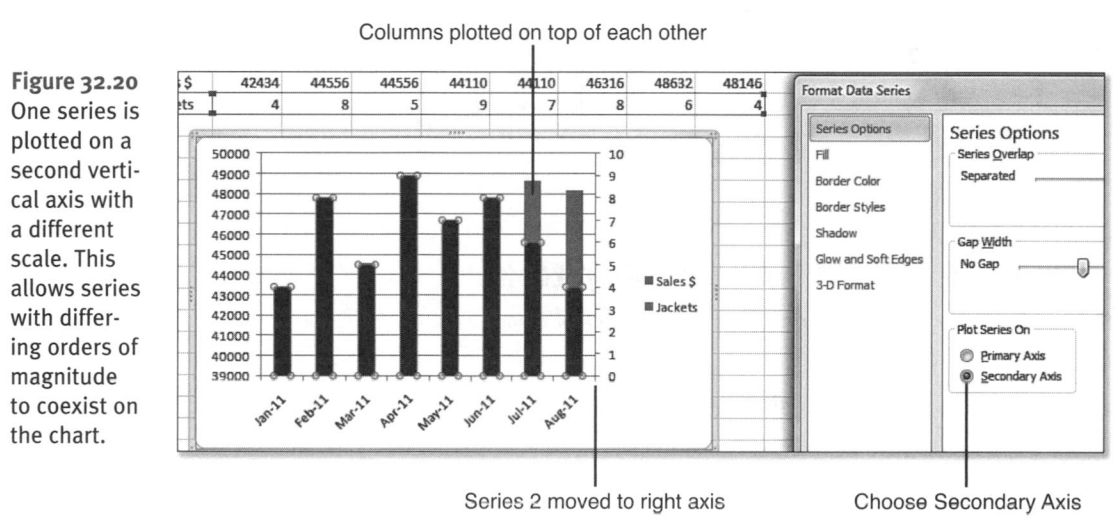

Columns plotted on top of each other

Figure 32.20
One series is plotted on a second vertical axis with a different scale. This allows series with differing orders of magnitude to coexist on the chart.

Series 2 moved to right axis   Choose Secondary Axis

4. While the second series is still selected, select Design, Change Chart Type, and then select a Line chart.

5. Optionally, use color to signify that the line applies to the right axis. To format the right axis, select Secondary Vertical Axis from the Current Selection drop-down. Choose a text fill color to match the color of the second series. Repeat to change the left axis to match the color of the first series.

In Figure 32.21, the legend is moved from the right to the top.

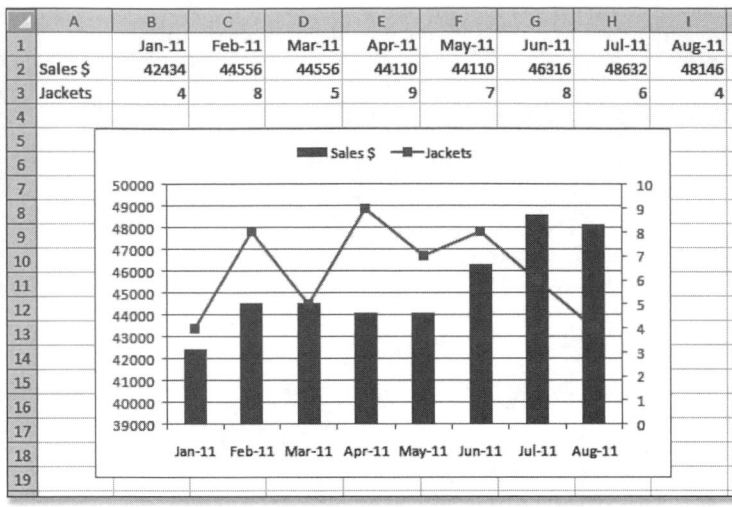

Figure 32.21
This chart shows sales in thousands and quantity in units.

Creating a Chart with One Keystroke

One of my favorite tricks in Excel is the trick of creating a chart by using one keystroke. Here's how you do this in Excel 2010:

1. Select the range of data to be charted.

2. To create a chart on a new chart sheet, press F11. Alternatively, to create a chart embedded on the current sheet, press Alt+F1. A new chart is created.

The new chart reflects the default chart style. In the default installation of Excel 2010, the default chart type is a clustered 2D column chart. You can change the default chart type by following these steps:

1. Build a chart of the desired chart type.

2. Select the chart.

3. From the Design tab, select Change Chart Type. The Change Chart Type dialog appears.

4. In the lower-left corner of the Change Chart Type dialog, click the Set As Default Chart button.

After you follow these steps, all future charts created with F11 or Alt+F1 will use this chart type.

Adding New Data to a Chart by Pasting

Even though this next trick has existed in Excel since 1997, not many people know about it—you can add new data to a chart by pasting. Suppose you have a chart showing data for several months. You have nicely formatted and customized the chart. You now have new data available. Instead of re-creating the chart, you can paste the new data to the existing chart.

Follow these steps to expand the chart by pasting new data on the chart:

1. Make sure the new data has a heading consistent with the old data. Note that if you accidentally enter the heading as Text instead of Date or vice versa, the trick will have unexpected results.

2. Select the new data including the heading.

3. Press Ctrl+C to copy the new data.

4. Select the chart.

5. Press Ctrl+V to paste the new data on the chart.

To watch a video of adding data to an existing chart, search for "Excel In Depth 32" at YouTube.

Adding New Data to a Chart by Using a Table

If you use Excel's new table functionality, charts are automatically updated when new data is added. This method works even if the chart is based on data that is not currently in a table. Follow these steps to make the data into a table and extend the chart:

1. Select a cell in the source data for the chart.

2. Type Ctrl+T to make the range into a table.

3. Confirm the location for the table. Excel applies a default table format to the table, as shown in Figure 32.22.

Figure 32.22
Converting the source data into a table.

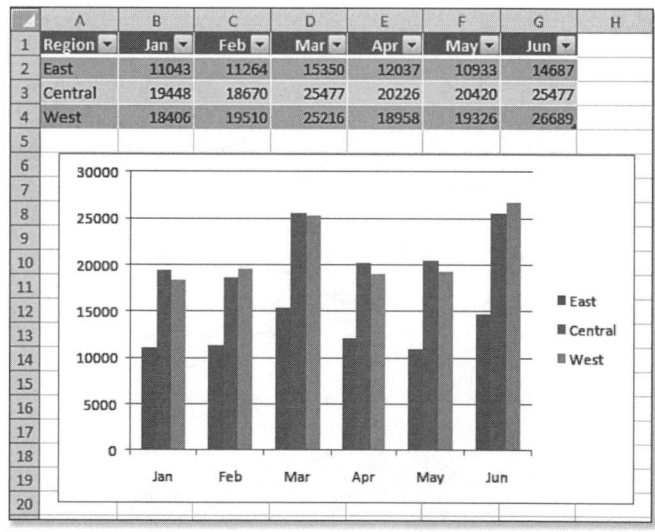

	A	B	C	D	E	F	G	H
1	Region	Jan	Feb	Mar	Apr	May	Jun	
2	East	11043	11264	15350	12037	10933	14687	
3	Central	19448	18670	25477	20226	20420	25477	
4	West	18406	19510	25216	18958	19326	26689	

4. In the blank column next to the table, type the heading for the next month. Excel automatically extends the table and adds the new month to the chart, as shown in Figure 32.23.

5. Type the values for the new column. Excel extends both the table and the chart.

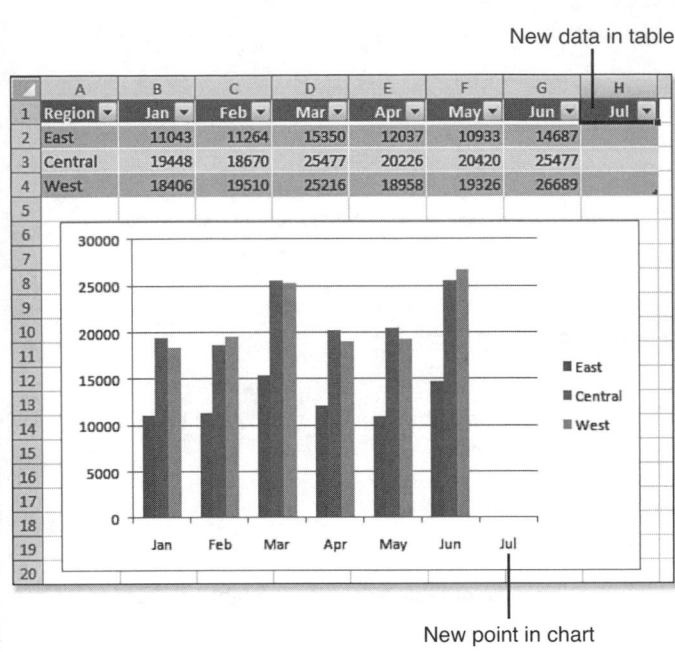

New data in table

New point in chart

Figure 32.23
When you type a new column heading, Excel extends the table and consequently the chart.

Adding Drop Lines to a Surface Chart

Surface charts can be hard to read. Excel draws a smooth line between adjacent data points. It is difficult for your eye to follow the label on the x-axis up to the point on the surface chart. For example, Figure 32.24 shows a surface chart. However, it is difficult to tell if the point for June 2002 is above or below 70%.

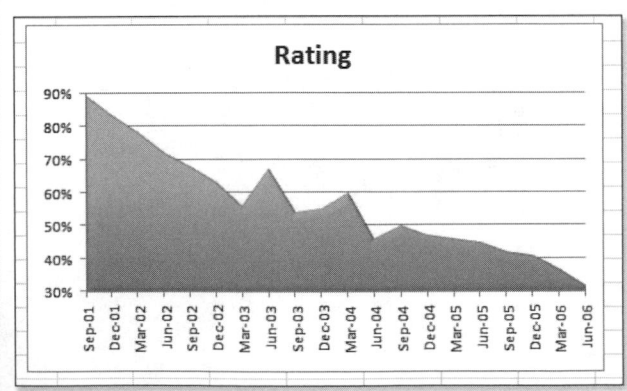

Figure 32.24
Surface charts can be difficult to read.

To make surface charts easier to read, you can add drop lines from each point on the surface chart in Excel 2010. Here's how you do it:

1. Select the chart.

2. From the Layout tab in the Analysis group, select Lines, Drop Lines. Excel draws a vertical line from the x-axis to the surface of the chart, as shown in Figure 32.25.

Figure 32.25
Vertical drop lines make it easier to figure out where each data point crosses the chart.

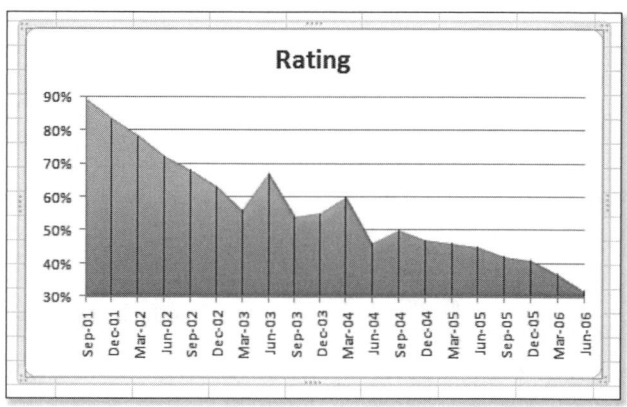

Predicting the Future by Using a Trendline

As you may recall, Chapter 15, "Using Trig, Matrix, and Engineering Functions," presented some fairly complicated functions for calculating linear regression lines. Instead of using those functions, it is simpler to plot the data on a chart and ask Excel to add a trendline.

A line chart shows progress toward a goal for the first eight days of a month, as shown in Figure 32.26. Excel can add a trendline to the chart and extend the trendline to predict the final goal. You can consider the trendline to be a predictor of what will happen if things continue to progress at the same pace. If the trendline after 30 days does not meet the goal, you need to start working harder.

Follow these steps to add a trendline to a chart:

1. Select a chart that contains data of past actuals.

2. From the Layout tab in the Analysis group, select the Trendline drop-down. As shown in Figure 32.27, although Excel offers four canned trendlines, you need to select the More Trendline Options to force the trendline to predict the future. The Format Trendline dialog appears.

3. In the Format Trendline dialog, enter a positive value in the Forecast Forward section. For this example, assume 22 days is appropriate.

4. Optionally, if you want to display a legend on the chart, type a custom name for the Trendline name.

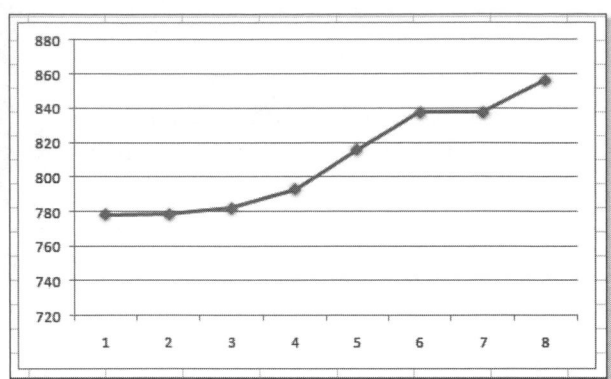

Figure 32.26
This simple chart plots historical data about what will happen in the future.

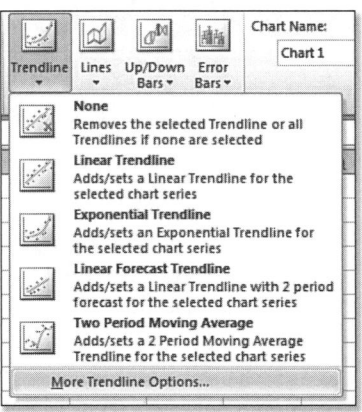

Figure 32.27
Select the historical series and then More Trendline Options.

5. Optionally, choose the Line Style category to change the line style to a dashed line. This helps indicate that the projection is not real data but is a mathematical projection of what could happen.

A new series is added to the chart, as shown in Figure 32.28. The series uses straight-line regression to calculate future data points.

Creating Stock Charts

Excel offers four varieties of stock market charts to track historical stock performance. Each variety requires a slightly different organization for the data. The order of the data must match the following requirements exactly:

- **High-Low-Close**—These charts require four columns of data: date, high, low, and close.

- **Open-High-Low-Close**—These charts require five columns of data: date, open, high, low, and close.

Figure 32.28
The projection line predicts that this book will have 1,000+ pages. Turn to the last page to see if it is correct.

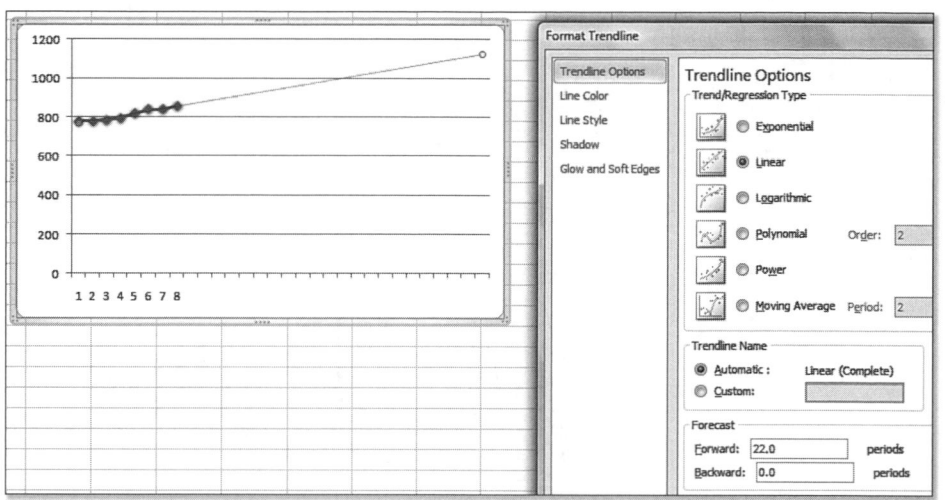

- **Volume-High-Low-Close**—These charts require five columns of data: date, volume, high, low, and close.

- **Volume-Open-High-Low-Close**—These charts require six columns of data: date, volume, open, high, low, and close.

To create a stock chart, follow these steps:

1. Import your data from http://finance.yahoo.com or another data source.

2. If necessary, cut and paste the columns into the proper sequence to match your desired chart type.

3. Sort the data by date, oldest to newest.

4. Select the data, including the headings.

5. From the Insert tab, select Charts, Other Charts, Stock, and then select the appropriate chart type to match your data.

6. If you prefer the volume columns to occupy the bottom half of the chart, format the left scale. Specify a maximum value about two times larger than the largest value. This keeps the volume data near the bottom of the chart.

The result, shown in Figure 32.29, is a chart similar to those published in the financial websites.

 tip

Stock traders use far more complex charts for their analyses. Add-ins are available to produce box-and-whisker charts, point and figure charts, and so on. Perform a Google search for the word Excel combined with the particular chart type to locate these add-ins.

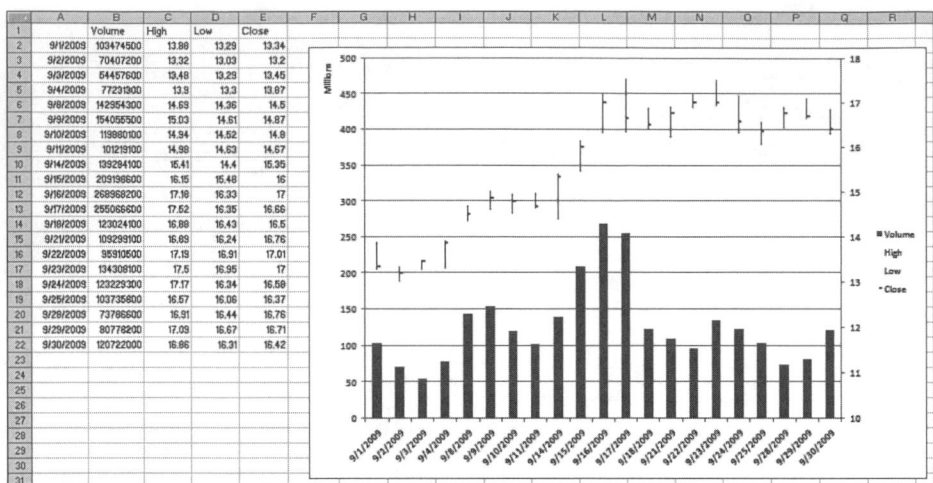

Figure 32.29
Excel creates
this stock
chart.

Dealing with Small Pie Slices

In many data series, a few pie slices take up 80 percent of the pie, and many tiny slices account for the rest of the pie. Typically, the last pie slices end up at the back of the pie where it is impossible to fit the labels, so no one can make out what they are.

One solution is to rotate the pie so that the smaller pie slices are near the front. Here's how you do it:

1. Enter one series of data. Sort the values from high to low.

2. Create a pie chart by using the 3D Pie type.

3. On the Labels group of the Layout tab, turn off the legend.

4. In the same group, select the Data Labels drop-down and then select More Data Label Options. Turn off the value and turn on Category Name and Percentage. Choose Best Fit.

5. Right-click in the pie chart and select Format Data Series. The Format Data Series dialog appears.

6. In the Format Data Series dialog, the first category is Angle of First Slice. Move this up to be between 150 and 160 to rotate the last slices to the right-front position. In this position, the smaller slices are in front, so there is more room for labels to appear near each other, as shown in Figure 32.30.

When you have several small data points at the end of a pie chart series, and you need to see all the smaller segments, you can change the chart type to a special type called *bar of pie*. In this type, the smallest few categories are exploded out and shown as a bar chart next to the pie.

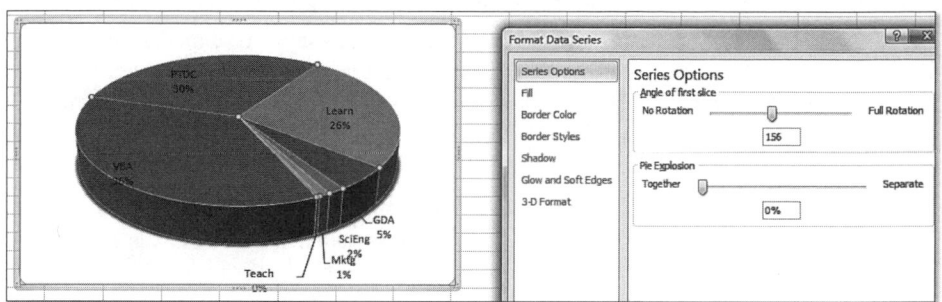

Figure 32.30
Adjusting the Angle of First Slice setting to around 150 moves the smaller final slices toward the right front of the pie.

To change an existing pie chart to a bar of pie chart, follow these steps:

1. Select the chart.

2. From the Type group of the Design tab, select Change Chart Type. The Change Chart Type dialog appears.

3. In the Change Chart Type dialog, select the last option for pie charts: Bar of Pie.

4. Click OK to close the dialog.

5. Right-click the chart and select Format Data Series. The Format Data Series dialog appears.

6. In the Format Data Series dialog, you have control over the number of values in the bar chart. For example, in Figure 32.31, the settings call for the last four items to be in the other bar chart. Note that the total of 285 for those four items is shown on the chart as Other 285. The bar chart breaks down the 285 by category.

Figure 32.31
In a bar of pie chart, the tiny slices are exploded so it is easy to see the details.

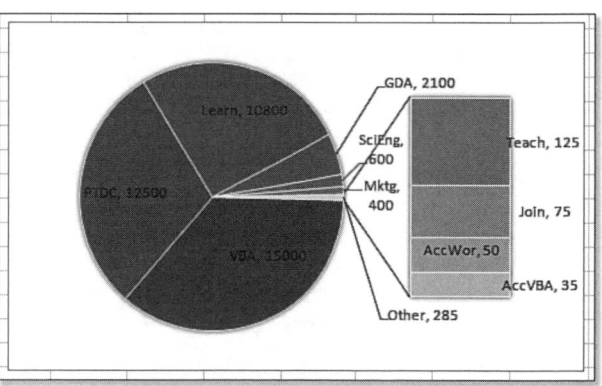

Displaying Three Variables by Using a Bubble Chart

Typically, a scatter chart or an XY chart shows points in a two-dimensional x,y-coordinate grid. This might be useful for exploring the relationship between two measures. By using a bubble chart, you can display the relationship between *three* variables. For example, in Figure 32.32, the chart compares used vehicle prices from the local newspaper. The table shows age in year, miles, and the asking price.

When you set up a bubble chart, the first column is plotted along the x-axis. The second column is plotted along the y-axis. The price becomes the size of the bubble at the intersection of each x,y coordinate.

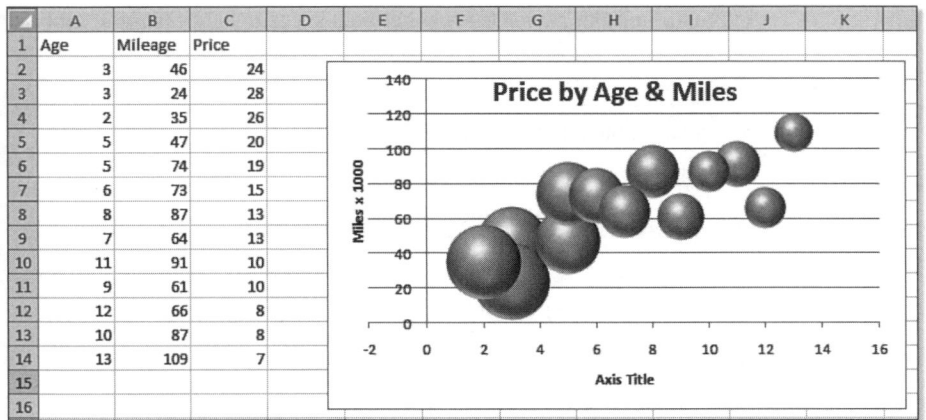

Figure 32.32
The size of the sphere at each intersection communicates the information about a third dimension. In this example, the bubble size represents relative price.

Changing the Location of a Chart

Charts can be embedded on a worksheet, or they can exist on their own sheets. To move a chart from one place to another, follow these steps:

1. Select the Design tab and then select Location, Move Chart. Excel displays the Move Chart dialog.

2. You can choose to place the object in an existing sheet or to move the chart to a new sheet.

Saving a Favorite Chart Style As a Template

Although Microsoft has provided great-looking built-in charts, you will likely design some great-looking charts of your own. After you have designed a chart, you can save it as a template. When you build new charts based on that template, all the settings for colors, fonts, effects, and chart elements are applied to the new data.

For all the power and glitz of Excel's built-in chart styles, the chart templates feature can save you massive amounts of time, such as if you routinely customize your charts to meet company standards.

Follow these steps to create a template:

1. Build a chart and customize it as necessary.

2. Select the chart. In the Type group of the Design tab, select Save As Template. Give the chart template a name. Excel saves the template with a .crtx file extension.

To create a chart by using your template, follow these steps:

1. Select the data you want to chart.

2. From the Insert tab, choose any of the Chart drop-downs and then select All Chart Types. The Create Chart dialog appears.

3. In the Create Chart dialog, select the Templates category.

4. Click the desired Template, if there is more than one.

5. Click OK. Excel creates the chart with all the custom formatting from the saved template.

If you like your template so much that you want all future charts to be based on the template, follow these steps to make the template your default style:

1. Select a chart based on the desired template.

2. From the Design tab, select Change Chart Type. The Create Chart dialog appears.

3. In the Create Chart dialog, select the Templates category.

4. Select the desired template.

5. In the lower-left corner of the Change Chart Type dialog, select Set as Default Chart.

In the future, you can create a chart that uses this template by following these steps:

1. Select the data you want to chart.

2. Press Alt+F1 to apply your default template.

Using Pivot Charts

Pivot tables were discussed in detail in Chapter 23, "Using Pivot Tables to Analyze Data." Pivot charts have been an underused component of pivot tables for several versions of Excel.

A *pivot chart* is a chart based on an underlying pivot table. As you sort, filter, and change the field layout of the pivot table, the associated chart updates automatically.

In Excel 2010, the pivot chart engine shares the same charting engine with the rest of Office. Style changes made to a pivot chart persist after you add new fields to the pivot chart.

 note

The process of creating and customizing charts every month used to be a time-consuming process. The capability to save every nuance of desired formatting as a template and then make the template the default for all future charts is something that would have made my job as a financial analyst far easier.

In Excel 2007, Microsoft experimented by moving the field buttons from the pivot chart to a PivotChart Filter pane. In Excel 2010, the Filter pane is gone and the controls return to the chart. However, you can use the Field Buttons drop-down on the Analyze tab to hide the buttons from the chart. Alternatively, you can right-click a button to access a menu to hide some or all of the buttons.

To create a pivot chart, follow these steps:

1. Select a single cell in your data.

2. From the Insert tab, select Tables, PivotTable, PivotChart. The Create PivotTable with PivotChart dialog appears.

3. Click OK to create a pivot chart on a new worksheet. A blank pivot chart is created and the PivotTable Field List appears.

4. Drop your primary chart field on the Axis Fields drop zone.

5. If you drop a field on the Legend Fields drop zone, it is treated as an additional data series in the chart. Therefore, you should drop a secondary chart field here.

6. Drag a summable field such as Revenue, to the Sum Values drop zone.

7. Select the chart. From the PivotDesign tab, click Chart Type. Choose either a clustered or stacked bar or column chart.

8. Optionally, move any filter fields to the Report Filter drop zone.

9. Optionally, apply a style to the chart by selecting Chart Styles from the PivotDesign tab.

 **note**

The PivotTable field list is similar to the one used in pivot tables, with two exceptions:

The Row Labels drop zone is called Axis Fields.

The Columns Labels drop zone is called Legend Fields.

Excel creates a chart for the selected fields, as shown in Figure 32.33. You can use the new Product drop-down on the chart to filter the chart to any specific product.

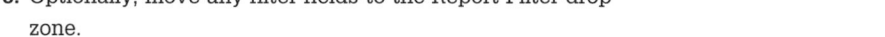

Figure 32.33
In Excel
2010, you
can pivot
a pivot
chart, and
it retains its
formatting
and styles.

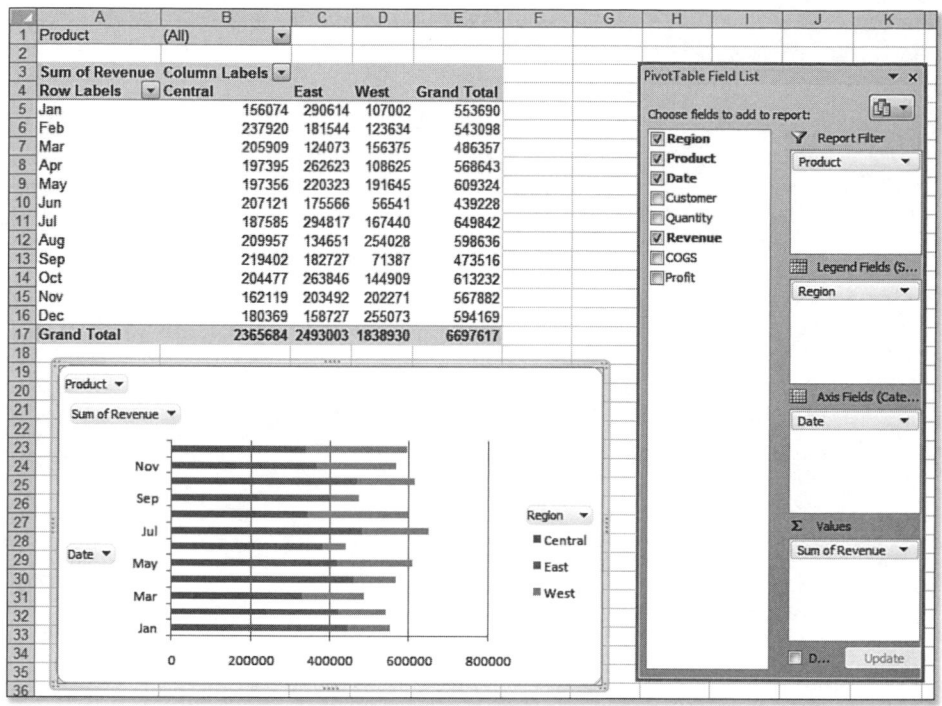

USING SPARKLINES

Edward Tufte wrote about small, intense, simple datawords in his 2006 book, *Beautiful Evidence*. Tufte called them sparklines and produced several examples where you could fit dozens of points of data in the space of a word. Six months later, the Excel team began planning for Excel 2010 and Tufte's concepts made it into Excel 2010.

Fitting a Chart into the Size of a Cell with Sparklines

Excel's implementation of sparklines offers line charts, column charts, and a win/loss chart. See Figure 33.1 for an example of each.

- **Win/Loss**—The 1951 Pennant Race in rows 7 & 8 show two examples of a Win/Loss chart. Each event (in this case, a baseball game) is represented by either an upward facing marker to indicate a win or a downward facing marker to indicate a loss. This type of chart shows winning streaks. The final three games were the playoff between the Dodgers and the Giants, with the Giants winning 2 games to 1.

- **Sparkline**—The sparkline in row 12 shows 120 monthly points of the Dow Jones Industrial Index showing the closing price for each month in one decade.

- **Sparkcolumns**—Rows 16 through 21 compare monthly high temperatures for various cities. The minimum and maximum values for each city are marked in a contrasting color. Curitiba, in the southern hemisphere, has its warmest month in February.

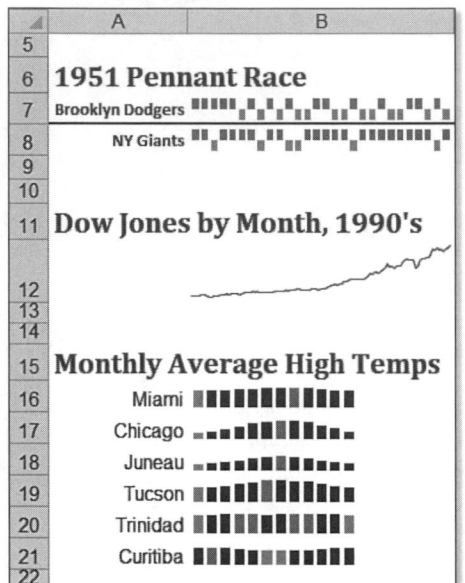

Figure 33.1
Excel 2010 offers three types of sparklines.

Sparklines can exist as a single cell (the Dow Jones example) or as a group of sparklines (the temperature example). When sparklines are created as a group, you can specify that all the sparklines should have the same scale or that they should be independent. There are times where each is appropriate.

The Sparkline feature offers the capability to mark the high point, the low point, the first point, the last point, and/or all negative points.

There is no built-in way to label sparklines. However, sparklines are drawn on a special drawing layer that was added to Excel 2007 to accommodate the data visualizations discussed in Chapter 31. This layer is transparent, so with some clever formatting, you can add some label information in the cell behind the sparkline.

Understanding How Excel Maps Data to Sparklines

Contrary to most examples that you see in the Microsoft demos, sparklines do not have to be created adjacent to the original data set.

Suppose that you have the 4-row by 10-column data set shown in Figure 33.2. This data shows four series of economic data. It should be used to create four sparklines.

The sparklines can be created in a four-row by one-column range, as shown in D3:D6 of Figure 33.3, or in a one-row by four-column range, as shown in A1:D1 of the same figure. When you specify a sparkline, you specify the source data and the target range. Given a 4x10 cell source data and a 1x4 or 4x1 target range, Excel figures out that it should create four sparklines.

Figure 33.2
Four series of economic indicators for a decade.

	2000	2001	2002	2003	2004	2005	2006	2007	2008	2009
Unemployment	4	4.7	5.8	6	5.5	5.1	4.6	4.6	5.8	9.3
GDP	9952	10286	10642	11142	11868	12638	13399	14078	14441	14242
New Construction	803	840	848	892	992	1103	1168	1151	1072	900
Bank Credit	5027	5210	5643	6011	6564	7259	8038	8844	9373	9104

Figure 33.3
The sparklines can be plotted in a row or a column, no matter whether the original data was in rows or columns.

	A	B	C	D
1	........▄█	...▄▄██	...▄██▄	....▄██
2				
3				⌒
4				⌒
5				⌒
6				⌒
7				

What if your original data set is perfectly square? This will occur when you have four rows by four columns, as shown in Figure 33.4.

Figure 33.4
If the original data set has the same number of rows and columns...

	2006	2007	2008	2009
Unemployment	4.6	4.6	5.8	9.3
GDP	13399	14078	14441	14242
New Construction	1168	1151	1072	900
Bank Credit	8038	8844	9373	9104

You then have the chance that Excel will choose to create the sparklines along the wrong axis (see Figure 33.5).

Figure 33.5
Excel might choose the wrong way to draw the sparklines.

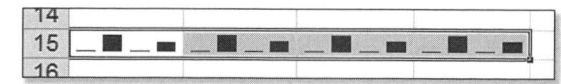

While those sparklines are selected, go to the Sparkline Tools Design tab of the Ribbon. Open the Edit Data drop-down and select Switch Row & Column (see Figure 33.6).

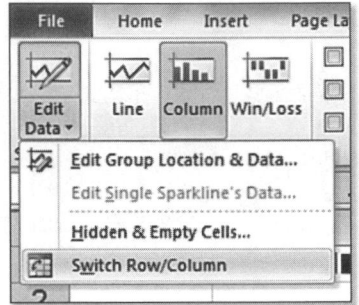

Figure 33.6
Excel offers a way to reverse the row and column.

The sparkline will reverse, as shown in Figure 33.7.

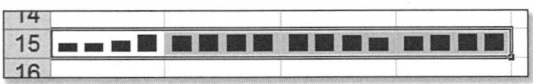

Figure 33.7
Excel is now plotting like values in each sparkline.

Creating a Group of Sparklines

The worksheet in Figure 33.8 includes a decade of leading economic indicators. Use the following steps to add sparklines to the table:

	A	B	C	D	E	F	G	H	I	J	K	L
3	Economic Indicators 2000-2009											
4			2000	2001	2002	2003	2004	2005	2006	2007	2008	2009
5	Unemployment		4	4.7	5.8	6	5.5	5.1	4.6	4.6	5.8	9.3
6	GDP		9952	10286	10642	11142	11868	12638	13399	14078	14441	14242
7	New Construction		803	840	848	892	992	1103	1168	1151	1072	900
8	Bank Credit		5027	5210	5643	6011	6564	7259	8038	8844	9373	9104
9												

Figure 33.8
Add space in your table for the sparklines.

1. Insert a blank column between columns A and B. This provides room for the sparklines to appear next to the labels in column A.

2. Select the data in C4:L8. Note that you should not include any headings in this selection.

3. On the Insert tab, select Column from the Sparkline Group. Excel displays the Create Sparklines dialog. This dialog is the same for all three types of sparklines. You have to specify the location of the data and the location where you

 tip

In step 1, you might find that you don't need to print the table of numbers, just the labels and sparklines will suffice.

want the sparklines. Because your data is 4 rows by 10 columns, the Location Range must be a 4-cell vector. You can either specify one row by four columns or four rows by one column.

4. Select B5:B8 as the location range, as shown in Figure 33.9.

Figure 33.9
Preselect the data range, and then specify the location range.

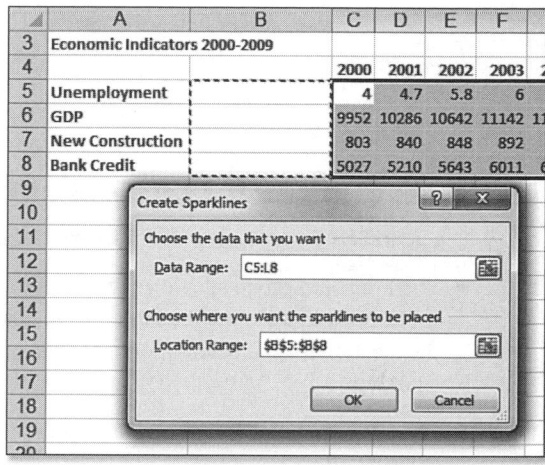

5. Click OK to create the default sparklines.

As shown in Figure 33.10, the sparklines have no markers. They are scaled independently of each other. The unemployment max of 9.3 reaches nearly to the top of cell B5, indicating the maximum for Unemployment is probably about 10. By contrast, the maximum for GDP in B6 is closer to 14,500.

Figure 33.10
Default sparklines have no markers and are autoscaled to fit the cell.

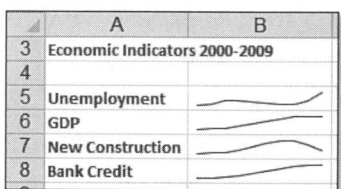

The Show group of the Sparkline toolbar allows you to mark certain points on the line. In Figure 33.11, the high point is marked with a dot. This one change adds a lot of information to the sparklines. New Construction peaked in 2006. GDP and Bank Credit peaked in 2008. Unemployment peaked in 2009. Did the drop in new construction in 2007 foretell the other items?

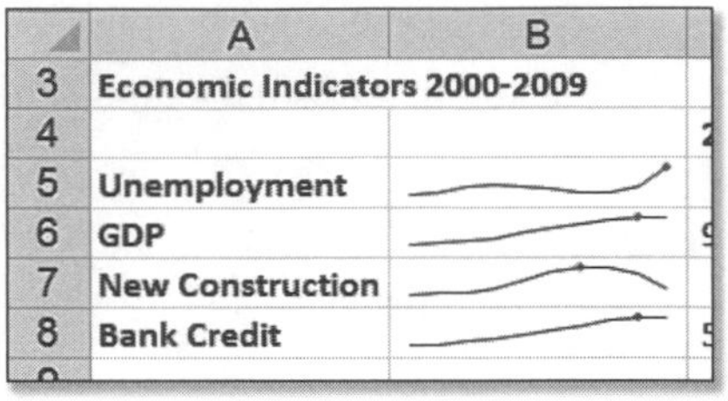

Figure 33.11
Adding a marker at the high point adds key information to the sparkline.

Built-In Choices for Customizing Sparklines

The Sparkline Tools Design tab offers several built-in choices for customizing sparklines.

- The Edit Data group allows you to respecify the data range for the source data and the location. If you have to add new data to existing sparklines, you can do so here. Generally, you would edit the location for the whole group, but the drop-down menu allows you to edit data for a single sparkline.

- The Type group allows you to switch between Line, Column, and Win/Loss charts.

- The Show group offers the second-most useful settings in the tab. There are six check boxes here that control which points should display markers in the sparkline:

    - High Point

    - Low Point

    - First Point

    - Last Point

    - Negative Points

    - All Points

- Here, you can choose to highlight the High Point, Low Point, First Point, or Last Points. Note that if there is a tie for High or Low point, both points in the tie will be marked. You can also choose to highlight all points and/or the negative points.

For sparklines, any item that you choose in the Show Group is drawn as a marker on the line. You can control the color for each of the six options using the Marker Color drop-down, discussed next.

For sparkcolumns, the markers are always shown for "All Points" so this check box is grayed out. Choosing any of the five other check boxes in the Show group will cause those particular columns to be drawn in a different color.

For Win/Loss, you will generally always choose Markers and Negative. This is how the losses show in a contrasting color from the wins.

In Figure 33.12, examples of the various options are shown.

In cell B3, the high, low, first, and last points are shown.

In cell B5, all markers are shown in the same color.

When you choose Markers and Negative, all points appear, but you can change the negative points to another color, as shown in cell B7.

In cells B11 & B13, the chosen markers are shown in a contrasting color.

Cells B9 & B15 are examples where the horizontal axis is shown. This helps to differentiate positive from negative. Note that the axis always appears at a zero location.

Figure 33.12
Use the Show Group to highlight certain points.

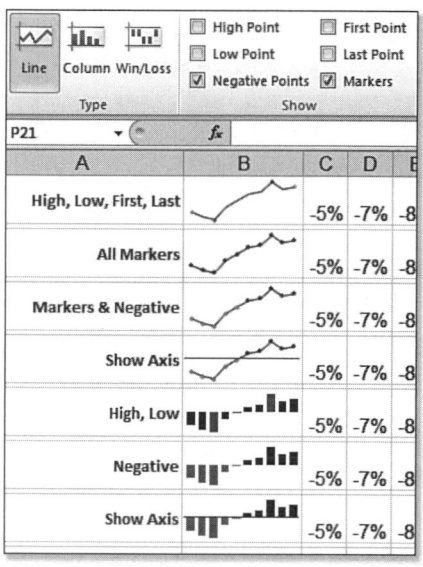

The Style gallery seems to be a huge waste of real estate. In the Office theme, it offers 36 ugly alternatives for sparkline color. This group also offers the Sparkline Color drop-down, which is the standard Excel 2010 color chooser. The color chosen here controls the line in a sparkline. You use the Marker Color drop-down to control the color of the High, Low, First, Last, Negative points, as well as the default color for regular markers. Figure 33.13 shows the Marker Color drop-down.

You use the Group group to ungroup a group of sparklines. Any changes that you make on the Design tab apply to all the sparklines in the group. This is usually a desired outcome. But, if you needed to mark the High Point in one line and the Low Point in another line, you would ungroup the sparklines.

You can also group sparklines or clear sparklines using icons in the Group group. The Axis drop-down appears in this group and contains the most important settings for sparklines. You will learn how to use the Axis drop-down in the next example.

 note

For sparklines, the sparkline color controls the color of the line. For sparkcolumn or the win/loss, the sparkline color controls the color of the columns.

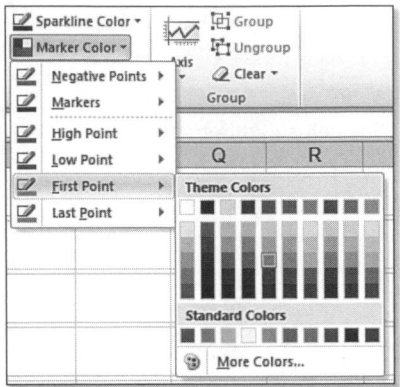

Figure 33.13
Control the color of the chosen markers in this drop-down.

Controlling Axis Values for Sparklines

Figure 33.14 shows a group of sparkcolumns showing the average high temperature for several cities. These cities are a mix of tropical and frigid cities.

The default behavior of sparklines is that each sparkline in the group gets its own scale. This worked for the varying economic indicators in Figure 33.8. However, it does not work here.

When the vertical axis scale is set to Automatic, you can never really know the high and low of the scale in use. If you study the data and the sparkline for Trinidad, it appears as if Excel has chosen a min point of 84.8 and a max point of 89. Without any scale, you might think that Trinidad in January is as cold as Chicago in January.

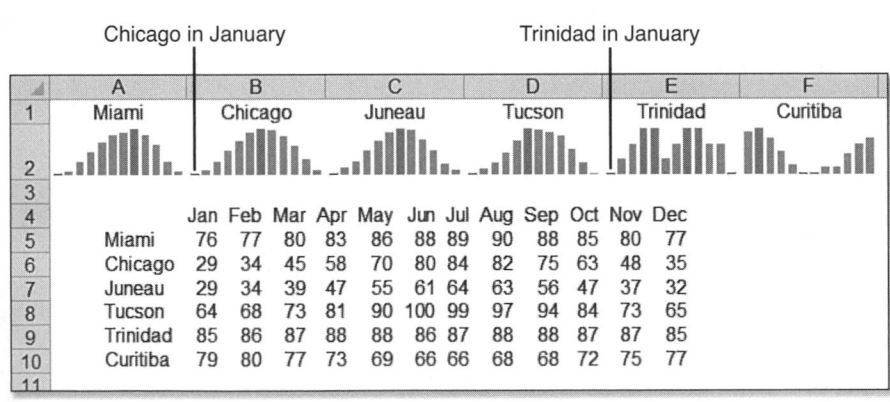

Figure 33.14
The automatic vertical scale assigned to each sparkline doesn't work in this example.

Chicago in January   Trinidad in January

	Jan	Feb	Mar	Apr	May	Jun	Jul	Aug	Sep	Oct	Nov	Dec
Miami	76	77	80	83	86	88	89	90	88	85	80	77
Chicago	29	34	45	58	70	80	84	82	75	63	48	35
Juneau	29	34	39	47	55	61	64	63	56	47	37	32
Tucson	64	68	73	81	90	100	99	97	94	84	73	65
Trinidad	85	86	87	88	88	86	87	88	88	87	87	85
Curitiba	79	80	77	73	69	66	66	68	68	72	75	77

Figure 33.15 shows the options available in the Axis drop-down on the right end of the Sparkline Tools Design tab. The important settings here are the choices for the Minimum Value and Maximum Value.

Figure 33.15
Control the vertical axis using this drop-down.

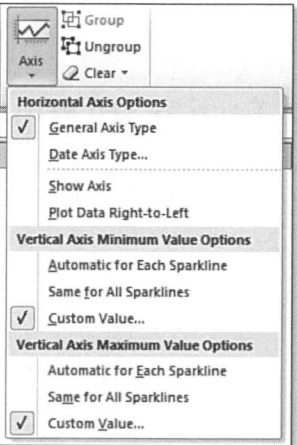

If you change the min and max to the setting of Same for All Sparklines, then all six sparklines in this group will have the same min and max scale. The sparklines in Figure 33.16 initially look better. Juneau is never as warm as Tucson. But you still do not know what the max and min values are. Take a close look at Chicago. It appears that the January high temperature is about zero, but the data table shows that the average high temperature in January is 29. You can estimate that these columns run from a min of 28 to a max of 101, based on looking through the data.

Figure 33.16
Force all sparklines to have the same vertical scale.

	A	B	C	D	E	F
1	Miami	Chicago	Juneau	Tucson	Trinidad	Curitiba
2						
3						
4		Jan Feb Mar Apr May Jun Jul Aug Sep Oct Nov Dec				
5	Miami	76 77 80 83 86 88 89 90 88 85 80 77				
6	Chicago	29 34 45 58 70 80 84 82 75 63 48 35				
7	Juneau	29 34 39 47 55 61 64 63 56 47 37 32				
8	Tucson	64 68 73 81 90 100 99 97 94 84 73 65				
9	Trinidad	85 86 87 88 88 86 87 88 88 87 87 85				
10	Curitiba	79 80 77 73 69 66 66 68 68 72 75 77				

My suggestion is to always visit the axis drop-down and set a custom min value and a custom max value. In Figure 33.17, the minimum is 0 and the maximum is 100.

 To see a demo of controlling sparkline axes, search for "Excel in Depth 33" at YouTube.

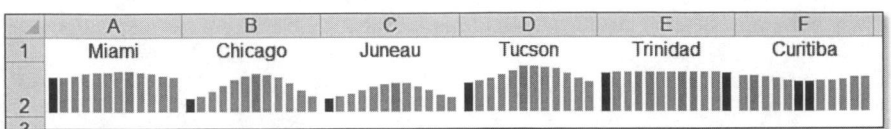

Figure 33.17
For absolute control, define a custom min and max value.

Setting Up Win/Loss Sparklines

The data for a Win/Loss sparkline is simple: Put a 1 (or any positive number) for a win. Put a -1 (or any negative number) for a loss. Put a zero to have no marker.

In Figure 33.18, you can see the data for a pair of Win/Loss sparklines. The 2 in cell F3 does not cause the marker to appear any taller than any of the 1s in the other cells.

Figure 33.18
Data sets for wins and losses are composed of 1s and -1s.

The data for the Win/Loss sparkcolumn chart does not have to be composed of 1s and negative 1s. Any positive and negative numbers will work.

In Figure 33.19, the data show the closing price for the Dow for a few month period. Column D calculates the daily change. The Win/Loss chart in rows 4 and 5 does not show the magnitude of the change, but instead focuses on how many days in a row had market gains vs. market losses.

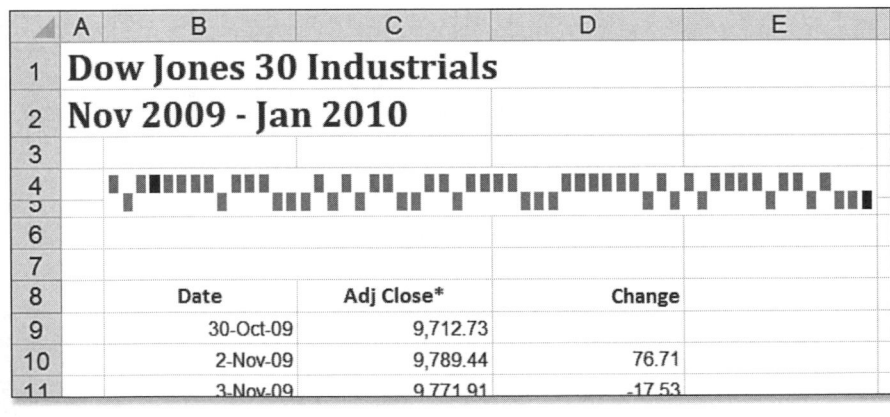

Figure 33.19
This chart focuses on how many days in a row were gains or losses. The magnitude of the change is not factored in.

Some notes about the chart in Figure 33.19:

- Cells B4:E5 are merged in order to show a larger sparkline.

- If you stretch a sparkcolumn or a win/loss chart out wide enough, gaps eventually show up between the columns. This helps to quantify the number of events in a streak.

- The final day is a darker color than the other losses. This is because the final day of the data set had a greater loss than any other point.

- The fourth day is a darker color than the other wins. This is the high point being marked in the data set.

Showing Detail by Enlarging the Sparkline and Adding Labels

The examples of sparklines created by Tufte in *Beautiful Evidence* almost always labeled the final point. Some examples included min and max values or a gray box to indicate the normal range of values.

Professor Tufte's definition of sparklines included the word "small." If you are going to be showing the sparklines on a computer screen, there is no reason that the sparklines have to stay small.

When you increase the height and width of the cell, the sparkline automatically grows to fill the cell. If you merge cells, the sparkline will fill the complete range of merged cells.

In Figure 33.20, the height of the cell is set to 56.25. This height allows for five rows of 8-point Calibri text to appear in the cell. To determine the optimum height for your font, type 1 Alt+Enter 2 Alt+Enter 3 Alt+Enter 4 Alt+Enter 5 in a cell. Use Home, Format, AutoFit Row Height.

The sparkline in cell B2 is set to have a custom minimum and a custom maximum that matches the minimum and maximum of the data set.

The label in cell A2 is right-justified 8-point Calibri font. The formula in A2 is =B9&REPT(CHAR(10),4)&B8. This formula concatenates the maximum value, four line feeds, and the minimum value. Ensure the Wrap Text icon is selected on the Home tab.

The labels in B3 are 10-point Calibri. Type J F M A M J J A S O N D in cell B3 and adjust the column width to fit the text.

Formulas in B10 and B13 calculate the range from the min to the max, and the quintile where the final value falls. The formula in C2 uses =REPT(CHAR(10),B13-1)&B11 to put the final label at about the right height to match the final point.

In Figure 33.21, the city labels are values typed in the same cell as the sparkcolumns. The max scale was set to 120 to make sure that there was room for the city name to appear. The Month abbreviations below the charts are "J F M A M J J A S O N D" in 6.5-point Courier New font.

 tip

After trying both 6-point and 7-point and not having the labels line up with the bars, I ended up using 6.5-point and adjusted the column widths until the columns lined up with the labels.

If you set a row height equal to 110, you can fit 10 lines of text in the cell using Alt+Enter. Even with a height of 55, you can fit five lines of text. This will allow the label for the final point to get near to the final point.

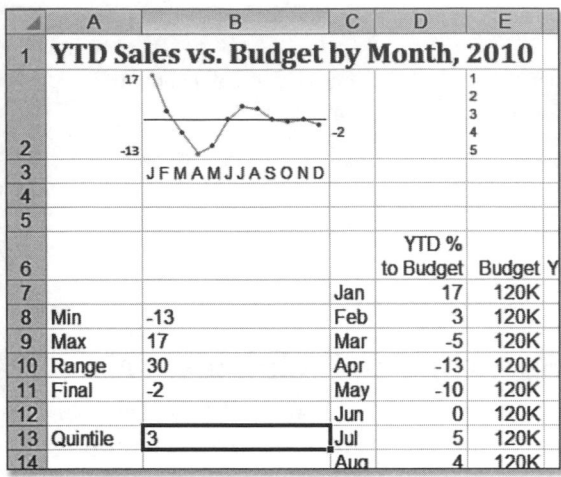

Figure 33.20
This sparkline has many labels, but they are all manually added outside of the sparkline.

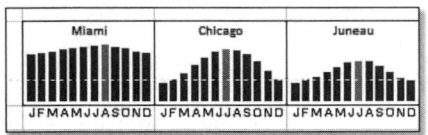

Figure 33.21
Labels are created by typing in a small font in the cell.

In Figure 33.22, a semitransparent gray box indicates the acceptable limits for a measurement. In this case, anything outside of 95 to 105% is sent for review. Those gray boxes are Shapes from the Insert tab.

Some tips when setting up the box:

1. Temporarily change the first two points in the first cell to be at the min and max for the box.

2. Increase the zoom to 400%.

3. Draw a rectangle in the cell.

4. Use the Drawing Tools Format tab to set the outline to None.

5. Under Shape Fill, select More Fill Colors. Choose a gray. Because shapes are drawn on top of the sparkline layer, drag the transparency slider up to about 70% transparent.

6. Use the resize handles to make sure the top and bottom of the box go through the first and second points of the line.

 tip
It is possible to copy sparklines. You have to copy both the sparkline and the data source in a single copy. If your copy range includes both elements, the sparkline will get pasted.

Figure 33.22
A gray box shows the acceptable range to help the reader locate items outside of the acceptable range.

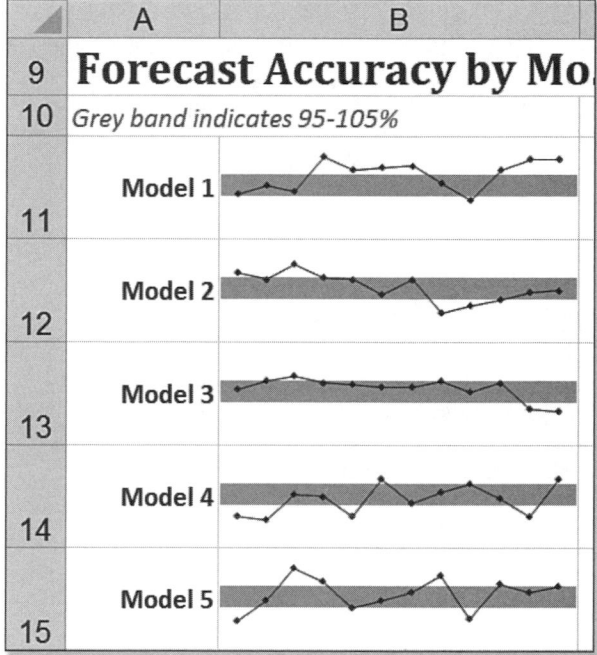

7. After getting the box sized appropriately, reset the first two data points back to their original values.

8. Copy the cell that contains the first box. Paste onto the other sparkline cells. Because the sparklines are not copied, only the box will be pasted.

Other Sparkline Options

You can choose how to deal with gaps in the data. Select Sparkline Tools Design, Edit Data, Hidden and Empty Cells to display the Hidden and Empty Cell Setting dialog as shown in Figure 33.23.

By default, any missing data in the source range is plotted as a gap, as shown in the top chart in Figure 33.23.

Alternatively, you can choose to plot the missing values as zero (center chart) or have Excel connect the data points with a straight line (bottom chart).

Also, by default, any data in hidden rows or columns will be removed from the sparkline. To keep the hidden data in the chart, select the Show Data in Hidden Rows and Columns check box in Figure 33.23.tip

In step 1, you might find that you don't need to print the table of numbers, just the labels and sparklines will suffice.

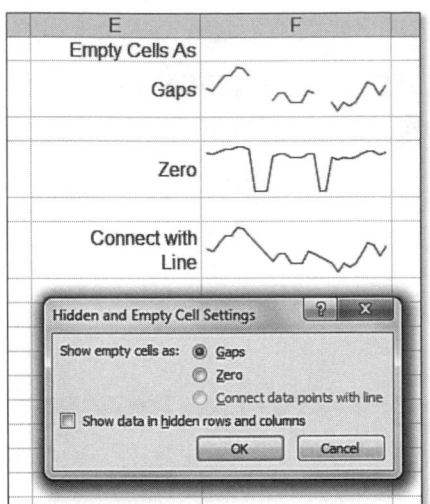

Figure 33.23
Choose how to deal with missing points.

USING SMARTART, SHAPES, WORDART, AND TEXT BOXES

Images and artwork provide an interesting visual break from tables of numbers in Excel 2010. Office 2010 provides four elements that can be used to illustrate a workbook:

- **SmartArt**—SmartArt is a collection of similar shapes, arranged to imply a process, groups, or a hierarchy. In legacy version of Excel, SmartArt was known as Diagrams. As in the past, you can add new shapes, reverse the order of shapes, and change the color of shapes. Office 2010 includes a text editor that allows for Level 1 and Level 2 text for each shape in a diagram. Many styles of SmartArt include the capability to add a small picture or logo to each shape.

- **Shapes**—Interesting shapes can be added to a document. Shapes can contain words. In fact, shapes are the only art objects in which the words can come from a cell on the worksheet. You can add glow, bevel, and 3D effects to shapes. In legacy versions of Excel, shapes were known as AutoShapes. Microsoft added some new shapes to Excel 2007, along with several formatting properties.

- **WordArt**—Present ordinary text it in a stylized manner. You can use WordArt to bend, rotate, and twist the characters in text. WordArt was redesigned completely in Excel 2007, which enabled you to add glow, bevel, and material effects.

- **Text boxes**—Allow text to flow in a defined area. The text box feature is excellent if you need to include paragraphs of body copy in a worksheet. A new feature added in Excel 2007 is the capability to have text flow through multiple columns in a single text box.

Using SmartArt

You use SmartArt to show a series of similar shapes, where each shape represents a related step, concept, idea, or grouping.

SmartArt in Excel 2010 is an enhanced version of business diagrams from legacy versions of Excel. In SmartArt, Microsoft addressed many of the shortcomings of business diagrams, including the following:

- Each shape has an associated text editor.

- Shapes can contain Level 1 text for headlines and Level 2 text for body copy.

- Some styles now allow shapes to include an image.

- Settings in SmartArt can automatically resize the text in all shapes to allow the longest text to fit.

- Quick Styles enables you to apply glow and bevels to an entire SmartArt diagram.

 **caution**

If you want to fine-tune the text in a particular box, select the SmartArt Tools from the Format tab to micromanage any element in the SmartArt. However, use caution because adjusting the built-in properties is a great way to ruin the look of the SmartArt.

The goal of SmartArt is to enable you to create a great-looking graphic with a minimum of effort. After you define a SmartArt image, you can change to any of the other 129 layouts by choosing the desired layout from the gallery. Text is carried from one layout to the next. Figure 34.1 shows four SmartArt styles:

- **Basic Process**—In this layout, all text is typed as Level 1.

- **Accent Process**—This layout puts the Level 1 text in the background and highlights the Level 2 text in the foreground boxes.

- **Picture Accent Process**—This layout gives equal weight to the Level 1 and Level 2 text. Pictures are added behind each shape.

- **Picture Accent List**—Unlike the process charts, a list chart does not include arrows to indicate a process.

Elements Common in Most SmartArt

A SmartArt style is a collection of two or more related shapes. In most styles, you can add additional shapes to illustrate a longer process. However, a few styles are limited to only n items. Each shape can contain a headline (Level 1 text), body copy (Level 2 text), and a graphic. Some of the 129 layouts show only Level 1 text. If you switch to a style that does not display Level 2 text and then back, the shape remembers the Level 2 text it had originally. After the file is saved and closed, the hidden text is removed.

 note

Thirty of the 129 SmartArt layouts can include pictures. A limitation in Excel 2007 required you to add pictures as the last step. This means that changing from one picture layout to another caused the pictures to be lost. Microsoft improved SmartArt in Excel 2010 to allow the pictures to remain as you change to different layouts.

Figure 34.1
Subtle differences in four of the 129 possible SmartArt layouts give more weight to either Level 1 or Level 2 text.

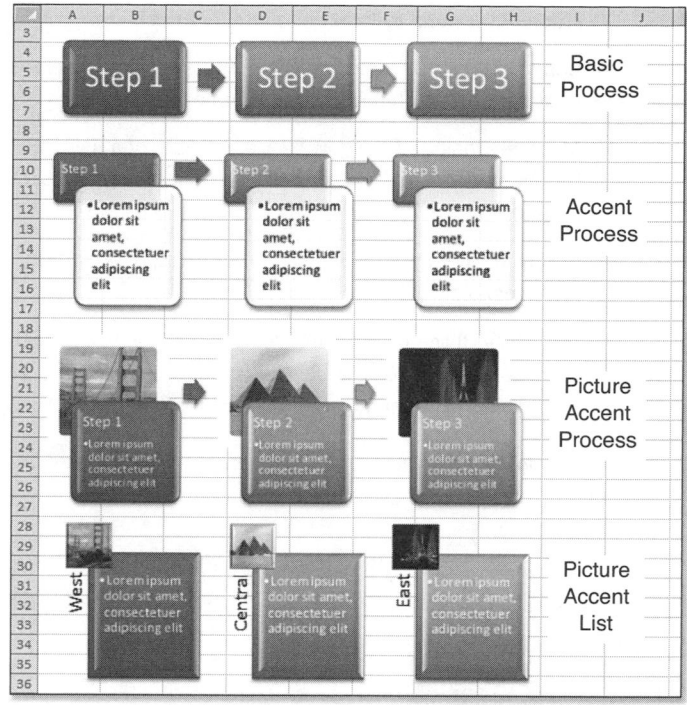

While you are editing SmartArt, a text pane that is slightly reminiscent of PowerPoint appears. You can type some bullet points into the text pane. If you demote a bullet point, the text changes from Level 1 text to Level 2 text. If you add a new Level 1 bullet point, Excel adds a new shape to the SmartArt.

Tour of the SmartArt Categories

The SmartArt gallery groups the 129 SmartArt layouts into the following eight broad categories:

- **List**—Designed to show a nonsequential list of information. Variations include horizontal, vertical, and bending lists. Some lists include chevrons, and some include pictures. In general, these styles do not include arrows between shapes.

- **Process**—Designed to show a sequential list of steps. Variations include horizontal, vertical, bending, equations, funnels, gears, and several varieties of arrows. Some process charts allow the inclusion of images. Most styles include arrows or other connectors in order to convey a sequence.

- **Cycle**—Designed to show a series of steps that repeat. It includes cycle charts, radial charts, a gear chart, and a pie chart.

- **Hierarchy**—Designed to show organization charts, decision trees, and other hierarchical relationships. Variations include horizontal, vertical, and with and without connecting lines.

- **Relationship**—Designed to show a relationship between items. Many of the layouts in this category are duplicated from the other seven categories.

- **Matrix**—Designed to show four quadrants of a list. The Titled Matrix layout offers a fifth block for an overall title. New in Excel 2010 is the Cycle Matrix that allows for Level 2 text outside the main blocks.

- **Pyramid**—Designed to show containment, overlapping, proportional, or interconnected relationships.

- **Picture**—All the layouts that contain pictures are repeated in this category. In Excel 2010, Microsoft added 16 new picture layouts that appear only in this category. Some of these picture layouts are appropriate only for pictures with little or no text.

Figure 34.2 shows one version of each of the eight categories.

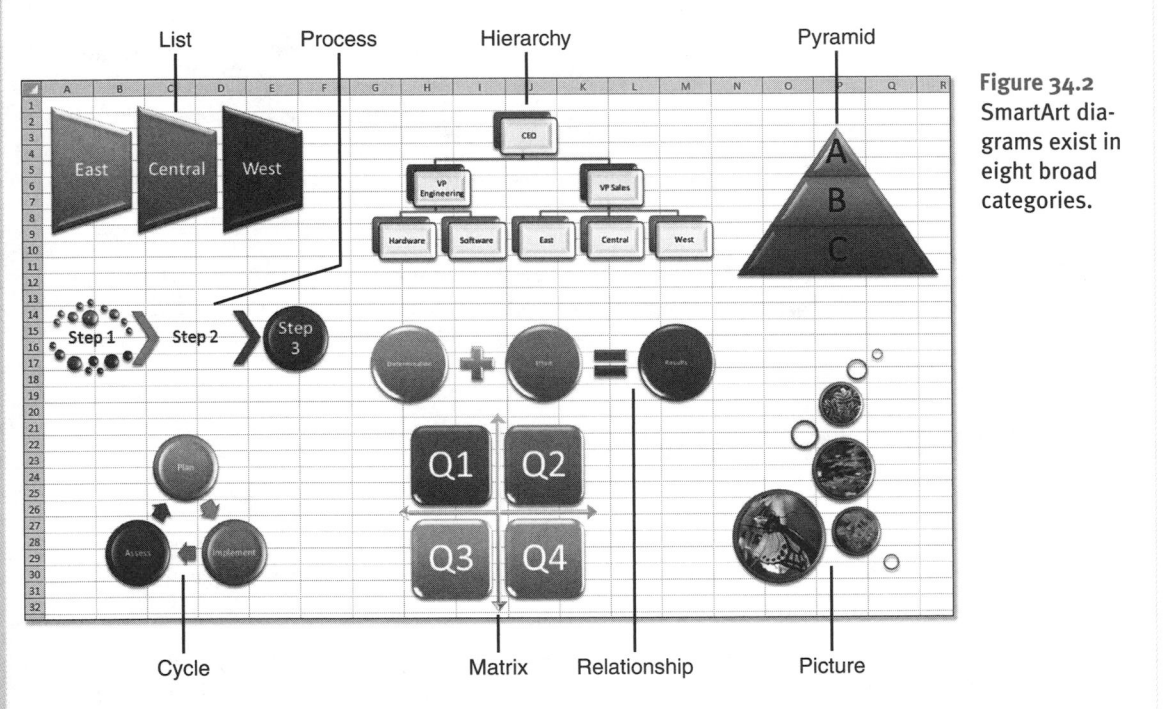

Figure 34.2
SmartArt diagrams exist in eight broad categories.

Inserting SmartArt

Although there are 129 different layouts of SmartArt, you follow the same basic steps to insert any SmartArt layout:

1. Select a cell in a blank section of the workbook.

2. From the Insert tab, select SmartArt from the Illustrations group. The Choose a SmartArt Graphic dialog appears.

3. Choose a category in the left side of the Choose a SmartArt Graphic dialog.

4. Click a SmartArt type in the center of the Choose a SmartArt Graphic dialog.

5. Read the description on the right side. This description tells you if the layout is good for Level 1 text, Level 2 text, or both. In Figure 34.3, the Vertical Chevron List layout is good for large amounts of Level 2 text.

Figure 34.3
The description for each style tells you whether a particular style is appropriate for Level 1 or Level 2 text.

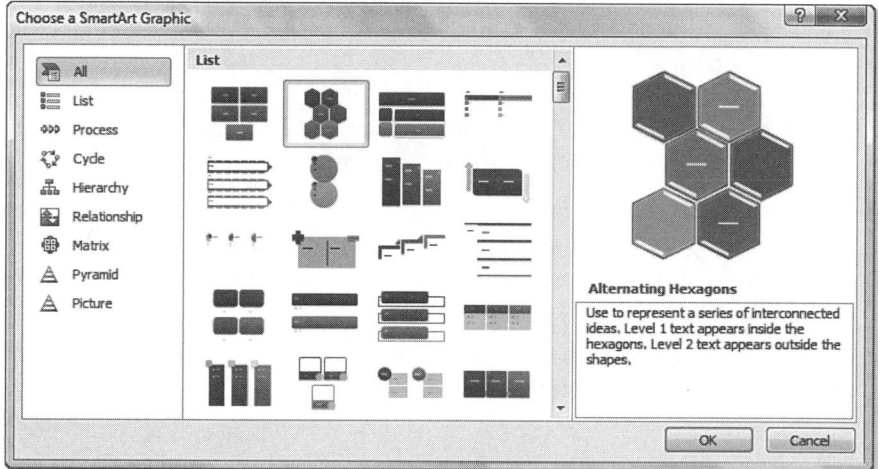

6. Repeat steps 4 and 5 until you find a style suitable for your content. Then click OK. Figure 34.4 shows an outline of the SmartArt drawn on the worksheet. The flashing insertion cursor is in the first item of the text pane. One element of the SmartArt is selected. When you type text at the flashing insertion point, it is added to the selected shape.

7. Fill in the text pane with text for your SmartArt. You can add, delete, promote, or demote items by using icons in the SmartArt Tools Design tab, Create Graphic group. The SmartArt updates as you type more text. In many cases, adding a new Level 1 item adds a new shape element to the SmartArt.

8. Add longer text to the SmartArt, and Excel shrinks the font size of all the elements to make the text fit. You can make the entire SmartArt graphic larger at any time by grabbing the resize handles in the corners of the SmartArt and dragging to a new size. After you resize the graphic, Excel resizes the text to make it fit in the SmartArt at the largest size possible.

9. The color scheme of the SmartArt initially appears in one color. To change the color scheme, select SmartArt Tools Design, SmartArt Styles, Change Colors. Excel offers several versions of monochrome styles and five styles of color variations for each shape.

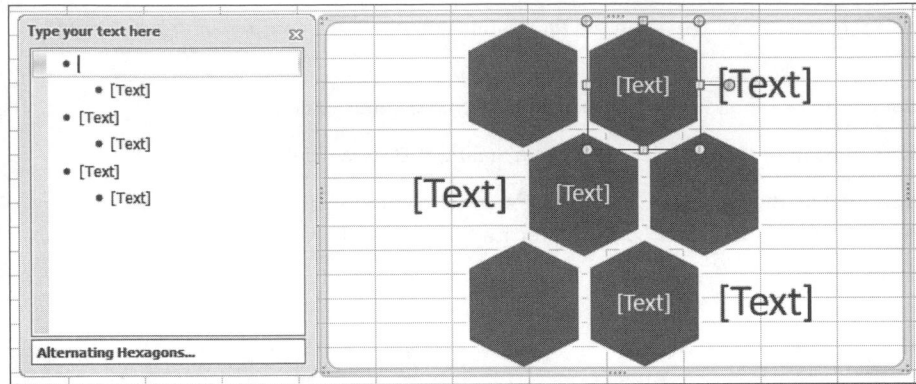

Figure 34.4
When you type in the text pane, the text is added to the selected element of the SmartArt.

10. Choose a basic or 3D style from the SmartArt Styles gallery. The Polished or Inset styles have a suitable mix of effects but are still readable.

11. Move the SmartArt to the proper location. Position the mouse over the border of the SmartArt, avoiding the eight Resize handles. The cursor changes to a four-headed arrow. Click and drag the SmartArt to a new location. If you drag the SmartArt to the left side of the worksheet, the text pane moves to the right of the SmartArt.

12. Click outside the SmartArt. Excel embeds the SmartArt graphic in the worksheet and hides the SmartArt tabs, as shown in Figure 34.5.

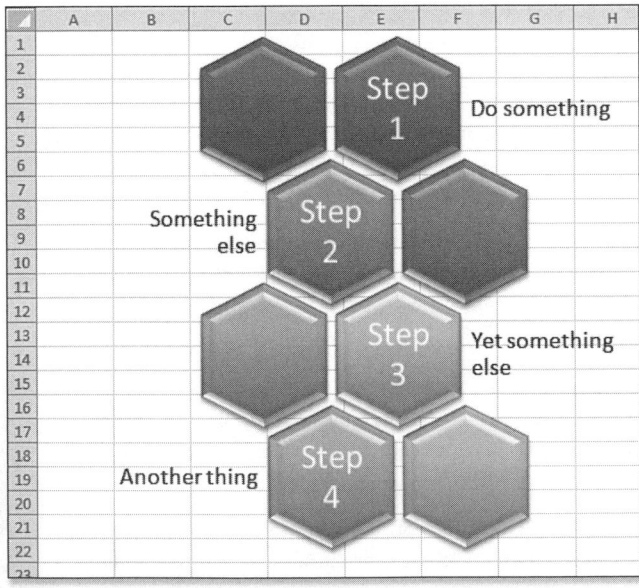

Figure 34.5
Click outside the SmartArt boundary to embed the completed SmartArt.

Changing Existing SmartArt to a New Style

There are a couple of ways you can change SmartArt to a new style:

- Left-click the SmartArt and then select SmartArt Tools, Layouts from the Design tab to choose a new layout. As shown in Figure 34.6, the Layouts drop-down initially shows only the styles that Excel thinks are a close fit to the current style. If you want to access the complete list of styles, you have to select More Layouts. The advantage of this method is that Live Preview shows the changes before you commit to a style. Figures 34.7 through 34.9 show other styles in Live Preview.

Figure 34.6
Grouped List provides a new shape for each bullet point in Level 2.

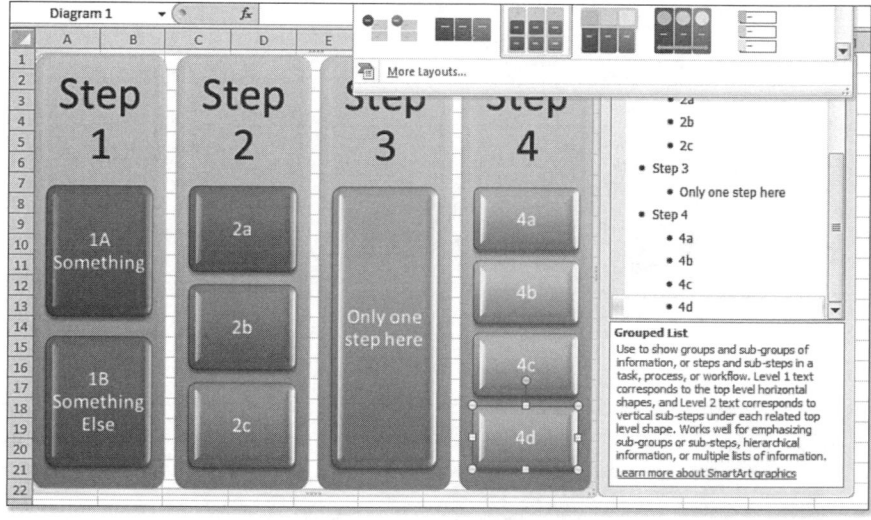

Figure 34.7
Captioned Pictures allocates a lot of space for images and minimal space for text.

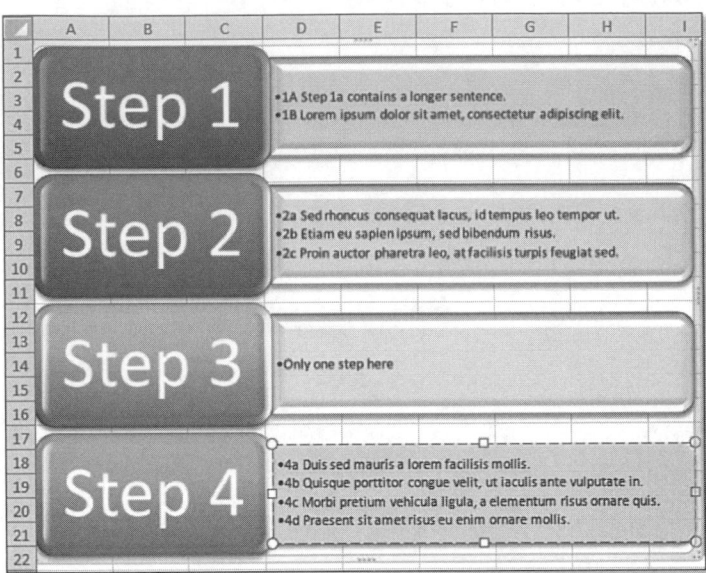

Figure 34.8
Vertical Block List is good for large amounts of Level 2 text.

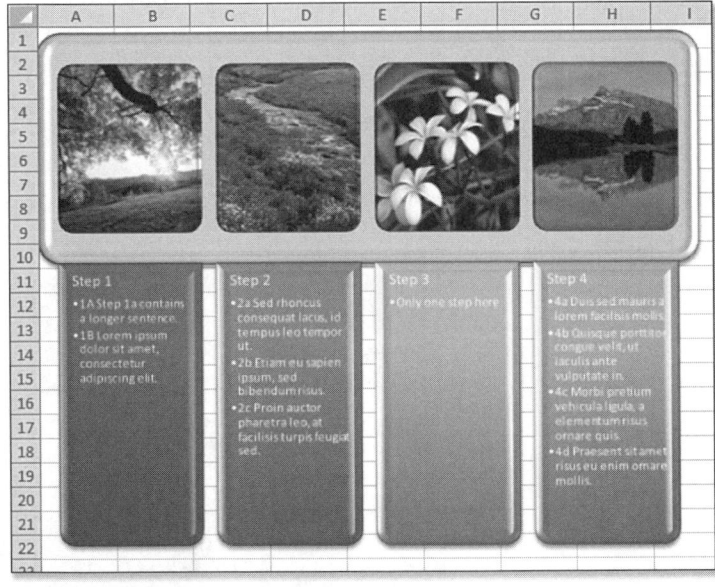

Figure 34.9
Horizontal Picture List can handle a balance of text and pictures.

- A faster way to access the complete list of styles is to right-click between two shapes in the SmartArt and select Change Layout from the context menu. This step is a little tricky because you cannot click an existing shape. Instead, you must click inside the SmartArt border, but on a portion of the SmartArt which is empty.

Micromanaging SmartArt Elements

The two tabs for SmartArt tools enable you to manage the SmartArt elements—the Design tab and the Format tab.

The Design tab enables you to change the overall design of the SmartArt. If you stay on the Design tab, Microsoft will make sure that your SmartArt looks good because it keeps the font for all Level 2 text consistent for all shapes and all the shapes proportional.

However, if you need to override some aspect of one shape, you can do so on the Format tab.

 caution

When you change any setting on the Format tab, Microsoft turns off the automatic formatting for the other elements. For this reason, changing a setting on the Format tab is a great way to make horrible-looking SmartArt. If you absolutely have to use the Format tab, you should first get your SmartArt as close as possible to the final version by using the Design tab.

Changing Text Formatting in One Element

In Automatic mode, Excel chooses a font size that is small enough to show the longest text completely. This can cause problems if you have one shape with long text and short text everywhere else. In this case, Excel chooses a small font size for the long text and then forces all the other items to have tiny text as well. In such a situation, you might want to override the text size for the shape that has the longest text. Excel then automatically resizes the font size in the remaining automatic shapes to be larger.

The mini toolbar is useful for making these changes. You select the text either directly in the shape or in the text pane. Immediately after you complete the selection, you should watch for an almost-transparent formatting box to appear. Then you immediately move the mouse to the box to prevent it from disappearing. You can then change the font size by using the drop-down in the mini toolbar. If you allow the mini toolbar to disappear, you can use the formatting tools on the Home tab to change the font size.

As shown in Figure 34.10, the long Level 2 text in step 4 was resized. Excel then calculated the proper text size for steps 1 through 3, resulting in the text in the top three shapes automatically growing to a larger font size.

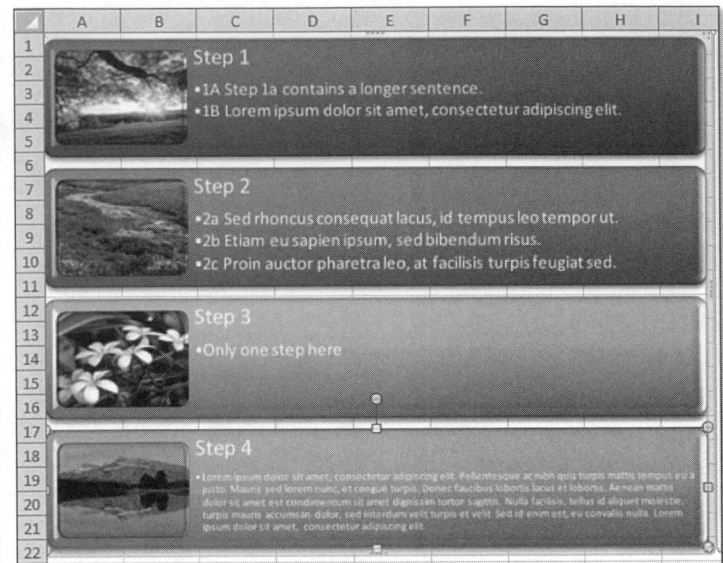

Figure 34.10
When you manually override the font size in the fourth shape, the text in the remaining three shapes automatically becomes larger.

Changing One Shape

You can edit many items for a SmartArt shape. To see how this works, click any shape in the SmartArt and then try the following:

- Use the green handle to rotate the shape.

- Use the resize handles to resize the shape.

- Use the move handle to nudge the shape.

- Select Shapes, Change Shape from the SmartArt Tools Format tab to change the shape completely.

- Select settings from the Shape Styles group to change fill, outline, and effects for the shape.

- Choose settings from the WordArt Styles group to change the text inside the shape.

- Right-click the shape and select Format Shape to have complete control over the shape.

In general, SmartArt created on the Design tab looks uniform and neat. When you move to the Format tab, the possibility for chaos arises. For example, the SmartArt in Figure 34.11 that was created in the Format tab contains mixed effects, font sizes, and rotation.

Controlling SmartArt Shapes from the Text Pane

The text pane represents a fantastic improvement over business diagrams in legacy versions of Excel. By using only the keyboard, you can add or delete shapes and promote or demote items.

Figure 34.11
After experimenting with the Format tab, select Reset Graphic on the Design tab to make the SmartArt uniform.

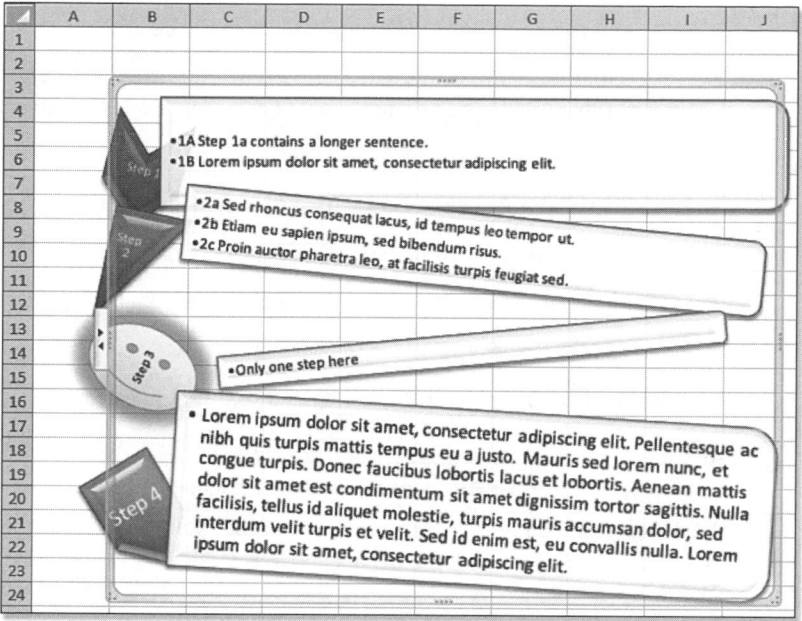

Further, the text pane has proofing tools such as spell check. Using the text pane is similar to creating bullet points in a PowerPoint slide.

Figure 34.12 shows a newly inserted pyramid SmartArt in Excel. By default, most new SmartArt diagrams have three shapes, but you can change that number by using the text pane.

Figure 34.12
A default SmartArt includes three shapes. You can edit the number of shapes by using the text pane.

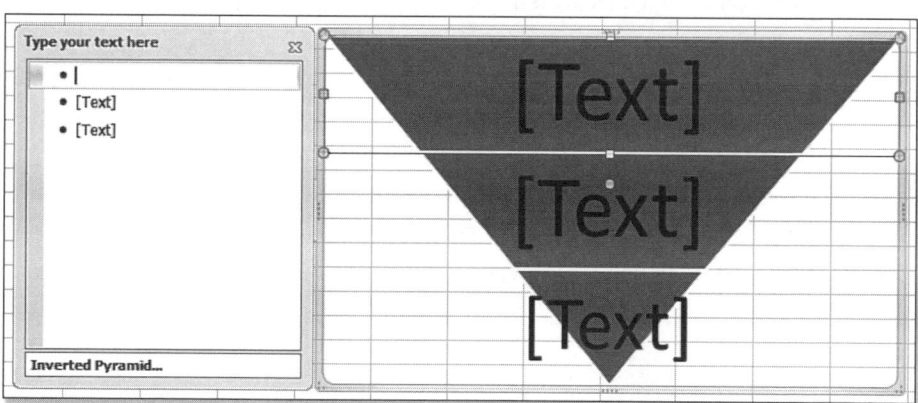

The following rules apply to the text pane for SmartArt:

- Press up-arrow or down-arrow keys to move from one line to another.

- Press the Enter key to insert a new line below the current line. The new line will be at the same level as the current line. Adding a new Level 1 line inserts a new shape in the SmartArt.

- Press the Tab key to demote Level 1 text to Level 2 text.

- Press Shift+Tab to promote Level 2 text to Level 1 text.

- Press the Backspace key on an empty line to delete the line.

- Press Delete at the end of any line to combine text from the next line with this line.

- Press End to move to the end of the current line.

- Press Home to move to the beginning of the current line.

As you add shapes, Excel continues to attempt to squeeze them into the default size. You can resize an entire piece of SmartArt by using the resize handles around the SmartArt.

Strictly as an example of how the text pane works, you can use the following steps to customize Figure 34.12 into Figure 34.13. This example illustrates how quickly you can change from the default SmartArt with three shapes to any number of shapes:

1. Type Shape 1 and then press Enter.

2. Type Subtext and then press Tab to demote the item. Next, press the down-arrow key to move to Text 2.

3. Type Shape 2 and then press Enter.

4. Type Point 1 and then press Tab and Enter.

5. Type Point 2 and then press Tab and the down-arrow key.

6. Type Shape 3 and then press Enter.

7. Type Point 3 and then press Tab and Enter.

8. Because Excel wants the next item to be Level 2 text, press Shift+Tab to promote this item.

9. Type Shape 4 and then press Enter. Type Shape 5 and then press Enter. Type Shape 6 and then press Enter. Type Shape 7 and then press Enter.

10. Type Point 4 and then press Tab, Enter, and Shift+Tab, and then type 8.

11. Using the mouse, resize the SmartArt so it is larger.

12. From the Quick Styles gallery on the Design tab, choose a color scheme.

The result is shown in Figure 34.13. As this example shows, by using only the keyboard and the text pane, you can quickly expand SmartArt and add Level 2 subpoints.

Figure 34.13
Add additional shapes and subpoints by using the text pane.

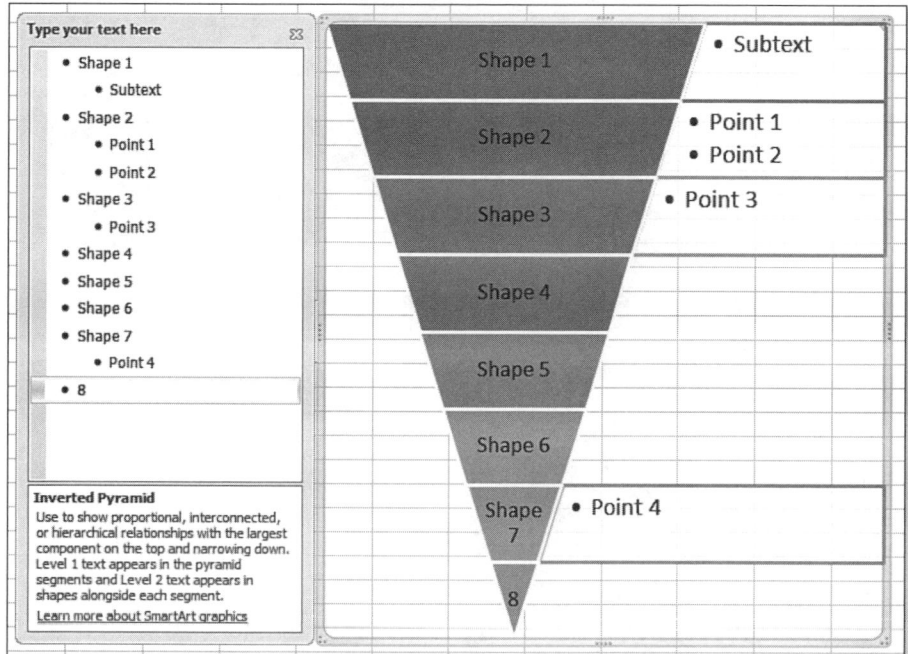

Adding Images to SmartArt

Thirty SmartArt layouts in the Picture category are designed to hold small images in addition to the text. In some of these styles, the picture is emphasized. However, in other pictures, the focus shifts to the text, and the picture is an accent.

When you select one of these styles, you can add text using the text pane and then specify pictures by clicking the picture icon inside each Level 1 shape. The SmartArt shows a picture icon next to bullet points in the text pane and in each shape, as shown in Figure 34.14.

You can click a picture icon to display the Insert Picture dialog. Then you can choose a picture and click Insert. Repeat this process to add each additional picture. The pictures are cropped automatically to fit the allotted area, as shown in Figure 34.15.

Clickable picture icons

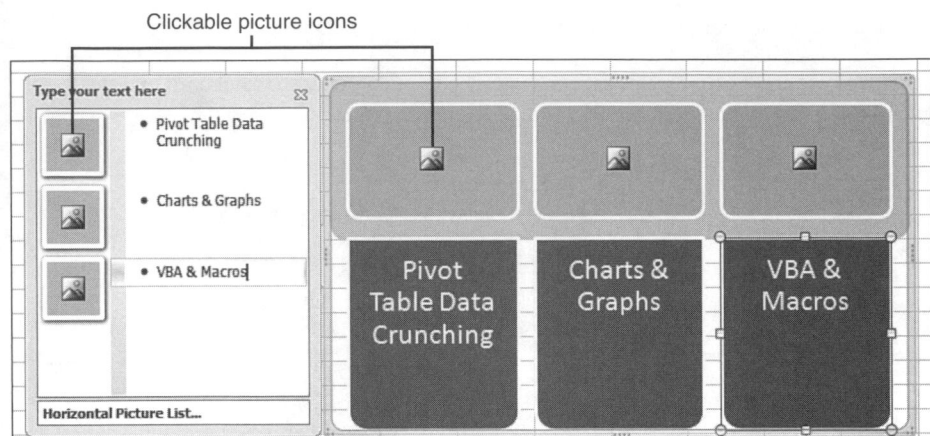

Figure 34.14
Each Level 1 bullet includes a picture placeholder.

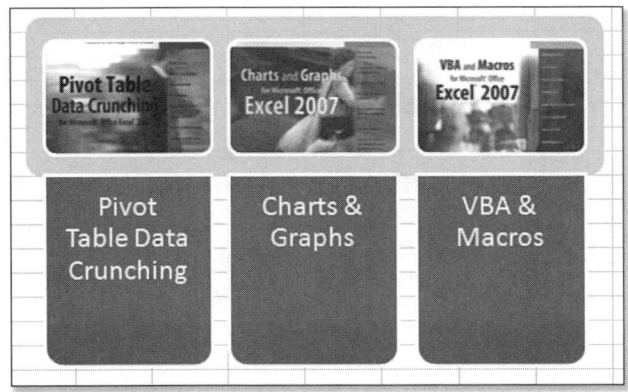

Figure 34.15
Pictures have been added to each shape.

■ After adding pictures, you can use all the formatting tools on the Picture Tools Format tab.

➡ *For details on the picture formatting tools, see Chapter 35, "Using Pictures and Clip Art."*

Special Considerations for Organizational Charts and Hierarchical SmartArt

Hierarchical SmartArt can contain more than two text levels. As you add more levels to the SmartArt, Excel continues to intelligently add boxes and resize them to fit.

Figure 34.16 shows a diagram created in the Hierarchy layout. In this layout, each level is assigned a different color.

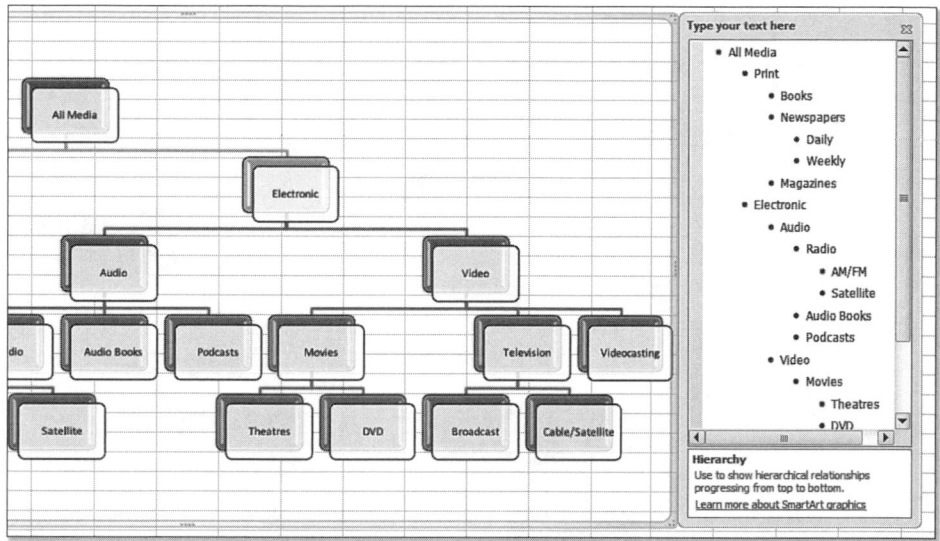

Figure 34.16
Hierarchical
SmartArt can
contain more
than two
levels.

Four styles in the Hierarchical category are organization charts. These layouts are used to describe reporting relationships in an organization. There are a few extra options in the ribbon for organization charts. For example, if you select the SmartArt Tools Design tab, the Add Shape drop-down includes the option Add Assistant, as shown in Figure 34.17. You can select this option to add an extra shape immediately below the selected level.

In the Create Graphic group of the Design tab, the Org Chart drop-down offers four options for showing the boxes within a group. First, you select the manager for the group. Then you select the appropriate type from the drop-down to affect all direct reports for the manager. Figure 34.18 illustrates the four options for Org Chart:

- **VP of Sales**—Shows a standard organization chart. The regions are arranged side by side.

- **VP of Manufacturing**—Includes a Right Hanging group that enables departments to be arranged vertically to the right of the line.

- **VP of Engineering**—Includes a Left Hanging group that enables departments to be arranged vertically to the left of the line.

- **CFO**—Includes a Both group that lists direct reports in two columns under the manager on both sides of the vertical line.

In each group, the assistant box is set off from the other boxes.

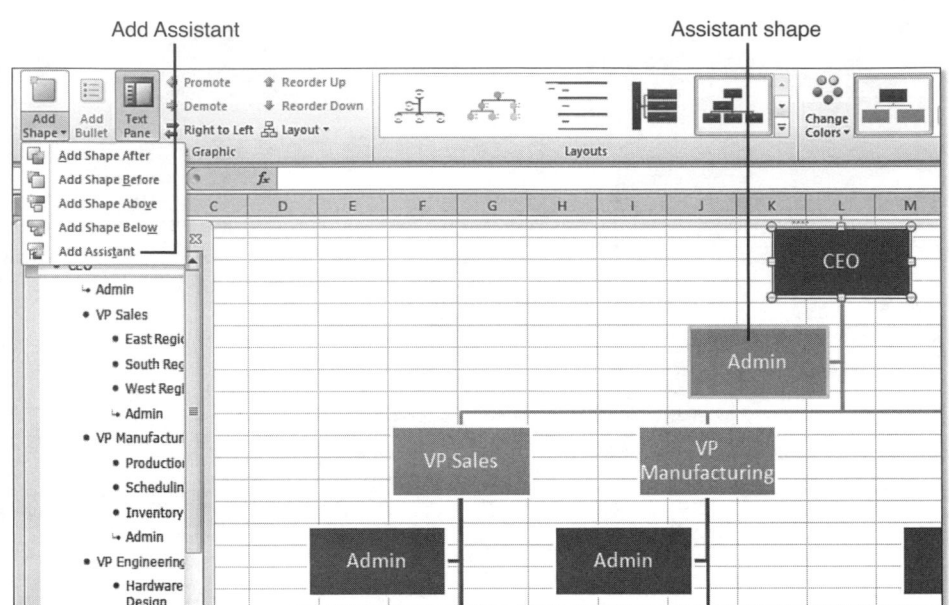

Figure 34.17
The Add Assistant selection adds a box for an administrative assistant below the selected shape.

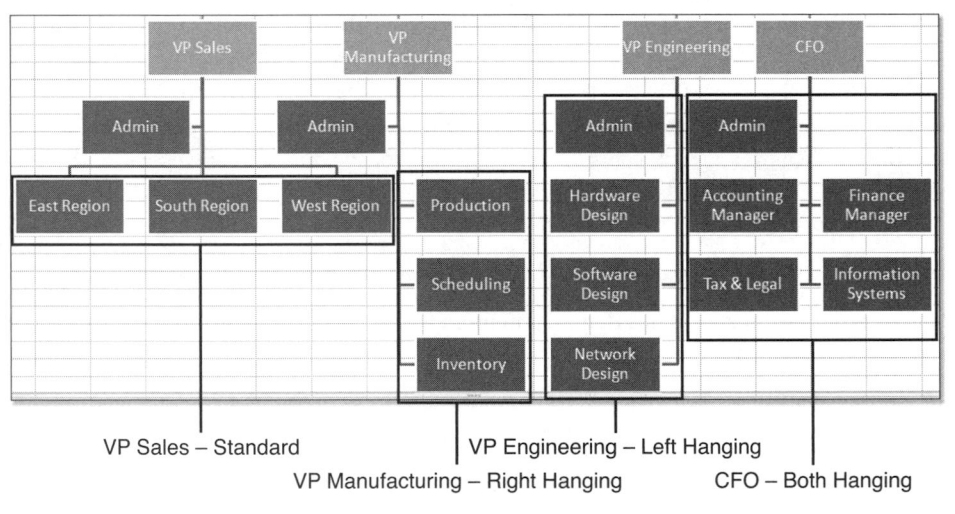

VP Sales – Standard

VP Manufacturing – Right Hanging

VP Engineering – Left Hanging

CFO – Both Hanging

Figure 34.18
Organization charts include additional options to control the arrangement of direct reports.

Using Limited SmartArt

Most of the SmartArt examples in the previous section are expandable, which means that new shapes are added to the SmartArt as you add Level 1 text. However, the following SmartArt styles cannot be expanded:

- The top-left image in Figure 34.19 shows a gear chart. Both the gear and funnel charts are limited to three items. If you add additional items to the text pane, each appears with a red X. These items do not display in the SmartArt, but they are stored temporarily in case you change to another SmartArt layout. When you save the workbook, the text associated with the fourth and subsequent shapes is deleted. This prevents you from inadvertently leaving hidden bullet points before sending the workbook to a client.

- Many of the arrow layouts in the Relationship category are limited to two shapes.

- The Matrix layouts are limited to four quadrants. Grid Matrix offers four quadrants plus a title, as shown in the center of Figure 34.19.

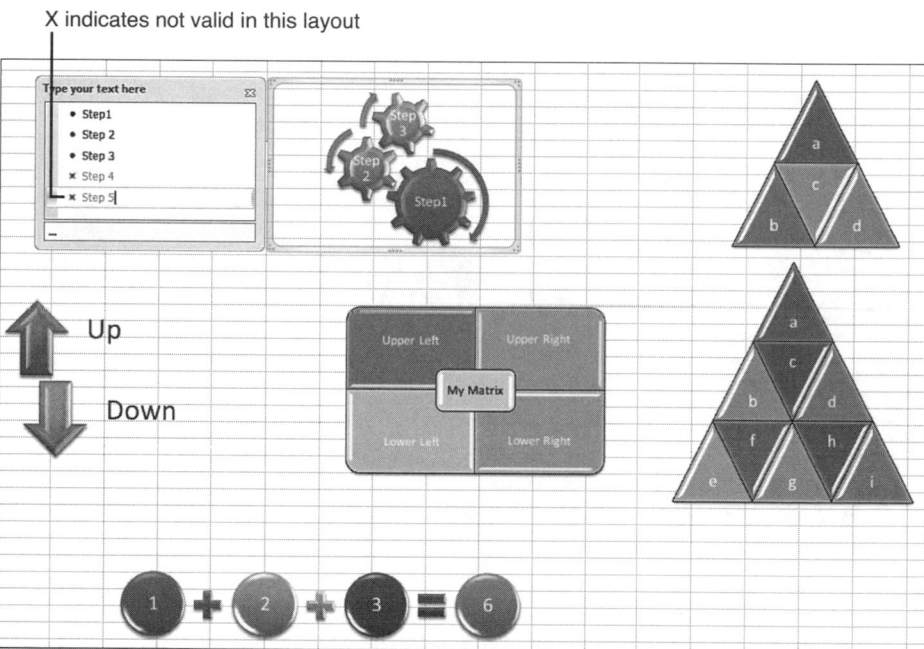

Figure 34.19
Arrows, gears, funnels, and matrix shapes have certain limitations on the number of shapes they can contain.

- The Segmented Pyramid style can be expanded, but it must contain 1, 4, 9, or 16 shapes. As soon as you add a fifth style to the SmartArt in the upper-left corner of the display, an entire row is added to the bottom of the pyramid, resulting in the SmartArt shown in the lower right of Figure 34.19.

■ The Equation style can be expanded, but the answer is always the last Level 1 item in the text pane.

Deciphering the Labeled Hierarchy Layouts

A few of the SmartArt layouts in Excel 2010 are somewhat confusing. For example, Figure 34.20 shows a Labeled Hierarchy Chart. In this layout, the first Level 1 text is shown in a box at the beginning of the diagram. All the subitems should be typed as Level 2 items below the first shape. After building all the boxes in the hierarchy, you should add an additional Level 1 item for each level in the diagram. These final Level 1 items will be used for the labels at the left side of the diagram.

First Level 1 is top shape

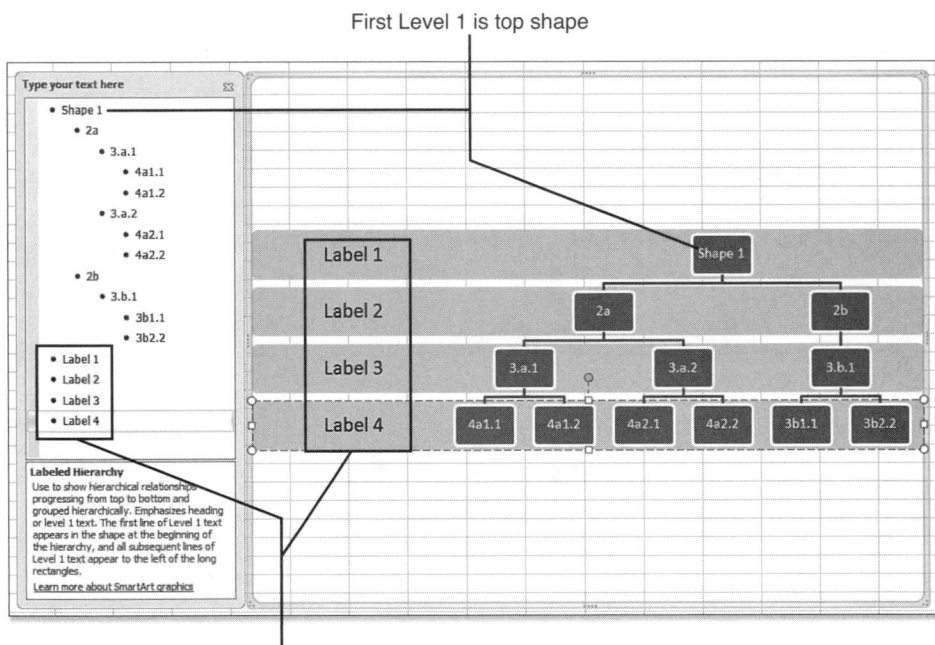

Figure 34.20
The Labeled Hierarchy layouts require extra Level 1 elements after the main part of the diagram to label each level.

Add additiontial Level 1 shape for Level Labels

Overall, SmartArt is a great addition to the Office family. The one real drawback related to using SmartArt in Excel is its inability to create dynamic SmartArt where the text for a shape is the result of a calculation.

The following section details how a regular shape can contain calculated text. The solution to creating dynamic SmartArt is to build SmartArt, then use the Convert to Shapes icon in the SmartArt Tools Design tab. You can then link the individual shapes to formula cells.

Using Shapes to Display Cell Contents

In legacy versions of Excel, shapes were known as AutoShapes. Beginning with Excel 2007, Microsoft added new shapes to the already long list of shapes available in AutoShapes. In addition, Excel 2010 shapes have some new formatting options, such as shadow, glow, and bevel.

Perhaps the best part of shapes is that you can tie the text on a shape to a worksheet cell. For example, in Figure 34.21, the shape is set to display the current value of Cell B26. Every time the worksheet is calculated, the text on the shape is updated.

Figure 34.21
Shapes can be set to display the current value of a cell.

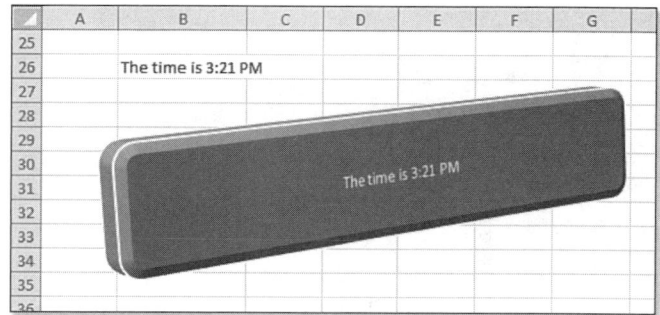

Follow these steps to insert a shape into a worksheet:

1. Select a blank area of the worksheet.

2. From the Insert tab, open the Shapes drop-down.

3. Select one of the 160 basic shapes, as shown in Figure 34.22.

4. The mouse pointer changes to a small crosshair. Click and drag in the worksheet to draw the shape.

5. Choose a color scheme from the Shapes Styles drop-down.

6. Select Shape Effects, Preset, and select an effect.

> 🔍 **note**
>
> If you want the shape to include a calculated value, skip step 9 and follow steps 10 through 12.

7. Look for a yellow diamond on the shape, which allows you to change the inflection point for the shape. For example, on the rounded rectangle, sliding the yellow diamond controls how wide the rounded corners are.

8. Look for a green circle on the outside of the shape. If necessary, drag this circle to rotate the shape.

9. To include static text in the shape, click in the middle of the shape and type the text. You can control the style by using the WordArt Styles drop-down. You can control text size and color by using the formatting buttons on the Home tab. The shape can include text from any cell, but it cannot perform a calculation.

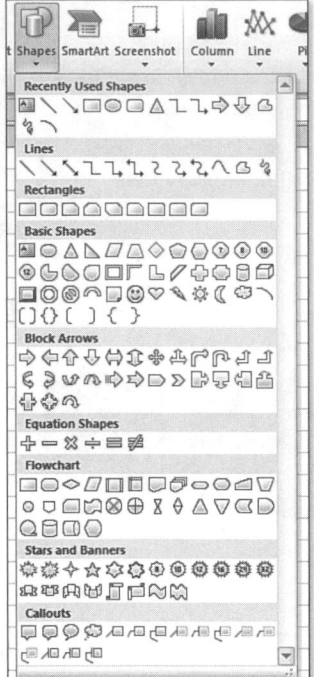

Figure 34.22
Choose from these shapes.

10. If desired, add a new cell that will format a message for the Shape. As shown in Figure 34.23, add the formula **="We are at "&TEXT(B13,"0%")&" of our goal!"** to an empty cell to convert the calculation in Cell B13 to a suitable message.

11. Click in the middle of the text box as you would if text was being added.

12. Click in the formula bar, type **=B14**, and then press Enter. As shown in Figure 34.23, the shape displays the results from the selected cell.

 To watch a video of converting SmartArt to shapes so you can add a formula to the shapes, search for "Excel In Depth 34" at YouTube.

Working with Shapes

The Drawing Tools section of the Format tab contains sections to change the shape style, fill, outline, effects, and WordArt effects.

In the Insert Shapes dialog, use the Edit Shape, Change Shape command to choose another shape style.

If you right-click a shape and select Format Shape, Excel displays the Format Shape dialog, with the fine-tuning settings Fill, Line, Line Style, Shadow, 3D Format, 3D Rotation, and Text Placement.

Figure 34.23
This shape picks up the formula from Cell B14 to show how a message changes with the worksheet.

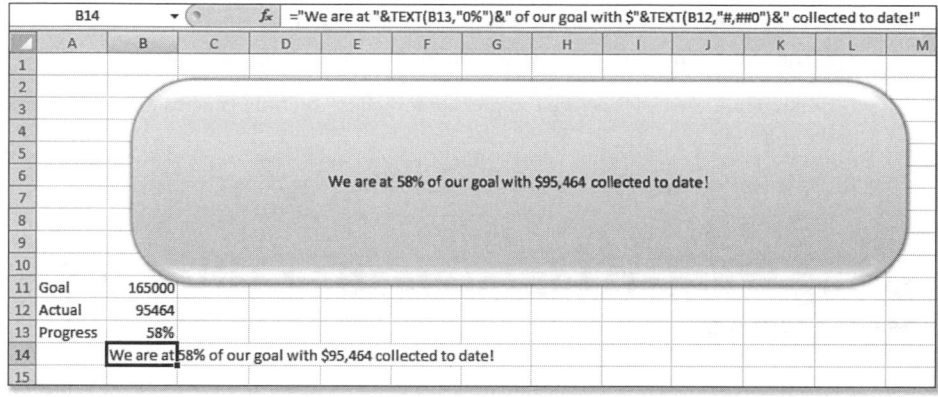

Using the Freeform Shape to Create a Custom Shape

Despite my friendly relationship with Microsoft, I have not convinced them to add the MrExcel logo to the Shapes gallery—yet. However, you can build any shape by using the Freeform line tools in the Shapes gallery.

After you create a shape, you can add 3D effects, glow, and so on. For example, you can enhance your company logo, as shown in Figure 34.24.

Figure 34.24
After this shape was created with the Freeform shape tool, it was enhanced using the Drawing Tools section of the Format tab.

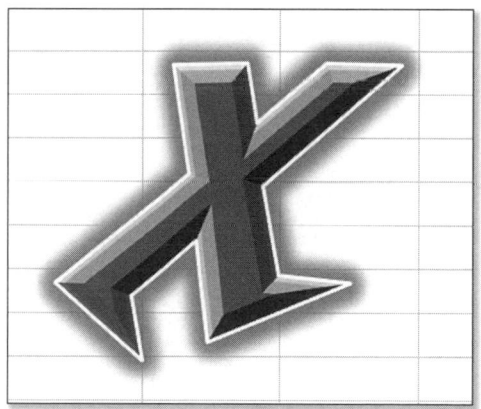

To create a custom shape, follow these steps:

1. Insert a picture of the shape that you can use as a guide to trace.

2. From the Insert tab, select the Shapes drop-down. In the Lines section, the last two shapes are Freeform and Scribble. Select the Freeform shape.

3. Click one corner of your logo.

4. Move the mouse to the adjacent corner of the logo and click again.

5. Repeat step 4 for each corner. If your logo has a curve, click several times around the perimeter of the curve. The more often you click, the better the curve will be.

6. When you arrive back at the original corner, click one final time to close the shape and complete the drawing.

7. Use the effect and fill settings to color and stylize the logo.

Using WordArt for Interesting Titles and Headlines

Even though WordArt was redesigned in Excel 2007, it is still best to use it sparingly, such as for a headline or title at the top of a page. It is best to use it for impressive display fonts to add interest to a report. However, you would not want to create an entire 20-page document in WordArt.

To use WordArt, follow these steps:

1. Select a blank section of the worksheet.

2. From the Insert tab, select the WordArt drop-down.

3. As shown in Figure 34.25, choose from the 30 WordArt presets in the drop-down. Do not worry that these presets seem less exciting than the WordArt in legacy versions of Excel. You will be able to customize the WordArt later.

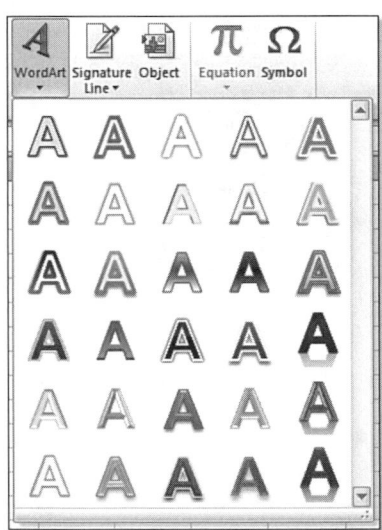

Figure 34.25
Excel offers 30 WordArt presets.

4. Excel adds the generic text Your Text Here in the preset WordArt you chose. Select this default text and then type your own text.

5. Select the text. Choose a new font style by using either the mini toolbar that appears or the Home tab.

6. Use the WordArt Styles group on the Drawing Tools Format tab to color the WordArt. To the right of the Styles drop-down are icons for text color and line color and a drop-down for effects. The Effects drop-down includes the flyout menus Shadow, Reflection, Glow, Soft Edges, Bevel, and 3D Rotation.

7. To achieve the old-style WordArt effects, from the Format tab select Drawing Tools, WordArt Styles, Text Effects, Transform, and then select a shape for the text. Figure 34.26 shows the WordArt with a Wave 1 transformation.

Figure 34.26
WordArt includes the Transform menu to bend and twist type.

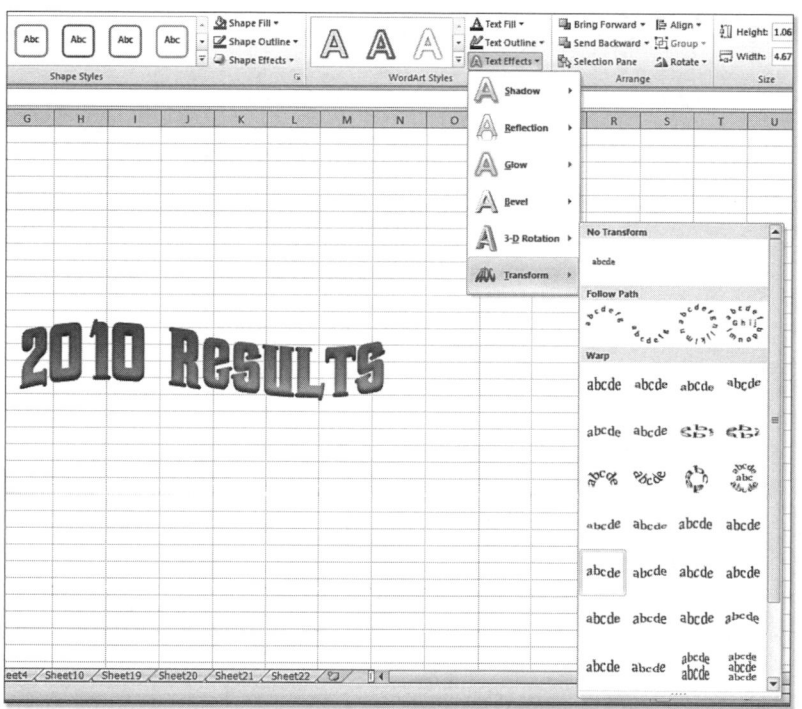

Using Text Boxes to Flow Long Text Passages

WordArt is perfect for short titles. However, it is not suitable for long text passages that you want to fit in a range. Figure 34.27 shows a series of sentences in a column that are of different lengths. You would like to have these sentences fit in a range from Column A through Column D.

You can solve this particular problem by following these steps:

1. Select a range to include the sentences and extend the range out to Column D.

2. Select the Home tab and then select Editing, Fill, Justify. Excel word wraps the sentences to fit the current widths of Columns A:D, as shown in Figure 34.28.

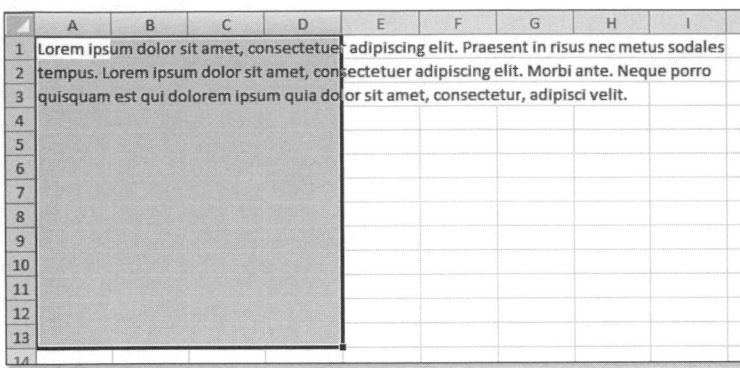

Figure 34.27
At times, you need Excel to act like a word processor.

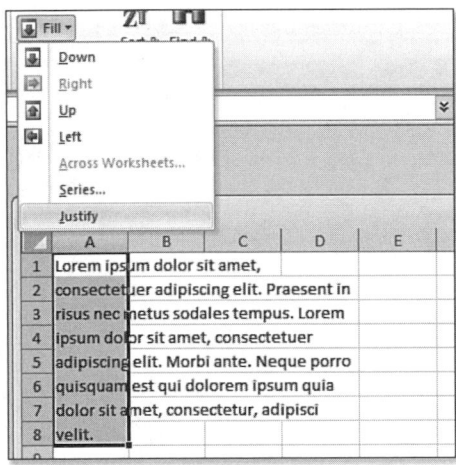

Figure 34.28
The Justify command wraps the text to the width of the range that was selected before the command was invoked.

To use a Text Box object to create two columns of text, follow these steps:

1. Select a blank section of the worksheet.

2. From the Insert tab, select Text, Text Box.

3. Drag in your document to draw a large text box on the worksheet.

4. Either type your text here or switch to Word, copy the text, and then switch back to Excel and paste the text.

⚠ caution

Using Justify is not perfect, because it was written over a decade ago when a cell could not contain more than 255 characters. For example, if you attempt to use the Justify command on a cell that contains more than 255 characters, the extra characters are truncated without any warning.

If you subsequently resize Column A, the text does not reflow. You have to use the Justify command again. In addition, if you change the font size of the text in Column A, you have to use the Justify command again.

If any cell in the input range contains more than 255 characters, the cell is truncated. This fatal flaw causes Justify to fail most often. To solve this problem, you use a Text Box object. This object has been improved in Excel 2010 to allow multiple columns in the text box.

5. Right-click the text box and select Exit Edit Mode.

6. Use the Font group on the Home tab to adjust the font size and face.

7. Right-click the text box and select Format Shape. The Format Shape dialog appears.

8. In the Format Shape dialog, select the Text Box category.

9. Adjust the margins and alignment, if desired.

10. Click the Columns button. The Columns dialog appears.

11. Choose two columns with nonzero spacing between them, as shown in Figure 34.29.

Figure 34.29
You can change the number of columns.

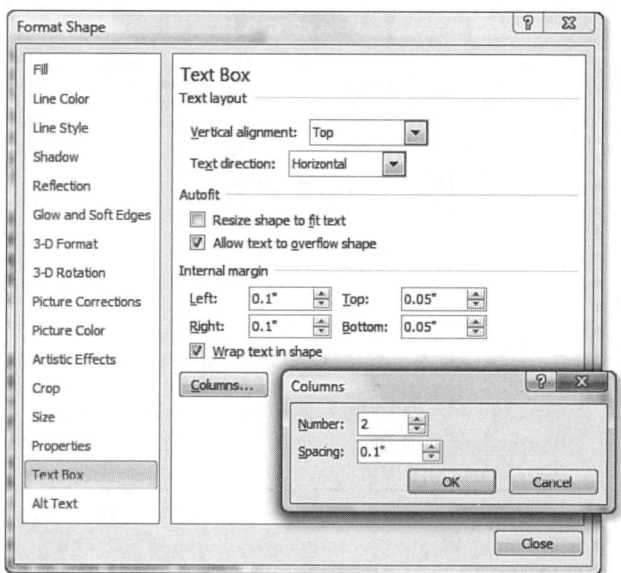

12. Click OK to close the Columns dialog. Click Close to close the Format Shape dialog. The result, as shown in Figure 34.30, is a text box that has two columns of text. As you change the size of the text, it automatically reflows to fit the desired columns.

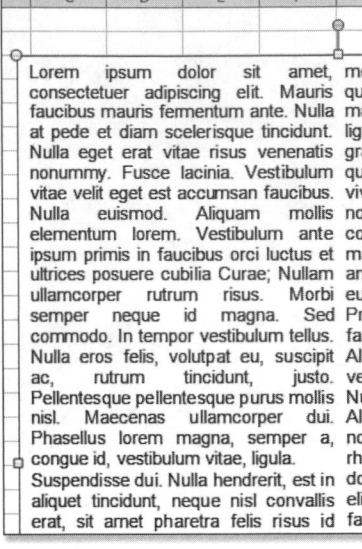

Figure 34.30
A text box can hold long passages of text.

Excel Troubleshooting: Eliminating Stray Drawing Objects

As you add multiple objects to one screen in an Excel workbook, you might find stray ghost objects left behind. It seems that when the selection box for the second shape overwrites the first shape, part of the shape is lost.

To solve this problem, scroll down the worksheet so that the shapes are not visible. When you scroll back up, Excel redraws the shapes correctly.

USING PICTURES AND CLIP ART

Excel worksheets have a tendency to be dominated by numbers. A picture can liven up a spreadsheet and add interest. The picture functionality in Excel 2010 is vastly improved over that in legacy versions of Excel.

Excel 2010 offers 28 quick picture styles and the tools to create thousands of additional effects.

When the spreadsheet was invented in 1979, accountants were amazed and thrilled with the simple black-and-white, numbers-only spreadsheets. The new image processing tools available in Excel 2010 elevate spreadsheets from simple tables of numbers to beautiful marketing showpieces.

Using Pictures on Worksheets

The first step in creating a great-looking picture is to insert a picture on a worksheet. To do so, follow these steps:

1. Select the cell where you want the upper-left corner of the picture to be positioned.

2. From the Insert tab, select Illustrations, Picture.

3. Browse to the folder that contains your pictures.

4. Choose the picture you want. Valid types of pictures include JPG, GIF, PNG, BMP, and many others. Click Insert.

When the picture is inserted, a new Picture Tools Format tab appears on the Ribbon, as shown in Figure 35.1.

Formatting with Picture Styles

For a quick way to make a picture look interesting, you can use one of the 28 presets in the Picture
Styles gallery. These presets include various combinations of rotation, shadow, frame, and shape.
Here's how you use them:

1. Select a picture. The Picture Tools tab appears.

2. To the right of the Picture Styles icon, select the drop-down arrow.

3. Hover over the 28 built-in styles until you find one that is suitable.

4. To apply the style, click the style in the gallery.

Figure 35.2 shows the gallery and several varieties of built-in picture styles.

Resizing and Cropping Pictures

One problem you might have when using a picture on a worksheet is that the image may be too
large. As digital cameras improve, it is becoming increasingly common for digital images to be 6, 7,
8, or more megapixels. These images are very large. For example, an image from a 3-megapixel camera occupies from A1 through Q41.

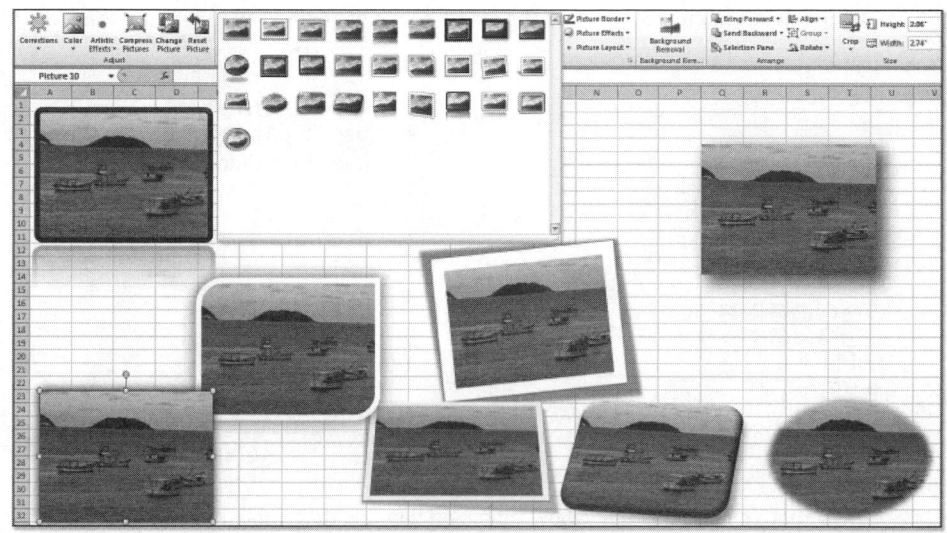

Figure 35.2
The Picture Styles gallery offers many quick alternatives for formatting pictures.

You can use the Zoom slider in the lower-right corner of the window to zoom out so that you can see the complete image. Then you can resize the picture. It is important that you resize the picture so that it remains proportional. The tools in the Format tab enable you to do this.

In the Picture Tools section of the Format tab, you can find Height and Width spin buttons in the Size group. Use either of them to resize an image. Any change you make to either spin button results in a proportional change to the other spin button as well.

You can also resize a picture by dragging one of the corner handles inward or outward.

Cropping a picture involves removing extraneous parts of the picture while in Crop mode. To crop a picture, follow these steps:

1. Select a picture.

2. Click the top half of the Crop icon in the Size group of the Picture Tools section of the Format tab. Eight crop handles appear on the edges and corner of the picture. Use the handles as follows:

   - To crop out one side of a picture, drag the center handle on that side inward toward the middle of the picture.

   - To crop both sides equally, hold down Ctrl while you drag the center handle on either side inward.

   - To crop equally on all four sides, hold down Ctrl while dragging one of the corner handles inward.

3. When the picture is cropped appropriately, click the Crop icon in the Picture Tools Format tab to exit Crop mode.

Excel 2010 offers a Crop to Shape tool. Click the bottom half of the Crop icon and open the Crop to Shape flyout menu. Excel offers the standard set of shapes, as shown in Figure 35.3.

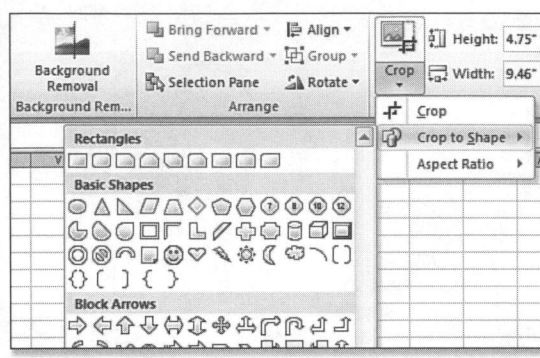

Figure 35.3
Use Crop to Shape to crop the photo into a particular shape.

Note that you can use the yellow inflection handles that appear on shapes to adjust the shape of the cropped area. However, the green rotation handle rotates the entire picture along with the shape. This seems to be an extremely limiting decision. If you need to crop to a right-triangle based on the top-right corner of the photo, it will not work.

The workaround is to start with a shape and then fill the shape with the photo. Follow these steps:

1. Select Insert, Shape.

2. Use green rotation handle to rotate the shape.

3. On the Drawing Tools Format tab, select Shape Fill, Picture. Choose a picture.

4. Press Ctrl+1 to access the format dialog for the shape.

5. Select the Fill category from the left navigation of the Format Shape dialog.

6. At the bottom of the dialog, clear Rotate with Shape. This is the setting that is missing if you start with a photo and crop to a shape.

Reducing a Picture's File Size

When you import a picture into a workbook, the file size of the workbook can increase dramatically. If you plan to view the image onscreen only, you can reduce the size of the picture to reduce the size of the workbook. Here's how you do it:

1. Select the picture.

2. In the Picture Tools Format tab, select Compress Pictures from the Adjust group. Excel displays the Compress Pictures dialog as shown in Figure 35.4.

3. If desired, click the Options button. Excel enables you to choose from four compression rates, as shown in Figure 35.4. You can also choose to discard the cropped portions of the photo.

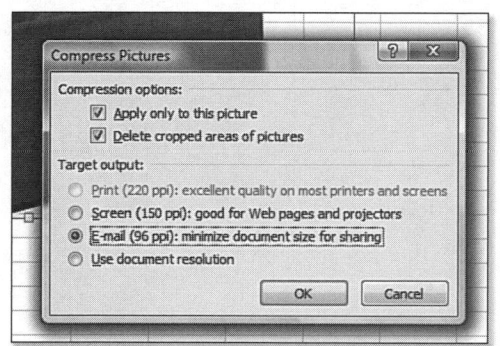

Figure 35.4
You use the Compress Pictures dialog to reduce file size.

Adjusting a Picture

The Adjust group of the Picture Tools Format tab in Excel 2010 offers three improved drop-down menus. Each menu offers various corrections to Sharpness, Brightness, Contrast, Color, and Visual Effects. The improvement is that the flyout menu shows thumbnails of your original image with the effect applied. Users who are better with numbers than graphic design will appreciate these menus.

Figure 35.5 shows the Corrections flyout menu. This menu combines the old Brightness and Contrast menus into a single grid. If you understand Brightness and Contrast, you can adjust these settings. For example, you may want -63% Brightness and +17% Contrast. Increasing the brightness makes an image lighter. Increasing the contrast makes the blacks blacker and the whites whiter. However, both of these adjustments cause the photograph to lose some detail.

In addition, you can use the Picture Correction Options at the bottom of the menu to access the Format Picture dialog with precise settings for all the options. The Corrections menu also adds a tool to Sharpen or Soften the photo.

Figure 35.6 shows the Color flyout menu. The top row changes color saturation. The second row changes the temperature of the photo. The remaining rows offer various changes to color, including Sepia, black and white, and so on.

Figure 35.7 shows the Artistic Effects flyout menu. All these effects are new in Excel 2010. You can make your photo look like a pencil sketch, a mosaic, a photocopy, and more. Figure 35.8 shows some of the more interesting artistic effects.

 tip

If the image you are working with is going to be printed in a glossy annual report, it would be better to use an image editing tool such as Photoshop. However, for the department staff meeting, Excel's options are good enough.

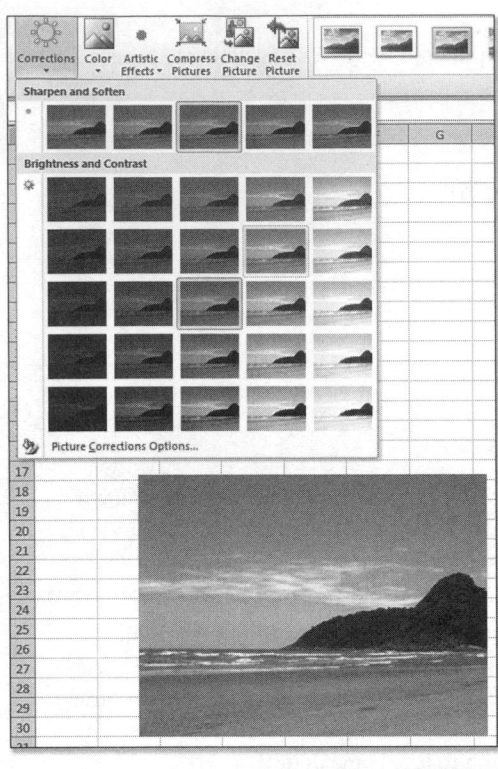

Figure 35.5
Adjust Brightness, Contrast, and Sharpness on the Corrections menu.

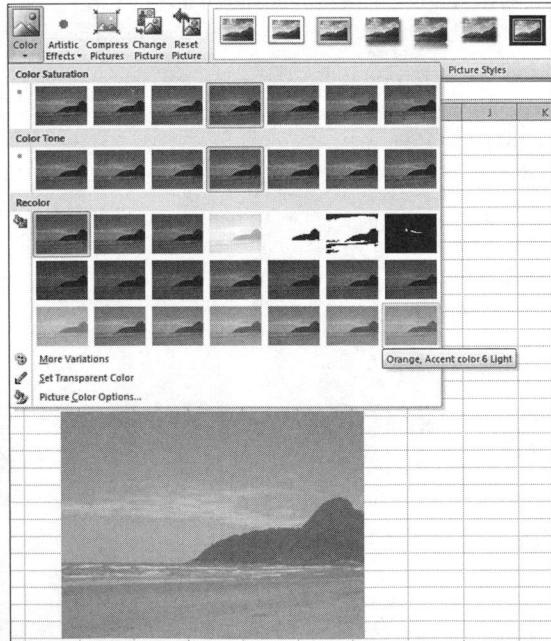

Figure 35.6
Change Saturation, Temperature, and color on the Color menu.

Figure 35.7
These artistic effects are new in Excel 2010.

Figure 35.8
The original photo is in the top left. Artistic effects make the photo look like an illustration.

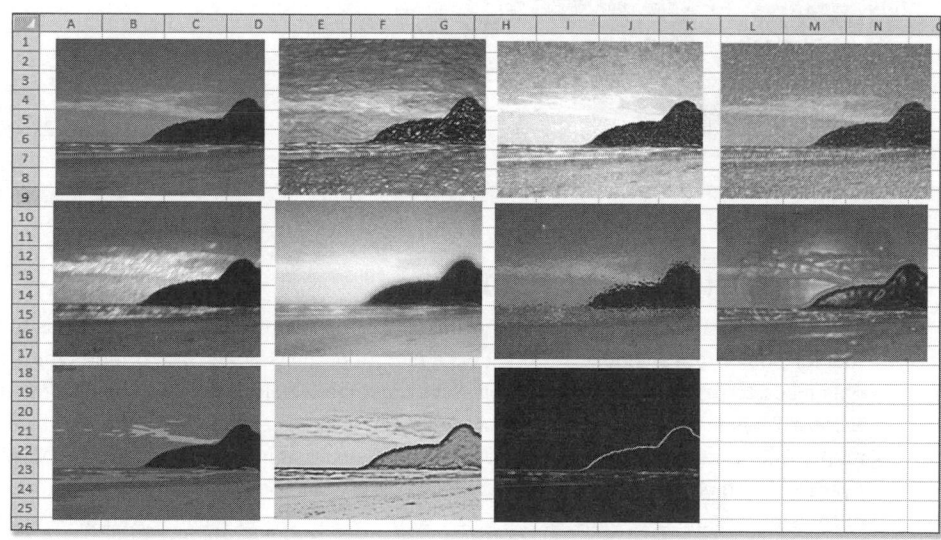

Adding Borders

The Border menu on the Picture Tools Format tab lets you add a border around an image. You can choose any color, various line thicknesses, and dashed-line effects.

Whereas the Artistic Effects are new in Excel 2010, the Picture Effects drop-down was the new eye candy in Excel 2007. The tools in this drop-down allow you to add bevel effects to an image. Figure 35.9 shows one preset.

Other menus here allow you to add a shadow, reflection, glow, or bevel.

 tip

If you want even more control over picture effects, look for a More option in most effects' drop-down menus. When you click this option, the Format Picture dialog appears, offering you complete control over fill, line, line style, shadow, 3D format, and 3D rotation.

Figure 35.9
Use Picture Effects to add 3D and bevel to your images.

Removing the Background

The old Set Transparent Color icon present in Excel 2007 and previous versions is not an effective tool for photographs. Figure 35.10 shows a picture of the Golden Gate Bridge where an attempt was made to remove the sky using the Set Transparent Color icon from the Color menu on the Picture Tools Format tab. This old tool would allow you to specify one color and have Excel remove all pixels of that color. In this photograph, there are too many colors in the sky. When you use the eyedropper to choose a color in the sky, you will be disappointed to discover that only a tiny portion of the sky is marked as transparent. The rest of the sky doesn't match your selected color exactly. Excel 2010 offers an amazing new tool to solve this problem, discussed next.

Excel 2010 offers a new Background Removal Tool. To use this tool, select an image and then select the Background Removal from the Picture Tools Format menu. Excel analyzes the picture and does a fairly decent job of predicting where the subject of the image is. Areas shown in purple will be removed from the photograph (see Figure 35.11).

Figure 35.10
Set Transparent Color uses too narrow of a range of colors around the selected color.

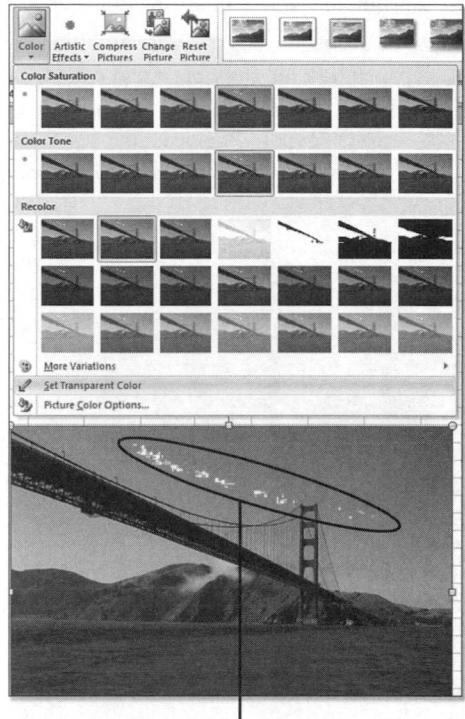

Only this narrow band of sky is set as transparent

Figure 35.11
Excel predicts which portions of the photograph's background should be removed.

You have a new Background Removal tab on the ribbon.

Your next step should be to adjust the bounding box around the subject in your photograph. If you change the bounding box to only surround the desired subject, Excel will re-scan the photograph and do a vastly improved job of choosing areas to include or exclude.

If Excel chooses to delete a portion of the photograph that you want to keep, you can select Mark to Include from the ribbon and click to remove purple from that section of the image. If Excel chooses to keep portions of the image, such as the sky behind two sections of the bridge tower, you can select Mark to Remove and click inside those areas of the picture. Figure 35.12 shows the image preview after adding some rocks along the left and removing the sky under the bridge.

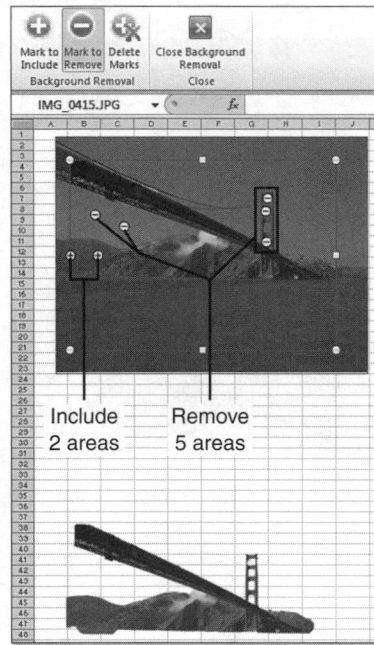

Figure 35.12
Use Mark to Include and Mark to Exclude to add or remove sections from the visible portion of the photo.

When you are finished, click Close Background Removal Tool. The background will be removed. You can now type in the cells behind the transparent portions of the photo, as shown in Figure 35.13.

 To watch a video of removing picture backgrounds, search for Excel In Depth 35 at YouTube.

Arranging Pictures

The Arrange group on the Picture Tools Format tab offers a rotation tool. You can use this tool to flip a portrait picture to landscape or vice versa. You can use the Bring Forward and Send Backward options to determine which of two overlapping pictures is displayed on top.

The Align option allows you to snap the pictures to a grid or to make sure that several images line up. To use the latter feature, you need to select the image that was placed last. Try this example:

1. Select Image3.

2. Ctrl+click Image2 and then Ctrl+click Image1.

3. Select Align, Align Left. The left edges of Image2 and Image3 move so they line up with the left edge of Image1.

All the available alignment options are shown in Figure 35.14. One interesting option here is View Gridlines, which was formerly tucked away on an obscure tab in the Options dialog.

> ### ☢ caution
> You cannot click Cell B8 in Figure 35.13 to select that cell, because the picture will be selected. To select Cell B8, click outside the boundary of the original picture and then use the arrow keys to move to the appropriate cell.

Figure 35.13
You can now see data in the former background of the photo.

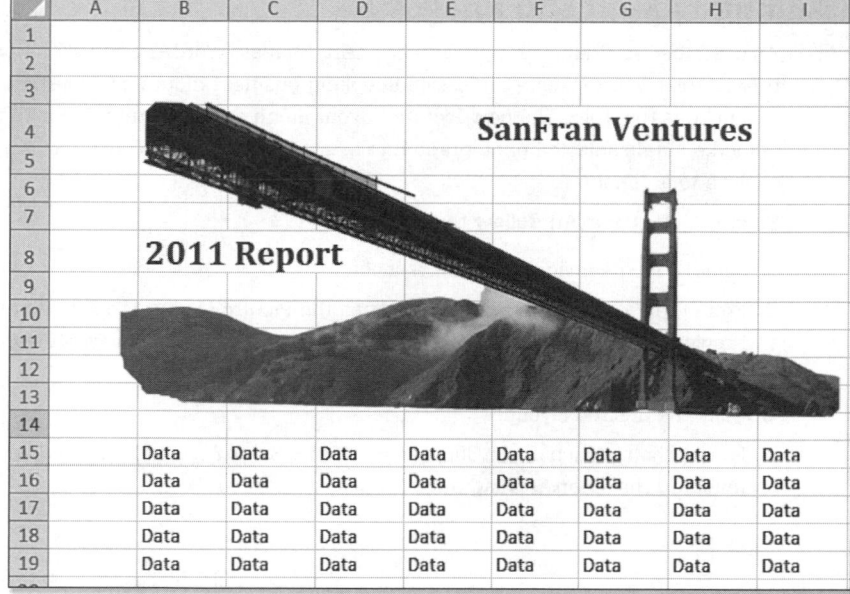

Figure 35.14
The Align drop-down allows you to line up multiple images with each other.

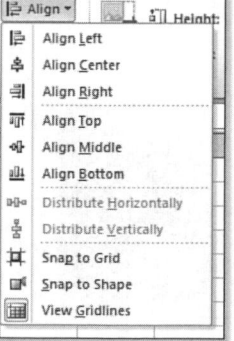

If you select multiple images and group them together by using the Group drop-down, you can then move the images, and their location relative to each other remains the same.

Displaying the Selection Pane

The selection and visibility pane lists all the images on the worksheet and allows you to make certain images invisible. To display the pane, select the Picture Tools Format tab and then select Arrange, Selection Pane.

A check box is located at the right of each image name. You can select this check box to toggle the visibility. The buttons Show All and Hide All allow you to show and hide all images.

Adding Captions to Images

As described in Chapter 34, "Using SmartArt, Shapes, WordArt, and Text Boxes," the SmartArt feature enables you to create professional-looking business diagrams. SmartArt mixes words, shapes, and images together. The new Picture Layout menu on the Picture Tools Format tab allows you to embed a single selected photograph into a SmartArt diagram. This effectively allows you to add a caption to an image.

To create the SmartArt, follow these steps:

1. Select a single image on the worksheet.

2. From the Picture Tools Format tab, open the Picture Layout tab (see Figure 35.15). Use Live Preview as you hover over various thumbnails. The various SmartArt layouts offer variations, such as emphasizing text and emphasizing pictures.

3. Click the desired layout.

4. Follow the instructions in Chapter 34, "Using SmartArt, Shapes, WordArt and Text Boxes," for finishing the SmartArt diagram.

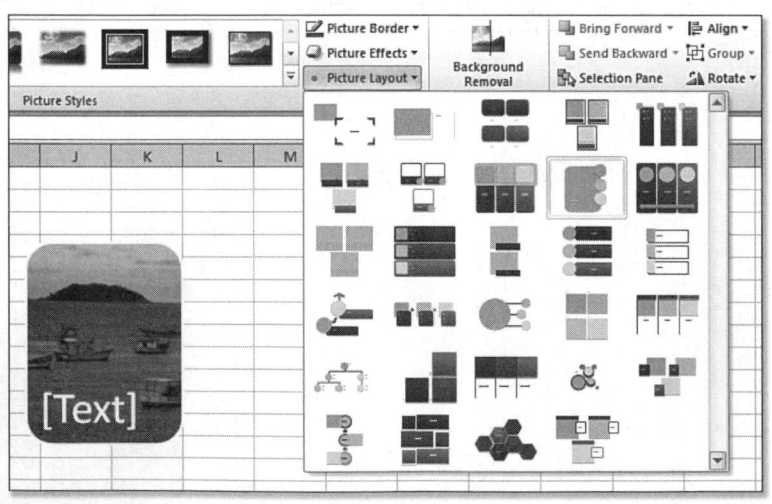

Figure 35.15
Add a caption to an image by converting the image to SmartArt.

Inserting Screen Clippings

If you need to grab an image of a Web page, a PDF file, or a PowerPoint slide, you can grab a screen capture of the entire window or a portion of the window.

To insert the entire window, follow these steps:

1. Open the other document in a program such as a browser or Acrobat reader.

2. Use the scrollbars to arrange the window so that the visible portion of the window includes the portion you want to insert as an image in Excel.

3. Switch back to Excel.

4. Position the cell pointer at the top left corner cell where the picture should be inserted.

5. From the Insert tab, open the Screenshot drop-down, as shown in Figure 35.16. Excel offers thumbnails of most open applications. Click an image to insert a picture of that window in the current Excel worksheet.

Figure 35.16
Insert another application window into Excel as an image.

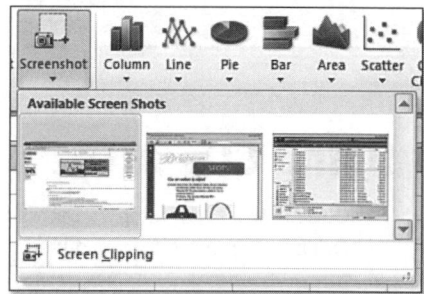

It is also possible to insert a portion of an open application window as a screenshot. However, this is a bit trickier. Follow these steps:

1. In Excel, position the cell pointer at the point where you want to insert the screen clipping.

2. Switch to the other application. The screen clipping tool always reverts back to the window used most recently before you switched back to Excel.

3. Switch back to Excel.

4. Select Insert, Screenshot, Screen Clipping. The screen will switch to the application from step 2 and the screen will gray out.

5. Using the mouse, draw a rectangle around the portion of the application window that you want to capture, as shown in Figure 35.17.

 note

Excel does not offer to insert screenshots of other open Excel workbooks in the Screenshot drop-down. One solution is to open a second instance of Excel. The Screenshot tool offers to insert a screenshot of the other instance of Excel. Alternatively, you can use the Paste as Picture, as described in the next tip.

Drag to un-gray a section of the window

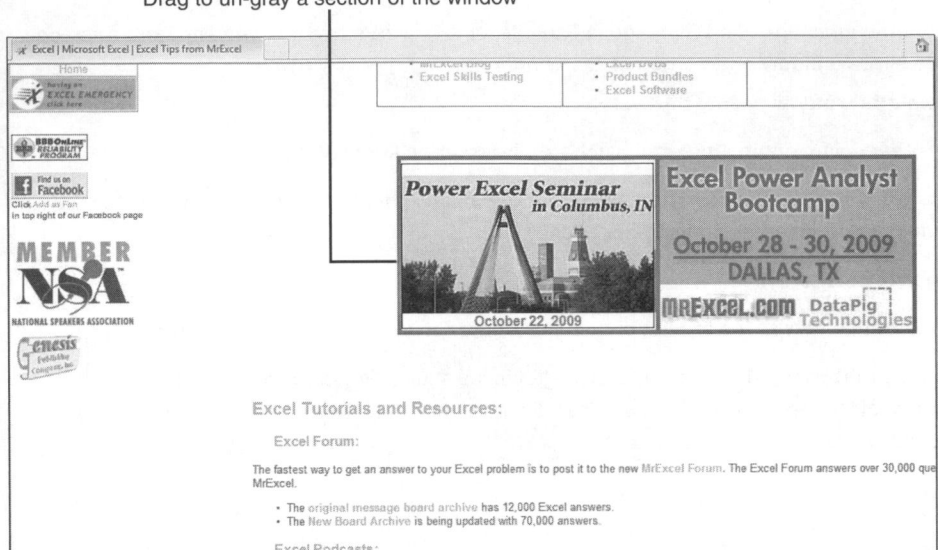

Figure 35.17
Select a portion of the other window to insert.

Using Clip Art

Clip art has been improved in Excel 2010. When you search for a piece of clip art, clips from Office Online are now automatically incorporated in your search results when you are connected to the Internet.

To add clip art to a worksheet, follow these steps:

1. Position the cell pointer near where you want the clip art to be inserted.

2. Select Insert, Clip Art Pane.

3. Type a keyword for the clip art in the Search For box, and then press Go.

4. You might be asked if you want to include results from Office Online. Click Yes. A gallery of matching clip art is displayed in the Clip Art pane.

5. Every clip art thumbnail has a drop-down available on the right side. Choose a drop-down to display a context menu, as shown in Figure 35.18. Select Insert to add the clip art at the active cell.

6. Resize the clip art as needed to fit the desired space.

The Clip Art context menu includes the following options:

- **Copy**—Use this option to copy the clip art to the clipboard.

- **Delete from Clip Organizer**—Use this option to delete any local copy of the clip art.

Figure 35.18
Select Insert to add clip art at the desired location.

- **Make Available Offline**—Use this option to copy the clip art from Clips Online to your computer.

- **Move to Collection**—Use this option to organize clip art on your computer.

- **Edit Keywords**—Use this option to add your own keywords to clip art. This is like tagging in Flickr.com.

- **Find similar style**—Use this option to narrow the results to similar images.

- **Preview/Properties**—Use this option to display the exact size of the clip art before you import it.

After you add clip art, you can resize it by dragging any of the resize handles around the selected clip art.

PRINTING

Printing Options in Excel 2010 move from the Print dialog used in legacy versions of Excel to a Print panel in the Backstage view. This panel combines the old Print dialog, the old Printer Properties dialog, the Find Printers dialog, and the old Print Preview into a single powerful screen of data.

Excel 2007 introduced a new Page Layout view that is light-years ahead of the Page Break Preview mode offered in legacy versions of Excel. This view allows you to type and edit headers and footers right on the worksheet. Excel offers support for different headers and footers on odd and even pages. In addition, it allows you to use a different header for the first page than for the rest of the document. Excel 2010 also supports the use of color, images, and more in headers and footers.

For those who share a printer, one minor change becomes a major change. In legacy versions of Excel, if you printed 20 copies of a one-page document, Excel sent 20 print jobs to the printer. This was a huge problem if your printer sent a banner page before each print job. Now, the software spools all 20 pages into a single print job, which eliminates the 19 extra banner pages.

Most of the major print options for controlling page setup are arranged in two groups on the Page Layout tab. There is also a new Header & Footer Tools Design tab dedicated to editing headers and footers in Page Layout view.

Printing from Backstage View

To access the Print tab, you can either select File, Print or press Ctrl+P. The new Print tab of the Backstage view appears, as shown in Figure 36.1.

The right side of the screen shows the Print Preview. As you update settings on the left side of the screen, the Print Preview will update, which allows you always to see the current print preview.

The left side of the screen starts with a very large Print button. Click this button to print the document. The spin button next to the Print button enables you to control the number of copies to print (see Figure 36.2).

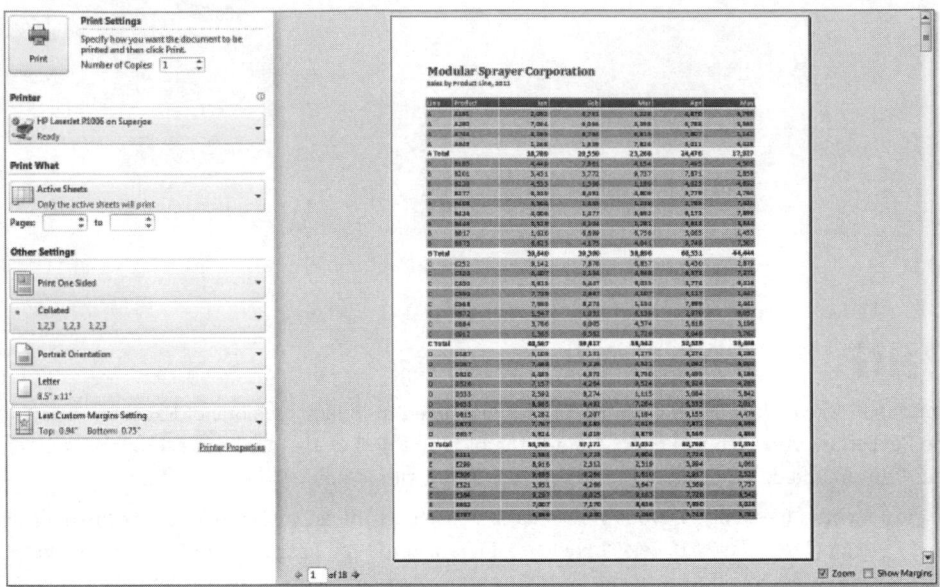

Figure 36.1
Print Preview and Print settings are combined in a single screen.

Print button

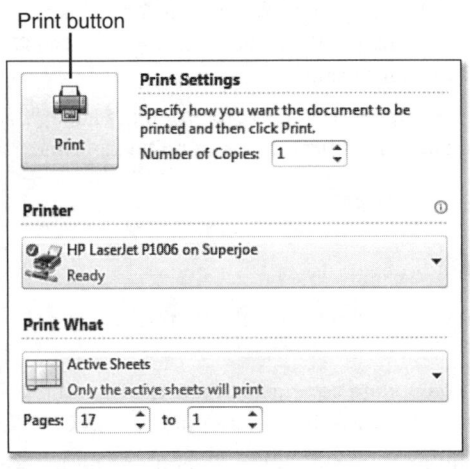

Figure 36.2
To print this document, click this button.

The rest of the left panel contains a new kind of gallery. You can see the current choice of the gallery without opening the gallery. If the correct Printer is already selected, there is no need to open the drop-down.

Choosing a Printer

When you open the Printer drop-down, Excel displays all the current printers and indicates if the printer is currently online and/or available. This handy improvement allows you to detect if the department printer is in a Paper Jam condition so you can print to a different printer (Figure 36.3).

Figure 36.3
The Printers gallery shows the status of each printer.

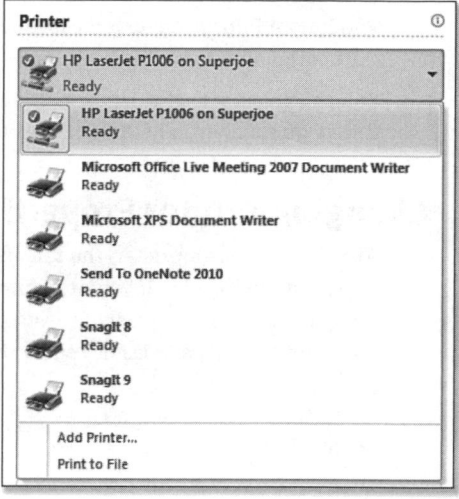

Choosing What to Print

As shown in Figure 36.4, the Print What gallery offers Active Sheets, Entire Workbook, Selection. You can further modify those settings by choosing Ignore Print Area.

Figure 36.4
Choosing what to print.

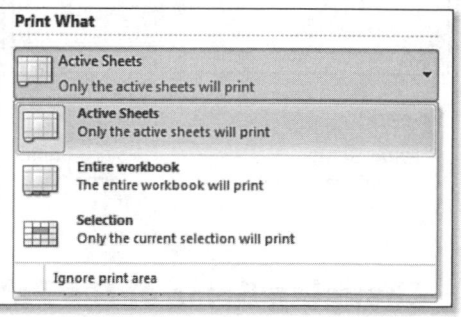

If you choose the Active Sheets option, the currently selected sheet will print. If you have specified a Print Area, only that range will print, otherwise, Excel prints the entire used range of the document. However, if you select multiple sheets in Group Mode, all the selected sheets will print.

If you choose the Entire Workbook option, all the nonhidden worksheets in the workbook will print. One advantage to this option is that the pages are numbered consecutively as the printout moves from Sheet1 to Sheet2.

Choosing the Selection option allows you to override the print area temporarily. However, if you need to print one small range of a large report, select that range and then choose the Selection option in the Print What gallery. This prevents you from having to change the Print Area twice.

The Ignore Print Area option causes Excel to ignore any print areas speficied previously. This causes the entire used area of the worksheet to be printed.

You can select specific pages to print using the Pages spin buttons. To print a single page, enter that page number in both the Pages and To boxes.

Changing Printer Properties

After you choose a printer, the remaining galleries on the left side of the Print panel are redrawn, as shown in Figure 36.5. If you are printing to an office printer that supports collating and stapling, use the galleries to select each of these options. If you are printing to a home printer that does not have these options, Excel does not show those galleries.

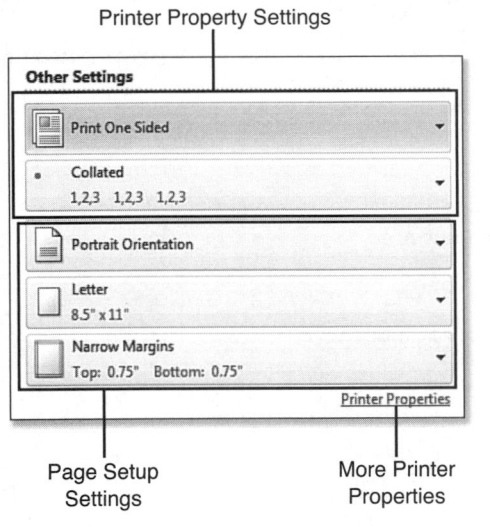

Printer Property Settings

Page Setup Settings

More Printer Properties

Figure 36.5
Other Settings include some Printer Properties and some Page Setup settings.

 **tip**

If a specific property does not appear, you can click the Printer Properties hyperlink at the bottom of the left panel to access the vendor-supplied Printer Property dialog box.

Changing Some of the Page Setup Settings

Even though it might seem like they are out of place, the last settings on the left side of the Backstage view are used to control Portrait versus Landscape, Paper Size, and Margins. If you change a setting here, it will also change in the Page Setup dialog.

If your initial reaction is to wonder why they repeated these settings here, you might also wonder why they did not also repeat your favorite Page Setup settings. Even though it is nice to switch from Portrait to Landscape here, it would also be nice to be able to change the Page Scaling or Rows to Repeat at Top here. However, this cannot be done because those settings require you to close Backstage view and to use the Page Layout tab of the Ribbon.

Using Print Preview Controls

The following Print Preview controls are available in the Print Preview side of the Backstage view (see Figure 36.6).

- To navigate to a new page, use the Left Arrow or Right Arrow icon in the lower left. You can also type a new page number in the page number text box and type Enter or Tab. The PgDn and PgUp controls still work, but only when you click the preview first.

- The Zoom check box feels like it is reversed. If you clear this check box, Excel will zoom in to a smaller section of your printout.

- Select the Show Margins check box to have Excel draw dragable margins in the page. Drag any of the margin lines to change the page margins. Drag any of the column handles to resize columns.

Figure 36.6
Print Preview controls.

Margin Handles   Column Handles

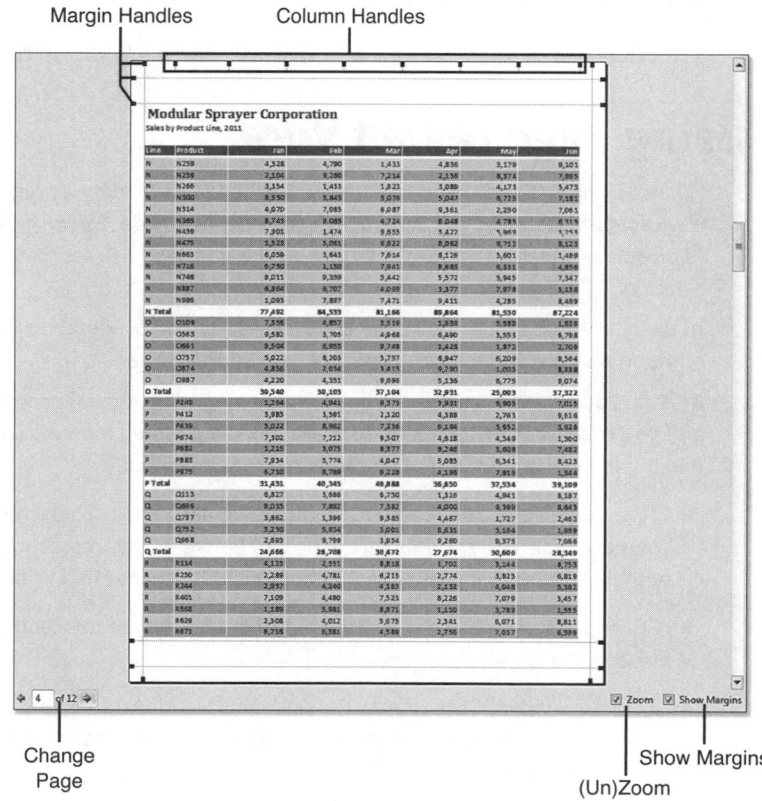

Change Page

Show Margins
(Un)Zoom

Closing Backstage View

To close Backstage view and return to your document, click any other ribbon tab. It is tempting to click the red "X" in the top right or the word "Close" in the left navigation. However, those will close your document instead of closing the Backstage view.

Printing Using Quick Print

Keyboard enthusiasts may be upset that in Excel 2010, Ctrl+P takes you to the Backstage view instead of performing a Quick Print. However, if you want to print with all the default settings, you need to add the Quick Print icon to the Quick Access Toolbar or Ribbon.

Follow these steps to add Quick Print to the Quick Access Toolbar:

1. Right-click the Quick Access Toolbar and select Customize Quick Access Toolbar. The Excel Options dialog box is displayed.

2. The left drop-down should start with Popular Commands. Click the Quick Print icon located in the left list box.

3. Click the Add button in the center of the dialog to move the Quick Print icon to the right list box.

4. Click OK to close the dialog.

You can now click using the Quick Print icon in the Quick Access Toolbar.

Using Page Layout View

When you open Excel, the default view is called Normal view. In legacy versions of Excel, your only choices were Normal view and Page Break Preview mode. However, beginning with Excel 2007, Microsoft added the Page Layout view, which works well when you are preparing a document for printing.

In Excel 2010, the three views are available either on the Workbook Views group of the View tab or on the right side of the status bar, as shown in Figure 36.7.

In Page Layout view, you have a fully functioning worksheet. For example, the formula bar works and you can scroll around the worksheet. However, listed next are the differences you will notice when you use Page Layout view compared to the Normal view.

- Whitespace appears to show the margins on each page. This is usually an advantage because you have a clear view of any page breaks between columns or rows. If you want to hide the white space, you can click the white space and choose Hide White Space.

- A ruler appears below the formula bar that you can use to change margins by dragging the gray areas of the ruler.

- Areas are marked Click to Add Header and Click to Add Footer. Whereas headers and footers are buried in legacy versions of Excel, in the Page Layout view of Excel 2010 it is obvious that headers and footers are available.

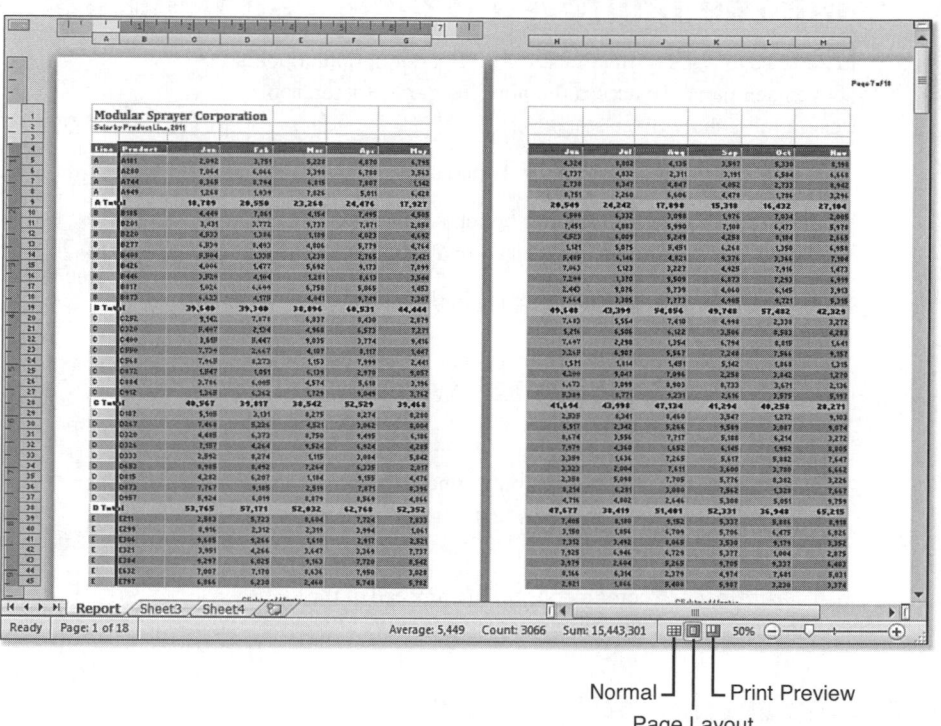

Figure 36.7
Buttons in the status bar make Page Layout view always available.

Normal ⏌   ⎇ Print Preview
Page Layout

- Areas outside the data area of a worksheet are marked with Click to Add Data. One of the problems with Page Break Preview mode is that areas outside the data area were grayed out. However, the Click to Add Data labels invite you to continue adding pages to your worksheet.

- The only disadvantage to Page Layout view is that Excel turns off your Freeze Panes settings in Page Layout view. Excel does this to emphasize that Print Titles are different from Freeze Panes.

Overall, the Page Layout view introduced in Excel 2007 is an excellent improvement over Page Break Preview mode. It practically makes the ubiquitous Print Preview icon obsolete. Even though Page Break Preview is still available, it is recommended that you try the Page Layout view when you are preparing to print.

 note

The worksheet in the figure has been zoomed to 50 percent to show multiple pages. This does not happen automatically when you enter Page Layout view.

 tip

Keep in mind that Excel does not restore the Freeze Panes settings when you return to Normal view.

➥ *To learn more about this topic, see the "Working with Page Breaks" section later in this chapter.*

 To watch a video tour of Page Layout view, search for Excel In Depth 36 at YouTube.

Using the Improved Headers and Footers

In Page Layout view, the Click to Add Header option appears above each page. To access the new Header & Footer Tools Design tab, follow these steps:

1. Select View, Workbook Views, Page Layout.

2. Click the Click to Add Header option above Row 1. You should see the new Header & Footer Tools Design tab.

3. Add either an auto header or a custom header.

   ➥ *Details about the auto header and custom header methods are included in the following sections of this chapter.*

4. To format a header, use the Font formatting options in the Home tab. Be sure to use these formatting tools while the header is displayed.

5. To exit Header/Footer mode, click in any cell of the worksheet.

Adding an Automatic Header

For a quick header or footer, you can click the Header or Footer drop-down in the Header & Footer Tools Design tab. The drop-down offers 16 different automatic headers, including various page numbering styles, the system date, your name, the sheet name, and the file path and filename.

 note

Note that the insertion cursor appears in a box in the center of the header area, as shown in Figure 36.8. There are light gray boxes around the left and right sections of the header area. You can click in any of these three boxes to add a header to the left, center, or right section of the header area.

 tip

To edit the left or right header directly, click to the left or right of the words Click to Add Header. When you hover over this section, a blue box appears that encourages you to click directly in a particular section of the header.

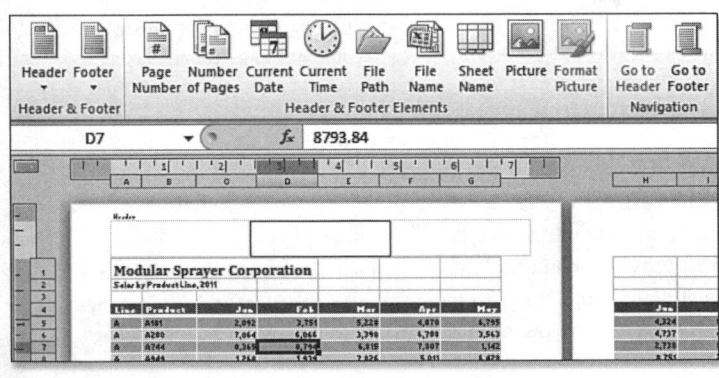

Figure 36.8
There are three faint sections in the header: left, center, and right.

As shown in Figure 36.9, some of the Header entries include values separated by commas. These entries put header values into the left, center, and right header sections.

Adding a Custom Header

You can type any text you want in the three header and footer areas. One of the automatic headers reads "Confidential," but you can customize this in any way dictated by your company. No matter what type of header you need, you can type it in the header by clicking in any header area and then typing the text that needs to be in the header. To start a new line, press Enter.

> **note**
>
> The process for adding footers is identical to the process for adding headers. Throughout the rest of this chapter, several sections include additional information about headers. Keep in mind that the identical instructions apply to footers.

Figure 36.9
To add a header, you can choose from the Header list.

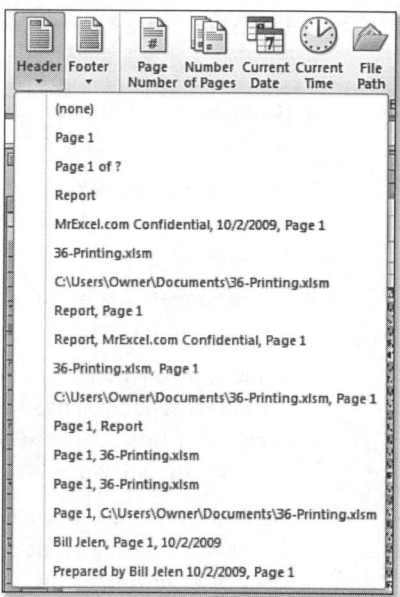

Excel enables you to add several fields to a header or a footer. Some fields will update automatically. For example, if you add the current date and time, the header will reflect the date and time whenever the worksheet is printed.

Icons for each field are located in the Header & Footer Elements group of the Header & Footer Tools Design tab. To add an element, click in a header or footer area, position the cursor in the proper place, and click the appropriate icon in the Ribbon. As long as the insertion cursor is in the header area, the screen displays the code for that field, such as &[Date] or &[Time]. When you click in another header section, you see the current value of the autotext field.

Inserting a Picture in a Header

You can add a picture to a header or footer. It can be either a small picture that prints in the header area or a large picture that extends below the header area and acts as a watermark behind the worksheet.

To add a picture to a header, follow these steps:

1. Select View, Page Layout View.

2. Click in the header area of the document.

3. From the Header & Footer Tools Design tab, select Header & Footer Elements, Picture. Excel displays the Insert Picture dialog.

4. Browse to the proper folder. Select a picture and click Insert. Excel adds the text &[Picture] to the header.

5. Click in the spreadsheet.

6. If you discover that the picture is too large, click in the header area.

7. From the Header & Footer Tools Design tab, select Header & Footer Elements, Format Picture. The Format Picture dialog appears.

8. In the Format Picture dialog, use the Size section to reduce the scale of the picture.

9. If you want your picture to appear as a watermark behind the spreadsheet, you need to lighten the picture. To do so, click the Picture tab of the Format Picture dialog. Change the Color drop-down to Washout.

10. None of the picture items in the header features Live Preview. To preview your picture, close the dialog box and then click outside the header. If the picture is not the way you want it, repeat steps 6 through 9 as necessary.

Using Different Headers and Footers in the Same Document

Excel 2010 allows the following four header and footer scenarios:

■ The same header/footer on all pages

■ One header/footer on page 1 and a different header/footer on all other pages

 note

If the company name listed in the Header drop-down is incorrect, it is difficult to change. You need to use RegEdit to access the Registry before you can make this change. Look for the RegCompany setting in HKEY_ LOCAL_MACHINE, SOFTWARE, Microsoft, Windows, Current Version, Installer, UserData, S-1-5-18, Products, ‹GUID›, InstallProperties. Note that GUID will be different depending on your version of Office. One brute-force method is to expand each product in the list, expand Installer, then look for the Display Name to find the correct product.

 tip

To include an ampersand in the header or footer, you must use the code &&. For example, to add the header Profit & Loss, type Profit && Loss.

 tip

Keep in mind that you will not actually see how large the picture will be until you click outside the header.

 note

If you use the spin button to change the height in the Scale section, the width is automatically changed as well, in order to keep the scale proportional.

- One header/footer on all odd pages and a different header/footer on all even pages

- One header/footer on page 1, a second header/footer on even pages, and a third header/footer on all odd pages from 3 on

Excel manages these scenarios by storing three headers for each worksheet. The first header is variously called the odd page header or the header. As you select and clear the options check boxes, the contents of each header remain constant, even though they might be used on different pages. Table 36.1 shows the details of each header option.

 tip

Although you cannot add to the automatic Header list, you can select an automatic header that is close to what you want and then customize it.

Table 36.1 Header Options

Different First Page	Different Odd & Even Pages	Odd Page Header	Even Page Header	First Page Header
Cleared	Cleared	Called the header and used on all pages	Not used	Not used
Cleared	Selected	Called the odd page header and used for pages 1, 3, 5, and so on	Called the even page header and used for pages 2, 4, 6, and so on	Not used
Selected	Cleared	Called the header and used on pages 2, 3, 4, and so on	Not used	Called the first page header and used for page 1
Selected	Selected	Called the odd page header and used for pages 3, 5, 7, and so on	Called the even page header and used for pages 2, 4, 6, and so on	Called the first page header and used for page 1

If you add a header in Page Layout view, it is known as the odd page header. In the default configuration, Excel displays the odd page header on all pages of the printout.

Excel has two other sets of headers that are initially hidden. One set is called the *first page header*. The other set is called the *Different First Page*, which you can select from the Options group on the Header & Footer Tools Design tab. When this option is used, Excel displays the first page header above page 1 and uses the odd page header everywhere else.

 tip

To minimize confusion, it is best to select the Options section check boxes Different First Page and Different Odd & Even before entering headers.

Scaling Headers and Footers

Settings in the Page Layout tab allow you to force a worksheet to fit a certain number of pages. If the scaling options require a 75 percent scale on Sheet1 and a 95 percent scale on Sheet2, your headings are scaled as well. This causes your page numbers to appear at a different point size in various sections of the report.

Excel offers an option to force all headers and footers to print at 100 percent scale, regardless of the zoom for the sheet. To select this option, from the Header & Footer Tools Design tab, select Options and clear the Scale with Document check box.

 caution

The Background icon is out of place in the Page Setup group of the Page Layout tab. Whereas every other setting in this group affects the printed page, the Background icon is only for the background on the displayed page. If you want to have a printed watermark appear behind your spreadsheet, you should use a large picture in the header.

Using the Page Setup and Sheet Options

Most of the page setup options are now in the Page Layout tab. The Page Setup, Scale to Fit, and Sheet Options groups reflect most of the items that used to be in the Page Setup dialog in legacy versions of Excel (see Figure 36.10).

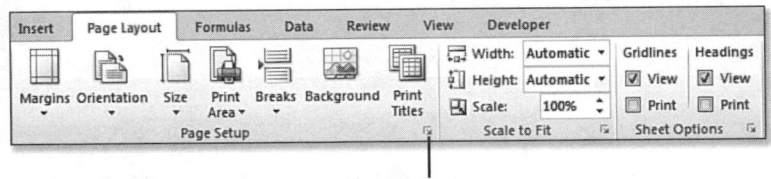

Dialog launcher

Figure 36.10
Page setup options are controlled from the Page Layout tab.

➡ *To review information on the Background icon, see the "Inserting a Picture in a Header" section earlier in this chapter.*

Adjusting Worksheet Margins

Following are three methods you can use to adjust worksheet margins:

- **Choose Page Layout, Margins**—This drop-down offers three settings: Normal, Wide, and Narrow. If you have previously used custom margins, another setting will appear with the last custom margins that you used. To apply one of these standard setups, choose the setup you want to use from the Margins drop-down, as shown in Figure 36.11. To apply a different custom margin, select Custom Margins from the bottom of this menu.

- **Use the Legacy Page Setup dialog**—When you click the dialog launcher icon in the bottom right of the Page Setup group, Excel displays the Page Setup dialog. As shown in Figure 36.12, use the Margins tab to adjust the margins at the top, left, right, and bottom, as well as the margins for the footer and header. The dialog used for this option in Excel 2010 is the same as in legacy versions of Excel (see Figure 36.12).

Figure 36.11
You can choose a quick setting for margins.

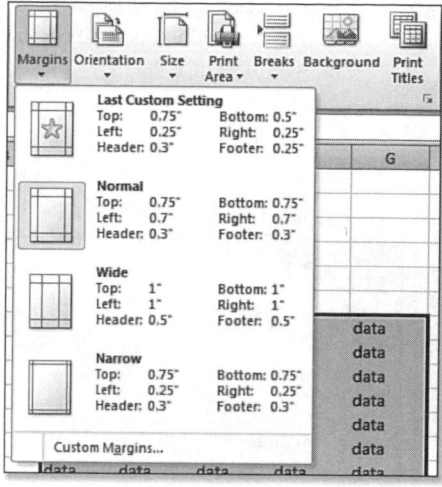

Figure 36.12
For control over each margin, use the Margins tab of the Page Setup dialog.

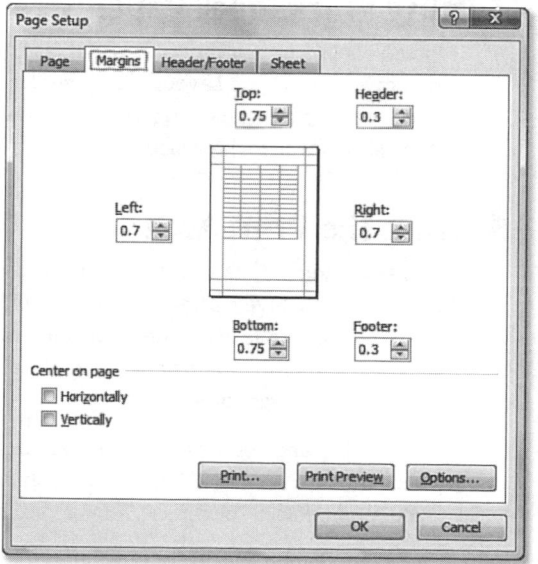

- **Choose View, Workbook Views, Page Layout View**—When you use this option, gray margins appear on each edge of the ruler. You can drag the gray margins in or out to decrease/increase the margin.

Adjusting Worksheet Orientation

Changing a report to print sideways, which is also referred to as *landscape*, takes just a couple of mouse clicks. From the Page Layout tab, select Page Setup to see the Orientation drop-down, which offers Portrait and Landscape options, as shown in Figure 36.13.

 tip
After you assign your favorite margins in the Page Setup dialog, they will be available later as the Last Custom Setting in the Margins drop-down.

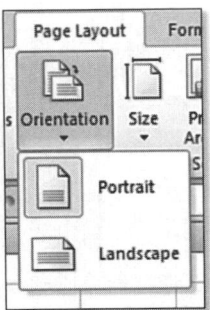

Figure 36.13
Print the report sideways by selecting the Landscape printing option.

Setting Worksheet Paper Size

You can choose from a variety of paper size options in the Size drop-down in the Page Layout tab, as shown in Figure 36.14. You can choose one paper size or select More from the bottom of the list to specify a new size.

 tip
Some paper sizes, such as 11"x17", are available only if your selected printer offers that size. If your default printer cannot print large-format paper, you should change the printer selection in the Backstage view and then return to the Page Setup dialog to select the larger-format paper.

Setting the Print Area

By default, Excel prints all the nonblank cells on a worksheet. Sometimes, you have a nicely formatted table of data to print, with some work cells in an out-of-the way location that you do not want to print. To prevent the work cells from being printed, follow these steps:

1. Select the range of cells to be included in the print range, such as Cells A1:Z99. Alternatively, you can print everything in certain columns. For example, you might select Columns C:X to be printed.

2. From the Page Layout tab, select Page Setup, Print Area, Set Print Area.

To clear the print area and to print everything on the worksheet, you can use the Clear Print Area option from the Set Print Area drop-down.

Figure 36.14
Select a built-in paper size or click More Paper Sizes to specify a custom size of paper.

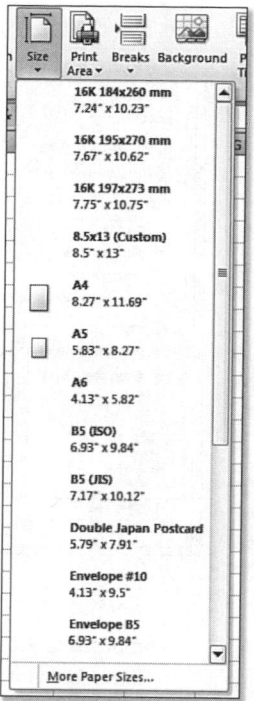

Occasionally, you will want to ignore the print areas and print everything on the worksheet. As described in the "Choosing What to Print" section earlier in this chapter, you can use the Ignore Print Areas setting.

Adding Print Titles

For reports that will span more than one page, you may want the headings from the report to print at the top of each page. Although the Print Titles icon was promoted to a large icon on the Page Layout tab in Excel 2007, this command leads back to the somewhat confusing Page Layout dialog, as shown in Figure 36.15. Suppose that you have a report that is two pages wide and several pages long. However, you notice that the printed page 2 of the printed report does not include title or column headings. If you want to have the titles and column headings repeat at the top of each row, you need to select 1:4 in the Rows To Repeat at Top option and A:B in the Columns To Repeat At Left option.

Scaling Options

You will often have worksheets in Excel that are a few columns too wide or a few rows too long to fit on a page. Legacy versions of Excel have included scaling options; however, it is not clear on the Page Layout tab how the scaling options work.

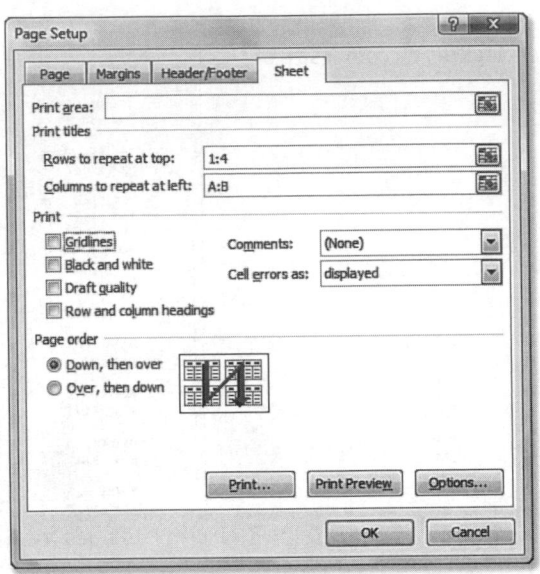

Figure 36.15
Use the Page Setup dialog to specify print titles to repeat on each page.

The Scale to Fit group on the Page Layout tab provides options for width, height, and a percentage scale. In most cases, you will change the height, width, or both to achieve the desired effect.

If your worksheet is a few columns too wide, change the Width drop-down to specify that the worksheet should fit on one page. If you have a report that is too tall, change the Height drop-down to specify that the worksheet should be one page tall. As shown in Figure 36.16, when you select either of these options, the Scale option is grayed out, but it still shows the scaling percentage used to make the report fit.

 note

To specify rows to repeat at top, you can either specify a single row using 1:1 or a range of rows using 1:4. Similarly, columns to repeat at left might be a single Column (A:A) or a range of Columns (A:B).

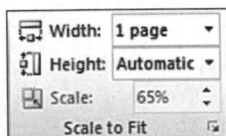

Figure 36.16
After you select Scale to Fit 1 Page wide, the Scale option is grayed out but shows the actual percentage scaling used.

Printing Gridlines and Headings

To print the gridlines on a worksheet, from the Page Layout tab select Sheet Options, Gridlines, Print.

You can also print the A-B-C column headings and 1-2-3 row headings. To do this, from the Page Layout tab, select Sheet Options, Headings, Print. This option is helpful when you are printing formulas and you need to see the cell address of each cell.

Working with Page Breaks

There are two varieties of page breaks: automatic and manual.

An *automatic page break* occurs when Excel reaches the bottom or right margin of a physical page. These page breaks change automatically as you add rows, delete rows, or even change the height of certain rows on the page.

Initially, automatic page breaks are not shown in the worksheet. However, after you go to Print Preview and return to Normal view, automatic page breaks are shown in the document using a thin dashed line. Automatic page breaks are also evident in Page Layout view and Page Break Preview mode.

You can manually insert page breaks at rows or columns where you want to start a new page. For example, you might want to insert a manual page break at the start of a new section in a report. A manual page break does not automatically change in response to changes in the worksheet rows.

 tip

If you plan to print multiple worksheets to produce a printed report, you should pay attention to the scaling percentage. If Sheet1 is scaled to 77 percent and Sheet2 is scaled to 82 percent, the characters on some pages of your report will appear larger than on other pages. You can manually set Sheet2 to 82 percent scaling to match the other worksheet.

Manually Adding Page Breaks

To add a page break manually at a certain row, follow these steps:

1. Select an entire row by clicking the row number that should be the first row on the new page. Alternatively, select the cell in column A in that row.

2. From the Page Layout tab, select Page Setup, Breaks, Insert Page Break.

 tip

Print Preview is automatically shown when you access the Print item in Backstage view. You can add a Print Preview icon to your Quick Access Toolbar that can be used as a shortcut to get to the Print pane of the Backstage view.

To add a page break manually at a certain column, follow these steps:

1. Select an entire column by clicking the number above the column that should be the first column on the new page. Alternatively, select Row 1 in that column.

2. From the Page Layout tab, select Page Setup, Breaks, Insert Page Break.

Manual Versus Automatic Page Breaks

In Normal view, a subtle visual difference exists between manual and automatic page breaks. For example, in Figure 36.17, an automatic page break occurs after Row 89, and a manual page break has been inserted after Row 97. The dashed line used to indicate a manual page break is more pronounced than the line used to indicate an automatic page break.

To see a better view of page breaks, you can select View, Page Break Preview to switch to Page Break Preview mode, as shown in Figure 36.18. In this mode, automatic page breaks are shown as dotted blue lines. Manual page breaks are shown as solid lines.

caution

If you insert a page break while the cell pointer is outside Row 1 or Column A, Excel simultaneously inserts a row page break and a column page break. This is rarely what you want. Make sure to select a cell in Column A to insert a row break or to select a cell in Row 1 to insert a column break.

Automatic Page Break

	A	B	C	D	E
87	J	J168	5,627	5,894	5,559
88	J	J177	5,342	4,088	2,585
89	J	J278	1,504	5,371	9,541
90	J	J354	9,006	3,544	2,057
91	J	J488	3,994	4,107	4,736
92	J	J552	1,784	5,047	2,925
93	J	J704	8,289	9,372	1,737
94	J	J737	3,820	1,861	3,307
95	J	J793	4,579	7,998	5,730
96	J	J905	2,910	8,802	1,780
97	J Total		46,856	56,084	39,958
98	K	K248	7,788	2,685	9,611
99	K	K297	8,258	1,216	3,933
100	K	K488	2,252	9,189	7,565
101	K Total		18,299	13,090	21,109

Manual Page Break

Figure 36.17
In Normal view, the page break indicator is bolder for manual page breaks.

Using Page Break Preview to Make Changes

An advantage of Page Break Preview mode is that while you are in this mode, you can move a page break by dragging the line associated with the page break. If you drag an automatic page break to expand the number of rows or columns on a page, Excel automatically changes the Scale percentage for all pages.

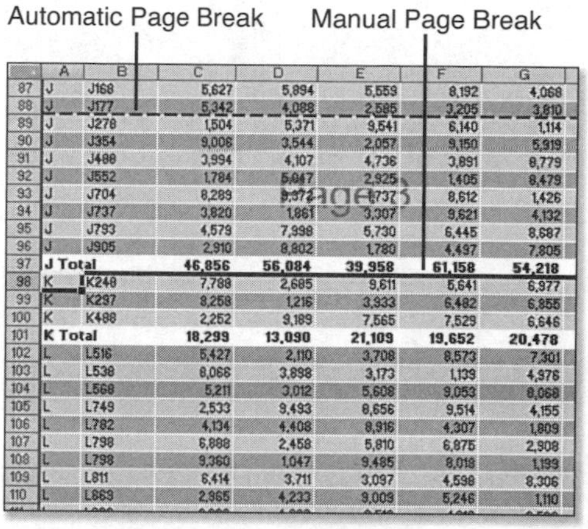

Figure 36.18

In Page Break Preview mode, automatic page breaks are shown using a dotted line and manual page breaks using a solid line.

Automatic Page Break   Manual Page Break

Removing Manual Page Breaks

To remove a manual page break for a row, follow these steps:

1. Position the cursor in the row below the page break.

2. From the Page Layout tab, select Page Setup, Breaks, Remove Page Break.

To remove a manual page break for a column, follow these steps:

1. Position the cursor in the column to the right of the page break.

2. From the Page Layout tab, select Page Setup, Breaks, Remove Page Break.

To remove all manual page breaks, from the Page Layout tab select Page Setup, Breaks, Reset All Page Breaks. Note that clearing the page breaks also resets the scaling back to 100%.

EXCEL WEB APP AND OTHER WAYS TO SHARE WORKBOOKS

I was a little upset when Microsoft removed the Publish with Interactivity option from Excel 2007. Yes, Microsoft offered the capability to publish the workbook to Excel Services, but you needed to have an IT department to figure out how to set up a SharePoint server to make that all work. In Excel 2010, the Office Web Apps provide an experience that runs circles around the old Publish with Interactivity option.

This chapter discusses publishing your workbook to Office Web Apps, to Excel Services, and good old methods of sending workbooks via email or creating PDF files.

This chapter also includes a discussion of sharing Excel data with other applications.

Sharing Workbooks with Others

After creating your workbooks in Excel, you will probably want to share those workbooks with co-workers, managers, or employees. Excel 2010 offers many more ways to share a workbook than ever before.

Using the Excel Web Application

Competition is a great driver of innovation at Microsoft. A few years ago, Google debuted a spreadsheet in a browser. It was limited to only 10,000 cells, but it was enough to kick Microsoft into gear to have a web-based spreadsheet as well.

Excel 2010 is available in a web version. Think of the web version as a great tool for sharing your workbooks with others and a place to collaborate; multiple people can be editing the same worksheet at the same time. It is also a great way to save a document on a virtual SkyDrive that you can access from home or from the road.

To use the Office Web Apps, you need a Windows Live ID. Sign up for Windows Live and enable your SkyDrive service, which provides 25GB of free storage available online.

Figure 37.1 shows an Excel 2010 workbook. This workbook includes many Excel 2010 features—such as slicers and a pivot table with row labels repeated. Some GetPivotData formulas that are out of view provide the data to create a chart.

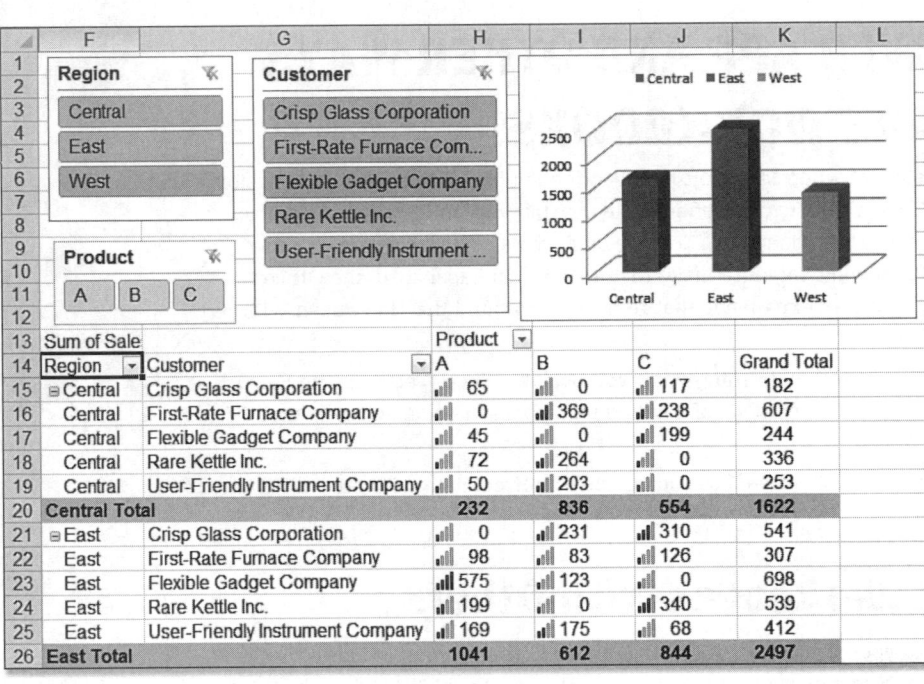

Figure 37.1
A workbook in the Excel client includes slicers, a pivot table, and a chart.

	Customer	A	B	C	Grand Total
Central	Crisp Glass Corporation	65	0	117	182
Central	First-Rate Furnace Company	0	369	238	607
Central	Flexible Gadget Company	45	0	199	244
Central	Rare Kettle Inc.	72	264	0	336
Central	User-Friendly Instrument Company	50	203	0	253
Central Total		**232**	**836**	**554**	**1622**
East	Crisp Glass Corporation	0	231	310	541
East	First-Rate Furnace Company	98	83	126	307
East	Flexible Gadget Company	575	123	0	698
East	Rare Kettle Inc.	199	0	340	539
East	User-Friendly Instrument Company	169	175	68	412
East Total		**1041**	**612**	**844**	**2497**

Publishing a Workbook to the Excel Web App

To publish this to the Excel Web App, use File, Save & Send, Save to Web. Choose one of your SkyDrive folders and then click Save As (see Figure 37.2).

After you have saved the file to the SkyDrive, use any browser to sign in to your Windows Live account. From the top navigation bar, select More, SkyDrive.

Figure 37.2
Saving to Windows Live is incorporated right into the Excel 2010 Backstage view.

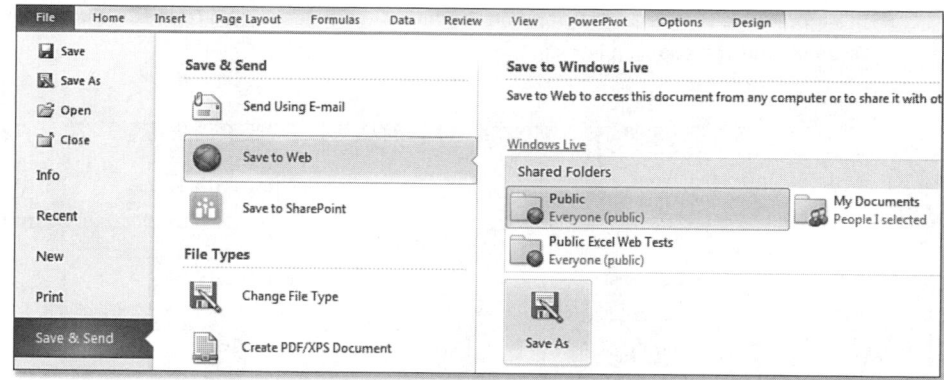

Locate the folder and double-click the file that you saved.

Select View, and you get a view of the spreadsheet in your browser! The chart shows up. The slicers show up. The icon sets show up. Microsoft did a nice job rendering the workbook in the browser (see Figure 37.3.).

Figure 37.3
Microsoft renders the worksheet in the browser.

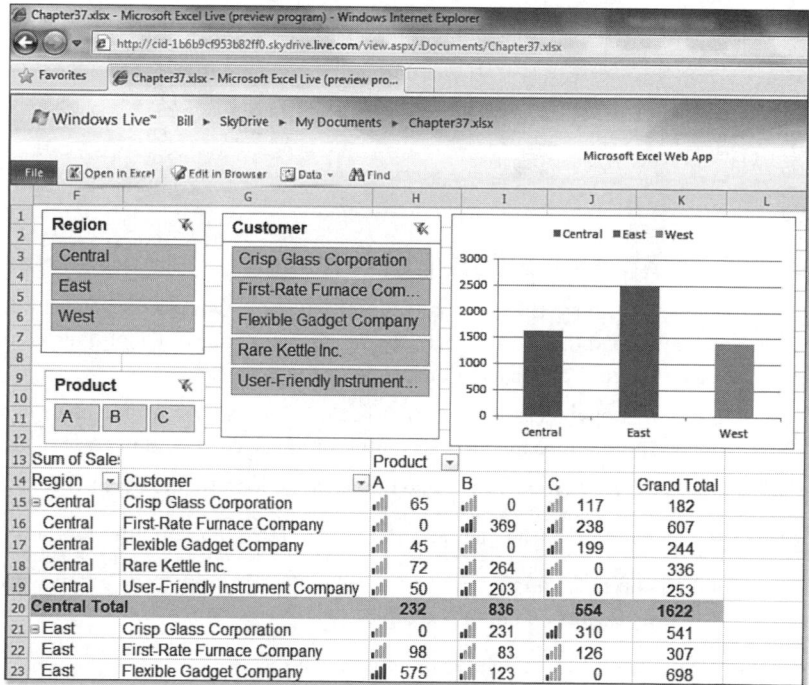

When you are in View mode, you can change the pivot table and the chart by using the slicers. In Figure 37.4, the Central region and Product C were deselected from the slicers. The pivot table redraws and the chart updates.

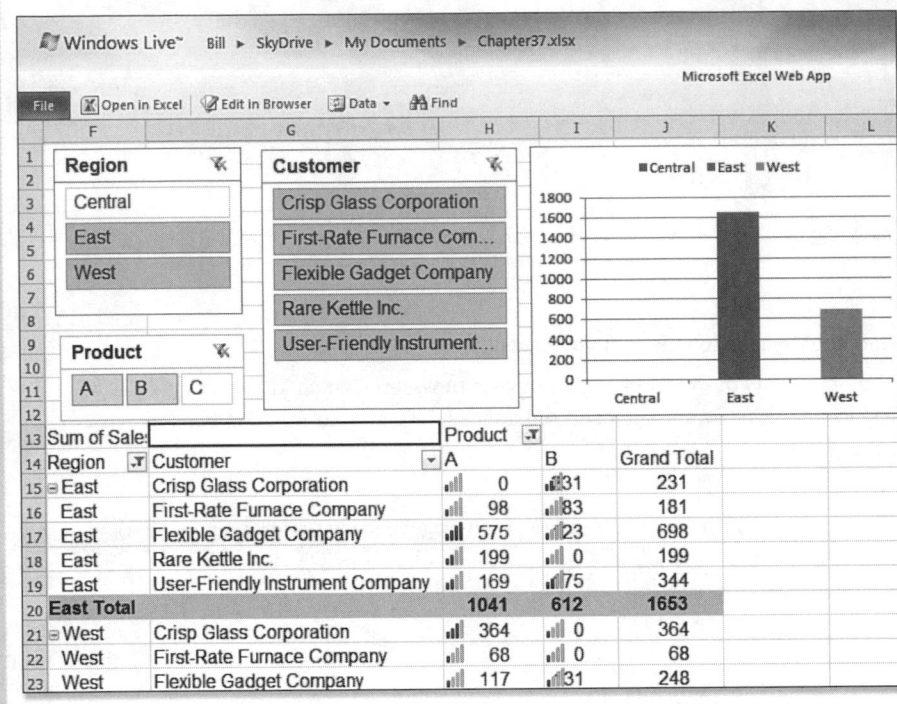

Figure 37.4
In View mode, the pivot table reacts to the slicers.

The Amazing Edit Button

Notice that above the spreadsheet are buttons to Open in Excel and Edit in Browser. Open in Excel will download the file and let you edit it in your copy of Excel. This is nicely integrated, but it is not that amazing. The amazing button is Edit in Browser.

In Edit mode, you can change data in the cells. As soon as you change a cell, that change is saved to the SkyDrive. You can edit cells, enter formulas, copy, and paste.

The Excel Web App has a Home tab in the Ribbon that allows the following:

- You can format the font, alignment, wrap text, and number format.

- You can make a range into an Excel table. After you have a table, you can use heading drop-downs to sort and filter the table.

- You can Insert or Delete columns or rows.

- You can use Find, Undo, and Redo.

Figure 37.5 shows the Home tab of the Excel Web app.

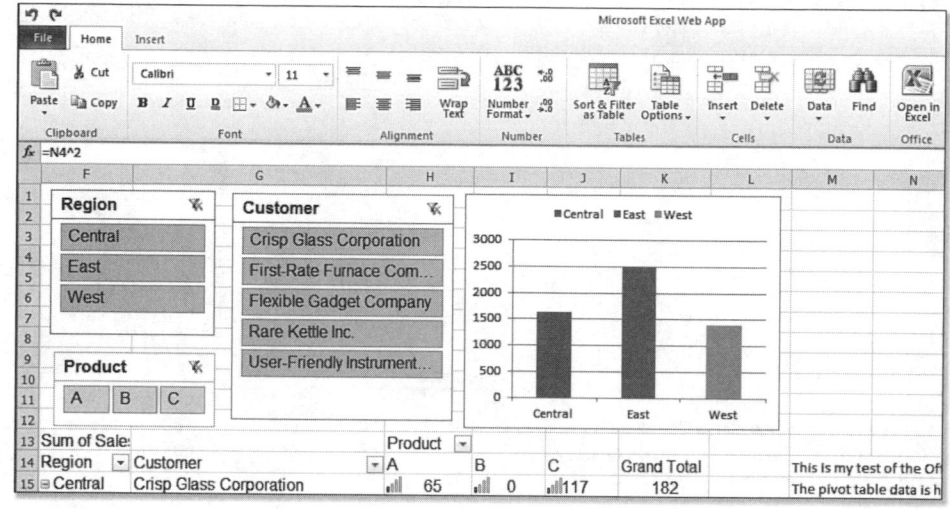

Figure 37.5
In Edit mode, the Home tab offers formatting and basic options.

As shown in the File menu, you can use Save As to save the workbook to the SkyDrive. You can download either a copy of the workbook or a snapshot of the workbook to your computer. (See Figure 37.6.)

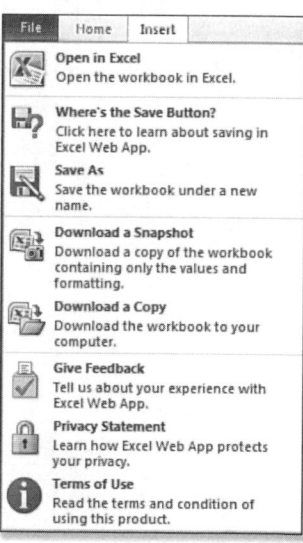

Figure 37.6
The File menu allows you to download a snapshot or the whole workbook to your computer.

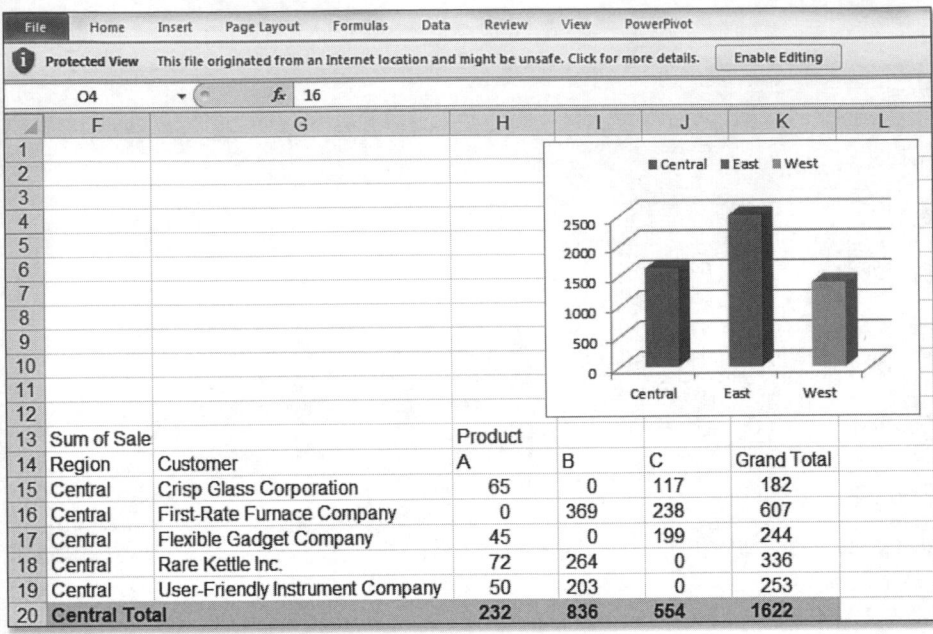

Figure 37.7
Download a snapshot and you will lose a lot of functionality.

 To see a demo of the Excel Web App, search for *"Excel In Depth 37"* at YouTube.

 note

The Excel Web application is evolving. For a version 1.0 product, it feels amazingly like the real Excel. They support slicers right out of the box. When I created the workbook used in this example, I purposely put in Excel 2010 features to see how the Excel Web application would react. It did amazingly well.

 caution

When you open a snapshot from the Web, the slicers are gone. The formulas are converted to values, as shown in Figure 37.7. If you download a copy to your computer, you have the full file.

Advantages of Creating a Client Version of Your Workbook

It is best to create your workbook in Excel and then upload to the SkyDrive. You can do many things in the client version of Excel 2010 that you cannot do in the web version. However, if you do those things in the Excel 2010 client, those features will work in the web version. Some examples follow:

- You cannot hide columns in the web version. However, you can hide them in the Excel client and they will remain hidden on the web. For example, in Figure 37.4 shown previously, the data for the pivot table is hidden in column A:E.

- You cannot set up pivot tables, slicers, or charts on the Web, but these elements that you create in the Excel 2010 client will render on the Web.

- Generate GetPivotData is not functional on the Web, but =GetPivotData functions that you create in the Excel client work on the Web.

- You cannot enter array formulas on the Web, but array formulas that you enter in the Excel client will work.

Some features will not work on the Web:

- Data Validation does not work on the Web.

- Links to external workbooks do not work on the Web.

- Worksheet protection does not work on the Web.

The mechanism for sharing the workbook on the web is provided by the SkyDrive service. The protection is at the folder level. Set up a folder. You can choose to share that folder with one email address, everyone in your Windows Live network, or the Public. You can choose whether people can view files or view and edit files (see Figure 37.8).

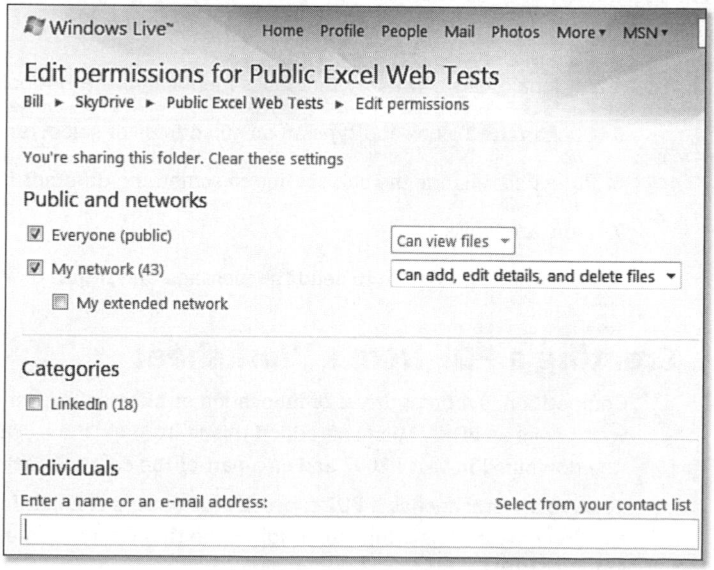

Figure 37.8
Choose to share a folder with specific people, your network, or everyone.

Windows Live™   Home Profile People Mail Photos More ▾ MSN ▾

Edit permissions for Public Excel Web Tests

Bill ▸ SkyDrive ▸ Public Excel Web Tests ▸ Edit permissions

You're sharing this folder. Clear these settings

Public and networks

☑ Everyone (public)   Can view files ▾

☑ My network (43)   Can add, edit details, and delete files ▾

☐ My extended network

Categories

☐ LinkedIn (18)

Individuals

Enter a name or an e-mail address: Select from your contact list

Sending a Workbook via Email

The fastest way to send a workbook via email is to send it directly from Excel. If Outlook is your default email client, this is easy to do. Follow these steps:

1. Open the workbook you want to send.

2. Arrange the window so it appears as you would like it to appear for your email recipient. This might mean scrolling explanatory notes into view or making some other adjustments.

3. From the File menu, select Save & Send, Send Using Email, Send as Attachment, as shown in Figure 37.9.

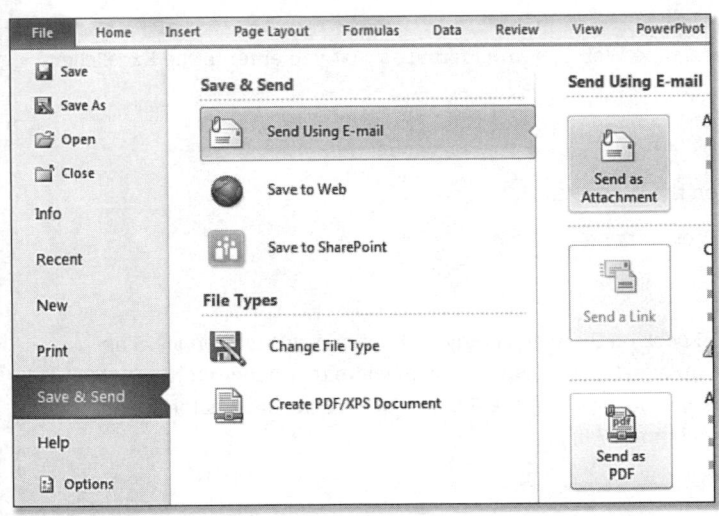

Figure 37.9
Send as Attachment.

4. Outlook opens a window that looks identical to the Outlook Send Mail window.

5. Click in the To box and type an email address or select email recipients.

6. If desired, change the subject line to something different from the filename.

7. Type any message.

8. Click the Send button to send the message and return to Microsoft Excel.

Creating a PDF from a Worksheet

Competition is a great driver of innovation at Microsoft. After OpenOffice started offering to save workbooks as PDFs, Microsoft added this feature to Office. The PDF functionality was available as a free download in Excel 2007 and as a part of the core product in Office 2010.

To save a worksheet as a PDF file, select File, Save & Send. In the center pane, select Create PDF/XPS Document. This brings up a right pane that offers Create PDF/XPS document, as shown in Figure 37.10.

caution

Although the Excel Message dialog box appears identical to the Outlook dialog box, it is actually a modal dialog box in Excel. This means that you cannot return to Excel until you have finished sending the email. If you need to look back to the Excel file to get information for the text of the email, you can try one of these two methods:

- Drag the Message dialog out of the way by dragging the title bar. This works if the information you need is in the visible portion of the Excel window.

- Click the Save button in the Message window to save the unsent message to the Outlook Inbox. Click the X in the upper-right corner of the Message window to return to Excel. You can now switch back and forth between Excel and Outlook to refer to specific values in any worksheet of the workbook.

Figure 37.10
Select to Create PDF/XPS.

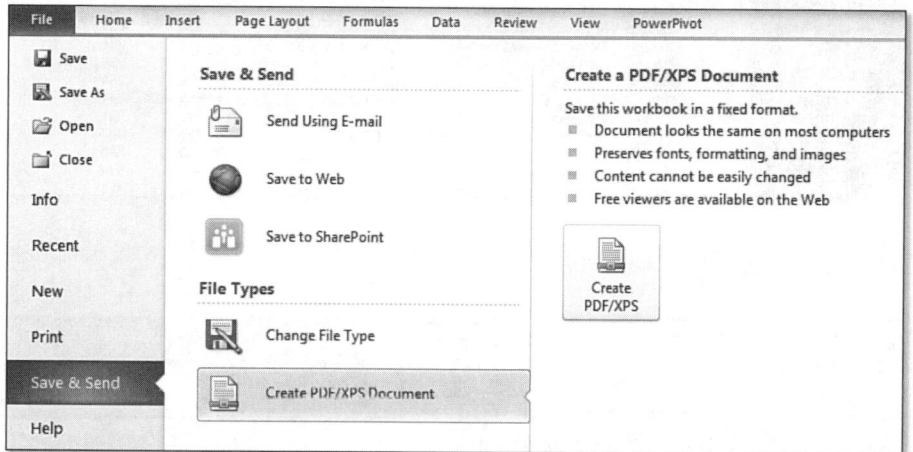

You have the option to save the file in a high-resolution format suitable for printing or a low-resolution format that is suitable for viewing onscreen. The PDF is shown in Figure 37.11.

In general, some PDFs contain data that can be selected, copied, and pasted to Excel. Other PDFs contain strange formatting that causes the paste back to Excel to render horribly.

You would think that a PDF file created by Microsoft would have the capability to paste back into Excel, but this is not the case. In Figure 37.12, the top left is the original data in Excel. The top right is the data in the PDF file created by Excel. The data in the bottom left is how that data was pasted back to Excel.

There is probably some bizarre real-world case where you need to unwind a range of data and this caution is really a tip in those 0.001% of the cases. For most people, however, this is an annoyance.

 tip

Think of creating a PDF file as printing to a PDF file. The data that is saved will follow the page setup settings, such as orientation, margins, rows to repeat at top, and the print area.

 tip

If you need to convert PDF data to Excel, check out my review of Able2Extract at www.mrexcel.com/tip107.shtm

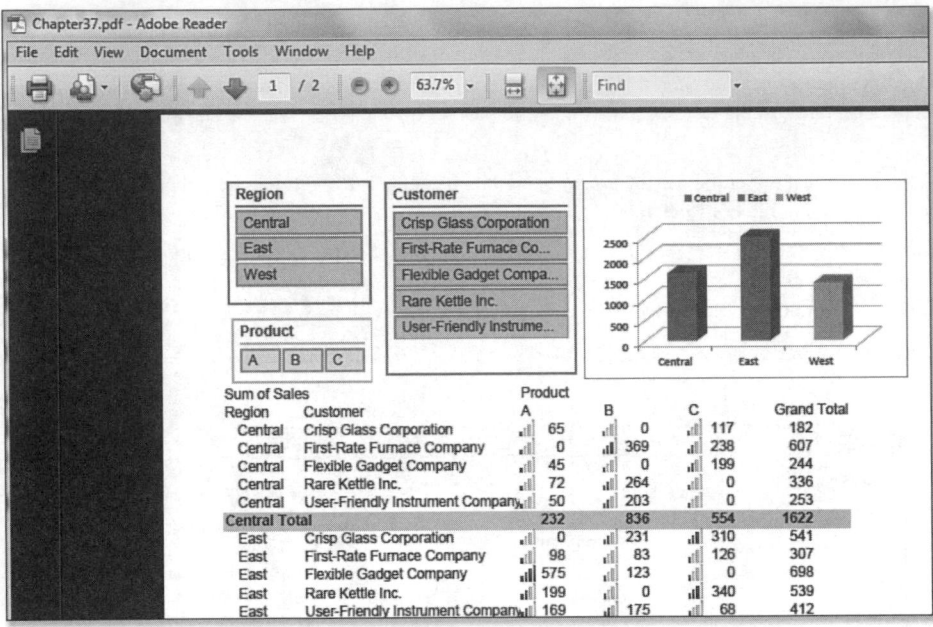

Figure 37.11
The PDF version of the worksheet has pictures of the chart, the icon sets, and even the slicers, although none of those are interactive in the PDF.

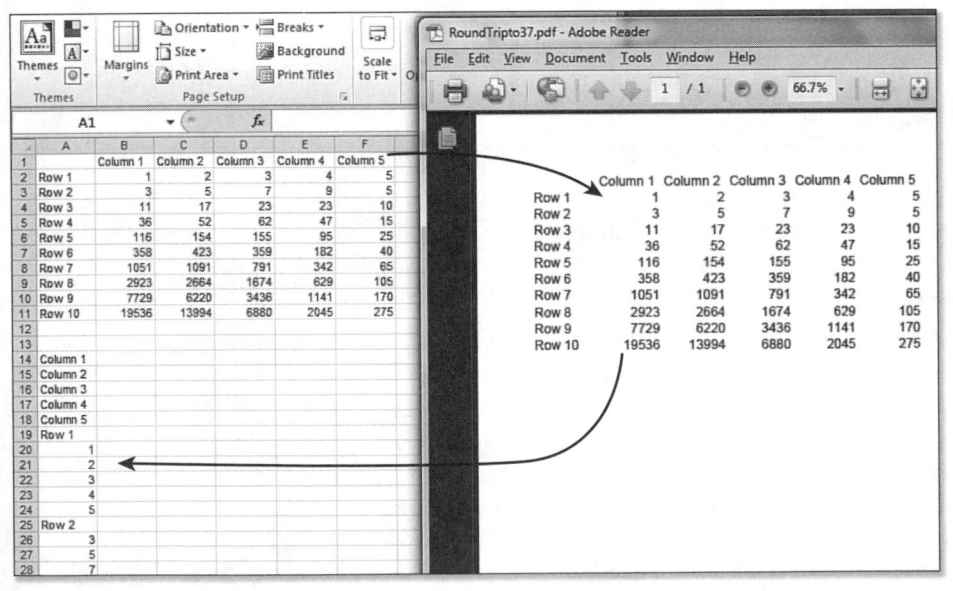

Figure 37.12
Don't try to copy the PDF data and paste back to Excel.

Publishing to Excel Services on SharePoint

Suppose that someone authors a spreadsheet using Excel 2010. This file is then saved to a SharePoint document library. Other people in the company could click the document in SharePoint. The person then sees a browser-based rendering of the spreadsheet that is somewhat interactive. This is the basic idea of Excel Services.

Behind the scenes, Excel Services opens the original spreadsheet. It refreshes any external data. It then builds a DHTML view of the spreadsheet that can be displayed in any modern browser.

Microsoft envisions that people will use Excel Services for three basic scenarios:

 tip
Although Adobe's PDF format is ubiquitous, you might consider starting to use Microsoft's new XPS file format. This format will compete with PDF. To save as XPS, you use the Save as Type drop-down to select XPS instead of PDF. An XPS reader ships with Vista and Windows 7. Others with earlier operating systems will have to download a free reader from Microsoft to open the files.

- Sharing spreadsheets through a browser

- Populating key indicator sections of executive dashboards

- Reusing logic encapsulated in Excel spreadsheets as a back end to any language that can speak web services

Defining Interactivity in Excel Services

People viewing a spreadsheet in SharePoint do not need to have Excel installed. In the browser, they have access to limited interactivity:

- They can scroll through the spreadsheet.

- They can access autofilter drop-downs or slicers to filter the data.

- They can access page field drop-downs in pivot tables.

- They can change certain cells that the author of the spreadsheet defined as workbook parameters.

The author of the spreadsheet must define parameters when saving the file to SharePoint. In addition, each parameter must be in a named cell.

Saving a Workbook to Excel Services

To save a file to Excel Services, follow these steps:

1. Identify any cells that you want to be changeable parameters in the browser.

2. For each parameter cell, select Formulas, Define Name and assign a name.

3. From the File menu, choose the Send and Save category, then select Save to SharePoint.

4. In the right pane of Backstage view, select Publish Options. Excel displays the Publish Options dialog.

5. In the Show tab of Publish Options, choose which worksheets should be published.

6. In the Parameters tab of the Publish Options dialog, select Add.

7. Choose each named range and/or slicer as shown in Figure 37.13. Click OK twice to close the dialogs.

8. Click Save As to save the workbook to a SharePoint library.

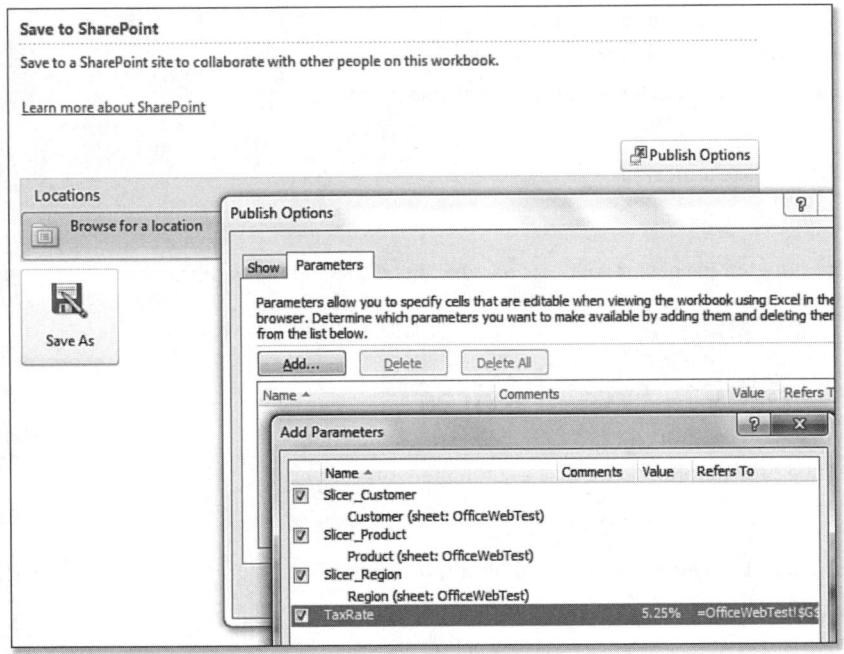

Figure 37.13
You define which named cells should be parameters in the SharePoint browser view of the workbook.

When this file is viewed in the browser, the Excel file provides support for recent features such as slicers, data bars, and conditional formatting.

Interacting with Other Office Applications

After authoring a worksheet in Excel, you might need to include its information in a PowerPoint presentation or a Word document. Or you might want to add portions of your spreadsheet in your OneNote notebook (assuming that your version came with OneNote). The collaborative nature of Office 2010 applications allow you to do this with ease.

In certain cases, you can utilize Excel data without ever opening the Excel file. If you have a list of addresses in Excel, you can access that list when doing a mail merge in Microsoft Word 2010. Excel can receive data from other Office applications. For example, you might author body copy in Word and then copy it to a text box in Excel. Data from Access can also be used as the source data for an external query in Excel or even for a pivot table.

Pasting Excel Data to Microsoft OneNote

Microsoft OneNote 2010 is being bundled as part of all editions of Microsoft Office except for the Starter Edition. This product was introduced in Office 2003 but was never bundled with any version of Office. Even though this is a fantastic product, it is not a product that many people were willing to spend $99 to buy. Now that OneNote is bundled with all versions of Office, it will finally get the exposure needed to allow more people to gravitate toward its capability to organize notes in one place.

In the initial release of OneNote, the capability to present tabular data was dismal. OneNote 2010 renders Excel worksheets in a tabular grid. OneNote offers several formatting options to choose from after pasting Excel data to OneNote:

■ In a default paste, the values from the Excel cells are pasted into a tabular grid. You lose icon sets and formulas.

■ Choose to keep text only and each cell is pasted after a Tab character. For those of you nostalgic for life in OneNote version 2003, use this paste option.

■ Select to Paste as a Picture and you get a perfect rendering of all icon sets, charts, and so on.

Figure 37.14 shows the default paste of an Excel range to OneNote.

Figure 37.14
Paste a range to OneNote.

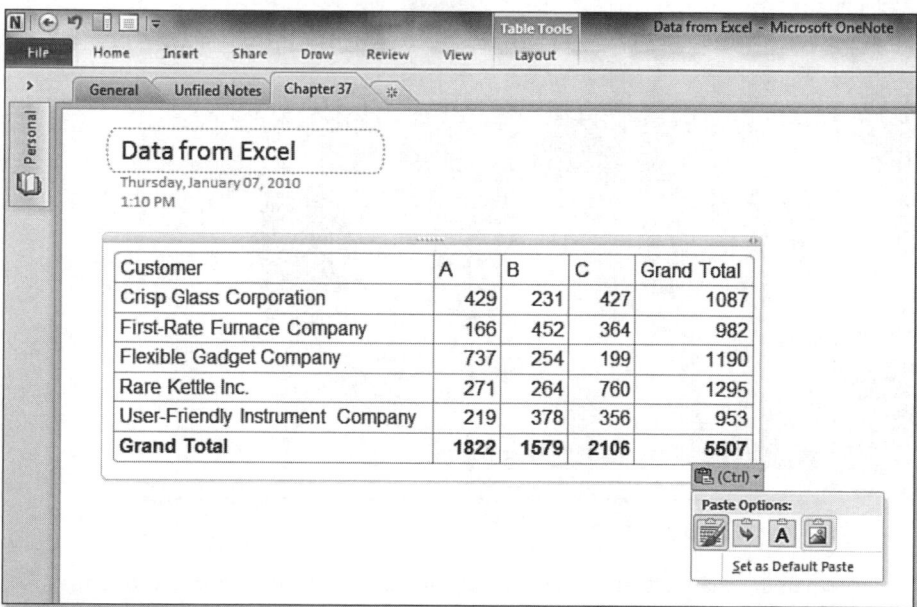

Customer	A	B	C	Grand Total
Crisp Glass Corporation	429	231	427	1087
First-Rate Furnace Company	166	452	364	982
Flexible Gadget Company	737	254	199	1190
Rare Kettle Inc.	271	264	760	1295
User-Friendly Instrument Company	219	378	356	953
Grand Total	**1822**	**1579**	**2106**	**5507**

Using Excel Charts in PowerPoint

The process of copying charts from Excel to PowerPoint works well in Office 2010. The resulting chart is completely editable in PowerPoint. In addition, changes to the slide theme change the look and feel of the chart.

To copy a chart to PowerPoint, follow these steps:

1. Prepare a blank slide in PowerPoint that is ready to accept the data from Excel.

2. Open the desired Excel workbook.

3. Select the chart to be copied.

4. Press Ctrl+C to copy the selected chart.

5. Switch back to PowerPoint.

6. From the Home tab, select Paste.

As shown in Figure 37.15, the chart is pasted to the slide. You can resize the chart to fill the area on the slide.

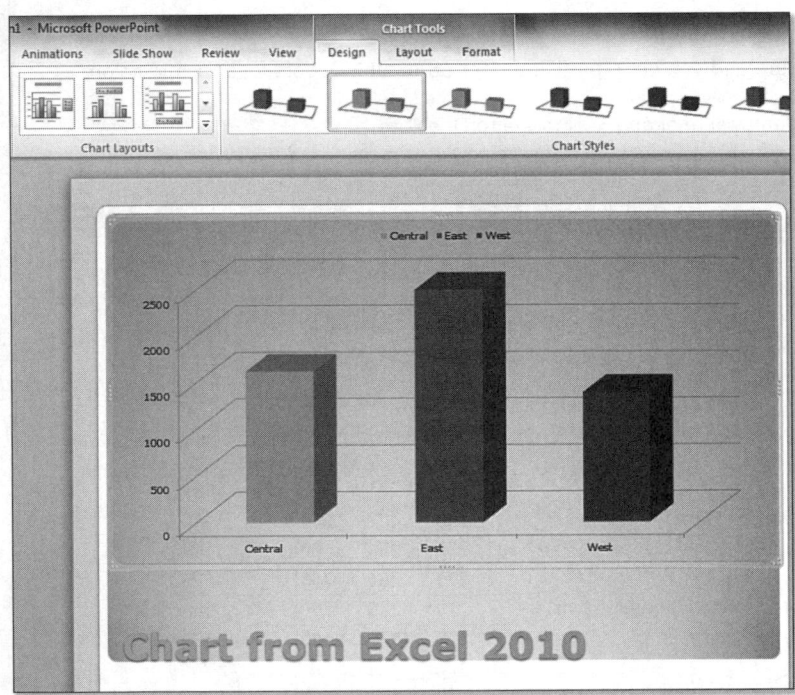

Figure 37.15
Charts pasted into PowerPoint have the same look and feel as in Excel, as well as the same user interface tabs on the Ribbon.

When the chart is selected in PowerPoint, three contextual Ribbon tabs offer the same chart experience as is available in Excel. For details on using the charting tools, see Chapter 32, "Using Excel Charts."

Creating Tables in Excel and Pasting to Word

Microsoft Word is excellent for typing body text. When you need to start creating tables in Word, however, the program is a bit confusing. If you are more comfortable with Excel than Word, it makes sense to switch to Excel, create and format a table, and then paste the table back to the Word document. This gives you better control over column widths, plus the possibility to provide formulas for calculating some of the content of the table.

To create a table for Word, using Excel, follow these steps:

1. Position the insertion cursor in Word at a point where the table should go.

2. Switch to Excel and create a blank workbook.

3. Type the data in columns in Excel.

4. If you use formulas to build rows of the table, it is best to convert the formulas to values before copying to Word. To do so, select the formulas and press Ctrl+C to copy. Then select Home, Paste, Paste Values.

5. If you have chosen a theme in Word, choose the identical theme in Excel.

6. Select the table and then select the Cells section of the Home tab and select Format, Width, AutoFit Selection.

7. Optionally, apply a table format.

> ➡ *To review how to apply a table format, refer back to Chapter 8, "Understanding Formulas."*

Select the table in Excel and then press Ctrl+C to copy. Switch to Word. From the Home tab, select Paste. An HTML representation of the table is pasted into Word. The column widths, alignment, font, font color, and fill copy perfectly from Excel.

Pasting Word Data to an Excel Text Box

Although Excel is great at handling tables of numbers, it does not have the editing tools needed to make it easy to handle body copy as well as in Word. If you want to be able to type paragraphs of text without needing to judge the length of each line, you should use Word to prepare the text and then paste it to a text box in Excel. You can follow these steps to build a section of body copy for use in Excel:

1. Switch to Microsoft Word and create a blank document.

2. Type the text. Use any formatting you like, such as underlining, bold, italic, font size, font changes, and so on.

3. Select the text in Word.

4. Press Ctrl+C to copy the selected text.

5. Switch to Excel.

6. On the Insert tab, select Text, Text Box.

7. Drag in the worksheet to define the shape of the text box.

8. When you release the mouse, the insertion point is at the start of the text box. Press Ctrl+V to paste.

9. By default, text boxes have a visible border. To remove the border, select Drawing Tools Format, Shape Styles, Shape Outline, No Outline.

10. If you need to resize or further format the text, select the text in the text box. The mini toolbar appears. If desired, change font size, style, and so on.

If you need to fine-tune the text box, follow these steps:

1. Click outside the text box.

2. Right-click the text box and select Format Shape. The Format Shape dialog appears.

3. In the Format Shape dialog, select the Text Box category.

4. Select an internal margin, select text alignment, add columns, or resize the shape to fit the text, as shown in Figure 37.16.

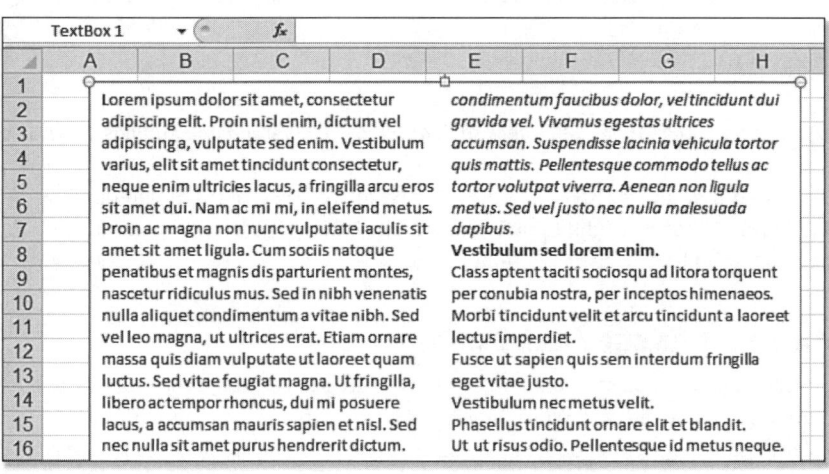

Figure 37.16
After copying Word text to a text box, you can use the formatting tools to fine-tune the text box.

Using Excel Data in a Word Mail Merge

Word's mail merge tools allow you to create a printed form letter that is customized to each person in an Excel list of names. For the best results, your Excel table should include columns for first name, last name, address line 1, address line 2.

Follow these steps to perform a mail merge in Word using Excel data:

1. Prepare your data in Excel. Include headings for each column. Do not include any blank columns or entirely blank rows.

2. To simplify the mail merge, select the range and press Ctrl+T to convert the range to a table. Be sure to specify that the table has headers.

3. Save and close the Excel workbook.

4. Open Microsoft Word.

5. Leave a few blank lines at the top for the address block and greeting.

6. Type the rest of the letter.

7. Select Mailings, Start Mail Merge, Step by Step Mail Merge Wizard. A Mail Merge task pane appears on the right side of the screen.

8. By default, step 1 of the task pane indicates that you are producing a letter. At the bottom of the task pane, click the hyperlink for Next: Starting Document.

9. In step 2 of the task pane, select to use the current document. Click Next: Select Recipients.

10. In step 3 of the task pane, select Use an Existing List and then select Browse. The Select Data Source dialog appears.

11. Open the Files of Type drop-down and select Excel Files (*.xlsx,*.xlsm,*.xlsb,*.xls).

12. Browse to your Excel file and click Open. The Select Table dialog appears.

13. In the Select Table dialog, Word selects the table in your document. Click OK to confirm. Word displays the Mail Merge Recipients dialog.

14. If desired, choose to filter or sort the list, as shown in Figure 37.17. Click OK to continue.

Figure 37.17
You preview the records from
Excel in this dialog.

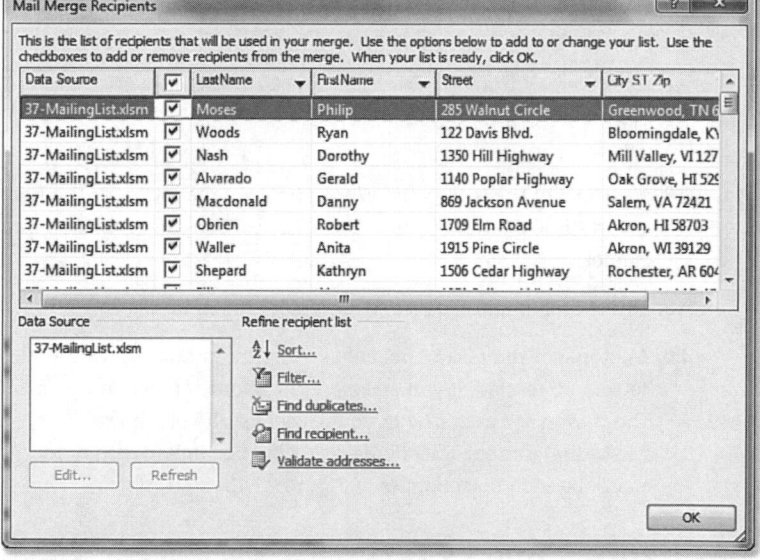

15. In the Mail Merge taskbar, click Next: Write Your letter.

16. In step 4 of the task pane, the instructions say to write your letter. This is the step where you insert placeholders from the Excel file. Click where you want a field to appear. In the Mailings tab, select Insert Merge Field and choose your field name. Word adds a field code to your document that looks like <<FirstName>> (see Figure 37.18). Repeat for each field.

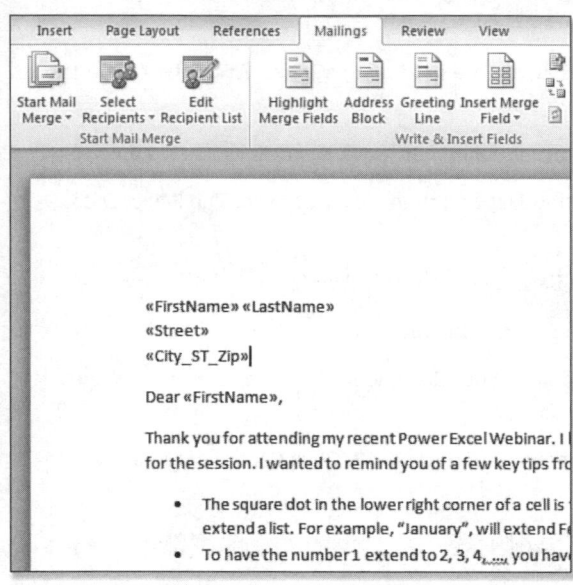

Figure 37.18
Add placeholders where the Excel data should go.

17. In the Mail Merge task pane, select Next: Preview Your Letters to proceed to step 5 of the task pane.

18. In step 5 of the task pane, Word previews the letter for the first recipient. You can format the inserted fields at this point. You can also use the >> button on the taskbar to browse through the names.

19. In the task pane, click Next: Complete the Merge.

20. In step 6 of the task pane, choose to print or edit individual letters, if needed. If you choose Print, Word sends one letter to the printer for each row in your Excel list. If you choose Edit Individual Letters, Excel creates a new document with a new page for each document (see Figure 37.19).

 note
Using Mail Merge in Word is a quick way to send customized letters to many recipients at once. The Mailings toolbar has options for creating envelopes and mailing labels as well. The steps for both of these document types are similar to those just provided for mail merges.

Building a Pivot Table from Access Queries

Microsoft Access is the database component of Microsoft Office. It is included in the Professional versions of Office 2010 but not with the Home edition of Microsoft Office.

Figure 37.19
Word produced 57 letters in less than a second.

> Philip Moses
> 285 Walnut Circle
> Greenwood, TN 67887
>
> Dear Philip,
>
> Thank you for attending my recent Power Exce
> for the session. I wanted to remind you of a few
>
> • The square dot in the lower right corne
>   extend a list. For example, "January" w

Before Excel 2007, many people occasionally encountered Access when they had more than 65,536 rows of data. Now that Excel can handle 1.1 million rows, there will be less casual use of Access.

Access is a *relational database*, which means that relationships can be defined between multiple tables, and these tables can be joined together in a query. In Figure 37.20, a query is defined in Access to join two tables. Calculated fields can calculate values from fields in each table.

Figure 37.20
This query joins multiple Access tables.

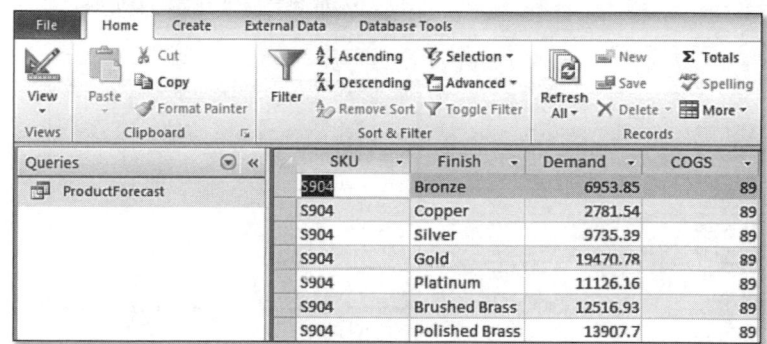

To use this data in an Excel pivot table, follow these steps:

1. Ensure that the Access database is saved in a trusted location. If you are unsure of trusted locations, go to Excel. Select File, Options, Trust Center, Trust Center Settings, Trusted Locations. If the location of the Access database is not in the list of trusted locations, select Add New Location.

2. In Excel, select Insert, PivotTable. The Create Pivot Table dialog appears.

3. In the Create Pivot Table dialog, select Use an External Data Source.

4. Click the Choose Connection button. The Existing Connections dialog appears.

5. In the Existing Connections dialog, click Browse for More.

6. Browse to and select your database. Click Open. The Select Table dialog appears.

7. The Select Table dialog offers all the available tables and views in the Access database. Note that queries in Access are shown as views. Click the desired view and click OK.

8. Click OK to create the pivot table. The Access data is now available as a regular pivot table cache.

The advantage of this method is that the data never has to be copied to Excel. In this case, two relatively small Access tables are joined into a larger query result. As shown in Figure 37.21, the pivot table presents results from the query without having to store the detailed data in Excel.

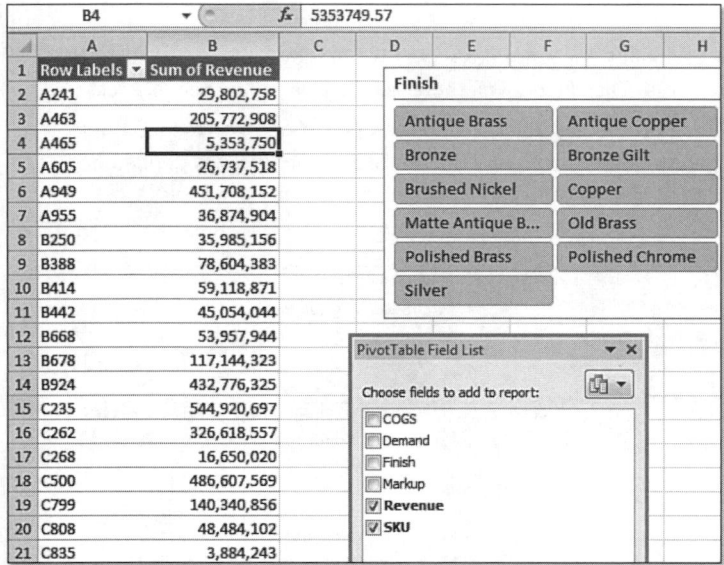

Figure 37.21
This pivot table creates a summary from thousands of virtual rows of data in Access without ever storing that data in the workbook.

SAVING TIME USING THE EASY-XL PROGRAM

My Easy-XL utility is designed to make complex data analysis tasks easy for anyone using Excel. Easy-XL adds 50 new commands to the Excel 2010 Ribbon. These commands are focused on letting even a casual Exceller summarize, join, pivot, merge, match, query, categorize, combine, split, and slice and dice data like an Excel guru.

If you are already an Excel guru, you might be thinking that you can already knock out VLOOKUP and SUMPRODUCT formulas with Advanced Filter queries to do many of the tasks in this chapter. Although this is true, why would you go through all that hassle when Easy-XL can do the task in a few clicks?

As a reader of this book, you receive a 90-day license to use Easy-XL. This should be enough time for you to get through your next big data emergency. Go through an annual budget cycle using Easy-XL to split workbooks, merge data, and summarize data, and you will wonder how you ever lived without it.

If you find that Easy-XL is for you, you can buy a full license at 25% off the normal price.

Downloading and Installing Easy-XL

Easy-XL works with all 32-bit versions of Excel for Windows from Excel 2000 up through Excel 2010. Easy-XL runs under Windows XP, Vista, or Windows 7. It does not run on the Macintosh platform. A 64-bit version of Easy-XL will be available in late 2010. To get started, visit this secret URL to download the software: www.easy-xl.com/excel2010indepth/.

You will download Easy-XL.msi. Make sure that Excel is closed. Double-click the installation file to install Easy-XL. When you load Excel, you should see a new Easy-XL tab in the Excel 2010 Ribbon (see Figure 38.1).

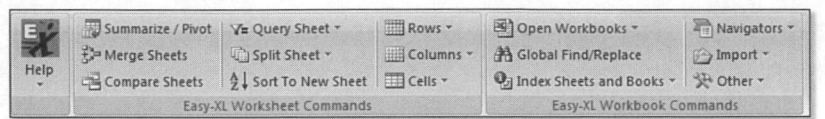

Figure 38.1
After installing Easy-XL, you should have this Ribbon tab.

Easy-XL Works Best with Tabular Data

Many of Easy-XL's powerful data analytics commands are looking for tabular data. This means field headings in row 1, no blank rows, and no blank columns.

To experiment with Easy-XL, you can load up the sample workbook that ships with Easy-XL. Select Easy-XL, Other, Open Easy-XL Sample Workbook. You will get a workbook with six data worksheets. The data worksheets contain databases of invoices, products, customers, and salespeople (see Figure 38.2).

	A	B	C	D	E	F	G	H	I	
	InvoiceNo	InvoiceDate	PaymentDate	CustomerNo	SalesPerson	ProductNo	Quantity	UnitPrice	Amount	Description
	20000	1/1/2011	3/6/2011	10220	8	8	4	299.00	1,196.00	Excel for Mac 20
	20001	1/1/2011	2/9/2011	10491	4	4	4	279.00	1,116.00	Excel version 20(
	20002	1/1/2011	2/22/2011	10704	3	1	3	299.90	899.70	Easy-XL From M
	20003	1/1/2011	2/9/2011	10430	5	54	4	199.00	796.00	Word version 200
	20004	1/1/2011	2/28/2011	10841	17	11	2	129.00	458.00	Expression Profe
	20005	1/1/2011	2/24/2011	10777	1	5	4	229.00	916.00	CCR DSS Toolki
	20006	1/1/2011	2/5/2011	10653	19	58	2	129.00	458.00	Windows® 7 Pro
	20007	1/1/2011	2/27/2011	10413	12	61	3	3,429.00	10,287.00	Application Cent(

Figure 38.2
Easy-XL includes this sample data set that you can use for learning the powerful Easy-XL features.

Doing Away with VLOOKUP

I love VLOOKUP. I don't know how anyone can live without knowing how to knock out VLOOKUPs with their eyes closed. However, Easy-XL allows someone who knows nothing about VLOOKUP to run circles around someone who solves problems with VLOOKUP.

The Invoice 2011 worksheet in the sample data set includes a customer number column. It does not contain customer name or any other customer information.

The sample workbook has a worksheet called Customer. This worksheet shows the customer name, address, city, and state for each customer number.

You want to merge data on these two sheets so that the customer name and state is included on the Invoices 2011 worksheet.

Follow these steps:

1. Start on the Invoices 2011 worksheet. Select Easy-XL, Merge Sheets. Excel displays a Select a Sheet to Merge with Invoices 2011 dialog.

2. Select Customers and click Select. Excel displays the Merge Sheets dialog.

3. In the Merge Sheets dialog, indicate that you want to group by the Customer Number field. In the right list box, select Contact Name and State. In the Merge Options section, select that you want Rows in Sheet1 that match a row in Sheet2 and also Rows in Sheet1 that don't match a row in Sheet2. The Merge dialog should look like Figure 38.3. Click OK.

Figure 38.3
Combine two fields from the Customer worksheet into the Invoices worksheet.

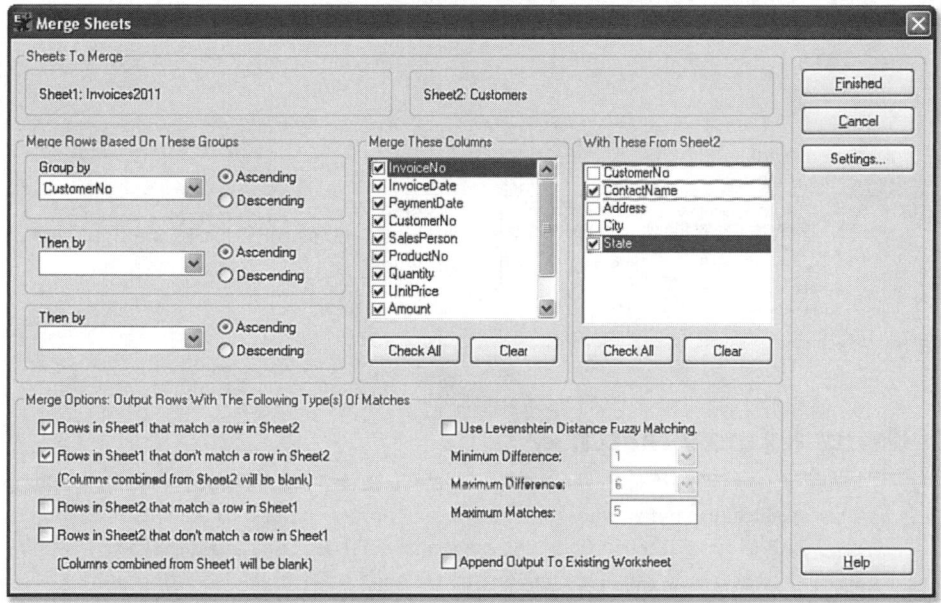

Easy-XL does several things. First, you will have a brand new worksheet called MergedInvoices2011. Second, a comment in cell A1 indicates how this sheet was created. This provides an audit trail of which worksheets were merged and how (see Figure 38.4). You will never get that level of detail with the VLOOKUP method.

If you scroll right, you will see that the data from the customer worksheet is added to new columns. The headings indicate that the data came from the Customer worksheet (see Figure 38.5). The results are no longer formulas; you don't have to worry about using Paste Special to convert the formulas to values.

Check the final rows in the data set. If any customers did not have a match in the customer worksheet, those records will appear with blank customer names at the end of the worksheet.

 To see a demo of using Easy-XL to merge worksheets, search for "Excel In Depth 38" at YouTube.

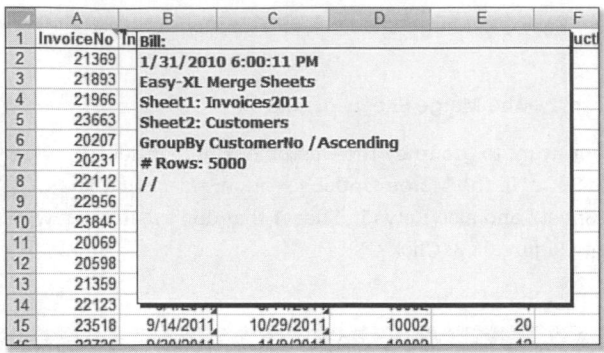

Figure 38.4
Easy-XL provides an audit trail
via cell comments.

	K	L	M
	Quarter	Customers.ContactName	Customers.State
	2	Kennedy Merrill	NS
	2	Kennedy Merrill	NS
	2	Kennedy Merrill	NS
	3	Kennedy Merrill	NS
	1	Kevon Cote De Neige	ON

Figure 38.5
The new data is appended to the right side of the new
worksheet.

Using a Fuzzy Match

When you match up data from two different sources, misspellings between the list commonly occur. This might happen if you are matching actual orders compared to a sales rep forecast. The sales reps tend to type abbreviations and have misspellings. The data from the company system tends to be spelled correctly because someone in accounts receivables is setting up the customers.

The Easy-XL Merge dialog box offers to do something called Levenshtein Distance Fuzzy Matching.

Suppose that you have two sheets, Forecast and Orders. Both sheets have a customer name and then a sales amount. The names don't match well enough; they have the usual amount of errors between them.

To perform a fuzzy match, follow these steps:

1. Start on the Sales sheet.

2. Select Easy-XL, Merge Sheets.

3. Select that you want to merge with the Forecast sheet.

4. In the Merge Sheets dialog, select Use Levenshtein Distance Fuzzy Matching. In that section, you should change the default settings. You want to allow Minimum Difference of zero. If you leave that setting at 1, exact matches are not reported. Use a Maximum Difference of 6. Set the Maximum Matches to 2 or 3. By using a high Maximum Difference, you run the risk of completely

different names being reported as a fuzzy match. By limiting the match to 2 or 3, you will get only the best 2 or 3 matches.

5. In the Merge Sheets dialog, select to Group by Customer. Select All columns in both worksheets. Select all the Merge Options check boxes in the lower left. Your dialog box should look like Figure 38.6. Click OK.

Figure 38.6
Select a fuzzy match.

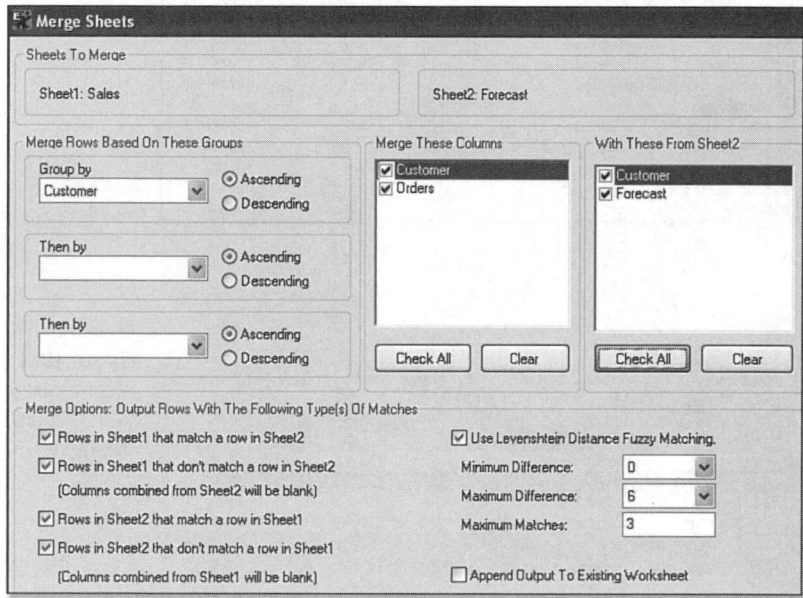

The initial results shown in Figure 38.7 are sorted by Difference. All the records at the top with a difference of 0 are exact matches. When you do a fuzzy match, you need to carefully go through the results to find the best result of each pair. Here is one way to go:

1. Select all the rows that have a match of 0 and apply a green fill color to those rows so that you know that they are likely the best match.

2. Sort all the rows by customer in column A.

3. Manually go through the list, keeping only one match for each customer in column A. You need to be careful while doing this. Consider Figure 38.8.

- In rows 2 and 4, the Difference column shows a 1. There were simple misspellings between A2 and B2.

- In row 6, the customers are considered a match even though one has an internal space and the other one doesn't.

	A	B	C	D	E	F
1	**Customer**	**Forecast.Customer**	**Difference**	**Orders**	**Forecast.Forecast**	**Tags**
2	Birds Eye	Birdseye	0	45186	3600 0	3
3	Cooper Tire	Cooper Tire	0	14095	800 0	4
4	FarmFresh	Farm Fresh	0	20870	1300 0	6
5	Hersheys Ice Cream	Hershey's Ice Cream	0	20987	1700 0	8
6	JayCo	JayCo	0	10860	700 0	9
7	King Sooper	King Sooper	0	37300	2200 0	10
8	Matrix	Matrix	0	41574	2900 0	11
9	Natl Semiconductor	Natl Semiconductor	0	30582	2400 0	12
10	Quaker Oats	Quaker Oats	0	38563	3100 0	13
11	Redbook	Redbook	0	11662	800 0	14
12	Target Stores	Target Stores	0	15002	1100 0	16
13	Vaseline	Vaseline	0	14252	900 0	18
14	Winnebago	Winnebago	0	42943	2600 0	19
15	Allen Bradley	Allen Bradly	1	19868	1200 0	2
16	Delta Airline	Delta Airlines	1	13218	1100 0	5
17	Sun Oil Co	Sunoco	2	26989	1600 0	15
18	Goodyear Tire	Cooper Tire	4	21205	800 0	7
19	Umbro	JayCo	4	17241	700 0	17

Figure 38.7
The best matches are shown at the top.

	A	B	C	D	E	F
1	**Customer**	**Forecast.Customer**	**Difference**	**Orders**	**Forecast.Forecast**	**Tags**
2	Allen Bradley	Allen Bradly	1	19868	1200 0	2
3	Birds Eye	Birdseye	0	45186	3600 0	3
4	Cooper Tire	Cooper Tire	0	14095	800 0	4
5	Delta Airline	Delta Airlines	1	13218	1100 0	5
6	FarmFresh	Farm Fresh	0	20870	1300 0	6
7	Goodyear Tire	Cooper Tire	4	21205	800 0	7
8	Goodyear Tire	Goodyear Tire & Rubber	6	21205	1700 0	7
9	Hersheys Ice Cream	Hershey's Ice Cream	0	20987	1700 0	8
10	JayCo	JayCo	0	10860	700 0	9
11	JayCo	Matrix	5	10860	2900 0	9
12	JayCo	Redbook	6	10860	800 0	9
13	King Sooper	King Sooper	0	37300	2200 0	10
14	Matrix	Matrix	0	41574	2900 0	11
15	Matrix	JayCo	5	41574	700 0	11
16	Matrix	Sunoco	6	41574	1600 0	11
17	Natl Semiconductor	Natl Semiconductor	0	30582	2400 0	12
18	Quaker Oats	Quaker Oats	0	38563	3100 0	13
19	Redbook	Redbook	0	11662	800 0	14
20	Redbook	JayCo	6	11662	700 0	14
21	Redbook	Sunoco	6	11662	1600 0	14
22	Sun Oil Co	Sunoco	2	26989	1600 0	15
23	Sun Oil Co	JayCo	6	26989	700 0	15
24	Sun Oil Co	Umbro	6	26989	1000 0	15
25	Target Stores	Target Stores	0	15002	1100 0	16
26	Umbro	JayCo	4	17241	700 0	17
27	Umbro	Matrix	5	17241	2900 0	17
28	Umbro	Redbook	5	17241	800 0	17

Figure 38.8
After a fuzzy match, you need to carefully look through the possible matches to find the best.

- In rows 7 and 8, the fuzzy match selected Cooper Tire as the best match for Goodyear Tire. Strictly from a blind data analysis point of view, both of those strings have "_oo_er Tire" in sequence and matches closer than Goodyear Tire & Rubber. In this case, you would keep row 8 and delete row 7.
- Rows 10 through 12 are interesting. You already have an exact match in row 10, so you will obviously keep that one. In row 11, though, the program is saying that "JayCo" and "Matrix" are

only off by 5 letters. Given that they both have an "a" in common and the second word has a stray "Mtrix," the fuzzy match is reporting this as a possible match. This could easily happen with any company name that is 5 or 6 characters.

- In Rows 26 through 28, the program comes up with possible matches for Umbro, but none of them are correct.

Go through the recordset, deleting the nonmatches.

When you are done, take a look through the Tags column. That tag is the original row number on the first worksheet. You should have no gaps in that range. If a gap exists, you need to get that value from the first worksheet and add it as a possible match.

note

When you match records from different sheets, the program expects the key fields to have the same headings on both worksheets. In Figure 38.8, change the heading in A1 to SalesCustomer and the heading in B1 to Customer.

Also, you are not sure that you have a complete list from the second worksheet. You should find any records on the Forecast worksheet that don't have a match on the FuzzyMatched Sales worksheet.

From the FuzzyMatchedSales worksheet, use Merge Sheets. Compare to the Forecast sheet, Group by Customer. In the lower left, choose only Rows in Sheet2 that don't match a row in Sheet1 (see Figure 38.9).

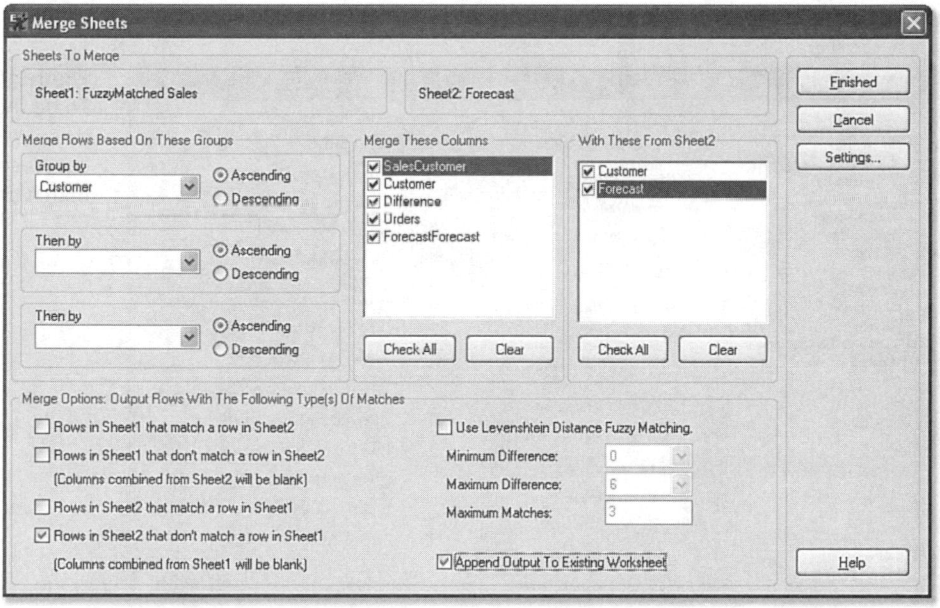

Figure 38.9
To be thorough, see if any forecast records exist that didn't match the sales.

[Screenshot of Merge Sheets dialog box]

Undoubtedly, the process of manually finding the best match for the fuzzy matches is tedious. However, without Easy-XL, it would have been nearly impossible to even come up with the fuzzy matched list.

Text to Columns on Steroids

Excel has had a text-to-columns feature for two decades. How could anyone improve on Excel's text to columns? Here are a few ways that Easy-XL has done it:

- When you are splitting a column into words, you can limit the maximum number of words that will result. A very common problem when splitting "FirstName LastName" into words are people with three names. "Mary Ellen Jelen" always ends up spilling into three columns instead of the expected two.

- The delimiter drop-down offers the usual delimiters, plus all 255 ASCII characters. If you have a data set with a strange delimiter, you can break the data, even if it is a delimiter that you can't type.

- If you need to grab the rightmost N characters from a column, you can do so with the Split from Right-hand Side check box.

- Easy-XL is very smart with date columns. You can choose to produce a year, month, day, and day of the week from a single date column.

In Figure 38.10, the invoice date column is being split into years, months, days, and days of the week.

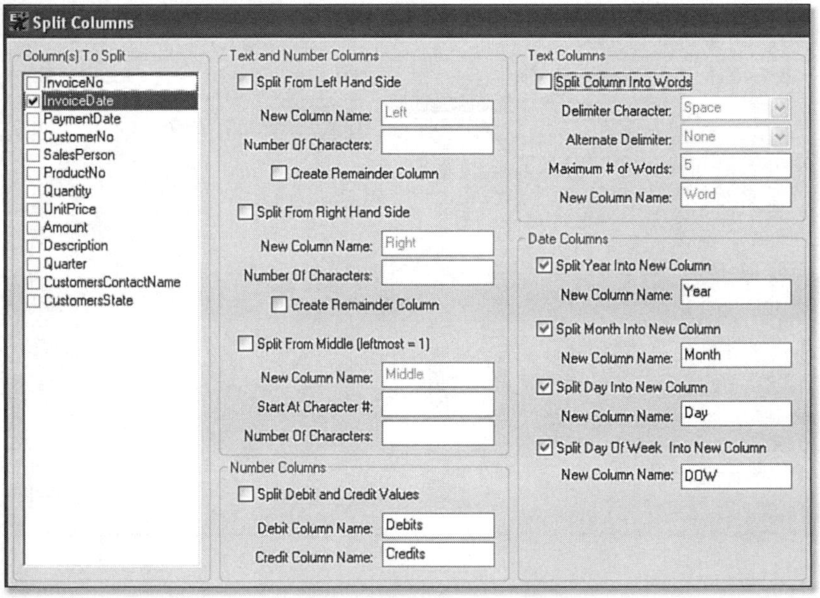

Figure 38.10
To be thorough, see if there were any forecast records that didn't match the sales.

The result is shown in Figure 38.11. Four new columns are added to the data set.

Figure 38.11
Easy-XL adds four new columns showing Year, Month, Day, and Day of Week.

B InvoiceDate	C InvoiceDate.DOW	D InvoiceDate.Day	E InvoiceDate.Month	F InvoiceDate.Year
4/10/2011	1	10	4	2011
5/19/2011	5	19	5	2011
5/24/2011	3	24	5	2011
9/25/2011	1	25	9	2011
1/16/2011	1	16	1	2011
1/17/2011	2	17	1	2011
6/4/2011	7	4	6	2011
8/4/2011	5	4	8	2011
10/8/2011	7	8	10	2011
1/6/2011	5	6	1	2011
2/13/2011	1	13	2	2011

Another common but difficult problem is people who have learned how to use Alt+Enter to move to a new line in a cell. Armed with this information, people will start storing name, address, city, and state all in one cell. Figure 38.12 shows a list of names and addresses stored in this way. When you type Alt+Enter, you are putting a character 10 in the cell. Using the regular Text to Columns wizard is tough, because you cannot type an ASCII character 10 into the Other delimiter field in step 2.

Figure 38.12
Break this data into columns.

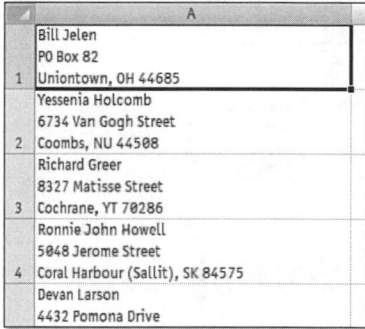

	A
1	Bill Jelen PO Box 82 Uniontown, OH 44685
2	Yessenia Holcomb 6734 Van Gogh Street Coombs, NU 44508
3	Richard Greer 8327 Matisse Street Cochrane, YT 70286
4	Ronnie John Howell 5048 Jerome Street Coral Harbour (Sallit), SK 84575
	Devan Larson 4432 Pomona Drive

To solve this problem, follow these steps:

1. Add a new row 1 with a heading of Name.

2. Select Easy-XL, Columns, Split Columns.

3. In the left list box, select Name.

4. In the top right, select Split Columns into Words.

5. Open the Delimiter drop-down. Scroll down to CHR(10), as shown in Figure 38.13.

6. Click OK.

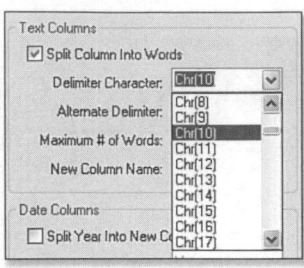

Figure 38.13
Select character 10 as the delimiter.

The result is that each line of column A is split into a new column. Because you did not change the maximum number of words from the default value of 5, Easy-XL created five new columns, even though all the records have only three lines of data (see Figure 38.14).

	A	B	C	D	E	N
1	Name	Name.Word.1	Name.Word.2	Name.Word.3	Name.Word.4	N
2	Bill Jelen PO Box 82 Uniontown, OH 44685	Bill Jelen	PO Box 82	Uniontown, OH 44685		
3	Yessenia Holcomb 6734 Van Gogh Street Coombs, NU 44508	Yessenia Holcomb	6734 Van Gogh Street	Coombs, NU 44508		
4	Richard Greer 8327 Matisse Street Cochrane, YT 70286	Richard Greer	8327 Matisse Street	Cochrane, YT 70286		
	Ronnie John Howell 5048 Jerome Street					

Figure 38.14
Easy-XL splits each line to a new column.

Sorting Columns Left to Right

After merging sheets, you might have columns in the wrong sequence. Easy-XL offers a utility for rearranging columns.

1. Select Easy-XL, Columns, Rearrange Columns. Easy-XL displays the Arrange Columns dialog with a complete list of columns.

2. Choose one column in the list and repeatedly click Move Up or Move Down to move the column.

3. Use the Rename button to create a new heading for the column.

4. Use the Format button to apply any formatting to the column.

5. Click OK.

Easy-XL rearranges the columns as you indicated.

Summarizing Data

Easy-XL offers several options for summarizing data.

Suppose that you want to see total sales by state. You've already added the state field in the merge data command. Follow these steps:

1. Select Easy-XL, Summarize/Pivot.

2. Select to Group by State.

3. Select to Include Grand Totals

4. Select to Summarize Quantity and Amount.

5. Click OK.

Easy-XL inserts a new worksheet titled Summary of Merged Invoices2011. This worksheet summarizes the 4999 rows on the original worksheet into a tight 16-row summary. For each state, the worksheet reports the number of records, the total quantity, and the total amount, as shown in Figure 38.15.

Figure 38.15
Easy-XL summarizes to one row per state.

	A	B	C	D
1	State	Count	Quantity.Total	Amount.Total
2	AB	338	1637	757,721.62
3	BC	384	2136	1,064,923.67
4	MB	466	2082	1,021,224.85
5	NB	371	1883	884,246.89
6	NL	303	1477	774,629.66
7	NS	545	2685	1,251,578.82
8	NT	429	2096	1,080,861.02
9	NU	377	1796	781,504.25
10	ON	330	1624	831,159.69
11	PE	375	1938	859,419.50
12	QC	425	2322	1,175,026.85
13	SK	287	1675	696,261.33
14	YT	366	1996	880,534.35
15		3	51	15,445.90
16	Totals	4999	25398	12074538.4
17				

Adding Statistics to the Report

One of the options in the Summarize/Pivot dialog is to add statistics. When you choose Select Fields, you are given a list of 30 statistics that you can add to the summary report (see Figure 38.16).

The result, shown in Figure 38.17, shows statistics for each state.

Many of those statistics are only mildly interesting to the data analyst, but would be highly interesting to the internal auditors.

note

Notice the hyperlinks in column B of Figure 38.15. Those aren't actual hyperlinks—there are not 14 new worksheets with data for each state—but if you click one of the hyperlinks, Easy-XL jumps into action and produces a report of the records that match that state.

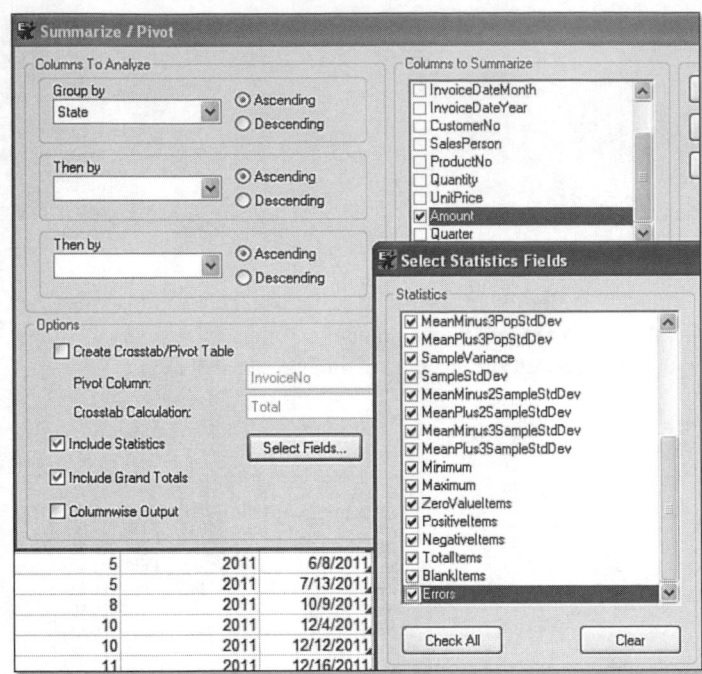

Figure 38.16
Choose statistics to add to the report.

	A	W	X	Y
1	State	Amount.Minimum	Amount.Maximum	Amount.ZeroValueItems
2	AB	131.00	24,540.00	0.00
3	BC	132.50	50,310.00	0.00
4	MB	131.00	33,540.00	0.00
5	NB	96.50	28,490.50	0.00
6	NL	144.00	44,720.00	0.00
7	NS	96.50	28,490.50	0.00
8	NT	96.50	32,720.00	0.00
9	NU	131.00	28,190.60	0.00
10	ON	139.00	33,540.00	0.00
11	PE	132.50	28,790.40	0.00
12	QC	131.00	50,310.00	0.00
13	SK	139.50	29,390.20	0.00
14	YT	118.50	27,950.00	0.00
15		358.00	12,295.90	0.00
16	Totals			

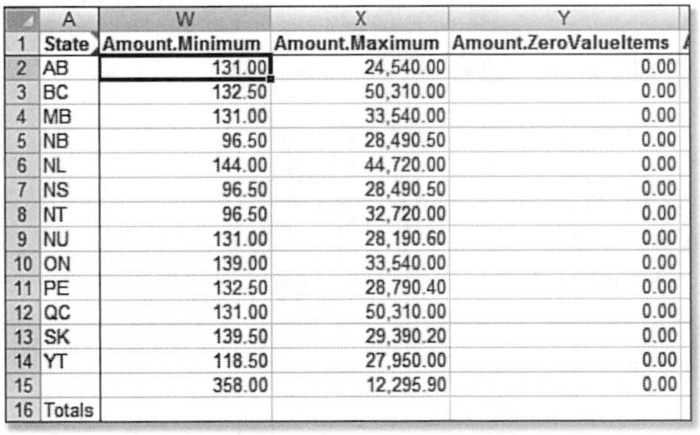

Figure 38.17
Add 30 statistics to the summary report.

Getting Quick Statistics

Select any range of cells. Right-click and select Easy-XL Quick Stats. A flyout menu appears that shows the total, min, max, median, number of positive values, number of negative values, number of errors, and so on as shown in Figure 38.18.

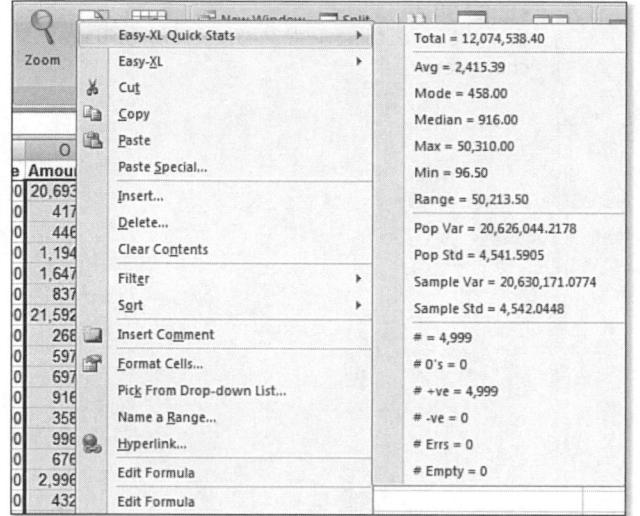

Figure 38.18
Quick statistics are a right-click away for any selection.

Transforming Data Instead of TRIM(), PROPER(), CLEAN()

Data cleansing is a task that many people run into frequently. VLOOKUPs don't work because of trailing spaces. Data from websites comes in with unprintable nonbreaking spaces. Names are in uppercase instead of proper case.

You can always add a new column, enter an =PROPER() function, copy down, copy, paste values, then cut and paste over the original data.

Or you can select the cells and use the Easy-XL flyout menu shown in Figure 38.19.

Adding Text to Cells

This book is nearly complete. Here is a task that I have been dealing with for 37 previous chapters. I have to produce a list of files used in the figures in the book. It is easy enough for me to use the Fill Handle to produce the list of filenames, as shown in Figure 38.20.

After I generate that list, I need to add ".tif" to each of those cells. Yes, you could use =A2& ".tif ", copy down, convert to values, cut, and paste. But it is so much easier to use Easy-XL, Cells, Fill Selected Cells, Fill with Text .tif, and then click Append to Cells, as shown in Figure 38.21.

After the command completes, the Fill Cells dialog stays open so that you can issue other commands. Click Finish when you are done.

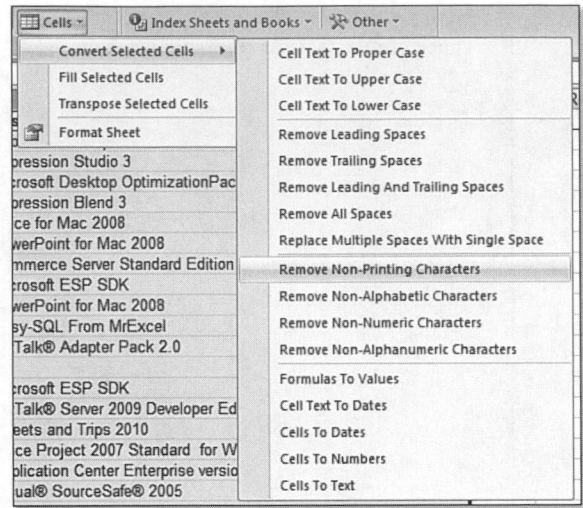

Figure 38.19
Convert case, remove spaces, remove garbage characters.

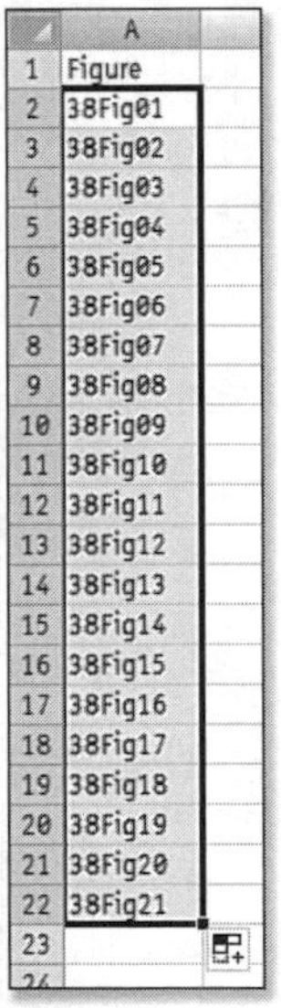

Figure 38.20
The fill handle did this.

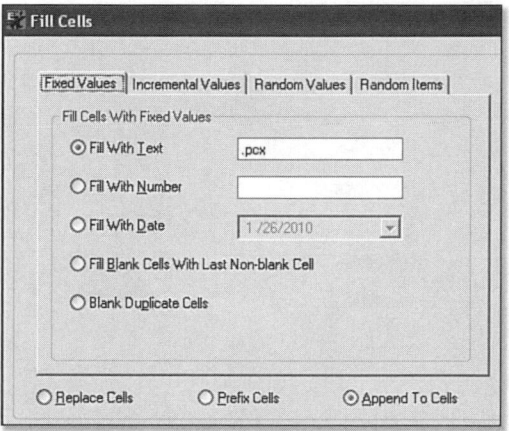

Figure 38.21
Append text to each cell.

Also, I've been appending .tif to cells for several days in a row. Easy-XL remembers the last settings that I used in this dialog. As soon as I select Fill Cells, the .tif is already filled in, as well as the Append to Cells setting.

Do you notice the Settings button in every dialog? If you have a particularly complex dialog box, you can save your settings and recall them later. The Settings button leads to a dialog where you can save settings for future use or load previous settings.

Filling in the Annoying Outline View

Create a pivot table with two column fields and the default presentation leaves a lot of blanks in the outer column field. Thankfully, you can override this in Excel 2010, but a lot of people are still using old versions of Excel and can't figure out how to fill in those blanks.

Use Easy-XL, Cells, Fill Selected Cells, Fill Blank Cells with Last Non-Blank Cell to fill in the outline view (see Figure 38.22).

There's More

There is still much more that can be done with Easy-XL:

- Split a worksheet out by group. Use Easy-XL, Split Sheet, by Group, and Easy-XL will put records from each state on a different worksheet.

- When Easy-XL offers Global Find and Replace, it really means Global. I had a series of 81 Excel files out on a network drive and I knew that one of those files had the record that I was looking for. I used Global Find, and Easy-XL looked through all the records in the folder until it found the data that I was looking for.

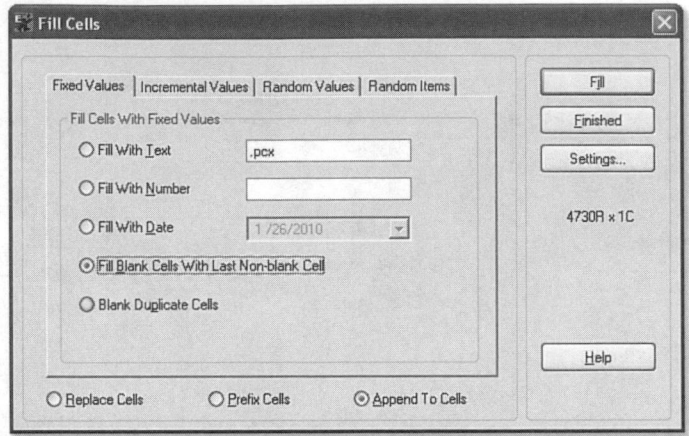

Figure 38.22
Fill in the annoying outline view.

- Use Import, File and Folder Listings to bring a list of files in a folder into Excel. You can sort, filter, and so on.

- Select to Index worksheets, and Easy-XL adds a new Index worksheet with hyperlinks to all of the worksheets in the workbook, plus a list of all cell comments in the workbook (see Figure 38.23).

	A	B	C	D	E
1	Sheet	Type	nRows	nCols	nCells
2	Invoices2011	Sheet	5,000	11	55,000
3	Sheet12	Sheet	4,731	1	4,731
4	Folder Listing	Easy-XL Folder Listing	60	17	1,020
5	Merged Invoices2011	Easy-XL Merge Sheets	5,000	17	85,000
6	Summary Of Merged Invoices2011	Easy-XL Group Summary	16	57	912
7	Invoices2010	Sheet	4,263	9	38,367
8	Products	Sheet	77	9	693
9	Customers	Sheet	1,001	7	7,007
10	SalesPeople2011	Sheet	27	8	216
11	SalesPeople2010	Sheet	25	8	200
12					
13		Total	20,200	144	193,146
14		Average	2,020	14	19,314
15		Max	5,000	57	85,000
16		Min	16	1	200
17					
18	Comments				
	Folder Listing (A1)	Bill: 1/31/2010 11:26:10 PM Easy-XL Folder Listing For C:\Documents and Settings\Bill G\Desktop\InDepth4*.*			
19		//			

Figure 38.23
Get a list of worksheets in the current workbook.

Deal with Fiscal Years

If you choose to Query Sheet, Query by Formula, you can build queries using built-in Excel functions, plus several new functions added by Easy-XL. These functions include Fiscal Quarter (see Figure 38.24).

Figure 38.24
Easy-XL adds some new functions to Excel.

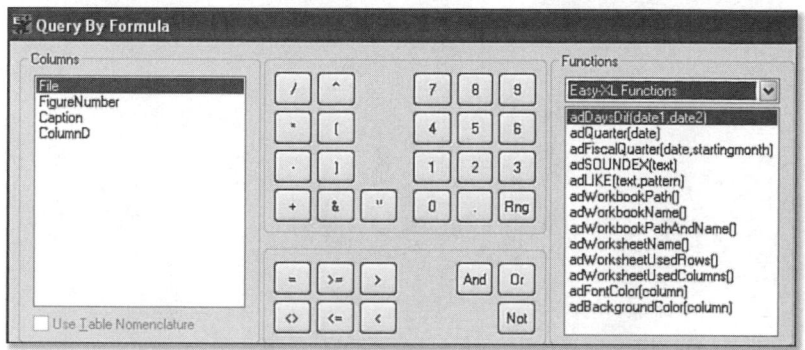

Record Easy-XL Commands into VBA Macros

At MrExcel.com, we have an active community of Excel enthusiasts. About one-third of the questions asked at the MrExcel message board deal with VBA Macros. Easy-XL is the only Excel add-in that will detect if the macro recorder is on and will write VBA code as you perform Easy-XL actions. This means that you can incorporate calls to Easy-XL into your VBA macros.

INDEX

FREE Online Edition

Your purchase of **Microsoft® Excel® 2010 In Depth** includes access to a free online edition for 45 days through the Safari Books Online subscription service. Nearly every Que book is available online through Safari Books Online, along with more than 5,000 other technical books and videos from publishers such as Addison-Wesley Professional, Cisco Press, Exam Cram, IBM Press, O'Reilly, Prentice Hall, and Sams.

SAFARI BOOKS ONLINE allows you to search for a specific answer, cut and paste code, download chapters, and stay current with emerging technologies.

Activate your FREE Online Edition at www.informit.com/safarifree

> **STEP 1:** Enter the coupon code: ZTIQFDB.

> **STEP 2:** New Safari users, complete the brief registration form.
> Safari subscribers, just log in.

If you have difficulty registering on Safari or accessing the online edition, please e-mail customer-service@safaribooksonline.com